The CRB Commodity Yearbook 2010

Commodity Research Bureau

WILEY
John Wiley & Sons, Inc.

Published by John Wiley & Sons, Inc., Hoboken, New Jersey
Published simultaneously in Canada.

For general information on our other products and services or for technical support, please contact our Customer Care Department within the United States at (800) 762-2974, outside the United States at (317) 572-3993 or fax (317) 572-4002.

Wiley also publishes its books in a variety of electronic formats. Some content that appears in print may not be available in electronic books. For more information about Wiley products, visit our web site at www.wiley.com.

ISBN 978-0-470-57477-5

Printed in the United States of America

10 9 8 7 6 5 4 3 2 1

Commodity Research Bureau
330 South Wells Street, Suite 612
Chicago, Illinois 60606-7110 USA
800.621.5271 or +1.312.554.8456
Fax: +1.312.939.4135
Website: www.crbtrader.com
Email: info@crbtrader.com

Contents

Acknowledgments

The editors wish to thank the following for source material:

Agricultural Marketing Service (AMS)
Agricultural Research Service (ARS)
American Bureau of Metal Statistics, Inc. (ABMS)
American Forest & Paper Association (AFPA)
The American Gas Association (AGA)
American Iron and Steel Institute (AISI)
American Metal Market (AMM)
Bureau of the Census
Bureau of Economic Analysis (BEA)
Bureau of Labor Statistics (BLS)
Chicago Board of Trade (CBT)
Chicago Mercantile Exchange (CME / IMM / IOM)
Coffee, Sugar & Cocoa Exchange (CSCE)
Commodity Credit Corporation (CCC)
Commodity Futures Trading Commision (CFTC)
The Conference Board
Economic Research Service (ERS)
Edison Electric Institute (EEI)
E D & F Man Cocoa Ltd
Farm Service Agency (FSA)
Federal Reserve Bank of St. Louis
Fiber Economics Bureau, Inc.
Florida Department of Citrus
Food and Agriculture Organization of the United Nations (FAO)
Foreign Agricultural Service (FAS)
Futures Industry Association (FIA)
International Cotton Advisory Committee (ICAC)
International Rubber Study Group (IRSG)
Johnson Matthey
Kansas City Board of Trade (KCBT)
Leather Industries of America
MidAmerica Commodity Exchange (MidAm)
Minneapolis Grain Exchange (MGE)
National Agricultural Statistics Service (NASS)
National Coffee Association of U.S.A., Inc. (NCA)
New York Cotton Exchange (NYCE / NYFE / FINEX)
New York Mercantile Exchange (NYMEX)
Commodity Exchange, Inc. (COMEX)
Oil World
The Organisation for Economic Co-Operation and Development (OECD)
Random Lengths
The Silver Institute
The Society of the Plastics Industry, Inc. (SPI)
United Nations (UN)
United States Department of Agriculture (USDA)
Wall Street Journal (WSJ)
Winnipeg Commodity Exchange (WCE)

The Commodity Price Trend

The Continuous Commodity Index (CCI) rallied sharply in 2009 and recovered a significant portion of the losses seen in 2008. The CCI index peaked at a record high of 615.04 in July 2008, bringing the 2001-08 bull market to a post-war record of +236.4%. The CCI index then plunged by an overall 48% to bottom out at a 4-year low of 322.53 in December 2008. The CCI index then rallied sharply during 2009 to post a new 1-year high and close the year up 33.4% at 484.42. Commodity prices rallied in 2009 due to (1) revived commodity demand with the global economic recovery that emerged mid-year, (2) strong GDP growth which reached 10.7% in China by Q4-2009, and (3) the dollar weakness seen during most of 2009 caused by financial institutions lightening up on the emergency dollar liquidity that they acquired during the financial crisis.

Five of the six CCI sub-sectors closed higher in 2009: Industrials +96.4%, Softs +63.5%, Energy +57.8%, Metals +43.1%, Meats +4.0%. The Grains sub-sector was the only one closing lower at –0.9%. The sub-sector changes noted above are calculated by simply taking the average of the percentage changes of the constituents in each sub-sector.

Energy

The CCI Energy sub-sector, which is composed of Crude Oil, Heating Oil, and Natural Gas, accounts for 18% of the overall CCI Index. The constituents in the Energy sub-sector on average in 2009 closed up +57.8%, more than reversing the previous year's decline of –46.1%. On a nearest-futures basis, crude oil in 2009 closed up +77.9%, gasoline closed up +103.6%, heating oil closed up +50.7%, and natural gas closed down –0.9%. Crude oil prices rallied sharply in the first half of 2009 due to improved demand and OPEC's sharp 16% production cut from mid-2008 through Q1-2009. Crude oil prices then traded basically sideways in the second half of 2009 as supply and demand both rose slowly and as inventories slowly declined. World oil demand rose by +3.6% from mid-2009 to the 20-month high posted in December 2009.

Grains

The CCI Grains and Oilseeds sub-sector, which is composed of Corn, Soybeans, and Wheat, accounts for 18% of the overall CCI Index. The constituents in the Grains and Oilseeds sub-sector on average closed down –0.9% in 2009, adding to the –20.2% decline seen in 2008. On a nearest-futures basis, corn in 2009 rose +1.8%, soybeans rose +6.9%, and wheat closed –11.3%. Corn traded in a sideways range during 2009 as usage grew and absorbed a record crop. Soybeans also saw a record crop, but firm demand kept carry-over inventories well below the 5-year average. Wheat prices were pressured in 2009 by a near-record global wheat crop and a substantial rise in the global carry-over.

Industrials

The CCI Industrials sub-sector, which is composed of Copper and Cotton, accounts for 12% of the overall Index. The constituents in the Industrials sub-sector on average showed a +96.4% rise in 2009, more than reversing the –40.9% decline seen in 2008. Copper closed sharply higher by +138.5% due to the reemergence of demand, particularly from China where GDP improved to +10.7% by Q4-2009. Cotton prices rallied +54.2% in 2009, more than reversing the –27.9% decline in 2008, due to strong Chinese demand and a tight supply situation with global cotton stocks falling to a 6-year low.

Livestock

The CCI Livestock sub-sector, which is composed of Live Cattle and Lean Hogs, accounts for 12% of the CCI Index. The constituents in the Livestock sub-sector on average closed up +4.0% in 2009 following the –2.7% decline seen in 2008. On a nearest-futures basis, cattle closed +0.1% while hogs closed +7.8%. Livestock prices were pressured in 2008 by weaker demand and by high feed and financing costs, which temporarily raised slaughter rates. On the bullish side, smaller herds were a supportive factor. Cattle prices were undercut in 2009 by weak exports but were supported by smaller herd sizes. Hog prices were hurt during mid-2009 by the swine flu epidemic, but then rallied sharply late in the year on smaller herds and tight supplies.

Precious Metals

The CCI Precious Metals sub-sector, which is composed of Gold, Platinum, and Silver, accounts for 17% of the overall Index. The constituents in the Precious Metals sub-sector on average closed up +43.1% in 2009, more than reversing the –19.0% decline seen in 2008. Bullish factors in 2009 centered on weakness in the dollar and fears of inflation with global central banks pursuing extraordinarily easy monetary policies to pull the global economy out of its worst post-war recession and to prevent any new crises from developing.

Softs

The CCI Softs sub-sector, which is composed of Cocoa, Coffee, Orange Juice, and Sugar #11, accounts for 23% of the CCI Index. The constituents in the Softs sub-sector on average in 2009 closed up +63.5%. All four commodities rose in 2009 with gains of +128.2% in sugar, +80.9% in orange juice, +23.4% in cocoa, and +421.3% in commodity. Tighter supply in the softs complex was the main bullish factor in 2009.

Continuous Commodity Index (CCI) (High, Low and Close 1967 = 100)

Year		Jan.	Feb.	Mar.	Apr.	May	June	July	Aug.	Sept.	Oct.	Nov.	Dec.	Range
2000	High	213.70	215.29	217.88	214.15	226.12	227.29	225.69	228.02	232.20	234.38	231.46	233.37	234.38
	Low	201.43	206.74	209.61	207.61	211.86	222.23	217.42	217.76	224.74	218.38	220.93	225.46	201.43
	Settle	210.46	208.78	214.37	211.03	222.27	223.93	218.61	227.41	226.57	219.28	229.79	227.83	----
2001	High	232.58	228.34	225.75	216.39	219.29	212.39	209.27	202.90	202.34	191.09	192.74	193.94	232.58
	Low	223.02	219.68	210.24	208.87	208.43	203.86	201.84	197.02	188.24	182.83	181.83	187.73	181.83
	Settle	224.12	221.78	210.26	214.50	209.00	205.56	202.70	199.63	190.49	185.66	192.66	190.61	----
2002	High	195.97	193.53	205.45	208.39	205.33	209.33	215.10	219.24	229.62	231.67	231.83	238.39	238.39
	Low	186.38	187.19	192.26	195.21	197.42	199.56	207.24	208.46	217.60	223.82	223.29	230.17	186.38
	Settle	187.29	192.33	204.92	201.16	204.20	209.29	210.97	219.20	226.53	228.91	230.64	234.52	----
2003	High	248.92	251.59	247.23	236.62	242.16	238.25	237.20	243.74	246.07	250.67	257.54	263.60	263.60
	Low	234.58	245.39	228.10	228.77	231.26	231.39	230.36	233.96	236.79	241.68	244.79	249.60	228.10
	Settle	248.45	247.25	232.15	232.53	235.55	233.78	234.21	243.70	243.66	247.58	248.44	255.29	----
2004	High	271.08	275.02	285.28	284.42	277.94	282.03	275.38	278.10	285.37	289.29	292.49	291.02	292.49
	Low	257.49	258.94	270.52	268.53	266.80	264.34	265.50	265.20	269.12	280.53	280.20	276.15	257.49
	Settle	262.57	274.73	283.77	272.54	277.25	265.94	267.78	276.50	284.98	283.70	290.94	283.90	----
2005	High	288.38	305.00	323.33	313.23	304.25	315.79	316.46	321.60	333.58	338.19	332.58	349.20	349.20
	Low	277.07	280.19	304.22	297.47	292.06	300.76	302.71	309.21	317.05	326.36	326.09	332.62	277.07
	Settle	284.75	305.00	313.57	303.74	300.83	306.91	315.24	318.99	333.33	326.68	332.49	347.89	----
2006	High	363.70	364.28	365.66	382.46	399.66	387.52	396.16	399.90	393.51	389.24	408.91	409.65	409.65
	Low	348.57	345.49	346.56	360.85	376.35	363.63	375.73	380.15	359.07	361.19	385.23	391.77	345.49
	Settle	363.30	353.27	361.91	379.53	379.80	385.63	391.49	390.95	370.10	383.92	408.79	394.89	----
2007	High	396.93	414.62	411.26	411.97	408.05	418.59	426.79	424.78	450.36	454.40	461.06	477.48	477.48
	Low	377.59	390.76	395.75	401.53	401.16	402.80	409.78	395.03	412.70	436.88	446.46	450.94	377.59
	Settle	394.37	410.64	407.45	403.54	407.58	410.36	424.52	413.49	447.56	454.29	451.26	476.08	----
2008	High	503.45	567.84	577.64	556.09	556.84	599.36	615.04	553.81	517.81	457.69	388.82	364.82	615.04
	Low	475.91	501.42	509.00	507.82	523.37	539.42	538.86	498.36	449.70	350.53	341.55	322.53	322.53
	Settle	503.27	565.65	516.38	536.23	541.30	595.98	548.86	516.47	452.42	369.56	361.74	363.06	----
2009	High	382.99	372.28	378.55	379.59	418.80	430.20	413.47	430.19	436.06	473.86	479.70	489.61	489.61
	Low	348.96	342.97	341.44	363.16	372.57	391.97	381.65	403.08	408.80	420.83	454.64	466.83	341.44
	Settle	364.50	352.45	368.83	371.55	417.04	398.76	413.41	415.49	430.67	452.69	479.22	484.42	----

Source: Thomson-Reuters

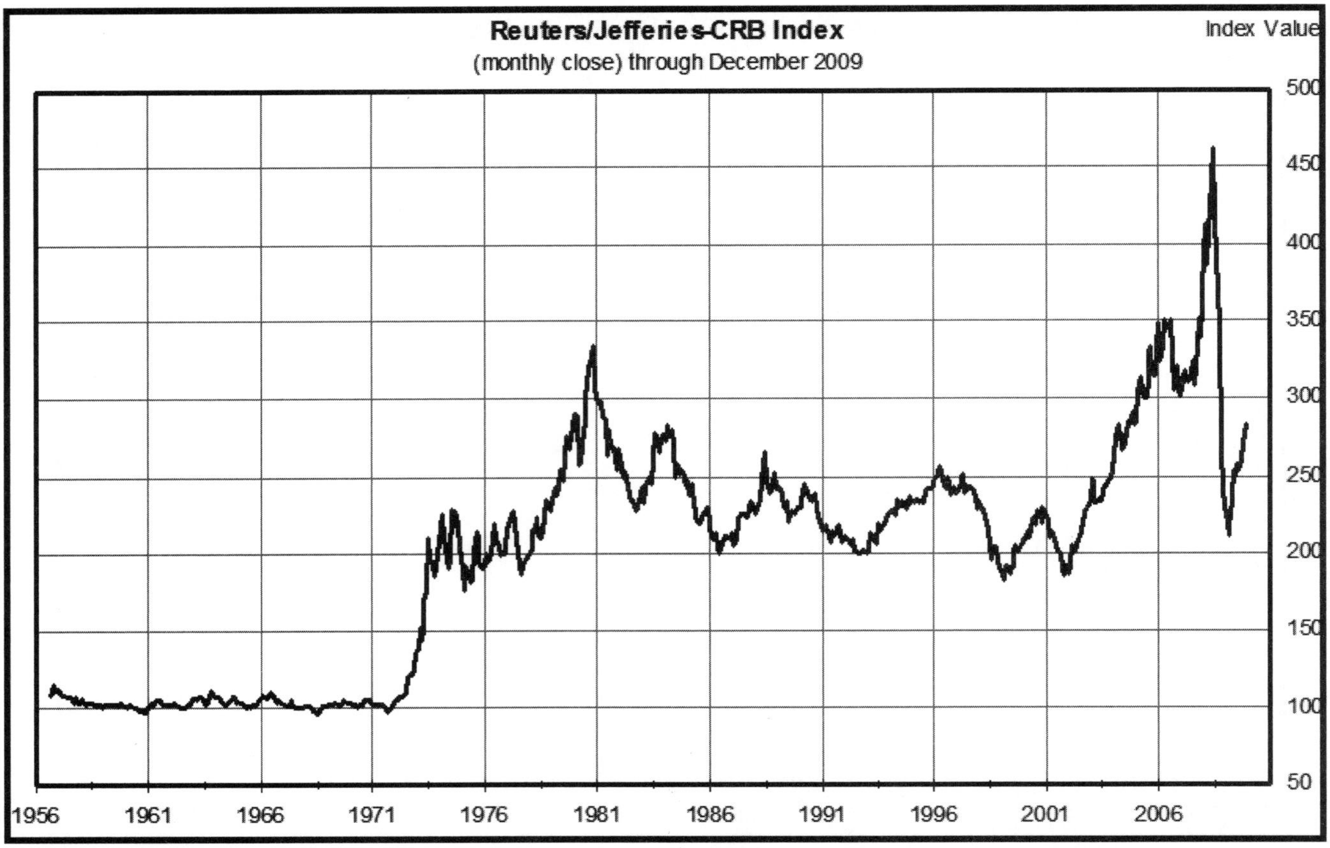
Reuters/Jefferies-CRB Index
(monthly close) through December 2009
Index Value
500
450
400
350
300
250
200
150
100
50
1956
1961
1966
1971
1976
1981
1986
1991
1996
2001
2006

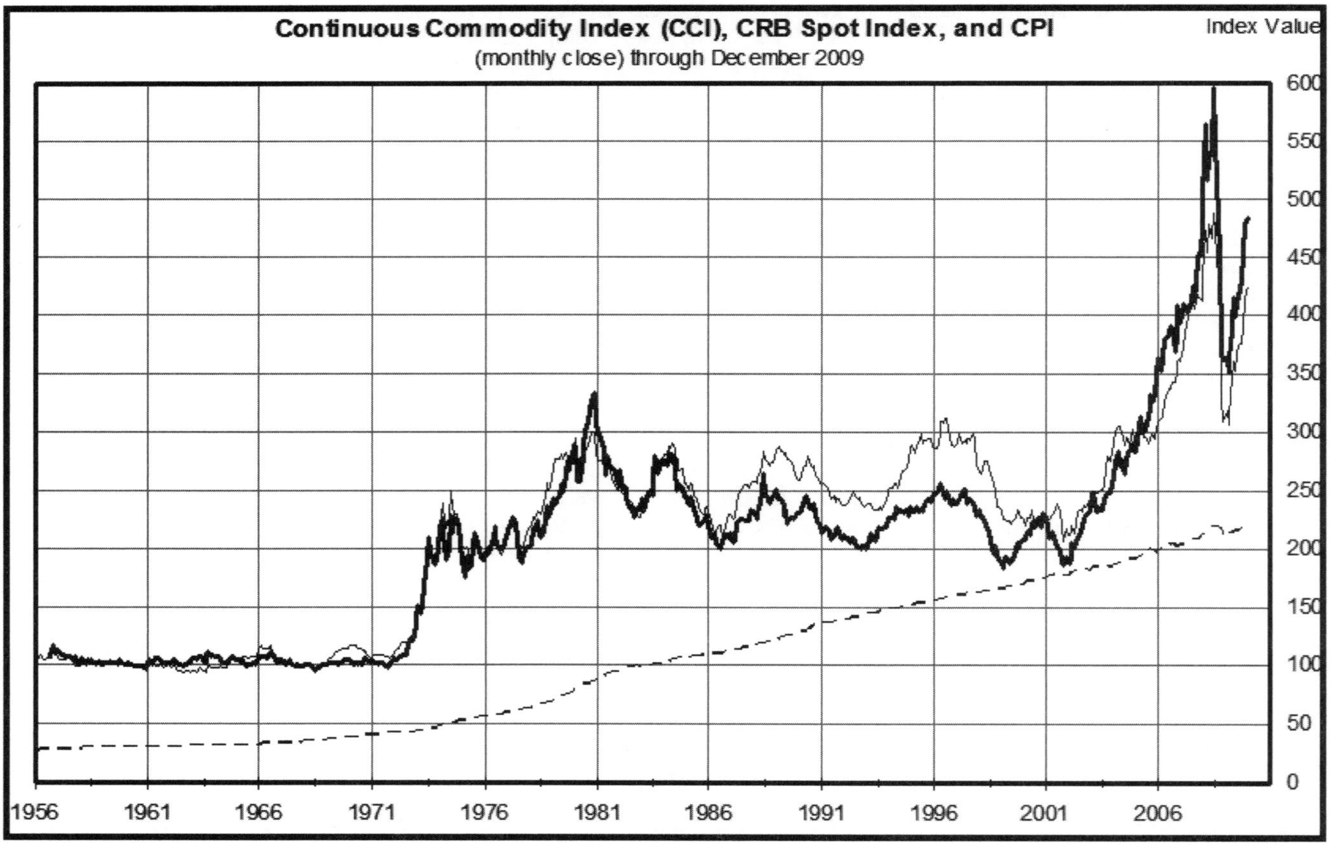
Continuous Commodity Index (CCI), CRB Spot Index, and CPI
(monthly close) through December 2009
Index Value
600
550
500
450
400
350
300
250
200
150
100
50
0
1956
1961
1966
1971
1976
1981
1986
1991
1996
2001
2006

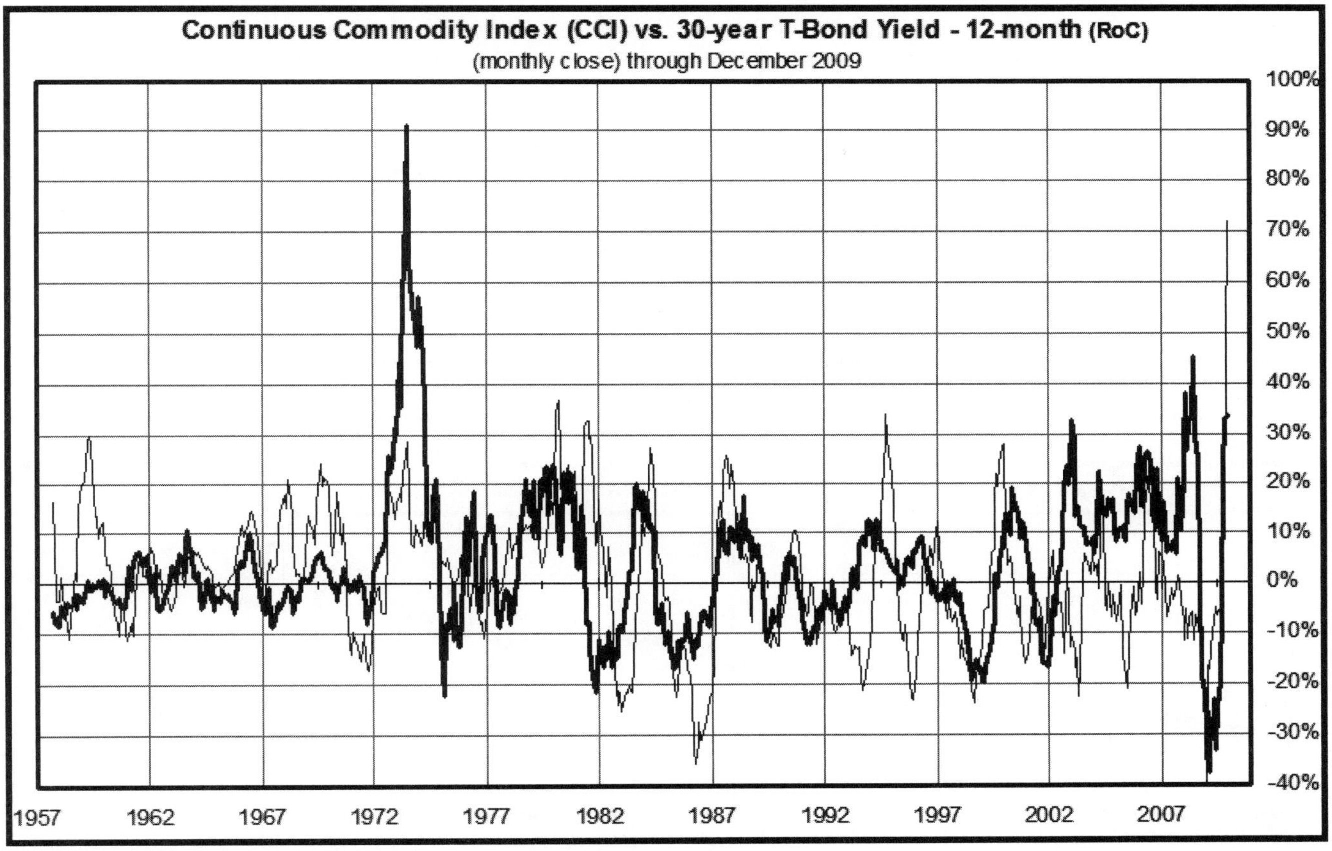
Continuous Commodity Index (CCI) vs. 30-year T-Bond Yield - 12-month (RoC)
(monthly close) through December 2009
100%
90%
80%
70%
60%
50%
40%
30%
20%
10%
0%
-10%
-20%
-30%
-40%
1957
1962
1967
1972
1977
1982
1987
1992
1997
2002
2007

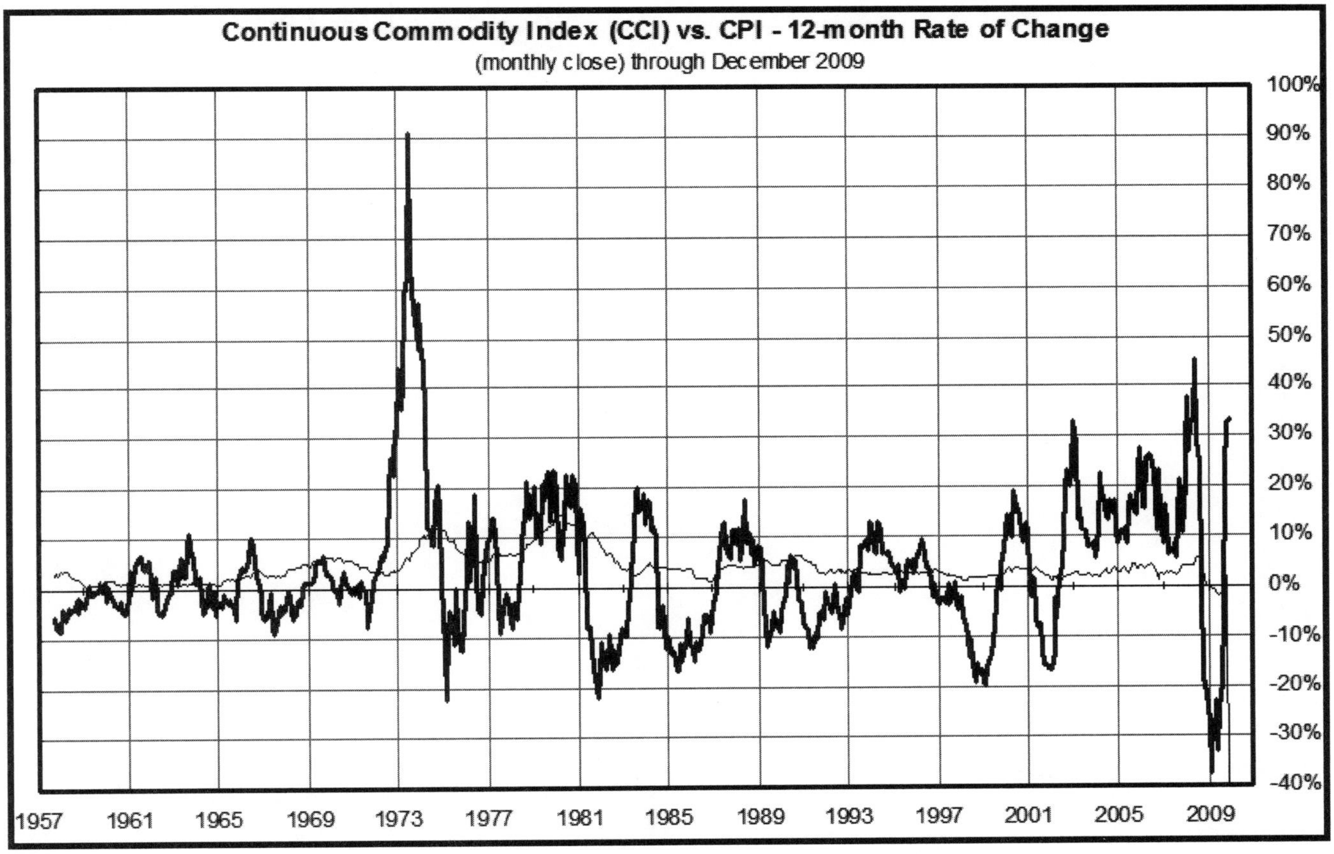
Continuous Commodity Index (CCI) vs. CPI - 12-month Rate of Change
(monthly close) through December 2009
100%
90%
80%
70%
60%
50%
40%
30%
20%
10%
0%
-10%
-20%
-30%
-40%
1957
1961
1965
1969
1973
1977
1981
1985
1989
1993
1997
2001
2005
2009

CRB INDICIES

CRB Metals Sub-Index (1967=100) (monthly close) through December 2009
Index Value
1,000
800
600
400
200
0
1947
1952
1957
1962
1967
1972
1977
1982
1987
1992
1997
2002
2007

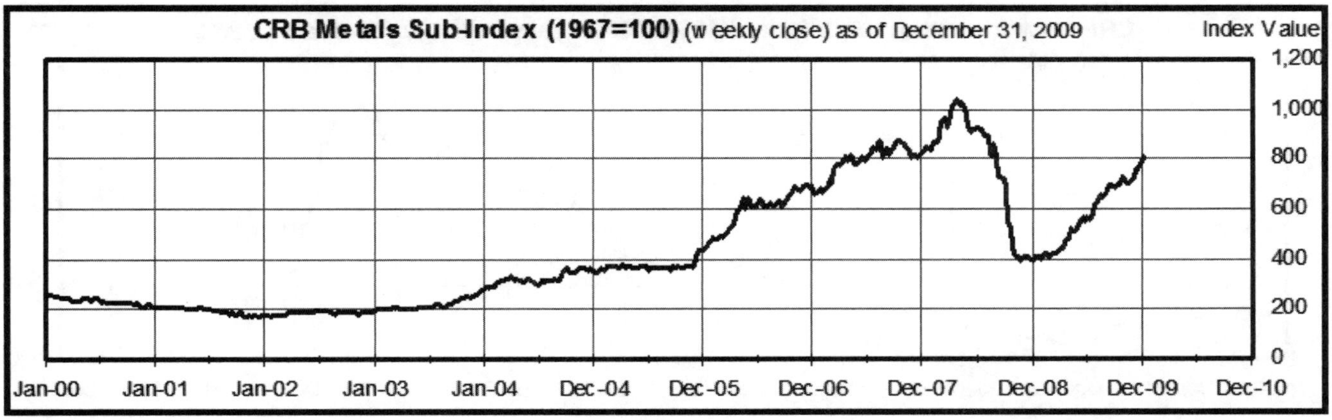
CRB Metals Sub-Index (1967=100) (weekly close) as of December 31, 2009
Index Value
1,200
1,000
800
600
400
200
0
Jan-00
Jan-01
Jan-02
Jan-03
Jan-04
Dec-04
Dec-05
Dec-06
Dec-07
Dec-08
Dec-09
Dec-10

CRB Textiles Sub-Index (1967=100) (monthly close) through December 2009
Index Value
350
300
250
200
150
100
50
1947
1952
1957
1962
1967
1972
1977
1982
1987
1992
1997
2002
2007

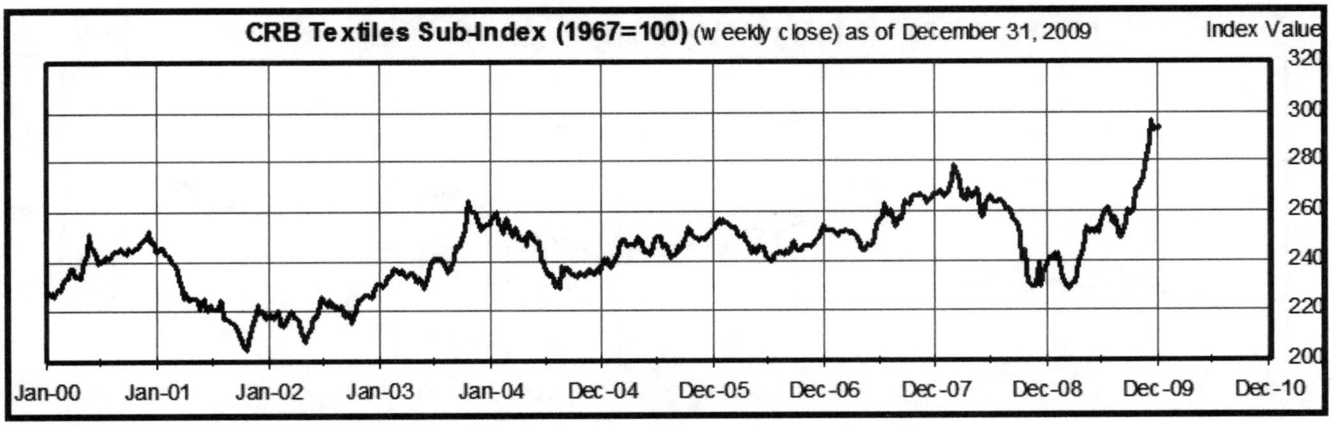
CRB Textiles Sub-Index (1967=100) (weekly close) as of December 31, 2009
Index Value
320
300
280
260
240
220
200
Jan-00
Jan-01
Jan-02
Jan-03
Jan-04
Dec-04
Dec-05
Dec-06
Dec-07
Dec-08
Dec-09
Dec-10

CRB Raw Industrials Sub-Index (1967=100) (monthly close) through December 2009
Index Value
600
500
400
300
200
100
0
1947
1952
1957
1962
1967
1972
1977
1982
1987
1992
1997
2002
2007

CRB Raw Industrials Sub-Index (1967=100) (weekly close) as of December 31, 2009
Index Value
600
500
400
300
200
Jan-00
Jan-01
Jan-02
Jan-03
Jan-04
Dec-04
Dec-05
Dec-06
Dec-07
Dec-08
Dec-09
Dec-10

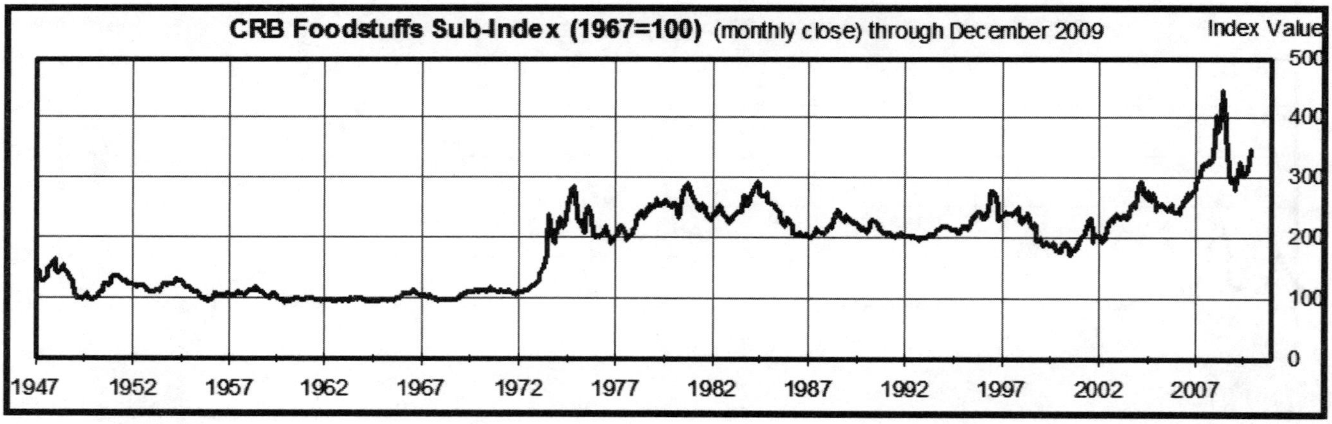
CRB Foodstuffs Sub-Index (1967=100) (monthly close) through December 2009
Index Value
500
400
300
200
100
0
1947
1952
1957
1962
1967
1972
1977
1982
1987
1992
1997
2002
2007

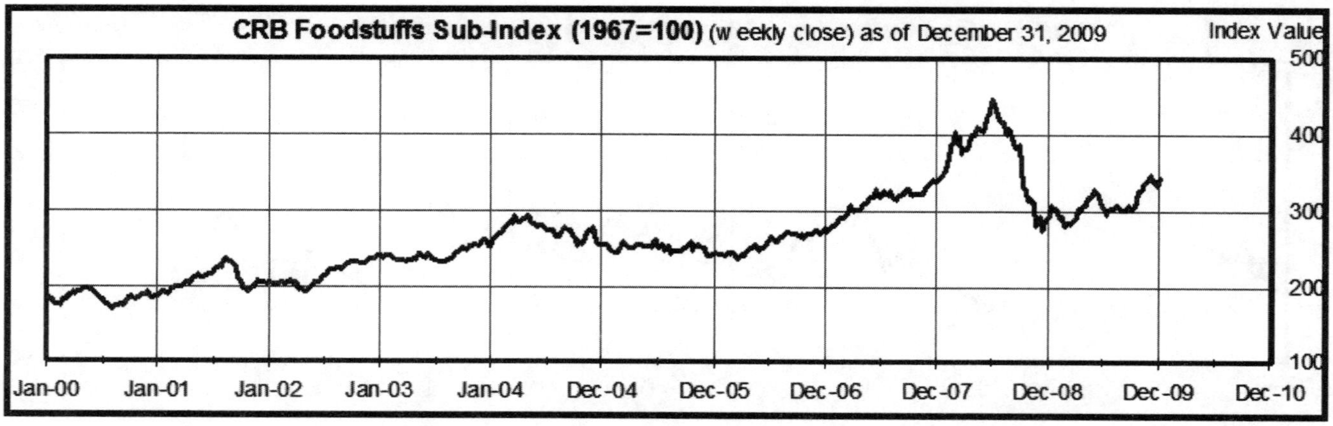
CRB Foodstuffs Sub-Index (1967=100) (weekly close) as of December 31, 2009
Index Value
500
400
300
200
100
Jan-00
Jan-01
Jan-02
Jan-03
Jan-04
Dec-04
Dec-05
Dec-06
Dec-07
Dec-08
Dec-09
Dec-10

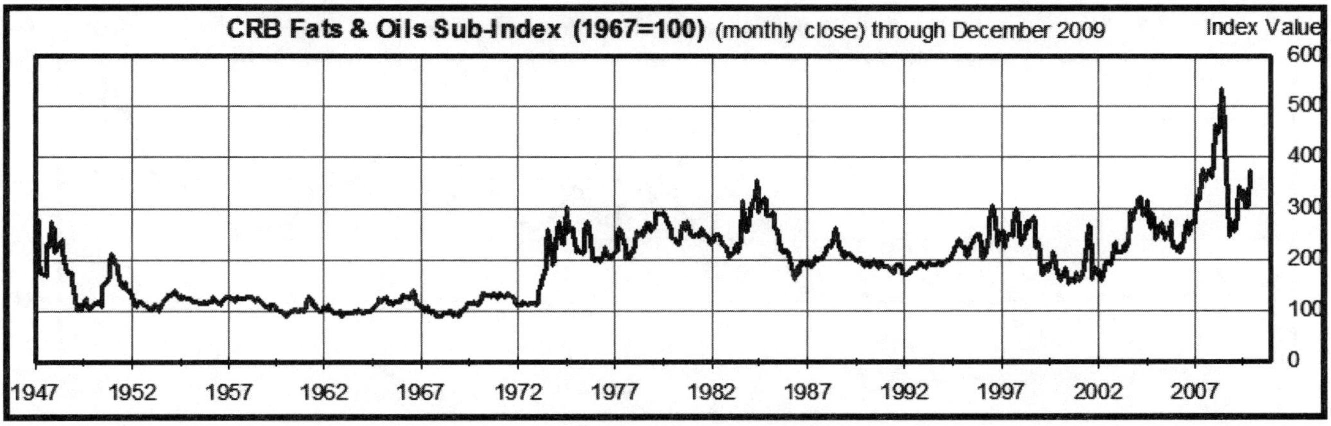
CRB Fats & Oils Sub-Index (1967=100) (monthly close) through December 2009
Index Value
600
500
400
300
200
100
0
1947
1952
1957
1962
1967
1972
1977
1982
1987
1992
1997
2002
2007

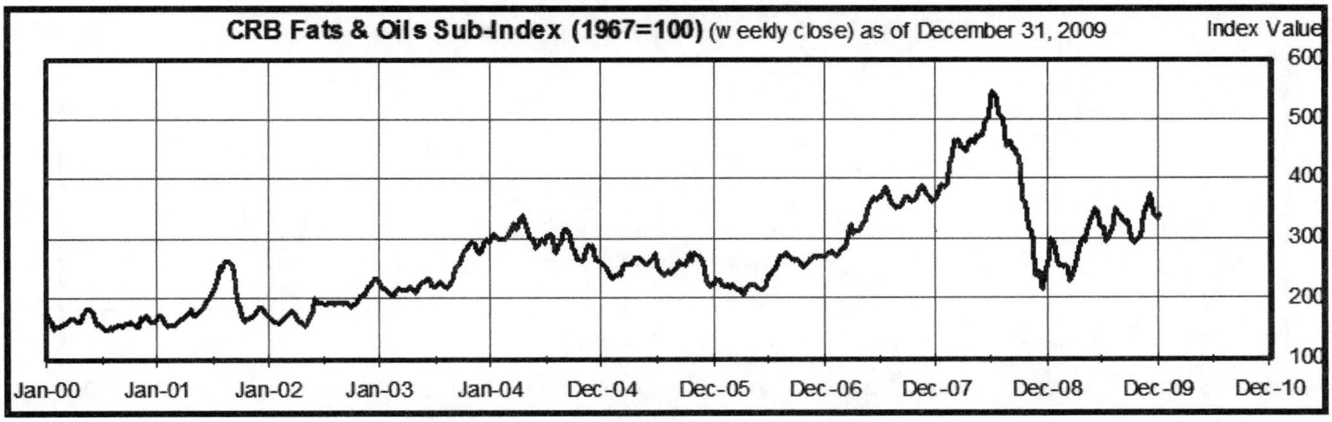
CRB Fats & Oils Sub-Index (1967=100) (weekly close) as of December 31, 2009
Index Value
600
500
400
300
200
100
Jan-00
Jan-01
Jan-02
Jan-03
Jan-04
Dec-04
Dec-05
Dec-06
Dec-07
Dec-08
Dec-09
Dec-10

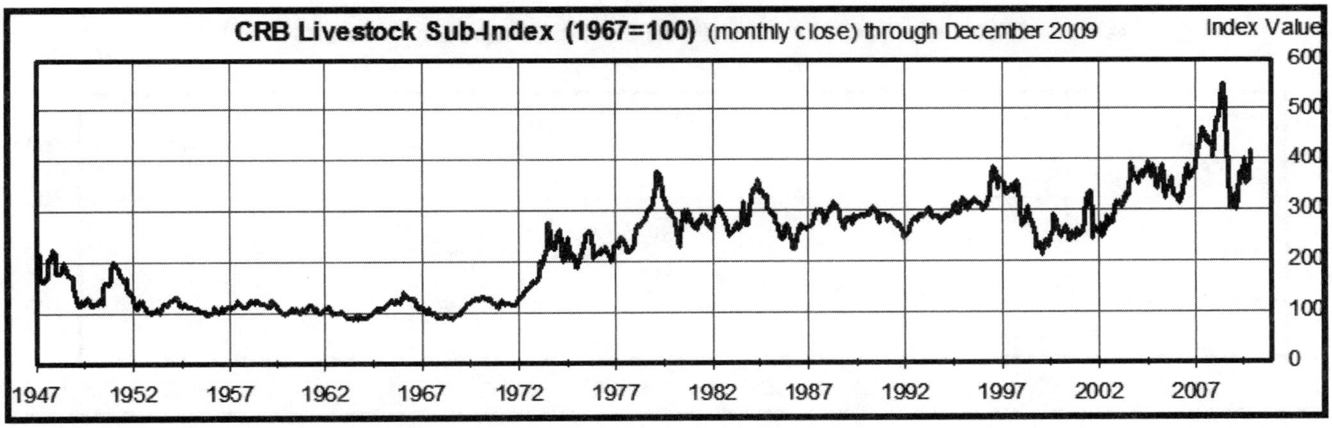
CRB Livestock Sub-Index (1967=100) (monthly close) through December 2009
Index Value
600
500
400
300
200
100
0
1947
1952
1957
1962
1967
1972
1977
1982
1987
1992
1997
2002
2007

CRB Livestock Sub-Index (1967=100) (weekly close) as of December 31, 2009
Index Value
600
500
400
300
200
Jan-00
Jan-01
Jan-02
Jan-03
Jan-04
Dec-04
Dec-05
Dec-06
Dec-07
Dec-08
Dec-09
Dec-10

CRB INDICIES

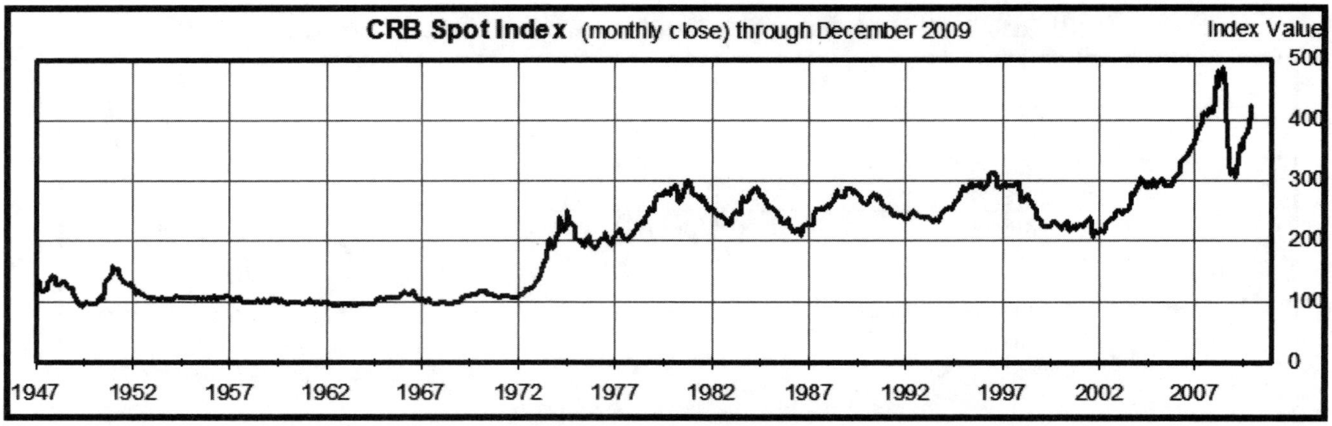

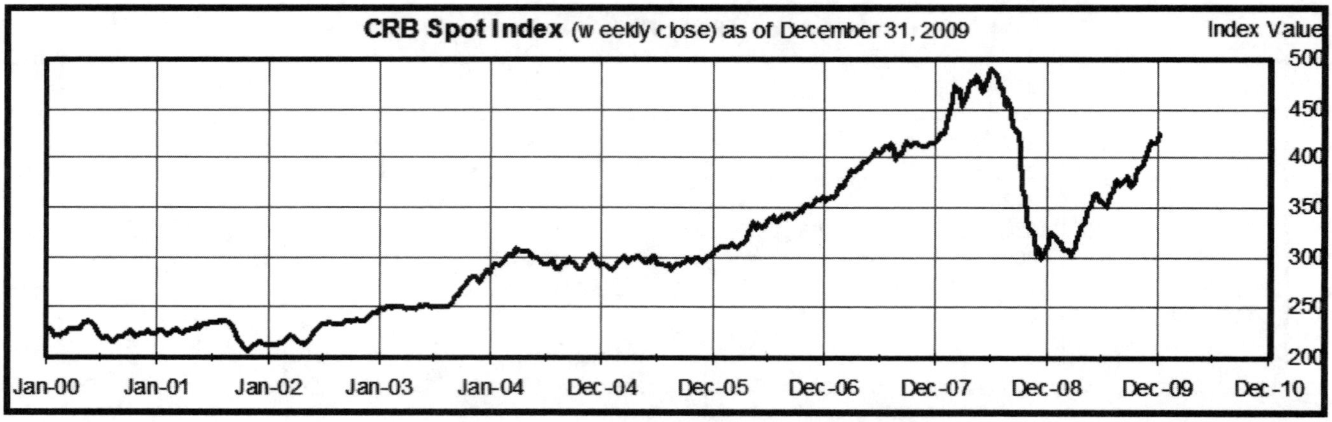

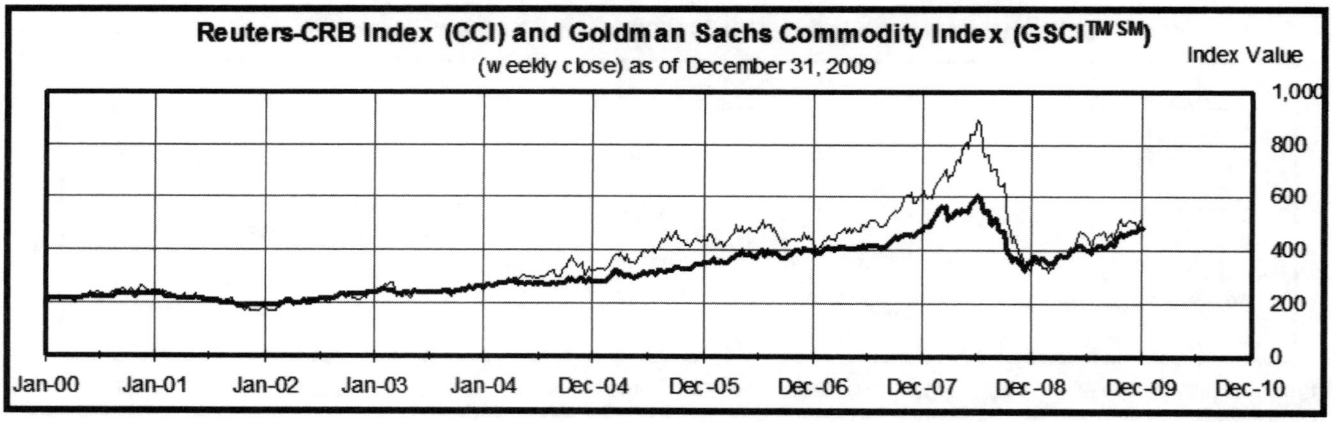

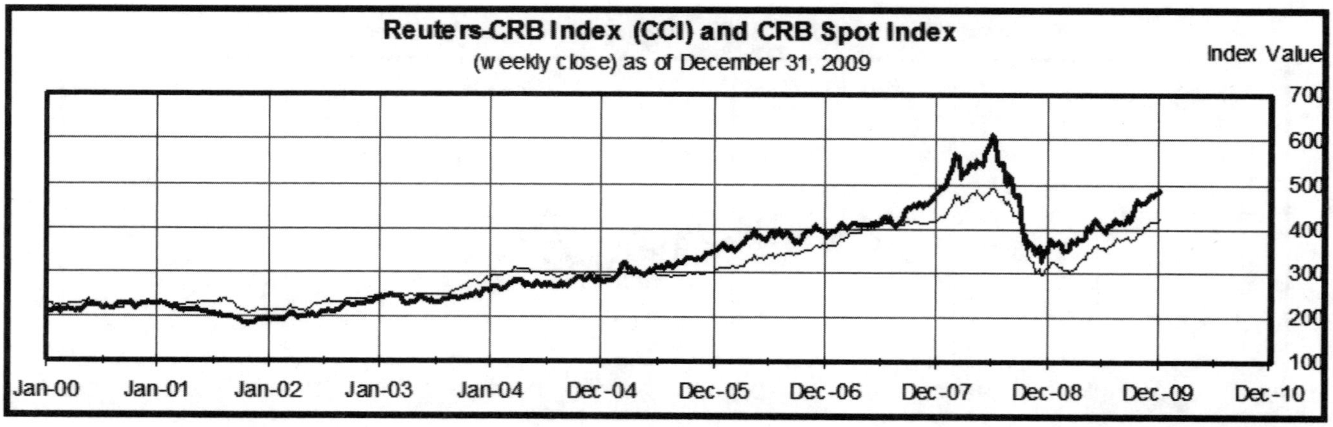

Continuous Commodity Index (CCI) (1967=100)

Year	Jan.	Feb.	Mar.	Apr.	May	June	July	Aug.	Sept.	Oct.	Nov.	Dec.	Average
2000	207.65	211.28	213.87	211.29	220.42	224.73	220.51	220.84	228.23	226.36	226.56	228.98	220.06
2001	228.30	223.42	218.06	213.43	214.69	208.37	204.98	200.18	195.34	186.20	188.42	190.42	205.98
2002	191.44	190.91	201.86	200.74	201.69	203.92	211.42	214.01	226.00	227.52	228.54	234.62	211.06
2003	242.04	247.89	237.81	231.73	237.38	235.11	234.05	238.13	241.44	246.15	250.66	258.44	241.74
2004	266.65	264.93	278.19	276.48	272.78	270.78	270.41	271.18	276.47	285.36	286.02	283.28	275.21
2005	282.96	289.01	312.70	305.26	298.11	308.07	311.47	315.00	324.05	333.46	330.39	343.83	312.86
2006	354.56	354.30	353.74	371.33	385.81	374.50	386.50	389.11	372.98	376.70	395.21	397.28	376.00
2007	386.38	400.96	403.41	405.99	404.24	410.22	418.88	411.65	432.37	446.95	453.23	467.28	420.13
2008	490.38	531.00	547.16	538.62	544.56	572.19	573.12	517.71	475.59	392.21	360.19	346.15	490.74
2009	364.14	356.43	358.81	372.81	399.62	410.96	400.35	417.38	421.88	450.93	466.10	479.51	408.24

Average. *Source: Thomson-Reuters*

Reuters/Jefferies-CRB Futures Index[1] (1967=100)

Year	Jan.	Feb.	Mar.	Apr.	May	June	July	Aug.	Sept.	Oct.	Nov.	Dec.	Average
2000	207.65	211.28	213.87	211.29	220.42	224.73	220.51	220.84	228.23	226.36	226.56	228.98	220.06
2001	228.30	223.42	218.06	213.43	214.69	208.37	204.98	200.18	195.34	186.20	188.42	190.42	205.98
2002	191.44	190.91	201.86	200.74	201.69	203.92	211.42	214.01	226.00	227.52	228.54	234.62	211.06
2003	242.04	247.89	237.81	231.73	237.38	235.11	234.05	238.13	241.44	246.15	250.66	258.44	241.74
2004	266.65	264.93	278.19	276.48	272.78	270.78	270.41	271.18	276.47	285.36	286.02	283.28	275.21
2005	282.96	289.01	312.70	305.26	298.11	306.97	308.04	318.76	326.19	326.44	315.27	327.58	309.77
2006	340.95	331.30	325.98	345.84	351.22	339.21	346.86	340.18	310.28	304.36	310.84	311.60	329.89
2007	292.18	305.63	309.03	314.35	310.77	314.32	320.89	308.89	323.89	336.20	349.82	349.36	319.61
2008	363.88	386.31	403.95	409.23	422.29	445.14	438.75	394.23	360.98	288.86	249.29	221.26	365.35
2009	224.69	212.16	215.45	222.70	241.36	255.94	244.10	260.66	253.92	269.88	274.27	276.58	245.98

Average. [1] New Calculation begins June 20, 2005. *Source: Thomson-Reuters*

Reuters/Jefferies-CRB Total Return Index[1] (01/02/1982=100)

Year	Jan.	Feb.	Mar.	Apr.	May	June	July	Aug.	Sept.	Oct.	Nov.	Dec.	Average
2000	122.59	128.50	132.60	128.43	139.10	144.80	143.12	147.23	155.89	155.00	157.45	158.74	142.79
2001	159.32	160.43	154.34	153.31	154.96	148.13	143.62	143.81	137.50	127.30	124.39	123.48	144.22
2002	123.82	124.53	135.70	138.03	138.93	138.66	143.23	145.91	153.53	153.91	151.63	161.51	142.45
2003	171.83	182.79	178.17	171.17	175.28	178.21	178.96	184.60	182.27	191.06	194.53	204.73	182.80
2004	213.15	215.30	226.72	227.21	234.19	230.03	232.57	236.76	238.75	254.24	248.91	241.10	233.24
2005	244.84	250.48	273.57	267.03	254.14	267.60	271.16	281.23	288.68	289.74	280.70	292.65	271.82
2006	305.70	298.05	294.39	313.52	319.76	310.00	318.32	313.52	287.18	282.84	290.08	291.98	302.11
2007	275.02	288.82	293.24	299.54	297.32	301.96	309.52	299.14	314.90	327.82	342.08	342.69	307.67
2008	357.92	380.80	398.78	404.43	417.85	441.16	435.51	391.90	359.36	287.82	248.68	220.56	362.06
2009	224.05	211.60	214.92	222.20	240.85	255.44	243.66	260.22	253.80	269.50	273.89	276.21	245.53

Average. [1] Theoretical data prior to June 20, 2005. *Source: Thomson-Reuters*

CRB INDICIES

CRB Metals Sub-Index (1967=100)

Year	Jan.	Feb.	Mar.	Apr.	May	June	July	Aug.	Sept.	Oct.	Nov.	Dec.	Average
2000	261.71	248.29	240.26	237.57	241.56	239.24	232.04	226.20	228.82	225.15	216.25	215.36	234.37
2001	212.47	212.90	210.59	204.94	205.14	205.60	197.04	188.09	181.32	179.50	172.96	173.80	195.36
2002	174.76	176.41	181.22	186.31	189.12	189.38	192.66	184.51	184.03	185.61	183.21	186.27	184.46
2003	199.71	204.17	206.72	202.78	205.57	207.77	212.24	214.09	220.24	240.20	248.49	266.70	219.06
2004	287.40	306.07	320.96	321.90	314.73	308.28	312.29	318.21	333.97	350.45	359.77	361.92	324.66
2005	355.95	364.50	371.99	371.31	365.83	369.32	361.39	363.75	364.70	369.68	370.47	425.84	371.23
2006	458.64	485.21	504.91	571.37	623.28	616.35	621.31	617.86	623.05	660.11	681.87	693.51	596.46
2007	668.94	691.71	761.81	798.96	798.65	803.29	834.00	840.13	835.06	868.19	828.50	812.12	795.11
2008	843.66	883.22	947.21	1,011.63	1,006.52	914.50	901.61	837.56	728.05	545.95	404.38	400.04	785.36
2009	409.17	416.80	421.44	455.21	410.21	552.61	591.59	651.17	688.67	704.55	716.43	767.81	565.47

Average. *Source: Commodity Research Bureau*

CRB Textiles Sub-Index (1967=100)

Year	Jan.	Feb.	Mar.	Apr.	May	June	July	Aug.	Sept.	Oct.	Nov.	Dec.	Average
2000	226.56	227.69	234.87	234.25	242.70	243.76	241.28	243.73	244.33	244.90	248.17	248.57	240.07
2001	244.74	241.84	233.40	225.97	224.47	222.12	222.44	218.55	214.74	207.79	215.86	218.99	224.24
2002	218.08	216.84	218.40	214.72	211.21	220.16	222.95	221.74	219.02	220.10	225.85	227.76	219.74
2003	231.25	235.31	235.04	234.64	231.66	235.24	240.88	237.50	244.30	256.99	257.59	254.25	241.22
2004	257.58	253.15	252.37	247.97	249.74	242.65	233.48	233.58	237.31	235.03	235.88	236.39	242.93
2005	239.93	240.36	247.12	247.73	246.60	244.69	247.21	243.08	246.64	251.24	248.96	250.83	246.20
2006	255.02	255.52	251.74	248.26	244.26	244.16	242.03	243.89	245.78	244.89	246.37	251.15	247.76
2007	252.50	251.35	251.91	248.99	245.40	250.72	260.09	256.51	261.58	264.79	265.79	265.28	256.24
2008	267.18	269.60	271.76	267.02	264.71	262.29	263.92	261.98	255.47	241.15	231.28	235.84	257.68
2009	241.13	237.01	229.83	240.05	252.00	253.03	258.94	253.52	257.42	265.67	280.85	296.96	255.53

Average. *Source: Commodity Research Bureau*

CRB Raw Industrials Sub-Index (1967=100)

Year	Jan.	Feb.	Mar.	Apr.	May	June	July	Aug.	Sept.	Oct.	Nov.	Dec.	Average
2000	267.85	260.91	260.39	258.23	265.37	261.78	255.19	255.69	258.81	257.29	252.58	256.00	259.17
2001	254.54	248.53	246.35	244.03	244.29	245.92	244.22	238.10	228.30	220.52	218.94	221.57	237.94
2002	219.05	222.33	231.03	230.38	231.81	243.72	245.38	240.53	240.77	240.68	243.04	248.21	236.41
2003	255.85	258.59	260.97	258.79	257.65	260.47	263.77	263.99	273.24	291.18	295.88	302.30	270.22
2004	312.24	309.54	316.77	318.52	312.98	308.40	308.84	307.54	315.25	315.13	320.52	322.65	314.03
2005	320.94	324.57	333.31	336.68	331.99	331.88	325.29	324.52	329.36	332.79	332.83	349.53	331.14
2006	363.05	371.00	372.08	385.69	400.62	399.97	403.50	403.90	403.19	415.76	426.67	434.25	398.31
2007	430.87	434.54	452.81	465.37	468.44	475.75	485.36	478.47	483.09	492.43	486.68	475.95	469.15
2008	487.92	502.29	522.98	534.29	532.30	517.02	517.29	495.17	460.96	392.49	329.86	317.83	467.53
2009	335.09	331.50	321.35	343.49	370.17	391.18	403.99	431.59	439.72	435.97	455.27	480.02	394.95

Average. *Source: Commodity Research Bureau*

CRB Foodstuffs Sub-Index (1967=100)

Year	Jan.	Feb.	Mar.	Apr.	May	June	July	Aug.	Sept.	Oct.	Nov.	Dec.	Average
2000	180.37	175.68	183.76	189.88	194.32	190.42	176.52	171.63	175.02	183.53	186.75	186.58	182.87
2001	189.68	192.93	200.48	203.57	210.24	213.09	222.61	232.42	224.06	199.51	200.24	203.40	207.69
2002	203.33	202.39	204.04	197.88	195.85	207.11	218.25	222.32	226.98	230.63	230.76	237.99	214.79
2003	238.60	237.01	234.16	234.55	239.15	239.53	232.81	234.30	244.69	251.04	255.36	257.99	241.60
2004	263.90	275.85	287.49	287.41	285.33	278.05	273.83	270.42	272.10	257.76	268.47	261.77	273.53
2005	252.84	246.44	253.58	252.19	254.21	255.43	251.31	247.65	249.22	253.37	252.74	242.54	250.96
2006	243.31	241.95	239.60	243.17	250.70	253.86	261.17	267.04	269.14	267.52	271.19	273.16	256.82
2007	275.31	286.30	297.37	299.85	311.98	320.79	322.44	319.95	325.01	322.19	325.40	337.97	312.05
2008	346.56	383.11	390.10	391.07	405.44	421.87	427.47	405.89	385.15	334.27	303.48	284.65	373.26
2009	299.83	286.21	284.71	302.35	316.81	318.81	301.83	304.44	305.01	314.86	338.56	339.54	309.41

Average. *Source: Commodity Research Bureau*

CRB Fats and Oils Sub-Index (1967=100)

Year	Jan.	Feb.	Mar.	Apr.	May	June	July	Aug.	Sept.	Oct.	Nov.	Dec.	Average
2000	171.15	154.77	161.97	165.37	177.74	171.57	152.26	153.11	157.52	160.41	165.44	167.35	163.22
2001	170.49	158.27	165.77	177.63	177.95	196.02	232.89	259.60	237.33	177.05	174.66	184.78	192.70
2002	169.64	165.91	177.34	167.61	164.38	193.38	193.29	192.85	193.20	193.90	211.97	230.05	187.79
2003	222.39	209.89	215.72	216.91	219.56	229.01	225.83	223.36	251.40	285.47	288.08	292.22	239.99
2004	305.30	300.47	318.53	330.54	302.31	295.32	304.60	290.52	302.51	267.12	279.42	271.36	297.33
2005	248.45	238.13	252.70	263.98	262.93	266.01	245.81	243.51	259.50	268.43	269.77	231.17	254.20
2006	231.10	221.46	217.14	214.75	222.03	221.97	247.09	271.97	267.18	257.29	264.75	270.94	242.31
2007	274.74	274.35	300.01	313.08	339.65	366.31	376.09	357.79	365.74	365.51	381.69	364.06	339.92
2008	381.95	418.92	459.52	457.65	467.23	498.89	526.26	467.08	443.38	366.91	283.76	238.42	417.50
2009	283.42	254.79	243.41	285.09	321.74	335.76	308.54	340.28	324.64	298.33	343.85	344.85	307.06

Average. *Source: Commodity Research Bureau*

CRB Livestock Sub-Index (1967=100)

Year	Jan.	Feb.	Mar.	Apr.	May	June	July	Aug.	Sept.	Oct.	Nov.	Dec.	Average
2000	261.83	245.67	252.65	258.44	268.41	260.53	241.72	238.62	245.35	252.78	240.45	259.65	252.18
2001	267.57	250.14	261.05	273.14	288.88	306.84	329.73	341.78	313.84	260.77	252.97	264.23	284.25
2002	251.61	260.32	274.95	257.32	256.33	289.40	288.22	279.03	274.13	276.94	288.86	313.14	275.85
2003	316.67	308.65	310.49	311.25	320.03	333.29	324.58	327.63	361.30	386.60	385.63	372.48	338.22
2004	372.16	353.19	362.41	369.65	369.31	374.28	395.48	392.33	395.40	365.68	373.69	370.63	374.52
2005	359.25	341.74	353.05	373.63	377.41	361.10	330.39	331.75	349.24	358.04	369.98	337.97	353.63
2006	331.93	328.72	320.09	314.72	327.28	340.29	359.18	388.13	384.78	366.35	364.05	372.08	349.80
2007	379.93	388.03	407.19	425.25	449.92	462.39	459.18	445.81	444.91	434.88	425.72	412.45	427.97
2008	417.36	451.42	468.41	483.09	510.01	522.82	556.10	526.98	492.24	426.75	342.41	288.42	457.17
2009	333.60	310.58	288.18	321.58	347.01	368.85	362.91	393.37	389.53	350.90	386.75	403.06	354.69

Average. *Source: Commodity Research Bureau*

CRB Spot Sub-Index (1967=100)

Year	Jan.	Feb.	Mar.	Apr.	May	June	July	Aug.	Sept.	Oct.	Nov.	Dec.	Average
2000	227.91	222.00	225.85	227.78	233.68	229.89	219.54	217.28	220.60	224.15	223.29	224.99	224.75
2001	225.75	224.13	226.51	226.66	229.81	231.98	235.20	235.83	226.62	211.72	211.15	214.01	224.95
2002	212.55	214.02	219.65	216.54	216.43	228.09	233.96	232.98	235.10	236.59	238.01	244.06	227.33
2003	248.72	249.60	249.73	248.66	250.00	251.77	250.71	251.49	261.25	274.11	278.66	283.38	258.17
2004	291.55	295.38	304.54	305.49	301.44	295.70	294.10	291.86	296.90	290.35	298.19	296.26	296.81
2005	291.19	290.08	298.13	299.24	297.73	298.26	292.80	290.63	293.94	297.75	297.48	301.05	295.69
2006	308.31	311.58	310.86	319.47	330.81	332.19	337.82	341.11	341.85	347.18	354.58	359.35	332.93
2007	358.84	366.47	381.36	388.90	396.79	405.08	410.71	405.97	410.96	414.11	412.79	413.88	397.16
2008	424.32	449.73	464.01	470.41	476.34	475.87	478.60	456.61	428.42	367.61	318.88	303.90	426.23
2009	320.03	312.26	305.91	326.11	347.44	359.84	358.67	374.28	378.72	381.73	403.44	416.74	357.10

Average. *Source: Commodity Research Bureau*

Goldman Sachs Commodity Index (GSCI) (12/31/1969=100)

Year	Jan.	Feb.	Mar.	Apr.	May	June	July	Aug.	Sept.	Oct.	Nov.	Dec.	Average
2000	200.140	211.150	214.190	200.420	219.110	230.070	222.130	230.880	247.730	243.670	251.820	244.790	226.342
2001	239.180	231.540	220.130	222.860	222.320	213.260	202.890	203.760	197.040	178.070	169.630	167.740	205.702
2002	168.970	172.750	193.580	199.870	200.650	197.070	203.120	208.760	223.690	222.700	212.180	230.030	202.781
2003	241.740	264.190	246.700	221.680	228.180	235.010	233.180	241.350	228.540	242.220	246.240	261.230	240.855
2004	269.180	266.230	280.100	284.060	303.190	292.630	298.970	308.010	315.290	356.700	341.120	314.250	302.478
2005	324.470	332.800	374.050	371.680	350.650	382.960	396.640	431.850	455.280	444.900	418.560	435.450	393.274
2006	442.120	422.490	427.470	469.730	477.930	471.650	490.320	485.650	434.560	431.130	442.050	444.620	453.310
2007	406.976	435.258	446.688	469.596	470.715	485.256	504.646	490.161	528.829	559.355	600.371	593.119	499.248
2008	606.714	638.875	689.259	717.944	778.146	832.309	818.904	716.837	644.004	496.045	405.956	338.266	640.272
2009	346.034	327.476	350.863	367.116	410.816	458.221	429.211	466.676	453.766	492.507	509.708	505.067	426.455

Average. *Source: Goldman Sachs*

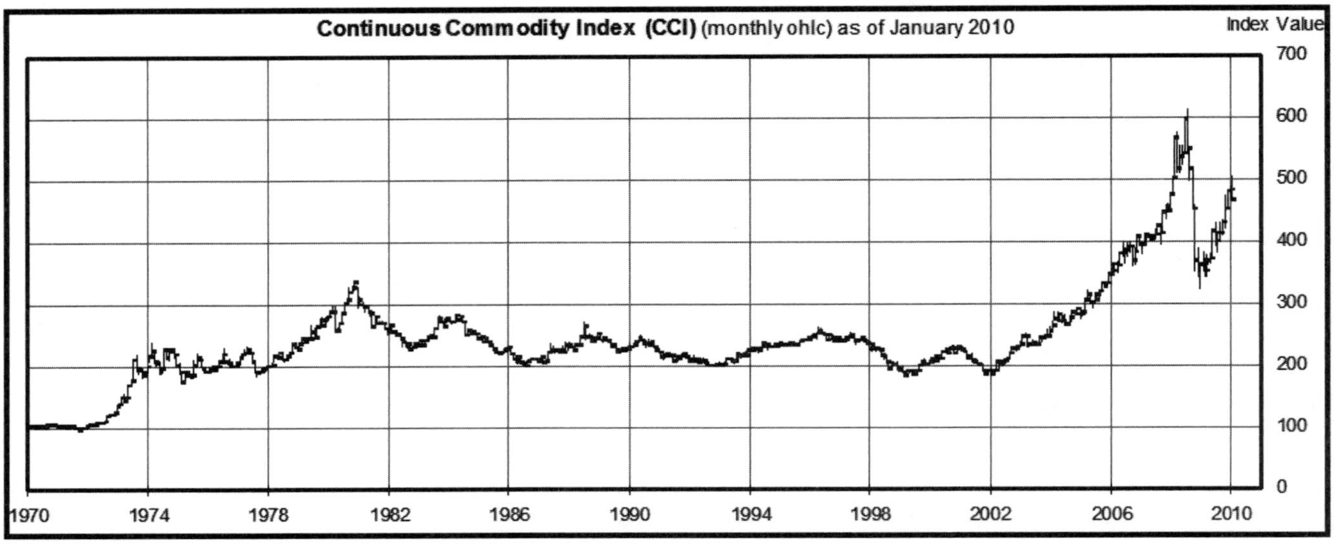

The Continuous Commodity Index (CCI) in 2009 showed a sharp recovery rally following the free-fall seen in the second half of 2008, which was caused mainly by the global financial crisis. The CCI index through January 2010 showed an overall rally of 56.5% from the 4-1/4 year low of 322.53 posted in December 2008. The CCI index on the December 2008 low had plunged by a total of 47.6% from the record high of 615.04 posted in July 2008.

On the record high posted in July 2008, the 2001-08 commodity bull market of +236.4% became the largest commodity bull market in post-war history, beating the previous record 1971-74 rally which totaled +146.7%. The 2001-08 commodity rally was also the longest-running rally at 81 months, far longer than 28 months for the second largest bull market of 1971-74. The 1971-74 and 1977-80 commodity bull markets were separated by two years of consolidation in 1975-76. If those two rallies are counted as one large bull market, then that bull market would be the largest in post-war history at 250.2%. However, the 2001-08 bull market of 236.4% was still close behind that two-stage 1971-80 rally.

The Continuous Commodity Index (CCI) in 2009 performed similarly to the RJ/CRB index, as illustrated by their parallel movement (see nearby chart). The RJ/CRB index was reformulated in June 2005 with a much heavier weighting on petroleum products of 33% versus the 12% weighting in the old CCI index. Strength in oil prices boosted the new CCI index in 2007, while strength in grain prices boosted the old CCI index.

The bull market in commodities abruptly ended in the latter half of 2008 when the U.S. housing and banking problems mushroomed into a financial crisis of global proportions. In the space of just five months, the CCI index plunged by 48% from the record high posted in July 2008 to the 4-1/4 year low posted in December 2008.

The plunge in commodity prices in late 2008 was due in part to extremely heavy long liquidation pressure by investors who had built up a huge long commodity position during the 2001-08 bull market. Investors during the crisis rushed to sell assets of all types in order to limit their losses and convert their portfolios into cash. Commodity prices were also hurt by the sharp rally in the dollar that occurred during the crisis since global financial institutions rushed into dollars for safety. Commodity prices were also pushed sharply lower in late 2008 as it became clear that the financial crisis would spark a serious global recession, thus undercutting demand for commodities.

Commodity Bull Markets Ranked by Percentage Gain of Continuous Commodity Index (CCI) (1960-2010[1])

	-------- Low --------		-------- High --------		Percent Rally	Rally Duration Months	Avg CPI (yr-yr%)
2001-08	Oct-01	182.83	Jul-08	615.04	236.4%	81	2.8%
1971-74	Oct-71	96.40	Feb-74	237.80	146.7%	28	4.9%
1977-80	Aug-77	184.70	Nov-80	337.60	82.8%	39	10.2%
1986-88	Jul-86	196.16	Jun-88	272.19	38.8%	23	3.2%
1992-96	Aug-92	198.17	Apr-96	263.79	33.1%	44	2.8%

[1] Data as of February 15, 2010. *Source: Commodity Research Bureau*

However, commodity prices in 2009 showed a sharp recovery from the 4-1/4 year low posted in December 2008. In fact the CCI index during the current recovery rallied by 57% and retraced 62% of the July-Dec 2008 plunge. The CCI index is currently in the upper third of the range established by the 2001-08 bull market and is far above the levels seen in 2001-06, illustrating that commodity prices are currently strong by any measure.

Commodity prices in 2009 were able to recover because of renewed demand, mainly from China, and because of dollar weakness during March-November 2009. China's GDP growth bottomed out at +6.2% in Q1-2009 and then improved substantially to a very strong +10.7% by Q4-2009. As for the dollar, the dollar index fell by a total of 17% from March 2009 through November 2009 as demand for emergency dollar liquidity dried up, and that dollar weakness provided support for commodity prices.

Looking ahead, commodity prices may be driven more by fundamental supply/demand factors in particular markets than by the external factors such as the dollar. The underlying fundamental picture for commodities should be moderately bullish in coming years. Commodity prices are likely to see underlying support as the global economic expansion gains traction and as demand strengthens for the raw materials to fuel global economic development.

Commodity prices are also likely to see continued strong investment demand from investors who now see commodities as a separate asset class and as an attractive investment theme tied to strong growth in the emerging countries such as China, India, Brazil and others. Investors in 2010 may pour even more cash into commodity investments than the record $60 billion amount they invested in 2009. The total amount of commodity assets under management in 2009 was at a massive $250 billion at the end of 2009, according to Barclay's Capital.

Commodity prices may also be boosted over the near-term by the market perception that the threat of deflation has now largely passed and that there is a serious threat of inflation in coming years if global central banks do not judiciously rein in their emergency liquidity measures.

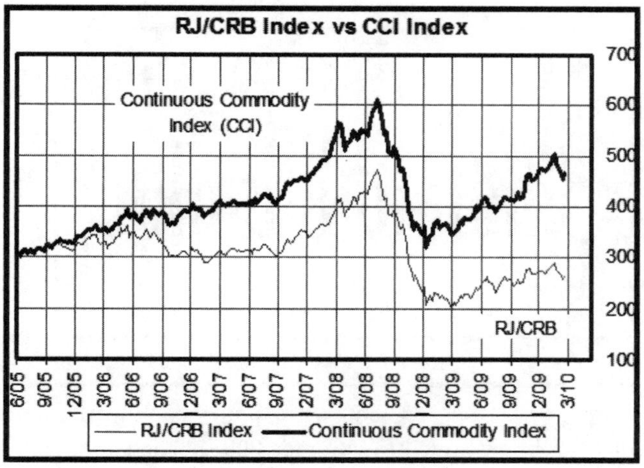

However, any further commodity rally may well be more of a slow upward grind than the moon shot that some investors are hoping for. Commodity prices may not get the help from a weak dollar they did during the 2001-08 bull market when the dollar index plunged by 39%. The weak dollar during that time frame provided a big boost for commodity prices since the weaker dollar meant higher prices for assets priced in terms of depreciated dollars.

The dollar is currently in a significantly stronger position than it was during the 2002-08 period, if only because the dollar is now at such a low level. The dollar index hit a record low in March 2008 and is still near the lowest levels seen since currencies started floating in the early 1970's. The dollar has already fallen to levels that have produced a big improvement in the U.S. trade deficit, excluding petroleum. In addition, the dollar has recently seen strength because of a lack of confidence in Europe with the big budget deficit problems in Greece, Portugal and Spain. A strong dollar in coming months would create bearish headwinds for commodity prices. Yet the underlying fundamentals for the commodity markets may be bullish enough to overcome any threat from a stronger dollar.

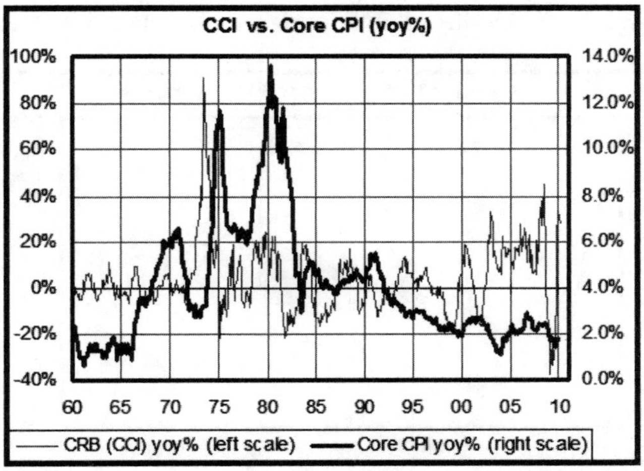

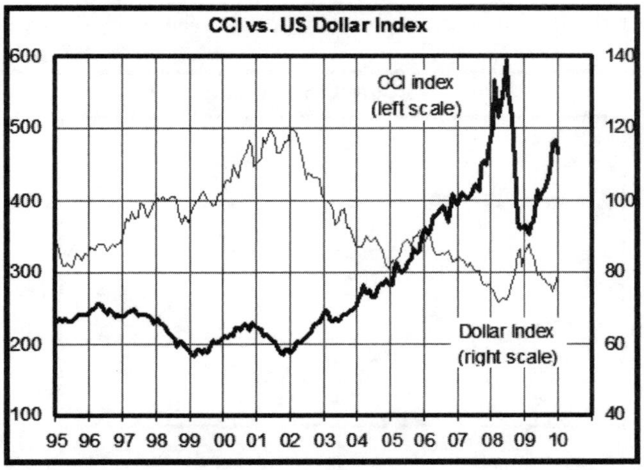

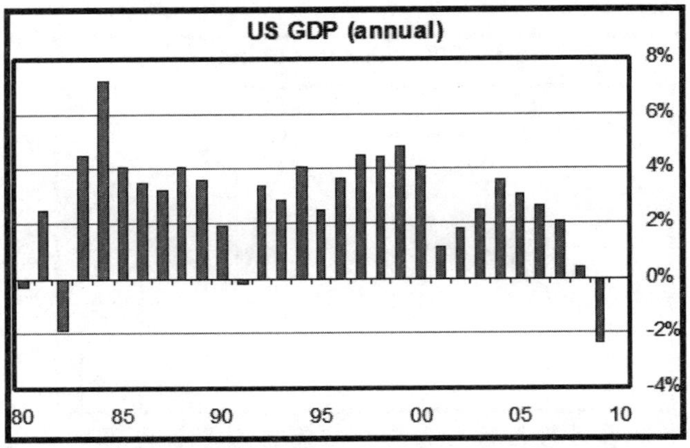

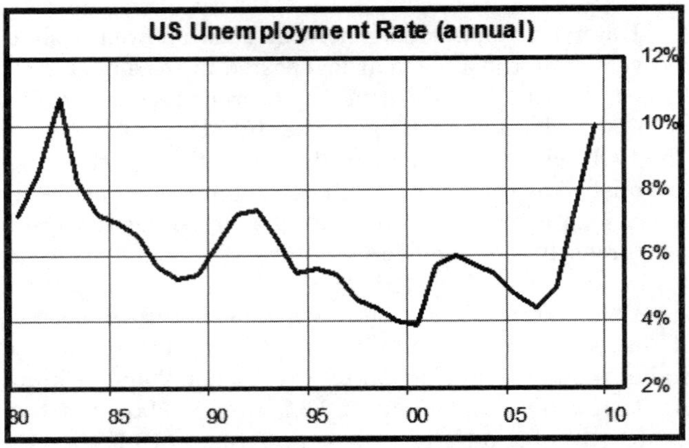

The U.S. recession, which officially began in December 2007, probably ended in summer 2009. The exact end of the recession is not likely to be officially determined by the National Bureau of Economic Research (NBER) for at least another year when more data is available and when the NBER can be sure that the U.S. economy does not fall back into a double-dip recession.

Based on GDP figures, the U.S. recession ended with the Q3-2009 GDP report, which rose by +2.2% and broke the string of four consecutive quarters of negative GDP growth. After the Q3-2009 report of +2.2%, U.S. GDP then rose sharply by +5.7% in Q4-2009. U.S. GDP on a peak-to-trough basis during the recession fell by a total of 3.8% from Q2-2008 through Q2-2009. That made the 2007-09 recession the worst U.S. recession in post-war history, edging out the 3.7% recession seen in 1957-58 and the 3.2% recession seen in 1973-75. For the full year of 2009, GDP fell by 2.4%.

While the U.S. recession may be over, the U.S. economy remains in generally poor shape. It is not difficult for the economic statistics to show some improvement given the extraordinary depths to which they had fallen. Even though the economic indicators are showing improvement, the economic recovery is likely to be slow and bumpy.

The labor market, for example, has not necessarily reached its worst levels. The unemployment rate in January fell by 0.3 points to 9.7% where it was down by a total of 0.4 points from the 27-year high of 10.1% posted in October 2009. The current cyclical peak of 10.1% was only 0.7 percentage points below the post-war record high for the unemployment rate of 10.8% posted in 1982. Even though the unemployment rate has fallen slightly, payroll jobs have yet to show a sustained increase. Payrolls fell by 20,000 in January, adding to December's 150,000 decline, to more than reverse the single-month 64,000 rise seen in November 2009. Payroll jobs over the 2-year period of January 2008 through January 2010 fell by a total of 8.4 million jobs. Recovering those jobs could take as long as 6 years if payroll growth shows the 10-year average monthly growth rate of 115,000 jobs seen prior to the 2007-09 recession.

The weak U.S. labor market is putting a heavy burden on the U.S. economy. The high level of unemployment is causing weak consumer confidence and spending since even U.S. consumers who still have a job remain worried about the job outlook. U.S. corporations during the financial crisis moved very quickly to lay off workers and reduce their expenses. The slash-and-burn approach of U.S. companies toward their employees creates tension for remaining employees that they might eventually lose their jobs in the next downturn or even sooner.

U.S. consumers are feeling a continued heavy burden from the housing market as well. Housing prices have dropped by a net 29% from the 2006 peak, causing severe damage to household balance sheets where the main asset is usually a home. Moreover, about one in five U.S. mortgage-holders was under water on his or her mortgage as of February 2010, according to Zillow.com. A homeowner that is underwater on his or her mortgage is trapped in the home and is paying off more debt than the home is worth. The high level of underwater mortgages, plus the high unemployment rate, has pushed the mortgage default rate and the foreclosure rates ever higher, thus throwing more

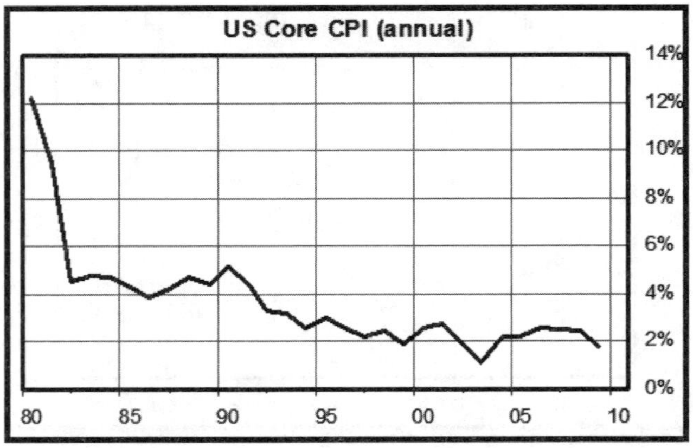

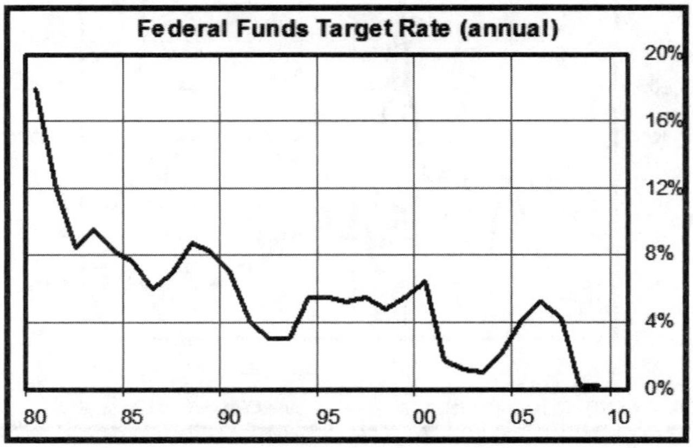

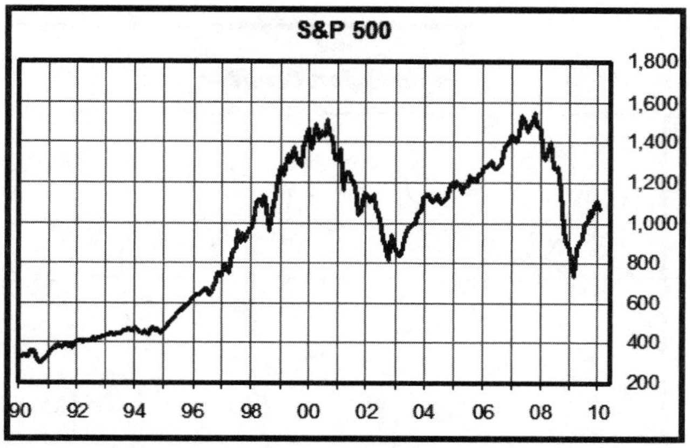

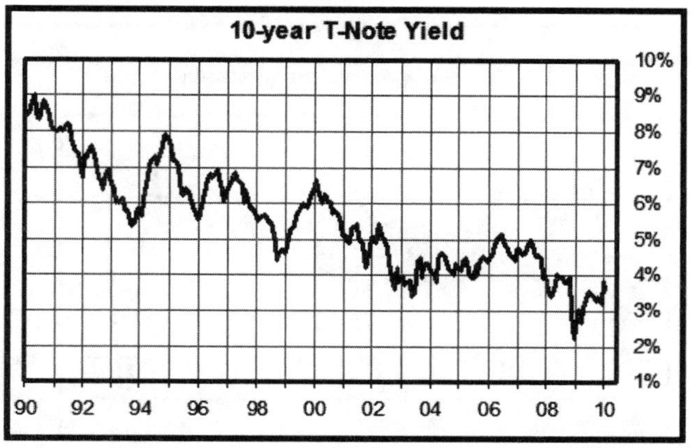

homes onto the market and keeping downward pressure on home prices. In fact, mortgage delinquencies in Q3-2009 were at a record 9.64% and mortgage foreclosures were at a record 4.47%, according to the Mortgage Bankers Association.

U.S. sales of existing homes have improved substantially from the multi-decade low of 4.49 million units posted in January 2009 and were at 5.45 million units in December 2009. However, roughly half of those purchases involved a distressed sale through a short sale or foreclosure, indicating that home buying demand remains weak except for homes that can be purchased at bargain basement prices. Moreover, the supply of homes on the market remained very high at 6.9 months in December 2009, down from the peak of 11.0 months posted in June 2008 but still far above the average of about 4.5 months seen before the housing crisis emerged. There are also a large number of people who would like to sell their homes when the market improves, meaning there is a big shadow-inventory of homes that are likely to come on the market in coming years. This suggests a continued heavy overhang of homes that will keep a lid on home prices in coming years and will keep downward pressure on household finances.

Despite these problems, most observers expect the U.S. economic recovery to continue. The market consensus is that U.S. GDP will grow by about +2.8% in all four quarters of 2010 and then improve to +3.0% in the first half of 2011 and +3.5% in the second half of 2011. The market consensus is that the U.S. economy will show sub-par growth over the next year due to continued instability in the banking system, weak consumer spending, and very cautious business spending and hiring.

Short-term U.S. interest rates have been extraordinarily low since the financial crisis emerged in September 2008. Most market observers expect short-term interest rates to remain very low through 2010. The market is expecting the Federal Reserve to keep its current federal funds rate in the current range of zero to 0.25% at least through summer 2010. The market is expecting only a 25 bp rate hike to 0.50% by the end of 2010 and an overall 150 bp rate hike to 1.75% by the end of 2011. The low funds rate should keep short-term rates anchored at low levels at least through 2010.

The longer end of the yield curve, on the other hand, has normalized to some extent. The 10-year T-note yield plunged to a record low of 2.04% in January 2009 but then moved higher in the first half of 2009 and traded sideways in the range of 3.0%-4.0% in the latter half of 2009. T-note yields are now back to where they were before the worst of the financial crisis emerged in September 2008. T-note yields have risen due to the economic recovery and concerns about whether the Fed will be successful in exiting its emergency liquidity measures without causing a surge in inflation.

The S&P 500 index in 2009 and early 2010 staged an impressive recovery rally after the debacle seen in 2008. Specifically, the S&P 500 rallied by 72% from the 13-year low posted in March 2008 to the 15-month high posted in January 2010. The stock market in February 2010 settled back on worries about government budget deficits and concern that the market may have gotten ahead of itself on earnings expectations. However, the forward price/earnings ratio for the S&P 500 in mid-February 2010 was relatively low at 13.8, indicating room on the upside for a renewed rally once the market gets more confidence about strengthening economic and earnings data.

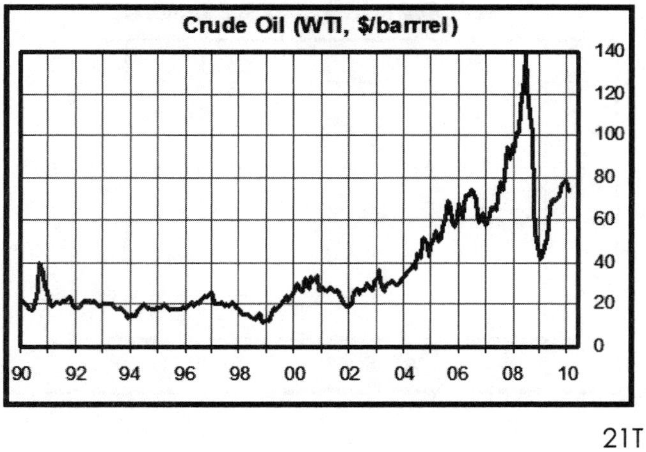

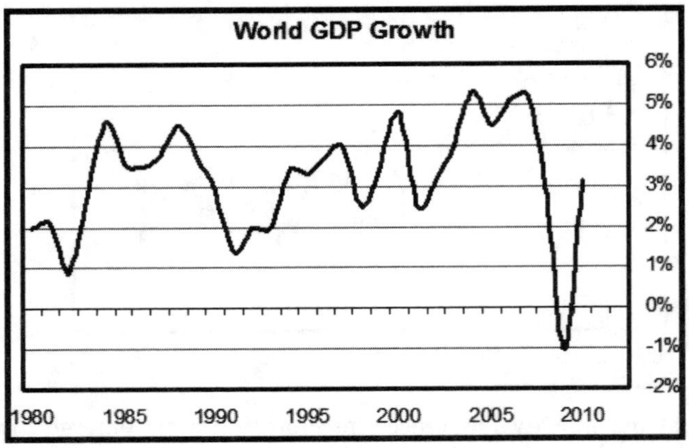

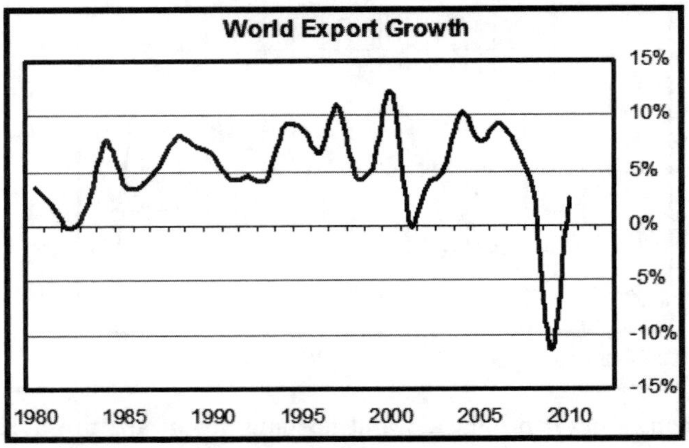

The global economy started to recover in the second half of 2009 after a global recession that lasted about a year. The World Bank estimates that the global economy declined by 1.1% in 2009, which was the first decline in the overall global economy in post-war history. However, the World Bank is expecting global economic growth to improve to +3.1% in 2010 and +4.2% in 2011, and then reach steady-state growth of about +4.5% in 2012.

The global financial crisis and recession decimated world trade. The World Bank estimates that world exports plunged by 11.4% in 2009. However, the World Bank expects exports to recover with growth of +2.6% in 2010. The World Bank expects imports to show +2.4% growth in 2010 after plunging by 12.4% in 2009. The recovery in trade has been a key engine for bringing the global economy out of recession.

The global recovery was sparked by aggressive monetary and fiscal stimulus measures. The U.S. Congress and the Obama Administration in February 2009 approved a $787 billion fiscal stimulus program. Europe instituted a 200 billion euro fiscal stimulus program and China instituted a $585 billion stimulus program. Most of those measures continued to have a positive impact into early 2010.

The markets are expecting the main G7 central banks to keep their low interest-rate policies in place at least until late 2010. The following interest rate targets were in place as of early 2010: U.S. zero to 0.25%, European Central Bank 1.00%, Bank of England 0.50% (the lowest in the bank's 315 year history), Canada 0.25%, and Japan 0.10%.

While interest rate targets remain low, global central banks are starting to cut back on their reserve injection programs. The Federal Reserve ended its Treasury purchase program in October 2009 and plans to end its mortgage security purchase program by March 2010. The European Central Bank does not plan to conduct any more 12-month lending operations and is moving back to normal money market operations by Q2-2010. The Chinese central bank in early 2010 had not yet raised interest rates but had announced two rounds of reserve ratio hikes to curb bank lending.

G7 bond yields rose in 2009 as the global economy recovered and as the threat of deflation faded. The average G7 10-year bond yield ended 2009 at 3.56%, up by 59 bp from 2.97% at the end of 2008. Poor budget finances took a toll on Italian and U.K. bond yields with relatively high yields of 4.63% and 4.0%, respectively, at the end of 2009. The G7 bond markets remain worried about the resolve of global central banks to exit their emergency liquidity measures without sparking a surge of inflation.

Global stock markets recovered sharply in 2009 as the global recession ended and as corporations did a remarkably good job in cutting expenses and preserving profits despite the worst recession in post-war history. The MSCI Developed World Stock index recovered by 49% from its low posted in February 2009.

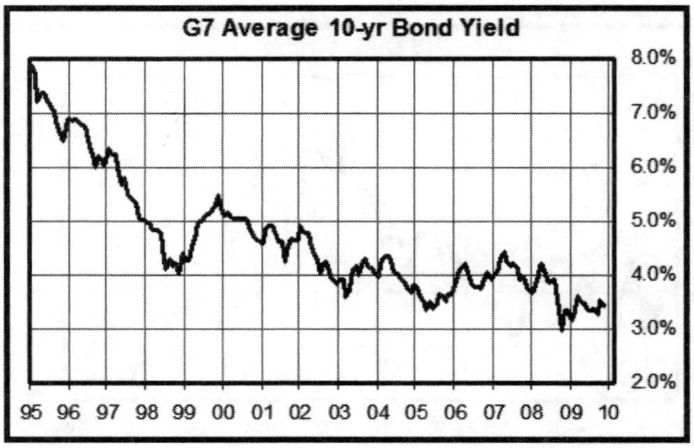

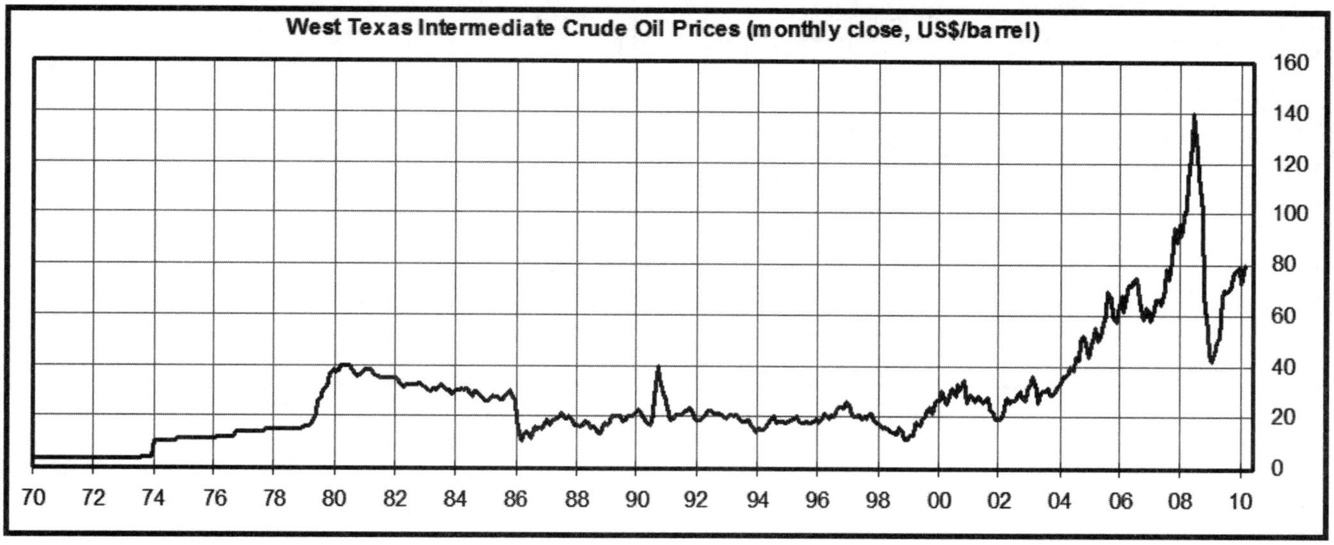

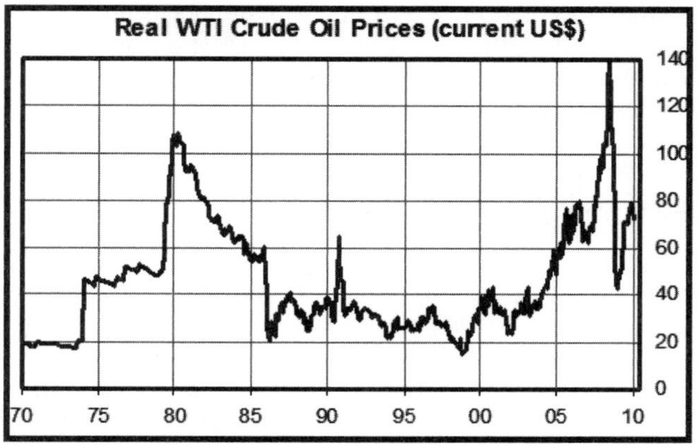

NYMEX West Texas Intermediate crude oil futures prices in 2009 partially recovered from the plunge seen in the second half of 2008 and traded in the narrow range of about $60-85 per barrel in the second half of 2009. Oil prices are now back within OPEC's target range after the sharp volatility seen in the past several years.

Oil prices from 2004 to 2008 more than quadrupled and hit a record high of $147 per barrel in July 2008. That rally was driven in its early stages by the overall bull market in commodities that was tied to the weak dollar and the emergence of strong demand from China and other developing nations. Oil prices in 2007 accelerated upward from the $60 area up to the record high of $147. That leg of the rally was supported, not only by developing country demand, but also by OPEC production cuts of 1.2 million barrels per day in November 2006 and another 500,000 bpd in February 2007. Oil prices in the first half of 2008 ran to the record high of $147.27 in July 2008 on a combination of a weak dollar and heavy speculative inflows of capital into the energy and commodity markets.

As oil prices during 2007 progressively rallied toward $100 per barrel, OPEC started boosting its production to take advantage of high oil prices and to try to curb the speculative fever. Moderate OPEC members such as Saudi Arabia also boosted production to try to prevent a world recession in response to the surge in oil prices. OPEC production (excluding Iraq) rose sharply by 15% starting in mid-2007 from 26.415 million barrels per day (bpd) to a peak of 30.315 million bpd in July 2008.

Finally in July 2008, the oil and commodity bubble burst and oil and commodity prices plunged through the end of 2008. The sell-off was initially due to the rally in the dollar that started in July 2008 and to emerging global economic weakness. World oil demand, in fact, fell by 4.7% from the peak of 86.9 million bpd in November 2007 to the 4-year low of 82.8 million bpd posted in May 2009. The oil and commodity sell-off was spurred on by heavy long

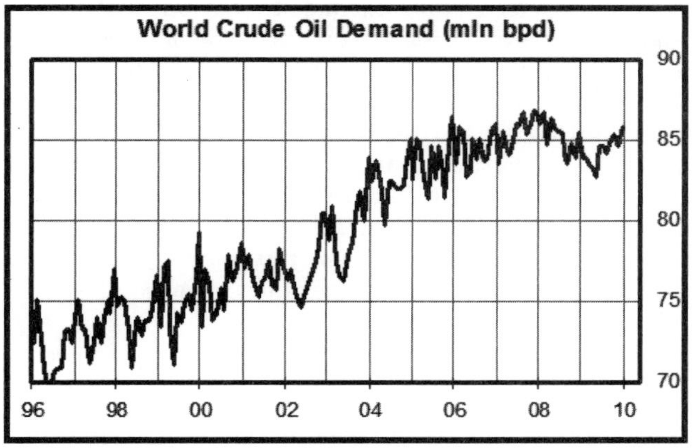

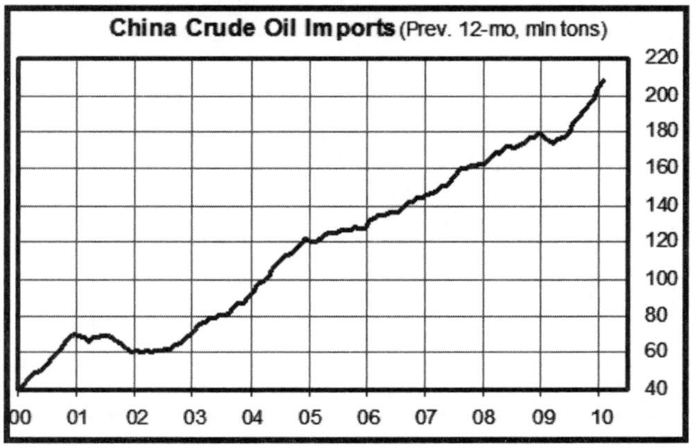

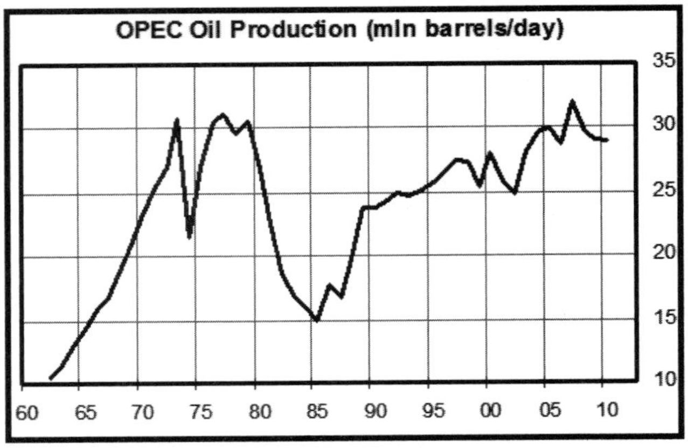

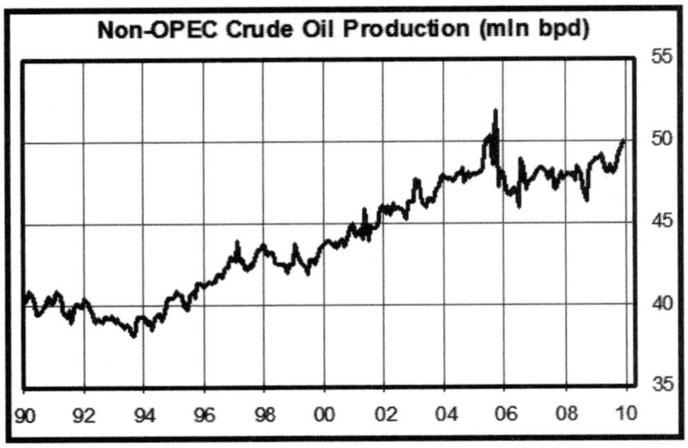

liquidation pressure by speculators who were washed out of their long positions by the financial crisis, which exploded in September 2008. Oil prices plunged to a 5-year low of $32.40 per barrel by December 2008.

OPEC responded to the free-fall in oil prices by slashing production. From the peak of 30.315 million bpd in July 2008, OPEC (ex-Iraq) cut production by 16.5% to 25.320 million bpd by March 2009. That production cut, combined with a small increase in demand stemming from gasoline prices below $2 per gallon, was finally enough to allow crude oil prices to stage a recovery rally in the first half of 2009.

Crude oil prices in the latter half of 2009 and early 2010 then traded sideways in the relatively narrow range of about $60-85 per barrel. As the U.S. and global economies recovered in the second half of 2009, oil demand strengthened by 3.6% from the 6-year low of 82.8 million bpd posted in May 2009 to the 20-month high of 85.8 million bpd posted in December 2009.

The improved demand seen in the latter half of 2009 did not boost oil prices, however, since OPEC members during the latter half of 2009 slowly boosted production to increase their revenues. Specifically, OPEC production (ex-Iraq) crept higher to a 1-year high of 26.65 million bpd by December 2009, which was up by 5.3% from the low of 25.32 million bpd seen in March 2009. OPEC implemented a 4.2 million bpd cut in its quota to 24.845 million bpd effective January 2009. However, OPEC members never even came close to cutting production to that level and OPEC members in early 2010 were over-producing by about 1.8 million bpd.

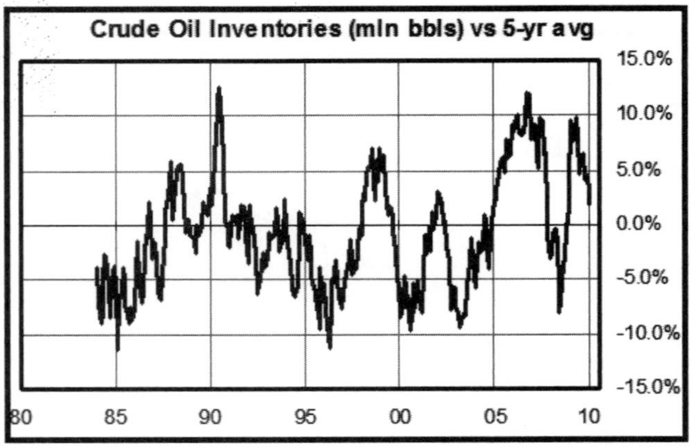

The stronger demand seen for oil in the latter half of 2009 was sufficient to absorb supplies and progressively push down inventories. U.S. oil inventories, which were 10.5% above their 5-year seasonal average in April 2009, fell during 2009 and were only 2% above their 5-year seasonal average by February 2010. The decline in inventories supported oil prices and allowed OPEC to slowly boost its production.

Looking ahead, crude oil prices may remain in a trading range near current levels over at least the next year but then see renewed strength once the global expansion kicks into full gear. It is important to remember that the OPEC cartel usually holds significant control over oil prices, mainly through production fine-tuning by Saudi Arabia. Right now, oil prices are right where OPEC wants them to be and OPEC is likely to enforce that range in coming months. Saudi Arabian Oil Minister Ali al-Naimi said in December 2009 when oil prices were in the high-$70 area that the oil price "is perfect." He said "investors, consumers and producers—they're all very happy." The Kuwaiti oil minister echoed those comments by saying that Kuwait is "comfortable" with the range of $70 to $80 for oil prices. OPEC wants to keep prices high enough to produce strong revenue for OPEC members, but not so high as to cause a global recession or to encourage large-scale switching to alternative energy sources.

The longer-term outlook for oil prices will become more bullish once the global expansion picks up steam. The reality is that most of the cheap oil has already been found in the earth's crust. Major new sources of oil can usually be found only in very remote places or under miles of ocean, or need to be extracted from oil shale or tar sands, which is an expensive process. The marginal cost of developing new oil supplies is in the neighborhood of $75-80 per barrel. Oil producers will only invest the huge sums of capital that are necessary to find new oil supplies if oil prices stay consistently above the cost of extracting new reserves plus a reasonable profit margin. Lagging supply is likely to become a major factor again once the global economic expansion gains steam, thus having the potential to push oil prices up from the current range.

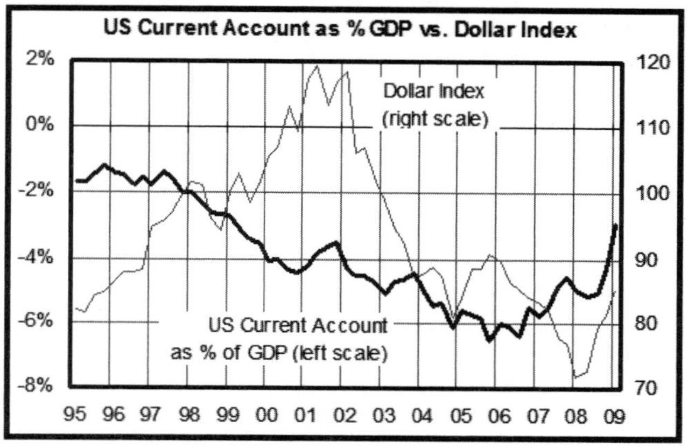

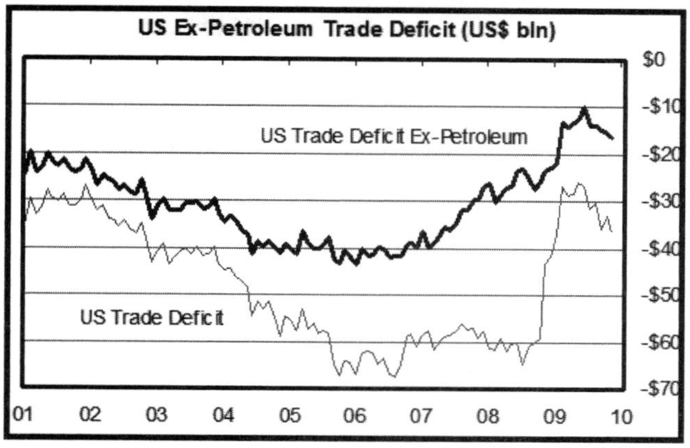

The U.S. dollar index is now back to where it was before the financial crisis sparked a temporary rally. The dollar index rallied sharply during the financial crisis as financial institutions and large investors fled into dollar liquidity in order to get through the financial crisis. The Federal Reserve during the financial crisis was forced to dramatically boost its currency swap lines with foreign central banks in order to ensure that there was adequate dollar liquidity in Europe, Asia and elsewhere. The dollar was also boosted during the financial crisis by U.S. investors who engaged in a wholesale dumping of overseas investments and brought their capital back home, thus forcing them to buy dollars to repatriate their capital.

The dollar index peaked in March 2009, however, and then spent most of the rest of 2009 in a downtrend. The dollar fell during 2009 as the financial crisis abated and as investors lightened up on their emergency dollar liquidity. The dollar also fell during 2009 as large traders used the dollar for the carry trade, borrowing cheap money in dollars and then selling those dollars to move into higher-yielding investments in other currencies.

The dollar's weakness finally ended in November 2009 when the dollar index bottomed out at 74.227, moderately above the record low of 70.698 posted in March 2008. The dollar index then rallied fairly sharply during December 2009 and January 2010, driven higher by short-covering, improved U.S. economic data, and weakness in the euro tied to budget crises in Greece, Portugal and Spain. The U.S. economic data in the latter half of 2009 was substantially stronger than in Europe or Japan, thus providing a boost for the dollar. U.S. GDP grew by a hefty +5.7% in Q4, stronger than +4.6% in Japan and much stronger than +0.4% in the Euro-Zone.

In the bigger picture, the dollar index may be in the process of bottoming out after the long bear market seen from 2002-2008. The dollar index is near the lowest levels seen since currencies started floating in 1973. The dollar has fallen by enough to spark a sharp improvement in the U.S. trade deficit, excluding petroleum, over the past several years. The U.S. trade deficit ex-petroleum posted a multi-decade low of $9.7 billion in June 2009, before slowly widening again in the latter half of 2009. However, the narrower U.S. trade deficit ex-petroleum suggests that the dollar has fallen far enough to bring the trade balance closer to zero by making exports less expensive and imports more expensive.

The problem for the U.S. trade deficit, however, is that the U.S. appetite for imported petroleum will continue for at least the next two decades regardless of the price of oil or the level of the dollar, thus keeping the overall U.S. trade deficit somewhat high. The U.S. trade deficit in petroleum was near $20 billion in November 2009, accounting for 55% of the overall U.S. trade deficit. The U.S. current account deficit has improved sharply to 3% of GDP from the peak of 5.2% of GDP seen in 2008. However, as long as the U.S. is running trade and current account deficits, dollars are flowing overseas and there is downward pressure on the dollar to the extent that overseas investors and financial

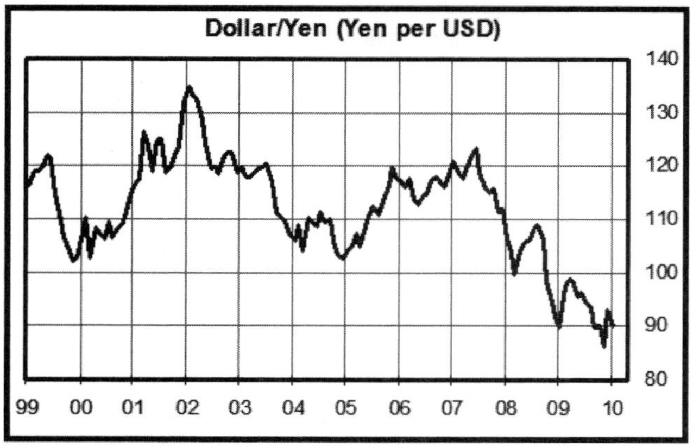

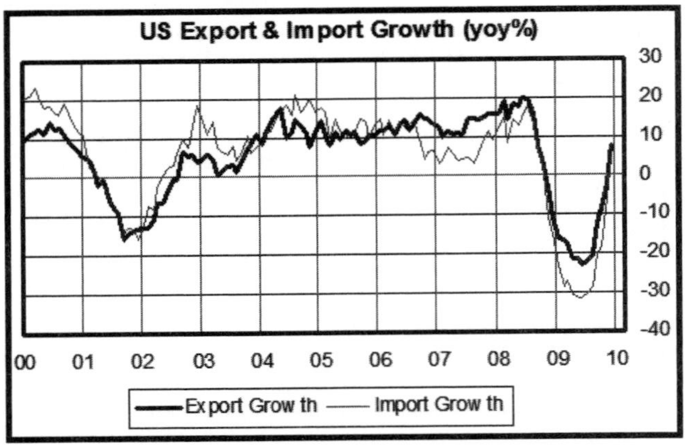

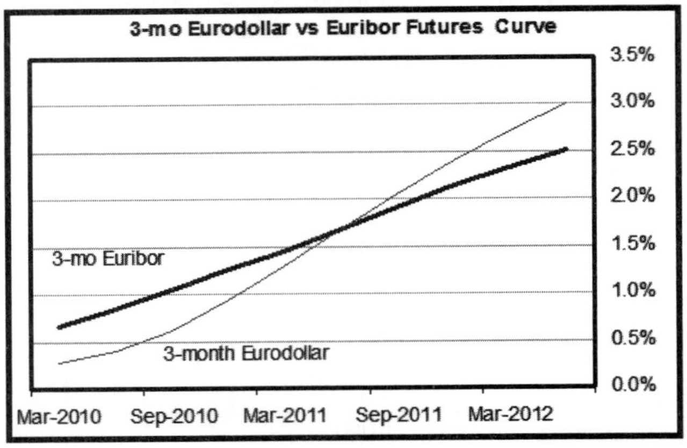

institutions do not want to hold the dollar. In short, the continued large U.S. trade deficit is likely to keep the dollar from showing any major rally.

Another long-term bearish factor for the dollar is that central banks would like to reduce their dollar risks by reducing the percentage of reserves that are held in dollars. In fact, the data already shows that the euro is gaining ground as a reserve currency. The percentage of reserves held in dollars fell to a record low of 61.6% in Q3-2009, down by 9.4 percentage points from 71.0% in 1999. Meanwhile, the percentage of reserves held in euros rose to a record high of 27.7%, up by 9.8 percentage points from 17.9% in 1999. The dollar will remain the primary global reserve currency in coming decades and its primacy was proven by the flight into dollars seen during the global financial crisis. Nevertheless, central banks are likely to slowly diversify their reserves away from dollars in coming years, thus providing a mildly bearish factor for the dollar over the long term.

The interest rate differential situation for the U.S. dollar is bearish versus the euro but bullish versus the yen. The U.S. 3-month Libor rate in mid-February 2010 was at 0.25%, which was well below the 3-month Euribor rate of 0.61% and therefore provided a bearish factor for the dollar versus the euro. The futures market indicates that the market consensus is that U.S. 3-month rates will remain below European rates until 2012. The European Central Bank (ECB) was less aggressive than the Fed in responding to the global financial crisis and that is a bullish factor for the euro. The ECB stopped cutting rates at 1.00% whereas the Fed cut its funds rate target to the range of zero to 0.25%. In addition, the ECB, unlike the Fed, did not engage in the quantitative easing move of buying government bonds and a huge amount of mortgage securities, which is another supportive factor for the euro versus the dollar. Against the yen, the dollar fares better on the interest rate differential situation since the Fed is likely to start raising interest rates well before the Bank of Japan does, thus providing a bullish factor for the dollar versus the yen.

The euro in early 2010 fell on concern about the debt crises in the so-called "PIGS" countries of Portugal, Ireland, Greece and Spain. Concern about Greece's massive budget deficit produced talk about the possible ejection of Greece from the Euro-Zone. While any breakup in the euro region is extremely unlikely, the fact remains that huge budget deficits in the PIGS countries illustrate that a lack of fiscal discipline is a key weakness of the concept of European Monetary Union. EU officials were forced to imply that Greece would receive some sort of bail-out if necessary, although officials refused to provide any details that might reduce the political will of Greek politicians to put their fiscal house in order. Tighter fiscal policy in southern Europe will put pressure on the ECB to keep its extraordinarily easy monetary policy in place longer than it might otherwise wish.

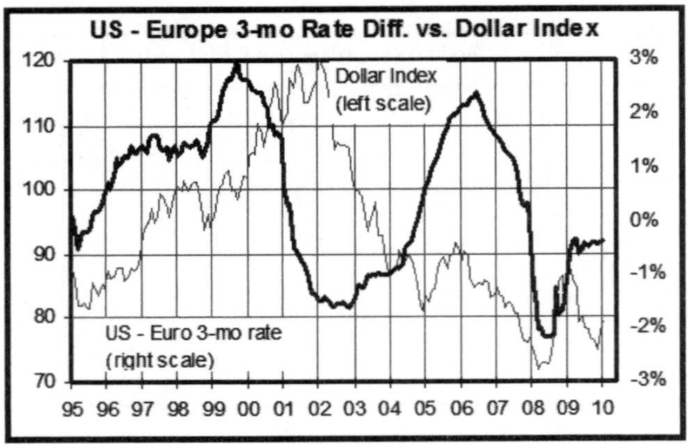

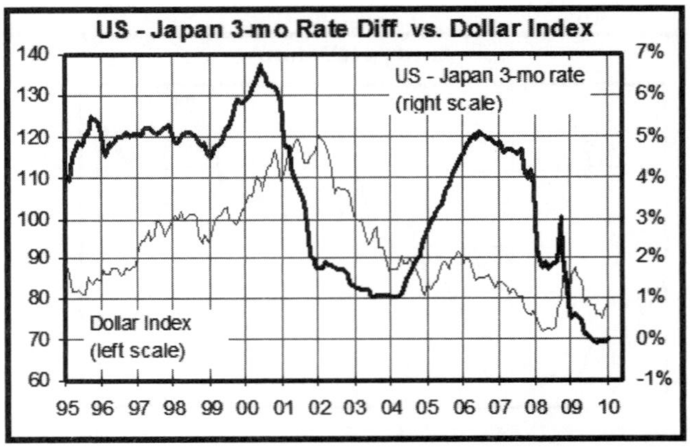

Central banks across the globe engaged in extraordinary measures to offset the effects of the financial crisis that started in 2006 with the meltdown in the U.S. mortgage and housing markets and ultimately mushroomed into a crisis of global proportions when Lehman Brothers was forced into bankruptcy on September 15, 2008. World GDP still has a long way to go to return to pre-recession levels, but the worst of the crisis is over and economic growth has resumed in most nations. The Bloomberg Financial Conditions Index, as seen in the chart below, shows that financial risk measures have largely returned to normal. However, the world's central banks now face the difficult problem of timing the withdrawal of their extraordinary stimulus measures.

During the Great Depression, the Federal Reserve was overly optimistic and tightened credit too soon, thus forcing the U.S. economy into a renewed slump. Federal Reserve Chairman Ben Bernanke, a student of the Depression, is well aware of that episode and recognizes the risks that tightening too soon in the current environment could spark a renewed financial crisis and push the U.S. and world economy back into recession. While U.S. GDP showed growth in the second half of 2009, the financial system is still fragile, government budget deficits have exploded, the U.S. housing crisis is not yet over, consumers are reluctant to spend money given the weak housing and labor markets, and businesses have little confidence in the macroeconomic outlook. The Fed, therefore, knows that it needs to withdraw liquidity very carefully, fast enough to prevent inflation but not so fast as to create a new financial crisis or push the U.S. economy back into recession.

The Fed responded aggressively to the financial crisis with a wide range of measures. The Fed started cutting its federal funds rate target in October 2007 from 5.25% when the housing crisis started to emerge. By February 2008 the Fed had cut the funds rate to 3.00% and by early 2009 the Fed cut the funds rate to the range of zero to 0.25%. After the financial crisis blew up into global proportions in September 2008, the Fed began a broad range of liquidity programs to lend money not only to banks, but also to securities firms and directly into the commercial paper and mortgage markets. The Fed, in a quantitative easing move, also purchased $300 billion in Treasury securities from March through September 2009, directly monetizing U.S. government debt and permanently injecting reserves into the banking system. The Fed in January 2009 also began a program of buying $1.25 trillion in agency mortgage-backed securities and about $175 billion of agency debt securities, a program that is due to be wrapped up by March 2010. That program kept mortgage rates down and helped to revive the mortgage securitization market. The Fed's liquidity measures caused the Fed's assets to quickly balloon from the normal level near $900 billion to the $2.3 trillion area by the end of 2008 (see chart on next page). The Fed's assets remained $1.0-1.4 trillion above normal all through 2009 and into early 2010.

The Fed's excess liquidity caused the monetary base, which is the basic stuff of bank lending, to soar by $1.2 trillion from late-2008 through early 2010 (see chart on the next page). Yet banks have not used those excess reserves to lend new money to customers because of the dearth of credit-worthy customers and because banks are still trying to rebuild their capital bases in order to get on a sound financial footing going forward. In fact, U.S. bank lending plunged by $730 billion from $7.34 trillion in October 2008 to $6.61 trillion by February 2010 and is still headed lower. On a year-on-year basis, U.S. bank lending collapsed to the –8% y/y area, the largest decline in bank lending seen in post-war history (see the chart below). The Fed is caught in a classic liquidity trap where its monetary policy is "pushing a string" since even a massive quantity of excess reserves has been unable to stimulate bank lending.

The Fed is clearly running a big risk if it keeps that excess liquidity in the financial system too long because it will eventually cause an asset bubble and a big inflation outbreak. The Fed is also running the risk of causing an upward spike in bond yields if the bond market suddenly loses confidence in the Fed's anti-inflation resolve. So far, inflation expectations remain under control at +2.3%, roughly where they were in 2006-07 before the crisis emerged (see chart on next page).

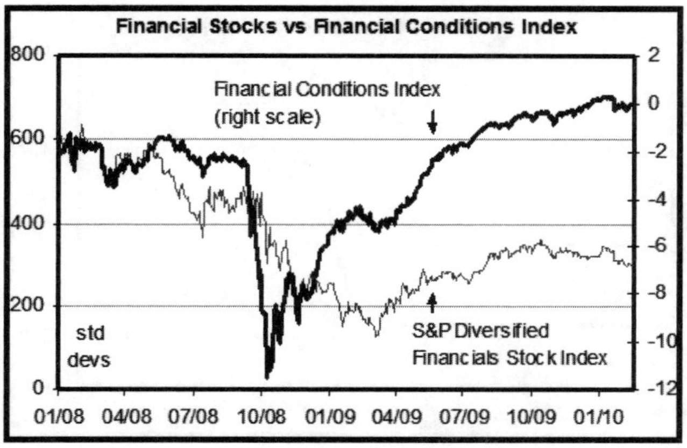

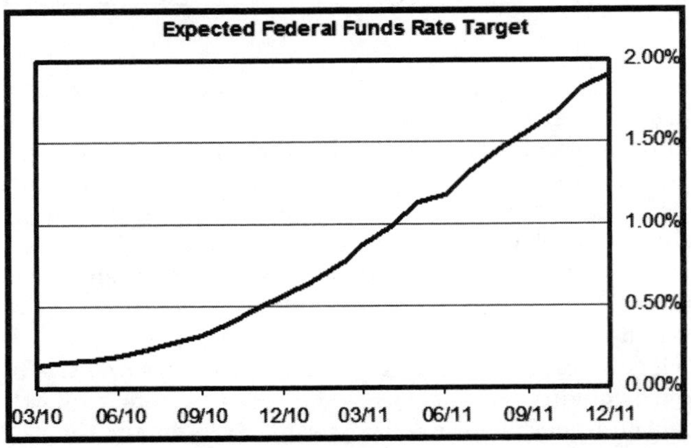

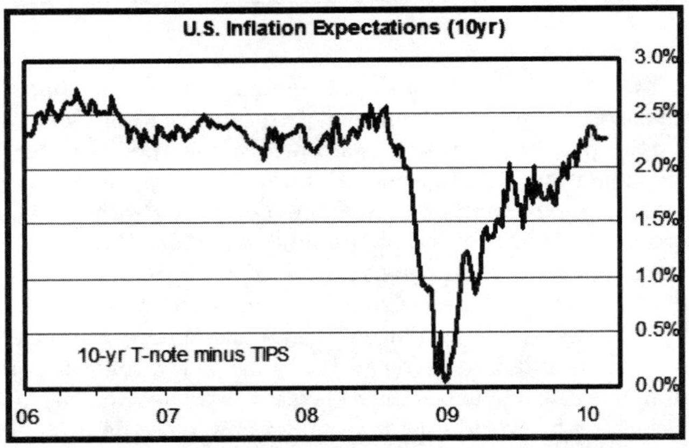

The Fed has so far been able to keep inflation expectations under control by ending some of its liquidity programs and publicly discussing its liquidity exit plan. Importantly, the Fed ended its quantitative easing program of buying government bonds in September 2009. The Fed plans to end its mortgage security purchase program in March 2010. In addition, the Fed on February 18, 2010, surprised the market by raising its discount rate by 25 bp to 0.75%, seeking to wean banks off emergency lending at the penalty discount rate and encourage those banks to return to the private market.

Fed Chairman Ben Bernanke in early February 2010 released testimony outlining the Fed's exit plan. The Fed indicated that it has no plans to raise the federal funds rate target in the near future, sticking to its language that rates would remain "exceptionally low" for an "extended period." The market as of February 2010 is not expecting the Fed to start raising the funds rate until late 2010. The Fed has already said that raising the funds rate target will come later after it first starts to drain excess liquidity from the banking system. The Fed plans to drain reserves via large reverse repo operations, where the Fed borrows cash from banks in return for collateral. The Fed also plans to drain reserves from the banking system by encouraging banks to deposit excess cash with the Fed in its deposit facility. Over time, these reserve draining operations, combined with the natural roll-off of various loan programs and a slow rise in deposit rates and the federal funds rate, will slowly return monetary policy to more normal levels and inflation risks will dissipate.

The European Central Bank (ECB) has also started its exit strategy. Most of the ECB's excess liquidity will be withdrawn automatically as the ECB's various lending operations expire and are not rolled over. In fact, the ECB's assets at the end of 2009 were already down by 9.5% to 1.9 trillion euros from 2.1 trillion euros at the beginning of the year. The ECB has already announced that there will be no more 12-month lending operations, which totaled 614 billion euros in 2009 and were instrumental in pushing down short-term rates. The ECB has also announced that it will end its emergency 6-month lending operations by March 2010 and will go back to its normal short-term operations of three months and less, which gives the ECB better control over reserve levels.

The ECB has also said that its guarantee of unlimited liquidity to the banking system will end on April 13, 2010, meaning the ECB will then go back to its normal system of rationing liquidity to meet its reserve, money supply, and interest rate targets. The ECB's program to buy 60 billion euros worth of covered bonds will end in June 2010. The ECB instituted that program to funnel liquidity into the covered bond market, which are bonds that are issued by banks to provide funds for mortgages and loans to public entities. The ECB as of February 2010 was about 60% through that program, having purchased 38 billion euros worth of covered bonds. Regarding interest rates, the market consensus is that the ECB will start raising its key 2-week refinancing rate from the 1.00% level starting in late 2010.

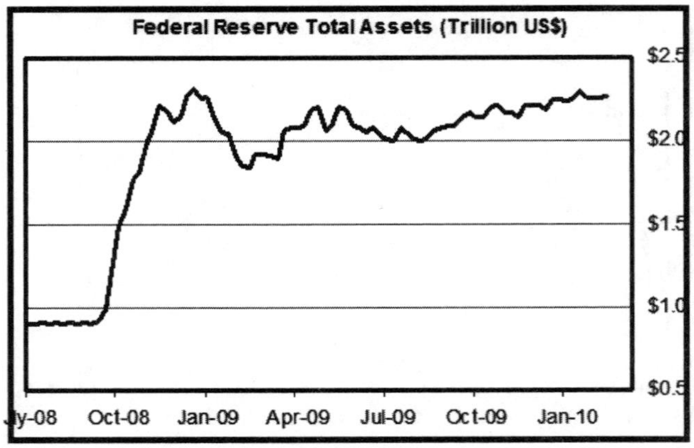

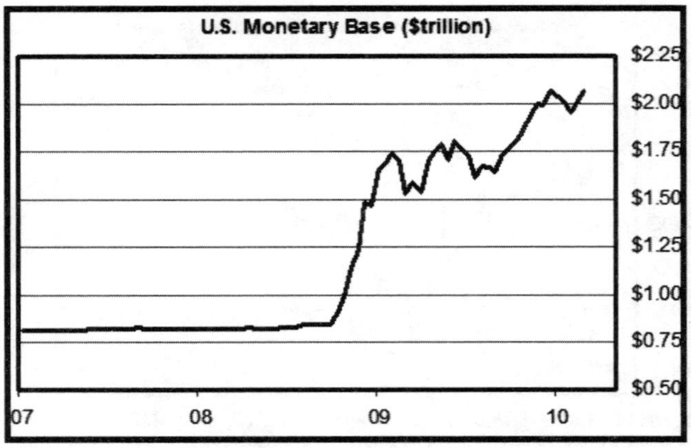

The U.S. Environmental Protection Agency (EPA) in February 2010 released its second Renewable Fuels Standard (RFS2), which specifies renewable fuel mandates for coming years. For 2010, the mandate requires that 12.95 billion gallons of renewable fuel be used by blenders, representing 8.25% of the overall U.S. fuel supply.

Almost all of the renewable fuel mandate for 2010 will be met by corn-based ethanol with a requirement of 12.0 billion gallons. The RFS2 mandate calls for only small quantities of cellulosic ethanol (100 million gallons) and other advanced biofuels, simply because those nascent industries are currently very limited in how much fuel they can produce. Cellulosic ethanol is ethanol that is produced from plant matter such as corn cobs, straw grass, etc. Cellulosic ethanol production is just coming out of the research stage with several pilot plants now operating around the U.S.

The RFS2 mandate for corn-based ethanol rises from 12.0 billion gallons in 2010 to a maximum of 15.0 billion gallons starting in 2015. The U.S. government has capped its corn-based ethanol mandate at 15.0 billion gallons simply because there is not enough land in the U.S. to grow more corn for ethanol without severely impacting the food supply. In the current 2009/10 marketing year, the USDA estimates that ethanol producers will use 4.3 billion bushels of corn, which represents 32.7% of the U.S. corn crop of 13.151 billion bushels. That means that nearly one-third of the U.S. corn crop is currently being used to produce ethanol rather than to supply the food chain. Yet corn prices remain subdued due to the record-sized corn crop this past summer.

The USDA estimates that the percentage of the corn crop used for ethanol will reach a maximum of about 35% in 2012 and then remain at that level. However, that assumes a steady increase in U.S. corn production due to trend increases in yield. If the U.S. corn crop does not increase, then the 15 billion gallon ethanol mandate would take as much as 40% of the U.S. corn crop.

The EPA's RFS2 mandate makes clear that the future of U.S. biofuel is cellulosic and other advanced biofuels and not corn-based ethanol. The requirement for advanced biofuels rises sharply from negligible quantities at present to 21 billion gallons by 2022. Combined with 15 billion gallons in corn-based ethanol, the total biofuel requirement is 36 billion gallons by 2022. The means that 20-22% of the U.S. fuel supply by 2022 will come from biofuels and will eliminate the need for 36 billion gallons of gasoline each year. Clearly biofuels are an important component of the U.S. energy policy of reducing dependence on foreign oil since biofuels are produced at home whereas the U.S. imports a net 57% of its petroleum.

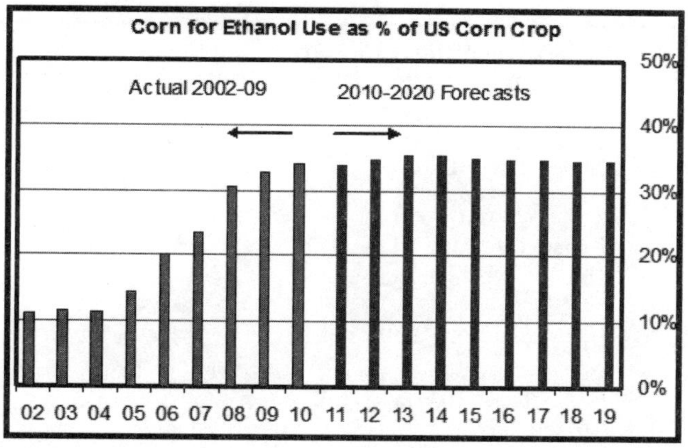

Biofuels are the major reason why some global oil company officials believe that the amount of gasoline they sell in the U.S. peaked in 2007 and will never again reach that level. U.S. gasoline usage is being diminished not only by biofuels but also by improved mileage and the advent of gasoline-electric hybrids and other alternative vehicles of the future including natural gas, electric and fuel cell vehicles.

The increasing use of biofuels in the U.S. fuel mix is also a key component of the U.S. government's policy of reducing greenhouse gas (GHG) emissions. The EPA's RFS2 report determined that corn-based ethanol reduces GHG emissions by 21% against a gasoline baseline and that cellulosic ethanol achieves a GHG reduction of 72-130% depending on feedstock and conversion process.

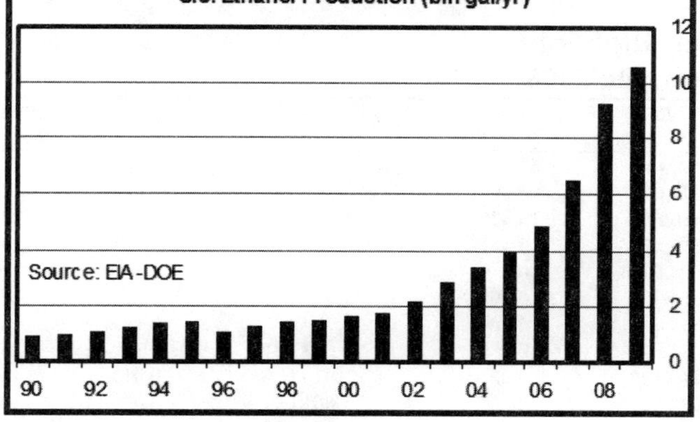

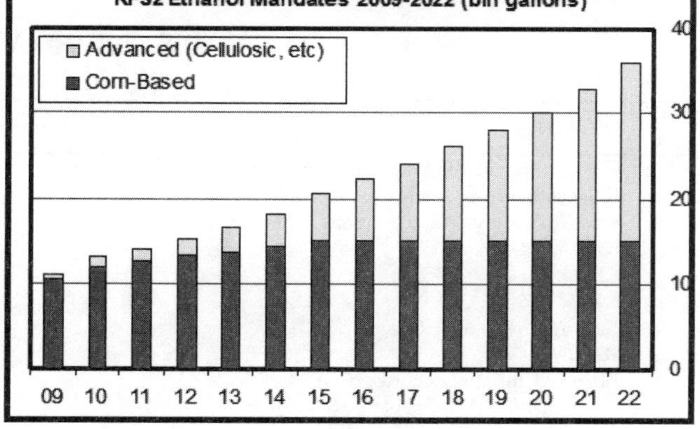

Volume - U.S.

U.S. Futures Volume Highlights
2009 in Comparison with 2008

2009 Rank	Top 50 Contracts Traded in 2009	2009 Contracts	%	2008 Contracts	%	2008 Rank
1	E-Mini S&P 500 Index, CME	556,314,143	19.50%	633,889,466	22.22%	1
2	Eurodollars (3-month), CME	437,585,193	15.34%	596,974,081	20.93%	2
3	T-Notes (10-year), CBT	189,852,019	6.66%	256,770,689	9.00%	3
4	Crude Oil, NYMEX	137,428,494	4.82%	134,674,264	4.72%	5
5	T-Notes (5-year), CBT	98,391,120	3.45%	168,127,469	5.89%	4
6	E-Mini NASDAQ 100, CME	77,972,143	2.73%	108,734,456	3.81%	6
7	T-Bonds (30-year), CBT	62,232,671	2.18%	89,464,546	3.14%	7
8	Euro FX, CME	54,393,644	1.91%	53,652,590	1.88%	11
9	Corn, CBT	50,948,804	1.79%	59,957,118	2.10%	9
10	T-Notes (2-year), CBT	48,158,948	1.69%	79,311,002	2.78%	8
11	Natural Gas, NYMEX	47,951,353	1.68%	38,730,519	1.36%	13
12	Mini ($5) Dow Jones Industrial Index, CBT	39,889,836	1.40%	55,348,312	1.94%	10
13	E-Mini Russell 2000 Index, ICE	38,686,673	1.36%	16,526,331	0.58%	26
14	Soybeans, CBT	35,758,855	1.25%	36,373,096	1.28%	15
15	Gold (100 oz.), COMEX Div. of NYMEX	35,139,541	1.23%	38,377,367	1.35%	14
16	Sugar #11, NYBOT	27,300,259	0.96%	27,019,704	0.95%	18
17	Henry Hub Swap, NYMEX	25,670,240	0.90%	31,401,575	1.10%	17
18	British Pound, CME	24,853,787	0.87%	20,497,378	0.72%	20
19	Japanese Yen, CME	22,749,569	0.80%	32,844,404	1.15%	16
20	Heating Oil #2, NYMEX	21,426,015	0.75%	19,583,052	0.69%	21
21	Gasoline, RBOB, NYMEX	21,159,516	0.74%	20,522,571	0.72%	19
22	Wheat, CBT	17,677,547	0.62%	19,011,928	0.67%	23
23	Soybean Oil, CBT	17,132,082	0.60%	16,928,361	0.59%	24
24	Australian Dollar, CME	16,732,682	0.59%	11,212,985	0.39%	32
25	Canadian Dollar, CME	15,481,166	0.54%	11,378,024	0.40%	31
26	Soybean Meal, CBT	12,880,767	0.45%	13,354,174	0.47%	28
27	Natural Gas Penultimate Swap, NYMEX	12,352,928	0.43%	12,352,928	0.43%	29
28	Swiss Franc, CME	10,618,630	0.37%	14,814,153	0.52%	27
29	S&P 500 Index, CME	10,435,912	0.37%	16,763,071	0.59%	25
30	Federal Funds (30-day), CBT	10,349,071	0.36%	19,434,295	0.68%	22
31	E-mini S&P MidCap 400 Index	9,133,223	0.32%	8,580,467	0.30%	35
32	Live Cattle, CME	8,797,033	0.31%	9,801,360	0.34%	33
33	Silver (5,000 oz)	7,990,528	0.28%	8,917,183	0.31%	34
34	Lean Hogs, CME	6,819,061	0.24%	8,505,138	0.30%	36
35	PJM Western Hub Day Ahead Off-Peak	6,810,613	0.24%	231,232	0.01%	
36	High Grade Copper, NYMEX	6,398,967	0.22%	4,618,074	0.16%	42
37	Mexican Peso, CME	4,298,939	0.15%	5,302,297	0.19%	40
38	Coffee "C", NYBOT	4,235,349	0.15%	5,446,516	0.19%	39
39	Nikkei 225 Index (JPY), CME	4,167,340	0.15%	4,769,567	0.17%	41
40	Rogers International TRAKRS, CME	3,686,161	0.13%	11,621,869	0.41%	30
41	Wheat, KCBT	3,660,343	0.13%	3,778,266	0.13%	44
42	Cotton #2, NYBOT	3,574,995	0.13%	6,162,963	0.22%	37
43	E-Mini Crude Oil, NYMEX	3,368,983	0.12%	5,641,145	0.20%	38
44	Cocoa, NYBOT	3,086,966	0.11%	3,592,268	0.13%	46
45	Nikkei 225 Index (USD), CME	2,935,616	0.10%	4,399,966	0.15%	43
46	PJM PSEG Day Ahead Off-Peak	2,801,488	0.10%	18,240	0.00%	
47	Single Stock Futures	2,624,496	0.09%	3,404,201	0.12%	
49	US Dollar Index	2,523,927	0.09%	1,825,326	0.06%	49
48	NEPOOL INTR HUB 5mw Day Ahead Off-Peak	2,433,442	0.09%			
50	Mini New York Gold	2,122,569	0.07%	675,114	0.02%	
	Top 50 Contracts	2,268,993,647	97.46%	2,751,321,101	96.45%	
	Contracts Below the Top 50	59,120,881	2.54%	101,284,123	3.55%	
	TOTAL	2,328,114,528	100.00%	2,852,605,224	100.00%	

* For 2008 Top 50 contracts totaled 2,803,617,668 including 5 contracts that are not among 2009's Top 50.

U.S. Futures Volume Highlights
2009 in Comparison with 2008

2009 Rank	EXCHANGE	2009 Contracts	%	2008 Contracts	%	2008 Rank
1	Chicago Mercantile Exchange (CME Group)	1,276,264,462	54.82%	1,612,884,857	56.54%	1
2	Chicago Board of Trade (CME Group)	587,977,047	25.26%	825,257,796	28.93%	2
3	New York Mercantile Exchange (CME Group)	362,426,620	15.57%	338,490,891	11.87%	3
4	ICE Futures U.S.	81,715,275	3.51%	63,433,647	2.22%	4
5	ELX	5,003,983	0.21%			
6	NYSE Liffe U.S.	4,474,734	0.19%	1,831,941	0.06%	7
7	Kansas City Board of Trade (KCBT)	3,660,343	0.16%	3,778,266	0.13%	6
8	OneChicago	2,983,148	0.13%	4,012,281	0.14%	5
9	Chicago Climate Exchange (CCFE)	1,246,123	0.05%	370,505	0.01%	10
10	Minneapolis Grain Exchange (MGE)	1,206,824	0.05%	1,361,067	0.05%	8
11	CBOE Futures Exchange (CFE)	1,155,969	0.05%	1,161,397	0.04%	9
	Total Futures	2,850,773,583	100.00%	2,644,564,674	100.00%	

Chicago Climate Futures Exchange (CCFE)

FUTURE	CONTRACT UNIT	2009	2008	2007	2006
CA Climate Action Registry-Climate Res		684			
Carbon Financial Instrument (CFI)		13,973	29,405	3,566	
Carbon Financial Instrument (CFI-US)		891			
Carbon Financial Instrument Offsets (CFI-		50			
Event Linked (IFEX)		4,499	10,373	2,321	
Event Linked (IFEX) FLW		1,860	2		
Nitrogen Financial Instrument - Annual		209,223	21,730	205	
Nitrogen Financial Instrument (NFI-OS)		808	1,348	3,465	
Renewable Energy Certificate Funds-		261			
Renewable Energy Certificate Funds-New		2,262			
Regional Greenhouse Gas Initiatives		693,863	17,043		
Sulfur Financial Instrument (SFI)		317,749	289,398	181,030	28,924
Total Futures		1,246,123	370,505	191,899	28,924

CBOE Futures Exchange (CFE)

FUTURE	CONTRACT UNIT	2009	2008	2007	2006	2005
CBOE Volatility Index (VIX)	100 USD x Index	1,144,858	1,088,105	1,046,475	434,478	128,927
CBOE Mini-Volatility Index (VM)		9,268				
CBOE S&P 500 12-Month Variance (VA)	50 USD per var pt	31	940	56	210	
DJIA Volatility Index (VXD)	100 USD x Index	1,019	40,706	43,555	38,892	9,546
Russell 2000 Volatility Index (RVX)		670	26,956	30,011		
S&P 500 3-Month Variance (VTI)	50 USD per point	123	2,078	9,302	3,787	5,033
Total Futures		1,155,969	1,161,397	1,136,295	478,424	177,632

Chicago Board of Trade (CBT)

FUTURE	CONTRACT UNIT	2009	2008	2007	2006	2005
Wheat	5,000 bu	17,677,547	19,011,928	19,582,706	16,224,871	10,114,098
Mini Wheat	1,000 bu	61,355	70,971	79,282	67,637	32,295
Corn	5,000 bu	50,948,804	59,957,118	54,520,152	47,239,893	27,965,057
Mini Corn	1,000 bu	203,474	219,562	156,210	162,545	102,292
Oats	5,000 bu	314,305	441,588	432,741	427,315	351,539
Soybeans	5,000 bu	35,758,855	36,373,096	31,726,316	22,647,784	20,216,137
Mini Soybeans	1,000 bu	466,367	475,231	540,940	581,047	495,313
Soybean Oil	60,000 lbs	17,132,082	16,928,361	13,170,914	9,488,524	7,676,130
Soybean Meal	100 tons	12,880,767	13,354,174	12,213,315	9,350,043	8,324,616
Rough Rice	200,000 lbs	277,065	362,565	358,905	321,330	228,502
T-Bonds (30-year)	100,000 USD	62,232,671	89,464,546	107,630,211	93,754,895	86,926,569
T-Notes (10-year)	100,000 USD	189,852,019	256,770,689	349,229,371	255,571,869	215,124,076
T-Notes (5-year)	100,000 USD	98,391,120	168,127,469	166,207,391	124,870,313	121,908,830
T-Notes (3-year)		268,622				
T-Notes (2-year)	200,000 USD	48,158,948	79,311,002	68,610,392	37,966,797	21,205,359
Interest Rate Swap (30-year)	100,000 USD	55,228	80,169	12,555		
Interest Rate Swap (10-year)	100,000 USD	871,074	1,004,309	848,372	520,090	655,711
Interest Rate Swap (7-year)	100,000 USD	21,957	320			
Interest Rate Swap (5-year)	100,000 USD	1,331,017	1,147,170	551,505	272,749	202,737
30-Day Federal Funds	5,000,000 USD	10,349,071	19,434,295	16,597,188	17,833,331	11,602,282
Ethanol	29,000 US Gallons	67,168	29,451	12,516	5,564	2,676
OTC Ethanol Forward Swap	14,500 US Gallons	270,596	249,147	60,729	42	
Ethanol Los Angeles Basis Swap	14,500 US Gallons	425	126			
Dow Jones Industrial Index ($25)	25 USD x Index	3,867	12,392	14,301	18,686	
Dow Jones Industrial Index ($10)	10 USD x Index	395,584	1,147,657	1,483,817	1,919,847	1,787,405
Mini Dow Jones Industrial Index ($5)	5 USD x Index	39,889,836	55,348,312	40,098,882	26,792,373	24,892,328
Dow Jones AIGER Index	100 x Index	97,223	73,445	51,651	5,990	
Total Futures		587,977,047	825,257,796	895,521,149	678,262,052	561,145,938

Chicago Mercantile Exchange (CME Group)

FUTURE	CONTRACT UNIT	2008	2007	2006	2005	2004
Live Cattle	40,000 lbs	8,797,033	9,801,360	8,587,973	8,209,698	5,833,556
Feeder Cattle	50,000 lbs	1,059,109	1,250,324	1,099,863	1,286,395	1,017,348
Lean Hogs	40,000 lbs	6,819,061	8,505,138	7,264,832	6,481,001	4,153,543
Pork Bellies, Frozen	40,000 lbs	27,852	56,705	68,409	107,564	124,418
Class III Milk	200,000 lbs	280,636	304,754	311,459	225,137	182,509
Class IV Milk	200,000 lbs	332	624	314	113	138
Nonfat Dry Milk	44,000 lbs	1,480	2,239	1,072	954	217
Deliverable Nonfat Dry Milk		2				
Butter	40,000 lbs	59	135	1,222	3,800	7,708
Cash Butter	20,000 lbs	16,983	17,495	20,067	18,673	2,337
Dry Whey		5,246	4,141	6,378		
Wood Pulp		3,364	8,740	1,038		
Random Lumber	100,000 bd ft	317,227	437,613	334,689	271,024	236,241
One Month LIBOR	3,000,000 USD	452,340	571,710	1,194,200	852,119	1,048,468
Eurodollar (3-month)	1,000,000 USD	437,585,193	596,974,081	621,470,328	502,077,391	410,355,384

Chicago Mercantile Exchange (CME Group) (continued)

FUTURE	CONTRACT UNIT	2008	2007	2006	2005	2004
E-Mini Eurodollar (5-year)		502	600	14,627	4,237	
Euroyen	1,000,000,000 JPY	40,879	122,917	561,220	662,653	200,958
3M Overnight Index Swaps (OIS)		16,159	15,358			
Australian Dollar	100,000	16,732,682	11,212,985	10,785,897	6,567,650	4,749,093
British Pound	62,500	24,853,787	20,497,378	20,799,827	16,099,540	8,769,751
Brazilian Real	100,000	30,398	67,168	127,879	94,514	23,144
Canadian Dollar	100,000	15,481,166	11,378,024	12,224,845	10,279,576	7,930,156
Czech Koruna		224	787	496	461	118
Euro FX	125,000	54,393,644	53,652,590	43,063,060	40,790,379	34,530,730
E-Mini Euro FX	62,500	664,350	774,078	491,401	386,850	642,857
Hungarian Forint	30,000,000	975	901	148	620	77
Israeli Shekel	1,000,000	7,495	3,014	3,070	113	
Japanese Yen	12,500,000	22,749,569	32,844,404	30,820,442	19,677,365	12,471,672
E-Mini Japanese Yen	6,250,000	28,906	24,657	19,116	9,203	4,887
Korean Won	125,000,000	1,411	268	2,312	5,867	
Mexican Peso	500,000	4,298,939	5,302,297	5,154,636	3,795,538	3,674,886
New Zealand Dollar	100,000	1,220,227	808,296	928,816	529,782	187,437
Norwegian Krone	227,000	11,652	7,327	10,289	6,461	3,966
Polish Zloty	500,000	19,848	20,554	25,977	23,899	15,046
Russian Ruble	2500000	162,314	213,341	173,613	125,762	45,835
South African Rand	500,000	77,848	99,413	84,376	70,491	63,379
Swedish Krona	193,600	5,396	2,436	12,374	4,618	1,884
Swiss Franc	125,000	10,618,630	14,814,153	14,478,658	11,470,031	7,784,498
Turkish Lira		12,011				
Australian Dollar / Canadian Dollar	200,000 AUD	3,582	2,762	1,749	6,708	1,797
Australian Dollar / Japanese Yen	200,000 AUD	3,493	1,088	44	19	836
Australian Dollar / New Zealand Dollar	200,000 AUD	281	1,346	903	39	1,990
British Pound / Japanese Yen	125,000 GBP	6,395	3,430	332	173	830
British Pound / Swiss Franc	125,000 GBP	2,610	702	3,031	6,151	3,209
Canadian Dollar / Japanese Yen	200,000 CAD	301	14	236	24	452
Chinese Renimibi / U.S. Dollar	1,000,000 CHR	7,024	16,790	8,179	5,407	
Swiss Franc / Japanese Yen	250,000 CHF	302	1,968	2,754	55	338
Euro / Australian Dollar	125,000 EUR	531	246	210	205	823
Euro / British Pound	125,000 EUR	125,657	73,554	80,232	42,053	39,069
Euro / Canadian Dollar	125,000 EUR	277	85	180	109	1,032
Euro / Czech Koruna	4,000,000 EUR	90	196	65		56
Euro / Hungarian Forint	30,000,000 EUR	189	193	78	1,050	10
Euro / Japanese Yen	125,000 EUR	219,109	320,060	365,895	272,182	123,805
Euro / Norwegian Krone	125,000 EUR	356	3,760	6,605	328	522
Euro / Polish Zloty	500,000	35,455	14,693	18,349	15,194	18,548
Euro / Swedish Krona	125,000 EUR	110	50	48	151	394
Euro / Swiss Franc	125,000 EUR	85,059	50,923	97,478	49,475	12,264
Euro / Turkish Lira		22,280				
E-Micro EUR/USD		424,726				
E-Micro GBP/USD		170,411				
E-Micro USD/CAD		39,809				
E-Micro USD/CHF		15,182				
E-Micro USD/JPY		94,508				
E-Micro AUD/USD		65,031				
S&P 500 Index	500 USD x Index	10,435,912	16,763,071	15,837,593	14,844,858	15,377,489
E-Mini S&P 500 Index	50 USD x Index	556,314,143	633,889,466	415,348,228	257,926,673	207,095,732
E-Mini S&P European		65	2,567			
E-mini S&P SmallCap 600 Index	100 USD x Index	66,471	107,039	28,894		
E-mini S&P MidCap 400 Index	100 USD x Index	9,133,223	8,580,467	7,352,427	5,528,263	4,885,430
S&P MidCap 400 Index	500 USD x Index	59,360	97,224	118,140	153,268	205,058
S&P Citigroup Growth	250 USD x Index	1,351	8,163	25,132	5,473	
S&P Citigroup Value	250 USD x Index	5,437	6,450	6,418	7,289	
E-Mini NASDAQ 100 Index	20 USD x Index	77,972,143	108,734,456	95,309,053	79,940,222	72,453,141
NASDAQ 100 Index	500 USD x Index	756,919	1,407,413	1,683,378	2,269,870	2,682,058
Nikkei 225 Index (USD)	5 USD x Index	2,935,616	4,399,966	3,421,085	2,809,839	1,886,270
Nikkei 225 Index (JPY)	5 USD x Index	4,167,340	4,769,567	3,290,909	2,126,654	952,618
S&P 500 Financial Sector	125 USD x Index	5,866	9,032	4,202		1,600
E-Mini MSCI EAFE	50 USD x Index	602,104	450,138	172,371	17,461	
E-mini MSCI Emerging Markets Index	50 USD x Index	324,722	171,064	26,793		
Technology SPCTR		8				
TRAKRS BXY	1 USD x Index	25,000	28,860	47,900	304,172	
TRAKRS PIMCO	1 USD x Index	792,148	3,668,906	8,712,135	24,471,474	
TRAKRS PIMCO SPTR	1 USD x Index	134,141	451,858	2,324,128	2,349,055	
Rogers International TRAKRS	1 USD x Index	3,686,161	11,621,869	17,651,395	26,486,999	36,081,429
HDD Weather	20 USD x Index	70,619	119,533	135,702	115,763	75,266
HDD Seasonal Weather Strips	20 USD x Index	3,550	6,600	12,350	13,675	50
CDD Weather	20 USD x Index	53,398	117,729	114,044	65,258	107,475
CDD Seasonal Weather Strips	20 USD x Index	2,900	3,610	7,300	8,450	
Euro HDD Weather	20 GBP x Index	16,950	4,625	3,625	3,435	7,302
Euro CAT Weather	20 GBP x Index	775	350	750	950	3,332

Chicago Mercantile Exchange (CME Group) (continued)

FUTURE	CONTRACT UNIT	2009	2008	2007	2006	2005
Euro HDD Seasonal Strip Weather	20 GBP x Index	300	2,850	1,750	1,225	
Euro CAT Seasonal Strip Weather		150				
Weekly Average Temperature	1,000 USD x Index	1,850	100	5		
CSI Housing Index	250 USD x Index	295	1,178	2,995	3,632	
Goldman Sachs Commodity Index	250 USD x Index	520,462	526,036	644,761	615,260	498,424
GSCI Excess Return Index	100 USD x Index	55,178	27,206	15,136	13,141	
S&P 500 ETF	100 shares	1,809	1,109	1,165	2,009	4,522
Russell 2000 ETF	200 shares	71	550	470	785	47
Nasdaq 100 ETF	200 shares	328	833	1,470	1,849	3,817
Total Futures		1,276,264,462	1,612,884,857	1,415,423,615	1,101,712,533	883,118,526

ELX Futures Exchange (ELX)

FUTURE	CONTRACT UNIT	2009
2-Year Treasury Note (ZTE)		1,075,171
5-Year Treasury Note (ZFE)		2,012,132
10-Year Treasury Note (ZNE)		1,322,429
30-Year Treasury Bond (ZBE)		594,251
Total Futures		5,003,983

ICE Futures U.S. (ICE)

FUTURE	CONTRACT UNIT	2008	2007	2006	2005	2004
Coffee 'C'	37,500 lbs	4,235,349	5,446,516	5,128,623	4,407,512	3,987,778
Sugar #11	112,000 lbs	27,300,259	27,019,704	21,263,799	15,100,721	13,007,072
Sugar #14	112,000 lbs	38,698	92,365	108,603	120,685	136,676
Sugar #16	112,000 lbs	66,719	250			
Cocoa	10 metric tons	3,086,966	3,592,268	3,335,283	3,169,202	2,582,927
Cotton #2	50,000 lbs	3,574,995	6,162,963	6,334,979	4,490,407	3,848,990
Orange Juice, Frozen Concentrate	15,000 lbs	656,995	710,512	845,792	923,696	902,019
US Dollar / Swedish Krona (Half Size)	100,000 USD	42,749	50,858			
US Dollar / Norwegian Krone (Half Size)	100,000 USD	30,359	48,976			
US Dollar / Czech Koruna (Half Size)	100,000 USD	31,581	12,711			
US Dollar / Hungarian Forint (Half Size)	100,000 USD	21,426	29,945			
US Dollar / South African Rand	100,000 USD	149,046	81,401	88,260	54,756	87,417
Canadian Dollar / Japanese Yen	200,000 CAD	6,719	13,078	20,463	13,215	9,238
Australian Dollar / US Dollar	100,000 AUD	2,858	4,920	17,666	29,069	39,578
Australian Dollar / Canadian Dollar	200,000 AUD	6,671	26,637	25,922	21,291	8,058
Australian Dolar / New Zealand Dollar	200,000 AUD	9,326	12,307	32,262	15,790	33,330
Australian Dollar / Japanese Yen	200,000 AUD	17,871	39,382	53,049	57,667	177,816
New Zealand Dollar / Japanese Yen	200,000 NZD	2,461	558	1,502	20	
New Zealand Dollar / US Dollar	200,000 NZD	8,156	45,134	61,657	53,413	70,364
Norwegian Krone / Japanese Yen		1,333				
Norwegian Krone / Swedish Koruna	500,000 NOK	29,257	38,021	20,866	15,172	11,797
Swiss Franc / Japanese Yen	200,000 CHF	15,721	76,734	74,148	65,275	66,907
Euro / US Dollar, Small	100,000 EUR	61,953	112,675	24,382	116,029	110,186
Euro / Australian Dollar	100,000 EUR	43,084	62,986	73,821	58,144	59,644
Euro / Canadian Dollar	100,000 EUR	12,746	21,972	43,266	26,477	12,179
Euro / Czech Koruna	100,000 EUR	25,233	16,204	49,442	17,533	21,525
Euro / Hungarian Forint	100,000 EUR	40,094	18,525	31,105	11,615	12,905
Euro / Japanese Yen	100,000 EUR	182,157	346,417	418,725	586,129	448,372
Euro / Swedish Krona	100,000 EUR	37,438	55,039	64,617	54,571	129,028
Euro / British Pound	100,000 EUR	105,056	169,921	241,409	304,382	253,818
Euro / Norwegian	100,000 EUR	18,857	52,084	58,664	44,635	55,945
Euro / South African Rand	100,000 EUR	117	244	318	163	
Euro / Swiss Franc	100,000 EUR	65,200	159,849	215,173	183,446	261,897
Million Australian Dollar / US Dollar	1,000,000 AUD	259	3			
Million Euro / Canadian Dollar		27				
Million Euro / US Dollar	1,000,000 EUR	3,062	4,804			
Million US Dollar / Swiss Franc	1,000,000 USD	102	49			
Million British Pound / US Dollar	1,000,000 GBP	250	327			
Million US Dollar / Japanese Yen	1,000,000 USD	4,780	1,783			
British Pound / Australian Dollar	125,000 GBP	6,271	8,104	5,994	10	
British Pound / Canadian Dollar	125,000 GBP	1,033	3,204	5,195	2	
British Pound / New Zealand Dollar	125,000 GBP	2,245	16			
British Pound / Norwegian Krone		383				
British Pound / South Africa Rand		4				
British Pound / Swedish Krona	125,000 GBP	4	254			
British Pound / Swiss franc	125,000 GBP	16,317	43,558	66,586	84,210	49,597
British Pound / Japanese Yen	125,000 GBP	25,686	46,231	111,274	148,696	156,444
Small British Pound / US Dollar	62,500 GBP	31,175	55,127	14,279	17,437	21,762
Small New Zealand Dollar / US Dollar		5,057				
Small US Dollar / Canadian Dollar	100,000 USD	3,587	6,572	14,672	18,910	15,624
Small US Dollar / Japanese Yen	100,000 USD	8,842	26,973	28,251	142,751	39,715
Small US Dollar / Swiss Franc	100,000 USD	5,853	9,462	17,866	64,417	28,262

ICE Futures U.S. (ICE) (continued)

FUTURE	CONTRACT UNIT	2009	2008	2007	2006	2005
US Dollar Index	1,000 USD x Index	2,523,927	1,825,326	1,099,800	1,168,486	1,159,938
Revised NYSE Composite Index	50 USD x Index	209	698	4,605	3,213	14,047
Russell 1000 Mini Index	50 USD x Index	445,752	177,768	81,432		
Russell 2000 Mini Index	500 USD x Index	38,686,673	16,526,331	57,540		
Reuters-CRB Futures Index (CCI)	500 USD x Index	15,973	19,185	19,973	14,312	9,144
RJ/CRB Futures Index	200 USD x Index	354	44	3	150	7,424
Total Futures		81,715,275	63,433,647	40,658,718	32,746,692	29,013,416

Kansas City Board of Trade (KCBT)

FUTURE	CONTRACT UNIT	2009	2008	2007	2006	2005
Wheat	5,000 bu	3,660,343	3,778,266	4,318,007	4,763,168	3,682,919
Total Futures		3,660,343	3,778,266	4,318,007	4,771,711	3,690,025

Minneapolis Grain Exchange (MGE)

FUTURE	CONTRACT UNIT	2009	2008	2007	2006	2005
Spring Wheat	5,000 bu	1,198,013	1,361,042	1,792,310	1,613,239	1,384,750
Hard Red Winter Wheat Index	5,000 bu	157	25	8	18	427
Soft Red Winter Wheat Index	5,000 bu	8,654				250
Total Futures		1,206,824	1,361,067	1,792,453	1,614,543	1,389,922

New York Mercantile Exchange (NYMEX)

FUTURE	CONTRACT UNIT	2009	2008	2007	2006	2005
Gold	100 oz	35,139,541	38,377,367	25,060,440	15,917,584	15,890,617
Platinum	50 oz	802,884	675,543	501,545	373,119	376,179
Palladium	100 oz	400,821	483,828	400,993	378,116	321,923
Silver	5,000 oz	7,990,528	8,917,183	6,817,137	5,433,063	5,536,351
Gold, E-mini		13,341				
Gold, miNY		59,900	20,034	10,988	313	
Silver, E-mini		660				
Silver, miNY		13,367	8,115	5,120	40	
Copper	25,000 lbs	6,398,967	4,618,068	3,753,168	3,281,312	3,950,842
Copper, miNY		5,987	4,890	4,927	77	
Hot-Rolled Steel		13,494	23			
Uranium		6,149	13,291	1,268		
Crude Oil, Physical	1,000 bbl	137,428,494	134,674,264	121,525,967	71,053,203	59,650,468
Crude Oil		1,139,308	1,360,899	625,839	820,579	
Crude Oil, miNY		3,368,983	5,641,145	5,185,214	9,323,467	
Brent Crude Oil, Last Day		31,708	465,056	506,075		
No. 2 Heating Oil, NY	42,000 gal	21,426,015	19,583,052	18,078,976	13,990,589	13,135,581
Heating Oil Financial		91,152	70,561	46,828	19,231	
Heating Oil, miNY		415	637	21,296	422,248	
NY Harbor RBOB Gasoline	42,000 gal	21,159,516	20,522,571	19,791,439	3,883,261	1,964
RBOB Gasoline, miNY		84	307	563	872	
Natural Gas, miNY		1,030,118	1,058,665	1,403,525	2,035,824	
Singapore 380 Fuel Oil		300	650	150		
REBCO Crude Oil Financial		182				
PJM Financially Settled Monthly - Peak		126,778	77,287	84,154	171,655	652,077
NYMEX Crude Oil MACI Index		539	23,742			
Natural Gas	10,000 MMBTU	47,951,353	38,730,519	29,786,318	23,029,988	19,142,549
1.5% Fuel Oil Barges FOB Rdam Swap		5				
3.5% Fuel Oil (Platts) CIF MED Swap		278				
AECO-C/NIT Basis Swap		86,888	533,158	860,885	1,317,291	1,247,570
PJM AER-Dayton Hub Monthly Electricity		4,000	12,258	4,262	8,026	18,020
PJM AER Dayton Hub Monthly Electricity		11,716	35,148	14,604	12,710	13,500
Algonquin City - gates Natural Gas Basis		1,924	214			
ANR - Louisiana Basis Swap		46,530	34,499	13,127	24,476	6,869
ANR - Oklahoma Basis		70,712	124,501	99,106	47,516	57,584
Central Appalacian Coal	1,500 tons	139,732	108,887	127,529	52,305	28,058
Argus Biodiesel RME FOB Rdam Swap		8,457				
Argus Gasoline Crack Spread SW		89,673	40,030	26,156	9,052	
Argus Gasoline NWE BALMO Swap		4,065	352			
Argus LLS vs WTI (Arg) T		843				
Argus Propane Far East Index Swap		2,220				
Argus Propane (Saudi Aramco) Swap		433	20			
Brent (ICE) Crude Oil BALMO Swap		4,619				
Brent (ICE) Calendar Swap		313,572	335,640	71,534	38,305	
Brent CFD (Platts) vs Front Month Swap		12,357				
Brent (CFD) Swap		61,632				
Brent Bullet Swap		276,532	114,701	42,053	20,432	
Carbon RGGI Emmissions		1,817				
Centerpoint Basis Swap		188,819	319,716	159,048	68,895	

New York Mercantile Exchange (NYMEX) (continued)

FUTURE	CONTRACT UNIT	2009	2008	2007	2006	2005
Centerpoint East Index		9,617	4,644	1,671	1,378	
Chicago Basis Swap		73,011	575,663	486,313	555,309	324,560
Chicago Ethanol Swap		15,169	15,617	4,590		
Chicago Index Swap		3,481	18,173	17,721	5,114	6,605
Chicago Natural Gas Swing Swap		3,064	4,001	3,205	572	991
Chicago Unleaded Gasoline vs RBOB		300				
CIG Basis Swap		42,065	117,473	100,525	245,305	181,241
CIG Rockies Natural Gas Index Swap		5,364	1,041			
CIG Rockies Natural Gas Swing Swap		726	62			
Cinergy Hub Off-Peak LMP Swap		32,146	27,524	10,202	24,076	9,780
Cinergy Hub LMP Swap-Peak		43,856	17,280	10,586	13,728	5,840
Cinergy Hub 5mw Day Ahead Off-Peak		604,840				
Cinergy Hub 5mw Day Ahead Peak		46,939				
Cinergy Hub 5mw Real-Time Off-Peak		236,576				
Cinergy Hub 5mw Real-Time Peak		15,321				
Columbia Gulf Mainline Basis Swap		99,036				
Columbia Gulf Mainline Natural Gas		556				
Columbia Gulf Onshore Basis		105,653	211,645	80,422	68,181	27,332
Conway Natural Gas (OPIS) Swap		220				
Conway Normal Butane (OPIS) Swap		362				
Conway Propane 5 decimals Swap		4,129				
Conway Propane (OPIS) Swap		7,808	672			
Crude Oil Last Day Financial Futures		130				
Crude Oil Monthly		15				
Dated Brent (Platts) Daily Swap		1,802				
Dated-to-Frontline Brent Swap		141,760	183,262	90,783	21,394	
Dawn Basis (Platts IFERC) Swap		100				
Demarc Natural Gas Index Swap		3,461	13,913	3,460	2,218	
Demarc Natural Gas Swing Swap		1,356	3,169	1,423	1,073	
Diesel 10ppm Barge FOB Rdam vs ICE		254				
Diesel 10ppm NEW Le Harve CIF Swap		5				
Diesel 10ppm NEW Le Harve vs ICE Gas		195				
Diesel 10ppm NEW Le Harve vs ICE Swap		25				
Dominion Transmission - Appalachian		297	2,240	1,994	3,344	3,832
Dominion Transmission - Appalachian		46,703	34,100	18,657	10,120	8,186
Dominion Transmission - Appalachian		102,937	229,043	458,950	433,304	459,360
Dubai Crude Oil BALMO Swap		3,774	2,276			
Dubai Crude Oil Calendar Swap		923,539	325,802	107,329	88,601	
Eastern Rail CSX Coal Swap		29,060	30,488	4,815		
East-West Fuel Oil Spread Swap		18,589	11,622	2,532	2,069	668
EIA Flat Tax On-Highway Diesel Swap		6,974				
EIA On-Highway Retail Diesel Swap		3,920	1,102			
Electric MISO Peak		800				
Electric NYISO Off-Peak		15,520				
El Paso/Permian Index Swap		42,447	46,469	34,194	16,710	11,740
El Paso/Permian Swing Swap		4,613	12,934	17,639	5,092	2,606
ERCOT HOU MCPE 50mw Daily Peak		5				
ERCOT HOU MCPE 50mw Off-Peak		22				
ERCOT HOU MCPE 50mw Peak		11,024				
ERCOT Houston ZMCPE 5mw Peak		1,275				
ERCOT North MCPE 50mw Daily Peak		39				
ERCOT North MCPE 50mw Off-Peak		33,558				
ERCOT North MCPE 50mw Peak		797				
ERCOT North Peak Swap		24				
ERCOT North ZMCPE 5mw Off-Peak		11,690				
ERCOT North ZMCPE 5mw Peak		4,285				
ERCOT South MCPE 50mw Peak		86				
ERCOT West MCPE 50mw Daily Off-Peak		9				
Ethanol T1 FOB Rdam Ex Duty Swap		2,427				
Ethanol T2 FOB Rdam Incl Duty Swap		300				
European 1% Fuel Oil BALMO Swap		1,886	815	15		
European 3.5% Fuel Oil Rdam BALMO		5,121	2,300	20		
European 3.5% Fuel Oil Spread Swap		740	282	53	5	
European Gasoil 10ppm Rdam Barges		42	116			
European Gasoil 10ppm Rdam Barges vs		4,789	2,850	436	27	
Europe 1% Fuel Oil Calendar Swap		24,162	24,565	8,048	3,047	1,382
Europe 1% Fuel Oil Rdam Calendar Swap		9,115	18,743	2,872	681	707
European 6.5% Fuel Oil MED Calendar		533	244	15	105	20
Europe 3.5% Fuel Oil Rotterdam Calendar		126,496	77,769	20,075	14,699	8,639
European Gasoil (ICE)		1,644				
European Naptha BALMO Swap		936	139	9		
European Naptha Crack Spread		110,560	34,053	13,268	2,332	
European Dated Brent Crude Oil Calendar		91,481	34,610	7,815	1,425	
European Jet Kero NWE Calendar Swap		782	250	71		
European Jet Kero Rdam Calendar Swap		6				

New York Mercantile Exchange (NYMEX) (continued)

FUTURE	CONTRACT UNIT	2009	2008	2007	2006	2005
European Naptha Calendar Swap		25,031	5,430	1,143	811	140
European Propane CIF ARA Swap		3,555	389			
FAME 0 Biodiesel FOB Rdam Swap		7,198				
Florida Gas, Zone 3 Natural Gas Index		668				
Florida Gas Transmission Zone 3 Basis		38,300	87,760	28,098	13,785	972
3.5% Fuel Oil Rdam Crack Swap		78,398	39,551	921	152	
1% Fuel Oil NWE Crack Spread Swap		9,042	5,322	1,385	95	
Fuel Oil (Platts) CAR CM		785				
1% Fuel Oil (Platts) Cargoes CIF NEW		210				
High-Low Sulfur Fuel Oil Spread Swap		21,931	14,528	2,860	1,701	592
Gas Euro-BOB OXY NWE Barges		12,549				
Gas Euro-BOB OXY NWE Barges Crack		15,321				
Gasoil 0.1 Barges FOB Rotterdam BALMO		1	3			
Gasoil 0.1 Barges FOB Rdam vs ICE Gasoil		137				
Gasoil 0.1 Cargoes CIF NEW Swap		104				
Gasoil 0.1 CIF MED		110				
Gasoil 0.1 CIF MED vs ICE Gasoil Swap		3,233	124			
Gasoil 0.1 CIF NW BALMO Swap		1	10	35	16	
Gasoil 0.1 Cargoes CIF NWE vs ICE Gasoil		1,294	773			
Gasoil 0.1 CIF MED vs ICE Gasoil BALMO		230				
Gasoil 0.1 Cargoes NWE vs ICE Gasoil		59				
Gasoil 0.1 Barges FOB Rdam vs ICE Gasoil		14,180	10,104			
Gasoil 0.1 Barges FOB Rdam Swap		1,833	965			
Gasoil 10ppm Cargoes CIF NEW vs ICE		495				
Gasoil 10ppm Cargoes CIF NWE Swap		351	42			
Gasoil 10ppm Cargoes CIF NWE vs ICE		9,233	1,968			
Gasoil (ICE) Bullet Swap		3,488	4,311	676		
Gasoil (ICE) Calendar Swap		14,669	6,791	220	419	
Gasoil Crack Spread Swap		257,528	190,522	14,287	14,040	
Gasoline Eurobob Oxy (Argus) NEW Barges		3				
Gasoline Up-Down (Argus) Swap		2,992	125			
Gasoline Up-Down BALMO Swap		697				
Gulf Coast Gasoline Crack Spread Swap		475				
Gulf Coast 3.0% Fuel Oil BALMO Swap		16,852	3,170			
Gulf Coast Gasoline Calendar Swap		3,473	7,283	6,142	21,921	3,352
Gulf Coast Heating Oil Calendar Swap		364	25	675	3,269	861
Gulf Coast Jet Fuel Calendar Swap		410	960	1,725	3,052	615
Gulf Coast Jet vs NY Harbor No 2 HO		97,772	27,511	6,470	2,427	6,137
Gulf Coast No 6 Fuel Oil 3.0% Sulfur Swap		683,433	180,907	53,150	27,673	21,515
Gulf Coast No 6 Fuel Oil Crack Swap		75,852	30,872	1,400	360	1,875
Gulf Coast ULSD Calendar Swap		7,538	3,506	305		
Gulf Coast ULSD Crack Spread Swap		106	825	325		
Gulf Coast Heating Oil (Argus) vs Heating		5,824				
Heating Oil Minute-Marker		147				
Heating Oil vs ICE Gasoil		72,340	16,561			
Henry Hub Basis Swap		309,092	287,216	264,818	467,158	337,152
Henry Hub Index Swap		187,879	187,463	207,234	332,129	271,791
Henry Hub Swap		25,670,240	31,401,575	16,207,044	24,157,726	10,406,462
Henry Hub Swing		19,156	66,875	73,750	37,243	85,830
Houston Ship Channel Basis Swap		595,698	787,312	1,088,654	1,696,435	778,513
Houston Ship Channel Index Swap		69,071	101,690	132,368	131,702	148,249
Houston Ship Channel Swing		4,903	41,940	19,333	10,247	6,384
ICE Brent-Dubai Swap		207,977	60,009	19,400	15,455	
ICE Gasoil BALMO Swap		40	114			
In Delivery Month CER		4,927				
In Delivery Month EUA		9,029				
ISO New England Off-Peak		27,468	20,279	11,258	25,445	41,573
ISO New England LMP Swap Peak		38,225	24,971	21,110	44,965	119,569
Japan C&F Naptha Crack Spread Swap		30	15			
Japan C&F Naptha Swap		32,132	5,114	195		
Japan Naptha BALMO Swap		201				
Jet AV Fuel (P) Car FM ICE Gas Swap		290				
European Jet Rotterdam Barges vs Gasoil		384	672			
European Jet CIF NWE vs Gasoil Swap		17,561	11,358	2,832	480	
Jet Fuel Barges FOB Rdam vs ICE Gasoil		5				
Jet Fuel Cargoes CIF NWE BALMO Swap		15	48			
Jet Fuel Cargoes CIF NEW vs ICE Gasoil		941				
Jet Fuel Up-Down BALMO CL		75				
Jet Up-Down (Argus) Swap		9,125				
Kern Opal Natural Gas Swing Swap		5,560	15,735	14,417	8,495	3,380
Los Angeles CARB Diesel (OPIS) Outright		259	25	25		
Los Angeles CARB Diesel (OPIS) Spread		13,142	5,189	25		
Los Angeles CARBOB (OPIS) Spread Swap		4,075	1,592			
Los Angeles Jet Fuel vs NYH #2 Heating		162	39	300	550	
Los Angeles Jet (OPIS) Spread Swap		33,572	6,425	775		

New York Mercantile Exchange (NYMEX) (continued)

FUTURE	CONTRACT UNIT	2009	2008	2007	2006	2005
LLS (Argus) Calendar Swap		200				
LLS (Argus) vs WTI Spread Calendar Swap		2,135	5,049			
LLS (Argus) vs WTI Spread Trade Month		512	902			
Los Angeles CARB Gasoline Swap (OPIS)		36				
Malin Basis Swap		14,897	251,130	327,357	533,176	682,135
Malin Natural Gas Swing Swap		724	2,402			
Mars (Argus) vs WTI Spread Calendar		1,500				
Mars (Argus) vs WTI Spread Trade Month		3,720	180			
Mars Blend Crude Oil		466				
MichCon Natural Gas Index Swap		5,413	1,414			
MichCon Natural Gas Swing Swap		62				
MichCon Basis Swap		173,256	283,962	289,738	484,925	158,667
Michigan Hub Off-Peak LMP Swap		116	448	60	280	240
Michigan Hub LMP Swap-Peak		246	28	620	1,040	
MISO 5mw Off-Peak		120,520				
MISO 5mw Peak		7,732				
Mont Belvieu Ethane 5 Decimals (OPIS)		38,404				
Mont Belvieu Ethane (OPIS) Swap		59,406	9,755			
Mont Belvieu Ethane (OPIS) BALMO		126				
Mont Belvieu Ethylene		1,530				
Mont Belvieu Isobutane (OPIS) Swap		1,056				
Mont Belvieu Isobutane 5 Deimal (OPIS)		90				
Mont Belvieu LDH Propane 5 Decimal		66,945				
Mont Belvieu LDH Propane (OPIS)		1,059				
Mont Belvieu Natural Gas (OPIS) Swap		39,797	9,920			
Mont Belvieu Natural Gas 5 Decimal		15,257				
Mont Belvieu Natural Gas (OPIS) BALMO		355				
Mont Belvieu Normal Butane 5 Decimal		28,214				
Mont Belvieu Normal Butane (OPIS)		148				
Mont Belvieu Normal Butane (OPIS) Swap		58,663	6,725			
Mont Belvieu Ethane (OPIS) BALMO Swap		390				
Mont Belvieu Natural Gas (OPIS) BLM		1,382				
Mont Belvieu Normal Butane (OPIS) BLM		2,196				
Mont Belvieu Propane (OPIS) BLM		1,797				
Natural Gas Penultimate Swap		11,038,692	12,352,928	10,117,889	7,973,290	2,751,455
NBP Henry Hub Basis Swap		150				
NEPOOL CNCTCT Day Ahead Off-Peak		1,194,942				
NEPOOL CONECTIC 5mw Day Ahead		66,666				
NEPOOL INTR HUB 5mw Day Ahead		2,433,442				
NEPOOL INTR HUB 5mw Day Ahead		140,169				
NE Maine HUB 5mw Day Ahead Off-Peak		75,404				
NE Maine HUB 5mw Day Ahead Peak		4,415				
NEPOOL NE Mass 5mw Day Ahead Off-		204,984				
NEPOOL NE Mass 5mw Day Ahead Peak		14,849				
NEPOOL SE Mass 5mw Day Ahead Off-		171,464				
NEPOOL SE Mass 5mw Day Ahead Peak		12,432				
NEPOOL W CNTR Mass 5mw Day Ahead		277,045				
NEPOOL W CNTR Mass 5mw Day Ahead		17,055				
New England Hub Daily Peak Swap		276	1,060	464	59,270	
New York 0.3% Fuel Oil HiPr (Platts) Swap		3,850	775			
New York Ethanol Swap		8,215	3,814	1,739		
New York Hub Zone G Peak Swap		320				
NGPL Mid-Continent Basis Swap		275,602	355,491	392,899	279,960	160,828
NGPL Mid-Continent Natural Gas Index		14,420	12,004	8,698	1,615	
NGPL Mid-Continent Natural Gas Swing		736	2,481	856	202	
NGPL STX Natural Gas Basis Swap		61,843	11,686			
NGPL STX Natural Gas Index Swap		1,592				
NGPL STX Natural Gas Swing Swap		60				
NGPL TEX/OK Basis Swap		430,388	524,326	675,365	1,119,784	401,241
NGPL TEX/OK Natural Gas Index Swap		33,584	43,322	14,304	3,537	
NGPL TEX/OK Natural Gas Swing Swap		2,349	1,299	2,569	472	
Northern Illinois Hub Monthly Peak		38,455	23,978	19,359	38,220	21,038
No 2 Heating Oil Up-Down Spread Calendar		20,285	8,762	3,735	4,193	1,848
Northern Natural Gas Demarcation Basis		177,130	334,235	278,478	162,381	73,501
Northern Natural Gas Ventura Basis Swap		259,500	361,503	353,186	306,787	207,843
Northern Illinois Hub Monthly Off-Peak		29,433	113,666	63,896	88,724	59,640
Northwest Rockies Basis Swap		293,089	792,219	1,040,846	1,408,279	1,261,653
NW Europe Gasoline Swap (Argus)		51,051	18,348	6,328	5,133	603
New York 0.7% Fuel Oil (Platts)		300				
New York 1% Fuel Oil vs Gulf Coast 3%		42,976	8,468			
New York 2.2% Fuel Oil (Platts) Swap		5,770				
New York 3.0% Fuel Oil Swap		2,293				
New York 0.3% Fuel Oil Swap		345	325			
NY Harbor Fuel Oil 1.0% Sulfur BALMO		5,375	1,161			
NY Harbor Heating Oil Calendar Swap		141,753	115,500	49,074	44,436	24,760

New York Mercantile Exchange (NYMEX) (continued)

FUTURE	CONTRACT UNIT	2009	2008	2007	2006	2005
NY Harbor Residual Fuel 1.0% Sulfur Swap		189,772	93,845	67,130	38,366	15,163
NY Harbor Residual Fuel Oil Crack Swap		6,672	5,255	11,464	4,877	4,700
NY Harbor No 2 Crack Spread Calendar		148,936	53,929	42,335	48,323	37,792
New York Heating Oil (Platts) vs NYMEX		1,895	50			
NY Harbor Conv Gasoline vs RBOB Swap		601	861	2,650	600	
NYISO Zone A LBMP Swap Peak		12,687	24,128	13,950	61,394	118,351
NYISO Zone A LBMP Swap Off-Peak		5,600	16,232	17,784	18,054	15,580
NYISO Zone G LBMP Swap Peak		10,459	15,500	16,990	50,385	62,913
NYISO Zone G LBMP Swap Off-Peak		10,050	22,442	26,608	13,568	8,060
NYISO Zone J LBMP Swap Peak		8,221	5,265	9,767	26,492	40,495
NYISO Zone J LBMP Swap Off-Peak		2,660	4,218	4,510	9,380	3,160
NYISO Zone A 5mw Day Ahead Off-Peak		284,962				
NYISO Zone A 5mw Day Ahead Peak		18,320				
NYISO Zone C 5mw Day Ahead Off-Peak		108,840				
NYISO Zone C 5mw Day Ahead Peak		8,555				
NYISO Zone G 5mw Day Ahead Off-Peak		154,380				
NYISO Zone G 5mw Day Ahead Peak		11,162				
NYISO Zone J 5mw Day Ahead Off-Peak		37,768				
NYISO Zone J 5mw Day Ahead Peak		7,512				
NY Jet Fuel (Argus) vs Heating Oil Swap		50				
NY Jet Fuel (Platts) vs Heating Oil Swap		1,150				
NYMEX ULSD vs NYMEX Heating Oil		558	510	100		
NY ULSD (Argus) vs Heating Oil Spread		530				
OneOk, OK Natural Gas Index Swap		1,020				
OneOk, OK Basis Swap		21,659				
OPIS Physical Ethane		475				
OPIS Physical LDH Propane		1,245				
OPIS Physical Natural Gas		4,535				
OPIS Physical Non-LDH Propane		1,405				
OPIS Physical Normal Nutane		5,676				
Panhandle Basis Swap		1,277,176	2,017,371	1,497,748	1,404,498	870,855
Panhandle Index Swap		24,002	37,250	31,609	9,444	6,171
Panhandle Swing Swap		6,264	21,182	8,493	3,634	2,780
El Paso Natural Gas Permian Basin Basis		152,858	432,177	521,914	520,763	306,329
Petro Outright Euro		80				
PG&E Citygate Natural Gas Index Swap		8,084	43,015	28,901	14,331	14,878
PG&E Citygate Natural Gas Swing Swap		1,283	12,387	9,100	2,960	4,147
PG&E Citygate Basis Swap		31,019	387,422	328,283	356,769	642,845
PJM AD Hub 5mw Real-Time Off-Peak		72,498				
PJM AD Hub 5mw Real-Time Peak		9,962				
PJM AECO Day Ahead Off-Peak		3,920				
PJM AECO Day Ahead Peak		308				
PJM BGE Day Ahead Off-Peak		823,697	3,800			
PJM BGE Day Ahead Peak		49,163				
PJM ComEd 5mw Day Ahead Off-Peak		149,456				
PJM ComEd 5mw Day Ahead Peak		10,144				
PJM Financially Settled Daily Peak		350	1,626	26,610	3,530	217,349
PJM Dayton Day Ahead Off-Peak		269,270	32,648			
PJM Dayton Day Ahead Peak		38,051	9,514			
PJM DPL Day Ahead Off-Peak		99,290	4,688			
PJM DPL Day Ahead Peak		5,635	512			
PJM Eastern Day Ahead Off-Peak		421,819	19,864			
PJM Eastern Day Ahead Peak		58,876	5,416			
PJM JCPL Zone Hub Off-Peak Cal-Mth Day		653,460	4,664			
PJM JCPL Zone Hub Peak Cal-Mth Day		44,379	1,516			
PJM Northern IL Hub 5mw Real-Time Off-		32,478				
PJM Northern IL Hub 5mw Real-Time Peak		465,914				
PJM Northern IL Hub Day Ahead Off-Peak		1,683,800	86,888			
PJM Northern IL Hub Day Ahead Peak		91,606	10,702			
PJM Off-Peak LMP Swap		61,397	68,172	50,940	83,734	85,922
PJM PECO Zone 5mw Peak Calendar		3,840				
PJM PEPCO Day Ahead Off-Peak		1,254,275	147,640			
PJM PEPCO Day Ahead Peak		97,197	7,690			
PJM PPL Day Ahead Off-Peak		332,772				
PJM PPL Day Ahead Peak		37,398				
PJM PSEG Day Ahead Off-Peak		2,801,488	18,240			
PJM PSEG Day Ahead Peak		203,264	5,690			
PJM Western Hub Day Ahead Off-Peak		6,810,613	231,232			
PJM Western Hub Day Ahead Peak		531,995	23,435			
PJM Western Hub Real-Time Off-Peak		1,727,213	202,312			
PJM Western Hub Real-Time Peak		98,311	11,905			
Premium Unld Gasoline 10ppm CIF FOB		10				
Premium Unld Gasoline 10ppm FOB MED		1,234				
Premium Unld Gasoline 10ppm CARGOE		37				
Premium Unld Gasoline 10ppm FOB		280				

New York Mercantile Exchange (NYMEX) (continued)

FUTURE	CONTRACT UNIT	2009	2008	2007	2006	2005
Premium Unld Gasoline 10ppm Rdam FOB		60				
Premium Unld Gasoline 10ppm FOB Swap		234				
Propane Non-LDH Mt Belvieu (OPIS)		315				
Propane Non-LDH Mt Belvieu (OPIS) Swap		3,390				
Mont Belvieu Propane (OPIS) Swap		110,757	54,323	5,386		
RBOB Calendar Swap		112,652	81,874	30,235	13,562	
RBOB Crack Spread Swap		151,414	83,269	57,793	13,254	
RBOB Gas		76,550				
RBOB Gasoline BALMO Swap		3,274				
RBOB Monthly (Late Priced)		348				
RBOB Up-Down Calendar Swap		93,703	53,431	22,724	6,169	
RBOB vs Heating Oil Swap		2,860	2,638	8,455	2,175	
Rockies Natural Gas Index Swap		29,993	26,500	19,440	29,994	8,562
San Juan Basis Swap		93,864	169,655	246,858	181,765	160,530
San Juan Natural Gas Index Swap		12,700	2,766	3,425	3,702	924
San Juan Natural Gas Swing Index		3,033	6,561	2,419	852	248
Singapore Fuel Oil 180cst BALMO Swap		5,762	2,085	90		
Singapore Fuel Oil 380cst BALMO Swap		929	514	15		
Singapore Fuel Oil 380cst Calendar Swap		5,982	3,662	2,142	461	118
Singapore Fuel Oil 180cst Calendar Swap		133,362	79,252	48,516	20,213	6,629
Singapore Fuel Oil Spread Swap		11,276	4,823	1,532	913	95
Singapore Gasoil BALMO Swap		28,166	15,214	425		
Singapore Gasoil Calendar Swap		321,662	128,359	52,955	13,484	305
Singapore Gasoil vs Rdam Gasoil Swap		69,019	37,975	18,564	5,610	
Singapore Jet Kerosene BALMO Swap		7,740	4,754	150		
Singapore Jet Kerosene vs Gasoil Spread		64,490	32,980	18,740	3,075	
Singapore Jet Kerosene Swap		81,705	36,688	20,045	4,898	
Singapore Jet Kero vs Gasoil BALMO		255				
Singapore Mogas 92 Unleaded BALMO		425				
Singapore Mogas 92 Unleaded Swap		11,224				
Singapore Naptha BALMO Swap		550	375			
Singapore Naptha Swap		13,887	25,374	9,955	2,750	150
SoCal Basis Swap		113,568	1,082,052	1,784,378	2,311,008	1,580,162
SoCal Index		20,713	121,780	121,263	53,086	23,512
SoCal Swing Swap		6,359	62,728	50,013	19,888	11,528
SONAT Basis Swap		72,505	130,742	36,106	18,722	8,966
Southern Star LA Natural Gas Index Swap		4,354				
Southern Star TX,OK,KS Natural Gas		4,304				
Sumas Basis Swap		6,652	63,684	83,641	205,978	429,597
Sumas Natural Gas Index Swap		1,654	3,810	6,727	14,976	13,088
Sumas Natural Gas Swing Swap		2,087	606	165	2,546	1,434
TC2 Rotterdam to USAC 37K		395	449	205	630	460
TC4 Singapore to Japan 30		305	445	10		30
TC5 Ras Tanura to Yokohama Freight		5,256	560	50		
TCO Basis Swap		110,615	236,679	394,285	333,867	316,053
TCO Natural Gas Index Swap		25,207	2,648			
TCO Natural Gas Swing Swap		208				
TD3 Middle Eastern Gulf to Japan 250K		651	460			
TD5 West Africa to USAC 1		105				
TD7 North Sea to Continent		10				
Tennessee 500 Leg Basis Swap		126,840	79,271	29,621	19,071	8,600
Tennessee 500 Leg Natural Gas Index		11,895	62			
Tennessee 500 Leg Natural Gas Swing Swap		60				
Tennessee 800 Basis Swap		6,426				
Tennessee Zone 0 Basis Swap		12,040	23,876	53,705	81,632	56,197
Tennesse Zone 0 Natural Gas Index Swap		7,777	2,804			
Tennesse Zone 0 Natural Gas Swing Swap		698				
TETCO ELA Basis		44,184	43,217	5,382	11,811	8,196
TETCO M-3 Natural Gas Index Swap		120,561	121,290	54,619	44,685	19,601
TETCO STX Natural Gas Swing Swap		584				
TETCO STX Basis Swap		12,289	37,702	51,664	69,669	36,481
TETCO STX Natural Gas Index Swap		7,388	2,195			
Texas Eastern ELA Natural Gas Swing		116				
Texas Eastern Zone M-3 Basis Swap		232,939	412,686	765,236	642,301	716,299
Texas Eastern Zone M-3 Swing Swap		2,830	2,059	10,643	2,394	498
Texas Eastern West Louisiana Natural Gas		6,878				
Texas Eastern West Louisiana Basis Swap		19,300				
Texas Gas Zone 1 Natural Gas		523				
Texas Gas Zone 1 Basis Swap		11,113				
Texas Gas Zone SL Basis Swap		81,101	71,598	46,454	49,163	10,640
Texas Gas Zone SL Natural Gas		232				
Texas Gas Zone 1 Basis Swap (Platts		124				
Texas Gas Zone 2 Natural Gas Index Swap		3,772				
Texas Gas Zone 2 Basis Swap		3,499				
Transco Zone 3 Basis Swap		73,501	157,593	126,442	58,349	92,944

New York Mercantile Exchange (NYMEX) (continued)

FUTURE	CONTRACT UNIT	2009	2008	2007	2006	2005
Transco Zone 3 Natural Gas Index Swap		12,980	9,215			
Transco Zone 4 Basis Swap		70,159	107,097	11,004	13,652	1,394
Transco Zone 4 Natural Gas Index		1,611				
Transco Zone 6 Basis Swap		94,997	165,105	545,492	313,674	529,577
Transco Zone 6 Natural Gas Index Swap		79,090	42,904	51,709	11,199	8,796
Transco Zone 6 Swing Swap		638	798	3,214	1,515	914
Trunkline, LA Basis Swap		10,210	31,481	17,364	7,001	3,972
Texas Gas Zone SL Natural Gas Index Swap		465				
ULSD 10ppm Cargoes CIF NWE BALMO		13	30			
ULSD 10ppm CIF MED Swap		146				
ULSD 10ppm CIF MED vs ICE Gasoil Swap		3,057	125			
ULSD 10ppm CIF NW BALMO Swap		4				
ULSD 10ppm CIF MED vs ICE Gasoil		334				
ULSD Up-Down (Argus) Swap		6,620				
ULSD Up-Down BALMO Swap		1,206				
Up Down GC ULSD vs NYMEX Heating Oil		228,195	105,423	19,834		
US Gulf Coast Unleaded 87 Crack Spread		8,045	10,724	8,517	19,933	5,876
Ventura Natural Gas Index Swap		6,267	17,671	12,748	2,508	
Ventura Natural Gas Swing Swap		426	3,131	610	434	
WAHA Basis Swap		425,807	624,817	727,707	611,795	338,241
WAHA Index Swap		101,880	71,755	72,219	26,784	26,923
WAHA Swing Swap		6,694	19,017	11,021	7,918	5,252
Western Rail Powder River Basin Coal Swap		24,085	28,340	10,680		
WTI-Brent (ICE) Bullet Swap		3,065	880	669	200	
WTI-Brent (ICE) Calendar Swap		107,192	240,916	60,008	35,343	
WTI Crude Oil Calendar Swap		1,057,843	847,658	489,274	377,086	41,931
WTS (Argus) vs WTI Spread Calendar Swap		3,600				
WTS (Argus) vs WTI Spread Trade Month		1,460	3,082			
NYMEX Columbian Peso		10,405				
Annual NOX 09		50	45			
Annual NOX 10		50	35			
Certified Emission Reduction		519	25,083			
EU Allowance		208	5,066			
Polyethylene		48				
Carbon RGGI Emissions		635	240			
Sulfur Dioxide (SO2) Emissions		30	5,034			
NYMEX Cocoa		1,318	2,222	1,769		
NYMEX Coffee		1,335	9,780	5,784		
NYMEX Cotton		1,764	8,495	7,407		
NYMEX Sugar #11		7,197	26,107	10,470	10	
Total Futures		362,426,620	338,490,891	277,408,465	216,252,995	166,608,057

NYSE LIFFE U.S.

FUTURE	CONTRACT UNIT	2009	2008
Gold	100 oz	1,467,450	847,778
Mini New York Gold	33.2 oz	2,122,569	675,114
Silver	5,000 oz	107,941	72,722
Mini New York Silver	1,000 oz	647,314	236,327
MSCI EAFE		75,697	
MSCI EM		49,373	
MSCI USA		4,390	
Total Futures		4,474,734	1,831,941

ONECHICAGO

FUTURE	CONTRACT UNIT	2009	2008	2007	2006	2005
Single Stock Futures		2,624,496	3,404,201	7,835,289	7,777,241	5,474,663
Exchange Traded Funds		101,660	299,547	51,034	9,124	14,162
Narrow-Based Equity Index		256,992	308,533	219,640	136,100	39,000
Total Futures		2,983,148	4,012,281	8,105,963	7,922,465	5,528,046

Total Volume

	2009	2008	2007	2006	2005
Total Futures	2,328,114,528	2,904,518,236	2,680,196,142	2,068,567,250	1,678,278,247
Precent Change	-19.85%	8.37%	29.57%	23.26%	24.60%

Options Traded on U.S. Securities Exchanges Volume Highlights
2009 in Comparison with 2008

2009 Rank	EXCHANGE	2009 Contracts	%	2008 Contracts	%	2008 Rank
1	Chicago Board of Options Exchange	1,134,764,209	31.41%	1,193,355,070	33.31%	1
2	International Securities Exchange	960,247,551	26.58%	1,007,661,590	28.13%	2
3	Nasdaq OMX PHLX[1]	606,456,252	16.79%	547,456,114	15.28%	3
4	NYSE-ARCA	421,349,395	11.66%	416,938,764	11.64%	4
5	NYSE-AMEX[2]	248,119,861	6.87%	207,285,283	5.79%	5
6	Boston Options Exchange	137,784,626	3.81%	178,650,541	4.99%	6
7	Nasdaq Options Market	103,912,524	2.88%	31,225,219	0.87%	7
	Total Options	**3,612,634,418**	**100.00%**	**3,582,572,581**	**100.00%**	

[1] Formerly Pacific Stock Exchange.

Options Traded on U.S. Futures Exchanges Volume Highlights
2009 in Comparison with 2008

2009 Rank	EXCHANGE	2009 Contracts	%	2008 Contracts	%	2008 Rank
1	Chicago Mercantile Exchange (CME Group)	199,818,921	53.36%	280,517,713	54.06%	1
2	Chicago Board of Trade (CME Group)	92,848,854	24.80%	135,519,960	26.12%	2
3	New York Mercantile Exchange (CME Group)	70,215,583	18.75%	85,014,980	16.38%	3
4	ICE Futures U.S.	11,309,749	3.02%	17,521,134	3.38%	4
5	Chicago Climate Futures Exchange (CCFE)	126,456	0.03%	113,817	0.02%	6
6	Kansas City Board of Trade (KCBT)	108,317	0.03%	187,658	0.04%	5
7	Minneapolis Grain Exchange (MGE)	25,137	0.01%	47,935	0.01%	7
8	NYSE Liffe U.S.	9,207	0.00%	5,602	0.00%	8
	Total Options	**374,462,224**	**100.00%**	**518,928,799**	**100.00%**	

*

Chicago Board of Trade (CBT)

OPTION	CONTRACT UNIT	2009	2008	2007	2006	2005
Wheat	5,000 bu	3,635,792	4,060,865	3,893,354	2,597,975	1,870,541
Corn	5,000 bu	14,435,687	20,992,582	14,691,277	11,317,388	6,257,027
Oats	5,000 bu	20,830	23,843	16,381	25,738	22,320
Soybeans	5,000 bu	9,555,840	9,806,935	8,215,582	6,042,797	6,817,588
Soybean Crush	50,000 bu	3,254	2,452	3,267	6,828	
Soybean Oil	60,000 lbs	1,255,304	1,458,568	1,277,884	902,096	682,825
Soybean Meal	100 tons	891,551	884,721	713,821	746,185	685,830
Rough Rice	200,000 lbs	15,674	26,681	23,374	26,868	17,834
Soybean Nearby + 2 Calendar Spread		603				
Corn Nearby + 2 Calendar Spread		186				
Wheat Nearby + 2 Calendar Spread		510				
Dec-July Wheat Calendar Spread		150				
July-Nov Soybean Calendar Spread		20,799				
Nov-Nov Soybean Calendar Spread		2,274				
July-Dec Corn Calendar Spread		50				
July-July Wheat Calendar Spread		451				
July-Dec Wheat Calendar Spread		320				
Ethanol Forward Month Swap		8,933	42,477	6,048		
T-Bonds (30-year)	100,000 USD	11,142,149	18,209,855	17,391,744	20,731,673	15,661,021
T-Notes (10-year)	100,000 USD	40,206,023	56,753,688	61,528,219	61,888,144	55,648,782
T-Notes (5-year)	100,000 USD	4,803,364	12,752,318	15,392,035	11,585,131	17,691,564
T-Notes (2-year)	200,000 USD	2,397,210	2,333,092	1,056,738	804,975	23,251
30-Day Federal Funds	5,000,000 USD	4,217,906	7,478,025	8,020,547	9,424,628	6,534,587
Flexible US T-Bonds		117,292	287,136	252,780	392,648	600,641
Flexible T-Notes (10-year)		7,550	12,575	910,609	311,295	259,295
Flexible T-Notes (2-year)		500				
Dow Jones Industrial Index	10 USD x Index	22,718	75,840	105,860	100,589	114,353
Mini ($5) Dow Jones Industrial Index	5 USD x Index	85,934	281,062	300,307	450,601	613,996
Total Options		92,848,854	135,519,960	134,047,704	127,622,361	113,505,455

Kansas City Board of Trade (KCBT)

OPTION	CONTRACT UNIT	2009	2008	2007	2006	2005
Wheat	5,000 bu	108,317	187,658	352,948	515,479	263,511
Total Options		108,317	187,658	352,948	515,479	263,511

VOLUME - U.S.

Chicago Mercantile Exchange (CME Group)

OPTION	CONTRACT UNIT	2009	2008	2007	2006	2005
Live Cattle	40,000 lbs	1,355,251	1,226,704	726,003	930,169	502,021
Feeder Cattle	50,000 lbs	74,777	99,911	106,587	156,292	142,253
Lean Hogs	40,000 lbs	651,731	512,159	321,258	225,013	198,274
Pork Bellies, Frozen	40,000 lbs	44	211	575	1,198	3,228
Class III Milk	200,000 lbs	153,513	167,779	94,640	85,713	71,431
Nonfat Dry Milk	44,000 lbs	59	60		116	
Mini BFP Milk	100,000 lbs	562	367	967	549	796
Dry Whey	44,000 lbs	862	670			
Cash Butter	20,000 lbs	223	322	17		
Random Lumber	100,000 bd ft	13,883	17,485	18,127	20,909	25,171
Eurodollar (3-month)	1,000,000 USD	117,553,569	187,341,383	313,032,284	268,957,052	188,001,048
Eurodollar Mid-Curve		43,369,605	40,883,014			
Eurdollar Calendar Spreads		1,400	11,752			
Treasury Matched Eurodollar Mid-Curve		107,128	287,662			
Australian Dollar	100,000	273,516	206,649	74,874	36,562	109,970
British Pound	62,500	465,413	565,050	352,736	158,473	146,893
Brazilian Real		1,455				
Canadian Dollar	100,000	465,264	380,894	530,023	375,257	231,329
Euro FX	125,000 EUR	2,207,616	2,696,811	1,801,681	1,849,119	2,100,595
Japanese Yen	12,500,000	758,564	850,340	929,733	544,716	419,232
Mexican Peso	500,000	158	768	51	371	1,284
Swiss Franc	125,000	112,861	198,694	78,675	47,984	50,107
Euro FX European	125,000 EUR	94,244	375,621	230,615	190,610	72,119
Euro / Swiss Franc		400				
Australian Dollar European		3,800				
British Pound European	62,500	61,434	89,910	98,323	18,191	
Canadian Dollar European	100,000	26,775	54,138	50,899	7,256	
Japanese Yen European	12,500,000 EUR	40,178	136,921	155,394	53,753	50,996
Swiss Franc European	125,000	20,423	37,868	30,079	6,773	
Nikkei 225	5 USD x Index	4,500	17,750	17,200	59,200	44,458
S&P 500 Index	500 USD x Index	10,350,127	16,378,218	19,458,815	15,785,802	9,810,489
E-Mini S&P 500 Index	50 USD x S&P Index	18,142,915	22,167,648	16,213,737	9,893,979	4,289,038
EOM S&P 500 Index	250 USD x Index	1,470,660	2,512,846	816,354	80,424	
EOM E-Mini S&P 500 Index	EOM x Index	845,519	1,028,368	950,829	147,471	
EOW1 S&P 500		153,184				
EOW1 E-mini S&P 500		88,404				
EOW2 S&P 500		114,594				
EOW2 E-mini S&P 500		82,869				
S&P MidCap 400 Index	500 USD x Index	50	441	400	435	670
E-Mini S&P MidCap 400 Index	100 USD x Index	5,272	5,507	235		
NASDAQ 100 Index	100 USD x Index	1,535	13,096	79,900	71,499	35,306
E-Mini NASDAQ 100 Index	20 USD x Index	440,634	542,497	742,395	317,765	110,093
CDD Weather	20 USD x Index	27,050	25,100	19,400	18,050	28,725
HDD Weather	20 USD x Index	40,250	50,850	63,835	75,277	16,400
HDD Seasonal Weather Strip	20 USD x Index	115,300	139,800	295,450	209,300	13,674
CDD Seasonal Weather Strip	20 USD x Index	98,950	245,850	258,350	97,200	
HDD Weather European		3,500				
Euro HDD Seasonal Weather	20 GBP x Index	3,000	4,200		2,000	33,625
Euro CAT Seasonal Strip Weather	20 GBP x Index	7,500	14,000	3,500		
Binary Seasonal Hurricane	1,000 USD x Index	3,000	4,600			
Binary Seasonal Hurricane Event 2		1,000				
Pacific Rim Dat SS Weather		4,400				
Total Options		199,818,921	280,517,713	360,005,823	301,551,501	207,233,185

Chicago Climate Futures Exchange (CCFE)

OPTION	CONTRACT UNIT	2009	2008	2007
CA Climate Action Registry-Climate Res		415		
Carbon Financial Instrument (CFI)		11,732	11,753	
Carbon Financial Instrument (CFI-US)		1,212		
Nitrogen Financial Instrument - Annual		13,800	6,500	
Regional Greenhouse Gas Initiatives (RGGI)		74,363	10,373	
Sulfur Financial Instrument (SFI)		24,934	85,190	91,858
Total Options		126,456	113,817	91,859

Minneapolis Grain Exchange (MGE)

OPTION	CONTRACT UNIT	2008	2007	2006	2005	2004
American Spring Wheat	5,000 bu	24,937	47,935	34,354	40,468	27,245
Soft Red Winter Wheat Index	5,000 bu	200				329
Total Options		25,137	47,935	34,354	40,491	32,464

ICE Futures U.S. (ICE)

OPTION	CONTRACT UNIT	2009	2008	2007	2006	2005
Coffee 'C'	37,500 lbs	1,427,032	2,826,331	2,999,648	2,785,053	2,370,161
Sugar #11	112,000 lbs	7,280,380	9,179,779	5,548,668	6,250,162	3,631,939
Sugar #11 Options on Futures Spreads		109,849	145,368	204,100	54,880	14,861
Cocoa	10 metric tons	318,805	376,444	370,429	377,905	512,259
Cotton #2	50,000 lbs	1,709,004	4,468,327	3,451,217	1,820,259	1,709,345
Orange Juice Frozen Concentrate	15,000 lbs	243,741	238,616	385,219	426,967	433,288
US Dollar Index	500 USD x Index	55,822	72,768	50,562	39,299	35,356
Russell 1000 Index Mini	100 USD x Index	7,798	877			
Russell 2000 Index Mini	100 USD x Index	157,126	73,634			
Reuters-CRB Futures Index (CCI)	500 USD x Index	192	892	435	6,320	1,539
Total Options		11,309,749	17,521,134	13,124,201	11,920,477	8,932,169

New York Mercantile Exchange (NYMEX)

OPTION	CONTRACT UNIT	2009	2008	2007	2006	2005
COMEX Copper	25,000 lbs	18,568	22,559	24,467	75,403	143,609
COMEX Gold	100 oz	4,755,427	4,392,737	3,554,858	3,708,573	2,889,803
COMEX Silver	5,000 oz	1,066,721	1,700,882	1,257,505	1,646,959	1,131,812
NYMEX Platinum	50 oz	20		300	321	404
Brent Crude Oil Average Price		137,549	92,549			
Brent Crude Oil European Style Look-Alike		18,562	31,181			
Brent Crude Oil American Style		2,410	8,904			
Central Appalachian Coal		255				
Cinergy Hub Peak Month		142,190	14,240	8,930		
Crude Oil 1-month CSO		719,802	1,016,327	1,851,827	1,209,952	440,234
Crude Oil APO		3,203,460	2,227,738	1,445,930	838,985	45,250
Crude Oil Physical		86,932	132,590	134,537	21,416	
Crude Oil European Style		1,507,042	3,580,861	1,879,999	379,250	119,218
Crude Oil	1,000 bbl	28,551,730	35,255,326	28,398,793	21,016,562	14,726,263
European Jet Kerosene NEW APO		10				
Heating Oil-Crude Oil Spread	1,000 bbl	6,238	824	5,783	29,862	82,505
Heating Oil Physical - European		11,479	112,488	32,438	1,525	24,339
Heating Oil	42,000 gal	686,270	781,003	620,761	595,427	983,388
Henry Hub Financial Last Day		16,892				
Heating Oil 1-month CSO		16,345	275		10,185	12,868
Heating Oil 3-month CSO		100				
Houston Ship Channel Pipe		8,800				
In Delivery Month EUA		1,250				
ISO New England Calendar-Month LMP		17,410	43,082	45,240		
Mont Belvieu Ethane (OPIS) APO		120				
Mont Belvieu Propane (OPIS) APO		5,435				
Mont Belvieu Natural Gas (OPIS) APO		720				
Mont Belvieu Normal Butane APO		555				
Natural Gas 1-month CSO Financial		15,874				
Natural Gas 1-month CSO		43,290	174,940	120,608	246,472	103,058
Natural Gas 3-month CSO Financial		52,855				
Natural Gas Option on Calendar Strip		3,240				
Natural Gas Physical		213,170	112,303	13,320	795	
Natural Gas Physical - European		25,309,214	31,158,326	29,921,068	19,515,968	6,968,569
Natural Gas Physical	10,000 MMBTU	1,135,135	2,336,287	5,051,879	9,581,663	9,168,354
Natural Gas 2-month CSO		150	2,300	950	1,150	1,525
Natural Gas 3-month CSO		10,877	26,605	14,233	24,556	3,175
Northern Illinois Calendar-Month LMP		2,160				
Northern Rockies Pipe		87,840	11,460	1,960		
NW Pipeline Rockies Basis		9,508				
NY Harbor Heating Oil Swap		661,036	240,362	60,471	18,868	8,302
NYISO Zone G 5mw Peak		69,120				
NYISO Zone J 5mw Peak		2,560				
NYMEX European Gasoil APO		9,957	96			
NYMEX European Style Gasoil		317				
Panhandle Basis		4,528				
Panhandle pipe		105,368	47,092			
Petrochemicals		645				
PJM Monthly Financially Settled Electricity		528,316	365,316	370,108	247,040	73,640
RBOB 1-Month CSO		32,381				
RBOB Calendar Swap		57,384	27,402	6,219	142	
RBOB Crack Spread		225	13,072	6,362	220	
RBOB Gasoline		680,635	884,839	1,016,963	82,176	
RBOB Gasoline European style		21,007	84,382	44,382	995	
Rotterdam 3.5% Fuel Oil CL		1,881				
San Juan Pipe		22,118	3,240			
Singapore Fuel Oil 180 CST		318				
Singapore Jet Fuel Calendar		3,023				
SoCal Pipe Swap		119,320	26,445			
Waha Basis		1,208				

New York Mercantile Exchange (NYMEX) (continued)

OPTION	CONTRACT UNIT	2009	2008	2007	2006	2005
WTI Crude Oil 12-month CSO		20,675	70,137	83,126	24,750	12,267
WTI Crude Oil 1-month CSO Financial		5,370				
Natural Gas Option on Summer Strip		1,000				
Carbon CER European		600	3,200			
Carbon EUA Emissions Euro		986	2,000			
Total Options		70,215,583	85,014,980	75,976,972	59,899,331	38,002,895

NYSE LIFFE U.S.

OPTION	CONTRACT UNIT	2009	2008
100 oz Gold		8,702	4,972
5,000 oz Silver		505	630
Total Options		9,207	5,602

Total Volume

	2009	2008	2007	2006	2005
Total Options	374,462,224	518,928,799	583,633,862	501,549,640	367,969,679
Percent Change	-27.84%	-11.09%	16.37%	36.30%	27.26%

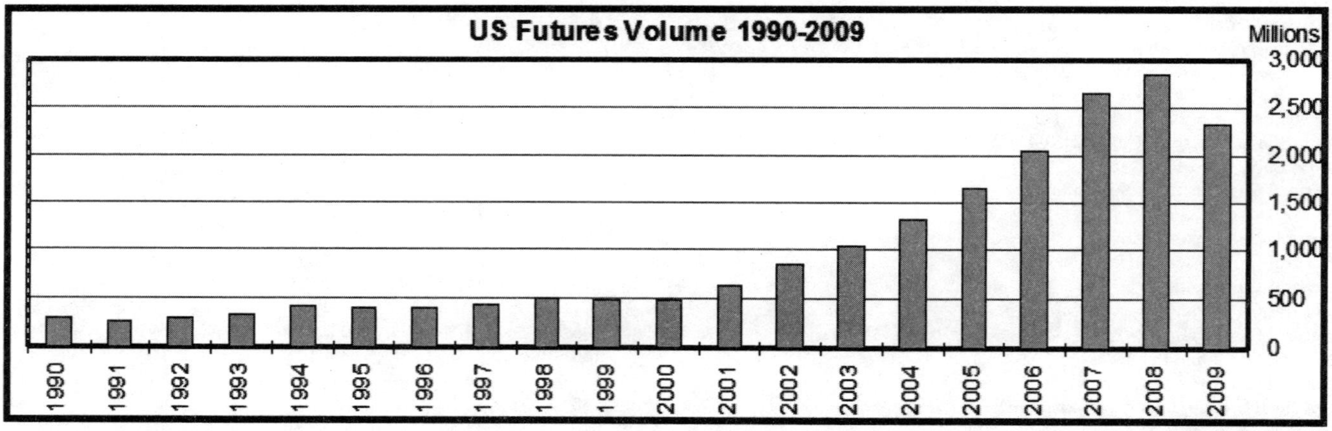

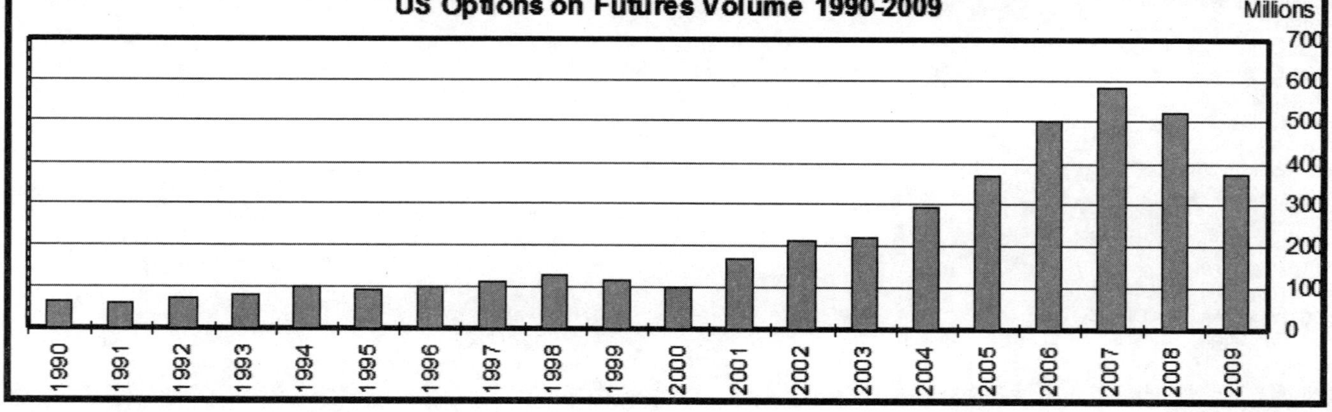

Volume - Worldwide

Athens Derivatives Exchange S.A. (ADEX), Greece

	2009	2008	2007
FTSE/Athex 20	2,371,733	2,808,788	2,588,908
All Futures on Individual Equities	5,037,065	3,713,266	3,101,602
Total Futures	**7,408,798**	**6,545,423**	**5,843,937**
FTSE/Athex 20	383,555	440,650	591,476
FTSE/Athex Mid 40	9	3,290	39,218
All Options on Individual Equities	67,590	182,757	106,913
Total Options	**451,154**	**626,697**	**737,607**

Australian Stock Exchange (ASX), Australia

	2009	2008	2007	2006	2005
S&P/ASX Index	396,723	309,499	238,823	110,769	106,237
All Futures on Individual Equities	777,732	971,261	706,656	693,683	490,238
Total Futures	**1,174,455**	**1,280,760**	**945,479**	**804,452**	**596,475**
S&P / ASX Index	3,486,914	2,819,582	1,797,754	1,170,793	1,163,213
All Options on Individual Equities	14,465,066	16,070,022	22,226,578	20,477,083	21,828,002
Total Futures	**17,951,980**	**18,889,604**	**24,024,332**	**21,647,876**	**22,991,215**

Bolsa de Mercadorias & Futuros (BM&F), Brazil

	2009	2008	2007	2006	2005
Arabica Coffee	596,435	760,761	724,319	528,462	485,902
Arabica Coffee Rollover	48,764	22,476			
Live Cattle	834,304	1,633,113	934,422	392,012	311,459
Live Cattle Rollover	1,418				
Ethanol	1	16,608	17,234		
Sugar Crystal	224	7,039	45,112	69,351	63,385
Corn	26,170	403,258	207,724	135,188	97,795
Corn Cash Settled	259,610	7,767			
Corn Cash Settled Rollover	1,966				
Soybean Futures	168,168	284,382	188,279	98,112	47,360
Gold Forward	176	520	283	308	668
Gold	640	1,280	2,100	3,180	2,640
Gold Spot	12,403	12,579	9,118	24,369	42,336
Bovespa Stock Index Futures	16,350,493	20,226,662	26,550,491	13,232,399	6,065,361
Bovespa Rollover	1,382,060	118,680			
Bovespa Mini Index	12,374,969	9,928,406	10,692,141	3,702,409	606,582
Interest Rate	151,958,184	166,983,583	221,627,417	161,654,736	121,249,186
Interest Rate Swap	71,545	547,146	91,503	192,356	260,404
Interest Rate x Exchange Rate Swap	368,853	449,784	483,342	398,757	382,326
Interest Rate x Reference Rate Swap	14,000	22,234	20,200	189,796	18,536
Interest Rate x Price Index Swap (formerly Inflation)	655,582	1,054,533	1,486,734	2,760,520	829,982
Exchange Rate Swap	27,883	43,007	54,887	26,443	21,035
Interest Rate x IBrX-50	3,901	9,254	10,467	7,448	776
ID x US Dollar Spread Futures	738,389	1,150,157	396,326	1,016,176	926,171
FRA on ID x US Dollar Spread	17,487,272	21,217,283	20,907,906	14,396,347	20,642,962
ID x US Dollar Spread Swap	256,434	336,560	44,049	145,943	232,609
ID x IPCA Spread	6,240	69,350	111,025	58,840	
CDS Brazil 5-Year	218	953			
Global 2040	3,409	48,533	94,845	57,590	232,883
US T-Note	26,291	107,576	73,123	630	
US Dollar	66,776,180	87,442,346	84,774,568	52,350,517	33,466,104
US Dollar Rollover	15,280,530	7,179,600			
Mini US Dollar	573,839	147,424	3,460,153	5,053,580	827,427
US Dollar forward points	3,157,515	3,488,158	2,850,000	1,648,807	908,062
Euro	75,265	37,550	2,725	70	
Euro (EBR)	11,905				
Total Futures	**289,551,236**	**323,770,173**	**375,885,135**	**258,466,105**	**187,850,634**
Gold on Actuals	369,564	363,867	193,380	119,378	149,932
Gold Exercise	61,234	47,630	38,115	19,492	28,540
US $ Denominated Arabica Coffee	8,459	48,166	80,523	30,602	22,341
US $ Denominated Arabica Coffee Exercise	3,427	6,687	3,444	2,370	1,662
Corn	1,808	4,590	1,132	3,119	
Corn Cash Settled	17,364	51			
Corn Cash Exercise	1,856				
Soybeans	6,611	6,616	7,184	1,345	
Soybeans, Exercise	296	1,434	741		
Live Cattle	46,001	75,622	5,108	987	71
Live Cattle, Exercise	14,678	4,328	1,147	251	
Bovespa Stock	1,714,845	1,229,734	727,015	26,625	6,344
Bovespa Stock Exercise	216,930	194,950	112,690	2,072	9,380
Bovespa Stock Volatility	19,325	85,270	40,230		
Interest Rate	4,545,435	7,317,364	1,886,247	945,250	268,819
Interest Rate (IDI) Exercise	962,310	1,511,261	273,500	18,080	147,840
Interest Rate (volatility)	1,455,990	3,724,645	2,436,765	933,445	539,825

Bolsa de Mercadorias & Futuros (BM&F), Brazil (continued)

	2009	2008	2007	2006	2005
Interest Rate (IDI)	40,174,869	13,915,878	12,316,359	9,279,101	2,058,806
IDI Index (exercise)	2,499,125	1,236,980	366,650	105,410	237,895
IDI Index (volatility)	5,894,010	1,823,370	3,068,460	1,848,810	351,575
Flexible Spot Interest Rate Index	159,582				
Flexible Bovespa Stock Index	622,374	469,747	323,459	199,557	85,279
US Dollar on Actuals	21,631,255	30,588,575	24,682,702	9,766,867	6,251,235
US Dollar Exercise	1,566,983	1,805,319	1,332,280	552,837	391,221
US Dollar Volatility	1,485,170	2,887,345	2,241,390	1,042,235	793,665
Flexible Currency	357,381	495,007	339,827	206,128	207,585
Total Options	**83,836,882**	**67,844,442**	**50,478,357**	**25,104,136**	**11,595,830**

BOVESPA, Brazil

	2009	2008	2007	2006	2005
Ibovespa Index	199,147	210,868	384,837	1,818,764	2,257,756
Exchange Traded Funds	242,863	17,063			
All Options on Individual Equities	546,547,550	350,046,567	367,305,446	285,699,806	266,362,631
Total Options	**546,989,560**	**350,274,498**	**367,690,283**	**287,518,570**	**268,620,460**

Budapest Stock Exchange (BSE), Hungary

	2009	2008	2007	2006	2005
Feed Corn	5,068	6,879	7,452	5,050	6,431
Feed Wheat	801	1,213	528	840	755
Euro Wheat	874	2,819	3,447	126	
Feed Barley	391	621	260	238	41
Soybean	24				
Sunflower Seed	1,874	1,942	564	1,235	1,499
Rapeseed	1,785	1,426	428	471	148
Ammonium Nitrate	9	164	10	4	1
Budapest Stock Index (BUX)	2,881,483	3,082,870	3,950,947	1,879,034	529,512
3-Month BUBOR	300		6,252		890
CHF/HUF	101,249	159,947	91,977	100,200	31,208
CZK/HUF	2,430	1,370	4,730	48,180	61,120
EUR/HUF	3,426,699	2,481,943	2,669,580	2,688,100	682,116
GBP/HUF	14,700	22,050	42,750	82,415	54,850
JPY/HUF	17,780	14,350	62,877	29,267	18,000
PLN/HUF	7,040	40	880	33,600	21,550
TRY/HUF	20,400	138,400	131,950	66,500	41,500
USD/HUF	700,606	1,446,993	1,152,754	814,635	494,057
AUD/JPY	5,550	3,300	2,700		
AUD/USD	29,400	150,650	32,940	46,400	950
CAD/JPY	1,000	1,500	12,700	19,000	34,900
CHF/JPY	3,750	2,750	5,050	19,050	46,000
GBP/CHF	35,200	188,850	102,456	388,770	395,540
GBP/JPY	116,050	328,270	1,353,100	361,450	368,703
GBP/SEK	15,500	32,300	83,050	242,950	100,600
GBP/USD	103,010	146,068	354,640	631,500	1,137,635
EURO/CHF	44,300	18,700	86,650	86,350	67,850
EURO/CZK	1,900	10,400	3,200	35,600	58,620
EURO/GBP	17,650	210,150	100,700	227,500	106,800
EURO/JPY	241,440	227,340	306,673	198,151	465,122
EURO/NOK	23,600	29,100	34,200	93,200	38,050
EURO/PLN	51,400	17,600	14,450	110,070	95,300
EURO/RON	35,750	20,300	3,500	16,400	29,100
EURO/RUB	400	8,350	7,700	19,600	
EURO/SEK	27,000	17,600	79,500	81,630	153,200
EURO/TRY	99,385	352,440	315,540	379,473	105,740
EURO/USD	416,160	999,736	1,555,406	1,117,803	1,112,158
NZD/JPY	16,800	5,000			
USD/CAD	34,120	78,332	251,316	345,405	17,750
USD/CHF	20,400	73,900	183,200	258,422	249,547
USD/CZK	400	2,300	11,500	6,700	11,400
USD/JPY	64,900	176,150	759,300	239,572	573,360
USD/MXN	900	900		3,400	
USD/NOK	2,200	1,000	25,900	2,200	
USD/PLN	7,800	4,600	52,600	8,600	57,500
USD/RUB	800	9,800	8,650	22,810	
USD/SEK	1,400	800	4,500	5,100	
USD/TRY	21,625	86,100	48,550	305,634	253,532
EUR (1 week)	493,066	360,950	594,650	910,300	12,300
GBP (1 week)	56,830	7,200	27,300	2,100	
USD (1 week)	140,290	111,920	71,500	24,000	12,500
AUD/USD (1 week)	12,800	800	87,000	500	
EUR/GBP (1 week)	31,100	4,900	17,000		

Budapest Stock Exchange (BSE), Hungary (continued)

	2009	2008	2007	2006	2005
EUR/JPY (1 week)	110,550	85,650	522,900	22,350	
EUR/PLN (1 week)	1,100	2,000	2,000	4,000	
EUR/USD (1 week)	429,700	189,250	330,900	100,690	
GBP/CHF (1 week)	33,773	27,300	8,100	13,200	
GBP/JPY (1 week)	189,750	231,400	432,000	25,700	
GBP/USD (1 week)	106,100	57,200	232,400	34,350	
USD/CAD (1 week)	40,850	84,700	362,040	22,100	
USD/CHF (1 week)	51,600	26,200	22,400	4,900	
USD/JPY (1 week)	45,000	23,400	29,500	3,000	
All Futures on Individual Equities	1,204,849	1,163,252	1,529,194	919,426	737,069
Total Futures	**11,570,661**	**12,958,135**	**18,221,627**	**13,656,165**	**9,322,332**
Feed Corn	75	225	496	527	365
Sunflower Seed	65	60	35	180	55
US Dollar	4,750	31,450	21,240	2,000	11,000
CHF	52,830	13,350	10,300		
EUR	155,350	130,559	126,766	205,000	92,200
EUR/JPY (HUF settlement)	1,000	2,900	16,850	500	
EUR/PLN (HUF settlement)	900	800		1,200	
EUR/TRY (HUF settlement)	1,250	31,066	54,635		
EUR/USD (HUF settlement)	6,600	26,958	23,100	514,901	
GBP/CHF (HUF settlement)	700	15,850	9,100	500	
USD/JPY (HUF settlement)	600	92,400	122,900	1,400	
USD/TRY	225	102	200		
Total Options	**224,345**	**411,290**	**606,601**	**1,026,764**	**160,617**

Central Japan Commodity Exchange (CJCE), Japan

	2009	2008	2007	2006	2005
Gasoline	984,956	1,745,785	3,635,329	4,953,168	11,972,407
Gas Oil	306	8,750	8,752	8,882	37,087
Kerosene	716,338	1,430,843	2,685,345	4,027,192	9,790,465
Hen Egg	486	6,362	7,077	12,275	65,142
Rubber (RSS3)	996	19,638	90,983	314,914	581,293
Rubber (TSR20)	306	8,776	11,620	34,031	212,805
Rubber Index	4,198	30,822	78,198	180,654	320,871
Gold	65,393				
Ferrous Scrap	223	5,856	5,885	17,899	84,465
Aluminum	308	9,534	15,016	75,659	459,244
Nickel	93	6,299	11,212	11,014	28,044
Total Futures	**1,773,603**	**3,272,665**	**6,549,417**	**9,635,688**	**23,551,823**

Dalian Commodity Exchange (DCE), China

	2009	2008	2007	2006	2005
Corn	16,744,088	59,918,460	59,436,742	64,976,076	21,859,732
No 1 Soybeans	42,507,076	113,681,550	47,432,721	8,897,061	40,035,707
No 2 Soybeans	32,048	42,791	21,107	1,925,226	541,093
Palm Oil	44,426,498	6,302,478	339,175		
Soybean Oil	94,836,881	43,695,993	13,283,866	10,333,006	
Soybean Meal	155,404,029	81,265,439	64,719,466	31,549,669	36,738,182
Linear Low Density Polyethylene (LLDPE)	44,752,979	13,252,982	381,836		
Polyvinyl Cloride (PVC)	18,078,662				
Total Futures	**416,782,261**	**318,159,693**	**185,614,913**	**117,681,038**	**99,174,714**

Dubai Mercantile Exchange (DME)

	2009	2008	2007
Oman Crude Oil	553,888	322,294	200,892
Total Futures	**553,888**	**330,379**	**223,174**

EUREX, Frankfurt, Germany

	2009	2008	2007	2006	2005
DAX	40,101,438	49,237,082	50,413,122	40,425,513	32,722,572
RDXxt USD RDX Extended Index	3,549	1,217	26		
OMX-Helsinki 25	148,333	186,127	100,795	33,860	41,761
DivDAX	1,803	22,679			
MDAX	297,724	595,273	824,809	395,550	72,351
MSCI Japan Index	426				
MSCI Russia Index	46,704	94,697			
TecDAX	245,270	435,556	585,377	515,891	269,354
DJ Global Titans 50	160	646	10,358	6,481	2,038
DAX - Kursindex Index Dividend	120				
DivDAX Index Dividend	8,030				
DJ Euro STOXX 50 Index Dividend	2,534,348	183,058			

EUREX, Frankfurt, Germany (continued)

	2009	2008	2007	2006	2005
DJ Euro STOXX 50 Index Dividend (Front Year)	4,493				
DJ Euro STOXX Select Dividend 30 Index Dividend	435				
SMI Index Dividend	2,576				
DJ Euro STOXX 50	333,407,299	432,298,342	327,034,149	213,514,918	139,983,083
DJ Euro STOXX Automobiles	84,664	212,427	142,146	83,868	82,203
DJ Euro STOXX Banks	437,131	651,855	640,667	225,960	233,955
DJ Euro STOXX Basic Resources	30,634	39,168	22,501	21,200	31,221
DJ Euro STOXX Chemicals	36,940	39,868	18,750	12,464	9,464
DJ Euro STOXX Construction	44,989	34,171	36,663	7,492	2,343
DJ Euro STOXX Financial Services	22,295	34,470	27,007	15,804	5,111
DJ Euro STOXX Food and Beverage	22,160	36,888	11,226	9,161	22,700
DJ Euro STOXX Healthcare	36,312	50,893	40,201	12,982	9,694
DJ Euro STOXX Industry Goods and Services	35,546	26,200	29,283	17,537	11,220
DJ Euro STOXX Insurance	192,823	234,726	153,642	192,065	169,198
DJ Euro STOXX Media	34,959	39,198	39,462	30,860	26,035
DJ Euro STOXX Energy	85,545	182,422	107,664	101,586	118,601
DJ Euro STOXX Non-Cyclical Goods and Services	21,120	21,440	15,420	8,326	5,910
DJ Euro STOXX Real Estate	2,413	2,742			
DJ Euro STOXX Media	28,668	27,085	18,399	2,441	9,568
DJ Euro STOXX Technology	89,955	171,420	153,129	210,081	218,982
DJ Euro STOXX Telecom	143,714	257,493	274,843	246,288	177,863
DJ Euro STOXX Cyclical Goods and Services	32,092	36,451	24,433	17,618	12,963
DJ Euro STOXX Utilities	109,173	117,898	74,923	107,036	75,356
DJ Euro STOXX Select Dividend 30 Index	132,793	103,422	21,118		
DJ STOXX 50	1,300,945	1,607,048	1,387,401	1,064,167	807,761
DJ STOXX Mid 200 Index	274,941	471,758	279,128	36,901	3,554
DJ STOXX Large 200 Index	101,477	140,741	9,866		
DJ STOXX Small 200 Index	199,440	279,477	21,848		
DJ STOXX 600	119,998	104,591	37,400	21,783	895
DJ STOXX 600 Automobiles & Parts	145,939	377,947	184,908	43,692	30,368
DJ STOXX 600 Banks	1,178,604	1,634,005	541,557	185,682	84,118
DJ STOXX 600 Basic Resources	491,332	441,871	214,640	90,361	30,441
DJ STOXX 600 Chemicals	75,880	89,156	72,184	18,340	3,861
DJ STOXX 600 Construction & Materials	69,729	144,268	85,996	11,482	4,103
DJ STOXX 600 Financial Services	28,542	69,389	96,472	14,349	9,695
DJ STOXX 600 Food & Beverage	212,780	175,795	85,753	91,537	24,807
DJ STOXX 600 Healthcare	366,782	379,849	305,236	171,262	117,720
DJ STOXX 600 Industrial G&S	306,558	285,522	174,806	81,265	21,844
DJ STOXX 600 Insurance	333,646	433,779	349,726	120,278	65,660
DJ STOXX 600 Media	201,928	273,233	74,664	25,242	14,955
DJ STOXX 600 Oil & Gas	490,611	534,071	387,825	146,585	35,459
DJ STOXX 600 Personal & Household Goods	101,473	60,153	15,092	21,262	7,187
DJ STOXX 600 Real Estate	34,407	17,321			
DJ STOXX 600 Retail	164,015	221,545	105,297	32,829	6,161
DJ STOXX 600 Technology	124,442	168,702	199,401	89,405	55,280
DJ STOXX 600 Telecom	396,821	386,335	268,292	164,519	112,686
DJ STOXX 600 Tracel & Leisure	158,307	113,510	86,329	25,622	9,706
DJ STOXX 600 Utilities	229,079	266,804	153,117	59,958	63,814
Swiss Leader index (SLI)	43,871	122,721	36,577		
Swiss Market Index (SMI)	12,135,437	17,658,178	14,391,903	11,369,444	8,639,822
Swiss Market Index Mid-Cap (SMIM)	80,081	99,254	152,977	29,643	4,638
Mini-Futures auf VSTOXX	14,576				
DJ Euro STOXX 50 (VSTOXX)	139	13,133	6,590	1,406	109
Swiss Government Bond (CONF)	279,720	407,583	360,355	334,314	372,385
Wuro-BTP	327,914				
Euro-BUND	180,755,004	257,827,619	338,319,416	319,889,369	299,287,916
Euro-BOBL	105,820,542	155,090,861	170,909,055	167,312,119	158,262,122
Euro-BUXL	925,627	1,155,127	1,582,859	1,265,079	470,831
3-Month Euribor	403,243	703,273	792,635	767,458	688,831
Euro-SCHATZ	125,607,110	174,226,719	181,101,310	165,318,779	141,228,207
CER	626				
CER MidDec	23				
EUA MidDec	876				
EU Allowance	22,117	80,084			
European Processing Potatoes	15,575				
Hogs	1,367				
London Potatoes	37				
Piglets	289				
DJ UBS Agriculture Sub-Index	5,552				
DJ UBS Commodity Index	14,177				
DJ UBS Energy Sub-Index	2,238				
DJ UBS Industrial Metals Sub-Index	308				
IPD UK Annual All Property Index	547				
Gold	4,154				
Silver	81				

EUREX, Frankfurt, Germany (continued)

	2009	2008	2007	2006	2005
Exchange Traded Funds	30	89	1,188	17,569	13,425
All Futures on Individual Equities	116,771,129	130,210,348	52,460,383	35,589,089	77,802
Total Futures	**928,766,700**	**1,231,646,824**	**1,146,081,579**	**960,631,763**	**784,896,954**
DAX	95,926,938	104,939,881	91,850,835	61,411,659	53,633,130
DAX 1st Friday Weekly	180,486	136,941	192,587	148,881	
DAX 2nd Friday Weekly	117,787	99,993	149,972	100,406	
DAX 3rd Friday Weekly	193,299	118,099	209,868	122,774	
DAX 4th Friday Weekly	68,591	41,279	74,790	49,821	
DAX 5th Friday Weekly	60,560	187,159	91,140	10,543	
MSCI Russia Index	28,424	4,057			
HEX 25	755	20	1,307	1,075	1,201
TecDAX	53,753	52,968	37,848	33,025	23,923
DJ Global Titans 50 Index	2		3	10	15
DJ Euro STOXX 50 Index	300,208,574	400,931,635	251,438,870	150,049,918	90,808,086
DJ Euro STOXX 50 Index - 1st Friday	72,606	36,992	149,414	90,475	
DJ Euro STOXX 50 Index - 2nd Friday	78,701	16,865	167,282	79,783	
DJ Euro STOXX 50 Index - 4th Friday	73,304	23,379	200,733	76,568	
DJ Euro STOXX 50 Index - 5th Friday	38,518	19,418	50,709	48,623	
DJ Euro STOXX Banks	32,571	103,585	644,500	105,512	119,125
DJ Euro STOXX Basic Resources	21	50	415	50	
DJ Euro STOXX Chemicals	12,317	5,899	12,790	1,540	458
DJ Euro STOXX Financial Services	1,511	1,575	5,381	2,000	250
DJ Euro STOXX Food and Beverage	1,200	104	3,486	2,000	17,910
DJ Euro STOXX Healthcare	74	502		2,460	5,250
DJ Euro STOXX Insurance	5,430	47,709	19,955	36,561	46,600
DJ Euro STOXX Media	2,000	5,408	16,559	7,300	22,492
DJ Euro STOXX Oil & Gas	1,652	14,544	17,870	108,053	90,726
DJ Euro STOXX Personal & Household Goods	10	165		906	
DJ Euro STOXX Technology	7,600	24,702	10,000	68,125	58,830
DJ Euro STOXX Telecom	9,741	51,047	40,018	49,856	113,758
DJ Euro STOXX Travel & Leisure	75	90	150	15,552	18,700
DJ Euro STOXX Utilities	15,989	13,781	62,494	87,546	33,230
DJ STOXX 50 Index	52,816	103,080	140,197	63,064	29,052
DJ STOXX 600 Index	16,113	37,529	30,593	4,208	
DJ STOXX 600 Automobiles & Parts	8,580	95,635	85,135	3,100	
DJ STOXX 600 Banks	245,012	535,531	377,343	30,701	10,887
DJ STOXX 600 Basic Resources	95,564	179,574	95,047	94,486	13,966
DJ STOXX 600 Chemicals	2,221	31,488	9,684	1,610	
DJ STOXX 600 Construction & Materials	1,018	60,216	50,582	305	
DJ STOXX 600 Financial Services	1,246	6,947	6,115	3,600	
DJ STOXX 600 Food & Beverage	1,384	29,802	623	568	
DJ STOXX 600 Healthcare	28,654	46,305	65,188	18,971	32,984
DJ STOXX 600 Industrial Goods & Services	57,026	111,988	142,189	41,602	1,360
DJ STOXX 600 Insurance	147,459	525,853	195,790	11,604	8,399
DJ STOXX 600 Media	5,990	15,632	10,744	5,206	310
DJ STOXX 600 Oil & Gas	39,455	173,140	89,956	55,822	29,824
DJ STOXX 600 Personal & Household Goods	706	4,587	7,063	320	
DJ STOXX 600 Retail	19,958	19,431			
DJ STOXX 600 Technology	1,550	11,612	11,539	4,081	600
DJ STOXX 600 Telecom	76,903	46,994	43,478	52,023	27,723
DJ STOXX 600 Travel & Leisure	9,208	922	9,653	18,761	486
DJ STOXX 600 Utilities	38,748	84,162	106,487	23,308	13,679
DJ Stoxx Small 200 Index	6,470	31,998	7,607		
DJ STOXX Mid 200 Index	11,251	112,858	172,017	52,899	1,584
Swiss Market Index (SMI)	4,094,103	5,588,591	5,773,269	3,948,593	4,134,470
Swiss Market Index (SMI) - 1st Friday	1		8,405	4,810	
Swiss Leader Index (SLI)	48,110	49,519	19,599		
Swiss Market Index Mid-Cap (SMIM)	54,287	49,610	44,920	14,616	
Euro-BUND	28,392,790	33,317,879	44,441,961	41,764,550	39,014,844
Euro-SCHATZ	16,215,924	20,438,378	19,085,515	17,344,245	11,546,405
Euro-BOBL	6,955,457	15,083,076	15,135,182	17,220,011	7,990,587
Gold	13,181				
Silver	106				
All Options on Austrian Equities	188,289	113,901	19,025		
All Options on Belgian Equities	104,865	31,017			
All Options on Dutch Equities	6,813,332	7,243,976	11,811,227	10,420,237	12,834,633
All Options on Exchange Traded Funds	5,515	330,944	31,730	15,732	42,278
All Options on French Equities	10,539,983	9,429,765	7,795,177	6,667,994	4,867,961
All Options on German Equities	186,930,541	234,948,892	214,969,289	180,695,967	162,437,728
All Options on Italian Equities	1,394,120	1,784,585	1,146,488	1,006,419	785,918
All Options on Russian Equities	59,885	179,672	22,398		
All Options on Scandinavian Equities	19,342,143	18,414,654	17,291,936	16,396,662	16,109,249
All Options on Spanish Equities	1,202,642	1,319,054	860,700	22,988	
All Options on Individual Swiss Equities	77,977,503	75,864,298	68,122,792	57,323,550	58,463,793
Total Options	**758,392,598**	**933,396,359**	**753,780,347**	**566,120,139**	**463,851,198**

Hong Kong Futures Exchange (HKFE), Hong Kong

	2009	2008	2007	2006	2005
Hang Seng Index	20,728,034	21,716,508	17,160,964	12,718,380	9,910,565
Mini Hang Seng Index	9,279,877	7,961,028	4,325,977	2,140,242	1,501,342
H-Shares Index	12,394,116	14,440,965	10,846,277	4,880,470	1,978,673
Mini H-Shares Index	799,894	318,395			
1-Month HIBOR	204	881	574	155	246
3-Month HIBOR	2,573	23,818	31,678	13,888	24,935
Gold	6,773	3,075			
All Futures on Individual Equities	271,766	257,015	351,514	102,010	13,069
Total Futures	**43,483,237**	**44,721,743**	**32,723,598**	**19,863,299**	**13,433,386**
Hang Seng Index	5,367,403	3,820,797	7,480,183	4,095,679	3,071,822
Mini Hang Seng Index	286,591	156,957	69,512	53,456	30,595
H-Shares Index	1,961,131	1,613,988	1,727,847	758,247	257,425
All Options on Individual Equities	47,439,896	54,692,865	45,982,968	18,127,353	8,722,393
Total Options	**55,055,021**	**60,284,993**	**55,262,088**	**23,042,616**	**12,089,621**

ICE Futures Canada (ICE), Canada

	2009	2008	2007	2006	2005
Canola (Rapeseed)	3,351,793	3,132,188	3,169,182	2,607,354	1,822,985
Western Barley	54,839	167,381	214,672	195,024	136,564
Total Futures	**3,406,632**	**3,299,999**	**3,430,324**	**2,868,933**	**2,047,183**
Canola	85,115	21,206	17,067	26,523	27,111
Total Options	85,115	21,211	**21,841**	**27,603**	**29,447**

ICE Futures Europe (ICE), United Kingdom

	2009	2008	2007	2006	2005
Brent Crude Oil	74,137,750	68,368,145	59,728,941	44,345,927	30,412,027
Brent Crude Oil (Quarters)	570	3	12	150	
Gas Oil (Monthly)	36,038,870	28,805,192	24,509,884	18,289,877	10,971,719
Gas Oil (Quarters)	204			300	
UK Natural Gas (Seasons)	907,470	279,930	136,740	42,660	11,520
UK Natural Gas (Quarters)	255,435	103,440	37,905	16,080	9,045
UK Natural Gas Monthly (NBP)	1,629,980	879,420	1,058,290	543,550	423,565
ECX EUA (Monthly)	3,775,621	1,991,276	980,780	452,359	94,348
ECX EUA (Daily)	38,214				
WTI Crude (Monthly)	46,393,671	51,091,712	51,388,362	28,672,639	
WTI Crude (Calendars)	360	12			
NYH (RBOB) Gasoline (Monthly)	4,965	26,356	14,805	9,692	
Gasoline (Quarters)	3	120			
Heating Oil (Monthly)	135,265	116,911	205,072	199,187	
ECX CER (Monthly)	766,349	507,779			
ECX CER (Daily)	3,780				
Rotterdam Coal (Monthly)	28,735	5,895	465	45	
Rotterdam Coal (Quarters)	135,240	24,720	3,870	630	
Rotterdam Coal (Seasons)	2,190	630		30	
Rotterdam Coal (Calendar)	255,420	70,860	4,500	120	
Richards Bay Coal (Monthly)	14,225	1,900	240	60	
Richards Bay Coal (Quarters)	44,265	8,880	525	15	
Richards Bay Coal (Calendar)	91,680	34,020	480		
Richards Bay Coal (Seasons)	210	30			
gCNewcastle Coal (Monthly)	4,625				
gCNewcastle Coal (Quarters)	18,210				
gCNewcastle Coal (Calendars)	39,240				
UK Base Electricity (Monthly)	895	370	990	3,155	2,500
UK Base Electricity (Quarters)	1,140	975	330	930	1,380
UK Base Electricity (Seasons)	16,830	2,790	1,920	3,870	8,190
Total Futures	**164,741,412**	**152,322,268**	**138,169,680**	**92,582,921**	**41,936,609**
Brent Crude Oil	212,341	121,024	74,056	33,249	44,421
ECX EUA	416,567	242,966	57,541	560	
ECX CER	91,130	69,565			
WTI Crude Oil	18,200	11,131	10,416		
Gasoil	213,884	183,179	159,263	104,320	74,055
Total Options	**952,122**	**627,865**	**301,276**	**138,129**	**118,476**

Italian Derivatives Market of the Italian Stock Exchange, Italy

	2009	2008	2007	2006	2005
MIB 30 Index	4,240,026	7,914,300	4,671,557	4,037,973	3,580,695
Mini FIB 30 Index	2,596,645	2,909,366	2,065,878	1,659,649	1,294,606
Electricity	5,188	634			
All Futures on Individual Equities	10,973,237	4,417,700	6,363,954	7,031,974	5,957,674
Total Futures	**17,815,096**	**15,242,000**	**13,101,389**	**12,729,596**	**10,832,975**
MIB 30 Index	2,821,434	3,630,359	3,658,686	2,819,916	2,597,830
All Options on Individual Equities	21,946,195	20,056,426	20,364,847	16,056,751	12,439,716
Total Options	**24,767,629**	**23,686,785**	**24,023,533**	**18,876,667**	**15,037,546**

JSE Securities Exchange of South Africa, Africa

	2009	2008	2007	2006	2005
White Maize (WMAZ)	687,472	859,920	956,026	865,549	806,639
Yellow Maize (YMAZ)	311,589	337,429	268,780	164,601	198,625
Corn	15,016				
WEAT	379,365	469,471	378,289	264,925	221,283
SUNS	127,807	165,088	64,402	68,882	78,093
SOYA	116,530	73,111	44,062	36,939	14,945
WOPT	18,371	80	14,500	18,913	
Gold	1,725				
Platinum	1,596				
Crude Oil	742				
FTSE/JSE Top 40 Index (ALSI)	12,145,844	15,924,693	16,150,010	13,483,033	10,103,226
FTSE/JSE Top 40 Index - Mini (ALMI)	10,876	450			
FTSE/JSE African Banks Index (J835)	56				
FTSE/JSE 25 Index (INDI)	3,058	25,723	22,845	20,259	40,066
FTSE/JSE Gold Mining Index (GLDX)	2,352	1,651	7,893	11,517	336
FTSE/JSE FINI 15 Index (FINI)	17,826	43,660	16,309	6,421	6,439
FTSE/JSE FNDI 30 Index (FNDI)	183,311	217,863	125,960	319,247	33,663
FTSE/JSE Capped Top 40 Index (CTOP)	11,420	47,687	19,977	106,003	
FTSE/JSE Shareholder Weighted Top 40 Index (DTOP)	4,361,957	3,037,960	2,359,997	1,321,011	460,071
FTSE/JSE SA Listed Property Index (SAPI)	200	370	684	12,245	6,184
FTSE/JSE RESI 20 Index	780	14,528	5,390	8,254	1,419
Can Do (CDAA)	10,619,562	1,128,772	736,044	219,211	
Kruger Rand (KGRD)	12	519	9,922	6,654	16,381
Dividend Futures	16,364,671	20,097,204	11,891,790	420,266	
IDX Futures	4,321,081	28,362			
IDX Dividend Futures	172,914	1,364,561			
All Futures on Individual Equities	88,791,925	431,212,627	265,493,735	69,665,994	24,455,924
Total Futures	**138,668,058**	**475,051,729**	**298,567,616**	**87,036,273**	**36,456,767**
White Maize (WMAZ)	182,400	455,403	471,727	368,404	344,269
Yellow Maize (YMAZ)	41,635	69,339	55,695	20,746	23,694
Corn	61				
WEAT	28,620	176,079	140,545	57,699	61,433
SUNS	7,108	21,073	5,983	9,179	21,115
SOYA	6,914	5,978	1,986	4,971	1,354
FTSE/JSE Top 40 Index (ALSI)	5,691,546	9,834,294	9,008,828	9,878,535	10,208,949
FTSE/JSE FNDI 30 Index (FNDI)	71,950	50,987	70,110	219,444	124,638
FTSE/JSE Shareholder Weighted Top 40 Index (DTOP)	4,975,451	4,722,544	4,026,943	1,540,221	1,226,005
CAN DO	1,247,761	3,604,877	2,978,981	73,454	
All Options on Individual Equities	15,670,869	19,591,351	14,312,446	5,751,833	2,799,774
Total Options	**27,924,315**	**38,532,275**	**31,074,787**	**18,011,251**	**14,861,408**

Kansai Commodities Exchange (KCE), Japan

	2009	2008	2007	2006	2005
Red Beans	4,750	4,362	4,362	8,491	13,760
US Soybeans	11,816	16,238	19,712	1,497	10,264
Corn	24,336	133,592	101,401	121,135	765,921
Raw Sugar	5,340	4,559	4,380	7,671	8,181
Raw Silk	504	358		1,446	6,346
Frozen Shrimp	5,789	5,853	6,248	66,651	511,944
Corn 75 Index	8,682	8,754	8,910	11,087	91,007
Coffee Index	8,683	8,903	11,248	59,627	269,269
Total Futures	**69,900**	**183,999**	**164,743**	**315,501**	**1,825,806**

Korea Futures Exchange (KFE), Korea

	2009	2008	2007	2006	2005
3-Year Treasury Bond	20,050,788	15,958,864	13,555,136	10,343,605	11,223,244
KOPSI 200*	83,117,030	64,835,148	47,758,294	46,611,008	43,848,706
STAR Index	490	13,325	21,919	107,538	103,619
Lean Hogs	13,703	16,258			
Gold	1,731	1,267	399		
US Dollar	41,161,819	6,672,438	5,752,134	3,104,641	2,667,005
Japanese Yen	272,531	104,012	271,043		
Euro	310,540	103,762	212,790		
All Futures on Individual Equities	36,971,510	11,293,134			
Total Futures	**181,900,142**	**99,007,894**	**67,571,815**	**60,169,114**	**57,883,098**
KOPSI 200 Index	2,920,990,655	2,766,474,404	2,709,844,077	2,414,422,952	2,535,201,692
All Options on Individual Equities	980	21	206	1,195	3,655
Total Options	**2,920,991,635**	**2,766,474,425**	**2,709,844,283**	**2,414,424,147**	**2,535,205,347**

London Metal Exchange (LME), United Kingdom

	2009	2008	2007	2006	2005
High Grade Primary Aluminium	46,988,069	48,307,389	40,229,693	36,418,131	30,426,465
Aluminium Alloy	427,452	582,398	492,868	444,738	501,960
North American Special Aluminium Alloy	920,336	1,519,811	1,236,484	1,031,411	1,001,412
Copper - Grade A	24,922,949	26,507,242	21,420,450	18,864,246	19,231,371
Standard Lead	5,983,323	6,188,753	4,697,862	4,568,140	4,061,819
Primary Nickel	6,717,299	5,202,609	3,792,788	4,177,557	3,482,593
Special High Grade Zinc	15,901,774	16,120,770	12,556,285	11,706,008	10,620,618
Far East Steel (MS)	447	2,760			
Mediterranean Steel (MS)	30,764	13,206			
Tin	4,567,915	1,410,450	1,293,722	1,283,897	1,095,031
LMEmini Copper Grade A	10	45	1,099	1,411	
Polypropylene	7	1,466	7,977	13,303	15,770
PE Europe	8	22	29		
PN North America	2,713	2,449	401		
LE Europe	26	80	16		
LA Asia	37	169			
LN North America	710	1,705	282		
Total Futures	**106,463,839**	**105,861,588**	**85,736,480**	**78,527,839**	**70,444,665**
High Grade Primary Aluminium	2,505,499	3,702,232	3,115,989	4,690,867	4,107,102
Aluminium Alloy	216,735	267,722	316,496	315	369,068
North American Special Aluminium Alloy	4,333	24,052	10,052	4,420	10,069
Copper - Grade A	1,624,350	1,987,291	2,027,181	1,850,993	2,091,198
Standard Lead	145,354	346,672	298,965	164,410	128,283
Primary Nickel	142,168	152,744	167,428	158,496	189,903
Special High Grade Zinc	712,526	715,970	1,111,080	1,335,184	1,011,429
Tin	33,562	67,716	18,407	17,315	14,012
Primary Aluminium TAPOS	55,149	37,748	43,621	93,540	129,657
Aluminium Alloy TAPOS	48	3,022	3,528	2,141	
Copper Grade A TAPOS	15,212	16,146	16,667	45,346	55,907
Lead TAPOS	3,065	9,411	3,210	3,335	8,116
Nickel TAPOS	3,541	11,347	35,220	14,502	12,610
Tin TAPOS	12	810	48	850	2,014
NASAA TAPOS	100	2,290	42	1,170	33,194
Special High Grade Zinc TAPOS	5,335	8,538	10,314	29,466	21,625
Total Options	**5,466,989**	**7,353,711**	**7,178,248**	**8,412,350**	**8,184,187**

Malaysia Derivatives Exchange, Malaysia

	2009	2008	2007	2006	2005
Crude Palm Oil (FCPO)	4,008,882	3,003,529	2,793,560	2,230,340	1,158,510
3-Month KLIBOR	126,690	195,203	239,314	272,502	162,592
5-Year Malaysian Gov't Securities (FMG5)	4,300	100	8,821	27,232	17,215
KLSE Composite Index (FKLI)	1,997,955	2,920,728	3,157,341	1,628,043	1,111,575
Total Futures	**6,137,827**	**6,120,032**	**6,202,686**	**4,161,024**	**2,459,745**

MEFF Renta Variable (RV), Spain

	2009	2008	2007	2006	2005
IBEX 35 Plus Index	5,436,989	7,275,299	8,435,258	6,408,961	4,591,196
Mini IBEX 35 Index	3,148,292	3,300,418	2,865,739	1,598,296	1,490,080
All Futures on Individual Equities	44,586,779	46,237,568	21,294,315	21,029,811	18,813,689
Total Futures	**53,172,060**	**56,813,285**	**32,595,312**	**29,037,068**	**24,894,965**
IBEX 35 Plus Index	4,357,260	8,286,224	5,670,773	5,510,621	4,407,465
All Options on Individual Equities	35,527,914	18,317,249	13,593,493	12,425,979	10,915,227
Total Options	**39,885,174**	**26,603,473**	**19,264,266**	**17,936,600**	**15,322,692**

Mercado a Termino de Buenos Aires (MATBA), Argentina

	2009	2008	2007	2006	2005
Wheat	25,921	37,243	41,781	41,200	34,863
Corn	15,144	22,269	32,012	18,310	10,535
Sunflower	99	101	135	206	824
Soybean	101,654	82,164	80,016	59,279	68,598
Total Futures	**142,818**	**141,873**	**154,069**	**118,995**	**114,820**
Wheat	2,584	1,449	5,243	7,934	7,074
Corn	356	1,538	4,068	5,021	569
Soybean	35,126	10,831	12,963	15,195	13,146
Total Options	**38,066**	**13,882**	**23,495**	**28,150**	**20,915**

Mexican Derivatives Exchange (MEXDER), Mexico

	2009	2008	2007	2006	2005
US Dollar	1,587,858	3,186,832	3,223,044	6,026,940	2,934,658
Euro FX	64,327	44,172	2,105	50,469	125
IPC Stock Index	1,130,528	1,085,663	951,955	620,557	410,565
CETE 91	4,877,430	4,087,066	2,812,500	3,290,100	4,509,002
TIIE 28	37,545,841	57,881,101	220,608,024	264,160,131	99,830,916
M3 Bond	216,150	43,000	36,500	28,600	
M10 Bond	2,613,021	3,005,307	1,182,069	471,879	284,460
M20 Bond	269,904				
10-Year Interest Rate Swap	67,144	170,949	25,332		
2-Year Interest Rate Swap	21,910				
Total Futures	**48,394,113**	**69,506,090**	**228,841,531**	**274,651,676**	**107,989,126**
MXN / USD	145	7	10	2,343	
IPC Stock Index	40,723	52,556	130,410	115,531	38,329
All Options on Individual Equities	345,718	577,452	78	448,120	149,091
Total Options	**386,586**	**637,600**	**130,498**	**565,994**	**188,150**

Montreal Exchange (ME), Canada

	2009	2008	2007	2006	2005
3-Month Bankers Acceptance (BAX)	7,668,781	9,958,833	15,237,958	16,702,302	11,157,298
S&P/TSX Composite Index Mini (SCF)	1,151				
5 Year Canadian Gov't Bond (CGF)	12,055				
10-Year Canadian Gov't Bond (CGB)	5,310,537	7,363,569	9,337,754	7,691,797	4,692,287
Canada Carbon Dioxide Equivalent Units (MCX)	43	1,179			
S&P Canada 60 Index (SXF)	4,157,917	4,575,352	3,885,872	3,064,695	2,234,406
Gold Index (SXA)	20	91,186	10,908	23,645	9,898
Banking Index (SXB)	94	24,129	9,014	140	266
Energy Index (SXY)	110	28,762	5,585	10,157	13,662
Total Futures	**17,150,708**	**22,043,015**	**28,493,454**	**27,578,059**	**18,240,633**
3-Month Bankers Acceptance (OBX)	234,861	282,190	748,991	605,806	377,370
10-Year Canadian Gov't Bond (OGB)	12,531	23,553	13,782	2,275	
US Dollar (USX)	29,902	23,795	34,889	31,262	7,264
S&P Canada 60 Index (SXO)	34,056	38,666	26,484	57,974	27,897
Claymore Global Agriculture (COW)	1,460	64			
Horizons BetaPro S&P/TSX Global Gold Bear Plus Fund	2,728				
Horizons BetaPro S&P/TSX Global Gold Bull Plus Fund	4,789				
Horizons BetaPro S&P/TSX 60 Bear Plus ETF (HXD)	13,137	3,896			
Horizons BetaPro S&P/TSX 60 Bull Plus ETF (HXU)	10,109	7,651			
i60 Index (XIU)	1,956,588	661,286	364,924	317,637	176,498
iShares DJ Canada Select Div Index Fund (XDV)	3,159				
iShares CDN S&P/TSX Capped Com Index Fund (XIC)	3,022				
iShares CDN S&P/TSX Capped REIT Index Fund (XRE)	1,978				
Horizons BetaPro NYMEX Crude Oil Bear Plus Fund	9,491				
Horizons BetaPro NYMEX Crude Oil Bull Plus Fund	75,439				
Horizons BetaPro S&P/TSX Capped Fin Bear Plus ETF	2,662				
Horizons BetaPro S&P/TSX Capped Fin Bull Plus ETF	2,553				
iShares CDN MSCI EAFE 100% Hedged to CAD $ Index	1,624				
iShares CDN S&P 500 Hedged to CAD $ Index Fund (XSP)	1,268				
Horizons BetaPro S&P/TSX Cap Energy Bear ETF (HEU)	634				
Horizons BetaPro S&P/TSX Cap Energy Bull ETF (HEU)	378				
Claymore Natural Gas Commodity ETF (GAS)	79,444				
iShares CDN DEX Corporate Bond Index Fund (XCB)	1,280				
iShares CDN DEX Short-term Bond Index Fund (XSB)	763				
Horizons BetaPro NYMEX Natural Gas Bear Plus Fund	451				
Horizons BetaPro NYMEX Natural Gas Bull Plus Fund	2,038				
CDN S&P/TSX Capped Gold Index Fund (XGD)	114,884	58,438	89,435	144,695	111,502
CDN S&P/TSX Capped Financials Index Fund (XFN)	356,040	195,820	101,499	130,730	99,079
CDN S&P/TSX Capped IT Index Fund (XIT)	2,110	3,248	14,989	10,018	7,942
CDN S&P/TSX Capped Materials Index Fund (XMA)	14,669	5,811	59,371	11,012	
CDN S&P/TSX Capped Energy Index Fund (XEG)	121,064	80,838	158,178	234,611	227,268
All Options on Individual Equities	14,507,261	14,633,599	12,634,060	11,416,758	9,409,938
Total Options	**17,602,373**	**16,021,887**	**14,248,756**	**12,962,778**	**10,444,758**

Moscow Interbank Currency Exchange (MICEX), Russia

	2009	2008	2007
Wheat	149,249	79,378	
EUR	54,369	96,000	2,000
US Dollar	17,752,959	131,699,407	85,331,934
EUR/USD	630		
3-Month MosPrime Rate	60	3,275	1,271
MICEX Index	396,289	25,716	49,568
All Futures on Individual Equities	954,685		
Total Futures	**19,308,241**	**131,905,458**	**85,386,473**

National Stock Exchange of India

	2009	2008	2007	2006	2005
S&P CNX Nifty Index	195,759,414	202,390,223	138,794,235	70,286,227	47,375,214
All Futures on Individual Equities	161,053,345	225,777,205	179,324,970	100,285,737	68,911,754
Total Futures	**356,812,759**	**428,167,428**	**318,119,205**	**170,571,964**	**116,286,968**
S&P CNX Nifty Index	321,265,217	150,916,778	52,707,150	18,702,248	10,140,239
All Options on Individual Equities	14,066,778	11,067,082	9,048,495	5,214,191	5,224,485
Total Options	**335,331,995**	**161,983,860**	**61,755,645**	**23,916,439**	**15,364,724**

NYSE-LIFFE

	2009	2008	2007	2006	2005
All Futures on Individual Equities	199,044,957				
All Futures on Individual Equities, Lisbon		413,987	894,753	584,957	413,315
All Futures on Individual Equities, United Kingdom		124,054,822	74,371,596	28,930,769	11,744,778
Total Futures	**199,044,957**	**124,468,809**	**75,266,349**	**29,515,726**	**12,158,093**
All Options on Individual Equities	170,870,365				
All Options on Individual Equities, Amsterdam		101,667,922	118,038,899	89,115,941	71,297,264
All Options on Individual Equities, Brussels		581,752	619,273	518,489	392,377
All Options on Individual Equities, United Kingdom		46,547,253	33,260,918	20,757,421	9,085,505
All Options on Individual Equities, Paris		35,308,480	34,233,628	45,160,159	183,560,708
Total Options	**170,870,365**	**184,105,407**	**186,152,718**	**155,552,010**	**264,335,854**

NYSE-LIFFE - Amsterdam, Netherlands

	2009	2008	2007	2006	2005
AEX Stock Index (FTI)	10,524,741	12,477,916	12,850,137	11,165,258	7,397,665
Euro/US Dollar (FED)	6,588	5,124	5,087	7,474	5,640
US Dollar/Euro (FDE)	829	1,394	918	1,333	1,795
Total Futures	**10,532,158**	**12,484,434**	**12,856,367**	**11,190,181**	**7,447,671**
Euro / US Dollar (EDX)	388,488	394,315	439,811	651,810	290,839
US Dollar / Euro	45,603	55,414	52,499	81,229	113,118
AEX Stock Index (AEX)	24,660,898	27,534,800	26,292,719	23,694,580	19,753,393
Total Options	**25,094,989**	**27,984,529**	**28,932,245**	**26,527,631**	**20,188,388**

NYSE-LIFFE - Brussels, Belgium

	2009	2008	2007	2006	2005
Bel 20 Index (BXF)	296,543	615,088	596,144	654,520	603,069
Total Futures	**296,543**	**615,088**	**596,144**	**654,520**	**603,069**
Bel 20 Index	10,192	15,404	133,467	127,000	117,795
Total Options	**10,192**	**15,404**	**133,467**	**127,000**	**117,795**

NYSE-LIFFE - Lisbon

	2009	2008	2007	2006	2005
PSI-20 Index	61,225	75,904	110,485	88,557	64,252
Total Futures	**61,225**	**75,904**	**110,485**	**88,557**	**64,252**

NYSE-LIFFE - Paris

	2009	2008	2007	2006	2005
Wheat #2	1,925,916	1,464,484	980,742	407,843	217,171
Corn	149,008	112,408	94,606	72,044	81,965
Rapeseed	812,779	680,765	438,849	238,594	211,281
CAC 40 Stock Index 10 Euro	41,940,487	49,242,000	44,668,975	33,405,804	25,011,372
CAC 40 Dividend Index	322				
FTSE EPRA Eurozone	28,659	12,265	3,742		
FTSE EPRA Europe	87,274	53,533	4,278		
FTSEurofirst 80	186,634	473,365	397,110	26,412	
FTSEurofirst 100	122	501	21,281	990	
Total Futures	**45,131,201**	**52,039,321**	**46,653,064**	**34,151,687**	**25,521,789**
Rapeseed	79,385	134,370	50,962	26,843	8,192
Wheat	655,099	325,464	129,365	41,398	9,810
Corn	5,720	3,738	4,656	1,818	1,622
CAC 40 Index, 10 EUR	6,126,542	8,628,618	9,793,350	6,633,635	2,802,039
Total Options	**6,866,746**	**9,092,220**	**9,982,198**	**6,705,070**	**33,891,553**

NYSE-LIFFE, United Kingdom

	2009	2008	2007	2006	2005
3-Month Short Sterling	104,073,092	104,572,875	119,675,947	83,003,622	68,029,052
3-Month Euroswiss	4,768,825	8,572,662	12,219,848	10,743,902	8,286,258
3-Month Euroyen Tibor	43,419	125,644	271,273	99,543	22
3-Month Eonia	135,594	31,322			
3-Month Euribor	192,859,090	228,487,462	221,411,485	202,091,612	166,682,115
3-Month Eurodollar	6,343	26,692	15,926	69,760	5,662,806
Short Gilt	30,680				
Medium Gilt	11,455				
Long Gilt	23,977,779	24,717,249	27,367,489	22,009,284	17,760,359
2-Year Swapnote EUR	452,362	703,608	512,872	274,459	322,212
5-Year Swapnote EUR	251,078	212,746	407,029	401,365	387,005
10-Year Swapnote EUR	76,200	104,460	273,961	405,011	434,759
Japanese Government Bond	50,953	105,584	173,810	140,487	101,127
FTSE 100 Index	38,515,933	42,314,080	33,535,934	25,120,880	21,522,583
FTSE 100 Dividend Index	667,052				
FTSE Eurotop 100 Index	9,882	13,907	27,352	32,694	74,667
MSCI Euro Index	3,684	5,964	6,360	18,036	21,114
MSCI Pan-Euro Index	358,168	641,354	835,603	701,066	521,591
FTSE Mid 250 Index	91,362	163,652	181,735	62,304	39,238
Index F Other Bclear	95,287				
Cocoa #7	3,218,726	3,577,010	3,319,396	3,095,346	2,690,105
Robusta Coffee	12,996	3,959,277	4,435,793	3,550,938	3,263,253
Robusta Coffee - 10 Tonne	2,514,457	207,443			
Wheat	114,133	131,358	128,073	76,239	65,324
White Sugar	1,852,702	1,654,446	2,091,654	1,668,674	1,497,150
Total Futures	**374,191,252**	**420,340,439**	**426,960,618**	**354,437,011**	**298,034,784**
3-Month Short Sterling	37,876,416	59,079,440	50,747,710	34,231,229	25,096,889
3-Month Sterling Mid-curve	12,109,210	12,994,233	4,330,981	3,212,817	3,173,334
3-Month Sterling 2-Year Mid-curve	10,550				
3-Month Euribor	121,612,383	106,730,522	74,276,297	48,176,163	44,138,922
3-Month Euribor Mid Curve	18,498,853	7,955,894	6,188,559	7,355,609	7,017,840
3-Month Euribor 2-Year Mid-curve	30,402				
Long Gilt	384,145				
FTSE 100 Index (ESX)	30,155,112	29,261,814	23,700,667	15,717,186	14,473,441
FTSE 100 Index FLEX	2,400,296	1,434,196	1,021,680	1,979,620	1,189,652
Other Bclear	34,992	57,250	13,697	16,700	
Cocoa	556,860	251,614	177,788	102,819	95,814
Robusta Coffee - 10 Tonne	192,398	48,987			
Wheat	656	523	5,284	2,320	3,070
White Sugar	50,195	224,977	254,307	81,647	81,598
Total Options	**223,912,468**	**218,508,097**	**161,381,797**	**111,353,733**	**95,563,612**

New Zealand Futures Exchange (NZFOE), New Zealand

	2009	2008	2007	2006	2005
3-Year Government Stock	2,510		30		
10-Year Government Stock	4,329	691	664	594	891
NZ 30-Day OCR Interbank	20				
90-Day Bank Bill	1,484,030	1,453,947	1,638,294	1,801,132	982,302
NZ Electricity (Otahuhu)	6				
NZ Electricity (Benmore)	52				
Total Futures	**1,490,947**	**1,454,638**	**1,638,988**	**1,801,726**	**983,223**
90-Day Bank Bill	3,100	1,850	4,450	24,190	2,850
Total Options	**3,100**	**4,450**	**12,050**	**24,301**	**2,850**

Osaka Securities Exchange (OSE), Japan

	2009	2008	2007	2006	2005
Nikkei 225 Index	25,368,919	35,546,016	30,084,781	25,151,924	17,909,404
Nikkei 225 Mini	104,738,309	95,446,729	49,107,059	6,348,382	
Nikkei 300 Index	405	35,509	81,907	153,439	141,534
US Dollar/Japanese Yen	243,611				
Euro/Japanese Yen	108,118				
British Pound/Japanese Yen	51,086				
Australian Dollar/Japanese Yen	52,858				
Swiss Franc/Japanese Yen	4,953				
Canadian Dollar/Japanese Yen	13,069				
New Zealand/Japanese Yen	7,567				
Euro/US Dollar	71,516				
British Pound/US Dollar	30,241				
Total Futures	**130,690,652**	**131,028,334**	**79,291,064**	**31,661,331**	**18,070,352**
Nikkei 225 Index	34,986,005	32,126,060	29,181,438	28,230,767	24,894,389
All Options on Individual Equities	408,752	534,954	444,149	753,937	1,206,987
Total Options	**35,394,757**	**32,661,014**	**29,625,747**	**28,985,106**	**26,101,912**

VOLUME - WORLDWIDE

OMX Exchanges, Sweden

	2009	2008	2007	2006	2005
3-Month STIBOR	12,923,736	16,929,736	14,892,134		
Policy Rate (RIBA)	1,040,006				
NASDAQ OMX Interest Rate Swap (NOIS)	1,250				
2-Year Swedish Gov't Bond Forward (R2)	2,096,471	4,049,661	3,568,792		
5-Year Swedish Gov't Bond Forward (R5)	1,179,563	1,366,872	1,930,006		
10-Year Swedish Gov't Bond Forward (R10)	885,565	892,169	798,640		
2-Year Nordea Hypotek Bond Forward (NBHYP2)	345,156	389,973	168,119		
5-Year Nordea Hypotek Bond Forward (NBHYP5)	202,314	186,936	118,052		
2-Year Spintab Bond Forward (SPA2)	176,791	215,937	154,457		
5-Year Spintab Bond Forward (SPA5)	240,372	226,499	178,072		
2-Year Stadshypotek Bond Forward (ST2)	257,681	674,731	386,189		
5-Year Stadshypotek Bond Forward (ST5)	331,842	294,279	328,507		
OMX Index	33,700,054	39,307,915	31,609,782	24,374,765	20,259,029
All Futures on Individual Equities	6,718,987	15,841,312	9,013,489	8,459,165	5,659,824
Total Futures	**60,099,788**	**80,376,020**	**63,376,025**	**45,039,885**	**34,142,225**
Interest Rate	1,170,505	629,000	685,010		
OMX Index	14,225,611	19,654,145	19,715,476	13,613,210	12,229,146
All Options on Individual Equities	28,775,091	42,767,407	59,660,819	64,514,641	57,138,565
Total Options	**44,171,207**	**63,050,552**	**80,061,305**	**78,127,851**	**69,367,711**

Oslo Stock Exchange (OSE), Norway

	2009	2008	2007	2006	2005
Forwards	1,173,476	1,637,407	2,630,772	3,615,036	1,796,570
OBX	9,041,941	9,195,919	4,755,934	2,429,235	562,591
Total Futures	**10,215,417**	**10,833,326**	**7,386,706**	**6,044,271**	**2,359,161**
OBX	746,589	1,460,422	1,797,651	1,331,023	515,538
All Options on Individual Equities	2,549,240	3,754,682	4,783,490	5,781,666	3,325,368
Total Options	**3,295,829**	**5,215,104**	**6,581,141**	**7,112,689**	**3,840,906**

Rosario Futures Exchange (ROFEX), Argentina

	2009	2008	2007	2006	2005
Wheat	267	106	405	1,039	41
Corn	88	208	294	538	8
Soybeans	26,047	17,421	40,000	556	504
Rosafe Soybean Index (ISR)	133,712	77,766	143,824	101,029	116,281
Rosafe Wheat Index (ITR)	1,840	5,631	10,661	5,061	
Rosafe Corn Index (IMR)	5,168	7,663	6,292	8,714	2,139
Badlar (BAR)	10	121			
US Dollar (DLR)	51,107,696	41,796,793	25,042,919	17,779,242	12,931,695
Euro (EC)	11,974	151,620	20	157,005	580
Total Futures	**51,286,802**	**42,092,168**	**25,249,072**	**18,053,184**	**13,051,248**
Rosafe Soybean Index (ISR)	53,114	24,986	36,972	24,229	44,307
Rosafe Wheat Index (ITR)	205	410	6,460	3,836	
Rosafe Corn Index (IMR)	626	2,762	1,845	6,750	2,969
Government Bond (DICP)	14,320	375			
US Dollar (DLR)	128,362	95,960	129,601	124,073	316,925
Total Options	**196,627**	**124,493**	**174,878**	**158,888**	**364,201**

Shanghai Metal Exchange, China

	2009	2008	2007	2006	2005
Copper	81,217,436	20,773,258	16,328,011	5,393,419	12,352,026
Aluminum	20,530,548	14,788,920	4,823,552	13,931,476	2,125,020
Zinc	32,253,386	23,538,897	10,215,449		
Steel Rebar	161,574,521				
Wire Rod	1,092,016				
Gold	3,406,233	3,890,467			
Rubber	89,035,959	46,461,103	42,191,727	26,047,061	9,503,158
Fuel Oil	45,753,969	30,810,540	12,005,094	12,734,045	9,809,550
Total Futures	**434,864,068**	**140,263,185**	**85,563,833**	**58,106,001**	**33,789,754**

Singapore Exchange (SGX), Singapore

	2009	2008	2007	2006	2005
Euroyen TIBOR	161,492	562,063	1,916,702	3,538,237	2,774,916
Mini Japanese Gov't Bond	694,655	831,196	1,457,309	1,427,458	1,241,616
Nikkei 225 Index	25,353,225	26,149,701	21,937,499	18,017,221	11,916,557
Nikkei 225 Index (USD)	666	3,154	10,913	871	
Mini Nikkei 225 Index	1,857	31,640	29,378		
Straits Times Index	2,916	2,734	22	4	546
FTSE/China A50 Index	1	34,232	12,349	8,932	
S&P CNX Nifty Index	7,115,255	12,435,118	750,361	134,445	9,910
MSCI Asia APEX 50 Index	659	6,658			

Singapore Exchange (SGX), Singapore

	2009	2008	2007	2006	2005
MSCI Singapore Index	3,947,690	4,635,517	4,012,860	2,214,521	1,707,865
MSCI Taiwan Index	15,718,096	16,913,325	13,611,314	10,824,249	8,100,202
Total Futures	**52,996,512**	**61,605,338**	**43,741,573**	**36,201,370**	**25,867,661**
MSCI Taiwan Index	9,901	385	16,010	29,642	1,293
MSCI Singapore Index	2,628				
Nikkei 225 Index	102,142	233,545	397,704	358,031	156,449
Total Options	**114,671**	**235,930**	**465,253**	**396,373**	**158,467**

Sydney Futures Exchange (SFE), Australia

	2009	2008	2007	2006	2005
SPI 200	9,538,554	10,174,823	8,407,052	6,516,247	5,597,066
30-Day Interbank Cash Rate	2,315,374	2,785,693	3,585,675	2,009,291	1,399,499
90-Day Bank Bills	14,435,474	20,192,284	22,682,851	19,501,781	16,119,237
3-Year Treasury Bonds	24,197,537	26,116,381	33,585,015	31,017,644	22,862,363
10-Year Treasury Bonds	10,072,494	13,188,549	19,169,641	15,051,399	11,021,452
10-Year Interest Rate Swaps	6,001				
d-cypha NSW Base Load Electricity	42,330	30,173	39,076	10,707	5,692
d-cypha QLD Base Load Electricity	28,811	30,469	36,357	9,532	2,956
d-cypha SA Base Load Electricity	1,751	2,191	4,372	2,127	1,322
d-cypha VIC Base Load Electricity	34,867	23,870	34,788	13,581	2,341
d-cypha NSW Peak Period Electricity	1,501	1,236	1,491	1,926	1,254
d-cypha QLD Peak Period Electricity	1,436	1,274	1,804	1,981	793
d-cypha SA Peak Period Electricity	105	251	338	110	161
d-cypha VIC Peak Period Electricity	1,774	2,538	4,089	5,038	4,104
d-cypha NSW Base $300 CAP	1,728	1,887	1,397	1,276	52
d-cypha QLD Base $300 CAP	2,734	1,625	902	986	595
d-cypha SA Base $300 CAP	232	101	260	62	
d-cypha VIC Base $300 CAP	3,085	3,621	2,422	1,590	308
Fine Wool	375	698	1,828	2,686	2,207
Greasy Wool	9,971	21,612	19,629	16,869	15,767
MLA/SFE Cattle	225	651	1,140	1,860	1,167
Total Futures	**60,696,359**	**72,580,096**	**87,595,681**	**74,204,335**	**57,091,807**
SPI 200	319,735	436,869	564,156	636,033	673,899
90-Day Bank Bills	33,146	287,103	774,472	182,663	244,940
3-Year Treasury Bond	446,182	326,323	466,507	856,723	477,764
Overnight 3-Year Treasury Bond	1,136,306	680,333	1,121,860	1,522,000	1,212,700
3-Year Bonds Intra-Day	430,590	288,288	472,047	576,935	508,754
10-Year Treasury Bonds	9,335	5,034	38,217	52,623	40,041
Overnight 10-Year Treasury Bond	2,250	1,200	19,115	76,909	57,700
d-cypha QLD Peak Period Electricity	30	30			
d-cypha SA Peak Period Electricity	50	20			
d-cypha VIC Peak Period Electricity	160	60	100	5	
Total Options	**2,377,784**	**2,025,460**	**3,525,481**	**3,915,771**	**3,233,159**

Taiwan Futures Exchange, Taiwan

	2009	2008	2007	2006	2005
TAIEX (TX)	24,625,062	19,819,775	11,813,150	9,914,999	6,917,375
Mini TAIEX (MTX)	13,926,904	9,058,436	2,964,042	1,760,583	1,088,523
Taiwan Stock Exchange Electronic Sector Index	1,166,622	1,356,290	1,004,603	1,459,821	1,179,643
Taiwan Stock Exchange Bank & Insurance Sector Index	1,482,264	1,285,074	909,383	786,477	909,621
Taiwan 50 Index	888	602	506	332	9,483
MSCI Taiwan Index (MSF)	466	1,425	1,132	9,894	
GreTai Securities Weighted Stock Index (GTF)	66,610	94,144	21,231		
Taiwan Stock Exch NonFin/NonElec SubIndex (XIF)	157,613	168,534	37,197		
10-Year Government Bond	103,949	471,508	151,247	40,675	2,887
30-Day Commercial Paper Interest Rate	13,149	114,558	36,243	1,022	217
Gold (GDF)	205	40,174	48,925	32,484	
NT Dollar Gold (TGF)	3,342,838	5,314,069			
Total Futures	**44,886,570**	**37,724,589**	**16,987,659**	**14,006,287**	**10,107,749**
TAIEX	72,082,548	92,757,254	92,585,637	96,929,940	80,096,506
TSE Electronic Sector Index	786,132	1,068,755	1,066,141	773,353	680,026
TSE Financial Sector Index	761,886	927,888	1,203,084	937,044	756,570
GreTai Securities Weighted Stock Index (GTO)	688,481	835,892	187,967		
Taiwan Stock Exch NonFin/NonElec SubIndex (XIO)	741,908	891,575	186,161		
MSCI Taiwan Index (MSO)	1,116,142	1,640,944	1,634,117	867,597	
DTB-demoninated Gold (TGO)	5,821,638				
All Options on Individual Equities	8,240,390	872,880	1,299,858	1,089,158	1,018,917
Total Options	**90,239,125**	**98,995,188**	**98,162,965**	**100,597,092**	**82,552,019**

Thailand Futures Exchange, Thailand

	2009	2008	2007
SET 50	2,522,465	2,099,098	1,228,238
Gold	311,591		
All Futures on Individual Equities	142,837	3,838	
Total Futures	**2,976,893**	**2,102,936**	**1,228,238**
SET 50	95,504	45,684	2,428
Total Options	**95,504**	**45,684**	**2,428**

Tel-Aviv Stock Exchange (TASE), Israel

	2009	2008	2007	2006	2005
TA-25 Index	43,025	29,694	19,802	32,474	10,910
TA-Banks Index	8,435				
Shekel-Dollar Rate	51,198	80			140
Shekel-Euro Rate	4,008				36
Total Futures	**106,666**	**29,774**	**20,445**	**57,334**	**11,086**
TA-25 Index	62,271,157	81,483,701	94,520,236	75,486,658	63,096,635
TA-Banks Index	73,937	72,486	87,445	56,273	36,781
Shekel-Dollar Rate	8,067,320	10,596,199	9,508,185	7,344,622	6,640,621
Shekel-Euro Rate	73,937	391,882	235,452	103,095	303,822
All Options on Individual Equities	321,228				
Total Options	**70,807,579**	**92,544,268**	**104,351,318**	**82,990,648**	**70,077,859**

Tokyo Commodity Exchange (TOCOM), Japan

	2009	2008	2007	2006	2005
Gold	11,913,502	15,163,975	18,203,194	22,228,198	17,958,240
Gold Mini	5,010,476	5,736,883	455,212		
Silver	111,775	301,216	536,583	858,153	817,624
Platinum	3,617,988	6,940,348	9,169,890	11,018,069	8,573,313
Platinum Mini	413,310	119,606			
Palladium	107,829	684,682	207,867	361,478	323,347
Aluminum	3,768	36,203	65,507	157,781	219,694
Gasoline	2,732,376	4,054,761	7,529,706	12,932,848	17,448,561
Kerosene	1,026,529	1,319,014	2,350,819	4,492,904	7,295,741
Crude Oil	624,307	755,520	1,489,018	1,961,190	1,981,389
Rubber	3,320,088	5,914,747	7,062,252	9,661,388	7,156,225
Total Futures	**28,881,948**	**41,026,955**	**47,070,048**	**63,672,011**	**61,780,446**

Tokyo International Financial Futures Exchange (TIFFE), Japan

	2009	2008	2007	2006	2005
3-Month Euroyen TIBOR	13,066,020	22,372,133	38,952,553	31,495,084	10,977,591
US Dollar / Japanese Yen	20,198,781	13,177,698	7,629,879		600
Euro / Japanese Yen	9,961,673	5,883,330	4,070,296		
British pound / Japanese Yen	16,266,521	7,634,056	6,041,471		
Australian Dollar / Japanese Yen	17,793,787	9,246,469	6,835,958		
Swiss Franc / Japanese Yen	183,224	768,754	669,032		
Canadian Dollar / Japanese Yen	467,812	1,334,653	2,005,416		
New Zealand Dollar / Japanese Yen	2,097,853	4,966,753	6,330,039		
South African Rand / Japanese Yen	860,162	48,086			
Norway Krone / Japanese Yen	27,956	1,948			
Hong Kong Dollar / Japanese Yen	21,825	2,014			
Sweden Krona / Japanese Yen	15,926	592			
Paland Zloty / Japanese Yen	217,530	22,335			
Euro / US Dollar	1,116,564	141,449			
British Pound / US Dollar	426,937	19,796			
British Pound / Swiss Franc	27,895	2,329			
US Dollar / Swiss Franc	75,115	11,313			
US Dollar / Canadian Dollar	45,869	3,939			
Australian Dollar / US Dollar	542,598	15,763			
Euro / Swiss Franc	20,485	1,100			
Euro / British Pound	88,194	10,453			
New Zealand Dollar / US Dollar	38,640	5,000			
Euro / Australian Dollar	24,891	2,351			
British Pound / Australian Dollar	59,698	1,087			
Total Futures	**83,645,956**	**65,675,700**	**72,535,144**	**31,508,764**	**11,057,134**
3-Month Euroyen	32,088	1,251,367	3,660,673	3,976,764	41,204
Total Options	**32,088**	**1,251,367**	**3,660,673**	**3,976,764**	**41,204**

Tokyo Grain Exchange (TGE), Japan

	2009	2008	2007	2006	2005
American Soybeans	2,320,782	910,992	1,247,786	1,259,515	2,050,803
Non-GMO Soybeans	189,020	2,899,301	12,280,932	9,885,557	10,964,812
Arabic Coffee	46,281	282,446	595,871	1,669,181	5,591,946
Azuki (Red Beans)	243,415	346,356	388,643	478,379	659,002
Corn	1,867,864	3,645,293	4,645,239	4,656,352	5,165,693
Raw Silk	2,169	2,923	3,096	14,170	113,938
Refined Sugar	690	2,862	2,862	2,896	2,860
Robusta Coffee	1,860	11,197	72,971	206,546	662,994
Raw Sugar	157,102	331,976	433,329	928,316	465,625
Total Futures	**4,829,183**	**8,433,346**	**19,674,560**	**19,116,748**	**25,957,307**

Tokyo Stock Exchange (TSE), Japan

	2009	2008	2007	2006	2005
10-Year Government Yen Bond	6,765,074	10,639,934	13,545,239	12,049,979	9,844,617
Mini 10-Year Government Yen Bond	46				
REIT Index	52,799	89,922			
TOPIX Stock Index	15,190,781	18,375,802	16,578,731	14,907,723	12,785,962
Mini TOPIX Stock Index	681,248	599,692			
TOPIX Core 30 Index	362,882	202,189			
Total Futures	**23,052,830**	**29,907,539**	**30,123,970**	**26,957,702**	**22,630,719**
TOPIX	52,523	62,045	19,555	18,354	20,004
10-Year Government Yen Bond	2,433,217	2,442,598	2,804,811	2,060,624	1,699,037
All Options on Individual Equities	662,813	88,256	145,449	190,876	
Total Options	**3,148,553**	**2,592,899**	**2,969,815**	**2,269,854**	**1,719,041**

Turkish Derivatives Exchange (TurkDEX), Turkey

	2009	2008	2007	2006	2005
Wheat	4	5,503			45
Gold	118,347	21,641	81	1,618	
ISE-100 Index	6,654	2,961	1,561	39,809	26,700
ISE-30 Index	65,393,094	40,332,007	17,015,352	2,203,916	143,572
US Dollar	13,687,292	13,979,082	7,832,542	4,393,609	1,594,157
Euro	225,314	131,210	17,067	204,807	64,558
Physically Delivered US Dollar	54				
Physically Delivered Euro	20				
T-Benchmark	564	420	401	4,104	
Total Futures	**79,431,343**	**54,472,835**	**24,867,033**	**6,848,087**	**1,832,871**

Warsaw Stock Exchange, Poland

	2009	2008	2007	2006	2005
WIG 20 Index	12,766,415	11,743,240	8,792,219	6,242,128	5,156,953
WIG 40 Index	30,182	25,349	15,819		
CHFPLN	9,418	5,669			
EURPLN	59,438	28,600	532	650	1,146
GBPPLN	1	71			
USDPLN	93,382	98,219	5,517	2,494	5,070
All Futures on Individual Equities	465,757	331,646	111,457	112,824	172,828
Total Futures	**13,424,593**	**12,233,935**	**8,936,225**	**6,386,377**	**5,378,517**
WIG20 Index	396,208	326,583	405,657	316,840	204,626
Total Options	**396,208**	**326,583**	**405,733**	**327,828**	**208,998**

Wiener Borse - Derivatives Market of Vienna, Austria

	2009	2008	2007	2006	2005
ATF Index	34,664	32,408	35,043	46,517	35,973
ATX Index	219,038	156,376	108,020	108,004	68,704
CeCe (5 Eastern European Indices)	13,362	59,692	89,335	65,953	63,722
All Futures on Individual Equities	6,053	6,981	11,199	12,371	23,748
Total Futures	**273,117**	**255,462**	**243,602**	**232,845**	**192,147**
ATF Index	3,993	3,236	8,117	1,938	2,496
ATX Index	14,821	22,894	28,067	23,462	34,631
All Options on Individual Equities	474,697	848,021	1,036,975	1,053,298	816,032
Total Options	**493,511**	**874,157**	**1,073,293**	**1,078,698**	**853,159**

Zhengzhou Commodity Exchange (ZCE), China

	2009	2008	2007	2006	2005
Cotton #1	8,534,688	5,400,835	2,955,235	2,084,541	10,870,825
Early Rice	1,950,083				
Rapeseed Oil	10,956,863	6,429,404	659,612		
White Sugar	146,063,344	165,485,978	45,468,481	29,342,066	
Strong Gluten Wheat	13,735,956	27,509,312	38,982,788	14,676,238	16,620,096
Hard White Winter Wheat	20,170	164,309	25,719	28,052	981,649
PTA	45,851,417	17,567,296	4,960,879	167,220	
Total Futures	**227,112,521**	**222,557,134**	**93,052,714**	**46,298,117**	**28,472,570**

Total Worldwide Volume

	2009	2008	2007	2006	2005
Total Futures	5,401,233,693	5,444,906,611	4,573,165,703	3,236,223,328	2,378,883,321
Percent Change	-0.80%	19.06%	41.31%	36.04%	9.75%
Total Options	5,533,857,416	5,259,609,949	4,862,456,753	4,050,032,450	4,066,769,167
Percent Change	5.21%	8.17%	20.06%	-0.41%	4.07%
Total Futures and Options	10,935,091,109	10,704,516,560	9,435,622,456	7,286,255,778	6,445,652,488
Percent Change	2.15%	13.45%	29.50%	13.04%	6.09%

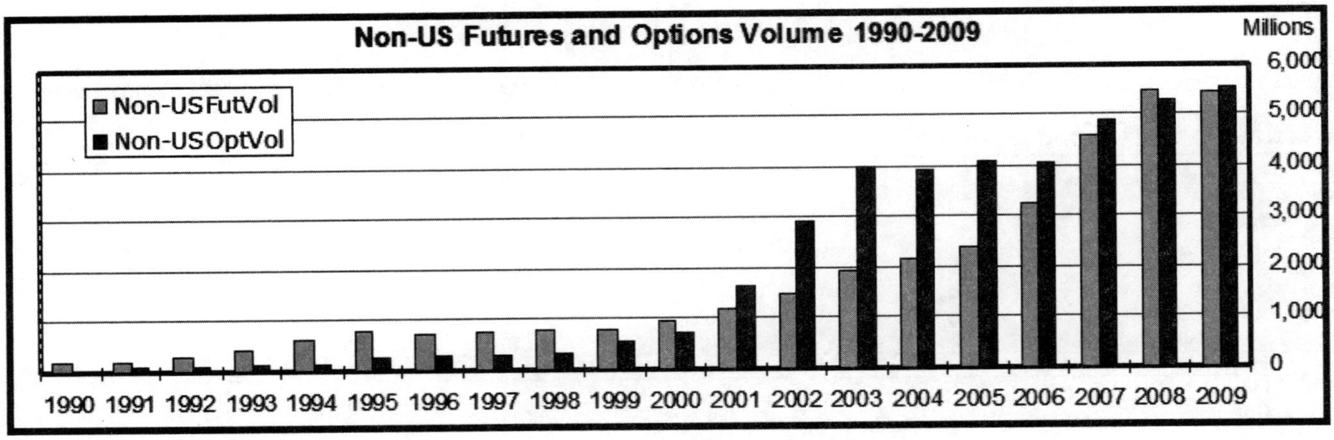

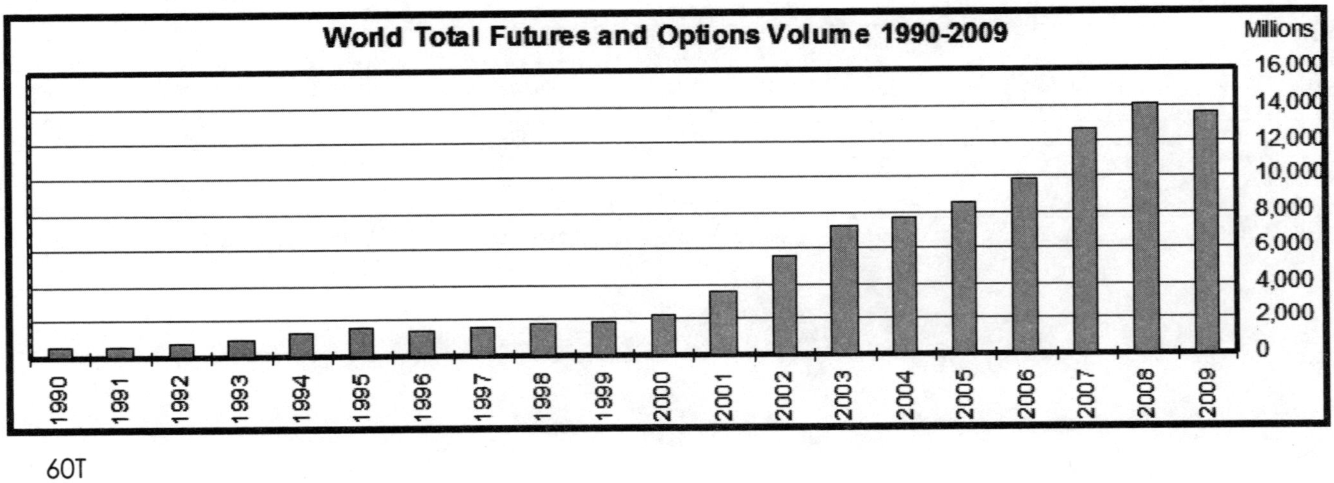

Commodity Research Bureau Product Overview

Price Data	
CRB DataCenter	End-of-day daily price files on futures, Commitments of Traders, options on futures, options volatility (implied/historic), equities and mutual funds. Available in various formats for direct upload to your chart/analysis software.
CRB InfoTech CD	The most comprehensive collection of commodity market information available anywhere, with decades of prices on over 600 cash, futures, foreign exchange, index markets, and option volatilities (implied/historic).
Custom Historical Data	Order a one-time package of price information according to your needs.

Charts	
CRB PriceCharts	Weekly 104-page magazine of charts on over 70 futures markets. Available in print and PDF formats.
PriceCharts.com	Over 400 pages of charts and technical studies covering the 77 major US, Europe, and Asia futures markets. Available in PDF format.
Wall Charts	Large poster-size charts on 35 futures markets with volume/open interest and Commitment of Traders data. Published annually each fall or on demand with your company logo.
Historical Desk Sets	Spiral-bound set of 86 charts on 48 markets with volume/open interest and Commitment of Traders data. Published each spring and fall.

Fundamental and Technical Research and Trading Systems	
Futures Market Service	Weekly 8-page newsletter on futures market fundamentals available in print or PDF formats.
Electronic Futures Trend Analyzer	Computerized daily trading system started in 1963 with specific entry and exit points for over 60 Futures Markets.

Books	
CRB Commodity Yearbook	Annual publication of fundamental data, including supply/demand and production/consumption and price data, on over 100 commodity markets. Concise introductory articles that describe the salient features of each commodity. Available as a hardcover book with CD.
CRB Encyclopedia of Commodity and Financial Prices	Concise introductory articles on the fundamental market factors moving commodity and financial prices, providing a valuable complement to understanding price behavior on the long-term historical price charts. Available as a hardcover book with CD.

Conversion Factors

Commonly Used Agricultural Weights and Measurements

Bushel Weights:
wheat and soybeans = 60 lbs.
corn, sorghum and rye = 56 lbs.
barley grain = 48 lbs.
barley malt = 34 lbs.
oats = 32 lbs.

Bushels to tonnes:
wheat and soybeans = bushels X 0.027216
barley grain = bushels X 0.021772
corn, sorghum and rye = bushels X 0.0254
oats = bushels X 0.014515

1 tonne (metric ton) equals:
2204.622 lbs.
1,000 kilograms
22.046 hundredweight
10 quintals

1 tonne (metric ton) equals:
36.7437 bushels of wheat or soybeans
39.3679 bushels of corn, sorghum or rye
45.9296 bushels of barley grain
68.8944 bushels of oats
4.5929 cotton bales (the statistical bale used by the USDA and ICAC contains a net weight of 480 pounds of lint)

Area Measurements:
1 acre = 43,560 square feet = 0.040694 hectare
1 hectare = 2.4710 acres = 10,000 square meters
640 acres = 1 square mile = 259 hectares

Yields:
wheat: bushels per acre X 0.6725 = quintals per hectare
rye, corn: bushels per acre X 0.6277 = quintals per hectare
barley grain: bushels per acre X 0.538 = quintals per hectare
oats: bushels per acre X 0.3587 = quintals per hectare

Commonly Used Weights

The troy, avoirdupois and apothecaries' grains are identical in U.S. and British weight systems, equal to 0.0648 gram in the metric system. One avoirdupois ounce equals 437.5 grains. The troy and apothecaries' ounces equal 480 grains, and their pounds contain 12 ounces.

Troy weights and conversions:
24 grains = 1 pennyweigh
20 pennyweights = 1 ounce
12 ounces = 1 pound
1 troy ounce = 31.103 grams
1 troy ounce = 0.0311033 kilogram
1 troy pound = 0.37224 kilogram
1 kilogram = 32.1507 troy ounces
1 tonne = 32,151 troy ounces

Avoirdupois weights and conversions:
27 11/32 grains = 1 dram
16 drams = 1 ounce
16 ounces = 1 lb.
1 lb. = 7,000 grains
14 lbs. = 1 stone (British)
100 lbs. = 1 hundredweight (U.S.)
112 lbs. = 8 stone = 1 hundredweight (British)
2,000 lbs. = 1 short ton (U.S. ton)
2,240 lbs. = 1 long ton (British ton)
160 stone = 1 long ton
20 hundredweight = 1 ton
1 lb. = 0.4536 kilogram
1 hundredweight (cwt.) = 45.359 kilograms
1 short ton = 907.18 kilograms
1 long ton = 1,016.05 kilograms

Metric weights and conversions:
1,000 grams = 1 kilogram
100 kilograms = 1 quintal
1 tonne = 1,000 kilograms = 10 quintals
1 kilogram = 2.204622 lbs.
1 quintal = 220.462 lbs.
1 tonne = 2204.6 lbs.
1 tonne = 1.102 short tons
1 tonne = 0.9842 long ton

U.S. dry volumes and conversions:
1 pint = 33.6 cubic inches = 0.5506 liter
2 pints = 1 quart = 1.1012 liters
8 quarts = 1 peck = 8.8098 liters
4 pecks = 1 bushel = 35.2391 liters
1 cubic foot = 28.3169 liters

U.S. liquid volumes and conversions:
1 ounce = 1.8047 cubic inches = 29.6 milliliters
1 cup = 8 ounces = 0.24 liter = 237 milliliters
1 pint = 16 ounces = 0.48 liter = 473 milliliters
1 quart = 2 pints = 0.946 liter = 946 milliliters
1 gallon = 4 quarts = 231 cubic inches = 3.785 liters
1 milliliter = 0.033815 fluid ounce
1 liter = 1.0567 quarts = 1,000 milliliters
1 liter = 33.815 fluid ounces
1 imperial gallon = 277.42 cubic inches = 1.2 U.S. gallons = 4.546 liters

Aluminum

Aluminum (symbol Al) is a silvery, lightweight metal that is the most abundant metallic element in the earth's crust. Aluminum was first isolated in 1825 by a Danish chemist, Hans Christian Oersted, using a chemical process involving a potassium amalgam. A German chemist, Friedrich Woehler, improved Oersted's process by using metallic potassium in 1827. He was the first to show aluminum's lightness. In France, Henri Sainte-Claire Deville isolated the metal by reducing aluminum chloride with sodium and established a large-scale experimental plant in 1854. He displayed pure aluminum at the Paris Exposition of 1855. In 1886, Charles Martin Hall in the U.S. and Paul L.T. Heroult in France simultaneously discovered the first practical method for producing aluminum through electrolytic reduction, which is still the primary method of aluminum production today.

By volume, aluminum weighs less than a third as much as steel. This high strength-to-weight ratio makes aluminum a good choice for construction of aircraft, railroad cars, and automobiles. Aluminum is used in cooking utensils and the pistons of internal-combustion engines because of its high heat conductivity. Aluminum foil, siding, and storm windows make excellent insulators. Because it absorbs relatively few neutrons, aluminum is used in low-temperature nuclear reactors. Aluminum is also useful in boat hulls and various marine devices due to its resistance to corrosion in salt water.

Futures and options on Primary Aluminum and Aluminum Alloy are traded on the London Metal Exchange. Aluminum futures are traded on the Tokyo Commodity Exchange (TOCOM), the Osaka Mercantile Exchange (OME), and the Shanghai Futures Exchange (SHFE). The London Metals Exchange aluminum futures contracts are priced in terms of dollars were metric tons.

Prices – The London Metals Exchange spot aluminum contract plunged by 61% from the record high of $3,271 per metric ton posted in July 2008 to a low of $1,269 in February 2009. Aluminum then recovered about one-half of those losses during the rest of 2009, closing 2009 at $2,197. The 2009 close was below the average of about $2,700 seen from 2006 through mid-2008 but still at a relatively high level well above the average of about $1500 seen during the 1990-2003 period.

Supply – World production of aluminum in 2009 fell b y -5.4% to 36.900 million metric tons, down from the 2008 record high of 36.900 million metric tons. The world's largest producers of aluminum are China with 35% of world production in 2009, Russia (9%), Canada (8%), U.S. (5%), and Australia (5%). U.S. production of primary aluminum in 2009 fell -34.4% yr/yr to 1.745 million metric tons. U.S. production of aluminum from secondary sources in 2008 (latest data) fell -11.5% yr/yr to 3.320 million metric tons.

Demand – World consumption of aluminum in 2001, the latest reporting year for the series, fell 4.8% yr/yr to 23.613 million metric tons, which was moderately below the record high of 24.811 million metric tons consumed in 2000. U.S. consumption of aluminum in 2009 fell 4.8% yr/yr to 3.610 million metric tons which was a four decade low.

Trade – U.S. exports in 2009 fell -21.7% yr/yr to 2.570 million metric tons, down from the 2008 record high of 3.280 million metric tons. U.S. imports of aluminum in 2009 fell -1.7% yr/yr to 4.130 million metric tons, down from the 2005 record high of 5.330 million metric tons. The U.S. was a net exporter in 2008 but in 2009 the U.S. relied on imports for 18% of its consumption.

World Production of Primary Aluminum In Thousands of Metric Tons

Year	Australia	Brazil	Canada	China	France	Germany	Norway	Russia	Spain	United Kingdom	United States	Vene-zuela	World Total
2000	1,769	1,277	2,373	2,800	441	644	1,026	3,245	366	305	3,668	571	24,300
2001	1,797	1,140	2,583	3,250	462	652	1,068	3,300	376	341	2,637	571	24,300
2002	1,836	1,318	2,709	4,300	463	653	1,096	3,347	380	344	2,707	605	26,100
2003	1,857	1,381	2,792	5,450	443	661	1,192	3,478	389	343	2,703	601	28,000
2004	1,890	1,460	2,590	6,670	451	668	1,320	3,590	398	360	2,516	624	29,900
2005	1,900	1,500	2,890	7,800	442	648	1,370	3,650	394	369	2,481	615	31,900
2006	1,930	1,610	3,050	9,360	442	516	1,330	3,720	349	360	2,284	610	33,900
2007	1,960	1,660	3,080	12,600	428	551	1,360	3,960	350	365	2,554	610	38,000
2008[1]	1,970	1,660	3,120	13,200	389	550	1,360	3,800	350	326	2,658	610	39,000
2009[2]	1,970	1,550	3,000	13,000	NA	520	1,200	3,300	NA	NA	1,710	550	36,900

[1] Preliminary. [2] Estimate. NA = Not available. *Source: U.S. Geological Survey (USGS)*

Production of Primary Aluminum (Domestic and Foreign Ores) in the U.S. In Thousands of Metric Tons

Year	Jan.	Feb.	Mar.	Apr.	May	June	July	Aug.	Sept.	Oct.	Nov.	Dec.	Total
2000	329	308	327	316	327	299	296	296	291	300	289	291	3,668
2001	256	220	232	225	229	215	214	212	206	214	208	205	2,637
2002	210	197	220	216	228	225	238	237	227	235	232	241	2,707
2003	242	220	238	225	228	221	226	225	217	224	215	221	2,702
2004	216	202	217	209	217	204	209	210	203	211	207	211	2,516
2005	209	191	214	211	214	206	210	208	199	207	204	208	2,481
2006	197	179	198	190	197	189	192	185	183	190	188	197	2,285
2007	202	185	217	209	210	209	219	220	216	224	220	225	2,556
2008	233	219	234	228	236	224	225	222	214	217	202	204	2,658
2009[1]	193	149	154	145	147	132	135	133	129	137	133		1,731

[1] Preliminary. *Source: U.S. Geological Survey (USGS)*

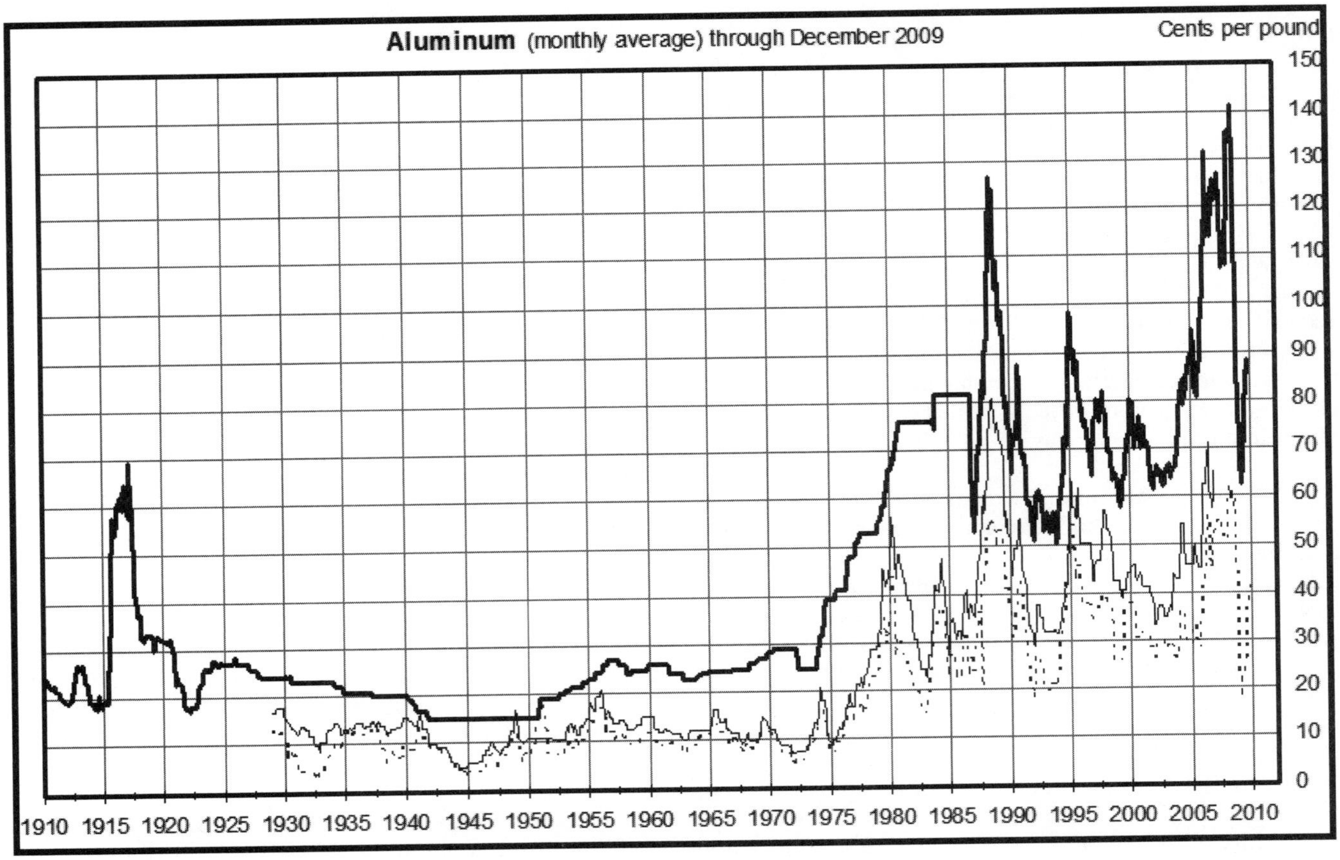

Salient Statistics of Aluminum in the United States In Thousands of Metric Tons

Year	Net Import Reliance as a % of Apparent Consumption	Production: Primary	Production: Secondary	Primary Shipments	Recovery from Scrap: Old	Recovery from Scrap: New	Apparent Consumption	Net Shipments[5] by Producers — Wrought Products: Plate, Sheet, Foil	Rolled Structural Shapes[3]	Extruded Shapes[4]	All	Castings: Permanent Mold	Die	Sand	All	Total All Net Shipments
1999	30	3,779	3,700	9,840	1,570	2,120	7,770	5,000	549	1,640	7,360	484	1,020	158	1,790	9,150
2000	33	3,668	3,450	9,830	1,370	2,080	7,530	4,840	592	1,640	7,240	549	991	152	1,850	9,080
2001	35	2,637	2,970	9,310	1,210	1,760	6,230	4,370	512	1,550	6,580	484	873	251	1,760	8,340
2002	39	2,707	2,930	9,640	1,170	1,750	6,320	4,450	559	1,550	6,710	693	1,280	279	2,450	9,160
2003	38	2,703	2,820	9,760	1,070	1,750	7,120	4,370	531	1,670	6,580	719	1,210	285	2,400	8,970
2004	39	2,516	3,030	10,400	1,160	1,870	6,570	4,750	579	1,810	7,140	735	1,250	221	2,370	9,510
2005	41	2,481	3,030	10,461	1,080	1,950	6,530	5,330	1,080	2,090	8,500	785	1,110	289	2,290	10,790
2006	31	2,284	3,540	10,500	1,250	2,280	5,980	4,690	608	192	5,490	754	1,170	335	2,310	7,800
2007	19	2,554	3,750	9,710	1,530	2,220	5,110	4,420	583	1,640	6,643	615	1,260	315	2,230	8,873
2008[1]	E	2,658	3,320		1,340	1,980	3,790	4,250	496	1,430	6,176	570	1,030	254	1,900	8,076

[1] Preliminary. [2] To domestic industry. [3] Also rod, bar & wire. [4] Also rod, bar, tube, blooms & tubing. [5] Consists of total shipments less shipments to other mills for further fabrication. *Source: U.S. Geological Survey (USGS)*

Supply and Distribution of Aluminum in the United States In Thousands of Metric Tons

Year	Apparent Consumption	Production: Primary	Production: From Old Scrap	Imports	Exports	Inventories - December 31 -: Private	Government[2]	Year	Apparent Consumption	Production: Primary	Production: From Old Scrap	Imports	Exports	Inventories - December 31 -: Private	Government[2]
1998	7,090	3,713	1,500	3,550	1,590	1,930	----	2004	6,570	2,516	1,160	4,720	1,820	1,470	----
1999	7,770	3,779	1,570	4,000	1,650	1,870	----	2005	6,530	2,481	1,080	5,330	2,370	1,430	----
2000	7,530	3,668	1,370	3,910	1,760	1,550	----	2006	5,980	2,284	1,250	5,180	2,820	1,410	----
2001	6,230	2,637	1,210	3,740	1,590	1,300	----	2007	5,110	2,554	1,530	4,490	2,840	1,400	----
2002	6,320	2,707	1,170	4,060	1,590	1,320	----	2008[1]	3,790	2,658	1,340	4,200	3,280	1,220	----
2003	7,120	2,703	1,070	4,130	1,540	1,400	----	2009[2]	3,610	1,710		4,130	2,570	920	----

[1] Preliminary. [2] Estimate. [3] National Defense Stockpile. [4] Less than 1/2 unit. *Source: U.S. Geological Survey (USGS)*

Aluminum Products Distribution of End-Use Shipments in the United States In Thousands of Metric Tons

Year	Building & Construction	Consumer Durables	Containers and Packaging	Electrical	Exports	Machinery and Equipment	Trans-portation	Other	Total
1999	1,470	760	2,320	739	1,330	661	3,600	293	11,200
2000	1,450	767	2,260	771	1,280	679	3,600	293	11,100
2001	1,500	681	2,250	686	902	641	3,190	367	10,200
2002	1,560	722	2,260	677	1,070	616	3,410	390	10,700
2003	1,560	689	2,240	653	905	659	3,540	415	10,700
2004	1,680	713	2,310	720	930	730	3,860	416	11,400
2005	1,671	708	2,320	746	1,125	741	3,939	336	11,586
2006	1,650	746	2,320	774	1,270	762	3,930	330	11,800
2007	1,410	664	2,230	762	1,450	736	3,580	359	11,200
2008[1]	1,180	607	2,230	700	1,490	688	2,830	334	10,000

[1] Preliminary. *Source: U.S. Geological Survey (USGS)*

World Consumption of Primary Aluminum In Thousands of Metric Tons

Year	Brazil	Canada	China	France	Germany	India	Italy	Japan	Rep. of Korea	Russia	United Kingdom	United States	World Total
1992	377.1	420.4	1,253.8	730.5	1,457.1	414.3	660.0	2,271.6	397.0	1,242.0	550.0	4,616.9	18,529.5
1993	378.9	492.5	1,339.9	667.2	1,150.7	475.3	554.0	2,138.3	524.8	657.0	540.0	4,877.1	18,122.6
1994	414.1	559.0	1,500.1	736.3	1,370.3	475.0	660.0	2,344.8	603.9	470.0	570.0	5,407.1	19,670.8
1995	500.6	611.9	1,941.6	743.8	1,491.3	581.0	665.4	2,335.6	675.4	476.0	620.0	5,054.8	20,480.9
1996	497.0	619.9	2,135.3	671.7	1,355.4	584.8	585.1	2,392.6	674.3	443.8	571.0	5,348.0	20,596.4
1997	478.6	628.2	2,260.3	724.2	1,558.4	553.4	671.0	2,434.3	666.3	469.2	583.0	5,390.0	21,721.8
1998	521.4	720.6	2,425.4	733.8	1,519.0	566.5	675.4	2,082.0	505.7	489.2	579.0	5,813.6	21,797.2
1999	463.1	777.2	2,925.9	774.2	1,438.6	569.5	735.3	2,112.3	814.0	562.8	496.8	6,203.3	23,323.0
2000	513.8	798.7	3,499.1	780.4	1,490.3	602.4	780.3	2,224.9	822.6	748.4	575.5	6,079.5	24,811.4
2001[1]	550.8	759.6	3,545.4	772.9	1,590.9	558.0	770.4	2,014.0	849.6	786.2	433.3	5,117.0	23,612.8

[1] Preliminary. *Source: American Metal Market (AMM)*

Salient Statistics of Recycling Aluminum in the United States

Year	Percent Recycled	New Scrap[1]	Old Scrap[2]	Recycled Metal[3]	Apparent Supply	New Scrap[1]	Old Scrap[2]	Recycled Metal[3]	Apparent Supply
		In Thousands of Metric Tons				Value in Millions of Dollars			
1998	38	1,950	1,500	3,440	9,040	2,810	2,160	4,970	13,100
1999	37	2,120	1,570	3,700	9,890	3,070	2,280	5,350	14,300
2000	36	2,080	1,370	3,450	9,610	3,420	2,260	5,670	15,800
2001	37	1,760	1,210	2,970	7,990	2,670	1,830	4,500	12,100
2002	36	1,750	1,170	2,930	8,070	2,510	1,680	4,190	11,500
2003	32	1,750	1,070	2,820	8,870	2,620	1,610	4,230	13,300
2004	33	1,870	1,160	3,030	9,080	3,460	2,140	5,600	16,800
2005	33	1,950	1,080	3,030	9,220	3,910	2,160	6,070	18,500
2006	39	2,300	1,260	3,560	9,010	6,140	3,370	9,520	24,100
2007	45	2,250	1,600	3,850	8,660	6,070	4,320	10,400	23,300

[1] Scrap that results from the manufacturing process. [2] Scrap that results from consumer products. [3] Metal recovered from new plus old scrap.
Source: U.S. Geological Survey (USGS)

Producer Prices for Aluminum Used Beverage Can Scrap In Cents Per Pound

Year	Jan.	Feb.	Mar.	Apr.	May	June	July	Aug.	Sept.	Oct.	Nov.	Dec.	Average
2000	58.58	62.90	61.50	56.85	54.50	54.50	56.50	57.00	57.00	56.20	53.50	53.50	56.88
2001	54.26	55.50	55.45	54.50	54.23	50.79	46.93	45.50	45.50	44.63	44.50	44.50	49.71
2002	44.50	44.66	47.21	49.41	48.68	48.50	46.89	45.06	46.36	47.07	49.76	50.29	47.37
2003	50.50	52.30	52.45	49.43	50.17	49.75	49.22	49.83	47.43	50.17	52.00	53.73	50.58
2004	57.44	61.64	61.65	63.00	57.85	60.00	62.23	60.57	59.48	62.07	61.45	63.81	60.93
2005	64.80	65.79	71.91	71.40	64.75	62.23	60.05	62.96	60.40	61.76	65.25	72.90	65.35
2006	81.03	85.76	85.13	91.08	99.41	83.50	83.40	82.74	80.70	79.66	83.90	85.00	85.11
2007	89.05	89.58	90.18	93.14	93.16	87.86	85.90	80.39	76.37	79.57	82.98	79.68	85.66
2008	82.81	90.35	100.19	100.09	97.52	98.88	98.75	88.83	79.38	63.43	55.67	46.33	83.52
2009	43.70	41.42	41.91	44.00	46.80	50.64	54.27	61.62	58.00	61.43	64.42	71.16	53.28

Source: American Metal Market (AMM)

Average Price of Cast Aluminum Scrap (Crank Cases) in Chicago[1] In Cents Per Pound

Year	Jan.	Feb.	Mar.	Apr.	May	June	July	Aug.	Sept.	Oct.	Nov.	Dec.	Average
2000	37.50	37.50	37.50	35.55	31.09	30.32	30.30	32.00	32.00	31.09	31.00	31.00	33.04
2001	31.00	31.00	31.00	31.00	31.00	31.00	28.29	28.00	28.00	28.00	26.40	26.00	29.25
2002	26.00	27.47	28.95	30.00	30.00	30.00	30.00	29.64	28.00	28.00	28.00	28.00	28.67
2003	28.10	30.00	30.00	29.00	29.00	27.90	26.68	26.00	26.00	26.00	26.00	26.00	27.56
2004	30.00	31.26	36.00	36.00	33.00	29.00	29.00	29.00	29.00	29.00	29.00	29.00	30.77
2005	29.00	29.00	31.61	33.00	31.33	28.00	28.00	28.00	28.00	28.00	28.00	39.71	30.14
2006	42.50	42.50	43.80	47.50	47.50	55.91	46.48	45.46	44.50	46.45	51.15	51.10	47.07
2007	52.50	52.50	54.00	55.50	55.50	53.07	52.50	52.50	51.34	50.50	50.50	50.50	52.58
2008	50.50	52.00	58.50	62.09	60.12	57.50	60.00	60.60	53.69	35.76	26.94	18.45	49.68
2009	17.50	17.50	22.27	22.50	22.50	22.50	24.55	27.50	37.50	37.50	37.50	42.24	27.63

[1] Dealer buying prices - prior to 1986 prices are for the New York area. Source: American Metal Market (AMM)

Aluminum Exports of Crude Metal and Alloys from the United States In Thousands of Metric Tons

Year	Jan.	Feb.	Mar.	Apr.	May	June	July	Aug.	Sept.	Oct.	Nov.	Dec.	Total
2000	18.7	27.2	30.2	21.9	24.4	22.4	20.5	24.2	20.5	20.7	20.7	21.6	273.0
2001	19.6	16.1	18.9	14.7	16.8	15.6	12.4	14.5	12.6	18.9	16.7	15.1	191.9
2002	17.1	15.2	15.6	16.4	19.4	18.3	15.0	15.5	17.5	19.8	19.4	16.4	205.6
2003	14.3	14.8	14.5	16.9	17.0	17.8	16.5	20.4	18.7	22.9	20.4	19.7	213.9
2004	18.2	20.8	24.3	25.2	25.1	27.6	23.7	23.0	28.3	26.9	28.0	27.4	298.5
2005	26.5	23.4	24.3	27.0	28.9	29.6	25.9	33.1	27.2	29.5	29.6	23.9	328.9
2006	40.0	26.0	30.5	29.4	38.8	25.3	23.7	32.0	26.1	25.8	27.0	22.0	346.6
2007	32.1	27.1	27.0	28.6	33.8	31.1	26.4	30.3	28.5	29.9	29.6	24.5	348.9
2008	30.8	26.8	26.4	30.4	28.4	27.6	25.9	26.4	27.4	25.3	17.3	15.6	308.3
2009[1]	15.9	15.9	12.7	14.8	24.7	24.9	24.6	24.7	24.4	28.0			252.7

[1] Preliminary. *Source: U.S. Geological Survey (USGS)*

Aluminum General Imports of Crude Metal and Alloys into the United States In Thousands of Metric Tons

Year	Jan.	Feb.	Mar.	Apr.	May	June	July	Aug.	Sept.	Oct.	Nov.	Dec.	Total
2000	246.0	213.0	206.0	211.0	233.0	234.0	250.0	206.0	189.0	186.0	181.0	137.0	2,490.0
2001	193.0	200.0	237.0	197.0	209.0	179.0	201.0	198.0	252.0	220.0	248.0	227.0	2,561.0
2002	272.0	205.0	223.0	221.0	221.0	263.0	228.0	279.0	235.0	196.0	264.0	186.0	2,793.0
2003	215.0	246.0	350.0	202.0	265.0	261.0	233.0	194.0	215.0	210.0	233.0	243.0	2,867.0
2004	211.0	288.0	248.0	254.0	282.0	309.0	297.0	225.0	279.0	286.0	272.0	294.0	3,245.0
2005	334.0	289.0	262.0	372.0	372.0	324.0	324.0	264.0	282.0	298.0	240.0	299.0	3,660.0
2006	348.0	247.0	289.0	353.0	315.0	298.0	249.0	315.0	289.0	259.0	233.0	241.0	3,436.0
2007	251.0	258.0	238.0	259.0	220.0	254.0	236.0	266.0	268.0	244.0	238.0	215.0	2,947.0
2008	240.0	208.0	247.0	238.0	237.0	263.0	227.0	204.0	229.0	249.0	219.0	233.0	2,794.0
2009/1	270.0	204.0	333.0	233.0	292.0	200.0	299.0	216.0	212.0	207.0			2,959.2

[1] Preliminary. *Source: U.S. Geological Survey (USGS)*

Average Open Interest of Aluminum Futures in New York In Contracts

Year	Jan.	Feb.	Mar.	Apr.	May	June	July	Aug.	Sept.	Oct.	Nov.	Dec.
2002	3,277	2,744	2,738	2,250	2,397	2,902	3,903	4,618	4,643	5,139	8,057	10,479
2003	9,573	9,163	6,960	7,190	7,686	8,529	8,402	8,445	7,655	7,283	8,434	9,427
2004	8,815	7,384	9,666	10,575	10,363	10,370	9,626	10,287	10,292	10,035	9,706	8,879
2005	8,183	8,487	7,464	6,612	5,654	5,061	4,359	3,223	3,225	2,676	2,232	1,670
2006	1,066	708	482	1,110	948	816	1,068	1,125	1,116	865	994	950
2007	608	614	491	450	415	368	329	276	237	194	156	132
2008	0	0	0	0	0	0	0	0	0	0	0	0

Source: CME Group; New York Mercantile Exchange (NYMEX)

Volume of Trading of Aluminum Futures in New York In Contracts

Year	Jan.	Feb.	Mar.	Apr.	May	June	July	Aug.	Sept.	Oct.	Nov.	Dec.	Total
2002	2,774	4,635	4,924	2,593	5,388	5,389	8,953	4,194	2,571	7,328	16,185	9,066	74,000
2003	12,565	9,625	8,163	5,440	10,567	8,463	11,797	9,451	5,119	6,222	8,536	11,542	107,490
2004	9,425	9,621	9,548	9,770	5,438	5,453	5,280	2,063	5,533	4,822	2,525	2,691	72,169
2005	5,294	2,829	3,244	2,627	2,613	1,832	1,247	902	1,625	623	3,135	2,520	28,491
2006	633	245	1,343	1,558	210	471	1,046	1,546	662	323	842	270	9,149
2007	94	332	82	28	2	56	84	19	25	0	1	0	723
2008	0	0	0	0	0	0	0	0	0	0	0	0	

Source: CME Group; New York Mercantile Exchange (NYMEX)

Antimony

Antimony (symbol Sb) is a lustrous, extremely brittle and hard crystalline semi-metal that is silvery white in its most common allotropic form. Antimony is a poor conductor of heat and electricity. In nature, antimony has a strong affinity for sulfur and for such metals as lead, silver, and copper. Antimony is primarily a byproduct of the mining, smelting and refining of lead, silver, and copper ores. There is no longer any mine production of antimony in the U.S.

The most common use of antimony is in antimony trioxide, a chemical that is used as a flame retardant in textiles, plastics, adhesives and building materials. Antimony trioxide is also used in battery components, ceramics, bearings, chemicals, glass, and ammunition.

Prices – Antimony prices in 2009 fell by -12.0% to 252.44 cents per pound, down from the 2008 record high average of 287.00 cents per pound. Antimony prices in 2009 were more than four times the 34-year low price of 66.05 cents per pound posted as recently as 1999. Bullish factors included stronger U.S. and global economic growth in 2008, the weak dollar, and tight supplies.

Supply – World mine production of antimony in 2009 rose by +9.4% to a record high of 197,000 metric tons. China accounted for 91% of world antimony production in 2008. After China, the only significant producers were Bolivia (1.8% of world production) and South Africa (1.4%). U.S. secondary production of antimony in 2008 fell by -11.5%yr/yr to 3,080 metric tons from 3,480 metric tons in 2007.

Demand – U.S. industrial consumption of antimony in 2008 (latest data available) fell -21.1% to 7,570 metric tons. Of the consumption in the U.S. in 2007, 42% was used for flame-retardants, 22 was used for metal products, and 35% was used for non-metal products.

Trade – The total U.S. gross weight of imports of antimony ore in 2008 (latest data available) fell by -8.6% to 286 metric tons. The antimony content of that ore fell by -27.4% to 164 metric tons. The gross weight of U.S. imports of antimony oxide rose by +0.4% to 26,200 metric tons. U.S. exports of antimony oxide in 2008 rose by +11.1% to 2,200 metric tons.

World Mine Production of Antimony (Content of Ore) In Metric Tons

Year	Australia	Bolivia	Canada	China[2]	Guatemala	Kyrgyzstan	Mexico[3]	Peru[4]	Russia	South Africa	Thailand	Turkey	World Total
2005	120	5,098	66	152,000	1,007	10	----	807	3,000	5,979	347	1,200	172,000
2006	1,600	5,460	226	153,000	----	50	----	810	3,500	4,362	1,409	1,100	174,000
2007[1]	1,010	3,881	162	163,000	1,000	10	----	810	3,500	3,354	----	1,200	180,000
2008[2]	1,500	3,500	97	180,000	1,000	10	----	810	3,500	2,800	----	1,300	197,000

[1] Preliminary. [2] Estimate. [3] Includes antimony content of miscellaneous smelter products. [4] Recoverable.
Source: U.S. Geological Survey (USGS)

Salient Statistics of Antimony in the United States In Metric Tons

	Avg. Price Cents/lb. C.i.F.	Production[3]			Imports for Consumption				Industry Stocks, December 31[3]				
		Primary[2]			Ore								
Year	U.S. Ports	Mine	Smelter	Secondary (Alloys)[2]	Gross Weight	Antimony Content	Oxide (Gross Weight)	Exports (Oxide)	Metallic	Oxide	Sulfide	Other	Total
2005	160.5	----	W	3,030	207	204	27,300	1,400	417	1,680	W	17	2,110
2006	238.0	----	W	3,520	205	153	27,700	1,680	421	1,690	W	15	2,120
2007[1]	257.3	W	W	3,480	313	226	26,100	1,980	470	1,410	W	18	1,900
2008[2]	279.5	----	W	3,080	286	164	26,200	2,200	217	1,050	W	357	1,620

[1] Preliminary. [2] Estimate. [3] Antimony content. [4] Including primary antimony residues & slag. W = Withheld proprietary data.
Source: U.S. Geological Survey (USGS)

Industrial Consumption of Primary Antimony in the United States In Metric Tons (Antimony Content)

	Metal Products						Non-Metal Products						
							Flame Retardents						
Year	Ammunition	Antimonial Lead[3]	Sheet & Pipe[4]	Bearing Metal & Bearings	Solder	Products	Plastics	Total	Ceramics & Glass	Pigments	Plastics	Total	Grand Total
2005	W	W	W	33	81	2,940	2,880	3,840	421	530	W	2,360	9,140
2006	W	W	W	20	61	3,000	2,810	3,810	258	215	W	3,600	10,400
2007	W	W	W	21	71	2,520	2,710	3,580	231	329	W	3,500	9,590
2008[1]	W	W	W	18	54	1,690	2,300	3,200	259	448	W	2,680	7,570

[1] Preliminary. [2] Estimated coverage based on 77% of the industry. W = Withheld proprietary data. *Source: U.S. Geological Survey (USGS)*

Average Price of Antimony[1] in the United States In Cents Per Pound

Year	Jan.	Feb.	Mar.	Apr.	May	June	July	Aug.	Sept.	Oct.	Nov.	Dec.	Average
2006	172.99	183.14	212.50	242.22	244.94	238.86	241.81	252.39	255.15	250.30	252.47	252.88	233.30
2007	252.88	252.88	252.26	251.75	251.75	250.42	249.74	258.55	254.24	255.39	258.24	258.55	253.89
2008	257.27	275.29	281.23	281.23	287.42	292.57	294.84	294.84	294.84	294.84	294.84	294.84	287.00
2009	294.84	294.84	202.98	198.35	200.77	212.06	235.57	265.46	276.69	278.14	292.57	277.04	252.44

[1] Prices are for antimony metal (99.65%) merchants, minimum 18-ton containers, c.i.f. U.S. Ports. *Source: American Metal Market (AMM)*

Apples

The apple tree is the common name of trees from the rose family, Rosaceae, and the fruit that comes from them. The apple tree is a deciduous plant and grows mainly in the temperate areas of the world. The apple tree is believed to have originated in the Caspian and Black Sea area. Apples were the favorite fruit of the ancient Greeks and Romans. The early settlers brought apple seeds with them and introduced them to America. John Champman, also known as Johnny Appleseed, was responsible for extensive planting of apple trees in the Midwestern United States.

Prices – The average monthly price of apples received by growers in the U.S.in 2009 fell by 37.8% yr/yr to 24.5 cents per pound.

Supply – World apple production in the 2009-10 marketing year rose +3.5% yr/yr to 62.046 million metric tons. The world's largest apple producers in 2009-10 were China (with 52% of world production), the European Union (19%), the U.S. (7%), and Russia (2%). U.S. apple production in 2009-10 rose +2.7% to a 5-year high of 4.505 million metric tons and far above the 2-decade low of 3.798 million metric tons posted in 2002-03.

Demand – The utilization breakdown of the 2008 apple crop showed that 65% of apples were for fresh consumption, 35% for canning, 16% for juice and cider, 2% for frozen apples, and 2% for dried apples. U.S. per capita apple consumption in 2008 was 16.2 pounds.

World Production of Apples[3], Fresh (Dessert & Cooking) In Thousands of Metric Tons

Year	Argentina	Canada	Chile	China	European Union	Japan	Mexico	New Zealand	Russia	South Africa	Turkey	United States	World Total
2004-05	1,200	381	1,120	23,675	----	755	573	504	1,500	659	2,300	4,687	46,085
2005-06	1,040	409	1,240	20,400	----	819	587	440	1,563	638	2,570	4,340	41,676
2006-07	1,100	403	1,250	26,059	11,134	832	510	454	1,250	710	2,458	4,414	54,484
2007-08	850	406	1,350	24,800	10,295	840	505	445	1,300	710	2,458	4,103	52,291
2008-09[1]	940	393	1,280	29,800	12,575	860	512	454	1,115	750	2,600	4,389	59,971
2009-10[2]	800	410	1,370	32,000	12,062	892	553	420	1,150	740	2,800	4,505	62,046

[1] Preliminary. [2] Estimate. NA = Not available. *Source: Foreign Agricultural Service, U.S. Department of Agriculture (FAS-USDA)*

Salient Statistics of Apples[2] in the United States

	-- Production --		- Growers Prices -		Utilization of Quantities Sold								Foreign Trade[4]			
						Processed[5]							Domestic			
Year	Total	Utilized	Fresh Cents/ lb.	Processing $/ton	Fresh	Canned	Dried	Frozen	Juice & Cider	Other[3]	Avg. Fram Price Cents/ lb.	Farm Value Million $	Exports Fresh	Dried[5]	Imports Fresh & Dried[5]	Fresh Per Capita Consumption Lbs.
			Millions of Pounds										Metric Tons			
2003	8,780	8,692	26.1	131.0	5,453	3,239	182	283	1,434	105	18.8	1,817.2	447.4	33.0	214.4	16.9
2004	10,412	10,333	18.2	107.0	6,619	3,714	201	256	1,870	78	13.6	1,403.0	607.4	32.4	119.2	18.8
2005	9,667	9,567	24.2	106.0	6,097	3,470	191	259	1,695	64	17.3	1,675.1	675.1		158.2	16.7
2006	9,823	9,730	31.6	129.0	6,309	3,422	253	272	1,550	61	22.7	2,236.1	638.3		194.1	17.7
2007	9,089	9,045	38.3	190.0	6,077	2,968	204	258	1,257	60	28.8	2,608.2	673.2		172.9	16.4
2008[1]	9,769	9,676	29.6	189.0	6,304	3,372	203	206	1,534	127	23.2	2,206.0	780.9		164.9	16.2

[1] Preliminary. [2] Commercial crop. [3] Mostly crushed for vinegar, jam, etc. [4] Year beginning July. [5] Fresh weight basis.
NA = Not available. Source: Economic Research Service, U.S. Department of Agriculture (ERS-USDA)

Price of Apples Received by Growers (for Fresh Use) in the United States In Cents Per Pound

Year	Jan.	Feb.	Mar.	Apr.	May	June	July	Aug.	Sept.	Oct.	Nov.	Dec.	Average
2004	30.4	30.0	30.4	29.8	29.6	30.1	30.0	26.8	26.8	26.1	24.5	22.2	28.1
2005	21.6	20.3	18.4	17.3	17.4	16.2	15.7	21.1	30.9	28.8	29.4	25.8	21.9
2006	21.7	20.6	19.8	19.3	18.9	22.9	42.3	35.9	42.0	36.2	36.1	31.0	28.9
2007	29.9	29.7	29.2	28.1	26.9	29.6	30.6	34.4	40.2	37.9	40.3	35.0	32.7
2008	35.5	34.8	34.4	33.8	36.2	41.2	44.6	53.7	50.6	42.5	36.0	29.3	39.4
2009[1]	27.2	23.7	22.1	20.8	18.5	18.1	17.8	25.6	33.5	31.0	28.1	27.2	24.5

[1] Preliminary. *Source: Economic Research Service, U.S. Department of Agriculture (ERS-USDA)*

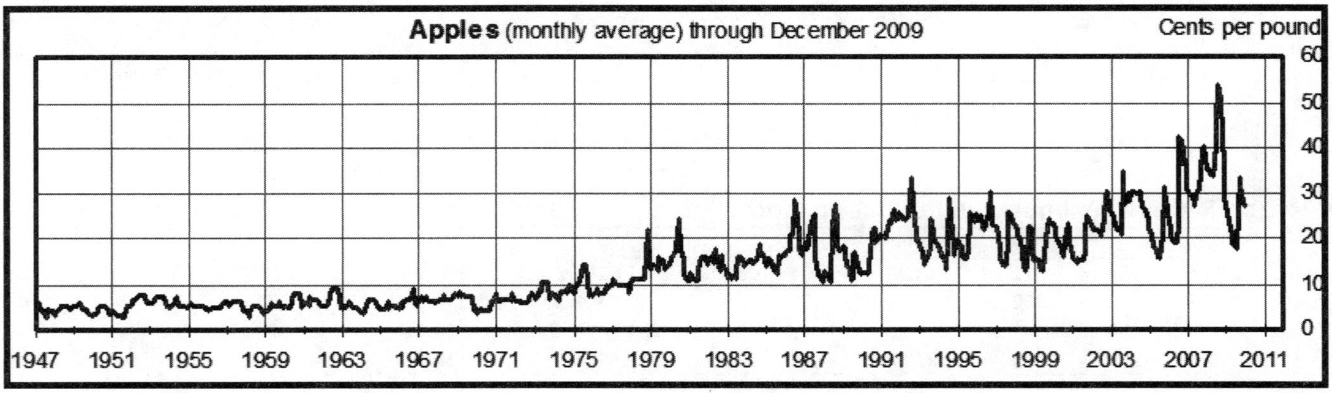

Arsenic

Arsenic (symbol As) is a silver-gray, extremely poisonous, semi-metallic element. Arsenic, which is odorless and flavorless, has been known since ancient times, but it wasn't until the Middle Ages that its poisonous characteristics first became known. Metallic arsenic was first produced in the 17th century by heating arsenic with potash and soap. Arsenic is rarely found in nature in its elemental form and is generally recovered as a by-product of ore processing. Recently, small doses of arsenic have been found to put some forms of cancer into remission. It can also help thin blood. Homoeopathists have successfully used undetectable amounts of arsenic to cure stomach cramps.

The U.S. does not produce any arsenic and instead imports all its consumption needs for arsenic metals and compounds. More than 95 percent of the arsenic consumed in the U.S. is in compound form, mostly as arsenic trioxide, which in turn is converted into arsenic acid. Production of chromated copper arsenate, a wood preservative, accounts for about 90% of the domestic consumption of arsenic trioxide. Three companies in the U.S. manufacture chromate copper arsenate. Another company used arsenic acid to produce an arsenical herbicide. Arsenic metal is used to produce nonferrous alloys, primarily for lead-acid batteries.

One area where there is increased consumption of arsenic is in the semiconductor industry. Very high-purity arsenic is used in the production of gallium arsenide. High speed and high frequency integrated circuits that use gallium arsenide have better signal reception and lower power consumption. An estimated 30 metric tons per year of high-purity arsenic is used in the production of semiconductor materials.

In the early 2000's, as much as 88% of U.S. arsenic production was used for wood preservative treatments, so the demand for arsenic was closely tied to new home construction, home renovation, and deck construction. However, the total demand for arsenic in 2004 dropped by 69% from 2003, and due to arsenic's toxicity and tighter environmental regulation; only 65% of that much smaller amount was used for wood preservative treatments. Since then the specific percentage used for wood preservative treatments is no longer available.

Supply – World production of white arsenic (arsenic trioxide) in 2008 fell by -5.4% to an 8-year low of 52,700 metric tons. The world's largest producer is China with about 47% of world production, followed by Chile with 19% of world production, Peru with 8%, Russia with 3%, and Mexico with 1%. China's production of arsenic was fairly constant at about 40,000 metric tons per year but that has dropped to about 25,000 to 30,000 in the last five years. The U.S. supply of arsenic in 2008 fell by -33.3% to a 31-year low of 5,186 metric tons.

Demand – U.S. demand for arsenic in 2008 fell by -21.8% to a record low of 4,130 metric tons. The use for arsenic is no longer available but in 2004 (latest data) about 65% was for wood preservatives, 10% was for non-ferrous alloys and electric usage, 10% was for glass, and 3% was for other uses.

Trade – U.S. imports of trioxide arsenic in 2008 (latest data available) fell by -31.5% to a record low of 6,320 metric tons from 12,400 metric tons in 2006. U.S. exports of trioxide arsenic in 2008 fell 57.8% to 1,050 metric tons, down further from the record high of 3,2703 metric tons in 2005.

World Production of White Arsenic (Arsenic Trioxide) In Metric Tons

Year	Belgium	Bolivia	Canada[4]	Chile	China	France	Germany	Mexico	Namibia[3]	Peru	Philippines	Russia	World Total
2001	1,000	846	250	11,500	39,500	1,000	200	2,381	----	2,800	----	1,500	63,000
2002	1,000	237	250	11,400	40,000	1,000	100	1,946	----	2,970	----	1,500	62,400
2003	1,000	276	250	11,600	40,000	----	----	1,729	----	4,640	----	1,500	69,700
2004	1,000	168	250	11,500	30,000	----	----	1,829	----	3,037	----	1,500	57,800
2005	1,000	120	250	11,700	30,000	----	----	1,664	----	3,150	----	1,500	60,000
2006	1,000	90	250	11,700	30,000	----	----	1,595	----	4,399	----	1,500	61,100
2007[1]	1,000	----	250	11,400	25,000	----	----	1,600	----	4,320	----	1,500	55,700
2008[2]	1,000	----	250	10,000	25,000	----	----	513	----	4,000	----	1,500	52,700

[1] Preliminary. [2] Estimate. [3] Output of Tsumeb Corp. Ltd. only. [4] Includes low-grade dusts that were exported to the U.S. for further refining.
Source: U.S. Geological Survey (USGS)

Salient Statistics of Arsenic in the United States (In Metric Tons -- Arsenic Content)

	Supply				Distribution		Estimated Demand Pattern						Average Price			
	Imports												Trioxide	Metal		
Year	Metal	Compounds	Industry Stocks Jan. 1	Total	Apparent Demand	Industry Stocks Dec. 31	Agricultural Chemicals	Glass	Wood Preservatives	Non-Ferrous Alloys & lectric	Other	Total	Mexican -- Cents/Pound	Chinese -- Cents/Pound	Imports Trioxide[3]	Exports
2001	1,030	23,900	----	24,930	24,900	----	----	750	21,900	1,000	250	24,900	----	----	31,500	57
2002	879	18,800	----	19,679	19,600	----	----	700	17,300	650	200	19,600	----	----	24,700	100
2003	990	20,800	----	21,790	21,600	----	----	660	19,200	660	200	21,600	----	----	27,300	173
2004	872	6,150	----	7,022	6,800	----	----	650	4,450	650	200	6,800	----	----	8,090	220
2005	812	8,330	----	9,142	5,870	----	----	NA	NA	NA	NA	5,870	----	----	11,000	3,270
2006	1,070	9,430	----	10,500	7,450	----	----	NA	NA	NA	NA	7,450	----	----	12,400	3,060
2007[1]	759	7,010	----	7,769	5,280	----	----	NA	NA	NA	NA	5,280	----	----	9,220	2,490
2008[2]	376	4,810	----	5,186	4,130	----	----	NA	NA	NA	NA	4,130	----	----	6,320	1,050

[1] Preliminary. [2] Estimate. [3] For Consumption. *Source: U.S. Geological Survey (USGS)*

Barley

Barley is the common name for the genus of cereal grass and is native to Asia and Ethiopia. Barley is an ancient crop and was grown by the Egyptians, Greek, Romans and Chinese. Barley is now the world's fourth largest grain crop, after wheat, rice, and corn. Barley is planted in the spring in most of Europe, Canada and the United States. The U.S. barley crop year begins June 1. It is planted in the autumn in parts of California, Arizona and along the Mediterranean Sea. Barley is hardy and drought resistant and can be grown on marginal cropland. Salt-resistant strains are being developed for use in coastal regions. Barley grain, along with hay, straw, and several by-products are used for animal feed. Barley is used for malt beverages and in cooking. Barley, like other cereals, contains a large proportion of carbohydrate (67%) and protein (12.8%). Barley futures are traded on the ICE Futures Canada (ICE) exchange, the London International Financial Futures and Options Exchange (LIFFE) and the Budapest Commodity Exchange.

Prices – The monthly average price for all barley received by U.S. farmers in the 2009-10 marketing year (through January 20010) fell by 9.9% yr/yr to $4.70 per bushel.

Supply – World barley production in the 2009-10 marketing year fell 3.1% yr/yr to 149.183 million metric tons. The world's largest barley crop of 179.038 million metric tons occurred in 1990-91. The world's largest barley producers are the European Union with 42% of world production in 2009-10, Russia (12%), Ukraine (8%), Canada (6%), Australia (6%), Turkey (4%), and the U.S. (3%).

U.S. barley production in the 2009-10 marketing year fell by 5.4% yr/yr to 237.323 million bushels and that is less than 40% of the record U.S. barley crop of 608.532 million bushels seen in 1986-87. U.S. farmers harvested 17.6% yr/yr fewer acres in 2009-10 at 3.113 million acres, not much more than the 2006-07 level of 2.951 million acres which was the lowest acreage since 1885. Barley yield in 2009-10 rose +14.8% yr/yr to a record high yield of 73.0 bushels per acre. Ending stocks for the 2009-10 marketing year rose +30.8% to 116.06 million bushels which is not too far below the 11-year high of 128.4 million bushels in 2004-05.

Demand – U.S. total barley disappearance in 2009-10 fell 9.5% yr/yr to 225.0 million bushels. About 72% of barley is used for food and alcoholic beverages, 22% for animal feed, and 3% for seed.

Trade – World exports of barley in 2009-10 fell by 14.5% yr/yr to 17.248 million metric tons. The largest world exporters of barley in 2008-09 were Australia with 22% of world exports, the European Union with 12%, Canada with 9%, and the U.S. with only 1%. The single largest importer of barley is Saudi Arabia with 7.500 million metric tons of imports in 2009-10, which is about 44% of total world imports.

World Barley Supply and Demand In Thousands of Metric Tons

	Exports						Imports			Utilization			Ending Stocks		
Year	Australia	Canada	European Union	Total Non-US	United States	Total	Saudi Arabia	Unaccounte	Total	Russia	United States	Total	Canada	United States	Total
2000-01	3,967	1,953	7,175	15,461	1,258	16,719	5,500	537	16,306	12,700	6,407	133,973	2,516	2,314	22,214
2001-02	4,676	1,149	4,188	16,733	575	17,308	6,000	489	16,800	14,250	5,661	136,203	2,047	2,006	28,850
2002-03	1,984	403	5,234	15,583	659	16,242	7,200	225	16,754	15,500	5,179	137,118	1,475	1,510	26,683
2003-04	6,398	1,839	2,641	15,969	409	16,378	7,000	444	15,297	18,600	4,990	145,283	2,102	2,619	22,528
2004-05	4,261	1,167	3,262	14,569	506	15,075	5,800	530	15,915	16,500	5,672	143,211	3,435	2,796	32,576
2005-06	5,267	2,257	3,311	17,661	606	18,267	7,100	660	17,544	15,500	4,570	140,109	3,289	2,350	27,993
2006-07	1,851	1,224	3,476	14,944	441	15,385	6,700	350	15,022	16,400	4,596	143,024	1,491	1,500	21,047
2007-08	3,386	3,046	3,803	14,565	902	15,467	7,400	455	15,748	15,050	4,324	134,918	1,568	1,485	19,217
2008-09[1]	3,500	1,483	3,597	19,885	288	20,173	7,600		19,783	17,100	5,127	143,059	2,843	1,932	30,171
2009-10[2]	3,800	1,500	2,000	17,030	218	17,248	7,500		16,807	17,100	4,789	146,713	2,463	2,527	31,851

[1] Preliminary. [2] Estimate. *Source: Foreign Agricultural Service, U.S. Department of Agriculture (FAS-USDA)*

World Production of Barley In Thousands of Metric Tons

Year	Australia	Belarus	Canada	China	European Union	India	Iran	Kazakhstan	Russia	Turkey	Ukraine	United States	World Total
2000-01	6,743	1,378	13,172	2,646	59,936	1,447	1,686	1,675	14,100	7,400	6,872	6,919	133,093
2001-02	8,280	1,700	10,846	2,893	58,767	1,432	2,423	2,200	19,500	6,900	10,186	5,407	143,347
2002-03	3,865	1,681	7,489	3,322	58,168	1,500	3,085	2,200	18,700	7,200	10,364	4,940	134,439
2003-04	10,387	1,800	12,164	2,717	55,818	1,410	2,908	2,100	18,000	6,900	6,850	6,059	142,209
2004-05	7,740	2,000	12,557	3,222	64,085	1,300	2,940	1,500	17,200	7,400	11,100	6,091	152,431
2005-06	9,483	1,800	11,678	3,400	54,752	1,200	2,857	1,500	15,800	7,600	9,000	4,613	136,271
2006-07	4,257	1,350	9,573	3,115	56,220	1,220	3,000	1,900	18,100	7,500	11,350	3,923	136,412
2007-08	7,160	1,700	10,984	2,785	57,545	1,330	3,000	2,500	15,650	6,000	6,000	4,575	132,725
2008-09[1]	7,669	2,000	11,781	2,900	65,459	1,230	2,000	1,800	23,100	5,600	12,600	5,230	153,930
2009-10[2]	8,300	1,650	9,520	3,100	61,965	1,500	2,600	2,600	18,000	6,000	12,000	4,949	149,183

[1] Preliminary. [2] Estimate. *Source: Foreign Agricultural Service, U.S. Department of Agriculture (FAS-USDA)*

Barley Acreage and Prices in the United States

Crop Year Beginning June 1	Acreage 1,000 Acres: Planted	Acreage 1,000 Acres: Harvested for Gain	Yield Per Harvested Acre (Bushels)	Seasonal Prices: Received by Farmers[3]: All	Received by Farmers[3]: Feed[4]	Received by Farmers[3]: Malting[4]	Portland No. 2 Western	Government Price Support Operations: National Average Loan Rate	Target Price	Put Under Support (mil. Bu.)	Percent of Production
				Dollars per Bushel							
2002-03	5,008	4,123	55.0	2.54	2.16	2.96	2.71	1.88	2.21	10.4	4.6
2003-04	5,348	4,727	58.9	2.90	2.27	3.07	2.74	1.88	2.21	17.9	6.4
2004-05	4,527	4,021	69.6	2.46	1.76	2.79	2.39	1.85	2.24	8.3	3.0
2005-06	3,875	3,269	64.8	2.54	1.89	2.80	2.44	1.85	2.24	12.0	5.7
2006-07	3,452	2,951	61.0	2.90	2.72	2.98	4.08	1.85	2.24	9.3	5.2
2007-08	4,018	3,502	60.0	4.14	4.42	4.00	5.71	1.85	2.24		
2008-09[1]	4,246	3,779	63.6	5.21	3.62	5.55	5.29				
2009-10[2]	3,567	3,113	73.0	4.68	2.58	5.08					

[1] Preliminary. [2] Estimate. [3] Excludes support payments. *Source: Economic Research Service, U.S. Department of Agriculture (ERS-USDA)*

Salient Statistics of Barley in the United States In Millions of Bushels

Crop Year Beginning June 1	Supply: Beginning Stocks	Supply: Production	Supply: Imports	Supply: Total Supply	Disappearance: Domestic Use: Food & Alcohol Beverage	Domestic Use: Seed	Domestic Use: Feed & Residual	Domestic Use: Total	Exports	Total Disappearance	Ending Stocks: Gov't Owned	Ending Stocks: Privately Owned	Ending Stocks: Total Stocks
2002-03	92.1	226.9	18.5	337.5	145.7	8.7	83.6	237.9	30.3	268.2	0	69.3	69.3
2003-04	69.3	278.3	20.6	368.3	147.5	7.4	74.3	229.2	18.8	247.9	0	120.3	120.3
2004-05	120.3	279.7	12.1	412.2	151.3	6.4	103.3	260.5	23.3	283.8	0	128.4	128.4
2005-06	128.4	211.9	5.4	345.7	152.2	5.7	52.0	209.9	27.8	237.8	0	107.9	107.9
2006-07	107.9	180.2	12.1	300.2	149.0	6.6	55.5	211.1	20.3	231.3	0	68.9	68.9
2007-08	68.9	210.1	29.2	308.2	161.6	7.0	30.0	198.6	41.4	240.0	0	68.2	68.2
2008-09[1]	68.2	240.2	29.0	337.4	163.0	6.0	66.5	235.5	13.2	248.7	0	88.7	88.7
2009-10[2]	88.7	227.3	25.0	341.1	163.1	6.9	50.0	220.0	5.0	225.0	0	116.1	116.1

[1] Preliminary. [2] Estimate. [3] Uncommitted inventory. [4] Includes quantity under loan & farmer-owned reserve. [5] Included in Food & Alcohol.
Source: Economic Research Service, U.S. Department of Agriculture (ERS-USDA)

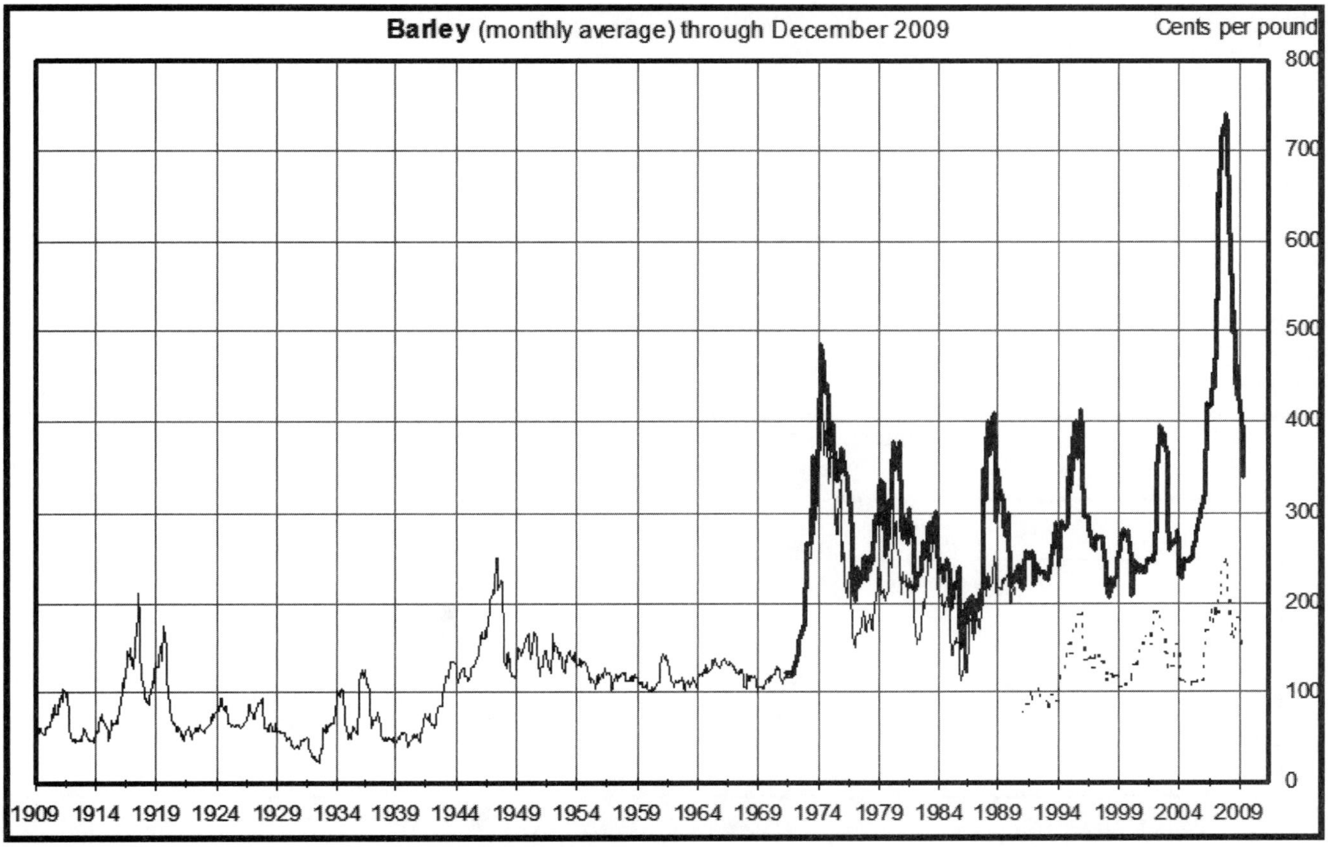

BARLEY

Average Price Received by Farmers for All Barley in the United States In Dollars Per Bushel

Year	June	July	Aug.	Sept.	Oct.	Nov.	Dec.	Jan.	Feb.	Mar.	Apr.	May	Average
2002-03	2.54	2.37	2.50	2.36	2.41	2.58	2.48	2.42	2.55	2.70	2.65	2.97	2.54
2003-04	2.77	2.71	2.70	2.53	2.76	2.92	2.93	3.03	3.09	3.11	3.07	3.12	2.90
2004-05	2.63	2.54	2.77	2.43	2.29	2.45	2.49	2.41	2.31	2.49	2.26	2.46	2.46
2005-06	2.54	2.37	2.50	2.36	2.41	2.58	2.48	2.42	2.55	2.70	2.65	2.97	2.54
2006-07	2.77	2.71	2.70	2.53	2.76	2.92	2.93	3.03	3.09	3.11	3.07	3.12	2.90
2007-08	3.30	3.46	3.55	4.05	4.53	4.31	4.44	4.35	4.38	4.18	4.56	4.52	4.14
2008-09	4.78	5.12	5.46	5.97	5.73	5.44	5.49	5.34	4.99	4.88	4.76	4.59	5.21
2009-10[1]	4.59	5.12	5.27	4.78	4.35	4.53	4.54	4.73	4.25				4.68

[1] Preliminary. *Source: National Agricultural Statistical Service, U.S. Department of Agriculture (NASS-USDA)*

Average Price Received by Farmers for Feed Barley in the United States In Dollars Per Bushel

Year	June	July	Aug.	Sept.	Oct.	Nov.	Dec.	Jan.	Feb.	Mar.	Apr.	May	Average
2002-03	1.83	1.88	2.05	2.23	2.26	2.32	2.14	2.17	2.20	2.30	2.20	2.33	2.16
2003-04	2.33	2.22	2.39	2.27	2.24	2.43	2.26	2.15	2.16	2.19	2.17	2.39	2.27
2004-05	2.20	2.21	1.83	1.64	1.58	1.78	1.66	1.65	1.60	1.67	1.56	1.71	1.76
2005-06	1.91	1.88	1.77	1.84	1.81	1.91	1.76	1.94	1.83	1.80	1.81	2.45	1.89
2006-07	2.08	2.04	2.06	2.31	2.68	2.84	2.79	3.11	3.15	3.19	3.20	3.20	2.72
2007-08	3.50	3.27	3.60	4.47	4.89	5.05	4.79	4.89	4.67	4.29	4.67	4.99	4.42
2008-09	5.49	4.72	4.54	4.46	3.82	3.43	3.00	2.90	2.63	2.73	2.67	2.99	3.62
2009-10[1]	3.15	2.88	2.48	2.14	2.33	2.51	2.63	2.64	2.49				2.58

[1] Preliminary. *Source: National Agricultural Statistical Service, U.S. Department of Agriculture (NASS-USDA)*

Average Open Interest of Western Feed Barley Futures in Winnipeg In Contracts

2002	9,771	10,653	11,255	11,113	11,141	11,068	11,271	13,046	13,845	12,172	9,000	8,027
2003	8,559	8,203	8,546	9,028	9,631	10,290	10,676	9,580	8,409	7,154	7,524	5,346
2004	6,731	6,881	6,262	9,779	10,497	9,930	9,992	9,743	11,140	11,956	12,786	10,916
2005	9,321	8,164	9,144	9,476	9,475	9,140	6,481	6,880	6,046	5,839	6,538	7,281
2006	8,179	10,505	10,719	12,131	12,543	12,762	12,948	13,680	14,938	16,026	13,803	14,620
2007	16,178	16,769	16,969	15,901	16,351	16,951	13,808	13,941	14,270	15,480	14,337	13,830
2008	14,224	15,626	15,758	14,304	14,394	13,462	12,975	12,052	10,528	9,502	8,462	8,486
2009	7,616	5,100	4,380	3,819	3,216	2,522	3,058	3,398	2,484	1,825	1,478	1,286
2007	16,178	16,769	16,969	15,901	16,351	16,951	13,808	13,941	14,270	15,480	14,337	13,830

Contract size = 20 tonnes. *Source: ICE Futures Canada (ICE)*

Volume of Trading of Western Feed Barley Futures in Winnipeg In Contracts

Year	Jan.	Feb.	Mar.	Apr.	May	June	July	Aug.	Sept.	Oct.	Nov.	Dec.	Total
2002	14,268	16,370	15,924	17,663	21,440	18,349	19,860	23,436	22,431	14,471	17,035	10,772	212,019
2003	10,555	18,933	13,069	18,879	13,900	15,153	13,293	29,799	19,438	18,937	17,768	10,977	200,701
2004	11,405	16,265	12,784	23,806	13,179	27,081	15,326	14,933	23,072	15,790	22,516	8,478	204,635
2005	15,452	12,171	19,849	9,325	16,469	14,741	4,100	11,815	7,573	12,665	8,452	3,952	136,564
2006	16,241	9,238	23,987	9,361	26,466	8,083	4,294	25,858	14,903	37,489	12,620	6,484	195,024
2007	24,784	10,380	21,229	12,525	21,161	23,044	11,151	20,457	27,030	27,072	11,926	3,913	214,672
2008	20,322	15,642	20,495	13,025	19,547	14,392	5,719	15,473	13,251	14,171	11,529	3,815	167,381
2009	11,518	6,580	5,388	6,579	3,955	3,876	1,887	4,910	3,222	4,064	950	1,910	54,839

Contract size = 20 tonnes. *Source: ICE Futures Canada (ICE)*

Bauxite

Bauxite is a naturally occurring, heterogeneous material comprised of one or more aluminum hydroxide minerals plus various mixtures of silica, iron oxide, titanium, alumina-silicates, and other impurities in trace amounts. Bauxite is an important ore of aluminum and forms by the rapid weathering of granite rocks in warm, humid climates. It is easily purified and can be converted directly into either alum or metallic aluminum. It is a soft mineral with hardness varying from 1 to 3, and specific gravity from 2 to 2.55. Bauxite is dull in appearance and may vary in color from white to brown. It usually occurs in aggregates in pea-sized lumps.

Bauxite is the only raw material used in the production of alumina on a commercial scale in the United States. Bauxite is classified according to the intended commercial application, such as abrasive, cement, chemical, metallurgical, and refractory. Of all the bauxite mined, about 95 percent is converted to alumina for the production of aluminum metal with some smaller amounts going to nonmetal uses as various forms of specialty alumina. Small amounts are used in non-metallurgical bauxite applications. Bauxite is also used to produce aluminum chemicals and is used in the steel industry.

Supply – World production of bauxite in 2009 fell -2.0% yr/yr to 201.000 million metric tons, down from the 2008 record high of 205.000 million metric tons. The world's largest producer of bauxite is Australia with 31% of the world's production in 2009, followed by China (18%), Brazil (14%), India (11%), Guinea (8%), and Jamaica (4%). Chinese production of bauxite has quadrupled in the past 10 years. India's bauxite production has also risen rapidly and is more than triple the amount seen 15 years ago.

Demand – U.S. consumption of bauxite in 2007 (latest data available) fell by –20.1% yr/yr to 9.780 million metric tons from 12.300 million metric tons in 2006. That was still well below the record high of 15.962 million metric tons seen in 1980. The alumina industry took 96% of bauxite production in 2007, or 9.430 million metric tons. According to 2004 data (the latest data available) the refractory industry usually takes about 1.4% of the U.S. bauxite supply, the abrasive industry takes about 0.2%, and the chemical industry takes the rest.

Trade – The U.S. relies on imports for almost 100% of its consumption needs. Domestic ore, which provides less than 1 percent of the U.S. requirement for bauxite, is mined by one company from surface mines in the states of Alabama and Georgia. U.S. imports of bauxite fell 25.0% yr/yr to 9.840 million metric tons in 2007, which was well below the record of 14.976 million metric tons seen in 1974. U.S. exports of bauxite in 2007 were negligible at 15,000 metric tons.

World Production of Bauxite In Thousands of Metric Tons

Year	Australia	Brazil	China	Greece	Guinea	Guyana[3]	Hungary	India	Jamaica[3]	Russia[3]	Sierra Leone	Suriname	Total
2000	53,802	13,866	9,000	1,991	15,700	2,471	1,047	7,562	11,127	4,200	----	3,610	136,000
2001	53,799	13,032	9,800	2,052	15,100	1,950	1,000	7,864	12,370	4,000	----	4,394	137,000
2002	54,135	13,260	12,000	2,492	15,300	1,690	720	9,647	13,120	4,500	----	4,002	144,000
2003	55,602	17,363	13,000	2,418	15,000	1,846	666	10,414	13,444	5,500	----	4,215	153,000
2004	56,593	20,950	17,000	2,444	15,254	1,506	647	11,285	13,296	6,000	----	4,052	164,000
2005	59,959	22,034	22,000	2,495	16,817	1,648	535	12,385	14,116	6,400	----	4,757	179,000
2006	61,780	22,055	27,000	2,163	18,784	1,558	538	13,940	14,865	6,600	1,071	4,924	192,000
2007	62,398	22,100	30,000	2,220	18,519	1,600	546	20,343	14,568	6,400	1,169	4,900	201,000
2008[1]	61,389	22,000	35,000	2,220	18,500	2,098	550	21,210	14,000	6,300	954	5,230	205,000
2009[2]	63,000	28,000	37,000	2,200	16,800	1,200		22,300	8,000	3,300		4,000	201,000

[1] Preliminary. [2] Estimate. [3] Dry Bauxite equivalent of ore processed. *Source: U.S. Geological Survey (USGS)*

Salient Statistics of Bauxite in the United States In Thousands of Metric Tons

	Net Import Reliance as a % of Apparent	Average Price F.O.B. Mine	Consumtion by Industry					Dry Equivalent			Stocks, December 31		
Year	Consumption	$ per Ton	Total	Alumina	Abrasive	Chemical	Re-fractoty	Imports[4]	Exports[3]	Con-sumption	Producers & Consumers	Gov't Owned	Total
1999	100	22	11,700	11,100	113	W	251	10,189	149	11,700	1,440	6,800	8,250
2000	100	23	10,800	10,100	111	W	160	8,550	133	10,800	1,300	5,710	7,000
2001	100	23	9,770	9,010	61	W	175	8,300	67	9,770	1,740	2,070	3,810
2002	100	20	9,980	9,290	52	W	115	7,340	27	9,980	1,280	1,770	3,050
2003	100	19	11,300	10,600	53	W	150	8,390	55	11,300	3,830	66	3,830
2004	100	22	13,600	12,500	53	W	260	9,640	42	13,600	3,120	----	3,120
2005	100	26	12,400	11,900	W	W	W	11,800	34	12,400	W	----	W
2006	100	28	12,300	11,800	W	W	W	11,600	20	12,300	W	----	W
2007[1]	100		10,200	9,830	W	W	W	9,840	15	10,200	W	----	W
2008[2]	100		9,550	9,310	W	W	W	10,500	14	9,550	W	----	W

[1] Preliminary. [2] Estimate. [3] Including concentrates. [4] For consumption. W = Withheld. *Source: U.S. Geological Survey (USGS)*

Bismuth

Bismuth (symbol Bi) is a rare metallic element with a pinkish tinge. Bismuth has been known since ancient times, but it was confused with lead, tin, and zinc until the middle of the 18th century. Among the elements in the earth's crust, bismuth is ranked about 73rd in natural abundance. This makes bismuth about as rare as silver. Most industrial bismuth is obtained as a by-product of ore extraction.

Bismuth is useful for castings because of the unusual way that it expands after solidifying. Some of bismuth's alloys have unusually low melting points. Bismuth is one of the most difficult of all substances to magnetize. It tends to turn at right angles to a magnetic field. Because of this property, it is used in instruments for measuring the strength of magnetic fields.

Bismuth finds a wide variety of uses such as pharmaceutical compounds, ceramic glazes, crystal ware, and chemicals and pigments. Bismuth is found in household pharmaceuticals and is used to treat stomach ulcers. Bismuth is opaque to X-rays and can be used in fluoroscopy. Bismuth has also found new use as a nontoxic substitute for lead in various applications such as brass plumbing fixtures, crystal ware, lubricating greases, pigments, and solders. There has been environmental interest in the use of bismuth as a replacement for lead used in shot for waterfowl hunting and in fishing sinkers. Another use has been for galvanizing to improve drainage characteristics of galvanizing alloys. Zinc-bismuth alloys have the same drainage properties as zinc-lead without being as hazardous.

Prices – The average price of bismuth (99.99% pure) in the U.S. in 2009 fell by -31.7% to $8.25 per pound, down from the 2007 record high of $13.32 per pound. Up until 2007 the prices were in the $3.00 to $5.00 per pound range.

Supply – World mine production of bismuth in 2008 rose +24.2% to a record high of 7,700 metric tons. The world's largest producer in 2008 was China with 65% of world production, followed by Mexico with 15%, Peru with 12%, and Canada with 1%. Regarding production of the refined metal in 2008 China had 80% of production, Mexico had 8%, Belgium had 5%, and Peru had 4%. The U.S. does not have any significant domestic refinery production of bismuth.

Demand – U.S. consumption of bismuth in 2008 fell –58.6% to 1,090 metric tons, down from the record high of 2,420 metric tons in 2004. In 2008 the consumed uses of bismuth were 55% for chemicals, 34% for metallurgical additives, 7% for fusible alloys, and 3% for other alloy uses.

Trade – U.S. imports of bismuth in 2008 fell -37.0% to 1,930 metric tons, down from the 2007 record high of 3,070 metric tons. Of U.S. imports, 38% came from Belgium and 26% came from Mexico. U.S. exports of bismuth and alloys in 2008 fell -11.0% yr/yr to 375 metric tons, down further from the 2001 record high of 541 metric tons.

World Production of Bismuth In Metric Tons (Mine Output=Metal Content)

	Mine Output, Metal Content						Refined Metal						
Year	Canada	China	Japan	Mexico	Peru	Total	Belgium	China	Kazakhastan[3]	Japan	Mexico	Peru	Total
2002	189	2,000	NA	1,126	1,000	4,600	1,000	3,000	130	474	1,126	568	6,700
2003	145	2,500	NA	1,064	1,000	5,100	1,000	5,000	130	513	1,064	600	8,700
2004	185	3,000	26	1,064	1,000	5,600	800	11,700	130	522	1,064	600	15,000
2005	185	3,000	23	970	952	5,400	800	10,600	120	463	970	600	14,000
2006	214	3,000	21	1,186	950	5,800	800	11,800	115	425	1,186	600	15,000
2007[1]	137	3,500	20	1,200	950	6,200	800	12,100	120	408	1,200	600	1,600
2008[2]	71	5,000	20	1,170	960	7,700	800	12,000	125	390	1,170	600	1,500

[1] Preliminary. [2] Estimate. *Source U.S. Geological Survey (USGS)*

Salient Statistics of Bismuth in the United States In Metric Tons

	Bismuth Consumed, By Uses								Imports from Metallic Bismuth from				Dealer Price
Year	Metallurgical Additives	Other Alloys & Uses	Fusible Alloys	Chemicals[3]	Total Consumption	Consumer Stocks Dec. 31	Exports of Metal & Alloys	Belgium	Mexico	Preu	Total	$ Per Pound
2002	388	50	1,070	813	2,320	111	131	724.0	518.0	19.5	1,930	3.14
2003	833	25	646	616	2,120	172	108	778.0	532.0	0.1	2,320	2.87
2004	1,110	22	703	584	2,420	167	109	793.0	495.0	39.8	1,990	3.35
2005	1,150	14	685	498	2,340	175	142	1,050.0	480.0	----	2,530	3.91
2006	1,050	12	260	660	1,990	125	311	876.0	552.0	17.6	2,300	5.04
2007[1]	1,130	45	709	744	2,630	138	421	1,020.0	420.0	3.7	3,070	14.07
2008[2]	375	38	75	597	1,090	228	375	509.0	40.0	55.7	1,930	12.73

[1] Preliminary. [2] Estimate. [3] Includes pharmaceuticals. *Source: U.S. Geological Survey (USGS)*

Average Price of Bismuth (99.99%) in the United States In Dollars Per Pound

Year	Jan.	Feb.	Mar.	Apr.	May	June	July	Aug.	Sept.	Oct.	Nov.	Dec.	Average
2006	4.63	4.63	4.63	4.63	4.63	4.63	4.63	4.63	4.63	4.63	4.63	4.63	4.63
2007	4.63	4.63	8.36	13.00	17.02	18.36	17.64	17.08	15.92	14.89	14.63	13.63	13.32
2008	13.00	12.35	12.00	12.00	14.94	13.70	12.75	12.21	10.50	10.50	10.50	10.50	12.08
2009	10.50	10.50	8.00	7.68	7.44	7.08	6.86	6.85	8.50	8.99	8.56	8.03	8.25

Source: American Metal Market (AMM)

Broilers

Broiler chickens are raised for meat rather than for eggs. The broiler industry was started in the late 1950's when chickens were selectively bred for meat production. Broiler chickens are housed in massive flocks mainly between 20,000 and 50,000 birds, with some flocks reaching over 100,000 birds. Broiler chicken farmers usually rear five or six batches of chickens per year.

After just six or seven weeks, broiler chickens are slaughtered (a chicken's natural lifespan is around seven years). Chickens marketed as pouissons, or spring chickens, are slaughtered after four weeks. A few are kept longer than seven weeks to be sold as the larger roasting chickens.

Prices – The average monthly price received by farmers for broilers (live weight) fell in 2009 by –3.0% yr/yr to 45.2 cents per pound. The average monthly price for wholesale broilers (ready-to-cook) in 2009 fell –2.6% to 77.60 cents per pound, down from the 2008 record high of 79.68 cents per pound.

Supply – Total production of broilers in 2009 fell by 3.7% yr/yr to 35.533 billion pounds. The number of broilers raised for commercial production in 2008 (latest data available) was up 1.2% yr/yr to a record high of 9.009 billion birds. The average live-weight per bird rose by +1.1% to 5.60 pounds, which was a new record high and was about 50% heavier than the average bird weight of 3.62 pounds seen in 1970, attesting to the increased efficiency of the industry.

Demand – U.S. per capita consumption of broilers in 2009 fell by -4.1% to 80.1 pounds (ready-to-cook) per person per year, down very slightly from the 2006 record high of 86.9. U.S. consumption of chicken has nearly doubled in the past two decades, up from 47.0 pounds in 1980, as consumers have increased their consumption of chicken because of the focus on low-carb diets and because chicken is a leaner and healthier meat than either beef or pork.

Broiler Supply and Prices in the United States

	Federally Inspected Slaughter					Per Capita	Prices	
Years and Quarters	Number (Million)	Average Weight (Pounds)	Liveweight Pounds (Mil. Lbs.)	Certified RTC[3] Weight (Mil. Lbs.)	Total Production RTC[3] (Mil. Lbs.)	Consumption RTC[3] Basis (Mil. Lnbs.)	Farm (Cents per Pound)	Georgia Dock[4] (Cents per Pound)
2004	8,762	5.27	46,097	34,064	34,063	84.2	45.17	74.69
2005	8,842	5.38	47,475	35,238	35,365	85.8	43.33	72.83
2006	8,838	5.47	48,333	35,750	35,500	86.5	38.92	68.25
2007	8,889	5.51	48,983	35,964	36,126	85.4	44.92	77.46
2008[1]	8,915	5.51	49,753	35,863	36,906	83.5	46.58	83.11
2009[2]	8,519	5.59	47,604	35,505	35,533	80.1	45.17	84.97
I	2,080	5.55	11,545	8,574	8,574	19.3	46.67	86.11
II	2,153	5.56	11,982	8,937	8,937	20.1	48.33	86.46
III	2,203	5.57	12,277	9,172	9,172	20.7	44.67	85.68
IV	2,083	5.66	11,801	8,822	8,850	20.0	41.00	81.64

[1] Preliminary. [2] Estimate. [3] Total production equals federal inspected slaughter plus other slaughter minus cut-up & further processing condemnation. [4] Ready-to-cook basis. *Source: Economic Research Service, U.S. Department of Agriculture (ERS-USDA)*

Salient Statistics of Broilers in the United States

	Commercial Production		Average			Total Chickens[3] Supply and Distribution							
						Production			Storage		Broiler	Consumption	
Year	Number (Mil. Lbs.)	Liveweight (Mil. Lbs.)	Liveweight Per Bird (Mil. Lbs.)	Average Price (cents Lb.)	Value of Production (Mil. $)	Federally Inspected (In Millions of Pounds)	Other Chickens (In Millions of Pounds)	Total (In Millions of Pounds)	Stocks January 1 (In Millions of Pounds)	Exports (In Millions of Pounds)	Feed Ratio (pounds)	Total (Mil. Lbs.)	Per Capita[4] (Pounds)
2002	8,591	44,059	5.13	30.5	13,437	31,895	547	32,442	720	4,941	5.5	27,467	80.50
2003	8,493	43,958	5.18	34.6	15,215	32,399	502	32,901	768	4,920	5.4	32,749	81.60
2004	8,741	45,796	5.24	44.6	20,446	33,699	504	34,203	611	4,783	5.9	34,063	84.30
2005	8,872	47,856	5.39	43.6	20,878	34,986	515	35,331	716	5,203	7.0	35,293	85.60
2006	8,868	48,830	5.51	36.3	17,739	35,120	525	35,461	926	5,205	6.2	36,325	87.90
2007[1]	8,907	49,331	5.54	43.6	21,514	35,739			750	5,801	5.1	29,827	85.00
2008[2]	9,009	50,441	5.60	45.8	23,112	36,505			743	5,900	3.7	30,800	87.00

Preliminary. [2] Estimate. [3] Ready-to-cook. [4] Retail weight basis. Source: Economic Research Service, U.S. Department of Agriculture (ERS-USDA)

Average Wholesale Broiler[1] Prices RTC (Ready-to-Cook) In Cents Per Pound

Year	Jan.	Feb.	Mar.	Apr.	May	June	July	Aug.	Sept.	Oct.	Nov.	Dec.	Average
2003	60.46	60.49	60.02	57.78	59.44	61.56	62.80	63.20	64.08	63.59	64.45	65.71	61.97
2004	68.66	74.96	75.94	76.40	79.54	82.00	81.59	75.44	70.07	68.79	68.08	68.01	74.12
2005	71.40	71.43	72.81	73.21	72.54	72.19	72.47	71.45	72.51	69.02	66.95	63.98	70.83
2006	63.13	63.19	61.77	58.91	59.57	64.44	67.10	68.26	68.18	65.16	65.93	66.48	64.34
2007	70.43	75.89	78.66	78.63	81.00	81.34	80.68	78.82	78.19	70.60	71.74	71.06	76.42
2008	75.91	78.79	79.51	77.84	81.58	82.48	84.60	79.34	77.98	77.65	78.51	82.01	79.68
2009[2]	81.90	80.17	77.01	76.39	82.96	86.22	82.95	74.50	72.81	71.00	71.76	73.56	77.60

[1] 12-city composite wholesale price. [2] Preliminary. *Source: Economic Research Service, U.S. Department of Agriculture (ERS-USDA)*

Butter

Butter is a dairy product produced by churning the fat from milk, usually cow's milk, until it solidifies. In some parts of the world, butter is also made from the milk of goats, sheep, and even horses. Butter has been in use since at least 2,000 BC. Today butter is used principally as a food item, but in ancient times it was used more as an ointment, medicine, or illuminating oil. Butter was first churned in skin pouches thrown back and forth over the backs of trotting horses.

It takes about 10 quarts of milk to produce 1 pound of butter. The manufacture of butter is the third largest use of milk in the U.S.. California is generally the largest producing state, followed closely by Wisconsin, with Washington as a distant third. Commercially finished butter is comprised of milk fat (80% to 85%), water (12% to 16%), and salt (about 2%). Although the price of butter is highly correlated with the price of milk, it also has its own supply and demand dynamics.

The consumption of butter has dropped in recent decades because pure butter has a high level of animal fat and cholesterol that have been linked to obesity and heart disease. The primary substitute for butter is margarine, which is produced from vegetable oil rather than milk fat. U.S. per capita consumption of margarine has risen from 2.6 pounds in 1930 to recent levels near 8.3 pounds, much higher than U.S. butter consumption.

Futures on butter are traded at the Chicago Mercantile Exchange (CME). The CME's butter futures contract calls for the delivery of 40,000 pounds of Grade AA butter and is priced in cents per pound.

Prices – The average monthly price of butter at the Chicago Mercantile Exchange in 2009 fell 15.1% yr/yr to 124.27 cents/pound. That is still down from the 2004 record high of 181.66 cents per pound, but higher than the 13-year low of 110.59 cents per pound posted in 2002.

Supply – World production of butter in 2009 rose +2.5% yr/yr to 8.017 million metric tons, down from the record high of 9.594 million metric tons in 2007. The world's largest producers of butter are India with 49% of the world production in 2009, the European Union with 26%, the United States with 9%, New Zealand with 5%, and Russia with 3%. Production of creamery butter by U.S. factories in 2009 fell -5.1% yr/yr to 1.568 billion pounds. The record high was 1.872 billion pounds in 1941.

Demand – Total commercial use of creamery butter in the U.S fell by -9.2% yr/yr to 1.559 billion pounds, down from last year's a record high of 1.716 billion pounds. That is about one-third higher that the commercial use of butter back in the 1950's. Cold storage stocks of creamery butter in the U.S. on December 1, 2009 rose +18.9% yr/yr to 142.661 million pounds.

Trade – World imports of butter in 2009 rose +1.1% yr/yr to 357,000 metric tons. U.S. imports of butter in 2009 were unchanged yr/yr at 5,000 metric tons. World exports of butter in 2009 rose +2.3% yr/yr to 699,000 metric tons. U.S exports in 2009 fell -41.9% yr/yr to 60,000 metric tons, down from last year's 16-year high of 105,000 metric tons.

Supply and Distribution of Butter in the United States In Millions of Pounds

	Supply				Distribution							93 Score	
					Domestic Disappearance			Department of Agriculture				AA Wholesale Price	
Year	Production	Cold Storage Stocks[3] Jan. 1	Imports	Total Supply	Total	Per Capita (Pounds)	Exports	Stocks[4] Jan. 1	Stocks[4] Dec 31	Removed by USDA Programs	Total Use	$ per Pound	
2000	1,274	25	32.400	1,331	1,329	4.5	7	0	0	8.9	1,289	----	1.1768
2001	1,237	24	75.000	1,336	1,268	4.4	18	0	0		1,275	----	1.6630
2002	1,355	56	34.800	1,446	1,293	4.4	8	0	1		1,288	----	1.1059
2003	1,242	158	32.200	1,432	1,307	4.5	9	1	6	29.1	1,332	----	1.1450
2004	1,250	100	50.600	1,400	1,326	4.6	26	6	0	-6.6	1,356	----	1.8166
2005	1,347	45	31.418	1,424	1,335		13	0			1,370	----	1.5484
2006	1,448	59	39.683	1,548	1,415		24				1,548	----	1.2360
2007[1]	1,533	109	37.478	1,678	1,435		88				1,678	----	1.3680
2008[2]	1,645	154	35.274	1,834	1,519		196				1,834		

[1] Preliminary. [2] Estimates. [3] Includes butter-equivalent. [4] Includes butteroil. [5] Includes stocks held by USDA.
Source: Economic Research Service, U.S. Department of Agriculture (ERS-USDA)

Quarterly Commercial Disappearance of Creamery Butter in the United States In Millions of Pounds

Year	First Quarter	Second Quarter	Third Quarter	Fourth Quarter	Total	Year	First Quarter	Second Quarter	Third Quarter	Fourth Quarter	Total
1998	289.0	276.3	255.3	308.6	1,137.0	2004	286.3	303.2	340.8	421.1	1,351.4
1999	299.3	316.4	318.3	374.8	1,308.8	2005	287.1	304.9	349.6	423.1	1,364.7
2000	300.8	286.9	332.3	380.6	1,300.6	2006	320.2	308.5	333.2	471.6	1,433.5
2001	290.9	278.4	316.1	397.0	1,282.4	2007	344.6	299.2	376.8	498.3	1,518.9
2002	313.5	263.5	317.4	393.4	1,287.8	2008	399.3	381.4	424.9	512.2	1,717.8
2003	304.2	275.4	317.2	411.8	1,308.6	2009[1]	372.9	374.0	353.4	458.7	1,559.0

[1] Preliminary. *Source: Economic Research Service, U.S. Department of Agriculture (ERS-USDA)*

World Production of Butter[3] In Thousands of Metric Tons

Year	Australia	Brazil	Canada	Egypt	European Union	India	Japan	Mexico	New Zealand	Russia	Ukraine	United States	World Total
2003	163	72	84	13	2,153	2,450	80	77	405	280	148	564	8,766
2004	132	75	84	12	2,164	2,600	80	88	418	270	138	568	8,792
2005	131	77	84	12	2,155	2,749	84	137	379	275	118	611	8,963
2006	129	79	75	10	2,035	3,050	80	200	390	290	105	657	9,167
2007	117	82	79	10	2,053	3,360	75	214	442	300	100	695	9,594
2008	111	84	85	----	2,040	3,690	72	180	422	305	85	746	7,820
2009[1]	134	76	82	----	2,090	3,910	80	165	428	280	72	700	8,017
2010[2]	129	78	82	----	2,060	4,160	80	170	412	290	70	708	8,239

[1] Preliminary. [2] Forecast. [3] Factory (including creameries and dairies) & farm. NA = Not available.
Source: Foreign Agricultural Service, U.S. Department of Agriculture (FAS-USDA)

Production of Creamery Butter in Factories in the United States In Millions of Pounds

Year	Jan.	Feb.	Mar.	Apr.	May	June	July	Aug.	Sept.	Oct.	Nov.	Dec.	Total
2002	140.1	124.2	127.7	131.6	125.5	95.8	94.4	88.9	92.8	102.6	103.9	127.6	1,355.1
2003	141.9	128.1	126.4	122.8	114.9	84.2	80.1	70.9	73.3	96.8	88.4	114.6	1,242.4
2004	129.3	108.6	100.4	100.3	110.1	99.2	92.6	90.3	94.2	104.4	101.4	118.8	1,249.7
2005	128.0	116.9	122.4	117.1	120.7	106.6	95.9	93.2	100.6	108.9	110.9	126.0	1,347.2
2006	149.8	136.8	141.7	127.7	128.6	101.1	94.7	88.9	104.3	119.1	118.1	137.6	1,448.5
2007	150.6	134.0	138.4	133.0	124.0	110.0	116.5	110.9	112.9	130.4	130.8	141.5	1,532.9
2008	168.8	146.8	151.9	150.1	142.6	119.8	114.2	115.7	121.0	130.0	133.7	156.3	1,651.1
2009[1]	174.7	145.7	147.2	142.5	139.4	125.5	114.3	100.9	94.6	112.9	120.5	150.8	1,568.9

[1] Preliminary. *Source: Economic Research Service, U.S. Department of Agriculture (ERS-USDA)*

Cold Storage Holdings of Creamery Butter in the United States, on First of Month In Millions of Pounds

Year	Jan.	Feb.	Mar.	Apr.	May	June	July	Aug.	Sept.	Oct.	Nov.	Dec.
2002	55.9	99.2	130.1	145.2	196.6	226.8	243.0	245.3	229.5	209.1	164.6	135.6
2003	157.8	204.8	239.9	249.0	263.7	298.0	301.4	283.9	253.9	207.2	170.2	122.5
2004	99.6	152.4	159.1	158.1	155.7	178.7	189.2	193.5	161.0	133.0	107.2	57.2
2005	45.0	77.2	110.9	132.4	164.5	178.0	179.6	176.7	148.9	124.1	98.1	60.4
2006	58.6	125.3	169.1	195.3	227.7	261.5	263.0	259.8	215.2	190.6	157.6	108.1
2007	108.6	148.7	185.4	193.1	245.9	270.2	273.0	271.5	260.9	240.3	196.6	143.2
2008	155.2	188.1	210.4	224.8	251.5	269.5	258.4	246.1	213.7	186.9	149.4	119.9
2009[1]	119.0	176.5	204.9	212.5	240.0	253.3	262.9	262.8	259.6	227.9	190.6	142.7

[1] Preliminary. *Source: Agricultural Statistics Board, U.S. Department of Agriculture (ASB-USDA)*

Average Price of Butter at Chicago Mercantile Exchange In Cents Per Pound

Year	Jan.	Feb.	Mar.	Apr.	May	June	July	Aug.	Sept.	Oct.	Nov.	Dec.	Average
2002	134.5	124.3	124.7	117.1	105.9	104.3	103.0	97.5	96.4	103.2	104.3	112.0	110.6
2003	108.2	104.1	109.2	109.1	109.2	111.4	119.9	117.1	117.3	118.5	120.6	129.7	114.5
2004	143.2	171.3	213.5	222.0	203.6	193.0	174.6	154.1	176.6	164.8	192.4	170.8	181.7
2005	157.8	161.5	155.3	149.3	140.4	153.1	162.1	168.6	169.9	162.0	142.6	135.5	154.8
2006	133.7	119.3	116.6	116.3	117.6	116.4	116.5	130.4	131.7	132.1	129.2	124.1	123.6
2007	122.5	121.9	132.2	137.3	148.3	150.2	149.1	144.6	137.8	130.2	135.9	131.9	136.8
2008	122.5	120.9	134.5	139.1	147.5	150.0	153.9	162.8	169.7	173.2	161.7	120.1	146.3
2009	111.0	111.0	117.7	120.4	125.3	122.4	123.5	120.1	122.0	128.3	150.1	139.7	124.3

Source: Economic Research Service, U.S. Department of Agriculture (ERS-USDA)

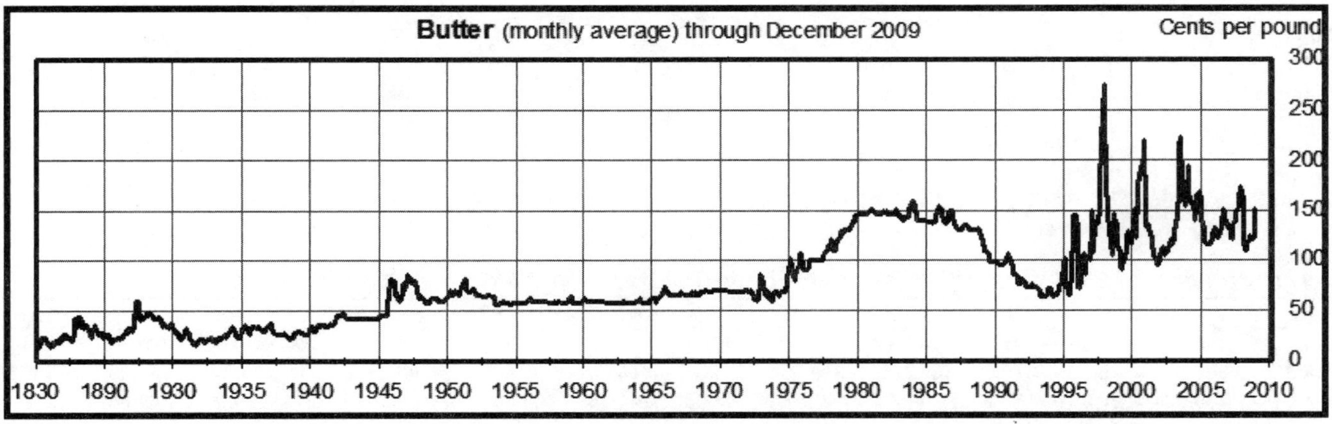

Cadmium

Cadmium (symbol Cd) is a soft, bluish-white, metallic element that can easily be shaped and cut with a knife. Cadmium melts at 321 degrees Celsius and boils at 765 degrees Celsius. Cadmium burns brightly in air when heated, forming the oxide CdO. In 1871, the German chemist Friedrich Stromeyer discovered cadmium in incrustations in zinc furnaces.

Rare greenockite is the only mineral bearing cadmium. Cadmium occurs most often in small quantities associated with zinc ores, such as sphalerite. Electrolysis or fractional distillation is used to separate the cadmium and zinc. About 80% of world cadmium output is a by-product from zinc refining. The remaining 20% comes from secondary sources and recycling of cadmium products. Cadmium recycling is practical only from nickel-cadmium batteries and from some alloys and dust from electric-arc furnaces.

Cadmium is used primarily for metal plating and coating operations in transportation equipment, machinery, baking enamels, photography, and television phosphors. It is also used in pigments and lasers, and in nickel-cadmium and solar batteries.

Prices – Cadmium prices for the 8 years up to 2005 were at severely depressed levels, reflecting the decreased demand for the substance. In 2005, however, cadmium prices rose very sharply by +172.7% to $1.50 cents per pound. In 2007 the price rose further to a 19-year high of $3.45 per pound. Since then in 2009 the price fell by -54.7% yr/yr to $1.22 per pound. The record high of $7.89 per pound was posted in 1988.

Supply – World cadmium production in 2009 fell by -4.1% yr/yr to 18,800 metric tons, but still above the 27-year low of 17,800 metric tons seen in 2002. The largest producer was China with 23% of total world production followed by Japan with 11%. The U.S produced only 3.7% of world. The U.S. production in 2009 fell 9.9% to 700 metric tons, which was the lowest level since 1932.

Demand – Consumption of cadmium has been declining fairly steeply in the last few years due to environmental concerns. U.S. cadmium consumption in 2009 fell by 58.6% yr/yr to 228 metric tons, which was the lowest since 1926. Of the total apparent consumption, about 75% is used for batteries, 12% for pigments, 8% for coatings and plating, 4% for nonferrous alloys, and 1% for other uses.

Trade – The U.S. in 2004 relied on imports for 20% of its cadmium usage, down from 38% as recently as 1998. U.S. imports of cadmium had plunged over the past 13 years but recovered to post a 6-year high in 2005 at 288 metric tons. That, however, was still far below the 1,110 metric tons seen as recently as 1994. In 2009 the U.S. imported 194 metric tons which was down -1.5% from 2008. U.S. exports of cadmium in 2009 rose by +60.1% yr/yr to 676 metric tons.

World Refinery Production of Cadmium In Metric Tons

Year	Australia	Belgium	Canada	China	Finland	Germany	Italy	Japan	Kazak-hstan	Mexico	United Kingdom	United States[3]	World Total
2002	370	117	1,706	2,440	4	422	391	2,444	1,300	1,382	422	1,280	17,800
2003	560	----	1,759	2,710	----	640	22	2,497	1,351	1,590	529	1,450	18,400
2004	347	----	1,880	2,800	----	640	10	2,233	1,900	1,615	532	1,480	18,600
2005	358	----	1,727	4,080	----	640	10	2,297	2,000	1,653	481	1,470	20,100
2006	329	----	2,090	3,790	----	640	10	2,287	2,000	1,401	416	723	19,900
2007	351	----	1,388	4,210	----	400	10	1,933	2,100	1,617	347	735	19,400
2008[1]	330	NA	1,300	4,300	NA	400	10	2,120	2,100	1,610	371	777	19,600
2009[2]	330	NA	1,150	4,300	NA	400	NA	1,990	2,100	1,580	NA	700	18,800

[1] Preliminary. [2] Estimate. [3] Primary and secondary metal. *Source: U.S. Geological Survey (USGS)*

Salient Statistics of Cadmium in the United States In Metric Tons of Contained Cadmium

Year	Net import Reliance As a % of Apparent Consumption	Production (Metal)	Producer Shipments	Cadmium Sulfide Production	Production Other Compounds	Imports of Cadmium Metal[3]	Exports[4]	Apparent Consumption	Industry Stocks Dec. 31[5]	New York Dealer Price $ Per Lb.
2002	E	1,280	1,470	33	----	81	264	1,700	1,360	.29
2003	E	1,450	1,200	----	----	112	615	1,020	1,430	.59
2004	20	1,480	1,410	----	----	263	154	1,840	1,170	.55
2005	E	1,470	1,680	----	----	288	686	699	1,540	1.50
2006	E	723	833	----	----	180	483	568	1,400	1.35
2007	E	735	692	----	----	316	424	585	1,440	3.45
2008[1]	E	777	774	----	----	197	421	550	1,460	2.69
2009[2]	E	700				194	676	228	1,450	1.22

[1] Preliminary. [2] Estimate. [3] For consumption. [4] Cadmium metal, alloys, dross, flue dust. [5] Metallic, Compounds, Distributors. [6] Sticks & Balls in 1 to 5 short ton lots of metal (99.95%). E = Net exporter. *Source: U.S. Geological Survey (USGS)*

Average Price of Cadmium (99.95%) in the United States In Dollars Per Pound

Year	Jan.	Feb.	Mar.	Apr.	May	June	July	Aug.	Sept.	Oct.	Nov.	Dec.	Average
2007	185.00	195.53	204.09	242.86	368.75	604.17	524.40	396.74	362.50	347.28	290.00	290.00	334.28
2008	301.90	315.00	315.00	315.00	315.00	315.00	315.00	306.67	280.00	280.00	280.00	280.00	301.55
2009	280.00	280.00	157.27	141.43	121.38	142.05	141.25	166.67	180.00	189.05	190.00	167.63	179.73

Source: American Metal Market (AMM)

Canola (Rapeseed)

Canola is a genetic variation of rapeseed that was developed by Canadian plant breeders specifically for its nutritional qualities and its low level of saturated fat. The term *Canola* is a contraction of "Canadian oil." The history of canola oil begins with the rapeseed plant, a member of the mustard family. The rape plant is grown both as feed for livestock and birdfeed. For 4,000 years, the oil from the rapeseed was used in China and India for cooking and as lamp oil. During World War II, rapeseed oil was used as a marine and industrial lubricant. After the war, the market for rapeseed oil plummeted. Rapeseed growers needed other uses for their crop, and that stimulated the research that led to the development of canola. In 1974, Canadian plant breeders from the University of Manitoba produced canola by genetically altering rapeseed. Each canola plant produces yellow flowers, which then produce pods. The tiny round seeds within each pod are crushed to produce canola oil. Each canola seed contains approximately 40% oil. Canola oil is the world's third largest source of vegetable oil accounting for 13% of world vegetable oils, following soybean oil at 32%, and palm oil at 28%. The rest of the seed is processed into canola meal, which is used as high protein livestock feed.

The climate in Canada is especially suitable for canola plant growth. Today, over 13 million acres of Canadian soil are dedicated to canola production. Canola oil is Canada's leading vegetable oil. Due to strong demand from the U.S. for canola oil, approximately 70% of Canada's canola oil is exported to the U.S. Canola oil is used as a salad oil, cooking oil, and for margarine as well as in the manufacture of inks, biodegradable greases, pharmaceuticals, fuel, soap, and cosmetics.

Canola futures and options are traded on the ICE Futures Canada (ICE) exchange. The futures contract calls for the delivery of 20 metric tons of canola and 5 contracts are together called a "1 board lot." The futures contract is priced in Canadian dollars per metric ton.

Prices – Canola prices on the ICE nearest-futures chart started 2009 at about CD$437 per metric ton and drifted lower to about CD$407 in February. The price then moved up to the year's high at about CD$477 and then moved lower the rest of the year to end the year at about CD$405 per metric ton. The price continued lower into 2010 to about CD$385 in February.

The average monthly wholesale price of canola oil in the Midwest in 2008 rose +35.4% yr/yr to 61.53 cents per pound, to post an 11-year high. The average monthly wholesale price of canola meal (delivery Pacific Northwest) in the 2009-10 crop year (through November 2009) fell by 20.0% to $199.30 per short ton.

Supply – World canola production in the 2009-10 marketing year rose by +2.2% yr/yr to a new record high of 59.385 million metric tons. The world's largest canola producers were the European Union with 36% of world production in 2009-10, China (22%), Canada (20%), and India (11%). U.S. production of canola and canola oil in 2009-10 rose +4.0% yr/yr to 682,000 metric tons. Regarding canola products, world production of canola oil in 2009-10 rose +7.6% to 21.926 million metric tons, which was a new record high. U.S. production of canola oil in 2009-10 fell -8.2% to 446,000 metric tons, down from the 2008-09 record high of 486,000 metric tons. World production of canola meal in 2009-10 rose +7.4% to a record high of 33.016 million metric tons.

Demand – World crush demand for canola in 2009-10 rose +7.6% yr/yr to 55.781 million metric tons, which was a new record high. World consumption of canola oil in 2009-10 rose +7.7% yr/yr to a new record high of 21.926 million metric tons. World consumption of canola meal in 2009-10 rose +6.9% to a record high of 32.769 million metric tons.

Trade – World canola exports in 2009-10 fell -18.7% to 10.085 million metric tons, world canola oil exports rose +10.0% to a record high of 2.608 million metric tons, and world canola meal exports rose +16.1% yr/yr to a record high of 3.888 million metric tons. World canola imports in 2009-10 fell -21.8% to 9.583 million metric tons, world canola oil imports fell -5.3% to 2.308 million metric tons, and world canola meal imports rose 2.3% to a record high of 3.623 million metric tons. Regarding U.S. canola trade, U.S. canola imports in 2009-10 fell -23.0% to 635,000 metric tons and U.S. exports fell -4.7% to 182,000 metric tons.

World Production of Canola (Rapeseed) In Thousands of Metric Tons

Year	Australia	Canada	China	Bangla-desh	Belarus	European Union	India	Pakistan	Romania	Russia	Ukraine	United States	World Total
2000-01	1,775	7,205	11,381	249	73	11,364	3,725	231		148	132	909	37,325
2001-02	1,756	5,017	11,331	238	95	11,585	4,500	221		140	135	908	36,010
2002-03	871	4,521	10,552	233	60	11,752	4,050	235		115	61	697	33,256
2003-04	1,703	6,771	11,420	218	55	11,185	6,800	238		192	51	686	39,428
2004-05	1,542	7,674	13,182	211	143	15,432	6,500	215		276	149	613	46,085
2005-06	1,419	9,483	13,052	191	150	15,523	7,000	181		303	285	718	48,504
2006-07	573	9,000	10,966	235	115	16,092	5,800	318		523	600	633	45,093
2007-08[1]	1,214	9,601	10,573	210	250	18,358	5,450	190		632	1,100	650	48,516
2008-09[2]	1,861	12,643	12,100	220	590	18,893	7,000	225		752	2,900	656	58,092
2009-10[3]	1,770	11,800	13,200	225	650	21,325	6,600	230		700	1,900	682	59,385

[1] Preliminary. [2] Estimate. [3] Forecast. *Source: Economic Research Service, U.S. Department of Agriculture (ERS-USDA); The Oil World*

Volume of Trading of Canola Futures in Winnipeg In 20 Metric Ton Units

Year	Jan.	Feb.	Mar.	Apr.	May	June	July	Aug.	Sept.	Oct.	Nov.	Dec.	Total
2000	137,528	182,744	163,038	169,807	168,164	152,358	79,071	91,762	146,890	208,639	154,727	204,045	1,858,773
2001	196,137	292,226	286,463	247,744	205,798	188,175	163,901	155,531	143,220	205,016	174,910	165,852	2,424,973
2002	164,945	179,753	166,889	159,981	133,202	139,256	132,524	174,527	131,034	170,873	105,661	169,477	1,828,122
2003	129,903	152,738	108,991	153,528	120,178	152,979	90,909	66,768	109,760	217,310	90,950	153,269	1,547,283
2004	145,339	204,567	178,516	192,429	120,218	128,843	73,417	97,483	113,368	175,776	110,922	196,094	1,736,972
2005	116,678	207,198	141,717	124,636	102,424	178,001	87,724	121,749	138,701	200,004	145,231	258,922	1,822,985
2006	195,189	240,070	237,537	229,470	211,688	238,967	129,433	145,133	212,164	284,033	191,676	291,994	2,607,354
2007	204,893	309,278	198,589	273,755	281,240	321,022	160,846	181,145	212,288	396,852	268,743	360,531	3,169,182
2008	368,963	388,180	307,536	318,641	209,631	290,152	172,089	170,596	220,479	293,978	126,273	265,670	3,132,188
2009	265,415	345,108	267,276	358,030	286,069	326,924	161,569	188,651	268,629	340,368	211,160	332,594	3,351,793

Contract size = 20 tonnes. *Source: ICE Futures Canada (ICE)*

Average Open Interest of Canola Futures in Winnipeg In 20 Metric Ton Units

Year	Jan.	Feb.	Mar.	Apr.	May	June	July	Aug.	Sept.	Oct.	Nov.	Dec.
2000	59,057	65,545	65,296	66,253	65,855	59,673	46,813	51,367	59,342	72,618	64,862	65,170
2001	57,537	73,539	88,111	78,143	77,425	84,315	72,430	70,137	67,275	71,651	65,580	66,884
2002	57,821	56,443	53,321	56,830	50,924	38,901	48,329	54,286	53,630	50,379	56,896	57,983
2003	52,818	54,749	55,369	53,480	50,549	49,930	47,479	45,314	44,510	49,008	45,423	48,655
2004	54,524	57,944	71,624	77,357	69,783	59,012	50,669	51,009	49,659	53,855	65,215	68,719
2005	64,147	75,090	65,205	63,514	54,341	53,390	57,706	56,305	65,700	68,186	66,117	87,246
2006	82,651	88,576	84,828	88,970	84,710	81,561	81,243	77,356	81,597	80,800	90,694	102,651
2007	103,317	103,250	94,001	102,050	114,244	124,321	117,967	111,470	121,589	122,965	146,879	156,698
2008	164,326	172,229	165,282	135,226	111,687	102,353	91,891	82,272	90,075	90,062	91,459	88,373
2009	88,487	100,072	97,016	104,423	111,922	109,921	94,574	104,426	95,168	99,968	93,108	99,736

Contract size = 20 tonnes. *Source: ICE Futures Canada (ICE)*

World Supply and Distribution of Canola and Products In Thousands of Metric Tons

Year	Canola Production	Canola Exports	Canola Imports	Canola Crush	Canola Ending Stocks	Canola Meal Production	Canola Meal Exports	Canola Meal Imports	Canola Meal Consumption	Canola Meal Ending Stocks	Canola oil Production	Canola oil Exports	Canola oil Imports	Canola oil Consumption	Canola oil Ending Stocks
2002-03	33,256	4,129	4,034	31,588	2,171	18,807	1,615	1,726	18,942	279	12,251	911	892	12,343	559
2003-04	39,428	5,491	5,148	36,414	2,099	21,786	2,478	2,491	21,429	649	14,092	1,324	1,356	14,286	397
2004-05	46,085	4,900	5,018	40,579	4,746	24,230	2,505	2,297	24,192	479	15,715	1,293	1,192	15,519	492
2005-06	48,504	6,984	6,684	44,616	5,506	26,574	2,687	2,558	26,330	594	17,296	1,667	1,477	16,934	664
2006-07	45,093	6,627	7,012	43,616	4,660	25,946	2,883	3,050	26,472	235	17,007	2,000	2,197	17,455	413
2007-08[1]	48,516	8,195	7,562	46,585	3,547	27,637	3,645	3,556	27,569	214	18,312	1,927	2,029	18,398	429
2008-09[2]	58,092	12,402	12,258	51,865	7,010	30,752	3,349	3,541	30,641	517	20,377	2,372	2,436	19,920	950
2009-10[3]	59,385	10,085	9,583	55,781	7,093	33,016	3,888	3,623	32,769	499	21,926	2,608	2,308	21,455	1,121

[1] Preliminary. [2] Estimate. [3] Forecast. *Source: Economic Research Service, U.S. Department of Agriculture (ERS-USDA); The Oil World*

Salient Statistics of Canola and Canola Oil in the United States In Thousands of Metric Tons

Year	Canola Supply: Stocks June 1	Canola Supply: Production	Canola Supply: Imports	Canola Supply: Total Supply	Canola Disappearance: Crush	Canola Disappearance: Exports	Canola Disappearance: Total[3]	Canola Oil Supply: Stocks Oct. 1	Canola Oil Supply: Production	Canola Oil Supply: Imports	Canola Oil Supply: Total Supply	Canola Oil Disappearance: Domestic	Canola Oil Disappearance: Exports	Canola Oil Disappearance: Total
2002-03	68	697	197	962	586	287	873	24	230	445	699	591	73	664
2003-04	72	686	244	1,002	640	305	945	35	277	555	867	699	126	825
2004-05	40	613	467	1,120	901	140	1,041	42	363	514	919	739	122	861
2005-06	60	718	518	1,296	1,030	157	1,187	58	381	726	1,165	831	214	1,045
2006-07	87	633	647	1,367	963	246	1,209	120	377	712	1,209	855	286	1,141
2007-08	135	650	874	1,659	1,050	423	1,473	68	442	1,017	1,527	1,309	158	1,467
2008-09[1]	158	656	825	1,639	1,218	191	1,409	60	486	1,050	1,596	1,272	249	1,521
2009-10[2]	203	682	635	1,520	1,210	182	1,392	75	446	1,171	1,692	1,475	160	1,635

[1] Preliminary. [2] Forecast. [3] Includes planting seed and residual. *Source: Economic Research Service, U.S. Department of Agriculture (ERS-USDA)*

Wholesale Price of Canola Oil in Midwest In Cents Per Pound

Year	Jan.	Feb.	Mar.	Apr.	May	June	July	Aug.	Sept.	Oct.	Nov.	Dec.	Average
2002	20.81	21.31	27.44	21.94	21.95	23.19	25.06	28.45	29.81	30.75	34.19	41.19	27.17
2003	24.30	28.88	27.63	27.44	28.13	27.13	26.56	26.30	28.44	31.88	32.67	33.92	28.61
2004	33.44	37.19	38.19	36.81	35.60	32.88	31.63	29.50	31.38	28.35	31.75	31.75	33.21
2005	29.80	28.88	31.38	31.00	31.25	33.00	31.95	29.75	30.50	31.50	30.88	28.81	30.73
2006	38.63	29.06	30.19	29.70	31.56	31.69	33.95	33.06	32.94	34.50	37.63	37.42	33.36
2007	38.56	40.06	38.95	38.44	40.44	42.56	45.00	44.25	48.00	50.38	57.30	61.50	45.45
2008	64.94	71.80	70.56	71.38	73.05	76.69	74.13	61.05	54.88	42.85	39.81	37.19	61.53
2009[1]	38.80	35.66	35.38	39.75	41.50	42.38	39.80	42.00	39.31	41.55	44.38	42.90	40.28

[1] Preliminary. *Source: Economic Research Service, U.S. Department of Agriculture (ERS-USDA)*

Average Price of Canola in Vancouver In Canadian Dollars Per Metric Ton

Year	Jan.	Feb.	Mar.	Apr.	May	June	July	Aug.	Sept.	Oct.	Nov.	Dec.	Average
2002	329.23	328.38	329.39	316.74	318.67	330.21	369.42	401.78	408.43	413.64	436.25	418.74	366.74
2003	396.78	380.81	351.97	362.89	344.59	333.48	322.64	319.37	324.07	338.93	343.65	338.57	346.48
2004	345.51	370.53	402.02	395.92	384.09	378.62	360.93	349.57	341.29	288.64	275.37	265.15	346.47
2005	261.56	250.02	270.29	273.13	275.58	286.78	279.45	259.58	240.30	235.00	233.21	226.39	257.61
2006	230.48	231.43	241.57	248.63	267.11	263.66	277.90	265.70	265.20	295.90	335.39	348.60	272.63
2007	354.09	357.65	350.26	348.36	357.87	368.11	372.55	380.70	401.35	402.61	417.23	453.82	380.38
2008	519.88	608.92	618.85	594.74	578.47	616.27	601.79	517.00	457.86	391.62	399.41	371.48	523.02
2009	413.77	416.13	409.67	428.95	459.08	461.29	422.69	429.38	394.03	377.19	377.74	389.42	414.95

Source: ICE Futures Canada; formerly Winnipeg Commodity Exchange (WCE)

Average Wholesale Price of Canola Meal, 36% Pacific Northwest In Dollars Per Short Ton

Year	Oct.	Nov.	Dec.	Jan.	Feb.	Mar.	Apr.	May	June	July	Aug.	Sept.	Average
2002-03	131.50	134.70	142.17	154.10	155.80	147.55	145.60	148.50	146.95	137.10	135.50	149.20	144.06
2003-04	169.65	187.19	181.35	201.07	205.50	228.65	214.40	200.03	189.00	192.09	146.99	145.55	188.46
2004-05	133.39	138.81	135.13	129.21	139.55	146.08	140.85	139.25	153.98	150.48	138.12	132.10	139.75
2005-06	130.13	139.55	158.06	150.05	143.94	134.74	136.04	136.59	139.63	137.83	143.28	136.38	140.52
2006-07	149.77	166.80	163.17	173.30	198.37	195.37	169.01	168.19	189.11	171.14	159.33	176.98	173.38
2007-08	167.24	192.25	226.30	276.78	285.83	276.85	268.14	258.75	293.20	310.19	239.88	220.42	251.32
2008-09	192.55	217.99	228.62	279.23	243.30	217.02	230.06	287.99	325.48	261.55	277.30	224.74	248.82
2009-10[1]	220.90	177.69	NA	248.63									215.74

[1] Preliminary. *Source: Economic Research Service, U.S. Department of Agriculture (ERS-USDA)*

Cassava

Cassava is a perennial woody shrub with an edible root. Cassava, which is also called manioc, mandioca, or yucca, grows in tropical and subtropical areas of the world. Cassava has been known since the 1500s and originates in Latin America. The cassava's starchy roots are a major source of dietary energy for more than 500 million people. Cassava is the highest producer of carbohydrates among staple crops, and it ranks fourth in food crops in developing countries. The leaves of the cassava plant are also edible and are relatively rich in protein and vitamins A and B.

Cassava is drought-tolerant and needs less soil preparation and weeding than other crops. Because cassava can be stored in the ground for up to 3 years, it also serves as a reserve food when other crops fail. The cassava is propagated by cuttings of the woody stem, thereby resulting in a low multiplication rate compared to crops propagated by true seeds.

One problem with cassava is the poisonous cyanides, which need to be destroyed before consumption. The cyanide content differs with each variety of cassava, but higher cyanide is usually correlated to high yields. The cyanide content can be destroyed through heat and various processing methods such as grating, sun drying, and fermenting.

Cassava is the primary source of tapioca. Cassava is also eaten raw or boiled, and is processed into livestock feed, starch and glucose, flour, and pharmaceuticals. One species of cassava has been successfully grown for its rubber.

Prices – The average price of tapioca (hard pellets, FOB Rotterdam) in 2008 (latest data) fell by -4.4% to $214 per metric ton, down from the record $224 per metric ton posted in 2007. The lower 2008 price is still more than double the record low of $82 in 2001.

Supply – World production of cassava in 2008 (latest data available) rose by +3.9% to a record high of 232.950 million metric tons. The world's largest producers of cassava in 2008 were Nigeria (with 19% of world production), Thailand (12%), Brazil (11%), and Indonesia (9.0%).

Trade – World exports of tapioca in 2008 (latest available) fell -35.7% to 4.092 million metric tons, down from the 2007 fifteen-year high of 6.360 million metric tons. Thailand accounted for 73% of world exports in 2008, followed by Vietnam with 21%, and Indonesia with 3%. The world's two main importers of tapioca in 2008 were China with 52% of world imports, the Republic of Korea with 24%, and the European Union with 16.

World Cassava Production In Thousands of Metric Tons

Year	Brazil	China	Ghana	India	Indonesia	Mozambique	Nigeria	Paraguay	Tanzania	Thailand	Uganda	Congo[2]	World Total
2001	22,577	3,873	8,966	6,768	17,055	5,975	32,068	3,568	4,336	18,396	5,265	15,436	182,181
2002	23,066	3,925	9,731	6,516	16,913	5,925	34,120	4,430	5,176	16,868	5,373	14,930	184,741
2003	21,961	4,015	10,239	5,426	18,524	6,150	36,304	4,669	3,962	19,718	5,450	14,945	191,322
2004	23,927	3,816	9,739	5,950	19,425	6,413	38,845	5,500	4,441	21,440	5,500	14,951	203,107
2005	25,872	4,016	9,567	7,463	19,321	6,500	41,565	4,785	5,539	16,938	5,576	14,974	207,086
2006	26,639	4,313	9,638	7,855	19,987	6,765	45,721	4,800	6,158	22,584	4,926	14,989	222,292
2007	26,541	4,362	9,650	8,232	19,988	5,039	43,410	4,800	6,600	26,916	4,456	15,004	224,132
2008[1]	25,878	4,362	9,650	9,054	21,593	5,039	44,582	4,800	6,600	27,566	5,072	15,019	232,950

[1] Estimate. [2] Formerly Zaire. *Source: Food and Agriculture Organization of the United Nations (FAO-UN)*

World Trade in Tapioca In Thousands of Metric Tons

	Exports					Imports						
Year	Costa Rica	Indonesia	Thailand	Vietnam	World Total	China	European Union	Japan	Korea	Philippines	Singapore	World Total
2001	9	177	4,494	409	5,140	1,950	2,915	20	445	17	19	5,475
2002	12	130	3,067	308	3,556	1,760	1,560	14	157	10	19	3,580
2003	14	42	3,994	681	4,785	2,368	1,869	21	247	6	19	4,624
2004	17	234	4,579	730	5,626	3,442	2,075	30	460	12	19	6,134
2005	18	230	3,028	545	3,889	3,335	362	23	265	----	21	4,062
2006	22	132	4,361	1,106	5,690	4,950	263	20	268	3	22	5,570
2007	25	210	4,798	1,252	6,360	4,625	1,325	27	302	----	21	6,503
2008[1]	76	135	2,984	844	4,092	1,976	619	37	900	----	21	3,770

[1] Estimate. [2] Intra-EU trade is excluded. *Source: The Oil World*

Prices of Tapioca, Hard Pellets, F.O.B. Rotterdam U.S. Dollars Per Tonne

Year	Jan.	Feb.	Mar.	Apr.	May	June	July	Aug.	Sept.	Oct.	Nov.	Dec.	Average
2001	83	80	77	78	80	82	84	84	87	83	84	84	82
2002	86	82	82	84	87	91	96	97	95	93	93	89	90
2003	91	92	95	96	101	101	103	108	114	134	138	143	110
2004	138	132	121	118	117	118	120	122	128	134	139	148	128
2005	147	149	153	145	142	130	----	----	----	----	----	----	144
2006	----	----	----	----	----	----	----	----	----	----	----	----	----
2007	165	169	164	171	185	203	229	273	317	299	265	247	224
2008	255	261	264	257	249	241	247	226	214	12	172	171	214

Source: The Oil World

Castor beans

Castor bean plants are native to the Ethiopian region of tropical east Africa. The seeds of the castor bean are used to produce castor oil. The average castor bean seed contains 35% to 55% oil. The oil is removed from the bean seeds by either pressing or solvent extraction. Castor oil is used in many products. In the U.S., the paint and varnish industry is the single largest market for castor oil. Castor oil is also used for coating fabrics, insulation, cosmetics, skin emollients, hair oils, inks, nylon plastics, greases, and hydraulic fluids.

Ricin is found in all parts of the castor bean plant, but the most concentrated amounts are found in the cake by-product after oil extraction. Ricin is one of the most deadly, naturally occurring poisons known. Ricin received attention when it was used in a subway attack in Japan in 1995 and again when it was sent to a Congressional office in an envelope in February 2004. One non-deadly use for ricin is for medical research where it is being studied for use as a potential treatment for cancer.

Supply – World production of castor-seed beans in the 2008-09 marketing year (the latest data available) rose by +3.6% to 1.415 million metric tons. The world's largest producer of castor-seed beans by far is India with 69% of world production in 2008-09 at 975,000 metric tons. The second and third largest producers are China with 14% of world production (200,000 metric tons) and Brazil with 9% of world production (123,000 metric tons).

Demand – U.S. consumption of castor oil in 2008-09 fell by -32.0% to 66.520 million pounds, down from the 2007-08 record high of 97.769 million pounds. The 2009-10 consumption is estimated to be only about 58 million pounds based on the first three months of the year.

World Production of Castorseed Beans In Thousands of Metric Tons

Year	Brazil	China	Ecuador	India	Mexico	Paraguay	Pakistan	Philippines	Sudan	Tanzania	Thailand	Former U.S.S.R.	Total
2001-02	100	260	4	610	1	13	3	4	1	3	9	2	1,044
2002-03	72	265	4	650	1	7	1	4	1	3	10	2	1,055
2003-04	78	258	4	720	1	10	10	4	1	3	10	2	1,154
2004-05	129	250	2	870	1	11	7	4	1	3	10	2	1,350
2005-06	162	220	2	930	1	12	8	4	1	3	11	2	1,418
2006-07[1]	92	190	3	820	1	9	8	4	1	3	11	2	1,210
2007-08[2]	94	170	3	990	1	10	8	4	1	3	11	2	1,366
2008-09[3]	123	200	3	975	1	13	8	4		4	11		1,415

[1] Preliminary. [2] Estimate. [3] Forecast. *Sources: Foreign Agricultural Service, U.S.Department of Agriculture (FAS-USDA); The Oil World*

Castor Oil Consumption[2] in the United States In Thousands of Pounds

Year	Oct.	Nov.	Dec.	Jan.	Feb.	Mar.	Apr.	May	June	July	Aug.	Sept.	Total
2003-04	2,072	1,836	1,779	1,526	1,251	2,241	2,396	2,250	1,905	1,542	2,382	2,366	23,546
2004-05	2,155	1,391	1,581	1,365	1,915	1,992	2,175	2,211	1,827	1,689	2,021	1,162	21,484
2005-06	1,389	1,761	1,654	1,602	1,610	1,426	1,457	1,766	1,899	1,516	1,768	1,379	19,227
2006-07	1,583	2,026	1,642	2,021	4,011	6,577	5,105	4,107	5,360	5,123	2,161	3,813	43,529
2007-08	2,616	4,583	W	7,664	7,890	7,942	9,327	9,190	9,101	10,361	11,406	9,542	97,769
2008-09	10,137	7,123	7,775	7,231	5,447	2,994	4,758	4,322	4,718	W	2,109	4,363	66,520
2009-10[1]	4,294	5,658	4,521										57,892

[1] Preliminary. [2] In inedible products (Resins, Plastics, etc.). W = Withheld. *Source: Bureau of the Census, U.S. Department of Commerce*

Castor Oil Stocks in the United States, on First of Month In Thousands of Pounds

Year	Oct.	Nov.	Dec.	Jan.	Feb.	Mar.	Apr.	May	June	July	Aug.	Sept.
2003-04	26,463	17,753	16,630	18,582	14,097	13,985	7,507	22,751	W	25,593	18,381	14,922
2004-05	34,525	31,608	24,287	19,476	32,641	25,318	27,876	19,098	31,493	22,919	15,963	35,604
2005-06	38,357	45,720	37,111	29,428	21,047	25,076	15,756	25,543	25,070	22,165	21,329	14,389
2006-07	39,635	24,055	18,780	43,896	30,734	46,850	58,989	50,455	49,276	46,715	37,668	26,019
2007-08	16,945	34,444	23,661	36,046	30,034	20,303	22,240	14,167	39,649	27,285	14,907	W
2008-09	W	W	47,243	38,349	56,845	50,612	38,987	32,208	42,361	34,222	25,908	25,111
2009-10[1]	28,817	21,217	20,504	22,096								

[1] Preliminary. W = Withheld proprietary data. *Source: Bureau of the Census, U.S. Department of Commerce*

Average Wholesale Price of Castor Oil No. 1, Brazilian Tanks in New York In Cents Per Pound

2002	47.50	47.50	47.50	47.50	47.50	47.50	47.00	47.00	47.00	47.00	47.00	47.00	47.25
2003	47.00	47.00	47.00	47.00	47.00	47.00	47.00	47.00	47.00	47.00	47.00	47.00	47.00
2004	47.00	47.00	47.00	47.00	47.00	47.00	47.00	47.00	47.00	47.00	47.00	48.00	47.08
2005	50.00	50.00	50.00	50.00	50.00	50.00	50.00	49.00	49.00	47.00	45.50	45.00	48.79
2006	45.00	45.00	44.00	43.00	43.00	43.00	43.00	43.00	44.00	44.00	44.00	43.50	43.71
2007	46.60	49.75	52.00	54.60	58.00	57.50	56.00	NA	60.00	60.00	60.00	60.29	55.89
2008	63.57	66.11	70.20	72.00	72.00	74.29	78.00	82.00	82.00	80.18	79.21	77.67	74.77
2009	76.00	72.58	70.00	69.00	67.00	64.45	64.09	65.00	65.00	67.00	67.00	70.64	68.15

Source: Foreign Agricultural Service, U.S.Department of Agriculture (FAS-USDA)

Cattle and Calves

The beef cycle begins with the cow-calf operation, which breeds the new calves. Most ranchers breed their herds of cows in summer, thus producing the new crop of calves in spring (the gestation period is about nine months). This allows the calves to be born during the milder weather of spring and provides the calves with ample forage through the summer and early autumn. The calves are weaned from the mother after 6-8 months and most are then moved into the "stocker" operation. The calves usually spend 6-10 months in the stocker operation, growing to near full-sized by foraging for summer grass or winter wheat. When the cattle reach 600-800 pounds, they are typically sent to a feedlot and become "feeder cattle." In the feedlot, the cattle are fed a special food mix to encourage rapid weight gain. The mix includes grain (corn, milo, or wheat), a protein supplement (soybean, cottonseed, or linseed meal), and roughage (alfalfa, silage, prairie hay, or an agricultural by-product such as sugar beet pulp). The animal is considered "finished" when it reaches full weight and is ready for slaughter, typically at around 1,200 pounds, which produces a dressed carcass of around 745 pounds. After reaching full weight, the cattle are sold for slaughter to a meat packing plant. Futures and options on live cattle and feeder cattle are traded at the Chicago Mercantile Exchange. Both the live and feeder cattle futures contracts trade in terms of cents per pound.

Prices – Live cattle futures prices, after posting a record high of 104.7 cents per pound in July 2008, fell sharply in late 2008 due to the financial crisis and the global recession. Cattle producers during the financial crisis ran into problems financing their herds and therefore sent cattle to slaughter in relatively high numbers, increasing the supply of beef on the market and pushing prices lower. The number of cattle on feed in 2009 fell by 0.4% to 22.2 million head, adding to the 4.7% decline seen in 2008. Live cattle prices then traded basically sideways in the range of about 80-90 cents through 2009, closing the year slightly higher by 1.8% at 86.0 cents. Cattle prices were able to stabilize in 2009 as demand picked up with the economic recovery that emerged in mid-2009. On the other hand, a major bearish factor during 2009 was a 48% decline in US live cattle exports to 55.83 million head as US cattle trade continued to be hurt by the perception of mad cow problems in the US, even though there has not been a case of mad cow in the US since 2006. Asian governments and consumers continue to resist importing or consuming US beef.

Supply – The world's number of cattle as of January 1, 2009 fell -2.1% to 956.690 million head, which is a 3-1/2 decade low. As of January 1, 2009 the number of cattle and calves on farms in the U.S. fell -1.6% to 94.491 million, which is the lowest level since the 1959 figure of 93.322. World production of beef and veal in 2009 fell -2.2% to 56.782 million metric tons (carcass weight equivalent) and the USDA is forecasting a drop of -0.7% to 56.405 million metric tons in 2010. U.S. commercial production of beef in 2009 fell -2.29% to 25.964 billion pounds and the USDA is forecasting a further drop of -1.9% in 2010.

Demand – World consumption of beef and veal in 2009 fell -2.3% to 56.116 million metric tons and the USDA is forecasting a further drop of 2.6% in 2010 to 55.972 million metric tons. U.S. consumption of beef and veal in 2009 fell -1.1% to 12.310 million metric tons and the USDA is forecasting a further drop of 1.2% in 2010 to 12.158 million metric tons.

Trade – U.S. imports of live cattle in 2009 fell by -15.5% to 1.930 million head, but remained well above the low levels seen when mad cow disease caused the U.S. to close the Canadian border to live cattle in 2003. U.S. exports of live cattle in 2009 fell by -48.1% yr/yr to 55.582 head, but still up from the multi-decade low of 21,607 in 2005 caused by cattle trading bans by key U.S. trading partners.

By weight, U.S. imports of beef in 2009 rose +6.54% to 2.703 billion pounds and the USDA is forecasting an increase of +3.4% to 2.795 billion pounds in 2010. U.S. exports of beef in 2009 fell by -1.4% to 1.861 billion pounds but the USDA is forecasting a rise of +9.6% to 2.040 billion pounds in 2010. That, however, remains far below the levels of about 2.5 billion pounds seen before mad cow disease hit in December 2003 and largely shut down U.S. beef exports.

World Cattle and Buffalo Numbers as of January 1 In Thousands of Head

Year	Argentina	Australia	Brazil	Canada	China	European Union	India	Mexico	Russia	South Africa	Ukraine	United States	World Total (Mil. Head)
2001	51,167	27,720	150,382	13,608	123,532	94,289	284,822	25,328	25,500	13,460	9,424	97,298	1,016.6
2002	52,369	27,870	156,314	13,752	118,092	93,234	285,124	25,349	24,510	13,505	9,433	96,723	1,019.1
2003	53,069	27,870	161,463	13,466	115,678	91,597	286,079	26,011	23,500	13,635	9,108	96,100	1,000.9
2004	53,968	26,640	165,492	14,555	114,344	90,375	283,103	25,199	22,285	13,540	7,712	94,403	995.0
2005	53,767	27,270	169,567	14,925	112,354	89,319	282,500	24,309	21,100	13,510	6,992	94,018	994.0
2006	54,266	27,782	172,111	14,655	109,908	89,672	282,300	23,669	19,850	13,790	6,514	96,342	996.1
2007	55,664	28,400	173,830	14,155	104,651	88,463	282,000	23,316	19,000	13,934	6,175	96,573	992.1
2008	55,662	28,040	175,437	13,895	105,948	89,043	281,700	22,850	18,370	14,082	5,491	96,035	987.8
2009[1]	54,260	27,321	179,788	13,180	105,722	88,945	281,400	22,700	17,900	14,195	5,079	94,491	977.3
2010[2]	50,158	27,436	185,243	12,820	104,900	88,630	281,100	22,168	17,464		4,950	93,000	956.7

[1] Preliminary. [2] Forecast. *Source: Foreign Agricultural Service, U.S. Department of Agriculture (FAS-USDA)*

Cattle Supply and Distribution in the United States In Thousands of Head

Year	Cattle & Calves on Farms Jan. 1	Imports	Calves Born	Total Supply	Livestock Slaughter - Cattle and Calves: Commercial: Federally Inspected	Other[3]	All Commercial	Farm	Total Slaughter	Deaths on Farms	Exports	Total Disappearance
1999	99,115	1,945	38,796	139,856	36,738	695	37,432	210	37,642	4,114	329	42,085
2000	98,198	2,187	38,631	139,016	36,720	658	37,378	210	37,588	4,097	481	42,166
2001	97,277	2,437	38,280	137,994	35,751	625	36,377	200	36,577	4,209	678	41,464
2002	96,704	2,503	38,224	137,431	36,139	641	36,780	190	36,970	4,076	243	41,289
2003	96,100	1,752	37,903	135,754	35,883	611	36,494	192	36,686	4,030	100	40,816
2004	94,888	1,374	37,505	133,767	32,979	592	33,571	189	33,760	4,003	30	37,792
2005	95,438	1,815	37,575	134,828	32,549	573	33,122	189	33,311	4,052	21	37,385
2006	96,702	2,289	37,519	136,509	33,844	566	34,410	187	34,597	4,167	50	38,813
2007[1]	97,003	2,495	36,759	136,257	34,465	557	35,022	187	35,209	4,251	66	39,526
2008[2]	96,669	2,092	36,113	134,873	34,747	580	35,327				110	

[1] Preliminary. [2] Estimate. [3] Wholesale and retail. *Source: Economic Research Service, U.S. Department of Agriculture (ERS-USDA)*

Beef Supply and Utilization in the United States

Years and Quarters	Beginning Stocks	Production: Commercial	Production: Total	Imports	Total Supply	Exports	Ending Stocks	Total Disappearance	Per Capita Disappearance: Carcass Weight	Retail Weight Total
2006	----	26,152	26,152	3,085	29,237	1,145	----	----	----	65.8
I	----	6,082	6,082	843	6,925	215	----	----	----	15.8
II	----	6,724	6,724	790	7,514	315	----	----	----	16.9
III	----	6,834	6,834	730	7,564	307	----	----	----	16.9
IV	----	6,513	6,513	722	7,235	308	----	----	----	16.3
2007	----	26,421	26,421	3,052	29,473	1,431	----	----	----	65.2
I	----	6,237	6,237	770	7,007	269	----	----	----	15.9
II	----	6,649	6,649	884	7,533	363	----	----	----	16.6
III	----	6,802	6,802	774	7,576	424	----	----	----	16.4
IV	----	6,733	6,733	624	7,357	375	----	----	----	16.2
2008	----	26,561	26,561	2,537	29,098	1,888	----	----	----	62.8
I	----	6,372	6,372	637	7,009	360	----	----	----	15.6
II	----	6,899	6,899	661	7,560	471	----	----	----	16.3
III	----	6,908	6,908	584	7,492	609	----	----	----	15.8
IV	----	6,382	6,382	655	7,037	448	----	----	----	15.1
2009[1]	----	25,954	25,954	2,703	28,657	1,861	----	----	----	61.4
I	----	6,248	6,248	704	6,952	384	----	----	----	15.3
II	----	6,602	6,602	751	7,353	471	----	----	----	15.7
III	----	6,689	6,689	623	7,312	496	----	----	----	15.6
IV	----	6,415	6,415	625	7,040	510	----	----	----	14.9
2010[2]	----	25,475	25,475	2,795	28,270	2,040	----	----	----	59.6
I	----	6,125	6,125	680	6,805	470	----	----	----	14.5
II	----	6,570	6,570	745	7,315	530	----	----	----	15.5
III	----	6,540	6,540	705	7,245	530	----	----	----	15.1
IV	----	6,240	6,240	665	6,905	510	----	----	----	14.5

[1] Preliminary. [2] Forecast. *Source: Economic Research Service, U.S. Department of Agriculture (ERS-USDA)*

United States Cattle on Feed in 13 States In Thousands of Head

Year	Number on Feed[3]	Placed on Feed	Marketings	Other Disappearance	Year	Number on Feed[3]	Placed on Feed	Marketings	Other Disappearance
2006	11,804	23,595	22,477	948	2008[1]	12,092	22,299	22,404	753
I	11,804	5,624	5,370	246	I	12,092	5,246	5,471	183
II	11,812	5,468	6,143	265	II	11,684	4,954	6,128	215
III	10,872	6,475	5,777	185	III	10,295	5,998	5,733	145
IV	11,385	6,028	5,187	252	IV	10,415	6,101	5,072	210
2007	11,974	23,400	22,461	821	2009[2]	11,234	22,201	21,684	743
I	11,974	5,309	5,395	244	I	11,234	5,344	5,243	173
II	11,644	5,384	6,041	250	II	11,162	4,629	5,812	227
III	10,737	6,156	5,761	165	III	9,752	6,364	5,496	146
IV	10,967	6,551	5,264	162	IV	10,474	5,864	5,133	197

[1] Preliminary. [2] Estimate. [3] Beginning of period. *Source: Economic Research Service, U.S. Department of Agriculture (ERS-USDA)*

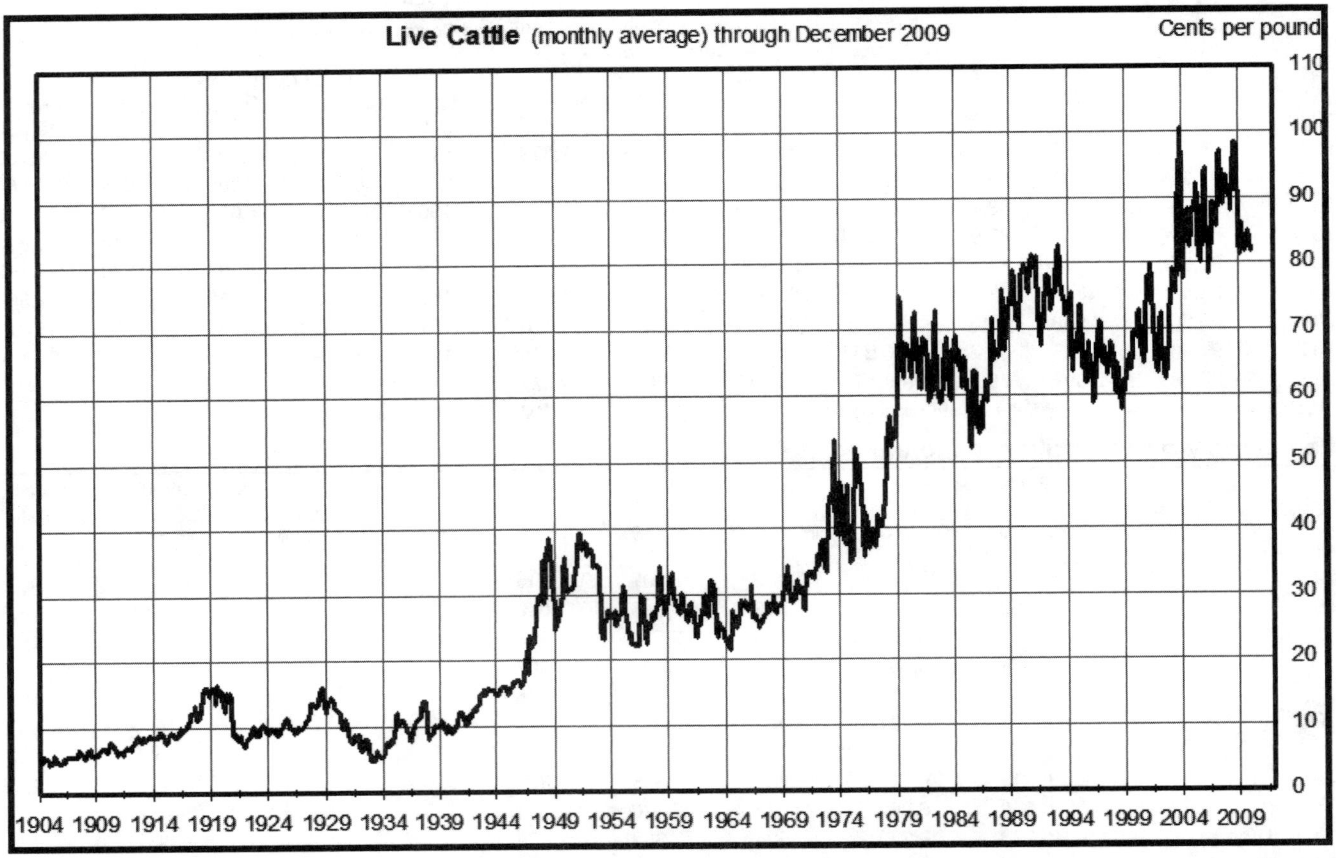

United States Cattle on Feed, 1000+ Capacity Feedlots[2], on First of Month In Thousands of Head

Year	Jan.	Feb.	Mar.	Apr.	May	June	July	Aug.	Sept.	Oct.	Nov.	Dec.
2000	9,752	9,885	9,695	9,593	9,391	9,411	8,959	8,812	8,972	9,502	10,192	10,213
2001	11,798	11,941	11,695	11,523	11,170	11,245	11,011	10,891	10,855	11,125	11,863	11,891
2002	11,565	11,572	11,518	11,587	10,971	10,990	10,507	10,109	10,159	10,452	10,785	10,946
2003	10,658	10,700	10,546	10,713	10,535	10,539	9,923	9,590	9,839	10,218	11,043	11,335
2004	11,253	11,138	10,987	10,763	10,375	10,640	10,132	9,868	9,988	10,502	11,334	11,334
2005	11,299	11,342	11,154	10,873	10,641	10,771	10,394	10,093	10,000	10,482	11,473	11,726
2006	11,804	12,110	12,023	11,812	11,559	11,187	10,872	10,822	10,986	11,385	11,969	11,973
2007	11,974	11,726	11,599	11,644	11,297	11,272	10,737	10,299	10,302	10,967	11,769	12,099
2008	12,092	11,966	11,853	11,684	11,135	10,815	10,295	9,869	9,997	10,415	10,972	11,346
2009[1]	11,234	11,288	11,228	11,162	10,822	10,407	9,752	9,637	9,879	10,474	11,134	11,277

[1] Preliminary. [2] 7 States through 2000. *Source: Economic Research Service, U.S. Department of Agriculture (ERS-USDA)*

United States Cattle Placed on Feed, 1000+ Capacity Feedlots[2] In Thousands of Head

Year	Jan.	Feb.	Mar.	Apr.	May	June	July	Aug.	Sept.	Oct.	Nov.	Dec.	Total
2000	1,931	1,606	1,736	1,470	1,998	1,413	1,674	2,091	2,286	2,387	1,678	1,440	21,710
2001	2,263	1,580	1,842	1,551	2,372	1,965	1,986	2,204	2,141	2,702	1,908	1,578	24,092
2002	2,179	1,810	1,963	1,463	2,267	1,644	1,840	2,228	2,194	2,396	1,982	1,610	23,576
2003	2,089	1,650	2,032	1,870	2,307	1,672	1,997	2,384	2,474	2,781	1,926	1,748	24,930
2004	1,754	1,612	1,810	1,600	2,370	1,647	1,719	2,102	2,375	2,701	1,743	1,834	23,267
2005	1,888	1,523	1,750	1,660	2,223	1,769	1,678	1,993	2,355	2,788	2,045	1,884	23,556
2006	2,199	1,588	1,837	1,619	1,903	1,946	1,958	2,290	2,227	2,430	1,884	1,714	23,595
2007	1,690	1,659	1,960	1,568	2,159	1,657	1,622	2,119	2,415	2,725	2,125	1,701	23,400
2008	1,787	1,723	1,736	1,536	1,900	1,518	1,656	2,061	2,281	2,438	2,016	1,647	22,299
2009[1]	1,858	1,678	1,808	1,600	1,638	1,391	1,863	2,113	2,388	2,474	1,844	1,546	22,201

[1] Preliminary. [2] 7 States through 2000. *Source: Economic Research Service, U.S. Department of Agriculture (ERS-USDA)*

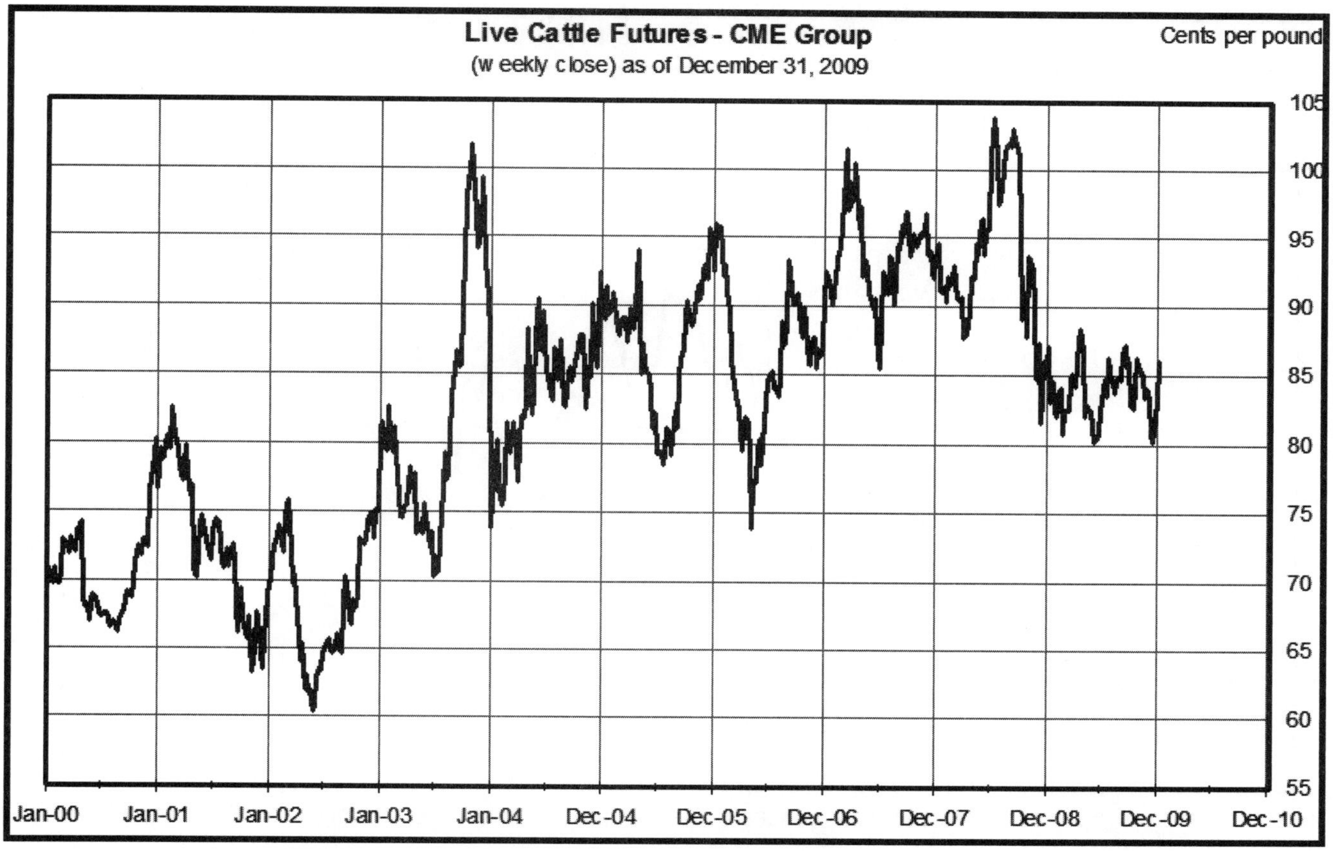

United States Cattle Marketings, 1000+ Capacity Feedlots[2] In Thousands of Head

Year	Jan.	Feb.	Mar.	Apr.	May	June	July	Aug.	Sept.	Oct.	Nov.	Dec.	Total
2000	1,747	1,749	1,764	1,601	1,863	1,828	1,784	1,895	1,708	1,647	1,568	1,500	20,654
2001	2,042	1,745	1,916	1,815	2,196	2,122	2,047	2,186	1,825	1,896	1,800	1,811	23,401
2002	2,083	1,801	1,825	1,996	2,171	2,076	2,193	2,135	1,848	1,979	1,731	1,799	23,637
2003	1,972	1,733	1,803	1,985	2,238	2,227	2,270	2,075	2,032	1,855	1,537	1,740	23,467
2004	1,775	1,694	1,967	1,891	2,026	2,085	1,925	1,926	1,800	1,803	1,635	1,777	22,304
2005	1,772	1,634	1,963	1,801	1,997	2,083	1,918	2,033	1,816	1,739	1,701	1,715	22,172
2006	1,810	1,602	1,958	1,785	2,160	2,198	1,950	2,067	1,760	1,765	1,797	1,625	22,477
2007	1,841	1,711	1,843	1,816	2,085	2,140	1,999	2,066	1,696	1,876	1,738	1,650	22,461
2008	1,853	1,776	1,842	2,010	2,140	1,978	2,037	1,884	1,812	1,814	1,575	1,683	22,404
2009[1]	1,737	1,682	1,824	1,871	1,952	1,989	1,935	1,815	1,746	1,755	1,635	1,743	21,684

[1] Preliminary. [2] 7 States through 2000. *Source: Economic Research Service, U.S. Department of Agriculture (ERS-USDA)*

Quarterly Trade of Live Cattle in the United States In Head

	Imports					Exports				
Year	First Quarter	Second Quarter	Third Quarter	Fourth Quarter	Total	First Quarter	Second Quarter	Third Quarter	Fourth Quarter	Total
2000	580,174	537,009	346,087	724,016	2,187,286	117,889	67,895	72,028	223,430	481,242
2001	701,347	611,570	444,604	679,194	2,436,715	111,458	75,632	67,042	194,563	448,695
2002	785,559	398,072	474,185	845,157	2,502,973	73,060	62,140	50,859	58,335	244,394
2003	630,381	409,239	142,296	569,980	1,751,896	36,692	34,152	11,114	16,860	98,818
2004	306,555	315,996	280,824	467,236	1,370,611	176	7,208	2,629	5,708	15,721
2005	336,216	348,368	342,661	788,293	1,815,538	5,580	6,446	5,977	3,604	21,607
2006	708,680	470,176	418,117	691,870	2,288,843	8,721	12,473	10,249	18,235	49,678
2007	629,157	518,173	462,359	885,276	2,494,965	13,723	15,112	10,441	27,107	66,383
2008	682,174	562,566	405,199	634,054	2,283,993	38,319	30,575	15,181	23,417	107,492
2009[1]	612,188	423,742	342,988	551,082	1,930,000	6,903	18,152	16,437	14,340	55,832

[1] Preliminary. *Source: Economic Research Service, U.S. Department of Agriculture (ERS-USDA)*

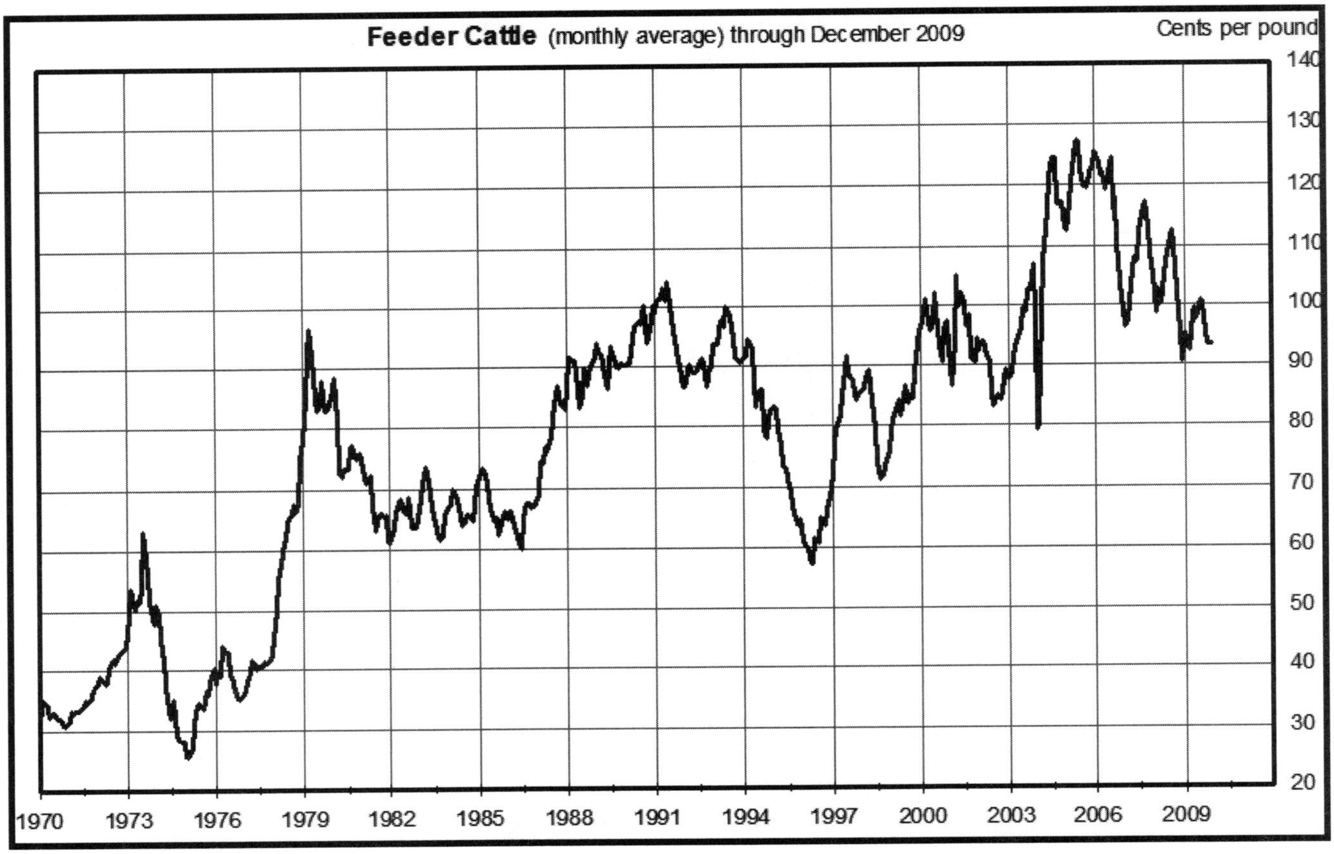

Average Slaughter Steer Price, Choice 2-4, Nebraska Direct (1100-1300 Lb.)[1] In Dollars Per 100 Pounds

Year	Jan.	Feb.	Mar.	Apr.	May	June	July	Aug.	Sept.	Oct.	Nov.	Dec.	Average
2003	77.18	78.77	77.52	79.24	79.50	76.73	76.89	81.74	90.59	105.50	101.88	90.75	84.69
2004	80.36	79.15	86.96	87.04	88.22	89.19	84.27	84.15	82.33	84.03	84.64	86.60	84.75
2005	87.77	87.73	91.78	91.98	88.83	83.06	79.37	80.80	85.19	87.40	90.32	93.08	87.28
2006	92.90	89.09	85.73	81.30	79.02	80.85	81.14	85.87	89.18	87.43	86.56	85.83	85.41
2007	86.75	88.68	96.39	98.04	95.50	86.81	89.09	91.49	93.49	91.69	93.37	90.50	91.82
2008	88.63	90.85	89.28	89.04	93.86	95.55	98.83	99.14	97.37	90.61	90.40	83.66	92.27
2009	81.60	79.68	81.66	87.02	85.27	81.31	82.72	82.48	83.13	83.53	83.43	80.34	82.68

Source: Economic Research Service, U.S. Department of Agriculture (ERS-USDA)

Average Price of Feeder Steers in Oklahoma City In Dollars Per 100 Pounds

Year	Jan.	Feb.	Mar.	Apr.	May	June	July	Aug.	Sept.	Oct.	Nov.	Dec.	Average
2003	87.76	88.84	91.31	92.94	93.58	96.04	99.28	99.15	102.68	102.63	106.87	98.09	96.60
2004	79.35	80.18	107.35	109.99	115.40	121.10	124.63	124.65	116.97	116.96	117.13	113.01	110.56
2005	112.40	116.87	120.48	126.77	127.13	126.91	122.73	119.96	119.61	120.29	122.84	122.75	121.56
2006	125.49	123.56	121.41	122.29	119.35	122.29	124.55	120.35	123.90	114.85	100.78	99.80	118.22
2007	96.54	97.50	103.38	107.97	107.74	107.65	112.29	116.30	117.20	112.79	108.80	105.13	107.77
2008	98.62	102.81	100.17	100.45	107.08	108.90	111.07	112.53	109.69	98.84	95.76	90.76	103.06
2009	95.57	93.19	92.47	98.05	99.58	97.74	100.65	100.39	97.75	93.56	93.33	93.29	96.30

Source: Economic Research Service, U.S. Department of Agriculture (ERS-USDA)

Federally Inspected Slaughter of Cattle in the United States In Thousands of Head

Year	Jan.	Feb.	Mar.	Apr.	May	June	July	Aug.	Sept.	Oct.	Nov.	Dec.	Total
2003	2,950	2,519	2,725	2,918	3,201	3,208	3,245	3,094	3,082	2,953	2,387	2,626	34,907
2004	2,527	2,381	2,818	2,654	2,792	2,949	2,745	2,775	2,689	2,693	2,492	2,642	32,156
2005	2,477	2,297	2,675	2,517	2,751	2,894	2,677	2,948	2,729	2,625	2,623	2,619	31,831
2006	2,591	2,302	2,806	2,566	2,993	3,116	2,795	3,089	2,721	2,803	2,797	2,566	33,145
2007	2,748	2,518	2,747	2,660	3,008	3,035	2,860	3,088	2,621	3,046	2,787	2,603	33,721
2008	2,847	2,598	2,684	2,914	3,095	2,912	3,017	2,866	2,842	2,933	2,475	2,623	33,805
2009[1]	2,668	2,479	2,681	2,724	2,806	2,936	2,878	2,738	2,766	2,829	2,556	2,704	32,765

[1] Preliminary. *Source: National Agricultural Statistics Service, U.S. Department of Agriculture (NASS-USDA)*

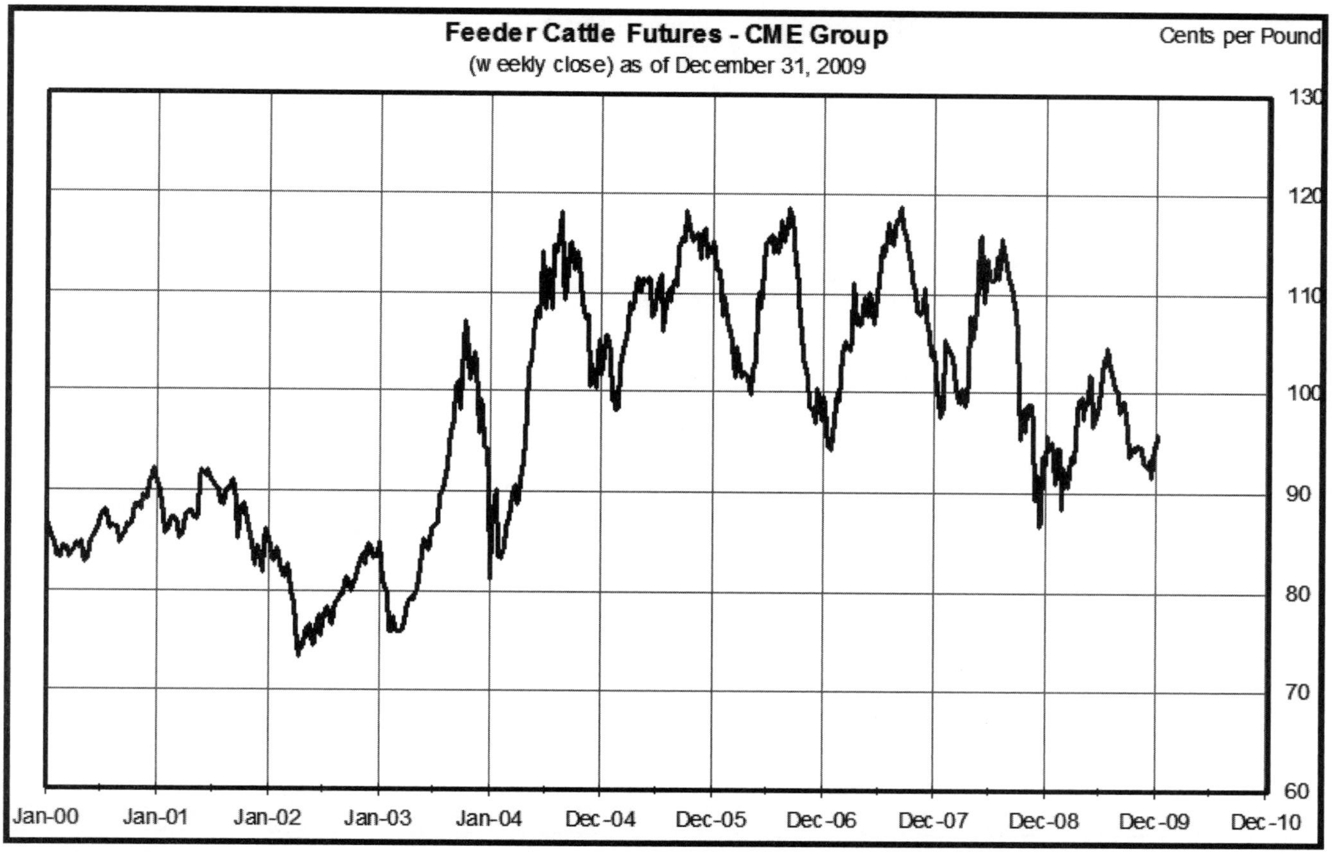

Average Open Interest of Live Cattle Futures in Chicago In Contracts

Year	Jan.	Feb.	Mar.	Apr.	May	June	July	Aug.	Sept.	Oct.	Nov.	Dec.
2000	128,918	123,980	123,925	122,596	117,834	106,196	116,266	120,526	123,945	123,517	131,773	132,239
2001	132,298	132,866	131,312	123,075	112,180	114,970	116,162	105,252	114,214	109,677	108,574	95,182
2002	93,589	91,566	98,176	98,343	98,846	91,129	93,541	92,966	109,651	111,338	121,671	116,588
2003	111,874	105,882	98,943	96,875	107,193	111,397	113,324	115,417	130,836	124,525	113,224	106,522
2004	98,752	99,491	112,449	124,930	128,727	126,481	114,656	109,588	104,928	109,832	112,709	123,483
2005	142,333	140,869	146,062	141,610	145,235	133,768	135,971	134,329	148,094	167,175	174,496	197,090
2006	225,313	220,947	220,042	240,567	261,496	235,783	231,914	213,918	214,583	205,776	211,814	224,501
2007	257,373	273,121	296,235	281,239	261,866	240,526	235,110	212,154	234,754	234,584	240,710	241,614
2008	252,555	273,397	276,043	285,956	298,370	298,937	300,862	278,808	265,436	227,860	215,054	211,836
2009	207,768	203,912	207,221	206,462	204,424	211,978	222,562	233,578	251,083	260,285	266,293	262,738

Contract size = 40,000 lbs. *Source: CME Group; Chicago Mercantile Exchange (CME)*

Volume of Trading of Live Cattle Futures Chicago In Thousands of Contracts

Year	Jan.	Feb.	Mar.	Apr.	May	June	July	Aug.	Sept.	Oct.	Nov.	Dec.	Total
2000	347,290	323,524	356,258	236,494	302,001	244,755	248,377	293,450	277,913	293,972	397,879	359,599	3,681,512
2001	511,050	357,474	385,581	302,829	348,294	289,093	318,564	324,614	340,969	403,101	403,009	294,695	4,279,273
2002	331,026	275,699	387,115	448,508	304,900	247,940	286,248	288,525	314,927	352,487	315,658	298,703	3,851,736
2003	378,862	343,931	334,007	306,713	391,477	311,239	449,966	319,677	473,218	469,405	324,732	332,862	4,436,089
2004	362,295	265,370	442,636	353,886	419,888	345,611	381,151	340,973	382,536	344,517	511,516	359,749	4,510,128
2005	519,794	395,847	598,171	377,494	503,753	405,687	506,253	406,010	569,040	438,631	627,585	485,291	5,833,556
2006	783,018	498,779	849,546	570,015	817,491	709,706	718,772	670,410	698,285	631,911	757,795	503,970	8,209,698
2007	907,155	663,121	1,046,653	575,800	814,423	513,667	849,053	634,475	724,467	638,942	761,870	458,347	8,587,973
2008	982,593	596,374	954,198	724,449	936,181	731,340	1,006,398	738,206	998,230	801,087	773,949	558,355	9,801,360
2009	819,482	616,769	789,335	641,323	721,536	617,848	855,383	657,909	854,593	739,683	844,321	638,851	8,797,033

Contract size = 40,000 lbs. *Source: CME Group; Chicago Mercantile Exchange (CME)*

Beef Steer-Corn Price Ratio[1] in the United States

Year	Jan.	Feb.	Mar.	Apr.	May	June	July	Aug.	Sept.	Oct.	Nov.	Dec.	Average
2002	36.1	38.1	38.2	37.0	35.3	34.0	31.2	28.3	27.4	29.3	31.5	32.3	33.2
2003	33.4	33.4	32.9	33.7	33.4	33.6	36.4	38.6	40.6	46.1	45.4	41.4	37.4
2004	35.7	31.5	32.0	30.8	32.3	33.6	36.4	38.9	40.7	42.6	44.0	45.0	37.0
2005	44.5	47.7	47.1	49.1	48.5	45.3	41.8	45.0	48.5	52.8	54.9	51.9	48.1
2006	51.0	48.3	45.0	42.3	39.8	41.2	42.1	43.8	43.3	36.7	31.3	29.6	41.2
2007	29.4	26.6	28.5	29.4	28.1	26.4	28.0	29.4	30.0	29.4	27.9	25.3	28.2
2008	23.5	20.8	19.8	17.9	18.2	17.6	19.0	19.0	19.8	21.3	21.3	20.9	19.9
2009[1]	19.7	21.7	21.8	23.0	22.1	21.1	23.7	25.6	26.3	23.4	23.4	23.3	22.9

[1] Bushels of corn equal in value to 100 pounds of steers and heifers. [2] Preliminary. *Source: Economic Research Service, U.S. Department of Agriculture*

Farm Value, Income and Wholesale Prices of Cattle and Calves in the United States

	January 1		Gross Income From	At Omaha				Feeder Heifers at	Cows, Boning	Cows, Com-	Wholesale Prices, Central U.S.		
				Steers		Heifers[4]							
	Per Head	Total	C & C[2]	Choice	Select	Select	Choice	Oklahoma City[5]	Utility Sioux Falls[6]	mercial Sioux Falls	Choice 700-850 lb.	Select 700-850 lb.	Cow[6], Canner, Cutter
Year	Dollars	Million $	Million $	Dollars per 100 Pounds									
2002	747	72,284	38,429	66.39	----	----	67.39	76.70	40.47	39.63	113.59	107.66	NA
2003	728	69,949	45,477	82.37	----	----	82.06	85.88	49.74	46.62	143.20	130.07	NA
2004	818	77,595	47,935	84.78	----	----	84.40	100.09	55.20	52.35	141.33	132.65	NA
2005	916	87,386	49,668	86.54	----	----	87.35	106.87	55.52	54.36	145.78	136.36	NA
2006	1,009	97,579	49,423	85.55	----	----	86.58	102.00	50.50	47.56	146.82	132.56	NA
2007	922	89,447	50,162					102.06	54.77	52.12	149.80	140.09	NA
2008[1]	987	95,401						96.85	57.75	54.92	153.17	147.68	NA

[1] Preliminary. [2] Excludes interfarm sales & Gov't. payments. Cash receipts from farm marketings + value of farm home consumption.
[3] 1,000 to 1,100 lb. [4] 1,000 to 1,200 lb. [5] 700 to 750 lb. [6] All weights.
Source: Economic Research Service, U.S. Department of Agriculture (NASS-USDA)

Average Price Received by Farmers for Beef Cattle in the United States In Dollars Per 100 Pounds

Year	Jan.	Feb.	Mar.	Apr.	May	June	July	Aug.	Sept.	Oct.	Nov.	Dec.	Average
2002	67.10	70.00	70.60	67.30	65.10	64.00	63.70	64.40	64.50	64.60	67.30	70.40	66.58
2003	73.20	73.90	72.60	74.50	75.50	74.90	75.80	79.30	84.90	91.50	93.40	90.40	79.99
2004	80.90	78.50	83.70	85.00	88.50	89.80	88.10	87.70	85.90	86.50	85.40	86.80	85.57
2005	89.40	88.80	91.00	93.70	92.10	88.00	85.00	84.40	88.00	90.40	90.80	93.30	89.58
2006	95.10	92.40	87.90	84.80	82.20	84.00	85.80	87.20	90.00	88.20	84.40	83.10	87.09
2007	84.30	86.10	91.60	93.70	92.80	88.80	89.00	91.40	93.10	90.90	89.90	89.20	90.07
2008	87.30	89.00	87.80	86.80	91.30	91.90	95.00	95.80	94.20	87.40	84.30	79.70	89.21
2009[1]	80.10	78.90	79.00	83.50	83.20	80.40	81.10	80.60	80.60	79.20	79.60	78.60	80.40

[1] Preliminary. *Source: National Agricultural Statistics Service, U.S. Department of Agriculture (NASS-USDA)*

Average Price Received by Farmers for Calves in the United States In Dollars Per 100 Pounds

Year	Jan.	Feb.	Mar.	Apr.	May	June	July	Aug.	Sept.	Oct.	Nov.	Dec.	Average
2002	102.00	105.00	105.00	101.00	99.50	96.50	92.40	94.90	92.40	92.00	91.90	95.30	97.33
2003	96.80	97.20	96.70	98.90	100.00	101.00	102.00	106.00	109.00	112.00	111.00	112.00	103.55
2004	110.00	111.00	115.00	117.00	121.00	125.00	130.00	131.00	128.00	126.00	123.00	122.00	121.58
2005	125.00	129.00	136.00	141.00	143.00	140.00	133.00	133.00	135.00	135.00	137.00	137.00	135.33
2006	141.00	143.00	139.00	137.00	134.00	135.00	137.00	136.00	136.00	128.00	119.00	116.00	133.42
2007	115.00	114.00	122.00	125.00	124.00	124.00	126.00	127.00	126.00	123.00	122.00	120.00	122.33
2008	117.00	120.00	118.00	116.00	120.00	118.00	114.00	117.00	113.00	106.00	105.00	98.90	113.58
2009[1]	106.00	104.00	107.00	110.00	112.00	110.00	110.00	110.00	107.00	104.00	105.00	105.00	107.50

[1] Preliminary. *Source: National Agricultural Statistics Board, U.S. Department of Agriculture (NASS-USDA)*

Federally Inspected Slaughter of Calves and Vealers in the United States In Thousands of Head

Year	Jan.	Feb.	Mar.	Apr.	May	June	July	Aug.	Sept.	Oct.	Nov.	Dec.	Total
2002	86	71	76	80	76	74	94	94	87	98	88	96	1,019
2003	92	81	83	77	74	72	83	78	80	85	76	95	976
2004	77	70	75	69	63	65	67	71	66	61	66	73	823
2005	66	61	67	60	57	58	57	64	60	54	55	59	718
2006	54	52	58	47	56	58	57	66	57	62	66	67	699
2007	73	66	70	56	58	60	62	65	55	64	58	60	745
2008	70	68	70	72	70	74	87	78	86	94	80	93	942
2009[1]	84	73	79	67	64	76	79	76	80	82	80	91	930

[1] Preliminary. *Source: Crop Reporting Board, U.S. Department of Agriculture (CRB-USDA)*

Cement

Cement is made in a wide variety of compositions and is used in many different ways. The best-known cement is *Portland cement*, which is bound with sand and gravel to create concrete. Concrete is used to unite the surfaces of various materials and to coat surfaces to protect them from various chemicals. Portland cement is almost universally used for structural concrete. It is manufactured from lime-bearing materials, usually limestone, together with clays, blast-furnace slag containing alumina and silica or shale. The combination is usually approximately 60 percent lime, 19 percent silica, 8 percent alumina, 5 percent iron, 5 percent magnesia, and 3 percent sulfur trioxide. To slow the hardening process, gypsum is often added. In 1924, the name "Portland cement" was coined by Joseph Aspdin, a British cement maker, because of the resemblance between concrete made from his cement and Portland stone. The United States did not start producing Portland cement in any great quantity until the 20th century. Hydraulic cements are those that set and harden in water. Clinker cement is an intermediate product in cement manufacture. The production and consumption of cement is directly related to the level of activity in the construction industry.

Prices – The average value (F.O.B. mill) of Portland cement in 2009 fell -2.9% yr/yr to $100 per ton, down from the e 2008 record high $103.00 per ton.

Supply – World production of hydraulic cement in 2009 fell -1.4% yr/yr to 2.800 billion tons, down from the 2008 record high of 2.900 billion metric tons. The world's largest hydraulic cement producers were China with 50% of world production in 2009, India (6%), U.S. (3%), and Japan (2%).

U.S. production of Portland cement in 2007 (latest data available) fell -1.8% yr/yr to 91.144, further down from the 2005 record high of 93.904 million tons. U.S. shipments of finished Portland cement from mills in the U.S. in 2009 fell 21.4% to 66.408 million metric tons, falling farther below the 2005 record high of 95.588 million metric tons.

Demand – U.S. consumption of cement in 2009 fell -23.7% to 93.800 million metric tons, falling farther below the 2005 record high of 128.260 million metric tons.

Trade – The U.S. relied on imports for 8% of its cement consumption in 2009. The two main suppliers of cement to the U.S. were Canada and a Mexico. U.S. exports of cement in 2009 fell -6.8% yr/yr to 800.000 million metric tons.

World Production of Hydraulic Cement In Thousands of Short Tons

Year	Brazil	China	France	Germany	India	Italy	Japan	Rep. of Korea	Russia	Spain	Turkey	United States	World Total
2002	38,027	725,000	19,437	31,009	115,000	41,722	71,828	55,514	37,700	42,417	32,577	91,266	1,850,000
2003	34,010	862,080	19,655	32,749	123,000	43,580	68,766	60,725	41,000	44,747	35,077	94,329	2,030,000
2004	34,413	970,000	20,962	31,854	130,000	45,343	67,376	56,955	45,700	45,593	38,796	99,015	2,190,000
2005	36,673	1,068,850	21,277	31,009	145,000	40,284	69,629	51,391	48,500	50,347	42,787	100,903	2,350,000
2006	39,540	1,236,770	22,540	33,630	160,000	47,814	69,942	53,971	54,700	54,033	47,499	99,712	2,600,000
2007	46,406	1,354,120	22,300	33,382	170,000	47,541	67,685	57,042	59,900	54,500	49,553	96,850	2,770,000
2008[1]	51,900	1,390,000	21,700	33,600	177,000	43,000	62,800	53,900	53,600	42,100	51,400	87,600	2,840,000
2009[2]	53,000	1,400,000	21,000	33,000	180,000	43,000	60,000	53,000	55,000	42,000	51,000	72,800	2,800,000

[1] Preliminary. [2] Estimate. *Source: U.S. Geological Survey (USGS)*

Salient Statistics of Cement in the United States

Year	Net Import Reliance as a % of Apparent Consumption	Production: Portland (1,000 Metric tons)	Production: Other[3]	Production: Total	Capacity Used at Portland Mills %	Shipments From Mills: Total (Mil. MT)	Shipments From Mills: Value[4] (Mil. $)	Average Value (F.O.B. Mill) $ per MT	Stocks at Mills Dec. 31 (1,000 Metric Tons)	Exports	Apparent Consumption	Imports for Consumption[5] by Country: Canada	Japan	Mexico	Spain	Total
2002	20	85,283	4,449	89,732	78.7	108,500	8,250	76.00	7,680	834	110,020	5,181	----	1,228	327	24,169
2003	20	88,106	4,737	92,843	78.5	111,000	8,340	75.00	6,610	837	114,090	6,319	----	891	355	23,959
2004	21	92,434	5,000	97,434	81.6	120,000	9,520	79.50	6,740	749	121,950	5,753	2	1,429	408	27,026
2005	23	93,904	5,415	99,319	82.3	128,000	11,700	91.00	7,450	766	128,260	5,404	4	2,173	236	33,261
2006	23	92,768	5,399	98,167	80.6	127,000	12,900	101.50	9,380	723	127,660	5,059	3	2,264	69	35,566
2007	17	91,144	4,320	95,464	78.2	114,000	11,800	104.00	8,890	886	116,800	5,326	5	1,684	29	22,468
2008[1]	12			86,310		99,000		103.00	8,360	858	96,700					11,610
2009[2]	8			71,800				100.00	12,000	800	73,800					

[1] Preliminary. [2] Estimate. [3] Masonry, natural & pozzolan (slag-line). [4] Value received F.O.B. mill, excluding cost of containers. [5] Hydraulic & clinker cement for consumption. [6] Less than 1/2 unit. *Source: U.S. Geological Survey (USGS)*

Shipments of Finished Portland Cement from Mills in the United States In Thousands of Metric Tons

Year	Jan.	Feb.	Mar.	Apr.	May	June	July	Aug.	Sept.	Oct.	Nov.	Dec.	Total
2003	5,486	4,560	6,483	8,009	8,288	8,492	9,064	8,829	8,755	9,781	6,987	6,348	91,082
2004	5,241	5,146	8,059	8,837	8,624	9,103	9,134	9,326	8,883	8,609	7,417	6,528	94,908
2005	5,337	5,732	7,498	8,316	9,102	9,595	8,305	9,604	8,847	8,870	8,065	6,317	95,588
2006	6,542	6,088	7,704	7,763	8,871	9,230	7,917	9,144	8,011	8,539	7,549	6,097	93,456
2007	5,574	5,207	7,241	7,697	9,082	8,869	8,693	9,426	8,218	9,182	7,890	5,189	92,268
2008	5,503	5,323	6,347	7,768	8,064	8,182	8,640	7,974	7,822	8,291	6,021	4,555	84,490
2009[1]	4,020	4,219	4,894	5,509	5,699	6,471	6,584	6,274	6,136	5,594	5,187	3,515	64,103

[1] Preliminary. *Source: U.S. Geological Survey (USGS)*

Cheese

Since prehistoric times, humans have been making and eating cheese. Dating back as far as 6,000 BC, archaeologists have discovered that cheese had been made from cow and goat milk and stored in tall jars. The Romans turned cheese making into a culinary art, mixing sheep and goat milk and adding herbs and spices for flavoring. By 300 AD, cheese was being exported regularly to countries along the Mediterranean coast.

Cheese is made from the milk of cows and other mammals such as sheep, goats, buffalo, reindeer, camels, yaks, and mares. More than 400 varieties of cheese exist. There are three basic steps common to all cheese making. First, proteins in milk are transformed into curds, or solid lumps. Second, the curds are separated from the milky liquid (or whey) and shaped or pressed into molds. Finally, the shaped curds are ripened according to a variety of aging and curing techniques. Cheeses are usually grouped according to their moisture content into fresh, soft, semi-soft, hard, and very hard. Many classifications overlap due to texture changes with aging.

Cheese is a multi-billion-dollar a year industry in the U.S. Cheddar cheese is the most common natural cheese produced in the U.S., accounting for 35% of U.S. production. Cheeses originating in America include Colby, cream cheese, and Monterey Jack. Varieties other than American cheeses, mostly Italian, now have had a combined level of production that easily exceeds American cheeses.

Prices – Average monthly cheese prices at the Chicago Mercantile Exchange in 2009 fell by fell by 30.2% yr/yr to 129.61 cents per pound, down from the 2008 record high of 185.58 cents per pound.

Supply – World production of cheese in 2009 rose +0.3% yr/yr to 14.358 million metric tons, down further from the 2007 record high of 21.440 million metric tons. The European Union is the world's largest producer of cheese with 47% of the total world production in 2009. The U.S. production was the next largest with 32% of the total. U.S. production of cheese in 2009 rose +2.7% to 10.105 billion pounds, which was a new record high.

Demand – U.S. consumption of cheese in 2007 (latest data available) rose +2.5% to 10.112 billion pounds. U.S. per capita cheese consumption in 2002 (latest data available) rose +2.0% to 30.60 pounds per person per year which is a new record high.

Trade – U.S. imports of cheese in 2005 (latest data available) fell -2.5% to 460 million pounds. U.S. exports of cheese in 2005 fell 4.9% to 128 million pounds, down from 2004's record high of 134 million pounds.

World Production of Cheese In Thousands of Metric Tons

Year	Argentina	Australia	Brazil	Canada	Egypt	European Union	Japan	Mexico	New Zealand	Russia	Ukraine	United States	World Total
2001	440	374	460	329	395	5,965	34	140	281	260	105	3,747	18,567
2002	370	413	470	350	410	6,106	36	145	312	340	129	3,877	19,125
2003	325	368	460	342	450	6,205	35	126	301	335	169	3,882	19,219
2004	370	389	470	345	455	6,481	35	134	305	350	224	4,025	20,019
2005	400	375	495	352	480	6,625	39	178	297	375	274	4,150	20,617
2006	480	362	528	291	408	6,801	40	182	292	405	210	4,320	21,002
2007	520	360	580	308	420	6,760	43	184	350	435	244	4,435	21,440
2008	525	344	607	285	----	6,800	47	188	292	430	249	4,506	14,313
2009[1]	534	325	614	280	----	6,730	45	225	294	445	250	4,575	14,358
2010[2]	543	325	648	295	----	6,800	45	231	306	460	245	4,574	14,514

[1] Preliminary. [2] Forecast. NA = Not available. *Source: Foreign Agricultural Service, U.S. Department of Agriculture (FAS-USDA)*

Supply and Distribution of All Cheese in the United States In Millions of Pounds

	Supply					Cheese 40-lb. Blocks Wisconsin Assembly Points	Distribution						
	Production								American Cheese		Domestic Disappearance		
Year	Whole Milk[2]	All Cheese[3]	Commercial Stocks Jan. 1	Imports[4]	Total Supply	(Cents/Lb.)	Exports & Shipments[5]	Gov't - Stocks Dec. 31	Removed by USDA Programs	Total Disappearance	American Cheese Donated	Total	Per Capita
1998	3,315	7,492	481	371	8,344	158.10	81	.6	8.2	7,797	----	7,664	27.70
1999	3,533	7,894	518	436	8,847	142.28	85	1.0	4.6	8,219	----	8,086	29.00
2000	3,642	8,258	621	416	9,295	116.14	105	2.3	28.0	8,555	----	8,406	29.80
2001	3,544	8,261	706	445	9,412	144.93	115	4.0	3.9	8,741	----	8,586	30.00
2002	3,691	8,547	659	475	9,681	118.22	119	2.7	15.8	8,933	----	8,819	30.60
2003	3,622	8,557	730	476	9,763	131.24	115	27.4	41.3	9,007			
2004	3,739	8,873	715	472	10,060	164.92	134	9.0	5.9	9,342			
2005	3,808	9,149	701	460	10,310	145.53	128			9,519			
2006	3,913	9,525	758			123.85				9,869			
2007[1]			817			175.78				10,112			

[1] Preliminary. [2] Whole milk American cheddar. [3] All types of cheese except cottage, pot and baker's cheese. [4] Imports for consumption. [5] Commercial. *Source: Economic Research Service, U.S. Department of Agriculture (ERS-USDA)*

Production of Cheese in the United States In Millions of Pounds

	American			Swiss,				Crean &				Total	Cottage Cheese		
Year	Whole Milk	Part Skim	Total	Including Block	Munster	Brick	Lim- burger	Neufchatel Cheese	Italian Varieties	Blue Mond	All Other Varieties	of All Cheese[2]	Lowfat	Curd[3]	Creamed[4]
1999	3,533	NA	3,533	221.0	80.3	8.1	.7	639.3	3,144.7	(5)	181.0	7,894	359.3	464.8	360.6
2000	3,642	NA	3,642	229.3	85.5	8.6	.6	687.4	3,288.9	(5)	219.7	8,258	363.7	461.0	371.5
2001	3,544	NA	3,544	245.5	82.2	8.7	.7	645.1	3,425.9	(5)	199.6	8,261	370.2	453.2	371.6
2002	3,691	NA	3,691	254.1	81.1	10.0	.7	686.2	3,470.0	(5)	229.8	8,547	374.3	436.6	374.2
2003	3,622	NA	3,622	264.7	79.4	9.8	.7	676.7	3,524.0	(5)	246.7	8,557	384.4	448.0	385.2
2004	3,739	NA	3,739	281.3	72.8	8.1	.9	699.1	3,661.6	(5)	268.1	8,873	396.4	464.0	382.4
2005	3,808	NA	3,808	300.1	77.9	8.9	.8	714.8	3,803.0	(5)	268.3	9,149	407.9	468.6	376.7
2006	3,913	NA	3,913	314.5	95.5	8.6	.8	756.2	3,972.9	(5)	281.5	9,525	409.2	459.0	368.8
2007	3,877	NA	3,877	313.7	103.6	7.4	.7	772.8	4,198.8	(5)	311.9	9,777	425.4	458.5	348.6
2008[1]	4,071	NA	4,071	307.8	118.3	6.7	.6	763.7	4,158.0	(5)	314.8	9,935	389.6	427.1	325.8

[1] Preliminary. [2] Excludes full-skim cheddar and cottage cheese. [3] Includes cottage, pot, and baker's cheese with a butterfat content of less than 4%. [4] Includes cheese with a butterfat content of 4 to 19 %. [5] Included in All Other Varieties. NA = Not available.
Source: Economic Research Service, U.S. Department of Agriculture ERS-USDA)

Average Price of Cheese, 40-lb. Blocks, Chicago Mercantile Exchange[2] In Cents Per Pound

Year	Jan.	Feb.	Mar.	Apr.	May	June	July	Aug.	Sept.	Oct.	Nov.	Dec.	Average
2000	114.6	111.6	112.2	110.7	110.6	120.0	125.2	125.5	133.4	109.4	107.5	113.0	116.1
2001	110.3	120.0	131.9	140.5	160.3	166.8	168.5	171.8	173.9	139.7	126.4	129.1	144.9
2002	132.4	120.8	121.3	124.5	120.1	113.0	108.9	115.8	120.4	119.5	108.9	113.1	118.2
2003	109.3	109.2	108.2	112.3	114.2	118.6	151.2	160.0	160.0	158.8	139.3	133.8	131.2
2004	130.6	139.6	182.0	216.9	199.3	171.1	144.9	157.3	157.0	151.7	169.6	159.2	164.9
2005	162.7	149.3	153.2	154.1	147.7	150.7	105.4	142.5	156.4	144.7	137.6	142.2	145.5
2006	133.4	119.9	116.4	116.5	118.6	119.2	116.3	123.5	129.3	123.5	137.5	132.2	123.8
2007	131.8	134.1	138.2	146.3	172.1	201.0	191.4	195.5	199.3	189.6	209.3	200.8	175.8
2008	182.6	200.2	182.3	188.3	209.8	203.5	196.7	174.0	187.6	179.6	171.0	151.3	185.6
2009[1]	108.3	121.7	124.6	120.5	113.9	113.5	115.2	134.7	132.9	147.1	157.9	165.0	129.6

[1] Preliminary. [2] Data through December 2001 are for Wholesale Price of Cheese, 40-lb. Blocks, Wisconsin Assembly Points.
Source: Economic Research Service, U.S. Department of Agriculture (ERS-USDA)

Production[2] of Cheese in the United States In Millions of Pounds

Year	Jan.	Feb.	Mar.	Apr.	May	June	July	Aug.	Sept.	Oct.	Nov.	Dec.	Total
2000	692.9	649.5	714.8	694.0	730.4	695.7	687.6	683.8	653.8	688.5	675.0	688.4	8,255
2001	680.3	625.3	713.7	670.2	706.8	678.5	676.0	660.0	641.8	682.1	691.2	703.1	8,129
2002	717.5	667.9	742.8	719.2	748.3	708.3	692.2	714.3	683.9	732.2	725.4	747.2	8,599
2003	714.8	648.6	730.3	718.8	737.0	712.3	718.3	700.1	708.7	740.0	710.0	758.9	8,598
2004	738.0	705.5	785.6	761.0	752.1	715.3	708.7	719.5	714.4	748.0	754.3	773.9	8,876
2005	754.0	704.6	797.5	754.8	783.9	764.5	739.5	757.4	745.5	760.4	766.1	798.9	9,127
2006	782.7	720.5	820.8	793.6	820.0	796.1	775.4	795.1	788.6	812.3	798.1	831.1	9,534
2007	822.9	754.1	840.5	803.8	824.6	792.6	799.5	797.0	777.2	825.8	815.2	847.3	9,700
2008	812.7	784.6	834.7	810.2	831.8	809.4	813.2	820.7	796.5	843.5	824.0	859.0	9,840
2009[1]	824.0	769.8	870.8	845.3	859.7	834.2	841.3	849.3	843.0	861.9	843.6	861.9	10,105

[1] Preliminary. [2] Excludes cottage cheese. *Source: National Agricultural Statistics Service, U.S. Department of Agriculture (NASS-USDA)*

Cold Storage Holdings of All Varieties of Cheese in the United States, on First of Month In Millions of Pounds

Year	Jan.	Feb.	Mar.	Apr.	May	June	July	Aug.	Sept.	Oct.	Nov.	Dec.
2000	621.3	728.1	757.2	765.1	794.0	811.4	828.1	870.3	839.9	780.9	732.0	696.0
2001	707.8	709.9	723.9	711.6	711.8	712.1	739.2	752.6	721.2	708.7	672.2	631.3
2002	660.0	693.6	720.3	731.7	765.6	789.0	797.6	833.6	801.5	753.9	720.4	697.1
2003	730.1	761.2	770.0	771.3	781.1	791.0	800.1	809.0	794.2	762.2	722.4	695.5
2004	724.4	756.9	766.1	759.5	767.6	804.5	842.0	870.0	811.5	790.7	756.1	704.3
2005	705.8	713.8	723.7	749.2	780.8	815.6	823.4	837.2	812.9	769.0	755.9	720.8
2006	758.2	765.0	782.8	810.7	832.8	863.3	876.0	898.9	862.3	843.1	810.2	784.8
2007	817.4	850.0	875.7	892.9	894.3	898.9	891.2	886.0	846.2	820.4	810.6	805.9
2008	798.3	781.4	801.0	824.3	855.9	881.3	902.5	902.8	880.3	834.2	829.0	818.6
2009[1]	852.0	882.4	875.1	894.6	914.5	958.2	972.5	988.0	984.9	983.9	969.2	961.7

Quantities are given in "net weight." [1] Preliminary. *Source: National Agricultural Statistics Service, U.S. Department of Agriculture (NASS-USDA)*

Chromium

Chromium (symbol Cr) is a steel-gray, hard, and brittle, metallic element that can take on a high polish. Chromium and its compounds are toxic. Discovered in 1797 by Louis Vauquelin, chromium is named after the Greek word for color, khroma. Vauquelin also discovered that an emerald's green color is due to the presence of chromium. Many precious stones owe their color to the presence of chromium compounds.

Chromium is primarily found in chromite ore. The primary use of chromium is to form alloys with iron, nickel, or cobalt. Chromium improves hardness and resistance to corrosion and oxidation in iron, steel, and nonferrous alloys. It is a critical alloying ingredient in the production of stainless steel, making up 10% or more of the final composition. More than half of the chromium consumed is used in metallic products, and about one-third is used in refractories. Chromium is also used as a lustrous decorative plating agent, in pigments, leather processing, plating of metals, and catalysts.

Supply – World production of chromium in 2009 fell -3.4% yr/yr to 23.000 million metric tons, down from the 2008 record high of 23.800 million metric tons. The world's largest producers of chromium in 2009 were South Africa with 42% of world production, India with 17%, and Kazakhstan with 16%. India has emerged as a major producer of chromium in the past two decades. India's 2009 production level of 3.900 million metric tons was more than ten times the level of 360,000 metric tons seen 20 years earlier. South Africa's production in 2009 at 9.600 million metric tons was down only -0.8% from the 2008 record high of 9.680 million metric tons and that is more than double the levels seen as recently as the early-1990s. Kazakhstan's production in 2009 of 3.600 million metric tons was down only -0.8% yr/yr and only slightly below the 2007 record high of 3.687 million metric tons. Zimbabwe's chromium production in 2007 (latest available data) was 663.593 metric tons. U.S. Government stocks of chromium as of Dec 31, 2006 (latest available data) fell 98.4% yr/yr to a record low of 1.160 metric tons.

Demand – Based on the most recently available data from 1994, the metallurgical and chemical industry accounts for 94% of chromium usage in the U.S., with the remaining 6% used by the refractory industry.

Trade – The U.S. relied on imports for a record low of 39% of its chromium consumption in 2009. That is well below the record high of 91% posted back in the 1970s. U.S. chromium imports in 2006 (latest available data) fell -3.3% yr/yr to 341,800 metric tons. U.S. exports of chromium in 2006 (latest available data) fell -1.6% yr/yr to 56.4 metric tons.

World Mine Production of Chromite In Thousands of Metric Tons (Gross Weight)

Year	Albania	Brazil	Cuba	Finland	India	Iran	Kazak-hstan	Mada-gascar	philip-pines	South Africa	Turkey	Zim-babwe	Total[1]
1999	71	458	52	597	1,473	255	2,406	----	20	6,817	770	653	14,200
2000	120	550	56	628	1,947	153	2,607	131	26	6,622	546	668	14,700
2001	130	409	50	575	1,678	145	2,046	24	27	5,502	390	780	12,200
2002	73	284	20	566	2,699	513	2,369	11	22	6,436	314	749	14,600
2003	98	377	33	549	2,210	97	2,928	45	34	7,405	229	637	15,500
2004	54	593	40	580	2,949	139	3,287	77	42	7,677	506	668	17,800
2005	66	617	34	571	3,255	224	3,581	141	38	7,552	688	615	18,900
2006	82	563	28	549	3,600	245	3,366	132	47	7,418	458	713	19,000
2007[1]	85	628	25	556	3,320	186	3,687	122	47	9,647	500	664	21,500
2008[2]	NA	NA	NA	NA	3,900	NA	3,630	NA	NA	9,680	NA	NA	23,800

[1] Preliminary. [2] Estimate. *Source: U.S. Geological Survey (USGS)*

Salient Statistics of Chromite in the United States In Thousands of Metric Tons (Gross Weight)

Year	Net Import Reliance as a % of Appearent Consumption	Production of Ferro-chromium	Exports	Imports for Con-sumption	Reexports	Consumption by -- Primary Consumer Group --- Total	Metal-lurgical & Chemical	Refractory	Government[5] Stocks, Dec. 31 - Metal-lurgical & Chemical	Refractory	Total Stocks	--- $/Metric Ton --- South Africa[3]	Turkish[4]
1998	80	W	55	383	----	W	W	W	W	W	159	68	145
1999	80	W	53	475	----	W	W	W	W	W	130	63	145
2000	77	W	86	453	----	W	W	W	396	241	637	60-65	140-150
2001	63	W	43	239	----	W	W	W	396	241	637	NA	NA
2002	69	W	29	263	----	W	W	W	78	126	204	NA	NA
2003	57	W	46	317	----	W	W	W	78	156	234	NA	NA
2004	64	W	35	326	----	W	W	W	46	88	135	NA	NA
2005	68	W	57	353	----	W	W	W	4	70	73	NA	NA
2006[1]	70	W	56	342	----	W	W	W	----	1	1	NA	NA
2007[2]	67	W	60	328	----	W	W	W	----	----	----	NA	NA

[1] Preliminary. [2] Estimate. [3] Cr_2O_3, 44% (Transvaal). [4] 48% Cr_2O_3. [5] Data through 1999 are for Consumer. W = Withheld.
Source: U.S. Geological Survey (USGS)

Coal

Coal is a sedimentary rock composed primarily of carbon, hydrogen, and oxygen. Coal is a fossil fuel formed from ancient plants buried deep in the Earth's crust over 300 million years ago. Historians believe coal was first used commercially in China for smelting copper and for casting coins around 1,000 BC. Almost 92% of all coal consumed in the U.S. is burned by electric power plants, and coal accounts for about 55% of total electricity output. Coal is also used in the manufacture of steel. The steel industry first converts coal into coke, then combines the coke with iron ore and limestone, and finally heats the mixture to produce iron. Other industries use coal to make fertilizers, solvents, medicine, pesticides, and synthetic fuels.

There are four types of mined coal: anthracite (used in high-grade steel production), bituminous (used for electricity generation and for making coke), sub-bituminous, and lignite (both used primarily for electricity generation).

Coal futures trade at the New York Mercantile Exchange (NYMEX). The contract trades in units of 1,550 tons and is priced in terms of dollars and cents per short ton.

Supply – U.S. production of bituminous coal in 2009 (annualized through November) fell -7.3% yr/yr to 1.084 billion tons, down from last year's record high of 1.169 billion tons.

Demand – U.S. consumption of coal in 2008 (latest data available) fell by -0.6% to 1.122 billion tons, down from last year's record high of 1.128 billion tons.

Trade – U.S. exports of coal in 2008 (latest data available) rose +37.8% yr/yr to an 11-year high of 81.519 million tons, and imports fell -5.9% yr/yr to 34.208 million tons, down from last year's record high of 36.347 million tons. The major exporting destinations for the U.S. are Canada and Europe.

World Production[3] of Coal (Monthly Average) In Thousands of Metric Tons

Year	Australia	Canada	China	Czech-Republic	Germany	India	Indonesia	Kazak-hstan	Poland	Russia	Ukraine	United Kingdom	United States
2000	19,958	2,817	70,782	1,238	3,111	25,802	6,402	5,960	8,598	14,292	6,749	2,600	65,220
2001	22,018	2,836	80,040	1,261	2,406	26,563	7,554	6,015	8,658	15,507	6,908	2,677	68,666
2002	23,123	2,468	92,339	1,206	2,197	27,938	8,588	6,493	8,642	15,198	5,163	2,499	66,565
2003	30,000	2,215	109,602	1,137	2,396	29,036	9,551	6,734	8,573	16,329	5,354	2,353	81,023
2004	31,250	2,438	130,434	1,109	2,429	31,438	11,021	6,922	8,436	17,495	4,947	2,089	92,953
2005	32,917	2,382	150,891	1,104	2,335	33,129	11,755	6,899	8,159	18,472	5,033	1,667	94,439
2006	33,583	2,492	171,288	1,111	1,980	35,088	12,571	7,631	7,935	19,468	5,135	1,506	96,782
2007	35,167	2,734	192,229	1,074	1,794	37,134	14,569	8,199	7,316	20,178	4,897	1,419	95,550
2008[1]	35,917	2,737	215,472	1,050	1,431	40,281	15,131	8,773	7,020	20,464	4,939	1,506	97,624
2009[2]	34,000	2,112	248,666	917	1,137	44,222	16,233	8,015	6,493	18,925	4,558	1,506	90,015

[1] Preliminary. [2] Estimate. [3] All grades of anthracite and bituminous coal, but excludes recovered slurries, lignite and brown coal.
Source: United Nations

Production of Bituminous & Lignite Coal in the United States In Thousands of Short Tons

Year	Alabama	Colorado	Illinois	Indiana	Kentucky	Montana	Ohio	Pennsyl-vania	Texas	West Virgina	Virgina	Wyoming	Total
1999	19,504	29,989	40,417	34,004	139,626	41,102	22,480	76,368	53,071	32,181	157,919	337,119	1,095,474
2000	19,324	29,137	33,444	27,965	130,688	38,352	22,269	74,619	49,498	32,834	158,257	338,900	1,073,612
2001	19,513	33,372	33,783	36,738	134,298	39,143	25,400	74,784	45,042	33,060	162,631	368,749	1,125,749
2002	19,062	35,103	33,358	35,513	124,388	37,386	21,157	67,104	45,247	30,126	150,222	373,161	1,092,916
2003	20,207	35,831	31,760	35,512	113,126	36,994	22,009	63,792	47,517	31,771	139,755	376,270	1,071,753
2004	22,329	39,870	31,912	35,206	114,743	39,989	23,222	66,023	45,863	31,647	148,017	396,493	1,110,393
2005	21,453	38,510	32,014	34,457	120,029	40,354	24,718	65,852	45,939	27,964	153,655	404,319	1,129,794
2006	18,830	36,322	32,729	35,119	120,848	41,823	22,722	64,500	45,548	29,740	152,374	446,742	1,162,750
2007[1]	19,522	36,384	32,857	35,003	115,530	43,390	22,575	63,621	41,948	25,462	153,522	453,568	1,145,067
2008[2]	20,782	33,728	31,967	36,070	118,986	44,278	25,506	62,992	38,472	24,820	159,378	467,456	1,168,663

[1] Preliminary. [2] Estimate. *Source: Energy Information Administration, U.S. Department of Energy (EIA-DOE)*

Production[2] of Bituminous Coal in the United States In Thousands of Short Tons

Year	Jan.	Feb.	Mar.	Apr.	May	June	July	Aug.	Sept.	Oct.	Nov.	Dec.	Total
2000	87,222	86,846	99,045	81,793	88,715	90,583	84,442	96,361	88,848	92,542	94,035	87,272	1,077,704
2001	96,721	86,802	99,176	89,954	94,840	92,657	89,037	99,048	88,985	99,529	93,736	88,234	1,118,719
2002	101,939	90,208	90,108	90,039	91,673	85,555	86,190	92,054	92,212	94,033	87,836	91,058	1,092,905
2003	92,649	82,130	88,976	89,202	90,435	88,348	88,301	89,355	90,344	93,928	84,155	94,154	1,071,977
2004	93,182	86,306	94,876	91,739	87,210	94,835	92,260	95,209	93,525	92,618	92,268	95,478	1,109,506
2005	92,804	89,039	102,178	93,296	90,168	95,374	91,930	97,907	95,493	93,532	94,842	92,774	1,129,337
2006	98,385	88,826	101,339	95,288	99,706	97,023	94,861	100,504	94,029	98,674	96,400	95,939	1,160,974
2007	99,221	88,084	97,490	92,923	96,867	95,432	92,884	100,493	92,288	98,691	96,769	93,010	1,144,152
2008	98,488	93,428	96,805	96,991	96,425	90,096	99,014	100,312	99,203	104,222	95,264	99,604	1,169,852
2009[1]	96,418	89,527	95,887	88,154	84,302	87,811	92,076	91,541	89,465	90,523	87,885	88,734	1,082,323

[1] Preliminary. [2] Includes small amount of lignite. *Source: Energy Information Administration, U.S. Department of Energy (EIA-DOE)*

Production[2] of Pennsylvania Anthracite Coal In Thousands of Short Tons

Year	Jan.	Feb.	Mar.	Apr.	May	June	July	Aug.	Sept.	Oct.	Nov.	Dec.	Total
2000	271	283	382	342	375	383	366	430	412	417	402	366	4,432
2001	302	275	323	283	300	297	328	358	318	375	349	173	3,681
2002	131	117	116	121	122	240	116	126	119	130	120	126	1,584
2003	108	98	98	115	114	107	97	95	101	130	111	116	1,290
2004	197	183	147	111	101	214	141	145	150	145	151	127	1,812
2005	133	129	149	137	135	157	125	140	135	156	179	127	1,704
2006	138	121	147	117	128	125	124	140	115	134	126	123	1,538
2007	141	125	139	125	133	134	120	135	116	134	141	128	1,568
2008	131	126	127	158	160	102	149	147	149	168	140	154	1,712
2009[1]	150	87	95	103	93	103	108	105	107	111	106	112	1,280

[1] Preliminary. [2] Represents production in Pennsylvania only. *Source: Energy Information Administration, U.S. Department of Energy (EIA-DOE)*

Salient Statistics of Coal in the United States In Thousands of Short Tons

Year	Production	Imports	Consumption	Exports: Brazil	Canada	Europe	Asia	Total	Total Ending Stocks[2]	Losses & Unaccounted For[3]
1999	1,100,431	9,089	1,038,648	4,442	19,826	22,508	9,157	58,476	188,590	-11,592
2000	1,073,612	12,513	1,084,094	4,536	18,769	24,969	6,702	58,489	140,282	938
2001	1,127,689	19,787	1,060,146	4,574	17,633	20,821	3,246	48,666	181,912	7,120
2002	1,094,283	16,875	1,066,355	3,538	16,686	15,574	1,735	39,601	192,127	4,039
2003	1,071,753	25,044	1,094,861	3,514	20,760	15,148	266	43,014	165,468	-4,403
2004	1,112,099	27,280	1,107,255	4,361	17,760	15,211	7,475	47,998	154,006	6,887
2005	1,131,498	30,460	1,125,978	4,199	19,466	18,825	5,082	49,942	144,304	9,092
2006	1,162,750	36,246	1,112,292	4,534	19,889	20,805	2,008	49,647	186,946	8,824
2007	1,146,635	36,347	1,127,998	6,512	18,389	27,119	1,202	59,163	192,758	4,085
2008[1]	1,171,483	34,208	1,121,714	6,380	22,979	40,306	5,269	81,519	199,202	9,756

[1] Preliminary. [2] Producer & distributor and consumer stocks, excludes stocks held by retail dealers for consumption by the residential and commercial sector. [3] Equals production plus imports minus the change in producer & distributor and consumer stocks minus consumption minus exports.
Source: Energy Information Administraion, U.S. Department of Energy (EIA-DOE)

Consumption and Stocks of Coal in the United States In Thousands of Short Tons

	Consumption								Stocks, Dec. 31			
	Electric Utilities				Industrial				Consumer			
Year	Anthracite	Bituminous	Lignite	Total	Coke Plants	Other Industrial[2]	Residential and Commercial	Total	Electric Utilities	Coke Plants	Other Industrials	Producers and Distributors
1999	686	815,909	77,525	940,922	28,108	64,738	4,878	1,038,647	141,604	1,943	5,569	39,475
2000	NA	781,821	75,794	985,821	28,939	65,208	4,127	1,084,095	102,296	1,494	4,587	31,905
2001	NA	NA	NA	964,433	26,075	65,268	4,369	1,060,146	138,496	1,510	6,006	35,900
2002	NA	NA	NA	977,507	23,656	60,747	4,445	1,066,355	141,714	1,364	5,792	43,257
2003	NA	NA	NA	1,005,116	24,248	61,261	4,236	1,094,861	121,567	905	4,718	38,277
2004	NA	NA	NA	1,016,268	23,670	62,195	5,122	1,107,255	106,669	1,344	4,842	41,151
2005	NA	NA	NA	1,037,485	23,434	60,340	4,719	1,125,978	101,237	2,615	5,582	34,971
2006	NA	NA	NA	1,026,636	22,957	59,472	3,227	1,112,292	140,964	2,928	6,506	36,548
2007	NA	NA	NA	1,045,141	22,715	56,615	3,526	1,127,998	151,221	1,936	5,624	33,977
2008[1]	NA	NA	NA	1,041,603	22,070	54,536	3,506	1,121,714	163,059	2,331	6,007	27,311

[1] Preliminary. [2] Including transportation. [3] Excludes stocks held at retail dealers for consumption by the residential and commercial sector.
Source: Energy Information Administration, U.S. Department of Energy (EIA-DOE)

Average Prices of Coal in the United States In Dollars Per Short Ton

	End-Use Sector				Exports				End-Use Sector				Exports		
Year	Electric Utilities	Coke Plants	Other Industrial[2]	Imports[3]	Steam	Metal-lurgical	Total Average[3]	Year	Electric Utilities	Coke Plants	Other Industrial[2]	Imports[3]	Steam	Metal-lurgical	Total Average[3]
1999	24.72	45.85	31.59	30.77	29.91	41.91	36.50	2004	27.30	61.50	39.30	37.52	42.03	63.63	54.11
2000	24.28	44.38	31.46	30.10	29.67	38.99	34.89	2005	31.22	83.79	47.63	46.71	47.64	81.56	67.10
2001	24.68	46.42	32.26	34.00	31.88	41.63	36.97	2006	34.26	92.87	51.67	49.10	46.25	90.81	70.93
2002	24.74	50.67	35.49	35.51	34.51	45.41	40.44	2007	NA	94.97	54.42	47.64	47.90	88.99	70.25
2003	25.29	50.63	34.70	31.45	26.94	44.55	35.98	2008[1]	NA	118.09	63.44	59.83	57.35	134.62	97.68

[1] Preliminary. [2] Manufacturing plants only. [3] Based on the free alongside ship (F.A.S.) value.
Source: Energy Information Administration, U.S. Department of Energy (EIA-DOE)

Trends in Bituminous Coal, Lignite and Pennsylvania Anthracite in the United States In Thousands of Short Tons

	Bituminous Coal and Lignite							Pennsylvania Anthracite					All Mines
	Production				Labor Productivity								
Year	Under-Ground	Surface	Total	Miners[1] Employed	Under-Ground - Short Tons Per Miner Per Hour	Surface - Short Tons Per Miner Per Hour	Average - Short Tons Per Miner Per Hour	Under-Ground	Surface	Total	Miners[1] Employed	Labor Productivity Short Tons Miner/Hr.	Labor Productivity Short Tons Miner/Hr.
1999	391,790	708,642	1,100,431	78,723	3.99	10.39	6.61	377	4,376	4,753	1,326	1.76	6.61
2000	373,659	699,953	1,073,612	72,748	4.15	11.01	6.99	301	4,271	4,572	1,272	1.89	6.99
2001	380,627	745,308	1,127,689	77,088	4.02	10.60	6.82	341	1,143	1,484	955	.81	6.82
2002	357,385	735,910	1,094,283	75,466	3.98	10.38	6.80	305	998	1,303	872	.78	6.80
2003	352,785	717,870	1,071,753	71,023	4.04	10.76	6.95	282	961	1,243	814	.82	6.95
2004	367,557	743,552	1,112,099	73,912	3.96	10.57	6.80	271	1,408	1,679	890	.97	6.80
2005	368,612	762,190	1,131,498	79,283	3.62	10.04	6.36	264	1,296	1,560	891	.95	6.36
2006	359,022	802,976	1,161,998	82,959	3.37	10.19	6.26	239	1,132	1,371	869	.95	6.26
2007	351,790	793,690	1,145,480	81,278	3.34	10.25	6.27	224	1,199	1,423	910	.89	6.27
2008	357,079	813,322	1,170,401	86,859	3.15	9.82	5.96	1,340	1,459	2,799	929	.91	5.96

[1] Excludes miners employed at mines producing less than 10,000 tons.
Source: Energy Information Administration, U.S. Department of Energy (EIA-DOE)

Average Mine Prices of Coal in the United States In Dollars Per Short Ton

	Average Mine Prices by Method			Average Mine Prices by Rank						All Coal
Year	Under-ground	Surface	Total	Lignite	Sub-bituminous	Bituminous	Anthracite[1]	Bituminous & Lignite FOB Mines[2]	Anthracite FOB Mines[2]	CIF[3] Electric Utility Plants
1999	24.33	12.37	16.63	11.04	6.87	23.92	35.13	23.92	35.13	24.72
2000	23.84	12.26	16.44	11.41	7.12	24.15	40.90	24.15	40.90	24.28
2001	25.37	13.18	17.38	11.52	6.67	25.36	47.67	25.36	47.67	24.68
2002	26.68	13.65	17.98	11.07	7.34	26.57	47.78	26.57	47.78	24.74
2003	26.71	13.42	17.85	11.20	7.73	26.73	49.55	26.73	49.55	25.29
2004	30.36	14.75	19.93	12.27	8.12	30.56	39.77	30.56	39.77	27.30
2005	36.42	17.37	23.59	13.49	8.68	36.80	41.00	36.80	41.00	31.22
2006	38.28	18.88	25.16	14.00	9.95	39.32	43.61	39.32	43.61	34.26
2007	40.29	19.41	26.20	14.89	10.69	40.80	52.24	40.80	52.24	36.06
2008	51.37	22.35	31.26	16.50	12.31	51.40	60.76	51.40	60.76	

[1] Produced in Pennsylvania. [2] FOB = free on board. [3] *CIF = cost, insurance and freight.* W = Withheld data.
Source: Energy Information Adminstration, U.S. Department of Energy (EIA-DOE)

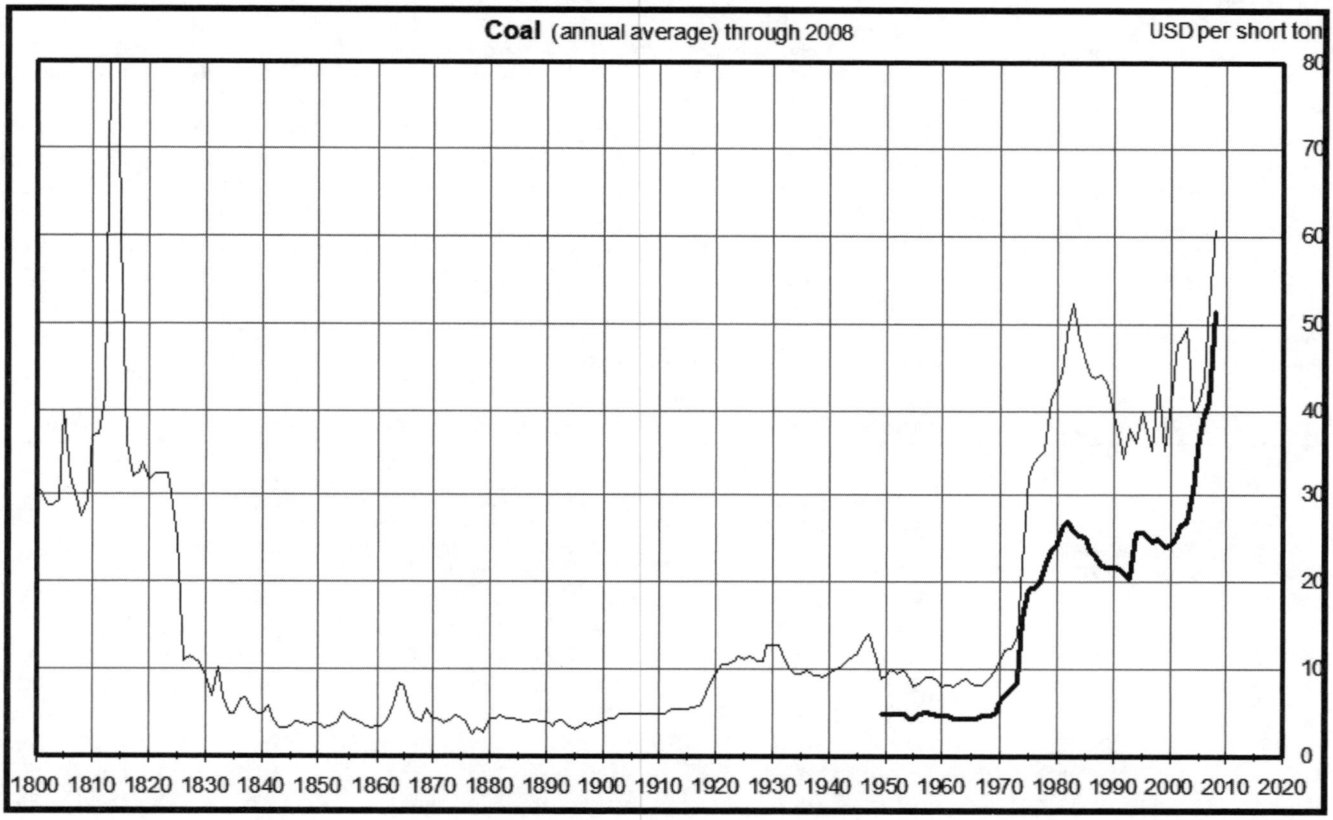

Cobalt

Cobalt (symbol Co) is a lustrous, silvery-white, magnetic, metallic element used chiefly for making alloys. Cobalt was known in ancient times and used by the Persians in 2250 BC to color glass. The name *cobalt* comes from the German word *kobalt* or *kobold*, meaning evil spirit. Miners gave cobalt its name because it was poisonous and troublesome since it polluted and degraded other mined elements, like nickel. In the 1730s, George Brandt first isolated metallic cobalt and was able to show that cobalt was the source of the blue color in glasses. In 1780, it was recognized as an element. Cobalt is generally not found in nature as a free metal and is instead found in ores. Cobalt is generally produced as a by-product of nickel and copper mining.

Cobalt is used in a variety of applications: high temperature steel alloys; fasteners in gas turbine engines; magnets and magnetic recording media; drying agents for paints and pigments; and steel-belted radial tires. Cobalt-60, an important radioactive tracer and cancer-treatment agent, is an artificially produced radioactive isotope of cobalt.

Prices – The price of cobalt in 2009 fell sharply by +53.9% to $18.00 per pound, down from the 2008 record high of $39.01 per pound, but still more than double the 20-year low of $6.91 per pound in 2002, just eight years ago.

Supply – World production of cobalt in 2009 fell by -18.3% to 62,000 metric tons, down from the 2008 record high of 75,800 metric tons. The world's largest cobalt mine producers are the Congo with 40% of world production in 2009, Australia (10%), Russia (10%), Australia (9%) and Canada (8%).

The U.S. does not specifically mine or refine cobalt although some cobalt is produced as a by-product of other mining operations. Imports, stock releases, and secondary materials comprise the U.S. cobalt supply. Secondary production includes extraction from super-alloy scrap, cemented carbide scrap, and spent catalysts. In the U.S. there are two domestic producers of extra-fine cobalt powder. One company produces the powder from imported primary metal and the other from recycled materials. There are only about seven companies that produce cobalt compounds. U.S. secondary production of cobalt in 2009 fell -11.9% yr/yr to 1,700 metric tons and remains well below the record high of 3,080 metric tons seen in 1998.

Demand – U.S. consumption of cobalt in 2009 fell by -33.7% yr/yr to 6,700 metric tons, but still below the 2005 record high of 11,800 metric tons. The largest use of cobalt by far was for super-alloys 35% of consumption in 2007 consumption. Other smaller-scaled applications for cobalt include cutting and wear-resistant materials (7.2%), magnetic alloys (3.5%), and welding materials (2.0%). Demand for some other uses is not available as proprietary information.

Trade – U.S. imports of cobalt in 2009 fell -31.8% to 7,300 metric tons, further below the 2006 record high of 11,600 metric tons. In 2009 the U.S. relied on imports for 75% of its cobalt consumption, which is down from the 99% level seen in the early 1970s.

World Mine Production of Cobalt In Metric Tons (Cobalt Content)

Year	Australia	Botswana	Canada	Cuba	Finland (Refinery)	France (Refinery)	Japan (Refinery)	New Caledonia	Norway (Refinery)	Russia	Congo[3]	Zambia	World Total
1999	4,100	331	5,323	2,537	10,000	300	480	1,100	4,500	3,900	7,000	5,640	32,700
2000	5,600	308	5,298	2,852	7,700	204	311	1,200	3,433	4,000	11,000	4,600	37,900
2001	6,300	325	5,326	3,425	8,100	199	350	1,400	3,314	4,600	12,000	8,000	44,800
2002	6,800	269	5,148	3,442	8,240	176	354	2,780	3,994	4,600	14,600	10,000	52,200
2003	6,000	294	4,327	3,274	7,989	181	379	2,602	4,556	6,100	14,800	11,300	52,900
2004	5,600	223	5,060	3,554	7,893	199	429	2,726	4,670	6,000	20,200	10,000	58,600
2005	5,600	326	5,767	3,768	8,171	280	471	1,769	5,021	6,300	24,500	9,300	63,400
2006	6,000	303	7,115	3,500	8,582	256	920	1,629	4,927	6,300	27,100	8,000	65,900
2007[1]	5,900	242	8,261	3,800	9,158	305	1,084	1,620	3,939	6,300	25,300	7,600	65,500
2008[2]	6,100		8,600	3,200				1,600		6,200	31,000	6,900	75,900

[1] Preliminary. [2] Estimate. [3] Formerly Zaire. *Source: U.S. Geological Survey (USGS)*

Salient Statistics of Cobalt in the United States In Metric Tons (Cobalt Content)

					Consumption by End Uses											
Year	Net Import Reliance As a % of Apparent Consumption	Cobalt Secondary Production	Processor and Consumer Stocks Dec. 31	Imports for Consumption	Ground Coat Frit	Stainless & Heat Resisting	Catalysts	Super-alloys	Tool Steel	Magnetic Alloys	Pigments	Drier in Paints, etc.	Cutting & Wear-Resistant Material	Welding Materials	Total Apparent Uses	Price $ Per Pound[4]
1999	73	2,720	738	8,150	W	W	W	3,830	W	794	W	W	755	291	10,700	17.02
2000	78	2,550	820	8,770	W	W	W	4,070	W	625	W	W	760	867	11,600	15.16
2001	76	2,780	852	9,410	W	W	W	4,850	W	472	W	W	720	661	11,800	10.55
2002	72	2,800	917	8,450	W	W	W	3,700	W	416	W	W	618	634	9,830	6.91
2003	79	2,130	649	8,080	W	W	W	3,400	W	282	W	W	662	632	10,000	10.60
2004	77	2,300	719	8,720	W	W	W	3,650	W	396	W	W	765	627	9,950	23.93
2005	83	2,030	705	11,100	W	W	W	4,140	W	343	W	W	762	227	11,800	15.96
2006	82	2,010	737	11,600	W	W	W	4,170	W	386	W	W	808	224	11,000	17.22
2007[1]	80	1,930	651	10,300	W	W	W	4,340	W	385	W	W	726	225	9,630	30.55
2008[2]	81	1,930		10,700											10,100	39.01

[1] Preliminary. [2] Estimate. [3] Or related usage. [4] Annual spot for cathodes. W = Withheld. *Source: U.S. Geological Survey (USGS)*

Cocoa

Cocoa is the common name for a powder derived from the fruit seeds of the cacao tree. The Spanish called cocoa "the food of the gods" when they found it in South America 500 years ago. Today, it remains a valued commodity. Dating back to the time of the Aztecs, cocoa was mainly used as a beverage. The processing of the cacao seeds, also known as cocoa beans, begins when the harvested fruit is fermented or cured into a pulpy state for three to nine days. The cocoa beans are then dried in the sun and cleaned in special machines before they are roasted to bring out the chocolate flavor. After roasting, they are put into a crushing machine and ground into cocoa powder. Cocoa has a high food value because it contains as much as 20 percent protein, 40 percent carbohydrate, and 40 percent fat. It is also mildly stimulating because of the presence of theobromine, an alkaloid that is closely related to caffeine. Roughly two-thirds of cocoa bean production is used to make chocolate and one-third to make cocoa powder.

Four major West African cocoa producers, the Ivory Coast, Ghana, Nigeria and Cameroon, together account for about two-thirds of world cocoa production. Outside of West Africa, the major producers of cocoa are Indonesia, Brazil, Malaysia, Ecuador, and the Dominican Republic. Cocoa producers like Ghana and Indonesia have been making efforts to increase cocoa production while producers like Malaysia have been switching to other crops. Ghana has had an ongoing problem with black pod disease and with smuggling of the crop into neighboring Ivory Coast. Brazil was once one of the largest producers of cocoa but has had problems with witches' broom disease. In West Africa, the main crop harvest starts in the September-October period and can be extended into the January-March period. Cocoa trees reach maturity in 5-6 years but can live to be 50 years old or more. During the course of a growing season, the cocoa tree will produce thousands of flowers but only a few will develop into cocoa pods.

Cocoa futures and options are traded on the ICE Futures U.S. (ICE) exchange and on the London International Financial Futures and Options Exchange (LIFFE). The futures contracts call for the delivery of 10 metric tons of cocoa and the contract is priced in US dollars per metric ton.

Prices – Cocoa futures prices on a nearest-futures basis fell sharply in the second half of 2008 due to the overall commodity plunge and the global financial crisis and recession. However, cocoa prices bottomed out at a 2-year low of $1,867 per metric ton in October 2008 and then rallied throughout 2009. Cocoa prices posted a 31-year high of $3,510 per metric ton in December 2009 and closed 2009 at $3,289 per metric ton, up 23.4% year-on-year. The record high for cocoa futures is $5379.2 per metric ton posted in July 1977. Bullish factors for cocoa that fueled the 2009 rally included (1) the general rally in commodity prices tied to the global economic recovery and dollar weakness, (2) improved demand with seasonal grindings in the 2009/10 marketing year up +2.5% after the sharp 6.9% decline seen in 2008/09, (3) the relatively low end-of-season stocks for 2009-10 of 1.6 million metric tons, which translated into a stocks-to-grinding ratio of 44.5%, the second lowest in the past 10 years (behind 42.2% in 2007-08), and (4) three straight years of production deficits in 2006-07, 2007-08 and 2008-09. Cocoa prices faded in early 2010 due to bearish factors including the forecast by the International Coffee Organization for a moderate-sized 150,000 metric ton surplus for the marketing year of 2009-10 (beginning October 1, 2009).

Supply – The world production of cocoa beans in the 2008-09 crop year (latest data available) rose +3.6% to a record high of 4.300 million metric tons. The world's largest cocoa producer by far is the Ivory Coast with 32% of total world production in 2008-09. The Ivory Coast's production in 2008-09, however, fell -1.0% yr/yr. After the Ivory Coast the major producers are Indonesia with 18% of total world production in 2008-09, Ghana with 16%, Nigeria with 12%, Brazil with 5%, and Cameroon with 4%. Closing stocks of cocoa in the 2009-10 crop year fell -1.1% yr/yr to 1.593 metric tons.

Demand – World seasonal grindings of cocoa in 2009/10 rose by +2.5% y/y to 3.579 million metric tons, recovering somewhat after the -6.9% decline seen in the recession year of 2008/09. Cocoa grindings hit a record high of 3.752 million metric tons in the 2007/08 marketing year. European is by far the largest global consumer of cocoa, consuming about 40% of the global crop.

Trade – U.S. imports of cocoa and cocoa products in 2009 (annualized through November) rose +2.2% yr/yr to 1.139 million metric tons, but still below the record high of 1.317 million metric tons in 2005.

World Supply and Demand Cocoa In Thousands of Metric Tons

Crop Year Beginning Oct. 1	Stocks Oct. 1	Net World Production[4]	Total Availability	Seasona Grindings	Closing Stocks	Stock Change	Stock/Consumption Ratio %
1999-00	1,469	3,077	4,546	2,960	1,564	96	52.9
2000-01	1,564	3,372	4,936	3,065	1,344	-220	43.9
2001-02	1,344	3,108	4,453	2,886	1,315	-29	45.6
2002-03	1,315	3,271	4,587	3,078	1,394	79	45.3
2003-04	1,394	3,579	4,973	3,238	1,682	288	51.9
2004-05	1,682	4,018	5,700	3,363	1,666	-16	49.5
2005-06	1,666	4,054	5,720	3,508	1,906	240	54.3
2006-07[1]	1,906	4,275	6,181	3,661	1,650	-256	45.1
2007-08[2]	1,650	4,150	5,800	3,752	1,579	-71	42.1
2008-09[3]	1,579	4,300	5,879	3,492	1,611	32	46.1

[1] Preliminary. [2] Estimate. [3] Forecast. [4] Obtained by adjusting the gross world crop for a one percent loss in weight.
Source: ED&F Man Cocoa Limited

COCOA

World Production of Cocoa Beans In Thousands of Metric Tons

Crop Year Beginning Oct. 1	Brazil	Cameroon	Colombia	Dominican Republic	Ecuador	Ghana	Indonesia	Ivory Coast	Malaysia	Mexico	Nigeria	Papau New Guinea	World Total
1999-00	124	115	37	28	92	435	428	1,404	37	31	180	46	3,054
2000-01	197	123	37	37	100	437	421	1,401	70	28	338	47	3,372
2001-02	186	122	36	45	76	390	428	1,212	58	47	340	39	3,108
2002-03	175	125	34	45	88	341	571	1,265	48	46	362	42	3,271
2003-04	170	155	42	47	88	497	573	1,352	36	50	385	43	3,579
2004-05	196	167	39	48	90	737	642	1,407	33	44	412	39	4,018
2005-06	209	179	37	31	94	740	643	1,360	28	36	441	48	4,054
2006-07[1]	212	165	35	46	88	734	769	1,372	32	38	485	51	4,275
2007-08[2]	202	179	40	42	86	615	740	1,384	35	30	500	47	4,150
2008-09[3]	208	188	45	42	94	700	793	1,370	30	28	500	49	4,300

[1] Preliminary. [2] Estimate. [3] Forecast. *Source: Food and Agricultural Organization of the United Nations (FAO-UN)*

World Consumption of Cocoa[4] In Thousands of Metric Tons

Crop Year Beginning Oct. 1	Canada	Brazil	European Union	Ghana	Indonesia	Ivory Coast	Japan	Malaysia	Singapore	Turkey	United States	Russia	World Total
1995-96	39	183	1,225	60	60	130	49	96	63	16	345	75	2,655
1996-97	35	180	1,203	68	72	145	53	103	61	16	394	74	2,730
1997-98	53	188	1,228	67	74	195	43	94	68	22	399	50	2,773
1998-99	42	191	1,186	65	83	210	47	109	63	22	406	48	2,757
1999-00	56	202	1,235	75	88	230	48	117	60	25	439	62	2,975
2000-01	58	195	1,263	80	91	285	49	121	59	39	445	67	3,072
2001-02	56	173	1,159	80	108	265	50	93	62	39	393	69	2,843
2002-03[1]	57	196	1,190	69	115	290	64	129	71	50	400	60	3,014
2003-04[2]	72	207	1,256	78	122	321	57	200	59	71	401	63	3,230
2004-05[3]	65	209	1,328	76	111	320	53	228	57	58	409	68	3,321

[1] Preliminary. [2] Estimate. [3] Forecast. [4] Figures represent the "grindings" of cocoa beans in each country. NA = Not available.
Source: ED&F Man Cocoa Limited

Imports of Cocoa Butter in Selected Countries In Metric Tons

Year	Australia	Austria	Belgium	Canada	France	Germany	Italy	Japan	Netherlands	Sweden	Switzerland	United Kingdom	United States
1998	18,000	5,954	25,722	17,000	43,721	76,059	8,950	15,371	25,624	7,403	19,856	33,355	65,307
1999	22,473	5,356	42,278	17,323	56,923	70,455	8,277	17,824	36,799	6,948	21,278	38,023	80,475
2000	20,590	4,325	51,826	22,009	54,197	72,014	12,071	21,695	37,261	6,010	19,922	38,770	94,648
2001	20,633	3,945	51,577	23,307	51,145	80,839	11,765	21,665	36,687	6,349	20,604	41,827	80,806
2002	20,800	3,777	48,992	24,397	63,814	82,313	12,099	20,212	47,562	6,401	21,545	46,912	84,788
2003	22,310	3,823	54,621	26,309	58,759	77,880	13,337	22,579	55,523	6,564	21,555	39,092	78,035
2004	23,514	4,536	56,328	27,646	70,386	79,155	13,891	22,166	63,657	6,668	22,960	50,593	94,890
2005	21,527	4,281	61,200	28,382	72,561	82,050	16,114	24,633	70,255	6,276	24,264	70,777	96,876
2006	19,172	4,729	68,173	23,803	75,572	82,726	16,285	25,603	82,864	5,774	25,725	48,447	96,455
2007[1]	15,845	4,367	75,283	31,301	78,858	85,113	20,973	24,417	70,598	3,441	27,265	48,911	86,258

[1] Preliminary. NA = Not available. *Sources: Food and Agricultural Organization of the United Nations (FAO)*

Imports of Cocoa Liquor and Cocoa Powder in Selected Countries In Metric Tons

	Cocoa Liquor						Cocoa Powder						
Year	France	Germany	Japan	lands	United Kingdom	United States	Denmark	France	Germany	Italy	Japan	Netherlands	United States
1998	70,883	9,121	1,144	12,534	3,813	21,894	3,816	25,091	38,742	17,164	9,151	17,237	128,771
1999	74,721	13,833	1,421	25,639	4,396	12,823	4,410	27,229	38,681	16,885	10,227	17,469	113,746
2000	67,812	14,295	1,618	33,815	8,529	10,902	3,661	37,165	39,498	18,249	11,765	29,044	130,610
2001	67,500	17,548	1,553	41,913	10,289	17,940	3,792	25,631	32,621	19,224	12,004	29,866	113,592
2002	64,820	28,100	1,193	46,369	14,038	22,215	2,895	35,128	39,871	19,642	10,859	54,422	126,443
2003	71,337	31,391	1,764	35,089	20,154	20,018	3,142	43,915	37,065	18,757	12,895	38,713	136,813
2004	72,057	42,975	2,773	40,847	17,753	20,758	3,447	44,213	35,460	19,538	14,973	38,692	147,392
2005	80,194	42,537	3,327	46,409	6,574	33,540	3,996	43,626	33,202	23,085	13,705	45,859	141,044
2006	86,767	43,918	14,684	43,885	6,541	24,359	3,053	39,833	41,050	22,485	15,831	34,770	145,820
2007[1]	58,344	39,985	7,659	48,960	6,725	20,357	3,106	41,030	47,480	28,241	16,218	35,979	158,132

[1] Preliminary. NA = Not available. *Source: Food and Agricultural Organization of the United Nations (FAO)*

Imports of Cocoa and Products in the United States In Thousands of Metric Tons

Year	Jan.	Feb.	Mar.	Apr.	May	June	July	Aug.	Sept.	Oct.	Nov.	Dec.	Total
2000	111	128	101	91	70	67	70	70	86	76	59	69	999
2001	108	97	77	47	68	61	80	78	76	86	92	118	989
2002	87	74	73	61	76	72	87	98	61	66	90	72	916
2003	115	74	92	71	68	74	95	82	79	95	85	116	1,046
2004	110	82	130	100	101	103	94	94	100	90	80	89	1,171
2005	129	109	156	108	104	93	91	104	84	97	113	129	1,317
2006	114	104	109	94	92	89	108	140	103	91	90	124	1,258
2007	111	121	110	102	82	76	83	83	84	95	76	106	1,130
2008	108	115	109	87	80	65	88	82	79	90	83	129	1,114
2009[1]	114	98	88	95	82	99	80	88	103	103	94		1,139

[1] Preliminary. *Source: Foreign Agricultural Service, U.S. Department of Agriculture (FAS-USDA)*

Visible Stocks of Cocoa in Port of Hampton Road Warehouses[1], at End of Month In Thousands of Bags

Year	Jan.	Feb.	Mar.	Apr.	May	June	July	Aug.	Sept.	Oct.	Nov.	Dec.
2000	469.7	448.4	571.7	583.4	711.1	672.4	720.3	925.2	921.4	839.7	762.9	816.0
2001	741.9	657.4	632.0	607.7	577.3	518.8	498.2	487.5	475.2	506.8	509.0	511.4
2002	504.7	462.8	436.7	424.0	383.8	353.4	327.4	273.3	255.4	194.8	181.5	169.9
2003	149.9	121.7	103.1	102.3	80.5	71.9	69.2	67.7	56.9	53.0	49.6	49.3
2004	48.6	47.8	47.5	47.5	44.3	43.9	41.2	40.4	40.1	38.0	38.0	36.8
2005	31.1	30.9	28.6	28.0	28.0	27.4	27.4	27.4	27.4	27.4	27.4	27.4
2006	18.3	17.9	17.6	17.3	17.3	17.3	17.3	17.3	17.1	17.1	17.1	17.1
2007	16.8	16.8	16.8	16.8	16.8	16.8	15.9	15.6	15.6	15.6	15.6	15.6
2008	15.6	15.6	15.6	15.6	15.8	15.8	15.8	15.8	15.8	15.6	15.6	15.6
2009	14.9	14.9	14.9	14.9	14.9	14.9	13.7	13.7	13.7	13.7	13.7	13.7

[1] Licensed warehouses approved by ICE. *Source: ICE Futures U.S. (ICE)*

Visible Stocks of Cocoa in Philadelphia (Del. River) Warehouses[1], at End of Month In Thousands of Bags

Year	Jan.	Feb.	Mar.	Apr.	May	June	July	Aug.	Sept.	Oct.	Nov.	Dec.
2000	1,619.0	1,801.7	2,466.4	2,582.0	2,581.6	2,363.7	2,168.3	2,101.6	2,105.1	2,039.1	1,697.4	1,589.4
2001	1,844.0	2,082.3	2,173.3	1,960.0	1,785.9	1,610.4	1,391.6	1,543.0	1,391.3	1,131.4	1,303.2	1,682.1
2002	1,701.5	1,876.7	1,849.3	1,708.0	1,746.4	1,689.5	1,793.1	1,832.7	1,750.9	1,334.5	1,162.7	1,250.6
2003	1,347.2	1,422.0	1,327.9	1,326.5	1,217.2	1,202.3	1,229.2	1,123.7	930.6	798.9	723.7	806.0
2004	1,294.9	1,061.5	1,259.1	1,187.1	1,238.8	1,342.0	1,432.6	1,529.3	1,366.4	1,569.4	1,312.8	1,335.7
2005	1,588.9	1,809.8	2,066.3	2,264.5	2,439.3	2,258.3	2,465.0	2,481.0	2,470.5	2,373.5	2,635.5	2,712.8
2006	2,888.5	2,828.9	3,018.9	3,208.9	3,095.0	2,913.8	3,005.2	3,404.0	3,382.1	3,307.2	3,135.3	3,293.0
2007	3,488.8	4,169.2	4,410.9	4,299.6	4,198.0	3,860.3	3,424.2	3,106.8	2,883.0	2,660.0	2,327.4	2,334.5
2008	2,435.5	2,679.8	2,920.4	2,787.6	2,733.9	2,486.3	2,223.6	2,110.8	1,717.5	1,571.2	1,390.4	1,533.4
2009	2,062.7	2,339.1	2,276.8	2,530.2	2,429.9	2,405.8	2,137.2	1,968.6	1,938.5	1,931.4	2,105.8	2,196.4

[1] Licensed warehouses approved by ICE. *Source: ICE Futures U.S. (ICE)*

Visible Stocks of Cocoa in New York Warehouses[1], at End of Month In Thousands of Bags

Year	Jan.	Feb.	Mar.	Apr.	May	June	July	Aug.	Sept.	Oct.	Nov.	Dec.
2000	1,633.7	1,689.5	1,926.9	2,049.8	1,926.7	1,789.6	1,632.2	1,383.7	1,323.7	1,234.8	1,100.0	1,019.4
2001	1,005.6	1,173.8	1,119.6	1,024.9	967.5	906.6	776.2	758.5	657.6	687.4	750.8	1,196.2
2002	1,088.9	870.8	892.0	816.1	739.1	736.0	640.9	553.6	670.1	525.7	473.1	554.8
2003	614.6	625.4	593.7	612.9	515.1	476.1	423.6	388.2	483.4	301.9	391.3	342.9
2004	229.9	415.2	616.1	579.9	712.7	680.1	676.3	596.1	486.3	334.5	272.0	209.6
2005	201.2	446.3	495.9	677.7	806.6	916.5	805.2	625.2	457.2	430.3	388.3	599.2
2006	758.4	971.5	894.9	818.3	759.3	691.8	618.7	685.8	654.2	649.1	528.0	502.8
2007	532.2	457.4	635.5	666.5	612.3	605.4	576.2	530.5	496.8	442.2	394.8	343.2
2008	422.4	411.1	574.4	618.7	614.0	554.4	527.9	434.6	396.1	375.6	323.1	242.5
2009	291.7	413.2	429.4	472.0	503.4	557.3	672.2	665.7	653.9	726.0	714.6	722.3

[1] Licensed warehouses approved by ICE. *Source: ICE Futures U.S. (ICE)*

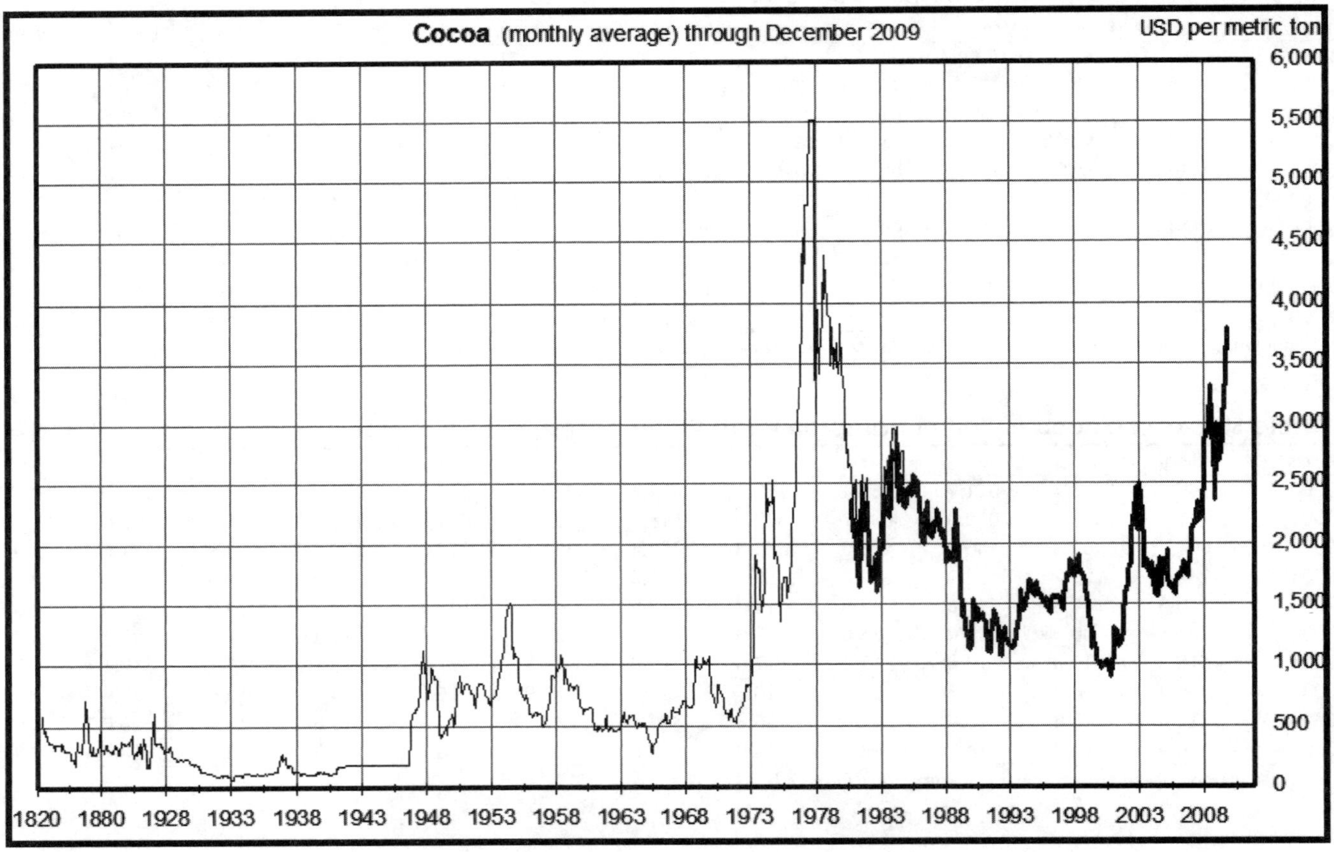

Average Cash Price of Cocoa, Ivory Coast in New York In Dollars Per Metric Ton

Year	Jan.	Feb.	Mar.	Apr.	May	June	July	Aug.	Sept.	Oct.	Nov.	Dec.	Average
2000	1,027	962	1,025	993	998	1,033	1,034	980	988	991	905	911	987
2001	1,093	1,299	1,290	1,244	1,281	1,146	1,152	1,200	1,183	1,288	1,439	1,543	1,263
2002	1,586	1,674	1,794	1,800	1,814	1,836	2,081	2,191	2,391	2,471	2,123	2,322	2,007
2003	2,483	2,506	2,258	2,232	1,996	1,818	1,803	1,843	1,877	1,713	1,737	1,832	2,008
2004	1,840	1,763	1,695	1,610	1,588	1,571	1,733	1,889	1,698	1,654	1,867	1,848	1,730
2005	1,740	1,827	1,950	1,744	1,656	1,687	1,625	1,626	1,640	1,598	1,585	1,670	1,696
2006	1,752	1,729	1,739	1,749	1,806	1,794	1,862	1,795	1,764	1,725	1,773	1,897	1,782
2007	1,883	1,996	2,120	2,169	2,214	2,225	2,361	2,185	2,242	2,198	2,251	2,396	2,187
2008	2,486	2,806	2,922	2,867	2,971	3,307	3,248	3,078	2,972	2,533	2,371	2,837	2,867
2009	2,985	2,977	2,781	2,830	2,699	2,892	3,047	3,186	3,427	3,634	3,596	3,782	3,153

Source: Economic Research Service, U.S. Department of Agriculture (ERS-USDA)

Average Open Interest of Cocoa Futures in New York In Contracts

Year	Jan.	Feb.	Mar.	Apr.	May	June	July	Aug.	Sept.	Oct.	Nov.	Dec.
2000	100,540	110,316	106,056	102,382	113,239	111,948	112,864	117,260	123,463	138,523	139,141	138,266
2001	132,711	119,459	114,036	102,275	107,008	111,224	104,473	99,280	92,235	96,204	93,088	92,326
2002	97,563	98,169	96,336	98,851	103,746	100,701	107,080	102,441	107,294	107,880	82,236	82,844
2003	96,375	91,944	83,625	83,230	95,307	96,813	89,846	78,197	76,468	86,392	99,038	94,010
2004	88,879	84,078	99,918	100,429	108,150	99,476	103,350	111,318	101,998	119,033	117,876	118,769
2005	117,091	115,007	144,055	124,417	124,925	128,203	126,388	129,562	118,468	132,629	131,733	123,302
2006	131,527	127,471	129,426	129,814	131,035	138,004	154,163	134,942	139,544	153,485	136,329	140,099
2007	145,503	152,358	172,846	157,373	154,649	148,608	167,565	134,823	123,171	133,362	137,208	165,522
2008	188,039	182,389	166,939	136,591	146,759	160,366	151,896	134,715	127,674	122,381	113,422	113,240
2009	119,496	118,145	114,051	111,859	117,027	114,792	112,079	112,935	121,226	133,635	129,171	129,296

Source: ICE Futures U.S. (ICE)

Volume of Trading of Cocoa Futures in New York In Contracts

Year	Jan.	Feb.	Mar.	Apr.	May	June	July	Aug.	Sept.	Oct.	Nov.	Dec.	Total
2000	156,812	231,562	232,803	186,837	147,072	267,470	124,906	191,849	111,740	174,216	186,515	98,266	2,110,048
2001	311,900	168,587	164,131	136,021	154,397	201,299	108,189	207,569	118,428	124,884	202,847	107,565	2,005,817
2002	155,699	187,550	129,833	217,590	160,364	220,289	176,450	209,249	138,394	207,310	162,982	114,270	2,079,980
2003	172,845	215,240	136,564	179,956	176,969	207,255	143,888	206,428	146,113	197,316	209,775	135,857	2,128,206
2004	174,684	180,693	181,667	244,946	174,452	238,201	219,018	260,025	146,090	150,443	290,227	128,604	2,389,050
2005	185,624	239,511	231,917	249,209	134,330	288,809	151,339	252,868	222,122	182,337	283,663	161,198	2,582,927
2006	235,410	264,557	201,604	295,814	244,032	333,275	331,108	313,591	174,246	264,490	308,782	202,293	3,169,202
2007	239,568	338,998	273,605	333,551	212,318	328,646	242,710	378,897	213,143	265,018	273,419	235,410	3,335,283
2008	322,864	434,965	316,509	328,981	293,874	353,593	280,275	345,973	197,765	313,220	228,699	175,550	3,592,268
2009	265,308	282,200	242,110	279,621	214,640	303,030	216,046	292,552	188,138	289,133	338,296	175,892	3,086,966

Source: ICE Futures U.S. (ICE)

Coconut Oil and Copra

Coconut oil and copra come from the fruit of the coconut palm tree, which originated in Southeast Asia. Coconut oil has been used for thousands of years as cooking oil, and is still a staple in the diets of many people living in tropical areas. Until shortages of imported oil developed during WWII, Americans also used coconut oil for cooking.

Copra is the meaty inner lining of the coconut. It is an oil-rich pulp with a light, slightly sweet, nutty flavor. Copra is used mainly as a source of coconut oil and is also used shredded for baking. High-quality copra contains about 65% to 72% oil, and oil made from the copra is called crude coconut oil. Crude coconut oil is processed from copra by expeller press and solvent extraction. It is not considered fit for human consumption until it has been refined, which consists of neutralizing, bleaching and deodorizing it at high heat with a vacuum. The remaining oil cake obtained as a by-product is used for livestock feed.

Premium grade coconut oil, also called virgin coconut oil, is oil made from the first pressing without the addition of any chemicals. Premium grade coconut oil is more expensive than refined or crude oil because the producers use only selected raw materials and there is a lower production yield due to only one pressing.

Coconut oil accounts for approximately 20% of all vegetable oils used worldwide. Coconut oil is used in margarines, vegetable shortening, salad oils, confections, and in sports drinks to boost energy and enhance athletic performance. It is also used in the manufacture of soaps, detergents, shampoos, cosmetics, candles, glycerin and synthetic rubber. Coconut oil is very healthy, unless it is hydrogenated, and is easily digested.

Prices – The average monthly price of coconut oil (crude) in 2008 rose +40.8% yr/yr to 58.69 cents per pound. The record high of 60.21 cents per pound was posted in 1984.

Supply – World production of copra in 2009 rose by +5.6% yr/yr to 5.219 million metric tons, but remains below the record high of 5.662 million metric tons posted in 2001. The world's largest producers of copra are the Philippines with 38% of world production, Indonesia with 30%, India with 13%, and Mexico with 4%. World production of coconut oil in the 2008-09 marketing year fell by -2.0% yr/yr to 3.083 million metric tons.

Demand – Virtually all of world production of copra goes for crushing into coconut meal and oil (over 99%). World consumption of coconut oil in 2008-09 fell by -2.8% yr/yr to 3.078 million metric tons, and still below the record high of 3.349 million metric tons in 2000-01.

Trade – Copra is generally crushed in the country of origin, meaning that less than 4% of copra itself is exported; the rest is exported in the form of coconut oil. World exports of coconut oil in 2008-09 fell by -10.1% yr/yr to 1.796 million metric tons, and still below the 2005-06 record high of 2.178 million metric tons.

World Production of Copra In Thousands of Metric Tons

Year	India	Indonesia	Ivory Coast	Malaysia	Mexico	Mozambique	Papua New Guinea	Philippines	Sri Lanka	Thailand	Vanuatu	Vietnam	World Total
2000	700	1,330	45	49	202	75	152	2,140	98	69	27	45	5,248
2001	690	1,185	45	47	198	75	95	2,790	113	60	30	41	5,662
2002	713	1,290	45	50	203	50	71	2,010	59	61	25	46	4,920
2003	690	1,260	45	51	185	55	85	2,406	50	68	25	49	5,267
2004	700	1,300	45	51	182	50	90	1,980	60	71	35	49	4,915
2005	660	1,460	45	48	184	50	112	2,100	67	72	30	50	5,197
2006	650	1,370	45	51	187	48	94	2,100	65	65	30	51	5,080
2007[1]	620	1,570	45	49	217	46	97	1,810	69	68	30	52	4,999
2008[2]	650	1,435	46	52	190	48	123	1,850	73	68	32	53	4,941
2009[3]	660	1,560	46	54	200	48	120	1,980	74	69	32	54	5,219

[1] Preliminary. [2] Estimate. [3] Forecast. *Source: The Oil World*

World Supply and Distribution of Coconut Oil In Thousands of Metric Tons

	Production							Consumption						Ending Stocks		
Year	India	Indonesia	Malaysia	Philippines	Total	Exports	Imports	European Union	India	Indonesia	Philippines	United States	Total	Philippines	United States	Total
1999-00	421	787	54	1,198	3,084	1,788	1,718	770	435	110	299	420	2,921	112	62	411
2000-01	419	700	48	1,731	3,496	2,159	2,173	751	439	277	348	437	3,349	60	118	572
2001-02	421	773	45	1,403	3,183	1,846	1,872	712	448	278	332	506	3,274	62	103	507
2002-03	418	758	41	1,425	3,180	1,958	1,991	786	454	273	352	384	3,301	53	98	418
2003-04	419	731	41	1,379	3,104	1,860	1,833	713	428	246	311	399	3,125	58	60	370
2004-05	402	881	42	1,263	3,151	2,116	2,067	814	421	175	253	361	3,069	73	110	402
2005-06	392	789	45	1,450	3,223	2,186	2,183	768	420	180	253	494	3,216	66	101	405
2006-07[1]	377	960	47	1,133	3,073	1,915	1,913	704	392	187	306	435	3,118	63	58	357
2007-08[2]	386	887	46	1,275	3,145	1,997	2,027	682	401	189	336	506	3,165	64	83	368
2008-09[3]	395	894	47	1,186	3,083	1,796	1,796	647	405	200	400	410	3,078	80	74	372

[1] Preliminary. [2] Estimate. [3] Forecast. *Source: The Oil World*

Supply and Distribution of Coconut Oil in the United States In Millions of Pounds

Year	--- Rotterdam --- Copra Tonne	Coconut Oil, CIF	Imports For Consumption	Stocks Oct. 1	Total Supply	Exports	-------- Disapearance -------- Total Domestic	Edible Products	Inedible Products	------ Production of Coconut Oil (Refined) ------ Total	Oct.-Dec.	Jan.-Mar.	April-June	July-Sept.
	------ $ U.S. ------													
1999-00	357	539	926	152	1,078	14	927	221	371	442.3	69.1	117.0	129.6	126.7
2000-01	208	323	1,100	136	1,236	8	968	237	297	534.9	135.7	128.3	146.9	124.0
2001-02	245	388	1,150	260	1,410	11	1,100	294	302	501.8	139.5	126.1	115.4	120.8
2002-03	286	450	866	226	1,092	28	1,205	305	310	546.7	128.8	137.0	155.6	125.2
2003-04	424	630	812	216	1,028	17	1,312	330	274	594.9	160.7	132.8	162.8	138.6
2004-05	431	636	936	131	1,067	29	1,374	341	280	623.3	153.7	157.5	160.8	151.3
2005-06	387	583	1,127	242	1,369	58	1,323	366	270	599.9	141.9	156.2	160.5	141.4
2006-07	537	812	892	222	1,114	26	1,443	339	309	654.6	162.6	152.2	165.4	174.4
2007-08[1]	867	1,306	1,196	129	1,325	28	1,383	373	447	627.4	139.9	165.9	161.1	160.5
2008-09[2]	486	728	915	132	1,047	31	1,293	364	394	586.6	147.6	131.1	122.8	185.2

[1] Preliminary. [2] Forecast. *Source: Bureau of Census, U.S. Department of Commerce*

Consumption of Coconut Oil in End Products (Edible and Inedible) in the United States In Millions of Pounds

Year	Jan.	Feb.	Mar.	Apr.	May	June	July	Aug.	Sept.	Oct.	Nov.	Dec.	Total
2000	49.4	44.0	52.7	54.6	51.4	56.5	49.1	56.2	54.7	44.1	44.3	43.0	600.0
2001	49.3	40.6	45.5	42.5	48.3	43.3	46.5	45.6	48.4	50.3	44.4	45.5	550.2
2002	55.4	41.3	50.8	59.3	53.9	46.4	50.7	51.8	45.9	54.3	56.1	49.4	615.4
2003	51.2	49.3	56.8	50.6	52.3	46.7	48.9	49.6	50.3	47.8	41.8	38.5	583.7
2004	50.0	51.7	58.5	54.6	48.5	55.6	52.9	55.1	48.9	48.2	64.3	51.7	640.0
2005	46.7	52.0	47.9	48.8	51.4	55.5	47.2	58.1	49.2	52.8	53.4	58.1	621.1
2006	70.4	62.7	50.4	47.5	50.7	51.6	43.1	51.6	43.8	49.6	44.4	40.8	606.4
2007	49.8	48.5	47.0	51.2	53.7	60.3	60.3	74.2	67.5	71.8	71.3	62.7	718.3
2008	63.6	72.1	64.8	74.4	69.7	70.4	65.8	67.6	65.8	63.0	63.6	53.6	794.5
2009[1]	67.9	62.8	60.2	66.9	66.9	27.6	36.5	28.1	29.4	32.8	32.1	30.6	541.8

[1] Preliminary. *Source: Bureau of Census, U.S. Department of Commerce*

Stocks of Coconut Oil (Crude and Refined) in the United States, on First of Month In Millions of Pounds

Year	Jan.	Feb.	Mar.	Apr.	May	June	July	Aug.	Sept.	Oct.	Nov.	Dec.
2000	93.6	123.6	100.1	99.6	102.3	104.0	137.7	163.6	161.4	136.4	178.1	161.6
2001	245.4	280.3	357.8	276.5	286.9	194.3	254.4	260.9	246.4	259.7	234.1	231.3
2002	245.9	238.8	249.6	251.3	233.5	231.6	303.3	301.6	245.8	226.5	273.8	264.1
2003	195.2	194.0	214.3	224.9	223.7	187.8	162.2	202.9	195.6	218.9	184.6	186.1
2004	167.2	160.3	192.6	181.7	131.4	108.7	90.6	132.8	149.2	131.3	147.7	182.5
2005	225.9	163.7	188.4	191.0	170.6	187.7	263.5	250.4	253.7	242.1	252.3	273.3
2006	268.3	236.9	224.5	227.3	260.2	229.1	213.8	214.4	204.7	224.5	179.2	180.2
2007	214.4	228.5	261.5	223.1	191.8	157.9	171.2	154.4	127.7	128.4	142.5	212.6
2008	205.6	192.9	180.9	191.9	223.9	203.9	187.8	181.5	180.4	182.2	163.3	174.6
2009[1]	164.1	183.7	215.6	167.2	143.9	138.0	134.8	133.2	102.3	182.3	159.0	154.7

[1] Preliminary. *Source: Bureau of Census, U.S. Department of Commerce*

Average Price of Coconut Oil (Crude) Tank Cars in New York In Cents Per Pound

Year	Jan.	Feb.	Mar.	Apr.	May	June	July	Aug.	Sept.	Oct.	Nov.	Dec.	Average
2000	40.88	32.94	28.81	26.63	24.25	21.90	19.63	18.58	16.40	16.81	17.50	15.70	23.34
2001	26.00	24.00	22.75	22.50	21.00	21.00	24.00	26.50	26.50	26.50	24.50	24.50	24.15
2002	16.38	17.38	17.25	18.75	20.05	21.13	21.06	21.35	28.50	28.25	27.13	26.00	21.94
2003	26.00	26.00	24.60	24.50	24.50	25.00	25.00	25.00	25.00	25.00	28.75	31.00	25.86
2004	32.00	33.38	34.56	39.20	45.00	46.00	46.00	46.00	39.25	32.65	31.25	31.25	38.05
2005	31.05	31.00	32.67	35.00	34.67	34.00	33.00	33.00	33.00	35.00	29.13	27.75	32.44
2006	27.75	27.75	27.75	27.75	27.75	27.75	27.75	27.75	29.25	30.75	32.25	34.95	29.10
2007	35.75	36.00	36.00	37.50	40.13	45.75	48.00	NA	42.50	45.16	45.38	46.32	41.68
2008	58.02	62.33	70.98	67.38	67.38	71.73	70.33	59.62	55.82	47.73	37.46	35.51	58.69
2009[1]	35.25	33.14	30.07	31.58	37.84	37.34	32.78	35.00	35.75	35.75	35.75	35.53	34.65

[1] Preliminary. *Source: Economic Research Service, U.S. Department of Agriculture (ERS-USDA)*

Coffee

Coffee is one of the world's most important cash commodities. Coffee is the common name for any type of tree in the genus madder family. It is actually a tropical evergreen shrub that has the potential to grow 100 feet tall. The coffee tree grows in tropical regions between the Tropics of Cancer and Capricorn in areas with abundant rainfall, year-round warm temperatures averaging about 70 degrees Fahrenheit, and no frost. In the U.S., the only areas that produce any significant amount of coffee are Puerto Rico and Hawaii. The coffee plant will produce its first full crop of beans at about 5 years old and then be productive for about 15 years. The average coffee tree produces enough beans to make about 1 to 1 ½ pounds of roasted coffee per year. It takes approximately 4,000 handpicked green coffee beans to make a pound of coffee. Wine was actually the first drink made from the coffee tree using the coffee cherries, honey, and water. In the 17th century, the first coffee house, also known as a "penny university" because of the price per cup, opened in London. The London Stock Exchange grew from one of these first coffee houses.

Coffee is generally classified into two types of beans: arabica and robusta. The most widely produced coffee is arabica, which makes up about 70 percent of total production. It grows mostly at high altitudes of 600 to 2,000 meters, with Brazil and Colombia being the largest producers. Arabic coffee is traded on the ICE Futures U.S. (ICE) exchange. The stronger of the two types is robusta. It is grown at lower altitudes with the largest producers being Indonesia, West Africa, Brazil, and Vietnam. Robusta coffee is traded on the LIFFE exchange.

Ninety percent of the world coffee trade is in green (unroasted) coffee beans. Seasonal factors have a significant influence on the price of coffee. There is no extreme peak in world production at any one time of the year, although coffee consumption declines by 12 percent or more below the year's average in the warm summer months. Therefore, coffee imports and roasts both tend to decline in spring and summer and pick up again in fall and winter.

The very low prices for coffee in 2000-03 created serious problems for coffee producers. When prices fall below the costs of production, there is little or no economic incentive to produce coffee. The result is that coffee trees are neglected or completely abandoned. When prices are low, producers cannot afford to hire the labor needed to maintain the trees and pick the crop at harvest. The result is that trees yield less due to reduced use of fertilizer and fewer employed coffee workers. One effect is a decline in the quality of the coffee that is produced. Higher quality Arabica coffee is often produced at higher altitudes, which entails higher costs. It is this coffee that is often abandoned. Although the pressure on producers can be severe, the market eventually comes back into balance as supply declines in response to low prices.

Coffee prices are subject to upward spikes in June, July and August due to possible freeze scares in Brazil during the winter months in the Southern Hemisphere. The Brazilian coffee crop is harvested starting in May and extending for several weeks into what are the winter months in Brazil. A major freeze in Brazil occurs roughly every five years on average.

Coffee futures are traded on the Bolsa de Mercadorias & Futuros (BM&F), the Tokyo Grain Exchange (TGE), the London International Financial Futures and Options Exchange (LIFFE), and the ICE Futures U.S. (ICE) exchange. Options are traded on the BM&F, the LIFFE and the ICE.

Prices – ICE Arabica coffee futures prices showed weakness during 2008 due to the financial crisis and the global recession, falling by 39% from the 11-year high of 166.75 cents per pound posted in February 2008. However, coffee prices bottomed out at a 2-1/2 year low of 101.60 cents per pound in December 2008 and then rallied through most of 2009. Coffee prices posted a new 1-1/2 year high in December 2009 and closed the year up 21% at 135.95 cents. Bullish factors in 2009 included (1) the global economic recovery, which boosted coffee demand, (2) the 14% y/y decline in Brazil's 2008-09 harvest, (3) the USDA's forecast for a 3.7% decline in 2009-10 world coffee production to 125.2 million bags, and (4) a sharp 15% decline in 2009-10 world ending stocks to 34.7 million bags, which would produce a record low in the stocks/supply ratio of 13.7% (data back to 1960). The tight supply situation was also illustrated by the fact that coffee supplies in exchange warehouses were at the lowest levels in a decade in late 2009. In addition, Brazil is expected to have near-zero inventories by spring 2010, meaning Brazil will have no buffer stocks to sell even at higher prices.

Supply – World coffee production in the 2009-10 marketing year (July-June) fell -3.7% yr/yr to 125.214 million bags (1 bag equals 60 kilograms or 132.3 pounds), down from last year's record high of 130.030 million bags. The decrease in production caused the 2009-10 ending stocks to fall -15.3% to 34,690 million bags.

Brazil is the world's largest coffee producer by far with 43.5 million bags of production in 2009-10, which was 35% of total world production. Other key producers include Vietnam with 14% of the world's production and with Columbia and Indonesia each with 7%. Brazil's coffee production in 2009-10 fell -15.5% y/y to 43.5 million bags. Vietnam has become a major coffee producer in recent years, boosting its production to 17.500 million bags in 2009-10, up from less than a million bags in 1990.

Demand – U.S. coffee consumption in 2009 fell -2.9% to 22.550 million bags, but still not far below the record high of 25.377 million bags seen in 1968.

Trade – World coffee exports in 2009-10 fell -10.9% yr/yr to 91.474 million bags, down from last year's record high of 102.710 million bags. The world's largest exporters of coffee in 2009-10 were Brazil with 27% of world exports, Vietnam with 18%, and Columbia with 9%. U.S. coffee imports in 2008 (latest data) was virtually unchanged from the previous year at 23.217 million bags. The all-time high of 24.549 million bags was posted in 1962. The key countries from which the U.S. imported coffee in 2008 were Brazil (which accounted for 21% of U.S. imports), Columbia (18%), Guatemala (8%), and Mexico (6%).

World Supply and Distribution of Coffee for Producing Countries In Thousands of 60 Kilogram Bags

Year	Beginning Stocks	Production	Imports	Total Supply	Total Exports	Bean Exports	Rst/Grn Exports	Soluble Exports	Domestic Use	Ending Stocks
2000-01	20,875	117,521	1,478	139,874	90,937	84,853	289	5,795	26,319	22,618
2001-02	22,618	111,518	1,647	135,783	88,292	81,739	337	6,216	27,774	19,717
2002-03	19,717	128,422	28,418	150,977	95,231	88,499	293	6,439	47,987	34,594
2003-04	34,594	111,561	71,715	182,140	91,172	83,758	317	7,097	97,886	42,807
2004-05	42,807	122,616	82,521	247,139	91,142	83,778	294	7,070	108,536	46,006
2005-06	46,006	116,951	83,155	242,277	87,036	80,187	350	6,499	114,858	38,611
2006-07	38,611	133,565	88,185	260,501	101,925	94,285	344	7,296	115,743	42,833
2007-08[1]	42,833	122,180	87,367	252,380	88,271	88,148	444	7,544	118,854	36,680
2008-09[2]	36,680	130,030	88,711	255,421	102,710	94,514	460	7,736	117,155	40,959
2009-10[3]	40,959	125,214	86,524	252,697	91,474	91,725			121,706	34,690

[1] Preliminary. [2] Estimate. [3] Forecast. 132.276 Lbs. Per Bag *Source: Foreign Agricultural Service, U.S. Department of Agriculture (FAS-USDA)*

World Production of Green Coffee In Thousands of 60 Kilogram Bags

Crop Year	Brazil	Colombia	Costa Rica	El Salvador	Ethiopia	Guatemala	India	Indonesia	Ivory Coast	Mexico	Uganda	Vietnam	World Total
2000-01	34,100	10,500	2,502	1,624	2,768	4,564	5,020	6,495	5,100	4,800	3,401	15,333	117,521
2001-02	35,100	11,950	2,338	1,610	3,756	3,530	5,010	6,160	3,568	4,200	3,158	12,833	111,518
2002-03	53,600	11,712	2,207	1,351	3,693	3,802	4,588	6,140	3,145	4,350	2,890	11,167	128,422
2003-04	33,200	11,053	2,106	1,343	3,875	3,671	4,508	6,000	2,689	4,428	2,599	15,000	111,561
2004-05	43,600	11,532	1,907	1,329	4,575	3,817	4,672	8,450	2,301	3,900	2,593	14,500	122,616
2005-06	36,100	11,953	1,751	1,387	4,000	3,605	4,617	9,450	1,962	4,000	2,159	16,335	116,951
2006-07	46,700	12,164	1,782	1,300	4,650	4,050	4,800	8,050	2,847	4,200	2,500	19,500	133,565
2007-08[1]	39,100	12,515	1,867	1,650	4,200	3,980	4,665	7,300	1,500	4,500	2,500	18,000	122,180
2008-09[2]	51,450	8,664	1,622	1,650	3,700	3,700	4,375	8,200	1,400	4,450	2,600	18,000	130,030
2009-10[3]	43,500	9,000	1,730	1,520	4,300	4,100	4,900	9,000	2,000	4,500	2,800	17,500	125,214

[1] Preliminary. [2] Estimate. [3] Forecast. 132.276 Lbs. Per Bag *Source: Foreign Agricultural Service, U.S. Department of Agriculture (FAS-USDA)*

World Exportable[4] Production of Green Coffee In Thousands of 60 Kilogram Bags

Crop Year	Brazil	Colombia	Ethiopia	Guatemala	Honduras	India	Indonesia	Ivory Coast	Mexico	Peru	Uganda	Vietnam	World Total
2000-01	19,676	9,460	1,418	4,414	2,470	3,702	5,536	4,045	3,822	2,664	3,075	14,667	90,937
2001-02	24,795	10,665	1,939	3,330	2,617	3,442	4,729	3,058	3,200	2,360	3,153	12,000	88,292
2002-03	29,396	10,478	2,277	3,500	2,438	3,567	4,801	5,166	3,400	2,575	2,810	11,176	95,231
2003-04	24,920	10,154	2,375	3,314	2,794	3,826	4,408	2,622	3,550	2,685	2,523	14,500	91,172
2004-05	27,920	11,032	2,625	3,451	2,450	2,790	4,600	1,984	2,107	3,306	2,489	13,992	91,142
2005-06	24,543	10,752	2,550	3,325	2,978	3,580	5,070	1,645	2,600	2,225	2,002	12,958	87,036
2006-07	29,260	11,237	2,775	3,700	3,248	3,664	4,710	2,691	2,720	4,430	2,700	18,600	101,925
2007-08[1]	21,710	11,378	2,200	3,642	3,594	2,937	5,340	1,201	2,300	3,832	2,440	17,100	88,271
2008-09[2]	33,340	7,464	1,600	3,365	3,295	2,472	6,447	1,085	2,250	3,905	2,500	16,936	102,710
2009-10[3]	24,850	7,900	2,100	3,765	3,661	3,000	6,730	1,690	2,300	3,780	2,700	16,385	91,474

[1] Preliminary. [2] Estimate. [3] Forecast. [4] Marketing year begins in October in some countries and April or July in others. Exportable production represents total harvested production minus estimated domestic consumption. 132.276 Lbs. Per Bag
Source: Foreign Agricultural Service, U.S. Department of Agriculture (FAS-USDA)

Coffee[2] Imports in the United States In Thousands of 60 Kilogram Bags

Year	Brazil	Colombia	Costa Rica	Republic	Ecuador	El Salvador	Ethiopia	Guatemala	Indonesia	Mexico	Peru	Venezuela	World Total
1999	4,847	3,418	783	80	461	550	77	2,149	724	3,276	766	372	21,787
2000	2,747	3,191	780	73	177	1,209	91	2,380	693	3,725	868	32	22,840
2001	3,007	3,272	915	50	230	507	80	2,040	887	2,057	692	4	20,490
2002	5,060	3,596	987	51	145	470	74	1,626	759	2,034	842	170	20,631
2003	5,321	3,883	914	80	133	569	101	2,023	966	1,510	807	180	21,694
2004	4,475	3,714	957	2	157	524	121	1,624	1,636	1,477	788	103	22,046
2005	4,464	4,090	920	2	74	406	177	1,752	1,599	1,285	587	0	21,791
2006	4,794	3,904	751	60	147	435	250	1,654	1,677	1,528	850	2	22,657
2007	4,968	4,064	823	35	123	565	234	1,815	1,122	1,495	919	25	23,215
2008[1]	4,971	4,245	952	35	40	657	349	1,901	1,351	1,427	963	93	23,217

[1] Preliminary. 132.276 Lbs. Per Bag *Source: Bureau of Census, U.S. Department of Commerce*

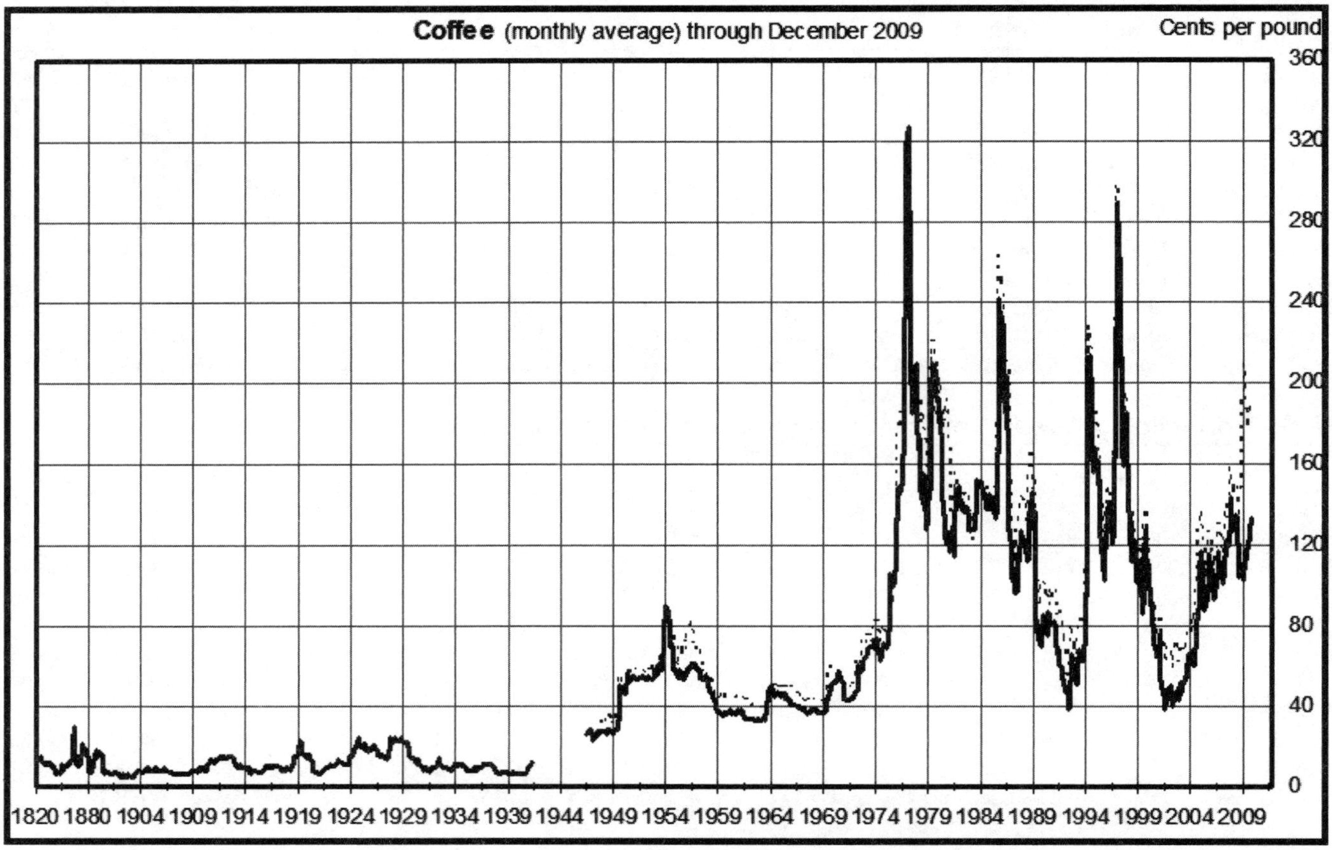

Monthly Coffee[2] Imports in the United States — In Thousands of 60 Kilogram Bags (132.276 Lbs. Per Bag)

Year	Jan.	Feb.	Mar.	Apr.	May	June	July	Aug.	Sept.	Oct.	Nov.	Dec.	Total
2000	2,189	2,092	2,416	2,003	2,199	1,960	1,912	1,815	1,598	1,583	1,546	1,527	22,840
2001	1,747	1,690	1,906	1,825	1,823	1,685	1,863	1,605	1,430	1,502	1,581	1,833	20,490
2002	1,652	1,364	1,613	1,697	1,672	1,547	1,802	1,794	1,850	1,877	1,807	1,958	20,631
2003	1,994	1,755	2,007	1,916	1,715	1,710	2,015	1,732	1,712	1,750	1,525	1,863	21,694
2004	1,813	1,635	1,967	1,862	2,049	2,034	1,784	1,766	1,708	1,684	1,798	1,947	22,047
2005	1,939	1,942	2,072	1,965	1,893	1,891	1,781	1,606	1,481	1,718	1,699	1,803	21,791
2006	1,852	1,647	2,042	1,672	2,007	1,916	1,780	2,091	2,089	1,894	1,834	1,833	22,657
2007	2,167	1,760	1,992	2,015	1,887	1,743	2,005	2,249	2,037	2,038	1,712	1,608	23,215
2008	1,987	1,867	2,117	2,073	2,002	1,945	1,980	1,851	1,977	1,863	1,542	2,012	23,217
2009[1]	1,872	1,679	1,996	1,980	2,041	2,196	2,357	1,895	1,662	1,604	1,389		22,550

[1] Preliminary. [2] Data through 1999 are for Green Coffee. *Source: Bureau of the Census, U.S. Department of Commerce*

Average Price of Brazilian[1] Coffee in New York — In Cents Per Pound

Year	Jan.	Feb.	Mar.	Apr.	May	June	July	Aug.	Sept.	Oct.	Nov.	Dec.	Average
2000	97.68	91.51	89.93	86.46	87.23	78.32	79.89	70.57	71.14	72.28	68.95	64.39	79.86
2001	62.38	62.50	60.35	55.11	57.19	51.86	46.43	46.49	42.42	38.63	42.28	41.60	50.60
2002	42.56	42.79	48.79	49.90	45.19	42.96	43.58	40.55	44.46	45.28	48.37	46.70	45.09
2003	49.14	48.54	43.77	48.71	51.06	47.11	49.64	52.88	55.19	53.51	54.15	56.92	50.89
2004	64.32	66.08	65.79	62.89	64.31	67.62	59.39	60.25	69.46	68.63	80.20	89.17	68.18
2005	94.00	108.05	117.03	112.82	111.89	105.08	94.66	95.66	87.02	94.54	99.35	96.23	101.36
2006	115.89	109.51	103.52	105.89	99.00	91.26	91.01	98.90	97.36	97.39	109.34	115.60	102.89
2007	111.99	109.78	102.34	100.84	99.66	105.89	105.25	112.47	116.43	120.95	118.99	124.06	110.72
2008	126.26	142.25	130.45	123.15	125.18	130.52	131.10	131.85	126.82	104.57	102.74	95.22	122.51
2009	101.43	100.45	97.48	101.46	113.13	109.81	104.55	114.01	114.12	122.84	126.21	131.23	111.39

[1] And other Arabicas. *Source: Foreign Agricultural Service, U.S. Department of Agriculture (FAS-USDA)*

Average Monthly Retail[1] Price of Coffee in the United States In Cents Per Pound

Year	Jan.	Feb.	Mar.	Apr.	May	June	July	Aug.	Sept.	Oct.	Nov.	Dec.	Average
2002	293.6	294.6	285.9	297.6	301.1	293.8	297.7	292.9	292.1	287.2	288.2	283.8	292.4
2003	299.9	292.4	293.3	300.8	293.7	293.1	294.4	292.1	291.9	282.5	277.9	287.5	291.6
2004	289.2	285.6	293.2	290.8	283.1	275.0	287.8	287.8	287.4	284.0	277.8	277.6	284.9
2005	304.9	294.0	300.9	324.0	332.9	341.6	333.4	342.8	337.6	344.7	329.3	323.5	325.8
2006	323.2	317.4	330.1	329.2	334.9	315.8	315.4	319.6	317.3	313.8	315.8	311.3	320.3
2007	328.8	345.6	347.5	343.7	330.8	340.7	352.9	349.7	NA	NA	360.7	368.5	346.9
2008	NA	NA	NA	NA	NA	NA	NA	NA	NA	NA	NA	NA	NA
2009	NA	NA	NA	NA	NA	NA	NA	NA	NA	NA	NA	NA	NA

[1] Roasted in 13.1 to 20 ounce cans. *Source: Foreign Agricultural Service, U.S. Department of Agriculture (FAS-USDA)*

Average Price of Colombian Mild Arabicas[1] in the United States In Cents Per Pound

Year	Jan.	Feb.	Mar.	Apr.	May	June	July	Aug.	Sept.	Oct.	Nov.	Dec.	Average
2002	63.46	65.64	71.16	70.17	63.44	60.86	59.60	58.98	62.49	66.54	72.83	67.92	65.26
2003	69.68	69.60	61.82	66.12	67.56	65.01	67.84	68.65	68.37	66.59	67.04	69.38	67.31
2004	76.61	79.34	80.12	77.08	80.61	85.62	78.27	78.85	85.71	85.52	95.63	106.48	84.15
2005	110.03	124.34	137.10	129.80	128.36	122.47	112.48	111.21	101.31	108.77	111.66	106.54	117.01
2006	129.64	123.17	117.00	119.87	113.03	106.84	109.45	116.22	112.26	113.73	126.23	132.85	118.36
2007	127.54	125.54	119.92	117.51	116.14	122.35	122.32	126.68	131.51	137.71	133.81	139.87	126.74
2008	143.37	161.30	151.48	142.41	143.51	150.60	151.56	154.23	150.20	133.37	133.40	134.72	145.85
2009	148.88	149.58	162.00	190.94	225.58	195.27	192.11	181.61	169.90	175.16	180.08	199.38	180.87

[1] ICO monthly and composite indicator prices on the New York Market, 1979 ICA Agreement basis. *Source: Foreign Agricultural Service, U.S. Department of Agriculture (FAS-USDA)*

Average Price of Other Mild Arabicas[1] in the United States In Cents Per Pound

Year	Jan.	Feb.	Mar.	Apr.	May	June	July	Aug.	Sept.	Oct.	Nov.	Dec.	Average
2002	57.34	60.51	66.38	65.78	58.45	55.12	53.07	52.02	57.58	64.05	70.15	64.75	60.43
2003	65.22	67.60	61.66	65.35	66.47	61.34	62.32	63.60	65.50	62.58	62.36	65.01	64.08
2004	74.25	77.51	77.29	74.24	76.40	82.24	73.64	72.99	81.22	79.90	89.88	102.19	80.15
2005	107.07	122.20	134.81	128.80	126.21	119.87	108.45	108.43	98.17	106.09	108.81	102.68	114.30
2006	124.26	118.46	112.20	114.65	107.96	101.21	102.77	112.13	109.36	110.91	123.57	129.93	113.95
2007	124.40	122.34	116.44	114.59	112.35	118.76	116.80	123.53	128.04	134.43	130.28	136.47	123.20
2008	139.10	158.03	148.07	138.06	139.32	144.90	145.13	146.03	141.50	122.04	120.76	116.87	138.32
2009	128.03	128.63	127.76	134.44	147.34	145.17	137.87	146.87	145.67	151.95	150.23	155.86	141.65

[1] ICO monthly and composite indicator prices on the New York Market, 1979 ICA Agreement basis. *Source: Foreign Agricultural Service, U.S. Department of Agriculture (FAS-USDA)*

Average Price of Robustas 1976[1] in the United States In Cents Per Pound

Year	Jan.	Feb.	Mar.	Apr.	May	June	July	Aug.	Sept.	Oct.	Nov.	Dec.	Average
2002	22.88	24.46	29.77	30.35	29.43	29.26	29.31	28.74	33.31	34.44	39.38	38.68	30.83
2003	42.75	42.35	38.26	38.68	38.90	35.33	36.71	37.92	38.76	37.32	36.05	37.59	38.39
2004	41.32	39.10	38.61	38.02	38.04	41.09	36.44	34.81	35.10	31.77	34.07	38.98	37.28
2005	39.63	44.61	50.70	53.32	58.66	62.96	60.57	55.60	50.07	50.84	54.72	58.79	53.37
2006	66.46	65.50	62.92	64.45	63.97	64.14	68.66	75.73	77.88	76.26	79.67	77.71	70.28
2007	80.55	80.97	78.95	81.64	86.06	94.76	93.47	88.51	93.61	97.34	92.28	91.37	88.29
2008	100.68	117.10	122.44	112.06	109.58	112.16	115.09	113.48	106.67	89.69	92.81	83.99	106.31
2009	85.77	81.66	77.48	76.50	77.00	75.88	74.83	75.04	77.31	76.68	73.08	74.68	77.16

[1] ICO monthly and composite indicator prices on the New York Market, 1979 ICA Agreement basis. *Source: Foreign Agricultural Service, U.S. Department of Agriculture (FAS-USDA)*

Average Price of Composite 1979[1] in the United States In Cents Per Pound

Year	Jan.	Feb.	Mar.	Apr.	May	June	July	Aug.	Sept.	Oct.	Nov.	Dec.	Average
2002	43.46	44.30	49.49	50.19	47.30	45.56	44.70	42.79	47.96	50.79	54.69	51.68	47.74
2003	54.04	54.07	49.61	51.87	53.19	48.90	50.89	52.22	54.10	51.72	49.81	52.44	51.91
2004	58.69	59.87	60.80	58.80	59.91	64.28	58.46	56.98	61.47	61.10	67.74	77.72	62.15
2005	79.35	89.40	101.44	98.20	99.78	96.29	88.48	85.31	78.79	82.55	85.93	86.85	89.36
2006	101.20	97.39	92.76	94.20	90.00	86.04	101.20	95.78	95.98	95.53	103.48	108.01	96.80
2007	105.81	104.18	100.09	99.30	100.09	107.03	106.20	107.98	113.20	115.71	114.43	118.16	107.68
2008	122.33	138.82	136.17	126.55	126.76	130.51	132.78	131.14	126.69	108.31	107.88	103.07	124.25
2009	108.39	107.60	105.87	111.61	123.05	119.05	112.90	117.45	116.40	121.09	119.67	124.96	115.67

[1] ICO monthly and composite indicator prices on the New York Market, 1979 ICA Agreement basis. *Source: Foreign Agricultural Service, U.S. Department of Agriculture (FAS-USDA)*

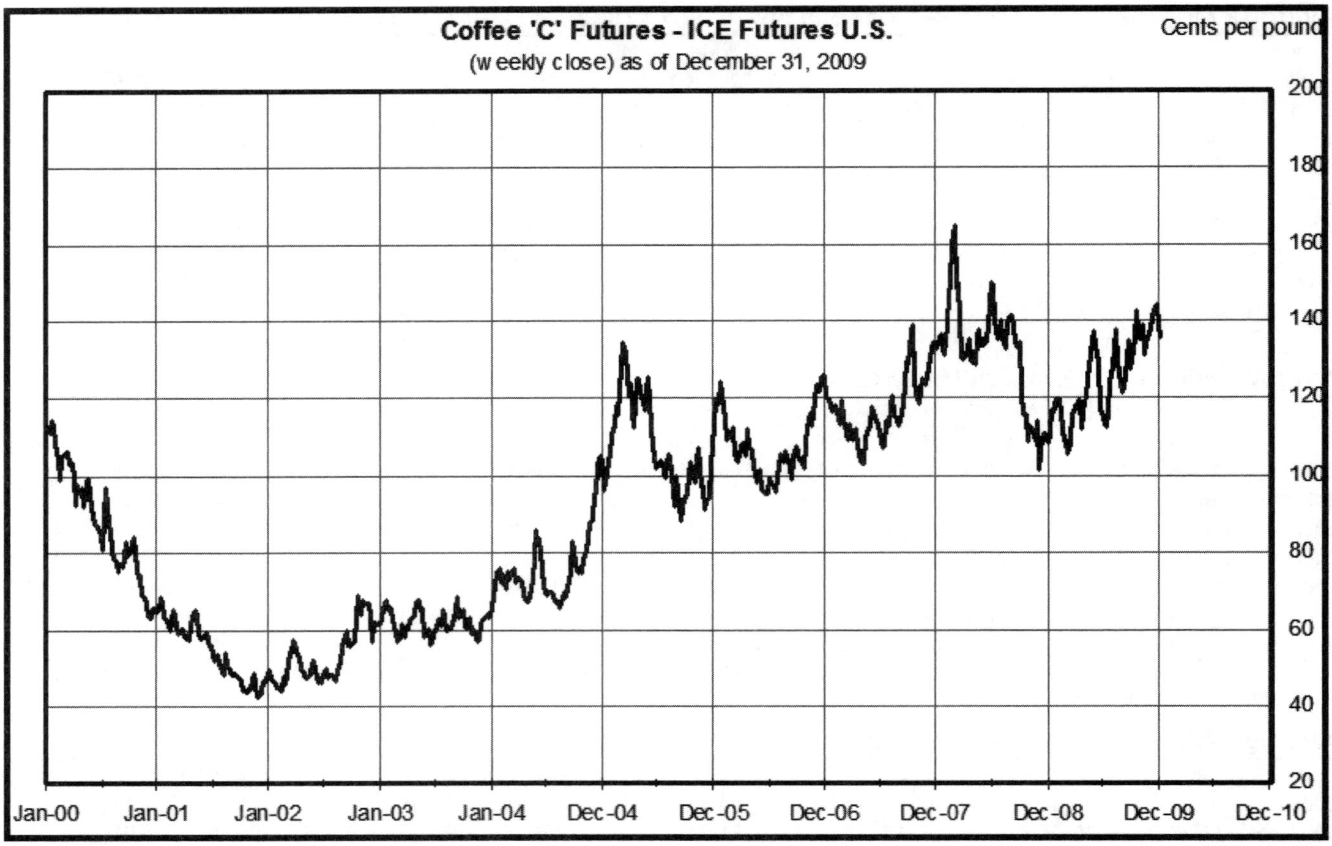

Average Open Interest of Coffee "C" Futures in New York In Contracts

Year	Jan.	Feb.	Mar.	Apr.	May	June	July	Aug.	Sept.	Oct.	Nov.	Dec.
2000	47,829	50,620	50,565	53,662	49,692	50,293	45,513	40,177	40,133	42,906	43,187	45,086
2001	48,914	53,050	58,111	57,722	53,481	58,311	57,888	57,243	55,674	58,345	55,317	53,953
2002	57,897	66,825	66,798	66,207	66,289	68,994	69,197	69,635	70,079	73,753	73,431	69,343
2003	69,508	71,682	76,934	77,954	72,716	72,155	72,110	68,259	73,809	79,038	81,253	76,670
2004	92,388	103,966	102,281	98,430	96,738	102,276	89,446	88,021	83,001	78,047	83,360	107,832
2005	102,163	107,715	117,419	105,245	96,063	94,139	93,303	89,662	85,518	86,489	81,525	81,234
2006	102,195	102,614	99,982	102,882	104,230	120,907	120,007	107,928	105,175	111,392	117,469	123,259
2007	128,158	132,849	141,033	146,723	159,011	157,086	168,019	163,288	162,445	173,426	158,146	160,331
2008	176,128	193,555	179,957	160,544	150,017	146,166	147,056	133,178	126,573	132,112	116,643	118,223
2009	129,577	130,101	135,143	134,290	134,827	127,263	107,711	100,880	97,935	114,065	118,016	123,699

Source: ICE Futures U.S. (ICE)

Volume of Trading of Coffee "C" Futures in New York In Contracts

Year	Jan.	Feb.	Mar.	Apr.	May	June	July	Aug.	Sept.	Oct.	Nov.	Dec.	Total
2000	158,962	232,174	166,970	224,266	177,753	218,467	198,975	175,868	119,304	163,399	187,230	111,593	2,134,961
2001	189,977	221,775	167,466	236,757	182,621	220,708	134,809	250,151	100,443	153,739	229,495	111,430	2,199,371
2002	201,327	279,966	229,764	295,701	159,670	225,177	174,567	254,563	232,255	250,483	236,307	178,728	2,718,508
2003	205,420	283,317	169,611	334,188	255,935	270,424	237,210	278,746	332,473	309,930	314,182	219,595	3,211,031
2004	389,864	397,656	301,270	395,552	324,849	467,887	247,439	366,171	305,196	280,733	424,146	292,540	4,193,303
2005	280,912	469,605	356,855	459,018	240,989	428,227	224,531	404,307	259,177	266,697	376,844	220,616	3,987,778
2006	357,994	416,964	326,256	429,249	322,932	476,542	289,027	481,870	238,953	313,459	492,904	261,362	4,407,512
2007	334,593	468,712	383,506	474,542	373,291	600,122	361,467	596,622	373,925	484,038	468,987	208,818	5,128,623
2008	419,096	729,397	515,528	556,002	354,887	642,074	317,917	512,002	381,241	384,451	383,346	250,575	5,446,516
2009	309,386	406,786	328,940	404,635	305,326	435,239	244,504	388,567	244,371	332,043	535,063	300,489	4,235,349

Source: ICE Futures U.S. (ICE)

Coke

Coke is the hard and porous residue left after certain types of bituminous coals are heated to high temperatures (up to 2,000 degrees Fahrenheit) for about 17 hours. It is blackish-gray and has a metallic luster. The residue is mostly carbon. Coke is used as a reducing agent in the smelting of pig iron and the production of steel. Petroleum coke is made from the heavy tar-like residue of the petroleum refining process. It is used primarily to generate electricity.

Supply – Production of petroleum coke in the U.S. in 2009 (annualized through April) fell 1.9% yr/yr to 293.115 million barrels. That was further down from the 2006 three-decade high of 309.980 and far below the U.S. production record of 369.305 million barrels posted back in 1957. U.S. stocks of coke at coke plants (Dec 31) in 2008 rose by +44.9% yr/yr to 916,000 short tons.

Trade – U.S. coke exports in 2008 rose +35.7% to an almost 3-decade high of 1.959 million tons, and over a third of those exports were to Canada. U.S. coke imports in 2008 rose by +46.5% yr/yr to 3.603 million short tons. About 17% of the imports were from Japan.

Salient Statistics of Coke in the United States In Thousands of Short Tons

	Coke and Breeze Production at Coke Plants — By Census Division									Exports		Imports	
Year	Middle Atlantic	East North Central	East South Central	Other	Total	Coke Total	Breeze Total	Consumption[2]	Producer and Distributor Stocks Dec. 31	Canada	Total	Japan	Total
2003	W	8,642	2,068	7,738	18,448	17,173	1,275	19,436	380	436	722	1,395	2,759
2004	W	8,614	2,104	7,356	18,074	16,909	1,165	22,492	351	596	1,319	943	6,873
2005	W	8,448	W	9,456	17,904	16,719	1,184	18,239	614	764	1,747	699	3,529
2006	W	8,439	W	9,112	17,551	16,404	1,147	18,784	685	840	1,616	838	4,068
2007	W	8,009	W	9,409	17,418	16,201	1,217	17,270	632	589	1,444	791	2,460
2008[1]	W	7,578	W	9,153	16,731	15,646	1,085	17,006	916	758	1,959	604	3,603

[1] Preliminary. [2] Equal to production plus imports minus the change in producer and distributor stocks minus exports.
W = Withheld. *Source: Energy Information Administration, U.S. Department of Energy (EIA-DOE)*

Production of Petroleum Coke in the United States In Thousands of Barrels

Year	Jan.	Feb.	Mar.	Apr.	May	June	July	Aug.	Sept.	Oct.	Nov.	Dec.	Total
2003	23,420	20,030	23,810	23,768	24,831	24,054	26,080	25,746	24,072	24,588	24,208	26,560	291,167
2004	25,640	22,380	24,025	25,086	26,789	25,874	26,263	26,151	24,259	25,899	25,897	27,599	305,862
2005	25,093	23,806	26,896	25,648	27,209	26,950	26,612	26,410	22,209	22,039	24,372	26,575	303,819
2006	26,180	23,706	25,722	24,987	26,690	26,128	26,372	26,395	26,300	25,957	25,048	26,495	309,980
2007	25,883	22,117	25,369	24,592	26,071	24,904	26,345	26,316	24,613	24,143	24,220	26,050	300,623
2008	25,862	22,994	24,616	24,100	25,432	25,801	26,691	25,993	21,350	24,796	25,196	25,875	298,706
2009[1]	25,902	21,991	25,071	24,741	24,402	25,339	25,205	24,862	24,364	23,823	22,490	23,857	292,047

[1] Preliminary. *Source: Energy Information Administration, U.S. Department of Energy (EIA-DOE)*

Coal Receipts and Average Prices at Coke Plants in the United States

	Coal Receipts at Coke Plants — By Census Division, in Thousands of Short Tons					Average Price of Coal Receipts at Coke Plants — By Census Division, In Dollars per Short Ton				
Year	Middle Atlantic	East North Central	East South Central	Other	Total	Middle Atlantic	East North Central	East South Central	Other	Total
2003	W	11,252	2,452	10,019	23,723	W	52.94	48.20	W	50.63
2004	W	11,591	2,710	9,795	24,096	W	63.30	59.16	W	61.50
2005	W	11,523	W	12,778	24,301	W	89.97	W	W	83.79
2006	W	11,488	W	11,865	23,353	W	99.48	W	W	92.87
2007	W	9,907	W	11,725	21,632	W	99.20	W	W	94.97
2008[1]	W	10,362	W	12,067	22,429	W	122.18	W	W	118.09

[1] Preliminary. W = Withheld. *Source: Energy Information Administration, U.S. Department of Energy (EIA-DOE)*

Coal Carbonized and Coke and Breeze Stocks at Coke Plants in the United States In Thousands of Short Tons

	Coal Carbonized at Coke Plants — By Census Division					Stocks at Coke Plants, Dec. 31 — By Census Division						
Year	Middle Atlantic	East North Central	East South Central	Other	Total	Middle Atlantic	East North Central	East South Central	Other	Total	Coke Total	Breeze Total
2003	W	11,410	2,541	10,297	24,248	W	233	135	144	512	380	132
2004	W	11,322	2,644	9,704	23,670	W	166	154	144	464	351	113
2005	W	11,064	W	12,370	23,434	W	363	W	383	746	614	132
2006	W	11,100	W	11,857	22,957	W	487	W	284	771	685	87
2007	W	10,486	W	12,229	22,715	W	414	W	296	710	632	78
2008[1]	W	10,228	W	11,842	22,070	W	658	W	335	993	916	77

[1] Preliminary. W = Withheld. *Source: Energy Information Administration, U.S. Department of Energy (EIA-DOE)*

Copper

The word copper comes from name of the Mediterranean island Cyprus that was a primary source of the metal. Dating back more than 10,000 years, copper is the oldest metal used by humans. From the Pyramid of Cheops in Egypt, archeologists recovered a portion of a water plumbing system whose copper tubing was found in serviceable condition after more than 5,000 years.

Copper is one of the most widely used industrial metals because it is an excellent conductor of electricity, has strong corrosion-resistance properties, and is very ductile. It is also used to produce the alloys of brass (a copper-zinc alloy) and bronze (a copper-tin alloy), both of which are far harder and stronger than pure copper. Electrical uses of copper account for about 75% of total copper usage, and building construction is the single largest market (the average U.S. home contains 400 pounds of copper). Copper is biostatic, meaning that bacteria will not grow on its surface, and it is therefore used in air-conditioning systems, food processing surfaces, and doorknobs to prevent the spread of disease.

Copper futures and options are traded on the London Metal Exchange (LME) and the New York Mercantile Exchange (NYMEX). Copper futures are traded on the Shanghai Futures Exchange. The NYMEX copper futures contract calls for the delivery of 25,000 pounds of Grade 1 electrolyte copper and is priced in terms of cents per pound.

Prices – NYMEX copper futures prices plunged by an overall 71% from the record high of $4.27 per pound posted in May 2008 to a 5-1/2 year low of $1.25 in December 2008 due to the financial crisis and the global recession. However, copper prices in 2009 then rallied sharply to post a 1-1/2 year high of $3.52 by January 2010. The main driver of the rally was the global economic recovery and particularly strong copper demand from China where GDP bottomed out at +6.2% in Q1-2009 and then improved to +10.7% by Q4-2009. Copper prices were also boosted in early 2009 by a big drawdown in copper inventories during spring and summer 2009.

Supply – World production of copper in 2009 rose by +2.6% yr/yr to 15.800 million metric tons, which was a new record high. The largest producer of copper was Chile with 34% of the world's production, followed by the U.S. with 8%, Peru with 8%, China with 6%, and Australia with 6%. U.S. production of refined copper in 2008 (latest data) fell -2.4% yr/yr to 1.279 million short tons, which was far below the record U.S. production level of 2.490 million short tons seen in 1998.

Demand – U.S. consumption of copper in 2007 (latest data) fell 7.1% yr/yr to 2.140 million metric tons. The primary users of copper in the U.S. in 2007 by class of consumer were wire rod mills with 75% of usage, brass mills with 22% of usage, and nominal use of 1% or less by each of foundries, ingot makers, and chemical plants.

Trade – U.S. exports of refined copper in 2008 fell by 29.6% to a 6-year low of 36,500 metric tons. U.S. imports of copper in 2008 fell by 14.0% yr/yr to 723,600 metric tons.

World Mine Production of Copper (Content of Ore) In Thousands of Metric Tons

Year	Australia	Canada[3]	Chile	China	Indonesia	Mexico	Peru	Poland	Russia	South Africa	United States[3]	Zambia	World Total[2]
2000	829.0	633.9	4,602.4	613	1,012.1	364.6	553.9	454.1	570	137.1	1,440	249.1	13,300
2001	871.0	633.5	4,739.0	605	1,081.0	371.1	722.3	474.0	600	141.9	1,340	312.0	13,700
2002	867.8	603.5	4,581.0	593	1,171.7	329.9	844.6	502.8	695	129.6	1,140	330.0	13,600
2003	839.6	557.1	4,904.2	620	1,005.8	355.7	862.6	505.0	675	89.5	1,120	378.0	13,800
2004	854.1	562.8	5,412.5	752	840.3	405.5	1,035.6	531.0	675	87.0	1,160	402.9	14,700
2005	916.3	595.4	5,320.5	777	1,065.0	429.1	1,009.9	512.0	700	88.6	1,140	432.0	15,000
2006	858.8	603.3	5,360.8	889	816.0	334.1	1,048.5	497.0	725	89.5	1,200	474.0	15,100
2007	871.0	589.1	5,557.0	946	772.9	358.0	1,190.3	452.0	740	97.0	1,170	528.0	15,400
2008[1]	886.0	607.0	5,330.0	950	651.0	247.0	1,270.0	430.0	750		1,310	546.0	15,400
2009[2]	900.0	520.0	5,320.0	960	950.0	250.0	1,260.0	440.0	750		1,190	655.0	15,800

[1] Preliminary. [2] Estimate. [3] Recoverable. *Source: U.S. Geological Survey (USGS)*

Commodity Exchange Inc. Warehouse Stocks of Copper, on First of Month In Thousands of Short Tons

Year	Jan.	Feb.	Mar.	Apr.	May	June	July	Aug.	Sept.	Oct.	Nov.	Dec.
2000	91.6	95.6	95.6	95.9	865.2	75.0	73.6	73.2	62.8	62.3	63.4	64.9
2001	64.7	79.3	90.0	105.1	126.5	150.9	165.1	176.1	186.8	199.6	211.0	236.5
2002	269.2	284.8	304.0	314.1	326.0	337.4	355.7	374.6	375.9	380.3	381.6	382.8
2003	399.3	395.2	373.7	362.7	351.2	336.7	320.5	310.6	303.9	299.0	294.4	288.1
2004	280.9	262.7	241.9	213.3	171.7	130.7	95.1	79.0	62.3	49.2	45.5	42.4
2005	48.2	45.8	46.8	43.3	30.1	22.0	15.3	11.0	9.3	7.2	3.7	3.7
2006	6.8	11.7	30.4	20.7	16.7	9.5	7.9	6.8	12.4	22.3	23.2	31.3
2007	34.0	36.2	37.0	36.4	33.7	27.2	22.1	21.8	20.7	20.1	19.0	18.0
2008	14.1	14.0	13.1	11.9	10.8	11.1	11.0	5.4	5.4	9.9	9.9	24.5
2009	NA	40.2	45.3	46.5	54.1	56.8	59.8	54.1	53.5	55.0	55.0	70.7

Source: CME Group; New York Mercantile Exchange (NYMEX)

Salient Statistics of Copper in the United States In Thousands of Metric Tons

	New Copper Produced						Imports[5]		Exports				Blister &	Apparent Consumption	
	From Domestic Ores			From		Secon-			Ore,			Primary	Material	Refined	Primary
			Refin-	Foreign	Total	dary Re-	Unmanu-		Concen-			Producers	in	Copper	& Old
Year	Mines	Smelters	eries	Ores	New	covery	factured	Refined	trate[6]	Refined[7]	COMEX	(Refined)	Solution	(Reported)	Copper[8]
1999	1,600	1,090	1,110	196	1,890	381	1,280	837	63	25	83	566	138	2,980	3,130
2000	1,450	1,000	865	163	1,580	358	1,350	1,060	107	94	59	345	122	3,020	3,090
2001	1,340	919	808	192	1,630	317	1,400	991	45	23	244	952	98	2,620	2,500
2002	1,140	683	725	116	1,440	190	1,230	927	23	27	362	1,030	44	2,370	2,610
2003	1,120	539	532	130	1,250	207	1,140	882	10	93	255	656	57	2,290	2,430
2004	1,160	542	531	140	1,260	191	1,060	807	24	118	44	134	51	2,410	2,550
2005	1,140	523	524	130	1,210	183	1,230	1,000	137	40	6	66	44	2,270	2,400
2006	1,200	501	531	144	1,210	150	1,320	1,070	108	106	31	196	19	2,110	2,190
2007[1]	1,170	617	702	62	1,280	157	1,100	829	134	51	14	133		2,140	2,270
2008[2]	1,310				1,230	166	934	724	301	37		190		2,020	2,020

[1] Preliminary. [2] Estimate. [3] Also from matte, etc., refinery reports. [4] From old scrap only. [5] For consumption. [6] Blister (copper content). [7] Ingots, bars, etc. [8] Old scrap only. W = Withheld. *Source: U.S. Geological Survey (USGS)*

Consumption of Refined Copper[3] in the United States In Thousands of Metric Tons

		By-Products					By Class of Consumer						Total
		Wire	Ingots and	Cakes			Wire Rod	Brass	Chemical	Ingot		Miscel-	Con-
Year	Cathodes	Bars	Ingot Bars	& Slabs	Billets	Other[4]	Mills	Mills	Plants	Makers	Foundries	laneous[5]	sumption
1998	2,600.0	W	30.7	76.2	W	184.0	2,170.0	659.0	1.1	5.4	19.2	31.8	2,890.0
1999	2,710.0	W	24.4	79.3	W	166.0	2,230.0	691.0	1.2	4.5	21.2	29.8	2,980.0
2000	2,730.0	W	23.8	101.0	W	175.0	2,240.0	723.0	1.2	4.6	24.3	32.5	3,030.0
2001	2,360.0	W	24.0	95.9	W	140.0	1,940.0	623.0	1.2	4.6	21.6	28.6	2,620.0
2002	2,140.0	W	22.8	72.6	W	126.0	1,710.0	593.0	1.0	4.6	19.8	35.7	2,370.0
2003	2,070.0	W	22.3	41.8	W	153.0	1,640.0	587.0	1.0	4.6	21.9	36.7	2,290.0
2004	2,160.0	W	21.4	57.0	W	173.0	1,780.0	573.0	1.2	4.6	21.0	35.2	2,410.0
2005	2,040.0	W	28.8	35.3	W	167.0	1,680.0	528.0	1.2	4.5	20.2	39.3	2,270.0
2006[1]	1,910.0	W	30.8	37.1	W	135.0	1,570.0	490.0	1.0	4.5	21.4	24.1	2,110.0
2007[2]	1,930.0	W	28.8	42.7	W	135.0	1,610.0	476.0	1.0	4.5	19.4	25.7	2,140.0

[1] Preliminary. [2] Estimate. [3] Primary & secondary. [4] Includes Wirebars and Billets. [5] Includes iron and steel plants, primary smelters producing alloys other than copper, consumers of copper powder and copper shot, and other manufacturers. W = Withheld.
Source: U.S. Geological Survey (USGS)

London Metals Exchange Warehouse Stocks of Copper, at End of Month In Thousands of Metric Tons

Year	Jan.	Feb.	Mar.	Apr.	May	June	July	Aug.	Sept.	Oct.	Nov.	Dec.
2000	807.3	824.1	755.4	697.8	605.7	553.4	487.8	449.2	401.5	380.9	349.4	357.4
2001	349.9	327.9	400.5	445.2	431.3	464.7	651.9	661.2	729.0	737.2	780.4	799.5
2002	855.5	910.9	950.9	973.8	958.3	892.1	893.6	896.6	870.6	863.2	862.8	855.9
2003	833.8	825.9	813.2	768.2	740.8	665.8	612.6	620.3	580.4	516.5	467.0	430.7
2004	358.2	281.6	187.5	151.3	132.3	101.5	87.7	111.3	91.8	77.9	59.8	48.9
2005	46.4	52.5	45.3	61.0	44.4	28.9	31.6	68.0	79.9	65.1	72.6	92.3
2006	96.0	115.3	120.7	117.6	111.2	93.6	100.6	125.4	116.9	135.2	156.8	190.7
2007	216.2	205.4	181.1	156.6	127.5	112.6	103.5	139.1	130.7	167.1	189.6	199.0
2008	177.9	141.4	111.3	110.1	124.0	122.4	144.6	173.8	199.1	238.0	291.3	240.7
2009[1]	491.3	536.8	501.9	398.8	312.1	265.8	282.2	300.0	346.2	372.2	441.1	

[1] Preliminary. *Source: American Bureau of Metal Statistics (ABMS)*

Copper Refined from Scrap in the United States In Thousands of Metric Tons

Year	Jan.	Feb.	Mar.	Apr.	May	June	July	Aug.	Sept.	Oct.	Nov.	Dec.	Total
1999	20.1	21.8	23.7	17.6	16.2	17.5	21.2	18.2	21.3	21.0	17.7	20.0	230.0
2000	19.4	18.6	25.8	22.5	22.1	15.4	11.7	19.7	14.1	14.3	19.7	15.6	208.0
2001	15.4	14.2	15.2	13.4	12.8	13.2	13.9	13.5	12.3	10.2	6.4	5.7	154.0
2002	7.1	6.2	7.2	7.6	8.2	7.8	7.0	7.6	7.1	6.3	5.1	3.9	81.1
2003	5.8	3.9	5.7	3.9	4.1	4.9	4.9	3.9	4.2	4.5	4.1	4.1	53.8
2004	4.2	3.9	4.3	4.4	4.2	4.5	4.1	3.9	4.7	4.5	4.2	4.0	50.8
2005	4.4	4.4	4.2	4.2	3.8	3.6	3.9	3.6	3.6	3.8	3.8	3.9	47.1
2006	3.8	3.7	3.8	3.7	3.7	3.7	3.7	3.7	3.8	3.7	3.7	3.8	44.8
2007	3.9	3.9	3.4	3.5	3.4	3.4	3.4	3.4	3.5	3.4	3.6	3.5	42.1
2008[1]	4.1	4.2	4.1	4.3	4.6	5.0	4.3	4.5	4.3	4.6	4.6	4.6	53.2

[1] Preliminary. *Source: U.S. Geological Survey (USGS)*

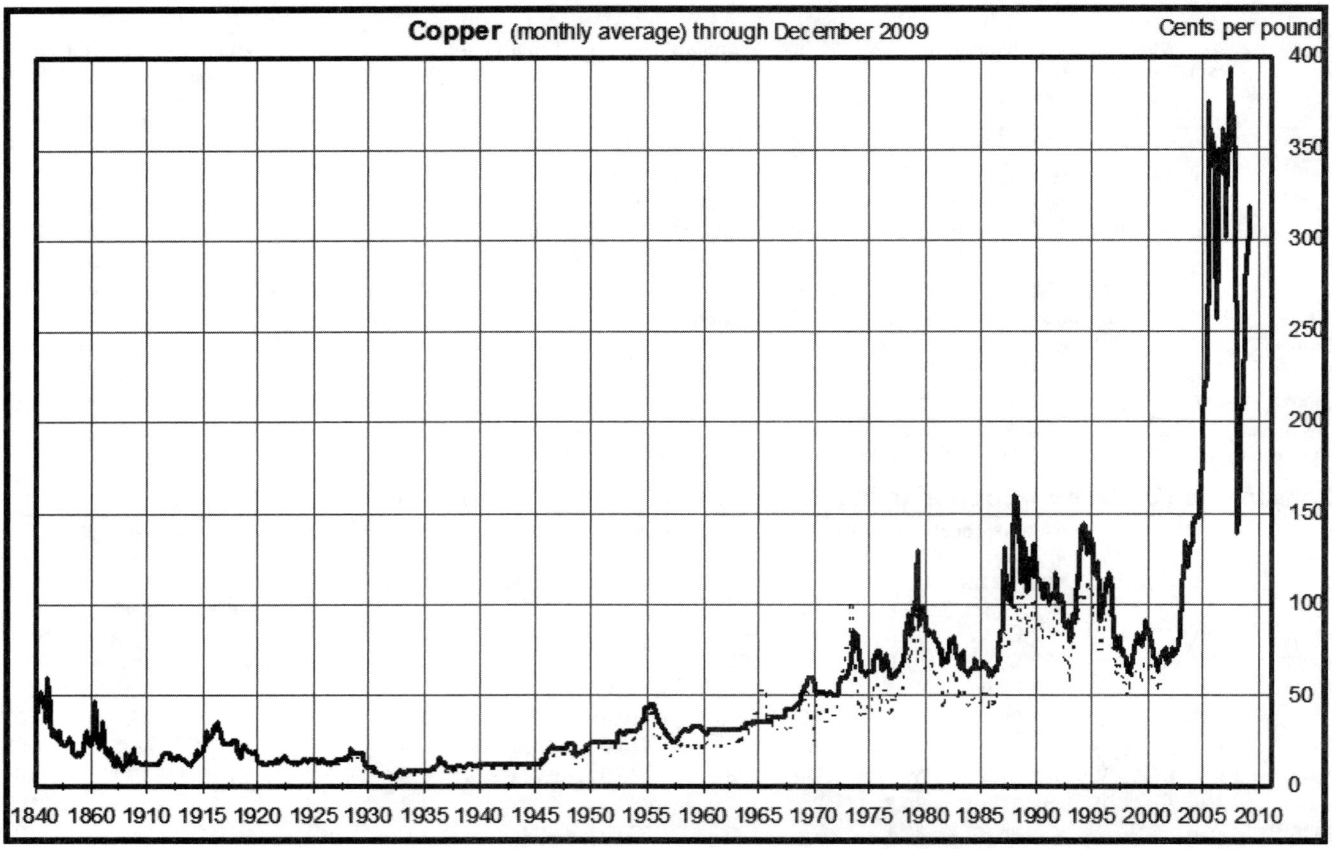

Average Open Interest of Copper Futures in New York In Contracts

Year	Jan.	Feb.	Mar.	Apr.	May	June	July	Aug.	Sept.	Oct.	Nov.	Dec.
2000	82,289	73,778	68,026	75,520	69,531	63,786	71,389	79,565	83,546	73,609	74,161	70,349
2001	77,952	76,721	78,034	83,647	72,970	85,495	83,690	88,782	87,004	88,166	85,809	68,981
2002	72,823	79,806	79,156	75,229	74,350	80,981	82,661	102,056	99,225	99,470	89,213	79,218
2003	81,820	81,499	72,484	85,485	77,704	81,509	82,868	94,517	92,768	106,924	103,218	90,208
2004	91,726	88,136	77,158	71,705	65,531	64,879	65,310	71,096	81,162	85,421	81,928	88,822
2005	85,363	96,537	116,004	120,138	98,240	106,218	109,156	109,481	102,652	106,829	110,972	104,062
2006	102,227	93,813	93,069	97,283	83,758	75,841	74,471	72,158	69,004	72,023	72,517	68,402
2007	69,972	70,373	69,324	78,919	80,834	79,257	88,691	78,113	72,469	86,909	78,385	71,626
2008	81,778	94,021	101,503	105,050	98,787	103,055	109,591	96,254	76,523	80,961	76,869	71,809
2009	82,402	85,831	90,636	103,517	106,511	111,555	111,849	118,935	117,782	127,204	146,612	149,621

Source: CME Group; New York Mercantile Exchange (NYMEX)

Volume of Trading of Copper Futures in New York In Contracts

Year	Jan.	Feb.	Mar.	Apr.	May	June	July	Aug.	Sept.	Oct.	Nov.	Dec.	Total
2000	220,488	276,374	195,668	261,971	232,971	241,854	187,453	283,328	171,080	243,342	266,051	197,544	2,778,124
2001	240,588	246,052	247,722	279,348	260,697	317,001	159,394	298,639	129,622	190,469	337,589	149,520	2,856,641
2002	217,598	233,704	164,747	254,259	218,091	267,201	263,395	303,642	195,637	232,731	276,492	179,789	2,807,286
2003	232,921	269,806	249,306	274,079	221,364	301,709	252,713	324,175	196,481	230,413	363,865	172,438	3,089,270
2004	213,536	385,848	265,312	340,236	203,906	280,882	208,415	310,299	212,082	245,011	317,220	207,878	3,190,625
2005	199,938	391,949	298,181	469,849	288,399	475,756	227,917	435,848	252,733	265,234	458,258	186,780	3,950,842
2006	234,295	401,404	284,478	406,984	260,422	321,626	182,175	310,023	189,405	216,369	320,780	153,351	3,281,312
2007	241,333	333,967	264,511	402,764	292,359	367,217	272,429	451,599	225,624	289,319	412,949	199,097	3,753,168
2008	345,506	459,539	298,485	466,514	344,500	462,033	382,095	463,234	349,533	403,803	414,380	228,444	4,618,066
2009	343,546	446,018	361,084	592,879	373,568	661,946	499,520	746,223	511,205	599,658	809,343	454,049	6,399,039

Source: CME Group; New York Mercantile Exchange (NYMEX)

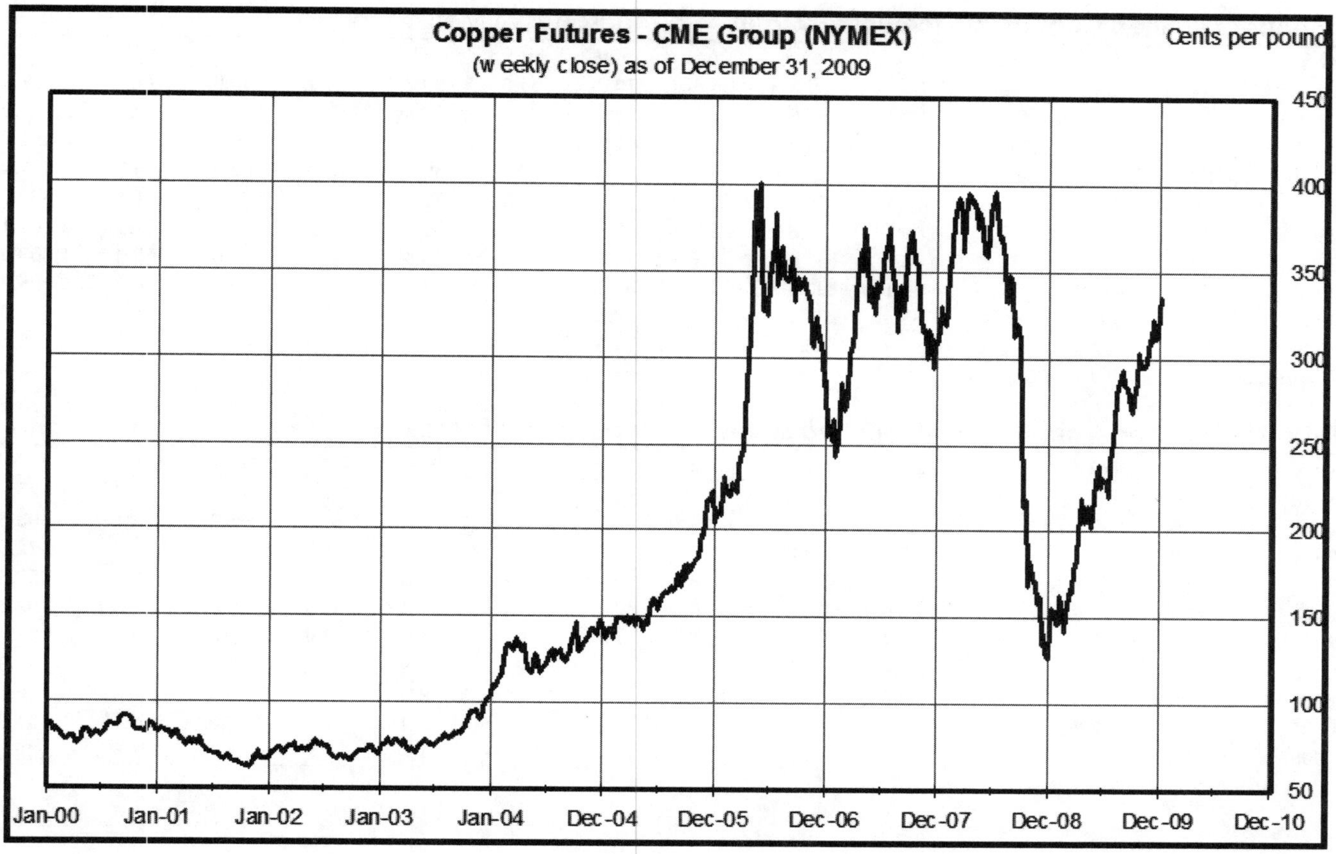

Producers' Price of Electrolytic (Wirebar) Copper, Delivered to U.S. Destinations In Cents Per Pound

Year	Jan.	Feb.	Mar.	Apr.	May	June	July	Aug.	Sept.	Oct.	Nov.	Dec.	Average
2000	96.83	94.41	91.63	89.32	94.80	92.74	95.81	98.67	103.49	99.63	95.25	98.92	95.96
2001	95.70	94.01	92.07	88.27	88.85	84.58	81.44	79.34	77.41	75.21	78.13	79.83	84.57
2002	81.79	84.23	86.60	85.11	85.22	88.23	84.44	79.82	79.71	80.16	84.57	75.56	82.62
2003	78.62	80.21	78.87	75.60	78.56	80.44	81.55	83.51	85.34	91.50	96.47	103.72	84.53
2004	113.93	129.91	139.96	135.82	129.44	129.11	134.34	135.50	138.74	142.01	147.99	151.88	135.72
2005	151.25	152.89	154.68	155.42	154.19	168.31	169.62	178.39	182.00	197.61	208.60	224.25	174.77
2006	225.07	230.74	238.31	302.74	382.65	346.65	368.49	359.91	353.01	345.83	322.45	307.00	315.24
2007	263.89	265.67	298.65	356.76	355.24	346.59	370.42	343.65	351.87	364.48	318.93	306.74	328.57
2008	325.53	364.78	385.98	399.96	383.39	375.08	382.31	349.89	320.54	224.32	174.59	145.09	319.29
2009	153.55	155.38	176.45	209.36	215.36	233.23	243.36	285.81	285.91	292.24	307.45	320.57	239.89

Source: American Metal Market (AMM)

Dealers' Buying Price of No. 2 Heavy Copper Scrap in Chicago In Cents Per Pound

Year	Jan.	Feb.	Mar.	Apr.	May	June	July	Aug.	Sept.	Oct.	Nov.	Dec.	Average
2000	50.00	50.00	50.00	49.15	49.00	49.00	49.30	52.65	54.60	55.00	52.65	51.00	51.04
2001	51.62	49.16	49.00	49.81	50.00	50.00	49.14	44.00	44.00	43.48	41.45	41.47	46.93
2002	41.00	41.00	41.00	41.00	41.00	41.00	41.00	41.00	41.00	41.00	41.00	41.00	41.00
2003	41.00	41.00	41.00	41.00	41.00	41.00	41.00	41.00	41.00	48.17	56.00	56.00	43.99
2004	56.65	69.00	69.00	69.32	76.00	76.00	76.64	90.00	90.00	90.00	90.00	90.00	78.55
2005	90.00	90.00	90.00	90.00	90.00	94.09	100.00	100.00	100.00	100.00	100.00	129.52	97.80
2006	137.50	137.50	139.46	145.00	145.00	171.36	175.25	185.89	184.10	192.09	192.85	183.30	165.78
2007	155.83	153.92	164.32	197.83	210.09	203.60	216.83	219.89	213.97	224.72	210.20	191.87	196.92
2008	198.21	210.00	238.21	246.82	247.02	237.50	240.00	233.93	226.07	141.85	97.50	87.02	200.34
2009	80.00	92.24	104.32	124.40	134.00	155.23	166.59	182.02	192.50	194.40	203.55	224.61	154.49

Source: American Metal Market (AMM)

Imports of Refined Copper into the United States In Thousands of Metric Tons

Year	Jan.	Feb.	Mar.	Apr.	May	June	July	Aug.	Sept.	Oct.	Nov.	Dec.	Total
1999	64.7	53.2	68.1	59.9	62.3	63.8	73.0	84.5	90.3	81.0	59.0	77.5	837.0
2000	84.9	67.8	85.5	92.1	83.6	84.5	89.4	83.0	98.6	112.0	100.0	73.7	1,060.0
2001	105.0	91.6	90.1	94.4	70.3	72.7	61.7	66.3	83.5	71.0	110.0	74.4	991.0
2002	82.5	87.8	53.0	92.6	59.9	76.2	80.3	90.5	69.9	79.0	82.0	73.0	927.0
2003	60.7	87.8	69.9	78.5	72.7	62.3	74.0	78.1	81.7	82.0	73.2	61.1	882.0
2004	55.4	48.8	70.7	59.3	70.8	51.3	83.9	78.7	91.7	68.4	77.0	51.1	807.1
2005	85.2	66.5	75.8	63.7	107.0	64.7	75.8	79.4	79.4	99.4	101.0	106.0	1,003.9
2006	138.0	108.0	80.1	69.1	100.0	94.1	91.4	101.0	106.0	96.4	58.3	56.5	1,098.9
2007	87.3	76.4	68.4	65.8	80.1	58.9	66.6	77.7	68.5	66.9	54.5	NA	841.2
2008[1]	58.6	57.8	53.6	59.8	63.6	48.9	77.5	86.9	54.5	49.7	51.0	61.7	723.6

[1] Preliminary. *Source: U.S. Geological Survey (USGS)*

Exports of Refined Copper from the United States In Thousands of Metric Tons

Year	Jan.	Feb.	Mar.	Apr.	May	June	July	Aug.	Sept.	Oct.	Nov.	Dec.	Total
1999	2.4	1.1	1.8	1.3	1.6	4.2	1.6	1.5	1.2	1.4	3.7	3.3	25.2
2000	1.6	5.3	22.0	12.2	18.1	12.8	6.7	4.4	2.9	4.3	1.2	2.1	93.6
2001	1.2	.9	.8	1.9	1.0	.8	1.7	2.6	1.2	4.6	5.3	.6	22.5
2002	.4	.7	3.2	.7	.8	6.8	7.7	2.6	1.3	.6	.5	1.5	26.6
2003	2.5	.8	1.5	.6	15.9	23.0	5.1	4.1	4.3	4.6	8.5	22.3	93.2
2004	11.0	18.5	23.9	28.4	3.7	2.7	5.5	9.4	.6	3.9	2.5	8.4	118.4
2005	4.5	3.2	2.8	1.9	7.2	4.3	3.0	2.7	1.8	3.3	3.3	3.0	40.9
2006	5.6	7.3	6.8	9.6	6.3	13.1	6.0	9.6	9.3	13.7	6.2	12.6	106.1
2007	3.1	2.7	5.1	3.6	3.9	6.6	3.6	3.4	5.4	7.1	3.0	NA	51.8
2008[1]	6.0	5.7	6.3	3.2	1.9	1.4	2.0	2.0	1.5	3.2	1.7	1.6	36.5

[1] Preliminary. *Source: U.S. Geological Survey (USGS)*

Stocks of Refined Copper in the United States, on First of Month In Thousands of Short Tons

Year	Jan.	Feb.	Mar.	Apr.	May	June	July	Aug.	Sept.	Oct.	Nov.	Dec.
2000	619.2	620.8	619.5	582.9	537.0	508.8	467.8	418.0	397.7	394.3	379.1	344.2
2001	383.8	408.4	416.2	481.9	552.6	585.7	626.7	733.1	767.4	895.6	916.6	985.7
2002	1,045.1	1,096.2	1,132.4	1,155.3	1,175.0	1,158.8	1,126.7	1,132.2	1,123.0	1,123.7	1,110.5	1,109.0
2003	1,119.8	109.7	1,038.8	1,042.1	998.3	959.8	891.8	848.9	855.6	825.5	761.2	768.0
2004	733.8	646.3	566.7	463.9	367.0	311.8	247.8	218.3	194.5	169.2	158.9	147.4
2005	145.8	151.0	143.4	134.4	129.3	116.2	105.3	98.5	83.0	68.2	56.8	59.4
2006	66.8	76.9	103.3	109.0	88.2	84.5	68.3	76.4	80.1	88.4	103.4	152.3
2007	194.9	222.1	216.8	197.7	165.8	130.7	114.3	118.8	114.0	110.3	115.0	123.8
2008	147.2	122.5	106.3	105.9	74.4	81.3	72.8	83.8	106.3	123.6	134.6	165.7
2009[1]	231.1	290.3	321.7	376.8	380.1	355.9	320.8	331.1	336.3	363.3	384.8	

Recoverable Copper Content. [1] Preliminary. *Source: American Bureau of Metal Statistics (ABMS)*

Stocks of Refined Copper Outside the United States, on First of Month In Thousands of Short Tons

Year	Jan.	Feb.	Mar.	Apr.	May	June	July	Aug.	Sept.	Oct.	Nov.	Dec.
2000	983.8	1,034.9	1,040.7	1,011.4	988.6	880.9	866.0	857.3	837.0	826.7	784.1	764.8
2001	795.0	999.5	986.4	971.2	995.7	969.4	1,000.8	1,091.0	1,108.7	1,083.3	1,021.0	1,104.5
2002	1,241.3	1,273.5	1,291.5	1,370.4	1,391.1	1,399.4	1,289.0	1,342.6	1,369.1	1,321.1	1,219.7	1,224.5
2003	1,238.8	2,147.6	1,188.0	1,216.3	1,147.4	1,109.8	1,129.2	1,139.9	1,150.9	1,140.2	1,170.8	1,157.1
2004	1,191.5	1,149.9	1,139.5	995.5	968.4	826.0	807.1	812.4	830.2	825.2	778.0	816.8
2005	833.8	802.2	929.8	848.0	758.2	771.3	822.6	786.4	846.9	774.3	803.4	805.0
2006	871.2	956.8	923.2	797.7	816.4	819.2	789.1	812.9	872.4	830.1	877.6	905.9
2007	1,016.2	969.5	966.6	994.3	973.0	873.8	893.9	845.9	880.9	894.4	884.8	860.7
2008	947.7	920.0	833.9	1,257.0	1,253.4	1,311.1	1,309.1	1,315.5	1,318.0	1,487.6	366.8	957.6
2009	931.3	1,155.7	1,125.6	1,024.3	853.1	788.4	817.5	752.9	864.3	943.0	962.3	

Recoverable Copper Content. *Source: American Bureau of Metal Statistics (ABMS)*

Production of Refined Copper in the United States In Thousands of Short Tons

Year	Jan.	Feb.	Mar.	Apr.	May	June	July	Aug.	Sept.	Oct.	Nov.	Dec.	Total
1999	185.0	178.0	220.0	198.0	186.0	175.0	163.0	161.0	172.0	172.0	157.0	162.0	2,130
2000	157.0	149.0	173.0	144.0	161.0	146.0	134.0	149.0	141.0	140.0	147.0	154.0	1,800
2001	155.0	144.0	156.0	145.0	155.0	157.0	146.0	143.0	148.0	149.0	152.0	150.0	1,800
2002	134.0	117.0	124.0	129.0	134.0	128.0	130.0	124.0	120.0	129.0	120.0	119.0	1,508
2003	124.0	110.0	118.0	98.7	98.8	106.0	110.0	110.0	112.0	108.0	101.0	111.0	1,308
2004	104.0	98.9	105.0	111.0	109.0	113.0	104.0	107.0	112.0	111.0	109.0	123.0	1,307
2005	102.0	102.0	104.0	105.0	109.0	101.0	100.0	102.0	103.0	104.0	108.0	115.0	1,255
2006	99.9	101.0	117.0	109.0	113.0	114.0	100.0	101.0	102.0	89.8	94.4	108.0	1,249
2007	101.0	97.1	116.0	113.0	116.0	112.0	116.0	117.0	108.0	120.0	91.5	103.0	1,311
2008[1]	110.0	107.0	108.0	102.0	107.0	102.0	98.0	107.0	108.0	110.0	107.0	113.0	1,279

Recoverable Copper Content. [1] Preliminary. *Source: U.S. Geological Survey (USGS)*

Production of Refined Copper Outside North America In Thousands of Short Tons

Year	Jan.	Feb.	Mar.	Apr.	May	June	July	Aug.	Sept.	Oct.	Nov.	Dec.	Total
2000	1,179.5	1,121.6	1,205.2	1,178.1	1,227.4	1,188.6	1,198.2	1,204.8	1,230.0	1,253.8	1,238.2	1,251.8	14,477
2001	1,279.1	1,188.0	1,316.5	1,243.6	1,295.9	1,241.7	1,269.8	1,296.1	1,247.1	1,308.5	1,299.8	1,318.5	15,305
2002	1,310.4	1,190.9	1,307.8	1,268.2	1,294.3	1,257.6	1,254.9	1,272.7	1,242.9	1,293.6	1,263.1	1,282.0	15,238
2003	1,274.4	1,188.2	1,283.9	1,244.3	1,292.2	1,253.9	1,289.6	1,272.9	1,268.6	1,320.6	1,302.4	1,349.4	15,340
2004	1,286.7	1,256.0	1,344.1	1,290.0	1,277.3	1,291.9	1,358.8	1,366.5	1,370.6	1,390.0	1,402.4	1,406.5	16,041
2005	1,407.9	1,252.0	1,388.1	1,343.0	1,390.5	1,389.3	1,402.3	1,409.2	1,407.9	1,429.0	1,444.8	1,493.6	16,758
2006	1,423.7	1,346.1	1,466.0	1,435.9	1,459.1	1,457.0	1,476.2	1,459.2	1,460.0	1,521.8	1,494.8	1,566.7	17,567
2007	1,568.4	1,443.8	1,541.9	1,502.0	1,520.9	1,483.0	1,491.6	1,501.0	1,531.9	1,549.1	1,570.6	1,601.4	18,306
2008	1,553.2	1,475.5	1,612.2	1,577.6	1,569.2	1,610.8	1,643.0	1,640.4	1,605.5	1,606.6	1,567.9	1,579.2	19,041
2009[1]	1,637.9	1,564.4	1,649.7	1,631.1	1,677.4	1,650.9	1,690.5	1,712.3	1,720.6	1,767.5	1,786.5		20,170

Recoverable Copper Content. [1] Preliminary. *Source: American Bureau of Metal Statistics (ABMS)*

Deliveries of Refined Copper to Fabricators in the United States In Thousands of Short Tons

Year	Jan.	Feb.	Mar.	Apr.	May	June	July	Aug.	Sept.	Oct.	Nov.	Dec.	Total
2000	166.8	161.3	176.3	157.0	173.7	161.3	145.2	149.7	150.6	154.8	149.8	162.7	1,909
2001	166.1	150.8	167.4	148.4	167.6	165.2	162.7	154.0	151.6	160.7	154.7	147.5	1,897
2002	152.1	126.0	140.7	149.3	148.6	136.2	147.9	141.1	129.5	141.6	124.5	129.7	1,667
2003	136.4	123.4	124.6	106.6	107.7	117.0	127.1	120.6	125.8	127.9	114.4	133.8	1,465
2004	126.4	131.1	137.6	137.7	130.9	143.5	133.3	132.9	136.8	129.3	128.8	137.5	1,606
2005	120.1	120.0	131.2	125.4	125.7	119.2	106.9	112.8	108.0	110.9	112.6	115.9	1,409
2006	124.8	110.3	131.5	121.9	121.8	132.7	117.5	119.9	112.7	95.5	95.6	100.5	1,385
2007	115.9	118.9	131.9	127.4	128.1	126.2	131.3	132.3	112.2	134.9	113.3	100.9	1,473
2008	134.1	118.8	123.2	114.7	111.6	120.8	105.4	118.3	121.4	129.7	109.4	110.6	1,418
2009[1]	117.6	105.0	104.3	99.4	97.6	105.7	115.3	110.1	100.6	101.6	105.0		1,268

Recoverable Copper Content. [1] Preliminary. *Source: American Bureau of Metal Statistics (ABMS)*

Deliveries of Refined Copper to Fabricators Outside the United States In Thousands of Short Tons

Year	Jan.	Feb.	Mar.	Apr.	May	June	July	Aug.	Sept.	Oct.	Nov.	Dec.	Total
1990	419.9	466.3	436.7	392.9	408.3	466.7	303.7	373.5	370.8	448.9	469.1	420.7	4,972
1991	405.0	404.4	391.5	361.2	406.3	433.5	368.5	323.4	420.7	499.1	391.4	483.4	4,807
1992	453.7	408.9	441.8	416.4	413.4	432.4	410.4	364.7	432.6	403.5	406.1	461.3	5,045
1993	427.9	392.9	452.3	361.7	422.2	442.6	384.4	347.9	387.5	414.8	463.4	458.5	4,956
1994	399.8	429.5	481.2	466.5	468.9	428.1	387.9	369.2	423.5	448.9	457.1	436.0	5,197
1995[2]	758.5	810.1	892.8	882.2	853.0	867.3	863.7	814.1	803.4	835.1	796.6	726.2	9,903
1996	875.2	859.4	934.3	907.2	816.7	950.7	908.3	817.4	911.5	1,056.0	922.7	918.3	10,878
1997	862.2	889.7	977.9	1,007.1	991.1	982.7	897.8	873.9	886.2	1,009.0	980.4	966.6	11,349
1998	1,091.7	973.8	1,062.0	1,055.5	995.7	1,014.8	986.8	924.8	913.3	987.9	982.1	1,023.0	12,011
1999[1]	314.5	745.5	NA	NA	NA	NA	NA	NA	NA	NA	NA	NA	6,360

Recoverable Copper Content. [1] Preliminary. [2] New reporting method beginning January 1995, includes crude copper deliveries.
Source: American Bureau of Metal Statistics (ABMS)

Corn

Corn is a member of the grass family of plants and is a native grain of the American continents. Fossils of corn pollen that are over 80,000 years old have been found in lake sediment under Mexico City. Archaeological discoveries show that cultivated corn existed in the southwestern U.S. for at least 3,000 years, indicating that the indigenous people of the region cultivated corn as a food crop long before the Europeans reached the New World. Corn is a hardy plant that grows in many different areas of the world. It can grow at altitudes as low as sea level and as high as 12,000 feet in the South American Andes Mountains. Corn can also grow in tropical climates that receive up to 400 inches of rainfall per year, or in areas that receive only 12 inches of rainfall per year. Corn is used primarily as livestock feed in the United States and the rest of the world. Other uses for corn are alcohol additives for gasoline, adhesives, corn oil for cooking and margarine, sweeteners, and as food for humans. Corn is the largest crop in the U.S., both in terms of the value of the crop and of the acres planted.

The largest futures market for corn is at the Chicago Board of Trade. Corn futures also trade at the Bolsa de Mercadorias & Futuros (BM&F) in Brazil, the Budapest Commodity Exchange, the Marche a Terme International de France (MATIF), the Mercado a Termino de Buenos Aires in Argentina, the Kanmon Commodity Exchange (KCE) in Korea, and the Tokyo Grain Exchange (TGE). The CBOT futures contract calls for the delivery of 5000 bushels of No. 2 yellow corn at par contract price, No. 1 yellow at 1-1/2 cents per bushel over the contract price, or No. 3 yellow at 1-1/2 cents per bushel below the contract price.

Prices – Corn futures prices in 2009 traded in the relatively narrow range of $3.00-$4.50 after the temporary upward spike to a record high of $7.6250 per barrel seen in June 2008. That upward spike was caused by the feverish commodity bubble in late-2007 and early-2008, which was eventually popped by the global financial crisis in September 2008. Corn prices are nevertheless still trading in a substantially higher range than the average price of $2.50 per bushel seen before 2006, mainly because of the huge demand for corn that started to emerge in 2006 from ethanol producers. The percentage of the corn crop used by ethanol producers, which was only 11% in the 2002-2004 period, quickly ramped up to a record high of 32.7% in the 2009/10 marketing year. That percentage will continue to climb to at least 35% in coming years due to the U.S. government's renewable fuel mandates. Other categories of demand for corn from the feed, food and export categories have also been strong, leading to a +5.4% compounded annual growth for corn usage in the 2006-09 period. Strong corn demand is likely to continue in coming years due to further increases in the U.S. corn-based ethanol mandate, the economic recovery, and a continued increase in food demand tied to improved living standards in the developing world. However, trend improvements in yield due to improved seeds and cultivation techniques are likely to allow the size of the corn crop to keep up with demand, thus keeping a relative balance between supply and demand. At present, there are adequate corn supplies given the good growing weather in the summer of 2009 and the record-sized crop of 13.151 billion bushels. The USDA is forecasting a similar-sized record crop for summer 2010 of 13.160 billion bushels that would help to keep corn prices under wraps.

Supply – World production of corn in the 2009-10 marketing year rose +0.6% to a new record high of 796.446 million metric tons. The world's largest corn producers are the U.S. with 42% of world production, China (19%), and Brazil (6%). Corn production in both China and Brazil has nearly doubled since 1980. Production in the U.S. over that same time frame has risen by about 50%. The world area harvested with corn in 2009-10 fell -1.1% yr/yr to 309.2 million hectares, down from the 13-year high of 318.0 million hectares in 2007-08. World ending stocks of corn and coarse grains in 2009-10 fell –4.5% to 180.2 million metric tons.

U.S. corn production estimate for the 2009-10 marketing year (Sep-Aug) rose by +8.8% yr/yr to a new record high of 13.151 billion bushels. U.S. farmers harvested a record high of 79.630 million acres of corn for grain usage in 2009-10, which was up +1.4% yr/yr. U.S. corn yield in 2009-10 rose +7.3% to a new record high of 165.2 bushels per acre. U.S. carry-over stocks on June 1, 2009 rose +5.8% to 4.261 billion bushels. The largest corn producing states in the U.S. in 2009 were Iowa with 19% of U.S. production, Illinois (16%), Nebraska (12%), Minnesota (10%), and Indiana (7%). The value of the U.S. corn crop in 2008-09 (latest data) was $47.378 billion.

Demand – World consumption of corn and rough grains in 2009-10 rose by +2.8% yr/yr to 1,102.4 million metric tons, which was a new record high. The U.S. distribution tables for corn show that in 2008-09 (latest data) the largest category of usage, aside from animal feed, is for ethanol production (alcohol fuel) with 4.000 billion bushels. That was up +33% from 2007-08 and is 75.0% of total non-feed usage. Corn usage for ethanol is more than five times the usage in 2000 and that usage category is likely to grow if there is a return of the high prices of crude oil and gasoline. After ethanol, the largest non-feed usage categories are for high fructose corn syrup (HFCS) with 9% of U.S. usage, corn starch (5%), glucose and dextrose sugars (5%), cereal and other corn products (4%), and alcoholic beverages (3%).

Trade – U.S. exports of corn in 2007-08 (latest data available) rose +12.1% yr/yr to 60.685 million metric tons, which is getting close to the record high of 61.417 million metric tons posted in 1979-80. The largest destination countries for U.S. corn exports are Japan, which accounted for 25% of U.S. corn exports in 2007-08, Mexico (16%), South Korea (14%), Taiwan (6%), Egypt (5%), and Canada (5%).

World Production of Corn or Maize In Thousands of Metric Tons

Crop Year Beginning Oct. 1	Argentina	Brazil	Canada	China	European Union	Egypt	India	Mexico	Romania	South Africa	United States	Ukraine	World Total
2000-01	15,400	41,536	6,827	106,000	50,089	5,636	12,068	17,917	4,800	8,040	251,854	3,848	591,382
2001-02	14,700	35,501	8,389	114,088	58,022	6,160	13,510	20,400	7,000	10,050	241,377	3,641	601,216
2002-03	15,500	44,500	8,999	121,300	57,660	6,000	11,100	19,280	7,300	9,675	227,767	4,180	602,954
2003-04	15,000	42,000	9,587	115,830	47,905	5,740	14,980	21,800	7,020	9,700	256,229	6,850	626,798
2004-05	20,500	35,000	8,837	130,290	66,471	5,840	14,180	22,050	12,000	11,716	299,876	8,800	714,919
2005-06	15,800	41,700	9,332	139,365	60,668	5,932	14,710	19,500	10,300	6,935	282,263	7,150	698,784
2006-07	22,500	51,000	8,990	151,600	53,829	6,149	15,100	22,350	8,500	7,300	267,503	6,400	712,380
2007-08[1]	22,000	58,600	11,649	152,300	47,555	6,174	18,960	23,600		13,164	331,177	7,400	791,871
2008-09[2]	12,600	51,000	10,592	165,900	62,701	6,217	19,290	24,226		12,567	307,142	11,400	791,617
2009-10[3]	15,000	51,000	9,560	155,000	56,126	6,300	18,500	22,000		11,500	334,052	10,500	796,446

[1] Preliminary. [2] Estimate. [3] Forecast. *Source: Foreign Agricultural Service, U.S. Department of Agriculture (FAS-USDA)*

World Supply and Demand of Coarse Grains In Millions of Metric Tons/Hectares

Crop Year Beginning Oct. 1	Area Harvested	Yield	Production	World Trade	Total Consumption	Ending Stocks	Stocks as % of Consumption[3]
2000-01	296.0	2.90	863.5	102.7	884.7	211.2	23.9
2001-02	300.9	3.00	896.1	100.5	908.8	198.5	21.8
2002-03	292.0	3.00	874.6	102.7	902.4	170.7	18.9
2003-04	306.1	3.00	915.6	102.6	944.7	141.7	15.0
2004-05	300.1	3.40	1,014.8	101.2	977.8	178.7	18.3
2005-06	300.8	3.30	978.8	108.5	992.7	164.7	16.6
2006-07	305.1	3.20	986.2	114.6	1,012.2	138.7	13.7
2007-08	318.0	3.40	1,077.1	128.9	1,056.5	159.3	15.1
2008-09[1]	312.6	3.50	1,101.7	109.8	1,072.3	188.7	17.6
2009-10[2]	309.2	3.50	1,093.9	110.8	1,102.4	180.2	16.3

[1] Preliminary. [2] Estimate. [3] Represents the ratio of marketing year ending stocks to total consumption. *Source: Foreign Agricultural Service, U.S. Department of Agriculture (FAS-USDA)*

Acreage and Supply of Corn in the United States In Millions of Bushels

Crop Year Beginning Sept. 1	Planted (In Thousands of Acres)	Harvested For Grain (In Thousands of Acres)	Harvested For Silage (In Thousands of Acres)	Yield Per Harvested Acre Bushels	Carry-over, Sept. 1 On Farms	Carry-over, Sept. 1 Off Farms	Supply: Beginning Stocks	Supply: Production	Supply: Imports	Supply: Total Supply
2000-01	79,551	72,440	6,082	136.9	793.0	924.5	1,718	9,915	7	11,693
2001-02	75,752	68,808	6,148	138.2	753.2	1,146.0	1,899	9,507	10	11,412
2002-03	78,894	69,330	7,122	129.3	586.8	1,009.6	1,596	8,967	14	10,578
2003-04	78,603	70,944	6,583	142.2	484.9	601.8	1,087	10,089	14	11,188
2004-05	80,930	73,632	6,103	160.4	438.0	520.1	958	11,807	11	12,775
2005-06	81,759	75,107	5,920	147.9	820.5	1,293.5	2,114	11,112	9	13,235
2006-07	78,327	70,648	6,477	149.1	749.5	1,217.7	1,967	10,531	12	12,510
2007-08	93,527	86,520	6,060	150.7	460.1	843.5	1,304	13,038	20	14,362
2008-09[1]	85,982	78,570	5,965	153.9	500.0	1,124.2	1,624	12,092	14	13,739
2009-10[2]	86,482	79,630	5,605	165.2	607.5	1,065.8	1,674	13,151	10	14,605

[1] Preliminary. [2] Estimate. *Source: Economic Research Service, U.S. Department of Agriculture (ERS-USDA)*

Production of Corn (For Grain) in the United States, by State In Million of Bushels

Year	Illinois	Indiana	Iowa	Kansas	Michigan	Minnesota	Missouri	Nebraska	Ohio	South Dakota	Texas	Wisconsin	Total
2000	1,668.6	810.3	1,728.0	412.1	241.8	964.3	396.1	1,014.3	485.1	425.6	235.6	363.0	9,915.1
2001	1,649.2	884.5	1,664.4	387.4	199.5	806.0	345.8	1,139.3	437.5	370.6	167.6	330.2	9,506.8
2002	1,471.5	631.6	1,931.6	301.6	234.0	1,051.9	283.5	940.8	264.3	308.8	202.3	391.5	8,966.8
2003	1,812.2	786.9	1,868.3	300.0	259.8	970.9	302.4	1,124.2	478.9	427.4	194.7	367.7	10,089.2
2004	2,088.0	929.0	2,244.4	432.0	257.3	1,121.0	466.6	1,319.7	491.4	539.5	233.5	353.6	11,807.2
2005	1,708.9	888.6	2,162.5	465.8	288.9	1,191.9	329.7	1,270.5	464.8	470.1	210.9	429.2	11,112.1
2006	1,817.5	844.7	2,050.1	345.0	286.7	1,102.9	362.9	1,178.0	470.6	312.3	175.5	400.4	10,531.1
2007	2,283.8	981.0	2,376.9	507.8	287.8	1,146.1	457.8	1,472.0	541.5	542.1	291.6	442.8	13,037.9
2008	2,130.1	873.6	2,188.8	486.4	295.3	1,180.8	381.6	1,393.7	421.2	585.2	253.8	394.6	12,091.6
2009[1]	2,065.0	933.7	2,438.8	598.3	310.8	1,251.3	446.8	1,575.3	546.4	719.1	254.8	448.3	13,151.1

[1] Preliminary. *Source: National Agricultural Statistics Service, U.S. Department of Agriculture (NASS-USDA)*

CORN

Quarterly Supply and Disappearance of Corn in the United States In Millions of Bushels

Crop Year Beginning Sept. 1	Supply				Disapperance: Domestic Use						Ending Stocks		
	Beginning Stocks	Pro-duction	Imports[3]	Total Supply	Food & Alcohol	Seed	Feed & Residual	Total	Exports[3]	Total Disap-pearance	Gov't Owned[4]	Privately Owned[5]	Total Stocks
2005-06	2,114	11,112	8.8	13,235	2,962	19.9	6,152	9,134	2,134	11,268			1,967
Sept.-Nov.	2,114	11,112	2.1	13,228	697	0	2,239	2,936	477	3,413			9,815
Dec.-Feb.	9,815	----	1.2	9,816	708	0	1,647	2,355	474	2,829			6,987
Mar.-May	6,987	----	4.1	6,991	754	19.5	1,294	2,067	562	2,630			4,362
June-Aug.	4,362	----	1.3	4,363	802	.4	973	1,776	620	2,396			1,967
2006-07	1,967	10,531	12.0	12,510	3,467	23.8	5,591	9,081	2,125	11,207			1,304
Sept.-Nov.	1,967	10,531	1.2	12,499	799	0	2,172	2,971	596	3,567			8,933
Dec.-Feb.	8,933	----	1.7	8,934	821	0	1,533	2,353	513	2,866			6,068
Mar.-May	6,068	----	5.5	6,074	895	23.4	1,127	2,045	495	2,540			3,533
June-Aug.	3,533	----	3.7	3,537	952	.3	760	1,712	521	2,233			1,304
2007-08	1,304	13,038	20.0	14,362	4,342	21.8	5,913	10,277	2,437	12,737			1,624
Sept.-Nov.	1,304	13,038	2.2	14,344	971	0	2,402	3,372	693	4,066			10,278
Dec.-Feb.	10,278	----	2.8	10,281	1,021	0	1,748	2,769	642	3,422			6,859
Mar.-May	6,859	----	9.7	6,868	1,144	20.7	1,082	2,247	583	2,840			4,028
June-Aug.	4,028	----	5.3	4,033	1,206	1.1	681	1,889	519	2,409			1,624
2008-09[1]	1,624	12,101	13.5	13,739	4,931	22.1	5,254	10,207	1,858	12,065			1,674
Sept.-Nov.	1,624	12,101	2.8	13,728	1,208	0	1,994	3,202	449	3,651			10,078
Dec.-Feb.	10,078	----	4.1	10,082	1,169	0	1,583	2,752	373	3,124			6,957
Mar.-May	6,957	----	5.1	6,962	1,216	20.5	967	2,204	497	2,701			4,261
June-Aug.	4,261	----	1.5	4,263	1,338	1.6	710	2,050	539	2,589			1,674
2009-10[2]	1,674	12,921	10.0	14,605	5,457	22.7	5,400	10,880	2,050	12,930			1,675
Sept.-Nov.	1,674	12,921	2.0	14,605	1,220	0	1,975	3,195	500	3,695			9,997

[1] Preliminary. [2] Estimate. [3] Uncommitted inventory. [4] Includes quantity under loan and farmer-owned reserve. *Source: Economic Research Service, U.S. Department of Agriculture (ERS-USDA)*

Corn Production Estimates and Cash Price in the United States

Year	Corn for Grain Production Estimates (In Thousands of Bushels)					St. Louis No. 2 Yellow	Omaha No. 2 Yellow	Gulf Ports No. 2 Yellow	Kansas City No. 2 White	Chicago No. 2 Yellow	Average Farm Price[2]	Value of Production (Mil. $)
	Aug. 1	Sept. 1	Oct. 1	Nov. 1	Final	Dollars Per Bushel						
2000-01	10,369,369	10,362,374	10,191,817	10,053,942	9,915,051	2.01	1.82	2.26	2.06	1.99	1.85	18,499
2001-02	9,266,397	9,238,356	9,429,543	9,545,513	9,506,840	2.15	1.95	2.35	2.20	2.13	1.98	18,888
2002-03	8,886,009	8,848,529	8,969,836	9,003,364	8,966,787	2.49	2.29	2.71	2.94	2.46	2.32	20,882
2003-04	10,064,452	9,944,418	10,207,141	10,277,932	10,089,222	2.49	2.29	2.94	2.66	2.66	2.50	24,477
2004-05	10,923,099	10,960,710	11,613,226	11,740,920	11,807,217	2.73	2.50	2.48	2.01	2.08	2.05	24,381
2005-06	10,349,841	10,638,661	10,857,440	11,032,105	11,112,072	2.13	1.82	2.69	2.11	2.10	2.01	22,198
2006-07	10,975,740	11,113,766	10,905,194	10,744,806	10,531,123	2.19	1.88	3.95	4.18	3.46	3.13	32,083
2007-08	13,053,617	13,307,999	13,318,102	13,167,741	13,037,875	3.60	3.33	5.54	5.19	4.98	4.45	54,667
2008-09	12,287,875	12,072,365	12,199,908	12,019,894	12,091,648	5.05	4.84	4.39	4.13	3.89	4.05	49,313
2009-10[1]	12,760,986	12,954,500	13,018,058	12,920,928	13,151,062	3.88	3.80	4.17	3.81	3.68	3.54	48,589

[1] Preliminary. [2] Season-average price based on monthly prices weigthed by monthly marketings.
Source: Economic Research Service, U.S. Department of Agriculture (ERS-USDA)

Distribution of Corn in the United States In Millions of Bushels

Crop Year Beginning Sept. 1	Food, Seed and Industrial Use								Livestock Feed[4]	Exports (Including Grain Equiv. of Products)	Domestic Disap-pearance	Total Utilization
	HFCS	Glucose & Dextrose	Starch	Alcohol: Fuel	Alcohol: Bev-rage[3]	Seed	Cereal & Other Products	Total				
2000-01	530	218	247	628	130	19.3	185	1,938	5,842	1,941.3	7,799	9,740
2001-02	541	217	246	706	131	20.1	186	2,046	5,864	1,904.8	7,911	9,815
2002-03	532	219	256	996	131	20.0	187	2,340	5,563	1,587.9	7,903	9,491
2003-04	530	228	271	1,168	132	20.6	187	2,537	5,793	1,899.8	8,330	10,230
2004-05	521	222	277	1,323	133	20.8	189	2,666	6,155	1,818.1	8,842	10,661
2005-06	529	229	275	1,603	135	19.9	190	2,961	6,152	2,133.8	9,134	11,268
2006-07	510	239	272	2,117	136	23.8	190	3,464	5,591	2,125.4	9,081	11,207
2007-08	490	236	262	3,049	135	21.8	192	4,387	5,938	2,435.8	10,302	12,737
2008-09[1]	466	230	232	3,677	134	22.1	192	4,953	5,350	1,750.0	10,390	12,140
2009-10[2]	460	225	230	4,300	134	22.7	193	5,565	5,250	1,900.0	10,660	12,560

[1] Preliminary. [2] Estimate. [3] Also includes nonfuel industrial alcohol. [4] Feed and waste (residual, mostly feed).
Source: Economic Research Service, U.S. Department of Agriculture (ERS-USDA)

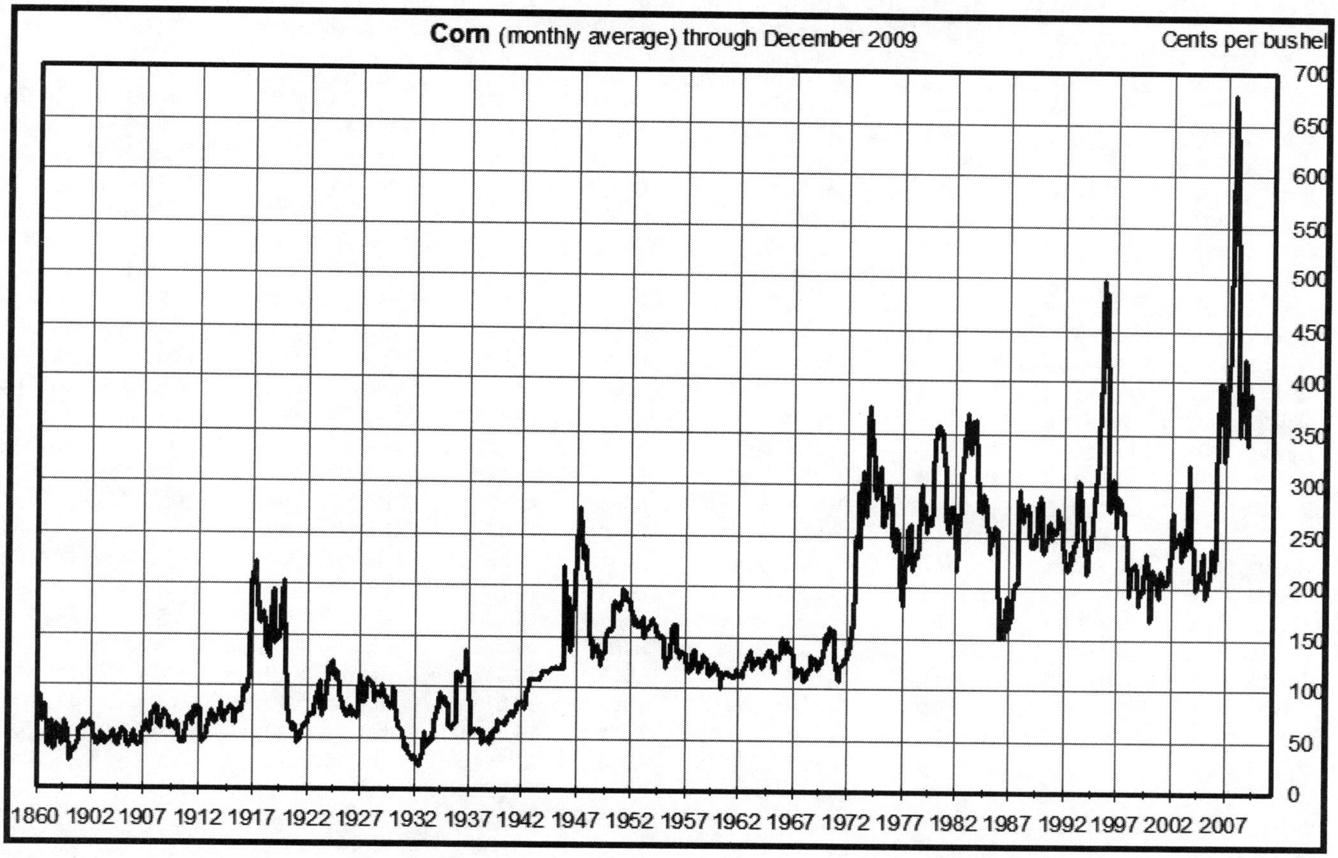

Average Cash Price of Corn, No. 2 Yellow in Central Illinois In Dollars Per Bushel

Year	Sept.	Oct.	Nov.	Dec.	Jan.	Feb.	Mar.	Apr.	May	June	July	Aug.	Average
2000-01	1.58	1.81	1.96	2.01	1.99	1.95	1.92	1.87	1.78	1.76	1.92	2.00	1.88
2001-02	1.94	1.84	1.90	1.97	1.95	1.92	1.92	1.89	1.96	2.04	2.22	2.50	2.00
2002-03	2.57	2.41	2.36	2.32	2.29	2.33	2.31	2.36	2.40	2.37	2.13	2.26	2.34
2003-04	2.25	2.11	2.26	2.38	2.52	2.73	2.89	3.03	2.90	2.76	2.26	2.17	2.52
2004-05	1.98	1.77	1.79	1.87	1.86	1.86	1.97	1.94	1.93	2.02	2.20	1.98	1.93
2005-06	1.75	1.67	1.75	1.89	1.98	2.07	2.04	2.18	2.22	2.15	2.22	2.07	2.00
2006-07	2.21	2.82	3.43	3.53	3.66	3.90	3.76	3.36	3.52	3.68	3.03	3.08	3.33
2007-08	3.15	3.28	3.66	4.03	4.55	4.91	5.15	5.59	5.58	6.55	5.97	5.04	4.79
2008-09	5.00	3.69	3.42	3.33	3.61	3.46	3.60	3.69	3.98	3.97	3.22	3.21	3.68
2009-10[1]	3.10	3.52	3.62	3.59									3.46

[1] Preliminary. *Source: Economic Research Service, U.S. Department of Agriculture (ERS-USDA)*

Average Cash Price of Corn, No. 2 Yellow at Gulf Ports[2] In Dollars Per Bushel

Year	Sept.	Oct.	Nov.	Dec.	Jan.	Feb.	Mar.	Apr.	May	June	July	Aug.	Average
2000-01	2.03	2.15	2.26	2.45	2.40	2.35	2.32	2.22	2.14	2.11	2.30	2.36	2.26
2001-02	2.27	2.19	2.28	2.35	2.34	2.30	2.28	2.21	2.29	2.37	2.53	2.79	2.35
2002-03	2.89	2.79	2.77	2.71	2.69	2.69	2.67	2.68	2.74	2.72	2.48	2.56	2.70
2003-04	2.63	2.65	2.75	2.85	2.95	3.12	3.27	3.39	3.29	3.13	2.66	2.64	2.94
2004-05	2.49	2.37	2.39	2.43	2.44	2.40	2.54	2.45	2.42	2.49	2.69	2.59	2.48
2005-06	2.47	2.58	2.44	2.61	2.61	2.72	2.67	2.74	2.81	2.78	2.90	2.92	2.69
2006-07	3.05	3.82	4.17	4.08	4.19	4.50	3.81	3.88	4.07	4.20	3.73	3.84	3.95
2007-08	4.05	4.17	4.35	4.58	5.25	5.59	5.99	6.26	6.18	7.29	6.74	5.97	5.54
2008-09	5.94	4.65	4.18	4.02	4.39	4.15	4.18	4.29	4.58	4.56	3.86	3.87	4.39
2009-10[1]	3.82	4.25	4.36	4.18	4.25								4.17

[1] Preliminary. [2] Barge delivered to Louisiana Gulf. *Source: Economic Research Service, U.S. Department of Agriculture (ERS-USDA)*

Weekly Outstanding Export Sales and Cumulative Exports of U.S. Corn In Thousands of Metric Tons

Marketing Year 2006/0007 Week Ending	Out-standing Sales	Cumu-lative Exports	Marketing Year 2007/0008 Week Ending	Out-standing Sales	Cumu-lative Exports	Marketing Year 2008/0009 Week Ending	Out-standing Sales	Cumu-lative Exports
Sep 06, 2007	15,761.7	904.2	Sep 04, 2008	11,883.8	199.3	Sep 03, 2009	12,131.4	537.0
Sep 13, 2007	16,919.9	1,778.3	Sep 11, 2008	11,346.4	1,062.1	Sep 10, 2009	11,934.6	1,699.4
Sep 20, 2007	17,414.7	2,981.4	Sep 18, 2008	10,900.0	2,056.3	Sep 17, 2009	11,569.5	2,737.7
Sep 27, 2007	17,340.6	4,206.1	Sep 25, 2008	10,302.6	3,220.2	Sep 24, 2009	11,827.8	3,702.9
Oct 04, 2007	18,468.1	5,398.3	Oct 02, 2008	10,435.2	4,045.5	Oct 01, 2009	11,205.5	4,847.1
Oct 11, 2007	19,158.2	6,503.3	Oct 09, 2008	10,486.9	4,918.6	Oct 08, 2009	11,167.2	5,516.8
Oct 18, 2007	19,421.3	7,760.5	Oct 16, 2008	10,522.9	5,672.2	Oct 15, 2009	10,584.1	6,334.8
Oct 25, 2007	18,806.4	9,010.7	Oct 23, 2008	10,332.9	6,275.3	Oct 22, 2009	10,284.3	7,001.7
Nov 01, 2007	18,788.3	10,533.9	Oct 30, 2008	10,185.9	6,893.6	Oct 29, 2009	10,140.1	7,709.9
Nov 08, 2007	18,642.4	12,043.6	Nov 06, 2008	9,732.8	7,702.2	Nov 05, 2009	9,870.5	8,468.0
Nov 15, 2007	19,111.3	13,420.3	Nov 13, 2008	9,410.7	8,458.1	Nov 12, 2009	9,540.2	9,151.2
Nov 22, 2007	19,513.3	14,859.8	Nov 20, 2008	9,110.1	9,224.0	Nov 19, 2009	10,135.9	9,779.1
Nov 29, 2007	19,044.3	16,387.9	Nov 27, 2008	8,523.5	10,154.5	Nov 26, 2009	9,915.4	10,658.6
Dec 06, 2007	19,144.2	17,432.0	Dec 04, 2008	8,763.6	10,843.1	Dec 03, 2009	10,056.6	11,365.1
Dec 13, 2007	19,082.5	18,662.1	Dec 11, 2008	8,665.9	11,553.3	Dec 10, 2009	10,507.3	12,141.5
Dec 20, 2007	19,243.4	19,924.6	Dec 18, 2008	8,386.0	12,384.6	Dec 17, 2009	11,684.4	12,556.2
Dec 27, 2007	18,803.5	21,065.3	Dec 25, 2008	8,053.8	12,986.7	Dec 24, 2009	11,593.4	13,419.8
Jan 03, 2008	18,496.3	21,979.3	Jan 01, 2009	7,702.9	13,598.2	Dec 31, 2009	11,160.1	14,217.8
Jan 10, 2008	19,363.1	23,481.8	Jan 08, 2009	7,307.4	14,209.9	Jan 07, 2010	10,829.3	14,875.9
Jan 17, 2008	19,623.4	24,816.6	Jan 15, 2009	7,709.4	14,893.9	Jan 14, 2010	11,603.8	15,711.8
Jan 24, 2008	20,019.7	26,308.0	Jan 22, 2009	8,078.4	15,632.6	Jan 21, 2010	11,974.3	16,243.6
Jan 31, 2008	19,799.4	27,549.9	Jan 29, 2009	8,497.0	16,378.2	Jan 28, 2010	11,774.5	17,366.6
Feb 07, 2008	19,586.3	28,695.4	Feb 05, 2009	9,473.4	16,945.6	Feb 04, 2010	11,913.9	17,970.5
Feb 14, 2008	19,316.2	30,106.9	Feb 12, 2009	9,894.4	17,856.9	Feb 11, 2010	12,236.3	18,598.2
Feb 21, 2008	18,669.7	31,354.7	Feb 19, 2009	9,571.6	18,628.6	Feb 18, 2010	11,397.0	19,838.7
Feb 28, 2008	17,985.6	32,686.8	Feb 26, 2009	9,455.4	19,536.7	Feb 25, 2010	11,103.1	20,894.1
Mar 06, 2008	17,692.1	33,749.1	Mar 05, 2009	9,478.4	20,606.1	Mar 04, 2010		
Mar 13, 2008	16,968.9	35,221.9	Mar 12, 2009	8,985.5	21,539.6	Mar 11, 2010		
Mar 20, 2008	16,312.3	36,511.0	Mar 19, 2009	9,400.4	22,316.0	Mar 18, 2010		
Mar 27, 2008	15,871.1	37,651.1	Mar 26, 2009	9,657.3	23,310.3	Mar 25, 2010		
Apr 03, 2008	15,090.3	38,905.8	Apr 02, 2009	9,663.6	24,366.8	Apr 01, 2010		
Apr 10, 2008	14,847.0	40,018.0	Apr 09, 2009	9,678.6	25,221.5	Apr 08, 2010		
Apr 17, 2008	14,512.4	41,127.9	Apr 16, 2009	9,866.0	26,248.4	Apr 15, 2010		
Apr 24, 2008	14,059.9	42,131.6	Apr 23, 2009	10,253.4	27,086.3	Apr 22, 2010		
May 01, 2008	13,459.6	43,069.1	Apr 30, 2009	10,052.0	27,876.3	Apr 29, 2010		
May 08, 2008	13,011.9	44,064.0	May 07, 2009	9,716.5	29,148.6	May 06, 2010		
May 15, 2008	12,775.0	44,808.1	May 14, 2009	9,691.7	29,856.9	May 13, 2010		
May 22, 2008	12,180.0	45,880.6	May 21, 2009	9,637.7	30,667.0	May 20, 2010		
May 29, 2008	11,725.0	46,865.7	May 28, 2009	9,386.1	31,523.1	May 27, 2010		
Jun 05, 2008	11,084.7	48,030.7	Jun 04, 2009	9,475.0	32,147.4	Jun 03, 2010		
Jun 12, 2008	10,340.6	49,117.7	Jun 11, 2009	9,424.4	32,965.2	Jun 10, 2010		
Jun 19, 2008	9,588.0	50,096.6	Jun 18, 2009	9,072.4	34,003.7	Jun 17, 2010		
Jun 26, 2008	8,724.4	51,286.1	Jun 25, 2009	9,485.0	34,746.2	Jun 24, 2010		
Jul 03, 2008	8,132.2	52,216.7	Jul 02, 2009	9,266.2	35,714.0	Jul 01, 2010		
Jul 10, 2008	7,811.3	52,905.7	Jul 09, 2009	8,996.4	36,683.5	Jul 08, 2010		
Jul 17, 2008	7,387.6	53,652.9	Jul 16, 2009	8,832.5	37,605.1	Jul 15, 2010		
Jul 24, 2008	6,215.7	54,887.9	Jul 23, 2009	7,837.1	39,059.1	Jul 22, 2010		
Jul 31, 2008	5,677.2	55,764.3	Jul 30, 2009	7,070.4	40,248.6	Jul 29, 2010		
Aug 07, 2008	5,124.0	56,703.4	Aug 06, 2009	6,653.8	41,206.4	Aug 05, 2010		
Aug 14, 2008	4,230.2	57,793.9	Aug 13, 2009	6,107.2	42,330.0	Aug 12, 2010		
Aug 21, 2008	3,711.7	58,615.4	Aug 20, 2009	5,097.9	43,605.0	Aug 19, 2010		
Aug 28, 2008	2,861.0	59,666.4	Aug 27, 2009	4,397.7	44,650.0	Aug 26, 2010		

Source: Foreign Agricultural Service, U.S. Department of Agriculture (FAS-USDA)

Average Price Received by Farmers for Corn in the United States In Dollars Per Bushel

Year	Sept.	Oct.	Nov.	Dec.	Jan.	Feb.	Mar.	Apr.	May	June	July	Aug.	Average
2000-01	1.61	1.74	1.86	1.97	1.98	1.96	1.96	1.89	1.82	1.76	1.87	1.90	1.86
2001-02	1.91	1.84	1.85	1.98	1.97	1.93	1.94	1.91	1.93	1.97	2.13	2.38	1.98
2002-03	2.47	2.34	2.28	2.32	2.33	2.34	2.33	2.34	2.38	2.34	2.17	2.15	2.32
2003-04	2.20	2.12	2.20	2.31	2.39	2.61	2.75	2.89	2.87	2.79	2.51	2.34	2.50
2004-05	2.20	2.14	2.05	2.04	2.12	1.95	2.02	2.00	1.98	2.03	2.11	1.95	2.05
2005-06	1.90	1.82	1.77	1.92	2.00	2.02	2.06	2.11	2.17	2.14	2.14	2.09	2.01
2006-07	2.20	2.55	2.88	3.01	3.05	3.44	3.43	3.39	3.49	3.53	3.32	3.26	3.13
2007-08	3.28	3.29	3.44	3.77	3.98	4.54	4.70	5.14	5.27	5.47	5.25	5.26	4.45
2008-09	5.01	4.37	4.26	4.11	4.36	3.87	3.86	3.85	3.97	4.03	3.60	3.33	4.05
2009-10[1]	3.25	3.61	3.65	3.59	3.66	3.45							3.54

[1] Preliminary. *Source: Economic Research Service, U.S. Department of Agriculture (ERS-USDA)*

Corn Price Support Data in the United States

Crop Year Beginning Sept. 1	National Average Loan Rate[3]	Target Price	Placed Under Loan	% of Production	Acquired by CCC	Owned by CCC Aug. 31	CCC Inventory As of Dec. 31: CCC Owned	CCC Inventory As of Dec. 31: Under CCC Loan	Quantity Pledged (Thousands of Bushels)	Face Amount (Thousands of Dollars)
	Dollars Per Bushel		Millions of Bushels							
2000-01	1.89	NA	1,394	14.1	27	8	36	----	1,393,947	2,562,172
2001-02	1.89	NA	1,395	14.7	0	6	24	----	1,394,561	2,557,874
2002-03	1.98	2.60	1,367	15.2	0	4	18	----	1,366,513	2,622,823
2003-04	1.98	2.60	1,327	13.2	1	0	16	----	1,326,884	2,555,183
2004-05	1.95	2.63	1,366	11.6	25	0			40,814	87,053
2005-06[1]	1.95	2.63	1,064	9.6	2	2			47,595	99,406
2006-07[2]	1.95	2.63							31,873	65,968
2007-08[2]	1.95	2.63								
2008-09[2]	1.95	2.63								
2009-10[2]	1.95	2.63								

[1] Preliminary. [2] Estimate. [3] Findley or announced loan rate. NA = Not available.
Source: National Agricultural Statistics Service, U.S. Department of Agriculture (NASS-USDA)

U.S. Exports[1] of Corn (Including Seed), By Country of Destination In Thousands of Metric Tons

Crop Year Beginning Oct. 1	Algeria	Canada	Egypt	Israel	Japan	Mexico	Rep. of Korea	Russia	Saudi Arabia	Spain	Taiwan	Venezuela	Total
1999-00	1,099	1,080	3,542	748	14,939	4,910	2,822	491	1,197	16	4,989	1,146	49,378
2000-01	1,180	2,797	4,116	621	14,091	5,928	3,109	26	1,003	0	4,894	1,152	48,192
2001-02	1,343	3,979	4,283	847	14,817	4,025	1,085	86	670	5	4,599	502	47,058
2002-03	1,009	3,811	2,904	313	14,384	5,220	272	0	222	0	4,139	651	40,780
2003-04	1,158	2,014	3,120	1,154	14,968	5,730	3,942	70	402	5	4,757	669	48,724
2004-05	1,036	2,210	3,738	393	15,036	5,935	2,210	13	126	14	4,446	90	45,262
2005-06	1,255	1,901	4,156	725	16,361	6,755	5,866	15	619	8	4,519	133	56,038
2006-07	940	2,142	3,522	844	14,840	8,886	3,873	9	540	3	4,213	514	54,159
2007-08	898	3,051	2,971	1,207	15,043	9,526	8,380	7	985	10	3,792	1,085	60,593
2008-09[2]	95	1,809	2,445	138	15,597	7,714	5,748	0	440	3	3,718	1,145	47,808

[1] Excludes exports of corn by-products. [2] Preliminary. *Source: Foreign Agricultural Service, U.S. Department of Agriculture (FAS-USDA)*

Stocks of Corn (Shelled and Ear) in the United States In Millions of Bushels

Year	On Farms: Mar. 1	On Farms: June 1	On Farms: Sept. 1	On Farms: Dec. 1	Off Farms: Mar. 1	Off Farms: June 1	Off Farms: Sept. 1	Off Farms: Dec. 1	Total Stocks: Mar. 1	Total Stocks: June 1	Total Stocks: Sept. 1	Total Stocks: Dec. 1
2000	3,300.0	2,029.8	793.0	5,550.0	2,301.9	1,556.1	924.5	2,972.2	5,601.9	3,585.9	1,717.5	8,522.2
2001	3,600.0	2,230.8	753.2	5,275.0	2,443.0	1,693.2	1,146.0	2,989.7	6,043.0	3,924.0	1,899.1	8,264.7
2002	3,355.0	2,020.6	586.8	4,800.0	2,440.3	1,576.3	1,009.6	2,838.0	5,795.3	3,596.9	1,596.4	7,638.0
2003	2,940.0	1,620.2	484.9	5,286.0	2,191.9	1,364.7	601.8	2,667.8	5,131.9	2,984.9	1,086.7	7,953.8
2004	3,030.0	1,540.0	438.0	6,144.0	2,241.5	1,430.1	520.1	3,308.5	5,271.5	2,970.1	958.1	9,452.5
2005	4,137.0	2,462.3	820.5	6,325.0	2,619.3	1,858.5	1,293.5	3,490.0	6,756.3	4,320.8	2,114.0	9,815.0
2006	4,055.0	2,350.5	749.5	5,627.0	2,932.3	2,011.2	1,217.7	3,305.7	6,987.3	4,361.7	1,967.2	8,932.7
2007	3,330.0	1,826.6	460.1	6,530.0	2,738.3	1,706.8	843.5	3,748.1	6,068.3	3,533.4	1,303.6	10,278.1
2008	3,780.0	1,970.9	500.0	6,482.0	3,078.7	2,057.1	1,124.2	3,590.1	6,858.7	4,028.0	1,624.2	10,072.1
2009[1]	4,085.0	2,205.4	607.5	7,445.0	2,869.1	2,056.0	1,065.8	3,488.7	6,954.1	4,261.4	1,673.3	10,933.7

[1] Preliminary. *Source: National Agricultural Statistics Service, U.S. Department of Agriculture (NASS-USDA)*

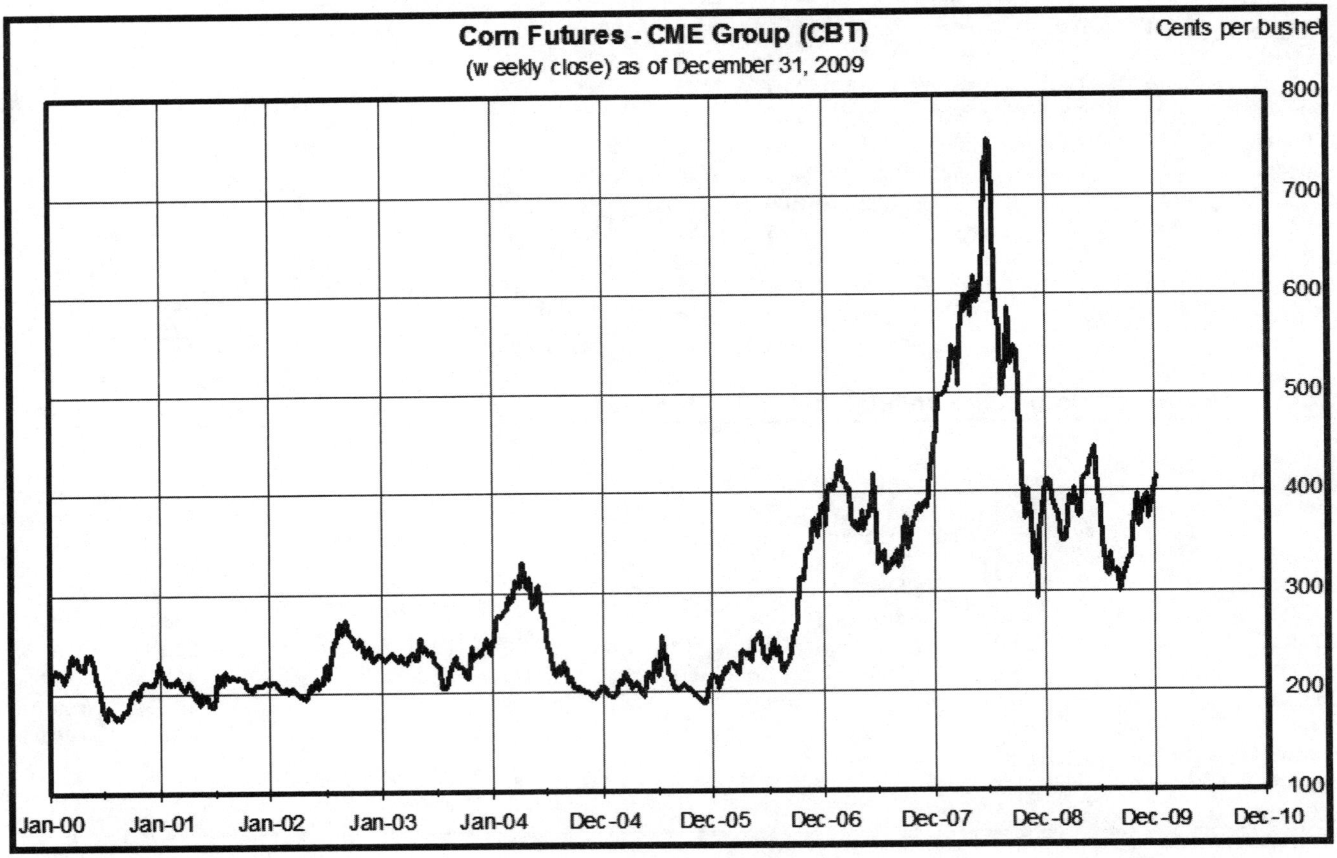

Volume of Trading of Corn Futures in Chicago In Thousands of Contracts

Year	Jan.	Feb.	Mar.	Apr.	May	June	July	Aug.	Sept.	Oct.	Nov.	Dec.	Total
2000	1,502.2	1,580.9	1,713.1	1,386.3	1,789.7	1,830.7	1,178.3	1,291.8	1,057.4	1,256.1	1,612.8	986.1	17,185.4
2001	1,397.2	1,197.4	1,329.5	1,518.7	1,173.2	1,612.1	2,023.5	1,549.0	1,072.3	1,223.3	1,741.2	891.4	16,728.7
2002	996.3	1,449.6	944.7	1,498.0	1,434.5	1,851.5	1,958.4	2,158.7	1,635.4	1,523.3	1,801.4	880.5	18,132.4
2003	1,204.0	1,559.1	1,156.9	1,633.1	1,657.0	1,951.2	1,499.3	1,830.6	1,389.7	2,057.7	1,815.9	1,364.3	19,118.7
2004	2,025.7	2,367.0	2,190.9	2,870.9	1,855.3	2,538.6	1,740.5	1,883.0	1,446.9	1,476.4	2,473.3	1,169.6	24,038.2
2005	1,467.8	2,680.8	2,278.1	2,519.1	2,188.3	3,446.1	2,626.0	2,993.6	1,618.5	1,504.2	2,892.2	1,750.3	27,965.1
2006	2,494.6	3,599.1	3,041.0	3,507.5	3,773.1	4,693.4	3,743.6	4,226.9	3,760.5	5,300.2	6,279.4	2,820.6	47,239.9
2007	5,166.5	5,111.6	4,959.0	6,095.4	4,519.9	6,090.9	4,035.7	4,344.1	3,128.9	3,306.5	4,615.6	3,145.9	54,520.2
2008	4,213.2	5,808.2	4,350.8	6,501.1	4,876.9	7,593.8	5,402.2	4,989.1	3,934.7	4,572.5	4,448.6	3,266.2	59,957.1
2009	3,041.3	4,487.1	3,684.9	4,567.6	4,151.8	5,636.8	4,765.8	4,441.8	3,153.8	4,374.0	5,509.1	3,134.9	50,948.8

Contract size = 5,000 bu. *Source: CME Group; Chicago Board of Trade (CBT)*

Average Open Interest of Corn Futures in Chicago In Thousands of Contracts

Year	Jan.	Feb.	Mar.	Apr.	May	June	July	Aug.	Sept.	Oct.	Nov.	Dec.
2000	446.0	478.9	482.1	487.8	476.9	445.0	392.0	387.3	356.6	398.0	454.9	414.9
2001	454.3	469.0	440.5	455.7	424.4	423.8	389.9	387.7	370.3	419.4	462.9	416.6
2002	459.3	464.4	431.9	430.7	411.3	430.9	458.1	509.1	501.5	485.9	497.0	450.0
2003	456.0	469.6	445.3	412.0	407.0	385.8	384.6	383.6	356.2	420.7	470.2	447.5
2004	544.0	641.4	678.0	704.9	637.4	621.9	566.5	562.2	548.8	606.3	639.5	588.9
2005	629.3	654.1	659.7	673.8	677.3	702.4	713.1	733.6	714.2	794.4	852.5	774.2
2006	875.3	1,048.8	1,066.0	1,176.0	1,288.2	1,327.8	1,360.2	1,347.2	1,302.1	1,312.6	1,405.7	1,381.5
2007	1,448.2	1,498.8	1,427.3	1,345.9	1,257.6	1,244.1	1,213.4	1,132.8	1,108.5	1,161.7	1,202.6	1,211.5
2008	1,383.2	1,463.1	1,421.8	1,445.3	1,409.2	1,396.1	1,279.9	1,170.4	1,050.9	995.5	967.6	820.5
2009	806.7	801.1	767.8	823.3	860.6	971.7	894.1	862.6	850.1	923.9	1,002.9	969.2

Contract size = 5,000 bu. *Source: CME Group; Chicago Board of Trade (CBT)*

Corn Oil

Corn oil is a bland, odorless oil produced by refining the crude corn oil that is mechanically extracted from the germ of the plant seed. High-oil corn, the most common type of corn used to make corn oil, typically has an oil content of 7% or higher compared to about 4% for normal corn. Corn oil is widely used as cooking oil, for making margarine and mayonnaise, and for making inedible products such as soap, paints, inks, varnishes, and cosmetics. For humans, studies have shown that no vegetable oil is more effective than corn oil in lowering blood cholesterol levels.

Prices –The average monthly price of corn oil (wet mill price in Chicago) in the 2008-09 marketing year (Oct-Sep) fell -52.8% yr/yr to 37.25 cents per pound, down from last year's record high of 69.37 cents per pound. Seasonally, prices tend to be highest around March/April and lowest late in the calendar year.

Supply – U.S. corn oil production in the 2007-08 marketing year (latest data) fell by -1.2% yr/yr to 2.560 billion pounds, down from the 2006-07 high of 2.590 billion pounds. Seasonally, production tends to peak around December and March and reaches a low in July. U.S. stocks in the 2007-08 marketing year (Oct 1) fell -9.5% yr/yr to 181 million pounds.

Demand – U.S. usage (domestic disappearance) in 2007-08 fell -0.2% to 1.856 billion pounds.

Exports – U.S. corn oil exports in 2007-08 fell -6.7% to 740 million pounds. U.S. corn oil imports in 2007-08 rose 4.7% to 45 million pounds.

Supply and Disappearance of Corn Oil in the United States In Millions of Pounds

	Supply				Disappearance						
Year	Stocks Oct. 1	Production	Imports	Total Supply	Baking and Frying Fats	Salad and Cooking Oil	Margarine	Total Edible Products	Domestic Disappearance	Exports	Total Disappearance
2002-03	104	2,453	65.6	2,623	W	W	W	W	1,615	888	2,503
2003-04	119	2,396	66.0	2,582	W	W	W	1,724	1,662	767	2,429
2004-05	153	2,396	49.1	2,598	W	1,466	W	1,690	1,653	789	2,442
2005-06	156	2,483	45.0	2,683	W	1,407	W	1,607	1,685	799	2,483
2006-07	200	2,560	43.1	2,803	W	1,335	W	1,735	1,831	793	2,624
2007-08[1]	179	2,507	45.2	2,731	W	1,722	W	1,606	1,756	769	2,525
2008-09[2]	205	2,475	45.0	2,725	W	1,731	W	1,591	1,705	770	2,475

[1] Preliminary. [2] Estimate. W = Withheld. *Source: Economic Research Service, U.S. Department of Agriculture (ERS-USDA)*

Production[2] of Crude Corn Oil in the United States In Millions of Pounds

Year	Oct.	Nov.	Dec.	Jan.	Feb.	Mar.	Apr.	May	June	July	Aug.	Sept.	Total
2003-04	209.1	196.5	193.2	201.0	182.9	195.8	200.0	197.7	210.7	204.3	205.2	200.1	2,397
2004-05	208.8	187.1	191.0	205.2	182.5	206.6	217.2	188.2	211.5	206.7	198.5	189.0	2,392
2005-06	207.5	199.9	200.3	209.2	184.8	217.6	191.7	218.7	206.7	215.3	222.0	209.0	2,483
2006-07	228.7	216.0	226.1	224.7	187.9	216.4	194.1	214.4	212.7	219.8	209.5	209.4	2,560
2007-08	213.5	213.0	214.0	205.4	193.7	222.5	190.7	220.9	193.7	214.9	217.3	207.3	2,507
2008-09	206.3	210.6	198.7	199.8	199.8	218.8	189.4	202.5	189.0	186.0	201.4	215.8	2,418
2009-10[1]	212.9	205.2	203.1										2,485

[1] Preliminary. [2] Not seasonally adjusted. *Source: Bureau of the Census, U.S. Department of Commerce*

Consumption Corn Oil, in Refining, in the United States In Millions of Pounds

Year	Oct.	Nov.	Dec.	Jan.	Feb.	Mar.	Apr.	May	June	July	Aug.	Sept.	Total
2003-04	W	W	W	W	W	W	134.6	W	152.8	W	W	W	1,724
2004-05	W	165.4	131.6	140.3	W	147.3	132.2	124.8	149.0	142.9	142.4	132.1	1,690
2005-06	148.4	140.4	140.3	148.4	123.4	128.0	110.8	145.2	138.9	121.6	131.6	130.0	1,607
2006-07	143.6	146.7	153.3	155.3	131.1	137.2	W	W	147.7	142.2	146.0	143.0	1,735
2007-08	155.2	W	133.8	119.5	119.2	143.8	124.2	142.9	109.7	131.8	150.3	141.8	1,606
2008-09	137.8	132.1	130.8	131.4	113.7	134.3	102.7	129.4	121.6	158.2	144.2	154.6	1,591
2009-10[1]	146.8	126.4	129.9										1,612

[1] Preliminary. W = Withheld proprietary data. *Source: Bureau of Census, U.S. Department of Commerce*

Average Corn Oil Price, Wet Mill in Chicago In Cents Per Pound

Year	Oct.	Nov.	Dec.	Jan.	Feb.	Mar.	Apr.	May	June	July	Aug.	Sept.	Average
2003-04	26.99	27.56	28.73	29.26	30.16	30.56	30.36	30.34	28.36	27.33	25.61	25.07	28.36
2004-05	23.10	24.24	26.67	27.41	27.58	28.08	29.29	30.65	30.73	30.01	28.83	27.75	27.86
2005-06	27.50	27.08	26.08	25.22	23.65	22.61	23.19	25.25	25.70	25.75	25.42	24.71	25.18
2006-07	24.70	26.47	28.05	28.05	28.66	29.08	29.93	31.56	34.71	37.25	39.61	43.61	31.81
2007-08	52.50	56.32	59.47	63.67	74.89	83.55	87.09	87.29	82.33	76.64	60.00	48.71	69.37
2008-09	34.76	31.06	26.88	25.19	29.05	29.64	31.31	37.23	39.57	36.30	35.23	36.83	32.75
2009-10[1]	37.59	38.12	40.02	40.34									39.02

[1] Preliminary. *Source: Economic Research Service, U.S. Department of Agriculture (ERS-USDA)*

Cotton

Cotton is a natural vegetable fiber that comes from small trees and shrubs of a genus belonging to the mallow family, one of which is the common American Upland cotton plant. Cotton has been used in India for at least the last 5,000 years and probably much longer, and was also used by the ancient Chinese, Egyptians, and North and South Americans. Cotton was one of the earliest crops grown by European settlers in the U.S.

Cotton requires a long growing season, plenty of sunshine and water during the growing season, and then dry weather for harvesting. In the United States, the Cotton Belt stretches from northern Florida to North Carolina and westward to California. In the U.S., planting time varies from the beginning of February in Southern Texas to the beginning of June in the northern sections of the Cotton Belt. The flower bud of the plant blossoms and develops into an oval boll that splits open at maturity. At maturity, cotton is most vulnerable to damage from wind and rain. Approximately 95% of the cotton in the U.S. is now harvested mechanically with spindle-type pickers or strippers and then sent off to cotton gins for processing. There it is dried, cleaned, separated, and packed into bales.

Cotton is used in a wide range of products from clothing to home furnishings to medical products. The value of cotton is determined according to the staple, grade, and character of each bale. Staple refers to short, medium, long, or extra-long fiber length, with medium staple accounting for about 70% of all U.S. cotton. Grade refers to the color, brightness, and amount of foreign matter and is established by the U.S. Department of Agriculture. Character refers to the fiber's diameter, strength, body, maturity (ratio of mature to immature fibers), uniformity, and smoothness. Cotton is the fifth leading cash crop in the U.S. and is one of the nation's principal agricultural exports. The weight of cotton is typically measured in terms of a "bale," which is deemed to equal 480 pounds.

Cotton futures and options are traded on the ICE Futures U.S. (ICE) exchange. Cotton futures are also traded on the Bolsa de Mercadorias & Futuros (BM&F). Cotton yarn futures are traded on the Central Japan Commodity Exchange (CCOM) and the Osaka Mercantile Exchange (OME). The ICE's futures contract calls for the delivery of 50,000 pounds net weight (approximately 100 bales) of No. 2 cotton with a quality rating of Strict Low Middling and a staple length of 1-and-2/32 inch. Delivery points include Texas (Galveston and Houston), New Orleans, Memphis, and Greenville/Spartanburg in South Carolina.

Prices – Cotton prices on the nearest-futures chart hit a 7-1/2 year low of 36.7 cents per pound in November 2008 due to the global financial crisis and expectations for a sharp drop in cotton demand due to the global recession. However, cotton prices in 2009 then staged a sharp rally during 2009 and early 2010, posting a new 2-year high of 83.3 cents in February 2010. That rally was sparked by a sharp 3-fold increase in Chinese demand for cotton due to the rebound in the Chinese economy and a much tighter supply situation for cotton. US cotton planting plunged during the summers of 2007 through 2009 due to competition for acres from corn and soybeans and due to generally weak global demand for cotton. The plunge in acreage resulted in very small US cotton crops of 12.82 million bales (-33% y/y) in 2008-09 and 12.40 million bales (-3% y/y) in 2009-10. Those small crops caused the US carry-over to drop sharply to a 14-year low of 3.30 million bales in 2009-10. On the world stage, global cotton production fell sharply in 2008-09 and 2009-10, thus causing world ending stocks to tighten to a 6-year low of 51.7 million metric tons in 2009-10.

Supply – World cotton production in 2009-10 fell -4.4% yr/yr to 102.713 million bales (480 pounds per bale), farther below the record high of 121.953 million bales seen in 2006-07. The world's largest cotton producers were China with 31% of world production in 2009-10, India with 23%, the U.S. with 12%, and Pakistan with 10%. World beginning stocks in 2009-10 fell 2.0% yr/yr to a record high of 60.925 million bales.

The U.S. cotton crop in 2009-10 fell by –3.2% yr/yr to 12.401 million bales, well down from the 2005-06 record high of 23.890 million bales. U.S. farmers harvested 7.691 million acres of cotton in 2009-10, up +1.6% yr/yr. The U.S. cotton yield in 2009-10 fell -4.8% to 774 pounds per acre, down from the 2007-08 record high of 879 pounds per acre. The leading U.S. producing states of Upland cotton are Texas with 43% of U.S. production in 2009, Georgia (16%), Arkansas (7%), North Carolina (7%), Missouri (5%), Mississippi (4%), and California (2%). U.S. production of cotton cloth has fallen sharply by almost half in the past decade due to the movement of the textile industry out of the U.S. to low-wage foreign countries. Specifically, U.S. production of cotton cloth in 2009 fell –21.3% yr/yr to a record low of 1.378 billion square yards, less than one-fourth of the production level seen in 1950.

Demand – World consumption of cotton in 2009-10 rose by +3.1% yr/yr to 111.905 million bales, but still below the 2006-07 record high of 121.979. Consumption of cotton continues to move toward countries with low wages, where the raw cotton is utilized to produce textiles and other cotton products. The largest consumers of cotton in 2009-10 were China (40% of world total), India (17%), and Pakistan (11%). U.S. consumption of cotton by mills in 2008-09 (latest data) fell –4.5% yr/yr to 4.400 million bales, and accounted for 25% of U.S. production. The remaining 75% of U.S. cotton production went for exports.

Trade – World exports of cotton in 2009-10 rose by +11.4% yr/yr to 33.661 million bales, but still below the 2005-06 record high of 44.584 million bales. The U.S. is the world's largest cotton exporter by far and accounts for 33% of world cotton exports. Key world cotton importers include Turkey with 10% of total world imports in 2009-10, Indonesia with 6%, Mexico with 4%, and Russia with 2%. U.S. cotton exports in 2007-08 (latest data) rose by +14.4% yr/yr to a new record high of 13.982 million bales. The main destinations for U.S. exports in 2007-08 were China (32%), Mexico (10%), Indonesia (9%), Taiwan (6%), and Thailand (3%).

Supply and Distribution of All Cotton in the United States In Thousands of 480-Pound Bales

Crop Year Beginning Aug. 1	Acre: Planted (1,000 Acres)	Acre: Harvested (1,000 Acres)	Yield Lbs./Acre	Supply: Beginning Stocks[3]	Supply: Production[4]	Supply: Imports	Supply: Total	Mill Use	Exports	Total	Unaccounted	Ending Stocks	Farm Price[5]	"A" Index Price[6]	Value of Production Million USD
2000-01	15,517	13,053	632	3,915	17,188	16	21,119	8,862	6,740	15,602	483	6,000	51.6	57.25	4,260.4
2001-02	15,769	13,828	705	6,000	20,303	21	26,324	7,696	11,000	18,696	-180	7,448	32.0	41.88	3,121.8
2002-03	13,958	12,417	665	7,448	17,209	67	24,724	7,273	11,900	19,173	-166	5,385	45.7	55.81	3,777.1
2003-04	13,480	12,003	730	5,385	18,255	45	23,685	6,266	13,758	20,024	-211	3,450	63.0	68.22	5,516.8
2004-05	13,659	13,057	855	3,450	23,251	29	26,730	6,691	14,436	21,127	-108	5,495	43.5	52.22	4,993.6
2005-06	14,245	13,803	831	5,495	23,890	28	29,413	5,871	17,549	23,420	76	6,069	49.7	56.19	5,695.2
2006-07	15,274	12,732	814	6,069	21,588	19	27,676	4,935	13,010	17,945	-252	9,479	48.4	59.22	5,013.2
2007-08	10,827	10,489	879	9,479	19,207	12	28,698	4,589	13,653	18,242	-412	10,044	61.1	73.02	5,652.9
2008-09[1]	9,471	7,569	813	10,044	12,815	0	22,859	3,587	13,276	16,863	-340	6,336	49.5	61.10	3,021.5
2009-10[2]	9,149	7,691	774	6,336	12,401	5	18,837	3,400	10,500	13,900	37	4,900	54-62		3,735.6

[1] Preliminary. [2] Estimate. [3] Excludes preseason ginnings (adjusted to 480-lb. bale net weight basis). [4] Includes preseason ginnings. [5] Marketing year average price. [6] Average of 5 cheapest types of SLM 1 3/32" staple length cotton offered on the European market.
Source: Economic Research Service, U.S. Department of Agriculture (ERS-USDA)

World Production of All Cotton In Thousands of 480-Pound Bales

Crop Year Beginning Aug. 1	Argentina	Australia	Brazil	Burkina	China	Egypt	Greece	India	Pakistan	Turkey	United States	Uzbekistan	Total
2000-01	758	3,700	4,312	525	20,300	965	2,035	10,931	8,379	3,600	17,188	4,400	89,098
2001-02	300	3,340	3,519	725	24,400	1,454	2,093	12,300	8,286	3,975	20,303	4,900	98,701
2002-03	290	1,680	3,890	750	25,200	1,331	1,715	10,600	7,972	4,179	17,209	4,600	90,976
2003-04	515	1,700	6,015	965	23,800	920	1,530	14,000	7,845	4,100	18,255	4,100	96,757
2004-05	675	3,000	5,900	1,180	30,300	1,356	1,800	19,000	11,138	4,150	23,251	5,200	121,504
2005-06	625	2,800	4,700	1,367	28,400	938	1,975	19,050	10,165	3,550	23,890	5,550	116,691
2006-07	800	1,350	7,000	1,300	35,500	975	1,400	21,800	9,900	3,800	21,588	5,350	121,953
2007-08	703	640	7,360	675	37,000	970	1,550	24,000	8,900	3,100	19,207	5,350	119,908
2008-09[1]	600	1,500	5,480	850	36,700	500	1,150	22,600	9,000	1,930	12,815	4,600	107,480
2009-10[2]	800	1,750	5,550	875	32,000	450	900	23,500	9,800	1,700	12,401	4,400	102,713

[1] Preliminary. [2] Estimate. *Source: Foreign Agricultural Service, U.S. Department of Agriculture (FAS-USDA)*

World Stocks and Trade of Cotton In Thousands of 480-Pound Bales

Crop Year Beginning Aug. 1	Beginning Stocks: United States	Beginning Stocks: Uzbekistan	Beginning Stocks: China	Beginning Stocks: World Total	Imports: Indonesia	Imports: Mexico	Imports: Russia	Imports: Turkey	Imports: World Total	Exports: United States	Exports: Uzbekistan	Exports: China	Exports: World Total
2000-01	3,915	738	22,378	51,079	2,650	1,865	1,650	1,758	26,227	6,740	3,450	442	26,200
2001-02	6,000	668	19,741	49,410	2,356	2,065	1,800	2,977	29,304	11,000	3,500	342	29,149
2002-03	7,448	918	18,848	54,530	2,228	2,330	1,650	2,265	30,187	11,900	3,400	751	30,457
2003-04	5,385	1,018	17,474	47,625	2,150	1,858	1,475	2,370	34,112	13,758	3,100	173	33,198
2004-05	3,450	923	18,983	48,082	2,200	1,810	1,450	3,414	33,839	14,436	3,950	30	35,014
2005-06	5,495	1,298	18,388	60,567	2,200	1,744	1,375	3,501	44,769	17,549	4,800	36	44,595
2006-07	6,069	1,248	22,536	62,371	2,200	1,353	1,325	4,029	38,055	13,010	4,500	88	37,266
2007-08	9,479	1,198	20,536	63,134	2,300	1,530	1,125	3,268	38,992	13,653	4,200	62	38,472
2008-09[1]	10,044	1,348	20,004	62,156	2,000	1,315	725	2,889	30,061	13,276	3,000	84	30,230
2009-10[2]	6,336	1,948	20,866	60,925	2,075	1,500	675	3,300	33,647	11,000	4,000	75	33,661

[1] Preliminary. [2] Estimate. *Source: Foreign Agricultural Service, U.S. Department of Agriculture (FAS-USDA)*

World Consumption of All Cottons in Specified Countries In Thousands of 480-Pound Bales

Crop Year Beginning Aug. 1	Bangladesh	Brazil	China	Egypt	India	Indonesia	Mexico	Pakistan	Russia	Thailand	Turkey	United States	Total
2000-01	1,001	4,025	22,725	773	13,544	2,500	2,125	8,125	1,600	1,685	5,167	8,379	90,819
2001-02	1,201	3,689	25,400	798	13,275	2,350	2,225	8,525	1,800	1,825	6,150	7,876	93,736
2002-03	1,552	3,585	28,950	913	13,300	2,300	2,125	9,425	1,650	1,975	6,300	7,439	97,611
2003-04	1,802	3,865	30,950	913	13,500	2,200	2,025	9,625	1,500	1,875	6,000	6,477	97,214
2004-05	2,205	4,160	37,250	963	14,800	2,200	2,125	10,525	1,425	2,125	7,100	6,799	107,844
2005-06	2,505	4,302	43,500	1,013	16,700	2,225	2,125	11,525	1,375	2,075	6,900	5,795	115,061
2006-07	3,210	4,423	48,000	1,013	18,100	2,225	2,125	12,025	1,325	1,975	7,300	5,187	121,979
2007-08	3,510	4,450	49,000	963	18,600	2,275	2,025	12,025	1,150	1,975	6,000	5,001	121,406
2008-09[1]	3,760	4,050	42,750	913	17,900	2,050	1,875	11,525	775	1,625	5,000	3,247	108,542
2009-10[2]	4,010	4,050	44,250	888	18,750	2,100	1,925	12,025	700	1,800	5,100	3,442	111,905

[1] Preliminary. [2] Estimate. *Source: Foreign Agricultural Service, U.S. Department of Agriculture (FAS-USDA)*

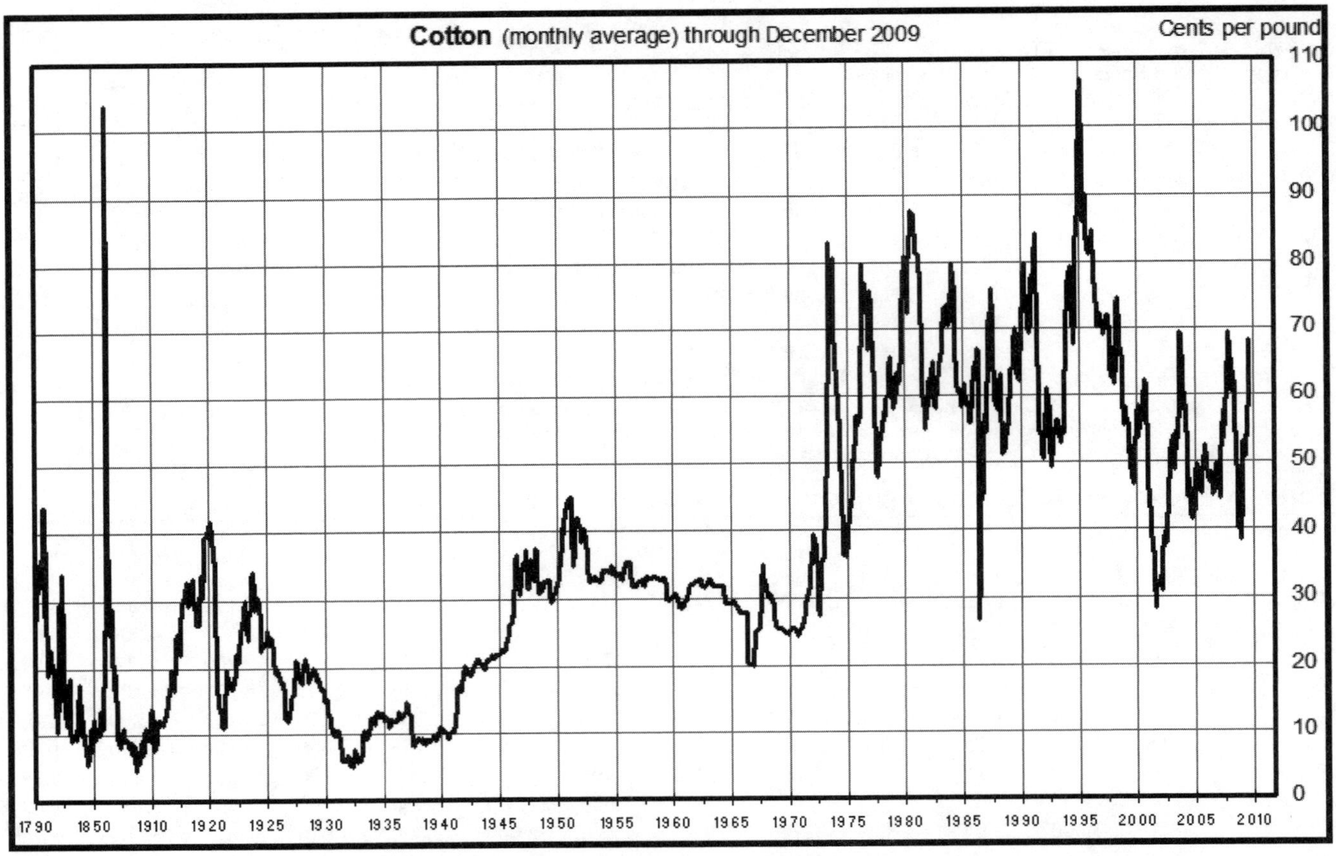

Average Spot Cotton Prices[2], C.I.F. Northern Europe In U.S. Cents Per Pound

Crop Year Beginning Aug. 1	Argentina "C"[3] 1 1/16"	Australia M 1 3/32"	Cotlook Index A	Cotlook Index B	Egypt Giza[4] 81	Greece M 1 3/32"	Mexico[5] M 1 3/32"	Pakistan Sind/ Punjab[6]	Tanzania AR[7] Type 3	Turkey Izmir[8] 1 3/32"	U.S. Calif. ACALA SJV[9]	U.S. Memphis Terr.[10] M 1 3/32"	U.S. Orleans/ Texas[11] M 1 1/32"
1990-1	77.06	85.58	82.90	77.80	177.43	84.24	84.46	77.19	89.62	81.32	92.84	88.13	80.35
1991-2	55.08	65.97	63.05	58.50	128.10	65.90	68.19	58.14	68.90	74.66	74.47	66.35	63.41
1992-3	64.31	64.01	57.70	53.70	99.24	56.92	----	52.66	62.24	----	68.37	63.08	58.89
1993-4	80.20	72.81	70.60	67.30	88.35	58.81	----	54.42	69.83	59.80	77.55	72.80	69.78
1994-5	101.88	81.05	92.75	92.40	93.70	88.64	82.65	73.75	----	----	106.40	98.67	95.70
1995-6	82.98	93.75	85.61	81.06	----	84.95	94.94	81.86	96.20	90.38	103.49	94.71	90.37
1996-7	79.71	83.24	78.59	74.80	----	75.85	79.60	73.37	79.22	----	89.55	82.81	79.77
1997-8	69.96	77.49	72.19	70.69	----	72.03	81.70	72.93	84.04	----	85.11	78.12	74.74
1998-9	57.19	66.48	58.94	54.26	----	58.66	65.78	----	72.70	----	78.57	74.20	70.95
1999-00[1]	----	61.97	52.85	49.55	----	51.71	56.43	----	55.67	----	68.76	66.29	55.67

[1] Preliminary. [2] Generally for prompt shipment. [3] 1-1/32" prior to January 20, 1984; 1-1/16" since. [4] Dendera until 1969/70; Giza 67 1969/70 until December 1983; Giza 69/75/81 until November 1990; Giza 81 since. [5] S. Brazil Type 5, 1-1/32" prior to 1968-69; 1-1/16" until 1987/88; Brazilian Type 5/6, 1-1/16" since. [6] Punjab until 1979/80; Sind SG until June 1984; Sind/Punjab SG until January 1985; Afzal 1" until January 1986; Afzal 1-1/32" since. [7] No. 1 until 1978/79; No. 1/2 until February 1986; AR' Mwanza No. 3 until January 1992; AR' Type 3 since. [8] Izmir ST 1 White 1-1/16" RG prior to 1981/82; 1-3/32" from 1981/82 until January 1987; Izmir/Antalya ST 1 White 1-3/32" RG since. [9] SM 1-3/32" prior to 1975/76; SM 1-1/8" since. [10] SM 1-1/16" prior to 1981/82; Middling 1-3/32" since. [11] Middling 1" prior to 1988/89; Middling 1-1/32" since.
Source: International Cotton Advisory Committee (ICAC)

Average Producer Price Index of Gray Cotton Broadwovens Index 1982 = 100

Year	Jan.	Feb.	Mar.	Apr.	May	June	July	Aug.	Sept.	Oct.	Nov.	Dec.	Average
2000	112.1	111.1	106.9	108.2	108.6	107.7	108.3	108.8	110.1	110.2	112.3	112.3	109.7
2001	112.8	113.1	113.1	112.7	112.8	112.9	113.2	112.9	112.9	112.0	111.2	111.1	112.6
2002	110.7	109.9	110.1	108.1	107.3	108.0	106.9	107.0	106.9	105.9	105.7	106.2	107.7
2003	105.7	105.2	105.0	105.9	106.0	106.7	107.2	109.1	110.1	111.0	110.6	108.9	107.6
2004	109.9	111.2	110.6	111.5	112.3	112.6	113.7	113.2	113.5	113.6	113.3	112.5	112.3
2005	112.6	112.0	111.9	111.8	111.2	111.2	111.1	111.2	111.2	111.3	110.9	111.1	111.5
2006	111.1	110.5	109.9	109.9	110.1	110.1	110.1	110.1	110.1	110.0	110.0	109.9	110.2
2007	110.0	109.9	109.9	110.1	109.8	109.9	109.9	109.9	109.9	110.0	109.9	109.9	109.9
2008	110.1	110.1	110.1	110.1	110.0	109.9	110.2	111.7	111.7	111.7	111.6	111.4	110.7
2009[1]	111.0	111.0	111.0	107.2	107.2	107.2	107.2	107.5	107.5	107.5	108.3	108.3	108.4

[1] Preliminary. *Source: Bureau of Labor Statistics (0337-01), U.S. Department of Commerce*

Average Price of SLM 1-1/16", Cotton/5 at Designated U.S. Markets   In Cents Per Pound (Net Weight)

Year	Aug.	Sept.	Oct.	Nov.	Dec.	Jan.	Feb.	Mar.	Apr.	May	June	July	Average
2000-01	59.33	60.62	60.54	62.16	61.04	56.66	54.10	47.22	42.19	40.02	37.38	37.48	51.56
2001-02	36.05	33.22	28.42	31.23	32.21	32.13	31.60	33.23	31.86	31.14	36.36	39.78	33.10
2002-03	39.20	37.91	39.62	44.98	46.38	48.60	51.35	53.82	53.38	48.94	50.92	54.45	47.46
2003-04	51.94	58.02	69.38	68.88	65.09	68.21	63.35	61.78	57.50	60.22	52.35	45.05	60.15
2004-05	44.92	47.48	44.55	42.62	41.68	43.21	42.90	48.19	49.58	48.57	45.92	47.78	45.62
2005-06	45.38	47.43	51.02	48.80	49.53	51.91	52.39	50.04	49.00	47.00	47.90	47.15	48.96
2006-07	48.65	46.80	45.15	46.32	49.85	49.90	48.77	49.21	46.97	44.62	50.35	57.50	48.67
2007-08	53.46	57.08	59.06	59.59	59.44	63.34	65.92	69.27	63.91	60.67	63.34	62.85	61.49
2008-09	60.93	56.72	46.90	39.83	42.07	44.87	41.81	38.53	45.11	52.92	50.80	53.98	47.87
2009-10[1]	53.77	55.78	59.19	64.90	68.11	65.93							61.28

[1] Preliminary. [2] Grade 41, leaf 4, staple 34, mike 35-36 and 43-49 , strength 23.5-26.4. *Source: Agricultural Marketing Service, U.S. Department of Agriculture (AMS-USDA)*

Average Spot Cotton, 1-3/32", Price (SLM) at Designated U.S. Markets[2]   In Cents Per Pound (Net Weight)

Year	Aug.	Sept.	Oct.	Nov.	Dec.	Jan.	Feb.	Mar.	Apr.	May	June	July	Average
2000-01	62.60	63.62	63.13	65.08	64.73	60.18	57.18	50.08	44.94	42.54	39.88	39.96	54.49
2001-02	38.88	36.11	31.55	34.03	34.82	34.55	34.08	36.04	34.84	34.03	39.31	42.86	35.93
2002-03	42.31	41.07	43.08	48.78	50.70	52.87	55.34	57.88	57.54	52.96	55.09	58.46	51.34
2003-04	55.87	61.76	73.27	72.63	68.90	71.96	67.34	66.42	63.11	65.97	57.99	51.11	64.69
2004-05	50.45	52.55	49.45	47.23	46.41	48.16	48.17	53.37	54.67	53.76	51.26	52.97	50.70
2005-06	50.59	52.81	56.01	53.78	54.47	56.69	57.16	55.03	54.07	52.02	52.97	52.35	54.00
2006-07	53.80	51.95	50.20	51.13	54.71	54.75	53.66	54.05	51.59	49.12	54.71	61.59	53.44
2007-08	57.53	61.15	63.08	63.71	63.50	67.22	69.73	72.68	67.25	63.99	66.67	66.17	65.22
2008-09	64.25	60.01	50.52	43.76	45.95	48.76	45.67	42.40	49.02	56.81	54.70	57.94	51.65
2009-10[1]	57.77	59.82	64.58	69.23	72.59								64.80

[1] Preliminary. *Source: Agricultural Marketing Service, U.S. Department of Agriculture (AMS-USDA)*

Average Spot Prices of U.S. Cotton,[2] Base Quality (SLM) at Designated Markets   In Cents Per Pound

Crop Year Beginning Aug. 1	Dallas (EastTex.-Okl.)	Fresno (San Joaquin Valley)	Greenville (South-east)	Greenwood (South Delta)	Lubbock (West Texas)	Memphis (North Delta)	Phoenix Desert (South-west)	Average
1999-00	50.49	56.67	53.81	53.34	50.12	53.34	48.79	52.36
2000-01	51.03	52.45	52.63	52.32	50.71	52.32	49.47	51.56
2001-02	32.59	34.64	33.02	33.24	32.39	33.24	32.60	33.10
2002-03	46.76	47.52	48.28	48.46	46.51	48.47	46.27	47.46
2003-04	59.95	59.71	60.80	60.85	59.71	60.78	59.23	60.15
2004-05	44.22	47.38	45.91	46.02	44.08	46.02	45.66	45.61
2005-06	47.69	50.06	49.65	49.63	47.78	49.67	48.26	48.96
2006-07	48.17	48.58	49.90	49.46	48.06	49.46	47.08	48.67
2007-08	60.89	60.57	63.95	62.67	60.64	62.67	59.07	61.50
2008-09[1]	47.08	49.10	48.97	47.99	46.93	47.99	47.03	47.87

[1] Preliminary [2] Prices are for mixed lots, net weight, uncompressed in warehouse.
Source: Agricultural Marketing Service, U.S. Department of Agriculture (AMS-USDA)

Average Price[1] Received by Farmers for Upland Cotton in the United States   In Cents Per Pound

Year	Aug.	Sept.	Oct.	Nov.	Dec.	Jan.	Feb.	Mar.	Apr.	May	June	July	Average
2000-01	51.4	50.6	55.5	58.0	57.8	52.1	48.5	41.1	42.6	40.9	39.2	38.9	49.8
2001-02	37.3	36.5	30.7	27.8	30.8	27.3	28.0	28.4	27.2	26.7	33.7	35.3	29.8
2002-03	33.0	35.2	39.4	43.0	44.3	45.5	46.5	48.6	45.4	45.9	45.5	46.3	43.2
2003-04	46.3	55.7	67.8	63.0	63.3	62.2	61.9	61.6	60.3	59.7	59.9	53.8	59.6
2004-05	53.7	49.3	50.6	43.2	39.3	38.5	38.3	40.3	41.4	39.6	41.9	41.1	43.1
2005-06	42.1	44.3	48.5	48.5	48.0	48.6	48.9	50.0	48.5	46.4	47.4	46.8	47.3
2006-07	45.8	47.3	45.9	47.4	49.0	49.4	47.4	46.4	46.3	44.0	45.4	45.2	46.6
2007-08	44.9	52.0	55.5	57.4	59.6	61.5	63.0	63.0	65.5	64.6	64.0	66.2	59.8
2008-09	58.5	61.1	58.8	54.8	53.3	46.0	41.2	41.0	45.3	46.4	46.4	47.2	50.0
2009-10[2]	47.7	55.0	56.7	58.5	62.8	60.6	61.7						57.6

[1] Weighted average by sales. [2] Preliminary. *Source: Agricultural Marketing Service, U.S. Department of Agriculture (AMS-USDA)*

COTTON

Purchases Reported by Exchanges in Designated U.S. Spot Markets[1] In Running Bales

Crop Year Beginning Aug. 1	Aug.	Sept.	Oct.	Nov.	Dec.	Jan.	Feb.	Mar.	Apr.	May	June	July	Market Total
2000-01	63,607	69,083	143,938	323,891	288,242	217,755	215,318	191,667	274,185	193,774	152,905	167,647	2,302,012
2001-02	118,000	94,697	214,785	644,860	225,869	289,778	180,362	278,853	84,259	155,391	143,422	93,489	2,523,765
2002-03	43,047	49,671	194,020	204,564	369,838	481,730	432,055	169,064	170,951	213,679	149,780	86,830	2,565,229
2003-04	125,240	245,295	273,028	167,285	321,083	417,090	267,237	167,357	62,031	70,979	79,061	58,400	2,254,086
2004-05	135,568	46,749	91,390	263,999	369,597	402,504	445,448	424,472	210,285	93,471	95,154	20,398	2,599,035
2005-06	67,318	63,884	138,910	220,961	363,287	434,818	183,744	183,273	62,703	73,726	117,934	60,708	1,971,266
2006-07	87,527	58,849	111,619	112,634	214,384	174,852	140,273	125,562	207,478	310,748	168,730	137,204	1,849,860
2007-08	85,183	133,709	126,008	149,748	197,651	359,180	303,523	95,053	104,513	64,281	119,022	46,555	1,784,426
2008-09	79,487	75,191	89,246	92,960	113,117	149,362	106,701	175,099	265,718	92,969	66,390		1,424,989
2009-10	34,279	54,457	83,790	179,007	199,006	75,580							1,252,238

[1] Seven markets. *Source: Agricultural Marketing Service, U.S. Department of Agriculture (AMS-USDA)*

Production of Cotton (Upland and American-Pima) in the United States In Thousands of 480-Pound Bales

	Upland												Total
Year	Alabama	Arizona	Arkansas	California	Georgia	Louisiana	sippi	Missouri	Carolina	Carolina	nessee	Texas	American-Pima
2000	543	791	1,425	2,210	1,663	911	1,711	540	1,429	379	710	3,940	389.1
2001	920	690	1,833	1,770	2,220	1,034	2,396	695	1,673	423	978	4,260	700.4
2002	570	613	1,669	1,460	1,578	739	1,935	610	806	131	818	5,040	678.3
2003	820	550	1,804	1,495	2,110	1,027	2,120	700	1,037	326	890	4,330	432.3
2004	814	723	2,089	1,790	1,797	885	2,346	830	1,360	390	984	7,740	745.6
2005	848	622	2,202	1,623	2,140	1,098	2,147	864	1,437	410	1,122	8,484	630.5
2006	675	556	2,525	779	2,334	1,241	2,107	985	1,285	433	1,368	5,800	765.4
2007	416	514	1,896	650	1,660	699	1,318	764	783	160	600	8,250	851.8
2008[1]	469	405	1,296	367	1,600	281	683	698	755	246	530	4,450	430.8
2009[2]	360	440	830	250	1,820	340	425	520	760	200	500	4,900	390.3

[1] Preliminary. [2] Forecast. *Source: Agricultural Statistics Board, U.S. Department of Agriculture (ASB-USDA)*

Cotton Production and Yield Estimates

	Forecasts of Production (1,000 Bales of 480 Lbs.[1])						Actual	Forecasts of Yield (Lbs. Per Harvested Acre)						Actual
Year	Aug.1	Sept.1	Oct. 1	Nov. 1	Dec. 1	Jan. 1	Crop	Aug.1	Sept.1	Oct. 1	Nov. 1	Dec. 1	Jan. 1	Yield
2000	19,159	18,315	17,485	17,510	17,399	----	17,188	648	622	620	622	619	----	632
2001	20,003	19,992	20,072	20,175	20,064	----	20,303	670	679	681	685	691	----	705
2002	18,439	18,134	18,070	17,815	17,375	----	17,209	675	675	674	665	648	----	665
2003	17,104	16,939	17,559	18,215	18,215	----	18,255	667	667	696	722	722	----	730
2004	20,183	20,895	21,545	22,545	22,815	----	23,251	727	758	782	818	828	----	855
2005	21,291	22,282	22,717	23,161	23,703	----	23,890	748	782	797	813	832	----	831
2006	20,431	20,345	20,659	21,299	21,297	----	21,588	765	762	774	798	798	----	814
2007	17,346	17,812	18,154	18,862	18,987	----	19,207	783	811	826	859	864	----	879
2008	13,767	13,846	13,711	13,528	13,613	----	12,815	842	849	849	837	843	----	813
2009	13,207	13,438	12,998	12,496	12,592	----	12,401	816	816	807	776	782	----	774

[1] Net weight bales. *Source: Agricultural Statistics Board, U.S. Department of Agriculture (ASB-USDA)*

Supply and Distribution of Upland Cotton in the United States In Thousands of 480-Pound Bales

Crop Year	Area			Supply				Disappearance				Farm
Beginning	Planted	Harvested	Yield	Beginning	Pro-		Total	Mill			Ending	Price[5]
Aug. 1	1,000 Acres		Lbs./Acre	Stocks[3]	duction	Imports	Supply	Use	Exports	Total	Stocks	Cents/ Lb.
2000-01	15,347	12,884	626	3,665	16,799	8	20,472	8,738	6,303	15,041	5,879	49.8
2001-02	15,499	13,560	694	5,879	19,603	6	25,488	7,592	10,603	18,195	7,120	29.8
2002-03	13,714	12,174	652	7,120	16,530	10	23,661	7,170	11,266	18,436	5,140	43.2
2003-04	13,301	11,826	723	5,140	17,823	4	22,967	6,204	13,220	19,424	3,384	59.6
2004-05	13,409	12,809	843	3,384	22,505	8	25,897	6,629	13,645	20,274	5,482	43.1
2005-06	13,975	13,534	825	5,482	23,260	9	28,751	5,820	17,029	22,849	5,991	47.3
2006-07	14,948	12,408	806	5,991	20,822	10	26,824	4,896	12,338	17,234	9,291	46.6
2007-08	10,535	10,201	864	9,291	18,355	6	27,652	4,553	12,820	17,373	9,888	59.8
2008-09[1]	9,297	7,400	803	9,888	12,385	0	22,272	3,558	13,044	16,602	6,031	50.0
2009-10[2]	9,008	7,552	763	6,031	12,011	3	18,163	3,370	9,950	13,320	4,806	57.6

[1] Preliminary. [2] Estimate. [3] Excludes preseason ginnings (adjusted to 480-lb. bale net weight basis). [4] Includes preseason ginnings.
[5] Marketing year average price. *Source: Economic Research Service, U.S. Department of Agriculture (ERS-USDA)*

Average Open Interest of Cotton #2 Futures in New York In Contracts

Year	Jan.	Feb.	Mar.	Apr.	May	June	July	Aug.	Sept.	Oct.	Nov.	Dec.
2000	63,987	67,720	69,788	56,038	54,058	48,024	53,621	63,069	73,735	67,767	65,017	62,931
2001	71,849	73,383	71,389	70,407	66,680	64,032	61,183	65,257	65,496	59,777	56,896	58,156
2002	64,096	64,572	63,451	63,827	67,601	65,848	74,892	72,612	69,554	71,526	82,802	74,685
2003	83,775	89,852	91,336	78,658	73,146	69,137	62,565	62,781	80,348	108,981	97,809	79,627
2004	93,191	81,871	84,600	89,082	81,988	79,310	77,029	75,449	69,514	76,556	86,280	84,409
2005	92,651	94,047	118,183	120,416	103,446	93,818	92,284	99,959	105,874	117,889	103,466	100,660
2006	118,234	129,108	129,728	141,156	165,386	170,190	161,719	166,806	178,539	184,002	170,275	164,797
2007	177,495	199,342	214,628	225,473	223,839	212,296	214,893	206,042	215,820	239,217	229,629	219,185
2008	264,235	279,240	286,505	259,800	258,309	239,935	219,979	216,387	211,933	177,277	146,431	127,380
2009	130,049	120,331	128,054	128,973	134,079	120,861	122,153	127,019	136,585	165,683	180,594	182,489

Contract size = 50,000 lbs. *Source: ICE Futures U.S. (ICE)*

Volume of Trading of Cotton #2 Futures in New York In Contracts

Year	Jan.	Feb.	Mar.	Apr.	May	June	July	Aug.	Sept.	Oct.	Nov.	Dec.	Total
2000	270,792	279,566	248,017	220,222	232,947	272,023	147,878	175,707	154,735	172,875	242,013	180,982	2,597,757
2001	267,930	270,876	237,356	215,903	175,808	214,513	132,065	118,685	98,947	152,702	258,847	116,033	2,259,665
2002	156,834	248,299	162,781	237,861	188,340	234,442	170,893	128,185	145,946	199,779	296,859	157,741	2,327,960
2003	202,615	267,234	217,791	325,627	249,314	271,822	164,027	127,080	283,988	422,132	356,052	148,310	3,035,992
2004	272,948	359,105	300,820	376,669	184,869	357,548	159,924	195,886	196,739	224,431	341,709	185,370	3,156,018
2005	356,817	407,277	317,486	465,210	306,971	456,584	171,139	189,584	271,268	290,650	408,580	207,424	3,848,990
2006	311,926	495,729	375,624	515,709	330,785	601,971	184,482	259,259	268,847	308,584	587,710	249,781	4,490,407
2007	366,579	713,894	375,964	765,244	439,838	745,901	428,059	445,099	435,529	520,221	759,829	338,822	6,334,979
2008	684,489	971,319	730,160	651,281	427,731	690,183	281,522	306,004	418,279	401,064	426,785	174,146	6,162,963
2009	276,977	326,853	272,091	373,379	274,983	372,124	187,347	177,989	228,815	347,989	509,375	227,073	3,574,995

Contract size = 50,000 lbs. *Source: ICE Futures U.S. (ICE)*

Daily Rate of Upland Cotton Mill Consumption[2] on Cotton-System Spinning Spindles in the United States
In Thousands of Running Bales

Crop Year Beginning Aug. 1	Aug.	Sept.	Oct.	Nov.	Dec.	Jan.	Feb.	Mar.	Apr.	May	June	July	Average
2000-01	36.4	35.6	34.5	33.0	34.4	33.5	31.9	31.8	30.6	29.7	27.6	28.6	32.3
2001-02	28.8	28.1	27.5	26.3	27.1	27.1	27.5	27.9	27.4	28.4	29.3	30.6	28.0
2002-03	28.0	28.3	27.9	27.4	27.2	26.5	26.8	26.4	26.0	25.0	24.3	24.7	26.5
2003-04	23.0	22.7	22.6	23.0	22.7	22.4	23.1	23.1	22.8	23.1	23.2	24.2	23.0
2004-05	25.1	25.1	24.9	24.4	25.2	24.8	23.7	23.7	24.0	23.6	25.2	24.4	24.5
2005-06	23.2	22.0	22.6	21.2	20.5	22.9	23.1	22.4	20.7	20.2	19.9	19.5	21.5
2006-07	18.9	18.8	18.5	W	W	W	W	W	W	W	W	W	18.7
2007-08	W	W	W	W	W	W	W	W	W	W	W	W	W
2008-09	W	W	W	W	W	W	W	W	W	W	W	W	W
2009-10[1]	W	W	W	W	W								

[1] Preliminary. [2] Not seasonally adjusted. W = Withheld. *Source: Bureau of the Census: U.S. Department of Commerce*

Consumption of American and Foreign Cotton in the United States
In Thousands of Running Bales

Year	Aug.	Sept.	Oct.	Nov.	Dec.	Jan.	Feb.	Mar.	Apr.	May	June	July	Total
2000-01	766	929	741	663	749	661	657	837	641	628	727	510	8,510
2001-02	616	751	600	521	563	541	580	759	575	594	754	571	7,425
2002-03	574	733	585	545	598	671	556	708	541	523	616	456	7,106
2003-04	476	599	482	468	504	478	475	609	461	473	582	446	6,053
2004-05	484	604	483	460	500	470	472	601	469	463	581	449	6,035
2005-06	454	574	472	415	438	452	476	593	430	422	531	381	5,637
2006-07	385	492	389	357	370	361	363	461	371	371	476	348	4,744
2007-08	358	467	366	343	362	423	341	402	346	333	430	329	4,499
2008-09	349	399	333	285	234	261	230	302	230	251	311	254	3,439
2009-10[1]	263	280	261	266	267								3,208

[1] Preliminary. *Source: Bureau of the Census, U.S. Department of Commerce*

Exports of All Cotton[2] from the United States
In Thousands of Running Bales

Year	Aug.	Sept.	Oct.	Nov.	Dec.	Jan.	Feb.	Mar.	Apr.	May	June	July	Total
2000-01	430	336	382	435	541	564	614	720	568	692	784	648	6,715
2001-02	612	824	678	649	927	964	1,042	1,225	999	842	1,067	679	10,505
2002-03	472	653	373	626	935	1,206	873	1,597	1,174	1,150	1,273	1,231	11,561
2003-04	810	555	446	758	1,116	1,194	1,238	1,869	1,453	1,117	1,576	1,021	13,154
2004-05	760	374	422	632	1,087	1,179	1,214	1,839	1,461	1,094	1,411	1,828	13,301
2005-06	1,407	742	533	763	1,236	946	1,541	2,195	1,758	1,725	1,906	1,903	16,655
2006-07	688	412	487	599	812	683	824	1,266	1,269	1,385	2,174	1,745	12,342
2007-08	1,116	1,337	883	977	781	981	945	955	1,096	1,360	1,292	1,427	13,150
2008-09	994	983	1,159	923	747	742	812	1,132	1,444	1,473	1,274	1,118	12,800
2009-10[1]	892	812	665	570									8,816

[1] Preliminary. *Source: Foreign Agricultural Service, U.S. Department of Agriculture (FAS-USDA)*

U.S. Exports of American Cotton to Countries of Destination
In Thousands of 480-Pound Bales

Crop Year Beginning Aug. 1	Canada	China	Hong Kong	Indo-nesia	Italy	Japan	Rep. of Korea	Mexico	Philip-pines	Taiwan	Thailand	United Kingdom	Total
1999-00	245	147	316	573	61	424	307	1,500	71	257	476	4	6,401
2000-01	322	124	287	558	52	355	489	1,760	42	237	367	1	6,740
2001-02	235	306	407	947	58	385	577	1,516	126	693	693	0	10,397
2002-03	303	1,840	364	869	81	380	480	1,777	104	592	556	4	11,607
2003-04	303	4,919	169	889	63	284	469	1,620	100	527	396	20	13,758
2004-05	305	4,085	274	1,138	75	301	643	1,589	110	846	711	60	14,436
2005-06	178	9,095	280	933	33	265	431	1,511	46	530	660	23	18,039
2006-07	101	3,641	238	928	36	265	307	1,200	39	456	429	0	12,219
2007-08[1]	40	4,491	177	1,261	62	376	361	1,432	26	838	390	0	13,972
2008-09[2]	19	3,776	184	1,052	23	158	302	1,320	52	616	436		13,211

[1] Preliminary. [2] Estimate. *Source: Foreign Agricultural Service, U.S. Department of Agriculture (FAS-USDA)*

Cotton[1] Government Loan Program in the United States

Crop Year Beginning Aug. 1	Support Price (Cents Per Lb.)	Target Price (Cents Per Lb.)	Put Under Support (Ths Bales)	% of Production	Acquired (Ths. Bales)	Owned July 31 (Ths. Bales)
2000-01	51.92	NA	8,837	51.4	69	5
2001-02	51.92	NA	13,655	67.3	31	2
2002-03	52.00	72.4	12,740	74.0	0	106
2003-04	52.00	72.4	10,466	57.3	16	0
2004-05	52.00	72.4	17,092	73.5	8	0
2005-06	52.00	72.4	17,783	74.4	181	11
2006-07	52.00	72.4	17,839	82.6	79	29
2007-08	52.00	72.4	14,636	76.2	169	14
2008-09	52.00	71.3	10,005	78.1	4	13
2009-10[2]	52.00	71.3	8,233	66.4		6

[1] Upland. [2] Preliminary. NA = Not applicable. *Source: Economic Research Service, U.S. Department of Agriculture (ERS-USDA)*

Production of Cotton Cloth[1] in the United States In Millions of Square Yards

Year	First Quarter	Second Quarter	Third Quarter	Fourth Quarter	Total
2000	1,075	1,129	1,111	1,079	4,395
2001	1,047	976	873	811	3,706
2002	893	912	894	825	3,524
2003	836	780	662	620	2,898
2004	648	644	640	614	2,547
2005	672	640	653	664	2,629
2006	583	609	551	487	2,230
2007	521	507	488	453	1,969
2008	447	460	451	393	1,751
2009[2]	336	357	340		1,378

[1] Cotton broadwoven goods over 12 inches in width. [2] Preliminary. *Source: Bureau of Census, U.S. Department of Commerce*

Cotton Ginnings[1] in the United States To: In Thousands of Running Bales

Crop Year	Aug. 1	Sept. 1	Sept. 15	Oct. 1	Oct. 15	Nov. 1	Nov. 15	Dec. 1	Dec. 15	Jan. 1	Jan. 15	Feb. 1	Total Crop
2000-01	245	842	1,454	3,264	5,930	9,221	11,546	13,657	15,364	16,097	16,518	16,648	16,742
2001-02	99	609	802	2,072	4,616	8,806	12,558	15,564	17,606	18,759	19,268	19,532	19,771
2002-03	56	538	898	1,656	3,520	6,697	9,265	12,368	14,392	15,654	16,285	16,576	16,710
2003-04	29	567	958	2,001	3,819	7,393	10,507	13,466	15,678	16,883	17,409	17,601	17,709
2004-05	48	563	1,157	2,227	4,788	8,758	12,019	14,754	17,072	18,925	20,155	21,249	22,556
2005-06	69	592	976	2,314	4,556	8,691	12,569	15,991	18,401	20,108	21,282	22,255	23,253
2006-07	23	406	996	2,572	5,039	8,604	11,833	15,139	17,657	19,212	20,062	20,559	20,998
2007-08	W	182	375	1,566	3,793	7,072	10,099	12,593	14,341	15,700	16,690	17,585	18,713
2008-09	13	335	476	797	2,027	4,358	6,800	8,928	10,463	11,572	12,094	12,370	12,462
2009-10[2]	5	143	175	293	567	2,193	4,962	7,874	9,733	10,819	11,390	11,715	

[1] Excluding linters. [2] Preliminary. W = Withheld. *Source: National Agricultural Statistics Service, U.S. Department of Agriculture (NASS-USDA)*

Fiber Prices in the United States In Cents Per Pound

Year		Cotton[1] Actual	Cotton[1] Raw[5] Equivalent	Rayon[2] Actual	Rayon[2] Raw[5] Equivalent	Polyester[3] Actual	Polyester[3] Raw[5] Equivalent	Price Ratios[4] In Percent Cotton/ Rayon	Price Ratios[4] In Percent Cotton/ Polyester
2000		64.06	71.17	97.58	101.65	57.08	59.46	70.0	119.1
2001		47.08	52.32	98.50	102.61	60.42	62.93	52.0	83.0
2002		45.56	50.63	97.83	101.91	61.17	63.72	50.0	79.0
2003		62.54	69.49	90.25	94.01	60.67	63.20	74.1	111.0
2004		60.42	67.13	99.08	103.21	62.67	65.28	66.5	103.5
2005		54.75	60.00	114.58	119.36	67.75	70.57	51.0	86.2
2006		56.70	63.00	113.00	117.71	69.00	71.86	53.5	88.0
2007		61.97	68.86	113.00	117.71	74.00	77.08	58.5	89.3
2008[6]		73.79	82.01	113.00	117.71	74.00	77.08	69.7	121.1
	Jan.	73.32	81.47	113.00	117.71	74.00	77.08	69.2	120.3
	Feb.	74.25	82.54	113.00	117.71	74.00	77.08	70.1	121.8
	Mar.	NA	NA	NA	NA	NA	NA	NA	NA
	Apr.	NA	NA	NA	NA	NA	NA	NA	NA
	May	NA	NA	NA	NA	NA	NA	NA	NA
	June	NA	NA	NA	NA	NA	NA	NA	NA
	July	NA	NA	NA	NA	NA	NA	NA	NA
	Aug.	NA	NA	NA	NA	NA	NA	NA	NA
	Sept.	NA	NA	NA	NA	NA	NA	NA	NA
	Oct.	NA	NA	NA	NA	NA	NA	NA	NA
	Nov.	NA	NA	NA	NA	NA	NA	NA	NA
	Dec.								

[1] SLM-1 1/16" at group B Mill points, net weight. [2] 1.5 and 3.0 denier, regular rayon staples. [3] Reported average market price for 1.5 denier polyester staple for cotton blending. [4] Raw fiber equivalent. [5] Actual prices converted to estimated raw fiber equivalent as follows: cotton, divided by 0.90, rayon and polyester, divided by 0.96. [6] Preliminary.
Source: Economic Research Service, U.S. Department of Agriculture (ERS-USDA)

Cottonseed and Products

Cottonseed is crushed to produce both oil and meal. Cottonseed oil is typically used for cooking oil and cottonseed meal is fed to livestock. Before the cottonseed is crushed for oil and meal, it is de-linted of its linters. Linters are used for padding in furniture, absorbent cotton swabs, and for the manufacture of many cellulose products. The sediment left by cottonseed oil refining, called foots, provides fatty acids for industrial products. The value of cottonseeds represents a substantial 18% of a cotton producer's income.

Prices – The average monthly price of cottonseed oil in 2009 fell by -45.0% yr/yr to 37.47 cents per pound, down from last year's record high of 68.09 cents per pound. The average monthly price of cottonseed meal in 2009 fell by -0.6% yr/yr to $263.60 per short ton, down from last year's record high of $265.22 per short ton.

Supply – World production of cottonseed in the 2008-09 marketing year fell –7.9% yr/yr to 40.273 million metric tons, down from the record high of 45.136 million metric tons posted in 2004-05. The world's largest cottonseed producers are China with 31% of world production, India with 24%, the U.S. with 10%, and Pakistan with 10%. U.S. production of cottonseed in the 2009-10 marketing year fell by –2.8% yr/yr to 4.178 million tons. U.S. production of cottonseed oil in 2009-10 fell by –7.2% yr/yr to 615 million pounds, down from the 12-year high of 957 million pounds posted in 2004-05. U.S. annualized production of cottonseed cake and meal for the first five months of the 2009-10 marketing year (Aug-Jul) fell by 29.7% yr/yr to 717,422 short tons.

Demand – U.S. cottonseed crushed (consumed) in the U.S. annualized for the first five months of the 2009-10 marketing year fell by –27.3% to a record low of 1.635 million tons, far below the levels of over 4 million tons seen in the 1970s.

Trade – U.S. exports of cottonseed in 2009-10 rose +83.3% to 350,000 short tons, while imports were zero.

World Production of Cottonseed   In Thousands of Metric Ton

Crop Year Beginning Oct. 1	Argentina	Australia	Brazil	China	Egypt	Greece	India	Mexico	Pakistan	Turkey	United States	Former USSR	World Total
2000-01	257	1,062	1,720	7,868	371	726	4,760	128	3,651	1,289	5,838	2,531	33,914
2001-02	102	1,054	1,407	9,476	527	743	5,372	152	3,610	1,354	6,761	2,749	37,365
2002-03	90	470	1,451	8,750	475	718	4,624	68	3,472	1,457	5,610	2,584	33,641
2003-04	159	494	2,390	8,651	338	611	6,018	115	3,416	1,337	6,046	2,442	36,131
2004-05	200	912	2,309	11,257	487	645	8,250	212	4,853	1,390	7,437	2,885	45,136
2005-06	187	770	1,816	10,240	399	677	8,200	221	4,428	1,230	7,414	3,102	42,891
2006-07	245	320	2,498	12,200	372	520	9,300	249	4,422	1,340	6,666	3,045	44,659
2007-08[1]	205	170	2,436	12,200	389	500	10,400	209	3,800	1,160	5,977	3,063	43,714
2008-09[2]	195	400	2,017	12,400	195	430	9,500	203	3,940	900	4,018	2,920	40,273

[1] Preliminary. [2] Estimate. *Source: The Oil World*

Salient Statistics of Cottonseed in the United States   In Thousands of Short Tons

Crop Year Beginning Aug. 1	Supply: Stocks	Supply: Production	Supply: Total Supply	Disappearance: Crush	Disappearance: Exports	Disappearance: Other	Disappearance: Total	Farm Price USD/Ton	Value of Production Mil. USD	Products Produced ---	Products Produced: Total
	In Thousands of Short Tons										
2001-02	427	7,452	8,206	2,791	274	4,742	7,807	91	667.3	876	1,294
2002-03	400	6,184	6,687	2,495	370	3,477	6,341	101	616.4	725	1,115
2003-04	347	6,665	7,013	2,643	354	3,595	6,592	117	779.0	874	1,244
2004-05	421	8,242	8,664	2,923	379	4,770	8,072	107	872.8	957	1,362
2005-06	592	8,172	8,764	3,010	523	4,630	8,163	96	779.5	951	1,372
2006-07	602	7,348	7,950	2,680	616	4,165	7,461	111	814.2	849	1,241
2007-08	489	6,589	7,080	2,706	599	3,132	6,437	162	1,069.8	856	1,262
2008-09[1]	643	4,300	4,943	2,250	191	1,989	4,429	230	992.4	663	934
2009-10[2]	514	4,178	4,692	1,850	350	2,167	4,267	200-260		615	895

[1] Preliminary. [2] Estimate. *Source: Economic Research Service, U.S. Department of Agriculture (ERS-USDA)*

Average Wholesale Price of Cottonseed Meal (41% Solvent)[2] in Memphis   In Dollars Per Short Ton

Year	Jan.	Feb.	Mar.	Apr.	May	June	July	Aug.	Sept.	Oct.	Nov.	Dec.	Average
2001	184.00	148.75	138.13	140.00	137.50	126.88	129.69	130.63	131.25	131.25	128.13	134.17	138.37
2002	133.13	125.00	131.88	124.30	120.88	137.50	151.50	159.75	156.38	150.10	150.00	156.00	141.37
2003	157.38	143.60	142.40	142.40	131.75	131.50	143.00	151.70	153.20	163.50	182.50	185.00	152.33
2004	188.00	193.00	205.10	219.67	203.00	185.40	177.50	156.20	142.75	126.75	119.00	117.00	169.45
2005	112.50	111.25	110.80	108.00	110.40	138.75	151.00	143.00	140.00	133.13	132.50	175.00	130.53
2006	172.50	152.50	148.75	144.38	131.50	135.00	132.50	134.50	139.00	132.40	131.88	152.50	142.28
2007	161.00	174.75	185.50	148.25	137.00	131.25	137.50	144.75	167.50	183.40	176.25	196.67	161.99
2008	273.60	292.00	245.00	230.00	240.50	293.25	333.00	290.00	292.00	238.75	225.00	229.50	265.22
2009[1]	237.50	236.25	213.00	212.50	236.25	306.00	305.00	315.00	308.00	250.00	260.00	283.75	263.60

[1] Preliminary. *Source: Economic Research Service, U.S. Department of Agriculture (ERS-USDA)*

Supply and Distribution of Cottonseed Oil in the United States In Millions of Pounds

Crop Year Beginning Oct. 1	Supply: Stocks	Supply: Production	Supply: Imports	Supply: Total Supply	Disappearance: Domestic	Disappearance: Exports	Disappearance: Total	Per Capita Consumption of Salad & Cooking Oils --- In Lbs. ---	Utilization Food Uses: Shortening	Utilization Food Uses: Salad & Cooking Oils	Utilization Food Uses: Total	Prices: U.S.[3] (Crude) --- $/Metric Ton ---	Prices: Rott[4] (Cif) --- $/Metric Ton ---
2003-04	36	874	0	910	690	111	801	40	167	295	462	688	752
2004-05	109	957	2.0	1,068	935	57	991	40	166	304	470	617	649
2005-06	76	951	1.0	1,028	860	67	927	43	213	389	602	649	669
2006-07	101	849	1.0	951	714	138	852	44	162	547	709	787	804
2007-08	99	856	0	956	623	186	809	50	166	567	733	1,622	1,648
2008-09[1]	147	663	0	810	497	192	690	53	W	637	637	820	822
2009-10[2]	121	615	0	736	466	185	651					876	

[1] Preliminary. [2] Estimate. [3] Valley Points FOB; Tank Cars. [4] Rotterdam; US, PBSY, fob gulf. W = Withheld.
Source: Economic Research Service, U.S. Department of Agriculture (ERS-USDA)

Consumption of Crude Cottonseed Oil, in Refining[2], in the United States In Millions of Pound

Year	Oct.	Nov.	Dec.	Jan.	Feb.	Mar.	Apr.	May	June	July	Aug.	Sept.	Total
2003-04	60.1	63.5	61.6	64.5	58.6	68.5	55.1	55.2	52.5	43.8	53.6	52.2	689.1
2004-05	60.0	66.4	67.0	73.7	69.2	66.8	72.6	52.9	64.7	57.0	71.8	55.2	777.1
2005-06	72.7	79.0	75.1	70.9	64.0	71.1	58.2	71.6	61.2	52.6	61.4	52.4	790.2
2006-07	65.7	55.7	61.4	63.9	55.3	63.7	60.1	63.6	54.1	56.3	56.5	55.6	711.9
2007-08	59.6	60.9	61.7	74.0	70.2	68.0	70.9	62.2	52.3	55.3	57.1	52.8	744.8
2008-09	47.2	56.4	63.5	58.3	58.4	57.5	44.0	48.1	50.6	36.9	39.3	37.5	597.6
2009-10[1]	32.6	46.2	47.1										503.3

[1] Preliminary. *Source: U.S. Bureau of Census, U.S. Department of Commerce*

Exports of Cottonseed Oil (Crude and Refined) from the United States In Thousands of Pounds

Year	Jan.	Feb.	Mar.	Apr.	May	June	July	Aug.	Sept.	Oct.	Nov.	Dec.	Total
2003	7,017	8,483	10,054	8,234	9,706	8,161	6,593	8,663	8,764	8,640	9,349	8,176	101,839
2004	14,203	8,982	8,321	10,399	9,632	10,720	7,931	9,891	4,617	5,669	7,619	7,507	105,492
2005	3,490	3,161	5,191	3,461	5,873	3,029	3,147	3,763	4,823	3,847	2,926	4,676	47,387
2006	5,084	5,724	5,410	7,738	5,519	6,640	7,539	6,608	5,755	8,827	9,377	14,365	88,586
2007	7,461	17,932	9,732	14,573	10,676	10,647	11,768	10,404	12,055	12,697	17,137	11,420	146,503
2008	11,089	21,546	25,577	11,565	12,436	17,019	17,441	11,300	17,263	22,083	20,819	18,611	206,747
2009[1]	14,423	20,981	15,258	19,313	12,296	14,087	12,070	10,915	11,370	8,506			167,062

[1] Preliminary. *Source: Economic Research Service, U.S. Department of Agriculture (ERS-USDA)*

COTTONSEED AND PRODUCTS

Cottonseed Crushed (Consumption) in the United States In Thousands of Short Tons

Year	Aug.	Sept.	Oct.	Nov.	Dec.	Jan.	Feb.	Mar.	Apr.	May	June	July	Total
2001-02	186.8	147.6	267.5	287.0	273.1	281.3	253.2	251.8	243.0	233.3	200.3	166.3	2,791
2002-03	195.1	131.4	207.8	242.5	236.6	274.5	224.5	230.4	241.5	203.6	179.4	127.4	2,495
2003-04	138.7	98.9	251.6	254.8	252.0	265.2	242.3	278.0	217.1	240.2	217.7	182.4	2,639
2004-05	193.8	141.0	247.9	260.3	263.5	283.1	266.3	270.2	287.7	221.0	266.6	221.6	2,923
2005-06	240.7	170.3	272.2	289.4	296.9	291.3	245.0	276.7	235.0	280.3	227.2	203.4	3,028
2006-07	204.8	158.2	252.4	223.3	236.7	251.2	222.5	249.1	230.8	243.2	204.6	203.3	2,680
2007-08	173.4	163.8	242.5	241.2	252.1	267.5	264.1	236.3	245.2	233.4	190.3	193.1	2,703
2008-09	202.3	147.4	175.2	206.5	230.0	234.3	217.6	206.5	170.7	168.1	158.1	133.2	2,250
2009-10[1]	107.1	92.8	131.2	169.2	180.9								1,635

[1] Preliminary. *Source: Economic Research Service, U.S. Department of Agriculture (ERS-USDA)*

Production of Cottonseed Cake and Meal in the United States In Thousands of Short Tons

Year	Aug.	Sept.	Oct.	Nov.	Dec.	Jan.	Feb.	Mar.	Apr.	May	June	July	Total
2001-02	83.9	70.8	118.5	126.5	118.2	129.0	112.5	115.0	109.2	107.9	96.3	73.7	1,261
2002-03	92.4	79.3	95.5	112.6	108.0	123.0	100.3	96.7	108.9	89.8	81.4	63.0	1,151
2003-04	74.9	59.5	112.3	111.0	112.5	113.9	105.1	123.4	94.2	104.7	97.7	91.0	1,200
2004-05	95.3	82.5	105.4	110.4	118.7	125.7	119.3	120.4	124.4	103.6	121.0	106.2	1,333
2005-06	116.4	91.1	109.6	134.6	129.3	128.8	108.2	119.4	104.5	129.3	107.2	99.0	1,377
2006-07	102.0	83.0	118.8	101.8	102.4	115.3	101.8	114.6	105.9	112.6	97.4	102.3	1,258
2007-08	81.3	87.3	112.5	111.0	111.9	125.6	119.9	116.3	110.4	103.2	86.8	90.7	1,257
2008-09	96.5	76.9	74.8	89.7	103.5	102.7	99.2	90.8	76.6	73.0	75.6	60.7	1,020
2009-10[1]	46.9	40.8	60.9	73.4	76.9								717

[1] Preliminary. *Source: Bureau of Census, U.S. Department of Commerce*

Production of Crude Cottonseed Oil[2] in the United States In Millions of Pounds

Year	Aug.	Sept.	Oct.	Nov.	Dec.	Jan.	Feb.	Mar.	Apr.	May	June	July	Total
2001-02	57.5	42.2	79.4	86.2	81.7	87.5	78.3	78.2	74.6	74.5	61.8	50.6	853
2002-03	60.2	53.7	62.8	72.1	67.9	80.8	65.6	66.7	71.0	59.9	52.8	39.9	753
2003-04	45.0	40.7	77.5	78.2	79.0	82.4	75.7	87.2	67.0	73.8	66.7	59.7	833
2004-05	68.6	58.1	77.1	82.2	81.4	88.7	83.4	84.3	90.7	71.3	81.6	69.5	937
2005-06	84.3	62.0	86.9	95.7	90.9	92.8	77.2	87.8	70.9	90.4	70.4	68.1	977
2006-07	68.4	59.2	77.1	71.7	73.9	78.6	67.1	78.1	72.5	77.2	65.2	66.7	856
2007-08	58.2	62.5	77.5	73.8	76.8	83.5	82.1	77.1	77.1	70.3	58.5	60.3	858
2008-09	64.4	55.0	49.4	64.4	71.2	70.4	68.4	65.9	53.4	57.2	53.5	42.7	716
2009-10[1]	34.5	27.2	38.3	54.1	55.2								502

[1] Preliminary. [2] Not seasonally adjusted. *Source: Bureau of Census, U.S. Department of Commerce*

Production of Refined Cottonseed Oil in the United States In Millions of Pounds

Year	Aug.	Sept.	Oct.	Nov.	Dec.	Jan.	Feb.	Mar.	Apr.	May	June	July	Total
2001-02	49.4	29.6	48.2	63.6	61.3	64.9	58.0	58.5	56.2	56.7	45.2	36.8	628
2002-03	52.7	47.1	48.3	59.2	55.7	66.5	55.6	56.8	58.9	49.4	42.4	31.7	624
2003-04	38.5	34.6	59.8	63.5	61.4	64.3	58.4	68.3	55.1	55.1	52.4	43.8	655
2004-05	53.4	52.0	59.7	66.1	66.9	73.4	68.8	66.6	72.3	52.7	64.6	56.6	753
2005-06	71.2	54.7	72.8	78.5	74.7	70.3	63.8	70.8	57.8	71.2	60.8	52.3	799
2006-07	61.0	52.0	65.2	55.3	61.1	63.5	55.3	62.9	58.9	63.5	54.0	56.1	709
2007-08	56.4	55.5	59.6	60.9	61.6	73.8	70.0	67.8	70.5	62.1	52.3	55.2	746
2008-09	56.9	52.6	46.9	56.3	63.2	57.9	58.1	57.2	43.7	47.9	50.3	36.7	628
2009-10[1]	39.2	37.5	32.6	46.2	47.1								486

[1] Preliminary. *Source: Bureau of the Census, U.S. Department of Commerce*

Stocks of Cottonseed Oil (Crude and Refined) in the U.S., at End of Month In Millions of Pounds

Year	Aug.	Sept.	Oct.	Nov.	Dec.	Jan.	Feb.	Mar.	Apr.	May	June	July
2001-02	97.7	91.8	113.8	112.9	109.8	124.9	120.3	106.9	110.3	97.3	82.7	61.8
2002-03	46.1	39.7	32.8	40.2	38.0	46.1	58.8	72.2	83.3	84.2	91.4	64.0
2003-04	50.5	36.0	51.9	56.1	68.7	85.9	100.6	117.6	116.8	125.7	121.0	123.0
2004-05	123.3	109.0	106.6	110.6	111.3	116.6	122.0	112.9	121.2	111.5	90.0	86.2
2005-06	90.6	76.4	69.0	76.1	74.0	84.0	99.0	108.5	103.3	110.8	105.8	95.6
2006-07	98.9	101.1	93.2	92.3	106.8	119.2	117.0	112.2	124.5	126.1	119.5	160.2
2007-08	132.9	105.8	92.8	91.6	94.9	114.3	138.4	143.5	156.1	161.4	158.7	143.1
2008-09	153.8	146.6	139.7	124.7	120.0	126.7	134.1	149.4	151.4	160.9	144.7	150.3
2009-10[1]	141.0	120.6	98.1	85.4	108.4							

[1] Preliminary. *Source: Bureau of the Census, U.S. Department of Commerce*

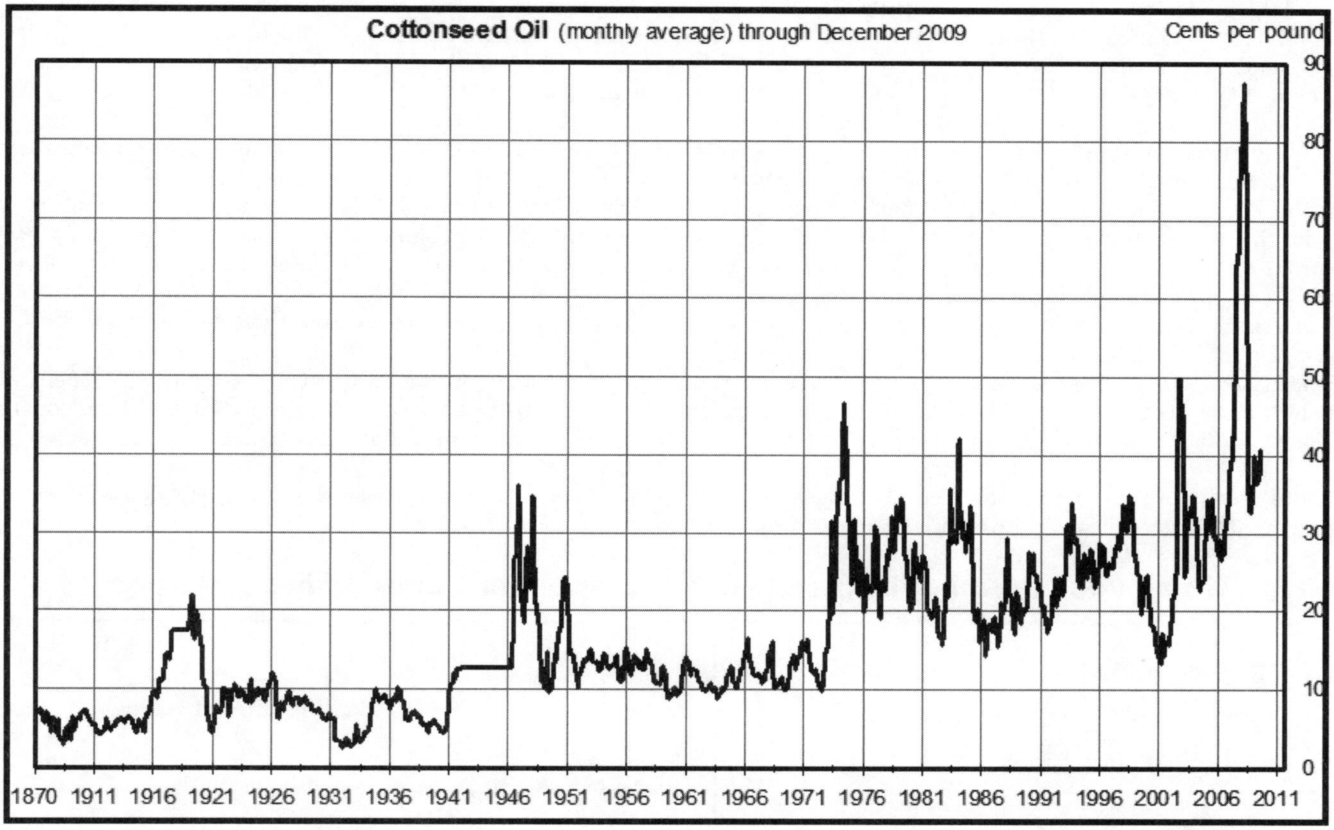

Average Price of Crude Cottonseed Oil, PBSY, Greenwood, MS.[1] in Tank Cars In Cents Per Pound

Year	Jan.	Feb.	Mar.	Apr.	May	June	July	Aug.	Sept.	Oct.	Nov.	Dec.	Average
2000	21.98	22.65	23.70	24.57	22.97	21.54	21.03	20.17	18.52	18.16	17.83	17.25	20.86
2001	16.24	15.20	15.53	14.03	14.53	13.27	16.78	17.18	15.78	14.44	15.91	16.07	15.41
2002	16.38	15.89	16.77	16.98	17.95	19.48	21.30	22.32	22.32	26.84	36.90	46.89	23.34
2003	49.82	49.90	47.52	44.57	42.33	28.69	24.38	25.51	29.64	32.93	32.24	33.26	36.73
2004	32.76	34.21	34.91	34.47	32.57	30.72	27.83	25.29	23.29	22.74	23.88	23.81	28.87
2005	23.70	24.38	28.19	29.80	30.63	33.13	34.15	30.44	31.25	34.44	34.09	30.50	30.39
2006	29.63	29.50	29.75	27.05	28.06	27.25	29.20	26.69	27.13	27.44	30.25	30.75	28.56
2007	31.00	32.69	33.00	34.38	37.75	40.00	42.44	42.15	46.56	52.20	63.60	66.63	43.53
2008	71.69	78.60	78.94	79.75	82.75	87.56	86.06	72.55	62.44	46.45	37.38	32.88	68.09
2009	35.70	33.19	32.63	37.38	39.90	38.75	36.55	39.13	36.44	37.90	40.69	41.40	37.47

Source: Economic Research Service, U.S. Department of Agriculture (ERS-USDA)

Exports of Cottonseed Oil to Important Countries from the United States In Thousands of Metric Tons

Year	Canada	Dominican Republic	Egypt	Guate-mala	Japan	Mexico	Nether-lands	El Salvador	Rep. of Korea	Turkey	Venez-uela	Total
2000	40.2	.0	0	0	7.6	7.9	.4	0	.1	0	0	58.5
2001	26.0	.0	0	.5	6.5	8.6	3.1	4.8	2.5	0	0	64.6
2002	36.4	0	3.0	0	5.4	6.9	0	1.8	4.7	.3	0	63.2
2003	33.6	0	0	0	3.5	7.2	0	.0	.7	0	0	46.2
2004	26.5	0	0	0	11.6	8.6	0	0	.0	0	0	47.9
2005	12.7	0	0	0	1.0	6.5	0	0	.1	0	0	21.5
2006	10.0	.0	0	.0	1.3	11.2	0	0	14.1	0	.1	40.2
2007	24.0	.1	0	0	7.1	11.6	0	0	17.3	0	.0	66.5
2008	40.8	.1	0	0	9.0	22.3	0	0	14.5	0	0	93.8
2009[1]	37.0	0	0	0	2.6	18.1	.1	.2	8.7	0	0	73.8

[1] Preliminary. *Source: Foreign Agricultural Service, U.S. Department of Agriculture (FAS-USDA)*

Continuous Commodity Index (CCI)

The Continuous Commodity Index (CCI) was first calculated by Commodity Research Bureau, Inc. in 1957 and made its inaugural appearance in the 1958 CRB Commodity Year Book.

The Index originally consisted of two cash markets and 26 futures markets which were traded on exchanges in the U.S. and Canada. It included barley and flaxseed from the Winnipeg exchange; cocoa, coffee "B", copper, cotton, cottonseed oil, grease wool, hides, lead, potatoes, rubber, sugar #4, sugar #6, wool tops and zinc from New York exchanges; and corn, oats, wheat, rye, soybeans, soybean oil, soybean meal, lard, onions, and eggs from Chicago exchanges. In addition to those 26, the Index also included the spot New Orleans cotton and Minneapolis wheat markets.

Like the Bureau of Labor Statistics spot index, the CCI is calculated to produce an unweighted geometric mean of the individual commodity price relatives. In other words, a ratio of the current price to the base year average price. Currently, 1967 is the base year the Index is calculated against (1967=100).

The formula considers all future delivery contracts that expire on or before the end of the sixth calendar month from the current date, using up to a maximum of five contracts per commodity. However, a minimum of two contracts must be used to calculate the current price, even if the second contract is outside the six-month window. Contracts are excluded when in their delivery period.

The 2009 closing value of 484.42 was 33.43 percent higher than the 2008 close of 363.06. 15 of the 17 component commodities finished higher for the year.

Futures and options on the CCI are traded on the ICE Futures U.S. (ICE) exchange.

Continuous Commodity Index (CCI) Component Commodities by Group

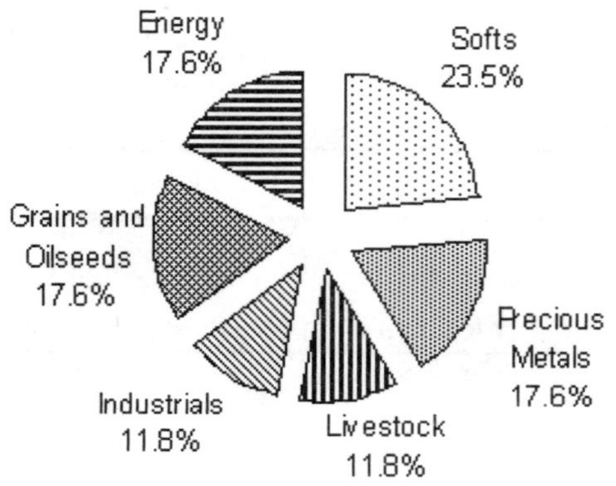

Group:	*Components*
Energy:	Crude Oil, Heating Oil, Natural gas
Grains and Oilseeds:	Corn, Soybeans, Wheat
Industrials:	Copper, Cotton
Livestock:	Live Cattle, Lean Hogs
Precious Metals:	Gold, Platinum, Silver
Softs:	Cocoa, Coffee, Orange Juice, Sugar #11

The Continuous Commodity Index (CCI) is computed using a three-step process:

1) Each of the Index's 17 component commodities is arithmetically averaged using the prices for all of the designated contract months which expire on or before the end of the sixth calendar month from the current date, except that: a) no contract shall be included in the calculation while in delivery; b) there shall be a minimum of two contract months for each component commodity (adding contracts beyond the six month window if necessary); c) there shall be a maximum of five contract months for each commodity (dropping the most deferred contracts to remain at five, if necessary). The result is that the Index extends six to seven months into the future depending on where one is in the current month. For example, live cattle's average price on October 30, 1995 would be computed as follows:

$$\text{Cattle Average} = \frac{\text{Dec. '96 + Feb. '97}}{2}$$

2) These 17 component averages are then geometrically averaged by multiplying all of the numbers together and taking the 17th root.

$$\text{Geometric Average} = \sqrt[17]{\text{Crude Avg. * Heating Oil Avg. * Sugar Avg....}}$$

3) The resulting average is divided by 30.7766, the 1967 base-year average for these 17 commodities. That result is then multiplied by an adjustment factor of .8486. This adjustment factor is necessitated by the nine revisions to the Index since its inception in 1957. Finally, that result is multiplied by 100 in order to convert the Index into percentage terms:

$$\text{CCI} = \frac{\text{Current Geometric Average}}{\text{1967 Geometric Avg. (30.7766) * .8486 * 100}}$$

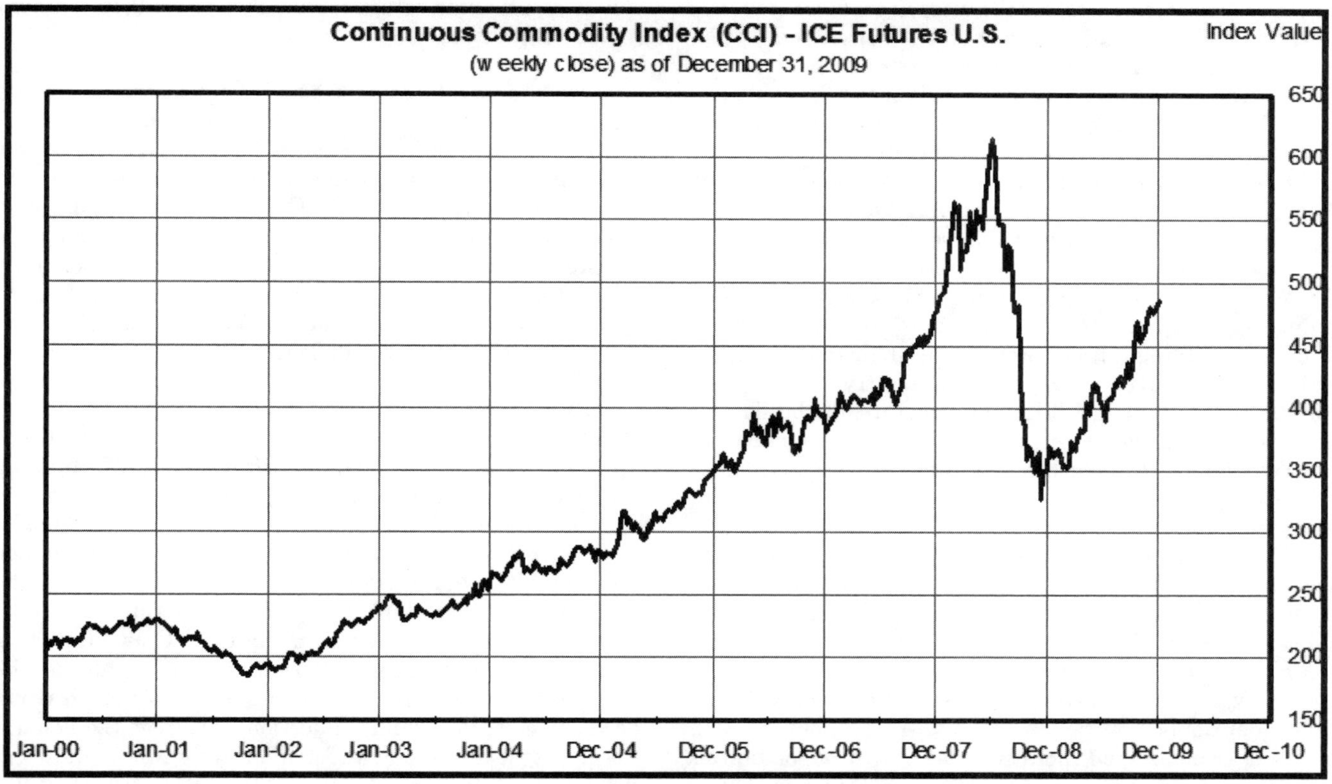

Average Open Interest of Continuous Commodity Index (CCI) in New York In Contracts

Year	Jan.	Feb.	Mar.	Apr.	May	June	July	Aug.	Sept.	Oct.	Nov.	Dec.
2000	3,487	3,525	3,271	3,117	3,155	2,737	2,104	1,640	1,551	1,632	1,544	1,438
2001	1,280	1,063	1,032	1,036	969	1,006	1,058	1,048	993	559	354	404
2002	422	514	458	384	400	412	489	399	583	646	684	710
2003	748	877	835	849	939	905	858	917	1,078	1,029	1,013	760
2004	838	870	942	704	357	305	413	412	539	600	581	604
2005	540	561	710	663	644	683	861	1,023	1,016	1,024	1,016	1,035
2006	1,045	1,025	998	1,061	1,045	964	939	919	935	948	955	959
2007	927	914	995	1,251	1,526	1,500	1,409	1,560	1,416	1,603	1,864	1,484
2008	1,349	1,355	1,241	1,159	1,168	1,226	1,329	1,302	1,435	1,677	1,541	1,392
2009	1,540	1,449	1,551	1,634	1,411	1,288	1,247	1,283	1,251	1,422	1,319	1,324

Contract size = $500. *Source: ICE Futures U.S. (ICE)*

Volume of Trading of Continuous Commodity Index (CCI) in New York In Contracts

Year	Jan.	Feb.	Mar.	Apr.	May	June	July	Aug.	Sept.	Oct.	Nov.	Dec.	Total
2000	14,975	6,760	3,941	7,582	7,402	8,924	2,023	3,973	1,333	2,122	3,254	1,205	63,494
2001	2,428	1,823	1,310	2,062	930	1,965	880	2,021	625	1,263	843	728	16,878
2002	1,251	1,231	896	1,472	785	1,191	1,217	915	1,100	1,654	1,430	1,141	14,283
2003	2,289	2,154	1,826	1,634	1,514	2,106	1,632	1,350	1,712	2,123	2,502	2,314	23,156
2004	2,477	1,695	3,169	2,672	1,209	1,618	792	1,341	759	813	1,630	979	19,154
2005	1,154	861	2,023	1,891	1,027	2,105	1,623	1,931	605	707	1,258	882	16,067
2006	2,231	1,114	1,017	1,836	1,563	1,323	927	1,020	892	461	1,220	708	14,312
2007	1,156	249	1,698	1,648	885	3,164	1,716	927	802	1,837	5,615	276	19,973
2008	1,888	1,454	2,139	2,186	745	1,758	2,162	1,311	1,408	499	2,692	943	19,185
2009	2,525	124	724	3,213	1,047	2,560	697	938	74	2,856	778	437	15,973

Contract size = $500. *Source: ICE Futures U.S. (ICE)*

Currencies

A currency rate involves the price of the base currency (e.g., the dollar) quoted in terms of another currency (e.g., the yen), or in terms of a basket of currencies (e.g., the dollar index). The world's major currencies have traded in a floating-rate exchange rate regime ever since the Bretton-Woods international payments system broke down in 1971 when President Nixon broke the dollar's peg to gold. The two key factors affecting a currency's value are central bank monetary policy and the trade balance. An easy monetary policy (low interest rates) is bearish for a currency because the central bank is aggressively pumping new currency reserves into the marketplace and because foreign investors are not attracted to the low interest rate returns available in the country. By contrast, a tight monetary policy (high interest rates) is bullish for a currency because of the tight supply of new currency reserves and attractive interest rate returns for foreign investors.

The other key factor driving currency values is the nation's current account balance. A current account surplus is bullish for a currency due to the net inflow of the currency, while a current account deficit is bearish for a currency due to the net outflow of the currency. Currency values are also affected by economic growth and investment opportunities in the country. A country with a strong economy and lucrative investment opportunities will typically have a strong currency because global companies and investors want to buy into that country's investment opportunities. Futures on major currencies and on cross-currency rates are traded primarily at the Chicago Mercantile Exchange.

Dollar –The dollar index rallied in the second half of 2008 and early 2009 due to (1) the global financial crisis, which caused investors and financial institutions to flee into dollar liquidity, and (2) capital repatriation by U.S. investors who dumped riskier foreign investments during the financial crisis. However, the U.S. dollar index peaked at a 3-2/3 year high of 89.624 in March 2009 and then fell during the rest of 2009. The dollar fell after the global stock markets bottomed out in March 2009 and staged an impressive recovery rally, thus causing investors to slowly sell some of the emergency dollar liquidity that they acquired during the crisis.

The dollar was also weak during 2009 due to extremely low U.S. interest rates with the Federal Reserve targeting the federal funds rate in the range of zero to 0.25%. Low interest rates discouraged capital from flowing into the U.S. In addition, large traders used the dollar for the carry trade, where they borrow cheap money in dollars and then sell those dollars in return for a higher-yielding investment in a foreign currency.

After the weakness in the dollar index seen during the later part of 2009, the dollar index hit bottom in November 2009 and then rallied in early 2010. That rally was sparked by the faster economic recovery in the U.S. than in Europe and Japan and by the Greek debt problems, which undercut the euro. The dollar was also supported by the long-term improvement in the U.S. trade deficit excluding petroleum, which suggested that the dollar had become cheap enough to force a closer balance in trade aside from the immovable petroleum deficit.

Euro – The euro, after falling sharply in the second half of 2008 due to the financial crisis, staged a sharp recovery during 2009 when financial institutions started lightening up on their emergency dollar liquidity. In addition, the euro is slowly gaining popularity among central banks as a currency in which to hold their foreign exchange reserves. The euro also saw strength in 2009 when the European Central Bank stopped cutting rates at 1.00% and kept its rates higher than the U.S., thus supporting the euro's interest rate differentials. In addition, the European Central Bank has already started drawing down its massive liquidity injections, whereas the Federal Reserve still has about $1.2 trillion in excess liquidity in the financial system. In early 2010, however, the euro fell sharply as Greece ran into serious budget troubles and had difficulty in selling its bonds, thus sparking talk that Greece, along with other high-deficit countries such as Spain and Portugal, might eventually be forced to stop using the euro and go back to using their original national currencies. However, the European Union came to the rescue to provide enough support to Greece to ease it through its budget difficulties and scotch talk of a euro breakup.

Yen – The yen generally strengthened during 2009 as the dollar fell when financial institutions lightened up on their emergency dollar liquidity. The yen in late 2009 posted a 15-year high against the dollar. The yen also received support during 2009 as Japanese corporations and investors repatriated profits and assets back home. Some pressure came off the yen in 2009 when some large traders used the dollar for the carry trade rather than the yen. The yen's strength in 2009 came despite major bearish factors for the yen such as the weak economic recovery and that the Bank of Japan kept targeting the overnight rate near 0.10%, thus causing poor Japanese interest rate differentials.

U.S. Dollars per British Pound

Year	Jan.	Feb.	Mar.	Apr.	May	June	July	Aug.	Sept.	Oct.	Nov.	Dec.	Average
2000	1.6395	1.6007	1.5810	1.5807	1.5084	1.5102	1.5082	1.4885	1.4341	1.4509	1.4252	1.4657	1.5161
2001	1.4767	1.4522	1.4438	1.4350	1.4268	1.4025	1.4149	1.4376	1.4646	1.4520	1.4358	1.4422	1.4403
2002	1.4314	1.4233	1.4233	1.4434	1.4601	1.4849	1.5566	1.5375	1.5562	1.5576	1.5718	1.5882	1.5029
2003	1.6184	1.6077	1.5832	1.5751	1.6230	1.6606	1.6242	1.5942	1.6141	1.6778	1.6899	1.7536	1.6352
2004	1.8223	1.8675	1.8273	1.8050	1.7888	1.8292	1.8433	1.8195	1.7932	1.8069	1.8608	1.9298	1.8328
2005	1.8783	1.8883	1.9034	1.8961	1.8538	1.8179	1.7518	1.7947	1.8078	1.7649	1.7355	1.7454	1.8198
2006	1.7665	1.7478	1.7446	1.7690	1.8693	1.8435	1.8451	1.8934	1.8858	1.8766	1.9124	1.9634	1.8431
2007	1.9585	1.9586	1.9479	1.9874	1.9834	1.9870	2.0344	2.0112	2.0202	2.0453	2.0709	2.0168	2.0018
2008	1.9692	1.9640	2.0012	1.9815	1.9662	1.9675	1.9897	1.8870	1.7997	1.6899	1.5290	1.4869	1.8526
2009	1.4484	1.4417	1.4197	1.4727	1.5460	1.6379	1.6387	1.6532	1.6312	1.6196	1.6610	1.6230	1.5661

Average. *Source: FOREX*

Volume of Trading of British Pound Futures in Chicago In Thousands of Contracts

Year	Jan.	Feb.	Mar.	Apr.	May	June	July	Aug.	Sept.	Oct.	Nov.	Dec.	Total
2000	199.6	179.8	270.9	138.9	133.3	225.8	136.2	155.9	245.1	100.7	100.7	152.5	2,039.3
2001	125.6	126.2	198.7	127.0	166.3	248.9	164.2	183.6	197.1	178.9	161.4	187.4	2,065.4
2002	182.0	168.2	230.4	168.2	174.1	239.8	133.3	138.3	185.3	177.5	160.9	198.0	2,155.9
2003	158.3	161.8	217.4	158.1	164.7	288.6	214.9	163.5	284.5	212.6	206.2	364.5	2,595.2
2004	310.3	291.6	470.3	293.1	282.5	427.8	373.4	367.1	471.4	405.4	348.4	635.2	4,676.5
2005	376.7	410.5	628.7	453.3	555.5	763.5	640.2	735.3	1,034.5	887.8	1,080.6	1,203.1	8,769.8
2006	1,013.7	1,012.0	1,479.2	1,207.6	1,465.1	1,262.1	963.1	1,262.2	1,486.2	1,387.1	1,563.9	1,997.4	16,099.5
2007	1,639.3	1,485.2	2,151.4	1,330.1	1,705.8	2,066.0	1,946.6	1,964.1	1,668.3	1,729.8	1,793.9	1,319.3	20,799.8
2008	1,541.0	1,442.5	1,886.1	1,979.0	1,633.7	2,058.8	1,896.4	1,805.7	2,151.8	1,584.1	1,240.3	1,278.1	20,497.4
2009	1,446.3	1,457.1	1,721.8	1,509.2	1,736.4	2,609.0	2,127.0	2,126.5	2,644.3	2,864.8	2,389.1	2,222.4	24,853.8

Contract size = 62,500 GBP. *Source: CME Group; Chicago Mercantile Exchange (CME)*

Average Open Interest of British Pound Futures in Chicago In Contracts

Year	Jan.	Feb.	Mar.	Apr.	May	June	July	Aug.	Sept.	Oct.	Nov.	Dec.
2000	37,192	45,329	51,645	41,488	51,965	43,009	30,766	36,320	42,781	30,978	34,627	32,913
2001	28,776	30,555	36,532	34,713	39,836	48,310	33,273	40,935	50,083	38,579	40,461	35,424
2002	26,450	31,023	30,474	39,952	46,178	47,355	38,138	31,320	31,513	29,599	40,901	36,671
2003	36,892	33,066	27,042	25,274	36,171	50,118	41,702	46,979	40,183	55,884	66,660	70,197
2004	61,694	68,173	51,968	43,830	45,843	53,615	68,262	71,503	60,274	66,565	87,487	86,572
2005	67,140	70,872	81,799	80,850	88,397	79,278	75,387	73,199	81,479	79,854	84,884	91,497
2006	83,051	97,226	83,641	83,275	106,555	98,417	91,563	129,334	120,737	106,288	145,026	157,837
2007	147,183	152,892	135,618	130,611	130,861	145,405	157,336	124,948	110,905	118,737	128,761	96,974
2008	87,465	94,154	98,154	109,464	158,836	126,688	100,775	105,857	112,717	110,761	113,147	93,313
2009	81,141	84,191	88,354	82,933	91,683	92,365	90,994	98,358	88,658	104,344	96,882	83,847

Contract size = 62,500 GBP. *Source: CME Group; Chicago Mercantile Exchange (CME)*

Canadian Dollars per U.S. Dollar

Year	Jan.	Feb.	Mar.	Apr.	May	June	July	Aug.	Sept.	Oct.	Nov.	Dec.	Average
2000	1.4480	1.4499	1.4600	1.4681	1.4944	1.4762	1.4778	1.4819	1.4841	1.5119	1.5425	1.5219	1.4847
2001	1.5021	1.5227	1.5579	1.5581	1.5403	1.5238	1.5294	1.5384	1.5665	1.5708	1.5934	1.5793	1.5486
2002	1.5996	1.5961	1.5872	1.5814	1.5491	1.5312	1.5447	1.5685	1.5747	1.5783	1.5715	1.5588	1.5701
2003	1.5395	1.5119	1.4752	1.4567	1.3819	1.3520	1.3801	1.3948	1.3638	1.3226	1.3128	1.3121	1.4003
2004	1.2967	1.3292	1.3282	1.3410	1.3774	1.3582	1.3225	1.3127	1.2880	1.2476	1.1958	1.2177	1.3013
2005	1.2248	1.2386	1.2157	1.2368	1.2553	1.2402	1.2239	1.2048	1.1781	1.1777	1.1813	1.1619	1.2116
2006	1.1573	1.1488	1.1571	1.1440	1.1094	1.1139	1.1287	1.1191	1.1161	1.1281	1.1365	1.1531	1.1343
2007	1.1757	1.1708	1.1687	1.1351	1.0948	1.0655	1.0512	1.0585	1.0260	0.9752	0.9680	1.0021	1.0743
2008	1.0114	1.0001	1.0031	1.0130	0.9999	1.0170	1.0133	1.0539	1.0582	1.1797	1.2204	1.2337	1.0670
2009	1.2244	1.2449	1.2638	1.2244	1.1502	1.1274	1.1225	1.0878	1.0812	1.0547	1.0587	1.0558	1.1413

Average. *Source: FOREX*

Volume of Trading of Canadian Dollar Futures in Chicago In Thousands of Contracts

Year	Jan.	Feb.	Mar.	Apr.	May	June	July	Aug.	Sept.	Oct.	Nov.	Dec.	Total
2000	184.2	182.5	280.9	155.0	162.8	295.5	166.0	188.5	241.2	161.6	150.3	265.8	2,434.1
2001	194.7	201.1	317.9	188.2	228.4	351.0	221.6	235.9	265.1	214.1	218.1	287.3	2,923.3
2002	222.9	191.5	338.3	249.6	222.2	358.7	278.8	204.2	279.1	245.3	207.4	324.4	3,122.3
2003	270.8	256.7	475.5	289.2	353.1	494.2	331.3	266.2	393.3	285.7	294.4	509.3	4,219.6
2004	380.7	328.0	516.3	380.3	337.1	504.0	366.5	419.4	640.8	512.0	499.5	726.8	5,611.3
2005	548.6	483.0	678.0	592.9	555.2	761.5	562.2	566.3	914.2	671.3	736.0	861.0	7,930.2
2006	695.1	648.6	1,040.9	654.9	816.6	1,043.4	658.3	811.0	1,073.7	805.8	960.8	1,070.4	10,279.6
2007	795.9	724.5	1,089.4	749.9	949.9	1,348.4	1,101.2	1,015.5	1,226.6	1,054.0	1,238.3	931.2	12,224.8
2008	960.2	957.8	1,202.2	948.1	958.2	1,151.9	932.0	966.4	1,240.9	812.9	601.8	645.8	11,378.0
2009	625.5	685.7	1,040.2	964.4	1,222.0	1,691.7	1,318.6	1,319.2	1,644.8	1,626.3	1,569.5	1,773.2	15,481.2

Contract size = 100,000 CAD. *Source: CME Group; Chicago Mercantile Exchange (CME)*

Average Open Interest of Canadian Dollar Futures in Chicago In Contracts

Year	Jan.	Feb.	Mar.	Apr.	May	June	July	Aug.	Sept.	Oct.	Nov.	Dec.
2000	66,374	64,528	58,621	60,389	76,444	69,033	67,198	65,370	65,779	81,995	77,746	65,452
2001	54,369	58,660	72,051	64,550	65,407	62,489	54,742	54,580	73,647	71,610	82,083	67,578
2002	68,927	72,132	70,484	68,120	81,574	86,250	74,347	63,116	63,605	57,031	60,648	71,852
2003	82,870	105,051	107,507	97,515	96,689	85,665	68,741	63,518	70,261	79,754	82,366	74,271
2004	74,577	64,032	61,981	72,750	84,356	68,458	73,164	83,483	97,486	112,648	110,035	81,976
2005	74,703	84,753	93,986	77,680	95,229	79,464	86,451	101,128	120,542	108,095	106,773	122,584
2006	103,427	118,978	103,066	92,541	114,587	107,605	89,443	91,591	112,788	99,209	121,729	146,474
2007	151,511	144,025	140,775	119,430	163,570	180,961	147,966	132,910	136,952	145,923	120,912	99,261
2008	86,448	99,650	109,567	103,486	115,665	103,145	95,618	120,175	116,163	103,135	94,297	66,313
2009	59,962	70,940	70,863	63,119	83,214	88,873	87,203	98,521	91,989	97,587	89,022	94,758

Contract size = 100,000 CAD. *Source: CME Group; Chicago Mercantile Exchange (CME)*

Euro[1] per U.S. Dollar

Year	Jan.	Feb.	Mar.	Apr.	May	June	July	Aug.	Sept.	Oct.	Nov.	Dec.	Average
2000	1.0135	.9842	.9644	.9450	.9080	.9496	.9394	.9042	.8706	.8533	.8554	.9004	.9240
2001	.9380	.9208	.9085	.8931	.8747	.8536	.8616	.9023	.9123	.9062	.8882	.8913	.8959
2002	.8828	.8706	.8767	.8866	.9179	.9567	.9924	.9781	.9810	.9818	1.0020	1.0210	.9456
2003	1.0636	1.0778	1.0795	1.0875	1.1580	1.1670	1.1374	1.1154	1.1260	1.1701	1.1714	1.2314	1.1321
2004	1.2604	1.2633	1.2263	1.1999	1.2013	1.2147	1.2265	1.2192	1.2226	1.2504	1.3001	1.3415	1.2439
2005	1.3110	1.3020	1.3178	1.2940	1.2685	1.2156	1.2049	1.2299	1.2246	1.2030	1.1796	1.1861	1.2448
2006	1.2121	1.1940	1.2033	1.2282	1.2773	1.2665	1.2693	1.2811	1.2734	1.2623	1.2893	1.3200	1.2564
2007	1.2989	1.3087	1.3249	1.3512	1.3511	1.3422	1.3720	1.3620	1.3918	1.4234	1.4681	1.4561	1.3709
2008	1.4722	1.4759	1.5527	1.5760	1.5560	1.5569	1.5765	1.4954	1.4367	1.3286	1.2723	1.3518	1.4709
2009	1.3253	1.2805	1.3074	1.3207	1.3675	1.4014	1.4087	1.4267	1.4565	1.4817	1.4926	1.4577	1.3939

Average. [1] Data through December 1998 are theoretical based on DEM * 1.95583. Source: FOREX

Volume of Trading of Euro FX Futures in Chicago In Thousands of Contracts

Year	Jan.	Feb.	Mar.	Apr.	May	June	July	Aug.	Sept.	Oct.	Nov.	Dec.	Total
2000	404.9	335.0	452.4	289.4	318.3	382.2	234.9	303.3	486.3	287.7	297.0	466.7	4,258.2
2001	453.5	373.2	556.4	368.3	407.7	585.3	425.1	494.7	533.9	533.6	545.0	781.1	6,057.8
2002	567.8	582.3	783.3	650.2	611.4	917.7	821.6	525.5	675.3	525.2	426.7	625.4	7,712.3
2003	610.6	749.2	977.9	785.5	902.7	1,103.8	866.2	824.5	1,112.4	1,069.6	958.9	1,232.6	11,193.9
2004	1,487.3	1,469.2	1,837.7	1,326.7	1,328.9	1,682.2	1,491.2	1,518.5	1,798.7	1,786.0	2,138.5	2,591.9	20,456.7
2005	2,646.0	2,266.4	2,772.9	2,992.0	2,771.6	3,656.1	2,732.6	2,765.1	3,206.6	2,613.6	3,164.2	2,943.6	34,530.7
2006	2,956.0	2,563.9	3,411.2	2,984.4	4,496.3	3,765.7	2,789.0	3,229.5	3,364.0	3,123.5	3,790.4	4,316.6	40,790.4
2007	3,701.9	3,032.1	4,427.3	2,979.1	3,337.4	3,877.6	3,560.5	4,074.2	3,286.6	3,831.5	3,793.1	3,161.6	43,063.1
2008	3,669.9	3,327.5	4,709.2	4,596.3	4,537.8	5,312.0	4,661.3	5,009.7	6,216.8	4,556.3	3,607.9	3,447.8	53,652.6
2009	3,574.5	3,903.4	4,564.5	3,155.7	3,758.9	5,261.4	4,675.6	4,220.4	5,123.9	5,429.9	5,419.9	5,305.7	54,393.6

Contract size = 125,000 EUR. *Source: CME Group; Chicago Mercantile Exchange (CME)*

Average Open Interest of Euro FX Futures in Chicago In Contracts

Year	Jan.	Feb.	Mar.	Apr.	May	June	July	Aug.	Sept.	Oct.	Nov.	Dec.
2000	63,124	68,413	61,180	59,110	67,644	63,361	57,723	69,561	77,617	73,314	79,577	92,730
2001	89,049	91,130	90,127	78,762	89,390	94,160	84,637	104,437	112,797	108,445	108,999	104,323
2002	100,258	108,955	113,075	112,413	136,660	135,364	112,462	101,992	99,365	85,462	103,156	108,602
2003	105,762	106,905	100,759	85,604	108,619	111,651	96,338	98,671	95,553	102,568	113,601	131,560
2004	125,879	133,690	115,712	112,361	138,193	120,281	140,430	160,315	121,180	136,959	202,074	175,374
2005	135,748	152,110	140,879	130,131	154,751	163,584	142,826	148,309	149,184	142,879	171,035	160,065
2006	133,092	150,085	152,674	166,920	196,057	177,700	155,865	173,151	155,567	152,410	182,079	214,241
2007	173,989	196,963	205,366	217,899	222,019	204,945	218,401	221,095	221,268	207,644	221,736	204,536
2008	179,767	206,661	200,084	178,993	211,068	193,878	170,675	153,423	163,948	180,955	169,315	144,926
2009	127,134	156,321	141,863	110,261	124,438	130,793	129,062	133,469	156,493	168,629	169,331	155,488

Contract size = 125,000 EUR. *Source: CME Group; Chicago Mercantile Exchange (CME)*

Japanese Yen per U.S. Dollar

Year	Jan.	Feb.	Mar.	Apr.	May	June	July	Aug.	Sept.	Oct.	Nov.	Dec.	Average
2000	105.29	109.49	106.34	105.65	108.19	106.15	108.03	108.06	106.79	108.39	108.94	112.18	107.79
2001	116.83	116.17	121.44	123.64	121.66	122.38	124.45	121.29	118.64	121.35	122.39	127.72	121.50
2002	132.77	133.50	131.11	130.75	126.29	123.25	118.02	119.04	120.88	123.92	121.50	121.83	125.24
2003	118.76	119.39	118.76	119.81	117.37	118.31	118.64	118.61	114.94	109.51	109.17	107.70	115.91
2004	106.38	106.70	108.51	107.61	112.05	109.44	109.46	110.24	110.10	108.81	104.71	103.79	108.15
2005	103.29	104.98	105.35	107.19	106.71	108.75	111.92	110.62	111.19	114.84	118.42	118.39	110.14
2006	115.53	117.92	117.31	116.97	111.77	114.65	115.69	115.95	117.14	118.61	117.28	117.43	116.35
2007	120.45	120.40	117.33	118.96	120.82	122.65	121.47	116.78	115.08	115.92	110.92	112.37	117.76
2008	107.71	107.11	100.80	102.69	104.33	106.88	106.87	109.41	106.62	100.15	96.80	91.13	103.37
2009	90.33	92.86	97.74	98.94	96.49	96.67	94.46	94.90	91.40	90.32	89.12	89.99	93.60

Average. *Source: FOREX*

Volume of Trading of Japanese Yen Futures in Chicago In Thousands of Contracts

Year	Jan.	Feb.	Mar.	Apr.	May	June	July	Aug.	Sept.	Oct.	Nov.	Dec.	Total
2000	433.9	299.1	569.7	250.5	265.8	427.4	248.8	285.9	367.1	213.9	222.7	405.2	3,990.0
2001	258.6	223.7	598.4	295.4	351.2	459.4	307.4	369.4	518.6	286.2	350.1	595.9	4,614.1
2002	415.7	417.5	630.8	391.7	318.5	461.7	301.2	234.2	499.2	349.5	255.4	535.8	4,811.1
2003	423.9	388.3	634.4	453.4	495.6	621.0	518.8	427.0	731.0	396.6	353.4	641.8	6,085.2
2004	410.1	484.9	741.8	516.4	415.5	685.8	487.5	490.7	807.6	629.6	650.5	1,074.9	7,395.3
2005	789.9	718.8	1,045.2	915.4	876.2	1,263.0	946.9	1,012.4	1,285.4	963.7	1,001.0	1,653.9	12,471.7
2006	1,221.1	1,128.7	1,950.5	1,385.9	1,890.9	1,905.3	1,317.9	1,395.9	1,965.8	1,525.1	1,852.8	2,137.5	19,677.4
2007	1,602.2	2,006.6	3,286.7	1,771.1	1,802.4	2,777.8	3,083.8	3,954.2	2,860.7	2,493.1	3,125.2	2,056.6	30,820.4
2008	3,013.2	2,558.7	3,384.5	2,632.6	2,502.9	3,193.9	2,898.0	2,428.9	3,446.2	3,117.8	1,937.5	1,730.2	32,844.4
2009	1,644.2	1,802.9	1,796.0	1,469.3	1,600.9	1,932.6	2,061.8	1,924.0	2,260.9	2,157.6	1,916.7	2,182.7	22,749.6

Contract size = 12,500,000 JPY. *Source: CME Group; Chicago Mercantile Exchange (CME)*

Average Open Interest of Japanese Yen Futures in Chicago In Contracts

Year	Jan.	Feb.	Mar.	Apr.	May	June	July	Aug.	Sept.	Oct.	Nov.	Dec.
2000	93,785	125,318	95,034	75,631	80,840	68,359	60,966	79,195	64,845	64,648	68,719	100,713
2001	89,680	90,652	109,536	96,244	89,377	82,838	93,430	107,588	102,710	75,096	97,368	137,756
2002	129,917	123,735	95,535	72,358	88,905	88,324	77,168	71,683	79,980	80,104	74,584	99,643
2003	116,574	107,929	101,809	81,168	107,090	102,507	107,450	125,884	149,978	152,368	138,799	147,255
2004	156,929	156,416	120,848	117,483	108,078	105,505	106,280	110,234	93,780	127,644	181,093	172,526
2005	164,708	155,593	132,268	134,802	172,574	164,580	161,763	170,290	159,227	186,631	202,939	191,591
2006	168,309	198,855	203,450	201,459	210,578	197,160	191,480	218,893	239,426	258,509	242,216	265,490
2007	312,252	338,933	246,715	234,352	303,537	347,031	302,278	272,937	227,242	225,047	202,361	195,324
2008	197,886	233,558	224,932	176,577	171,298	171,516	185,657	207,309	168,119	142,938	128,891	130,118
2009	112,194	108,893	90,828	79,142	86,624	81,378	95,456	80,087	119,014	118,478	123,821	110,809

Contract size = 12,500,000 JPY. *Source: CME Group; Chicago Mercantile Exchange (CME)*

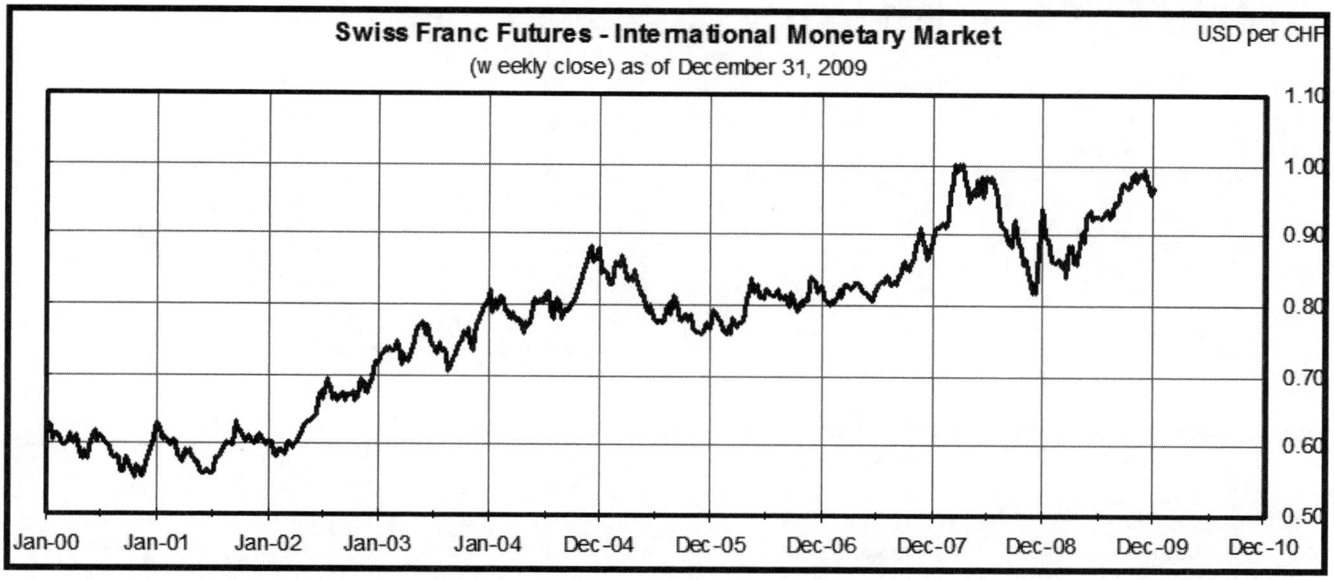

Swiss Francs per U.S. Dollar

Year	Jan.	Feb.	Mar.	Apr.	May	June	July	Aug.	Sept.	Oct.	Nov.	Dec.	Average
2000	1.5888	1.6326	1.6624	1.6638	1.7151	1.6422	1.6503	1.7146	1.7564	1.7727	1.7772	1.6778	1.6878
2001	1.6296	1.6681	1.6903	1.7115	1.7525	1.7842	1.7564	1.6791	1.6338	1.6337	1.6501	1.6569	1.6872
2002	1.6710	1.6972	1.6741	1.6527	1.5868	1.5389	1.4731	1.4968	1.4929	1.4922	1.4647	1.4360	1.5564
2003	1.3748	1.3609	1.3617	1.3770	1.3091	1.3196	1.3597	1.3813	1.3741	1.3234	1.3314	1.2627	1.3446
2004	1.2425	1.2458	1.2773	1.2954	1.2818	1.2501	1.2458	1.2625	1.2624	1.2338	1.1702	1.1455	1.2428
2005	1.1802	1.1906	1.1763	1.1955	1.2183	1.2663	1.2935	1.2626	1.2657	1.2872	1.3100	1.3056	1.2460
2006	1.2781	1.3056	1.3044	1.2822	1.2185	1.2319	1.2362	1.2319	1.2440	1.2597	1.2351	1.2102	1.2532
2007	1.2438	1.2385	1.2179	1.2128	1.2217	1.2329	1.2076	1.2034	1.1847	1.1743	1.1229	1.1397	1.2000
2008	1.1001	1.0894	1.0116	1.0141	1.0443	1.0363	1.0278	1.0843	1.1091	1.1429	1.1923	1.1393	1.0826
2009	1.1280	1.1635	1.1540	1.1472	1.1057	1.0810	1.0784	1.0677	1.0399	1.0218	1.0117	1.0304	1.0858

Average. *Source: FOREX*

Volume of Trading of Swiss Franc Futures in Chicago In Thousands of Contracts

Year	Jan.	Feb.	Mar.	Apr.	May	June	July	Aug.	Sept.	Oct.	Nov.	Dec.	Total
2000	326.2	313.1	385.3	252.1	247.7	301.2	214.6	216.6	344.5	176.2	185.4	267.3	3,230.2
2001	193.5	203.0	280.3	168.7	191.6	326.0	257.6	229.4	261.8	227.5	238.2	297.3	2,874.8
2002	195.3	183.2	281.3	211.5	208.1	297.0	187.2	218.5	323.1	237.6	207.8	271.6	2,822.1
2003	236.1	289.9	412.7	256.9	277.8	384.9	315.0	252.1	349.9	237.2	283.8	300.5	3,596.7
2004	216.1	230.1	359.6	260.0	255.7	370.9	331.4	313.7	404.5	428.3	329.0	568.4	4,067.8
2005	444.3	389.1	575.5	605.0	521.4	753.4	546.4	596.4	888.8	765.9	797.1	901.2	7,784.5
2006	803.5	745.9	1,129.0	837.5	1,011.3	993.3	771.2	1,014.8	1,046.8	919.6	1,078.1	1,118.9	11,470.0
2007	994.4	998.5	1,418.5	959.4	1,100.0	1,507.0	1,660.0	1,588.2	1,113.7	1,129.8	1,067.3	941.8	14,478.7
2008	1,090.5	1,082.4	1,311.8	1,350.7	1,362.8	1,789.1	1,650.0	1,330.3	1,578.9	1,042.4	574.0	651.3	14,814.2
2009	677.7	624.5	813.9	641.5	731.2	1,094.1	844.8	727.0	1,015.2	1,098.5	1,206.6	1,143.5	10,618.6

Contract size = 125,000 CHF. *Source: CME Group; Chicago Mercantile Exchange (CME)*

Average Open Interest of Swiss Franc Futures in Chicago In Contracts

Year	Jan.	Feb.	Mar.	Apr.	May	June	July	Aug.	Sept.	Oct.	Nov.	Dec.
2000	55,660	69,983	57,703	41,732	46,159	41,727	36,894	50,595	57,439	47,313	48,870	55,982
2001	50,121	44,405	46,470	41,641	53,265	60,943	53,687	60,986	61,689	48,962	53,445	46,771
2002	35,116	44,388	45,434	38,248	55,039	54,573	42,060	38,102	37,675	35,796	48,951	50,107
2003	56,268	57,099	50,008	37,451	53,642	49,688	41,489	50,677	52,641	54,259	62,584	60,475
2004	45,259	42,950	41,250	38,563	38,024	48,654	51,116	40,256	33,539	47,200	74,988	70,330
2005	51,858	56,240	50,827	41,322	55,995	78,794	72,596	67,489	66,009	75,088	91,072	98,443
2006	80,904	107,509	101,445	82,280	98,416	89,254	67,127	69,406	83,545	97,034	89,039	74,522
2007	83,176	103,073	70,627	66,246	89,737	121,557	108,394	118,597	100,948	73,433	81,366	73,025
2008	67,993	67,786	71,972	60,528	65,029	58,511	56,337	61,521	53,448	39,448	42,315	31,420
2009	26,083	32,701	33,518	28,613	34,585	40,027	35,918	39,324	49,537	51,736	52,912	41,890

Contract size = 125,000 CHF. *Source: CME Group; Chicago Mercantile Exchange (CME)*

United States Merchandise Trade Balance[1] In Millions of Dollars

Year	Jan.	Feb.	Mar.	Apr.	May	June	July	Aug.	Sept.	Oct.	Nov.	Dec.	Total
2000	-34,116	-34,708	-37,215	-36,934	-36,910	-37,827	-38,091	-36,839	-39,682	-40,205	-38,955	-39,360	-452,423
2001	-39,161	-34,648	-38,815	-37,270	-34,690	-35,760	-35,633	-34,458	-35,660	-35,034	-34,095	-31,534	-427,215
2002	-33,407	-31,405	-31,865	-39,875	-39,229	-37,590	-46,642	-44,082	-43,241	-45,583	-44,076	-45,303	-482,298
2003	-43,619	-38,301	-43,538	-46,145	-43,275	-43,882	-51,798	-45,166	-49,478	-51,812	-42,937	-47,345	-547,296
2004	-46,104	-42,621	-50,545	-52,314	-49,848	-60,221	-60,068	-60,752	-57,766	-62,556	-66,320	-56,294	-665,409
2005	-57,625	-54,860	-56,700	-60,386	-61,475	-64,686	-66,999	-70,417	-73,183	-77,869	-72,663	-65,876	-782,739
2006	-71,633	-59,128	-64,704	-65,823	-73,714	-72,255	-79,974	-81,111	-72,571	-74,119	-69,312	-62,916	-847,260
2007	-67,295	-57,212	-64,452	-68,035	-68,731	-68,149	-78,155	-72,928	-67,668	-78,690	-75,543	-64,133	-830,991
2008	-71,512	-63,333	-62,719	-74,791	-71,830	-75,003	-90,199	-75,456	-76,249	-76,431	-52,175	-50,554	-840,252
2009[2]	-44,980	-29,962	-34,698	-39,138	-34,223	-41,358	-50,914	-44,957	-50,718	-48,330	-49,759	-48,007	-517,044

[1] Not seasonally adjusted. [2] Preliminary. *Source: Bureau of Economic Analysis, U.S. Department of Commerce (BEA)*

Index of Real Trade-Weighted Dollar Exchange Rates for Total Agriculture[3] (2000 = 100)

Year		Jan.	Feb.	Mar.	Apr.	May	June	July	Aug.	Sept.	Oct.	Nov.	Dec.
2003	U.S. Markets	109.1	110.1	110.0	108.9	105.6	105.5	106.3	107.4	106.3	104.5	103.9	102.7
	U.S. Competitors	115.9	115.4	115.0	113.0	107.8	106.9	108.6	110.6	109.4	106.2	105.5	102.2
2004	U.S. Markets	101.5	102.2	103.0	103.6	106.0	105.0	103.9	103.7	103.3	102.0	99.5	98.2
	U.S. Competitors	100.4	100.6	102.8	103.9	105.4	104.9	103.5	103.7	103.2	101.4	98.4	95.9
2005	U.S. Markets	98.5	98.7	98.4	99.8	99.7	100.2	100.7	100.0	100.6	101.6	101.3	100.1
	U.S. Competitors	97.0	97.2	96.7	98.2	98.8	101.1	102.0	100.6	101.3	102.4	102.6	101.7
2006	U.S. Markets	99.2	99.4	99.9	100.0	98.6	100.2	100.1	99.2	98.9	98.6	97.7	97.0
	U.S. Competitors	100.7	101.1	101.1	100.1	97.8	99.3	99.1	98.0	97.9	97.6	95.8	93.9
2007	U.S. Markets	98.2	98.2	98.2	97.6	97.0	96.9	95.7	95.6	94.2	92.3	91.4	91.7
	U.S. Competitors	95.0	94.7	94.3	92.8	92.4	92.7	90.9	91.7	90.2	87.7	86.1	86.3
2008	U.S. Markets	91.3	90.3	89.0	88.9	89.4	89.9	89.4	90.5	92.1	97.1	97.5	95.8
	U.S. Competitors	85.9	85.1	82.6	81.9	82.5	82.8	82.1	84.8	88.3	94.8	97.4	93.8
2009[1]	U.S. Markets	97.1	100.0	101.5	98.3	95.5	95.3	94.7	93.5	92.8	91.4	90.8	90.5
	U.S. Competitors	95.9	98.9	98.4	96.0	92.8	91.2	90.7	89.2	87.9	86.2	85.5	86.3
2010[2]	U.S. Markets	90.3	91.2	90.8	90.5	90.4	90.3	90.3	90.3	90.2	90.1	90.0	89.9
	U.S. Competitors	87.1	89.4	89.5	89.8	90.4	91.2	92.1	93.0	93.6	94.3	95.0	95.8

[1] Not seasonally adjusted. [2] Preliminary. *Source: Bureau of Economic Analysis, U.S. Department of Commerce (BEA)*

United States Balance on Current Account[1] In Millions of Dollars

Year	First Quarter	Second Quarter	Third Quarter	Fourth Quarter	Annual
2000	-87,401	-100,735	-117,474	-111,816	-417,426
2001	-95,855	-98,341	-114,132	-89,942	-398,270
2002	-90,999	-115,988	-127,907	-124,258	-459,152
2003	-122,391	-131,081	-141,420	-126,628	-521,520
2004	-123,556	-157,375	-170,803	-179,396	-631,130
2005	-158,108	-181,503	-198,940	-210,132	-748,683
2006	-180,648	-204,742	-229,889	-188,268	-803,547
2007	-179,330	-191,631	-186,532	-169,080	-726,573
2008	-156,501	-189,674	-205,680	-154,213	-706,068
2009[2]	-86,517	-98,375	-124,052		-411,925

[1] Not seasonally adjusted. [2] Estimate. *Source: Bureau of Economic Analysis, U.S. Department of Commerce (BEA)*

Merchandise Trade and Current Account Balances[1] In Billions of Dollars

	Merchanise Trade Balance					Current Account Balance				
Year	Canada	Germany	Japan	Switzerland	United Kingdom	Canada	Germany	Japan	Switzerland	United Kingdom
2001	41.2	38.4	26.1	12.6	-34.6	16.3	.2	89.0	20.9	-30.4
2002	32.4	93.4	51.2	18.4	-42.2	12.6	41.0	112.6	25.0	-27.9
2003	32.5	98.2	69.3	21.4	-42.7	10.6	47.8	136.2	43.6	-30.0
2004	42.7	137.9	89.0	25.1	-59.5	22.9	126.8	171.6	48.8	-45.6
2005	42.5	147.0	63.3	25.0	-77.7	21.6	141.6	166.0	52.2	-59.2
2006	32.2	167.4	54.5	32.4	-76.7	17.9	189.9	171.5	59.8	-81.1
2007	27.3	237.9	73.3	44.8	-90.1	14.3	265.5	212.8	43.4	-75.3
2008	25.3	228.7	6.4	56.1	-70.3	9.2	244.5	157.4	11.4	-42.7
2009[2]	-25.8	119.9	-2.4	49.1	-48.5	-39.8	133.7	125.9	43.3	-57.8
2010[3]	-34.6	136.8	3.5	56.5	-37.1	-51.5	161.7	145.5	54.3	-56.8

[1] Not seasonally adjusted. [2] Estimate. [3] Projection. *Source: Organization for Economic Cooperation and Development (OECD)*

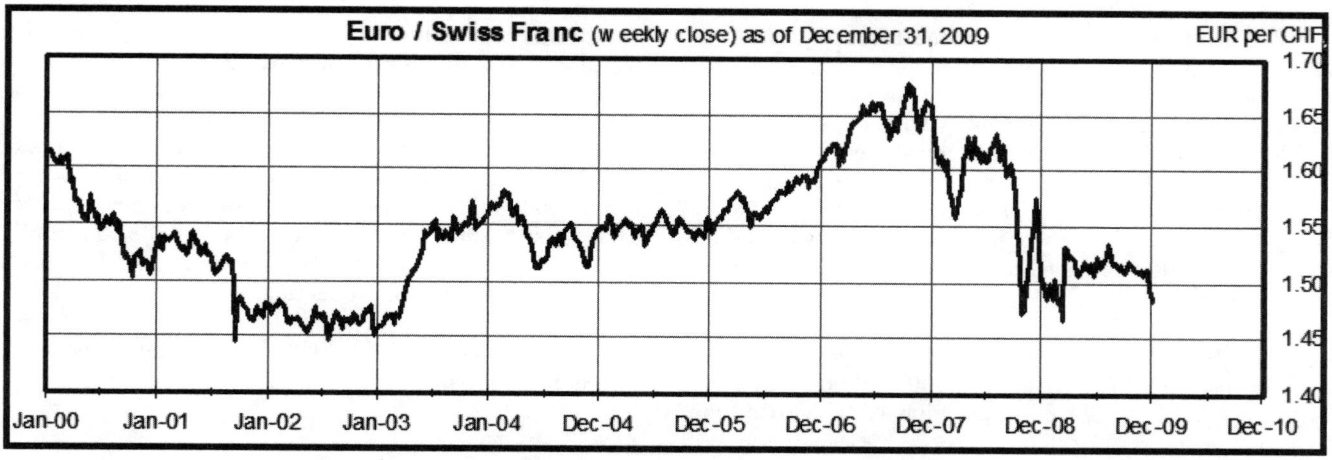
Euro / Swiss Franc (weekly close) as of December 31, 2009
EUR per CHF
1.70
1.65
1.60
1.55
1.50
1.45
1.40
Jan-00 Jan-01 Jan-02 Jan-03 Jan-04 Dec-04 Dec-05 Dec-06 Dec-07 Dec-08 Dec-09 Dec-10

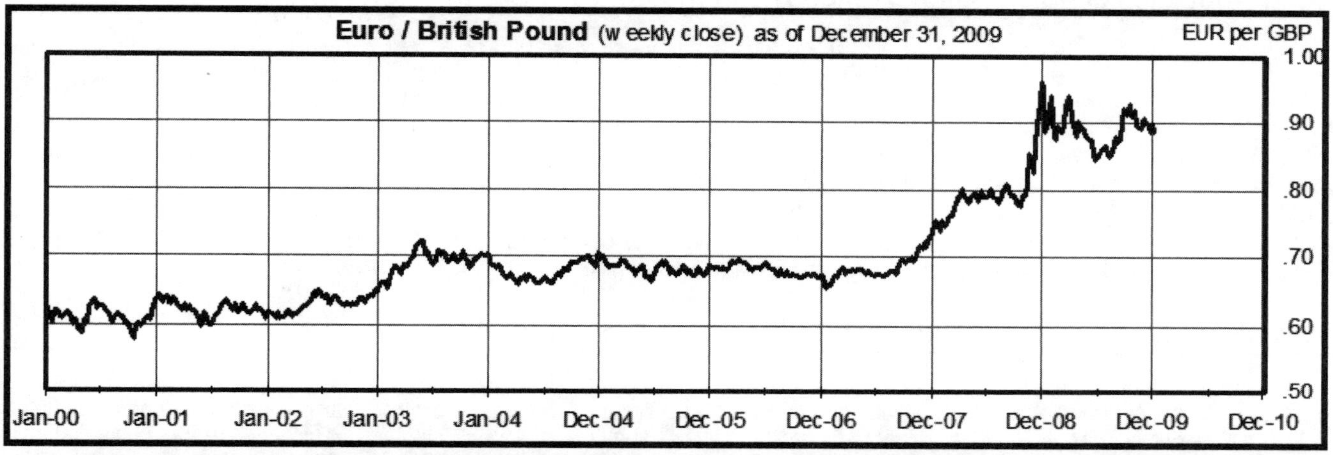
Euro / British Pound (weekly close) as of December 31, 2009
EUR per GBP
1.00
.90
.80
.70
.60
.50
Jan-00 Jan-01 Jan-02 Jan-03 Jan-04 Dec-04 Dec-05 Dec-06 Dec-07 Dec-08 Dec-09 Dec-10

Japanese Yen / British Pound (weekly close) as of December 31, 2009
JPY per GBP
280
240
200
160
120
80
Jan-00 Jan-01 Jan-02 Jan-03 Jan-04 Dec-04 Dec-05 Dec-06 Dec-07 Dec-08 Dec-09 Dec-10

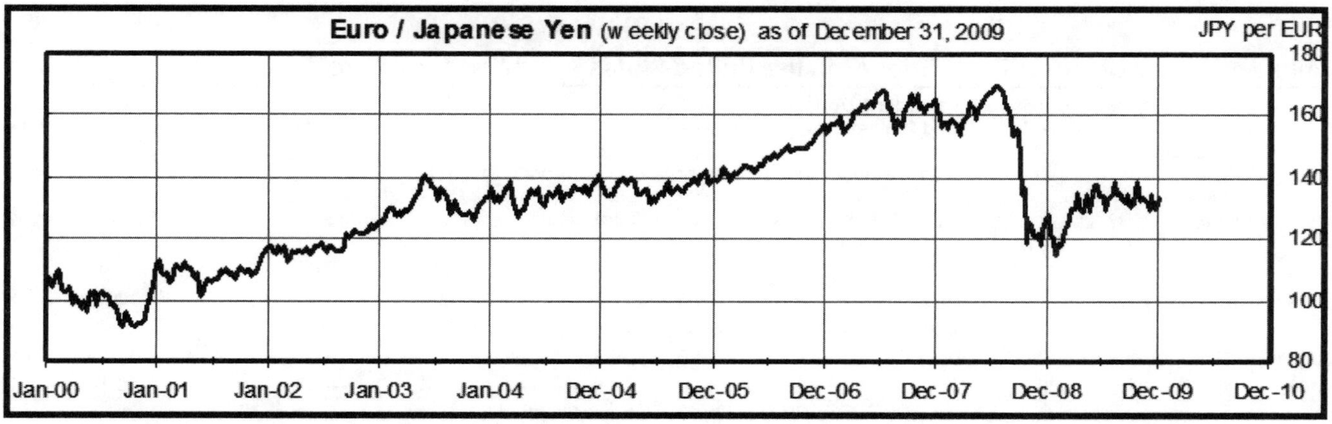
Euro / Japanese Yen (weekly close) as of December 31, 2009
JPY per EUR
180
160
140
120
100
80
Jan-00 Jan-01 Jan-02 Jan-03 Jan-04 Dec-04 Dec-05 Dec-06 Dec-07 Dec-08 Dec-09 Dec-10

Diamonds

The diamond, which is the mineral form of carbon, is the hardest, strongest natural material known on earth. The name *diamond* is derived from **adamas**, the ancient Greek term meaning "invincible." Diamonds form deep within the Earth's crust and are typically billions of years old. Diamonds have also have been found in and near meteorites and their craters. Diamonds are considered precious gemstones but lower grade diamonds are used for industrial applications such as drilling, cutting, grinding and polishing.

Supply – World production of natural gem diamonds in 2009 rose by +4.5% yr/yr to 90.900 million carats, but still down from the 2006 record high of 93.800 million carats (one carat equals 1/5 gram or 200 milligrams). The world's largest producers of natural gem diamonds are Botswana with 35% of world production in 2009, Russia with 24%, Australia with 8%, Angola with 9%, South Africa with 6%, and the Congo with 6%. World production of natural industrial diamonds in 2008 was up +0.4% yr/yr to 77.000 million carats. World production of synthetic diamonds in 2008 was up +0.4% yr/yr to 568.000 million carats. The main producer of synthetic diamonds was the U.S. with 46% of world production.

Trade – The U.S. in 2009 relied on net imports for 78% of its consumption of natural diamonds.

World Production of Natural Gem Diamonds In Thousands of Carats

Year	Angola	Australia	Botswana	Brazil	Central African Republic	China	Dem Rep. of Congo[3]	Ghana	Namibia	Russia	Suerra Leone	South Africa	World Total
2003	5,130	13,981	22,800	400	250	100	5,400	724	1,481	20,000	233	5,144	87,800
2004	5,490	6,058	23,300	300	263	100	5,900	725	2,004	23,700	318	5,800	88,400
2005	6,400	8,577	23,900	300	300	100	7,000	810	1,902	23,000	395	6,400	92,900
2006	8,300	7,305	24,000	300	340	100	5,700	780	2,400	23,400	360	6,100	93,800
2007[1]	8,700	231	25,000	300	370	100	5,400	720	2,200	23,300	360	6,100	92,600
2008[2]	8,100	273	25,000	200	400	100	5,400	520	1,500	21,900	220	5,200	87,000

[1] Preliminary. [2] Estimate. [3] Formerly Zaire. *Source: U.S. Geological Survey (USGS)*

World Production of Natural Industrial Diamonds[4] In Thousands of Carats

Year	Angola	Australia	Botswana	Brazil	Central African Republic	China	Ghana	Russia	Leone	South Africa	Vene-zuela	Dem. Rep of Congo[3]	World Total
2003	570	17,087	7,600	600	83	955	21,600	180	13,000	274	7,540	24	69,900
2004	610	18,172	7,800	600	88	960	23,600	180	15,200	374	8,500	60	76,700
2005	680	25,730	8,000	600	80	960	28,200	200	15,000	274	9,400	69	90,400
2006	880	21,915	8,000	600	85	965	22,800	190	15,000	252	9,100	70	80,300
2007[1]	970	18,960	8,000	600	47	970	21,800	180	15,000	240	9,100	70	76,700
2008[2]		18,000	8,000			1,000	23,000		15,000		9,000		77,000

[1] Preliminary. [2] Estimate. [3] Formerly Zaire. *Source: U.S. Geological Survey (USGS)*

World Production of Synthetic Diamonds In Thousands of Carats

Year	Belarus	China	Czech Republic	France	Greece	Ireland	Japan	Russia	South Africa	Sweden	Ukraine	United States	World Total
2002	25,000	17,000	5	3,000	----	60,000	34,000	80,000	60,000	20,000	8,000	222,000	529,000
2003	25,000	17,000	5	3,000	----	60,000	34,000	80,000	60,000	20,000	8,000	236,000	543,000
2004	25,000	17,000	5	3,000	----	60,000	34,000	80,000	60,000	20,000	8,000	252,000	559,000
2005	25,000	17,000	5	3,000	----	60,000	34,000	80,000	60,000	20,000	8,000	256,000	563,000
2006[1]	25,000	18,000	5	3,000	----	60,000	34,000	80,000	60,000	20,000	8,000	258,000	566,000
2007[2]	25,000	18,000	5	3,000	----	60,000	34,000	80,000	60,000	20,000	8,000	260,000	568,000

[1] Preliminary. [2] Estimate. *Source: U.S. Geological Survey (USGS)*

Salient Statistics of Industrial Diamonds in the United States In Millions of Carats

	Bort, Grit & Powder & Dust — Natural and Synthetic								Stones (Natural)						Net
	--- Production ---														
Year	Manu-factured Diamond	Secon-dary	Imports for Con-sumption	Exports & Reexports	In Manu-factured Products	Gov't Sales	Apparent Con-sumption	Price Value of Imports $/Carat	Secondary Pro-duction	Imports for Con-sumption	Exports & Reexports	Gov't Sales	Apparent Con-sumption	Price Value of Imports $/Carat	Net Import Reliance % of Con-sumption
2004	252.0	4.6	240.0	86.0	----	----	411.0	.25	[3]	1.8	.5	.4	2.1	7.77	80
2005	256.0	4.6	284.0	92.0	----	----	453.0	.27	[3]	2.1	[3]	----	2.2	13.91	77
2006	258.0	34.2	371.0	90.0	----	----	573.0	.22	[3]	2.2	[3]	[3]	2.8	12.61	80
2007	260.0	34.4	411.0	107.0	----	----	598.0	.19	[3]	3.1	----	[3]	3.5	11.54	89
2008[1]	261.0	33.9	492.0	116.0	----	----	670.0	.15	----	3.2	[3]	.5	4.1	12.89	92
2009[2]	260.0	33.9	229.0	73.8	----	----	449.0	.16	----	1.3	----	----	1.7	12.18	78

[1] Preliminary. [2] Estimate. [3] Less than 1/2 unit. *Source: U.S. Geological Survey (USGS)*

Eggs

Eggs are a low-priced protein source and are consumed worldwide. Each commercial chicken lays between 265-280 eggs per year. In the United States, the grade and size of eggs are regulated under the federal Egg Products Inspection Act (1970). The grades of eggs are AA, A, and B, and must have sound, whole shells and must be clean. The difference among the grades of eggs is internal and mostly reflects the freshness of the egg. Table eggs vary in color and can be determined by the color of the chicken's earlobe--white earlobes lay white eggs, reddish--brown earlobes lay brown eggs, etc. In the U.S., egg size is determined by the weight of a dozen eggs, not individual eggs, and range from Peewee to Jumbo. Store-bought eggs in the shell stay fresh for 3 to 5 weeks in a home refrigerator, according to the USDA.

Eggs are primarily used as a source of food, although eggs are also widely used for medical purposes. Fertile eggs, as a source of purified proteins, are used to produce many vaccines. Flu vaccines are produced by growing single strains of the flu virus in eggs, which are then extracted to make the vaccine. Eggs are also used in biotechnology to create new drugs. The hen's genetic make-up can be altered so the whites of the eggs are rich in tailored proteins that form the basis of medicines to fight cancer and other diseases. The U.S. biotech company Viragen and the Roslin Institute in Edinburgh have produced eggs with 100 mg or more of the easily-extracted proteins used in new drugs to treat various illnesses including ovarian and breast cancers.

Prices – The average monthly price of all eggs received by farmers in the U.S. in 2009 fell by 22.8% yr/yr to 82.2 cents per dozen, which down from last year's record high.

Supply – World egg production in 2008, the latest reporting year, was 1,144.0 billion eggs. The world's largest egg producers at that time were China with 40% of world production, the U.S. with 8%, Japan with 4%, Mexico with 4%, Russia with 3%, and Brazil with 3%. U.S. egg production in 2009 rose +0.2% to 90.296 billion eggs, but still down from the 2006 record high of 90.895. The average number of hens and pullets on U.S. farms in 2009 fell by -0.1% yr/yr to 339.341 million, down further from the 2006 record high of 348.719 million.

Demand – U.S. consumption of eggs in 2009 rose +0.4% yr/yr to 6.341 billion dozen eggs. That was down from the 2006 record high of 6.468 billion dozen, but still up about 20% from ten years earlier, reflecting sharply higher egg consumption due to the popularity of a low-carbohydrate diet since eggs are high in protein. U.S. per capita egg consumption in 2009 fell 0.6% yr/yr to 247.5 eggs per year per person. Per capita egg consumption was at a high of 277.2 eggs in 1970, then fell sharply in the 1990s to a low of 174.9 in 1995, and then began rebounding in 1997 to current levels of about 250 eggs per year.

Trade – U.S. imports of eggs in 2009 fell -11.6% yr/yr to 12.9 million dozen eggs. U.S. exports of eggs in 2009 rose by +6.75% yr/yr to 220.2 million dozen eggs, well below the record export level of 253.1 million dozen eggs in 1996.

World Production of Eggs In Millions of Eggs

Year	Brazil	China	France	Germany	Italy	Japan	Mexico	Russia	Spain	Ukraine	United Kingdom	United States	World Total
2000	30,189	378,239	17,317	14,400	12,252	42,257	35,759	33,911	11,742	8,675	9,804	84,402	963,482
2001	30,783	383,074	16,940	14,167	12,830	41,985	37,843	35,002	11,928	9,553	10,332	85,884	983,928
2002	30,951	393,179	16,480	14,262	12,855	42,157	38,012	36,106	13,113	11,159	10,272	87,216	1,008,455
2003	31,423	403,660	16,598	12,588	12,838	42,173	37,451	36,296	13,722	11,380	10,116	87,473	1,022,819
2004	32,319	410,015	15,757	12,353	13,054	41,346	40,033	35,562	15,213	11,883	10,704	89,091	1,043,033
2005	33,499	420,951	15,502	12,028	12,896	41,377	40,494	36,691	13,122	12,955	10,608	90,027	1,066,458
2006	35,207	418,718	15,138	12,137	12,500	41,611	45,801	37,651	13,142	14,122	10,166	90,877	1,087,935
2007[1]	35,584	436,664	14,640	11,974	12,500	43,050	45,817	37,559	12,590	13,978	9,920	91,101	1,118,177
2008[2]	36,500	454,955	14,640	12,103	12,500	42,567	46,744	37,831	12,590	14,809	10,277	90,151	1,144,356

[1] Preliminary. [2] Forecast. [3] Selected countries. *Source: Food and Agricultural Organization of the United Nations (FAO)*

Salient Statistics of Eggs in the United States

	--- Hens & Pullets ---		Rate	----- Eggs -----							----- Consumption -----	
Year	On Farm Dec. 1[3]	Average Number During Year	of Lay Per Layer During Year[4]	Total Produced	Price in cents Per Dozen	Value of Production[5] Million USD	Total Egg Production	Imports[6]	Exports[6]	Used for Hatching	Total	Per Capita Eggs[6]
	----- Thousands -----		(Number)	----- Millions -----			---------- Million Dozen ----------					Number
2001	338,628	335,012	256	85,745	62.2	4,446	7,187	8.9	190.0	964.2	6,043	252.7
2002	339,827	339,024	257	87,252	58.9	4,281	7,270	15.0	174.0	961.3	6,150	256.0
2003	340,979	338,393	259	87,473	73.2	5,333	7,299	13.3	146.0	959.4	6,204	255.7
2004	344,278	341,956	261	89,091	71.4	5,299	7,450	12.7	167.6	988.1	6,306	257.3
2005	347,917	343,792	262	90,027	54.0	4,049	7,538	8.5	203.3	996.7	6,345	255.8
2006	348,719	347,880	263	91,328	58.2	4,432	7,650	8.6	202.1	992.2	6,468	257.8
2007	344,492	346,498	263	91,101	88.5	6,719	7,587	13.6	250.3	1,016.3	6,335	250.1
2008[1]	339,643	339,131	266	90,040	109.0	8,225	7,509	14.6	206.3	994.9	6,316	248.9
2009[2]	339,341	337,376	268	90,359			7,517	11.4	239.5	950.3	6,341	247.5

[1] Preliminary. [2] Forecast. [3] All layers of laying age. [4] Number of eggs produced during the year divided by the average number of all layers of laying age on hand during the year. [5] Value of sales plus value of eggs consumed in households of producers. 6/ Shell-egg equivalent of eggs and egg products. *Source: National Agricultural Statistics Service, U.S. Department of Agriculture (NASS-USDA)*

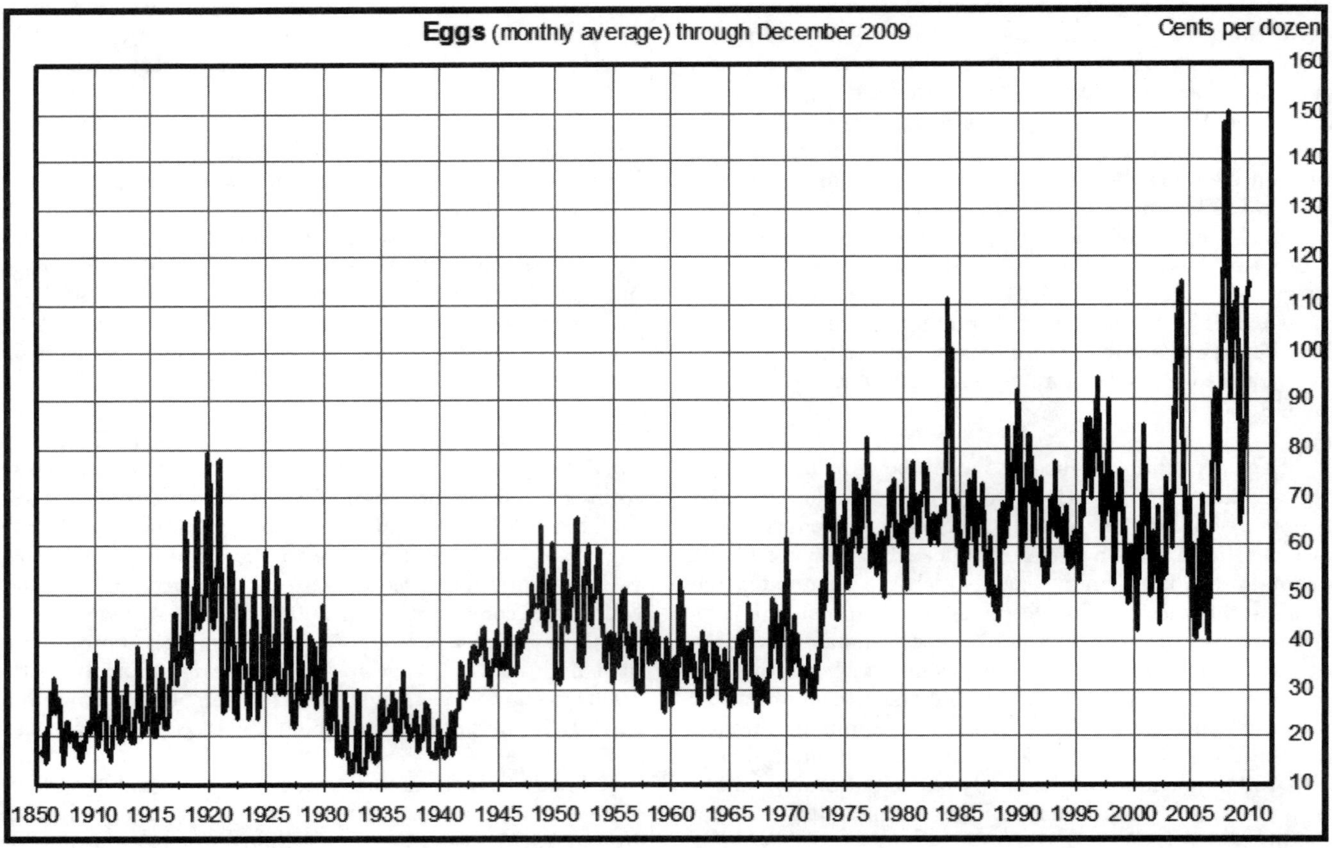

Average Price Received by Farmers for All Eggs in the United States In Cents Per Dozen

Year	Jan.	Feb.	Mar.	Apr.	May	June	July	Aug.	Sept.	Oct.	Nov.	Dec.	Average
2000	57.8	67.8	56.9	64.7	52.0	61.8	56.5	66.4	59.2	66.8	72.0	80.7	63.6
2001	67.2	68.2	69.1	65.0	55.2	55.0	54.0	56.6	55.5	59.9	64.1	59.0	60.7
2002	62.3	55.9	68.5	52.2	50.5	62.1	60.8	66.4	57.1	56.0	70.7	62.8	60.4
2003	63.6	59.3	68.7	68.6	58.7	67.2	68.7	80.8	77.6	83.8	102.0	86.8	73.8
2004	92.6	87.5	110.0	76.7	62.6	77.3	64.0	52.6	53.8	49.4	60.4	65.4	71.0
2005	55.8	55.1	52.6	47.4	45.6	45.2	52.7	47.1	63.6	51.1	65.0	71.9	54.4
2006	61.0	49.5	67.0	51.2	42.7	54.7	43.5	55.0	53.4	54.1	81.2	80.7	57.8
2007	91.5	78.1	82.8	72.9	78.0	73.4	94.5	86.6	107.0	93.5	126.0	136.0	93.4
2008	129.0	131.0	138.0	103.0	86.8	106.0	84.1	96.3	99.6	102.0	102.0	99.9	106.5
2009[1]	103.0	80.9	81.6	92.3	61.3	59.5	70.9	75.9	74.8	80.3	101.0	105.0	82.2

[1] Preliminary. *Source: Economic Research Service, U.S. Department of Agriculture (ERS-USDA)*

Average Wholesale Price of Shell Eggs (Large) Delivered, Chicago In Cents Per Dozen

Year	Jan.	Feb.	Mar.	Apr.	May	June	July	Aug.	Sept.	Oct.	Nov.	Dec.	Average
2000	54.97	59.65	52.93	61.71	42.59	55.18	52.80	64.39	58.08	66.45	74.26	84.90	60.66
2001	68.52	64.45	69.00	66.12	50.61	49.81	52.83	55.46	50.21	57.41	62.50	58.05	58.75
2002	60.43	52.00	68.00	47.23	43.73	56.40	53.02	57.16	53.20	54.43	74.00	66.38	57.17
2003	69.57	65.39	71.05	68.83	59.10	68.76	72.39	88.26	86.21	92.07	113.16	101.09	79.66
2004	105.10	103.89	115.00	86.88	67.28	70.00	63.12	59.45	55.81	53.79	60.36	69.83	75.88
2005	54.78	60.26	48.32	42.00	41.57	40.72	51.38	42.78	61.19	48.38	62.41	70.21	52.00
2006	65.40	46.08	65.11	57.11	41.32	56.14	40.30	57.46	54.97	55.64	84.38	87.65	59.30
2007	91.75	92.71	89.23	80.00	83.55	69.60	99.95	97.37	117.50	101.89	128.93	147.70	100.02
2008	144.55	142.70	150.15	115.23	90.64	107.33	95.43	100.07	108.98	103.85	110.50	109.50	114.91
2009[1]	113.40	92.29	85.64	99.26	64.55	72.41	73.55	85.69	80.17	86.14	110.75	114.41	89.86

[1] Preliminary. *Source: National Agricultural Statistics Service, U.S. Department of Agriculture (NASS-USDA)*

Total Egg Production in the United States In Millions of Eggs

Year	Jan.	Feb.	Mar.	Apr.	May	June	July	Aug.	Sept.	Oct.	Nov.	Dec.	Total
2000	7,157	6,648	7,234	7,013	7,104	6,801	7,061	7,104	6,854	7,130	7,027	7,287	84,420
2001	7,226	6,524	7,336	7,099	7,240	6,992	7,195	7,221	7,044	7,347	7,191	7,420	85,835
2002	7,264	6,581	7,417	7,105	7,297	7,126	7,347	7,356	7,147	7,412	7,226	7,451	86,729
2003	7,390	6,665	7,424	7,187	7,327	7,105	7,403	7,367	7,112	7,439	7,326	7,554	87,299
2004	7,386	6,901	7,547	7,358	7,513	7,289	7,557	7,538	7,344	7,659	7,482	7,721	89,295
2005	7,626	6,928	7,738	7,407	7,572	7,346	7,563	7,528	7,348	7,665	7,514	7,793	90,028
2006	7,727	6,980	7,843	7,543	7,637	7,401	7,645	7,647	7,430	7,678	7,549	7,815	90,895
2007	7,675	6,951	7,806	7,472	7,622	7,380	7,599	7,594	7,393	7,726	7,542	7,808	90,568
2008	7,646	7,114	7,675	7,373	7,564	7,367	7,599	7,551	7,339	7,625	7,490	7,778	90,121
2009[1]	7,678	6,903	7,737	7,472	7,607	7,360	7,590	7,593	7,376	7,696	7,569	7,827	90,408

[1] Preliminary. *Source: National Agricultural Statistics Service, U.S. Department of Agriculture (NASS-USDA)*

Per Capita Disappearance of Eggs[4] in the United States In Number of Eggs

Year	First Quarter	Second Quarter	Third Quarter	Fourth Quarter	Total	Total Consumption (Million Dozen)	Year	First Quarter	Second Quarter	Third Quarter	Fourth Quarter	Total	Total Consumption (Million Dozen)
1999	62.7	62.8	63.8	66.2	255.7	5,817	2005	63.4	63.0	63.5	65.0	255.8	6,345
2000	64.5	64.0	64.2	65.6	252.1	5,955	2006	64.1	63.7	63.9	64.7	257.8	6,468
2001	64.5	64.2	64.7	66.6	252.7	6,043	2007	62.2	61.7	62.4	63.8	250.1	6,335
2002	62.4	62.6	64.0	64.6	256.0	6,150	2008[1]	61.8	61.3	62.0	63.8	248.9	6,316
2003	62.6	63.0	63.8	65.3	255.7	6,204	2009[2]	62.0	61.4	61.4	62.8	247.5	
2004	63.7	63.9	64.1	65.5	257.3	6,306	2010[3]	61.0	61.3	61.7	62.9	246.8	

[1] Preliminary. [2] Estimate. [3] Forecast. *Source: Economic Research Service, U.S. Department of Agriculture (ERS-USDA)*

Egg-Feed Ratio[1] in the United States

Year	Jan.	Feb.	Mar.	Apr.	May	June	July	Aug.	Sept.	Oct.	Nov.	Dec.	Average
2000	8.9	11.3	8.0	9.9	6.4	9.5	9.2	12.9	10.3	12.2	13.1	15.0	10.6
2001	10.9	11.4	11.6	11.3	8.6	8.5	7.9	8.4	8.5	10.3	11.5	9.3	9.9
2002	10.2	8.4	11.6	7.4	6.7	9.5	7.5	7.9	7.1	6.6	10.5	8.9	8.5
2003	9.0	8.0	9.5	9.3	6.9	8.8	9.8	12.7	11.6	12.6	15.7	12.2	10.5
2004	12.9	10.7	13.2	7.8	6.0	6.6	5.9	5.6	6.5	5.8	8.8	9.8	8.3
2005	7.2	7.4	6.3	5.2	4.6	4.4	5.9	5.1	9.3	6.6	10.3	11.3	7.0
2006	8.5	5.9	9.8	6.3	4.2	7.1	4.6	7.5	6.9	6.4	10.6	10.1	7.3
2007	11.7	8.4	9.1	7.6	8.1	6.4	10.7	9.5	12.3	10.2	13.9	13.9	10.2
2008	12.7	11.1	11.8	7.4	5.8	7.3	5.4	6.6	7.7	8.9	9.4	9.2	8.6
2009[1]	9.0	7.0	7.2	8.3	4.2	3.8	5.6	6.5	6.7	7.2	9.9	10.3	7.1

[1] Pounds of laying feed equivalent in value to one dozen eggs. [2] Preliminary. *Source: Economic Research Service, U.S. Department of Agriculture (ERS-USDA)*

Hens and Pullets of Laying Age (Layers) in the United States, on First of Month In Thousands

Year	Jan.	Feb.	Mar.	Apr.	May	June	July	Aug.	Sept.	Oct.	Nov.	Dec.
2000	328,307	328,767	330,876	330,807	327,597	325,012	324,843	326,240	325,212	327,219	329,092	332,410
2001	332,107	335,449	336,131	337,472	336,755	333,522	332,274	332,148	333,417	336,573	337,549	338,625
2002	339,423	338,465	337,478	337,376	336,131	335,547	335,236	335,717	336,561	337,923	338,350	339,827
2003	340,752	341,019	340,080	339,645	336,678	335,611	333,925	334,381	334,248	334,103	336,528	339,989
2004	338,272	338,774	340,479	342,879	342,305	343,233	342,392	342,522	343,405	344,794	345,267	344,278
2005	347,273	348,412	349,117	344,759	342,346	341,247	338,424	338,674	339,984	341,803	343,789	347,917
2006	349,763	349,930	350,452	350,453	346,809	343,596	341,733	340,728	342,309	343,946	345,090	348,719
2007	349,192	348,563	349,081	347,280	343,835	341,057	339,373	340,648	340,604	341,322	343,909	344,492
2008	345,535	343,891	342,666	341,320	340,318	339,867	337,416	335,094	335,396	333,534	336,301	339,643
2009[1]	341,373	341,388	340,260	340,604	338,850	334,499	332,227	332,015	332,524	334,652	336,024	339,341

[1] Preliminary. *Source: National Agricultural Statistics Service, U.S. Department of Agriculture (NASS-USDA)*

Eggs Laid Per Hundred Layers in the United States In Number of Eggs

Year	Jan.	Feb.	Mar.	Apr.	May	June	July	Aug.	Sept.	Oct.	Nov.	Dec.	Average
2000	2,178	2,016	2,186	2,130	2,177	2,093	2,169	2,181	2,101	2,173	2,125	2,193	2,144
2001	2,165	1,943	2,178	2,106	2,160	2,100	2,166	2,170	2,103	2,180	2,130	2,188	2,132
2002	2,143	1,947	2,198	2,110	2,173	2,125	2,190	2,188	2,119	2,192	2,139	2,189	2,143
2003	2,168	1,957	2,184	2,125	2,180	2,122	2,215	2,203	2,128	2,218	2,166	2,223	2,157
2004	2,182	2,032	2,209	2,148	2,192	2,126	2,207	2,198	2,134	2,220	2,170	2,234	2,171
2005	2,192	1,986	2,230	2,156	2,215	2,162	2,234	2,218	2,155	2,236	2,172	2,234	2,183
2006	2,210	1,994	2,238	2,164	2,212	2,160	2,240	2,239	2,165	2,228	2,176	2,234	2,188
2007	2,200	1,993	2,242	2,162	2,226	2,169	2,235	2,229	2,168	2,255	2,191	2,255	2,194
2008	2,218	2,072	2,244	2,163	2,224	2,175	2,260	2,252	2,194	2,277	2,216	2,283	2,215
2009[1]	2,249	2,023	2,269	2,196	2,256	2,204	2,281	2,284	2,209	2,292	2,238	2,304	2,234

[1] Preliminary. *Source: National Agricultural Statistics Service, U.S. Department of Agriculture (NASS-USDA)*

Egg-Type Chicks Hatched by Commercial Hatcheries in the United States In Thousands

Year	Jan.	Feb.	Mar.	Apr.	May	June	July	Aug.	Sept.	Oct.	Nov.	Dec.	Total
2000	34,181	34,659	38,877	36,653	41,185	37,268	33,240	34,328	36,325	36,080	32,438	35,178	430,412
2001	36,728	37,836	41,015	42,789	42,655	40,822	38,651	34,987	37,140	35,825	32,355	31,870	452,673
2002	35,655	34,473	36,985	38,096	38,760	35,144	35,581	35,689	35,742	32,157	31,154	32,113	421,549
2003	33,521	30,474	36,775	37,820	37,630	36,602	35,578	33,199	35,763	34,812	30,241	33,588	416,003
2004	35,155	31,923	37,545	37,466	38,347	37,508	34,919	36,854	36,631	34,866	38,758	37,332	437,304
2005	38,291	34,427	41,701	38,049	38,792	35,034	34,897	38,700	33,623	35,461	32,285	35,917	437,177
2006	35,159	33,409	38,805	35,435	39,744	37,406	32,727	35,611	36,873	36,162	31,554	33,183	426,068
2007	36,195	36,739	38,561	39,254	38,080	40,641	35,952	36,930	35,327	36,332	36,232	35,866	446,109
2008	40,256	38,534	41,954	42,329	41,826	40,928	37,250	35,578	37,111	40,198	34,187	37,091	467,242
2009[1]	38,083	36,861	40,137	40,621	37,774	43,453	36,282	37,160	40,001	37,406	34,897	39,655	462,330

[1] Preliminary. *Source: National Agricultural Statistics Service, U.S. Department of Agriculture (NASS-USDA)*

Cold Storage Holdings of Frozen Eggs in the United States, on First of Month In Millions of Pounds[2]

Year	Jan.	Feb.	Mar.	Apr.	May	June	July	Aug.	Sept.	Oct.	Nov.	Dec.
2000	10.1	17.6	14.8	14.0	12.8	13.5	14.1	14.4	14.9	14.4	16.6	15.4
2001	15.0	16.9	15.5	14.6	15.9	15.8	14.4	16.7	17.8	17.7	15.5	13.9
2002	13.7	13.1	13.9	11.7	10.2	11.1	12.7	12.9	13.2	13.2	13.1	11.2
2003	13.5	15.3	17.1	17.0	15.7	17.7	18.0	18.6	18.0	16.6	16.9	14.9
2004	18.0	21.3	21.1	19.2	20.9	20.6	18.3	16.7	17.3	18.7	17.9	17.3
2005	19.1	18.6	17.9	18.5	18.9	17.7	19.7	19.6	19.9	18.8	17.6	17.6
2006	21.0	22.5	24.5	20.8	23.3	21.0	22.1	23.6	21.6	19.0	16.3	17.1
2007	16.5	17.2	15.7	14.6	14.3	15.2	17.4	17.5	18.5	17.7	17.6	15.2
2008	14.7	12.0	16.7	16.3	16.0	12.4	16.1	21.1	20.8	21.9	22.4	21.3
2009[1]	22.6	22.6	22.1	20.3	18.2	21.7	21.7	22.6	22.6	21.6	22.9	21.2

[1] Preliminary. [2] Converted on basis 39.5 pounds frozen eggs equals 1 case. *Source: National Agricultural Statistics Service, U.S. Department of Agriculture (NASS-USDA)*

Electric Power

The modern electric utility industry began in the 1800s. In 1807, Humphry Davy constructed a practical battery and demonstrated both incandescent and arc light. In 1831, Michael Faraday built the first electric generator proving that rotary mechanical power could be converted into electric power. In 1879, Thomas Edison perfected a practical incandescent light bulb. The electric utility industry evolved from gas and electric carbon-arc commercial and street lighting systems. In 1882, in New York City, Thomas Edison's Pearl Street electricity generating station established the industry by displaying the four key elements of a modern electric utility system: reliable central generation, efficient distribution, successful end use, and a competitive price.

Electricity is measured in units called watts and watt-hours. Electricity must be used when it is generated and cannot be stored to any significant degree. That means the power utilities must match the level of electricity generation to the level of demand in order to avoid wasteful over-production. The power industry has been deregulated to some degree in the past decade and now major utility companies sell power back and forth across major national grids in order to meet supply and demand needs. The rapid changes in the supply-demand situation mean that the cost of electricity can be very volatile.

Electricity futures trade at the New York Mercantile Exchange (NYMEX). The futures contract is a financially settled contract, which is priced based on electricity prices in the PJM western hub at 111 delivery points, mainly on the utility transmission systems of Pennsylvania Electric Co. and the Potomac Electric Co. The contract is priced in dollars and cents per megawatt hours.

Supply – U.S. electricity production in 2009 (annualized through September) fell -4.1% yr/yr to 2.369 trillion kilowatt-hours. That was well below the record high of 3.212 trillion kilowatt-hours in 1998 and indicated that recent electricity production has been reduced by more efficient production and distribution systems, and to some extent by conservation of electricity by both business and residential consumers.

U.S. electricity generation in 2006 (latest data available) required the use of 2.478 trillion cubic feet of natural gas (+16.1% yr/yr), 753 million tons of coal (1.0% yr/yr), and 54 million barrels of fuel oil (-45.5% yr/yr).

In terms of kilowatt-hours, coal is the most widely used source of electricity production in the U.S. accounting for 60% of electricity production in 2008, followed by nuclear (17%), hydro (9%), natural gas (13%), and fuel oil (0.9%). Alternative sources of fuel for electricity generation that are gaining favor include geothermal, biomass, solar, wind, etc. but so far account for only 0.5% of total electricity production in the U.S.

Demand – Residential use of electricity accounts for the largest single category of electricity demand with usage of 1.352 trillion kilowatt hours in 2006 (latest data) accounting for 35% of overall usage. Business users in total use more electricity than residential users, but business users are broken into the categories of commercial with 34% of usage and industrial with 27% of usage.

World Electricity Production (Monthly Average) In Millions of Kilowatt Hours

Year	Australia	Canada	China	Germany	India	Italy	Japan	Rep. of Korea	Russia	South Africa	Ukraine	United Kingdom	United States
2000	15,712	58,337	109,426	46,417	41,725	22,986	78,391	22,200	73,117	17,557	14,287	28,484	316,845
2001	15,548	56,576	118,439	47,107	42,434	23,242	77,742	23,768	74,031	17,508	14,414	29,414	311,387
2002	15,646	57,873	133,513	47,211	44,141	23,638	77,139	25,500	74,078	18,142	14,477	29,220	321,538
2003	15,564	56,294	153,229	49,060	52,773	24,386	76,661	26,856	76,158	19,267	15,030	35,006	307,250
2004	16,095	56,844	176,169	44,439	48,968	24,975	71,574	28,472	77,562	20,648	15,180	34,924	316,000
2005	16,870	49,559	199,780	48,840	51,125	25,754	72,667	30,357	79,355	20,673	15,505	33,377	336,499
2006	19,077	48,758	229,119	45,030	54,309	26,037	74,906	31,773	82,619	21,150	16,115	33,272	337,747
2007	18,958	50,265	265,047	43,565	57,933	26,070	82,731	33,594	84,656	21,957	16,272	30,170	346,626
2008[1]	19,793	50,143	282,692	43,565	59,874	26,393	82,572	35,389	86,429	21,524	15,982	29,605	342,513
2009[2]	19,345	48,065	301,774	38,922	62,509	23,930	75,962	36,253	80,964	20,828	13,901	27,969	329,729

[1] Preliminary. [2] Estimate. NA = Not avaliable. *Source: United Nations*

Installed Capacity, Capability & Peak Load of the U.S. Electric Utility Industry In Thousands of Megawatts (Nameplate)

		Type of Prime Mover				Type of Ownership										
Year	Total Electric Utility Industry	Hydro	Gas Turbine & Steam	Nuclear Power	Internal Combustion	Investor	Cooperative	Sub-total Gov't.	Municipal Utilities	Federal	Power Districts, State Projects	Capability at Winter Peak Load	Non-Coincident Winter Peak Load	Capacity Margin Non-Co-incident Peak Load (%)	Total Electric Utility Industry Generation (Mil. kWh)	Annual Peak Load Factor (%)
1990	735.1	87.2	531.1	108.0	8.7	568.8	26.3	139.9	40.1	65.4	34.4	696.8	484.8	20.4	2,901.3	60.4
1991	740.0	88.7	534.1	108.4	8.8	573.0	26.5	140.5	40.4	65.6	34.5	703.2	486.4	20.2	2,935.6	60.9
1992	741.7	89.7	534.5	107.9	9.6	572.9	26.0	142.7	41.6	66.1	35.0	707.8	493.6	21.1	2,934.4	61.1
1993	744.7	90.2	536.9	107.8	9.8	575.2	26.1	143.4	41.8	66.1	35.5	712.0	522.4	17.1	3,043.9	61.0
1994	764.0	90.3	537.9	107.9	9.9	574.8	26.4	144.7	42.0	66.3	36.4	715.1	518.9	16.7	3,088.7	61.2
1995	769.0	91.1	541.6	107.9	9.9	578.7	27.1	144.8	42.2	65.9	36.6	727.7	545.4	13.2	3,194.2	59.8
1996	463.0	91.0	546.6	109.0	9.9	582.2	27.2	147.1	43.0	67.2	36.9	740.5	554.1	27.7	3,284.1	61.0
1997	775.9	92.5	549.7	107.6	10.0	582.5	28.0	149.4	43.8	68.9	36.7	743.8	529.9	26.0	3,329.4	61.3
1998	778.6	91.2	522.1	104.8	10.2	531.3	32.5	164.5	50.5	68.7	45.3	835.3	567.6	25.7	3,457.4	62.0
1999[1]	775.9	89.8	476.3	102.3	9.6	483.7	34.6	159.6	50.2	68.7	40.7	848.9	570.9	26.7	3,530.0	61.2

[1] Preliminary. *Source: Edison Electric Institute (EEI)*

Available Electricity and Energy Sales in the United States In Billions of Kilowatt Hours

	Net Generation									Sales to Ultimate Customer							
		Electric Utility Industry															
Year	Total[2]	Hydro	Natural Gas	Coal	Fuel Oil	Nuclear	Other Sources[3]	Total	Total Million $	Total	Residential	Interdepartmental	Commercial	Industrial	Street & highway Lighting	Other Public Auth.	Railways & Railroads
1999	3,174	299.9	296.4	1,768	86.9	725.0	3.7	3,695	219,896	3,484	1,145	[4]	1,002.0	1,058	15.9	107.0	[4]
2000	3,015	253.2	290.7	1,697	72.2	705.4	2.2	3,802	233,163	3,592	1,192	[4]	1,055.2	1,064	[4]	109.5	[4]
2001	2,630	197.8	264.4	1,560	78.9	534.2	2.2	3,737	247,343	3,557	1,202	[4]	1,083.1	997	[4]	113.2	[4]
2002	2,549	242.3	229.6	1,515	59.1	507.4	3.8	3,858	249,411	3,632	1,265	[4]	1,104.5	990	[4]	105.6	[4]
2003	2,462	249.6	187.0	1,500	69.9	458.8	4.2	3,883	259,767	3,662	1,276	[4]	1,198.7	1,012	[4]	NA	[4]
2004	2,505	245.5	199.7	1,514	73.7	475.7	4.5	3,971	270,119	3,716	1,292	[4]	1,230.4	1,018	[4]	NA	[4]
2005	2,475	245.6	238.2	1,485	69.7	436.3	5.6	4,055	298,003	3,811	1,359	[4]	1,275.1	1,019	[4]	NA	[4]
2006	2,484	261.9	282.1	1,471	40.9	425.3	7.3	4,065	326,506	3,817	1,352	[4]	1,299.7	1,011	[4]	NA	[4]
2007	2,504	226.7	313.8	1,491	33.3	427.6	9.7	4,157	343,703	3,924	1,392	[4]	1,336.3	1,028	[4]	NA	[4]
2008[1]	2,469	224.6	314.2	1,472	21.8	424.2	11.4	4,110	363,650	3,906	1,380	[4]	1,336.0	1,009	[4]	NA	[4]

[1] Preliminary. [2] Includes internal combustion. [3] Includes electricity produced from geothermal, wood, waste, wind, solar, etc. [4] Included in Other.
NA = Not available. *Source: Edison Electric Institute (EEI)*

Electric Power Production by Electric Utilities in the United States In Millions of Kilowatt Hours

Year	Jan.	Feb.	Mar.	Apr.	May	June	July	Aug.	Sept.	Oct.	Nov.	Dec.	Total
1999	275,230	239,825	258,678	238,969	255,266	281,233	318,745	307,835	261,347	243,212	235,129	258,205	3,173,674
2000	265,991	237,324	241,397	227,031	253,890	268,128	279,421	286,682	245,137	228,389	226,765	255,229	3,015,383
2001	236,467	199,802	211,942	197,499	215,508	233,622	253,400	258,901	214,236	204,307	192,518	211,742	2,629,946
2002	215,684	187,929	200,833	194,038	208,436	227,940	248,962	241,449	215,408	201,705	194,205	212,868	2,549,457
2003	217,338	189,944	193,305	181,914	200,634	212,297	234,888	234,675	201,966	192,198	189,362	213,758	2,462,281
2004	221,782	198,675	193,763	182,744	207,224	219,767	235,266	227,785	209,507	197,320	191,813	219,585	2,505,231
2005	212,654	185,283	196,136	178,408	197,082	221,116	239,381	238,790	211,139	193,687	188,255	212,914	2,474,845
2006	204,976	192,304	197,249	184,803	204,107	223,950	243,526	242,624	200,655	193,321	189,435	206,705	2,483,655
2007	218,288	197,329	197,229	184,017	202,783	218,554	234,728	246,147	209,641	197,285	189,498	208,631	2,504,130
2008[1]	220,619	198,266	195,810	184,352	203,149	227,204	239,761	229,255	201,218	187,502	185,444		2,479,178

[1] Preliminary. *Source: Energy Information Administration, U.S. Department of Energy (EIA-DOE)*

Use of Fuels for Electric Generation in the United States

	Consumption of Fuel									
Year	Coal (Thousand ShortTons)	Fuel Oil (Thousand Barrels)	Gas (Million Cubic Feet)	Total Fuel in Coal Equivalent[3]	Net Generation by Fuels[4] (Million Kilowatt Hour)	Pounds of Coal Per Kilowatt Hour (Pounds)	Cost of Fossil-Fuel at Elec. Utilities (Cents/MMBTU)	Average Cost of Fuel Per Kilowatt Hour (In Cents)	Heat Rate BTU Per Kilowatt Hour	Cost Per Million BTU Consumed (In Cents)
1997	900,361	125,146	2,968,453	1,103,037	2,148,756	1.005	152.2	1.53	10,081	152.2
1998	910,867	178,614	3,258,054	1,147,317	2,226,860	.996	143.8	1.49	10,360	143.8
1999	894,120	143,830	3,113,419	1,113,614	2,150,989	1.012	144.1	1.48	10,301	144.1
2000	859,335	120,129	3,043,094				173.8			
2001	806,269	126,367	2,686,287				173.0			
2002	767,803	88,595	2,259,684				151.5			
2003	757,384	105,319	1,763,764							
2004	772,224	103,793	1,809,443							
2005	761,349	98,223	2,134,859							
2006[1]	753,390	53,529	2,478,396							

[1] Preliminary. [2] 42-gallon barrels. [3] Coal equivalents are calculated on the basis of Btu instead of generation data. [4] Excludes wood & waste fuels.
Source: Edison Electric Institute (EEI)

Ethanol

World Production of Ethanol In Millions of Gallons

Year	Brazil	China	France	Germany	India	Russia	Saudi Arabia	South Africa	Spain	Thailand	United Kingdom	United States	World Total
2004	3,989	964	219	71	462	198	79	110	79	74	106	3,535	10,770
2005	4,227	1,004	240	114	449	198	32	103	93	79	92	4,264	12,150
2006	4,491	1,017	251	202	502	171	52	102	122	93	74	4,855	13,489
2007[1]	5,019	486			53					79		6,499	13,102
2008[2]	6,472	502			66					90		9,000	17,335

[1] Preliminary. [2] Estimate. *Source: Renewable Fuels Association*

Salient Statistics of Ethanol in the United States

Year	Ethanol Plants	Ethanol Production Capacity (mgy)	Plants Under Con-struction	Capacity Under Construction (mgy)	Farmer Owned Plants	Farmer Owned Capacity (mgy)	Percent of Total Capacity Farmer	Farmer Owned UC Plants	Farmers Owned UC Capacity	Percent of Total UC Capacity	States with Ethanol Plants
2001	56	1,921.9	5	64.7	21	473.0	25	3	60	71	18
2002	61	2,347.3	13	390.7	25	645.6	28	10	335	86	19
2003	68	2,706.8	11	483.0	28	796.6	29	8	318	66	20
2004	72	3,100.8	15	598.0	33	1,041.1	34	12	447	75	19
2005	81	3,643.7	16	754.0	40	1,388.6	38	10	450	60	18
2006	95	4,336.4	31	1,778.0	46	1,677.1	39	4	187	11	20
2007	110	5,493.4	76	5,635.5	46	1,677.1	39	4	187	11	21
2008[1]	139	7,888.4	61	5,536.0	49	1,948.6	28	13	771	12	21
2009[2]	170	10,569.4	24	2,066.0							26

[1] Preliminary. [2] Estimate. *Source: Renewable Fuels Association*

Production of Fuel Ethanol in the United States In Thousands of Barrels Per Day

Year	Jan.	Feb.	Mar.	Apr.	May	June	July	Aug.	Sept.	Oct.	Nov.	Dec.	Average
2001	115	116	113	108	108	110	112	113	116	121	126	124	115
2002	135	122	128	126	129	123	128	136	145	159	166	176	139
2003	177	169	175	179	175	181	178	180	190	188	194	207	183
2004	211	212	214	218	221	222	218	225	226	226	232	232	221
2005	241	245	243	238	237	249	258	260	261	269	275	280	255
2006	288	302	301	289	293	318	316	329	333	333	343	356	317
2007	375	386	384	391	406	418	421	434	441	452	479	489	423
2008	510	518	561	562	598	585	614	647	640	647	668	656	601
2009[1]	630	647	640	641	669	694	728	727	725	741	786	788	701

[1] Preliminary. *Source: Energy Information Administration, U.S. Department of Energy (EIA-DOE)*

Production of Fuel Ethanol in the United States In Thousands of Barrels

Year	Jan.	Feb.	Mar.	Apr.	May	June	July	Aug.	Sept.	Oct.	Nov.	Dec.	Total
2001	3,574	3,249	3,500	3,226	3,339	3,310	3,472	3,515	3,470	3,743	3,794	3,836	42,028
2002	4,189	3,429	3,968	3,788	4,007	3,705	3,970	4,203	4,342	4,939	4,965	5,451	50,956
2003	5,497	4,734	5,430	5,384	5,426	5,440	5,529	5,589	5,685	5,829	5,806	6,423	66,772
2004	6,551	6,155	6,648	6,525	6,857	6,648	6,749	6,977	6,766	7,007	6,946	7,229	81,058
2005	7,461	6,847	7,530	7,135	7,357	7,463	8,007	8,050	7,841	8,335	8,259	8,676	92,961
2006	8,935	8,463	9,333	8,663	9,086	9,531	9,791	10,235	10,088	10,512	10,442	11,215	116,294
2007	11,621	10,795	11,892	11,716	12,573	12,553	13,083	13,581	13,402	14,221	14,568	15,258	155,263
2008	16,058	15,527	17,527	17,152	18,756	17,651	19,040	20,059	19,338	20,048	20,139	20,342	221,637
2009[1]	19,545	18,120	19,837	19,220	20,752	20,822	22,577	22,552	21,751	22,956	23,592		252,790

[1] Preliminary. *Source: Energy Information Administration, U.S. Department of Energy (EIA-DOE)*

Stocks of Fuel Ethanol in the United States In Thousands of Barrels

Year	Jan.	Feb.	Mar.	Apr.	May	June	July	Aug.	Sept.	Oct.	Nov.	Dec.
2001	2,811	2,771	2,691	2,936	3,172	4,152	3,503	4,226	4,438	3,783	4,038	4,298
2002	4,828	4,757	5,691	5,853	5,994	6,188	6,070	6,212	6,485	6,530	6,009	6,200
2003	6,933	5,943	6,549	6,528	6,507	6,753	6,975	6,744	7,256	7,201	6,472	5,978
2004	5,830	5,469	5,578	5,433	5,796	5,345	5,971	6,367	6,641	6,664	6,414	6,002
2005	6,142	6,261	6,605	6,861	6,810	6,064	5,926	5,398	5,317	5,591	5,723	5,563
2006	6,099	7,268	8,626	8,990	7,767	6,675	7,706	9,133	9,725	9,723	9,232	8,760
2007	8,656	8,765	8,539	8,807	8,966	9,171	9,866	11,011	11,555	11,449	11,218	10,535
2008	11,383	11,173	12,288	12,572	13,297	13,323	13,448	14,771	16,110	15,214	15,286	14,226
2009[1]	14,186	15,688	15,652	14,845	13,999	13,903	14,294	15,001	15,688	15,080	15,518	

[1] Preliminary. *Source: Energy Information Administration, U.S. Department of Energy (EIA-DOE)*

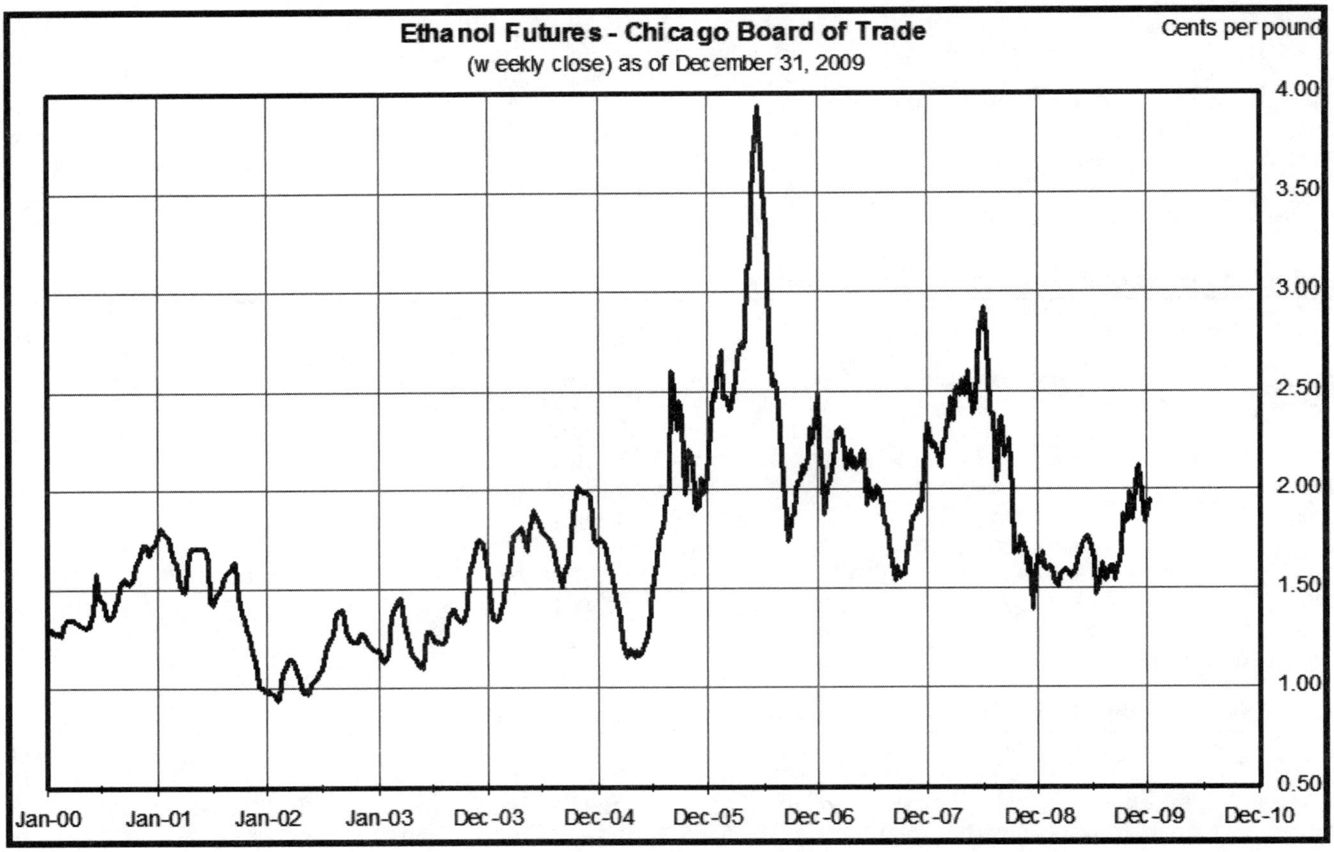

Average Price of Ethanol in the United States[1] In Dollars Per Gallon

Year	Jan.	Feb.	Mar.	Apr.	May	June	July	Aug.	Sept.	Oct.	Nov.	Dec.	Average
2000	1.285	1.275	1.331	1.329	1.314	1.471	1.402	1.405	1.533	1.558	1.687	1.696	1.441
2001	1.783	1.737	1.579	1.571	1.707	1.646	1.457	1.551	1.593	1.375	1.188	1.012	1.517
2002	0.979	0.973	1.125	1.070	0.982	1.046	1.156	1.330	1.335	1.238	1.263	1.210	1.142
2003	1.151	1.278	1.427	1.269	1.131	1.242	1.234	1.262	1.388	1.381	1.645	1.716	1.344
2004	1.423	1.398	1.666	1.791	1.753	1.862	1.762	1.624	1.585	1.878	1.995	1.812	1.712
2005	1.733	1.597	1.365	1.237	1.221	1.405	1.786	2.031	2.695	2.511	2.130	1.916	1.802
2006	1.967	2.428	2.450	2.475	2.903	3.597	3.208	2.668	2.148	1.815	2.045	2.234	2.495
2007	2.144	1.899	2.185	2.159	2.169	2.089	1.970	1.849	1.581	1.523	1.739	1.950	1.938
2008	2.188	2.129	2.316	2.455	2.485	2.535	2.642	2.224	2.150	1.846	1.648	1.493	2.176
2009	1.518	1.488	1.461	1.497	1.553	1.673	1.585	1.535	1.540	1.798	1.984	1.962	1.633

[1] Northeast and Northwest Iowa. *Source: Agricultural Marketing Service, U.S. Department of Agriculture (AMS-USDA)*

Volume of Trading of Ethanol Futures in Chicago In Contracts

Year	Jan.	Feb.	Mar.	Apr.	May	June	July	Aug.	Sept.	Oct.	Nov.	Dec.	Total
2005	----	----	350	119	222	61	155	321	227	390	559	272	2,676
2006	443	508	329	421	330	686	1,141	365	779	348	97	117	5,564
2007	191	526	945	1,153	784	1,163	792	969	704	966	1,436	2,887	12,516
2008	1,889	1,045	1,634	2,594	1,956	2,843	2,156	3,556	2,969	2,857	2,327	3,625	29,451
2009	2,969	2,116	7,158	4,673	4,031	5,535	4,707	4,843	7,439	6,530	6,521	10,646	67,168

Source: CME Group; Chicago Board of Trade (CBT)

Month-End Open Interest of Ethanol Futures in Chicago In Contracts

Year	Jan.	Feb.	Mar.	Apr.	May	June	July	Aug.	Sept.	Oct.	Nov.	Dec.
2005	----	----	246	215	88	39	61	208	301	461	759	778
2006	774	856	860	900	745	735	829	599	474	442	396	322
2007	402	478	593	623	842	1,227	1,100	1,378	1,326	1,642	1,853	2,141
2008	2,328	2,245	2,257	1,862	2,053	2,659	2,763	2,447	2,641	3,055	3,114	2,935
2009	3,146	3,228	4,644	4,145	4,381	4,174	3,877	4,631	4,940	5,575	5,933	6,904

Source: CME Group; Chicago Board of Trade (CBT)

Fertilizer

Fertilizer is a natural or synthetic chemical substance, or mixture, that enriches soil to promote plant growth. The three primary nutrients that fertilizers provide are nitrogen, potassium, and phosphorus. In ancient times, and still today, many commonly used fertilizers contain one or more of the three primary ingredients: manure (containing nitrogen), bones (containing small amounts of nitrogen and large quantities of phosphorus), and wood ash (containing potassium).

At least fourteen different nutrients have been found essential for crops. These include three organic nutrients (carbon, hydrogen, and oxygen, which are taken directly from air and water), three primary chemical nutrients (nitrogen, phosphorus, and potassium), and three secondary chemical nutrients (magnesium, calcium, and sulfur). The others are micronutrients or trace elements and include iron, manganese, copper, zinc, boron, and molybdenum.

Prices – The average price of ammonia, a key source of ingredients for fertilizers, fell by -57.6% yr/yr in 2009 to $250 per metric ton, down from last year's record high of $590 per metric ton. The average price of phosphate rock in the U.S. in 2006 (latest data available) rose by +3.1% yr/yr to a record high of $30.52 per metric ton. The average price of potash in the U.S. in 2009 rose by +17.1% yr/yr to a record high of $820.00 per metric ton.

Supply – World production of nitrogen (as contained in ammonia) in 2009 was unchanged from the 2008 record high of 133.000 million metric tons. The world's largest producers of nitrogen in 2009 were China with 33% of world production, India (8%), Russia (8%), and the U.S. (6%). U.S. nitrogen production in 2009 fell -1.9% to 7.700 million metric tons.

World production of phosphate rock, basic slag and guano in 2009 fell -1.9% yr/yr to 158.000 million metric tons. The world's largest producers of phosphate rock in 2009 were China (with 35% of world production), U.S. (17%), Morocco (15%), and Russia (6%). U.S. production in 2009 fell -9.9% y/y to 27.2 million metric tons.

World production of marketable potash in 2009 fell -28.6% yr/yr to 25.0 million metric tons, down from last year's record high of 35.0 million metric tons. The world's largest producers of potash in 2009 were Canada with 26% of world production, Belarus (15%), Russia (14%), and Germany (9%). U.S. production of potash in 2009 fell -23.6% yr/yr to 840,000 metric tons.

Demand – U.S. consumption of nitrogen in 2007 (latest data) rose +9.1% yr/yr to a 7-year high of 12.000 million metric tons. U.S. consumption of phosphate rock in 2009 fell -18.7% yr/yr to a 4 decade low of 25.700 million metric tons. U.S. consumption of potash in 2009 fell -54.5% yr/yr to 3.1 million metric tons, down from 2004's 12-year high of 6.000 million metric tons.

Trade – U.S. imports of nitrogen in 2009 fell -16.0% yr/yr to 5.060 million metric tons and the U.S. relied on imports for 40% of consumption. U.S. imports of phosphate rock in 2009 fell 34.6%% yr/yr to an 11-year low of 1.800 million metric tons. U.S. imports of potash in 2009 fell -58.6% to a 4-decade low of 2.400 million metric tons, and imports accounted for 73% of U.S. consumption.

World Production of Ammonia In Thousands of Metric Tons of Contained Nitrogen

Year	Canada	China	France	Germany	India	Indonesia	Japan	Mexico	Netherlands	Poland	Russia	United States	Total
2001	3,439	28,200	1,380	2,522	10,081	3,655	1,318	548	1,989	1,735	8,690	9,120	105,000
2002	3,700	30,200	1,172	2,560	9,827	4,200	1,192	559	2,053	1,311	8,600	10,300	109,000
2003	3,662	31,500	1,153	2,803	10,048	4,250	1,061	439	1,750	1,906	9,100	8,450	110,000
2004	4,107	34,770	1,120	2,741	10,718	4,120	1,101	560	1,970	1,984	9,800	8,990	117,000
2005	4,100	37,850	1,206	2,789	10,800	4,400	1,083	423	1,700	2,080	10,000	8,340	122,000
2006	4,100	40,660	616	2,718	10,900	4,300	1,091	487	1,800	2,007	10,500	8,190	126,000
2007	4,498	42,480	800	2,746	11,000	4,400	1,114	487	1,800	1,995	10,500	8,540	132,000
2008[1]	4,781	44,000	800	2,819	11,100	4,500	1,110	625	1,800	2,000	10,425	7,850	133,000
2009[2]	4,500	44,000	NA	2,800	11,100	4,600	1,000	NA	1,800	2,000	10,400	7,700	133,000

[1] Preliminary. [2] Estimate. *Source: U.S. Geological Survey (USGS)*

Salient Statistics of Nitrogen[3] (Ammonia) in the United States In Thousands of Metric Tons

Year	Net Import Reliance As a % of Apparent Consumption	Production[3] (Fixed): Fertilizer	Production[3] (Fixed): Non-fertilizer	Production[3] (Fixed): Total	Imprts[4] (Fixed)	Exports	Nitrogen[5] Compounds: Produced	Nitrogen[5] Compounds: Consumption	Stocks, Dec. 31: Ammonia	Stocks, Dec. 31: Fixed Nitrogen Compounds	Ammonia Consumption (Apparent)	Average Price ($/Metric Ton): Urea FOB Gulf[6] Coast	Average Price ($/Metric Ton): Urea FOB Corn Belt	Average Price ($/Metric Ton): Ammonium Nitrate: FOB Corn Belt	Average Price ($/Metric Ton): Ammonia FOB Gulf Coast
2001	31	8,190	929	9,120	4,550	647	7,852	10,600	261	1,340	13,200	104-108	130-135	120-130	183
2002	29	9,300	1,030	10,300	4,670	437	9,937	11,000	286	1,140	14,500	128-132	150-160	120-130	137
2003	39	7,490	961	8,450	5,720	400	9,122	11,000	195	476	13,900	192-195	215-225	190-195	245
2004	38	8,470	524	8,990	5,900	381	9,258	11,900	298	590	14,400	225-230	255-270	195-210	274
2005	42	7,450	884	8,340	6,520	525	9,099	11,300	254	605	14,400	260-267	300-325	265-270	304
2006	41	7,270	921	8,190	5,920	194	9,083	11,000	201	485	14,000	265-280	295-305	250-260	302
2007	43	7,610	930	8,540	6,530	145	9,485	12,000	157	407	15,000	435-445	465-490	590-620	350
2008[1]	42	6,960	893	7,850	6,020	192	8,722	11,900	368	990	13,500	190-210	270-330	450-650	120
2009[2]	40			7,700	5,060	50			300		12,800				

[1] Preliminary. [2] Estimate. [3] Anhydrous ammonia, synthetic. [4] For consumption. [5] Major downstream nitrogen compounds. [6] Granular.
Source: U.S. Geological Survey (USGS)

World Production of Phosphate Rock, Basic Slag & Guano In Thousands of Metric Tons (Gross Weight)

Year	Brazil	China	Egypt	Israel	Jordan	Morocco	Russia	Senegal	Syria	Togo	Tunisia	United States	World Total
2000	4,725	19,400	1,096	4,110	5,526	21,463	11,100	1,738	2,166	1,370	8,339	38,600	132,000
2001	4,805	21,000	972	3,511	5,843	21,983	10,500	1,708	2,043	1,067	8,144	31,900	126,000
2002	5,084	23,000	1,550	4,091	7,179	23,028	10,700	1,551	2,483	1,271	7,461	36,100	136,000
2003	5,584	25,200	2,183	3,708	6,650	23,338	11,000	1,765	2,414	1,471	7,890	35,000	138,000
2004	5,690	25,500	2,219	3,290	6,188	26,675	11,000	1,580	2,883	1,115	8,051	35,800	143,000
2005	5,450	30,400	2,144	3,236	6,375	28,788	11,000	1,455	3,500	1,350	8,220	36,100	150,000
2006	5,930	38,600	2,200	2,949	5,805	27,000	11,000	584	3,664	1,650	7,801	30,100	151,000
2007	6,000	45,400	2,200	3,100	5,540	27,000	11,000	600	3,700	800	7,800	29,700	156,000
2008[1]	6,200	50,700	3,000	3,090	6,270	25,000	10,400	700	3,220	800	8,000	30,200	161,000
2009[2]	6,000	55,000	3,300	3,000	6,000	24,000	9,000	700	3,000	800	7,000	27,200	158,000

[1] Preliminary. [2] Estimate. *Source: U.S. Geological Survey (USGS)*

Salient Statistics of Phosphate Rock in the United States In Thousands of Metric Tons

Year	Mine Production	Marketable Production	Value Million Dollars	Imports for Consumption	Exports	Apparent Consumption	Producer Stocks, Dec. 31	Avg. Price FOB Mine $/Metric Ton	Avg. Price of Florida & N. Carolina - $/Met. Ton - FOB Mine (-60% to +74%) - Domestic	Export	Average
2000	163,000	38,600	$932	1,930	299	39,000	8,170	$24.29	$24.14	$40.38	$24.29
2001	130,000	31,900	$856	2,500	9	35,300	7,510	$26.82	$26.82	W	$26.81
2002	154,000	36,100	$993	2,700	62	37,400	8,860	$27.47	$27.69	W	$27.69
2003	153,000	35,000	$946	2,400	64	38,800	7,540	$27.01	$26.95	W	$26.95
2004	146,000	35,800	$995	2,500	----	39,000	7,220	$27.79	$27.76	NA	$27.76
2005	151,000	36,100	$1,070	2,630	----	37,800	6,970	$29.61	$29.67	NA	$29.60
2006	111,000	30,100	$919	2,420	----	32,600	7,070	$30.49	W	NA	$30.52
2007	126,000	29,700	$1,520	2,670	----	33,800	4,970	$51.10	W	NA	$51.36
2008[1]		30,000		2,754		31,600	6,335	$76.76			
2009[2]		26,500		1,800		25,700	8,000	$50.00			

[1] Preliminary. [2] Estimate. *Source: U.S. Geological Survey (USGS)*

World Production of Marketable Potash In Thousands of Metric Tons (K_2O Equivalent)

Year	Belarus	Brazil	Canada	China	France	Germany	Israel	Jordan	Russia	Spain	United Kingdom	United States	World Total
2000	3,786	352	9,202	380	320	3,407	1,750	1,160	3,700	653	600	1,300	27,000
2001	3,700	319	8,237	385	244	3,549	1,770	1,180	4,300	471	532	1,200	26,400
2002	3,800	337	8,515	450	130	3,472	1,950	1,191	4,400	481	540	1,200	27,100
2003	4,230	416	9,104	650	----	3,564	1,960	1,194	5,465	594	1,040	1,100	29,900
2004	4,600	403	10,100	770	----	3,627	2,140	1,180	6,405	590	547	1,200	32,100
2005	4,844	405	10,140	1,500	----	3,664	2,224	1,115	7,131	575	439	1,200	33,800
2006	4,605	403	8,518	1,800	----	3,625	2,190	1,036	6,610	580	420	1,100	31,400
2007	4,972	405	11,112	2,000	----	3,600	2,200	1,090	6,600	580	427	1,100	34,600
2008[1]	4,970	471	10,500	2,750	----	3,280	2,300	1,220	6,730	435	427	1,100	35,000
2009[2]	3,850	500	6,500	2,750	----	2,300	2,000	1,100	3,600	400	400	840	25,000

[1] Preliminary. [2] Estimate. *Source: U.S. Geological Survey (USGS)*

Salient Statistics of Potash in the United States In Thousands of Metric Tons (K_2O Equivalent)

Year	Net Import Reliance As a % of Apparent Consumption	Production	Sales by Producers	Value Million Dollars	Imports for Consumption	Exports	Apparent Consumption	Producer Stocks Dec. 31	Dollars per Ton: Avg Value of Product	Avg Value of K_2O Equiv	Avg. Price[3] (Metric Ton)
2000	80	1,300	1,200	290.0	4,600	367	5,600	----	110.00	230.00	157.50
2001	80	1,200	1,100	260.0	4,540	366	5,300	----	110.00	230.00	165.00
2002	80	1,200	1,200	280.0	4,620	371	5,400	----	110.00	230.00	155.00
2003	80	1,100	1,200	280.0	4,720	329	5,600	----	110.00	230.00	170.00
2004	80	1,200	1,300	340.0	4,920	233	6,000	----	125.00	270.00	200.00
2005	80	1,200	1,200	410.0	4,920	200	5,900	----	165.00	350.00	280.00
2006	79	1,100	1,100	410.0	4,470	332	5,200	----	170.00	375.00	290.00
2007	81	1,100	1,200	480.0	4,970	199	5,900	----	185.00	400.00	400.00
2008[1]	84	1,100			5,800	116	6,800	----			700.00
2009[2]	73	840			2,400	142	3,100	----			820.00

[1] Preliminary. [2] Estimate. [3] Unit of K_2O, standard 60% muriate F.O.B. mine. *Source: U.S. Geological Survey (USGS)*

Fish

Fish are the primary source of protein for a large portion of the world's population. The worldwide yearly harvest of all sea fish (including aquaculture) is between 85 and 130 million metric tons. There are approximately 20,000 species of fish, of which 9,000 are regularly caught. Only 22 fish species are harvested in large amounts. Ground-fish, which are fish that live near or on the ocean floor, account for about 10% of the world's fishery harvest, and include cod, haddock, pollock, flounder, halibut and sole. Large pelagic fish such as tuna, swordfish, marlin, and mahi-mahi, account for about 5% of world harvest. The fish eaten most often in the United States is canned tuna.

Rising global demand for fish has increased the pressure to harvest more fish to the point where all 17 of the world's major fishing areas have either reached or exceeded their limits. Atlantic stocks of cod, haddock and blue-fin tuna are all seriously depleted, while in the Pacific, anchovies, salmon and halibut are all over-fished. Aquaculture, or fish farming, reduces pressure on wild stocks and now accounts for nearly 20% of world harvest.

Supply – The U.S. grand total of fishery products rose +1.7% to a record high of 20.966 billion pounds in 2006 (latest data). The U.S. total domestic catch in 2006 fell by -2.3% to 9.489 billion pounds, and that comprised 45% of total U.S. supply. Of the U.S. total domestic catch in 2006, 71% of the catch was finfish for human consumption, 18% of the catch was a variety of fish for industrial use, and 12% was shellfish for human consumption. The principal species of U.S. fishery landings in 2006 were Pollock (with 3.414 billion pounds landed), Menhaden (1.304 billion pounds), Pacific Salmon (663 million pounds), Flounder (446 million pounds), and Sea Herring (365 million pounds).

About 30% of the fish harvested in the world are processed directly into fishmeal and fish oil. Fishmeal is used primarily in animal feed. Fish oil is used in both animal feed and human food products. World fishmeal production in the 2008-09 marketing year fell by -0.2% to 5.186 million metric tons. World production of fish oil in 2008-09 fell -3.7% to 1.017 million metric tons. Peru and Chile are by far the world's largest producers of fishmeal and fish oil.

Trade – U.S. imports of fishery products in 2006 (latest data) rose +5.3% yr/yr to a record high of 11.477 billion pounds, comprising 55% of total U.S. supply.

					Domestic Catch					Imports				
	Grand	For Human Food		For Industrial		Percent of Grand	For Human Food		For Industrial		Percent of Grand	For Human Food		For Industrial
Year	Total	Finfish	Shellfish[3]	Use[4]	Total	Total	Finfish	Shellfish[3]	Use[4]	Total	Total	Finfish	Shellfish[3]	Use[4]
2002	19,028	11,770	4,237	3,022	9,397	49.4	6,013	1,192	2,193	9,631	50.6	5,757	3,045	829
2003	19,850	12,617	4,570	2,663	9,507	47.9	6,388	1,133	1,986	10,343	52.1	6,229	3,437	677
2004	20,413	12,959	4,689	2,765	9,683	47.4	6,641	1,153	1,889	10,730	52.6	6,318	3,536	876
2005	20,612	13,567	4,588	2,457	9,707	47.1	6,914	1,084	1,710	10,905	52.9	6,653	3,505	747
2006	20,960	13,484	5,110	2,366	9,483	45.2	6,671	1,171	1,641	11,477	54.8	6,813	3,939	725
2007	20,561	13,339	4,914	2,308	9,309	45.3	6,415	1,075	1,819	11,252	54.7	6,925	3,838	489
2008[1]	19,252	12,347	4,742	2,163	8,326	43.2	5,590	1,043	1,692	10,927	56.8	6,757	3,699	471

[1] Preliminary. [2] Live weight, except percent. [3] For univalue and bivalues mollusks (conchs, clams, oysters, scallops, etc.) the weight of meats, excluding the shell is reported. [4] Fish meal and sea herring. *Source: Fisheries Statistics Division, U.S. Department of Commerce*

Fisheries -- Landings of Principal Species in the United States In Millions of Pounds

	Fish									Shellfish					
Year	Cod, Atlantic	Flounder	Halibut	Herring, Sea	Man-haden	Pollock	Salmon, Pacific	Tuna	Whiting	Clams (Meats)	Crabs	Lobsters American	Oysters (Meats)	Scallops (Meats)	Shrimp
2002	29	373	82	214	1,751	3,349	567	49	18	130	308	82	34	53	317
2003	24	365	80	287	1,599	3,372	674	62	19	128	332	74	37	56	315
2004	16	360	80	265	1,498	3,365	739	57	19	119	316	88	39	65	309
2005	14	419	76	303	1,244	3,426	899	44	17	106	299	88	34	57	261
2006	13	446	71	290	1,307	3,414	664	50	12	111	340	93	34	59	320
2007	17	483	70	233	1,484	3,085	885	51	14	116	294	81	38	59	281
2008[1]	19	663	67	259	1,341	2,298	658	48	14	108	325	82	30	54	257

[1] Preliminary. *Source: National Marine Fisheries Service, U.S. Department of Commerce*

U.S. Fisheries: Quantity & Value of Domestic Catch & Consumption & World Fish Oil Production

	Disposition										
Year	Fresh & Frozen	Canned	Cured	For Meal, Oil, etc.	Total	For Human Food	For Industrial Products	Ex-vessel Value[3]	Average Price	Fish Per Capita Consumption	World[2] Fish Oil Production
	Millions of Pounds							Million $	Cents /Lb.	Pounds	1,000 Tons
2002	6,826	652	117	1,802	9,397	7,205	2,192	3,092	32.9	NA	946
2003	7,266	498	119	1,624	9,507	7,521	1,986	3,347	35.2	NA	1,006
2004	7,488	552	137	1,506	9,683	7,794	1,889	3,756	38.8	NA	1,128
2005	7,776	563	160	1,208	9,707	7,997	1,710	3,942	40.6	NA	979
2006	7,627	573	117	1,166	9,483	7,809	1,680	4,024	42.1	NA	1,014
2007	7,450	514	121	1,224	9,309	7,466	1,766	4,192			1,067
2008[1]	6,538	336	138	1,313	8,325	6,633	1,692	4,383			1,044

[1] Preliminary. [2] Crop years on a marketing year basis. [3] At the Dock Prices. Source: Fisheries Statistics Division, U.S. Department of Commerce

Imports of Seafood Products into the United States In Thousands of Pounds

	Fresh			Fresh &	Frozen			Canned &	Fresh &				
Year	Atlantic Salmon	Pacific Salmon[2]	Shrimp	Frozen Trout	Atlantic Salmon	Pacific Salmon[2]	Shrimp	Prepared Salmon[3]	Prepared Shrimp[4]	Oysters[5]	Mussels[6]	Clams[7]	Tilapia[8]
2000	7,095	119,366	19,908	10,658	12,844	620,890	159,254	9,453	140,865	89,202	20,790	43,118	27,791
2001	7,294	132,601	17,592	8,387	10,515	714,340	217,270	11,513	169,225	124,312	18,438	39,973	31,485
2002	9,752	149,083	23,063	6,629	18,354	729,903	257,175	16,417	217,629	148,034	19,084	45,696	30,507
2003	9,044	132,801	22,462	8,776	27,309	879,924	272,802	25,312	234,834	198,955	22,283	43,275	34,416
2004	8,580	121,724	22,396	7,917	40,860	871,856	264,586	24,632	271,199	249,167	23,120	50,817	31,111
2005	7,171	142,244	22,514	5,052	42,270	870,595	275,501	25,672	301,534	297,639	22,912	51,662	32,912
2006	10,215	171,848	20,905	5,137	52,161	920,922	257,970	27,456	385,701	348,707	24,599	50,796	34,454
2007[1]	11,679	178,932	17,583	6,596	52,688	913,977	265,404	30,490	317,811	383,065	24,040	53,104	30,638

[1] Preliminary. [2] Also contains salmon with no specific species noted. [3] Includes smoked and cured salmon. [4] Shrimp, canned, breaded, or prepared. [5] Oysters fresh or prepared. [6] Mussels fresh or prepared. [7] Clams, fresh or prepared. [8] Tilapia, frozen whole fish plus fresh and frozen fillets.
Source: Bureau of the Census, U.S. Department of Commerce

Exports of Seafood Products From the United States In Thousands of Pounds

	Fresh			Fresh &	Frozen			Canned &	Fresh &			
Year	Atlantic Salmon	Pacific Salmon[2]	Shrimp	Frozen Trout	Atlantic Salmon	Pacific Salmon[2]	Shrimp	Prepared Salmon[3]	Prepared Shrimp[4]	Oysters[5]	Mussels[6]	Clams[7]
2000	1,818	15,798	39,393	299	161,785	15,158	99,206	14,759	3,230	1,568	4,483	7,250
2001	1,080	18,431	25,198	84	167,558	13,956	128,154	14,320	3,932	1,424	4,232	9,273
2002	1,163	8,444	29,884	84	132,605	13,899	116,419	15,519	3,928	1,179	11,285	10,049
2003	2,600	11,388	39,846	99	155,256	16,395	121,038	16,172	5,905	1,340	10,071	13,443
2004	1,180	13,995	34,249	197	187,954	12,730	138,455	14,620	7,688	924	12,506	16,909
2005	972	11,760	18,965	379	261,124	9,105	146,064	13,026	7,852	1,026	10,523	25,591
2006	875	8,759	19,869	106	219,019	7,544	137,538	12,944	6,241	2,525	12,257	29,110
2007[1]	797	7,255	15,671	257	300,340	8,565	138,950	14,137	6,192	1,886	12,467	24,141

[1] Preliminary. [2] Also contains salmon with no specific species noted. [3] Includes smoked and cured salmon. [4] Shrimp, canned, breaded, or prepared. [5] Oysters fresh or prepared. [6] Mussels fresh or prepared. [7] Clams, fresh or prepared. *Source: Bureau of the Census, U.S. Department of Commerce*

World Production of Fish Meal In Thousands of Metric Tons

Year	Chile	Spain	Denmark	European Union	Former USSR	Iceland	Japan	Norway	Peru	South Africa	Thailand	United States	World Total
2001-02	766.0	95.5	308.2	562.8	72.9	307.9	318.0	222.9	1,688.1	115.7	390.9	349.8	6,212.4
2002-03	858.9	98.0	238.9	495.8	71.8	268.5	326.0	199.2	1,344.6	115.3	398.8	322.4	5,770.4
2003-04	929.7	83.4	255.9	520.4	61.3	214.6	319.0	234.2	1,842.2	136.6	404.3	305.0	6,245.9
2004-05	886.1	53.2	231.2	472.8	59.6	202.1	318.0	155.6	1,949.2	121.3	407.9	308.1	6,100.3
2005-06	857.2	43.4	213.7	449.4	64.0	137.7	309.0	162.4	1,493.3	72.7	430.0	305.1	5,515.1
2006-07[1]	816.7	40.9	164.8	403.3	67.3	149.6	295.0	173.1	1,385.1	88.6	429.0	302.0	5,309.8
2007-08[2]	720.0	35.0	161.9	396.2	70.3	140.0	300.0	135.9	1,474.4	80.7	401.5	255.1	5,197.9
2008-09[3]	735.0	33.0	165.0	395.2	75.3	126.0	290.0	138.0	1,430.0	82.0	400.0	285.0	5,185.6

[1] Preliminary. [2] Estimate. [3] Forecast. *Source: The Oil World*

World Production of Fish Oil In Thousands of Metric Tons

Year	Canada	Chile	China	Denmark	Iceland	Japan	Norway	Peru	Africa	Former USSR	United States	World Total	Fish Oil CIF [4] $ Per Tonne
2001-02	4.3	140.2	22.5	104.1	84.6	64.7	61.2	162.2	5.3	2.9	103.9	935.0	593
2002-03	4.5	152.1	18.3	112.9	122.0	65.6	51.6	208.0	5.4	3.5	89.6	1,017.2	560
2003-04	4.8	176.5	14.0	107.4	74.2	68.1	40.5	263.5	7.1	3.6	81.9	1,036.0	648
2004-05	5.2	182.3	12.0	74.7	59.1	65.8	29.7	342.2	7.1	3.7	77.6	1,045.6	716
2005-06	5.0	179.0	12.1	75.0	51.6	68.5	36.1	287.4	7.5	3.8	62.7	1,000.2	792
2006-07[1]	5.2	186.4	13.0	52.6	53.4	66.9	41.5	327.9	4.5	3.9	71.4	1,040.9	885
2007-08[2]	5.4	177.7	12.5	57.0	66.0	67.0	42.9	284.6	4.0	4.0	81.3	1,055.4	1,612
2008-09[3]	5.2	175.0	14.0	59.0	58.0	65.0	38.0	275.0	4.4	4.0	80.0	1,016.8	915

[1] Preliminary. [2] Estimate. [3] Forecast. [4] Any origin, N.W. Europe. *Source: The Oil World*

Monthly Production of Catfish--Round Weight Processed--in the United States In Thousands of Pounds (Live Weight)

Year	Jan.	Feb.	Mar.	Apr.	May	June	July	Aug.	Sept.	Oct.	Nov.	Dec.	Total
2002	52,551	52,856	58,340	50,694	52,902	49,450	52,363	54,383	53,366	56,576	50,072	48,048	631,601
2003	55,523	55,461	65,007	57,105	58,424	52,441	54,089	54,153	51,885	57,652	51,246	48,518	661,504
2004	53,849	54,173	60,272	53,896	52,324	50,155	51,055	53,295	51,329	52,396	49,536	48,170	630,450
2005	53,856	51,720	57,117	50,306	51,552	49,626	47,241	50,686	47,151	49,034	46,674	45,707	600,670
2006	50,703	49,145	56,315	43,126	42,865	41,214	45,528	51,736	47,296	50,788	45,680	41,735	566,131
2007	46,079	44,083	45,477	37,954	38,867	37,275	39,168	42,626	39,519	45,890	40,307	39,001	496,246
2008	45,992	47,634	47,908	45,018	44,326	43,265	42,583	40,985	39,057	43,344	36,869	32,616	509,597
2009[1]	36,406	37,702	44,912	40,768	39,925	39,370	40,966	39,490	36,408	40,191	36,211	33,751	466,100

[1] Preliminary. *Source: Economic Research Service, U.S. Department of Agriculture ERS-USDA)*

Average Price Paid to Producers for Farm-Raised Catfish in the United States In Cents Per Pound (Live Weight)

Year	Jan.	Feb.	Mar.	Apr.	May	June	July	Aug.	Sept.	Oct.	Nov.	Dec.	Average
2002	54.9	55.5	56.5	56.1	57.4	58.8	59.0	58.2	57.6	56.8	56.0	54.4	56.8
2003	52.9	54.4	58.5	63.0	61.8	58.6	56.4	55.2	56.0	56.7	61.0	62.9	58.1
2004	66.8	70.3	72.3	72.8	72.0	68.9	68.2	68.3	68.3	69.5	68.9	69.0	69.6
2005	72.5	73.1	73.3	72.5	72.2	72.1	72.3	72.4	72.4	72.4	72.4	72.6	72.5
2006	72.7	72.9	74.5	78.5	79.6	80.7	81.2	81.1	83.2	83.6	83.7	83.8	79.6
2007	83.7	83.8	83.8	84.1	84.0	81.7	76.2	73.1	69.7	68.2	66.6	65.0	76.7
2008	65.8	68.8	74.3	75.7	77.6	79.4	81.8	82.7	82.7	82.5	82.3	82.1	78.0
2009[1]	81.0	77.0	77.3	76.3	76.2	76.3	77.1	76.9	77.2	76.8	76.5	76.3	77.1

[1] Preliminary. *Source: Economic Research Service, U.S. Department of Agriculture (ERS-USDA)*

Sales of Fresh Catfish in the United States In Thousands of Pounds

Year	Jan.	Feb.	Mar.	Apr.	May	June	July	Aug.	Sept.	Oct.	Nov.	Dec.	Total
Whole													
2001	3,516	3,242	4,260	3,644	3,271	3,166	3,233	3,204	3,174	3,294	2,865	2,803	39,672
2002	3,713	3,656	3,826	3,373	3,644	3,313	3,477	3,733	3,418	3,822	3,031	2,986	41,992
2003	3,833	3,785	4,339	3,643	3,692	3,266	3,553	3,510	3,233	3,231	2,798	2,693	41,576
2004	3,205	3,266	3,808	3,001	2,853	2,707	2,875	3,002	2,861	3,076	2,950	2,704	36,308
2005	3,111	3,177	3,402	2,938	2,679	2,765	2,686	2,673	2,687	2,546	2,615	2,784	34,063
2006[1]	3,195	3,331	4,024	2,940	2,795	2,464	2,716	2,711					36,264
Fillets[2]													
2001	4,884	6,112	6,751	5,709	5,587	5,122	5,191	5,313	5,264	5,273	4,463	4,489	64,158
2002	5,684	6,132	6,010	5,236	5,682	5,093	5,327	5,442	5,317	5,420	4,447	4,119	63,909
2003	5,362	5,158	6,715	5,700	6,364	5,737	5,984	6,013	5,308	6,082	5,187	4,710	68,320
2004	5,964	6,455	6,815	5,887	5,688	5,500	5,559	5,483	4,865	4,992	4,336	4,162	65,706
2005	5,274	5,615	5,795	4,979	5,274	4,987	4,714	4,998	4,848	5,072	4,291	4,209	60,056
2006[1]	5,160	5,109	6,090	5,077	4,653	4,446	4,279	4,447					58,892
Other[3]													
2001	1,443	1,292	2,156	1,309	1,282	1,298	1,375	1,436	1,449	1,430	1,223	1,252	16,945
2002	1,526	1,446	1,375	1,356	1,732	1,527	1,576	1,569	1,441	1,596	1,165	1,205	17,514
2003	1,668	1,532	1,599	1,458	1,472	1,319	1,425	1,366	1,473	1,361	1,138	1,134	16,945
2004	1,435	1,518	1,567	1,426	1,299	1,248	1,181	1,173	1,228	1,263	1,152	1,095	15,585
2005	1,300	1,295	1,370	1,271	1,204	1,130	1,097	1,128	1,084	1,121	965	900	13,865
2006[1]	1,126	1,024	1,214	987	915	807	863	879					11,723

[1] Preliminary. [2] Includes regular, shank and strip fillets; excludes breaded products. [3] Includes steaks, nuggets and all other products not reported.
Source: Economic Research Service, U.S. Department of Agriculture (ERS-USDA)

Prices of Fresh Catfish in the United States In Dollars Per Pound

Year	Jan.	Feb.	Mar.	Apr.	May	June	July	Aug.	Sept.	Oct.	Nov.	Dec.	Average
Whole													
2001	1.59	1.68	1.63	1.65	1.65	1.62	1.59	1.55	1.53	1.49	1.42	1.37	1.56
2002	1.36	1.35	1.30	1.34	1.36	1.37	1.35	1.32	1.32	1.28	1.24	1.25	1.32
2003	1.28	1.30	1.35	1.37	1.36	1.39	1.33	1.33	1.34	1.36	1.40	1.43	1.35
2004	1.49	1.53	1.57	1.60	1.60	1.57	1.57	1.58	1.56	1.59	1.51	1.57	1.56
2005	1.64	1.64	1.61	1.61	1.61	1.58	1.58	1.57	1.58	1.63	1.55	1.50	1.59
2006[1]	1.53	1.49	1.54	1.65	1.70	1.74	1.72	1.76					1.64
Fillets[2]													
2001	2.80	2.79	2.80	2.80	2.80	2.78	2.77	2.75	2.69	2.63	2.60	2.55	2.73
2002	2.52	2.49	2.49	2.51	2.53	2.55	2.55	2.54	2.54	2.52	2.49	2.47	2.52
2003	2.44	2.45	2.44	2.49	2.51	2.50	2.48	2.48	2.49	2.49	2.50	2.54	2.48
2004	2.59	2.62	2.71	2.73	2.74	2.74	2.73	2.73	2.74	2.76	2.77	2.77	2.72
2005	2.81	2.75	2.85	2.87	2.86	2.85	2.84	2.83	2.83	2.84	2.84	2.84	2.83
2006[1]	2.86	2.87	2.89	2.98	3.08	3.14	3.18	3.20					3.03
Other[3]													
2001	1.64	1.68	1.57	1.64	1.69	1.64	1.61	1.57	1.52	1.59	1.59	1.53	1.61
2002	1.53	1.57	1.54	1.51	1.45	1.51	1.51	1.50	1.54	1.48	1.55	1.46	1.51
2003	1.40	1.41	1.51	1.53	1.47	1.54	1.52	1.58	1.50	1.58	1.60	1.64	1.52
2004	1.63	1.70	1.71	1.78	1.78	1.78	1.62	1.76	1.69	1.72	1.70	1.71	1.72
2005	1.67	1.67	1.74	1.71	1.77	1.78	1.72	1.68	1.64	1.65	1.60	1.65	1.69
2006[1]	1.64	1.63	1.65	1.75	1.73	1.86	1.86	1.85					1.75

[1] Preliminary. [2] Includes regular, shank and strip fillets; excludes breaded products. [3] Includes steaks, nuggets and all other products not reported.
Source: Economic Research Service, U.S. Department of Agriculture (ERS-USDA)

Flaxseed and Linseed Oil

Flaxseed, also called linseed, is an ancient crop that was cultivated by the Babylonians around 3,000 BC. Flaxseed is used for fiber in textiles and to produce oil. Flaxseeds contain approximately 35% oil, of which 60% is omega-3 fatty acid. Flaxseed or linseed oil is obtained through either the expeller extraction or solvent extraction method. Manufacturers filter the processed oil to remove some impurities and then sell it as unrefined. Unrefined oil retains its full flavor, aroma, color, and naturally occurring nutrients. Flaxseed oil is used for cooking and as a dietary supplement as well as for animal feed. Industrial linseed oil is not for internal consumption due to possible poisonous additives and is used for making putty, sealants, linoleum, wood preservation, varnishes, and oil paints.

Prices – The average monthly price received by U.S. farmers for flaxseed in the 2009-10 marketing year (through January 2010) fell by -34.2% yr/yr to $7.88 per bushel, further down from the 2007-08 record high of $13.54 per bushel.

Supply – World production of flaxseed in the 2008-09 marketing year rose by +11.4% yr/yr to 2.157 million metric tons, but still below the 9-year high of 2.864 million metric tons in 2005-06. The world's largest producer of flaxseed is Canada with 44% of world production in 2008-09, followed by the China (23%), India (7%), the U.S. (7%), and the former USSR (6%). U.S. production of flaxseed in 2009-10 rose +29.9% to 7.423 million bushels, but still well below the record high of 19.695 million bushels in 2005-06. North Dakota is by far the largest producing state of flaxseed and accounted for 95.0% of flaxseed production in 2009, followed by South Dakota with 2.3% of production and Montana with 2.2% of production

World production of linseed oil in 2008-09 fell by -4.0% yr/yr to 606.5 million metric tons. The world's largest producers of linseed oil are China (with 24% of world production in 2008-09), Belgium (18%), the U.S. (17%), and India (8%). U.S. production of linseed oil in 2007-08 fell by –9.1% yr/yr to 212 million pounds.

Demand – U.S. distribution of flaxseed in 2007-08 fell by –19.4% yr/yr to 14.160 million bushels. The breakdown was 77% for crushing into meal and oil, 14% for exports, 4.7% for seed, and 4.6% for residual. U.S. consumption of linseed oil (inedible products) in the 2009-10 marketing year (through November 2009) fell by -13.9% yr/yr to 120.387 million pounds.

Trade – U.S. exports of flaxseed in 2007-08 rose by +11.8% yr/yr to 2.000 million bushels. U.S. imports of flaxseed in 2007-08 rose by +34.2% yr/yr to a 10-year high of 7.312 million bushels.

World Production of Flaxseed   In Thousands of Metric Tons

Crop Year	Argentina	Australia	Bangladesh	Canada	China	Egypt	France	Hungary	India	Romania	United States	Former USSR	World Total
1999-00	47	9	46	1,100	404	30	34	2	289	3	200	42	2,868
2000-01	22	9	48	775	520	30	38	1	240	1	273	74	2,361
2001-02	16	9	50	770	273	26	23	1	240	2	291	82	1,980
2002-03	11	9	50	750	409	15	17	1	200	2	301	60	1,974
2003-04	29	9	3	835	450	22	11	1	230	2	265	85	2,169
2004-05	36	10	3	592	460	31	13	2	200	3	263	98	2,008
2005-06	54	10	3	1,150	475	28	25	3	210	----	480	105	2,864
2006-07[1]	38	7	9	1,060	480	27	43	2	200	----	280	140	2,566
2007-08[2]	13	8	8	720	480	27	34	2	190	----	150	98	1,937
2008-09[3]	16	8	8	950	500	27	13	2	150	----	145	123	2,157

[1] Preliminary. [2] Estimate. [3] Forecast. *Source: The Oil World*

Supply and Distribution of Flaxseed in the United States   In Thousands of Bushels

Crop Year Beginning June 1	Planted (1,000 Acres)	Harvested (1,000 Acres)	Yield Per Acre (Bushels)	Supply: Beginning Stocks	Supply: Production	Supply: Imports	Supply: Total Supply	Distribution: Seed	Distribution: Crush	Distribution: Exports	Distribution: Residual	Distribution: Total
1999-00	387	381	20.6	2,158	7,864	6,629	16,651	434	11,500	201	2,735	14,884
2000-01	536	517	20.8	1,767	10,730	2,849	15,346	474	12,000	1,017	572	14,038
2001-02	585	578	19.8	1,308	11,455	1,904	14,667	635	10,000	2,386	753	13,774
2002-03	784	703	16.9	893	11,863	2,901	15,657	482	10,500	3,181	416	14,579
2003-04	595	588	17.9	1,078	10,516	4,580	16,174	424	11,260	2,516	686	14,886
2004-05	523	516	20.3	1,288	10,471	5,413	17,069	796	13,600	1,510	301	16,206
2005-06	983	955	20.6	863	19,695	4,256	24,814	659	16,400	3,780	440	21,279
2006-07[1]	813	767	14.4	3,535	11,019	5,447	20,001	287	14,900	1,789	582	17,557
2007-08[2]	354	349	16.9	2,444	5,896	7,312	15,660	659	10,850	2,000	651	14,160
2008-09[3]	354	340	16.8		5,716							

[1] Preliminary. [2] Estimate. [3] Forecast. NA = not avaliable. *Source: Economic Research Service, U.S. Department of Agriculture (ERS-USDA)*

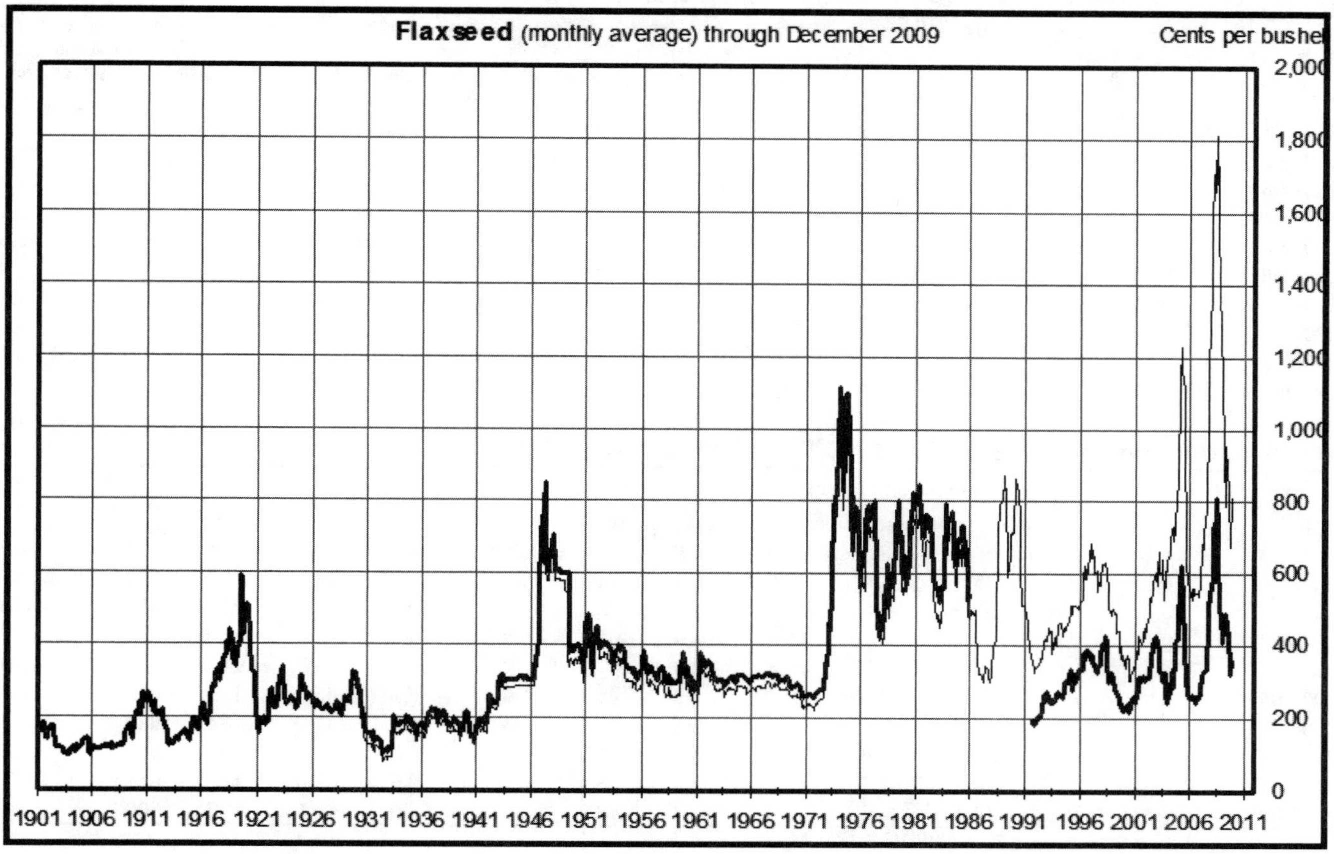

Production of Flaxseed in the United States, by States In Thousands of Bushels

Year	Minnesota	North Dakota	South Dakota	Montana[2]	Total	Year	Minnesota	North Dakota	South Dakota	Montana[2]	Total
2000	198	9,975	361	196	10,730	2005	132	18,165	480	918	19,695
2001	52	10,900	323	180	11,455	2006	126	10,368	228	297	11,019
2002	64	11,560	44	195	11,863	2007	72	5,548	96	180	5,896
2003	161	9,990	144	221	10,516	2008	69	5,491	84	72	5,716
2004	51	9,840	135	342	10,471	2009[1]	63	7,032	168	160	7,423

[1] Preliminary. [2] Data through 1999 are "Other". *Source: National Agricultural Statistics Service, U.S. Department of Agriculture (NASS-USDA)*

Factory Shipments of Paints, Varnish and Lacquer in the United States In Millions of Dollars

Year	First Quarter	Second Quarter	Third Quarter	Fourth Quarter	Total	Year	First Quarter	Second Quarter	Third Quarter	Fourth Quarter	Total
2000	4,073.1	4,573.5	4,082.0	3,474.7	16,203	2005	4,061.1	5,268.4	4,953.6	4,254.9	18,538
2001	3,625.0	4,345.4	4,094.5	3,652.6	15,718	2006	4,626.5	5,408.8	5,050.5	4,305.7	19,392
2002	3,729.9	4,440.7	4,251.4	3,600.7	16,023	2007	4,311.4	5,483.2	5,245.9	4,277.0	19,318
2003	3,981.5	4,671.8	4,374.7	3,905.8	16,934	2008	4,203.2	5,151.7	5,189.8	3,876.5	18,421
2004	4,306.1	5,000.1	4,843.2	4,104.7	18,254	2009[1]	3,446.6	4,248.1	4,182.3		15,836

[1] Preliminary. *Source: Bureau of the Census, U.S. Department of Commerce*

Consumption of Linseed Oil (Inedible Products) in the United States In Millions of Pounds

Year	July	Aug.	Sept.	Oct.	Nov.	Dec.	Jan.	Feb.	Mar.	Apr.	May	June	Average
2002-03	11.7	9.6	10.0	7.0	5.7	7.3	6.8	6.4	8.7	8.5	6.6	6.7	94.9
2003-04	7.9	6.9	6.0	6.8	3.5	5.0	5.6	7.3	6.0	7.7	8.1	8.2	79.1
2004-05	7.3	7.3	6.7	5.6	4.8	5.1	3.7	4.8	4.9	4.0	5.7	4.7	64.6
2005-06	4.8	4.5	4.2	3.7	2.7	2.7	3.9	3.8	4.9	3.3	5.9	6.0	50.5
2006-07	4.4	5.8	5.7	3.5	3.7	2.8	3.6	4.3	4.2	5.0	6.8	7.2	56.8
2007-08	8.6	W	W	W	W	W	5.8	W	W	W	W	W	86.4
2008-09	W	W	W	W	W	W	W	9.7	18.0	10.2	10.3	10.2	139.9
2009-10[1]	10.0	W	10.1	10.1	9.8	W							120.4

[1] Preliminary. W = Withheld. *Source: Bureau of the Census, U.S. Department of Commerce*

Supply and Distribution of Linseed Oil in the United States In Millions of Pounds

Crop Year Beginning June 1	Supply: Stocks June 1	Supply: Production	Supply: Total	Disappearance: Exports	Disappearance: Domestic	Disappearance: Total	Average Price at Minneapolis Cents/Lb.
1999-00	48	224	285	74	162	236	35.8
2000-01	49	234	295	73	179	252	36.0
2001-02	43	195	249	50	167	218	38.1
2002-03	31	205	249	70	149	219	39.9
2003-04	30	220	265	76	169	245	42.0
2004-05	20	265	301	107	149	256	59.5
2005-06	45	320	375	98	232	330	54.0
2006-07	45	291	344	76	217	293	44.4
2007-08[1]	52	228	292	74	191	265	66.0
2008-09[2]	27	188	225	76	114	190	86.5-89.5

[1] Preliminary. [2] Forecast. *Source: Economic Research Service, U.S. Department of Agriculture (ERS-USDA)*

World Production and Price of Linseed Oil In Thousands of Metric Tons

Year	Argentina	Bangladesh	Belgium	China	Egypt	Germany	India	Japan	United Kingdom	United States	Former USSR	World Total	Rotterdam Ex-TankUSD $/Tonne
1999-00	13.1	12.6	68.8	118.3	15.0	73.6	85.9	23.8	34.1	124.9	7.9	709.4	413
2000-01	6.2	12.9	75.2	133.0	23.0	63.4	74.7	21.1	17.0	114.7	16.4	669.0	378
2001-02	3.8	13.5	95.0	75.3	15.6	57.3	72.4	18.9	9.9	95.7	20.7	584.1	454
2002-03	2.1	7.5	92.1	111.4	15.1	64.4	63.3	8.6	5.9	105.5	15.1	582.4	679
2003-04	2.3	0.6	119.6	124.0	11.3	66.6	67.7	7.5	6.7	103.8	17.1	624.1	757
2004-05	6.9	0.6	97.9	127.0	12.0	37.9	62.7	6.8	3.5	135.5	16.3	622.0	1,191
2005-06	13.1	2.6	97.9	137.6	14.8	65.2	63.7	5.7	3.5	147.7	16.2	689.8	686
2006-07	5.0	4.3	135.9	146.6	16.5	59.3	61.7	6.2	5.3	140.3	13.0	722.0	809
2007-08[1]	2.8	2.8	120.0	148.1	12.1	53.6	58.4	4.6	2.8	107.6	12.2	631.8	1,635
2008-09[2]	2.8	2.3	110.4	146.0	11.9	55.4	48.2	3.6	3.9	105.5	13.5	606.5	965

[1] Preliminary. [2] Forecast. *Source: The Oil World*

Average Price Received by Farmers for Flaxseed in the United States In Dollars Per Bushel

Year	July	Aug.	Sept.	Oct.	Nov.	Dec.	Jan.	Feb.	Mar.	Apr.	May	June	Average
2000-01	3.25	3.05	3.10	3.17	3.39	4.45	3.42	3.43	3.90	3.68	3.91	4.10	3.57
2001-02	4.28	4.09	4.10	4.21	4.33	4.55	4.22	4.75	4.75	4.80	5.02	5.29	4.53
2002-03	5.38	5.27	5.55	5.76	6.04	5.92	5.71	6.25	6.47	6.57	6.05	6.02	5.92
2003-04	6.38	5.30	5.43	5.77	6.02	6.15	6.08	6.39	6.53	7.01	7.10	7.23	6.28
2004-05	7.33	6.90	7.19	7.36	8.62	8.42	8.89	10.90	11.40	12.30	11.60	11.20	9.34
2005-06	10.40	6.28	6.10	6.05	5.94	5.81	5.64	5.59	5.31	5.56	5.59	5.40	6.14
2006-07	5.47	5.50	5.46	5.41	5.38	5.73	6.03	6.39	6.79	6.72	7.08	7.81	6.15
2007-08	8.14	8.64	9.55	11.60	12.90	13.10	13.50	16.00	17.50	16.60	16.90	18.00	13.54
2008-09	18.10	16.50	15.60	12.60	12.60	11.50	11.00	9.98	9.29	7.90	9.03	9.58	11.97
2009-10[1]	8.28	8.14	6.79	6.78	8.15	8.41	8.42	8.70					7.96

[1] Preliminary. *Source: National Agricultural Statistics Service, U.S. Department of Agriculture (NASS-USDA)*

Stocks of Linseed Oil (Crude and Refined) at Factories and Warehouses in the U.S. In Millions of Pounds

Year	July 1	Aug. 1	Sept. 1	Oct. 1	Nov. 1	Dec. 1	Jan. 1	Feb. 1	Mar. 1	Apr. 1	May 1	June 1
2000-01	39.5	42.5	41.3	54.3	58.7	87.0	61.6	50.1	50.5	51.2	39.2	44.8
2001-02	29.1	30.2	22.6	38.4	32.4	29.9	33.4	36.6	26.8	33.4	32.3	31.1
2002-03	27.8	17.7	12.8	21.8	30.5	29.0	31.9	35.9	34.6	36.2	33.7	33.7
2003-04	30.2	27.2	22.3	78.5	42.0	35.0	40.0	43.4	37.6	32.9	24.5	19.9
2004-05	15.1	15.8	8.0	13.0	17.1	26.9	31.3	35.4	35.4	41.0	43.9	47.2
2005-06	38.1	24.8	14.1	33.9	31.1	21.0	29.4	38.4	42.2	32.2	25.5	29.8
2006-07	22.2	27.9	21.6	23.6	28.4	33.5	38.5	41.5	44.9	44.3	49.6	51.6
2007-08	41.5	44.4	49.5	39.4	50.3	49.9	34.3	22.8	37.1	28.0	35.6	26.5
2008-09	22.4	26.1	31.8	28.5	30.3	37.7	37.6	47.5	43.1	39.7	58.3	60.5
2009-10[1]	48.7	49.4	70.3	28.3	41.7	34.9	41.7					

[1] Preliminary. *Source: Bureau of the Census, U.S. Department of Commerce*

Wholesale Price of Raw Linseed Oil at Minneapolis in Tank Cars In Cents Per Pound

Year	Jan.	Feb.	Mar.	Apr.	May	June	July	Aug.	Sept.	Oct.	Nov.	Dec.	Average
2000-01	36.00	36.00	36.00	36.00	36.00	36.00	36.00	36.00	36.00	36.00	36.00	32.00	35.67
2001-02	35.50	38.00	39.00	39.00	39.00	39.00	39.00	39.00	39.00	39.00	39.65	40.35	38.79
2002-03	40.00	38.00	41.00	31.75	41.00	41.00	41.00	41.00	41.00	41.00	41.19	41.75	39.97
2003-04	41.75	41.75	42.00	42.75	43.13	43.25	42.60	40.00	40.00	40.00	45.00	45.50	42.31
2004-05	48.50	50.00	55.00	57.20	60.00	58.17	60.80	64.00	66.00	73.75	75.00	75.00	61.95
2005-06	75.00	75.00	75.00	48.75	42.75	43.50	42.40	42.00	42.38	42.94	43.10	42.35	51.26
2006-07	43.30	43.25	43.44	43.83	44.00	44.38	44.60	44.67	46.00	46.10	46.50	47.75	44.82
2007-08	49.00	NA	65.67	70.00	72.64	75.00	77.43	77.16	85.55	86.00	86.10	89.14	75.79
2008-09	93.18	95.71	90.00	87.86	87.21	85.82	86.35	83.42	82.59	80.00	77.00	75.36	85.38
2009-10[1]	73.27	70.29	70.00	70.00	70.00	70.00							70.59

[1] Preliminary. *Source: Economic Research Service, U.S. Department of Agriculture (ERS-USDA)*

Average Price of Linseed Meal (34% protein) at Minneapolis In Dollars Per Ton

Year	Jan.	Feb.	Mar.	Apr.	May	June	July	Aug.	Sept.	Oct.	Nov.	Dec.	Average
2000-01	115.10	106.50	95.70	110.00	113.80	121.30	140.00	130.00	121.90	116.30	116.80	110.00	116.45
2001-02	135.00	135.60	111.30	114.00	122.50	124.40	123.70	119.20	114.50	112.80	112.50	113.50	119.92
2002-03	127.50	143.80	127.10	114.00	113.10	112.50	118.40	120.10	133.00	126.70	125.00	127.30	124.04
2003-04	129.10	130.60	125.20	139.90	178.80	162.30	166.30	174.40	193.60	197.80	181.80	151.80	160.97
2004-05	139.80	112.40	112.40	99.50	114.60	109.10	111.60	109.90	109.80	104.00	96.00	116.00	111.26
2005-06	159.40	157.80	99.00	100.40	113.60	118.00	127.30	130.20	129.00	126.60	119.10	116.90	124.78
2006-07	111.50	101.10	92.80	100.80	118.10	123.30	134.20	156.40	156.30	149.00	135.10	132.00	125.88
2007-08	135.80	123.90	131.40	170.20	184.60	186.80	242.70	250.00	247.10	253.70	240.30	265.40	202.66
2008-09	273.70	231.30	200.00	160.80	164.00	189.60	248.80	270.00	231.90	233.50	263.10	250.00	226.39
2009-10[1]	226.90	217.00	195.20	185.00	220.00	256.50							216.77

[1] Preliminary. *Source: Economic Research Service, U.S. Department of Agriculture (ERS-USDA)*

Volume of Trading of Flaxseed Futures in Winnipeg In Contracts

Year	Jan.	Feb.	Mar.	Apr.	May	June	July	Aug.	Sept.	Oct.	Nov.	Dec.	Total
1995	10,707	15,819	10,676	15,315	12,569	9,235	6,579	5,922	11,790	11,051	15,064	7,798	132,525
1996	9,617	8,301	4,110	13,531	10,855	7,997	6,517	4,153	5,430	11,126	7,532	10,720	99,889
1997	7,640	6,486	7,123	10,912	6,256	7,851	7,662	7,081	20,967	23,418	20,049	15,311	140,756
1998	15,713	19,906	8,275	9,060	5,231	7,642	4,468	4,062	7,328	13,085	13,824	6,958	115,552
1999	4,855	8,922	4,383	8,460	5,241	5,891	4,863	2,833	5,852	12,078	7,710	7,345	78,433
2000	9,022	9,340	9,292	12,604	7,372	7,393	2,676	2,525	9,822	11,915	14,436	7,819	100,040
2001	8,232	6,428	6,928	7,117	6,514	6,745	4,344	2,620	5,242	7,291	4,689	6,326	72,476
2002	2,990	2,838	2,519	3,832	3,320	3,018	1,153	810	777	3,030	955	344	25,586
2003	333	724	412	368	452	738	343	96	491	273	183	25	4,438
2004	35	10	15	0	0	0	0	0	15	0	0	15	90

Source: Winnipeg Commodity Exchange (WCE)

Fruits

A fruit is any seed-bearing structure produced from a flowering plant. A widely used classification system divides fruit into fleshy or dry types. Fleshy fruits are juicy and include peaches, mangos, apples, and blueberries. Dry fruits include tree nuts such as almonds, walnuts, and pecans. Some foods that are commonly called vegetables, such as tomatoes, squash, peppers and eggplant, are technically fruits because they develop from the ovary of a flower.

Worldwide, over 430 million tons of fruit are produced each year and are grown everywhere except the Arctic and the Antarctic. The tropics, because of their abundant moisture and warm temperatures, produce the most diverse and abundant fruits. Mexico and Chile produce more than half of all the fresh and frozen fruit imported into the U.S. In the U.S., the top three fruits produced are oranges, grapes, and apples. Virtually all U.S. production of almonds, pistachios, and walnuts occurs in California, which leads the U.S. in tree nut production.

Prices – Overall fruit prices were fairly strong in 2008 with the fresh fruit Consumer Price Index (CPI) rising +4.9% to 345.5 and the processed fruit CPI index rising +8.3% to 135.6. Individual fruit prices, however, were mixed in 2007: Red Delicious Apples (+18.4% to $1.320 per pound), bananas (+19.4% to 60.9 cents per pound), Anjou pears (+4.6% to $1.331 per pound), Thompson seedless grapes (+5.8% to $2.212 per pound), lemons (+8.0% to $2.006 per pound), grapefruit (+0.2% to $0.966 per pound), navel oranges (-13.1% to $1.116 cents per pound), and Valencia oranges (-5.4% to $1.016 per pound).

Supply – U.S. commercial production of selected fruits in 2007 rose +11.3% to 30.205 million short tons. By weight, oranges accounted for 33% of that U.S. fruit production figure, followed by grapes at 24%, and apples at 16%. The value of U.S. fruit production in 2008 fell -4.2% yr/yr to $18.060 billion.

Demand – U.S. per capita fresh fruit consumption in 2008 rose +3.15% to 100.44 pounds per year, but remained below the 2004 record high of 102.46. The highest per capita consumption categories for non-citrus fruits in 2008 were bananas (25.06 pounds) and apples (16.17 pounds). Per capital consumption of citrus fruits were lemons (1.97 pounds) oranges (9.91 pounds), grapefruit (3.16 pounds), Tangerines & Tangelos (3.08 pounds). The utilization breakdown for 2008 shows that total U.S. non-citrus fruit was used for fresh fruit (41%), wine (22%), dried fruit (14%), canned fruit (8%), juice (7%), and frozen fruit (4%). The value of utilized non-citrus fruit production in 2008 fell -2.7% yr/yr to $11.134 billion.

Commercial Production for Selected Fruits in the United States In Thousands of Short Tons

Year	Apples	Cherries[2]	Cranberries	Grapes	Grapefruit	Lemons	Nectarines	Oranges	Peaches	Pears	Pineapple[3]	Prunes & Plums	Strawberries	Tangelos	Tangerines	Total All Fruits
2002	4,262	213	285	7,339	2,424	801	300	12,374	1,268	890	320	736	942	97	420	33,163
2003	4,397	359	310	6,644	2,063	1,026	273	11,545	1,260	934	300	803	1,078	105	382	31,985
2004	5,220	390	309	6,240	2,165	798	269	12,872	1,307	878	220	325	1,107	45	417	33,012
2005	4,853	386	312	7,814	1,018	870	251	9,251	1,185	823	212	476	1,161	70	335	29,549
2006	4,912	425	345	6,378	1,232	980	232	9,020	1,010	842	185	813	1,202	63	417	28,390
2007	4,545	437	328	7,057	1,627	798	283	7,625	1,127	873	NA	405	1,223	56	361	27,145
2008[1]	4,885	355	393	7,303	1,548	619	303	10,076	1,133	871	NA	544	1,266	68	527	30,205

[1] Preliminary. [2] Sweet and tart. [3] Utilized production. *Source: Economic Research Service, U.S. Department of Agriculture (ERS-USDA)*

Utilized Production for Selected Fruits in the United States In Thousands of Short Tons

	Utilized Production				Value of Production			
	Citrus[2]	Noncitrus	Tree nuts[3]	Total	Citrus[2]	Noncitrus	Tree nuts[3]	Total
Year	In Thousands of Short Tons				In Thousands of Dollars			
2002	16,194	17,122	1,448	34,764	2,610,559	8,137,640	2,078,670	12,826,869
2003	15,180	16,848	1,458	33,486	2,259,976	8,434,610	2,472,480	13,167,066
2004	16,360	16,823	1,524	34,706	2,485,052	8,553,060	3,527,904	14,566,016
2005	11,573	18,272	1,467	31,312	2,303,425	9,805,757	4,175,893	16,285,075
2006	11,744	16,816	1,598	30,158	2,738,361	10,510,417	3,680,383	16,929,161
2007	10,467	17,048	2,000	29,515	3,147,755	11,438,971	4,272,279	18,859,005
2008[1]	12,838	17,642	2,141	32,622	3,240,271	11,133,614	3,685,938	18,059,823

[1] Preliminary. [2] Year harvest was completed. [3] Tree nuts on an in-shell equivalent.
Source: Economic Research Service, U.S. Department of Agriculture (ERS-USDA)

Annual Average Retail Prices for Selected Fruits in the United States In Dollars Per Pound

Year	Red Delicious Apples	Bananas	Anjou Pears	Thompson Seedless Grapes	Lemons	Grapefruit	Oranges: Navel	Oranges: Valencias
2002	.948	.508	.997	1.887	1.391	.648	.836	.565
2003	.980	.509	NA	1.899	1.317	.723	.838	.575
2004	1.043	.495	NA	2.059	1.235	.819	.859	.691
2005	.949	.492	1.114	2.078	1.411	.998	.996	.897
2006	1.067	.500	1.133	2.246	1.529	1.114	1.087	1.001
2007	1.115	.510	1.273	2.092	1.857	.964	1.284	1.074
2008[1]	1.320	.609	1.331	2.212	2.006	.966	1.116	1.016

[1] Estimate. *Source: Economic Research Service, U.S. Department of Agriculture (ERS-USDA)*

Utilization of Noncitrus Fruit Production, and Value in the United States 1,000 Short Tons (Fresh Equivalent)

Year	Utilized Production	Fresh	Processed: Canned	Dried	Juice	Frozen	Wine	Other Processed	Value of Utilized Production $1,000
1999	17,347	6,691	1,986	2,154	1,887	717	3,351	244	8,077,404
2000	18,854	7,015	1,812	3,023	1,712	691	4,130	191	7,883,036
2001	16,740	6,488	1,859	2,290	1,462	665	3,568	169	7,918,636
2002	17,122	6,549	1,727	2,582	1,251	591	3,999	138	8,137,640
2003	16,848	6,672	1,762	2,293	1,295	716	3,582	219	8,434,610
2004	16,823	7,168	1,710	1,425	1,418	685	3,819	290	8,553,060
2005	18,272	7,188	1,575	2,101	1,555	712	4,551	277	9,805,757
2006	16,816	6,930	1,400	2,219	1,256	710	3,726	235	10,510,417
2007	17,048	7,013	1,453	2,030	1,277	748	3,921	278	11,438,971
2008[1]	17,642	7,254	1,375	2,388	1,321	679	3,944	289	11,133,614

[1] Preliminary. *Source: Economic Research Service, U.S. Department of Agriculture (ERS-USDA)*

Average Price Indexes for Fruits in the United States

Year	Index of all Fruit & Nut Prices Received by Growers (1990-92=100)	Producer Price Index (1982 = 100): Fresh Fruit	Dried Fruit	Canned Fruits and Juices	Frozen Fruits and Juices	Consumer Price Index (1982-84 = 100): Fresh Fruit	Processed Fruit
1999	115	103.6	122.9	137.0	106.1	266.3	105.4
2000	98	91.4	122.4	139.5	108.9	258.3	106.9
2001	109	97.7	120.3	143.3	111.9	265.1	109.0
2002	105	91.5	120.7	141.7	112.5	270.2	111.6
2003	106	84.1	122.1	142.3	115.7	279.1	113.7
2004	124	104.9	NA	143.1	113.3	286.8	114.0
2005	128	102.8	NA	148.1	112.4	297.4	118.4
2006	154	111.0	NA	153.0	119.7	315.2	121.5
2007	158	123.4	NA	156.9	138.5	329.5	125.2
2008[1]	147	122.9	NA	167.5	146.7	345.5	135.6

[1] Estimate. NA = Not availavle. *Source: Economic Research Service, U.S. Department of Agriculture (ERS-USDA)*

Fresh Fruit: Per Capita Consumption[1] in the United States In Pounds

Year	Cutrus Fruit: Oranges	Tangerines & Tangelos	Lemons	Grapefruit	Total	Noncitrus Fruit: Apples	Apricots	Avocados	Bananas	Cherries	Cran-berries
1999	8.38	2.30	2.61	5.75	20.37	18.50	.12	1.92	30.70	.63	.11
2000	11.74	2.86	2.44	5.09	23.51	17.46	.15	2.21	28.45	.60	.14
2001	11.87	2.72	2.96	4.84	23.90	15.61	.08	2.50	26.64	.77	.13
2002	11.73	2.55	3.34	4.62	23.34	16.01	.09	2.34	26.78	.70	.11
2003	11.88	2.71	3.33	4.09	23.78	16.91	.13	2.75	26.18	.92	.10
2004	10.78	2.76	3.12	4.13	22.64	18.81	.12	3.06	25.79	.99	.11
2005	11.41	2.50	2.95	2.64	21.59	16.67	.13	3.48	25.20	.87	.09
2006	10.24	2.69	4.15	2.31	21.63	17.74	.08	3.59	25.13	1.07	.09
2007	7.46	2.56	2.81	2.84	17.93	16.41	.16	3.50	25.98	1.22	.10
2008[2]	9.91	3.08	1.97	3.16	20.60	16.17	.13	3.83	25.06	1.00	.10

[1] All data on calendar-year basis except for citrus fruits; apples, August; grapes and pears, July; grapefruit, September; lemons, August of prior year; all other citrus, November. [2] Preliminary. *Source: Economic Research Service, U.S. Department of Agriculture (ERS-USDA)*

Fresh Fruit: Per Capita Consumption[1] in the United States In Pounds

Year	Noncitrus Fruit Continued: Grapes	Kiwifruit	Mangos	& Peaches	Pears	Pineapples	Papaya	Prunes	Straw-berries	Total Noncitrus	Total Fruit
1999	7.97	.52	1.62	5.29	3.53	3.03	.62	1.28	4.57	80.72	101.09
2000	7.44	.56	1.75	5.30	3.40	3.22	.68	1.19	4.86	77.68	101.19
2001	7.38	.44	1.79	5.16	3.25	3.16	.78	1.33	4.21	73.58	97.49
2002	8.42	.38	1.97	5.23	3.06	3.82	.79	1.26	4.65	75.99	99.33
2003	7.66	.38	2.06	5.17	3.08	4.40	.87	1.24	5.29	77.53	101.32
2004	7.80	.41	2.02	5.15	2.96	4.43	1.03	1.12	5.48	79.81	102.46
2005	8.60	.45	1.88	4.83	2.91	4.91	.94	1.11	5.83	78.34	99.93
2006	7.60	.47	2.10	4.58	3.19	5.21	1.04	1.02	6.14	79.62	101.25
2007	8.02	.44	2.11	4.47	3.09	5.02	1.08	1.01	6.27	79.45	97.38
2008[2]	8.53	.48	2.11	5.07	3.12	5.08	.98	.92	6.45	79.84	100.44

[1] All data on calendar-year basis except for citrus fruits; apples, August; grapes and pears, July; grapefruit, September; lemons, August of prior year; all other citrus, November. [2] Preliminary. *Source: Economic Research Service, U.S. Department of Agriculture (ERS-USDA)*

Gas

Natural gas is a fossil fuel that is colorless, shapeless, and odorless in its pure form. It is a mixture of hydrocarbon gases formed primarily of methane, but it can also include ethane, propane, butane, and pentane. Natural gas is combustible, clean burning, and gives off a great deal of energy. Around 500 BC, the Chinese discovered that the energy in natural gas could be harnessed. They passed it through crude bamboo-shoot pipes and then burned it to boil sea water to create potable fresh water. Around 1785, Britain became the first country to commercially use natural gas produced from coal for streetlights and indoor lights. In 1821, William Hart dug the first well specifically intended to obtain natural gas and he is generally regarded as the "father of natural gas" in America. There is a vast amount of natural gas estimated to still be in the ground in the U.S. Natural gas as a source of energy is significantly less expensive than electricity per Btu.

Natural gas futures and options are traded on the New York Mercantile Exchange (NYMEX). The NYMEX natural gas futures contract calls for the delivery of natural gas representing 10,000 million British thermal units (mmBtu) at the Henry Hub in Louisiana, which is the nexus of 16 intra-state and inter-state pipelines. The contract is priced in terms of dollars per mmBtu. NYMEX also has basic swap futures contracts available for 30 different natural gas pricing locations versus the benchmark Henry Hub location. Natural gas futures are also listed in London on the ICE Futures Europe (ICE) exchange.

Prices – NYMEX natural gas futures on the nearest-futures chart in early 2009 extended the sharp sell-off seen in the latter half of 2008, posting a new 8-year low of $2.408 in September 2009. Natural gas futures then rebounded mildly higher in late 2009 to close the year virtually unchanged on the year at $5.572.

Supply – U.S. recovery of natural gas in 2009 rose +2.2% to a record high of 26,320 billion cubic feet. The top U.S. producing states for natural gas in 2009 were Texas with 31% of U.S. production, Wyoming with 11% and Oklahoma with 8%, Louisiana with 7%, and New Mexico with 6%. In 2009 the world's largest natural gas producers were the U.S. with 1,907,653 terajoules of monthly average marketed production and Russia with 1,593,279 terajoules. The next closest producer was Canada with 473,442 terajoules.

Demand – U.S. - delivered consumption of natural gas in 2009 fell -1.66% yr/yr to 22,841 billion cubic feet, of which about 30% was delivered to electrical utility plants, 27% to industrial establishments, 21% to residences, and 14% to commercial establishments.

Trade – U.S. imports of natural gas (consumed) in 2009 fell -6.82% yr/yr to 3,713 billion cubic feet, further down from the 2007 record high of 4,608 billion cubic feet. U.S. exports of natural gas in 2009 rose +4.23% yr/yr to a record high of 1,048 billion cubic feet.

World Production of Natural Gas (Monthly Average Marketed Production[3]) In Terajoule[4]

Year	Australia	Canada	China	Germany	Indonesia	India	Italy	Mexico	Netherlands	Romania	Russia	United Kingdom	United States
2000	92,746	588,447	90,287	59,164	267,707	94,783	54,289	178,861	178,989	38,254	1,898,046	377,565	1,812,716
2001	96,523	550,463	98,431	60,463	258,122	91,063	48,008	171,940	192,180	40,422	1,887,953	370,237	1,848,810
2002	96,841	553,183	106,720	61,147	280,939	92,568	46,190	168,675	186,206	38,004	1,934,011	361,414	1,792,367
2003	99,771	534,434	111,352	61,441	289,371	89,570	42,812	174,733	178,853	38,831	2,016,895	358,798	1,726,221
2004	104,731	537,643	132,281	55,108	282,364	83,996	39,760	177,650	232,485	41,725	2,055,061	333,492	1,564,674
2005	108,249	547,204	163,802	55,089	267,057	92,451	38,167	187,151	218,699	40,959	2,065,477	307,775	1,636,149
2006	115,535	551,543	193,124	55,557	279,573	101,144	34,670	208,018	191,741	33,977	2,134,095	277,025	1,682,950
2007	115,541	540,070	223,107	49,895	292,656	101,150	30,839	230,885	189,494	34,001	2,116,869	251,428	1,745,050
2008[1]	113,672	507,412	261,162	51,470	266,429	102,793	28,893	265,820	210,393	32,374	1,862,664	242,892	1,861,274
2009[2]	124,343	473,442	277,124	49,116	274,662	115,378	25,778	269,896	181,709	31,315	1,593,279	207,991	1,907,652

[1] Preliminary. [2] Estimate. [3] Compares all gas collected & utilized as fuel or as a chemical industry raw material, including gas used in oilfields and/or gasfields as a fuel by producers. [4] Terajoule = 10 to the 12th power Joule = approximately 10 to the 9th power BTU. *Source: United Nations*

Marketed Production of Natural Gas in the United States, by States In Million Cubic Feet

Year	Alaska	California	Colorado	Kansas	Louisiana[2]	Michigan	Mississippi	Mexico	Oklahoma	Texas[2]	Wyoming	Total
2000	458,995	376,580	752,985	525,729	1,455,014	296,556	88,558	1,695,295	1,612,890	5,282,104	1,088,328	20,197,511
2001	471,440	377,824	817,206	480,145	1,502,086	275,036	107,541	1,689,125	1,615,384	5,282,723	1,363,879	20,570,295
2002	463,301	360,205	937,245	454,901	1,361,751	274,476	112,980	1,632,080	1,581,606	5,141,075	1,453,957	19,884,780
2003	489,757	337,216	1,011,285	418,893	1,350,399	236,987	133,901	1,604,015	1,558,155	5,243,567	1,539,318	19,974,360
2004	471,899	319,919	1,079,235	397,121	1,353,249	259,681	63,353	1,632,539	1,655,769	5,067,315	1,592,203	19,517,491
2005	487,282	317,637	1,133,086	377,229	1,296,048	261,112	52,923	1,645,166	1,670,137	5,276,401	1,639,317	18,927,095
2006	444,724	315,209	1,202,821	371,044	1,361,119	365,294	60,531	1,609,223	1,688,985	5,548,022	1,816,201	19,409,674
2007	433,485				1,365,333			1,517,922	1,783,682	6,123,180	2,047,882	20,196,346
2008	398,442				1,377,396			1,446,204	1,913,029	6,920,996	2,274,850	21,239,516
2009[1]	396,897				1,606,558			1,405,315	1,865,048	6,907,312	2,354,214	22,032,718

[1] Preliminary. *Source: Energy Information Administration, U.S. Department of Energy (EIA-DOE)*

World Production of Natural Gas Plant Liquids Thousand Barrels per Day

Year	Algeria	Canada	Mexico	Saudi Arabia	Russia	United States	Persian Gulf[2]	OAPEC[3]	OPEC-12[4]	OPEC-11[4]	World
2001	250	709	433	1,051	237	1,868	1,721	2,029	2,225	2,304	6,763
2002	270	698	408	1,095	246	1,880	1,797	2,137	2,326	2,403	6,872
2003	280	724	418	1,220	390	1,719	1,972	2,312	2,473	2,548	7,134
2004	292	658	442	1,310	456	1,809	2,100	2,437	2,634	2,702	7,382
2005	295	645	426	1,460	457	1,717	2,282	2,639	2,874	2,930	7,630
2006	310	685	427	1,427	417	1,739	2,289	2,678	2,955	2,999	7,773
2007	342	728	396	1,440	426	1,783	2,313	2,748	3,031	3,083	7,921
2008	357	676	365	1,434	422	1,784	2,339	2,783	3,088		7,887
2009[1]	345	635	370	1,427	423	1,886	2,370	2,791	3,102		7,982

Average. [1] Preliminary. [2] Bahrain, Iran, Iraq, Kuwait, Qatar, Saudi Arabia, and the United Arab Emirates. [3] Organization of Arab Petroleum Exporting Countriess: Algeria, Iraq, Kuwait, Libya, Qatar, Saudi Arabia, and the United Arab Emirates. [4] OPEC-12: Organization of the Petroleum Exporting Countries: Algeria, Angola, Indonesia, Iran, Iraq, Kuwait, Libya, Nigeria, Qatar, Saudi Arabia, the United Arab Emirates, and Venezuela. OPEC-11 does not include Angola. *Source: Energy Information Administration, U.S. Department of Energy (EIA-DOE)*

Recoverable Reserves and Deliveries of Natural Gas in the United States In Billions of Cubic Feet

Year	Gross With-drawals	Recoverable Reserves of Natural Gas Dec. 31[2]	Deliveries: Residential	Commercial	Electric Utility Plants[3]	Industrial	Total	Lease & Plant Fuel	Used as Pipline Fuel	Heating Value BTU per Cubic Foot
2001	24,501	183,460	4,771	3,023	5,342	7,344	22,239	1,119	625	1,028
2002	23,941	186,946	4,889	3,144	5,672	7,507	23,007	1,113	667	1,027
2003	24,119	189,044	5,079	3,179	5,135	7,150	22,277	1,122	591	1,031
2004	23,970	192,513	4,869	3,129	5,464	7,243	22,389	1,098	566	1,027
2005	23,457	204,385	4,827	2,999	5,869	6,597	22,011	1,112	584	1,029
2006	23,535	211,085	4,368	2,832	6,222	6,512	21,685	1,142	584	1,028
2007	24,664	237,726	4,722	3,013	6,841	6,648	23,097	1,226	621	1,029
2008	25,754	244,700	4,872	3,136	6,668	6,650	23,227	1,224	648	
2009[1]	26,320		4,764	3,114	6,887	6,138	22,841	1,270	637	

[1] Preliminary. [2] Estimated proved recoverable reserves of dry natural gas. [3] Figures include gas other than natural (impossible to segregate); therefore, shown separately from other consumption. *Source: Energy Information Administration, U.S. Department of Energy (EIA-DOE)*

Gas Utility Sales in the United States by Types and Class of Service In Trillions of BTUs

Year	Total Utility Sales	Number of Customers (Millions)	Class of Service: Resi-dental	Commer-cial	Industrial	Electric Generation	Other	Revenue - Million $ From Sales to Customers: Total	Resi-dental	Commer-cial	Industrial	Electric Generation	Other
1998	8,781	61.5	4,534	2,063	1,370	810	5	47,084	30,130	11,020	4,189	1,726	20
1999	8,975	60.8	4,622	2,067	1,553	729	5	47,202	30,095	10,731	4,715	1,641	21
2000	9,232	61.3	4,741	2,077	1,698	709	6	59,243	35,828	13,338	7,432	2,612	33
2001	8,667	61.4	4,525	2,053	1,461	620	8	69,150	42,454	16,848	7,513	2,286	49
2002	8,864	62.0	4,589	2,055	1,748	459	13	57,112	35,062	13,512	6,840	1,639	59
2003	8,927	62.6	4,722	2,125	1,672	397	11	72,606	43,664	17,349	9,478	2,048	68
2004	8,766	63.3	4,566	2,075	1,763	351	12	79,929	47,275	18,689	11,230	2,653	83
2005[1]	8,848	64.4	4,516	2,056	1,654	610	12	96,909	55,680	22,653	13,751	4,718	107
2006[2]	8,222	65.0	4,117	1,861	1,576	606	62	91,928	53,961	21,557	12,006	3,921	484

[1] Preliminary. [2] Estimate. *Source: American Gas Association (AGA)*

Salient Statistics of Natural Gas in the United States

Year	Supply (In Billions of Cubic Feet): Marketed Production	Extraction Loss	Dry Production	Storage With-drawals	Imports (Consumed)	Total Supply	Disposition: Consumption	Exports	Added to Storage	Total Disposition	Average Price Delivered to Customers (Dollars Per Thousand Cubic Feet): Well-head Price	Imports	Exports	Resi-dential	Com-mercial	Indus-trial	Electric Utilities
2001	24,501	954	19,616	2,344	3,977	26,697	22,239	373	3,510	26,697	4.00	4.43	4.19	9.63	8.43	5.24	4.61
2002	23,941	957	18,928	3,180	4,015	26,767	23,007	516	2,713	26,767	2.95	3.14	3.41	7.89	6.63	4.02	3.68
2003	24,119	876	19,099	3,161	3,944	26,963	22,277	680	3,358	26,963	4.88	5.17	5.54	9.63	8.40	5.89	5.57
2004	24,055	927	18,591	3,088	4,259	26,985	22,389	854	3,202	26,985	5.46	5.81	6.09	10.75	9.43	6.53	6.11
2005	23,457	876	18,051	3,057	4,341		22,011	729	3,002		7.33	8.12	7.59	12.70	11.34	8.56	8.47
2006	23,535	906	18,504	2,493	4,186		21,685	724	2,924		6.39	6.88	6.83	13.73	12.00	7.87	7.11
2007	24,664	930	19,266	2,688	4,608		23,097	822	3,080		6.25	6.87	6.92	13.08	11.34	7.68	7.31
2008[1]	25,754	953	20,286		3,984		23,227	1,006			7.96	8.70	8.60	13.89	12.23	9.67	9.26
2009[2]	26,320	938	21,095		3,713		22,841	1,048			3.71			11.98	9.75	5.27	

[1] Preliminary. [2] Estimate. *Source: Energy Information Administration, U.S. Department of Energy (EIA-DOE)*

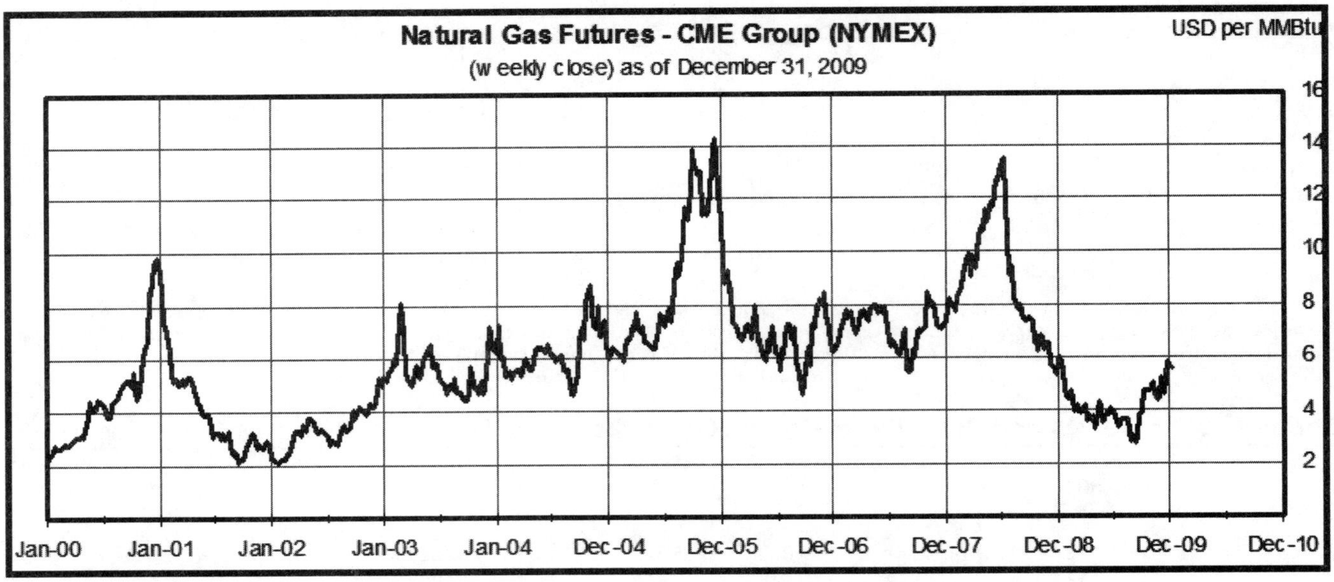

Average Price of Natural Gas at Henry Hub In Dollars Per MMBtu

Year	Jan.	Feb.	Mar.	Apr.	May	June	July	Aug.	Sept.	Oct.	Nov.	Dec.	Average
2000	2.42	2.65	2.79	3.03	3.58	4.28	3.96	4.41	5.11	5.02	5.54	8.95	4.31
2001	8.18	5.62	5.16	5.16	4.21	3.71	3.11	2.95	2.15	2.45	2.35	2.43	3.96
2002	2.25	2.31	3.03	3.42	3.49	3.22	2.98	3.09	3.55	4.12	4.04	4.75	3.35
2003	5.49	7.41	6.08	5.27	5.81	5.83	5.03	4.97	4.61	4.66	4.47	6.13	5.48
2004	6.17	5.39	5.38	5.71	6.30	6.29	5.93	5.44	5.11	6.39	6.15	6.64	5.91
2005	6.13	6.13	6.91	7.22	6.48	7.15	7.63	9.46	11.87	13.42	10.28	13.05	8.81
2006	8.65	7.54	6.90	7.16	6.23	6.19	6.22	7.14	4.90	5.84	7.36	6.73	6.74
2007	6.60	7.92	7.10	7.59	7.63	7.35	6.21	6.23	6.08	6.78	7.15	7.13	6.98
2008	7.98	8.54	9.44	10.13	11.28	12.68	11.06	8.25	7.67	6.73	6.67	5.81	8.85
2009	5.23	4.52	3.95	3.50	3.83	3.81	3.39	3.15	3.01	4.02	3.70	5.33	3.95

Source: Energy Information Administration, U.S. Department of Energy (EIA-DOE)

Volume of Trading of Natural Gas Futures in New York In Thousands of Contracts

Year	Jan.	Feb.	Mar.	Apr.	May	June	July	Aug.	Sept.	Oct.	Nov.	Dec.	Total
2000	1,388.8	1,470.9	1,505.0	1,179.3	1,822.2	1,853.7	1,331.4	1,483.9	1,510.2	1,594.9	1,759.5	975.1	17,875.0
2001	1,044.4	1,044.6	1,131.7	1,144.8	1,632.5	1,536.9	1,350.3	1,510.9	901.1	1,639.7	1,891.7	1,639.6	16,468.1
2002	1,942.5	1,668.6	2,381.1	2,421.7	2,281.4	1,911.7	2,266.1	2,115.6	1,990.0	2,103.4	1,569.2	1,706.4	24,357.8
2003	2,134.4	1,909.1	1,362.4	1,321.3	1,521.7	1,584.8	1,543.7	1,315.3	1,503.7	1,948.9	1,376.6	1,515.2	19,037.1
2004	1,162.1	1,125.1	1,420.3	1,443.1	1,587.5	1,588.5	1,508.8	1,724.1	1,885.6	1,458.3	1,320.0	1,218.6	17,441.9
2005	1,442.2	1,490.4	1,653.3	1,586.0	1,504.1	1,931.9	1,528.4	2,044.4	1,587.6	1,433.1	1,449.5	1,491.7	19,142.5
2006	1,609.9	1,833.9	1,682.2	1,911.6	2,272.5	1,920.6	1,786.2	2,428.7	2,017.7	1,935.1	1,799.6	1,832.0	23,030.0
2007	2,597.6	2,417.5	1,922.6	2,163.2	2,266.2	2,683.7	2,346.7	3,049.9	2,468.5	3,044.3	2,452.0	2,374.2	29,786.3
2008	2,921.9	3,330.7	2,983.6	3,382.9	3,168.0	3,379.1	4,274.0	3,756.1	3,458.5	3,151.7	2,539.9	2,384.3	38,730.5
2009	2,343.7	2,780.6	2,989.9	2,493.1	3,479.0	4,486.6	3,979.4	4,445.9	5,597.7	5,594.7	4,413.7	5,347.2	47,951.4

Source: CME Group; New York Mercantile Exchange (NYMEX)

Average Open Interest of Natural Gas Futures in New York In Contracts

Year	Jan.	Feb.	Mar.	Apr.	May	June	July	Aug.	Sept.	Oct.	Nov.	Dec.
2000	262,845	266,826	295,176	313,739	342,455	347,353	330,604	339,025	373,654	369,448	389,363	377,470
2001	364,532	346,343	360,032	380,632	421,145	456,512	473,675	497,972	494,475	488,187	455,766	415,882
2002	458,924	491,215	527,765	559,413	556,277	526,016	494,133	437,285	419,532	413,312	393,953	391,424
2003	415,642	420,329	367,673	354,154	365,838	366,610	357,299	343,622	354,568	352,685	356,622	340,756
2004	322,762	312,475	322,366	338,786	382,160	366,135	373,853	378,787	393,477	392,626	383,712	387,605
2005	401,829	405,692	458,013	479,880	480,318	472,631	498,440	524,235	544,165	551,121	545,270	551,444
2006	545,165	582,231	634,072	700,588	795,375	851,655	883,492	938,024	940,339	931,949	903,355	889,759
2007	905,449	839,142	761,701	747,721	752,596	787,099	823,127	776,747	778,512	749,480	789,360	843,361
2008	881,812	942,089	906,497	875,484	885,165	946,673	963,953	922,474	915,638	859,278	744,821	702,918
2009	693,269	708,968	652,412	649,925	678,413	709,236	737,506	731,555	713,822	709,965	713,612	719,561

Source: CME Group; New York Mercantile Exchange (NYMEX)

Gasoline

Gasoline is a complex mixture of hundreds of lighter liquid hydrocarbons and is used chiefly as a fuel for internal-combustion engines. Petroleum crude, or crude oil, is still the most economical source of gasoline with refineries turning more than half of every barrel of crude oil into gasoline. The three basic steps to all refining operations are the separation process (separating crude oil into various chemical components), conversion process (breaking the chemicals down into molecules called hydrocarbons), and treatment process (transforming and combining hydrocarbon molecules and other additives). Another process, called hydro treating, removes a significant amount of sulfur from finished gasoline as is currently required by the state of California.

Octane is a measure of a gasoline's ability to resist pinging or knocking noise from an engine. Most gasoline stations offer three octane grades of unleaded fuel—regular at 87 (R+M)/2, mid-grade at 89 (R+M)/2, and premium at 93 (R+M)/2. Additional refining steps are needed to increase the octane, which increases the retail price. This does not make the gasoline any cleaner or better, but yields a different blend of hydrocarbons that burn more slowly.

In an attempt to improve air quality and reduce harmful emissions from internal combustion engines, Congress in 1990 amended the Clean Air Act to mandate the addition of ethanol to gasoline. Some 2 billion gallons of ethanol are now added to gasoline each year in the U.S. The most common blend is E10, which contains 10% ethanol and 90% gasoline. Auto manufacturers have approved that mixture for use in all U.S. vehicles. Ethanol is an alcohol-based fuel produced by fermenting and distilling crops such as corn, barley, wheat and sugar.

Unleaded gasoline futures and options trade at the New York Mercantile Exchange (NYMEX). The NYMEX gasoline futures contract calls for the delivery of 1,000 barrels (42,000 gallons) of unleaded gasoline in the New York harbor and is priced in terms of dollars and cents per gallon.

Prices – NYMEX gasoline futures prices fluctuated less in 2009 than they did in 2008. The price started the year at about \$1.05 per gallon and rallied to a high of \$2.04 in early June. From there until the end of the year the price moved in a range between about \$2.04 and \$1.65 per gallon. The price at the end of the year was about \$2.05.

The average monthly retail price of regular unleaded gasoline in 2009 (through November) fell 28.8% yr/yr to \$2.33 per gallon. The average monthly retail price of unleaded premium motor gasoline in the U.S. in 2009 (through November) fell -26.3% to \$2.58 per gallon. The average monthly refiner price of finished aviation gasoline to end users in 2009 (through September) fell 27.4% yr/yr to \$2.35 per gallon.

Supply – U.S. production of gasoline in 2009 (through November, annualized) rose +2.0% yr/yr to 8.720 million barrels per day. Gasoline stocks in October of 2009 were 79.2 million barrels, down from 98.3 million barrels in December of 2008.

Demand – U.S. consumption of finished motor gasoline in 2009 (through November, annualized) rose +0.22% yr/yr to 9.007 million barrels per day, but still below 2007's record high of 9.284 million barrels per day.

Production of Finished Motor Gasoline in the United States In Thousand Barrels per Day

Year	Jan.	Feb.	Mar.	Apr.	May	June	July	Aug.	Sept.	Oct.	Nov.	Dec.	Average
2000	7,798	7,658	8,032	8,130	8,398	8,550	8,320	8,251	8,358	8,031	8,394	8,298	8,186
2001	7,888	7,822	8,011	8,450	8,651	8,637	8,481	8,277	8,381	8,446	8,366	8,301	8,312
2002	8,160	8,117	8,072	8,626	8,729	8,661	8,665	8,666	8,320	8,190	8,738	8,734	8,475
2003	7,870	7,800	7,724	8,161	8,311	8,293	8,320	8,355	8,228	8,253	8,450	8,540	8,194
2004	7,956	7,979	8,102	8,233	8,447	8,336	8,370	8,357	7,993	8,384	8,346	8,659	8,264
2005	8,157	8,194	8,119	8,549	8,475	8,589	8,352	8,326	8,129	7,953	8,468	8,503	8,318
2006	8,189	7,969	7,765	8,032	8,613	8,957	8,624	8,610	8,465	8,210	8,335	8,567	8,361
2007	8,348	8,012	8,101	8,122	8,491	8,686	8,504	8,547	8,320	8,276	8,353	8,501	8,355
2008	8,516	8,495	8,373	8,560	8,700	8,564	8,523	8,513	7,855	8,889	8,722	8,850	8,547
2009[1]	8,445	8,429	8,668	8,761	8,742	9,042	8,903	8,755	8,779	8,620	8,776		8,720

[1] Preliminary. *Source: Energy Information Administration, U.S. Department of Energy (EIA-DOE)*

Disposition of Finished Motor Gasoline, Total Product Supplied in the United States In Thousand Barrels per Day

Year	Jan.	Feb.	Mar.	Apr.	May	June	July	Aug.	Sept.	Oct.	Nov.	Dec.	Average
2000	7,653	8,291	8,305	8,375	8,661	8,824	8,642	8,921	8,518	8,417	8,384	8,670	8,472
2001	8,099	8,234	8,532	8,575	8,706	8,690	9,023	8,953	8,557	8,655	8,677	8,585	8,610
2002	8,227	8,607	8,655	8,766	9,078	9,140	9,143	9,313	8,687	8,814	8,829	8,893	8,848
2003	8,414	8,525	8,602	8,838	9,042	9,170	9,192	9,411	8,926	9,108	8,946	9,011	8,935
2004	8,705	8,838	9,024	9,126	9,179	9,322	9,357	9,327	9,015	9,097	9,055	9,206	9,104
2005	8,813	8,861	8,994	9,128	9,278	9,373	9,534	9,537	8,915	9,036	9,115	9,296	9,157
2006	8,839	8,911	9,054	9,154	9,308	9,478	9,607	9,564	9,236	9,267	9,244	9,338	9,250
2007	8,886	9,006	9,178	9,215	9,434	9,491	9,640	9,582	9,254	9,236	9,229	9,251	9,284
2008	8,810	8,866	9,066	9,112	9,251	9,110	9,150	9,134	8,497	9,024	8,904	8,927	8,988
2009[1]	8,690	8,816	8,866	8,948	9,087	9,224	9,300	9,250	8,897	9,016	8,987		9,007

[1] Preliminary. *Source: Energy Information Administration, U.S. Department of Energy (EIA-DOE)*

Average Spot Price of Unleaded Gasoline in New York In Cents Per Gallon

Year	Jan.	Feb.	Mar.	Apr.	May	June	July	Aug.	Sept.	Oct.	Nov.	Dec.	Average
2000	70.43	81.30	89.11	73.15	89.06	96.18	86.76	86.97	96.04	94.71	93.94	73.66	85.94
2001	83.32	82.56	78.18	94.95	92.37	71.85	68.31	77.18	75.00	59.79	51.34	51.85	73.89
2002	54.30	55.41	69.64	74.66	70.32	71.65	76.62	76.75	78.36	82.34	76.08	80.56	72.22
2003	87.56	99.62	95.51	80.08	76.16	80.65	87.17	100.42	90.41	87.12	87.33	88.37	88.37
2004	99.66	104.63	109.12	112.02	133.98	115.70	122.65	120.89	126.17	137.75	126.96	106.90	118.04
2005	123.85	122.42	143.90	147.06	137.06	151.02	158.89	191.13	214.78	170.87	147.73	159.88	155.72
2006	173.39	149.98	175.87	214.62	204.68	206.50	223.99	203.23	158.42	152.00	158.71	166.70	182.34
2007	141.63	164.55	193.58	210.05	224.09	218.30	213.51	199.83	209.72	216.93	242.33	232.69	205.60
2008	233.09	238.37	249.09	277.45	309.23	329.79	315.86	290.20	280.69	190.84	129.29	97.18	245.09
2009	115.11	121.66	128.84	137.77	169.79	190.79	174.74	193.01	178.43	192.30	198.63	192.00	166.09

Source: Energy Information Administration, U.S. Department of Energy (EIA-DOE)

Volume of Trading of Gasoline, RBOB[1] Futures in New York In Contracts

Year	Jan.	Feb.	Mar.	Apr.	May	June	July	Aug.	Sept.	Oct.	Nov.	Dec.	Total
1999	561.5	619.7	876.4	741.5	721.1	737.7	822.0	800.4	751.3	705.1	748.8	615.7	8,701.2
2000	693.6	721.9	921.6	730.0	927.5	838.5	650.6	677.2	641.2	635.7	612.1	595.1	8,645.2
2001	825.2	701.2	809.2	981.0	1,056.5	895.0	737.3	790.8	581.9	664.9	613.3	567.2	9,223.4
2002	795.0	744.7	942.7	1,019.3	985.2	834.5	967.8	893.6	867.6	1,105.0	865.9	958.4	10,979.7
2003	1,054.1	968.7	1,010.9	909.0	933.7	944.0	987.5	1,021.5	943.0	877.1	760.8	761.6	11,172.1
2004	956.1	998.7	1,169.2	1,169.0	1,203.8	1,194.5	1,027.0	1,177.7	1,052.9	983.7	849.0	995.9	12,777.5
2005	974.6	1,000.9	1,193.5	1,252.5	1,060.2	1,104.7	1,103.2	1,341.3	1,221.3	999.2	928.1	989.0	13,168.4
2006	1,149.6	1,233.0	1,259.1	1,079.6	1,122.7	1,039.8	939.8	1,145.5	891.4	839.6	838.1	966.0	12,504.2
2007	1,172.9	1,272.2	1,722.5	1,826.7	2,134.5	1,811.8	1,770.2	1,872.8	1,627.3	1,706.1	1,531.3	1,343.2	19,791.4
2008	1,660.6	1,887.5	2,111.9	1,986.3	1,917.6	1,854.4	1,621.6	1,667.7	1,774.1	1,452.9	1,193.4	1,306.4	20,434.6

[1] Data thru September 2005 are Unleaded, October 2005 thru December 2006 are Unleaded and RBOB.
Source: CME Group; New York Mercantile Exchange

Average Open Interest of Gasoline, RBOB[1] Futures in New York In Contracts

Year	Jan.	Feb.	Mar.	Apr.	May	June	July	Aug.	Sept.	Oct.	Nov.	Dec.
1999	105,532	113,683	111,449	110,531	107,644	102,927	113,619	120,468	120,328	111,758	109,428	96,652
2000	89,049	103,586	105,448	105,133	103,831	96,772	80,886	66,598	74,735	80,446	88,509	92,041
2001	117,540	126,762	124,631	124,162	111,576	103,058	101,249	92,156	87,841	102,414	115,699	126,634
2002	136,795	139,191	133,649	129,274	120,224	114,663	106,463	94,648	95,754	100,427	105,175	109,737
2003	117,558	124,288	113,380	98,627	96,405	93,285	95,433	99,394	85,457	90,007	95,002	105,919
2004	125,207	141,837	150,573	146,375	148,782	138,248	140,691	146,532	147,088	150,643	138,280	153,907
2005	162,432	161,603	172,012	166,620	145,587	148,482	156,730	156,282	140,270	134,833	138,659	144,396
2006	157,562	173,978	168,067	165,233	150,913	138,578	146,173	135,367	131,771	124,963	128,906	135,085
2007	161,557	161,335	166,936	170,675	172,870	183,443	189,084	184,342	188,954	196,730	206,392	208,238
2008	230,032	253,303	241,781	250,852	264,988	256,220	238,170	219,229	198,263	162,480	172,267	194,234

[1] Data thru September 2005 are Unleaded, October 2005 thru December 2006 are Unleaded and RBOB.
Source: CME Group; New York Mercantile Exchange

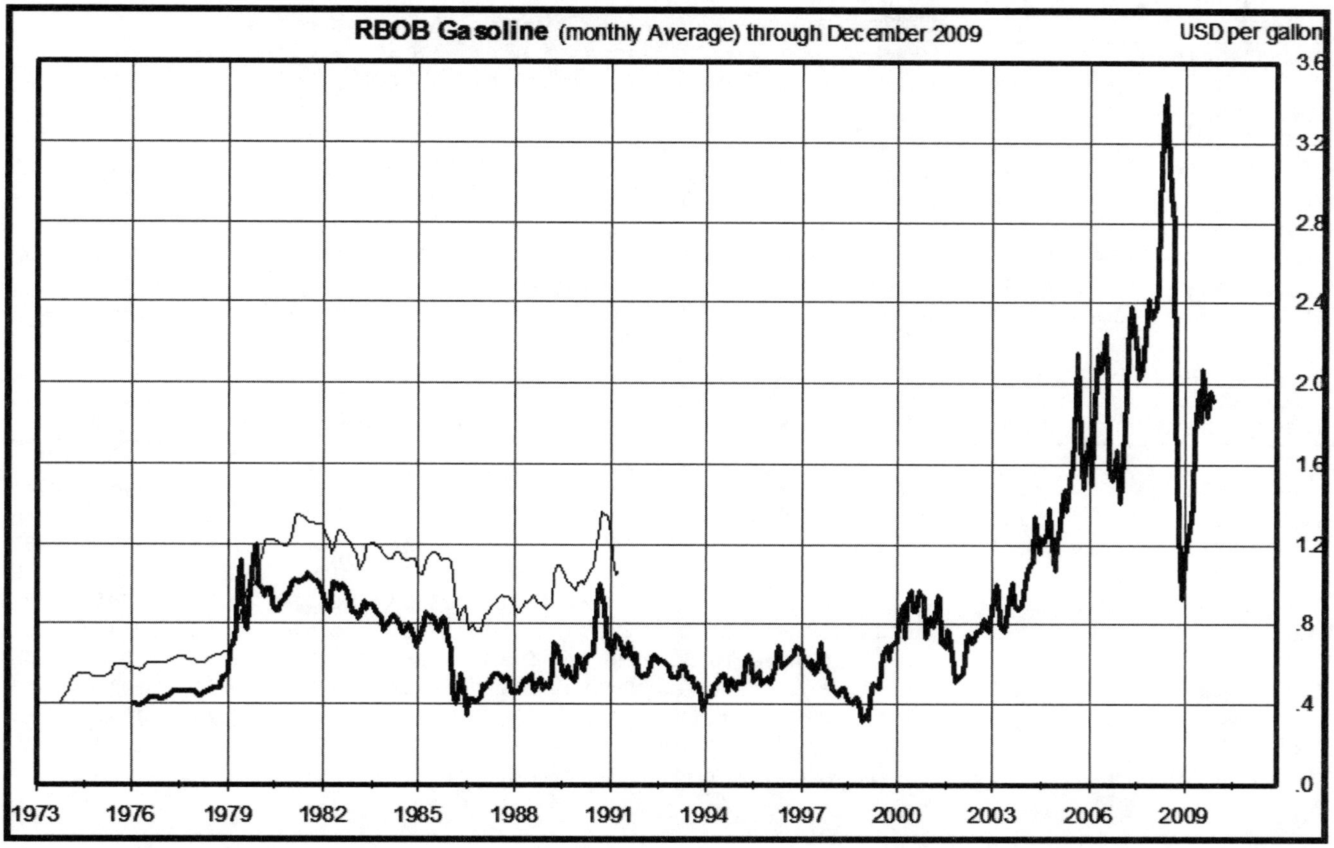

Stocks of Finished Gasoline[2] on Hand in the United States, at End of Month In Millions of Barrels

Year	Jan.	Feb.	Mar.	Apr.	May	June	July	Aug.	Sept.	Oct.	Nov.	Dec.
2000	165.3	156.4	157.1	160.6	162.2	164.5	164.6	151.0	154.2	147.4	156.7	153.0
2001	158.7	154.6	144.7	150.3	160.1	169.4	162.3	150.6	158.0	160.2	161.2	161.5
2002	169.7	165.5	159.8	167.0	168.3	167.6	164.8	157.3	157.4	148.2	158.0	161.9
2003	157.2	151.1	144.7	151.4	155.2	153.0	150.1	145.2	146.1	140.4	146.3	146.9
2004	138.7	133.5	132.1	133.1	137.2	140.2	140.5	137.9	135.7	138.4	141.5	143.2
2005	144.8	148.4	137.8	141.6	141.0	141.9	135.1	125.0	128.1	130.0	132.9	135.0
2006	142.2	137.9	124.2	115.4	121.5	119.1	117.9	116.6	120.5	112.8	113.8	116.1
2007	125.0	115.7	108.8	108.5	114.7	116.7	114.4	110.7	112.3	107.7	108.8	110.0
2008	117.4	119.9	110.6	106.2	106.0	107.3	102.3	97.8	92.6	95.9	96.9	98.3
2009[1]	95.4	88.0	88.2	87.6	83.9	87.9	87.1	86.1	84.2	79.2	83.2	

[1] Preliminary. [2] Includes oxygenated and other finished. *Source: Energy Information Administration, U.S. Department of Energy (EIA-DOE)*

Average Refiner Price of Finished Motor Gasoline to End Users[1] in the United States In Cents Per Gallon

Year	Jan.	Feb.	Mar.	Apr.	May	June	July	Aug.	Sept.	Oct.	Nov.	Dec.	Average
2000	91.7	98.7	113.1	108.7	110.3	121.3	117.3	110.3	117.5	115.5	113.5	106.3	110.6
2001	106.8	106.7	103.9	117.7	130.1	120.7	103.2	102.5	1,009.2	89.9	76.9	68.5	103.2
2002	70.6	71.8	87.2	100.4	99.9	99.1	100.3	100.1	100.1	104.0	101.2	98.1	94.7
2003	106.0	122.1	130.0	120.1	110.0	109.3	110.6	123.1	126.5	115.0	109.5	106.5	115.7
2004	117.3	125.6	133.8	139.6	156.9	154.4	148.3	145.1	145.0	158.6	155.1	141.3	143.4
2005	139.5	146.8	163.7	180.3	171.4	172.1	185.0	208.0	241.7	226.2	182.4	173.9	182.6
2006	187.2	183.3	198.3	233.1	245.8	243.6	252.8	248.6	207.6	178.9	178.8	186.8	212.1
2007	179.1	184.2	213.8	240.5	266.9	256.9	248.8	232.0	233.7	235.0	261.4	255.2	234.0
2008	257.3	256.9	278.4	298.4	331.6	357.9	356.7	327.8	320.7	253.4	161.3	121.6	276.8
2009[2]	135.7	146.9	150.3	160.0	185.6	218.7	206.7	215.7	208.6	210.4	217.2		186.9

[1] Excludes aviation and taxes. [2] Preliminary. *Source: Energy Information Administration, U.S. Department of Energy (EIA-DOE)*

Average Retail Price of Unleaded Premium Motor Gasoline[2] in the United States In Cents per Gallon

Year	Jan.	Feb.	Mar.	Apr.	May	June	July	Aug.	Sept.	Oct.	Nov.	Dec.	Average
2000	148.6	155.1	172.3	169.8	168.2	178.6	177.3	168.9	176.4	174.4	173.8	167.9	169.3
2001	165.7	167.1	163.8	174.8	193.4	188.1	169.5	163.6	172.6	156.0	142.7	131.2	165.7
2002	132.3	133.0	145.0	162.2	162.5	160.8	160.7	162.0	161.9	164.3	164.3	158.9	157.8
2003	166.6	182.8	192.4	184.6	172.9	170.0	171.0	180.8	191.1	178.9	172.4	168.6	177.7
2004	177.9	185.8	194.9	201.2	218.6	222.5	213.0	209.1	208.2	221.5	220.3	208.0	206.8
2005	201.7	210.5	225.1	246.8	240.3	236.5	250.2	270.1	313.0	300.1	256.0	239.3	249.1
2006	252.1	251.9	260.3	296.7	316.9	313.9	321.9	320.7	281.9	249.3	245.9	255.0	280.5
2007	250.1	250.9	281.8	309.3	334.8	328.1	320.0	301.8	302.1	303.7	330.7	326.4	303.3
2008	329.1	327.2	350.2	369.0	400.3	431.9	435.0	404.5	394.0	343.2	243.3	195.1	351.9
2009[1]	203.6	218.2	219.7	230.9	251.1	288.3	280.6	288.7	284.5	282.6	291.7	288.2	260.7

[1] Preliminary. [2] Including taxes. *Source: Energy Information Administration, U.S. Department of Energy (EIA-DOE)*

Average Retail Price of Unleaded Regular Motor Gasoline[2] in the United States In Cents per Gallon

Year	Jan.	Feb.	Mar.	Apr.	May	June	July	Aug.	Sept.	Oct.	Nov.	Dec.	Average
2000	130.1	136.9	154.1	150.6	149.8	161.7	159.3	151.0	158.2	155.9	155.5	148.9	151.0
2001	147.2	148.4	144.7	156.4	172.9	164.0	148.2	142.7	153.1	136.2	126.3	113.1	146.1
2002	113.9	113.0	124.1	140.7	142.1	140.4	141.2	142.3	142.2	144.9	144.8	139.4	135.8
2003	147.3	164.1	174.8	165.9	154.2	151.4	152.4	162.8	172.8	160.3	153.5	149.4	159.1
2004	159.2	167.2	176.6	183.3	200.9	204.1	193.9	189.8	189.1	202.9	201.0	188.2	188.0
2005	182.3	191.8	206.5	228.3	221.6	217.6	231.6	250.3	292.7	278.5	234.3	218.6	229.5
2006	231.5	231.0	240.1	275.7	294.7	291.7	299.9	298.5	258.9	227.2	224.1	233.4	258.9
2007	227.4	228.5	259.2	286.0	313.0	305.2	296.1	278.2	278.9	279.3	306.9	302.0	280.1
2008	304.7	303.3	325.8	344.1	376.4	406.5	409.0	378.6	369.8	317.3	215.1	168.9	326.6
2009[1]	178.7	192.8	194.9	205.6	226.5	263.1	254.3	262.7	257.4	256.1	266.0	262.1	235.0

[1] Preliminary. [2] Including taxes. *Source: Energy Information Administration, U.S. Department of Energy (EIA-DOE)*

Average Retail Price of All-Types[2] Motor Gasoline[3] in the United States In Cents per Gallon

Year	Jan.	Feb.	Mar.	Apr.	May	June	July	Aug.	Sept.	Oct.	Nov.	Dec.	Average
2000	135.6	142.2	159.4	156.1	155.2	166.6	164.2	155.9	163.5	161.3	160.8	154.4	156.3
2001	152.5	153.8	150.3	161.7	181.2	173.1	156.5	150.9	160.9	144.2	132.4	120.0	153.1
2002	120.9	121.0	132.4	149.3	150.8	148.9	149.6	150.8	150.7	153.5	153.4	147.7	144.1
2003	155.7	168.6	179.1	170.4	158.7	155.8	156.7	167.1	177.1	164.6	157.8	153.8	163.8
2004	163.5	171.5	180.9	187.5	205.0	208.3	198.2	194.1	193.4	207.2	205.3	192.6	192.3
2005	186.6	196.0	210.7	232.5	225.7	221.8	235.7	254.8	296.9	283.0	238.7	223.0	233.8
2006	235.9	235.4	244.4	280.1	299.3	296.3	304.6	303.3	263.7	231.9	228.7	238.0	263.5
2007	232.1	233.3	263.9	290.9	317.6	310.0	301.3	283.3	283.9	284.3	311.8	306.9	284.9
2008	309.6	308.3	330.7	349.1	381.3	411.5	414.2	383.8	374.9	322.5	220.8	174.2	331.7
2009[1]	183.8	197.9	200.0	210.7	231.4	268.1	259.4	267.7	262.6	261.3	270.9	267.1	240.1

[1] Preliminary. [2] Also includes types of motor oil not shown separately. [3] Including taxes. *Source: Energy Information Administration, U.S. Department of Energy (EIA-DOE)*

Average Refiner Price of Finished Aviation Gasoline to End Users[2] in the United States In Cents per Gallon

Year	Jan.	Feb.	Mar.	Apr.	May	June	July	Aug.	Sept.	Oct.	Nov.	Dec.	Average
2000	118.7	119.5	129.1	124.3	126.8	139.8	142.6	NA	138.2	134.9	134.9	126.1	130.6
2001	128.5	129.2	124.5	134.9	150.9	145.1	134.6	136.3	142.4	125.3	119.4	115.8	132.3
2002	111.8	110.6	122.6	129.8	128.9	127.3	139.2	136.9	139.1	143.0	141.8	139.8	128.8
2003	139.7	W	W	W	139.8	145.1	151.9	162.2	158.9	150.8	W	146.6	149.4
2004	W	W	W	177.4	194.4	192.3	185.4	184.9	187.8	195.5	187.0	176.7	186.8
2005	173.8	186.7	201.5	221.7	212.1	211.6	223.0	238.6	280.8	270.8	218.6	219.3	221.5
2006	239.1	232.4	247.3	286.9	301.3	305.7	310.3	305.8	253.2	238.5	235.3	234.9	265.9
2007	217.9	228.5	262.7	296.9	309.6	297.8	305.3	282.3	290.0	285.5	306.7	297.5	281.7
2008	298.7	295.4	329.6	335.8	361.5	396.5	392.9	379.2	383.7	297.5	223.0	181.4	322.9
2009[1]	185.7	196.1	196.4	215.0	242.3	270.7	260.7	276.3	268.4	269.3	283.9		242.3

[1] Preliminary. [2] Excluding taxes. NA = Not available. W = Withheld proprietary data. *Source: Energy Information Administration, U.S. Department Energy (EIA-DOE)*

Gold

Gold is a dense, bright yellow metallic element with a high luster. Gold is an inactive substance and is unaffected by air, heat, moisture, and most solvents. Gold has been coveted for centuries for its unique blend of rarity, beauty, and near indestructibility. The Egyptians mined gold before 2,000 BC. The first known, pure gold coin was made on the orders of King Croesus of Lydia in the sixth century BC.

Gold is found in nature in quartz veins and secondary alluvial deposits as a free metal. Gold is produced from mines on every continent with the exception of Antarctica, where mining is forbidden. Because it is virtually indestructible, much of the gold that has ever been mined still exists above ground in one form or another. The largest producer of gold in the U.S. by far is the state of Nevada, with Alaska and California running a distant second and third.

Gold is a vital industrial commodity. Pure gold is one of the most malleable and ductile of all the metals. It is a good conductor of heat and electricity. The prime industrial use of gold is in electronics. Another important sector is dental gold where it has been used for almost 3,000 years. Other applications for gold include decorative gold leaf, reflective glass, and jewelry.

In 1792, the United States first assigned a formal monetary role for gold when Congress put the nation's currency on a bimetallic standard, backing it with gold and silver. Under the gold standard, the U.S. government was willing to exchange its paper currency for a set amount of gold, meaning the paper currency was backed by a physical asset with real value. However, President Nixon in 1971 severed the convertibility between the U.S. dollar and gold, which led to the breakdown of the Bretton Woods international payments system. Since then, the prices of gold and of paper currencies have floated freely. U.S. and other central banks now hold physical gold reserves primarily as a store of wealth.

Gold futures and options are traded at the New York Mercantile Exchange. Gold futures are traded on the Bolsa de Mercadorias and Futuros (BM&F) and on the Tokyo Commodity Exchange (TOCOM), the Chicago Board of Trade (CBOT) and the Korea Futures Exchange (KOFEX). The NYMEX gold futures contract calls for the delivery of 100 troy ounces of gold (0.995 fineness), and the contract trades in terms of dollars and cents per troy ounce.

Prices – NYMEX gold futures prices on a nearest-futures basis initially fell in late 2008 when the financial crisis emerged due to the flight-to-quality rally in the dollar and concerns about deflation. However, gold prices bottomed out at a 2-1/2 year low of $681 in October 2008 and then rallied sharply through 2009 to post a record high of $1226 in December 2009 due to inflation fears sparked by the massive liquidity injections by the G7 central banks. The Federal Reserve and the Bank of England also engaged in quantitative easing by buying government bonds, joining the Bank of Japan in its long-standing bond-buying program. The markets remain nervous that the world's central banks will not be aggressive enough in removing that liquidity, thus running the risk of causing a surge in inflation within the next year or two.

Supply – World mine production of gold rose +4.0% yr/yr to 2.350 million kilograms in 2009, and was still below the record high of 2.570 million kilograms seen in 1999 and 2000 (1 kilogram = 32.1507 troy ounces). The world's largest producers of gold in 2009 were China with 13% of world production, followed by South Africa (9%), the U.S (9%), Australia (9%), and Russia (8%).

Gold mine production has been moving lower in most major gold-producing countries such as South Africa, Australia, and the U.S. For example, South Africa's production of 210,000 kilograms in 2009 was down -1.4% yr/yr and that was about one-third the production levels of more than 600,000 kilograms seen in the 1980s and early 1990s. On the other hand, China's gold production in 2009 rose +5.3 to a record 300,000 kilograms. U.S. gold mine production in 2009 fell 9.9% yr/yr to 210,000 kilograms, which was the lowest production level since 1988. U.S. refinery production of gold from domestic and foreign ore sources in 2009 rose +1.2% yr/yr to 170,000 kilograms. U.S. refinery production of gold from secondary scrap sources in 2009 rose +5.0% yr/yr to 190,000 kilograms.

Demand – U.S. consumption of gold in 2009 fell -3.4% to 170,000 kilograms. The most recent data available from the early 1990s showed that 71% of that gold demand came from jewelry and the arts, 22% from industrial uses, and 7% from dental uses.

Trade – U.S. exports of gold (excluding coinage) in 2009 fell -32.2% yr/yr to 385,000 kilograms, down from the 16-year high of 568,000 kilograms seen in 2008. U.S. imports of gold for consumption in 2009 rose +47.2% yr/yr to 340,000 kilograms, down slightly from the 2005 level of 341,000 kilograms, which was a 22-year high.

World Mine Production of Gold In Kilograms (1 Kilogram = 32.1507 Troy Ounces)

Year	Australia	Brazil	Canada	Chile	China	Ghana	Indonesia	Papua New Guinea	Russia	South Africa	United States	Uzebistan	World Total
2001	280,100	42,884	158,875	42,673	185,000	68,341	166,091	67,043	152,500	394,800	335,000	87,000	2,560,000
2002	266,100	41,662	151,904	38,688	192,000	69,271	142,238	61,379	168,411	398,523	298,000	90,000	2,530,000
2003	282,000	40,416	140,861	38,954	205,000	70,749	141,019	67,832	170,068	373,300	277,000	90,000	2,540,000
2004	259,000	47,596	129,478	39,986	215,000	63,139	91,710	73,670	163,148	337,223	258,000	93,000	2,420,000
2005	262,000	38,293	119,549	40,447	225,000	66,852	130,620	68,483	164,186	294,671	256,000	90,000	2,480,000
2006	247,000	40,075	103,513	42,100	245,000	69,817	93,176	58,349	159,340	272,128	252,000	85,000	2,370,000
2007	246,000	40,100	101,440	41,527	275,000	77,349	117,851	58,000	156,912	252,344	238,000	85,000	2,340,000
2008[1]	215,000	50,000	95,000	39,000	285,000	75,000	60,000	62,000	176,000	213,000	233,000	85,000	2,260,000
2009[2]	220,000	50,000	100,000	40,000	300,000	85,000	100,000	65,000	185,000	210,000	210,000	85,000	2,350,000

[1] Preliminary. [2] Estimate. *Source: U.S. Geological Survey (USGS)*

Salient Statistics of Gold in the United States In Kilograms (1 Kilogram = 32.1507 Troy Ounces)

		- Refinery Production -					-------- Stocks, Dec. 31 ---------				----------- Consumption -----------			
Year	Mine Production	Value Million $	Domestic & Foreign Ores	Secondary (Old Scrap)	Exports, Excluding Coinage	Imports for Consumption	Treasury Department[3]	Futures Exchange	Industry	Official World Reserves[4]	Dental	Industrial[5]	Jewelry & Arts	Total
2000	353,000	3,180.0	197,000	81,600	547,000	223,000	8,140,000	52,900	9,300	33,000	----	----	----	183,000
2001	335,000	2,940.0	191,000	82,700	489,000	194,000	8,120,000	38,000	3,670	33,000	----	----	----	179,000
2002	298,000	2,980.0	196,000	78,100	257,000	217,000	8,140,000	63,900	3,490	32,200	----	----	----	163,000
2003	277,000	3,250.0	194,000	89,100	352,000	249,000	8,140,000	97,100	3,590	31,800	----	----	----	183,000
2004	258,000	3,400.0	222,000	91,700	257,000	283,000	8,140,000	180,000	1,080	31,400	----	----	----	185,000
2005	256,000	3,670.0	195,000	81,300	324,000	341,000	8,140,000	211,000	2,040	30,800	----	----	----	183,000
2006	252,000	4,910.0	181,000	89,100	389,000	263,000	8,140,000	234,000	2,000	30,400	----	----	----	185,000
2007	238,000	5,350.0	176,000	135,000	519,000	170,000	8,140,000	229,000	1,140	29,900	----	----	----	180,000
2008[1]	233,000		168,000	181,000	568,000	231,000	8,140,000				----	----	----	176,000
2009[2]	210,000		170,000	190,000	385,000	340,000	8,140,000				----	----	----	170,000

[1] Preliminary. [2] Estimate. [3] Includes gold in Exchange Stabilization Fund. [4] Held by market economy country central banks and governments and international monetary orgainzations. [5] Including space and defense. NA = Not available. *Source: U.S. Geological Survey (USGS)*

Monthly Average Gold Price (Handy & Harman) in New York Dollars Per Troy Ounce

Year	Jan.	Feb.	Mar.	Apr.	May	June	July	Aug.	Sept.	Oct.	Nov.	Dec.	Average
2000	284.26	299.60	286.39	279.75	275.10	285.73	281.01	274.44	273.53	270.00	266.05	271.68	278.96
2001	265.58	261.99	263.03	260.56	272.07	270.23	267.53	272.40	283.78	283.06	276.49	275.98	271.06
2002	281.47	295.40	294.06	302.68	314.08	321.81	313.51	310.18	319.49	316.56	319.14	333.21	310.13
2003	356.91	359.60	340.55	328.25	355.03	356.35	351.01	359.91	379.07	378.92	389.13	407.44	363.51
2004	414.09	404.52	405.99	403.96	383.94	392.73	398.08	400.86	405.45	420.46	438.21	442.20	409.21
2005	424.39	423.15	433.91	429.23	422.53	430.66	424.33	438.03	456.52	469.90	474.87	510.01	444.79
2006	549.27	555.02	557.09	610.41	673.97	596.15	634.89	632.10	596.76	585.78	627.12	629.38	604.00
2007	630.97	664.43	655.30	679.20	667.86	655.40	665.83	665.21	714.79	749.73	806.68	803.20	696.55
2008	890.47	923.25	966.30	909.70	886.29	889.49	940.16	838.30	830.30	806.62	754.95	816.09	870.99
2009[1]	859.98	943.20	924.27	890.50	927.34	945.67	937.76	949.34	996.76	1043.16	1122.03	1132.99	972.75

[1] Preliminary. *Source: U.S. Geological Survey (USGS)*

Volume of Trading of Gold Futures in New York (COMEX) In Thousands of Contracts

Year	Jan.	Feb.	Mar.	Apr.	May	June	July	Aug.	Sept.	Oct.	Nov.	Dec.	Total
2000	616.4	833.5	767.7	362.2	701.5	625.5	532.5	374.4	403.2	424.9	625.7	349.0	6,616.5
2001	755.2	483.3	766.6	438.1	971.6	481.4	578.3	547.4	341.0	481.4	573.6	367.4	6,785.3
2002	733.6	613.2	717.7	559.8	1,089.6	775.5	998.9	585.8	621.8	669.0	844.8	808.5	9,018.2
2003	1,260.1	1,007.5	987.6	667.8	1,160.3	824.3	1,191.7	837.5	1,034.0	1,091.3	1,397.3	776.3	12,235.5
2004	1,581.3	962.6	1,649.5	1,202.9	1,344.8	960.6	1,405.0	953.0	944.9	1,067.2	1,864.7	1,053.2	14,989.6
2005	1,502.3	944.4	1,599.0	858.1	1,451.7	1,240.0	1,432.4	1,234.4	1,380.2	1,174.0	1,852.7	1,221.5	15,890.6
2006	2,018.8	1,162.7	2,052.7	1,302.9	2,071.0	1,148.6	1,487.2	804.5	884.7	857.1	1,284.7	842.7	15,917.6
2007	1,929.8	1,455.9	2,195.9	1,405.2	2,336.6	1,610.8	2,292.2	1,710.7	2,024.6	2,584.4	3,837.1	1,677.2	25,060.4
2008	4,041.7	2,617.6	3,901.8	2,765.5	3,328.0	2,624.0	4,269.9	3,066.1	4,109.4	3,045.1	2,687.1	1,921.1	38,377.4
2009	3,073.0	2,444.2	3,385.0	1,808.4	2,766.7	2,305.0	2,846.2	1,815.6	2,831.4	3,216.7	4,564.3	4,083.1	35,139.5

Source: CME Group; New York Mercantile Exchange (NYMEX)

Average Open Interest of Gold in New York (COMEX) In Thousands of Contracts

Year	Jan.	Feb.	Mar.	Apr.	May	June	July	Aug.	Sept.	Oct.	Nov.	Dec.
2000	149,606	158,026	160,325	155,188	162,516	144,099	133,087	126,893	132,731	132,546	134,630	113,830
2001	134,401	142,673	126,558	120,111	118,426	116,788	114,098	116,687	125,907	125,639	114,238	111,622
2002	124,222	142,763	142,638	159,892	190,845	174,123	166,042	146,596	167,620	162,456	164,581	191,594
2003	221,495	210,247	186,656	176,033	191,459	198,808	199,741	224,694	284,906	258,238	275,346	277,183
2004	283,813	238,816	256,873	274,898	250,963	225,001	239,579	237,940	259,181	306,522	344,665	329,669
2005	277,112	263,191	301,758	283,546	277,469	275,508	268,068	304,000	339,269	356,526	334,562	331,527
2006	348,949	338,851	331,223	350,380	336,735	288,309	316,969	309,186	320,850	330,152	346,141	335,204
2007	350,958	387,321	372,781	377,094	405,645	401,337	379,066	339,923	394,400	479,735	530,775	500,409
2008	556,302	487,373	471,320	418,693	435,847	401,914	460,178	382,302	378,216	321,545	290,706	280,402
2009	331,891	359,420	376,201	341,491	366,468	382,960	380,301	383,826	454,286	493,909	522,556	504,102

Source: CME Group; New York Mercantile Exchange (NYMEX)

Commodity Exchange, Inc. (COMEX) Depository Warehouse Stocks of Gold In Thousands of Troy Ounces

Year	Jan. 1	Feb. 1	Mar. 1	Apr. 1	May 1	June 1	July 1	Aug. 1	Sept. 1	Oct. 1	Nov. 1	Dec. 1
2000	1,219.4	1,392.9	1,373.9	1,968.1	1,966.7	1,900.6	1,890.1	2,012.6	1,961.1	1,918.1	1,865.5	1,863.6
2001	1,701.2	1,775.3	1,653.7	1,302.4	858.3	864.2	891.3	901.1	793.6	824.3	1,164.6	1,425.7
2002	1,220.3	1,186.7	1,285.7	1,322.3	1,372.3	1,764.1	1,850.7	1,835.6	1,915.0	1,892.4	1,994.9	2,046.5
2003	2,056.5	2,159.8	2,262.4	2,383.9	2,460.7	2,474.9	2,675.1	2,743.8	2,729.4	2,822.6	2,912.1	3,058.9
2004	3,122.2	3,324.0	3,476.9	3,677.1	4,142.0	4,391.8	4,399.6	4,657.0	4,880.1	5,122.4	5,334.7	5,374.3
2005	5,795.6	5,962.6	5,913.9	5,960.7	6,156.7	6,036.6	5,751.0	5,713.8	6,008.5	6,737.1	6,351.5	6,614.3
2006	6,657.7	7,320.9	7,518.9	7,426.6	7,334.4	7,796.0	8,031.2	8,199.0	7,980.8	7,695.2	7,565.8	7,491.1
2007	7,534.5	7,459.2	7,487.2	7,302.5	7,624.8	7,633.1	7,276.1	7,130.5	7,077.1	7,211.9	7,346.7	7,366.1
2008	7,492.5	7,588.0	7,371.3	7,623.1	7,760.4	7,588.9	7,611.6	8,266.0	8,442.8	8,594.9	8,171.8	8,540.3
2009	NA	8,556.8	8,635.9	8,508.6	8,322.6	8,725.8	8,893.4	9,144.6	9,173.0	9,316.2	9,316.2	9,508.9

Source: CME Group; New York Mercantile Exchange (NYMEX)

Central Gold Bank Reserves In Millions of Troy Ounces

	Industrial Countries															
Year	Belgium	Canada	France	Germany	Italy	Japan	Netherlands	Switzerland	United Kingdom	United States	Industrial Total	Developing Oil	Developing Non-Oil	IMF[2]	Bank for Int'l Settlements	World Total
2000	8.3	1.2	97.2	111.5	78.8	24.5	29.3	77.8	15.7	261.6	796.5	41.6	112.0	103.4	6.5	1,060.1
2001	8.3	1.1	97.2	111.1	78.8	24.6	28.4	70.7	11.4	262.0	791.3	42.3	111.3	103.4	6.5	1,054.7
2002	8.3	0.6	97.2	110.8	78.8	24.6	27.4	61.6	10.1	262.0						1,042.1
2003	8.3	0.1	97.2	110.6	78.8	24.6	25.0	52.5	10.1	261.5						1,024.3
2004	8.3	0.1	96.0	110.4	78.8	24.6	25.0	43.5	10.0	261.6						1,007.7
2005	7.3	0.1	90.9	110.2	78.8	24.6	22.3	41.5	10.0	261.6						988.4
2006	7.3	0.1	87.4	110.0	78.8	24.6	20.6	41.5	10.0	261.5						976.7
2007	7.3	0.1	83.7	109.9	78.8	24.6	20.0	36.8	10.0	261.5						960.5
2008	7.3	0.1	80.1	109.7	78.8	24.6	19.7	33.4	10.0	261.5						954.6
2009[1]	7.3	0.1	78.3	109.5	78.8	24.6	19.7		10.0	261.5						

[1] Preliminary. [2] International Monetary Fund. *Source: American Metal Market (AMM)*

Mine Production of Recoverable Gold in the United States In Kilograms

Year	Arizona	California	Idaho	Montana	Nevada	Alaska	Colorado	South Dakota	New Mexico	Utah	Other States	Total
1999	786	17,500	W	7,540	9,310	16,200	W	10,300	W	W	279,364	341,000
2000	442	17,200	W	9,310	268,000	15,600	W	8,230	W	W	34,218	353,000
2001	W	13,800	W	W	253,000	16,700	W	W	W	W	51,500	335,000
2002	W	9,180	W	W	240,000	W	W	W	W	W	48,820	298,000
2003	W	4,270	W	W	227,000	W	W	W	W	W	45,730	277,000
2004	W	3,260	W	W	216,000	W	W	W	W	W	38,740	258,000
2005	W	W	W	W	212,000	W	W	W	W	W	44,200	256,000
2006	W	W	W	W	206,000	W	W	W	W	W	45,800	252,000
2007	W	W	W	W	186,000	W	W	W	W	W	52,400	238,000
2008[1]	W	W	W	W	175,000	W	W	W	W	W	54,200	229,000

[1] Preliminary. W = Withheld proprietary data, included in "Other States." *Source: U.S. Geological Survey (USGS)*

Consumption of Gold, By End-Use in the United States In Kilograms

	Jewelry and the Arts				Industrial					
Year	Gold-Filled & Other	Electro-plating	Karat Gold	Total	Dental	Gold-Filled & Other	Electro-plating	Karat Gold	Total	Grand Total
1989	7,364	1,283	60,877	69,524	7,927	15,723	20,684	1,215	37,621	115,078
1990	8,132	429	69,952	78,514	8,700	12,725	17,251	1,020	30,996	118,216
1991	3,848	373	79,875	84,096	8,485	8,102	12,624	1,068	21,793	114,375
1992	3,546	581	79,381	83,508	6,543	8,802	10,476	1,082	20,360	110,410
1993	3,530	373	61,700	65,600	6,170	9,470	9,090	1,100	19,700	91,400
1994	3,650	369	49,700	53,700	5,430	7,450	9,470	96	17,000	76,100
1995	NA	NA	NA	NA	NA	NA	NA	NA	NA	NA
1996	NA	NA	NA	NA	NA	NA	NA	NA	NA	NA
1997	NA	NA	NA	NA	NA	NA	NA	NA	NA	NA
1998	NA	NA	NA	NA	NA	NA	NA	NA	NA	NA

[1] Preliminary. NA = Not available. *Source: U.S. Geological Survey (USGS)*

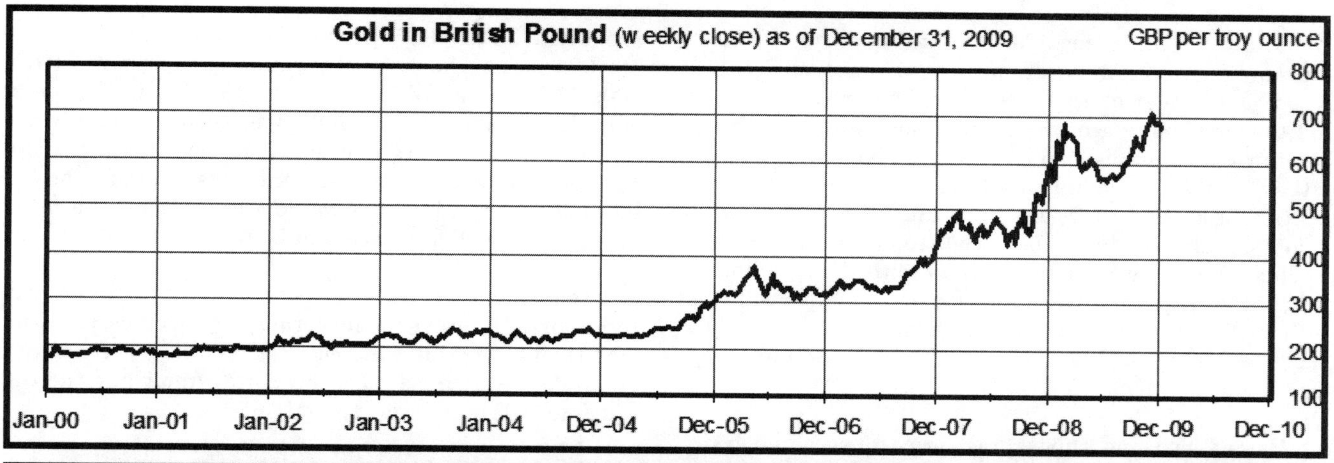
Gold in British Pound (weekly close) as of December 31, 2009
GBP per troy ounce
800
700
600
500
400
300
200
100
Jan-00
Jan-01
Jan-02
Jan-03
Jan-04
Dec-04
Dec-05
Dec-06
Dec-07
Dec-08
Dec-09
Dec-10

Gold in Euro (weekly close) as of December 31, 2009
EUR per troy ounce
900
800
700
600
500
400
300
200
Jan-00
Jan-01
Jan-02
Jan-03
Jan-04
Dec-04
Dec-05
Dec-06
Dec-07
Dec-08
Dec-09
Dec-10

Gold in Japanese Yen (weekly close) as of December 31, 2009
JPY per troy ounce
1,200
1,000
800
600
400
200
Jan-00
Jan-01
Jan-02
Jan-03
Jan-04
Dec-04
Dec-05
Dec-06
Dec-07
Dec-08
Dec-09
Dec-10

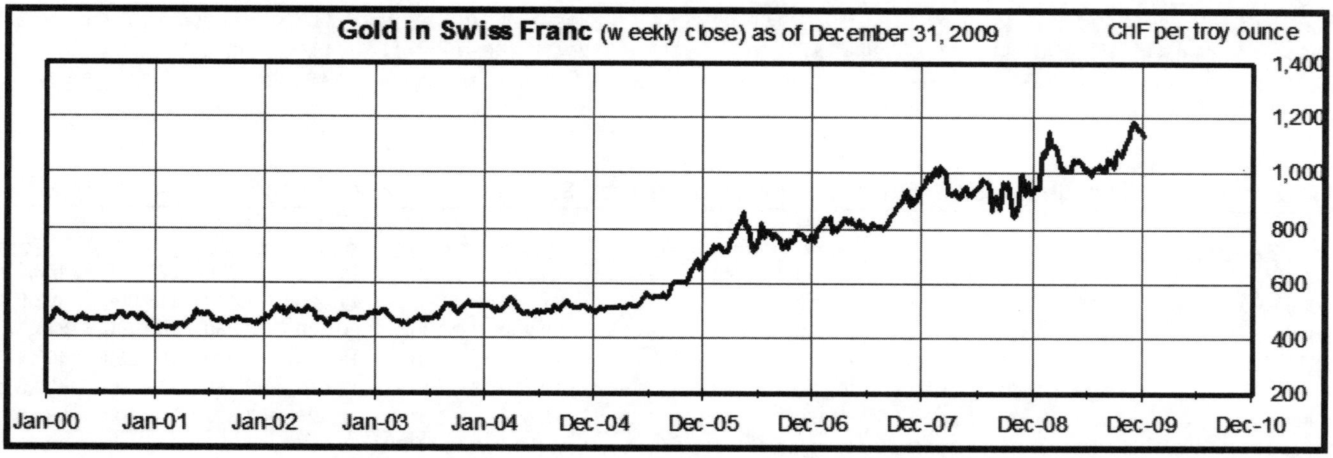
Gold in Swiss Franc (weekly close) as of December 31, 2009
CHF per troy ounce
1,400
1,200
1,000
800
600
400
200
Jan-00
Jan-01
Jan-02
Jan-03
Jan-04
Dec-04
Dec-05
Dec-06
Dec-07
Dec-08
Dec-09
Dec-10

Grain Sorghum

Grain sorghums include milo, kafir, durra, feterita, and kaoliang. Grain sorghums are tolerant of drought by going into dormancy during dry and hot conditions and then resuming growth as conditions improve. Grain sorghums are a staple food in China, India, and Africa but in the U.S. they are mainly used as livestock feed. The two key U.S. producing states are Texas and Kansas, each with about one-third of total U.S. production. U.S. sorghum production has become more popular with the breeding of dwarf grain sorghum hybrids which are only about 3 feet tall (versus up to 10 feet tall for wild sorghum) and are easier to harvest with a combine. The U.S. sorghum crop year begins September 1.

Prices – The monthly average price for sorghum grain received by U.S. farmers in the 2009-10 (Sep 09-Aug 10), annualized through Jan 2010 fell by -5.0% yr/yr to $5.62 per hundred pounds. The value of U.S. grain sorghum production in the 2008-09 marketing year (latest data) fell 12.7% to $1.682 billion.

Supply – World production of sorghum in the 2009-10 marketing year is forecasted to fall 3.4% to 62.349 million metric tons, falling farther below the 13-year high of 66.289 million metric tons posted in 2007-08. U.S. grain sorghum production in 2009-10 is forecasted to fall -18.9% yr/yr to 382.983 million bushels. Sorghum acreage harvested in 2009-10 is forecasted to fall 24.1% to 5,520 million acres, only slightly above the 2006-07 figure of 4.937 acres which was the smallest sorghum acreage since the late 1930s. Yield will be better in 2009-10 and is estimated to be 69.4 bushels per acre, but that would still be below the record high of 73.2 bushels per acre in 2007-08.

Demand – World utilization (consumption) of grain sorghum in the 2009-10 marketing year is forecasted to fall -2.9% to 62.617 million metric tons. The biggest consumers are Mexico utilizing 15% of the world supply and the U.S. utilizing 10% of the world supply.

Trade – World exports of sorghum in the 2009-10 marketing year is forecasted to fall -3.4% to 5.966 million metric tons, down further from the 21-year high of 9.730 million metric tons seen in207-08. U.S. exports in 2009-10 are forecasted to fall -2.4% yr/yr to 3.556 million metric tons, and that accounted for 60% of total world exports. Argentina is the world's other major exporter with 1.0 million metric tons of exports in 2009-10, accounting for 17% of total world exports. Major world importers are Mexico and Japan.

World Supply and Demand of Grain Sorghum In Thousands of Metric Tons

	Exports				Imports					Utilization				Ending Stocks		
Crop Year	Argentina	Non-U.S.	U.S.	Total	Japan	Mexico	Unaccounted	Total	Total Production	China	Mexico	U.S.	Total	Non-U.S.	U.S.	Total
2004-05	351	728	4,675	5,403	1,374	2,931	147	5,262	58,810	2,300	9,300	6,254	58,904	3,396	1,446	4,842
2005-06	197	442	4,936	5,378	1,393	3,029	176	5,335	59,582	2,300	8,600	4,818	59,211	3,502	1,668	5,170
2006-07	1,083	1,587	3,876	5,463	1,276	1,954	406	4,839	57,469	2,050	8,100	4,012	57,653	3,548	814	4,362
2007-08[1]	1,223	2,700	7,030	9,730	1,084	1,156	525	9,679	66,289	2,000	7,200	5,081	65,255	4,005	1,340	5,345
2008-09[2]	1,100	2,531	3,643	6,174	1,629	2,496		6,020	64,543	2,000	8,600	8,308	64,514	3,830	1,390	5,220
2009-10[3]	1,000	2,410	3,556	5,966	1,600	2,700		5,975	62,349	1,850	9,200	6,096	62,617	3,495	1,466	4,961

[1] Preliminary. [2] Estimate. [3] Forecast. *Source: Foreign Agricultural Service, U.S. Department of Agriculture (FAS-USDA)*

Salient Statistics of Grain Sorghum in the United States

Crop Year Beginning Sept. 1	Acreage Planted[4] for All Purposes (1,000 Acres)	For Grain: Acreage Harvested (1,000 Acres)	For Grain: Production (1,000 Bushels)	For Grain: Yield Per Harvested Acre (Bushels)	For Grain: Price in Cents Per Bushel	For Grain: Value of Production (Million $)	For Silage: Acreage Harvested (1,000 Acres)	For Silage: Production (1,000 Tons)	For Silage: Yield Per Harvested Acre (Tons)	Sorghum Grain Stocks Dec. 1: On Farms (1,000 Bushels)	Dec. 1: Off Farms	June 1: On Farms	June 1: Off Farms
2004-05	7,486	6,517	453,650	69.8	179	843.5	352	4,763	13.5	78,700	203,505	16,000	97,170
2005-06	6,454	5,736	392,933	68.7	186	737.0	311	4,218	13.6	55,000	235,376	12,650	102,213
2006-07	6,522	4,937	277,538	56.2	329	883.2	347	4,642	13.4	38,100	174,094	5,380	69,490
2007-08[1]	7,712	6,792	497,445	73.2	408	1,925.3	392	5,246	13.4	51,400	239,850	7,000	94,019
2008-09[2]	8,284	7,271	472,342	65.0	320	1,681.6	408	5,646	13.8	54,400	243,290	12,000	90,215
2009-10[3]	6,633	5,520	382,983	69.4	310-350		254	3,680	14.5	48,000	202,295		

[1] Preliminary. [2] Estimate. [3] Forecast. *Source: Foreign Agricultural Service, U.S. Department of Agriculture (FAS-USDA)*

Production of All Sorghum for Grain in the United States, by States In Thousands of Bushels

Year	Arkansas	Colorado	Illinois	Kansas	Louisiana	Mississippi	Missouri	Nebraska	New Mexico	Oklahoma	South Dakota	Texas	Total
2004	4,704	5,400	8,938	220,400	5,200	1,422	15,660	33,615	4,232	14,400	6,300	127,100	453,650
2005	4,960	3,410	7,636	195,000	8,712	----	9,880	21,750	4,365	11,520	4,420	111,000	392,933
2006	5,100	3,380	6,408	145,000	8,352	----	8,075	19,200	2,100	6,800	2,880	62,400	277,538
2007	20,640	5,550	6,237	209,350	23,275	9,775	9,600	22,560	3,000	12,320	7,800	159,250	497,445
2008	10,120	4,500	7,828	214,500	9,570	5,822	7,760	19,110	3,440	13,950	7,360	158,600	472,342
2009[1]	2,923	6,750	2,952	224,400	5,330	770	3,698	13,020	2,300	12,320	7,320	98,400	382,983

[1] Preliminary. *Source: National Agricultural Statistics Service, U.S. Department of Agriculture (NASS-USDA)*

Quarterly Supply and Disappearance of Grain Sorghum in the United States In Millions of Bushels

Crop Year Beginning Sept. 1	Supply: Beginning Stocks	Supply: Production	Supply: Imports[3]	Supply: Total Supply	Disappearance – Domestic Use: Food & Alcohol	Domestic Use: Seed	Domestic Use: Feed & Residual	Domestic Use: Total	Exports[3]	Total Disappearance	Ending Stocks: Gov't Owned[4]	Ending Stocks: Privately Owned[5]	Ending Stocks: Total Stocks
2006-07	65.7	276.8	.1	342.6	45.0	1.0	112.9	157.9	152.6	310.5			32.1
Sept.-Nov.	65.7	276.8	0	342.5	13.2	0	80.7	93.9	36.4	130.3			212.2
Dec.-Feb.	212.2	----	.0	212.2	13.2	0	13.9	27.1	42.9	70.0			142.2
Mar.-May	142.2	----	0	142.2	13.8	.6	18.3	32.1	35.2	67.4			74.9
June-Aug.	74.9	----	.0	74.9	4.7	.4	.1	4.8	38.1	42.9			32.1
2007-08	32.1	497.4	.0	529.5	34.1	1.1	164.9	200.0	276.7	476.8			52.8
Sept.-Nov.	32.1	497.4	.0	529.5	8.5	0	136.1	144.6	93.7	238.3			291.3
Dec.-Feb.	291.3	----	.0	291.3	8.5	0	5.9	14.4	91.0	105.3			185.9
Mar.-May	185.9	----	.0	185.9	8.7	.6	17.9	27.2	57.7	84.9			101.0
June-Aug.	101.0	----	.0	101.0	8.4	.5	5.1	13.9	34.3	48.3			52.8
2008-09[1]	52.8	472.3	.1	525.2	94.1	.9	232.1	327.1	143.4	470.5			54.7
Sept.-Nov.	52.8	472.3	.1	525.2	27.3	0	156.0	183.4	44.2	227.5			297.7
Dec.-Feb.	297.7	----	.0	297.7	27.3	0	32.4	59.7	32.2	91.9			205.9
Mar.-May	205.9	----	0	205.9	27.8	.5	39.6	68.0	35.7	103.6			102.2
June-Aug.	102.2	----	0	102.2	11.7	.4	4.0	16.1	31.4	47.5			54.7
2009-10[2]	54.7	383.0	0	437.7	89.0	1.0	150.0	240.0	140.0	380.0			57.7
Sept.-Nov.	54.7	383.0	0	437.7	22.0	0	119.4	141.4	46.0	187.4			250.3

[1] Preliminary. [2] Estimate. [3] Uncommitted inventory. [4] Includes quantity under loan and farmer-owned reserve. *Source: Economic Research Service, U.S. Department of Agriculture (ERS-USDA)*

Average Price of Sorghum Grain, No. 2, Yellow in Kansas City In Dollars Per Hundred Pounds (Cwt.)

Year	Sept.	Oct.	Nov.	Dec.	Jan.	Feb.	Mar.	Apr.	May	June	July	Aug.	Average
2002-03	4.86	4.70	4.72	4.62	4.52	4.43	4.07	4.24	4.12	4.06	3.71	4.00	4.34
2003-04	4.15	4.18	4.50	4.61	4.71	4.88	5.18	5.37	4.94	4.67	3.92	3.75	4.57
2004-05	3.45	3.21	3.17	3.21	3.13	3.23	3.44	3.30	3.36	3.56	3.90	3.53	3.37
2005-06	3.22	3.08	2.93	3.30	3.46	3.58	3.65	3.79	4.03	3.90	4.15	3.79	3.57
2006-07	3.82	5.07	5.97	6.03	6.36	6.72	6.38	5.69	5.97	6.09	5.33	5.50	5.75
2007-08	5.68	5.60	6.13	7.34	8.36	8.86	9.13	9.70	9.65	11.63	10.10	8.37	8.38
2008-09	8.43	5.92	5.49	5.19	5.67	5.48	5.51	5.76	6.37	6.29	4.66	4.75	5.79
2009-10[1]	4.81	5.49	5.72	6.44	5.81	5.56							5.64

[1] Preliminary. *Source: Economic Research Service, U.S. Department of Agriculture (ERS-USDA)*

Exports of Grain Sorghum, by Country of Destination from the United States In Metric Tons

Year	Canada	Ecuador	Ethiopia	Israel	Japan	Jordan	Mexico	South Africa	Spain	Sudan	Turkey	World Total
2002-03	5,921	91	48,000	65,725	1,035,634	0	3,150,014	43,918	266,892	5,880	0	4,690,875
2003-04	8,025	210	54,320	105,170	889,054	0	2,814,386	156	267,691	11,430	0	4,626,171
2004-05	5,270	0	53,540	26,654	1,088,171	0	2,883,335	2,000	167,896	116,577	0	4,474,017
2005-06	4,227	0	31,500	16,177	1,193,039	0	3,004,518	30,398	131,995	211,021	0	4,929,700
2006-07	3,999	0	4,100	54,533	674,824	0	1,914,111	0	1,018,325	299,650	0	4,333,212
2007-08[1]	5,775	0	27,600	137,284	505,919	125	1,150,231	45,498	1,929,955	303,818	0	6,653,444
2008-09[2]	4,987	0	28,170	0	313,518	0	2,486,966	41,000	0	268,160	0	3,596,941

[1] Preliminary. [2] Estimate. *Source: Economic Research Service, U.S. Department of Agriculture (ERS-USDA)*

Grain Sorghum Price Support Program and Market Prices in the United States

Year	Price Support Operations – Price Support: Quantity (Million Cwt.)	Price Support: % of Production	Aquired by CCC (Million Cwt.)	Owned by CCC at Year End (Million Cwt.)	Basic Loan Rate (Dollars Per Bushel)	Target Price (Dollars Per Bushel)	Findley Loan Rate (Dollars Per Bushel)	Effective Base[3] (Million Acres)	Participation Rate[4] % of Base	No. 2 Yellow ($ Per Cwt.): Kansas City	Texas High Plains	Los Angeles	Gulf Ports
2002-03	3.7	1.8	0	0	3.54	2.54	1.98	12.1	----	4.34	4.69	----	5.01
2003-04	3.5	1.5	0	0	3.54	2.54	1.98	12.1	----	4.57	5.01	----	5.45
2004-05	5.5	2.1	.2	0	3.48	2.57	1.95	12.0	----	3.37	3.95	----	4.42
2005-06	5.4	2.4	0	0	3.48	2.57	1.95	11.9	----	3.57	3.84	----	5.04
2006-07	1.9	1.2	0	0	3.48	2.57	1.95	11.8	----	5.75	6.09	----	7.39
2007-08[1]	1.8				3.48	2.57	1.95	11.7	----	8.38	8.49	----	9.81
2008-09[2]	4.5					2.57	1.95	11.6	----	5.79	5.44	----	7.18

[1] Preliminary. [2] Estimate. [3] National effective crop acreage base as determined by ASCS. [4] Percentage of effective base acres enrolled in acreage reduction programs. 5/ Beginning with the 1996-7 marketing year, target prices are no longer applicable. *Source: Economic Research Service, U.S. Department of Agriculture (ERS-USDA)*

Hay

Hay is a catchall term for forage plants, typically grasses such as timothy and Sudan-grass, and legumes such as alfalfa and clover. Alfalfa and alfalfa mixtures account for nearly half of all hay production. Hay is generally used to make cured feed for livestock. Curing, which is the proper drying of hay, is necessary to prevent spoilage. Hay, when properly cured, contains about 20% moisture. If hay is dried excessively, however, there is a loss of protein, which makes it less effective as livestock feed. Hay is harvested in virtually all of the lower 48 states.

Prices – The average monthly price of hay received by U.S. farmers in the first nine months of the 2009-10 marketing year (May 2009 through April 2010) as of January 2010 fell by -21.2% yr/yr to $117.22 per ton, down from last year's record high of $148.75 per ton. The farm production value of hay produced in 2008-09 (latest data available) was $18.777 million.

Supply – U.S. hay production in 2009-10 rose +0.80% yr/yr to 147,442 million tons. U.S. farmers harvested 59.755 million acres of hay in 2009-10, down -0.66% yr/yr. The yield in 2009-10 was 2.47 tons per acre, below the 2004-05 record high of 2.55. U.S. carryover (May 1) in 2009-10 rose +2.22% to 22.065 million tons.

The largest hay producing states in the U.S. for 2009 were California, (with 5.9% of U.S. hay production), Texas (5.6%), Missouri (5.5%), South Dakota (3.6), Oklahoma (3.6%), Nebraska (4.2%), Idaho (3.8%), and Minnesota (3.6%).

Salient Statistics of All Hay in the United States

Crop Year Beginning May 1	Acres Harvested (1,000 Acres)	Yield Per Acre (Tons)	Production	Carry-over May 1	Disappearance	Supply	Disappearance	Animal Units Fed[3] (Millions)	Farm Price ($ Per Ton)	Farm Production Value Million $	Alfalfa (Certified)	Timothy	Red Clover	Sudan-grass
			Millions of Tons			Per Animal Unit In Tons					Retail Price Paid by Farmers for Seed, April 15 Dollars Per Cwt.			
2004-05	61,944	2.55	158.1	25.9	156.4	2.60	2.21	71.3	92.1	12,212	291.00	110.00	145.00	55.60
2005-06	61,637	2.44	150.5	27.8	NA	2.50	2.20	72.4	98.4	12,585	281.00	105.00	174.00	57.40
2006-07	60,632	2.32	140.8	21.3	NA	2.26	2.05	73.1	111.1	13,634	286.00	106.00	177.00	50.20
2007-08	61,006	2.41	146.9	15.0		2.26	1.96		130.8	16,842	292.00	112.00	202.00	56.70
2008-09[1]	60,152	2.43	146.3	21.6		2.36	2.05		148.7	18,777				
2009-10[2]	59,755	2.47	147.4	22.1					116.2					

[1] Preliminary. [2] Estimate. [3] Roughage-consuming animal units fed annually. NA = Not available.
Source: Economic Research Service, U.S. Department of Agriculture (ERS-USDA)

Production of All Hay in the United States, by States In Thousands of Tons

Year	California	Idaho	Iowa	Minnesota	Missouri	New York	North Dakota	Ohio	Oklahoma	South Dakota	Texas	Wisconsin	Total
2004	9,220	5,350	6,240	5,895	9,420	6,423	3,666	3,232	5,958	6,870	12,295	4,880	158,122
2005	9,206	5,382	5,860	6,055	6,718	6,945	5,646	3,630	5,084	7,560	9,140	4,470	150,461
2006	9,568	5,505	5,189	5,679	6,944	5,588	3,137	3,421	3,556	4,180	8,675	5,264	140,783
2007	9,042	5,345	4,944	4,240	7,528	6,185	5,063	2,804	6,858	7,275	14,740	4,392	146,901
2008	9,414	5,588	5,330	5,265	8,820	6,232	4,118	2,802	5,536	7,840	9,211	4,810	146,270
2009[1]	8,632	5,528	4,002	5,250	8,040	6,235	5,240	2,876	5,278	7,830	8,250	4,430	147,442

[1] Preliminary. *Source: Agricultural Statistics Board, U.S. Department of Agriculture (ASB-USDA)*

Hay Production and Farm Stocks in the United States In Thousands of Short Tons

Year	Production: Alfalfa & Mixtures	All Others	All Hay	Corn for Silage[1]	Sorghum Silage[1]	Farm Stocks: May 1	Dec. 1
2004	75,375	82,747	158,122	107,293	4,776	25,947	114,489
2005	75,610	74,851	150,461	106,486	4,218	27,758	105,181
2006	70,548	70,235	140,783	105,294	4,612	21,345	96,400
2007	69,880	77,021	146,901	106,229	5,246	14,990	104,089
2008	70,180	76,090	146,270	111,619	5,646	21,585	103,658
2009[2]	71,030	76,412	147,442	108,209	3,680	22,065	107,222

[1] Not included in all tame hay. [2] Preliminary. *Source: Agricultural Statistics Board, U.S. Department of Agriculture (ASB-USDA)*

Mid-Month Price Received by Farmers for All Hay (Baled) in the United States In Dollars Per Ton

Year	May	June	July	Aug.	Sept.	Oct.	Nov.	Dec.	Jan.	Feb.	Mar.	Apr.	Average
2004-05	101.0	95.2	90.4	92.2	91.4	92.8	88.7	86.0	87.8	88.2	92.6	99.4	92.1
2005-06	107.0	102.0	99.7	99.7	99.0	97.7	91.7	92.0	93.1	95.8	97.5	105.0	98.4
2006-07	113.0	109.0	107.0	106.0	108.0	109.0	106.0	110.0	109.0	113.0	119.0	124.0	111.1
2007-08	138.0	131.0	131.0	124.0	127.0	128.0	129.0	127.0	126.0	129.0	133.0	147.0	130.8
2008-09	168.0	161.0	164.0	163.0	161.0	156.0	149.0	138.0	135.0	131.0	129.0	129.0	148.7
2009-10[1]	131.0	163.0	116.0	109.0	107.0	106.0	107.0	107.0	109.0	107.0			116.2

[1] Preliminary. [2] Marketing year average. *Source: Economic Research Service, U.S. Department of Agriculture (ERS-USDA)*

Heating Oil

Heating oil is a heavy fuel oil that is derived from crude oil. Heating oil is also known as No. 2 fuel oil and accounts for about 25% of the yield from a barrel of crude oil. That is the second largest "cut" after gasoline. The price to consumers of home heating oil is generally comprised of 42% for crude oil, 12% for refining costs, and 46% for marketing and distribution costs (Source: EIA's Petroleum Marketing Monthly, 2001). Generally, a $1 increase in the price of crude oil translates into a 2.5-cent per gallon rise in heating oil. Because of this, heating oil prices are highly correlated with crude oil prices, although heating oil prices are also subject to swift supply and demand shifts due to weather changes or refinery shutdowns.

The primary use for heating oil is for residential heating. In the U.S., approximately 8.1 million households use heating oil as their main heating fuel. Most of the demand for heating oil occurs from October through March. The Northeast region, which includes the New England and the Central Atlantic States, is most reliant on heating oil. This region consumes approximately 70% of U.S. heating oil. However, demand for heating oil has been dropping as households switch to a more convenient heating source like natural gas. In fact, demand for heating oil is down by about 10 billion gallons/year from its peak use in 1976 (Source: American Petroleum Institute).

Refineries produce approximately 85% of U.S. heating oil as part of the "distillate fuel oil" product family, which includes heating oil and diesel fuel. The remainder of U.S. heating oil is imported from Canada, the Virgin Islands, and Venezuela.

Recently, a team of Purdue University researchers developed a way to make home heating oil from a mixture of soybean oil and conventional fuel oil. The oil blend is made by replacing 20% of the fuel oil with soybean oil, potentially saving 1.3 billion gallons of fuel oil per year. This soybean heating oil can be used in conventional furnaces without altering existing equipment. The soybean heating oil is relatively easy to produce and creates no sulfur emissions.

The "crack-spread" is the processing margin earned when refiners buy crude oil and refine it into heating oil and gasoline. The crack-spread ratio commonly used in the industry is the 3-2-1, which involves buying 1 heating oil contract and 2 gasoline futures contracts, and then selling 3 crude oil contracts. As long as the crack spread is positive, it is profitable for refiners to buy crude oil and refine it into products. The NYMEX has a crack-spread calculator on their web site at www.NYMEX.com.

Heating oil futures and options trade at the New York Mercantile Exchange (NYMEX). The heating oil futures contract calls for the delivery of 1,000 barrels of fungible No. 2 heating oil in the New York harbor. In London, gas/oil futures and options are traded on the ICE Futures Europe (ICE) exchange.

Prices – NYMEX heating oil futures prices on the nearest-futures chart started the year 2009 at around $1.48 per gallon and rallied to a high at the end of the year of $2.12 in December. After a spike to 220.03 in January of 2010 the priced moved lower.

Supply – U.S. production of distillate fuel oil in 2009 (through November, annualized) fell by 8.8% yr/yr to 3.598 million barrels per day, down from the record high of 4.198 million barrels per day in 2007. Stocks of distillate fuel oil in November 2009 were 169.9 million barrels. U.S. production of residual fuel in 2009 (through November, annualized) fell by -4.0% yr/yr to an average of 595,000 barrels per day, which less than half the production levels of well over 1 million barrels per day produced in the 1970s. U.S. stocks of residual fuel oil as of January 1, 2009 rose +0.3% to 38.7 million barrels from 38.6 million barrels a year earlier.

Demand – U.S. usage of distillate fuel oil in 2009 (through November, annualized) fell -8.2% yr/yr to 3.598 million barrels per day, further down from 2007's record high of 4.198 million barrels per day.

Trade – U.S. imports of distillate fuel oil in 2009 (through November, annualized) rose +6.0% to an average of 226,000 barrels per day, down from the 2006 record high of 365,000 barrels per day. U.S. exports of distillate fuel oil in 2007 (latest data) rose by +2.7% yr/yr to a 13-year high average of 221 barrels per day. U.S. imports of residual fuel oil in 2007 (latest data) rose +5.1% yr/yr to 368,000 barrels per day, which was less than a third of the levels of over 1 million barrels per day seen back in the 1970s. U.S. exports of residual fuel oil in 2007 (latest data) rose +9.2% to 309,000 barrels per day, which was a new record high.

Average Price of Heating Oil #2 In Cents Per Gallon

Year	Jan.	Feb.	Mar.	Apr.	May	June	July	Aug.	Sept.	Oct.	Nov.	Dec.	Average
2000	91.32	94.37	77.29	75.32	75.88	78.32	78.14	89.13	98.87	97.46	102.70	94.08	87.74
2001	84.30	78.55	74.17	78.02	77.11	75.74	69.88	73.41	71.65	62.63	54.37	52.60	71.04
2002	53.52	54.03	63.52	66.60	66.54	64.50	67.79	69.81	77.25	76.55	72.14	81.70	67.83
2003	90.09	112.84	99.70	79.75	74.31	75.95	79.03	81.61	73.54	81.97	83.35	89.04	85.10
2004	97.91	91.19	90.88	91.87	101.65	99.41	109.42	116.86	125.73	148.55	138.16	127.32	111.58
2005	132.01	134.26	155.44	152.35	140.89	161.20	163.71	180.75	196.50	188.75	168.67	170.32	162.07
2006	174.99	163.68	177.70	198.27	197.17	191.76	192.30	198.25	169.17	154.53	165.00	167.85	179.22
2007	151.99	169.48	174.05	186.30	188.47	200.31	206.99	198.36	218.06	228.32	258.79	257.54	203.22
2008	255.64	264.17	306.80	322.96	361.64	379.99	375.67	317.16	290.76	222.44	185.15	138.93	285.11
2009	146.43	127.78	128.30	135.95	147.87	174.72	163.18	186.59	173.05	193.34	198.48	197.22	164.41

Source: Energy Information Administration, U.S. Department of Energy (EIA-DOE)

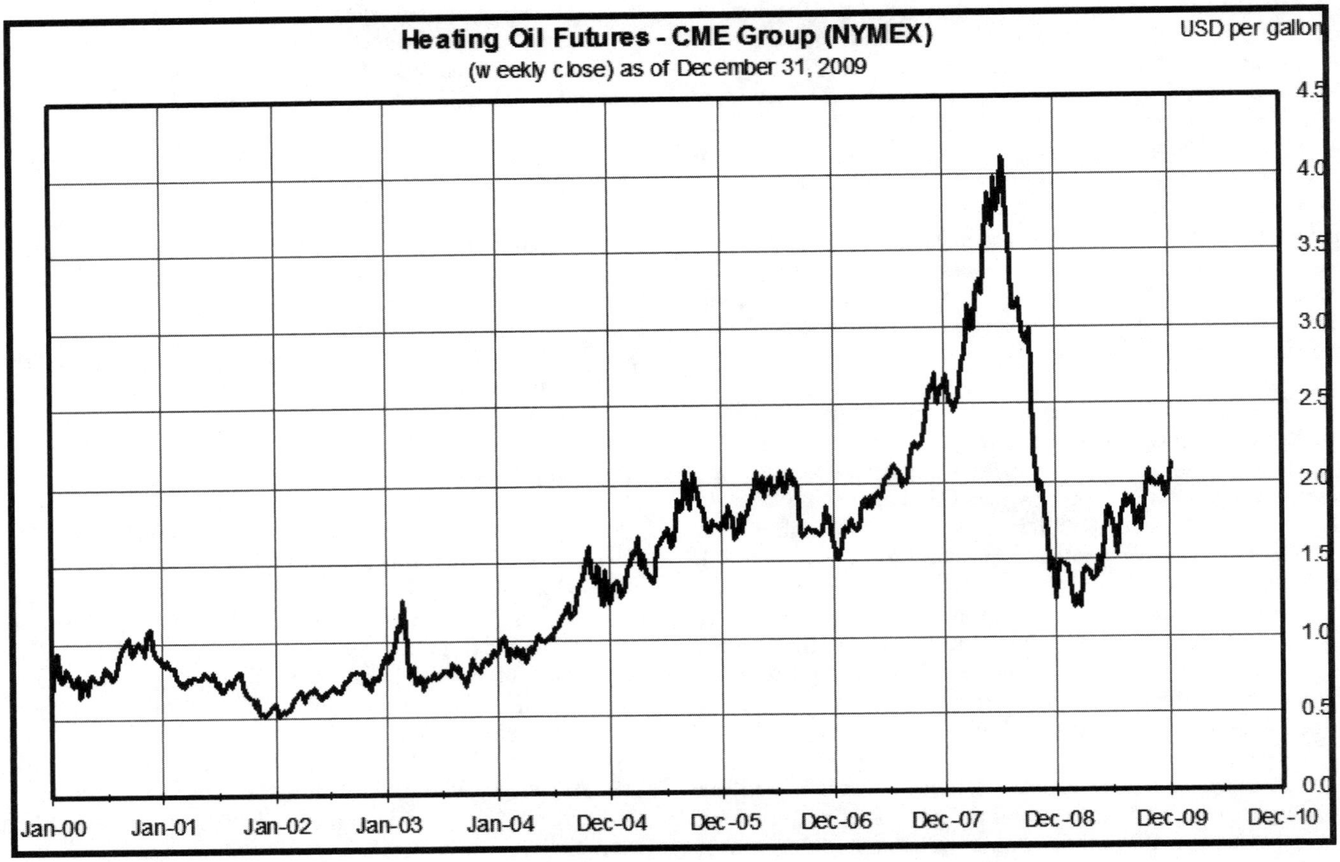

Average Open Interest of Heating Oil #2 Futures in New York In Contracts

Year	Jan.	Feb.	Mar.	Apr.	May	June	July	Aug.	Sept.	Oct.	Nov.	Dec.
2000	135,431	132,407	108,646	100,389	117,055	129,872	153,914	169,092	177,997	168,388	155,475	142,145
2001	138,980	127,219	120,899	127,395	130,328	141,436	149,577	145,605	145,692	155,540	162,392	153,850
2002	166,824	173,110	160,205	144,936	139,979	136,201	131,742	141,084	147,692	153,739	161,137	156,268
2003	178,932	174,224	134,616	111,706	118,822	124,675	127,273	146,821	150,893	156,142	145,857	145,555
2004	153,794	145,924	161,945	174,618	176,784	167,331	193,291	206,099	197,783	188,843	176,298	163,629
2005	155,528	152,479	174,437	179,923	176,770	185,831	182,710	185,185	174,229	172,772	178,199	178,008
2006	170,094	165,627	168,415	170,955	171,732	169,123	179,773	185,648	208,848	221,942	228,152	216,033
2007	219,690	219,715	209,805	208,829	210,128	224,289	239,109	218,913	235,403	232,165	224,475	209,578
2008	202,976	220,716	230,646	227,140	224,480	218,004	223,645	221,733	212,561	212,981	224,465	224,359
2009	237,894	252,753	261,552	259,008	260,646	283,068	294,270	308,022	311,296	312,653	322,505	309,113

Source: CME Group; New York Mercantile Exchange (NYMEX)

Volume of Trading of Heating Oil #2 Futures in New York In Thousands of Contracts

Year	Jan.	Feb.	Mar.	Apr.	May	June	July	Aug.	Sept.	Oct.	Nov.	Dec.	Total
2000	914.0	770.3	645.2	556.1	673.3	705.9	663.0	1,004.4	954.9	878.1	939.0	927.3	9,631.4
2001	914.4	650.7	758.0	728.6	722.8	849.9	712.9	745.8	694.0	853.8	835.5	798.1	9,264.5
2002	998.5	810.8	885.5	844.1	789.8	720.1	798.8	866.0	794.4	1,017.9	1,039.5	1,129.9	10,695.2
2003	1,340.1	1,158.9	965.9	757.7	811.6	802.9	849.9	891.3	1,118.5	1,095.5	817.3	971.8	11,581.7
2004	1,153.8	1,059.7	1,139.9	1,007.8	910.0	1,100.5	920.7	1,105.7	1,060.8	1,148.6	1,112.7	1,164.4	12,884.5
2005	1,090.6	1,046.1	1,204.2	1,062.5	999.7	1,193.5	1,058.5	1,150.4	1,165.1	1,019.5	1,009.5	1,136.0	13,135.6
2006	1,157.5	1,131.2	1,121.7	974.8	1,185.1	1,114.0	1,027.1	1,166.1	1,235.9	1,291.1	1,228.6	1,357.5	13,990.6
2007	1,655.6	1,507.5	1,370.3	1,326.0	1,462.2	1,605.8	1,478.9	1,579.8	1,394.7	1,687.2	1,544.1	1,467.0	18,079.0
2008	1,611.7	1,726.3	1,763.3	1,639.2	1,825.3	1,651.9	1,571.3	1,641.9	1,578.0	1,646.4	1,297.3	1,630.4	19,583.1
2009	1,789.0	1,513.1	1,670.1	1,633.3	1,644.5	1,809.7	2,004.2	1,652.6	1,777.3	1,975.9	1,921.9	2,035.1	21,426.8

Source: CME Group; New York Mercantile Exchange (NYMEX)

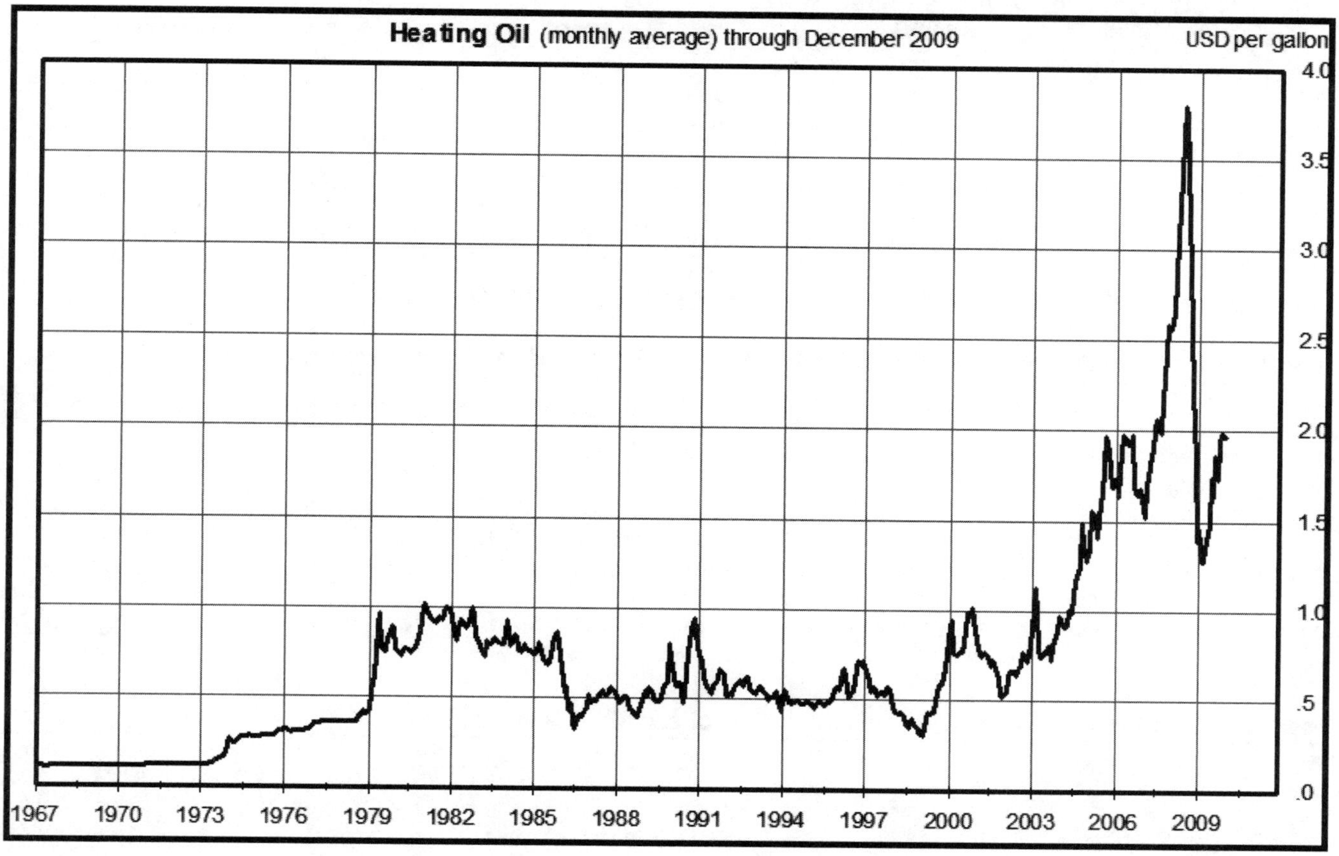

Stocks of Distillate and Residual Fuel in the United States, on First of Month In Millions of Barrels

													Residual Fuel --- Oil Stocks ---	
Year	Jan.	Feb.	Mar.	Apr.	May	June	July	Aug.	Sept.	Oct.	Nov.	Dec.	Jan. 1	July 1
2000	124.1	106.7	105.2	96.0	100.1	105.4	106.4	112.9	111.0	115.3	116.5	121.1	35.8	37.0
2001	118.0	118.2	117.0	105.0	104.9	107.1	113.9	125.2	122.0	127.0	128.9	138.9	36.2	41.7
2002	144.5	137.8	130.0	123.0	122.6	127.4	130.9	133.4	130.6	126.9	121.4	124.4	41.0	32.7
2003	134.1	112.6	97.7	98.6	97.2	106.7	112.2	118.0	126.5	131.3	132.1	136.1	31.3	35.3
2004	136.5	122.8	112.2	104.4	101.5	107.5	114.3	121.9	130.8	123.1	118.3	123.2	37.8	37.5
2005	126.3	121.4	116.4	104.5	104.5	111.0	118.8	132.0	139.4	127.7	124.8	133.8	42.4	37.4
2006	136.0	139.4	135.6	120.5	116.5	124.0	129.9	137.5	145.1	149.3	142.8	140.6	37.4	43.2
2007	143.7	139.5	123.2	119.7	120.9	124.8	123.4	130.6	133.5	133.6	133.9	134.4	42.4	36.1
2008	133.5	131.0	117.6	107.8	107.1	113.9	121.7	130.9	133.0	127.7	127.6	135.9	38.6	41.6
2009[1]	146.0	143.4	146.1	143.6	148.2	155.2	160.0	161.1	165.0	172.2	169.9	171.3	38.7	37.0

[1] Preliminary. *Source: Energy Information Administration; U.S. Department of Energy (EIA-DOE)*

Production of Distillate Fuel Oil in the United States In Thousand Barrels per Day

Year	Jan.	Feb.	Mar.	Apr.	May	June	July	Aug.	Sept.	Oct.	Nov.	Dec.	Average
2000	3,123	3,348	3,342	3,533	3,650	3,481	3,520	3,678	3,844	3,774	3,785	3,872	3,580
2001	3,609	3,612	3,483	3,650	3,652	3,702	3,837	3,654	3,625	3,796	3,968	3,744	3,695
2002	3,508	3,498	3,360	3,647	3,709	3,679	3,561	3,538	3,536	3,380	3,768	3,922	3,592
2003	3,403	3,459	3,732	3,796	3,833	3,728	3,673	3,730	3,721	3,750	3,800	3,845	3,707
2004	3,592	3,446	3,550	3,874	3,857	3,956	3,902	3,981	3,625	3,808	4,004	4,159	3,813
2005	3,777	3,797	3,874	4,028	4,179	4,274	4,236	4,108	3,570	3,585	3,966	4,044	3,953
2006	3,840	3,941	3,736	3,833	4,105	4,107	4,065	4,234	4,300	4,090	4,070	4,159	4,040
2007	4,256	4,582	4,334	4,214	4,068	4,114	4,026	4,146	4,161	4,213	4,074	4,193	4,198
2008	4,192	4,281	4,161	4,106	3,931	3,763	3,688	3,659	3,740	4,182	3,872	3,783	3,947
2009[1]	4,075	3,915	3,732	3,460	3,421	3,550	3,464	3,383	3,459	3,677	3,549	3,704	3,616

[1] Preliminary. *Source: Energy Information Administration; U.S. Department of Energy (EIA-DOE)*

Imports of Distillate Fuel Oil in the United States In Thousand of Barrels per Day

Year	Jan.	Feb.	Mar.	Apr.	May	June	July	Aug.	Sept.	Oct.	Nov.	Dec.	Average
2002	298	248	234	219	193	204	188	205	196	350	373	496	267
2003	325	503	460	246	287	337	299	375	352	281	241	305	333
2004	370	507	449	267	275	324	283	313	272	243	319	292	326
2005	353	344	257	264	281	236	243	263	275	507	486	435	329
2006	552	388	292	297	437	297	361	363	438	307	288	355	365
2007	352	334	360	322	272	273	318	346	261	288	245	241	301
2008	309	249	249	266	188	180	181	109	195	166	203	262	213
2009[1]	368	327	268	166	206	244	191	166	205	177	163	264	229

[1] Preliminary. *Source: Energy Information Administration, U.S. Department of Energy (EIA-DOE)*

Exports of Distillate Fuel Oil from the United States In Thousand of Barrels per Day

Year	Jan.	Feb.	Mar.	Apr.	May	June	July	Aug.	Sept.	Oct.	Nov.	Dec.	Average
2001	67	77	75	107	146	120	113	140	152	99	132	202	119
2002	109	279	67	68	74	93	44	119	127	96	114	171	112
2003	119	132	161	139	162	101	103	80	43	62	81	100	107
2004	72	86	99	92	100	163	113	120	88	101	102	176	109
2005	49	102	165	192	199	227	189	163	108	109	92	65	138
2006	123	156	120	200	229	187	231	191	456	291	252	149	215
2007	253	202	155	167	227	240	243	311	274	173	188	NA	221
2008[1]	NA	NA	NA	NA	NA	NA	NA	NA	NA	NA	NA	NA	NA

[1] Preliminary. *Source: Energy Information Administration, U.S. Department of Energy (EIA-DOE)*

Disposition of Distillate Fuel Oil, Total Product Supplied in the United States In Thousand of Barrels per Day

Year	Jan.	Feb.	Mar.	Apr.	May	June	July	Aug.	Sept.	Oct.	Nov.	Dec.	Average
2002	3,940	3,714	3,750	3,821	3,679	3,587	3,683	3,728	3,730	3,808	3,929	3,934	3,776
2003	4,301	4,362	4,001	3,951	3,651	3,781	3,680	3,752	3,871	3,945	3,824	4,037	3,927
2004	4,334	4,232	4,152	4,145	3,840	3,888	3,827	3,887	4,065	4,104	4,058	4,176	4,059
2005	4,223	4,202	4,349	4,101	4,037	4,038	3,854	4,020	4,116	4,079	4,061	4,339	4,118
2006	4,159	4,308	4,395	4,065	4,072	4,019	3,950	4,162	4,141	4,315	4,180	4,268	4,170
2007	4,256	4,582	4,334	4,214	4,068	4,114	4,026	4,146	4,161	4,213	4,074	4,193	4,198
2008	4,192	4,281	4,161	4,106	3,931	3,763	3,688	3,659	3,740	4,182	3,872	3,783	3,947
2009[1]	4,075	3,915	3,732	3,460	3,421	3,550	3,464	3,383	3,459	3,677	3,549	3,704	3,616

[1] Preliminary. *Source: Energy Information Administration, U.S. Department of Energy (EIA-DOE)*

Production of Residual Fuel Oil in the United States In Thousands of Barrels per Day

Year	Jan.	Feb.	Mar.	Apr.	May	June	July	Aug.	Sept.	Oct.	Nov.	Dec.	Average
2002	625	613	617	601	582	540	566	583	607	593	648	641	601
2003	658	683	652	632	729	666	632	663	662	640	616	686	660
2004	656	659	635	701	668	648	618	631	617	610	703	723	656
2005	701	691	619	598	645	673	614	594	555	530	642	674	628
2006	670	635	644	643	580	645	658	652	619	597	624	656	635
2007	667	650	656	658	647	628	708	698	698	689	694	676	672
2008	588	643	662	710	734	695	584	579	485	575	588	597	620
2009[1]	582	572	584	476	606	614	588	632	606	673	626	575	595

[1] Preliminary. *Source: Energy Information Administration, U.S. Department of Energy (EIA-DOE)*

Supply and Disposition of Residual Fuel Oil in the United States

	Supply		Disposition				
Year	Total Production	Imports	Stock Change	Exports	Product Supplied	Ending Stocks (Million Barrels)	Average Sales to End Users[3] (Cents per Gallon)
	In Tousands of Barrels Per Day						
2000	696	352	1	139	909	36	60.2
2001	721	295	13	191	811	41	53.1
2002	601	249	-27	177	700	31	56.9
2003	660	327	18	197	772	38	69.8
2004	655	426	12	205	865	42	73.9
2005	628	530	-14	251	920	37	104.8
2006	635	350	14	283	689	42	121.8
2007[1]	669	368	-13	309	742	38	

[1] Preliminary. [2] Less than +500 barrels per day and greater than -500 barrels per day. [3] Refiner price excluding taxes.
Source: Energy Information Administration, U.S. Department of Energy (EIA-DOE)

Hides and Leather

Hides and leather have been used since ancient times for boots, clothing, shields, armor, tents, bottles, buckets, and cups. Leather is produced through the tanning of hides, pelts, and skins of animals. The remains of leather have been found in the Middle East dating back at least 7,000 years.

Today, most leather is made of cowhide but it is also made from the hides of lamb, deer, ostrich, snakes, crocodiles, and even stingray. Cattle hides are the most valuable byproduct of the meat packing industry. U.S. exports of cowhides bring more than $1 billion in foreign trade, and U.S. finished leather production is worth about $4 billion.

Prices – The average monthly price of wholesale cattle hides (packer heavy native steers FOB Chicago) in 2008 fell -10.8% yr/yr to 80.75 cents per pound, down from last year's record high of 90.53 cents per pound.

Supply – World production of cattle and buffalo hides in 2005 (latest data available) rose by +2.9% yr/yr to a record high of 8.769 million metric tons. The world's largest producers of cattle and buffalo hides in 2005 were the U.S. with 11% of world production, Brazil with 10%, and Argentina with 5%. U.S. new supply of cattle hides from domestic slaughter in 2004 (latest data available) fell 7.8% yr/yr to 32,728 million hides, which is far below the record high of 43.582 million hides posted in 1976. U.S. production of leather footwear has been dropping off sharply in recent years due to the movement of production offshore to lower cost producers. U.S. production of leather footwear in 2003 (latest data available) fell -46% yr/yr to 22.3 million pairs and was a mere 4% of the 562.3 million pairs produced in 1970.

Demand – World consumption of cowhides and skins in 2000, the last reporting year for the series, rose +1.4% to 4,774 metric tons, which was a record high for the data series, which goes back to 1984. The world's largest consumers of cowhides and skins in 2000 were the U.S. with 13.0% of world consumption, Italy (10.6%), Brazil (8.9%), Mexico, (6.0%), Argentina (6.0%), and South Korea (5.9%).

Trade – U.S. net exports of cattle hides in 2004 (latest data available) fell –4.3% yr/yr to 17.388 million hides from the 15-year high of 21.750 million hides posted in 2001. The total value of U.S. leather exports in 2004 rose +16.8% yr/yr to $1.344 billion. The largest destinations for U.S. exports in 2008 were South Korea (which took 15% of U.S. exports), Mexico (7%), Taiwan (5%), Thailand (3%), and Italy (2%). World imports of cowhides and skins in 2000 (latest data available) rose +2.8% yr/yr to a record high of 2,058 metric tons. The world's largest importers of cowhides and skins in 2000 were South Korea (with 13% of world imports in 2000), Italy (11%) and Taiwan (7%).

World Production of Cattle and Buffalo Hides In Thousands of Metric Tons

Year	Argentina	Australia	Brazil	Canada	Colombia	France	Germany	Italy	Mexico	Russia	United Kingdom	United States	World Total
1999	364	241	667	98	86	151	162	145	170	229	64	1,099	8,001
2000	372	238	670	96	82	150	152	143	175	232	68	1,116	8,184
2001	348	254	725	95	76	150	153	130	178	220	61	1,031	8,008
2002	345	243	750	96	72	160	151	132	178	224	65	1,054	8,158
2003	375	248	770	88	72	157	141	130	180	229	63	1,046	8,280
2004	429	243	792	111	80	150	145	128	191	223	66	962	8,376
2005	428	255	850	112	86	150	132	126	192	203	68	949	8,455
2006	402	255	886	104	85	150	135	125	197	183	68	949	8,544
2007[1]	405	255	914	96	88	150	132	126	199	180	68	949	8,591
2008[2]	405	255	914	96	94	150	132	125	199	182	68	949	8,615

[1] Preliminary. [2] Forecast. *Source: Food and Agricultural Organization of the United Nations (FAO-UN)*

Salient Statistics of Hides and Leather in the United States In Thousands of Equivalent HIdes

	New Supply of Cattle hides – Domestic Slaughter				Wholesale Prices – Cents Per Pound		Production			Wholesale Leather Indicies – Upper		Footwear	
Year	Federally Inspected	Uninspected[4]	Total Production	Net Exports	Heavy Native Cows[2]	Heavy Native[3] Steers	All U.S. Tanning	Cattle-hide	Value of Leather Exports ($1,000)	Men	Women	Production[5]	Exports
	Thousands of Equivalent Hides						In 1,000 Equiv. Hides			(1982 = 100)		Million Pairs	
1996	36,583	177	36,760	18,626	92.15	86.4	18,769	18,135	950,510	152.4	132.1	127,315	23,726
1997	35,567	751	36,492	17,562	90.99	86.1	19,592	18,930	1,145,664	156.4	132.2	124,444	21,958
1998	34,787	677	35,637	15,937	75.45	69.5	20,297	19,706	1,289,547	158.0	132.4	108,536	19,009
1999	36,150	664	36,320	15,700	73.80	73.1	21,342	20,620	1,137,534	157.0	133.0	78,581	18,176
2000	36,246	615	36,416	19,670	83.41	81.2	17,332	16,746	1,125,957	157.2	133.6	58,870	20,157
2001	34,771	599	35,370	21,750	85.52	89.8	14,212	13,779	1,221,131	158.4	133.8	55,600	19,472
2002	35,120	614	35,734	19,484	85.73	82.3		16,403	1,161,944	158.8	133.5	41,100	21,582
2003	34,907	590	35,493	18,177	88.34	83.8		17,470	1,150,212	161.4	132.1	22,300	21,319
2004[1]	32,156		32,728	17,388		82.2		15,492	1,344,017	161.7	129.2		21,464
2005[1]										163.5	132.1		

[1] Preliminary. [2] Central U.S., heifers. [3] F.O.B. Chicago. [4] Includes farm slaughter; diseased & condemned animals & hides taken off fallen animals.
[5] Other than rubber. *Sources: Leather Industries of America (LIA); Bureau of Labor Statistics, U.S. Department of Commerce (BLS)*

HIDES AND LEATHER

Production of All Footwear (Shoes, Sandals, Slippers, Athletic, Etc.) in the United States In Millions of Pairs

Year	First Quarter	Second Quarter	Third Quarter	Fourth Quarter	Total	Year	First Quarter	Second Quarter	Third Quarter	Fourth Quarter	Total
1994	42.5	40.8	40.1	39.5	163.0	1999	26.7	26.1	24.5	21.7	78.5
1995	37.2	38.3	34.8	36.7	147.0	2000	----	----	----	----	58.8
1996	33.2	31.8	29.7	33.2	128.0	2001	----	----	----	----	55.6
1997	31.4	33.1	28.6	30.6	124.4	2002	----	----	----	----	41.1
1998	32.8	31.8	29.3	28.6	108.5	2003[1]	----	----	----	----	22.3

[1] Preliminary. *Source: Bureau of the Census, U.S. Department of Commerce*

Average Factory Price[2] of Footwear in the United States In Dollars Per Pair

Year	First Quarter	Second Quarter	Third Quarter	Fourth Quarter	Total	Year	First Quarter	Second Quarter	Third Quarter	Fourth Quarter	Total
1994	25.77	23.60	21.49	22.44	23.22	1999	23.33	22.70	19.90	19.50	21.19
1995	19.61	21.46	25.37	21.26	21.79	2000	----	----	----	----	24.14
1996	23.65	22.78	22.14	20.38	22.07	2001	----	----	----	----	25.66
1997	22.42	21.56	22.21	22.24	22.11	2002	----	----	----	----	24.12
1998	24.39	24.21	20.27	19.78	21.84	2003[1]	----	----	----	----	45.95

[1] Preliminary. [2] Average value of factory shipments per pair. *Source: Bureau of the Census, U.S. Department of Commerce*

Imports and Exports of All Cattle Hides in the United States In Thousands of Hides

	----- Imports -----		---------- U.S. Exports - by Country of Destination ----------										
Year	Total	From Canada	Total	Canada	Italy	Japan	Rep of Korea	Mexico	Portugal	Romania	Spain	Taiwan	Thailand
1999	1,906	1,742	17,621	829	738	1,252	6,038	2,723	46	0	262	2,863	343
2000	1,972	1,876	21,658	875	1,163	1,529	7,673	2,196	37	0	189	2,844	562
2001	1,721	1,615	23,471	716	920	1,343	7,602	1,647	54	0	159	2,751	888
2002	1,298	1,227	20,784	837	1,099	584	5,812	1,470	14	0	189	2,145	914
2003	2,934	1,888	19,139	530	779	483	4,784	1,257	6	0	63	1,982	788
2004	7,342	6,165	18,795	346	417	468	4,218	1,419	4	0	16	1,842	684
2005	3,698	2,888	19,231	141	568	334	4,048	1,288	2	0	8	1,730	652
2006	2,175	1,602	20,059	57	523	277	3,455	1,225	5	0	41	1,902	441
2007	1,924	1,182	17,687	91	191	234	2,867	1,243	3	0	44	1,260	724
2008[1]	1,722	1,100	15,157	111	246	150	2,240	1,045	0	0	99	749	428

[1] Preliminary. *Source: Leather Industries of America*

Imports of Bovine Hides and Skins by Selected Countries In Metric Tons

Year	Brazil	Canada	Hong Kong	Italy	Japan	Mexico	Portugal	Rep. of Korea	Spain	Taiwan	Turkey	United States	World Total
1992	11	17	80	131	188	71	32	385	26	91	28	65	1,266
1993	21	26	81	141	188	71	39	372	35	94	37	57	1,426
1994	16	28	95	243	139	60	56	356	29	112	17	49	1,556
1995	33	35	100	250	152	30	43	342	42	112	43	57	1,715
1996	20	34	79	263	123	71	42	341	33	124	50	60	1,692
1997	13	39	64	254	114	96	37	323	44	140	68	60	1,985
1998	10	42	71	249	96	110	39	229	44	142	45	59	1,876
1999[1]	8	34	91	215	95	115	42	254	29	142	55	57	2,002
2000[2]	8	36	93	220	95	115	43	260	30	142	60	57	2,058

[1] Preliminary. [2] Forecast. *Source: Foreign Agricultural Service, U.S. Department of Agriculture (FAS-USDA)*

Exports of Bovine Hides and Skins by Selected Countries In Metric Tons

Year	Australia	Brazil	Canada	Germany	Hong Kong	Italy	Netherlands	New Zealand	Poland	Russia	United Kingdom	United States	World Total
1992	144	71	74	38	75	9	66	31	17	28	19	610	1,261
1993	142	76	87	40	76	7	35	21	5	150	25	581	1,374
1994	96	84	79	24	93	10	37	22	2	216	22	455	1,271
1995	85	148	90	34	100	10	47	22	2	195	22	510	1,351
1996	93	174	97	33	72	20	47	28	3	212	24	506	1,423
1997	115	216	97	35	60	16	48	27	3	210	25	473	1,475
1998	111	220	86	31	69	24	32	28	6	202	17	443	1,400
1999[1]	115	230	83	28	90	7	30	30	7	190	15	436	1,389
2000[2]	108	250	85	31	92	8	25	30	7	170	15	427	1,399

[1] Preliminary. [2] Forecast. *Source: Foreign Agricultural Service, U.S. Department of Agriculture (FAS-USDA)*

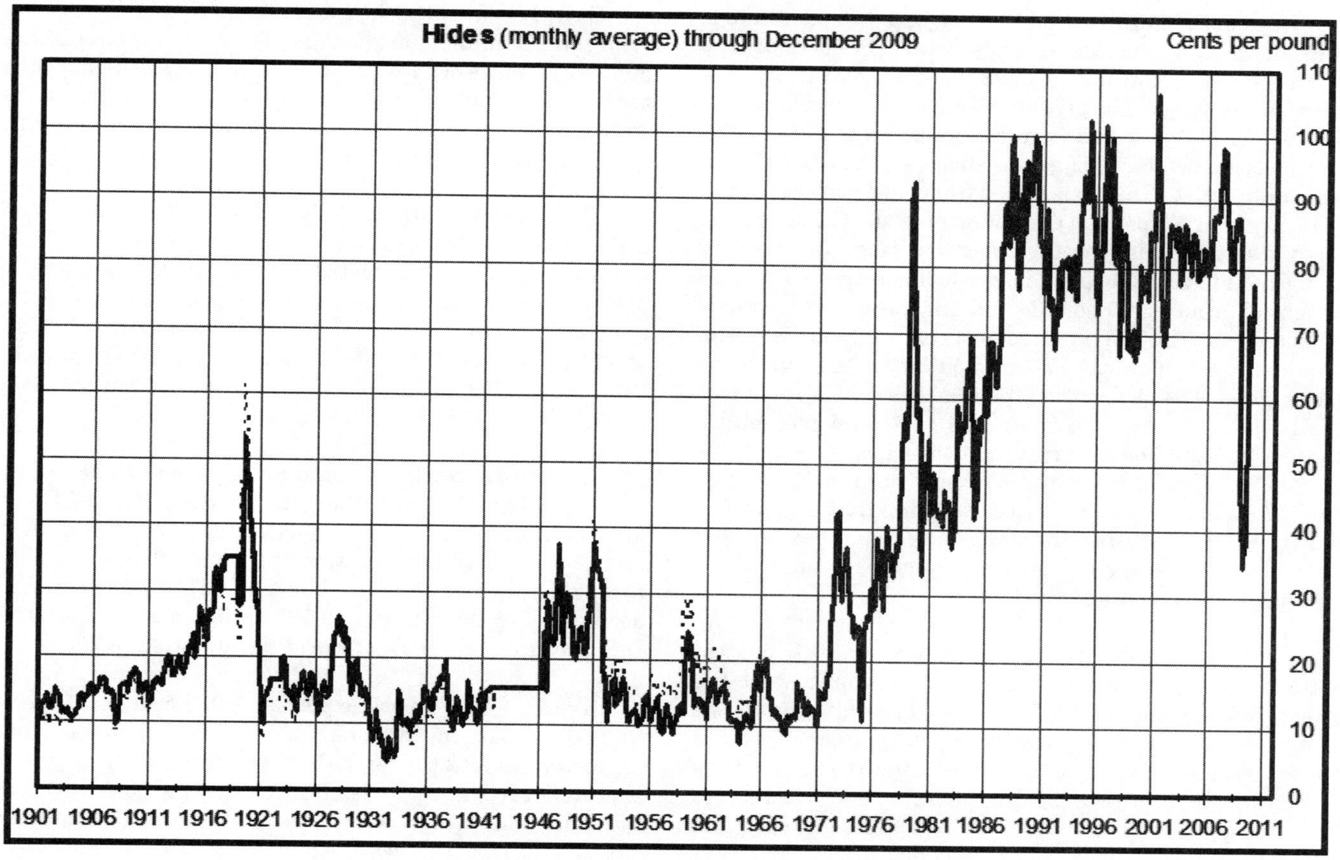

Utilization of Bovine Hides and Skins by Selected Countries In Metric Tons

Year	Argentina	Brazil	Colombia	Germany	Italy	Japan	Mexico	Rep. of Korea	Spain	Taiwan	Turkey	United States	World Total
1992	298	382	97	129	435	229	231	400	98	91	90	528	3,977
1993	302	510	94	100	435	226	232	385	98	94	95	554	4,322
1994	304	505	96	83	550	200	226	374	94	112	85	536	4,282
1995	300	493	89	79	570	191	200	355	98	112	100	523	4,365
1996	308	461	91	80	615	165	230	353	95	124	110	548	4,332
1997	332	387	89	101	570	150	251	347	106	140	120	572	4,609
1998	285	412	91	100	540	135	275	265	108	142	100	603	4,584
1999[1]	300	415	89	102	500	130	280	280	104	142	110	623	4,707
2000[2]	285	425	89	103	505	130	285	283	108	142	120	623	4,774

[1] Preliminary. [2] Forecast. *Source: Foreign Agricultural Service, U.S. Department of Agriculture (FAS-USDA)*

Wholesale Price of Hides (Packer Heavy Native Steers) F.O.B. Chicago In Cents Per Pound

Year	Jan.	Feb.	Mar.	Apr.	May	June	July	Aug.	Sept.	Oct.	Nov.	Dec.	Average
2000	75.92	76.29	77.86	78.83	79.24	75.18	77.25	81.64	85.60	84.89	84.41	85.31	80.20
2001	85.33	84.12	93.02	102.64	106.19	97.31	87.59	77.28	73.51	70.58	73.30	69.16	85.00
2002	68.23	72.39	80.41	83.21	84.32	86.72	84.43	85.77	85.84	85.75	83.35	85.18	82.13
2003	83.77	85.81	86.04	85.81	79.42	77.64	80.53	84.09	86.78	86.13	85.89	86.05	84.00
2004	85.17	81.79	82.89	79.15	80.16	82.43	85.11	84.54	85.05	82.23	81.42	78.02	82.33
2005	78.14	80.90	79.04	80.45	79.49	83.07	82.70	81.78	80.58	80.44	80.07	79.03	80.47
2006	79.28	81.01	83.86	84.95	87.76	88.07	87.93	87.15	88.29	88.08	88.81	90.50	86.31
2007	93.75	95.85	95.66	98.13	97.68	93.19	87.36	86.95	86.14	83.08	84.72	83.83	90.53
2008	79.55	79.43	82.79	85.58	85.82	87.01	87.55	87.49	85.10	85.31	78.38	44.98	80.75
2009	43.75	43.09	34.55	36.22	38.33	46.84	53.76	73.02	68.86	65.35	74.23	77.51	54.63

Source: National Agricultural Statistics Service, U.S. Department of Agriculture (NASS-USDA)

Hogs

Hogs are generally bred twice a year in a continuous cycle designed to provide a steady flow of production. The gestation period for hogs is 3-1/2 months and the average litter size is 9 pigs. The pigs are weaned at 3-4 weeks of age. The pigs are then fed so as to maximize weight gain. The feed consists primarily of grains such as corn, barley, milo, oats, and wheat. Protein is added from oilseed meals. Hogs typically gain 3.1 pounds per pound of feed. The time from birth to slaughter is typically 6 months. Hogs are ready for slaughter at about 254 pounds, producing a dressed carcass weight of around 190 pounds and an average 88.6 pounds of lean meat. The lean meat consists of 21% ham, 20% loin, 14% belly, 3% spareribs, 7% Boston butt roast and blade steaks, and 10% picnic, with the remaining 25% going into jowl, lean trim, fat, miscellaneous cuts, and trimmings. Futures on lean hogs are traded at the Chicago Mercantile Exchange. The futures contract is settled in cash based on the CME Lean Hog Index price, meaning that no physical delivery of hogs occurs. The CME Lean Hog Index is based on the 2-day average net price of slaughtered hogs at the average lean percentage level.

Prices – Lean hog futures prices on the nearest futures chart fell sharply in late 2008 along with the rest of the commodity markets due to the financial crisis and the ensuing global recession. The financial crisis caused producers to trim their herds and take more hogs to market, thus pressuring hog prices. Lean hog futures traded sideways in the first half of 2009 as supply and demand stabilized. Hog prices fell sharply to a new 7-year low in August 2009 due to a collapse in US pork exports from fears about H1NI flu, otherwise known as swine flu. US pork exports were down 19% y/y in January through August 2009. However, hog prices then rallied sharply going into late 2009 and early 2010 as herds were trimmed and supplies tightened. US producers by late 2009 cut the size of the breeding herd to the smallest level since 1973. Lean hog futures prices ended 2009 at 65.70 cents per pound, which was up 7.9% from the 2008 close of 60.875 cents per pound.

Supply – World pork production in 2009 rose +1.7% yr/yr to 100.236 million metric tons. The USDA is forecasting another increase of +1.6% in 2010 to 101.883 million metric tons. The world's largest pork producers are China with 48% of world production in 2009, the European Union with 22%, and the U.S. with 10%.

U.S. pork production in 2009 fell -1.4% to 10.446 million metric tons, and is forecasted by the USDA to fall another -2.4% to 10.185 million metric tons in 2010. The number of hogs and pigs on U.S. farms in 2009 (Dec 1) fell by -2.0% to 65.807 million, down from the more than 6-decade high of 68.117 in 2007. The federally-inspected hog slaughter in the U.S. in 2009 fell -2.4% to 112.611, down from the 2008 record high of 115.421 million head.

Demand – World consumption of pork in 2009 rose by +1.7% yr/yr to 100.022 million metric tons. The USDA is forecasting an increase of +1.8% in 2010 to 101.867 million metric tons. U.S. consumption of pork in 2009 rose +1.4% to 8.925 million metric tons, but the USDA is forecasting a decrease of -2.4% in 2010 to 8.557 million metric tons. The U.S. accounted for 8.9% of world consumption in 2009.

Trade – World pork exports in 2009 fell -11.1% yr/yr to 5.465 million metric tons, but the USDA is forecasting an increase of +2.6% for 2010. The world's largest pork exporters are the U.S. with 34% of world exports in 2009, the European Union with 23%, Canada with 21%, and Brazil with 12%. U.S. pork exports in 2009 fell -10.9% yr/yr to 1.887 million metric tons but the USDA is forecasting a rise of +6.9% in 2010 to 2.018 million metric tons.

World pork imports in 2009 fell -10.0% to 5.323 million metric tons, but the USDA is forecasting a rise of +1.7% to 5.412 million metric tons in 2010. The world's largest pork importers are Japan, which accounted for 23% of world imports in 2009, Russia (14%), Mexico (11%), South Korea (7%), and the U.S. (7%).

Salient Statistics of Pigs and Hogs in the United States

	Pig Crop						Value of Hogs on Farms, Dec. 1-					Hogs Slaughtered, Thousand Head				
	Spring[3]			Fall[4]								Commercial				
Year	Sows Farrowed (1,000 Head)	Pig Crop (1,000 Head)	Pigs Per Litter	Sows Farrowed (1,000 Head)	Pig Crop (1,000 Head)	Pigs Per Litter	$ Per Head	Total Million $	Hog Marketings (1,000 Head)	Quantity Produced (Live Wt.) (Mil. Lbs.)	Value of Production (Million $)	Federally Inspected	Other	Total	Farm	Total
2000	5,683	50,087	8.81	5,727	50,660	8.85	77.0	4,542	118,418	25,717	10,791	96,436	1,540	97,976	130	98,106
2001	5,619	49,472	8.81	5,767	51,031	8.85	77.0	4,590	119,262	25,884	11,430	96,528	1,434	97,962	120	98,082
2002	5,776	50,858	8.81	5,716	50,820	8.89	71.0	4,231	124,013	26,274	8,691	98,915	1,348	100,263	115	100,378
2003	5,655	50,029	8.85	5,773	51,462	8.91	67.0	4,025	124,383	26,260	9,663	99,685	1,233	100,931	116	101,047
2004	5,706	50,737	8.89	5,793	52,043	8.98	103.0	6,303	127,563	26,689	13,072	102,361	1,103	103,463	114	103,577
2005	5,716	51,330	8.98	5,818	52,635	9.05	92.0	5,672	129,056	27,416	13,607	102,519	1,063	103,582	109	103,690
2006	5,768	52,242	9.06	5,862	53,376	9.11	89.0	5,586	132,262	28,149	12,702	103,689	1,048	104,737	105	104,842
2007	5,935	54,266	9.14	6,312	58,608	9.28	73.0	4,917	137,519	29,606	13,468	108,138	1,034	109,172	106	109,278
2008[1]	6,123	57,019	9.31	6,103	58,011	9.51			149,078	31,384	14,435	115,421	1,026	116,446	106	116,553
2009[2]	6,029	57,564	9.55	5,939	57,610	9.70						112,611	973	113,584		113,584

[1] Preliminary. [2] Estimate. [3] December-May. [4] June-November. *Source: Economic Research Service, U.S. Department of Agriculture (ERS-USDA)*

World Hog Numbers in Specified Countries as of January 1   In Thousands of Head

Year	Brazil	Canada	China	European Union	Japan	Rep. of Korea	Mexico	Philip-pines	Russia	Taiwan	Ukraine	United States	World Total
2001	32,440	13,576	416,336	158,765	9,788	7,350	9,372	11,715	15,780	7,495	7,652	59,110	773,889
2002	32,710	14,375	419,505	158,250	9,612	7,856	9,302	11,816	16,570	7,165	8,317	59,722	781,697
2003	32,655	14,745	417,762	160,486	9,725	8,110	9,284	12,218	17,000	6,794	9,204	59,554	785,949
2004	32,081	14,725	413,818	158,970	9,724	8,367	9,389	12,518	17,200	6,779	7,321	60,453	781,054
2005	32,323	14,810	421,234	156,973	9,600	8,044	9,068	12,139	16,500	6,819	6,466	60,982	785,946
2006	32,938	15,110	433,191	159,115	9,620	8,098	8,911	13,041	16,550	7,172	7,052	61,463	804,551
2007	33,147	14,907	418,504	161,526	9,759	8,518	9,021	13,693	17,180	7,092	8,055	62,516	797,126
2008	32,947	13,810	439,895	159,732	9,745	8,742	9,401		18,187		7,020	68,177	772,659
2009[1]	33,892	12,180	462,913	152,960	9,899	8,223	9,310		19,562		6,526	67,148	784,794
2010[2]	35,122	10,632	485,005	149,250	9,900	8,200	9,500		20,230		7,150	65,150	802,339

[1] Preliminary. [2] Forecast. *Source: Foreign Agricultural Service, U.S. Department of Agriculture (FAS-USDA)*

Hogs and Pigs on Farms in the United States on December 1   In Thousands of Head

Year	Georgia	Illinois	Indiana	Iowa	Kansas	Minne-sota	Missouri	Nebraska	North Carolina	Ohio	South Dakota	Wisconsin	Total
2000	380	4,150	3,350	15,100	1,520	5,800	2,900	3,050	9,300	1,490	1,320	610	59,138
2001	315	4,250	3,200	15,400	1,570	5,800	3,000	2,900	9,800	1,430	1,290	540	59,804
2002	345	4,150	3,250	15,500	1,530	6,100	2,950	3,000	9,700	1,440	1,330	520	59,554
2003	295	4,000	3,100	15,900	1,650	6,500	2,950	2,900	10,000	1,520	1,280	480	60,444
2004	275	4,100	3,200	16,300	1,710	6,500	2,900	2,850	9,900	1,450	1,340	430	60,975
2005	270	4,000	3,250	16,600	1,790	6,600	2,700	2,850	9,800	1,560	1,490	430	61,449
2006	245	4,200	3,350	17,300	1,840	6,900	2,800	3,050	9,500	1,690	1,270	450	62,490
2007	265	4,350	3,700	19,400	1,880	7,700	3,150	3,350	10,200	1,830	1,460	440	68,177
2008	235	4,350	3,550	19,900	1,740	7,500	3,150	3,350	9,700	1,940	1,280	360	67,148
2009[1]	210	4,350	3,650	19,300	1,810	7,400	3,100	3,150	9,700	2,020	1,170	360	65,807

[1] Preliminary. *Source: National Agricultural Statistics Service, U.S. Department of Agriculture (NASS-USDA)*

Hog-Corn Price Ratio[2] in the United States

Year	Jan.	Feb.	Mar.	Apr.	May	June	July	Aug.	Sept.	Oct.	Nov.	Dec.	Average
2000	19.3	20.2	20.5	23.3	22.9	25.6	29.5	28.8	25.8	23.8	19.8	20.2	23.3
2001	18.8	20.0	23.5	25.3	27.7	29.7	27.6	26.6	23.7	21.8	18.9	16.8	23.4
2002	19.1	19.9	18.6	16.6	17.2	18.2	18.4	13.4	10.7	13.2	12.2	13.1	15.9
2003	14.2	14.7	14.9	14.9	17.4	19.2	19.7	18.4	18.0	17.3	15.8	14.8	16.6
2004	15.4	16.3	17.2	16.4	19.7	20.3	22.7	23.6	24.9	24.4	27.1	25.7	21.1
2005	25.1	26.0	25.3	25.6	27.7	24.4	23.6	26.2	26.0	25.8	24.6	23.1	25.3
2006	20.4	21.1	20.8	19.6	22.2	25.1	23.5	24.7	22.2	18.2	15.6	14.5	20.7
2007	14.0	13.8	13.1	14.0	15.2	15.4	15.7	15.7	14.3	12.9	11.0	10.5	13.8
2008	9.3	9.3	8.6	8.6	10.5	9.8	10.3	11.5	10.5	11.1	9.6	10.2	9.9
2009[1]	9.8	11.3	11.3	11.5	11.2	10.7	12.0	11.2	11.6	10.5	11.0	12.5	11.2

[1] Preliminary. [2] Bushels of corn equal in value to 100 pounds of hog, live weight. *Source: Economic Research Service, U.S. Department of Agriculture (ERS-USDA)*

Cold Storage Holdings of Frozen Pork[2] in the United States, on First of Month   In Millions of Pounds

Year	Jan.	Feb.	Mar.	Apr.	May	June	July	Aug.	Sept.	Oct.	Nov.	Dec.
2000	415.4	481.4	523.5	534.7	532.1	537.9	495.5	478.5	455.6	439.5	438.6	445.6
2001	411.5	471.4	468.3	432.3	432.6	421.5	374.1	339.5	332.6	366.9	430.6	432.7
2002	465.0	503.9	510.9	531.5	567.7	548.0	497.8	472.2	464.4	480.2	489.8	463.9
2003	468.5	512.7	519.7	530.5	520.0	499.7	460.0	440.7	430.2	435.2	446.8	438.9
2004	470.7	504.1	477.1	447.3	448.6	412.8	373.0	366.8	382.1	413.8	423.1	436.3
2005	482.9	496.8	538.2	540.2	562.8	511.2	488.6	442.9	408.5	425.6	440.7	431.3
2006	421.3	527.7	528.0	505.0	520.0	477.0	412.6	417.8	415.6	458.4	488.4	468.5
2007	442.5	484.3	483.2	494.8	528.5	492.0	467.9	455.9	458.3	484.9	494.8	474.6
2008	458.7	574.9	611.8	657.3	663.4	579.4	530.1	505.3	502.7	526.2	528.0	526.7
2009[1]	555.6	606.9	624.5	594.1	612.3	584.5	577.9	539.7	530.1	528.7	516.3	482.8

[1] Preliminary. [2] Excludes lard. *Source: Economic Research Service, U.S. Department of Agriculture (ERS-USDA)*

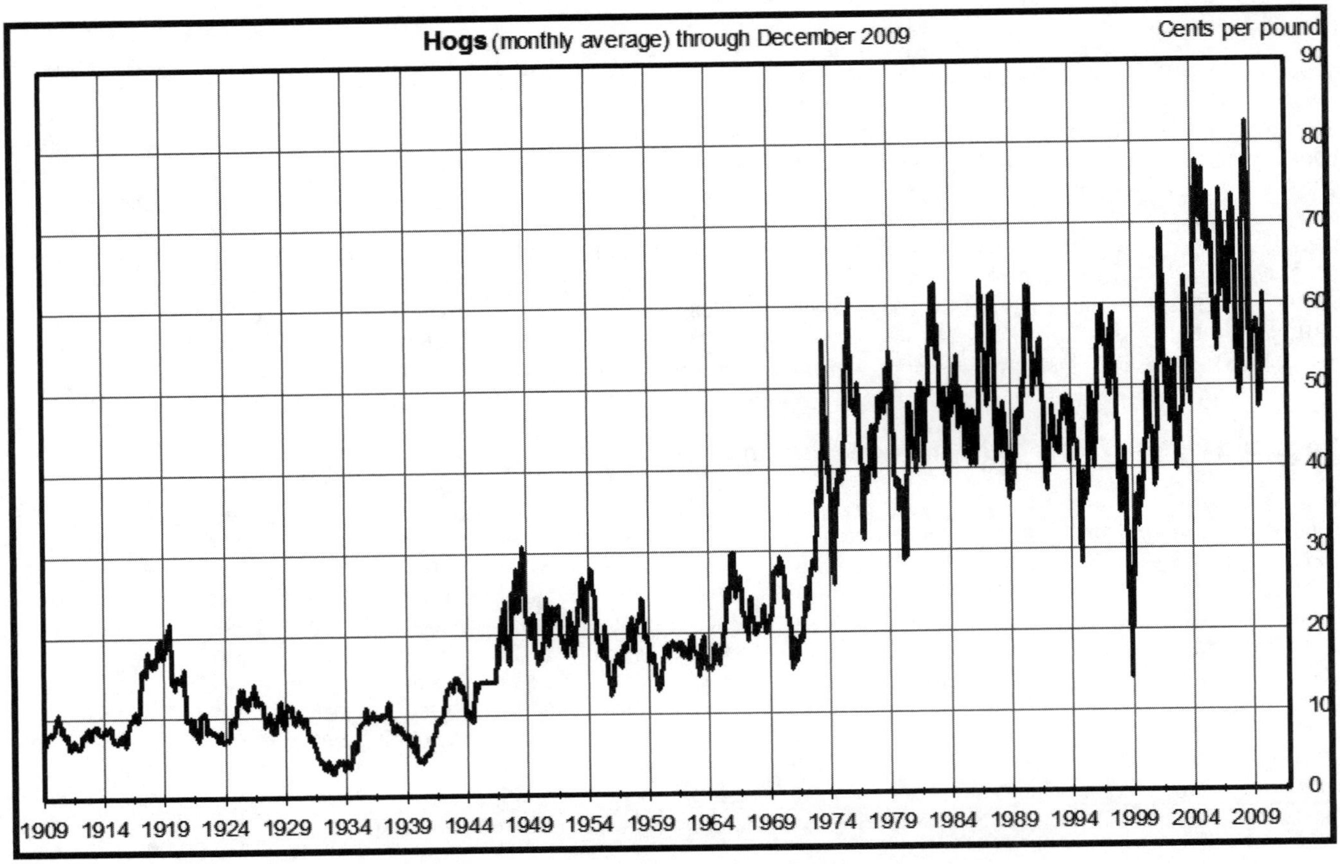

Average Price of Hogs, National Base 51-52% lean In Dollars Per Hundred Pounds (Cwt.)

Year	Jan.	Feb.	Mar.	Apr.	May	June	July	Aug.	Sept.	Oct.	Nov.	Dec.	Average
2000	38.32	41.58	43.52	49.59	50.21	51.48	50.45	45.35	43.49	43.09	37.84	41.40	44.69
2001	38.61	41.47	48.41	49.28	52.34	54.53	53.75	52.47	46.93	41.27	35.49	35.14	45.81
2002	40.16	40.65	37.47	32.97	34.64	37.32	40.53	34.00	26.98	31.69	29.99	32.35	34.90
2003	34.39	35.64	36.11	36.42	43.62	47.88	44.98	41.90	41.82	38.63	36.02	36.02	39.45
2004	39.02	45.21	48.30	48.34	58.45	57.95	58.21	56.19	55.34	53.68	56.23	53.15	52.51
2005	53.36	51.11	51.30	51.00	55.40	49.86	49.96	51.60	49.98	47.49	37.70	44.81	49.46
2006	41.37	43.17	43.34	41.45	49.00	54.90	51.89	53.32	50.28	47.57	45.97	44.84	47.26
2007	44.04	48.60	45.47	48.43	54.40	54.82	52.39	52.01	46.61	41.96	36.95	39.40	47.09
2008	36.77	42.74	39.40	45.06	57.75	54.71	56.48	62.56	52.76	47.06	38.90	39.80	47.83
2009[1]	41.43	42.43	42.47	42.83	43.18	42.21	42.74	36.56	37.41	37.65	40.12	45.82	41.24

[1] Preliminary. *Source: Economic Research Service, U.S. Department of Agriculture (ERS-USDA)*

Average Price Received by Farmers for Hogs in the United States In Cents Per Pound

Year	Jan.	Feb.	Mar.	Apr.	May	June	July	Aug.	Sept.	Oct.	Nov.	Dec.	Average
2000	36.8	39.9	41.7	47.4	48.3	48.9	48.3	43.8	41.6	41.4	36.8	39.8	42.9
2001	37.2	39.2	45.9	47.8	50.4	52.2	51.7	50.8	45.2	40.2	35.0	33.3	44.1
2002	37.7	38.5	36.0	31.7	33.2	35.8	39.2	31.9	26.5	30.8	27.8	30.3	33.3
2003	33.0	34.3	34.7	34.8	41.3	45.0	42.7	39.6	39.7	36.7	34.7	34.2	37.6
2004	36.8	42.6	47.2	47.4	56.6	56.7	57.1	55.3	54.8	52.2	55.6	52.4	51.2
2005	53.2	50.7	51.2	51.1	54.9	49.5	49.8	51.0	49.4	47.0	43.5	44.3	49.6
2006	40.7	42.6	42.8	41.3	48.2	53.8	50.2	51.6	48.9	46.5	44.9	43.5	46.3
2007	42.7	47.5	44.9	47.3	53.1	54.3	52.2	51.3	46.8	42.4	37.9	39.6	46.7
2008	37.2	42.2	40.3	44.4	55.3	53.4	54.3	60.7	52.6	48.5	40.7	41.9	47.6
2009[1]	42.8	43.8	43.8	44.1	44.5	43.3	43.2	37.4	37.7	37.8	40.2	45.0	42.0

[1] Preliminary. *Source: Economic Research Service, U.S. Department of Agriculture (ERS-USDA)*

Quarterly Hogs and Pigs Report in the United States, 10 States In Thousands of Head

Year[2]	Inventory[3]	Breeding[3]	Market[3]	Farrowings	Pig Crop
2000	59,342	6,234	53,109	11,410	100,747
I	59,342	6,234	53,109	2,798	24,522
II	57,782	6,190	51,593	2,885	25,565
III	59,117	6,234	52,884	2,889	25,548
IV	59,495	6,246	53,250	2,838	25,112
2001	59,138	6,270	52,868	11,385	100,503
I	59,138	6,270	52,868	2,748	23,963
II	57,524	6,232	51,292	2,870	25,509
III	58,603	6,186	52,417	2,878	25,539
IV	59,777	6,158	53,619	2,889	25,492
2002	59,804	6,209	53,594	11,492	101,677
I	59,804	6,209	53,594	2,835	24,857
II	59,256	6,230	53,026	2,941	26,001
III	60,391	6,208	54,183	2,883	25,725
IV	60,753	6,051	54,702	2,833	25,094
2003	59,554	6,058	53,496	11,429	101,491
I	59,554	6,058	53,496	2,769	24,400
II	58,183	6,027	52,156	2,886	25,629
III	59,602	6,026	53,576	2,918	25,974
IV	61,009	5,938	55,071	2,856	25,488
2004	60,444	6,009	54,434	11,499	102,781
I	60,444	6,009	54,434	2,836	25,105
II	59,520	5,961	53,558	2,870	25,633
III	60,698	5,937	54,760	2,905	26,162
IV	61,519	5,962	55,556	2,888	25,881
2005	60,975	5,969	55,005	11,535	103,965
I	60,975	5,969	55,005	2,835	25,343
II	59,699	5,941	53,757	2,882	25,986
III	60,732	5,977	54,754	2,918	26,449
IV	61,846	5,972	55,873	2,900	26,187
2006	61,449	6,011	55,438	11,629	105,618
I	61,449	6,011	55,438	2,841	25,662
II	60,326	6,025	54,301	2,927	26,580
III	61,687	6,060	55,627	2,912	26,519
IV	62,914	6,079	56,835	2,949	26,857
2007	62,490	6,087	56,402	12,248	112,873
I	62,490	6,087	56,402	2,905	26,395
II	61,896	6,149	55,746	3,030	27,870
III	63,947	6,169	57,777	3,133	29,095
IV	67,275	6,208	66,708	3,180	29,513
2008	68,177	6,233	61,944	12,226	115,030
I	68,177	6,233	61,944	3,071	28,388
II	67,218	6,200	61,018	3,052	28,631
III	67,400	6,131	61,269	3,075	29,240
IV	68,196	6,061	62,135	3,028	28,771
2009[1]	67,148	6,062	61,087	11,968	115,174
I	67,148	6,062	61,087	3,011	28,552
II	65,819	5,992	59,828	3,018	29,012
III	66,809	5,968	60,842	2,965	28,777
IV	66,826	5,875	60,952	2,974	28,833

[1] Preliminary. [2] Quarters are Dec. preceding year-Feb.(I), Mar.-May(II), June-Aug.(III) and Sept.-Nov.(IV).
[3] Beginning of period. *Source: National Agricultural Statistics Service, U.S. Department of Agriculture (NASS-USDA)*

Federally Inspected Hog Slaughter in the United States In Thousands of Head

Year	Jan.	Feb.	Mar.	Apr.	May	June	July	Aug.	Sept.	Oct.	Nov.	Dec.	Total
2000	8,010	7,955	8,695	7,108	7,816	7,823	7,235	8,481	7,992	8,746	8,633	7,943	96,436
2001	8,521	7,491	8,207	7,722	7,836	7,368	7,333	8,247	7,687	9,210	8,610	8,298	96,528
2002	8,552	7,400	7,879	8,321	8,215	7,425	7,957	8,425	8,384	9,276	8,548	8,534	98,915
2003	8,680	7,587	8,069	8,238	7,715	7,665	8,008	7,951	8,466	9,547	8,506	9,254	99,685
2004	8,704	7,805	8,942	8,567	7,494	8,415	8,008	8,616	8,897	8,883	8,881	9,150	102,361
2005	8,402	8,031	8,858	8,369	7,939	8,470	7,582	8,888	8,778	9,027	9,038	9,138	102,519
2006	8,834	7,978	9,148	7,884	8,450	8,256	7,805	8,991	8,738	9,541	9,276	8,788	103,689
2007	9,281	8,040	9,119	8,389	8,680	8,218	8,312	9,296	8,683	10,555	9,964	9,601	108,138
2008	10,474	9,297	9,579	9,911	8,981	8,801	9,373	9,170	9,878	10,654	9,250	10,053	115,421
2009[1]	9,846	8,840	9,574	9,353	8,379	9,101	9,062	9,250	9,848	10,230	9,385	9,742	112,611

[1] Preliminary. *Source: National Agricultural Statistics Service, U.S. Department of Agriculture (NASS-USDA)*

Average Live Weight of all Hogs Slaughtered Under Federal Inspection In Pounds Per Head

Year	Jan.	Feb.	Mar.	Apr.	May	June	July	Aug.	Sept.	Oct.	Nov.	Dec.	Average
2000	262	262	263	263	264	263	260	258	260	263	266	265	262
2001	265	264	264	265	264	264	261	258	262	267	269	268	264
2002	268	267	267	268	267	266	261	259	261	264	268	268	265
2003	268	267	268	268	268	266	263	261	263	268	270	269	267
2004	269	268	268	268	266	265	263	263	266	267	270	270	267
2005	270	270	271	271	270	269	265	263	265	269	272	272	269
2006	273	272	272	272	271	267	264	262	267	269	272	271	269
2007	271	270	271	270	269	267	265	264	267	270	273	272	269
2008	273	271	271	270	268	266	263	261	266	270	271	271	268
2009[1]	272	272	272	272	272	270	268	268	270	272	272	270	271

[1] Preliminary. *Source: National Agricultural Statistics Service, U.S. Department of Agriculture (NASS-USDA)*

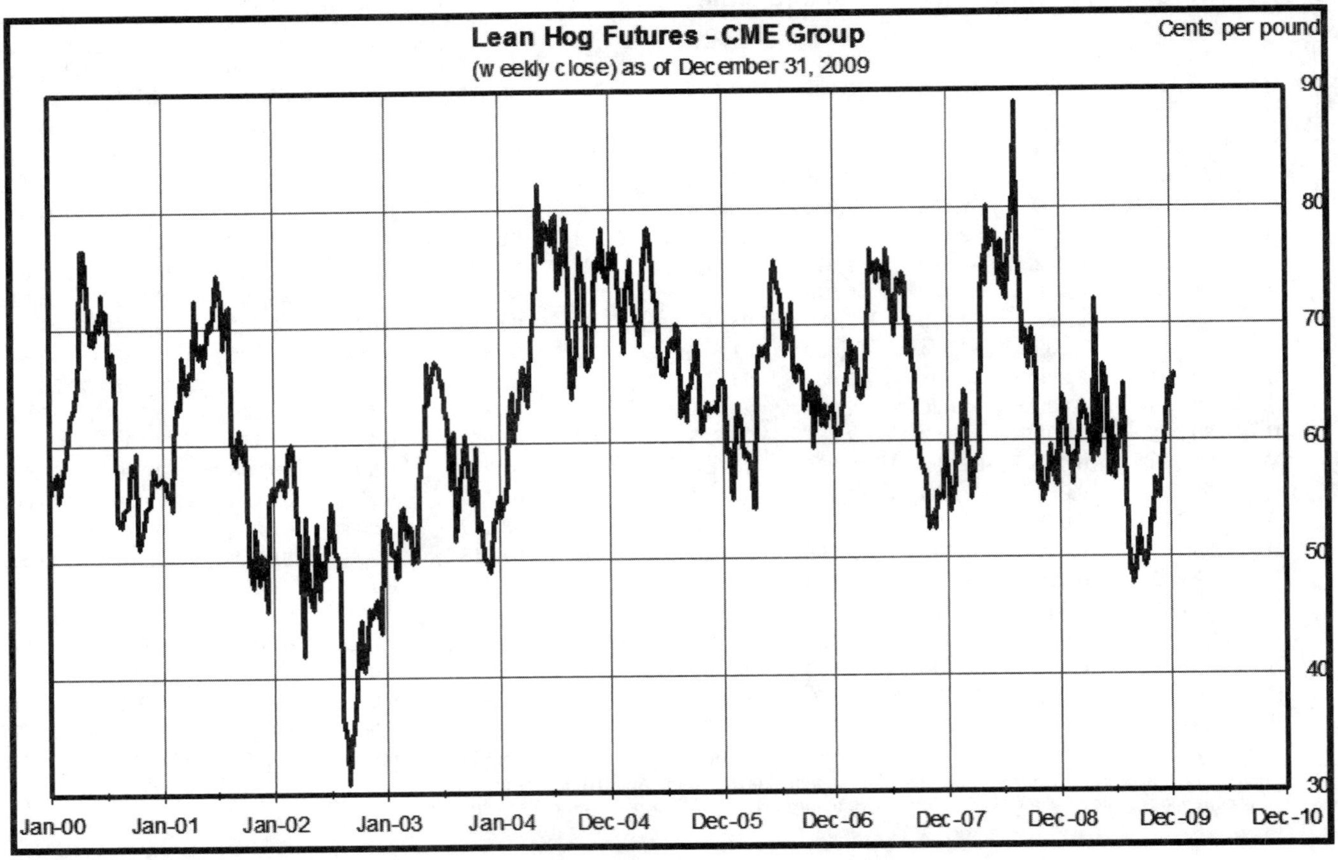

Average Open Interest of Lean Hog Futures in Chicago In Contracts

Year	Jan.	Feb.	Mar.	Apr.	May	June	July	Aug.	Sept.	Oct.	Nov.	Dec.
2000	49,209	54,094	57,472	68,535	64,938	54,208	45,730	38,233	38,802	38,254	40,075	45,141
2001	41,425	41,892	48,381	45,296	41,910	45,715	51,661	47,760	42,072	36,983	32,821	27,687
2002	28,720	31,662	33,056	33,472	33,161	28,719	29,338	32,030	36,136	35,245	42,852	43,974
2003	40,660	39,862	40,446	37,883	43,672	47,338	39,706	37,700	49,469	46,295	43,552	43,352
2004	46,380	55,058	63,889	77,756	80,271	81,370	79,860	84,840	86,092	86,423	94,336	98,328
2005	102,580	97,550	95,841	94,008	96,662	91,871	97,160	95,841	107,617	113,754	116,005	124,492
2006	133,258	144,506	145,020	144,250	157,259	158,276	157,899	165,781	176,336	174,971	188,965	179,057
2007	174,424	182,146	178,296	174,233	176,897	177,274	174,144	176,425	175,093	179,402	204,475	206,458
2008	212,644	227,377	219,938	232,309	252,497	242,588	238,162	231,283	206,602	171,506	168,129	159,600
2009	137,693	122,594	126,377	134,363	143,493	135,606	131,683	130,844	143,952	152,820	164,819	174,739

Source: Chicago Mercantile Exchange (CME)

Volume of Trading of Lean Hog Futures in Chicago In Contracts

Year	Jan.	Feb.	Mar.	Apr.	May	June	July	Aug.	Sept.	Oct.	Nov.	Dec.	Total
2000	175,399	186,352	231,532	158,765	218,222	235,036	172,725	145,849	146,240	142,240	153,043	146,404	2,111,807
2001	183,493	159,020	197,004	142,892	165,220	184,421	198,503	164,712	152,178	177,601	163,798	129,497	2,018,339
2002	145,266	120,994	168,929	196,956	163,816	158,074	166,064	140,154	174,797	167,065	165,039	164,106	1,931,260
2003	186,436	137,479	186,511	156,370	209,740	210,901	199,782	124,677	232,705	207,247	164,190	148,117	2,164,155
2004	212,420	170,270	249,205	211,501	295,271	304,279	315,197	215,233	356,295	242,204	376,823	255,488	3,204,186
2005	347,467	237,079	380,658	287,828	412,655	398,201	354,819	315,949	391,121	295,817	421,714	310,235	4,153,543
2006	561,152	319,827	597,852	356,950	658,973	826,312	578,656	478,837	577,375	533,532	649,293	342,242	6,481,001
2007	687,585	449,649	721,014	423,223	620,985	744,799	865,371	559,139	591,564	485,066	730,036	386,401	7,264,832
2008	800,566	527,093	809,724	736,404	796,703	938,662	968,358	617,855	781,563	506,765	576,326	445,119	8,505,138
2009	614,928	390,054	593,621	503,180	620,260	727,565	644,070	510,721	657,827	540,591	590,062	426,182	6,819,061

Source: Chicago Mercantile Exchange (CME)

Honey

Honey is the thick, supersaturated sugar solution produced by bees to feed their larvae. It is composed of fructose, glucose and water in varying proportions and also contains several enzymes and oils. The color of honey varies due to the source of nectar and age of the honey. Light colored honeys are usually of higher quality than darker honeys. The average honeybee colony can produce more than 700 pounds of honey per year but only 10 percent is usually harvested by the beekeeper. The rest of the honey is consumed by the colony during the year. American per capita honey consumption is 1 pound per person per year. Honey is said to be humanity's oldest sweet, and beeswax the first plastic.

Honey is used in many ways, including direct human consumption, baking, and medicine. Honey has several healing properties. Its high sugar content nourishes injured tissues, thus enhancing faster healing time. Honey's phytochemicals create a form of hydrogen peroxide that cleans out the wound, and the thick consistency protects the wound from contact with air Honey has also proven superior to antibiotic ointments for reducing rates of infection in people with burns.

Prices – U.S. average domestic honey prices in 2008 (latest data) rose by +30.9% to a record high of 141.0 cents per pound. The value of U.S. honey production in 2008 rose +42.0% to $226.814 million, but stayed well below the 2003 record high of $253.106 million.

Supply – World production of honey in 2008 (latest data available) rose +2.1% to 1.496 million metric tons, not far below the 2006 record high of 1.512 million metric tons. The major producer of honey by far is China with 367,219 metric tons in 2008 which is 25% of total world production. Other major producers in 2008 were Argentina with 81,000 metric tons, the U.S. with 72,965 metric tons, Russia with 57,440 metric tons, and Mexico with 55,271 metric tons.

U.S. production of honey in 2008 (latest data) rose +8.4% to 160.861 million pounds, remaining well below the 14-year high of 220.339 million pounds posted in 2000. Stocks fell by 4.2% to 50.445 million pounds in 2008 (Jan 1), but stayed well above the 25-year low of 39.4 million pounds posted in 2002. Yield per colony in 2008 rose +15.2% to 69.9 pounds per colony. The number of colonies in 2008 fell by -5.8% to a record low of 2.301 million.

Trade – U.S. imports of honey in 2008 (latest data) fell by -0.7% to 231.4 million pounds, down from the 2006 record high of 277.7 million pounds. U.S. exports of honey are generally small and in 2008 they totaled only 10.1 million pounds, which was only 6.3% of U.S. production.

World Production of Honey In Metric Tons

Year	Argentina	Australia	Brazil	Canada	China	Germany	Japan	Mexico	Russia	United States	Total
2002	83,000	18,000	23,995	37,072	267,830	14,620	3,300	58,890	49,400	77,890	1,283,709
2003	75,000	16,000	30,022	34,602	294,721	23,691	3,300	57,045	48,048	82,431	1,334,163
2004	80,000	16,000	32,290	34,241	297,987	25,575	3,300	56,917	52,666	83,272	1,369,788
2005	110,000	16,000	33,750	36,109	299,527	21,232	3,300	50,631	52,123	72,927	1,410,317
2006	105,000	17,500	36,194	48,353	337,578	25,199	3,300	55,970	55,678	70,238	1,511,560
2007	81,000	18,000	34,747	31,489	357,220	18,266	3,300	55,459	53,655	67,286	1,465,634
2008[1]	81,000	18,000	34,747	28,112	367,219	15,727	3,300	55,271	57,440	72,965	1,496,416

[1] Preliminary. NA = Not available. *Source: Food and Agricultural Organization of the United Nations (FAO)*

Salient Statistics of Honey in the United States In Millions of Pounds

Year	Number of Colonies (1,000)	Yield Per Colony (Pounds)	Stocks Jan. 1	Total U.S. Production	Imports for Consumption	Domestic Disappearance	Exports	Total Supply	Program Activity: Placed Under Loan	Program Activity: CCC Take Over	Program Activity: Net Gov't. Expenditure[3] (Million $)	Domestic Avg. Price All Honey - Cents Per Pound -	National Avg. Price Support - Cents Per Pound -	Per Capita Consumption (Pounds)
2004	2,556	71.8	61.2	183.6	178.6	----	7.8	423.4	----	----	----	106.9	----	----
2005	2,413	72.4	62.5	174.8	233.0	----	7.6	470.3	----	----	----	91.8	----	----
2006	2,393	64.7	60.5	154.9	277.7	----	7.0	493.1	----	----	----	103.6	----	----
2007	2,443	60.7	52.6	148.3	233.0	----	8.3	434.0	----	----	----	107.7	----	----
2008[1]	2,342	69.9	51.2	163.8	231.4	----	10.1	446.3	----	----	----	142.1	----	----
2009[2]	2,462	58.5	37.2	144.1		----			----	----	----	144.5	----	----

[1] Preliminary. [2] Forecast. [3] Fiscal year. *Source: Economic Research Service, U.S. Department of Agriculture (ERS-USDA)*

Production and Yield of Honey in the United States

Year	Production in Thousands of Pounds: California	Florida	Minnesota	North Dakota	South Dakota	Total	Value of Production ($1,000)	Yield Per Colony in Pounds: California	Florida	Minnesota	North Dakota	South Dakota	Average
2004	17,550	20,090	10,125	30,420	22,575	183,582	196,259	45	98	75	78	105	71.8
2005	30,000	13,760	8,880	33,670	17,380	174,818	160,428	75	86	74	91	79	72.4
2006	19,760	13,770	10,000	25,900	10,575	154,907	160,484	52	81	80	74	47	64.7
2007	13,600	11,360	8,840	31,080	13,260	148,341	159,763	40	71	68	74	52	60.8
2008	18,360	11,850	9,516	36,000	21,375	163,789	232,744	51	79	78	90	95	69.9
2009[1]	11,715	10,200	7,930	34,650	17,820	144,108	208,236	33	68	65	77	66	58.5

[1] Preliminary. *Source: National Agricultural Statistics Service, U.S. Department of Agriculture (NASS-USDA)*

Interest Rates - U.S.

U.S. interest rates can be characterized in two main ways, by credit quality and maturity. Credit quality refers to the level of risk associated with a particular borrower. U.S. Treasury securities, for example, carry the lowest risk. Maturity refers to the time at which the security matures and must be repaid. Treasury securities carry the full spectrum of maturities, from short-term cash management bills, to T-bills (4-weeks, 3-months, and 6-months), T-notes (2-year, 3-year, 5-year and 10-year), and 30-year T-bonds. The most active futures markets are the Treasury note and bond futures traded at the Chicago Board of Trade (CBOT) and the Eurodollar futures traded at the Chicago Mercantile Exchange (CME).

Prices – T-note prices spiked higher in late 2008 due to the global financial crisis, which had been brewing for two years but then exploded into international proportions with the bankruptcy of Lehman Brothers in mid-September 2008. T-note prices during the crisis rallied sharply on flight to quality and the deep economic recession that resulted from the financial crisis. However, T-note prices in the first half of 2009 fell back and returned to the area seen before the Lehman crisis. T-note prices fell in the first half of 2009 as the Federal Reserve got the financial crisis under control and the stock market rallied, thus causing flight-to-quality demand for T-notes to dry up. In addition, the U.S. recession ended in summer 2009 and GDP turned positive in the second half of 2009, thus putting additional downward pressure on T-note prices. T-note prices then staged a mild rally later in 2009 due to bumpy economic data and assurances from the Federal Reserve that a rate hike was a long time away.

The Fed started cutting its federal funds target rate in September 2007 from the 5.25% level as the U.S. housing and mortgage security crisis started to emerge. The Fed cut the funds rate sharply by a total of 325 bp to 2.00% by April 2008. When the Lehman Brothers bankruptcy occurred in September 2008, the Fed cut the funds rate further to 1.00% in October 2008 and then to the range of zero to 0.25% in December 2008. The funds rate remained in the range of zero to 0.25% all through 2009 and into early 2010. As of early 2010, the market consensus was that the Fed would leave the funds rate at zero to 0.25% at least through mid-2010 and then raise the funds rate very slowly to 1.00% by May 2011 and to 2.00% by February 2012.

The extremely low funds rate target of zero to 0.25% kept short-term rates locked at very low levels all through 2009. The 3-month Libor rate fell sharply from the 5.40% area in mid-2007 to 0.25% by mid-2009. The 2-year T-note yield during 2009 traded just below 1.00%. However, the 10-year T-note yield in 2009 reversed the plunge seen during the crisis and by early 2010 was trading at 3.60% as the market discounted a return to normal inflation levels over a 10-year time horizon. The low 2-year yield, combined with the more normalized 10-year yield, meant that the yield curve was very steep all through 2009. The yield curve, as defined by the 10-year T-note yield minus the 2-year T-note yield, rose sharply from near zero in mid-2007 to a record high of 280 basis points by early 2010. That steep yield curve was a big help for banks, which could profit by borrowing money at low short-term rates and then lend it out at higher long-term rates.

U.S. Producer Price Index[2] for All Commodities 1982 = 100

Year	Jan.	Feb.	Mar.	Apr.	May	June	July	Aug.	Sept.	Oct.	Nov.	Dec.	Average
2000	128.3	129.8	130.8	130.7	131.6	133.8	133.7	132.9	134.7	135.4	135.0	136.2	132.7
2001	140.0	137.4	135.9	136.4	136.8	135.5	133.4	133.4	133.3	130.3	129.8	128.1	134.2
2002	128.5	128.4	129.8	130.8	130.8	130.9	131.2	131.5	132.3	133.2	133.1	132.9	131.1
2003	135.3	137.6	141.2	136.8	136.7	138.0	137.7	138.0	138.5	139.3	138.9	139.5	138.1
2004	141.4	142.1	143.1	144.8	146.8	147.2	147.4	148.0	147.7	150.0	151.4	150.2	146.7
2005	150.9	151.6	153.7	155.0	154.3	154.3	156.3	157.6	162.2	166.2	163.7	163.0	157.4
2006	164.3	161.8	162.2	164.3	165.8	166.1	166.8	167.9	165.4	162.2	164.6	165.6	164.8
2007	164.0	166.8	169.3	171.4	173.3	173.8	175.1	172.4	173.5	174.7	179.0	178.6	172.7
2008	181.0	182.7	187.9	190.9	196.6	200.5	205.5	199.0	196.9	186.4	176.8	170.9	189.6
2009[1]	171.2	169.3	168.1	169.1	170.8	174.1	172.5	175.0	174.1	175.3	177.7	178.1	172.9

[1] Preliminary. [2] Not seasonally adjusted. *Source: Bureau of Labor Statistics, U.S. Department of Commerce (BLS)*

U.S. Consumer Price Index[2] for All Urban Consumers 1982-84 = 100

Year	Jan.	Feb.	Mar.	Apr.	May	June	July	Aug.	Sept.	Oct.	Nov.	Dec.	Average
2000	168.8	169.8	171.2	171.3	171.5	172.4	172.8	172.8	173.7	174.0	174.1	174.0	172.2
2001	175.1	175.8	176.2	176.9	177.7	178.0	177.5	177.5	178.3	177.7	177.4	176.7	177.1
2002	177.1	177.8	178.8	179.8	179.8	179.9	180.1	180.7	181.0	181.3	181.3	180.9	179.9
2003	181.7	183.1	184.2	183.8	183.5	183.7	183.9	184.6	185.2	185.0	184.5	184.3	184.0
2004	185.2	186.2	187.4	188.0	189.1	189.7	189.4	189.5	189.9	190.9	191.0	190.3	188.9
2005	190.7	191.8	193.3	194.6	194.4	194.5	195.4	196.4	198.8	199.2	197.6	196.8	195.3
2006	198.3	198.7	199.8	201.5	202.5	202.9	203.5	203.9	202.9	201.8	201.5	201.8	201.6
2007	202.4	203.5	205.4	206.7	207.9	208.4	208.3	207.9	208.5	208.9	210.2	210.0	207.3
2008	211.1	211.7	213.5	214.8	216.6	218.8	220.0	219.1	218.8	216.6	212.4	210.2	215.3
2009[1]	211.1	212.2	212.7	213.2	213.9	215.7	215.4	215.8	216.0	216.2	216.3	215.9	214.5

[1] Preliminary. [2] Not seasonally adjusted. *Source: Bureau of Labor Statistics, U.S. Department of Commerce (BLS)*

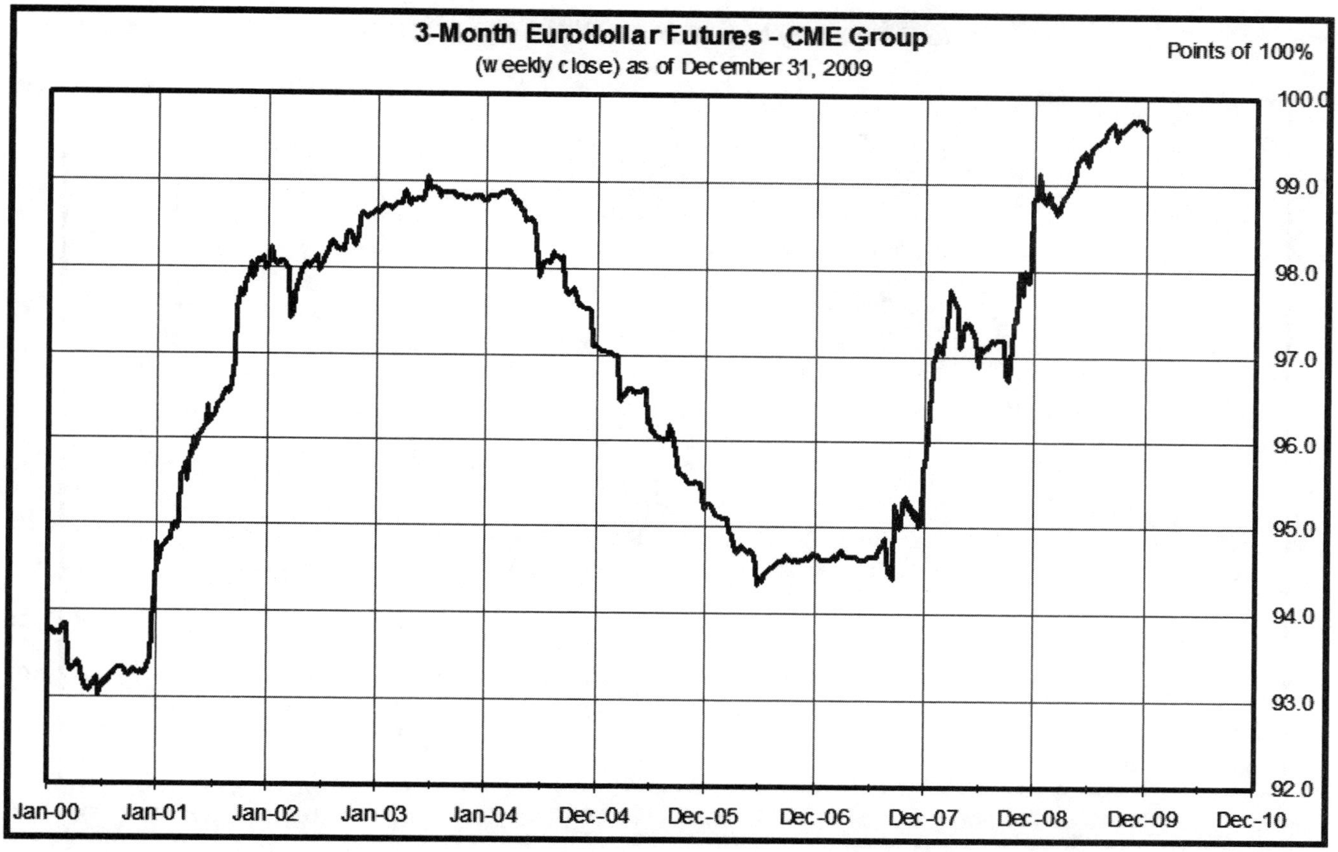

Volume of Trading of 3-month Eurodollar Futures in Chicago In Thousands of Contracts

Year	Jan.	Feb.	Mar.	Apr.	May	June	July	Aug.	Sept.	Oct.	Nov.	Dec.	Total
2000	8,379.6	9,723.0	10,197.8	10,171.8	10,261.3	9,791.3	7,384.8	7,009.6	8,204.6	9,276.4	7,561.4	10,152.3	108,115
2001	17,515.1	12,908.4	15,478.5	15,191.7	15,691.1	14,309.9	12,673.1	14,947.9	16,776.2	14,139.1	21,150.1	13,234.4	184,015
2002	19,487.1	14,491.2	17,986.7	17,946.9	18,717.5	17,931.8	20,366.9	17,757.9	15,309.9	18,495.9	13,348.6	10,240.5	202,081
2003	13,534.2	12,314.9	18,275.3	15,392.9	19,403.0	21,162.6	18,732.5	18,724.3	18,817.0	20,004.3	15,431.9	16,978.2	208,771
2004	20,808.8	16,042.4	22,583.6	26,673.6	25,548.9	28,067.1	25,114.4	24,859.3	32,283.0	25,737.3	27,945.3	21,920.2	297,584
2005	27,793.8	28,549.2	34,472.4	42,437.2	36,599.9	37,997.0	26,794.7	32,920.8	45,483.5	35,148.8	34,775.7	27,382.0	410,355
2006	35,602.4	34,218.0	47,463.8	37,752.2	44,154.6	45,443.4	36,794.1	45,126.7	45,180.3	46,453.5	42,700.7	41,187.7	502,077
2007	43,204.2	46,365.8	63,154.7	39,567.7	50,305.2	58,372.0	53,290.3	77,539.0	49,528.8	45,862.8	53,795.1	40,484.5	621,470
2008	70,787.1	59,378.2	60,956.1	56,371.5	48,683.4	60,086.5	54,178.8	36,521.6	58,497.7	40,508.5	24,515.5	26,489.2	596,974
2009	31,370.9	29,422.6	35,280.3	29,706.3	34,665.5	51,021.4	40,062.0	36,483.1	39,604.4	40,397.6	32,914.4	36,656.6	437,585

Source: CME Group; International Monetary Market (IOM), division of the Chicago Mercantile Exchange (CME)

Average Open Interest of 3-month Eurodollar Futures in Chicago In Thousands of Contracts

Year	Jan.	Feb.	Mar.	Apr.	May	June	July	Aug.	Sept.	Oct.	Nov.	Dec.
2000	2,971.3	3,261.4	3,138.7	3,156.6	3,331.7	3,272.1	3,160.3	3,225.7	3,181.8	3,067.2	3,201.1	3,349.7
2001	3,576.4	3,878.6	4,117.4	4,109.3	4,316.3	4,471.7	4,452.4	4,753.5	4,567.8	4,524.0	4,950.8	4,559.1
2002	4,592.0	4,937.0	4,727.9	4,411.6	4,421.0	4,295.5	4,123.7	4,482.4	4,243.4	4,237.9	4,553.7	4,072.5
2003	4,007.1	4,500.1	4,517.3	4,448.6	5,098.7	5,514.2	5,218.4	5,277.9	5,034.1	4,935.4	5,024.2	4,936.1
2004	5,128.0	5,624.1	5,640.5	5,602.2	6,060.0	6,117.3	6,026.7	6,236.3	5,992.8	5,968.9	6,527.8	6,706.7
2005	7,163.3	7,858.5	8,124.1	8,244.1	8,604.5	8,045.7	7,416.0	8,044.7	8,054.2	8,471.9	9,264.8	9,145.1
2006	8,833.5	9,574.0	9,586.0	9,679.6	10,126.2	9,995.4	9,572.4	10,153.9	9,949.4	9,809.8	10,345.5	10,201.1
2007	9,682.3	10,400.5	10,847.9	10,827.1	11,895.5	11,285.2	11,166.9	11,416.3	10,782.6	10,019.4	10,631.2	10,515.5
2008	11,033.0	11,206.7	10,356.6	9,225.3	9,282.5	9,266.0	9,589.0	9,882.1	8,953.0	8,141.7	8,286.9	7,389.1
2009	6,772.8	6,857.6	6,371.3	6,055.5	6,480.5	6,383.2	6,540.1	6,748.5	6,659.5	6,937.8	7,382.3	6,876.4

Source: CME Group; International Monetary Market (IOM), division of the Chicago Mercantile Exchange (CME)

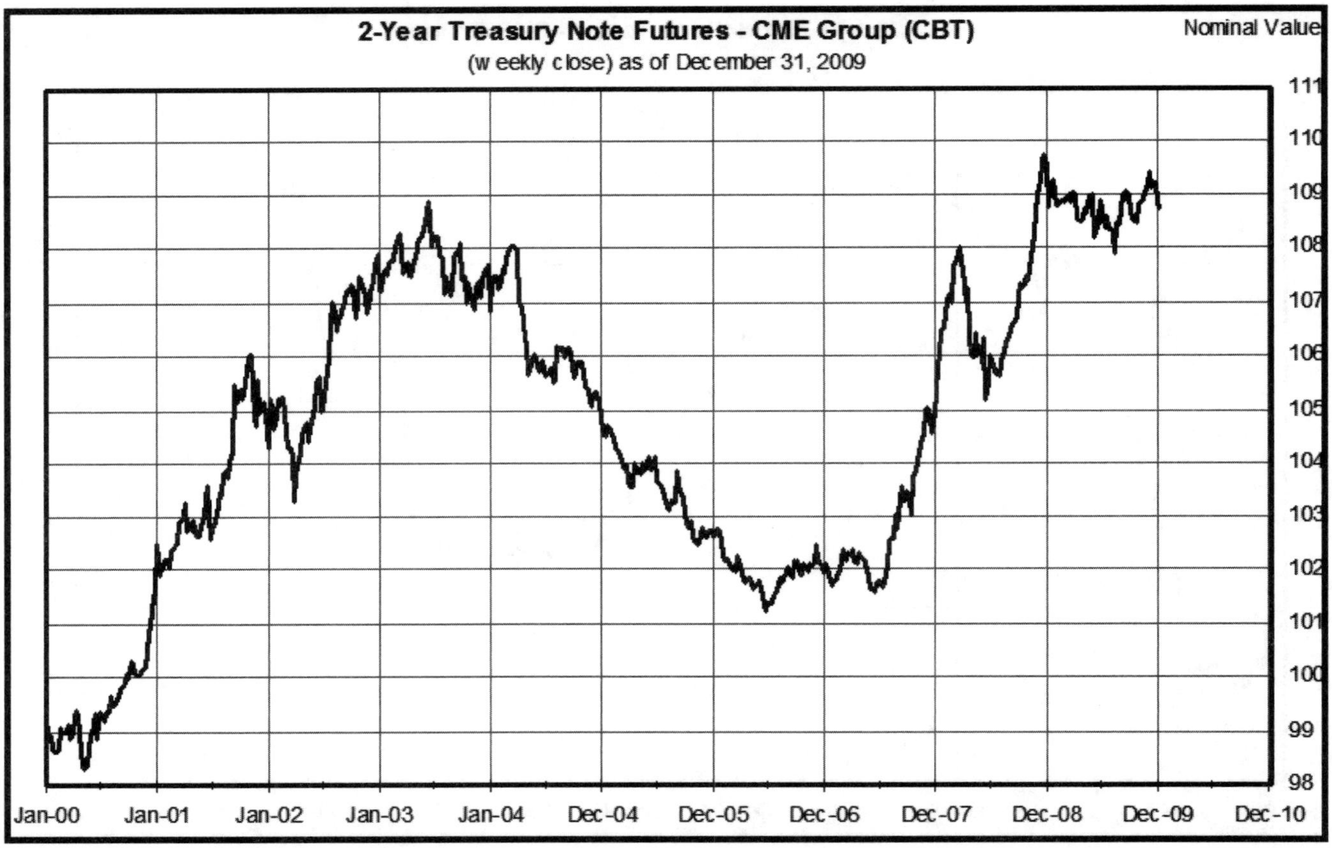

Volume of Trading of 2-Year U.S. Treasury Note Futures in Chicago In Thousands of Contracts

Year	Jan.	Feb.	Mar.	Apr.	May	June	July	Aug.	Sept.	Oct.	Nov.	Dec.	Total
2000	51.5	159.3	97.9	76.9	160.2	105.2	43.0	181.0	107.4	97.4	287.6	126.5	1,494
2001	174.6	299.2	160.9	194.8	274.0	163.3	93.4	316.4	198.1	122.9	303.8	160.6	2,462
2002	195.0	332.9	290.4	159.2	377.0	242.9	177.0	377.0	253.0	174.8	387.2	232.3	3,199
2003	146.8	392.9	292.5	153.3	513.9	339.2	274.1	514.0	522.8	281.1	496.7	488.5	4,416
2004	310.4	829.8	630.0	462.4	872.2	788.8	406.7	1,009.9	1,014.5	678.0	1,393.3	1,058.5	9,455
2005	953.7	1,997.5	1,706.1	1,548.3	2,306.3	1,811.4	1,153.0	2,144.2	2,118.0	1,344.1	2,451.5	1,671.3	21,205
2006	2,053.3	3,223.3	3,206.5	2,090.0	4,690.9	2,837.1	2,525.1	4,461.0	2,768.3	2,422.9	4,826.4	2,862.0	37,967
2007	2,892.6	5,666.6	5,321.4	3,128.3	7,197.4	5,495.7	4,793.7	10,567.2	4,788.1	4,771.2	8,849.7	5,138.5	68,610
2008	7,526.1	10,092.8	7,515.4	5,102.6	8,195.6	7,207.2	6,366.1	7,529.6	8,126.5	5,355.3	4,067.9	2,225.8	79,311
2009	2,117.4	3,797.2	2,486.1	2,219.7	4,409.0	3,818.7	3,094.7	5,931.9	3,915.7	5,012.4	7,205.5	4,150.6	48,159

Source: CME Group; Chicago Board of Trade (CBT)

Average Open Interest of 2-Year U.S. Treasury Note Futures in Chicago In Thousands ofContracts

Year	Jan.	Feb.	Mar.	Apr.	May	June	July	Aug.	Sept.	Oct.	Nov.	Dec.
2000	34.3	43.0	44.5	43.8	49.0	51.2	55.8	53.4	47.9	53.3	60.9	77.9
2001	82.2	79.4	81.7	72.5	66.2	63.6	56.6	73.0	74.4	65.4	72.7	71.3
2002	86.5	103.3	103.6	87.9	102.0	105.9	99.4	108.0	110.4	108.1	115.5	113.6
2003	107.1	114.2	123.9	109.0	120.3	118.8	112.1	149.1	151.9	144.6	149.0	156.5
2004	161.9	195.2	186.8	172.4	198.9	210.7	191.7	207.1	216.4	205.5	221.6	248.5
2005	287.3	345.7	329.6	307.0	341.5	372.9	362.3	371.1	364.4	351.3	357.3	363.2
2006	437.8	489.3	469.0	489.5	607.6	541.1	595.1	701.4	683.6	680.7	698.4	716.0
2007	764.5	826.7	896.3	1,003.3	1,125.5	965.1	1,016.8	985.4	902.3	993.1	1,043.6	997.3
2008	1,101.2	1,313.0	1,187.3	1,110.0	1,166.8	972.5	895.4	922.6	783.7	735.0	648.0	503.4
2009	505.7	495.1	473.4	487.5	514.2	535.3	627.8	741.6	772.4	935.2	1,052.2	911.8

Source: CME Group; Chicago Board of Trade (CBT)

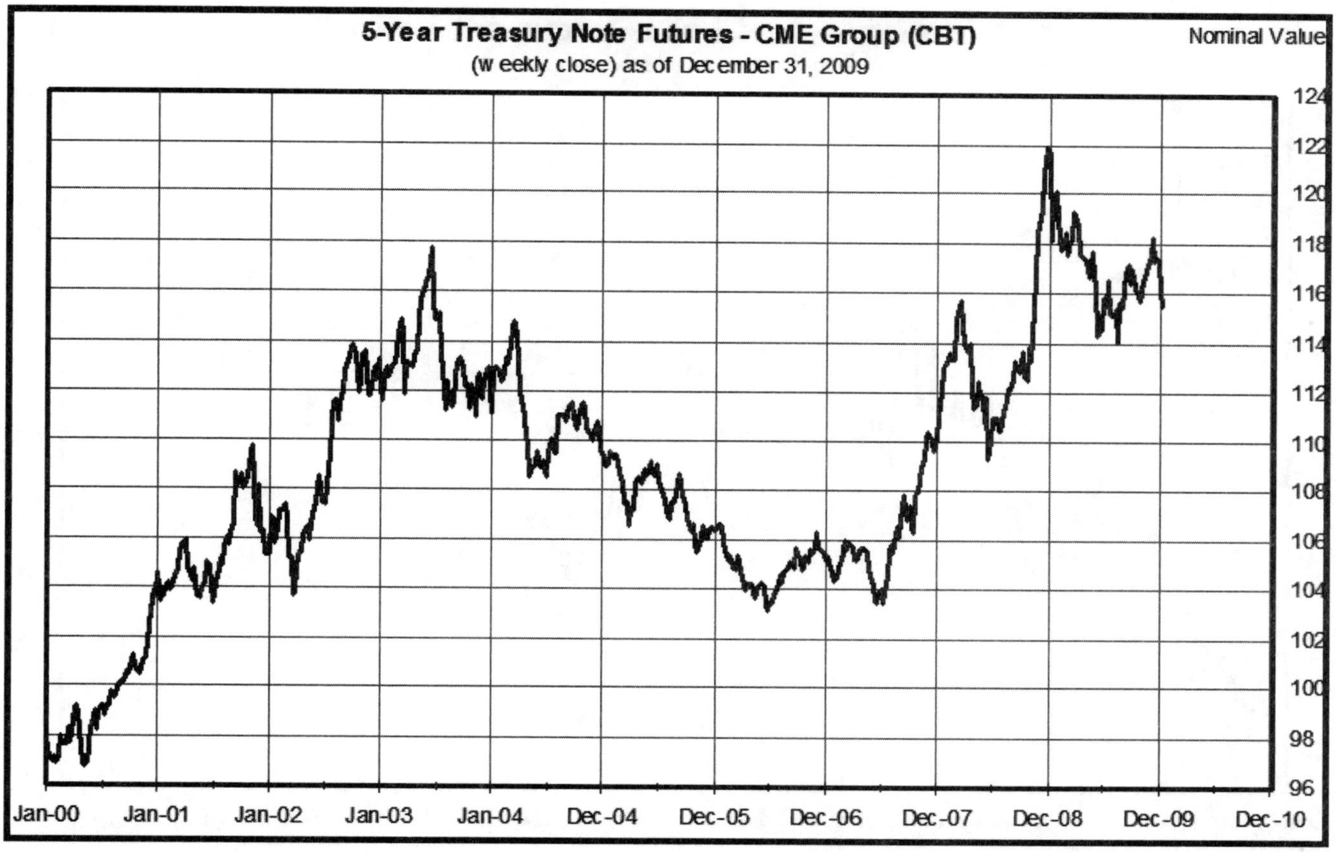

Volume of Trading of 5-Year U.S. Treasury Note Futures in Chicago In Thousands of Contracts

Year	Jan.	Feb.	Mar.	Apr.	May	June	July	Aug.	Sept.	Oct.	Nov.	Dec.	Total
2000	1,800.5	2,873.8	2,010.0	1,707.8	2,548.4	1,757.3	1,188.9	2,253.3	1,515.5	1,774.2	2,259.7	1,642.6	23,332
2001	2,422.8	2,591.5	2,281.2	2,062.8	3,221.5	2,264.0	1,702.0	2,697.4	2,617.3	2,525.7	4,052.5	2,683.6	31,122
2002	2,867.9	3,826.0	3,848.2	3,092.4	4,637.6	4,095.7	4,437.4	5,354.4	4,859.3	5,026.7	5,013.2	3,453.2	50,512
2003	4,435.6	5,178.5	5,533.7	4,623.6	7,267.6	6,165.7	6,462.6	7,090.2	7,453.9	6,364.3	6,885.3	6,285.6	73,746
2004	5,856.9	7,388.8	7,775.6	7,793.1	10,979.4	9,458.2	7,109.8	10,656.0	10,311.6	7,686.2	11,036.9	9,416.8	105,469
2005	7,797.7	11,168.4	11,848.9	10,720.3	12,320.4	9,164.3	7,698.0	12,662.9	10,999.9	8,510.5	11,996.4	7,021.1	121,909
2006	9,388.4	12,141.7	11,865.2	7,869.8	12,971.9	9,368.7	8,102.0	13,347.5	9,369.3	8,730.9	13,423.5	8,291.5	124,870
2007	9,208.6	14,410.2	14,156.0	8,372.3	15,673.4	13,243.1	13,001.7	22,354.8	11,376.0	12,495.6	21,271.6	10,644.1	166,207
2008	15,479.7	20,790.4	17,424.0	12,474.7	17,616.2	14,904.3	14,514.1	15,085.6	16,979.1	10,079.8	8,057.9	4,721.7	168,127
2009	4,821.3	8,349.9	17,424.0	5,837.7	9,658.3	8,314.8	8,034.1	10,588.0	8,259.3	9,242.9	10,231.8	7,664.7	108,427

Source: CME Group; Chicago Board of Trade (CBT)

Average Open Interest of 5-Year U.S. Treasury Note Futures in Chicago In Thousands of Contracts

Year	Jan.	Feb.	Mar.	Apr.	May	June	July	Aug.	Sept.	Oct.	Nov.	Dec.
2000	387.0	475.5	420.8	417.9	428.2	379.6	402.7	405.1	372.8	373.7	381.4	380.2
2001	377.7	392.0	374.5	376.9	436.3	422.0	461.0	483.3	451.4	463.2	554.6	491.1
2002	507.2	576.2	585.6	632.2	656.4	594.9	554.9	652.8	655.0	662.5	720.7	692.8
2003	685.1	743.2	777.8	835.5	856.3	827.5	781.7	840.4	737.0	819.4	925.6	880.1
2004	874.2	1,008.1	987.2	1,043.0	1,145.4	1,118.5	1,217.3	1,322.5	1,168.1	1,099.4	1,290.7	1,318.7
2005	1,160.2	1,237.0	1,325.0	1,383.0	1,320.9	1,127.9	1,247.7	1,450.3	1,190.2	1,342.0	1,397.6	1,126.8
2006	1,105.1	1,404.8	1,238.0	1,257.2	1,326.0	1,264.7	1,258.3	1,409.8	1,341.3	1,413.8	1,484.4	1,423.8
2007	1,468.1	1,499.6	1,481.0	1,614.9	1,763.5	1,601.5	1,586.9	1,648.0	1,564.9	1,666.1	1,932.4	1,841.2
2008	1,940.6	2,101.2	1,923.8	1,850.9	1,851.0	1,669.6	1,574.5	1,600.7	1,483.4	1,378.1	1,267.1	1,057.8
2009	965.5	964.7	897.8	812.7	860.8	774.2	761.1	831.9	800.3	770.9	854.0	831.6

Source: CME Group; Chicago Board of Trade (CBT)

Volume of Trading of 10-year U.S. Treasury Note Futures in Chicago In Thousands of Contracts

Year	Jan.	Feb.	Mar.	Apr.	May	June	July	Aug.	Sept.	Oct.	Nov.	Dec.	Total
2000	3,557.0	4,974.7	3,750.4	3,529.7	4,711.6	3,706.0	2,580.9	4,459.8	3,779.5	3,824.3	4,513.6	3,313.1	46,701
2001	4,632.8	4,915.3	4,500.5	4,299.4	5,483.3	4,083.8	3,493.1	5,683.1	4,389.7	4,144.8	7,270.1	4,689.8	57,586
2002	5,539.7	6,407.2	6,520.6	5,463.3	8,309.1	7,547.7	8,980.8	10,590.5	8,529.1	11,198.8	9,679.2	7,020.2	95,786
2003	9,120.6	10,746.5	11,320.5	9,377.2	13,817.0	12,149.5	15,285.0	14,248.7	13,706.7	13,586.9	12,474.5	10,912.2	146,745
2004	13,608.5	14,569.4	16,984.0	16,478.4	17,785.8	15,184.2	12,954.3	17,419.5	18,467.8	16,622.0	21,006.4	15,038.9	196,119
2005	13,901.3	19,565.4	21,132.8	19,487.3	22,688.8	16,778.7	13,894.5	20,120.1	18,348.2	15,357.3	20,705.4	13,144.2	215,124
2006	17,188.6	21,262.7	22,739.9	17,241.5	26,174.6	20,311.2	16,645.2	24,796.6	22,125.2	20,602.6	28,413.8	18,070.1	255,572
2007	21,492.5	30,367.2	30,210.2	18,529.8	34,343.9	37,171.0	32,361.3	38,785.6	24,375.6	25,280.4	36,890.7	19,421.3	349,229
2008	28,924.8	33,426.2	23,331.5	19,043.9	27,414.0	22,591.8	22,903.0	21,069.7	23,265.1	15,101.1	11,826.6	7,873.1	256,771
2009	9,778.0	14,548.1	15,116.1	11,893.7	17,309.8	16,994.6	16,420.7	19,292.8	16,099.0	19,268.8	19,037.2	14,093.3	189,852

Source: CME Group; Chicago Board of Trade (CBT)

Average Open Interest of 10-year U.S. Treasury Note Futures in Chicago In Thousands of Contracts

Year	Jan.	Feb.	Mar.	Apr.	May	June	July	Aug.	Sept.	Oct.	Nov.	Dec.
2000	595.2	653.8	571.9	615.6	621.4	583.9	608.4	602.1	547.6	564.6	555.2	508.9
2001	550.3	541.6	560.0	595.1	628.7	512.1	550.2	627.3	610.4	590.3	662.0	559.9
2002	572.9	643.9	679.6	699.1	806.5	793.0	877.6	958.3	888.7	970.2	938.0	751.6
2003	772.9	896.9	914.9	897.1	968.1	993.6	1,009.5	1,032.5	856.2	985.7	1,140.7	965.0
2004	1,145.9	1,320.6	1,312.9	1,347.7	1,392.4	1,300.3	1,348.2	1,456.6	1,503.6	1,626.9	1,767.4	1,642.0
2005	1,671.3	1,888.6	1,980.2	2,003.5	2,140.8	1,869.0	1,859.3	1,992.8	1,749.4	1,677.7	1,778.6	1,635.6
2006	1,700.0	1,990.4	2,048.7	2,259.7	2,321.0	2,054.2	2,087.1	2,265.3	2,271.5	2,408.2	2,398.2	2,236.0
2007	2,343.6	2,367.3	2,294.0	2,586.9	2,878.3	2,853.9	2,871.5	2,820.5	2,269.5	2,497.2	2,661.6	2,313.2
2008	2,431.2	2,517.6	2,179.8	2,073.7	2,144.6	1,978.8	1,802.6	1,835.2	1,658.2	1,385.2	1,226.4	1,074.2
2009	1,034.9	1,027.6	1,007.0	1,010.0	1,132.3	1,070.9	1,056.2	1,139.7	1,120.2	1,239.1	1,327.5	1,203.9

Source: CME Group; Chicago Board of Trade (CBT)

Volume of Trading of 30-year U.S. Treasury Bond Futures in Chicago   In Thousands of Contracts

Year	Jan.	Feb.	Mar.	Apr.	May	June	July	Aug.	Sept.	Oct.	Nov.	Dec.	Total
2000	7,966.4	8,157.4	5,378.6	5,282.3	5,972.9	4,458.6	3,080.0	4,709.9	4,529.2	4,460.4	5,072.8	3,682.3	62,751
2001	5,123.0	5,545.9	5,196.3	4,584.0	6,022.2	4,233.2	3,347.0	4,965.6	4,331.0	4,598.6	6,746.4	3,886.0	58,579
2002	4,132.7	4,721.1	4,504.8	3,932.8	5,191.4	4,722.2	5,157.9	5,666.5	4,534.5	5,190.1	4,722.8	3,605.6	56,082
2003	3,625.3	4,840.9	5,106.9	3,795.0	7,188.4	5,896.2	6,352.1	6,198.0	5,738.4	5,121.8	4,823.4	4,835.2	63,522
2004	5,025.4	5,762.8	6,687.9	5,983.2	6,463.8	5,556.9	4,540.1	6,343.5	7,638.7	5,658.6	7,374.2	5,914.0	72,949
2005	6,134.8	8,973.5	8,573.7	7,293.5	8,558.9	7,407.2	5,367.0	7,771.3	7,193.6	6,450.4	7,928.8	5,274.0	86,927
2006	7,044.8	8,511.6	8,980.6	6,969.2	10,354.4	7,564.5	5,854.2	8,736.7	7,553.9	6,375.1	9,461.6	6,348.2	93,755
2007	7,108.8	10,060.2	10,338.3	6,108.4	10,578.5	11,338.4	9,452.1	11,439.3	6,864.4	7,232.1	11,146.2	5,963.6	107,630
2008	9,667.3	11,646.2	8,739.1	5,835.3	9,173.4	7,176.8	7,429.4	7,521.6	7,830.0	5,559.1	5,267.6	3,618.7	89,465
2009	3,805.9	6,062.7	4,525.5	3,224.8	6,465.1	5,192.0	4,995.2	7,238.3	4,297.6	5,133.4	6,978.4	4,313.9	62,233

Source: CME Group; Chicago Board of Trade (CBT)

Average Open Interest of 30-year U.S. Treasury Bond Futures in Chicago   In Contracts

Year	Jan.	Feb.	Mar.	Apr.	May	June	July	Aug.	Sept.	Oct.	Nov.	Dec.
2000	637,023	612,298	530,957	503,412	434,771	390,928	394,075	440,437	402,156	399,880	443,282	445,386
2001	413,244	479,165	519,987	509,558	503,194	455,799	458,613	531,098	525,972	567,177	602,647	478,418
2002	468,455	520,573	479,939	463,100	472,778	458,020	427,896	465,971	496,815	467,440	459,877	440,225
2003	420,797	506,910	487,277	449,286	566,887	596,186	554,632	521,928	423,995	443,177	489,185	471,848
2004	488,484	571,445	557,595	488,921	553,721	512,566	517,893	594,905	584,416	594,353	640,026	634,008
2005	674,170	792,247	749,403	710,061	735,910	665,235	579,724	600,565	595,736	586,653	618,647	574,121
2006	601,094	662,314	622,927	739,601	858,812	760,240	760,749	813,905	763,092	737,070	810,426	803,020
2007	816,747	903,121	852,305	875,810	949,173	980,004	988,995	991,513	915,693	948,940	1,022,623	947,588
2008	1,033,106	1,041,505	979,695	893,308	941,317	879,149	891,111	880,157	877,623	756,790	731,186	754,687
2009	726,062	733,323	712,813	708,243	724,577	706,818	696,641	727,674	749,290	739,723	777,241	704,259

Source: CME Group; Chicago Board of Trade (CBT)

U.S. Federal Funds Rate In Percent

Year	Jan.	Feb.	Mar.	Apr.	May	June	July	Aug.	Sept.	Oct.	Nov.	Dec.	Average
2000	5.46	5.73	5.85	6.02	6.27	6.53	6.54	6.50	6.52	6.51	6.51	6.40	6.24
2001	5.98	5.49	5.31	4.80	4.21	3.97	3.77	3.65	3.07	2.49	2.09	1.82	3.89
2002	1.73	1.74	1.73	1.75	1.75	1.75	1.73	1.74	1.75	1.75	1.34	1.24	1.67
2003	1.24	1.26	1.25	1.26	1.26	1.22	1.01	1.03	1.01	1.01	1.00	0.98	1.13
2004	1.00	1.01	1.00	1.00	1.00	1.03	1.26	1.43	1.61	1.76	1.93	2.16	1.35
2005	2.28	2.50	2.63	2.79	3.00	3.04	3.26	3.50	3.62	3.78	4.00	4.16	3.21
2006	4.29	4.49	4.59	4.79	4.94	4.99	5.24	5.25	5.25	5.25	5.25	5.24	4.96
2007	5.25	5.26	5.26	5.25	5.25	5.25	5.26	5.02	4.94	4.76	4.49	4.24	5.02
2008	3.94	2.98	2.61	2.28	1.98	2.00	2.01	2.00	1.81	0.97	0.39	0.16	1.93
2009	0.15	0.22	0.18	0.15	0.18	0.21	0.16	0.16	0.15	0.12	0.12	0.12	0.16

Source: Bureau of Economic Analysis, U.S. Department of Commerce (BEA)

U.S. Municipal Bond Yield[1] In Percent

Year	Jan.	Feb.	Mar.	Apr.	May	June	July	Aug.	Sept.	Oct.	Nov.	Dec.	Average
2000	6.08	6.00	5.83	5.75	6.00	5.80	5.63	5.51	5.56	5.59	5.54	5.22	5.71
2001	5.10	5.18	5.13	5.27	5.29	5.20	5.20	5.03	5.09	5.05	5.04	5.25	5.15
2002	5.16	5.11	5.29	5.22	5.19	5.09	5.02	4.95	4.74	4.88	4.95	4.85	5.04
2003	4.90	4.81	4.76	4.74	4.41	4.33	4.74	5.10	4.92	4.89	4.73	4.65	4.75
2004	4.61	4.55	4.41	4.82	5.07	5.05	4.87	4.70	4.56	4.49	4.52	4.48	4.68
2005	4.41	4.35	4.57	4.46	4.31	4.23	4.31	4.32	4.29	4.48	4.57	4.46	4.40
2006	4.37	4.41	4.44	4.58	4.59	4.60	4.61	4.39	4.27	4.30	4.14	4.11	4.40
2007	4.23	4.22	4.15	4.26	4.31	4.60	4.56	4.64	4.51	4.39	4.46	4.42	4.40
2008	4.27	4.64	4.93	4.70	4.58	4.69	4.68	4.69	4.86	5.50	5.23	5.56	4.86
2009	5.07	4.90	4.99	4.78	4.56	4.81	4.72	4.60	4.24	4.20	4.37	4.21	4.62

[1] 20-bond average. *Source: Bureau of Economic Analysis, U.S. Department of Commerce (BEA)*

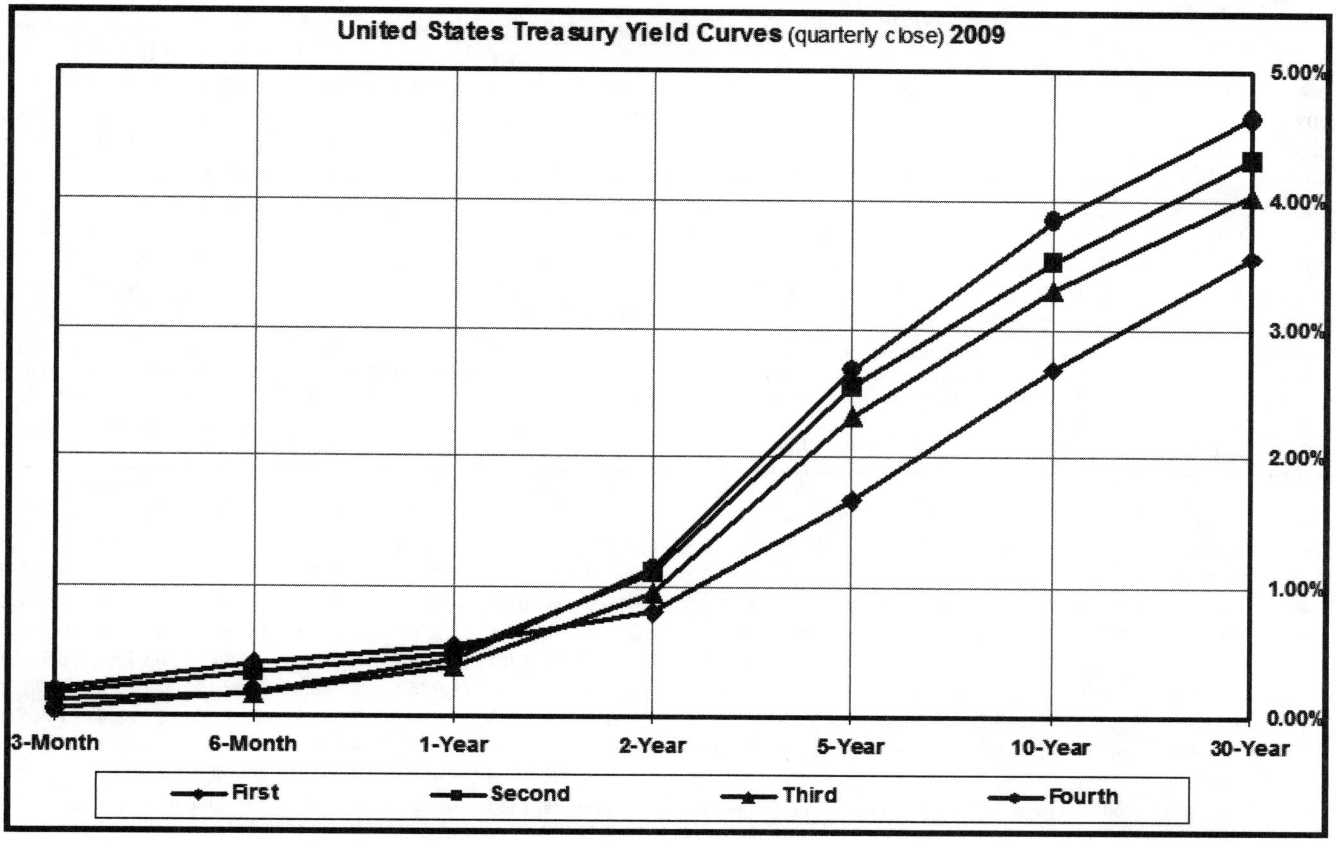

U.S. Industrial Production Index[1] 1997 = 100

Year	Jan.	Feb.	Mar.	Apr.	May	June	July	Aug.	Sept.	Oct.	Nov.	Dec.	Average
2000	143.6	144.3	145.2	146.3	147.2	147.9	147.6	148.7	148.8	146.3	145.8	145.1	145.7
2001	143.9	143.5	142.9	142.0	141.6	140.3	140.4	140.0	138.5	137.7	108.8	108.3	111.5
2002	109.0	109.2	109.6	110.1	110.4	110.8	111.6	111.3	111.2	111.0	111.2	110.6	111.0
2003	111.2	111.6	110.8	110.1	110.0	110.0	110.8	110.9	111.5	111.8	112.7	112.9	110.9
2004	113.2	114.4	114.1	114.7	115.5	115.1	115.9	116.0	105.1	105.8	106.0	106.7	103.6
2005	106.9	107.4	107.3	107.2	107.4	108.3	108.3	108.6	107.2	107.1	108.2	109.2	106.9
2006	109.1	109.4	110.0	110.9	110.9	111.9	112.3	112.5	112.2	112.0	111.5	112.2	111.2
2007	111.7	112.5	110.4	111.0	111.0	111.4	112.0	112.0	112.3	111.8	112.3	112.4	111.7
2008	112.6	112.3	112.0	111.4	111.2	111.3	111.3	109.8	105.2	106.8	106.1	102.4	109.4
2009[2]	100.1	99.3	97.7	97.2	96.2	95.8	96.9	98.3	98.9	99.1	99.7	100.3	98.3

[1] Total Index of the Federal Reserve Index of Quantity Output, seasonally adjusted. [2] Preliminary. *Source: Bureau of Economic Analysis, U.S. Department of Commerce (BEA)*

U.S. Gross National Product, National Income, and Personal Income In Billions of Constant Dollars[1]

	Gross Domestic Product					National Income					Personal Income				
Year	First Quarter	Second Quarter	Third Quarter	Fourth Quarter	Total	First Quarter	Second Quarter	Third Quarter	Fourth Quarter	Total	First Quarter	Second Quarter	Third Quarter	Fourth Quarter	Total
2000	9,710	9,949	10,018	10,130	9,951	8,810	8,896	9,006	9,044	8,939	8,380	8,507	8,644	8,707	8,559
2001	10,165	10,301	10,305	10,373	10,286	9,184	9,210	9,157	9,189	9,185	8,859	8,881	8,881	8,912	8,883
2002	10,499	10,602	10,702	10,767	10,642	9,305	9,381	9,418	9,531	9,409	8,978	9,061	9,075	9,127	9,060
2003	10,888	11,008	11,256	11,417	11,142	9,614	9,757	9,899	10,090	9,840	9,195	9,321	9,419	9,578	9,378
2004	11,597	11,778	11,951	12,145	11,868	10,281	10,445	10,642	10,769	10,534	9,680	9,847	9,999	10,223	9,937
2005	12,380	12,517	12,742	12,916	12,638	11,020	11,157	11,360	11,559	11,274	10,239	10,387	10,578	10,741	10,486
2006	13,184	13,348	13,453	13,612	13,399	11,838	11,966	12,093	12,228	12,031	11,027	11,204	11,337	11,505	11,268
2007	13,796	13,997	14,180	14,338	14,078	12,254	12,421	12,482	12,635	12,448	11,707	11,823	11,946	12,100	11,894
2008	14,374	14,498	14,547	14,347	14,441	12,662	12,664	12,781	12,434	12,635	12,142	12,293	12,287	12,234	12,239
2009[2]	14,178	14,151	14,242	14,463	14,259	12,209	12,218	12,350		12,259	11,953	12,049	12,084	12,203	12,072

[1] Seasonally adjusted at annual rates. [2] Preliminary. *Source: Bureau of Economic Analysis, U.S. Department of Commerce (BEA)*

U.S. Money Supply M1[2] In Billions of Dollars

Year	Jan.	Feb.	Mar.	Apr.	May	June	July	Aug.	Sept.	Oct.	Nov.	Dec.	Average
2000	1,121.9	1,109.3	1,108.3	1,113.5	1,105.8	1,103.3	1,103.0	1,100.4	1,099.1	1,098.7	1,092.4	1,087.7	1,103.6
2001	1,097.5	1,101.5	1,109.9	1,115.0	1,119.6	1,126.4	1,139.8	1,149.8	1,204.0	1,165.9	1,171.6	1,182.2	1,140.3
2002	1,190.4	1,190.7	1,193.2	1,185.8	1,189.3	1,192.2	1,199.6	1,185.9	1,194.6	1,203.8	1,209.4	1,220.4	1,196.3
2003	1,226.3	1,238.6	1,239.2	1,248.3	1,268.1	1,280.3	1,287.9	1,294.1	1,296.8	1,297.3	1,298.2	1,306.9	1,273.5
2004	1,305.3	1,321.9	1,330.5	1,332.0	1,331.7	1,342.6	1,340.3	1,353.2	1,361.2	1,360.9	1,376.5	1,377.1	1,344.4
2005	1,365.8	1,372.9	1,373.0	1,357.6	1,365.4	1,378.5	1,366.5	1,376.1	1,377.5	1,374.7	1,377.9	1,375.3	1,371.8
2006	1,380.2	1,380.6	1,384.5	1,380.0	1,386.3	1,372.8	1,368.5	1,368.8	1,361.5	1,369.1	1,372.4	1,367.9	1,374.4
2007	1,374.0	1,367.1	1,369.1	1,379.2	1,380.8	1,364.6	1,368.6	1,371.8	1,372.4	1,379.0	1,375.5	1,375.8	1,373.2
2008	1,381.1	1,387.0	1,389.7	1,392.1	1,391.5	1,398.1	1,415.1	1,400.0	1,459.5	1,472.7	1,518.1	1,594.7	1,433.3
2009[1]	1,573.8	1,562.1	1,564.3	1,592.7	1,593.0	1,641.0	1,649.9	1,648.3	1,660.9	1,673.8	1,685.6	1,693.4	1,628.2

[1] Preliminary. [2] *M1* -- The sum of currency held outside the vaults of depository institutions, Federal Reserve Banks, and the U.S. Treasury; travelers checks; and demand and other checkable deposits issued by financial institutions (except demand deposits due to the Treasury and depository institutions), minus cash items in process of collection and Federal Reserve float. Seasonally adjusted. *Source: Board of Governors of the Federal Reserve System*

U.S. Money Supply M2[2] In Billions of Dollars

Year	Jan.	Feb.	Mar.	Apr.	May	June	July	Aug.	Sept.	Oct.	Nov.	Dec.	Average
2000	4,661.5	4,678.7	4,706.6	4,758.6	4,752.4	4,765.6	4,780.4	4,814.8	4,846.3	4,864.9	4,874.1	4,917.9	4,785.2
2001	4,972.7	5,009.8	5,068.8	5,130.3	5,133.8	5,172.8	5,206.5	5,238.2	5,348.8	5,340.9	5,383.1	5,434.1	5,203.3
2002	5,463.5	5,491.2	5,502.6	5,507.1	5,529.8	5,553.1	5,602.2	5,638.8	5,662.7	5,714.6	5,759.3	5,785.9	5,600.9
2003	5,811.3	5,848.8	5,864.7	5,909.4	5,962.4	6,001.0	6,055.3	6,102.0	6,081.9	6,067.1	6,067.9	6,073.7	5,987.1
2004	6,074.3	6,115.5	6,155.3	6,193.3	6,262.5	6,275.3	6,280.2	6,305.4	6,340.1	6,364.8	6,400.2	6,415.2	6,265.2
2005	6,413.9	6,431.3	6,447.2	6,452.3	6,469.1	6,501.9	6,529.4	6,561.4	6,596.5	6,627.6	6,654.6	6,679.2	6,530.4
2006	6,719.4	6,746.9	6,762.6	6,787.5	6,805.4	6,840.3	6,875.9	6,905.8	6,935.6	6,995.0	7,031.4	7,079.5	6,873.8
2007	7,115.4	7,133.9	7,167.2	7,219.3	7,253.2	7,279.1	7,311.8	7,371.3	7,410.8	7,443.7	7,472.2	7,509.4	7,307.3
2008	7,542.3	7,631.7	7,691.6	7,716.3	7,739.0	7,751.1	7,802.7	7,790.6	7,898.2	8,014.7	8,065.3	8,241.6	7,823.8
2009[1]	8,302.6	8,340.7	8,392.7	8,343.7	8,416.1	8,442.2	8,436.6	8,413.3	8,452.4	8,481.4	8,509.0	8,524.3	8,421.3

[1] Preliminary. [2] *M2* -- M1 plus savings deposits (including money market deposit accounts) and small-denomination (less than $100,000) time deposits issued by financial institutions; and shares in retail money market mutual funds (funds with initial investments of less than $50,000), net of retirement accounts. Seasonally adjusted. *Source: Board of Governors of the Federal Reserve System*

U.S. Money Supply M3[2] In Billions of Dollars

Year	Jan.	Feb.	Mar.	Apr.	May	June	July	Aug.	Sept.	Oct.	Nov.	Dec.	Average
1997	5,013.2	5,041.7	5,080.2	5,119.8	5,147.1	5,177.4	5,235.8	5,291.4	5,332.3	5,376.3	5,417.1	5,460.5	5,224.4
1998	5,508.8	5,541.3	5,611.5	5,647.3	5,686.9	5,728.4	5,750.0	5,815.0	5,882.0	5,953.7	6,010.1	6,051.9	5,765.6
1999	6,080.7	6,129.5	6,133.6	6,172.3	6,201.0	6,237.7	6,269.0	6,299.1	6,323.0	6,378.4	6,464.1	6,551.8	6,270.0
2000	6,605.5	6,642.2	6,704.0	6,767.3	6,776.9	6,823.6	6,875.2	6,945.0	7,003.5	7,027.0	7,038.3	7,117.6	6,860.5
2001	7,237.2	7,308.5	7,372.0	7,507.8	7,564.1	7,644.7	7,691.9	7,696.3	7,853.2	7,897.8	7,973.0	8,035.4	7,648.5
2002	8,063.9	8,109.3	8,117.3	8,142.6	8,175.1	8,190.8	8,244.2	8,298.1	8,331.5	8,368.9	8,498.8	8,568.0	8,259.0
2003	8,588.1	8,628.7	8,648.8	8,686.0	8,741.9	8,791.6	8,888.7	8,918.2	8,906.5	8,896.8	8,880.3	8,872.3	8,787.3
2004	8,930.2	9,000.3	9,080.7	9,149.6	9,243.8	9,275.7	9,282.7	9,314.4	9,351.8	9,359.4	9,395.1	9,433.0	9,234.7
2005	9,487.2	9,531.6	9,565.3	9,620.9	9,665.0	9,725.3	9,762.4	9,864.6	9,950.8	10,032.0	10,078.5	10,154.0	9,786.5
2006[1]	10,242.8	10,298.7	Discontinued										10,270.8

[1] Preliminary. [2] *M3* -- M2 plus large-denomination ($100,000 or more) time deposits; repurchase agreements issued by depository institutions; Eurodollar deposits, specifically, dollar-denominated deposits due to nonbank U.S. addresses held at foreign offices of U.S. banks worldwide and all banking offices in Canada and the United Kingdom; and institutional money market mutual funds (funds with initial investments of $50,000 or more). Seasonally adjusted. *Source: Board of Governors of the Federal Reserve System*

U.S. Money Supply MZM[2] In Billions of Dollars

Year	Jan.	Feb.	Mar.	Apr.	May	June	July	Aug.	Sept.	Oct.	Nov.	Dec.	Average
2000	4,374.4	4,385.3	4,420.9	4,469.5	4,465.4	4,478.6	4,510.5	4,554.2	4,599.4	4,621.5	4,633.1	4,686.7	4,516.6
2001	4,776.7	4,874.0	4,960.9	5,059.7	5,113.4	5,191.9	5,248.2	5,272.3	5,437.4	5,515.0	5,594.9	5,675.9	5,226.7
2002	5,714.3	5,760.2	5,780.5	5,801.7	5,832.1	5,854.6	5,904.8	5,933.2	5,945.5	5,983.3	6,105.0	6,157.9	5,897.8
2003	6,169.7	6,203.0	6,207.8	6,236.6	6,276.9	6,323.4	6,428.2	6,449.8	6,432.8	6,413.4	6,402.9	6,383.3	6,327.3
2004	6,389.7	6,430.5	6,479.0	6,522.0	6,598.9	6,606.8	6,599.4	6,612.4	6,631.5	6,636.7	6,664.8	6,667.3	6,569.9
2005	6,647.9	6,647.9	6,644.8	6,641.0	6,640.0	6,668.3	6,695.2	6,720.8	6,757.6	6,790.0	6,808.9	6,838.5	6,708.4
2006	6,875.0	6,887.5	6,891.8	6,910.4	6,923.5	6,959.5	6,989.6	7,014.6	7,043.7	7,108.1	7,154.1	7,233.5	6,999.3
2007	7,251.9	7,273.3	7,323.8	7,397.3	7,462.7	7,518.6	7,592.5	7,726.0	7,856.3	7,972.7	8,071.4	8,150.6	7,633.1
2008	8,196.2	8,405.9	8,544.1	8,612.1	8,663.7	8,709.7	8,765.8	8,750.3	8,795.8	8,843.0	8,969.3	9,198.6	8,704.5
2009[1]	9,329.3	9,397.8	9,469.4	9,453.0	9,560.3	9,591.9	9,594.8	9,556.3	9,591.6	9,591.2	9,592.4	9,575.6	9,525.3

[1] Preliminary. [2] *MZM* (money, zero maturity): M2 minus small-denomination time deposits, plus institutional money market mutual funds (that is, those included in M3 but excluded from M2). The label MZM was coined by William Poole (1991); the aggregate itself was proposed earlier by Motley (1988). Seasonally adjusted. *Source: Board of Governors of the Federal Reserve System*

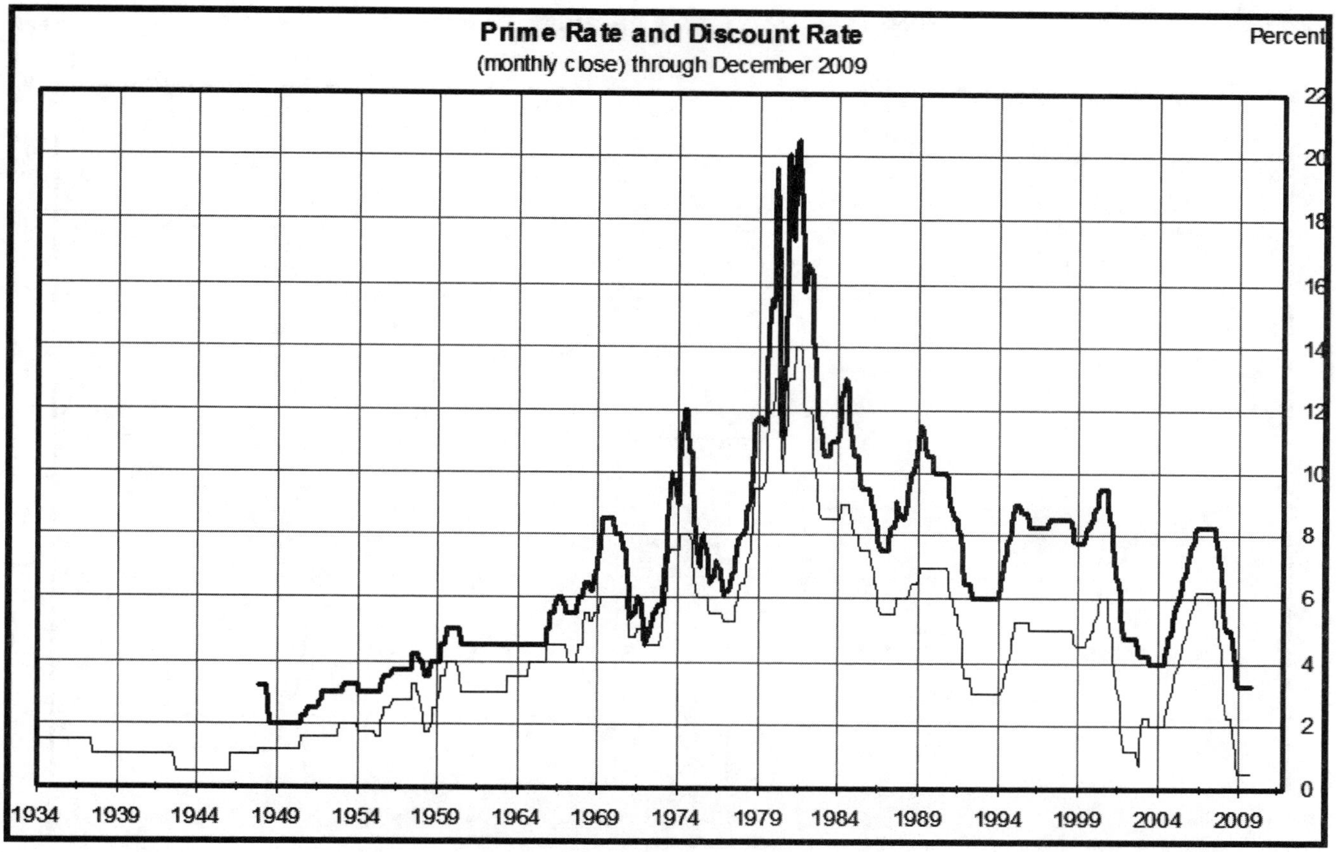
Prime Rate and Discount Rate
(monthly close) through December 2009
Percent
22
20
18
16
14
12
10
8
6
4
2
0
1934 1939 1944 1949 1954 1959 1964 1969 1974 1979 1984 1989 1994 1999 2004 2009

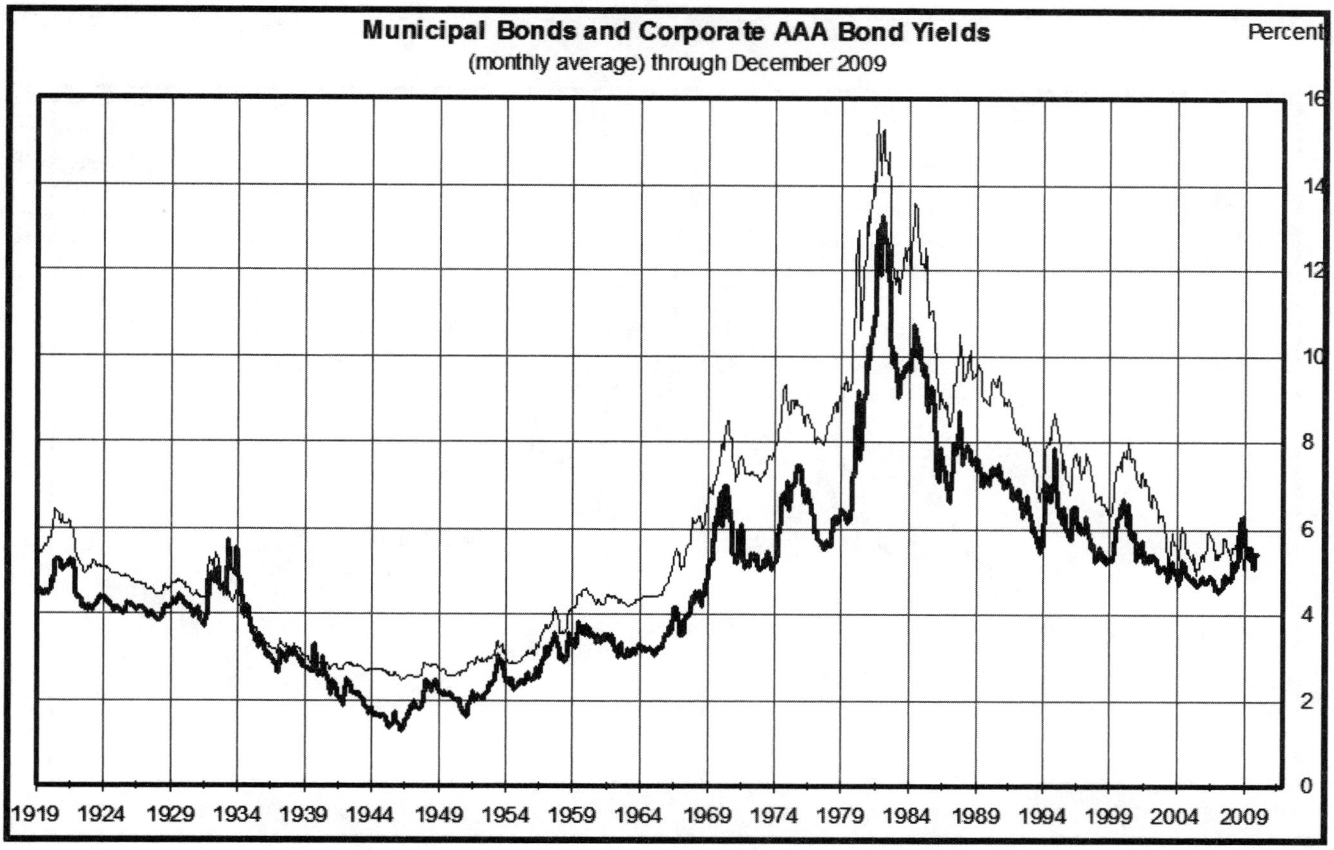
Municipal Bonds and Corporate AAA Bond Yields
(monthly average) through December 2009
Percent
16
14
12
10
8
6
4
2
0
1919 1924 1929 1934 1939 1944 1949 1954 1959 1964 1969 1974 1979 1984 1989 1994 1999 2004 2009

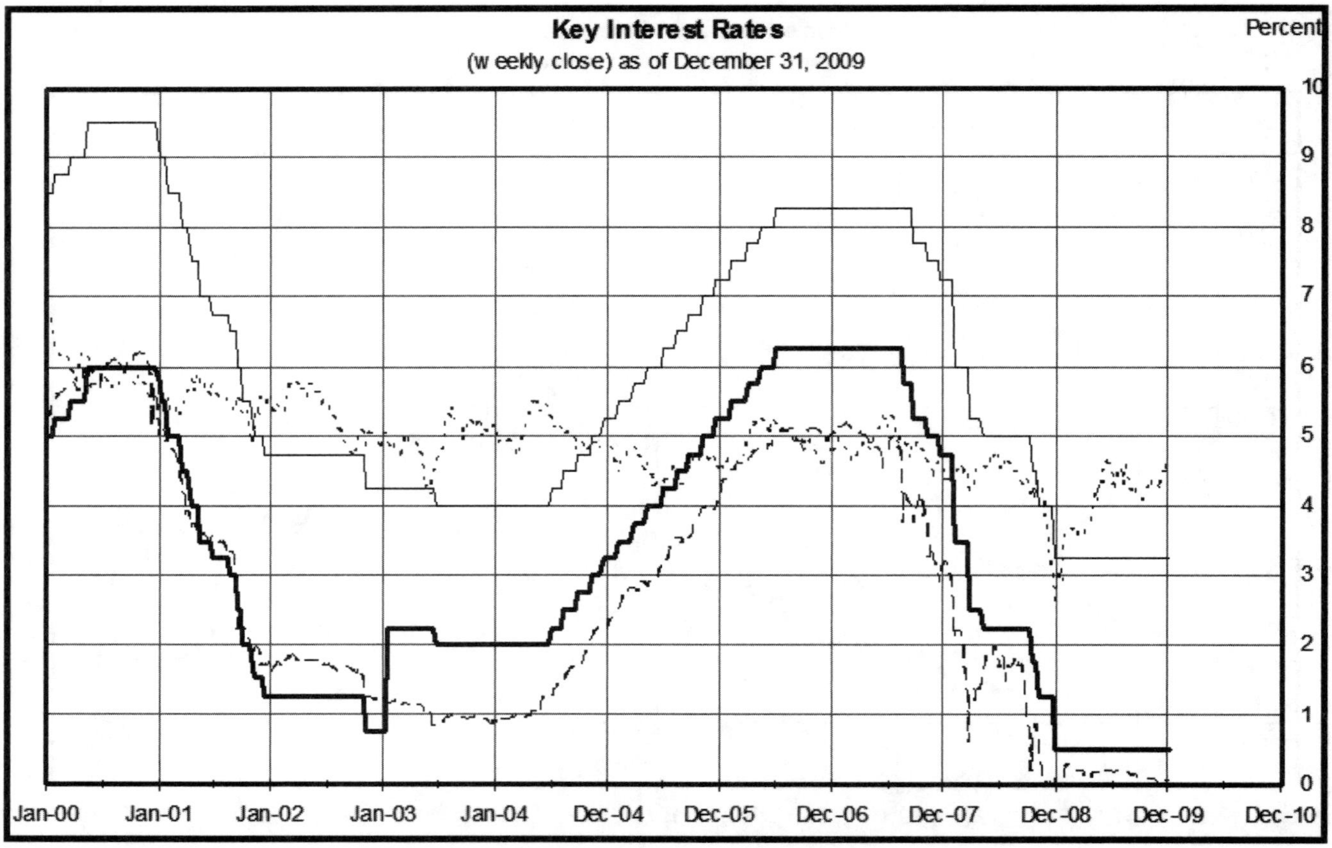
Key Interest Rates
(weekly close) as of December 31, 2009
Percent
10
9
8
7
6
5
4
3
2
1
0
Jan-00
Jan-01
Jan-02
Jan-03
Jan-04
Dec-04
Dec-05
Dec-06
Dec-07
Dec-08
Dec-09
Dec-10

5-Year Treasury Note Yield
(monthly average) through December 2009
Percent
18
16
14
12
10
8
6
4
2
0
1953
1957
1961
1965
1969
1973
1977
1981
1985
1989
1993
1997
2001
2005
2009

Interest Rates - Worldwide

Interest rate futures contracts are widely traded throughout the world. The most popular futures contracts are generally 10-year government bonds and the 3-month interest rate contracts. In Europe, futures on German interest rates are traded at the all-electronic Eurex Exchange in Frankfurt. Futures on UK interest rates are traded at the Liffe Exchange in London. Futures on Canadian interest rates are traded at the Montreal Exchange. Futures on Japanese interest rates are traded at the Singapore Exchange (Simex) and at the Tokyo Stock Exchange. A variety of other interest rate futures contracts are traded throughout the rest of the world (please see the front of this Yearbook for a complete list).

Euro-Zone – The Eurex 10-year Euro Bund futures contract, after topping out in January 2009 on the financial crisis that started in September 2008, sold off fairly sharply during spring but then recovered through most of the rest of the year to close 2009 down -3.65 points. The 10-year Bund yield hit a record low of 2.85% in January 2009 and then spent the rest of the year consolidating mildly above that level, finally closing 2009 at 3.39%, up 44 basis points. The 3-month Euribor interbank lending rate fell sharply during 2009 to hit a record low of 0.66% by the end of 2009.

In response to the financial crisis that emerged in September 2008, the European Central Bank (ECB) cut its key 2-week refinancing rate by a total of 325 basis points from 4.25% in September 2008 to 1.00% by May 2009. The ECB then left its refinancing rate unchanged at 1.00% all through 2009. The market consensus as of early 2010 was that the ECB would leave the refinancing rate at 1.00% until early 2011.

The ECB at the start of the crisis flooded the banking system with reserves and the ECB's assets ballooned by 600 billion euros in late 2008. However, the 3-month Euribor rate did not start falling substantially until later in the year after the ECB conducted three 12-month bank lending operations that totaled a massive 614 billion euros. The ECB during the crisis followed a policy of providing banks with all the liquidity they required, thus ensuring that no banks would be caught short of cash and fall into danger of default. The ECB in March 2010 extended the promise of unlimited bank lending until October 2010. The ECB in late 2009 and early 2010 also purchased 60 billion euros worth of covered bonds, thus funneling liquidity to banks that sell covered bonds to fund mortgages and lending to public institutions.

Euro-Zone GDP growth was negative for five consecutive quarters from Q2-2008 through Q2-2009. Euro-Zone GDP finally turned positive to +0.4% q/q in Q3-2009 but then lost steam with a gain of only +0.1% q/q in Q4-2009. The Euro-Zone faced difficulty in early 2010 when Greece ran into serious budget problems and talk arose about the possibility of a Greek sovereign bond default. The European Union had to step in with an implicit promise of providing a financial backstop for Greece should the need arise. Nevertheless, the Greek problems caused weakness in the euro and also forced the ECB to maintain its dovish monetary policy longer than it might otherwise have desired.

UK – The Liffe 10-year Gilt futures contract hit a record high in March 2009 but then steadily fell during the rest of 2009 to finally close the year down -9.02 points. The 10-year gilt yield hit a record low of 3.02% in December 2008 and then rose during 2009 to close the year up 100 basis points at 4.02%. The 3-month UK Libor rate fell sharply in late 2008 and during the first three quarters of 2009, closing 2009 down -216 basis points at 0.61%. The Bank of England (BOE) slashed its base rate by a total of 525 bp from 5.75% in November 2007 to 0.50% by March 2009, which was the lowest rate in the BOE's 315-year history. In addition to cutting interest rates, the BOE instituted a quantitative easing program of buying 200 billion pounds of government bonds. The UK economy was hit particularly hard by the global financial crisis. UK GDP showed six consecutive quarters of negative growth from Q2-2008 through Q3-2009, finally showing a modest increase of +0.3% q/q in Q4-2009. Looking ahead, the BOE is forecasting GDP growth in 2010 of only +1.4%.

Canada – The Montreal Exchange's Canadian 10-year government note futures contract posted a record high in March 2009 and then spent most of the rest of 2009 trending lower, finally closing the year down 8.92 points. The 10-year Canadian bond yield hit a record low of 2.52% in January 2009 and then moved higher during the year to close the year up +6 basis points at 3.23%. The 3-month Canadian interbank lending rate fell sharply in late 2008 and all during 2009, closing the year down -212 basis points at 0.47%. The Bank of Canada slashed its overnight lending rate from 4.50% in November 2007 to 0.50% by March 2009 and the rate then stayed at 0.50% through early 2010. Canadian real GDP growth, which is reported on a monthly basis, was negative on a month-on-month basis from August 2008 through May 2009, but then turned positive for the remainder of 2009 except for one month August 2009. The market consensus as of early 2010 was that Canada's GDP would grow by +2.6% in 2010 and then +3.4% in 2011.

Japan – The SGX 10-year JGB futures showed some weakness early in 2009 but then rallied in the latter part of the year to close mildly higher by 1.73 points. The 10-year JGB government bond yield in 2009 traded in a relatively narrow range in the low 1% area and closed the year up +13 basis points at 1.30%. The Bank of Japan started cutting its overnight benchmark rate from 0.50% in September 2008 to 0.10% by December and the overnight remained at 0.10% through 2009 and into early 2010. The Bank of Japan also pursued an aggressive government bond program in order to force reserves into the banking system. Japan's real GDP growth was negative for four consecutive quarters from Q2-2008 through Q1-2009. Japan's GDP was choppy in the later part of 2009 at +5.2% in Q2, zero in Q3, and +4.6% in Q4. Japan's economy was clearly helped by the quick recovery in the Chinese economy, which bottomed out at +6.2% in Q1-2009 and then recovered to +10.7% by Q4-2009. Looking ahead, the market consensus as of early 2010 was for Japanese GDP to grow by a weak +1.8% in both 2010 and 2011, which will likely force the BOJ to maintain its extremely easy monetary policy.

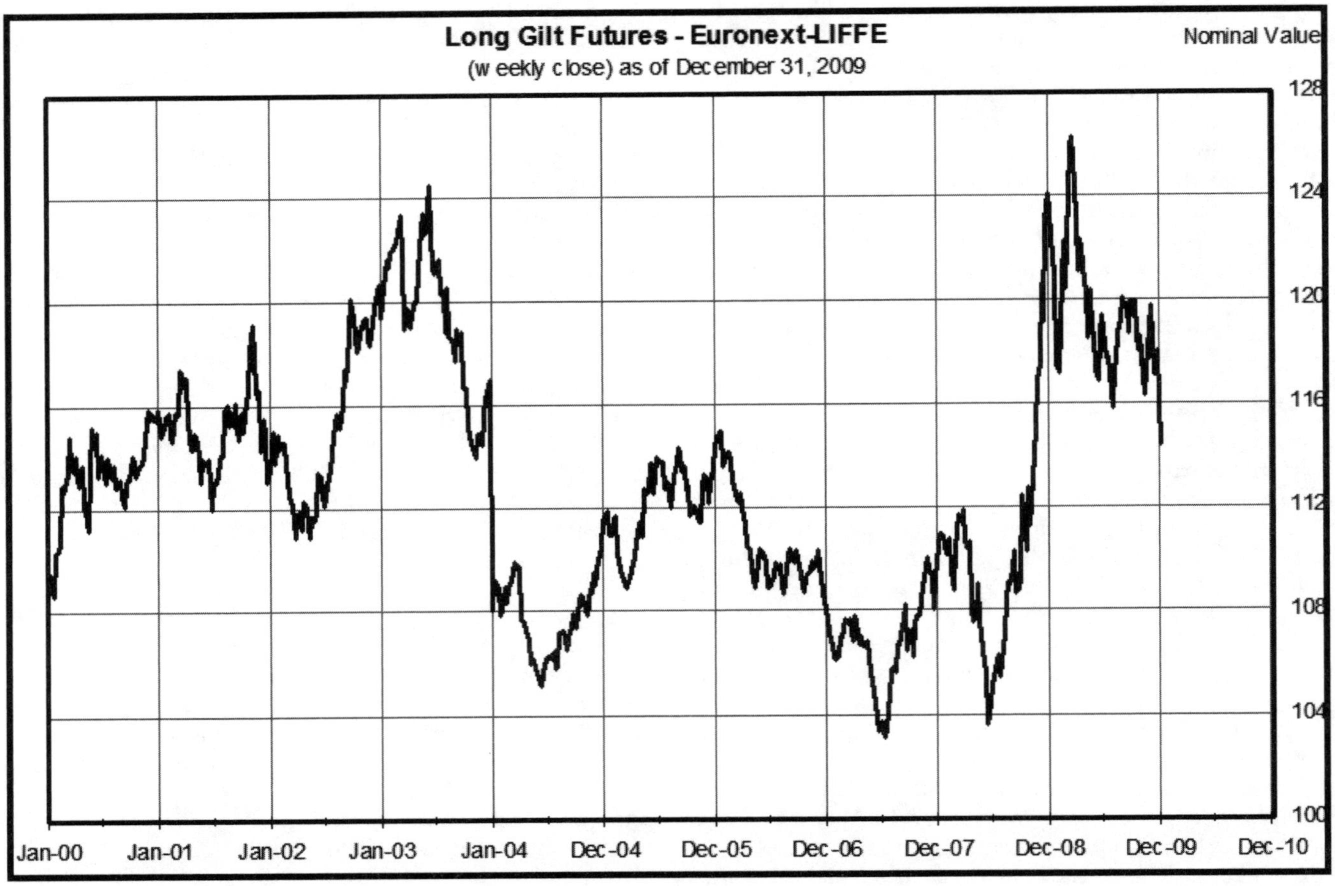
Long Gilt Futures - Euronext-LIFFE
(weekly close) as of December 31, 2009
Nominal Value
128
124
120
116
112
108
104
100
Jan-00
Jan-01
Jan-02
Jan-03
Jan-04
Dec-04
Dec-05
Dec-06
Dec-07
Dec-08
Dec-09
Dec-10

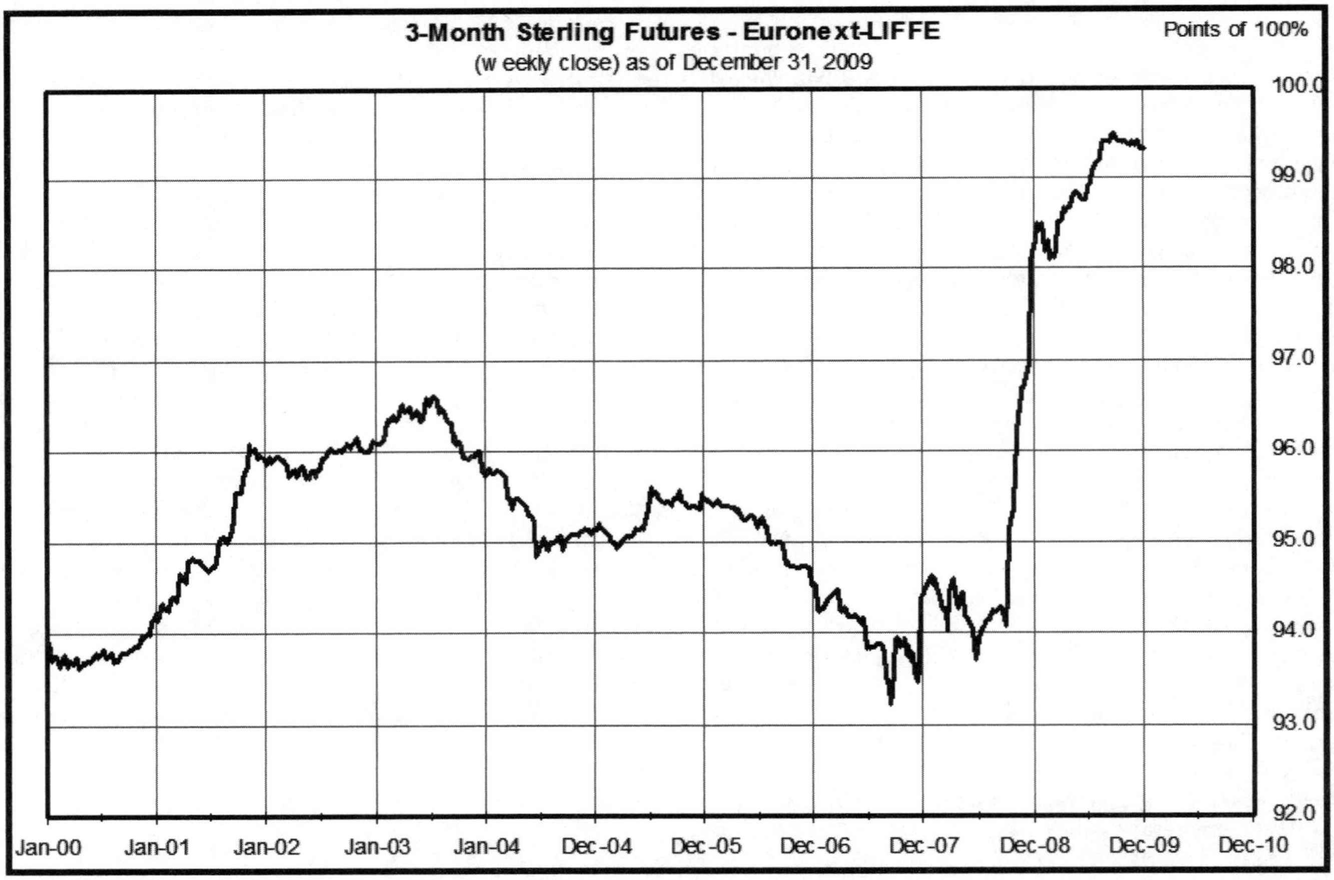
3-Month Sterling Futures - Euronext-LIFFE
(weekly close) as of December 31, 2009
Points of 100%
100.0
99.0
98.0
97.0
96.0
95.0
94.0
93.0
92.0
Jan-00
Jan-01
Jan-02
Jan-03
Jan-04
Dec-04
Dec-05
Dec-06
Dec-07
Dec-08
Dec-09
Dec-10

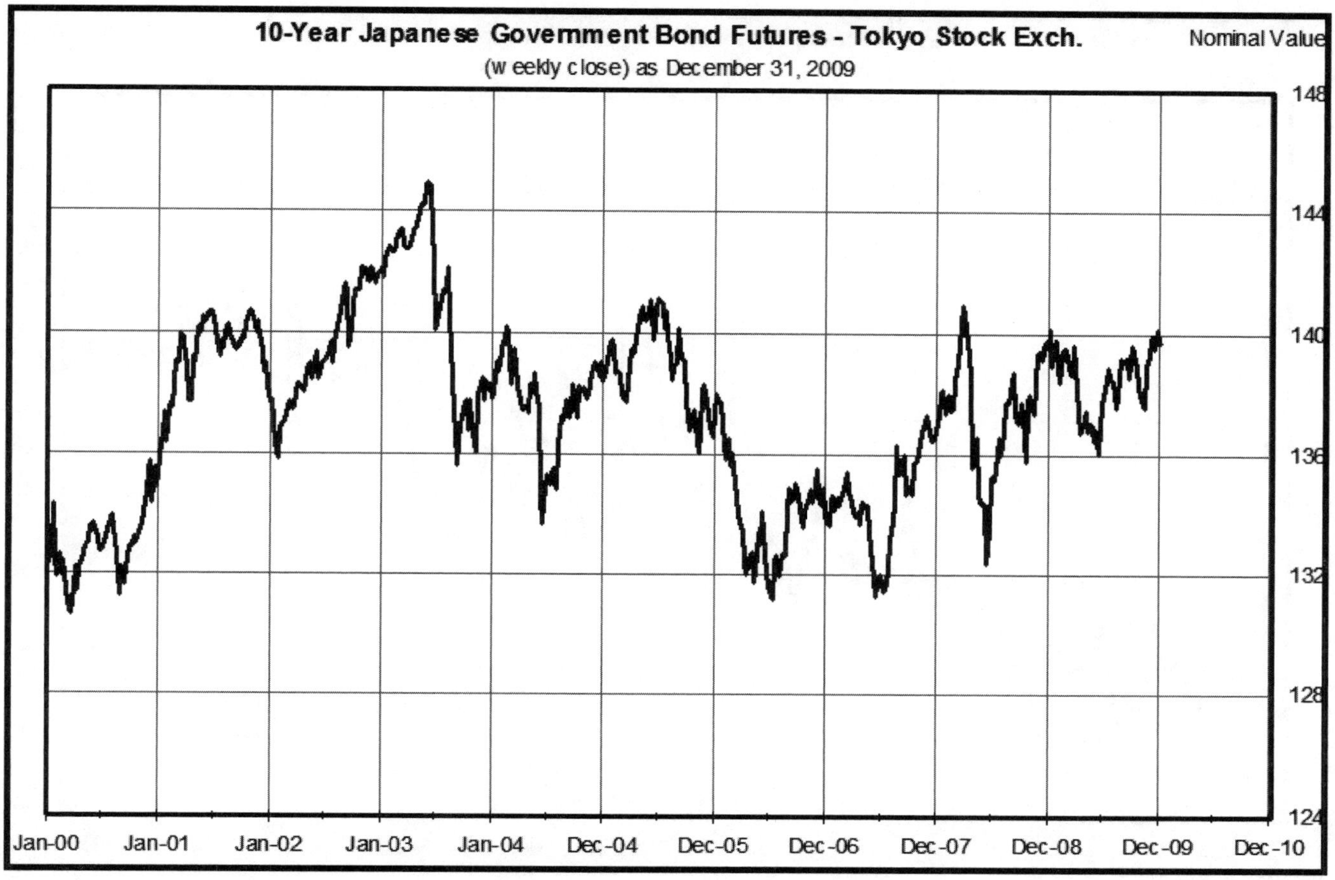
10-Year Japanese Government Bond Futures - Tokyo Stock Exch.
(weekly close) as December 31, 2009
Nominal Value
148
144
140
136
132
128
124
Jan-00
Jan-01
Jan-02
Jan-03
Jan-04
Dec-04
Dec-05
Dec-06
Dec-07
Dec-08
Dec-09
Dec-10

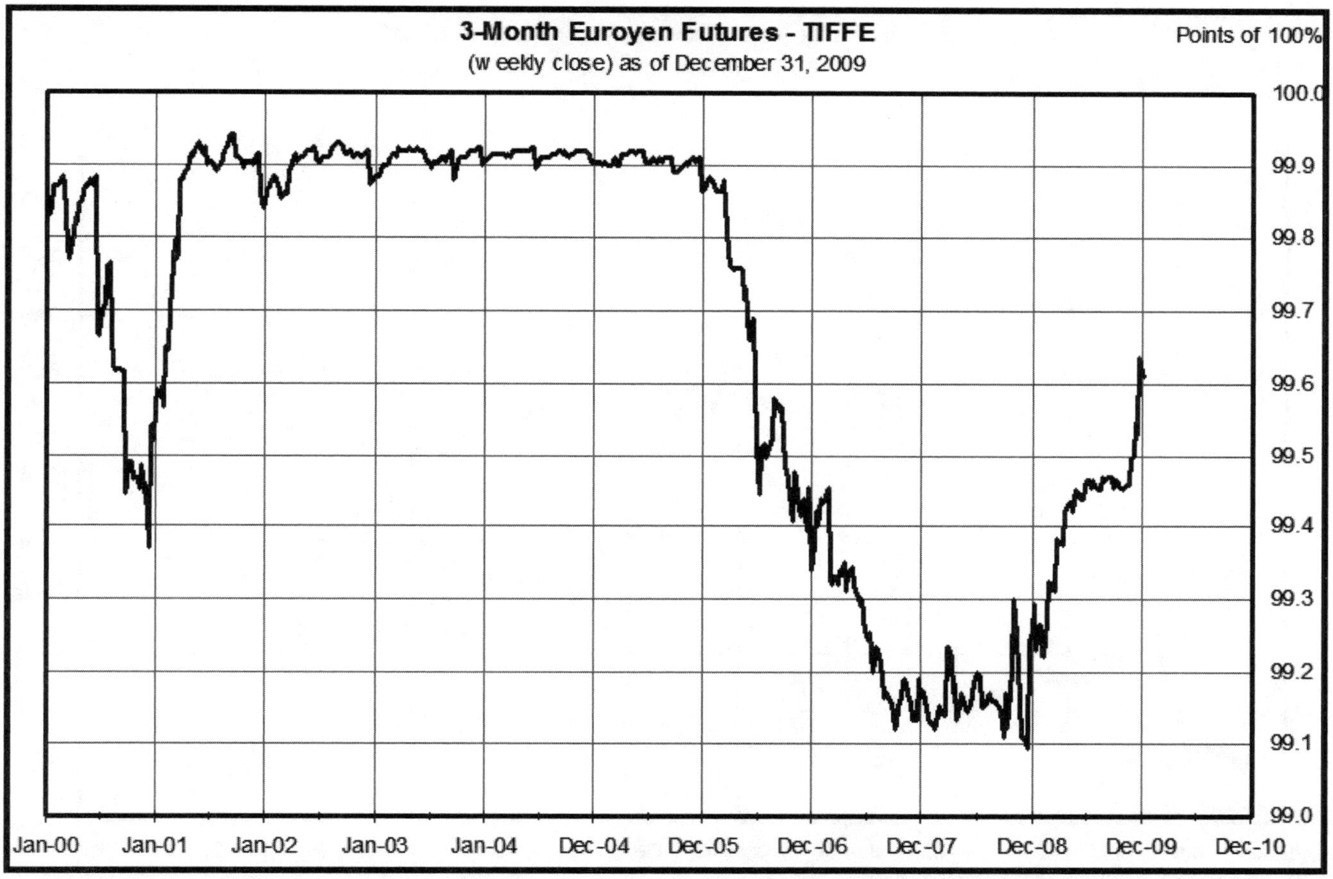
3-Month Euroyen Futures - TIFFE
(weekly close) as of December 31, 2009
Points of 100%
100.0
99.9
99.8
99.7
99.6
99.5
99.4
99.3
99.2
99.1
99.0
Jan-00
Jan-01
Jan-02
Jan-03
Jan-04
Dec-04
Dec-05
Dec-06
Dec-07
Dec-08
Dec-09
Dec-10

10-Year Canadian Government Bond Futures - Montreal Exch.
(weekly close) as of December 31, 2009
Nominal Value
132
128
124
120
116
112
108
104
100
96
Jan-00
Jan-01
Jan-02
Jan-03
Jan-04
Dec-04
Dec-05
Dec-06
Dec-07
Dec-08
Dec-09
Dec-10

3-Month Canadian Bankers' Acceptance Futures - Montreal Exch.
(weekly close) as of December 31, 2009
Points of 100%
100.0
99.5
99.0
98.5
98.0
97.5
97.0
96.5
96.0
95.5
95.0
94.5
94.0
93.5
Jan-00
Jan-01
Jan-02
Jan-03
Jan-04
Dec-04
Dec-05
Dec-06
Dec-07
Dec-08
Dec-09
Dec-10

Australia -- Economic Statistics Percentage Change from Previous Period

Year	Real GDP	Nominal GDP	Real Private Consump-tion	Real Public Consump-tion	Grossed Fixed Invest-ment	Real Total Domestic Demand	Real Exports of Goods & Services	Real Imports of Goods & Services	Consumer Prices[1]	Unem-ployment Rate
2002	4.0	7.0	3.8	3.0	17.0	6.3	.2	10.9	3.0	6.3
2003	3.4	6.3	3.6	3.7	9.3	6.2	-1.6	10.7	2.8	5.9
2004	3.2	7.5	5.9	3.9	6.9	5.4	4.6	15.3	2.3	5.4
2005	3.1	7.5	3.0	3.0	8.7	4.7	2.4	8.4	2.7	5.0
2006	2.6	7.4	3.2	3.2	4.8	2.9	3.3	7.3	3.5	4.8
2007	4.2	8.4	4.4	2.4	9.5	6.1	3.2	12.1	2.3	4.4
2008	2.3	8.9	2.6	4.0	9.6	4.1	3.8	11.1	4.4	4.2
2009[1]	.8	.8	1.5	2.4	-3.1	-.4	2.3	-10.2	1.6	5.7
2010[3]	2.4	4.3	1.5	2.3	2.9	2.5	6.3	6.1	2.4	6.3

[1] National accounts implicit private consumption deflator. [2] Estimate. [3] Projection. *Source: Organization for Economic Co-operation and Development (OECD)*

Canada -- Economic Statistics Percentage Change from Previous Period

Year	Real GDP	Nominal GDP	Real Private Consump-tion	Real Public Consump-tion	Grossed Fixed Invest-ment	Real Total Domestic Demand	Real Exports of Goods & Services	Real Imports of Goods & Services	Consumer Prices[1]	Unem-ployment Rate
2002	2.9	4.0	3.6	2.5	1.6	3.2	1.2	1.7	2.3	7.6
2003	1.9	5.2	3.0	3.1	6.2	4.5	-2.3	4.1	2.8	7.6
2004	3.1	6.4	3.3	2.0	7.8	4.1	5.0	8.0	1.9	7.2
2005	3.0	6.4	3.7	1.4	9.3	4.9	1.9	7.1	2.2	6.8
2006	2.9	5.5	4.1	3.0	6.9	4.3	.8	4.7	2.0	6.3
2007	2.5	5.8	4.6	3.3	3.7	4.3	1.1	5.8	2.1	6.0
2008	.4	4.4	3.0	3.7	.9	2.4	-4.7	.8	2.4	6.1
2009[1]	-2.7	-4.5	-.1	2.5	-8.7	-2.8	-14.0	-13.3	.4	8.3
2010[3]	2.0	4.3	2.3	2.7	4.4	3.8	5.2	11.4	1.3	8.7

[1] National accounts implicit private consumption deflator. [2] Estimate. [3] Projection. *Source: Organization for Economic Co-operation and Development (OECD)*

France -- Economic Statistics Percentage Change from Previous Period

Year	Real GDP	Nominal GDP	Real Private Consump-tion	Real Public Consump-tion	Grossed Fixed Invest-ment	Real Total Domestic Demand	Real Exports of Goods & Services	Real Imports of Goods & Services	Consumer Prices[1]	Unem-ployment Rate
2002	1.1	3.5	2.3	1.9	-1.7	1.1	1.4	1.6	1.9	7.9
2003	1.1	3.0	2.1	2.0	2.2	1.8	-1.2	1.3	2.2	8.5
2004	2.3	3.9	2.3	2.2	3.3	2.9	3.7	6.4	2.3	8.8
2005	1.9	4.0	2.5	1.3	4.5	2.7	3.4	6.3	1.9	8.9
2006	2.4	4.9	2.6	1.3	4.4	2.7	5.0	5.9	1.9	8.8
2007	2.3	4.8	2.4	1.5	6.5	3.1	2.5	5.4	1.6	8.0
2008	.3	2.8	1.0	1.1	.4	.6	-.6	.6	3.2	7.4
2009[1]	-2.3	-1.3	.6	1.5	-6.8	-2.2	-11.0	-10.0	.1	9.1
2010[3]	1.4	1.9	.3	1.3	-.3	1.0	4.7	2.9	1.0	9.9

[1] National accounts implicit private consumption deflator. [2] Estimate. [3] Projection. *Source: Organization for Economic Co-operation and Development (OECD)*

Germany -- Economic Statistics Percentage Change from Previous Period

Year	Real GDP	Nominal GDP	Real Private Consump-tion	Real Public Consump-tion	Grossed Fixed Invest-ment	Real Total Domestic Demand	Real Exports of Goods & Services	Real Imports of Goods & Services	Consumer Prices[1]	Unem-ployment Rate
2002	.0	1.4	-.8	1.5	-6.1	-2.0	4.3	-1.4	1.4	8.3
2003	-.2	.9	.1	.4	-.3	.6	2.4	5.3	1.0	9.2
2004	.7	1.7	-.2	-.7	-1.3	-.5	9.3	6.5	1.8	9.7
2005	.9	1.6	.4	.4	1.1	.1	8.0	6.9	1.9	10.5
2006	3.4	3.9	1.4	1.0	8.6	2.4	13.4	12.2	1.8	9.8
2007	2.6	4.6	-.3	1.7	5.3	1.1	7.8	5.0	2.3	8.3
2008	1.0	2.5	.2	2.0	2.3	1.5	2.4	3.9	2.8	7.2
2009[1]	-4.9	-4.0	.8	2.3	-8.7	-1.5	-14.4	-8.2	.2	7.6
2010[3]	1.4	1.6	-.5	1.5	1.3	.4	7.2	5.1	1.0	9.2

[1] National accounts implicit private consumption deflator. [2] Estimate. [3] Projection. *Source: Organization for Economic Co-operation and Development (OECD)*

Italy -- Economic Statistics   Percentage Change from Previous Period

Year	Real GDP	Nominal GDP	Real Private Consump-tion	Real Public Consump-tion	Grossed Fixed Invest-ment	Real Total Domestic Demand	Real Exports of Goods & Services	Real Imports of Goods & Services	Consumer Prices[1]	Unem-ployment Rate
2002	.5	3.7	.2	2.4	3.7	1.3	-2.8	.2	2.6	8.7
2003	.1	3.2	1.0	1.9	-.9	.8	-1.5	1.6	2.8	8.6
2004	1.4	4.0	.8	2.2	1.5	1.3	3.6	3.3	2.3	8.1
2005	.8	2.9	1.2	1.9	1.4	1.0	2.0	2.7	2.2	7.8
2006	2.1	4.0	1.3	.5	3.2	2.0	6.5	6.2	2.2	6.8
2007	1.5	3.9	1.2	1.0	1.6	1.3	4.0	3.3	2.0	6.2
2008	-1.0	1.8	-.9	.6	-2.9	-1.3	-3.7	-4.5	3.5	6.8
2009[1]	-4.8	-2.5	-1.9	1.7	-12.6	-3.6	-20.3	-15.8	.7	7.6
2010[3]	1.1	2.1	.7	.7	.6	1.0	1.4	1.0	.9	8.5

[1] National accounts implicit private consumption deflator. [2] Estimate. [3] Projection. *Source: Organization for Economic Co-operation and Development (OECD)*

Japan -- Economic Statistics   Percentage Change from Previous Period

Year	Real GDP	Nominal GDP	Real Private Consump-tion	Real Public Consump-tion	Grossed Fixed Invest-ment	Real Total Domestic Demand	Real Exports of Goods & Services	Real Imports of Goods & Services	Consumer Prices[1]	Unem-ployment Rate
2002	.3	-1.3	1.1	2.4	-4.9	-.4	7.5	.9	-.9	5.4
2003	1.4	-.2	.4	2.3	-.5	.8	9.2	3.9	-.2	5.3
2004	2.7	1.6	1.6	1.9	1.4	1.9	13.9	8.1	.0	4.7
2005	1.9	.7	1.3	1.6	3.1	1.7	7.0	5.8	-.6	4.4
2006	2.0	1.1	1.5	.4	.5	1.2	9.7	4.2	.2	4.1
2007	2.3	1.7	.7	1.9	.8	1.2	8.4	1.5	.1	3.9
2008	-.7	-1.6	.6	.8	-5.0	-.9	1.8	.9	1.4	4.0
2009[1]	-5.3	-5.3	-.7	1.1	-12.8	-3.4	-25.1	-14.7	-1.2	5.2
2010[3]	1.8	.1	1.2	2.3	-.8	1.1	10.8	5.9	-.9	5.6

[1] National accounts implicit private consumption deflator. [2] Estimate. [3] Projection. *Source: Organization for Economic Co-operation and Development (OECD)*

Switzerland -- Economic Statistics   Percentage Change from Previous Period

Year	Real GDP	Nominal GDP	Real Private Consump-tion	Real Public Consump-tion	Grossed Fixed Invest-ment	Real Total Domestic Demand	Real Exports of Goods & Services	Real Imports of Goods & Services	Consumer Prices[1]	Unem-ployment Rate
2002	.4	.9	.1	1.2	-.5	.1	-.1	-1.1	.6	3.2
2003	-.2	.8	.9	1.9	-1.2	.5	-.5	1.3	.6	4.3
2004	2.5	3.1	1.6	.8	4.5	1.9	7.9	7.3	.8	4.4
2005	2.6	2.8	1.7	1.2	3.8	1.8	7.8	6.6	1.2	4.4
2006	3.6	5.8	1.6	.3	4.7	1.6	10.0	6.5	1.1	4.0
2007	3.6	6.2	2.4	.5	5.2	1.3	9.5	6.0	.7	3.6
2008	1.8	4.0	1.7	-.1	.4	.4	2.9	.4	2.4	3.5
2009[1]	-1.9	-1.6	1.2	2.3	-2.9	1.7	-12.5	-8.2	-.6	4.3
2010[3]	.9	1.4	1.2	1.1	1.1	.0	3.4	2.1	.6	4.9

[1] National accounts implicit private consumption deflator. [2] Estimate. [3] Projection. *Source: Organization for Economic Co-operation and Development (OECD)*

United Kingdom -- Economic Statistics   Percentage Change from Previous Period

Year	Real GDP	Nominal GDP	Real Private Consump-tion	Real Public Consump-tion	Grossed Fixed Invest-ment	Real Total Domestic Demand	Real Exports of Goods & Services	Real Imports of Goods & Services	Consumer Prices[1]	Unem-ployment Rate
2002	2.1	5.3	3.5	3.5	3.6	3.2	1.0	4.9	1.3	5.2
2003	2.8	6.0	3.0	3.4	1.1	2.9	1.8	2.2	1.4	5.0
2004	3.0	5.5	3.1	3.0	5.1	3.5	5.0	6.9	1.3	4.8
2005	2.2	4.2	2.2	2.0	2.4	2.1	7.9	7.1	2.0	4.8
2006	2.9	5.7	1.5	1.6	6.5	2.4	11.3	8.8	2.3	5.4
2007	2.6	5.5	2.1	1.2	7.8	3.0	-2.8	-.7	2.3	5.4
2008	.6	3.5	1.2	2.5	-3.3	.3	1.0	-.8	3.6	5.7
2009[1]	-4.7	-3.6	-3.0	2.8	-16.1	-5.5	-10.6	-13.3	2.1	8.0
2010[3]	1.2	2.8	-.2	3.3	-5.2	.3	4.4	.9	1.7	9.3

[1] National accounts implicit private consumption deflator. [2] Estimate. [3] Projection. *Source: Organization for Economic Co-operation and Development (OECD)*

Iron and Steel

Iron (symbol Fe) is a soft, malleable, and ductile metallic element. Next to aluminum, iron is the most abundant of all metals. Pure iron melts at about 1535 degrees Celsius and boils at 2750 degrees Celsius. Archaeologists in Egypt discovered the earliest iron implements dating back to about 3000 BC, and iron ornaments were used even earlier.

Steel is an alloy of iron and carbon, often with an admixture of other elements. The physical properties of various types of steel and steel alloys depend primarily on the amount of carbon present and how it is distributed in the iron. Steel is marketed in a variety of sizes and shapes, such as rods, pipes, railroad rails, tees, channels, and I-beams. Steel mills roll and form heated ingots into the required shapes. The working of steel improves the quality of the steel by refining its crystalline structure and making the metal tougher. There are five classifications of steel: carbon steels, alloy steels, high-strength low-alloy steels, stainless steel, and tool steels.

Prices – In 2009 the average wholesale price for No. 1 heavy-melting steel scrap in Chicago fell by -41.9% to $206.33 per metric ton. That was down from last year's record high of $354.89.

Supply – World production of iron ore in 2009 rose by +3.6% to 2.300 billion metric tons, which was a new record high. The world's largest producers of iron ore are China (with 39% of world production), Brazil (with 17%), and Australia (with 16%). The U.S. accounted for only 1.3.0% of world iron ore production in 2009. World production of raw steel (ingots and castings) in 2009 fell -17.3 % yr/yr to 1,100 million metric tons, with the largest producers being China (with 50% of world production), Japan (with 7%), and the U.S. (with 5%). U.S. production of steel ingots in 2006 (latest data available) rose by +5.7% to an 8-year high of 108.621 million short tons. U.S. production of pig iron (excluding ferro-alloys) in 2009 (annualized through June) was down 49.3% to 17.500 million short tons.

Demand – U.S. consumption of ferrous scrap and pig iron fell –0.4% yr/yr in 2007 (latest data available) to 102.800 million metric tons which is the lowest level since 1986. The largest consumers of ferrous scrap and pig iron were the manufacturers of pig iron and steel ingots and castings with 89% of consumption at 91.200 million metric tons in 2007. Iron foundries and miscellaneous users accounted for 10% of consumption and manufacturers of steel castings (scrap) accounted for 1% of consumption.

Trade – The U.S. imported 9.250 million metric tons of iron ore in 2008, down 1.6% yr/yr from 9.400 million metric tons in 2007. The bulk of U.S. iron ore imports came from Canada (64% with 5.900 million metric tons) and Brazil (28% with 2.620 million metric tons).

World Production of Raw Steel (Ingots and Castings) In Thousands of Metric Tons

Year	Brazil	Canada	China	France	Germany	Italy	Japan	Rep. of Korea	Russia	Ukraine	United Kindom	United States	World Total
2000	27,865	15,900	128,500	21,002	46,376	26,544	106,444	43,107	59,098	31,780	15,022	102,000	850,000
2001	26,718	16,300	151,630	19,431	44,775	26,483	102,866	43,852	59,030	33,110	13,610	90,100	853,000
2002	29,605	16,300	182,370	20,524	44,999	25,930	107,745	45,390	59,777	34,538	11,718	91,600	907,000
2003	31,150	15,928	222,340	19,803	44,809	26,832	110,511	46,310	62,710	36,900	13,128	93,700	974,000
2004	32,918	16,305	272,450	20,770	46,374	28,317	112,718	47,521	65,646	38,740	13,766	99,700	1,060,000
2005	31,631	15,327	353,240	19,481	44,524	29,061	112,471	47,820	66,186	38,636	13,210	94,900	1,140,000
2006	30,900	15,493	419,150	19,857	47,224	31,550	116,266	48,455	70,816	40,899	13,931	98,200	1,250,000
2007	31,800	15,569	489,240	19,252	48,550	31,990	120,203	51,517	72,389	42,830	14,300	98,100	1,340,000
2008[1]	34,000	NA	500,000	18,000	46,000	30,000	119,000	53,000	69,000	37,000	14,000	92,000	1,330,000
2009[2]	24,000	NA	550,000	12,000	29,000	18,000	79,000	47,000	55,000	28,000	9,000	56,000	1,100,000

[1] Preliminary. [2] Estimate. *Source: U.S. Geological Survey (USGS)*

Average Wholesale Prices of Iron and Steel in the United States

	No. 1 Heavy Melting Steel Scrap		Pittsburg Prices								
				Sheet Bars							
Year	Pittsburg	Chicago	Hot Rolled	Hot Rolled	Cold Finished	Hot Rolled Strip	Carbon Steel Plates	Cold Rolled Strip	Galvanized Sheets	Rail Road Steel Scrap[2]	Used Steel Cans[3]
	$ Per Gross Ton		Cents Per Pound							$ Per Gross Ton	
2000	103.73	96.07	15.67	----	23.08	----	15.69	----	21.38	150.00	82.23
2001	79.34	74.17	11.71	----	22.76	----	12.94	----	16.41	NA	68.52
2002	101.06	89.92	16.46	----	23.26	----	----	----	22.00	NA	66.71
2003	128.32	113.82	14.80	----	25.15	----	----	----	20.08	----	116.21
2004	221.05	220.13	30.84	----	38.67	----	----	----	36.69	----	192.80
2005	199.10	196.75	27.83	----	44.96	----	----	----	33.77	----	172.00
2006	222.39	225.21	29.78	----	44.02	----	----	----	38.09	----	212.63
2007	250.98	262.80	26.89	----	45.26	----	----	----	38.25	----	244.65
2008	365.62	357.88	44.56	----	61.67	----	----	----	54.91	----	314.63
2009[1]	204.21	206.14	24.60	----	42.10	----	----	----	34.23	----	121.84

[1] Preliminary. [2] Specialties scrap. [3] Consumer buying prices. NA = Not available. *Source: American Metal Market (AMM)*

Salient Statistics of Steel in the United States In Thousands of Short Tons

Year	Pig Iron Production	Producer Price Index for Steel Mill Products (1982=100)	Raw Steel Production: By Type of Furnace: Basic Oxygen	Open Hearth	Electric[2]	Stainless	Carbon	Alloy	Total	Net Shipments Steel Mill Products	Total Steel Products: Exports	Imports
1997	54,679	116.4	61,053	----	47,508	2,382	95,933	10,246	108,561	105,858	7,369	34,389
1998	53,164	113.8	59,686	----	49,067	2,214	97,054	9,484	108,752	102,420	5,520	41,520
1999	51,002	105.3	57,722	----	49,673	2,086	98,694	5,421	107,395	106,201	5,426	35,731
2000	52,787	108.4	59,485	----	52,756	2,104	102,141	5,379	111,903	109,050	6,529	37,957
2001	46,424	101.3	52,204	----	47,118	1,836	92,946	4,666	99,322	99,448	6,144	30,080
2002	44,341	104.8	50,114	----	51,564	1,894	92,518	4,779	101,679	99,191	6,009	32,686
2003	43,122	109.5	50,942	----	48,751	1,952	98,772	4,901	99,693	105,625	8,220	23,125
2004	44,731	147.2	50,613	----	58,456	2,073	105,161	4,851	109,069	112,085	7,933	35,808
2005	40,036	159.7	45,231	----	57,599	1,903	96,636	4,935	102,830	103,474	9,393	32,108
2006[1]	41,781	174.1	46,802	----	61,838	2,081	101,572	4,956	108,640	108,609	9,728	45,272

[1] Preliminary. [2] Includes crucible steels. *Sources: American Iron & Steel Institute (AISI); U.S. Geological Survey (USGS)*

Production of Steel Ingots, Rate of Capability Utilization[1] in the United States In Percent

Year	Jan.	Feb.	Mar.	Apr.	May	June	July	Aug.	Sept.	Oct.	Nov.	Dec.	Average
2000	89.7	89.4	91.2	92.0	91.3	89.6	85.3	83.5	82.7	81.0	75.1	72.0	85.2
2001	77.6	82.3	81.8	82.9	81.5	81.6	79.8	80.4	80.5	77.5	73.5	65.9	78.8
2002	84.5	88.4	86.7	90.3	89.4	92.5	86.8	91.0	94.0	90.8	86.8	83.9	88.8
2003	83.1	87.3	85.0	87.8	81.1	86.2	78.9	78.3	80.7	82.8	82.8	81.9	83.0
2004	88.0	90.9	93.8	93.3	92.9	94.4	93.5	95.0	97.3	97.5	94.8	91.5	93.6
2005	90.9	92.9	88.4	89.2	84.2	79.8	77.1	81.3	86.4	89.3	88.1	85.0	86.1
2006	85.6	89.5	92.8	91.4	92.5	92.1	88.7	88.7	91.2	86.2	81.5	75.0	87.9
2007	78.2	87.8	86.3	85.0	88.4	88.6	87.0	87.7	86.5	88.5	88.5	88.1	86.7
2008	90.3	91.6	89.7	90.3	91.1	90.3	88.8	90.4	84.5	70.5	50.7	40.9	80.8
2009[2]	42.6	45.5	42.9	40.8	42.8	46.9	52.4	57.7	62.1	62.3	61.4		50.7

[1] Based on tonnage capability to produce raw steel for a full order book. [2] Preliminary. *Sources: American Iron and Steel Institute (AISI); U.S. Geological Survey (USGS)*

Production of Steel Ingots in the United States In Thousands of Short Tons

Year	Jan.	Feb.	Mar.	Apr.	May	June	July	Aug.	Sept.	Oct.	Nov.	Dec.	Total
1997	8,735	8,266	9,175	8,882	9,048	8,662	8,692	8,818	9,006	9,128	9,116	9,071	107,488
1998	9,510	9,087	9,839	9,524	9,483	8,863	8,832	9,194	8,548	8,681	7,710	8,013	107,643
1999	8,422	7,837	8,854	8,643	8,914	8,413	8,619	8,993	8,650	9,574	9,357	9,604	105,882
2000	9,838	9,170	10,009	9,843	10,097	9,592	9,411	9,213	8,830	8,978	8,054	7,982	111,015
2001	8,475	8,122	8,932	8,685	8,832	8,550	8,459	8,525	8,263	8,125	7,226	6,695	98,889
2002	8,050	7,609	8,261	8,214	8,401	8,414	8,510	8,918	8,916	9,015	8,340	8,329	100,976
2003	8,617	8,175	8,817	8,692	8,047	8,534	8,163	8,096	8,026	8,514	8,347	8,414	100,442
2004	8,656	8,400	9,268	8,901	9,163	9,006	9,164	9,314	9,234	9,551	8,989	8,660	108,305
2005	9,123	8,419	9,028	8,757	8,543	7,837	7,896	8,330	8,562	9,032	8,629	8,599	102,754
2006[1]	8,918	8,506	9,770	9,382	9,811	9,458	9,324	9,320	9,282	8,922	8,169	7,760	108,621

[1] Preliminary. *Source: American Iron and Steel Institute (AISI)*

Shipments of Steel Products[1] by Market Classifications in the United States In Thousands of Short Tons

Year	Appliances Utensils & Cutlery	Automotive	Containers, Packaging & Shipping Materials	Construction Including Maint.	Contractors Products	Electrical Equipment	Export	Machinery, Industrial Equip. & Tools	Oil and Gas	Rail Transportation	Steel for Converting & Processing[2]	Steel Service Center & Distributors	All Other[3]	Total Shipments
1997	1,635	15,251	4,163	15,885	[5]	2,434	2,610	2,355	3,811	1,410	11,263	27,800	17,241	105,858
1998	1,729	15,842	3,829	15,289	[5]	2,255	2,556	2,147	2,649	1,657	9,975	27,751	16,741	102,420
1999	1,712	15,639	3,768	14,685	[5]	2,260	2,292	1,547	1,544	876	7,599	21,439	32,840	106,201
2000	1,530	14,697	3,684	14,763	[5]	2,039	2,752	1,513	2,268	994	7,753	22,537	35,093	109,624
2001	1,675	12,767	3,193	16,339	[5]	1,694	2,281	1,210	2,134	720	7,462	23,887	26,086	99,448
2002	1,734	12,562	3,251	15,729	[5]	1,336	1,844	1,137	1,658	751	7,201	22,828	29,160	99,191
2003	1,891	11,937	2,949	14,403	[5]	1,200	2,572	1,108	1,800	799	6,798	24,266	35,905	105,628
2004	1,919	12,527	2,978	15,114	[5]	1,139	2,426	1,332	2,043	957	7,295	25,385	38,969	112,085
2005	1,895	13,031	2,504	15,858	[5]	1,088	2,592	1,300	2,056	1,019	7,559	23,213	31,359	103,474
2006[4]	1,781	14,003	2,535	17,544	[5]	1,228	3,068	1,360	2,459	1,242	8,531	23,706	31,153	108,609

[1] All grades including carbon, alloy and stainless steel. [2] Net total after deducting shipments to reporting companies for conversion or resale.
[3] Includes agricultural; bolts, nuts rivets & screws; forgings (other than automotive); shipbuilding & marine equipment; aircraft; mining, quarrying & lumbering; other domestic & commercial equipment machinery; ordnance & other direct military; and shipments of non-reporting companies.
[4] Preliminary. [5] Included in Construction. *Source: American Iron and Steel Institute (AISI)*

Net Shipments of Steel Products[2] in the United States In Thousands of Short Tons

Year	Cold Finished Bars	Rails & Accessories	Wire Drawn	Tin Mill Products	Plates Cut & Coils	Sheet & Strip[3] Galv, Hot Dipped	Hot Rolled Bars	Pipe & Tubing	Structural Shapes & Steel Piling	Reinforcing Bars	Hot Rolled Sheets	Cold Rolled Sheets	Carbon	Alloy	Stainless
1997	1,809	875	619	4,057	8,855	12,439	8,153	6,548	6,029	6,188	18,221	13,322	97,509	6,282	2,067
1998	1,780	938	725	3,714	8,864	13,481	8,189	5,409	5,595	5,909	15,715	13,185	94,536	5,847	2,037
1999	1,775	646	611	3,771	8,200	14,870	8,078	4,772	5,995	6,183	17,740	13,874	98,694	5,421	2,086
2000	1,756	783	579	3,742	8,898	14,917	7,901	5,385	7,402	6,893	19,236	14,802	102,141	5,379	2,104
2001	1,369	630	481	3,202	8,349	14,310	7,032	5,377	6,789	6,976	18,866	12,352	92,314	4,789	1,837
2002	1,404	789	733	3,419	8,769	14,944	6,581	4,809	6,729	6,359	19,243	12,673	92,518	4,779	1,894
2003	1,426	739	684	3,513	9,230	15,221	6,486	4,597	7,437	7,970	22,218	13,485	98,772	4,901	1,952
2004	1,520	843	428	3,247	10,740	16,306	7,181	5,328	7,812	8,274	23,106	14,762	105,161	4,851	2,073
2005	1,495	920	560	2,874	10,274	15,249	6,674	5,096	8,070	7,464	20,569	12,793	97,884	5,183	1,903
2006[1]	1,487	1,016	603	2,880	10,827	16,358	7,595	5,426	8,652	7,419	20,862	13,281	101,572	4,956	2,081

[1] Preliminary. [2] All grades, including carbon, alloy and stainless steel. *Source: American Iron and Steel Institute (AISI)*

World Production of Pig Iron (Excludes Ferro-Alloys) In Thousands of Metric Tons

Year	Belgium	Brazil	China	France	Germany	India	Italy	Japan	Russia	Ukraine	United Kingdom	United States	World Total
2000	8,472	27,952	131,010	13,621	30,846	21,321	11,223	81,071	44,618	25,700	10,891	47,900	616,000
2001	7,732	27,623	155,540	12,004	29,184	21,900	10,650	78,836	44,980	26,400	9,861	42,125	624,086
2002	8,053	29,667	170,850	13,217	29,427	24,315	9,736	80,979	46,060	27,560	8,561	40,200	653,000
2003	7,813	32,036	213,660	12,756	29,481	26,550	10,604	82,092	48,368	29,570	10,228	40,600	719,000
2004	8,224	34,579	251,850	13,198	30,018	25,117	10,664	82,974	50,427	31,000	10,180	42,300	773,000
2005	7,254	34,382	343,750	12,705	28,854	27,125	11,423	83,058	49,175	30,747	10,236	37,200	858,000
2006	7,516	34,975	412,450	13,013	30,360	28,300	11,535	84,270	51,683	32,926	10,736	37,900	942,000
2007	6,576	35,500	469,440	12,426	31,150	28,800	11,100	86,771	51,523	35,647	11,000	36,300	1,010,000
2008[1]		35,000	471,000	12,000	29,000		11,000	86,000	48,000	31,000	11,000	34,000	932,000
2009[2]		22,000	540,000	7,000	17,000		5,000	61,000	40,000	25,000	7,000	18,000	860,000

[1] Preliminary. [2] Estimate. *Source: U.S. Geological Survey (USGS)*

Production of Pig Iron (Excludes Ferro-Alloys) in the United States In Thousands of Short Tons

Year	Jan.	Feb.	Mar.	Apr.	May	June	July	Aug.	Sept.	Oct.	Nov.	Dec.	Total
2000	4,571	4,325	4,793	4,741	4,887	4,577	4,454	4,387	4,262	4,138	3,675	3,781	52,591
2001	3,808	3,691	4,255	4,183	4,278	4,143	4,048	4,121	3,920	3,837	3,202	2,965	46,451
2002	3,493	3,308	3,616	3,480	3,584	3,612	3,854	3,983	4,006	4,018	3,710	3,677	44,341
2003	3,832	3,631	3,906	3,810	3,381	3,569	3,395	3,253	3,289	3,527	3,530	3,733	42,856
2004	3,682	3,524	4,018	3,749	3,670	3,633	3,590	3,839	3,818	3,940	3,668	3,389	44,520
2005	3,773	3,592	4,030	3,397	3,395	2,962	2,895	3,183	3,127	3,237	3,310	3,135	40,036
2006	3,519	3,421	3,765	3,612	3,816	3,667	3,540	3,525	3,544	3,403	3,059	2,909	41,780
2007	2,850	2,610	3,040	3,010	3,130	3,120	3,080	3,010	3,010	3,200	2,940	3,160	36,160
2008	2,900	3,110	3,280	3,240	3,210	3,020	3,090	3,290	2,900	2,770	2,040	1,690	34,540
2009[1]	1,450	1,510	1,630	1,410	1,370	1,380							17,500

[1] Preliminary. *Source: American Iron and Steel Institute*

Salient Statistics of Ferrous Scrap and Pig Iron in the United States In Thousands of Metric Tons

	Consumption: Ferrous Scrap & Pig Iron Charged To												Stocks, Dec. 31 Ferrous Scrap & Pig Iron at Consumers		
	Mfg. of Pig Iron & Steel Ingots & Castings			Iron Foundries & Misc. Users			Mfg. of Steel Castings	All Uses							
Year	Scrap	Pig Iron	Total	Scrap	Pig Iron	Total	(Scrap)	Ferrous Scrap	Pig Iron	Grand Total	Imports of Scrap[2]	Exports of Scrap[3]			Total
1998	58,000	49,000	107,000	13,000	1,200	14,200	2,000	73,000	50,000	123,000	3,060	5,570	5,300	570	5,870
1999	56,000	48,000	104,000	13,000	1,100	14,100	1,900	71,000	49,000	120,000	3,360	5,000	5,450	724	6,174
2000	59,000	49,000	108,000	13,000	1,200	14,200	2,200	74,000	50,000	124,000	3,040	5,230	5,320	930	6,250
2001	56,700	46,900	103,600	12,000	1,100	13,100	2,200	71,000	48,000	119,000	2,630	7,440	4,880	787	5,667
2002	56,400	42,500	98,900	11,000	1,500	12,500	1,800	69,000	44,000	113,000	3,130	8,950	4,930	754	5,684
2003	55,200	39,700	94,900	4,460	655	5,115	2,680	61,900	41,000	102,900	3,480	10,800	4,410	381	4,791
2004	57,100	38,000	95,100	8,490	1,020	9,510	1,330	66,500	39,100	105,600	4,660	11,800	5,400	722	6,122
2005	54,600	36,900	91,500	9,010	1,090	10,100	1,810	65,400	38,000	103,400	3,840	13,000	4,970	665	5,635
2006	54,500	36,700	91,200	9,370	857	10,227	1,640	65,600	37,600	103,200	4,820	14,900	4,610	700	5,310
2007[1]	54,600	36,500	91,100	9,080	1,290	10,370	1,380	65,000	37,800	102,800	3,700	16,500	4,410	784	5,194

[1] Preliminary. [2] Includes tinplate and terneplate. [3] Excludes used rails for rerolling and other uses and ships, boats, and other vessels for scrapping.
Source: U.S. Geological Survey (USGS)

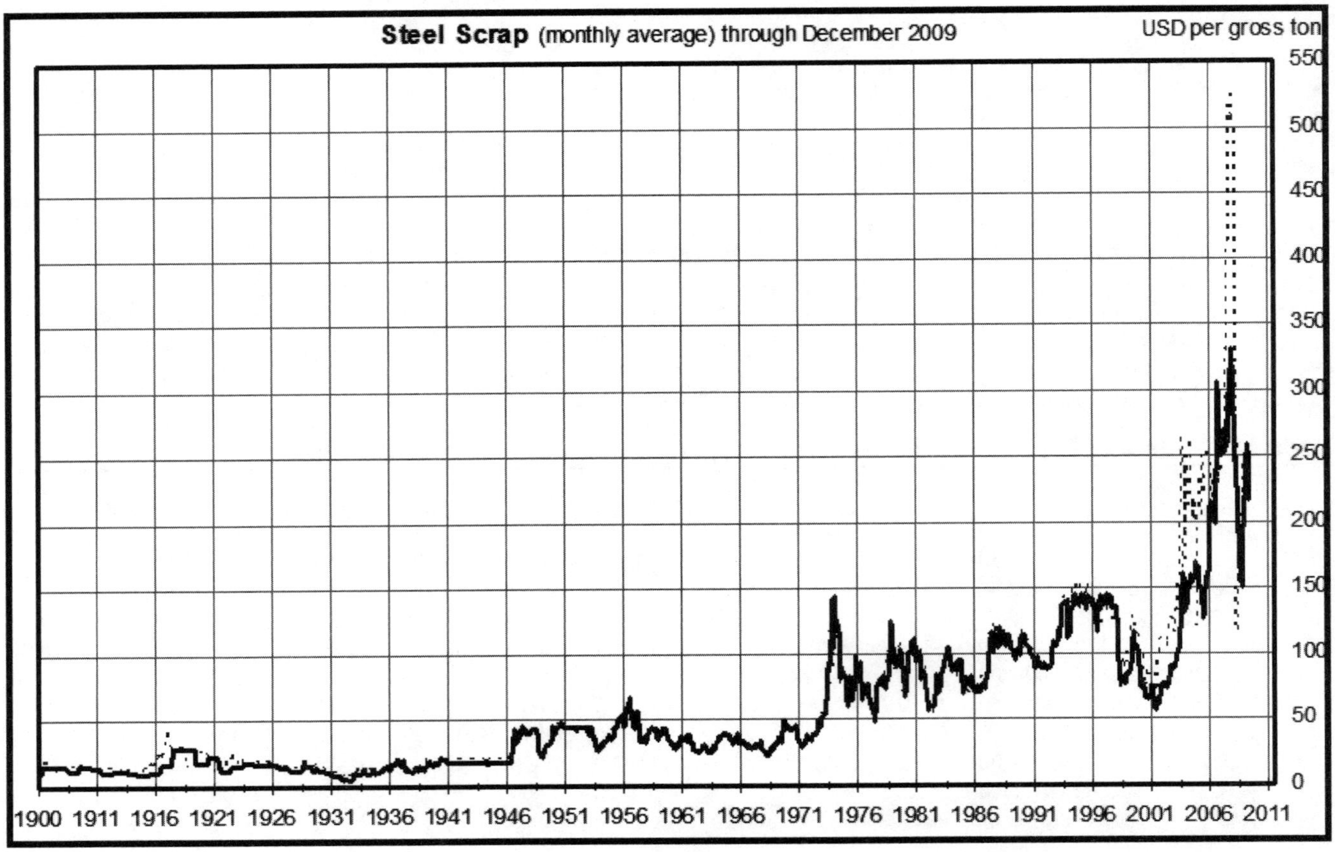

Consumption of Pig Iron in the United States, by Type of Furance or Equipment In Thousands of Metric Tons

Year	Open Hearth	Electric	Cupola	Basic Oxygen Process	Air & Other Furnace	Direct Casting	Total
1999	----	3,100	520	45,000	W	36	49,000
2000	----	2,900	530	47,000	W	35	50,000
2001	----	2,700	500	45,000	W	36	48,000
2002	----	3,200	520	40,000	W	36	44,000
2003	----	2,310	792	37,900	W	36	41,000
2004	----	3,030	354	35,700	W	36	39,100
2005	----	3,040	528	34,400	W	36	38,000
2006	----	3,380	435	33,800	W	36	37,600
2007[1]	----	3,980	401	33,400	8	36	37,800
2008[2]	----	W	W	30,500	W	W	33,600

[1] Preliminary. [2] Estimate. W = Withheld. *Source: U.S. Geological Survey (USGS)*

Wholesale Price of No. 1 Heavy Melting Steel Scrap in Chicago In Dollars Per Metric Ton

Year	Jan.	Feb.	Mar.	Apr.	May	June	July	Aug.	Sept.	Oct.	Nov.	Dec.	Average
2000	120.50	111.10	110.50	108.15	101.50	94.59	92.50	92.50	92.50	82.59	72.80	74.20	96.07
2001	83.55	74.50	74.50	74.50	73.23	72.50	75.93	76.50	76.50	72.54	67.50	67.50	74.17
2002	70.21	75.03	75.50	85.05	93.09	97.10	97.50	97.50	100.50	98.85	93.50	93.50	89.78
2003	96.93	101.97	105.07	105.50	101.69	96.88	101.05	116.79	122.02	122.50	138.22	159.74	114.03
2004	187.75	219.92	250.85	224.55	181.90	180.00	222.50	249.32	217.38	237.62	248.00	223.57	220.28
2005	203.00	190.00	190.00	217.14	180.95	124.32	135.50	189.78	241.19	204.29	246.25	242.43	197.07
2006	222.70	237.76	237.07	245.00	249.23	249.23	245.25	204.41	207.25	202.55	197.90	203.55	225.16
2007	225.24	252.37	305.00	291.90	255.36	254.71	250.71	257.04	268.74	265.65	252.10	273.42	262.69
2008	334.00	338.70	352.57	482.73	513.10	498.10	510.45	466.43	313.62	188.00	91.67	169.29	354.89
2009	183.00	176.68	157.73	150.00	179.25	185.00	230.00	244.29	257.86	244.76	216.32	251.05	206.33

Source: American Metal Market (AMM)

World Production of Iron Ore[3] In Thousands of Metric Tons (Gross Weight)

Year	Australia	Brazil	Canada	China	India	Mauritania	Russia	South Africa	Sweden	Ukraine	United States	Venezula	World Total
2000	167,935	212,576	35,427	223,000	75,950	11,345	86,630	33,707	20,557	55,883	63,089	17,353	1,078,746
2001	181,553	201,430	27,119	220,000	79,200	10,302	82,500	34,757	19,486	54,650	46,192	16,902	1,046,430
2002	187,198	214,560	30,902	231,000	86,400	9,553	84,236	36,484	20,300	58,900	51,600	16,684	1,100,000
2003	212,981	230,707	33,322	261,000	99,100	10,377	91,760	38,086	21,500	62,498	48,600	17,954	1,210,000
2004	233,994	261,696	28,596	320,000	120,600	10,674	96,980	39,322	22,300	65,550	54,700	19,196	1,360,000
2005	261,855	281,462	30,387	420,000	140,000	10,752	96,764	39,542	23,300	68,570	54,300	20,000	1,540,000
2006	275,098	317,800	33,543	601,000	160,000	10,658	102,000	41,326	23,300	74,000	52,700	23,000	1,820,000
2007	299,009	354,674	32,834	707,000	180,000	11,817	105,000	42,083	24,700	77,900	52,500	23,000	2,030,000
2008[1]	342,000	355,000	31,000	824,000	220,000	11,000	100,000	49,000	24,000	73,000	54,000	21,000	2,220,000
2009[2]	370,000	380,000	27,000	900,000	260,000	11,000	85,000	53,000	18,000	56,000	26,000	16,000	2,300,000

[1] Preliminary. [2] Estimate. [3] Iron ore, iron ore concentrates and iron ore agglomerates. *Source: U.S. Geological Survey (USGS)*

Salient Statistics of Iron Ore[3] in the United States In Thousands of Metric Tons

Year	Net Import Reliance As a % of Apparent Consumption	Production Total	Production Lake Superior	Production Other Regions	Shipments	Value Million $ (at Mine)	Average Value $ at Mine Per Ton	Stock, Dec. 31 Mines	Stock, Dec. 31 Consuming Plants	Stock, Dec. 31 Lake Erie Docks	Imports	Exports	Consumption	Total
2000	19	63,100	62,983	NA	61,000	1,560.0	25.57	9,150	16,800	2,860	15,700	6,150	76,500	420.0
2001	15	46,200	46,100	NA	50,600	1,210.0	23.87	3,800	12,300	1,960	10,700	5,610	65,700	293.0
2002	11	51,600	51,500	NA	51,500	1,340.0	26.04	4,090	12,400	1,820	12,500	6,750	59,700	313.0
2003	11	48,600	NA	NA	46,100	1,490.0	32.30	4,910	10,900	1,630	12,600	6,770	61,600	328.0
2004	6	54,700	NA	NA	54,900	2,080.0	37.92	3,930	NA	NA	11,800	8,400	64,500	371.0
2005	4	54,300	NA	NA	53,200	2,370.0	44.50	2,040	NA	NA	13,000	11,800	60,100	532.0
2006	8	52,700	NA	NA	52,700	2,840.0	53.88	1,650	NA	NA	11,500	8,270	58,200	611.0
2007	E	52,500	NA	NA	50,900	3,040.0	59.64	2,090	NA	NA	9,400	9,310	54,800	543.0
2008[1]	E	53,600	NA	NA	56,000		70.43		NA	NA	9,200	11,100	51,900	
2009[2]	E	26,000	NA	NA			70.00		NA	NA	4,000	5,000	28,000	

[1] Preliminary. [2] Estimate. [3] Usable iron ore exclusive of ore containing 5% or more manganese and includes byproduct ore.
NA = Not available. *Source: U.S. Geological Survey (USGS)*

U.S. Imports (for Consumption) of Iron Ore[2] In Thousands of Metric Tons

Year	Australia	Brazil	Canada	Chile	Mauritania	Peru	Sweden	Venezuela	Total
1999	694	5,540	6,860	69	----	63	421	327	14,300
2000	755	6,090	7,990	135	----	40	250	349	15,700
2001	576	4,260	4,530	711	----	71	70	87	10,700
2002	567	5,750	5,540	319	----	86	44	49	12,500
2003	128	4,980	6,970	296	----	77	88	21	12,600
2004	3	5,020	5,830	244	----	56	111	262	11,800
2005	1	4,180	7,510	270	----	33	133	148	13,000
2006	8	4,530	6,240	283	----	52	3	23	11,500
2007	----	3,210	5,520	279	----	140	141	58	9,400
2008[1]	----	2,620	5,900	215	----	59	88	68	9,250

[1] Preliminary. [2] Including agglomerates. [3] Less than 1/2 unit. *Source: U.S. Geological Survey (USGS)*

Iron Ore Stocks[2] in the United States, at End of Month In Thousands of Metric Tons

Year	Jan.	Feb.	Mar.	Apr.	May	June	July	Aug.	Sept.	Oct.	Nov.	Dec.
2000	6,847	11,027	13,209	12,227	11,508	11,258	10,358	10,143	10,022	9,519	9,127	9,146
2001	10,712	13,176	14,681	13,839	11,558	9,364	7,433	6,367	6,345	5,659	4,789	3,803
2002	4,980	6,810	8,270	7,740	7,270	6,330	5,020	4,080	3,420	3,290	3,540	3,210
2003	4,640	7,790	10,100	9,500	8,180	7,080	6,550	6,160	5,820	5,640	5,240	3,860
2004	4,220	7,260	8,780	8,360	7,660	7,080	5,670	4,500	3,470	3,850	3,700	2,990
2005	4,060	6,770	8,410	7,690	7,730	7,370	7,420	7,240	6,550	5,840	6,250	5,750
2006	6,750	9,620	11,900	11,100	10,800	10,100	9,353	8,760	8,090	8,120	7,590	5,880
2007	7,330	10,100	11,800	11,000	10,300	9,870	9,340	8,700	7,950	7,660	7,110	6,490
2008	6,930	9,820	12,400	11,300	9,950	9,370	8,170	6,910	6,110	5,800	5,830	6,630
2009[1]	8,670	10,900	12,500	12,300	10,600	9,010	7,410					

[1] Preliminary. [2] Through August 1997 includes mines, plants and loading docks plus furnace yards and receiving/transfer docks; Beginning September 1997 includes mines, plants and loading docks. *Source: U.S. Geological Survey (USGS)*

Lard

Lard is the layer of fat found along the back and underneath the skin of a hog. The hog's fat is purified by washing it with water, melting it under constant heat, and straining it several times. Lard is an important byproduct of the meatpacking industry. It is valued highly as cooking oil because there is very little smoke when it is heated. However, demand for lard in cooking is declining because of the trend toward healthier eating. Lard is also used for medicinal purposes such as ointments, plasters, liniments, and occasionally as a laxative for children. Lard production is directly proportional to commercial hog production, meaning the largest producers of hogs are the largest producers of lard.

Prices – The average monthly wholesale price of lard in 2009 (through December) fell by 31.9% to 28.81 per pound, down from last year's record high of 39.34 cents per pound.

Supply – World production of lard in the 2008-09 marketing year rose by +0.64% yr/yr to 7.782 million metric tons, which was a new record high. The world's largest lard producers were China (with 42% of world production), the U.S (8%), Germany (7%), Brazil (5%), the former USSR (5%), Spain (4%), and Poland (3%). U.S. production of lard in 2008-09 fell -3.4% yr/yr to 1.289 billion pounds.

Demand – U.S. consumption of lard in 2009 fell -40.8% to 290.356 million pounds, down from last year's record high of 490.602 million pounds. The current level of consumption is less than 20% of the consumption of 1.574 billion pounds in 1971.

Exports – U.S. exports of lard in 2007-08 latest data available) rose by +1.4% to 73.0 million pounds, and accounted for only 6% of U.S. production.

World Production of Lard In Thousands of Metric Tons

Year	Brazil	Canada	China	France	Germany	Italy	Japan	Poland	Romania	Spain	United States	Ex-USSR	World Total
2000-01	336.8	112.6	2,832.1	155.7	415.2	195.9	62.3	239.5	72.7	264.9	488.6	314.8	6,748.6
2001-02	361.4	112.1	2,920.9	157.4	422.3	199.3	61.8	252.0	76.9	263.9	508.1	324.6	6,963.7
2002-03	350.2	124.2	3,040.4	156.2	433.7	204.8	59.3	272.5	60.1	280.9	510.0	346.0	7,166.8
2003-04	337.2	127.0	3,154.3	155.5	439.5	208.3	59.3	257.7	69.4	273.4	531.7	334.1	7,308.2
2004-05	344.2	127.4	3,317.8	153.4	456.9	199.2	59.4	243.8	58.9	278.1	532.4	315.3	7,476.2
2005-06	368.9	126.5	3,371.0	151.3	471.3	200.9	55.9	266.4	66.7	282.1	541.3	326.1	7,649.1
2006-07[1]	382.5	126.1	3,181.3	152.2	501.2	207.7	54.2	270.9	76.2	300.5	552.7	363.3	7,630.8
2007-08[2]	393.0	123.7	3,192.7	153.0	520.1	208.7	54.7	249.9	75.0	308.5	605.3	378.5	7,732.2
2008-09[3]	403.6	123.0	3,297.7	146.7	507.2	207.0	54.2	247.0	72.7	297.9	584.8	383.9	7,782.0

[1] Preliminary. [2] Estimate. [3] Forecast. *Source: The Oil World*

Supply and Distribution of Lard in the United States In Millions of Pounds

	Supply			Disappearance							
Year	Production	Stocks Oct. 1	Total Supply	Domestic	Baking or Frying Fats	Margarine[3]	Exports	Total Disap-pearance	Direct Use	Per Capita (Lbs.)
2000-01	1,058.0	26.7	1,087.0	557.5	W	12.0	173.9	731.4	221.1	0.8
2001-02	1,058.0	16.2	1,077.0	626.7	W	6.0	103.3	730.0	325.4	1.1
2002-03	1,083.0	13.6	1,105.0	670.9	W	7.0	84.2	755.2	370.3	1.3
2003-04	1,090.0	10.5	1,108.0	639.6	W	16.0	117.3	756.9	368.5	1.3
2004-05	1,117.0	13.3	1,136.0	487.8	W	6.0	289.2	777.0	220.2	0.7
2005-06	1,193.3	13.8	1,207.1	694.8	W	3.0	93.8	788.6	459.7	1.5
2006-07	1,218.5	9.4	1,227.9	718.5	W	W	71.9	790.4	498.6	1.7
2007-08[1]	1,334.4	14.2	1,348.6	756.8	W	W	72.9	829.7	486.7	1.6
2008-09[2]	1,289.3	13.9	1,303.2	800.9	W	W	81.4	882.3	310.3	1.0

[1] Preliminary. [2] Forecast. [3] Includes edible tallow. W = Withheld.
Source: Economic Research Service, U.S. Department of Agriculture (ERS-USDA)

Consumption of Lard (Edible and Inedible) in the United States In Millions of Pounds

Year	Jan.	Feb.	Mar.	Apr.	May	June	July	Aug.	Sept.	Oct.	Nov.	Dec.	Total
2000	27.3	25.7	29.1	23.3	30.3	27.6	24.4	31.3	31.1	32.6	29.6	31.7	343.9
2001	27.8	22.2	28.3	24.5	22.5	23.3	21.8	27.1	23.2	27.9	26.7	24.4	299.8
2002	26.4	26.1	21.8	26.7	24.8	21.2	22.9	26.4	23.6	26.4	28.1	28.7	303.2
2003	22.6	22.3	23.4	21.4	23.3	24.0	23.0	21.4	22.5	24.3	20.2	21.0	269.5
2004	22.9	25.8	25.9	23.9	23.5	22.0	19.1	19.7	21.3	22.4	21.9	19.9	268.1
2005	19.0	15.4	21.4	18.7	19.9	20.4	18.9	19.5	20.1	19.7	22.2	17.9	233.1
2006	15.7	16.4	20.6	21.4	20.2	16.7	14.9	17.7	17.8	18.9	22.3	20.9	223.4
2007	21.6	16.2	22.2	19.7	20.5	20.8	22.8	23.9	22.8	31.1	29.7	31.4	282.8
2008	34.8	32.2	44.6	50.7	50.8	44.4	47.8	39.7	44.0	37.5	31.7	32.2	490.6
2009[1]	23.4	17.3	26.8	26.0	26.3	25.8	21.3	20.5	25.4	32.4	29.9	15.1	290.4

[1] Preliminary. *Source: Bureau of the Census, U.S. Department of Commerce*

Average Wholesale Price of Lard--Loose, Tank Cars, in Chicago In Cents Per Pound

Year	Jan.	Feb.	Mar.	Apr.	May	June	July	Aug.	Sept.	Oct.	Nov.	Dec.	Average
2000	15.66	12.38	11.99	11.96	12.68	12.64	10.32	10.35	11.14	13.04	12.06	12.14	12.20
2001	13.57	11.92	11.07	12.09	11.84	13.38	18.05	24.11	22.00	13.04	13.18	14.92	14.93
2002	12.69	12.50	13.07	12.42	11.38	14.64	14.60	15.00	15.21	14.39	16.28	18.42	14.22
2003	18.61	17.11	16.85	16.72	17.29	18.90	18.93	20.08	23.98	27.50	26.40	25.18	20.63
2004	26.50	25.83	23.77	22.58	21.31	22.50	27.53	32.06	32.38	27.95	27.26	26.50	26.35
2005	22.10	18.30	17.71	20.72	22.95	21.30	18.08	17.75	20.97	27.38	27.76	18.60	21.14
2006	17.16	16.44	16.82	18.00	17.13	17.63	22.21	29.91	31.86	23.55	20.78	22.58	21.17
2007	23.00	23.82	30.75	27.71	28.60	32.64	36.00	35.77	36.00	35.09	33.78	32.66	31.32
2008	33.01	38.33	46.00	43.04	42.27	44.93	52.82	46.50	41.73	37.07	26.40	20.00	39.34
2009	25.36	20.31	19.49	23.36	29.00	30.06	27.63	32.20	29.73	25.75	30.07	28.75	26.81

Source: Economic Research Service, U.S. Department of Agriculture (ERS-USDA)

Cold Storage Holdings of all Lard[1] in the United States, on First of Month In Millions of Pounds

Year	Jan.	Feb.	Mar.	Apr.	May	June	July	Aug.	Sept.	Oct.	Nov.	Dec.
2000	26.7	27.8	29.2	30.1	20.2	22.5	18.9	19.3	17.3	17.4	16.3	16.8
2001	16.0	14.9	14.9	17.9	13.7	13.1	10.3	12.4	11.8	13.6	13.0	11.7
2002	13.2	18.0	16.4	16.5	20.3	22.4	18.9	18.3	12.0	10.5	14.6	11.3
2003	10.5	14.0	19.6	18.7	16.5	13.5	11.9	9.7	8.4	9.3	10.1	12.4
2004	13.3	19.8	18.6	20.3	20.5	15.0	12.9	10.8	10.3	11.8	11.4	13.2
2005	13.7	14.6	20.6	19.0	17.8	12.3	12.0	12.3	12.5	13.0	12.2	14.7
2006	9.6	11.5	13.7	13.6	9.3	9.9	13.0	12.4	13.0	11.5	16.1	16.0
2007	16.4	14.9	13.3	18.5	10.9	14.6	11.3	12.8	11.0	9.2	14.6	18.8
2008	14.0	22.4	20.4	22.9	23.0	19.5	22.7	13.6	18.0	17.8	16.1	20.4
2009[2]	12.1	13.6	15.4	16.2	14.5	18.8	17.3	21.6	20.5	26.7	18.5	15.4

[1] Stocks in factories and warehouses (except that in hands of retailers). [2] Preliminary. *Source: Bureau of the Census, U.S. Department of Commerce*

Lead

Lead (symbol Pb) is a dense, toxic, bluish-gray metallic element, and is the heaviest stable element. Lead was one of the first known metals. The ancients used lead in face powders, rouges, mascaras, paints, condiments, wine preservatives, and water supply plumbing. The Romans were slowly poisoned from lead because of its diverse daily usage.

Lead is usually found in ore with zinc, silver, and most often copper. The most common lead ore is galena, containing 86.6% lead. Cerussite and angleside are other common varieties of lead. More than half of the lead currently used comes from recycling.

Lead is used in building construction, bullets and shot, tank and pipe lining, storage batteries, and electric cable sheathing. Lead is used extensively as a protective shielding for radioactive material (e.g., X-ray apparatus) because of its high density and nuclear properties. Lead is also part of solder, pewter, and fusible alloys.

Lead futures and options trade at the London Metal Exchange (LME). The LME lead futures contract calls for the delivery of 25 metric tons of at least 99.970% purity lead ingots (pigs). The contract is priced in U.S. dollars per metric ton. Lead first started trading on the LME in 1903.

Prices – The price of lead at the beginning of 2009 was about $1,000 per metric ton. The price then rallied steadily all year to a high of about $2,300 in late December. In January of 2010 the price moved higher to about $2,500 per metric ton but then moved sharply lower to less than $2,000 per metric ton in February 2010.

Supply – World smelter production of lead (both primary and secondary) in 2008 (the latest data available) rose +4.7% yr/yr to 8.620 million metric tons to post a new record high production level. The world's largest smelter producers of lead (both primary and secondary) are China with 37% of world production in 2008, followed by the U.S. with 15%, Germany with 5%, and with the UK, Australia, Canada, Japan, each with 3%.

U.S. mine production of recoverable lead fell -8.1% yr/yr to a 13-year low of 399,000 metric tons in 2008 (latest data available). Missouri was responsible for 90% of U.S. production, with the remainder produced mainly by Idaho and Montana. Lead recovered from scrap in the U.S. (secondary production) fell -5.9% yr/yr in 2009 (through November, annualized) to 1.148 million metric tons, down from the 2008 record high of 1.220 metric tons. The amount of lead recovered from scrap is more than twice the amount of lead produced in the U.S. from mines (primary production). The value of U.S. secondary lead production in 2008 (latest data available) fell by -5.6% to $3.040 billion, down from last year's record high of $3.220 billion.

Demand – U.S. lead consumption in 2009 (through November, annualized) fell -11.1% to 1.426 million metric tons, which was a 14-year low. The record level of U.S. lead consumption was 1.680 million metric tons posted in 1999.

Trade – The U.S. relied on imports for 8% of its lead consumption in 2001 but has been a net exporter ever since. U.S. imports of lead pigs and bars in 2008 (latest data available) rose + 17.5% yr/yr to 309,000 metric tons. U.S. lead exports in 2008 were comprised of ore concentrate (277,000 metric tons), scrap (175,000 metric tons), unwrought lead (81,000 metric tons), and wrought lead (7,530 metric tons).

World Smelter (Primary and Secondary) Production of Lead In Thousands of Metric Tons

Year	Australia[3]	Belgium[4]	Canada[3]	China[2]	France	Germany	Italy	Japan	Mexico[3]	Spain	United Kingdom[3]	United States	World Total
2000	251.8	118.0	284.8	1,100.0	258.0	414.5	235.0	311.7	253.2	120.0	337.2	1,470	6,650
2001	303.0	96.0	230.9	1,200.0	238.0	373.4	203.0	302.4	253.5	98.0	366.0	1,390	6,600
2002	304.0	88.0	251.6	1,330.0	204.0	379.9	205.0	285.8	237.2	116.0	374.6	1,360	6,800
2003	295.0	65.0	223.4	1,580.0	96.7	356.9	246.0	295.3	247.5	102.0	364.6	1,380	6,990
2004	268.0	63.0	241.2	1,940.0	105.6	359.2	202.0	282.9	217.4	105.6	245.9	1,280	7,040
2005	263.0	83.4	230.2	2,387.0	105.0	341.7	211.5	274.6	226.5	110.0	304.4	1,300	7,580
2006	233.0	54.0	250.5	2,720.0	104.2	321.5	190.5	279.4	212.5	110.0	307.7	1,310	7,890
2007[1]	229.0	117.2	236.7	2,790.0	104.2	405.1	210.0	276.3	212.0	110.0	300.0	1,300	8,230
2008[2]	248.0	117.2	259.1	3,200.0	92.0	415.0	211.8	276.8	199.8	110.0	294.0	1,280	8,620

[1] Preliminary. [2] Estimate. [3] Refinded & bullion. [4] Includes scrap. *Source: U.S. Geological Survey (USGS)*

Consumption of Lead in the United States, by Products In Metric Tons

Year	Ammunition	Bearing Metals	Pipes, Traps & Bends[2]	Cable Covering	Calking Lead	Casting Metals	Other Metal Products[3]	Total Other Oxides[4]	Sheet Lead	Solder	Storage Battery: Grids, Post, etc.	Storage Battery: Oxides	Brass and Bronze	Total Consumption
2000	63,700	1,490	2,010	W	1,140	35,100	25,800	52,400	23,800	11,500	796,000	690,000	3,670	1,720,000
2001	53,600	837	2,370	W	927	31,800	17,100	43,900	22,400	6,120	655,000	694,000	2,590	1,550,000
2002	57,600	406	2,250	W	1,060	34,800	24,200	51,900	25,600	6,450	554,000	641,000	2,730	1,440,000
2003	48,800	13,500	1,550	W	822	31,700	9,730	35,600	24,400	6,310	523,000	642,000	2,810	1,390,000
2004	61,500	1,300	W	W	W	17,900	W	25,700	31,600	7,440	657,000	630,000	2,390	1,480,000
2005	61,300	1,180	1,220	W	W	30,400	22,200	14,100	29,100	8,370	579,000	705,000	2,100	1,490,000
2006	65,700	1,240	1,440	W	W	29,900	23,400	16,000	28,400	7,280	586,000	710,000	3,130	1,490,000
2007	69,400	1,410	1,230	W	W	31,500	23,600	15,800	28,600	7,220	640,000	738,000	2,870	1,570,000
2008[1]	71,900	1,250	1,270	W	W	20,100	22,500	10,700	26,600	6,880	583,000	709,000	2,460	1,470,000

[1] Preliminary. [2] Including building. [3] Including terne metal, type metal, and lead consumed in foil, collapsible tubes, annealing, plating, galvanizing and fishing weights. [4] Includes paints, glass and ceramic products, and other pigments and chemicals. W = Withheld.
Source: U.S. Geological Survey (USGS)

Salient Statistics of Lead in the United States In Thousands of Metric Tons

Year	Net Import Reliance as a % of Apparent Consumption	Production of Refined Lead From: Domestic Ores[3]	Production of Refined Lead From: Foreighn Ores[3]	Production of Refined Lead From: Total Primary	Total Value of Refined Million $	Secondary Lead Recovered: As Soft Lead	Secondary Lead Recovered: In Antimonial Lead	Secondary Lead Recovered: In Other Alloys	Secondary Lead Recovered: Total	Total Value of Secondary Million USD	Stocks, Dec. 31: Primary	Stocks, Dec. 31: Consumer[4]	Average Price Cents Per Pound: New York	Average Price Cents Per Pound: London
1999	20	350.0	W	350.0	337.0	635.0	444.0	18.1	1,110.0	1,070.0	12.3	78.7	43.72	22.78
2000	13	341.0	W	341.0	328.0	651.0	428.0	36.8	1,130.0	1,090.0	18.6	106.0	43.57	20.57
2001	8	290.0	W	290.0	279.0	734.0	291.0	75.9	1,100.0	1,060.0	W	100.0	43.64	21.58
2002	E	262.0	W	262.0	252.0	754.0	289.0	72.8	1,120.0	1,070.0	W	111.0	43.56	20.52
2003	E	245.0	W	245.0	236.0	829.0	303.0	4.2	1,140.0	1,110.0	W	84.6	43.76	23.34
2004	E	148.0	W	148.0	143.0	841.0	283.0	3.0	1,130.0	1,370.0	W	59.0	55.14	40.19
2005	E	143.0	W	143.0		869.0	271.0	4.5	1,150.0	1,550.0	W	46.8	61.03	44.23
2006	E	153.0	W	153.0		948.0	200.0	12.4	1,160.0	1,980.0	W	54.8	77.40	58.00
2007[1]	E	123.0	W	123.0		1,020.0	160.0	2.4	1,180.0	3,220.0	W	39.0	123.84	117.00
2008[2]	E	135.0	W	135.0		1,000.0	140.0	2.4	1,150.0	3,040.0	W	56.5	120.00	94.80

[1] Preliminary. [2] Estimate. [3] And base bullion. [4] Also at secondary smelters. W = Withheld. E = Net exporter.
Source: U.S. Geological Survey (USGS)

U.S. Foreign Trade of Lead In Thousands of Metric Tons

Year	Exports: Ore Concentrate	Exports: Unwrought Lead[3]	Exports: Wrought Lead[4]	Exports: Scrap	Exports: Ash & Residues[5]	Imports for Consumption: Ores, Flue Dust or Fume & Mattes	Imports for Consumption: Base Bullion	Imports for Consumption: Pigs & Bars	Imports for Consumption: Reclaimed Scrap, Etc.	Imports for Consumption: Value Million $	General Import From: Ore, Flue, Dust & Matte: Australia	General Import From: Ore, Flue, Dust & Matte: Canada	General Import From: Ore, Flue, Dust & Matte: Peru	General Import From: Pigs & Bars: Canada	General Import From: Pigs & Bars: Mexico	General Import From: Pigs & Bars: Peru
1999	93.5	23.4	13.9	117.0	1.4	12.3	0.1	311.0	----	196.5	0.1	1.2	8.8	198.0	27.2	6.9
2000	117.0	21.4	27.2	71.6	11.3	31.2	0.1	356.0	0.0	217.1	----	(/6)	10.8	216.0	18.4	1.8
2001	181.0	17.0	17.7	108.0	14.2	2.2	----	271.0	10.2	166.8	----	----	----	167.0	12.4	2.3
2002	241.0	31.4	11.7	106.0	----	0.0	----	210.0	2.6	124.9	----	----	----	172.0	7.5	----
2003	253.0	92.1	30.5	92.8	----	----	----	175.0	4.2	111.9	----	----	----	167.0	8.3	----
2004	292.0	58.6	23.8	56.3	----	----	----	197.0	4.8	235.3	----	----	----	166.0	8.8	7.3
2005	390.2	45.5	19.0	67.3	----	----	----	298.0	3.3	334.8	----	----	----	190.0	15.2	23.9
2006	297.6	52.7	15.8	120.9	----	----	0.5	331.0	1.6	450.8	----	----	----	222.0	15.8	34.6
2007[1]	300.0	51.8	4.6	129.0	----	----	2.0	263.0	2.4	591.4	----	----	----	208.0	35.6	16.5
2008[2]	277.0	81.0	7.5	175.0	----	----	2.7	309.0	1.3	681.6	----	----	----	219.0	58.1	10.6

[1] Preliminary. [2] Estimate. [3] And lead alloys. [4] Blocks, pigs, etc. [5] Less than 1/2 unit. *Source: U.S. Geological Survey (USGS)*

Annual Mine Production of Recoverable Lead in the United States In Metric Tons

Year	Total	Idaho	Missouri	Montana	Other States	Missouri's % of Total
1999	503,000	W	464,000	7,950	31,200	92%
2000	449,000	W	410,000	W	38,700	91%
2001	454,000	W	423,000	W	30,900	93%
2002	440,000	W	428,000	W	12,300	97%
2003	449,000	W	432,000	W	17,200	96%
2004	430,000	W	407,000	W	23,400	95%
2005	426,000	W	397,000	W	29,500	93%
2006	419,000	W	393,000	W	26,100	94%
2007[1]	434,000	W	400,000	W	34,200	92%
2008[2]	399,000	W	360,000	W	38,600	90%

[1] Preliminary. [2] Estimate. W = Withheld, included in Other States. *Source: U.S. Geological Survey (USGS)*

Mine Production of Recoverable Lead in the United States In Thousands of Metric Tons

Year	Jan.	Feb.	Mar.	Apr.	May	June	July	Aug.	Sept.	Oct.	Nov.	Dec.	Total
2000	35.1	36.7	43.0	37.5	37.4	37.8	33.0	36.8	36.8	32.4	38.8	36.9	447.0
2001	42.9	37.8	39.4	33.7	35.0	32.2	38.2	39.6	32.4	39.5	32.1	35.4	450.0
2002	39.5	35.5	41.2	36.1	39.3	36.1	35.0	39.6	33.2	34.8	34.1	34.2	438.6
2003	33.7	34.9	38.5	36.2	38.8	39.2	41.3	38.0	38.3	37.2	34.0	33.9	444.0
2004	33.4	32.8	33.5	35.1	31.2	33.1	33.8	36.9	36.9	36.2	35.0	31.8	409.7
2005	31.1	31.1	34.6	35.2	33.4	41.4	39.5	37.4	38.2	37.9	34.6	37.9	432.3
2006	36.7	33.3	38.1	33.6	33.4	33.9	36.6	36.3	37.0	38.0	35.0	29.6	421.5
2007	38.1	33.9	36.7	31.6	36.9	34.5	38.7	41.3	34.6	39.4	31.5	37.1	434.3
2008	38.0	36.9	36.1	33.0	31.0	34.4	37.8	34.2	33.8	29.1	27.8	33.7	405.8
2009[1]	33.8	30.5	32.8	34.7	33.6	33.7	29.9	35.7	35.6	36.9	34.0		404.9

[1] Preliminary. *Source: U.S. Geological Survey (USGS)*

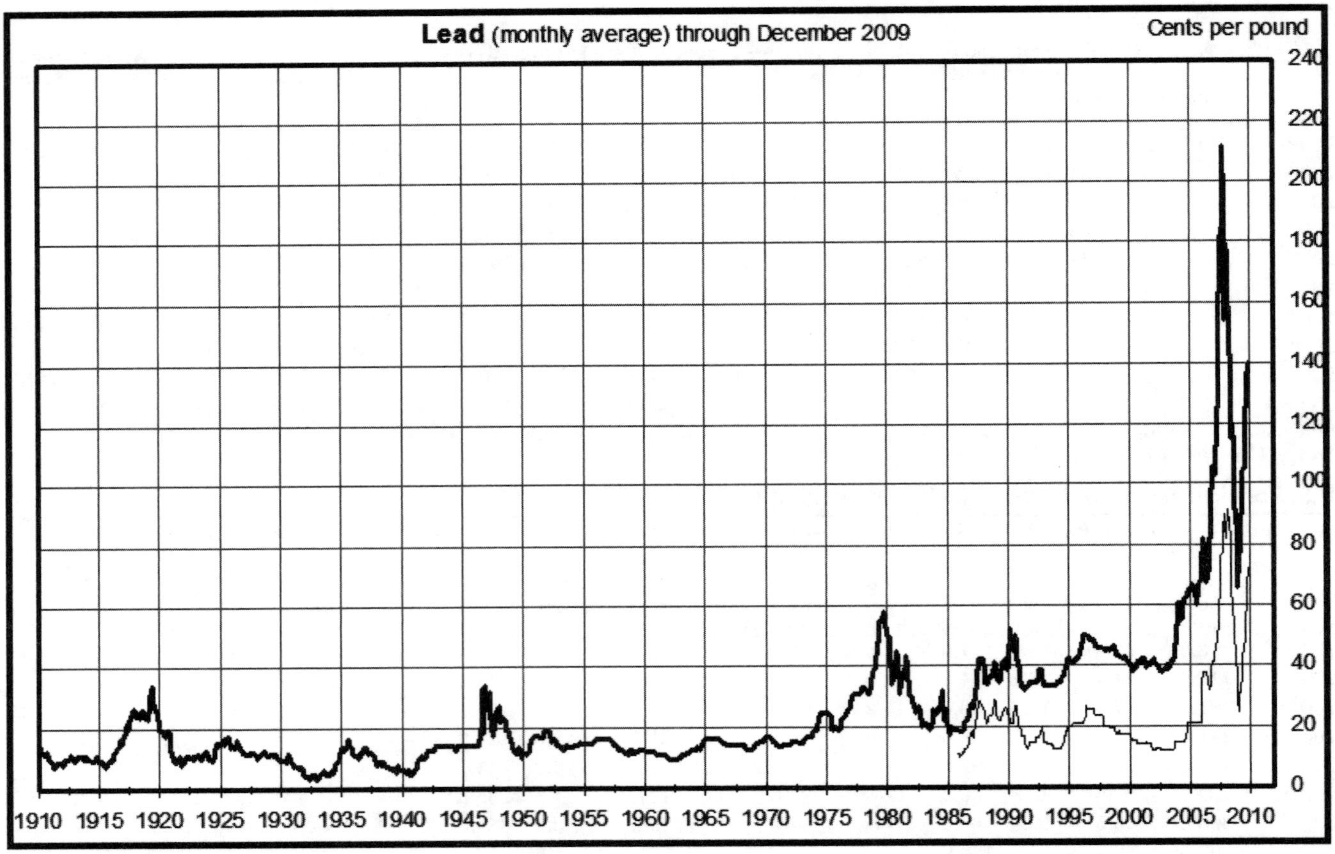

Average Price of Pig Lead, U.S. Primary Producers (Common Corroding)[1] In Cents Per Pound

Year	Jan.	Feb.	Mar.	Apr.	May	June	July	Aug.	Sept.	Oct.	Nov.	Dec.	Average
2000	45.00	45.00	45.00	45.00	45.00	45.00	45.00	45.00	45.00	45.00	45.00	45.00	45.00
2001	45.00	45.00	45.00	45.00	45.00	45.00	45.00	45.00	45.00	45.00	45.00	45.00	45.00
2002	45.00	45.00	45.00	45.00	45.00	45.00	45.00	45.00	45.00	45.00	45.00	45.00	45.00
2003	23.14	24.65	23.81	23.13	24.56	24.77	26.93	26.05	27.23	30.16	32.09	35.46	26.83
2004	38.48	44.79	45.30	39.93	42.44	45.16	48.20	47.46	48.08	48.01	49.54	49.75	45.60
2005	50.46	52.20	54.00	53.25	53.41	53.26	47.22	47.53	49.76	54.01	54.68	59.63	52.45
2006	66.16	67.16	63.28	61.58	61.16	51.92	56.07	61.48	69.24	77.64	82.09	86.22	67.00
2007	83.62	88.42	94.72	98.73	103.14	117.95	148.17	148.47	153.50	175.59	159.80	124.81	124.74
2008	125.37	146.72	141.77	134.92	106.42	88.93	93.68	92.49	90.49	73.02	65.52	49.58	100.74
2009	57.27	55.74	61.81	67.86	70.02	80.87	81.05	91.57	104.06	105.75	109.61	110.96	83.05

[1] New York Delivery. *Source: American Metal Market*

Refiners Production[1] of Lead in the United States In Metric Tons

Year	Jan.	Feb.	Mar.	Apr.	May	June	July	Aug.	Sept.	Oct.	Nov.	Dec.	Total
2000	NA	NA	NA	NA	NA	NA	NA	NA	NA	NA	NA	NA	341,000
2001	NA	NA	NA	NA	NA	NA	NA	NA	NA	NA	NA	NA	290,000
2002	NA	NA	NA	NA	NA	NA	NA	NA	NA	NA	NA	NA	262,000
2003	NA	NA	NA	NA	NA	NA	NA	NA	NA	NA	NA	NA	245,000
2004	NA	NA	NA	NA	NA	NA	NA	NA	NA	NA	NA	NA	NA
2005	NA	NA	NA	NA	NA	NA	NA	NA	NA	NA	NA	NA	143,000
2006	NA	NA	NA	NA	NA	NA	NA	NA	NA	NA	NA	NA	143,000
2007	NA	NA	NA	NA	NA	NA	NA	NA	NA	NA	NA	NA	NA
2008	NA	NA	NA	NA	NA	NA	NA	NA	NA	NA	NA	NA	NA
2009[2]	NA	NA	NA	NA	NA	NA	NA	NA	NA	NA	NA		NA

[1] Represents refined lead produced from domestic ores by primary smelters plus small amounts of secondary material passing through these smelters. Includes GSA metal purchased for remelt. [2] Preliminary. NA = Not available. *Source: U.S. Geological Survey (USGS)*

Total Stocks of Lead[1] in the United States at Refiners, at End of Month In Metric Tons

Year	Jan.	Feb.	Mar.	Apr.	May	June	July	Aug.	Sept.	Oct.	Nov.	Dec.
2000	NA	NA	NA	NA	NA	NA	NA	NA	NA	NA	NA	18,600
2001	NA	NA	NA	NA	NA	NA	NA	NA	NA	NA	NA	NA
2002	NA	NA	NA	NA	NA	NA	NA	NA	NA	NA	NA	NA
2003	NA	NA	NA	NA	NA	NA	NA	NA	NA	NA	NA	NA
2004	NA	NA	NA	NA	NA	NA	NA	NA	NA	NA	NA	NA
2005	NA	NA	NA	NA	NA	NA	NA	NA	NA	NA	NA	NA
2006	NA	NA	NA	NA	NA	NA	NA	NA	NA	NA	NA	NA
2007	NA	NA	NA	NA	NA	NA	NA	NA	NA	NA	NA	NA
2008	NA	NA	NA	NA	NA	NA	NA	NA	NA	NA	NA	NA
2009[2]	NA	NA	NA	NA	NA	NA	NA	NA	NA	NA	NA	

[1] Primary refineries. [2] Preliminary. NA = Not available. *Source: U.S. Geological Survey (USGS)*

Total[1] Lead Consumption in the United States In Thousands of Metric Tons

Year	Jan.	Feb.	Mar.	Apr.	May	June	July	Aug.	Sept.	Oct.	Nov.	Dec.	Total
2000	139.0	139.0	139.0	139.0	140.0	140.0	135.0	141.0	139.0	139.0	136.0	132.0	1,660
2001	145.0	135.0	133.0	130.0	138.0	136.0	135.0	136.0	142.0	146.0	138.0	138.0	1,652
2002	132.0	131.0	133.0	142.0	142.0	144.0	143.0	145.0	141.0	145.0	142.0	133.0	1,673
2003	134.0	129.0	126.0	120.0	121.0	121.0	121.0	122.0	123.0	127.0	122.0	125.0	1,491
2004	119.0	118.0	119.0	119.0	117.0	119.0	118.0	118.0	117.0	117.0	117.0	119.0	1,417
2005	125.0	117.0	109.0	108.0	134.0	130.0	124.0	129.0	126.0	126.0	126.0	126.0	1,480
2006	124.0	130.0	129.0	128.0	128.0	128.0	125.0	126.0	127.0	128.0	126.0	126.0	1,525
2007	130.0	128.0	129.0	128.0	131.0	139.0	131.0	134.0	132.0	137.0	132.0	127.0	1,578
2008	140.0	136.0	130.0	135.0	135.0	141.0	134.0	129.0	134.0	136.0	127.0	126.0	1,603
2009[2]	123.0	119.0	116.0	124.0	116.0	117.0	116.0	115.0	118.0	122.0	121.0		1,426

[1] Represents total consumption of primary & secondary lead as metal, in chemicals, or in alloys. [2] Preliminary. *Source: U.S. Geological Survey (USGS)*

Lead Recovered from Scrap in the United States In Thousands of Metric Tons (Lead Content)

Year	Jan.	Feb.	Mar.	Apr.	May	June	July	Aug.	Sept.	Oct.	Nov.	Dec.	Total
2000	91.0	88.0	91.1	91.4	90.5	91.3	88.6	95.1	94.0	96.0	95.4	93.7	1,110.0
2001	90.3	90.4	86.7	92.6	93.7	93.6	90.4	95.1	93.9	96.7	94.6	94.6	1,112.6
2002	89.3	82.3	88.2	93.1	93.9	93.6	88.0	96.1	93.3	97.5	95.0	95.7	1,106.0
2003	95.7	83.6	86.2	85.1	94.0	94.8	95.7	93.9	93.3	102.0	93.7	95.2	1,113.2
2004	94.0	94.2	96.3	97.9	94.4	96.6	97.4	96.3	94.8	96.8	94.9	95.4	1,149.0
2005	94.4	95.1	86.8	86.8	87.1	94.6	94.7	94.8	93.0	95.9	96.4	92.4	1,112.0
2006	90.2	96.7	97.4	98.2	99.5	95.7	94.9	97.0	95.6	98.4	98.4	95.9	1,157.9
2007	99.0	96.5	98.6	93.5	94.5	100.0	103.0	103.0	101.0	104.0	104.0	94.6	1,191.7
2008	104.0	98.2	102.0	100.0	105.0	102.0	92.0	102.0	91.7	100.0	122.0	101.0	1,219.9
2009[1]	97.3	99.0	101.0	90.2	91.6	93.8	97.0	97.2	90.9	96.3	98.0		1,148.0

[1] Preliminary. *Source: U.S. Geological Survey (USGS)*

Domestic Shipments[1] of Lead in the United States, by Refiners In Thousands of Short Tons

Year	Jan.	Feb.	Mar.	Apr.	May	June	July	Aug.	Sept.	Oct.	Nov.	Dec.	Total
1989	29.3	28.5	32.2	35.7	45.1	36.4	32.8	41.5	40.0	44.2	40.2	31.1	437.1
1990	39.3	33.9	39.1	33.5	38.4	32.9	32.6	38.9	36.6	38.9	37.9	31.7	433.7
1991	35.4	33.8	34.3	39.8	33.9	26.0	31.8	37.9	35.1	35.7	28.7	26.7	399.2
1992	31.3	23.9	30.4	26.3	25.6	27.2	27.3	28.7	26.3	28.5	26.3	21.7	323.5
1993	24.6	23.6	32.5	30.0	31.3	35.1	28.9	34.0	35.5	35.5	31.7	33.5	376.2
1994	35.9	32.8	35.2	32.7	34.7	36.7	31.6	33.4	34.8	34.3	34.0	33.3	409.3
1995	36.5	30.3	35.1	31.1	33.7	31.9	28.6	40.3	34.9	40.9	33.2	29.8	406.4
1996	37.2	32.4	29.5	30.2	29.4	26.7	27.7	33.5	30.1	33.5	28.1	27.6	366.0
1997[2]	31.5	27.8	24.7	35.2	39.2	36.1	33.4	29.4	26.4	31.5	30.4	28.1	377.8
1998[2]	Data no longer available.												

[1] Includes GSA metal. [2] Preliminary. *Source: American Metal Market (AMM)*

Lumber and Plywood

Humans have utilized lumber for construction for thousands of years, but due to the heaviness of timber and the manual methods of harvesting, large-scale lumbering didn't occur until the mechanical advances of the Industrial Revolution. Lumber is produced from both hardwood and softwood. Hardwood lumber comes from deciduous trees that have broad leaves. Most hardwood lumber is used for miscellaneous industrial applications, primarily wood pallets, and includes oak, gum, maple, and ash. Hardwood species with beautiful colors and patterns are used for such high-grade products as furniture, flooring, paneling, and cabinets and include black walnut, black cherry, and red oak. Wood from cone-bearing trees is called softwood, regardless of its actual hardness. Most lumber from the U.S. is softwood. Softwoods, such as southern yellow pine, Douglas fir, ponderosa pine, and true firs, are primarily used as structural lumber such as 2x4s and 2x6s, poles, paper and cardboard.

Plywood consists of several thin layers of veneer bonded together with adhesives. The veneer sheets are layered so that the grain of one sheet is perpendicular to that of the next, which makes plywood exceptionally strong for its weight. Most plywood has from three to nine layers of wood. Plywood manufacturers use both hard and soft woods, although hardwoods serve primarily for appearance and are not as strong as those made from softwoods. Plywood is primarily used in construction, particularly for floors, roofs, walls, and doors. Homebuilding and remodeling account for two-thirds of U.S. lumber consumption. The price of lumber and plywood is highly correlated with the strength of the U.S. home-building market.

The forest and wood products industry is dominated by Weyerhaeuser Company (ticker symbol WY), which has about $20 billion in annual sales. Weyerhaeuser is a forest products conglomerate that engages not only in growing and harvesting timber, but also in the production and distribution of forest products, real estate development, and construction of single-family homes. Forest products include wood products, pulp and paper, and containerboard. The timberland segment of the business manages 7.2 million acres of company-owned land and 800,000 acres of leased commercial forestlands in North America. The company's Canadian division has renewable, long-term licenses on about 35 million acres of forestland in five Canadian provinces. In order to maximize its long-term yield from its acreage, Weyerhaeuser engages in a number of forest management activities such as extensive planting, suppression of non-merchantable species, thinning, fertilization, and operational pruning.

Lumber futures and options are traded on the Chicago Mercantile Exchange (CME). The CME's lumber futures contract calls for the delivery of 111,000 board feet (one 73 foot rail car) of random length 8 to 12 foot 2 x 4s, the type used in construction. The contract is priced in terms of dollars per thousand board feet.

Prices – CME lumber futures prices opened in 2009 at about $170 but moved sharply lower to about $140 early in March. From there the price rose to about $215 in June only to fall to about $164 in October. From there the price moved sharply higher to $225 late November only to fall to about $209 by year's end. In 2010 the price moved sharply higher to about $270 in early February 2010.

Supply – The U.S. led the world in the production of industrial round wood but in 2008 (latest data) production fell -11.1% yr/yr to 336.611 million cubic meters, followed by Canada with 152.638 million cubic meters (-20.2% yr/yr), and Russia with 136.700 million cubic meters (-15.60% yr/yr). The U.S. also led the world in the production of plywood with 10.376 million cubic meters of production in 2008 (-16.3% yr/yr), followed by Russia with 2.583 million cubic meters (-7.0% yr/yr), and then Canada with 2.225 million cubic meters (15.7% yr/yr). U.S. softwood lumber production in latest data from the series of 2006 (latest data annualized through November) fell 4.4% yr/yr to 38.503 billion board feet.

Demand – U.S. consumption of softwood lumber in 2006, the last full reporting year, fell by 1.9% yr/yr to 63.080 billion board feet.

Trade – U.S. total lumber imports in 2006, the last full reporting year, fell 1.8% to 25.285 billion board feet, down from last year's record high. U.S. imports of hardwood in 2006 fell by 3.1% to 1,042 million board feet. U.S. imports of softwood in 2006 fell by 1.7% to 24.214 billion board feet. The leading softwood import was spruce with 1.730 billion board feet of imports in 20065, followed by cedar at 721 million board feet.

Total U.S. exports of lumber in 2006 (latest data) rose +3.6% yr/yr to 2.779 billion board feet, which is a 6-year high. The record high was 4.528 billion board feet in 1988. U.S. exports of hardwood in 2006 rose by +21.7% yr/yr to 1.797 billion board feet. U.S. exports of softwood in 2006 rose by 9.5% yr/yr to 982 million board feet. The largest types of U.S. softwood exports in 2006 were southern pine with 232 million board feet of exports, Ponderosa white pine (114 million board feet), and Douglas Fir (76 million board feet). The world's largest exporter of plywood in 2007 was Russia with 1.503 million cubic meters of exports, followed by Finland with 1.229 million cubic meters, and Canada with 964,000 thousand cubic meters.

World Production of Industrial Roundwood by Selected Countries In Thousands of Cubic Meters

Year	Austria	Canada	Czech Republic	Finland	France	Germany	Poland	Romania	Russia	Spain	Sweden	Turkey	United States
1999	10,988	190,988	13,363	49,593	33,237	35,063	22,842	9,484	94,600	13,160	52,800	10,065	423,298
2000	10,416	198,918	13,501	50,147	43,440	51,088	24,489	10,116	105,800	12,721	57,400	10,429	420,619
2001	10,562	182,945	13,364	47,727	37,471	36,502	23,375	9,806	117,800	13,276	57,300	9,976	403,212
2002	11,810	195,211	13,534	48,529	32,736	37,755	24,995	12,092	118,600	13,850	60,700	11,191	404,958
2003	13,719	176,799	13,960	49,246	30,540	45,415	27,204	12,537	126,600	14,075	61,200	10,729	405,613
2004	12,943	205,273	14,411	49,281	31,289	48,657	29,337	12,794	130,600	14,235	61,400	11,225	418,131
2005	12,786	200,247	14,285	47,116	28,253	50,905	28,531	11,542	138,000	13,351	92,300	11,202	423,456
2006	14,430	185,196	16,333	45,521	28,592	54,000	28,767	9,454	144,600	14,109	58,700	12,253	412,134
2007[1]	16,521	191,205	16,738	51,406	29,817	68,029	32,461	11,572	162,000	12,546	72,300	13,674	378,771
2008[2]	16,772	152,638	14,307	45,965	27,651	46,806	30,470	9,517	136,700	14,325	63,100	13,864	336,611

[1] Preliminary. [2] Estimate. NA = Not available. *Source: Food and Agriculture Organization of the United Nations (FAO-UN)*

LUMBER AND PLYWOOD

Lumber Production and Consumption in the United States In Millions of Board Feet

	Production						Domestic Consumption						
Year	California Redwood	Inland Region	Southern Pine	West Coast	Other Softwood	Total Softwood	Inland Region	California Redwood	Southern Pine	West Coast	Other Softwood	Softwood Imports	Total Softwood
1998	1,391	7,298	16,151	7,797	2,040	34,677	7,256	1,409	15,788	7,502	1,567	18,686	52,209
1999	1,325	7,580	16,922	8,625	2,153	36,605	7,445	1,358	16,525	8,115	1,641	19,178	54,262
2000	1,320	7,078	16,672	8,782	2,115	35,967	6,926	1,257	16,374	8,300	1,629	19,449	53,934
2001	1,121	6,563	16,094	8,764	2,035	34,577	6,490	1,132	15,937	8,471	1,724	20,075	53,828
2002	1,035	6,759	16,686	9,244	2,106	35,830	6,641	1,056	16,571	8,966	1,832	20,986	56,050
2003	977	6,716	16,841	9,904	2,151	36,591	6,709	976	16,759	9,585	1,751	21,188	56,969
2004	1,049	6,742	18,050	10,934	2,300	39,075	6,600	1,021	17,935	10,705	1,971	23,584	61,819
2005	1,048	21,386	18,986	11,599	2,139	40,458	6,635	1,060	18,829	11,346	1,781	24,626	64,279
I	280	1,789	4,725	2,914	542	10,250	1,712	246	4,615	2,708	455	5,632	15,368
II	265	16,394	4,939	2,928	548	10,374	1,690	283	4,934	2,948	472	6,685	17,014
III	271	1,692	4,731	2,877	535	10,106	1,709	291	4,720	2,844	446	6,297	16,308
IV	232	1,511	4,591	2,880	514	9,728	1,524	240	4,560	2,846	408	6,012	15,589
2006[1]	972	6,404	19,560	11,700	2,156	40,792	6,320	760	18,772	11,332	1,680	24,212	63,080
I	243	1,601	4,890	2,925	539	10,198	1,580	190	4,693	2,833	420	6,053	15,770
II													
III													

[1] Preliminary. *Source: American Forest & Paper Association (AFPA)*

U.S. Housing Starts: Seasonally Adjusted Annual Rate In Thousands

Year	Jan.	Feb.	Mar.	Apr.	May	June	July	Aug.	Sept.	Oct.	Nov.	Dec.	Average
2000	1,636	1,737	1,604	1,626	1,575	1,559	1,463	1,541	1,507	1,549	1,551	1,532	1,573
2001	1,600	1,625	1,590	1,649	1,605	1,636	1,670	1,567	1,562	1,540	1,602	1,568	1,601
2002	1,698	1,829	1,642	1,592	1,764	1,717	1,655	1,633	1,804	1,648	1,753	1,788	1,710
2003	1,853	1,629	1,726	1,643	1,751	1,867	1,897	1,833	1,939	1,967	2,083	2,057	1,854
2004	1,911	1,846	1,998	2,003	1,981	1,828	2,002	2,024	1,905	2,072	1,782	2,042	1,950
2005	2,144	2,207	1,864	2,061	2,025	2,068	2,054	2,095	2,151	2,065	2,147	1,994	2,073
2006	2,273	2,119	1,969	1,821	1,942	1,802	1,737	1,650	1,720	1,491	1,570	1,649	1,812
2007	1,409	1,480	1,495	1,490	1,415	1,448	1,354	1,330	1,183	1,264	1,197	1,037	1,342
2008	1,083	1,100	993	1,001	971	1,078	933	849	822	763	655	556	900
2009[1]	488	574	521	479	551	590	593	581	586	524	580	557	552

[1] Preliminary. Total Privately owned. *Source: Bureau of the Census, U.S. Department of Commerce*

Stocks (Gross) of Softwood Lumber in the United States, on First of Month In Millions of Board Feet

Year	Jan.	Feb.	Mar.	Apr.	May	June	July	Aug.	Sept.	Oct.	Nov.	Dec.
1997	3,973	4,019	4,113	4,067	3,963	4,017	3,915	3,871	3,875	3,927	3,925	3,865
1998	3,884	3,970	4,048	4,062	4,158	4,084	NA	NA	NA	NA	NA	NA
1999	3,519	3,595	3,688	3,726	3,698	3,581	3,512	3,485	3,533	3,491	3,562	3,536
2000	3,639	3,704	3,811	3,887	3,960	2,738	3,902	3,936	3,878	3,848	3,957	3,875
2001	3,919	3,864	4,013	3,951	4,095	3,955	NA	3,961	3,938	4,076	4,100	4,248
2002	4,784	3,735	3,826	3,756	3,273	3,316	3,242	3,230	3,136	3,098	3,173	3,127
2003	3,175	3,177	3,202	3,249	3,308	3,211	3,075	3,085	3,081	3,158	3,076	3,055
2004	2,904	2,904	2,904	2,873	2,966	2,966	2,966	2,966	3,030	3,030	3,031	2,450
2005	2,912	2,994	3,076	3,056	2,866	2,687	2,554	2,641	2,497	2,986	3,059	2,913
2006[1]	3,004	3,100	3,111	2,978	2,952	2,925	2,918	2,917	2,956	2,960	2,954	

[1] Preliminary. NA = Not available. *Source: American Forest & Paper Association (AFPA)*

Lumber (Softwood)Production in the United States In Millions of Board Feet

Year	Jan.	Feb.	Mar.	Apr.	May	June	July	Aug.	Sept.	Oct.	Nov.	Dec.	Total
1997	3,012	2,791	2,866	3,149	2,890	3,027	3,097	2,889	2,905	3,094	2,536	2,487	34,743
1998	2,767	2,760	2,928	3,084	2,647	3,051	3,079	2,930	2,953	3,167	2,667	2,754	34,787
1999	2,783	2,921	3,190	3,227	3,071	3,318	3,115	3,054	2,992	3,096	2,954	2,795	36,516
2000	3,020	3,128	3,474	3,058	3,276	3,249	2,730	2,971	2,839	3,041	2,761	2,342	35,889
2001	2,832	2,457	2,918	2,928	NA	3,032	2,812	3,240	2,743	3,188	2,740	2,372	34,104
2002	3,019	2,761	3,074	3,284	3,126	3,200	3,104	3,128	2,862	3,386	2,599	2,482	36,025
2003	2,971	2,801	2,937	2,994	2,931	3,109	3,088	2,981	3,052	3,335	2,793	2,740	35,732
2004	3,037	2,978	3,380	3,434	3,021	3,329	3,227	3,271	3,147	3,321	3,082	2,931	38,158
2005	3,233	3,169	3,596	3,486	3,339	3,535	3,248	3,490	3,385	3,574	3,180	3,052	40,287
2006[1]	3,511	3,216	3,550	3,294	3,360	3,420	3,195	3,349	2,877	3,154	2,368		38,503

[1] Preliminary. *Source: American Forest & Paper Association (AFPA)*

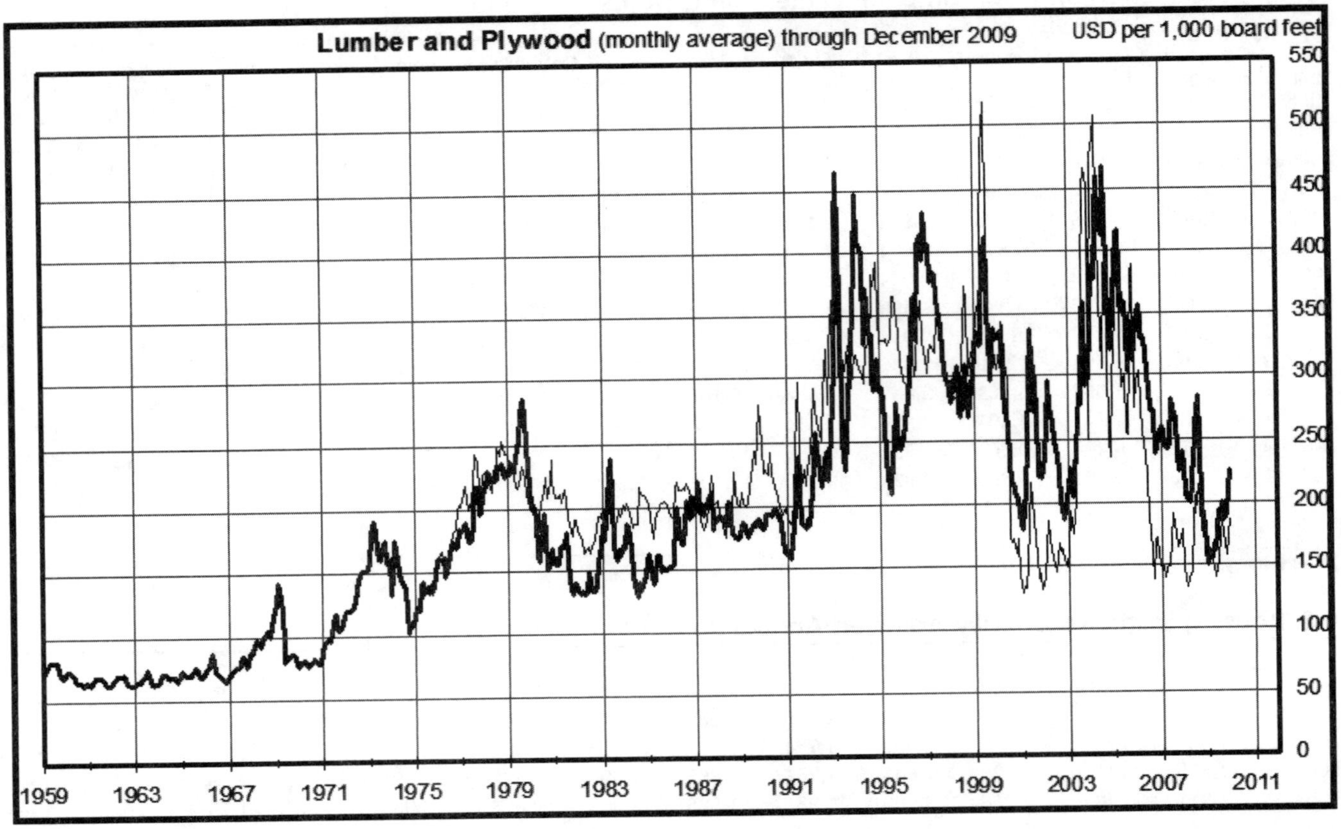

Lumber (Softwood) Shipments in the United States In Millions of Board Feet

Year	Jan.	Feb.	Mar.	Apr.	May	June	July	Aug.	Sept.	Oct.	Nov.	Dec.	Total
1997	2,966	2,697	2,890	3,253	2,834	3,126	3,139	2,885	2,852	3,096	2,598	2,461	34,797
1998	2,685	2,685	2,863	3,019	2,684	3,175	3,132	2,963	2,948	3,205	2,703	2,865	34,927
1999	2,689	2,829	3,177	3,227	3,071	3,383	3,141	3,004	3,037	3,021	2,944	2,691	36,214
2000	2,953	3,039	3,394	2,974	3,292	3,309	2,686	3,027	2,871	2,931	2,752	2,444	35,672
2001	2,859	2,372	2,981	2,974	NA	2,961	2,936	3,279	2,644	3,166	2,732	2,396	34,145
2002	3,032	2,815	3,049	3,212	3,064	3,260	3,234	3,111	2,858	3,299	2,675	2,501	36,110
2003	3,018	2,742	2,843	3,134	2,969	3,173	3,209	3,137	3,030	3,413	2,787	2,722	36,177
2004	3,067	2,840	3,262	3,582	3,061	3,385	3,485	3,372	3,086	3,345	3,135	2,964	38,584
2005	3,264	3,087	3,506	3,506	3,542	3,696	3,389	3,512	3,413	3,542	3,145	3,196	40,798
2006[1]	3,423	3,122	3,536	3,280	3,386	3,447	3,202	3,349	2,838	3,151	2,374		38,300

[1] Preliminary. *Source: American Forest & Paper Association (AFPA)*

Imports and Exports of Lumber in the United States, by Type In Millions of Board Feet

	Imports[2]								Exports[2]						
	Softwood								Softwood						
Year	Cedar	Douglas Fir	Hem-lock	Pine	Spruce	Total	Total Hard-wood	Total Lumber	Douglas Fir	Hem-lock	Pond-erosa/ White Pine	South-ern Pine	Total	Total Hard-wood	Total Lumber
1997	586	264	250	314	1,040	18,014	465	18,506	436	105	122	299	1,820	1,281	3,189
1998	514	417	268	363	849	18,686	589	19,306	252	39	113	279	1,265	1,119	2,601
1999	591	426	259	449	803	19,178	708	19,903	249	54	140	326	1,431	1,242	2,867
2000	694	455	184	450	812	19,449	795	20,268	232	46	116	298	1,355	1,319	2,822
2001	667	471	199	365	838	20,075	645	20,737	168	26	86	232	968	1,222	2,351
2002	648	385	69	445	1,046	20,986	739	21,774	111	19	83	205	848	1,219	2,313
2003	536	356	53	472	854	21,188	794	22,023	96	18	100	132	948	1,236	2,368
2004	630	570	67	580	1,183	23,483	995	24,499	88	19	93	156	821	1,496	2,533
2005	637	494	76	439	1,769	24,626	1,075	25,738	93	19	112	235	897	1,477	2,682
2006[1] I	180	88	31	100	432	6,054	261	6,321	19	3	29	58	246	449	695
II															
III															

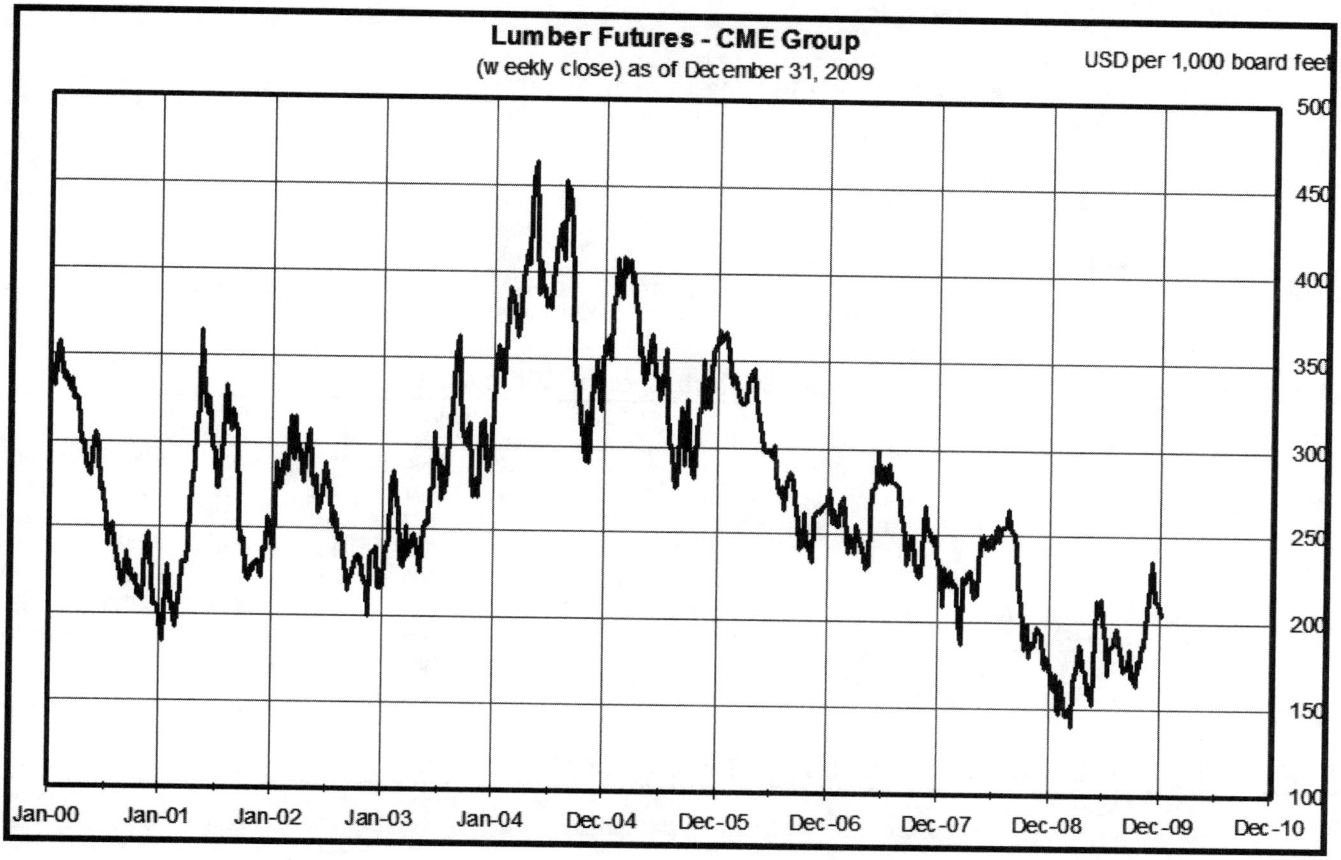

Average Open Interest of Random Lumber Futures in Chicago In Contracts

Year	Jan.	Feb.	Mar.	Apr.	May	June	July	Aug.	Sept.	Oct.	Nov.	Dec.
2000	3,004	3,131	2,728	3,175	3,171	3,218	3,064	3,638	3,845	4,277	4,208	4,405
2001	4,605	4,494	3,654	3,644	3,867	3,733	2,612	2,949	2,148	2,102	2,173	2,416
2002	2,106	2,382	2,441	2,011	1,502	2,136	1,879	2,265	2,654	2,974	3,315	3,249
2003	3,238	3,222	2,521	2,804	2,937	3,188	2,370	2,827	3,492	3,033	1,824	1,887
2004	2,884	3,996	3,790	5,414	5,436	5,042	5,123	6,216	4,667	3,826	3,489	3,540
2005	3,759	5,169	5,040	4,705	3,463	3,576	3,401	4,227	3,913	3,883	4,713	5,202
2006	5,893	5,144	4,084	4,959	4,586	5,449	5,317	6,429	5,912	6,351	6,121	7,018
2007	6,466	7,807	7,684	8,680	7,726	8,206	7,130	7,666	6,493	9,356	8,960	9,731
2008	9,827	13,134	13,385	14,637	14,801	14,275	14,417	14,016	12,110	9,466	7,744	8,084
2009	7,912	7,937	6,852	7,732	7,815	9,039	7,910	8,873	9,248	9,593	10,174	9,557

Contract size = 110,000 board feet. *Source: CME Group; Chicago Mercantile Exchange (CME)*

Volume of Trading of Random Lumber Futures in Chicago In Contracts

Year	Jan.	Feb.	Mar.	Apr.	May	June	July	Aug.	Sept.	Oct.	Nov.	Dec.	Total
2000	19,871	19,486	18,936	16,136	21,003	18,057	16,636	16,563	19,037	17,155	20,706	17,582	221,168
2001	21,567	15,076	24,561	22,458	23,681	18,878	15,210	16,440	12,882	11,608	11,989	12,490	206,840
2002	15,328	13,239	16,401	13,910	12,427	11,950	12,046	10,154	13,518	13,442	15,828	16,180	164,423
2003	24,241	17,533	17,027	11,573	20,132	21,840	21,097	22,418	22,891	19,387	12,480	13,272	223,891
2004	17,921	17,713	22,544	25,743	19,951	17,190	22,672	20,902	24,238	17,111	17,271	19,617	242,873
2005	20,838	20,257	24,595	20,360	17,338	17,115	16,244	19,590	22,895	15,896	23,404	17,709	236,241
2006	26,803	19,152	18,504	21,358	21,619	23,959	21,568	23,800	22,618	24,804	22,385	24,454	271,024
2007	26,214	28,328	24,741	26,433	31,540	28,545	23,462	28,610	24,841	33,876	29,738	28,361	334,689
2008	31,401	43,338	37,899	50,586	37,909	38,362	41,612	40,693	32,155	36,226	20,277	27,155	437,613
2009	18,478	29,930	22,193	25,349	24,351	34,027	24,340	29,548	22,271	33,768	21,817	31,155	317,227

Contract size = 110,000 board feet. *Source: CME Group; Chicago Mercantile Exchange (CME)*

LUMBER AND PLYWOOD

Production of Plywood by Selected Countries In Thousands of Cubic Meters

Year	Austria	Canada	Finland	France	Germany	Italy	Japan	Poland	Romania	Russia	Spain	Sweden	United States
2001	186	2,026	1,140	509	321	488	2,771	242	79	1,590	380	106	15,417
2002	186	2,176	1,240	459	285	520	2,735	261	90	1,821	360	87	15,307
2003	186	2,206	1,300	415	245	511	3,024	289	94	1,978	370	75	14,870
2004	186	2,344	1,350	435	283	485	3,149	342	117	2,246	375	71	14,833
2005	195	2,322	1,305	415	236	390	3,212	361	126	2,556	557	92	14,449
2006	178	2,252	1,415	431	235	334	3,314	385	188	2,614	468	92	13,651
2007[1]	258	2,639	1,410	378	229	420	3,073	440	107	2,777	450	72	12,402
2008[2]	268	2,225	1,265	360	204	421	2,586	395	90	2,583	250	75	10,376

[1] Preliminary. [2] Estimate. NA = Not available. *Source: Food and Agricultural Organization of the United Nations (FAO-UN)*

Imports of Plywood by Selected Countries In Thousands of Cubic Meters

Year	Austria	Belgium	Canada	Denmark	France	Germany	Italy	Japan	Nether-lands	Sweden	Switzer-land	United Kingdom	United States
2001	138	526	520	250	358	954	425	5,021	600	157	143	1,300	3,009
2002	156	505	489	254	349	905	558	5,119	541	152	128	1,297	3,890
2003	180	572	509	394	363	1,103	558	4,221	527	161	130	1,253	4,249
2004	144	624	350	413	383	1,214	581	5,122	542	164	140	1,474	5,900
2005	140	521	690	371	411	1,142	532	4,732	526	189	145	1,456	6,181
2006	140	610	685	402	445	1,314	575	5,046	603	197	128	1,497	6,393
2007[1]	172	672	1,827	389	459	1,516	588	4,064	608	240	126	1,624	4,397
2008[2]	133	633	2,111	143	503	1,274	530	3,583	635	192	131	1,490	3,059

[1] Preliminary. [2] Estimate. NA = Not available. *Source: Food and Agricultural Organization of the United Nations (FAO-UN)*

Exports of Plywood by Selected Countries In Thousands of Cubic Meters

Year	Austria	Baltic States	Belgium	Canada	Finland	France	Germany	Italy	Nether-lands	Poland	Russia	Spain	United States
2001	286	232	378	1,030	1,009	200	232	125	57	128	1,032	88	530
2002	240	238	371	1,056	1,117	190	167	204	43	138	1,157	82	523
2003	262	245	436	1,017	1,172	187	200	208	32	149	1,201	88	512
2004	265	255	474	1,027	1,234	192	265	201	46	171	1,438	114	525
2005	287	253	423	1,118	1,173	196	287	146	40	177	1,527	117	503
2006	311	282	470	950	1,250	225	321	239	60	137	1,577	124	492
2007[1]	285	318	386	964	1,229	227	368	295	55	148	1,503	162	443
2008[2]	278	197	470	835	1,083	223	320	184	51	133	1,326	213	506

[1] Preliminary. [2] Estimate. NA = Not available. *Source: Food and Agricultural Organization of the United Nations (FAO-UN)*

Imports of Industrial Roundwood by Selected Countries In Thousands of Cubic Meters

Year	Austria	Belgium	Canada	Finland	France	Germany	Italy	Norway	Poland	Portugal	Spain	Sweden	United States
2001	7,493	4,505	7,557	11,869	1,994	3,493	5,211	2,772	882	1,109	4,128	9,505	2,430
2002	7,289	2,653	6,941	12,586	1,993	2,623	4,703	2,561	726	901	3,374	9,705	2,687
2003	7,498	2,667	6,615	12,869	2,250	2,519	4,323	2,722	663	468	3,191	9,021	2,551
2004	8,812	2,879	5,961	12,961	2,175	2,227	4,614	2,866	943	364	2,973	9,398	2,437
2005	8,629	3,188	6,274	16,031	2,344	3,005	4,755	3,145	2,009	362	3,640	8,686	3,569
2006	9,102	3,284	5,787	14,655	2,601	3,669	4,486	2,333	1,814	335	3,841	6,664	2,922
2007[1]	8,722	4,094	5,100	12,942	3,181	4,692	4,299	2,539	2,088	746	3,965	7,364	2,242
2008[2]	7,550	3,251	4,609	13,371	2,346	4,130	3,478	1,808	1,868	521	2,860	6,781	1,430

[1] Preliminary. [2] Estimate. NA = Not available. *Source: Food and Agricultural Organization of the United Nations (FAO-UN)*

Exports of Industrial Roundwood by Selected Countries In Thousands of Cubic Meters

Year	Canada	Czech Republic	Estonia	France	Germany	Hungary	Latvia	Lithuania	Russia	Slovakia	Sweden	Switzer-land	United States
2001	3,835	2,276	3,482	5,116	4,906	1,227	3,990	1,314	31,693	1,550	1,303	3,149	11,412
2002	4,471	2,302	3,132	4,244	4,907	1,210	4,225	1,420	36,800	1,187	1,755	1,970	11,067
2003	5,004	2,955	3,029	4,111	4,592	1,366	3,922	1,378	37,518	1,034	1,520	1,748	10,288
2004	3,899	2,858	2,297	3,851	5,589	1,137	4,136	1,178	41,553	1,142	1,522	1,741	10,402
2005	5,592	2,942	1,806	3,862	6,819	871	3,919	1,131	48,020	1,691	3,095	1,416	9,815
2006	4,640	2,679	1,606	3,695	7,557	1,095	3,419	1,061	50,900	1,218	3,004	1,727	9,638
2007[1]	3,560	2,384	1,502	3,966	7,674	1,054	3,690	1,671	49,100	1,457	3,808	2,005	9,949
2008[2]	2,838	1,906	1,469	3,505	6,712	661	3,193	1,171	36,784	2,192	2,349	1,155	10,200

[1] Preliminary. [2] Estimate. NA = Not available. *Source: Food and Agricultural Organization of the United Nations (FAO-UN)*

Magnesium

Magnesium (symbol Mg) is a silvery-white, light, and fairly tough, metallic element and is relatively stable. Magnesium is one of the alkaline earth metals. Magnesium is the eighth most abundant element in the earth's crust and the third most plentiful element found in seawater. Magnesium is ductile and malleable when heated, and with the exception of beryllium, is the lightest metal that remains stable under ordinary conditions. First isolated by the British chemist Sir Humphrey Davy in 1808, magnesium today is obtained mainly by electrolysis of fused magnesium chloride.

Magnesium compounds, primarily magnesium oxide, are used in the refractory material that line the furnaces used to produce iron and steel, nonferrous metals, glass, and cement. Magnesium oxide and other compounds are also used in the chemical, agricultural, and construction industries. Magnesium's principal use is as an alloying addition for aluminum. These aluminum-magnesium alloys are used primarily in beverage cans. Due to their lightness and considerable tensile strength, the alloys are also used in structural components in airplanes and automobiles.

Prices – The average price of magnesium in 2009 fell -23.5% to $2.59 per pound, down from last year's record high of $3.38 per pound.

Supply – World primary production of magnesium in 2009 fell -15.1% yr/yr to 577,000 metric tons, down further from 2007's record high of 751,000 metric tons. The current level of magnesium production has more than doubled since the mid-1970s when 1976's production was 249,367 metric tons.

The world's largest primary producers of magnesium in 2009 were China with 470,000 metric tons, Russia with 30,000 metric tons, and Brazil with 15,000 metric tons. The U.S. production amount is not available because it is considered proprietary data but is probably less than about 50,000 metric tons. China's production has increased over the past 10 years from 70,500 metric tons in 1998 to 470,000 metric tons in 2009 but that was down from its record high of 625,000 in 2007. By 2006 Canada's production had grown by more than seven-fold from the mid-1980s, but that fell sharply in 2007 by -75% to 16,300 metric tons. Russia's production is less than half of what it was in the mid 1980s.

Demand – Total U.S. consumption of primary magnesium in 2008 fell 19.0% to 58,427 from 72,147 metric tons. U.S. consumption of magnesium for structural products in 2008 fell -50.6% yr/yr to 13,127 metric tons. Of the structural product consumption category, 81% was for castings and the remaining 19% was for wrought products. U.S. consumption of magnesium for aluminum alloys rose +9.4% yr/yr in 2008 to 35,000 metric tons. The consumption of magnesium for other uses fell by -24.3% yr/yr in 2008 to 10,300 metric tons.

Trade – U.S. exports of magnesium in 2009 rose +11.1% yr/yr to 16,000 metric tons, up from the 2005 record low of 9,650 metric tons. U.S. imports of magnesium in 2009 fell -40.0% yr/yr to 50,000 metric tons.

World Production of Magnesium (Primary and Secondary) In Metric Tons

	Primary Production								Secondary Production				
Year	Brazil	Canada	China	France	Norway	Russia	United States	Total	Japan	United Kingdom	United States	Former USSR	Total
2004	6,000	54,000	442,000	----	----	45,000	W	595,000	----	----	----	----	----
2005	6,000	50,000	470,000	----	----	45,000	W	622,000	----	----	----	----	----
2006	6,000	65,000	520,000	----	----	35,000	W	675,000	----	----	----	----	----
2007	18,000	16,300	625,000	----	----	37,000	W	751,000	----	----	----	----	----
2008[1]	15,000	----	559,000	----	----	37,000	W	671,000	----	----	----	----	----
2009[2]	15,000	----	470,000	----	----	30,000	W	570,000	----	----	----	----	----

[1] Preliminary. [2] Estimate. W = Withheld. *Source: U.S. Geological Survey (USGS)*

Salient Statistics of Magnesium in the United States In Metric Tons

	Production								Domestic Consumption of Primary Magnesium					
		Secondary							Structural Products					
Year	Primary (Ingot)	New Scrap	Old Scrap	Total	Total Exports[3]	Imports for Consumption	Stocks Dec. 31[4]	Price $ Per Pound[5]	Castings	Wrought	Total	Aluminum Alloys	Other Uses	Total
2004	W	W	20,500	72,000	11,800	98,600	W	1.58	48,629	2,240	50,869	33,900	16,400	50,300
2005	W	W	19,400	72,900	9,650	84,700	W	1.23	34,024	2,890	36,914	30,300	14,800	45,100
2006	W	W	21,700	75,800	12,300	75,300	W	1.40	26,007	2,410	28,417	33,700	15,400	49,100
2007	W	W	23,500	83,000	14,800	71,800	W	2.25	23,727	2,820	26,547	32,000	13,600	45,600
2008[1]	W	W	22,300	76,000	14,400	83,300	W	3.15	10,647	2,480	13,127	35,000	10,300	45,300
2009[2]	W	W		75,000	16,000	50,000	W	2.40						

[1] Preliminary. [2] Estimate. [3] Metal & alloys in crude form & scrap. [4] Estimate of Industry Stocks, metal. [5] Magnesium ingots (99.8%), f.o.b. Valasco, Texas. [6] Distributive or sacrificial purposes. W = Withheld proprietary data. *Source: U.S. Geological Survey (USGS)*

Average Price of Magnesium In Dollars Per Pound

Year	Jan.	Feb.	Mar.	Apr.	May	June	July	Aug.	Sept.	Oct.	Nov.	Dec.	Average
2005	1.60	1.57	1.57	1.57	1.54	1.48	1.40	1.40	1.33	1.32	1.29	1.25	1.44
2006	1.25	1.18	1.18	1.16	1.16	1.16	1.16	1.16	1.20	1.21	1.29	1.33	1.20
2007	1.42	1.56	1.58	1.62	1.65	1.65	1.65	1.65	1.65	1.98	2.09	2.20	1.73
2008	2.89	3.08	3.27	3.39	3.55	3.55	3.55	3.55	3.55	3.50	3.43	3.22	3.38
2009	3.13	2.99	2.83	2.73	2.73	2.73	2.52	2.35	2.30	2.25	2.23	2.23	2.59

Source: American Metal Market (AMM)

Manganese

Manganese (symbol Mn) is a silvery-white, very brittle, metallic element used primarily in making alloys. Manganese was first distinguished as an element and isolated in 1774 by Johan Gottlieb Gahn. Manganese dissolves in acid and corrodes in moist air.

Manganese is found in the earth's crust in the form of ores such as rhodochrosite, franklinite, psilomelane, and manganite. Pyrolusite is the principal ore of manganese. Pure manganese is produced by igniting pyrolusite with aluminum powder or by electrolyzing manganese sulfate.

Manganese is used primarily in the steel industry for creating alloys, the most important ones being ferromanganese and spiegeleisen. In steel, manganese improves forging and rolling qualities, strength, toughness, stiffness, wear resistance, and hardness. Manganese is also used in plant fertilizers, animal feed, pigments, and dry cell batteries.

Prices – The average monthly price of ferromanganese (high carbon, FOB plant) fell by 56.6% yr/yr in 2009 to $1,282.62 per gross ton, down from last year's record high of $2,953.84 per gross ton. The 2009 price, however, is still about three times the 22-year low price of $447.44 per gross ton posted as recently as 2001.

Supply – World production of manganese ore in 2007 (latest data available) rose by +8.8% to 35.7 million metric tons, which was a record high. That was well above the record low of 17.8 million metric tons posted in 1999. The world's largest producers of manganese ore are China with 28% of world production in 2007, South Africa with 17%, Australia with 15%, Brazil with 5%, and the Ukraine with 5%. China's production in 2007 was up +20.0% yr/yr at 10.000 million metric tons.

Demand – U.S. consumption of manganese ore in 2009 rose +6.2% to 410,000 metric tons, up further from the 2007 record low of 351,000 metric tons. U.S. consumption of ferromanganese in 2009 fell -50.7% yr/yr to 150,000 metric tons, far below the 12-year high of 315,000 metric tons posted in 2004. The 2009 figure is about 15% of the U.S. consumption in the early 1970s.

Trade – The U.S. still relies on imports for 100% of its manganese consumption, as it has since 1985. U.S. imports of manganese ore for consumption in 2009 fell -47.5% yr/yr to 300,000 metric tons, which is a 16-year low. U.S. imports of ferromanganese for consumption in 2009 fell -77.7% yr/yr to a record low of 100,000 metric tons. U.S. imports of silico-manganese in 2009 fell 64.4% yr/yr to a 25-year low of 130,000 metric tons. The primary sources of U.S. imports of manganese ore in 2006 were Gabon with 44% imports, South Africa with 34%, and Australia with 5%.

World Production of Manganese Ore In Thousands of Metric Tons (Gross Weight)

Year	Australia[2] 37-53[4]	Brazil 37[4]	China 20-30[4]	Gabon 45-53[4]	Georgia[5] 29-30[4]	Ghana 32-34[4]	India 10-54[4]	Kazakhstan[5] 29-30[4]	Mexico 27-50[4]	South Africa 30-48+[4]	Ukraine[5] 30-35[4]	Other	World Total
1998	1,500	1,940	5,300	2,092	----	537	1,557	634	510	3,044	2,226	522	19,900
1999	1,892	1,656	3,190	1,908	----	639	1,500	980	459	3,122	1,985	458	17,800
2000	1,614	1,925	3,500	1,743	----	896	1,550	1,136	435	3,635	2,741	433	19,600
2001	2,069	1,970	4,300	1,791	----	1,077	1,600	1,387	277	3,266	2,700	490	20,900
2002	2,189	2,529	4,500	1,856	----	1,136	1,553	1,792	245	3,322	2,470	526	22,100
2003	2,564	2,544	4,600	2,000	----	1,509	1,650	2,361	320	3,501	2,591	547	24,200
2004	3,431	3,143	5,500	2,460	----	1,597	1,776	2,318	377	4,282	2,362	612	27,900
2005	3,136	3,200	7,500	2,859	----	1,715	2,386	2,208	369	4,612	2,260	724	31,000
2006	4,556	3,128	8,000	3,000	----	1,600	2,084	2,531	346	5,213	1,606	741	32,800
2007[1]	5,289	1,866	10,000	3,300	----	1,600	2,300	2,482	350	5,996	1,720	818	35,700

[1] Preliminary. [2] Metallurgical Ore. [3] Concentrate. [4] Ranges of percentage of manganese. *Source: U.S. Geological Survey (USGS)*

Salient Statistics of Manganese in the United States In Thousands of Metric Tons (Gross Weight)

Year	Net Import Reliance As a % of Apparent Consumption	Manganese Ore (35% or More Manganese): Imports for Consumption	Exports	Consumption	Stocks Dec. 31[3]	Ferromanganese: Imports for Consumption	Exports	Consumption	Avg Price Mn. Metallurgical Ore $/Lg. Ton Unit[4]	Silicomanganese: Exports	Imports
2000	100	447	10	486	226	312	8	300	2.39	1.9	378.0
2001	100	358	9	425	138	251	9	266	2.44	3.6	269.0
2002	100	427	15	360	151	275	9	253	2.30	0.5	247.0
2003	100	347	18	398	156	238	11	248	2.41	0.6	267.0
2004	100	451	123	441	159	429	9	315	2.89	0.5	422.0
2005	100	656	13	368	337	255	14	286	4.39	0.9	327.0
2006	100	572	2	365	153	358	22	297	3.22	0.9	400.0
2007	100	602	29	351	114	315	29	272	3.10	3.3	414.0
2008[1]	100	571	48	386	285	448	23	304	12.15		365.0
2009[2]	100	300	19	410	110	100	28	150	5.77		130.0

[1] Preliminary. [2] Estimate. [3] Including bonded warehouses; excludes Gov't stocks; also excludes small tonnages of dealers' stocks.
[4] 46-48% Mn, C.I.F. U.S. Ports. *Source: U.S. Geological Survey (USGS)*

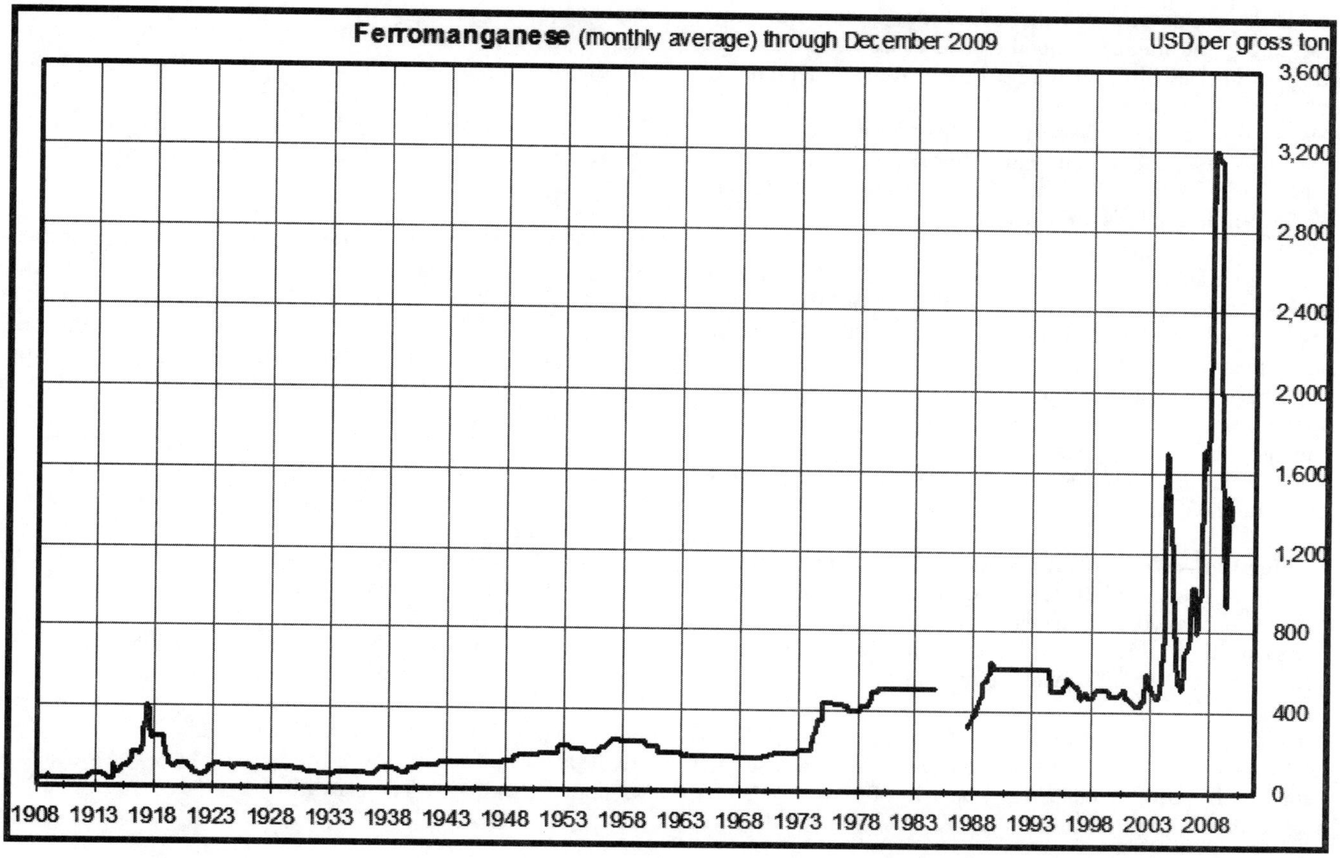

Imports[3] of Manganese Ore (20% or More Mn) in the United States In Metric Tons (Mn Content)

Year	Australia	Brazil	Gabon	Mexico	Morocco	South Africa	Total	Customs Value ($1,000)
1998	18,700	12,100	94,900	14,600	----	13,800	160,000	27,800
1999	23,500	1	142,000	9,130	----	39,100	224,000	37,200
2000	18,100	3,250	188,000	3,250	----	----	219,000	32,100
2001	18,000	3,480	158,000	1,720	----	17,400	199,000	28,000
2002	18,400	12,900	140,000	1,100	----	41,800	214,000	29,200
2003	12,900	7	123,000	1,520	----	36,900	175,000	27,000
2004	27,700	----	188,000	1,640	----	13,200	234,000	37,700
2005	21,300	7,020	252,000	4,320	----	33,100	334,000	58,200
2006[1]	12,800	5,800	120,000	1,320	----	91,200	270,000	53,900
2007[2]	34,900	20,000	170,000	3,670	----	53,600	298,000	57,600

[1] Preliminary. [2] Estimate. [3] Imports for consumption. *Source: U.S. Geological Survey (USGS)*

Average Price of Ferromanganese[1] In Dollars Per Gross Ton -- Carloads

Year	Jan.	Feb.	Mar.	Apr.	May	June	July	Aug.	Sept.	Oct.	Nov.	Dec.	Average
2000	482.50	482.50	482.50	482.50	482.50	482.50	501.63	505.00	509.00	510.00	510.00	477.50	492.40
2001	473.93	467.89	460.00	454.29	450.00	450.00	446.90	444.57	430.79	430.00	430.00	430.00	447.44
2002	430.00	430.00	437.14	447.73	449.55	456.75	481.82	556.14	597.00	589.67	552.89	518.93	495.64
2003	509.52	510.00	502.38	497.61	492.50	481.79	477.27	470.00	478.57	497.83	516.67	559.76	499.49
2004	610.00	790.00	1,382.61	1,700.00	1,700.00	1,674.43	1,490.34	1,488.64	1,500.00	1,371.43	1,207.50	1,019.52	1,327.87
2005	904.50	818.68	739.46	651.67	586.19	547.39	528.13	512.07	522.14	550.24	597.75	694.05	637.69
2006	707.25	712.50	737.50	759.00	764.55	870.23	987.50	1,025.00	1,021.25	946.25	836.25	790.00	846.44
2007	834.29	930.00	949.55	1,000.00	1,074.43	1,633.33	1,705.00	1,620.00	1,620.00	1,656.96	1,700.00	1,785.53	1,375.76
2008	1,978.57	2,262.75	2,734.29	3,145.45	3,200.00	3,200.00	3,175.00	3,150.00	3,150.00	3,150.00	3,150.00	3,150.00	2,953.84
2009	2,225.00	1,300.00	1,300.00	1,038.10	950.00	928.18	955.45	1,071.43	1,344.52	1,481.67	1,431.84	1,365.26	1,282.62

[1] Domestic standard, high carbon, FOB plant, carloads. *Source: American Metal Market (AMM)*

Meats

U.S. commercial red meat includes beef, veal, lamb, and pork. Red meat is a good source of iron, vitamin B12, and protein, and eliminating it from the diet can lead to iron and zinc deficiencies. Today, red meat is far leaner than it was 30 years ago due to newer breeds of livestock that carry less fat. The leanest cuts of beef include tenderloin, sirloin, and flank. The leanest cuts of pork include pork tenderloin, loin chops, and rib chops.

The USDA (United States Department of Agriculture) grades various cuts of meat. "Prime" is the highest USDA grade for beef, veal, and lamb. "Choice" is the grade designation below Prime for beef, veal, and lamb. "Commercial" and "Cutter" grades are two of the lower designations for beef, usually sold as ground meat, sausage, and canned meat. "Canner" is the lowest USDA grade designation for beef and is used primarily in canned meats not sold at retail.

Supply – World meat production in 2009 rose +0.28% to a new record high of 157.018 million metric tons. China was the world's largest meat producer in 2009 with 54.264 million metric tons of production (up +2.9% yr/yr), accounting for 35% of world production.

U.S. production of meat in 2008 (latest data) rose by +3.6% yr/yr to 50.567 billion pounds, which was a new record high. U.S. production of beef in 2008 rose 0.6% yr/yr to 26.682 billion pounds, which will be just moderately below the record of 27.192 billion pounds in 2002. Beef accounted for 53.0% of all U.S. meat production. U.S. production of pork in 2008 rose +7.3% yr/yr to a new record high of 23.554 billion pounds. Pork accounts for 47.0% of U.S. meat production. Veal accounts for only 0.3% of U.S. meat production, and lamb and mutton account for only 0.4% of U.S. meat production.

Demand – U.S. per capita meat consumption in 2008 rose by 0.9% to 119.0 pounds per person per year, but that is only slightly above the 2006/7 record low of 117 pounds per person reflecting the trend towards eating more chicken and fish and the availability of meat substitutes. Per capita beef consumption in 2008 was unchanged at 65.0 pounds per person per year, which was about half the record high of 127.5 pounds seen in 1976. Per capita pork consumption in 2008 rose by +4.0% to 53.0 pounds per person per year from he record low of 49.0 pounds posted in 2006. Per capita consumption of veal is negligible at .5 pounds per person and lamb/mutton consumption is also negligible at 1.0 pound per person.

Trade – World red meat exports in 2009 fell -7.8% to 12.575 million metric tons, down from the 2008 record high of 13.637 million metric tons. The world's largest red meat exporters will be the U.S. with 21% of world exports in 2009, Brazil with 18%, Canada with 13%, the European Union with 11%, and Australia with 11%.

World Total Meat Production[4] In Thousands of Metric Tons

Year	Argentina	Australia	Brazil	Canada	China[4]	European Union	India	Mexico	New Zealand	Russia	South Africa	United States	World Total
2001	2,838	2,428	9,125	2,855	45,603	29,300	----	2,990	624	3,320	776	20,674	139,225
2002	2,865	2,496	9,805	3,007	46,450	29,928	----	2,810	635	3,370	770	21,356	142,983
2003	2,950	2,492	9,945	2,934	47,811	30,016	----	3,050	729	3,380	756	21,095	144,908
2004	3,308	2,475	10,575	3,280	49,014	29,998	----	3,050	749	3,315	801	20,574	147,453
2005	3,388	2,487	11,302	3,235	51,234	29,766	----	2,920	711	3,260	829	20,710	150,703
2006	3,310	2,572	11,855	3,077	52,272	29,941	----	2,708	699	3,235	876	21,539	153,611
2007	3,515	2,558	12,293	3,024	49,012	31,046	----	2,752	657	3,280	828	22,058	152,944
2008	3,370	2,507	12,039	3,074	52,337	30,686	----	2,761	695	3,375	826	22,762	156,578
2009[1]	3,425	2,435	12,058	3,090	54,264	30,000	----	2,775	684	3,485	832	22,262	157,018
2010[2]	3,025	2,421	12,539	2,935	55,830	29,850	----	2,805	675	3,555	838	21,816	158,288

[1] Preliminary. [2] Forecast. [3] Data through 2000, includes beef, veal, pork, sheep and goat meat. Beginning 2001, excludes sheep and goat.
[4] Predominately pork production. *Source: Foreign Agricultural Service, U.S. Department of Agriculture (FAS-USDA)*

Production and Consumption of Red Meats in The United States

	Beef			Veal			Lamb & Mutton			Pork (Excluding Lard)			All Meats		
Year	Commercial Production - Million Pounds -	Consumption Total - Million Pounds -	Consumption Per Capita Lbs.	Commercial Production - Million Pounds -	Consumption Total - Million Pounds -	Consumption Per Capita Lbs.	Commercial Production - Million Pounds -	Consumption Total - Million Pounds -	Consumption Per Capita Lbs.	Commercial Production - Million Pounds -	Consumption Total - Million Pounds -	Consumption Per Capita Lbs.	Commercial Production - Million Pounds -	Consumption Total - Million Pounds -	Consumption Per Capita Lbs.
1999	26,493	26,936	68.0	235	235	1.0	248	358	1.0	19,308	18,954	53.0	46,284	46,483	122.0
2000	26,888	27,338	68.0	225	225	1.0	234	354	1.0	18,952	18,643	51.0	46,299	46,560	121.0
2001	26,212	27,026	66.0	205	204	1.0	227	368	1.0	19,160	18,492	50.0	45,804	46,089	118.0
2002	27,192	27,877	68.0	205	204	1.0	223	381	1.0	19,685	19,146	52.0	47,305	47,608	121.0
2003	26,339	27,000	65.0	202	204	0.6	203	367	1.0	19,966	19,436	52.0	46,710	47,006	118.0
2004	24,650	27,750	66.0	176	177	0.6	200	373	1.0	20,529	19,437	51.0	45,555	47,737	119.0
2005	24,787	27,754	66.0	165	164	0.6	191	355	1.0	20,705	19,112	50.0	45,848	47,385	117.0
2006	26,256	28,137	66.0	156	155	0.5	190	356	1.0	21,074	19,048	49.0	47,675	47,696	117.0
2007[1]	26,523	28,144	65.0	145	144	0.5	188	384	1.0	21,962	19,763	51.0	48,817	48,435	118.0
2008[2]	26,682	28,127	65.0	150	153	0.5	181	367	1.0	23,554	20,686	53.0	50,567	48,333	119.0

[1] Preliminary. [2] Estimate. [3] Forecast. *Source: Economic Research Service, U.S. Department of Agriculture (ERS-USDA)*

Total Red Meat Imports[3] (Carcass Weight Equivalent) of Principal Countries In Thousands of Metric Tons

Year	Brazil	Canada	European Union	Egypt	Hong Kong	Japan	Rep of Korea	Mexico	Philip-pines	Russia	Taiwan	United States	World Total
2001	44	421	449	147	294	2,004	385	732	136	1,130	93	1,866	8,923
2002	77	431	563	178	308	1,805	606	828	155	1,507	116	1,945	9,938
2003	62	395	593	127	339	1,924	620	752	149	1,416	144	1,901	10,276
2004	52	228	694	173	364	1,903	457	754	185	1,333	134	2,168	10,686
2005	48	290	810	215	351	2,000	595	755	160	1,730	129	2,096	11,533
2006	28	325	842	313	366	1,832	708	829	160	1,774	128	1,848	11,757
2007	30	413	676	361	392	1,896	755	854	179	1,924	120	1,823	12,314
2008	29	424	521	195	464	1,926	725	943	205	2,190	141	1,528	12,843
2009[1]	30	440	520	150	490	1,882	665	900	153	1,450	170	1,627	11,762
2010[2]	25	490	540	175	503	1,888	695	955	163	1,530	175	1,694	12,069

[1] Preliminary. [2] Forecast. [3] Data through 2000, includes beef, veal, pork, sheep and goat meat. Beginning 2001, excludes sheep and goat.
Source: Foreign Agricultural Service, U.S. Department of Agriculture (FAS-USDA)

Total Red Meat Exports[3] (Carcass Weight Equivalent) of Principal Countries In Thousands of Metric Tons

Year	Argentina	Australia	Brazil	Canada	China	Denmark	France	India	Ireland	Nether-lands	New Zealand	United States	World Total
2001	168	1,446	1,078	1,347	276	1,580	365	483	7	100	1,727	145	9,060
2002	345	1,424	1,462	1,521	344	1,573	411	475	7	187	1,841	225	10,170
2003	382	1,318	1,765	1,388	433	1,578	432	548	10	227	1,921	282	10,672
2004	616	1,431	2,231	1,575	589	1,665	492	594	10	127	1,198	354	11,373
2005	755	1,444	2,606	1,680	578	1,396	617	577	12	91	1,525	418	12,321
2006	553	1,490	2,723	1,558	629	1,502	681	530	9	24	1,878	461	12,727
2007	535	1,454	2,919	1,490	431	1,426	678	496	9	52	2,075	386	12,733
2008	424	1,455	2,426	1,623	281	1,929	672	533	12	24	2,973	361	13,637
2009[1]	562	1,435	2,200	1,605	263	1,410	675	525	13	17	2,672	310	12,575
2010[2]	392	1,398	2,570	1,590	265	1,360	700	517	13	17	2,855	360	12,814

[1] Preliminary. [2] Forecast. [3] Data through 2000, includes beef, veal, pork, sheep and goat meat. Beginning 2001, excludes sheep and goat.
Source: Foreign Agricultural Service, U.S. Department of Agriculture (FAS-USDA)

United States Meat Imports by Type of Product In Metric Tons

	Beef and Veal			Lamb, Mutton and Goat, Except Canned	Pork			Variety Meats, Fresh or Frozen	Other Livestock Meats NSE	
Year	Fresh	Frozen	Other Pre-pared or Preserved		Fresh and Chilled	Frozen	Other Pre-pared or Preserved			Total
1996	227,874	412,805	66,719	33,009	125,220	58,336	72,650	32,579	13,744	1,042,934
1997	262,985	469,949	63,181	37,848	126,061	65,000	72,903	44,317	14,215	1,156,457
1998	295,820	527,063	68,884	51,630	146,965	70,227	76,230	47,031	13,058	1,296,907
1999	337,899	542,524	82,669	50,209	188,556	77,638	84,207	51,640	13,625	1,428,966
2000	336,117	608,737	73,750	59,968	229,395	91,446	92,672	57,388	14,281	1,563,753
2001	368,529	618,897	73,713	66,785	240,275	84,687	83,724	62,541	16,723	1,615,873
2002	400,484	586,500	84,640	73,863	276,639	90,423	91,379	55,384	19,401	1,678,713
2003	285,772	612,569	85,439	77,546	293,169	107,749	107,964	47,688	21,367	1,639,263
2004	387,758	717,942	92,123	82,930	266,583	109,915	96,840	33,776	55,737	1,843,604
2005[1]	406,431	669,935	96,181	83,957	266,544	93,063	78,594	41,067	25,426	1,761,198

[1] Preliminary. NSE = Not specified elsewhere. *Source: Foreign Agricultural Service, U.S. Department of Agriculture (FAS-USDA)*

United States Meat Exports by Type of Product In Metric Tons

	Beef and Veal			Lamb and Mutton, Fresh or Frozen	Pork			Variety Meats, Fresh, Chilled or Frozen	Other Meats	
Year	Fresh	Frozen	Other Pre-pared or Preserved		Fresh and Chilled	Frozen	Other Pre-pared or Preserved			Total
1996	273,276	324,329	14,577	2,478	101,975	166,057	32,190	495,343	434,759	1,844,984
1997	316,534	359,460	15,227	2,545	134,706	151,121	31,215	469,789	435,258	1,915,854
1998	346,403	352,050	17,966	2,528	147,006	209,135	37,907	495,643	423,980	2,032,618
1999	370,184	414,458	19,323	2,219	160,910	225,492	40,463	524,325	455,561	2,212,935
2000	395,588	417,538	21,791	2,184	208,055	185,240	36,915	604,738	503,942	2,372,990
2001	393,105	362,972	23,932	2,770	227,807	247,461	44,494	685,063	513,969	2,501,573
2002	407,599	393,836	27,232	3,042	235,547	231,274	69,030	592,185	619,491	2,579,236
2003	430,071	390,543	37,572	2,909	237,129	257,360	69,693	598,726	567,565	2,591,568
2004	114,966	20,458	9,068	3,671	352,173	298,786	74,963	456,480	189,127	1,519,691
2005[1]	173,337	31,714	19,027	4,885	404,601	401,115	75,096	497,346	274,990	1,882,111

[1] Preliminary. *Source: Foreign Agricultural Service, U.S. Department of Agriculture (FAS-USDA)*

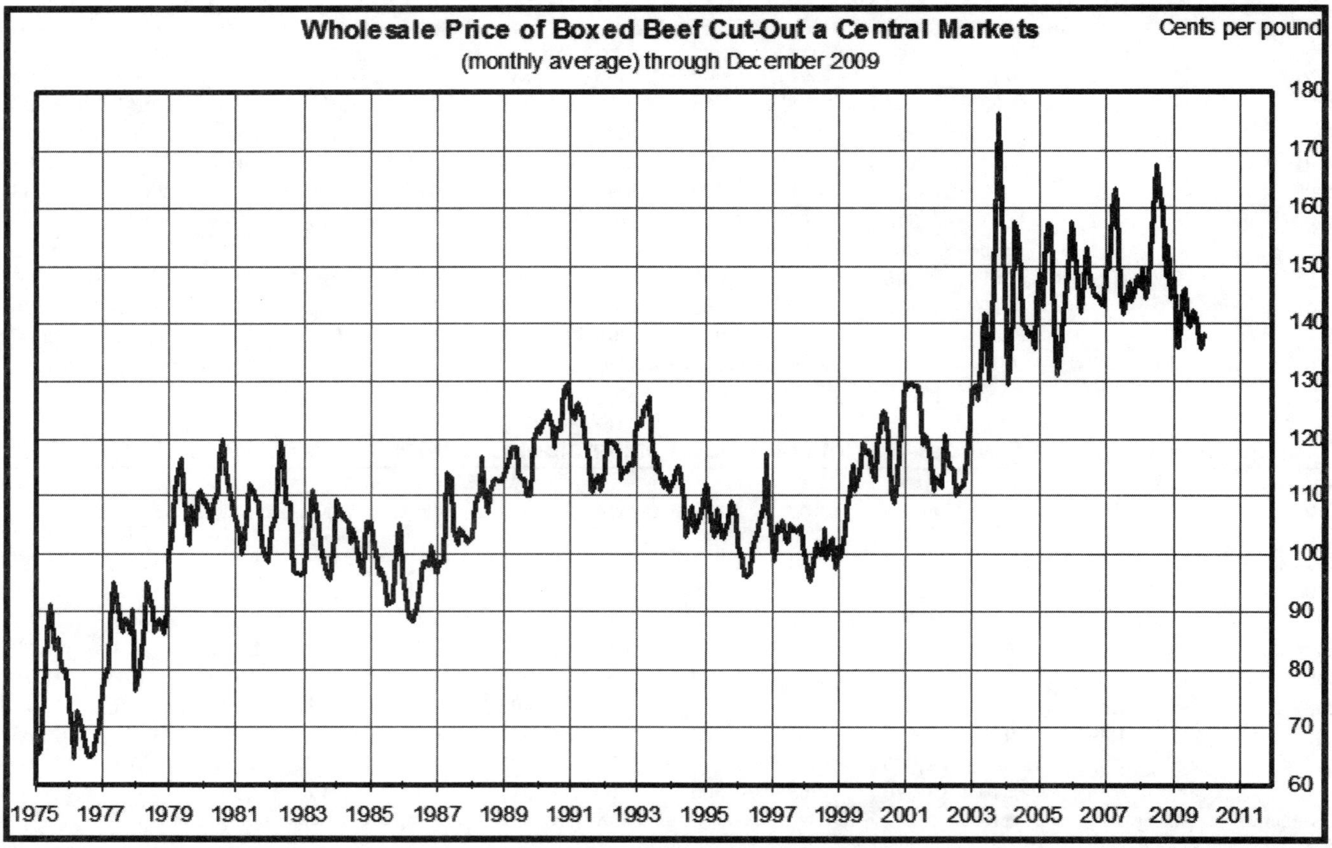

Exports and Imports of Meats in the United States (Carcass Weight Equivalent)[3]

Year	Exports: Beef and Veal	Exports: Lamb and Mutton	Exports: Pork[3]	Exports: All Meat	Imports: Beef and Veal	Imports: Lamb and Mutton	Imports: Pork[3]	Imports: All Meat
1997	2,136	5	1,044	3,185	2,343	83	634	3,061
1998	2,171	6	1,230	3,407	2,643	112	705	3,461
1999	2,412	5	1,277	3,694	2,873	112	827	3,813
2000	2,468	5	1,287	3,760	3,032	130	965	4,127
2001	2,269	7	1,559	3,835	3,163	146	951	4,260
2002	2,448	7	1,612	4,067	3,218	160	1,071	4,448
2003	2,518	7	1,717	4,242	3,006	168	1,185	4,359
2004	460	9	2,181	2,650	3,679	180	1,099	4,959
2005[1]	644	9	2,683	3,336	3,587	179	1,002	4,768
2006[2]	680	8	2,785	3,473	3,560	175	960	4,695

[1] Preliminary. [2] Estimate. [3] Includes meat content of minor meats and of mixed products.
Source: Economic Research Service, U.S. Department of Agriculture (FAS-USDA)

Average Wholesale Prices of Meats in the United States In Cent Per Pound

Year	Composite Retail Price of Beef, Choice, Grade 3	Composite Retail Price of Pork[3]	Wholesale Value[4] Beef	Wholesale Value[4] Pork	Net Farm Value[5] of Pork	Cow Beef Canner & Cutter, Central US	Boxed Beef Cut-out, Choice1-3, Central US 550-700 Lb.	Pork Carcass Cut-out, U.S., No. 2	Lamb Carcass, Choice-Prime, E. Coast, 55-65 lbs.	Pork[6] Loins, Central US 14-18 lbs.	Skinned Ham, Central US 17-20 lbs.	Pork Bellies, Central US 12-14 lbs.
2000	306.42	258.20	182.27	114.50	79.40	72.57	117.51	64.07	177.78	117.13	60.85	77.46
2001	337.73	269.39	192.12	117.80	81.30	79.50	122.61	66.83	148.96	116.97	64.86	78.61
2002	331.53	265.75	180.02	100.70	61.90	NA	114.42	53.49	151.28	97.98	47.52	69.91
2003	374.62	265.82	222.90	107.40	69.60	NA	143.58	58.87	185.21	100.96	45.48	86.42
2004	406.53	279.16	218.90	127.40	92.10	NA	142.15	73.53	189.08	117.14	64.98	99.35
2005	409.22	282.69	226.10	124.90	88.00	NA	145.78	69.84	209.88	113.22	64.07	81.46
2006	397.02	280.72	228.17	121.38	83.27	NA	146.82	67.62	199.10	104.46	64.04	82.81
2007	415.85	287.03	231.08	121.44	81.98	NA	149.80	67.54	215.96	104.17	57.96	88.97
2008[1]	432.45	293.65	235.04	124.73	82.48	NA	153.17	69.24	226.63	106.63	63.52	69.86
2009[2]	425.98	291.97	217.18	111.19	71.56	NA	140.77	58.13	225.45	92.81	51.34	60.91

[1] Preliminary. [2] Estimate. [3] Sold as retail cuts (ham, bacon, loin, etc.). [4] Quantity equivalent to 1 pound of retail cuts.
[5] Portion of gross farm value minus farm by-product allowance. *Source: Economic Research Service, U.S. Department of Agriculture (ERS-USDA)*

Average Wholesale Price of Boxed Beef Cut-Out[1], Choice 1-3, at Central US In Cents Per Pound

Year	Jan.	Feb.	Mar.	Apr.	May	June	July	Aug.	Sept.	Oct.	Nov.	Dec.	Average
2000	114.74	112.59	118.42	123.45	124.88	123.30	115.85	111.20	108.68	112.58	118.05	126.41	117.51
2001	129.78	128.87	129.58	128.93	129.03	126.82	118.93	120.20	119.30	115.93	110.95	113.04	122.61
2002	111.99	111.53	120.54	116.61	115.14	114.06	109.88	110.93	111.83	111.64	116.41	122.45	114.42
2003	128.59	128.77	126.35	133.03	141.44	141.16	130.13	139.91	156.64	176.06	167.15	153.71	143.58
2004	138.60	129.29	141.34	157.53	155.70	148.54	140.27	139.33	137.82	138.45	135.64	143.31	142.15
2005	148.93	143.02	150.66	157.34	156.82	140.02	131.19	132.85	137.97	144.30	148.81	157.49	145.78
2006	155.60	149.71	144.94	141.83	147.45	153.09	147.01	146.22	144.69	144.79	143.64	142.92	146.82
2007	149.15	149.54	159.23	163.23	160.20	145.59	141.47	144.51	146.99	144.09	145.39	148.25	149.80
2008	146.41	149.63	144.42	147.47	156.07	159.10	167.33	162.31	159.56	148.03	153.29	144.42	153.17
2009[2]	147.68	136.03	135.91	144.42	146.22	140.22	139.59	142.13	140.94	137.15	140.60	138.35	140.77

[1] Data through 2004: 550-750 pounds; beginning 2005: 600-900 pounds. [2] Preliminary. *Source: Economic Research Service, U.S. Department of Agriculture (ERS-USDA)*

Production (Commercial) of All Red Meats in the United States In Millions of Pounds (Carcass Weight)

Year	Jan.	Feb.	Mar.	Apr.	May	June	July	Aug.	Sept.	Oct.	Nov.	Dec.	Total
2000	3,784	3,767	4,044	3,460	3,878	3,941	3,644	4,113	3,861	4,096	3,919	3,619	46,126
2001	3,935	3,761	3,761	3,506	3,881	3,758	3,643	4,060	3,664	4,264	3,970	3,813	46,016
2002	4,081	3,501	3,677	3,902	4,018	3,813	4,016	4,141	3,873	4,382	3,908	3,859	47,171
2003	4,075	3,496	3,705	3,845	3,944	3,948	4,046	3,913	4,007	4,155	3,524	3,876	46,534
2004	3,713	3,404	3,944	3,713	3,597	3,928	3,708	3,878	3,905	3,921	3,770	3,931	45,412
2005	3,648	3,423	3,879	3,622	3,714	3,963	3,616	4,100	3,933	3,926	3,942	3,954	45,719
2006	3,890	3,485	4,111	3,614	4,048	4,120	3,782	4,245	3,933	4,182	4,136	3,862	47,408
2007	4,091	3,615	4,013	3,753	4,075	4,028	3,940	4,026	3,864	4,614	4,300	4,059	48,378
2008	4,416	3,968	4,090	4,297	4,223	4,050	4,252	4,097	4,273	4,530	3,872	4,162	50,230
2009[1]	4,169	3,825	4,142	4,084	3,919	4,162	4,124	4,077	4,262	4,391	3,963	4,148	49,264

[1] Preliminary. *Source: Economic Research Service, U.S. Department of Agriculture (ERS-USDA)*

Cold Storage Holdings of All[2] Meats in the United States, on First of Month In Millions of Pounds

Year	Jan.	Feb.	Mar.	Apr.	May	June	July	Aug.	Sept.	Oct.	Nov.	Dec.
2000	748.3	853.1	913.9	934.3	951.3	963.5	926.7	896.2	881.0	871.1	868.0	883.0
2001	836.2	907.8	852.6	787.9	771.4	772.5	742.2	717.4	732.6	775.3	849.0	880.9
2002	946.8	982.6	970.7	961.9	996.6	973.0	918.0	912.6	950.7	997.8	1,038.9	997.7
2003	1,011.5	1,015.2	978.2	951.9	926.8	901.5	847.5	825.0	817.3	832.1	836.9	828.1
2004	879.0	953.7	926.9	879.4	883.6	829.3	797.9	807.7	841.9	886.1	889.2	912.6
2005	979.0	965.0	953.2	928.0	908.5	847.0	847.8	850.8	842.9	884.9	900.1	882.1
2006	877.2	1,012.4	987.3	959.8	979.1	940.8	880.9	915.5	918.2	969.4	994.0	1,009.9
2007	946.6	977.3	963.4	943.5	970.3	925.7	919.7	943.5	958.7	991.8	1,003.2	968.4
2008	961.6	1,047.5	1,072.6	1,106.9	1,103.9	1,024.5	983.8	960.5	970.9	1,009.4	1,027.8	1,037.8
2009[1]	1,078.5	1,096.2	1,084.9	1,045.3	1,050.6	1,030.1	1,043.1	1,014.7	980.2	984.0	968.4	936.8

[1] Preliminary. [2] Includes beef and veal, mutton and lamb, pork and products, rendered pork fat, and miscellaneous meats. Excludes lard.
Source: Economic Research Service, U.S. Department of Agriculture (ERS-USDA)

Cold Storage Holdings of Frozen Beef in the United States, on First of Month In Millions of Pounds

Year	Jan.	Feb.	Mar.	Apr.	May	June	July	Aug.	Sept.	Oct.	Nov.	Dec.
2000	314.2	350.9	369.0	378.2	396.1	401.1	405.1	391.5	398.8	405.7	404.4	411.8
2001	401.7	410.9	360.2	332.6	315.3	325.1	340.8	351.4	373.2	382.8	395.1	427.6
2002	460.7	455.5	439.0	410.5	405.7	401.8	396.9	416.5	461.8	494.9	525.2	512.6
2003	524.6	482.4	441.9	403.1	389.7	385.1	371.5	368.2	371.0	379.8	375.2	373.8
2004	395.1	434.4	435.0	416.8	421.2	402.8	411.8	427.0	446.0	457.2	452.6	463.3
2005	484.3	453.3	400.2	372.3	329.4	318.2	342.1	385.2	410.6	438.8	439.2	429.9
2006	434.4	465.9	440.6	436.2	441.3	446.3	449.1	479.2	484.5	491.9	485.7	520.3
2007	482.1	470.6	458.9	427.2	417.3	411.5	430.3	467.7	480.9	486.7	488.0	475.3
2008	482.5	450.8	436.5	426.7	416.4	420.4	428.1	430.8	441.2	454.5	471.0	481.6
2009[1]	492.6	462.5	435.5	425.9	410.7	417.9	434.8	444.8	420.1	428.9	427.7	430.9

[1] Preliminary. *Source: Economic Research Service, U.S. Department of Agriculture (ERS-USDA)*

Mercury

Mercury (symbol Hg) was known to the ancient Hindus and Chinese, and was also found in Egyptian tombs dating back to 1500 BC. The ancient Greeks used mercury in ointments, and the Romans used it in cosmetics. Alchemists thought mercury turned into gold when it hardened.

Mercury, also called quicksilver, is a heavy, silvery, toxic, transitional metal. Mercury is the only common metal that is liquid at room temperatures. When subjected to a pressure of 7,640 atmospheres (7.7 million millibars), mercury becomes a solid. Mercury dissolves in nitric or concentrated sulfuric acid, but is resistant to alkalis. It is a poor conductor of heat. Mercury has superconductivity when cooled to sufficiently low temperatures. It has a freezing point of about –39 degrees Celsius and a boiling point of about 357 degrees Celsius.

Mercury is found in its pure form or combined in small amounts with silvers, but is found most often in the ore cinnabar, a mineral consisting of mercuric sulfide. By heating the cinnabar ore in air until the mercuric sulfide breaks down, pure mercury metal is produced. Mercury forms alloys called amalgams with all common metals except iron and platinum. Most mercury is used for the manufacture of industrial chemicals and for electrical and electronic applications. Other uses for mercury include its use in gold recovery from ores, barometers, diffusion pumps, laboratory instruments, mercury-vapor lamps, pesticides, batteries, and catalysts. A decline in mercury production and usage since the 1970s reflects a trend for using mercury substitutes due to its toxicity.

Prices – The average monthly price of mercury in 2009 rose by +7.4% yr/yr to $616.09 per flask (34.5 kilograms), but that is still below the 2005 record high price of $774.04.

Supply – World mine production of mercury in 2009 fell by -3.0% yr/yr to 1,280 metric tons. The record low of 1,150 metric tons was posted in 2006. The world's largest miners of mercury are China with 63% of world production and Kyrgyzstan with 20%. China's production in 2009 was 800 metric tons. China's production was as high as 1,140 metric tons as recently as 2004. China's record high production of 1,200 metric tons was posted in 1989 and its record low of 190 metric tons was posted in 2001. Spain is also a large producer but their data has not been available since 2004.

Demand – The breakdown of domestic consumption of mercury by particular categories is no longer available. However, as of 1997 records showed that chlorine and caustic soda accounted for 46% of U.S. mercury consumption, followed by wiring devices and switches (17%), dental equipment (12%), electrical lighting (8%), and measuring control instruments (7%). Substitutes for mercury include lithium and composite ceramic materials.

Trade – U.S. foreign trade in mercury has been relatively small but U.S. imports of mercury in 2009 rose by +22.6% yr/yr to 190 metric tons from 2007's 6-year low of 67 metric tons. U.S. imports were mostly from Chile and Peru. U.S. exports of mercury in 2009 fell by -4.4% to 700 metric tons, well up from 2007's 11-year 9-year low of 84 metric tons.

World Mine Production of Mercury In Metric Tons (1 tonne = 29.008216 flasks)

Year	Algeria	China	Finland	Kyrgyzstan	Mexico	Spain	Tajikistan	Russia	Ukraine	United States	World Total
2000	216	200	76	257	15	500	40	50	NA	NA	1,360
2001	321	190	71	300	15	500	40	50	----	NA	1,500
2002	307	495	51	300	15	727	20	50	NA	NA	1,980
2003	176	610	25	300	15	500	30	50	----	NA	1,730
2004	73	1,140	24	300	15	250	30	50	----	NA	1,900
2005	4	1,100	20	200	6	----	30	50	----	NA	1,520
2006	----	760	20	250	8	----	30	50	----	NA	1,150
2007	----	800	20	250	8	----	30	50	----	NA	1,200
2008[1]	----	800	20	250	21	----	30	50	----	NA	1,320
2009[2]	----	800	NA	250	NA	----	NA	NA	----	NA	1,280

[1] Preliminary. [2] Estimate. [4] Less than 1/2 unit. NA = Not available W = Withheld. *Source: U.S. Geological Survey (USGS)*

Salient Statistics of Mercury in the United States In Metric Tons

		Secondary Production						
Year	Producing Mines	Industrial	Government[3]	NDS[4] Shipments	Consumer & Dealer Stocks, Dec. 31	Industrial Demand	Exports	Imports
2001	NA	NA	----	----	NA	NA	108	100
2002	NA	NA	----	----	40	NA	201	209
2003	NA	NA	----	----	94	72	287	46
2004	NA	NA	----	----	62	91	278	92
2005	NA	NA	----	----	38	40	319	212
2006	NA	NA	----	----	19	38	390	94
2007	NA	NA	----	----	18	31	84	67
2008[1]	NA	NA	----	----	24	NA	732	155
2009[2]	NA	NA	----	----	NA	NA	700	190

[1] Preliminary. [2] Estimate. [3] Secondary mercury shipped from the Department of Energy. [4] National Defense Stockpile. NA = Not available. E = Net exporter. *Source: U.S. Geological Survey (USGS)*

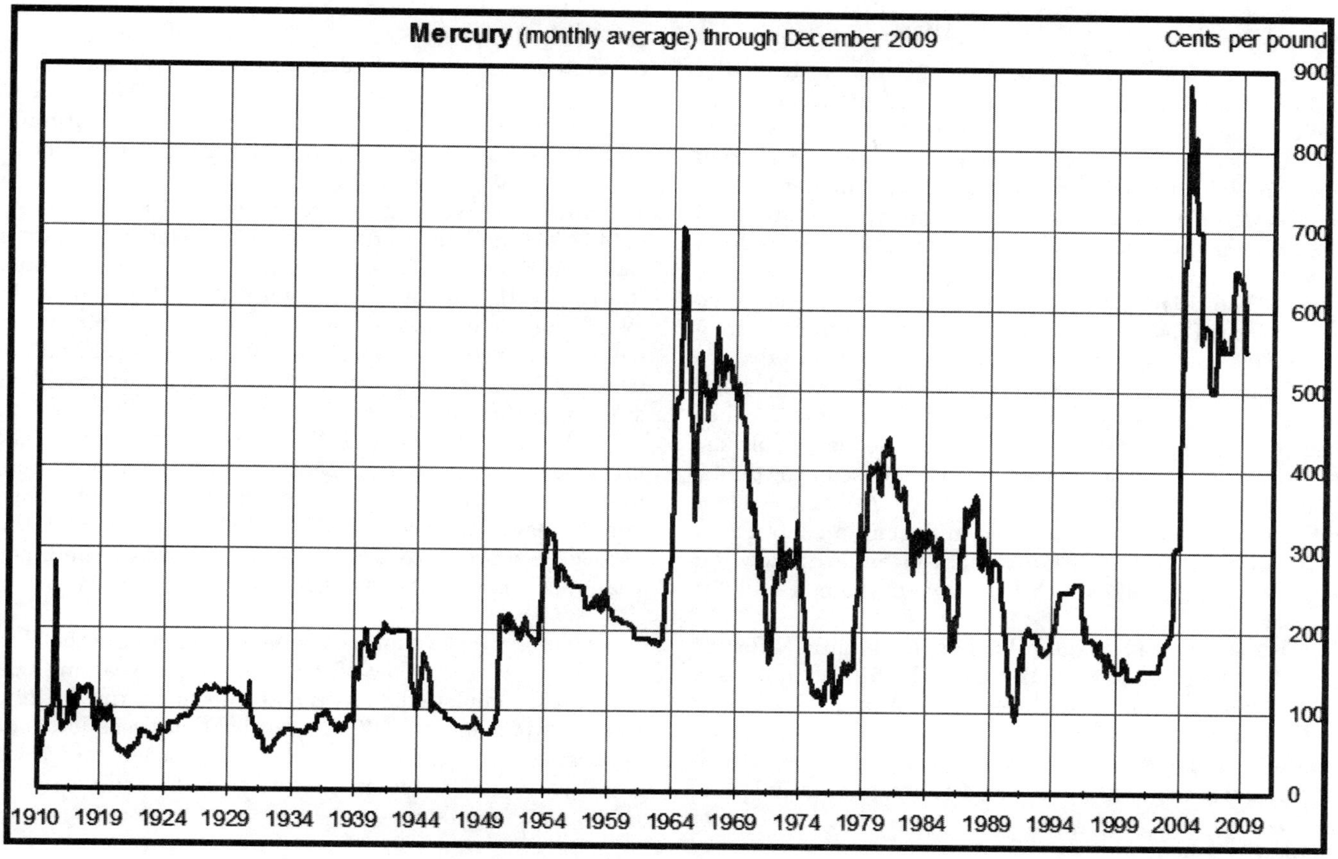

Average Price of Mercury in New York In Dollars Per Flask of 76 Pounds (34.5 Kilograms)

Year	Jan.	Feb.	Mar.	Apr.	May	June	July	Aug.	Sept.	Oct.	Nov.	Dec.	Average
2000	150.00	157.88	167.50	167.50	167.50	158.23	142.00	142.00	142.00	142.00	142.00	142.00	151.90
2001	142.00	142.00	142.00	142.00	142.00	143.71	154.00	154.00	154.00	154.00	154.00	154.00	148.12
2002	154.00	154.00	154.00	154.00	154.00	154.00	154.00	154.00	154.00	154.00	154.00	154.00	154.00
2003	165.43	175.00	175.00	175.00	185.23	187.50	187.50	187.50	187.50	187.50	195.63	200.00	184.07
2004	200.00	256.25	297.61	305.00	305.00	305.00	305.00	305.00	417.05	485.12	649.24	650.00	373.36
2005	678.57	747.50	867.39	873.81	850.00	817.05	759.52	750.00	813.64	730.95	700.00	700.00	774.04
2006	700.00	700.00	691.30	552.50	574.02	582.50	582.50	582.50	582.50	576.59	513.64	500.00	594.84
2007	500.00	500.00	500.00	500.00	500.00	573.81	600.00	600.00	572.50	550.00	550.00	550.00	541.36
2008	550.00	550.00	550.00	550.00	550.00	550.00	550.00	550.00	590.91	600.00	645.00	650.00	573.83
2009	650.00	647.00	640.00	640.00	642.86	640.00	640.00	640.00	603.18	550.00	550.00	550.00	616.09

Source: American Metal Market (AMM)

Mercury Consumed in the United States In Metric Tons

Year	Batteries[3]	Chlorine & Caustic Soda	Catalysts, Misc.	Dental Equip.	Electrical Lighting[3]	General Lab Use	Measuring Control Instrument	Paints	Wiring Devices & Switches[3]	Other Uses	Grand Total
1989	250	379	40	39	31	18	87	192	141	32	1,212
1990	106	247	29	44	33	32	108	14	70	38	720
1991	18	184	26	41	39	30	90	6	71	49	554
1992	13	209	20	42	55	28	80	----	82	92	621
1993	10	180	18	35	38	26	65	----	83	103	558
1994	6	135	25	24	27	24	53	----	79	110	483
1995	----	154	----	32	30	----	43	----	84	93	436
1996[1]	----	136	----	31	29	----	41	----	49	86	372
1997[2]	----	160	----	40	29	----	24	----	57	36	346
	Data No Longer Available										

[1] Preliminary. [2] Estimate. W = Withheld proprietary data. *Source: U.S. Geological Survey (USGS)*

Milk

Evidence of man's use of animal milk as food was discovered in a temple in the Euphrates Valley near Babylon, dating back to 3,000 BC. Humans drink the milk produced from a variety of domesticated mammals, including cows, goats, sheep, camels, reindeer, buffaloes, and llama. In India, half of all milk consumed is from water buffalo. Camels' milk spoils slower than other types of milk in the hot desert, but the vast majority of milk used for commercial production and consumption comes from cows.

Milk directly from a cow in its natural form is called raw milk. Raw milk is processed by spinning it in a centrifuge, homogenizing it to create a consistent texture (i.e., by forcing hot milk under high pressure through small nozzles), and then sterilizing it through pasteurization (i.e., heating to a high temperature for a specified length of time to destroy pathogenic bacteria). Condensed, powdered, and evaporated milk are produced by evaporating some or all of the water content. Whole milk contains 3.5% milk fat. Lower-fat milks include 2% low-fat milk, 1% low- fat milk, and skim milk, which has only 1/2 gram of milk fat per serving.

The Chicago Mercantile Exchange has three different milk futures contracts: Milk Class III which is milk used in the manufacturing of cheese, Milk Class IV which is milk used in the production of butter and all dried milk products, and Nonfat Dry Milk which is used in commercial or consumer cooking or to reconstitute nonfat milk by the consumer. The Milk Class III contract has the largest volume and open interest.

Prices – The average monthly price received by farmers for all milk sold to plants in 2009 fell by 30.0% yr/yr to $12.81 per hundred pounds, down further from the 2007 record high of $19.13. The average monthly price received by farmers for fluid grade milk in 2009 also fell by 30.0% yr/yr to $12.81 per hundred pounds. The average monthly price received by farmers for manufacturing grade milk in 2009 fell by 32.6% to $12.12 per hundred pounds.

Supply – World milk production in 2009 fell -0.6% to 432.538 million metric tons. The biggest producers were the European Union with 31% of world production, the U.S. with 20%, and India with11%. U.S. 2009 milk production in pounds fell -0.4% yr/yr to 189.259 billion pounds, down from last year's record high of 189.992 billion pounds. The number of dairy cows on U.S. farms has fallen sharply in the past 3 decades from the 12 million seen in 1970. In 2009, there were 9.200 million dairy cows on U.S. farms, down +1.3% yr/yr. Dairy farmers have been able to increase milk production even with fewer cows because of a dramatic increase in milk yield per cow. In 2009, the average cow produced a record 20,571 pounds of milk per year, more than double the 9,751 pounds seen in 1970.

Demand – Per capita consumption of milk in the U.S. fell to a new record low of 206 pounds per year in 2002 (the latest complete data available), down sharply by 26% from 277 pounds in 1977. The utilization breakdown for 2002 shows the largest manufacturing usage categories are cheese (64.504 billion pounds of milk) and creamery butter (30.250 billion pounds).

Trade – U.S. imports of milk in 2009 rose to +15.4% yr/yr to 4.500 billion pounds, but still well below the record high of 5.716 billion pounds posted in 2001.

World Fluid Milk Production (Cow's Milk) In Thousands of Metric Tons

Year	Argentina	Australia	Brazil	China	European Union	India	Japan	Mexico	New Zealand	Russia	Ukraine	United States	World Total
2003	7,950	10,636	22,860	17,463	135,069	36,500	8,400	9,784	14,346	33,000	13,400	77,289	541,446
2004	9,250	10,377	23,317	22,606	133,969	37,500	8,329	9,874	15,000	32,000	13,787	77,534	546,305
2005	9,500	10,429	24,250	27,534	134,672	37,520	8,285	9,855	14,500	32,000	13,423	80,255	553,359
2006	10,200	10,395	25,230	31,934	132,206	41,000	8,137	10,051	15,200	31,100	12,890	82,455	558,453
2007	9,550	9,870	26,750	35,252	132,604	42,890	8,007	10,657	15,640	32,200	11,997	84,211	568,283
2008	10,100	9,500	27,820	34,300	133,848	44,500	7,982	10,909	15,141	32,500	11,524	86,179	434,961
2009[1]	10,100	9,670	28,795	28,445	133,800	45,865	7,900	11,132	16,601	32,500	11,300	85,820	432,538
2010[2]	10,300	9,570	30,235	31,290	134,000	47,670	7,850	11,355	17,021	32,800	10,961	85,230	438,942

[1] Preliminary. [2] Forecast. *Source: Foreign Agricultural Service, U.S. Department of Agriculture (FAS-USDA)*

Salient Statistics of Milk in the United States In Millions of Pounds

Year	Number of Milk Cows on Farms3 (Thousands)	Supply: Production: Per Cow[4] (Pounds)	Supply: Production: Total[4]	Supply: Beginning Stocks[5]	Supply: Imports	Supply: Total Supply	Utilization: Exports[5]	Utilization: Domestic: Fed to Calves	Utilization: Domestic: Humans	Utilization: Total Use	Average Farm Price Received Per Cwt.: All Milk, Wholesale	Average Farm Price Received Per Cwt.: Milk Eligible for Fluid Market	Average Farm Price Received Per Cwt.: Milk, Manufacturing Grade	Per Capita Consumption[6] (Fluid Milk in Lbs)
2002	9,139	18,608	170,063	7,259	5,103	182,425	----	959	168,944	169,903	12.10	12.10	10.92	206
2003	9,083	18,761	170,394	9,891	5,040	185,325	----	964	169,276	170,240	12.52	12.53	11.77	
2004	9,010	18,958	170,805	8,333	5,278	184,416	----	956	169,699	170,655	16.04	16.04	15.41	
2005	9,040	19,577	176,989	7,154	5,071	189,214	3,300	987	175,788	180,075	15.14	15.14	14.45	
2006	9,112	19,951	181,798	8,007	4,981	194,786	3,400	943	180,700	185,043	12.91	12.92	12.28	
2007	9,158	20,266	185,602	9,500	4,638	199,740	5,700	952	184,565	191,217	19.13	19.13	18.18	
2008[1]	9,315	20,396	189,992	10,355	3,900	204,247	8,700	949	188,914	198,563	18.30	18.28	17.98	
2009[2]	9,200	20,576	189,320	10,000	4,500	203,820	4,000				12.81	12.81	12.12	

[1] Preliminary. [2] Estimate. [3] Average number on farms during year including dry cows, excluding heifers not yet fresh. [4] Excludes milk sucked by calves. [5] Government and commercial. [6] Product pounds of commercial sales and on farm consumption.
Source: Economic Research Service, U.S. Department of Agriculture (ERS-USDA)

Milk-Feed Price Ratio[1] in the United States In Pounds

Year	Jan.	Feb.	Mar.	Apr.	May	June	July	Aug.	Sept.	Oct.	Nov.	Dec.	Average
2001	3.08	3.03	3.24	3.29	3.41	3.74	3.60	3.62	3.75	3.55	3.29	2.99	3.38
2002	3.03	3.00	2.89	2.81	2.64	2.54	2.34	2.27	2.30	2.46	2.44	2.44	2.60
2003	2.40	2.35	2.27	2.25	2.19	2.21	2.60	2.89	3.16	3.23	3.05	2.89	2.62
2004	2.70	2.60	2.80	3.11	3.15	3.12	2.96	2.93	3.22	3.27	3.57	3.67	3.09
2005	3.45	3.50	3.35	3.18	2.93	2.87	2.93	3.08	3.27	3.42	3.45	3.28	3.23
2006	3.17	2.93	2.70	2.48	2.32	2.35	2.33	2.48	2.61	2.53	2.44	2.43	2.56
2007	2.45	2.33	2.39	2.51	2.54	2.88	3.16	3.19	3.19	3.10	3.05	2.85	2.80
2008	2.65	2.24	2.07	1.88	1.81	1.88	1.90	1.81	1.90	2.02	2.01	1.92	2.01
2009[1]	1.60	1.51	1.57	1.58	1.47	1.45	1.57	1.78	1.98	2.09	2.23	2.42	1.77

[1] Pounds of 16% protein mixed dairy feed equal in value to one pound of whole milk. [2] Preliminary. *Source: Economic Research Service, U.S. Department of Agriculture (ERS-USDA)*

Milk Production[2] in the United States In Millions of Pounds

Year	Jan.	Feb.	Mar.	Apr.	May	June	July	Aug.	Sept.	Oct.	Nov.	Dec.	Total
2001	13,998	12,894	14,375	14,078	14,646	13,957	13,877	13,564	13,129	13,611	13,305	13,902	165,497
2002	14,304	13,229	14,864	14,580	15,118	14,317	14,196	14,128	13,467	13,866	13,478	14,211	170,063
2003	14,584	13,441	15,044	14,634	15,003	14,328	14,263	14,015	13,468	13,898	13,470	14,164	170,394
2004	14,402	13,595	14,762	14,519	15,012	14,293	14,405	14,215	13,619	14,070	13,610	14,303	170,805
2005	14,614	13,530	15,206	15,047	15,697	15,087	14,978	14,896	14,260	14,611	14,209	14,854	176,989
2006	15,343	14,238	15,966	15,538	16,068	15,324	15,168	15,061	14,481	14,857	14,523	15,231	181,798
2007	15,605	14,321	16,132	15,763	16,180	15,476	15,714	15,525	14,871	15,370	15,013	15,632	185,602
2008	15,976	15,176	16,458	16,125	16,707	15,942	15,995	15,757	15,129	15,615	15,212	15,900	189,992
2009[1]	16,135	14,754	16,485	16,148	16,805	15,935	16,018	15,737	15,038	15,420	15,070	15,775	189,320

[1] Preliminary. [2] Excludes milk sucked by calves. *Source: Economic Research Service, U.S. Department of Agriculture (ERS-USDA)*

Milk Cows[2] in the United States In Thousands of Head

Year	Jan.	Feb.	Mar.	Apr.	May	June	July	Aug.	Sept.	Oct.	Nov.	Dec.	Total
2001	9,169	9,143	9,117	9,110	9,116	9,117	9,109	9,096	9,088	9,086	9,106	9,122	9,114
2002	9,117	9,109	9,110	9,132	9,149	9,166	9,158	9,157	9,145	9,147	9,146	9,150	9,139
2003	9,147	9,145	9,141	9,125	9,104	9,097	9,087	9,072	9,061	9,034	9,005	8,994	9,083
2004	8,985	8,993	9,002	8,999	8,991	9,014	9,028	9,029	9,025	9,023	9,021	9,013	9,010
2005	9,000	8,996	9,009	9,030	9,042	9,050	9,053	9,060	9,066	9,060	9,056	9,063	9,040
2006	9,081	9,088	9,106	9,116	9,129	9,139	9,119	9,114	9,107	9,107	9,111	9,126	9,112
2007	9,135	9,136	9,142	9,132	9,138	9,144	9,153	9,159	9,166	9,181	9,196	9,217	9,158
2008	9,276	9,287	9,295	9,307	9,318	9,321	9,335	9,331	9,323	9,324	9,333	9,334	9,315
2009[1]	9,312	9,289	9,283	9,282	9,270	9,228	9,191	9,162	9,123	9,094	9,085	9,082	9,200

[1] Preliminary. [2] Includes dry cows, excludes heifers not yet fresh. *Source: Economic Research Service, U.S. Department of Agriculture (ERS-USDA)*

Milk Per Cow[2] in the United States In Pounds

Year	Jan.	Feb.	Mar.	Apr.	May	June	July	Aug.	Sept.	Oct.	Nov.	Dec.	Total
2001	1,527	1,410	1,577	1,545	1,607	1,531	1,523	1,491	1,445	1,498	1,461	1,524	18,158
2002	1,569	1,452	1,632	1,597	1,652	1,562	1,550	1,543	1,473	1,516	1,474	1,553	18,608
2003	1,594	1,470	1,646	1,604	1,648	1,575	1,570	1,545	1,486	1,538	1,496	1,575	18,761
2004	1,603	1,512	1,640	1,613	1,670	1,586	1,596	1,574	1,509	1,559	1,509	1,587	18,958
2005	1,624	1,504	1,688	1,666	1,735	1,668	1,656	1,643	1,572	1,613	1,569	1,639	19,577
2006	1,690	1,567	1,753	1,705	1,760	1,676	1,663	1,653	1,590	1,631	1,594	1,669	19,951
2007	1,708	1,567	1,765	1,726	1,771	1,692	1,717	1,695	1,622	1,674	1,633	1,696	20,266
2008	1,722	1,634	1,771	1,733	1,793	1,710	1,713	1,689	1,623	1,675	1,630	1,703	20,396
2009[1]	1,733	1,588	1,776	1,740	1,812	1,726	1,744	1,718	1,649	1,695	1,658	1,737	20,576

[1] Preliminary. [2] Excludes milk sucked by calves. *Source: Economic Research Service, U.S. Department of Agriculture (ERS-USDA)*

Average Price Received by Farmers for All Milk (Sold to Plants) In Dollars Per Hundred Pounds (Cwt.)

Year	Jan.	Feb.	Mar.	Apr.	May	June	July	Aug.	Sept.	Oct.	Nov.	Dec.	Average
2001	13.20	13.00	13.90	14.60	15.50	16.20	16.20	16.50	17.10	15.60	14.40	13.50	14.98
2002	13.40	13.10	12.70	12.50	12.10	11.50	11.10	11.30	11.60	12.10	11.90	11.90	12.10
2003	11.70	11.40	11.00	11.00	11.00	11.00	12.10	13.30	14.50	15.00	14.40	13.80	12.52
2004	13.20	13.60	15.40	18.10	19.30	18.20	16.10	14.90	15.50	15.60	16.20	16.40	16.04
2005	15.90	15.50	15.60	15.20	14.70	14.40	14.80	14.80	15.30	15.60	15.10	14.80	15.14
2006	14.50	13.50	12.60	12.10	11.90	11.90	11.70	12.00	13.00	13.60	13.90	14.20	12.91
2007	14.50	14.90	15.60	16.60	18.00	20.20	21.60	21.60	21.80	21.40	21.90	21.50	19.13
2008	20.50	19.10	18.10	18.00	18.30	19.30	19.30	18.40	18.20	17.80	17.10	15.50	18.30
2009[1]	13.30	11.60	11.80	11.90	11.60	11.30	11.30	12.00	12.90	14.20	15.30	16.50	12.81

[1] Preliminary. *Source: Economic Research Service, U.S. Department of Agriculture (ERS-USDA)*

Molybdenum

Molybdenum (symbol Mo) is a silvery-white, hard, malleable, metallic element. Molybdenum melts at about 2610 degrees Celsius and boils at about 4640 degrees Celsius. Swedish chemist Carl Wilhelm Scheele discovered molybdenum in 1778.

Molybdenum occurs in nature in the form of molybdenite and wulfenite. Contributing to the growth of plants, it is an important trace element in soils. Approximately 70% of the world supply of molybdenum is obtained as a by-product of copper mining. -Molybdenum is chiefly used as an alloy to strengthen steel and resist corrosion. It is used for structural work, aircraft parts, and forged automobile parts because it withstands high temperatures and pressures and adds strength. Other uses include lubricants, a refractory metal in chemical applications, electron tubing, and as a catalyst.

Prices – The average monthly U.S. merchant price of molybdic oxide in 2009 fell by -62.0% yr/yr to $11.31 per pound. That was the lowest in five years, far below the 2005 record high of $32.70 per pound but still over four times higher than the 2001 record low of $2.37.

Supply – World production of molybdenum in 2009 fell by -8.3% yr/yr to 200,000 metric tons, down from last year's record high of 212,000 metric tons. The 15-year low of 122,000 metric tons was seen in 2002. The world's largest producers of molybdenum are China with 39% of world production in 2009, the U.S. with 25%, and Chili with 16%.

U.S. production of molybdenum concentrate in 2009 fell -10.6% yr/yr to 50,000 metric tons, but still sell above the 26-year low of 32,300 metric tons posted in 2002. U.S. production of molybdenum primary products in 2007 (latest data) rose +1.6% to 31,100 metric tons, with 29,500 metric tons of that production in molybdic oxide and 1,600 metric tons in molybdenum metal powder.

Demand – U.S. consumption of molybdenum concentrate in 2007 (latest data available) fell by 1.1% yr/yr to 43,900 metric tons, but remained well above the 13-year low of 21,200 metric tons posted in 2002. U.S. consumption of molybdenum concentrate has more than doubled over the last 13 years. U.S. consumption of molybdenum primary products fell by -9.1% yr/yr in 2009 to 19,000 metric tons.

Trade – U.S. imports of molybdenum concentrate for consumption in 2007 rose +13.8% yr/yr to 12,400 metric tons, well above the 13-year low of 4,710 metric tons posted in 2002.

World Mine Production of Molybdenum In Metric Tons (Contained Molybdenum)

Year	Armenia	Canada[3]	Chile	China	Iran	Kazakhstan	Mexico	Mongolia	Peru	Russia	United States	Uzbekisten	World Total
2003	2,763	9,092	33,374	31,000	2,200	230	3,524	1,793	9,561	2,900	33,500	500	131,000
2004	2,950	9,519	41,883	38,500	1,800	230	3,730	1,141	14,246	2,900	41,500	500	159,000
2005	3,000	7,935	48,041	40,000	2,476	230	4,246	1,188	17,325	3,000	58,000	575	186,000
2006	3,900	7,842	43,278	43,900	2,500	250	2,516	1,404	17,209	3,100	59,800	600	187,000
2007	4,080	12,000	44,912	59,800	2,600	400	6,159	1,300	16,737	3,300	57,000	600	209,000
2008[1]	4,250	7,720	33,700	81,000	3,800	400	7,810	2,000	16,700	3,600	55,900	500	218,000
2009[2]	4,000	7,200	32,000	77,000	3,100	400	7,200	3,000	15,000	3,400	50,000	400	200,000

[1] Preliminary. [2] Estimate. [3] Shipments. *Source: U.S. Geological Survey (USGS)*

Salient Statistics of Molybdenum in the United States In Metric Tons (Contained Molybdenum)

	Concentrate							Primary Products[4]							
		Shipments						Net Production				Shipments			
Year	Production	Total (Including Exports)	Value Million $	For Exports	Consumption	Imports For Consumption	Stocks Dec. 31[3]	Grand Total	Molybdic Oxide[5]	Molybdenum Metal Powder	Avg Price Value $ / Kg.[6]	Domestic Destinations	To Oxide for Exports, Gross Weight	Consumption	Producer Stocks, Dec. 31
2002	32,300	32,300	232.0	----	21,200	4,710	3,870	10,500	10,000	513	8.27	27,500	1,670	15,300	4,300
2003	33,500	33,600	324.0	----	27,500	5,190	2,520	11,800	11,000	760	11.75	30,100	2,580	16,400	2,760
2004	41,500	42,000	1,420.0	----	38,700	8,780	2,610	24,300	23,400	868	36.73	39,300	5,280	17,400	2,840
2005	58,000	57,900	NA	----	46,600	11,900	3,620	29,800	28,700	1,050	70.11	46,700	14,600	18,900	3,770
2006	59,800	60,100	NA	----	44,400	10,900	2,120	30,600	29,000	1,620	54.62	51,000	11,600	19,000	3,210
2007[1]	57,000	57,100	NA	----	43,900	12,400	2,630	31,100	29,500	1,620	66.79	48,700	14,900	21,000	3,140
2008[2]	55,900	57,800	NA	----	44,000	10,200	1,760	33,400	31,800	1,640	62.99	51,200	16,700	20,900	3,850

[1] Preliminary. [2] Estimate. [3] At mines & at plants making molybdenum products. [4] Comprises ferromolybdenum, molybdic oxide, & molybdenum salts & metal. [5] Includes molybdic oxide briquets, molybdic acid, molybdenum trioxide, all other. [6] U.S. producer price per kilogram of molybdenum oxide contained in technical-grade molybdic oxide. W = Withheld proprietary data. E = Net exporter. *Source: U.S. Geological Survey (USGS)*

US Merchant Price of Molybdic Oxide In Dollars Per Pound

Year	Jan.	Feb.	Mar.	Apr.	May	June	July	Aug.	Sept.	Oct.	Nov.	Dec.	Average
2003	3.63	3.74	4.62	5.20	5.20	5.77	5.86	5.60	5.84	6.25	6.25	6.25	5.35
2004	7.63	8.15	8.93	13.11	14.00	15.03	15.75	16.70	18.27	19.50	22.66	27.50	15.60
2005	33.00	30.15	33.59	34.79	36.41	38.32	32.79	30.00	31.93	32.33	30.33	28.72	32.70
2006	23.70	24.54	23.12	22.93	24.82	26.31	26.01	25.60	26.96	26.02	25.41	25.50	25.08
2007	25.22	25.53	27.77	28.52	30.05	33.71	32.23	31.39	23.00	32.00	32.80	32.63	29.57
2008	32.74	32.88	32.88	32.88	32.88	32.88	32.88	33.17	33.75	33.75	15.58	10.62	29.74
2009	9.78	9.61	9.03	8.55	9.08	10.34	11.56	17.35	15.24	13.22	10.86	11.15	11.31

Source: American Metal Market (AMM)

Nickel

Nickel (symbol Ni) is a hard, malleable, ductile metal that has a silvery tinge that can take on a high polish. Nickel is somewhat ferromagnetic and is a fair conductor of heat and electricity. Nickel is primarily used in the production of stainless steel and other corrosion-resistant alloys. Nickel is used in coins to replace silver, in rechargeable batteries, and in electronic circuitry. Nickel plating techniques, like electro-less coating or single-slurry coating, are employed in such applications as turbine blades, helicopter rotors, extrusion dies, and rolled steel strip.

Nickel futures and options trade at the London Metal Exchange (LME). The nickel futures contract calls for the delivery of 6 metric tons of primary nickel with at least 99.80% purity in the form of full plate, cut cathodes, pellets or briquettes. The contract is priced in terms of U.S. dollars per metric ton.

Prices – Nickel prices varied widely during 2009. Nickel started the year at about $13,000 per metric ton in the midst of a sharp downturn from the record high of $54,200 per metric ton in June 2007. The price fell to about $9,500 in March/April and then rallied to a high of about $21,000 per metric ton in July. From there, with brief dips in August and again in late November, prices moved lower to end the year 2009 at about $19,000 per metric ton.

Supply – World mine production of nickel in 2009 fell -8.9% yr/yr to 1.430 million metric tons, further down from the 2007 record high production of 1.660 million metric tons. The current levels are more than double the production seen in 1970. The world's largest mine producers of nickel in 2008 were Russia (with 19% of world production), Canada (13%), Indonesia (13%), Australia (12%), and New Caledonia (7%). In 2007 (latest data available) U.S. secondary nickel production fell -9.9% to 93,780 metric tons but still well up from the 6-year low of 81,200 metric tons in 2001.

Demand – U.S. consumption of nickel in 2007 (latest data available) fell -11.2% to 184,795 metric tons, down from last year's record high of 208,000 metric tons. The primary U.S. nickel consumption use is for stainless and heat-resisting steels, which accounted for 65% of U.S. consumption in 2005. Other consumption uses were super alloys (11%), nickel alloys (10%), electro-plating anodes (6%), alloy steels (4%), copper base alloys (3%), and chemicals (2%).

Trade – The U.S. relied on imports for 18% of its nickel consumption in 2009, down from 64% in 1998. U.S. imports of primary and secondary nickel in 2009 fell -23.0% to a record low of 114,800 metric tons. U.S. exports of primary and secondary nickel in 2009 fell -6.1% to 99,680 metric tons.

World Mine Production of Nickel In Metric Tons (Contained Nickel)

Year	Australia[3]	Botswana	Brazil	Canada	China	Republic	Greece	Indonesia	New Caledonia	Philippines	Russia	South Africa	Total
2003	190,210	38,230	44,928	163,244	61,000	45,253	21,410	144,000	112,013	19,537	259,161	40,842	1,330,000
2004	174,700	35,163	51,886	186,694	75,600	46,000	21,700	136,000	118,279	16,973	268,545	39,851	1,360,000
2005	191,710	39,305	74,198	199,932	72,700	53,124	23,210	135,000	111,939	22,555	277,177	42,392	1,460,000
2006	175,177	38,000	82,492	232,948	82,100	47,516	21,670	157,000	102,986	56,463	276,985	41,599	1,560,000
2007	160,457	38,000	58,317	254,784	85,000	47,125	21,190	229,000	125,221	68,075	279,773	37,877	1,660,000
2008[1]	200,000	38,000	58,500	260,000	68,400	31,300	18,600	193,000	103,000	83,900	277,000	31,700	1,570,000
2009[2]	167,000	36,000	56,700	181,000	84,300	----	14,000	189,000	107,000	85,000	266,000	34,000	1,430,000

[1] Preliminary. [2] Estimate. [3] Content of nickel sulfate and concentrates. *Source: U.S. Geological Survey (USGS)*

Salient Statistics of Nickel in the United States In Metric Tons (Contained Nickel)

	Net Import Reliance As a % of Apparent Consumption	- Production -		Nickel Consumed[1], By Uses									Stocks, Dec. 31		Primary & Secondary		
Year		Plant[4]	Secondary[5]	Alloy Sheets	Cast Iron	Copper Base Alloys	Electroplating Anodes	Nickel Alloys	Stainless & Heat Resisting Steels	Super Alloys	Chemicals	Apparent Consumption	At Consumer Plants	At Producer Plants	Exports	Imports	Avg. Price LME $/Lb.
2002	46	----	99,250	3,920	427	5,280	12,300	14,200	135,000	12,600	1,280	197,000	11,540	6,150	45,920	130,110	3.07
2003	45	----	100,800	3,730	591	5,200	11,400	14,600	114,000	13,400	2,400	165,000	11,680	8,040	53,630	136,500	4.37
2004	49	----	103,300	3,770	306	5,990	11,900	15,400	115,000	15,700	6,270	183,000	11,570	6,580	56,300	154,800	6.27
2005	48	----	101,420	4,020	179	6,090	11,300	18,800	131,000	18,000	2,030	196,000	12,910	5,940	63,230	158,500	6.69
2006	49	----	103,100	4,170	201	7,010	10,700	19,600	136,000	20,000	1,930	208,000	13,480	6,450	67,350	173,300	11.00
2007[2]	21	----	93,780	6,890	215	5,710	10,300	17,900	121,000	19,900	2,880	121,000	13,640	3,990	116,100	141,200	16.88
2008[3]	33												12,900	4,050	106,200	149,100	9.57

[1] Exclusive of scrap. [2] Preliminary. 3/ Estimate. [4] Smelter & refinery. [5] From purchased scrap (ferrous & nonferrous).
W = Withheld proprietary data. NA = Not available. *Source: U.S. Geological Survey (USGS)*

Average Price of Nickel[1] in the United States In Cents Per Pound

Year	Jan.	Feb.	Mar.	Apr.	May	June	July	Aug.	Sept.	Oct.	Nov.	Dec.	Average
2005	696.18	733.52	773.94	772.25	813.21	788.04	707.58	720.47	692.83	610.92	594.54	657.44	713.41
2006	705.36	718.05	716.83	854.01	994.34	996.93	1,273.06	1,461.61	1,424.67	1,545.18	1,511.97	1,629.01	1,152.59
2007	1,734.23	1,930.47	2,172.62	2,378.64	2,476.96	2,002.41	1,618.56	1,342.03	1,425.77	1,489.95	1,477.33	1,254.00	1,775.25
2008	1,328.12	1,341.80	1,475.21	1,376.29	1,243.11	1,094.23	986.01	929.79	870.45	612.68	551.36	501.41	1,025.87
2009	575.83	535.25	501.88	567.31	610.15	720.34	766.47	950.67	860.98	912.94	862.14	850.66	726.22

[1] Plating material, briquettes. *Source: American Metal Market (AMM)*

Oats

Oats are seeds or grains of a genus of plants that thrive in cool, moist climates. There are about 25 species of oats that grow worldwide in the cooler temperate regions. The oldest known cultivated oats were found inside caves in Switzerland and are believed to be from the Bronze Age. Oats are usually sown in early spring and harvested in mid to late summer, but in southern regions of the northern hemisphere, they may be sown in the fall. Oats are used in many processed foods such as flour, livestock feed, and furfural, a chemical used as a solvent in various refining industries. The oat crop year begins in June and ends in May. Oat futures and options are traded on the Chicago Board of Trade (CBOT).

Prices – Oat prices on the CBOT weekly nearest futures chart started the year 2008 at about $3.30 per bushel, and moved higher to close at $3.91 per bushel in March. Oats then moved lower to $3.34 before rallying to the year's high at $4.55 per bushel at the end of June. From there the price moved steadily lower to end the year at about $2.30 per bushel. The down move continued into early 2009 with the price reaching about $1.75 per bushel in March 2009.

Regarding cash prices, the average monthly price received by farmers for oats in the U.S. in the first eight months of the 2008-09 marketing year (i.e., June 2008 to May 2009) rose +10.5% yr/yr to $3.13 per bushel.

Supply – World oat production in 2008-09 rose +4.6% yr/yr at 26.741 million metric tons, up from the record low of 23.163 in 2006-07. World annual oat production in the past three decades has dropped very sharply from levels above 50 million metric tons in the early 1970s. The world's largest oat producers are the European Union with 33% of world production in 2008-09, Russia with 22%, Canada with 16%, the U.S. with 5%, and Australia with 4%.

U.S. oat production in the 2008-09 marketing year fell by –3.2% yr/yr to 88.635 million bushels, which was a new record low. U.S. oat production has fallen sharply from levels mostly above 1 billion bushels seen from the early 1900s into the early 1960s. U.S. farmers harvested only 1.395 million acres of oats in 2008-09, which was down –7.3% from the previous year and posted a new record low. That is down from the almost 40 million acres harvested back in the 1950s. The oat yield in 2008-09 rose +4.3% to 63.5 bushels per acre. Oat stocks in the U.S. as of December 2008 were up +21.7% yr/yr to a 5-year high for December. The largest U.S. oat-producing states in 2006 were the states of Wisconsin (with 13% of U.S. production), Minnesota (13%), South Dakota (10%), Texas (6%), Iowa (6%), and Pennsylvania (5%).

Demand – U.S. usage of oats in 2008-09 fell -0.4% yr/yr to a record low of 198.0 million bushels. Regarding U.S. usage of oats in 2008-09, 60.6% was for feed and residual, 33.4% for food, alcohol and industrial, 4.5% for seed, and 1.5% for exports.

Trade – U.S. exports of oats rose +3.1% to a mere 3.0 million bushels in 2008-09. U.S. imports of oats in 2008-09 fell -10.8% yr/yr to 110.0 million bushels, down from last year's record high of 123.29 million bushels.

World Production of Oats In Thousands of Metric Tons

Crop Year	Argentina	Australia	Belarus	Brazil	Canada	China	European Union	Norway	Turkey	Ukraine	United States	Russia	World Total
2000-01	645	1,050	495	330	3,389	600	8,783	397	6,000	314	881	2,165	25,977
2001-02	645	1,434	530	277	2,691	600	8,491	330	7,700	265	1,116	1,707	27,033
2002-03	500	957	575	390	2,911	600	9,680	279	5,700	290	943	1,684	25,599
2003-04	348	2,018	500	413	3,377	600	9,019	333	5,200	270	925	2,096	26,244
2004-05	508	1,283	770	433	3,467	600	9,146	367	4,950	270	1,000	1,679	25,679
2005-06	350	1,690	600	517	3,283	600	7,968	279	4,550	270	800	1,667	23,807
2006-07	400	748	550	475	3,852	600	7,768	248	4,900	210	700	1,357	23,043
2007-08[1]	470	1,502	600	475	4,696	600	8,634	276	5,400	200	550	1,313	25,921
2008-09[2]	290	1,205	900	475	4,273	600	8,865	328	5,800	200	950	1,294	26,369
2009-10[3]	500	1,260	800	475	2,800	600	8,581	245	5,000	210	900	1,351	23,955

[1] Preliminary. [2] Estimate. [3] Forecast. *Source: Foreign Agricultural Service, U.S. Department of Agriculture (FAS-USDA)*

Official Oats Crop Production Reports in the United States In Thousands of Bushels

Year	July 1	Aug. 1	Sept. 1	Oct. 1	Dec. 1	Final	Year	July 1	Aug. 1	Sept. 1	Oct. 1	Dec. 1	Final
1998	183,201	177,211	----	----	----	165,768	2004	121,860	127,950	----	----	----	115,695
1999	----	162,096	----	----	----	145,628	2005	131,314	127,819	----	----	----	114,878
2000	151,380	152,745	----	----	----	149,165	2006	110,322	107,423	----	----	----	93,522
2001	132,150	135,445	----	----	----	117,024	2007	100,921	98,341	----	----	----	90,430
2002	147,584	142,580	----	----	----	116,002	2008	92,872	89,897	----	----	----	89,135
2003	147,895	151,345	----	----	----	144,383	2009[1]	91,277	91,960	----	----	----	93,081

[1] Preliminary. *Source: National Agricultural Statistics Service, U.S. Department of Agriculture (NASS-USDA)*

Oat Stocks in the United States In Thousands of Bushels

Year	On Farms Mar. 1	On Farms June 1	On Farms Sept. 1	On Farms Dec. 1	Off Farms Mar. 1	Off Farms June 1	Off Farms Sept. 1	Off Farms Dec. 1	Total Stocks Mar. 1	Total Stocks June 1	Total Stocks Sept. 1	Total Stocks Dec. 1
2000	53,300	36,000	101,200	86,900	48,500	40,031	49,177	57,237	101,800	76,031	150,377	144,137
2001	55,800	32,050	74,800	58,100	54,128	40,677	41,592	56,117	109,928	72,727	116,392	114,217
2002	40,200	28,650	70,500	52,500	53,158	34,552	41,212	51,284	93,358	63,202	111,712	103,784
2003	35,000	20,600	82,100	64,400	47,879	29,233	49,637	54,900	82,879	49,833	131,737	119,300
2004	45,600	27,500	74,300	60,400	49,414	37,348	41,458	44,513	95,014	64,848	115,758	104,913
2005	43,500	25,350	71,700	60,100	38,946	32,592	41,803	35,617	82,446	57,942	113,503	95,717
2006	42,200	25,190	60,800	53,000	32,673	27,376	39,284	45,889	74,873	52,566	100,084	98,889
2007	33,900	18,400	53,650	43,100	37,158	32,198	34,710	51,331	71,058	50,598	88,360	94,431
2008	31,000	16,100	52,800	42,600	47,988	50,674	66,296	72,322	78,988	66,774	119,096	114,922
2009[1]	30,200	17,480	54,500	43,200	65,250	66,619	73,875	67,262	95,450	84,099	128,375	110,462

[1] Preliminary. *Source: National Agricultural Statistics Service, U.S. Department of Agriculture (NASS-USDA)*

Supply and Utilization of Oats in the United States In Millions of Bushels

Crop Year Beginning June 1	Acreage Planted (1,000 Acres)	Acreage Harvested (1,000 Acres)	Yield Per Acre (Bushels)	Production	Imports	Total Supply	Feed & Residual	Food, Alcohol & Industrial	Seed	Exports	Total Use	Ending Stocks	Farm Price (Dollars Per Bushel)	Findley Loan Rate (Dollars Per Bushel)	Target Price (Dollars Per Bushel)
2000-01	4,473	2,325	64.2	149.2	106.0	332.0	189.0	57.0	11.0	1.7	259.0	73.0	1.10	1.16	NA
2001-02	4,403	1,905	61.4	117.0	96.0	286.3	148.3	59.2	12.8	2.8	223.1	63.2	1.59	1.21	NA
2002-03	4,995	2,058	56.4	116.0	95.1	274.3	149.9	60.2	11.8	2.6	224.5	49.8	1.81	1.35	1.40
2003-04	4,597	2,220	65.0	144.4	89.7	284.0	143.7	62.4	10.5	2.5	219.1	64.9	1.48	1.35	1.40
2004-05	4,085	1,787	64.7	115.7	90.3	270.9	136.3	63.0	11.0	2.7	212.9	57.9	1.48	1.33	1.44
2005-06	4,246	1,823	63.0	114.9	91.2	264.0	135.7	62.9	10.8	2.1	211.4	52.6	1.63		
2006-07	4,168	1,566	59.8	93.5	106.2	252.3	125.0	64.5	9.7	2.6	201.7	50.6	1.87		
2007-08	3,763	1,504	60.1	90.4	123.3	264.3	120.3	66.0	8.4	2.9	197.6	66.8	2.63		
2008-09[1]	3,247	1,400	63.7	89.1	114.6	270.5	108.6	66.1	8.3	3.4	186.4	84.1	3.15		
2009-10[2]	3,404	1,379	67.5	93.1	95.0	272.2	125.0	66.1	8.9	3.0	203.0	74.2	2.00-2.20		

[1] Preliminary. [2] Forecast. [3] Less than 500,000 bushels. NA = Not available.
Source: Economic Research Service, U.S. Department of Agiculture (ERS-USDA)

Production of Oats in the United States, by States In Thousands of Bushels

Year	Illinois	Iowa	Michigan	Minnesota	Nebraska	New York	North Dakota	Ohio	Pennsylvania	South Dakota	Texas	Wisconsin	Total
2000	4,015	12,060	4,800	22,320	1,890	3,900	19,845	6,840	8,265	13,420	4,300	19,040	149,165
2001	3,200	9,100	3,520	12,600	3,660	5,520	14,880	6,205	7,475	7,800	7,200	12,480	117,024
2002	3,285	13,300	4,160	14,840	2,365	4,160	12,600	3,355	7,015	5,400	6,160	15,000	116,002
2003	4,450	10,790	5,250	18,815	6,570	4,410	21,240	3,960	6,490	15,640	6,300	15,410	144,383
2004	2,450	10,080	4,420	13,300	3,400	3,250	14,080	3,150	6,050	13,940	6,400	13,650	115,695
2005	3,160	9,875	4,575	12,710	4,380	4,050	14,160	3,600	6,050	12,960	4,730	13,760	114,878
2006	3,080	8,360	4,030	11,200	2,025	4,958	4,920	4,125	7,040	5,415	3,700	14,490	93,522
2007	1,488	4,757	3,080	10,800	2,135	3,480	15,340	3,100	4,480	9,360	4,000	10,720	90,430
2008	2,100	4,875	3,960	11,900	2,450	4,224	6,630	3,500	4,640	8,760	5,000	11,780	89,135
2009[1]	1,625	6,175	3,465	12,070	2,070	4,620	11,220	3,375	4,880	6,570	2,820	13,260	93,081

[1] Preliminary. *Source: National Agricultural Statistics Service, U.S. Department of Agriculture (NASS-USDA)*

Average Cash Price of No. 2 Heavy White Oats in Toledo In Dollars Per Bushel

Year	Jan.	Feb.	Mar.	Apr.	May	June	July	Aug.	Sept.	Oct.	Nov.	Dec.	Average
1996-97	NQ	2.45	2.34	2.19	2.02	1.96	1.96	1.99	2.16	2.26	2.12	2.08	2.14
1997-98	2.12	1.79	1.84	1.80	1.77	NQ	NQ	NQ	NQ	NQ	NQ	NQ	1.86
1998-99	NQ	NQ	NQ	NQ	NQ	NQ	NQ	NQ	NQ	NQ	NQ	NQ	NQ
1999-00	NQ	NQ	NQ	NQ	NQ	NQ	NQ	NQ	NQ	NQ	NQ	NQ	NQ
2000-01	NQ	NQ	NQ	NQ	NQ	NQ	NQ	NQ	NQ	NQ	NQ	NQ	NQ
2001-02	NQ	NQ	NQ	NQ	NQ	NQ	NQ	NQ	NQ	NQ	NQ	NQ	NQ
2002-03	NQ	NQ	NQ	NQ	NQ	NQ	NQ	NQ	NQ	NQ	NQ	NQ	NQ
2003-04	NQ	NQ	NQ	NQ	NQ	NQ	NQ	NQ	NQ	NQ	NQ	NQ	NQ
2004-05	NQ	NQ	NQ	NQ	NQ	NQ	NQ	NQ	NQ	NQ	NQ	NQ	NQ
2005-06[1]	NQ	NQ	NQ										

[1] Preliminary. NQ = No quotes. *Source: Economic Research Service, U.S. Department of Agriculture (ERS-USDA)*

Volume of Trading in Oats Futures in Chicago In Contracts

Year	Jan.	Feb.	Mar.	Apr.	May	June	July	Aug.	Sept.	Oct.	Nov.	Dec.	Total
2000	27,073	43,332	29,707	31,653	38,647	50,461	30,885	42,814	21,846	21,476	48,890	15,406	402,190
2001	26,377	38,040	24,903	41,482	20,516	41,926	50,440	22,883	31,252	50,580	53,578	38,877	440,854
2002	41,516	46,435	30,662	51,889	32,386	39,229	35,217	29,647	23,968	32,847	35,412	15,932	415,140
2003	26,149	31,892	27,766	26,022	20,442	24,113	23,230	21,562	26,658	33,621	30,273	27,170	318,898
2004	33,743	34,605	55,216	49,746	38,951	35,356	25,451	31,023	32,322	25,443	33,942	20,650	416,448
2005	26,439	35,921	36,808	35,199	24,696	33,748	28,353	26,134	17,708	27,080	32,687	26,766	351,539
2006	25,667	40,534	30,437	35,799	39,362	42,812	35,751	30,790	25,700	43,724	51,304	25,435	427,315
2007	42,231	41,327	41,259	46,054	31,288	43,157	32,977	30,240	24,565	29,484	48,488	21,671	432,741
2008	44,184	61,469	44,478	47,918	37,813	52,116	27,923	32,074	19,009	31,829	23,978	18,797	441,588
2009	17,494	34,259	19,035	34,277	25,365	41,961	19,370	24,801	20,076	29,720	29,328	18,319	314,005

Source: CME Group; Chicago Board of Trade (CBT)

Average Open Interest of Oats in Chicago In Contracts

Year	Jan.	Feb.	Mar.	Apr.	May	June	July	Aug.	Sept.	Oct.	Nov.	Dec.
2000	15,343	17,521	17,719	18,183	176,686	16,178	15,550	15,225	13,176	13,985	14,377	14,119
2001	14,093	15,060	14,873	14,962	14,875	13,695	11,861	11,707	10,059	12,111	14,453	12,142
2002	12,640	13,137	11,833	10,976	9,047	10,381	10,230	10,970	9,881	9,550	9,134	6,008
2003	6,929	6,715	5,945	6,135	5,833	5,640	5,811	5,958	6,261	6,194	6,268	5,122
2004	6,284	6,314	10,018	12,988	11,903	11,339	10,293	9,153	6,669	7,010	7,753	6,724
2005	7,691	8,482	7,346	8,110	7,746	7,686	7,779	6,721	5,847	6,914	7,565	9,385
2006	10,200	11,697	10,960	10,961	13,529	14,128	13,965	11,620	11,178	13,483	14,714	13,818
2007	16,176	18,406	19,178	19,255	18,061	17,909	14,824	13,387	14,158	14,251	13,223	10,914
2008	13,696	14,812	14,764	15,097	15,957	16,802	16,667	15,027	14,740	15,495	15,108	16,848
2009	16,519	16,927	14,367	15,142	13,304	14,380	13,805	13,649	13,684	13,526	13,593	11,976

Source: CME Group; Chicago Board of Trade (CBT)

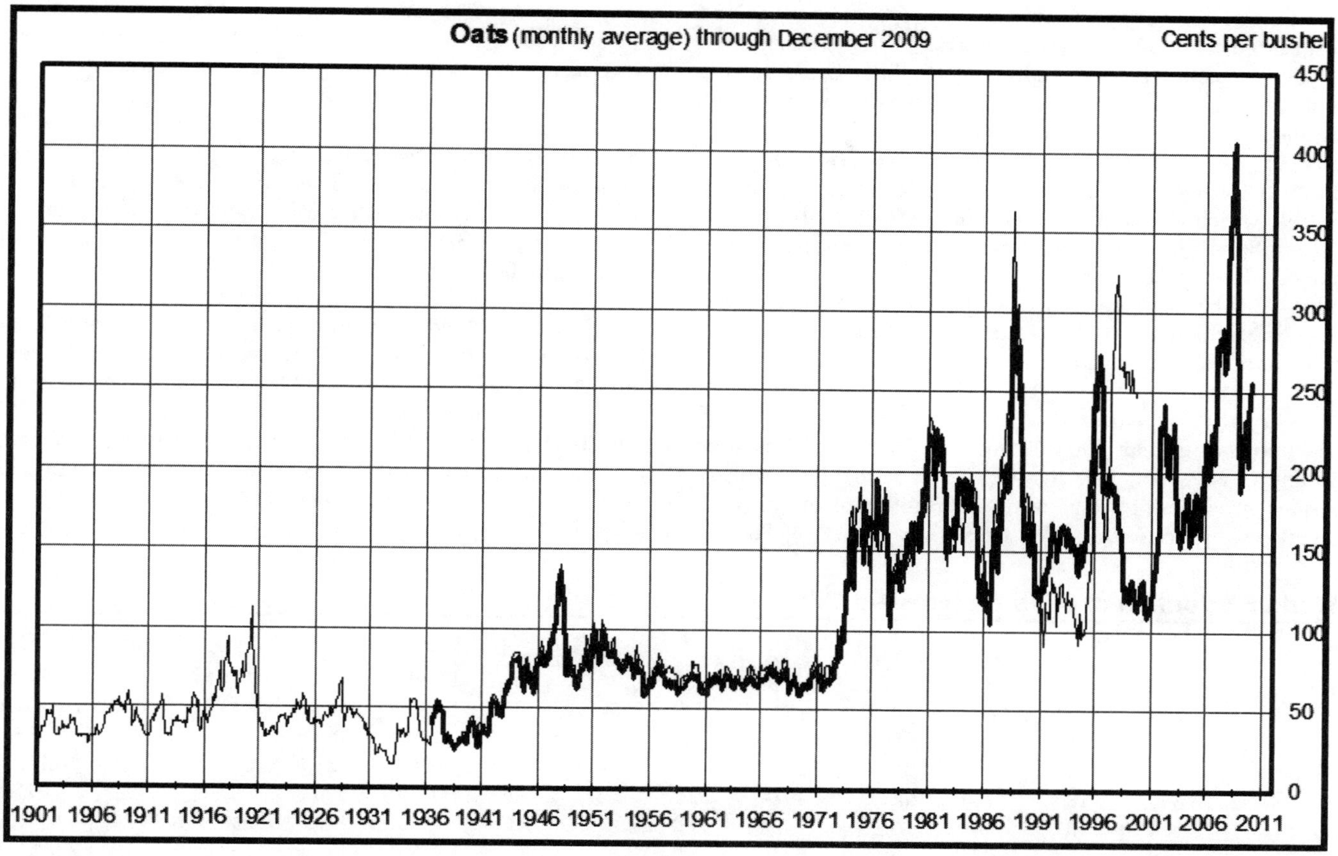

Average Cash Price of No. 2 Heavy White Oats in Minneapolis In Dollars Per Bushel

Year	Jan.	Feb.	Mar.	Apr.	May	June	July	Aug.	Sept.	Oct.	Nov.	Dec.	Average
2000-01	.73	.72	.69	.68	.70	.72	.70	.70	.75	.77	.80	.82	.73
2001-02	.83	.95	1.08	1.04	1.29	1.41	1.48	1.41	1.47	1.51	1.31	1.29	1.26
2002-03	1.40	1.24	1.23	1.36	1.36	1.33	1.36	1.44	1.28	1.28	1.22	1.08	1.30
2003-04	1.05	NQ	.98	1.01	1.00	.99	1.04	.99	1.14	1.08	1.22	1.08	1.05
2004-05	1.04	.96	.99	1.11	1.01	1.04	1.13	1.18	1.15	1.16	1.13	.99	1.07
2005-06	.99	1.20	1.12	1.09	1.16	1.16	1.37	1.33	1.29	1.23	1.25	1.33	1.21
2006-07	1.38	1.41	1.29	1.36	1.52	1.69	1.76	1.74	1.66	1.78	1.76	1.73	1.59
2007-08	1.81	1.68	1.63	1.67	NQ	1.74	2.43	2.02	2.28	3.18	2.35	2.47	2.12
2008-09	2.54	2.60	NQ	NQ	NQ	1.33	1.33	1.36	1.18	1.23	1.26	1.45	1.59
2009-10[1]	1.46	1.35	1.33	1.27	1.46	1.60	1.60	1.53					1.45

[1] Preliminary. NQ = No qoute. *Source: Economic Research Service, U.S. Department of Agriculture (ERS-USDA)*

Average Price Received by Farmers for Oats in the United States In Dollars Per Bushel

Year	Jan.	Feb.	Mar.	Apr.	May	June	July	Aug.	Sept.	Oct.	Nov.	Dec.	Average
2000-01	1.24	1.08	.93	.95	1.08	1.22	1.14	1.21	1.28	1.24	1.28	1.28	1.16
2001-02	1.38	1.32	1.25	1.39	1.64	1.79	1.92	1.93	1.91	1.99	1.99	1.99	1.71
2002-03	1.95	1.69	1.67	1.80	1.80	1.91	1.95	2.04	2.11	2.08	1.98	1.95	1.91
2003-04	1.83	1.46	1.39	1.39	1.44	1.29	1.58	1.48	1.58	1.60	1.63	1.70	1.53
2004-05	1.61	1.36	1.32	1.42	1.45	1.51	1.60	1.64	1.67	1.73	1.65	1.64	1.55
2005-06	1.75	1.59	1.49	1.54	1.59	1.64	1.73	1.73	1.82	1.82	1.75	1.85	1.69
2006-07	1.90	1.78	1.67	1.70	1.77	2.05	2.01	2.20	2.35	2.40	2.46	2.49	2.07
2007-08	2.54	2.32	2.24	2.47	2.45	2.63	2.69	2.88	3.19	3.43	3.47	3.63	2.83
2008-09	3.56	3.44	3.16	3.29	3.26	3.00	3.12	2.77	2.69	2.77	2.37	2.64	3.01
2009-10[1]	2.44	2.03	1.86	1.81	2.03	2.02	2.23	2.18	2.13				2.08

[1] Preliminary. *Source: National Agricultural Statistics Service, U.S. Department of Agriculture (NASS-USDA)*

Olive Oil

Olive oil is derived from the fruit of the olive tree and originated in the Mediterranean area. Olives designated for oil are picked before ripening in the fall. Olive picking is usually done by hand. The olives are then weighed and washed in cold water. The olives, along with their oil-rich pits, are then crushed and kneaded until a homogeneous paste is formed. The paste is spread by hand onto metal plates, which are then stacked and pressed hydraulically to yield a liquid. The liquid is then centrifuged to separate the oil. It takes 1,300 to 2,000 olives to produce 1 quart of olive oil. The best olive oil is still produced from the first pressing, which is usually performed within 24 to 72 hours after harvest and is called *extra virgin* olive oil.

Supply – World production of olive oil (pressed oil) in the marketing year 2008-09 rose +2.0% to 2.976 million metric tons, which was a new record high. The world's largest producers of olive oil in 2008-09 were Spain (with 38 of world production), Italy (20%), Greece (13%), Tunisia (6%), Turkey (6%), and Syria (5%). Production levels in the various countries vary considerable from year-to-year depending on various weather and crop conditions.

Demand – World consumption of olive oil in the 2008-09 marketing year rose +1.0% yr/yr to a new record high of 3.065 million metric tons. The U.S. is the world's largest consumer of olive oil with 8.6% of world consumption in 2008-09. The U.S. consumption of olive oil set a new record high of 265,000 metric tons.

Trade – World olive oil imports in 2008-09 fell -2.8% to 710,700 metric tons. The U.S. was the world's largest importer in 2008-09 with 265,000 metric tons, representing 37% of world imports. World olive oil exports in 2008-09 fell -1.3% to 710,200 metric tons. The world's largest exporters were Italy (with 27% of world exports), Tunisia (18%), Spain (23%), and Turkey (7%).

World Production of Olive Oil (Pressed Oil) In Thousands of Metric Tons

Crop Year	Algeria	Argentina	Greece	Italy	Jordan	Libya	Morocco	Portugal	Spain	Syria	Tunisia	Turkey	World Total
2000-01	26.5	3.0	467.0	508.0	29.5	4.0	39.5	28.5	1,040.0	183.0	141.0	197.5	2,742.7
2001-02	25.5	10.0	388.3	500.0	16.0	7.0	66.0	36.7	1,468.0	104.0	40.0	71.0	2,791.1
2002-03	15.0	11.0	449.0	620.0	30.0	6.5	48.5	31.9	949.4	184.5	76.0	187.0	2,698.0
2003-04	69.5	13.5	332.0	470.0	21.0	6.5	110.0	38.2	1,566.0	121.5	296.0	80.0	3,178.1
2004-05	33.5	18.0	470.0	785.0	49.0	12.5	54.0	46.7	1,034.0	195.0	139.5	157.0	3,077.6
2005-06	32.0	23.0	455.5	635.0	23.0	9.0	81.0	35.5	887.0	110.0	236.5	119.0	2,710.6
2006-07[1]	21.5	16.5	398.0	532.0	39.0	11.0	81.0	51.3	1,139.0	171.5	182.5	174.5	2,928.7
2007-08[2]	24.0	25.0	336.0	510.0	22.5	13.0	86.4	37.9	1,360.0	108.0	220.0	78.0	2,917.9
2008-09[3]	35.0	21.0	400.0	605.0	18.0	15.0	97.2	54.0	1,140.0	135.0	164.5	167.0	2,975.8

[1] Preliminary. [2] Estimate. [3] Forecast. *Source: The Oil World*

World Imports and Exports of Olive Oil (Pressed Oil) In Thousands of Metric Tons

	Imports							Exports					
Crop Year	Australia	Brazil	Italy	Japan	Spain	United States	World Total	Greece	Italy	Spain	Tunisia	Turkey	World Total
2000-01	29.5	24.7	110.5	29.6	13.3	212.5	549.1	6.3	194.1	97.9	101.0	77.5	543.8
2001-02	26.4	24.0	50.8	31.2	6.6	218.0	491.6	9.4	199.0	116.8	33.0	37.3	470.0
2002-03	32.0	21.1	70.1	31.4	16.6	220.1	536.5	10.4	197.3	118.4	42.9	60.8	532.9
2003-04	30.5	23.2	178.2	33.1	49.1	244.8	721.6	9.3	199.9	123.0	197.0	55.9	725.9
2004-05	28.9	25.7	154.6	32.8	40.7	248.7	719.1	8.9	217.0	125.1	119.9	88.4	725.7
2005-06	32.7	26.0	136.6	30.2	51.1	242.0	700.0	9.8	203.6	114.6	109.7	56.0	685.5
2006-07[1]	42.1	36.6	154.1	32.0	71.3	262.5	800.0	17.8	208.6	148.5	211.0	47.2	809.5
2007-08[2]	27.8	42.9	119.4	30.4	41.8	264.5	731.2	12.0	197.9	158.8	180.0	18.3	719.6
2008-09[3]	28.0	43.4	104.0	30.3	34.0	265.0	710.7	18.0	195.0	160.0	125.0	50.0	710.2

[1] Preliminary. [2] Estimate. [3] Forecast. *Source: The Oil World*

World Consumption and Ending Stocks of Olive Oil (Pressed Oil) In Thousands of Metric Tons

	Consumption							Ending Stocks					
Crop Year	Brazil	Morocco	Syria	Tunisia	Turkey	United States	World Total	European Union	Morocco	Syria	Tunisia	Turkey	World Total
2000-01	24.7	49.6	121.6	61.3	79.9	205.5	2,751.0	568.6	16.0	97.2	34.0	50.0	833.3
2001-02	24.0	61.1	111.6	38.4	73.7	211.5	2,750.6	709.0	25.3	86.5	3.0	12.0	895.4
2002-03	21.1	64.2	117.7	31.7	91.6	218.7	2,797.3	535.0	19.0	130.9	4.6	47.0	799.6
2003-04	23.2	69.8	133.4	59.2	61.8	225.3	2,924.9	791.0	35.0	95.0	45.0	10.0	1,048.6
2004-05	25.7	62.4	142.8	55.8	65.7	235.9	2,933.5	964.7	11.0	105.0	9.0	13.0	1,186.1
2005-06	26.0	60.4	135.8	57.8	66.1	232.7	2,880.1	863.7	3.0	37.0	79.0	8.0	1,031.2
2006-07[1]	36.6	69.8	126.3	44.4	95.4	244.2	3,006.2	782.6	16.0	27.0	9.0	40.0	944.1
2007-08[2]	42.9	78.0	107.4	44.9	85.0	259.0	3,034.8	736.6	22.0	7.0	6.5	14.8	838.8
2008-09[3]	43.4	83.0	117.0	44.0	95.0	265.0	3,065.4	628.7	20.0	10.0	4.0	36.9	749.7

[1] Preliminary. [2] Estimate. [3] Forecast. *Source: The Oil World*

Onions

Onions are the bulbs of plants in the lily family. Onions can be eaten raw, cooked, pickled, used as a flavoring or seasoning, or dehydrated. Onions rank in the top 10 vegetables produced in the U.S. in terms of dollar value. Since 1629, onions have been cultivated in the U.S., but are believed to be indigenous to Asia.

The two main types of onions produced in the U.S. are yellow and white onions. Yellow varieties comprise approximately 75% of all onions grown for bulb production in the U.S. Onions that are planted as a winter crop in warm areas are milder in taste and odor than onions planted during the summer in cooler regions.

Prices – Onion prices in 2009 averaged $12.20 per hundred pounds, down -2.4% from $12.50 in 2008. Monthly onion prices were weak in early 2009 at a low of $6.49 per hundred pounds in March, moved up to a high of $22.00 in June, but then faded to end the year at $7.83 per hundred pounds.

Supply – U.S. production in 2009 fell -0.2% to 7.497 billion pounds, still below the 2004 record high of 8.307 billion pounds. The farm value of the U.S. production crop in 2009 fell 3.3% to $843.570 million, down from the 2006 record high of $1.084 billion. U.S. farmers harvested a 17-year low of 148,560 acres in 2009, down –3.2% yr/yr. The yield per acre in 2009 was 505 pounds per acre.

Demand – U.S. per capita consumption of onions in 2009 rose +5/1% to 22.8 pounds.

Trade – U.S. exports of fresh onions in 2008 totaled 612 million pounds, and imports totaled 714 million pounds.

Salient Statistics of Onions in the United States

Crop Year	Harvested Acres	Yield Per Acre	Production 1,000 Cwt.	Price Per Cwt.	Farm Value $1,000	Jan. 1 Pack Frozen	Anual Pack Frozen	Imports Canned	Exports (Fresh)	Imports (Fresh)	Per Capita[3] Utilization -- Lbs., Farm Weight -- All	Fresh
						---- In Millions of Pounds ----						
2003	160,090	442	73,636	13.70	929,274	39.5	207.2	10.3	679.0	646.1	21.4	19.5
2004	169,150	491	83,065	9.06	671,626	38.6	218.2	10.5	620.1	689.3	23.4	21.9
2005	165,220	445	73,504	12.40	848,798	39.9		22.9	667.2	659.2	22.0	20.9
2006	163,780	444	73,066	16.10	1,084,099	48.1			658.8	643.2	21.7	19.9
2007	160,080	497	79,638	11.10	816,061	44.9			550.8	902.5	22.7	21.6
2008[1]	153,490	489	75,120	12.50	872,113	39.4			612.0	714.2	21.7	20.2
2009[2]	148,560	505	74,970	12.20	843,570	36.2					22.8	21.5

[1] Preliminary. [2] Forecast. [3] Includes fresh and processing. *Source: Economic Research Service, U.S. Department of Agiculture (ERS-USDA)*

Production of Onions in the United States In Thousands of Hundredweight (Cwt.)

	Spring				Summer										
Crop Year	Arizona	California	Texas	Total (All)	California	Colorado	Idaho	Michigan	Minnesota	Mexico	New York	Oregon, Malheur	Texas	Total (All)	Grand Total
2003	750	3,675	3,520	10,133	14,700	3,696	5,880	1,152	65	----	3,808	7,198	----	63,230	73,363
2004	800	3,586	3,875	12,031	13,200	5,500	8,008	986	----	----	5,200	8,658	----	71,034	83,065
2005	920	3,800	4,650	11,575	12,240	4,180	6,080	754	----	----	3,808	7,360	----	61,929	73,504
2006	490	3,279	4,104	11,128	13,515	3,800	5,076	650	----	----	4,224	6,084	----	62,049	73,177
2007	495	3,015	3,120	9,870	12,325	3,157	6,825	988	----	----	3,780	9,828	----	69,768	79,638
2008	660	2,860	2,403	9,498	13,303	2,850	6,192	1,008	----	----	4,141	8,662	----	65,622	75,120
2009[1]	576	2,460	3,003	8,559	14,287	3,015	6,512	1,330	----	----	4,141	8,176	----	66,411	74,970

[1] Preliminary. *Source: Agricultural Statistics Board, U.S. Department of Agriculture (ASB-USDA)*

Cold Storage Stocks of Frozen[2] Onions in the United States, on First of Month In Thousands of Pounds

Year	Jan.	Feb.	Mar.	Apr.	May	June	July	Aug.	Sept.	Oct.	Nov.	Dec.
2004	38,632	32,515	34,080	36,724	39,364	41,525	37,408	34,845	34,888	35,826	38,098	39,789
2005	39,865	40,428	44,191	48,695	50,579	47,418	45,605	47,231	44,834	40,718	43,751	45,690
2006	48,106	52,207	55,141	54,638	54,276	53,331	45,724	43,707	47,176	47,636	50,175	48,731
2007	44,919	42,027	45,810	46,244	40,350	32,240	34,663	30,966	36,734	39,096	37,653	37,929
2008	39,438	40,120	43,487	44,181	39,503	42,726	45,115	41,242	42,324	42,786	41,006	40,102
2009[1]	36,192	35,247	34,714	32,696	32,860	33,258	31,005	31,252	34,647	36,935	40,862	42,488

[1] Preliminary. *Source: National Agricultural Statistics Service, U.S. Department of Agriculture (NASS-USDA)*

Average Price Received by Growers for Onions in the United States In Dollars Per Hundred Pounds (Cwt.)

Year	Jan.	Feb.	Mar.	Apr.	May	June	July	Aug.	Sept.	Oct.	Nov.	Dec.	Season Average
2004	18.20	21.30	12.80	20.80	18.10	16.50	16.40	13.40	11.30	9.22	9.01	8.58	9.06
2005	6.29	5.61	6.13	18.20	19.70	17.80	14.00	11.10	13.10	12.90	14.00	12.30	12.40
2006	11.70	8.04	7.45	15.10	15.60	17.00	16.80	13.70	12.30	10.90	11.10	16.60	16.10
2007	22.10	26.20	35.00	55.20	24.20	24.60	15.40	10.80	5.57	4.47	4.70	4.39	11.10
2008	4.13	3.15	2.53	10.60	23.90	17.60	13.10	8.52	10.50	10.70	10.50	13.40	12.50
2009[1]	9.47	8.44	6.49	16.40	21.50	22.00	15.40	12.10	10.50	8.64	8.40	7.93	12.20

[1] Preliminary. *Source: Economic Research Service, U.S. Department of Agriculture (ERS-USDA)*

Oranges and Orange Juice

The orange tree is a semi-tropical, non-deciduous tree, and the fruit is technically a hesperidium, a kind of berry. The three major varieties of oranges include the sweet orange, the sour orange, and the mandarin orange (or tangerine). In the U.S., only sweet oranges are grown commercially. Those include Hamlin, Jaffa, navel, Pineapple, blood orange, and Valencia. Sour oranges are mainly used in marmalade and in liqueurs such as triple sec and curacao.

Frozen Concentrated Orange Juice (FCOJ) was developed in 1945, which led to oranges becoming the main fruit crop in the U.S.. The world's largest producer of orange juice is Brazil, followed by Florida. Two to four medium-sized oranges will produce about 1 cup of juice, and modern mechanical extractors can remove the juice from 400 to 700 oranges per minute. Before juice extraction, orange oil is recovered from the peel. Approximately 50% of the orange weight is juice, the remainder is peel, pulp, and seeds, which are dried to produce nutritious cattle feed.

The U.S. marketing year for oranges begins December 1 of the first year shown (e.g., the 2005-06 marketing year extends from December 1, 2005 to November 30, 2006). Orange juice futures prices are subject to upward spikes during the U.S. hurricane season (officially June 1 to November 30), and the Florida freeze season (late-November through March).

Frozen concentrated orange juice future and options are traded on the ICE Futures U.S. (ICE) exchange. The ICE orange juice futures contract calls for the delivery of 15,000 pounds of orange solids and is priced in terms of cents per pound.

Prices – ICE orange juice futures prices in early 2009 extended the plunge from the 31-year high of 209.50 cents per pound posted in February 2007 (which was just 10.5 cents shy of the record high of 220 cents posted in November 1977) and posted a 5-1/2 year low of 64.60 cents in February 2009. That sell-off was driven by the lack of hurricane damage during the 2007 through 2009 hurricane seasons and by a rebound in Florida orange production in 2007/08 and 2008/09 after poor crops seen in the previous three years due to hurricane damage. However, prices rallied through the rest of 2009 due to tighter supplies and the 17% y/y decline in the 2009/10 Florida orange crop.

Supply – World production of oranges in the 2009-10 marketing year fell -0.4% y/y to 52.181 million metric tons, down from the 2008-09 record high of 52.376 million metric tons. The world's largest producers of oranges in 2008-09 were Brazil with 34% of world production, followed by the U.S. (14%), and Mexico (7%).

U.S. production of oranges in 2008-09 (latest data) fell -9.3% y/y to 212.609 million boxes (1 box equals 90 lbs.) Florida's production in 2008-09 fell -4.6% y/y to 162.400 million boxes and California's production fell -21.8% to 48.500 million boxes.

World Production of Oranges In Thousands of Metric Tons

Year	Argentina	Australia	Brazil	Egypt	Greece	Italy	Mexico	Morocco	South Africa	Spain	Turkey	United States	World Total
2000-01	913	437	14,729	1,610	976	1,800	3,885	693	1,119	2,688	1,070	11,139	44,588
2001-02	780	633	18,360	1,696	1,076	1,724	4,020	720	1,263	2,822	1,250	11,290	49,828
2002-03	700	407	15,382	1,734	1,145	1,723	3,734	800	1,148	2,950	1,250	10,527	45,829
2003-04	750	453	19,054	1,740	550	1,835	3,901	705	1,113	3,052	1,250	11,734	50,805
2004-05	770	547	16,565	1,775	764	2,105	4,000	813	1,038	2,691	1,300	8,419	45,493
2005-06	840	470	17,993	1,800	1,017	2,261	4,157	784	1,167	2,376	1,445	8,212	47,453
2006-07	990	419	18,482	1,830			4,248	721	1,412		1,536	6,917	49,327
2007-08[1]	940	403	16,850	2,759			4,297	732	1,410		1,427	9,141	51,207
2008-09[2]	700	430	17,422	3,500			4,140	790	1,526		1,560	8,344	52,376
2009-10[3]	840	440	17,750	3,570			3,900	815	1,600		1,580	7,444	52,181

[1] Preliminary. [2] Estimate. [3] Forecast. NA = Not available. *Source: Foreign Agricultural Service, U.S. Department of Agriculture (FAS-USDA)*

Salient Statistics of Oranges & Orange Juice in the United States

	Production[4]					Florida Crop Processed				Frozen Concentrated Orange Juice - Florida			
Year	California	Florida	Total U.S.	Farm Price $	Farm Value	Frozen Concen-trates	Chilled Products	Total Pro-cessed	Yield Per Box Gallons[5]	Carry-in	Pack	Total Supply	Total Season Movement
	Million Boxes			Per Box	Million $	Million Boxes				In Millions of Gallons (42 Deg. Brix)			
1999-00	64.0	233.0	299.8	5.56	1,666.1	134.2	90.1	226.7	1.5	105.2	254.0	359.2	239.7
2000-01	54.5	223.3	280.9	5.88	1,682.8	124.1	89.6	215.9	1.6	112.6	245.2	357.8	226.0
2001-02	51.5	230.0	283.8	6.37	1,846.2	136.0	85.9	223.2	1.6	128.3	253.2	381.5	249.9
2002-03	62.0	203.0	267.0	5.80	1,564.7	102.1	92.5	196.0	1.5	120.2	203.3	323.5	200.1
2003-04	50.5	242.0	294.6	5.88	1,774.5	139.7	93.4	233.6	1.6	124.0	249.7	373.7	213.8
2004-05	64.5	149.8	216.5	6.68	1,475.4	54.3	88.5	143.9	1.6	151.8	86.3	238.1	175.2
2005-06	61.0	147.7	210.8	8.60	1,829.9	51.9	88.7	141.7	1.6	107.8	85.2	193.0	160.8
2006-07[1]	46.0	129.0	177.3	12.56	2,216.5	48.0	74.5	123.4	1.6	67.2	79.6	146.8	149.2
2007-08[2]	62.0	170.2	234.4	9.36	2,198.8	80.8	84.7	165.5	1.7	52.1	135.6	187.7	137.7
2008-09[3]	48.5	162.4	212.6	9.03	1,950.5	72.5	82.6	156.1	1.7	108.1	121.5	229.6	146.8

[1] Preliminary. [2] Estimate. [3] Forecast. 4/ Fruit ripened on trees, but destroyed prior to picking not included. [5] 42 deg. Brix equivalent.
Source: Economic Research Service, U.S. Department of Agriculture (ERS-USDA); Florida Department of Citrus

Average Open Interest of Frozen Concentrated Orange Juice Futures in New York In Contracts

Year	Jan.	Feb.	Mar.	Apr.	May	June	July	Aug.	Sept.	Oct.	Nov.	Dec.
2000	23,727	24,647	19,684	22,475	23,456	27,087	27,386	30,272	30,090	32,328	30,192	30,757
2001	28,852	28,011	28,073	27,794	24,199	24,428	22,591	22,073	17,789	18,026	21,506	19,275
2002	15,716	16,593	18,515	22,328	23,498	26,581	28,137	33,206	27,323	23,758	22,651	23,461
2003	25,080	26,588	22,707	21,466	20,634	23,794	25,467	26,518	27,788	30,767	31,575	36,336
2004	36,079	35,325	32,806	36,112	34,704	42,299	39,970	38,259	39,877	38,990	33,342	36,072
2005	33,821	33,619	30,008	32,523	26,171	28,730	32,221	29,034	23,603	28,602	34,966	35,795
2006	30,485	35,479	36,603	36,617	34,418	29,180	27,169	29,872	29,515	30,852	29,873	28,342
2007	29,484	28,370	32,312	29,430	28,830	31,917	30,457	29,540	28,335	29,599	26,608	27,412
2008	24,919	26,603	29,806	32,831	32,102	33,136	28,353	31,133	29,112	31,060	28,254	28,802
2009	27,889	28,234	26,905	27,982	29,370	31,608	30,602	31,281	28,806	30,805	29,677	34,210

Contract size = 15,000 lbs. *Source: ICE Futures U.S. (ICE)*

Volume of Trading of Frozen Concentrated Orange Juice Futures in New York In Contracts

Year	Jan.	Feb.	Mar.	Apr.	May	June	July	Aug.	Sept.	Oct.	Nov.	Dec.	Total
2000	45,680	78,532	33,617	71,024	50,475	80,372	46,548	67,312	38,485	64,831	45,966	89,362	712,204
2001	46,655	66,561	27,994	63,012	38,447	66,773	40,870	64,860	22,246	68,364	23,376	48,338	577,496
2002	31,709	50,898	30,316	58,644	37,283	52,238	45,316	78,111	36,053	71,635	24,111	61,443	577,757
2003	45,945	63,224	23,926	70,846	35,791	64,209	27,056	73,792	40,782	87,055	42,084	78,005	652,715
2004	52,908	86,600	41,941	99,532	45,741	123,815	105,220	118,021	65,655	89,064	56,502	85,438	970,437
2005	54,140	85,349	57,557	87,595	40,785	94,913	61,610	92,195	46,868	117,355	50,098	113,574	902,039
2006	65,978	98,034	82,293	92,312	73,517	87,429	63,429	84,160	50,871	95,955	54,975	74,743	923,696
2007	70,773	84,076	63,417	87,759	59,937	84,150	50,721	78,502	48,392	103,218	45,539	69,308	845,792
2008	57,421	78,860	52,166	80,331	43,942	70,780	51,859	67,402	41,353	78,327	29,013	59,058	710,512
2009	28,514	63,757	31,766	67,156	30,396	81,964	56,197	65,286	40,276	86,071	28,426	77,186	656,995

Contract size = 15,000 lbs. *Source: ICE Futures U.S. (ICE)*

Cold Storage Stocks of Orange Juice Concentrate[2] in the U.S., on First of Month — In Millions of Pounds

Year	Jan.	Feb.	Mar.	Apr.	May	June	July	Aug.	Sept.	Oct.	Nov.	Dec.
2000	1,330.7	1,540.6	1,632.7	1,857.9	1,812.5	1,965.6	2,037.9	1,843.7	1,457.7	1,346.6	1,169.4	1,202.0
2001	1,382.0	1,610.8	1,825.1	1,735.5	1,872.2	2,061.8	2,035.6	1,913.2	1,691.1	1,537.7	1,398.9	1,406.7
2002	1,571.7	1,721.3	1,770.9	1,794.4	1,886.0	1,982.8	1,934.0	1,870.9	1,680.9	1,543.6	1,409.6	1,471.2
2003	1,673.6	1,851.9	1,833.4	1,856.6	1,936.8	2,102.6	2,021.2	1,848.9	1,672.2	1,529.9	1,335.6	1,428.5
2004	1,585.8	1,613.0	1,646.1	1,790.5	1,987.6	2,128.7	2,075.7	1,953.4	1,823.3	1,644.2	1,516.8	1,458.0
2005	1,468.8	1,553.8	1,578.9	1,578.2	1,652.4	1,668.1	1,548.8	1,501.6	1,397.3	1,243.3	1,139.9	1,027.5
2006	1,044.7	1,065.9	1,076.8	1,005.7	1,087.5	1,157.7	1,104.1	1,002.6	888.8	776.0	714.3	650.3
2007	678.2	726.0	751.1	825.1	901.5	960.7	909.7	849.1	761.2	620.4	582.2	563.7
2008	682.5	837.8	942.4	1,031.9	1,210.6	1,442.7	1,514.9	1,424.9	1,319.4	1,199.7	1,086.0	1,034.6
2009[1]	1,088.0	1,193.2	1,249.5	1,272.0	1,385.2	1,461.0	1,485.7	1,370.5	1,282.6	1,217.6	1,115.8	1,126.7

[1] Preliminary. [2] Adjusted to 42.0 degrees Brix equivalent (9.896 pounds per gallon). Source: Agricultural Statistics Board, U.S. Department of Agriculture (ASB-USDA)

Producer Price Index of Frozen Orange Juice Concentrate — 1982 = 100

Year	Jan.	Feb.	Mar.	Apr.	May	June	July	Aug.	Sept.	Oct.	Nov.	Dec.	Average
2000	110.0	108.9	108.0	107.1	106.9	106.6	105.4	104.8	101.5	100.4	99.8	99.1	104.9
2001	98.9	99.2	98.3	96.8	96.8	97.4	97.3	97.2	97.3	97.3	99.6	102.5	98.2
2002	103.0	102.9	103.1	102.9	102.8	103.2	103.2	103.5	107.4	107.4	109.7	110.2	104.9
2003	110.2	110.2	110.7	110.4	108.5	109.4	109.1	108.9	107.1	106.6	105.1	103.0	108.3
2004	103.4	103.2	102.7	101.6	101.6	101.6	98.9	98.9	98.9	98.9	103.3	103.3	101.4
2005	103.3	103.3	105.0	109.0	109.0	109.0	109.3	109.3	108.1	107.9	108.4	126.4	109.0
2006	138.3	142.1	150.1	160.9	161.0	164.1	172.3	174.8	185.4	197.6	208.9	208.7	172.0
2007	198.1	191.7	198.5	179.6	187.7	184.1	173.6	171.5	152.9	159.3	162.6	168.2	177.3
2008	168.0	166.6	160.0	159.2	159.3	159.6	126.0	121.8	121.4	116.8	115.2	124.3	141.5
2009[1]	124.6	124.4	124.4	117.6	125.0	118.0	118.0	119.8	119.1	130.0	130.0	137.6	124.0

[1] Preliminary. NA = Not avaliable. *Source: Bureau of Labor Statistics, U.S. Department of Labor (BLS)*

Average Price Received by Farmers for Oranges (Equivalent On-Tree) in the U.S. — In Dollars Per Box

Year	Jan.	Feb.	Mar.	Apr.	May	June	July	Aug.	Sept.	Oct.	Nov.	Dec.	Average
2000	3.35	3.18	3.24	4.20	4.39	4.34	2.45	0.35	0.29	1.43	3.20	2.95	2.78
2001	2.85	3.20	4.93	4.84	4.64	4.47	4.63	5.01	6.20	4.99	2.90	3.20	4.32
2002	3.75	4.05	4.64	4.65	4.47	4.00	4.06	6.61	5.33	5.18	3.11	3.23	4.42
2003	3.00	3.14	4.17	4.43	4.43	4.41	3.91	4.27	2.80	2.78	2.32	2.55	3.52
2004	2.45	3.02	3.68	3.68	3.60	4.13	8.85	8.49	15.85	20.87	5.34	3.27	6.94
2005	3.39	3.69	4.84	4.80	5.11	5.43	6.55	4.90	4.29	4.04	5.90	4.46	4.78
2006	5.16	5.27	5.78	6.44	7.13	7.05	6.56	12.03	17.96	13.89	6.95	7.28	8.46
2007	8.25	8.11	10.58	10.62	11.12	11.07	8.95	8.81	7.84	9.60	8.14	5.80	9.07
2008	5.77	5.83	6.20	6.40	7.01	6.75	5.79	4.78	5.92	5.57	7.53	5.39	6.08
2009[1]	5.74	6.04	5.06	6.48	6.79	7.19	8.31	8.58	13.02	11.47	11.57	5.94	8.02

[1] Preliminary. [2] Data thru 1984 are for wholesale oranges (Calif.) F.O.B. packed fresh. *Source: Economic Research Service, U.S. Department of Agriculture (ERS-USDA)*

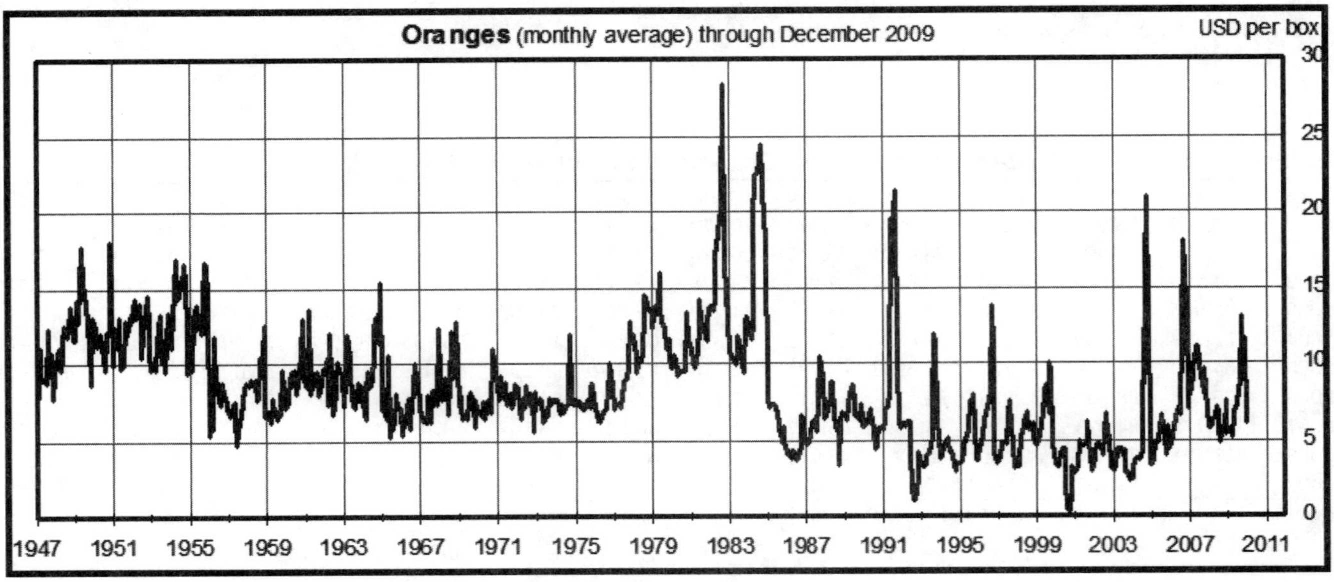

Palm Oil

Palm oil is an edible vegetable oil produced from the flesh of the fruit of the oil palm tree. The oil palm tree is a tropical palm tree that is a native of the west coast of Africa and is different from the coconut palm tree. The fruit of the oil palm tree is reddish, about the size of a large plum, and grows in large bunches. A single seed, the palm kernel, is contained in each fruit. Oil is extracted from both the pulp of the fruit (becoming palm oil) and the kernel (palm kernel oil). About 1 metric ton of palm kernel oil is obtained for every 10 metric tons of palm oil.

Palm oil is commercially used in soap, ointments, cosmetics, detergents, and machinery lubricants. It is also used worldwide as cooking oil, shortening, and margarine. Palm kernel oil is a lighter oil and is used exclusively for food use. Crude palm oil and crude palm kernel oil are traded on the Kuala Lumpur Commodity Exchange.

Prices – The monthly average wholesale price of palm oil (CIF, bulk, U.S. ports) in 2008 (latest data) rose by +14.7% yr/yr to 48.09 cents per pound, which was a new record high.

Supply – World production of palm oil in the 2008-09 marketing year rose by +4.7% to 44.480 million metric tons. World palm oil production has grown by over twenty times the production level of 1.922 million metric tons seen back in 1970. Indonesia and Malaysia are the world's two major global producers of palm oil. Indonesian production rose +7.3% to a record high of 20.250 million metric tons in 2008-09 and Indonesian production accounted for 46% of world production. Malaysian production in 2008-09 rose +1.1% to a record high of 17.760 million metric tons and Malaysian production accounted for 40% of world production. Other smaller global producers include Thailand with 2.7% of world production, Nigeria with 1.9%, and Columbia with (1.8%).

Demand – U.S. total disappearance of palm oil in 2008-09 rose +16.0% yr/yr to 1.090 million metric tons which was a new record high.

Trade – World palm oil exports in 2008-09 rose by +7.6% to 35.330 million metric tons, which was a new record high. The world's largest exporters are Malaysia with a 45% share of world exports and Indonesia also with a 45% share. World palm oil imports in 2008-09 rose +7.1% to 35.220 million metric tons. The world's largest importers are China with a 17% share of world imports and India also with a 17% share.

World Production of Palm Oil In Thousands of Metric Tons

Crop Year	Brazil	Cameroon	Colombia	Costa Rica	Ecuador	Ghana	Indonesia	Ivory Coast	Malaysia	Nigeria	Papua New Guinea	Thailand	World Total
1999-00	105	136	513	136	228	109	6,855	283	10,492	735	300	533	21,266
2000-01	109	138	561	147	199	108	7,775	211	11,940	763	334	601	23,773
2001-02	115	143	517	131	231	109	9,060	260	11,856	774	338	606	25,041
2002-03	128	142	537	148	265	111	10,370	245	13,180	782	310	669	27,811
2003-04	138	145	614	173	272	284	11,970	284	13,418	789	344	724	30,139
2004-05	155	152	653	170	316	292	13,560	291	15,195	798	330	709	33,651
2005-06	171	159	700	187	320	300	15,520	302	15,486	815	315	795	36,182
2006-07[1]	179	169	752	199	409	304	16,730	313	15,294	830	417	989	37,764
2007-08[2]	215	182	779	204	404	316	18,880	295	17,567	812	399	1,123	42,484
2008-09[3]	242	183	793	213	439	324	20,250	319	17,760	853	458	1,218	44,480

[1] Preliminary. [2] Estimate. [3] Forecast. *Source: The Oil World*

World Trade of Palm Oil In Thousands of Metric Tons

	Imports							Exports					
Crop Year	China	Germany	India	Netherlands	Pakistan	United Kingdom	Total	Hong Kong	Indonesia	Malaysia	Guinea	Singapore	Total
1999-00	1,474	431	3,482	780	1,086	558	14,759	130	3,898	9,051	292	251	14,628
2000-01	2,147	497	3,856	907	1,191	607	17,356	180	4,617	10,707	334	228	17,340
2001-02	2,600	592	3,233	1,101	1,333	721	18,590	302	6,094	10,758	332	217	18,917
2002-03	3,167	562	4,110	1,132	1,442	776	21,467	209	7,167	12,133	329	253	21,531
2003-04	3,570	646	3,574	1,174	1,405	819	23,459	154	8,706	12,186	336	227	23,474
2004-05	4,319	766	3,342	1,438	1,683	869	26,312	59	9,862	13,585	322	223	26,160
2005-06	5,182	662	2,820	1,589	1,728	885	28,053	14	11,590	13,718	317	206	28,130
2006-07[1]	5,543	711	3,664	1,710	1,743	734	29,450	27	12,465	13,768	406	185	29,630
2007-08[2]	5,559	654	5,019	2,011	1,813	635	32,900	11	14,100	15,041	384	199	32,845
2008-09[3]	6,150	820	6,000	2,080	1,820	585	35,220	16	15,870	15,900	444	190	35,330

[1] Preliminary. [2] Estimate. [3] Forecast. *Source: The Oil World*

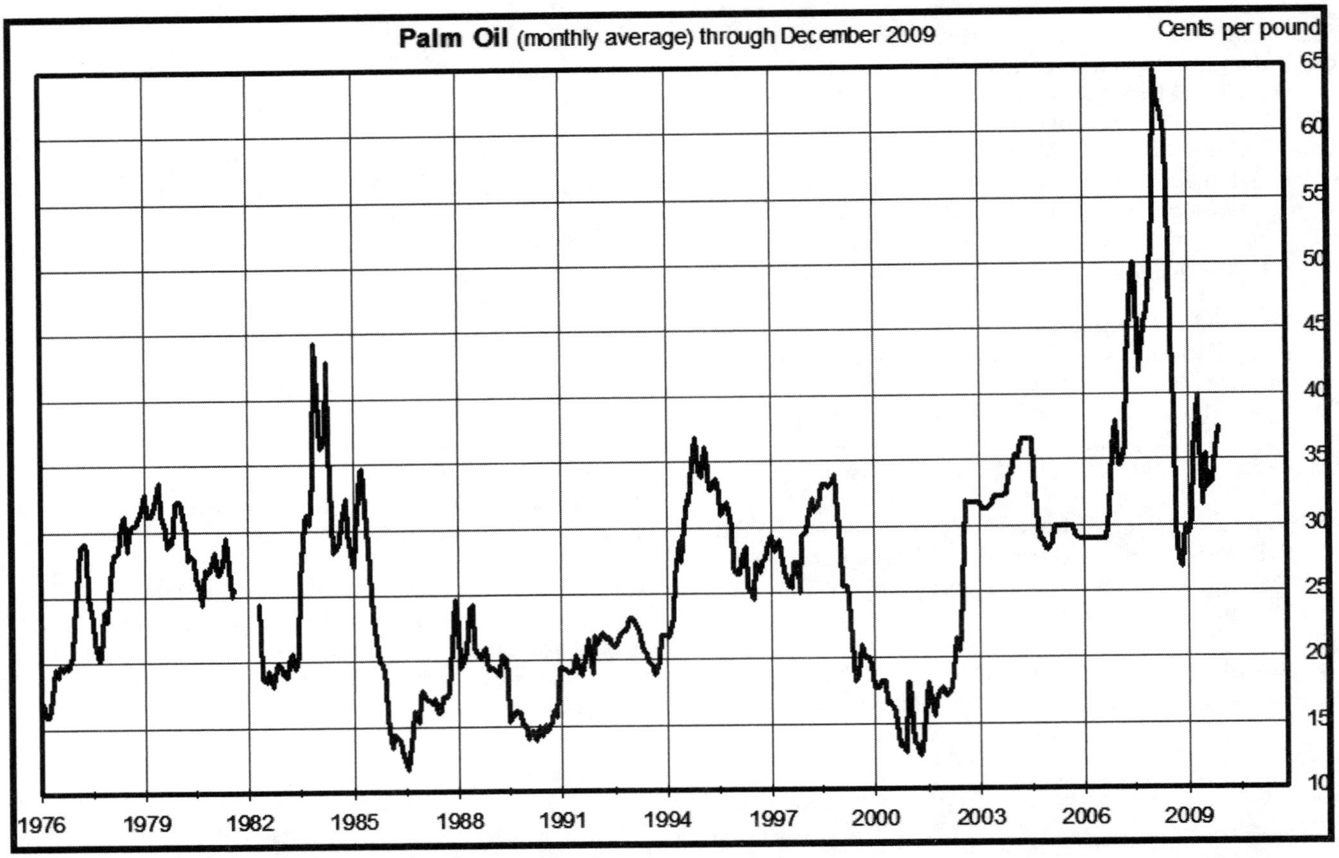

Supply and Distribution of Palm Oil in the United States In Thousands of Metric Tons

Crop Year Beginning Oct. 1	Stocks Oct. 1	Imports	Total Supply	Consumption: Edible Products	Consumption: Inedible Products	Consumption: Total End Products	Total Disap-pearance	Exports	Prices: U.S. Import Value[4]	Prices: Malaysia, F.O.B., RBD	Prices: Palm Kernel Oil, Malaysia, C.I.F Rotterdam
				In Millions of Pounds					U.S. $ Per Metric Ton		
1999-00	21.1	156.6	177.7	W	55.0	W	148.5	3.4	----	338	533
2000-01	25.7	175.5	201.2	W	36.0	W	167.7	6.0	----	272	313
2001-02	27.5	217.2	244.7	W	22.6	75.1	214.4	6.2	----	359	379
2002-03	24.1	174.4	198.5	W	W	76.7	168.5	8.1	----	428	439
2003-04	22.1	281.5	303.6	51.9	37.5	67.9	226.4	13.1	----	489	619
2004-05	64.0	349.0	413.0	62.3	W	62.3	319.4	17.2	----	420	638
2005-06	76.4	603.8	680.2	436.4	W	436.4	555.6	30.6	----	452	583
2006-07[1]	94.0	692.0	786.0	568.5	W	568.5	635.8	58.7	----	685	768
2007-08[2]	91.5	954.7	1,046.2	789.3	W	789.3	939.9	37.7	----	1053	1248
2008-09[3]	68.6	1,160.0	1,228.6	973.6	W	973.6	1,090.0	52.6	----	567	611

[1] Preliminary. [2] Estimate. [3] Forecast. [4] Market value in the foreign country, excluding import duties, ocean freight and marine insurance.
W = Withheld. *Sources: The Oil World; Economic Research Service, U.S. Department of Agriculture (ERS-USDA)*

Average Wholesale Palm Oil Prices, CIF, Bulk, U.S. Ports In Cents Per Pound

Year	Jan.	Feb.	Mar.	Apr.	May	June	July	Aug.	Sept.	Oct.	Nov.	Dec.	Average
2000	18.65	17.66	17.73	18.21	18.12	16.52	16.85	16.23	15.90	13.19	13.56	12.75	16.28
2001	18.05	18.05	13.50	13.50	12.50	13.00	15.50	18.00	16.75	15.60	16.85	17.45	15.73
2002	17.75	17.06	17.30	17.75	18.85	21.44	20.50	21.85	32.00	31.75	31.75	31.75	23.31
2003	31.75	31.75	31.35	31.25	31.25	31.75	32.25	32.25	32.25	32.25	32.44	33.75	32.02
2004	34.00	35.38	35.25	36.40	36.50	36.50	36.50	36.50	34.00	30.00	29.00	29.00	34.09
2005	28.20	28.00	28.67	30.00	30.00	30.00	30.00	30.00	30.00	30.00	29.25	29.00	29.43
2006	29.00	29.00	29.00	29.00	29.00	29.00	29.00	29.00	29.00	29.00	31.00	35.75	29.73
2007	38.00	34.50	34.50	36.00	42.38	48.63	50.00	NA	41.67	43.19	46.20	46.20	41.93
2008	51.48	54.66	64.63	61.96	61.90	59.70	55.41	44.43	38.52	30.11	27.41	26.91	48.09
2009	29.98	29.32	30.32	35.46	39.86	36.45	31.40	35.39	32.90	33.24	34.66	37.53	33.88

Source: Economic Research Service, U.S. Department of Agriculture (ERS-USDA)

Paper

The earliest known paper that is still in existence was made from cotton rags around 150 AD. Around 800 AD, paper made its appearance in Egypt but was not manufactured there until 900 AD. The Moors introduced the use of paper to Europe, and around 1150, the first papermaking mill was established in Spain, followed by England in 1495, and the U.S. in 1690.

During the 17th and 18th centuries, the increased usage of paper created a shortage of cotton rags, which were the only source for papermaking. The solution to this problem lead to the introduction of the ground-wood process of pulp-making in 1840 and the first chemical pulp process 10 years later.

Today, the paper and paperboard industries, including newsprint, are sensitive to the economic cycle. As the economy strengthens, paper use increases, and vice versa.

Prices – The average monthly index price (1982 = 100) for paperboard in 2009 fell -4.8% yr/yr to 207.50, down from last year's record index high of 217.9. The average monthly producer price index of standard newsprint paper in 2009 fell by -14.5% to 126.6, down from the 12-year high of 151.8 posted in 2006.

Supply – U.S. production of paper and paperboard in 2008 (latest data) fell -4.5% yr/yr to 80.178 million metric tons. The U.S. is the world's largest producer of paper and paperboard by far, followed by Germany with 22.842 million metric tons and Canada with 15.773 million metric tons.

U.S. production of newsprint fell by –2.4% yr/yr to a record low of 414.6 metric tons per month in 2005 which is the latest data available. U.S. production of newsprint is second in the world, after Canada, which had production of 657.167 metric tons per month in 2005.

Production of Paper and Paperboard by Selected Countries In Thousands of Metric Tons

Year	Austria	Canada	Finland	France	Germany	Italy	Netherlands	Norway	Russia/3	Spain	Sweden	United Kingdom	United States
2003	4,565	19,964	13,058	9,939	19,310	9,491	3,339	2,186	6,377	5,437	11,062	6,455	80,712
2004	4,852	20,462	14,036	10,255	20,391	9,667	3,459	2,294	6,830	5,526	11,589	6,442	82,084
2005	4,950	19,498	12,391	10,332	21,679	9,999	3,471	2,223	7,126	5,697	11,775	6,241	83,697
2006	5,213	18,189	14,189	10,006	22,656	10,008	3,367	2,109	7,434	6,898	12,066	5,454	84,317
2007	5,199	17,367	14,709	9,871	23,317	10,112	3,224	2,010	7,581	6,713	12,361	5,228	83,916
2008[1]	5,153	15,773	13,549	9,420	22,842	9,467	2,977	1,900	7,676	7,048	12,374	4,983	80,178

[1] Preliminary. *Source: Food and Agriculture Organization of the United Nations (FAO-UN)*

Production of Newsprint by Selected Countires (Monthly Average) In Thousands of Metric Tons

Year	Australia	Brazil	Canada	China	Finland	France	Germany	India	Japan	Rep. of Korea	Russia/3	Sweden	United States
2004	35.200	11.093	648.000	249.950	60.200	93.160	186.795	59.300	307.933	145.398	164.835	220.800	424.700
2005	NA	11.075	657.167	284.133	47.867	92.349	226.016	74.700	309.967	135.868	165.318	213.000	414.600
2006	NA	11.257	NA	333.967	NA	92.463	225.895	85.100	314.271	137.859	166.051	211.400	NA
2007	NA	11.640	NA	369.117	NA	90.655	218.606	84.310	317.042	138.792	164.875	214.075	NA
2008[1]	NA	12.349	NA	387.108	NA	90.307	227.865	95.501	306.701	133.334	165.642	210.342	NA
2009[2]	NA		NA	403.550	NA		204.288	78.203	286.940	124.783	166.824	200.323	NA

[1] Preliminary. [2] Estimate. NA = Not available. *Source: United Nations*

Index Price of Paperboard (1982 = 100)

Year	Jan.	Feb.	Mar.	Apr.	May	June	July	Aug.	Sept.	Oct.	Nov.	Dec.	Average
2003	166.8	166.5	164.4	163.5	163.6	163.4	162.5	162.5	160.5	159.9	159.6	159.7	162.7
2004	157.8	157.4	157.5	162.2	165.5	170.0	175.2	178.5	179.2	179.4	180.1	179.3	170.2
2005	179.7	180.0	180.1	180.7	180.9	176.6	174.6	168.5	168.5	168.6	174.1	173.9	175.5
2006	175.3	184.0	184.3	184.3	193.7	196.7	196.8	197.2	197.5	197.7	198.4	197.5	192.0
2007	198.0	198.1	198.2	199.0	198.8	198.7	199.0	199.1	203.1	209.5	209.2	209.4	201.7
2008	209.7	209.8	209.7	209.7	209.7	210.3	211.5	226.0	229.5	230.0	229.6	229.1	217.9
2009[1]	224.6	221.3	216.7	211.8	205.3	203.0	202.8	202.0	202.4	198.3	198.2	195.6	206.8

[1] Preliminary. *Source: Bureau of Labor Statistics, U.S. Department of Commerce (BLS) (0914)*

Producer Price Index of Standard Newsprint (1982 = 100)

Year	Jan.	Feb.	Mar.	Apr.	May	June	July	Aug.	Sept.	Oct.	Nov.	Dec.	Average
2003	106.1	107.4	106.3	110.2	112.6	112.5	111.0	114.3	116.8	118.1	114.6	115.0	112.1
2004	116.5	116.7	118.8	122.4	125.0	126.0	125.6	125.7	125.8	129.5	129.8	132.4	124.5
2005	130.3	131.9	131.6	132.8	133.2	135.9	138.8	141.4	152.2	143.5	144.9	145.6	138.5
2006	148.8	148.0	150.5	149.8	152.0	153.7	154.3	153.3	153.9	153.7	151.9	151.3	151.8
2007	150.3	146.1	145.0	143.1	127.9	127.5	125.8	124.1	122.5	121.8	121.1	124.4	131.6
2008	125.8	129.6	133.4	136.2	142.7	146.5	151.0	156.1	158.6	162.4	167.6	166.1	148.0
2009[1]	162.3	158.9	153.0	141.1	129.6	120.3	107.5	105.3	105.5	105.2	105.1	114.1	125.7

[1] Preliminary. *Source: Bureau of Labor Statistics, U.S. Department of Commerce (BLS) (0913-02)*

Peanuts and Peanut Oil

Peanuts are the edible seeds of a plant from the pea family. Although called a nut, the peanut is actually a legume. Ancient South American Inca Indians were the first to grind peanuts to make peanut butter. Peanuts originated in Brazil and were later brought to the U.S. via Africa. The first major use of peanuts was as feed for pigs. It wasn't until the Civil War that peanuts were used as human food when both Northern and Southern troops used the peanut as a food source during hard times. In 1903, Dr. George Washington Carver, a talented botanist who is considered the "father of commercial peanuts," introduced peanuts as a rotation crop in cotton-growing areas. Carver discovered over 300 uses for the peanut including shaving cream, leather dye, coffee, ink, cheese, and shampoo.

Peanuts come in many varieties, but there are four basic types grown in the U.S.: Runner, Spanish, Valencia, and Virginia. Over half of Runner peanuts are used to make peanut butter. Spanish peanuts are primarily used to make candies and peanut oil. Valencia peanuts are the sweetest of the four types. Virginia peanuts are mainly roasted and sold in and out of the shell.

Peanut oil is extracted from shelled and crushed peanuts through hydraulic pressing, expelled pressing, or solvent extraction. Crude peanut oil is used as a flavoring agent, salad oil, and cooking oil. Refined, bleached and deodorized peanut oil is used for cooking and in margarines and shortenings. The by-product called press cake is used for cattle feed along with the tops of the plants after the pods are removed. The dry shells can be burned as fuel.

Prices – The average monthly price received by farmers for peanuts (in the shell) in the first six months of the 2009-10 marketing year (i.e., Aug 2009-Jul 2010) fell -2.4% to 22.4 cents per pound. The record high is 34.7 cents posted in 1990-91. The average monthly price of peanut oil in the 2008-09 marketing year (through December 2009) fell -25.8% yr/yr to 51.80 cents per pound, down from the 2007-08 record high of 100.92 per pound. The average monthly price of peanut meal (50% Southeast Mills) fell by –8.0% yr/yr in 2006-07 (through February 2007, which is the latest data available) to a record low of $98.40 per short ton.

Supply – World peanut production in 2009-10 fell by -9.8% to 30.805 million metric tons, down from the 2008-09 record high of 34.151 million metric tons. The world's largest peanut producers are China with 41% of world production, India with 16%, U.S. with 5%, and Nigeria with 5%. U.S. peanut production in the 2009-10 marketing year fell by -28.6% to 3.688, down from the last year's record high of 5.148 billion pounds.

U.S. farmers harvested 1.507 million acres of peanuts in 2009-10, down -28.3% yr/yr. That was down from the 16-year high harvest of 1.629 million acres in 2005-06. U.S. peanut yield in 2009-10 fell -0.4% yr/yr to 3,412 pounds per acre, down from last year's record high. The largest peanut producing states in the U.S.in 2009 are Georgia (with 48% of U.S. production), Texas (15%), Alabama (13%), Florida (9%), and North Carolina (7%). U.S. crude peanut oil production in 2009 fell -9.7% to 143.837 million pounds, which was only about 40% of the record high level of 358,195 million pounds posted in 1996.

Demand – U.S. disposition of peanuts in 2007-08 fell by -3.3% yr/yr to 4.033 billion pounds. Of that disposition, 62% of the peanuts went for food, 15% for exports, 13% for crushing into peanut oil, and 10% for seed, loss and residual. The most popular type of peanut grown in the U.S. is the Runner peanut with 88% of U.S. production in 2008-09. This was followed by the Virginia peanut with 10% of production and the Spanish peanut far behind with only 2% of production. Peanut butter is a primary use for Runner and Virginia peanuts. It accounts for 62% of Runner peanut usage and 58% of Virginia peanut usage. In a poor third place, only about 5% of Spanish peanuts are used for peanut butter. Snack peanuts is also a key usage category and accounts for 31% of Spanish peanut usage, 28% of Virginia peanut usage, and 19% of Runner peanut usage. Candy accounts for 39% of Spanish peanut usage, 18% of Runner peanut usage, and 14% of Virginia peanut usage.

Trade –U.S. exports of peanuts in 2007-08 fell by -2.2% yr/yr to 590 million pounds. U.S. imports of peanuts fell by –5.2% yr/yr in 2007-08 to 55 million pounds.

World Production of Peanuts (in the Shell) In Thousands of Metric Tons

Crop Year	Argentina	Burma	China	India	Indonesia	Nigeria	Senegal	South Africa	Sudan	Thailand	United States	Zaire	World Total
2000-01	564	634	14,437	5,700	1,040	1,470	1,003	186	370	132	1,481	382	31,423
2001-02	517	731	14,415	7,600	1,033	1,490	903	120	370	107	1,940	368	33,816
2002-03	316	756	14,818	5,400	1,086	1,510	260	60	370	112	1,506	355	30,862
2003-04	420	878	13,420	7,700	1,130	1,510	445	115	370	113	1,880	360	32,834
2004-05	585	916	14,340	7,000	1,150	1,520	573	85	370	114	1,945	364	33,606
2005-06	510	910	14,340	6,300	1,170	1,520	703	93	370	114	2,209	365	33,218
2006-07	575	910	12,887	5,385	1,200	1,520	460	77	850	117	1,571	370	30,722
2007-08	625	1,000	13,027	6,800	1,150	1,550	331	118	850	114	1,666	370	32,388
2008-09[1]	580	1,000	14,286	6,250	1,250	1,550	450	128	850	115	2,342	370	34,151
2009-10[2]	550	1,000	12,720	5,000	1,250	1,550	625	115	850	115	1,673	370	30,805

[1] Preliminary. [2] Estimate. *Source: Foreign Agricultural Service, U.S. Department of Agriculture (FAS-USDA)*

Salient Statistics of Peanuts in the United States

Crop Year Beginning Aug. 1	Acreage Planted (1,000 Acres)	Acreage Harvested for Nuts (1,000 Acres)	Average Yield Per Acre In Lbs.	Production (1,000 Lbs)	Season Farm Price (Cents Lb.)	Farm Value (Million Dollars)	Exports: Unshelled (In Thousands of Pounds)	Exports: Shelled (In Thousands of Pounds)	Imports: Unshelled (In Thousands of Pounds)	Imports: Shelled (In Thousands of Pounds)
2000-01	1,536.8	1,336.0	2,444	3,265,505	27.4	896.1	527,200	----	215,626	----
2001-02	1,541.2	1,411.9	3,029	4,276,704	23.4	1,000.5	699,700	----	202,808	----
2002-03	1,353.0	1,291.7	2,571	3,321,040	18.2	599.7	489,900	----	75,372	----
2003-04	1,344.0	1,312.0	3,159	4,144,150	19.3	799.4	515,900	----	38,088	----
2004-05	1,430.0	1,394.0	3,076	4,288,200	18.9	813.6	491,000	----	36,863	----
2005-06	1,657.0	1,629.0	2,989	4,869,860	17.3	843.4	491,000	----	32,100	----
2006-07	1,243.0	1,210.0	2,863	3,464,250	17.7	612.8	603,000	----	61,000	----
2007-08	1,230.0	1,195.0	3,130	3,740,650	20.5	758.6	750,000	----	73,000	----
2008-09[1]	1,534.0	1,507.0	3,426	5,162,400	23.0	1,193.6	727,000	----	86,000	----
2009-10[2]	1,195.0	1,081.0	3,412	3,688,350	21.0-22.6	835.2	725,000	----	60,000	----

[1] Preliminary. [2] Estimate. *Source: Economic Research Service, U.S. Department of Agriculture (ERS-USDA)*

Supply and Disposition of Peanuts (Farmer's Stock Basis) & Support Program in the United States

Crop Year Beginning Aug. 1	Supply: Production	Supply: Imports	Supply: Stocks Aug. 1	Supply: Total	Disposition: Exports	Disposition: Crushed for Oil	Disposition: Seed, Loss & Residual	Disposition: Food	Disposition: Total Disappearance	Support Price (Cents Per Lb.)	Additional (Cents Per Lb.)	Amount Put Under Support: Quantity (Mil. Lbs.)	Amount Put Under Support: % of Production
	In Millions of Pounds												
2001-02	4,277	203	1,097	5,576	700	693	482	2,225	4,100	30.50	6.6	----	----
2002-03	3,321	75	1,476	4,873	490	857	410	2,241	3,998	NA	NA	----	----
2003-04	4,144	38	875	5,057	516	536	429	2,456	3,936	NA	NA	----	----
2004-05	4,288	37	1,121	5,446	491	393	547	2,600	4,031	NA	NA	----	----
2005-06	4,870	32	1,415	6,317	491	542	501	2,616	4,150	NA	NA	----	----
2006-07	3,464	61	2,167	5,692	603	513	471	2,585	4,172	NA	NA	----	----
2007-08	3,741	73	1,520	5,265	750	496	471	2,517	4,234	NA	NA	----	----
2008-09[1]	5,162	86	1,031	6,280	727	445	407	2,571	4,150	NA	NA	----	----
2009-10[2]	3,688	60	2,130	5,878	725	456	420	2,654	4,255	NA	NA	----	----

[1] Preliminary. [2] Estimate. *Source: Economic Research Service, U.S. Department of Agriculture (ERS-USDA)*

Production of Peanuts (Harvested for Nuts) in the United States, by States In Thousands of Pounds

Crop Year	Alabama	Florida	Georgia	New Mexico	North Carolina	Oklahoma	South Carolina	Texas	Virgina	Total
2000	271,180	213,710	1,328,400	54,990	338,250	120,600	29,500	698,500	210,375	3,265,505
2001	532,325	250,100	1,711,620	67,044	356,475	197,890	30,600	895,900	234,750	4,276,704
2002	379,800	197,800	1,313,000	54,000	210,000	159,600	19,140	868,000	119,700	3,321,040
2003	508,750	345,000	1,863,000	45,900	320,000	98,000	57,800	810,000	95,700	4,144,150
2004	557,200	364,000	1,817,800	59,500	367,500	102,300	112,200	803,700	104,000	4,288,200
2005	613,250	410,400	2,130,000	66,500	288,000	107,910	168,000	975,000	66,000	4,869,860
2006	407,500	300,000	1,598,500	43,200	268,800	62,700	168,000	514,750	54,400	3,464,250
2007	400,350	321,300	1,622,400	32,000	261,000	57,800	173,600	691,900	52,500	3,740,650
2008	675,500	448,000	2,329,000	25,600	358,900	63,000	265,200	834,900	80,400	5,162,400
2009[1]	471,500	336,000	1,782,650	21,700	244,200	42,900	148,800	542,500	44,400	3,688,350

[1] Preliminary. *Source: Agricultural Statistics Board, U.S. Department of Agriculture (ASB-USDA)*

Supply and Reported Uses of Shelled Peanuts and Products in the United States In Thousands of Pounds

Crop Year Beginning Aug. 1	Shelled Peanuts Stocks, Aug. 1: Edible	Shelled Peanuts Stocks, Aug. 1: Oil Stock[2]	Shelled Peanuts Production: Edible	Shelled Peanuts Production: Oil Stock[2]	Reported Used (Shelled Peanuts - Raw Basis), Edible Grades Used In: Candy[3]	Snack[4]	Sandwich Spread	Butter[5]	Other Products	Total	Shelled Peanuts Crushed[6]	Crude Oil Production	Cake & Meal Production
2000-01	707,672	14,463	1,939,736	337,324	355,610	361,516	----	753,239	19,998	1,490,363	411,558	178,523	230,099
2001-02	680,850	16,648	2,090,776	485,092	349,729	360,916	----	818,927	17,284	1,546,856	521,173	230,791	296,874
2002-03	504,186	24,231	1,983,016	611,627	354,232	344,913	----	828,529	24,379	1,552,053	644,194	285,685	356,888
2003-04	603,529	17,686	2,439,231	390,893	365,983	414,588	----	901,637	15,930	1,698,138	402,958	172,977	226,995
2004-05	621,190	17,686	2,357,314	246,663	389,696	450,781	----	938,514	22,547	1,801,538	295,769	126,249	172,668
2005-06	501,868	15,305	2,411,471	357,600	376,777	454,324	----	974,223	12,092	1,817,416	407,817	181,085	232,868
2006-07	510,097	21,499	2,415,495	347,243	373,684	415,131	----	993,445	9,397	1,791,657	385,375	166,450	223,537
2007-08	528,918	33,401	2,291,603	319,186	320,467	425,166	----	1,012,263	10,676	1,768,572	372,980	158,144	211,733
2008-09[1]	431,593	39,508	2,442,345	253,778	316,275	367,478	----	1,102,698	9,840	1,796,291	334,296	142,666	190,748

[1] Preliminary. [2] Includes straight run oil stock peanuts. [3] Includes peanut butter made by manufacturers for own use in candy. [4] Formerly titled "Salted Peanuts." [5] Includes peanut butter made by manufacturers for own use in cookies and sandwiches, but excludes peanut butter used in candy. [6] All crushings regardless of grade. *Source: National Agricultural Statistics Service, U.S. Department of Agriculture (NASS-USDA)*

Shelled Peanuts (Raw Basis) Used in Primary Products, by Type In Thousands of Pounds

Crop Year Beginning Aug. 1	Virginia Candy[2]	Virginia Peanuts	Virginia Butter[3]	Virginia Total	Runner Candy[2]	Runner Peanuts	Runner Butter[3]	Runner Total	Spanish Candy[2]	Spanish Peanuts	Spanish Butter[3]	Spanish Total
1999-00	23,173	100,384	73,926	200,804	315,467	278,440	690,564	1,300,393	16,313	15,297	7,614	40,208
2000-01	19,101	100,650	102,050	225,072	320,304	247,739	643,229	1,227,156	16,205	13,127	7,960	38,135
2001-02	26,640	97,046	106,573	233,356	303,668	250,079	702,454	1,269,776	19,421	13,791	9,900	43,724
2002-03	26,930	75,100	77,018	183,226	312,192	257,259	734,844	1,323,846	15,110	12,555	16,667	44,981
2003-04	23,580	68,257	88,053	181,559	328,560	333,198	805,852	1,481,457	13,843	13,133	7,732	35,122
2004-05	25,466	70,216	112,027	209,411	349,437	367,671	824,876	1,562,692	14,793	12,894	1,611	29,435
2005-06	25,738	81,617	123,402	231,893	335,748	361,176	849,176	1,557,025	15,291	11,531	W	28,498
2006-07	29,542	75,858	113,689	220,196	329,806	328,167	869,014	1,535,250	14,335	11,104	W	36,211
2007-08	27,909	71,059	125,497	225,445	279,564	344,551	878,026	1,511,807	12,994	9,556	W	31,321
2008-09[1]	26,342	52,925	110,737	191,770	276,212	303,730	981,546	1,569,531	13,721	10,823	W	34,990

[1] Preliminary. [2] Includes peanut butter made by manufacturers for own use in candy. [3] Includes peanut butter made by manufacturers for own use in cookies and sandwiches, but excludes peanut butter used in candy.
Source: National Agricultural Statistics Service, U.S. Department of Agriculture (NASS-USDA)

Production, Consumption, Stocks and Foreign Trade of Peanut Oil in the United States In Millions of Pounds

Crop Year Beginning Aug. 1	Production: Crude	Production: Refined	Consumption: In Refining	Consumption: In End Products	Stocks, Dec. 31: Crude	Stocks, Dec. 31: Refined	Imports for Consumption	Exports
2000-01	222.1	206.3	258.9	277.3	23.1	1.9	19.5	5.5
2001-02	278.5	179.1	291.9	282.5	8.2	1.7	----	----
2002-03	267.7	166.3	W	277.6	52.9	3.5	----	----
2003-04	180.7	115.8	W	203.8	23.0	1.8	----	----
2004-05	135.7	91.0	W	181.9	40.3	2.4	----	----
2005-06	188.0	119.9	W	152.1	15.4	3.7	----	----
2006-07	173.8	115.1	W	W	35.5	5.6	----	----
2007-08	168.7	111.2	W	W	14.1	1.8	----	----
2008-09[1]	150.8	99.9	W	W	17.6	3.0	----	----
2009-10[2]	152.5	99.4	W	W	18.1	2.1	----	----

[1] Preliminary. [2] Forecast. W = Withheld. *Source: Bureau of the Census, U.S. Department of Commerce*

Production of Crude Peanut Oil in the United States In Millions of Pounds

Year	Jan.	Feb.	Mar.	Apr.	May	June	July	Aug.	Sept.	Oct.	Nov.	Dec.	Total
2000	35.2	32.1	27.4	31.9	30.4	28.0	24.1	28.8	21.5	25.4	16.4	15.2	316.3
2001	17.3	15.7	20.1	15.3	12.4	19.1	16.3	16.7	12.9	17.1	13.8	25.6	202.4
2002	24.8	25.5	32.8	28.5	33.8	24.3	22.6	27.7	27.2	26.5	24.9	20.2	319.0
2003	21.7	16.6	19.4	20.5	20.0	23.2	19.8	17.3	18.3	24.1	15.6	13.2	229.6
2004	12.6	15.7	13.0	14.7	11.8	13.7	10.7	9.8	5.8	10.0	11.9	12.6	142.4
2005	14.4	13.1	9.9	11.3	13.3	14.6	8.9	14.5	11.3	15.3	16.4	17.7	160.8
2006	W	16.5	W	15.6	18.1	15.6	15.7	19.7	16.2	18.0	14.4	10.1	191.8
2007	14.3	12.8	14.3	14.9	9.7	15.2	14.1	17.7	19.0	17.3	12.0	14.0	175.3
2008	14.9	6.0	14.3	14.2	13.8	12.6	13.0	11.8	14.6	17.8	12.4	13.9	159.2
2009[1]	13.8	6.8	14.1	12.2	11.9	12.2	9.4	10.9	12.5	15.1	13.6	11.5	143.8

[1] Preliminary. W = Withheld. *Source: Bureau of the Census, U.S. Department of Commerce*

Average Price of Peanut Meal 50% Southeast Mills In Dollars Per Short Ton

Year	Jan.	Feb.	Mar.	Apr.	May	June	July	Aug.	Sept.	Oct.	Nov.	Dec.	Average
2000-01	118.00	118.00	118.00	142.50	120.00	118.00	110.75	112.50	NA	123.50	130.50	126.25	121.64
2001-02	115.00	111.25	100.00	102.50	100.00	105.00	110.00	105.00	NA	130.00	135.00	136.88	113.69
2002-03	NA	130.00	122.50	118.50	114.25	124.00	125.00	135.00	135.00	135.75	130.00	130.00	127.27
2003-04	147.10	161.00	163.25	163.35	168.75	200.40	226.00	237.50	204.00	199.33	143.33	133.00	178.92
2004-05	100.38	99.25	93.50	93.25	99.25	112.00	122.75	137.25	145.25	140.83	132.50	109.00	115.43
2005-06	105.50	102.50	100.88	NA	114.50	113.50	113.17	113.33	107.13	107.50	100.00	98.75	106.98
2006-07	98.50	98.50	98.00	98.50	98.50	NA	NA	NA	NA	NA	NA	NA	98.40
2007-08	NA	NA	NA	NA	NA	NA	NA	NA	NA	NA	NA	NA	NA
2008-09	NA	NA	NA	NA	NA	NA	NA	NA	NA	NA	NA	NA	NA
2009-10[1]	NA	NA	NA	NA									

[1] Preliminary. NA = Not available. *Source: Agricultural Marketing Service, U.S. Department of Agriculture (AMS-USDA)*

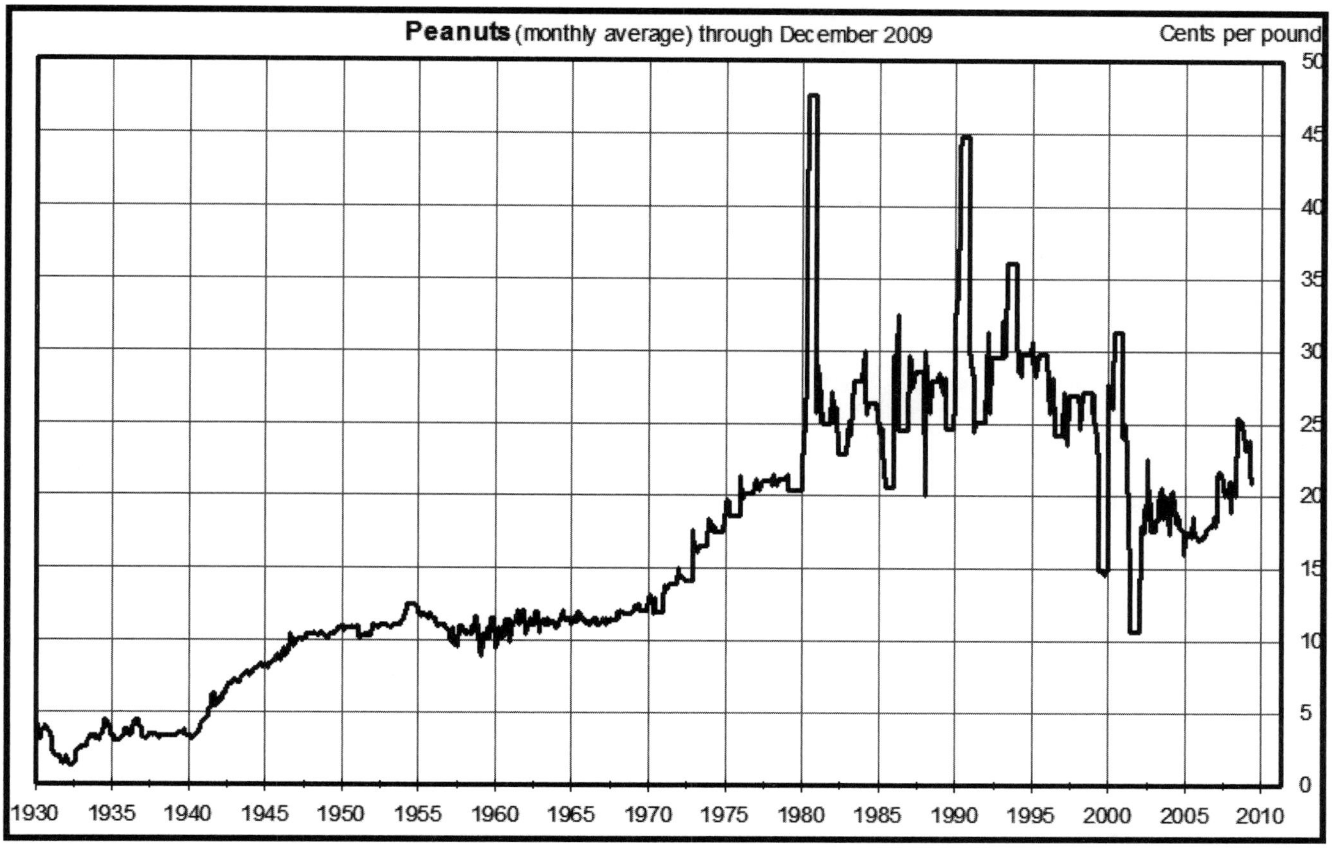

Average Price Received by Farmers for Peanuts (in the Shell) in the United States In Cents Per Pound

Year	Jan.	Feb.	Mar.	Apr.	May	June	July	Aug.	Sept.	Oct.	Nov.	Dec.	Average[1]
2000-01	NQ	27.7	26.5	26.1	27.3	31.4	NQ	NQ	NQ	NQ	NQ	NQ	27.8
2001-02	24.1	24.9	22.8	21.0	19.5	13.5	10.7	NQ	NQ	NQ	NQ	NQ	19.5
2002-03	NQ	17.9	17.9	18.0	17.5	19.1	19.6	22.6	18.4	19.6	17.7	NQ	18.8
2003-04	NQ	18.3	18.5	18.4	19.6	20.6	18.9	18.6	19.8	20.6	20.3	17.4	19.2
2004-05	19.0	19.2	20.1	20.3	18.3	18.9	18.6	18.5	18.0	17.8	17.6	16.0	18.5
2005-06	17.0	17.0	17.4	17.5	17.4	17.3	18.6	16.9	17.4	17.3	17.0	17.0	17.3
2006-07	17.0	17.3	17.2	17.2	17.6	17.8	17.8	17.8	18.3	17.9	18.1	18.7	17.7
2007-08	18.0	18.6	21.4	21.7	21.3	21.6	21.0	20.7	20.0	20.4	20.1	21.1	20.5
2008-09	18.9	21.0	20.6	20.1	21.7	23.9	25.3	25.4	25.2	24.7	24.7	23.4	22.9
2009-10[2]	23.2	23.3	23.8	21.8	21.5	20.6	21.4						22.2

[1] Weighted average by sales. [2] Preliminarly. NQ = No quote. *Source: National Agricultural Statistics Service, U.S. Department of Agriculture (NASS-USDA)*

Average Price of Domestic Crude Peanut Oil (in Tanks) F.O.B. Southeast Mills In Cents Per Pound

Year	Jan.	Feb.	Mar.	Apr.	May	June	July	Aug.	Sept.	Oct.	Nov.	Dec.	Average
2000-01	34.63	35.50	36.40	37.25	37.00	35.90	34.00	33.00	33.00	33.00	34.00	34.00	34.81
2001-02	36.25	37.00	37.00	35.00	28.00	27.50	27.00	27.00	30.00	34.00	35.20	36.25	32.52
2002-03	NA	42.00	43.67	45.75	46.00	47.00	50.25	52.75	56.60	58.25	60.00	60.67	51.18
2003-04	61.60	63.25	64.50	65.00	61.67	60.00	60.00	56.50	NA	56.00	53.75	55.00	59.75
2004-05	55.00	55.00	55.67	56.00	55.00	50.00	50.00	53.25	52.50	52.38	52.25	50.06	53.09
2005-06	45.50	45.50	45.00	42.50	42.50	42.50	42.50	42.50	43.75	45.00	47.30	49.25	44.48
2006-07	52.67	52.50	50.00	49.25	46.25	48.20	52.63	55.63	62.56	69.63	70.00	73.00	56.86
2007-08	76.75	93.20	98.50	97.33	99.00	100.00	104.38	104.80	107.00	110.00	110.00	110.00	100.91
2008-09	97.00	90.00	85.25	79.10	75.00	62.50	58.75	56.60	57.00	60.70	62.00	54.00	69.83
2009-10[1]	51.20	52.00	52.20	59.00									53.60

[1] Preliminary. NA = Not available. *Source: Agricultural Marketing Service, U.S. Department of Agriculture (AMS-USDA)*

Pepper

The pepper plant is a perennial climbing shrub that originated in India and Sri Lanka. Pepper is considered the world's most important spice and has been used to flavor foods for over 3,000 years. Pepper was once considered so valuable that it was used to ransom Rome from Attila the Hun. Black pepper alone accounts for nearly 35% of the world's spice trade. Unlike many other popular herbs and spices, pepper can only be cultivated in tropical climates. The pepper plant produces a berry called a peppercorn. Both black and white pepper are obtained from the same plant. The colors of pepper are determined by the maturity of the berry at harvest and by different processing methods.

Black pepper is picked when the berries are still green and immature. The peppercorns are then dried in the sun until they turn black. White pepper is picked when the berries are fully ripe and bright red. The red peppercorns are then soaked, washed to remove the skin of the berry, and dried to produce a white to yellowish-white peppercorn. Black pepper has a slightly hotter flavor and stronger aroma than white pepper. Piperine, an alkaloid of pyridine, is the active ingredient in pepper that makes it hot.

Black pepper oil is obtained from crushed berries using solvent extraction. Black pepper oil is used in the treatment of pain, chills, flu, muscular aches, and in some perfumes. It is also helpful in promoting digestion in the colon.

The world's key pepper varieties are known by their place of origin. Popular types of pepper include Lampong Black and Muntok White from Indonesia, Brazilian Black, and Malabar Black and Tellicherry from India.

Prices – The average monthly price for black pepper in 2007 (latest data through June) rose sharply by +55.8% to 161.8 cents per pound, way up from the 14-year low of 75.6 cents per pound in 2004. The average monthly price for white pepper in 2007 (latest data) rose sharply by +40.9% to 216.4 cents per pound, but that was still only 61% of the record high of 356.5 cents seen in 1998.

Trade – The world's largest exporters of pepper in 2007 (latest data) were Vietnam (with 83,000 metric tons of exports), India (47,464), Brazil (38,679), Indonesia (38,447), and Malaysia (15,165). U.S. imports of black pepper in 2008 (latest data) fell -2.6% yr/yr to 49,626 metric tons. The primary source of U.S. imports of black pepper in 2008 was Indonesia which accounted for 41% of U.S. imports, followed by India with 20%, and Brazil with 17%. Imports from Malaysia have dropped by over 95% since 2003. U.S. imports of white pepper in 2008 rose by +25.1% yr/yr to 6,960 metric tons. The primary source of U.S. imports of white pepper was Indonesia, which accounted for 69% of U.S. imports, followed by Malaysia with 5%, Brazil with 1%, and China with 1%.

World Exports of Pepper (Black and White) and Prices in the United States In Metric Tons

	Exports (In Metric Tons)								New York Spot Prices (Cents Per Pound) Indonesian		Indian		
Year	Brazil	India	Indo-nesia	Mada-gascar	Malaysia	Mexico	Sri Lanka	Vietnam	Lampong Black	Muntok White	Brazilian Black	Malabar Black	Telli-cherry[2]
1998	17,249	32,859	38,723	339	18,717	3,365	5,493	15,100	239.5	356.5	239.5	239.5	286.6
1999	19,617	35,635	36,293	619	21,804	4,026	3,754	34,800	254.5	334.9	254.5	254.5	296.3
2000	20,469	19,125	47,502	588	23,684	4,534	4,855	36,400	228.1	227.1	228.1	228.1	282.6
2001	36,975	19,641	53,432	811	25,537	4,658	2,161	57,000	116.2	132.6	116.2	116.2	179.3
2002	38,230	21,066	63,214	880	22,840	4,344	7,915	78,400	92.9	120.6	92.9	92.9	127.8
2003	38,972	15,319	51,546	863	18,346	3,861	7,740	73,900	85.8	139.3	85.8	85.8	128.8
2004	43,003	15,429	32,364	1,243	19,788	5,785	4,852	111,000	75.6	120.9	75.6	75.6	118.8
2005	38,424	21,470	34,531	1,229	18,097	15,415	8,131	109,000	76.0	116.0	76.0	76.0	109.9
2006	42,200	35,499	36,953	1,776	16,610	6,593	7,596	115,000	103.9	153.5	103.9	103.9	136.4
2007[1]	38,679	47,464	38,447	1,892	15,165	4,081	6,940	83,000	161.8	216.4	161.8	161.8	

[1] Preliminary. [2] Extra bold. NA = not avaliable. *Source: Foreign Agricultural Service, U.S. Department of Agriculture (FAS-USDA)*

United States Imports of Unground Pepper from Specified Countries In Metric Tons

	Black Pepper							White Pepper					
Year	Brazil	India	Indonesia	Malaysia	Sing-apore	Sri Lanka	Total	Brazil	China	Indonesia	Malaysia	Sing-apore	Total
1999	7,093	24,931	8,429	2,392	525	441	47,591	32	451	5,202	420	342	6,789
2000	7,853	10,981	15,713	4,148	306	516	43,539	15	210	6,345	185	215	7,311
2001	11,699	7,998	19,606	2,957	508	279	48,749	48	7	5,807	120	161	6,365
2002	11,300	7,407	13,638	3,213	110	564	50,155	18	73	6,559	103	219	7,207
2003	13,792	4,950	16,370	1,416	163	504	51,124	198	180	4,567	224	904	6,758
2004	15,606	2,039	13,210	97	25	187	50,925	472	98	4,034	192	422	7,290
2005	13,935	3,828	13,502	144	50	269	52,152	460	73	4,134	192	300	7,248
2006	15,622	7,272	12,941	249	90	342	55,523	615	106	3,809	419	344	7,805
2007	14,148	14,763	14,201	162	75	281	50,934	122	121	3,991	520	140	5,564
2008[1]	8,224	9,699	20,180	35	126	665	49,626	88	82	4,783	381	36	6,960

[1] Preliminary. *Source: Foreign Agricultural Service, U.S. Department of Agriculture (FAS-USDA)*

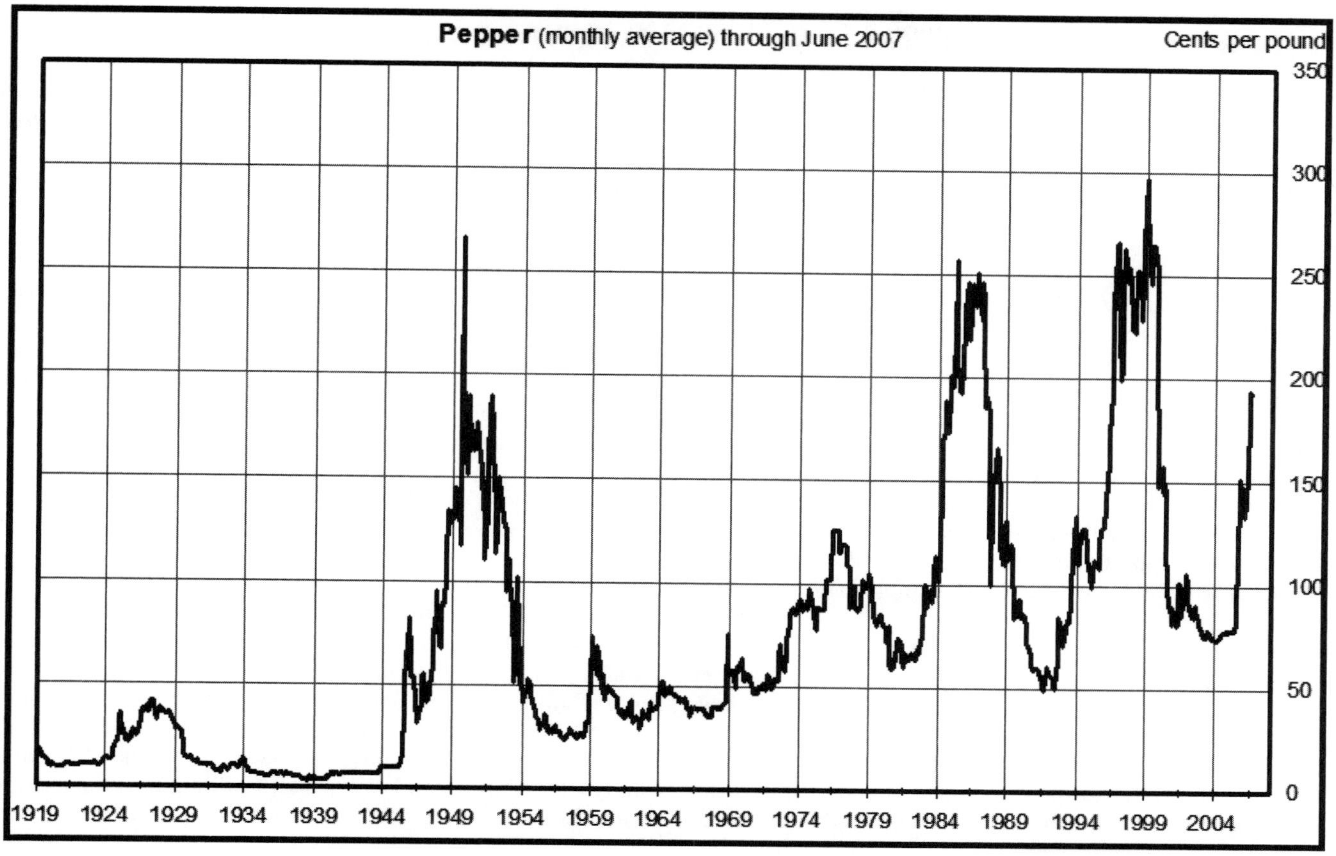

Average Black Pepper in New York (Brazilian)   In Cents Per Pound

Year	Jan.	Feb.	Mar.	Apr.	May	June	July	Aug.	Sept.	Oct.	Nov.	Dec.	Average
1998	199.4	205.5	243.8	262.8	262.8	247.5	253.0	253.8	246.3	243.0	231.3	225.0	239.5
1999	222.5	225.8	252.5	248.0	252.5	250.0	229.0	249.3	263.8	282.0	297.5	281.0	254.5
2000	260.0	256.3	246.0	260.0	265.0	265.0	263.8	252.5	205.0	167.5	147.5	149.0	228.1
2001	157.5	146.3	144.0	150.0	143.8	123.0	97.3	87.0	90.0	89.3	81.6	85.3	116.2
2002	85.0	80.0	81.4	100.5	101.0	92.0	84.8	86.8	93.5	103.5	106.0	100.8	92.9
2003	93.8	89.0	88.5	85.5	83.8	89.0	90.0	86.6	83.5	81.6	80.0	78.0	85.8
2004	78.0	75.5	75.5	75.4	77.3	78.0	76.8	75.0	75.0	74.2	73.3	73.0	75.6
2005	73.0	73.0	73.8	75.2	75.5	77.0	77.0	77.0	77.6	78.0	77.0	77.4	76.0
2006	78.0	78.0	77.8	78.5	80.0	80.4	89.0	112.7	146.0	152.0	139.5	134.3	103.9
2007	132.5	136.0	137.2	177.5	194.5	193.0							161.8

NA = Not available.   *Source: Foreign Agricultural Service, U.S. Department of Agriculture (FAS-USDA)*

Average White Pepper in New York (Indonesian)[1]   In Cents Per Pound

Year	Jan.	Feb.	Mar.	Apr.	May	June	July	Aug.	Sept.	Oct.	Nov.	Dec.	Average
1998	348.0	346.3	362.5	390.0	393.0	358.8	354.0	356.3	348.8	340.0	340.0	340.0	356.5
1999	361.3	355.0	365.0	355.0	352.5	335.0	310.0	313.8	325.0	327.0	316.3	303.0	334.9
2000	295.0	293.8	264.0	253.8	246.3	242.0	226.3	227.5	205.0	171.3	150.0	150.0	227.1
2001	159.0	151.3	144.0	133.8	130.0	127.0	122.5	129.6	128.0	125.5	120.0	120.0	132.6
2002	111.3	100.3	95.6	108.8	108.0	105.0	104.5	118.8	130.0	154.0	157.5	153.0	120.6
2003	152.4	148.8	150.0	150.0	142.6	133.0	133.0	138.2	137.5	133.6	127.5	125.0	139.3
2004	118.0	118.0	125.8	130.0	130.0	125.0	127.0	120.5	119.0	113.8	109.5	114.6	120.9
2005	119.0	118.0	118.0	116.4	115.0	115.0	115.0	115.0	115.2	115.0	115.0	115.0	116.0
2006	115.0	117.5	125.0	125.0	125.0	126.2	145.0	160.0	210.0	212.5	192.5	188.8	153.5
2007	191.3	195.0	197.0	225.0	245.0	245.0							216.4

[1] Muntok White.   *Source: Foreign Agricultural Service, U.S. Department of Agriculture (FAS-USDA)*

Petroleum

Crude oil is petroleum that is acquired directly from the ground. Crude oil was formed millions of years ago from the remains of tiny aquatic plants and animals that lived in ancient seas. Ancient societies such as the Persians, 10th century Sumatrans, and pre-Columbian Indians believed that crude oil had medicinal benefits. Around 4,000 BC in Mesopotamia, bitumen, a tarry crude, was used as caulking for ships, as a setting for jewels and mosaics, and as an adhesive to secure weapon handles. The walls of Babylon and the famed pyramids were held together with bitumen, and Egyptians used it for embalming. During the 19th century in America, an oil find was often met with dismay. Pioneers who dug wells to find water or brine, were disappointed when they struck oil. It wasn't until 1854, with the invention of the kerosene lamp, that the first large-scale demand for petroleum emerged. Crude oil is a relatively abundant commodity. The world has produced approximately 650 billion barrels of oil, but another trillion barrels of proved reserves have yet to be extracted. Crude oil was the world's first trillion-dollar industry and accounts for the single largest product in world trade.

Futures and options on crude oil trade at the New York Mercantile Exchange (NYMEX) and at the ICE Futures Europe (ICE) exchange. The NYMEX trades two main types of crude oil: light sweet crude oil and Brent crude oil. The light sweet futures contract calls for the delivery of 1,000 barrels of crude oil in Cushing, Oklahoma. Light sweet crude is preferred by refiners because of its low sulfur content and relatively high yield of high-value products such as gasoline, diesel fuel, heating oil, and jet fuel. The Brent blend crude is based on a light, sweet North Sea crude oil. Brent blend crude production is approximately 500,000 barrels per day, and is shipped from Sullom Voe in the Shetland Islands.

Prices – NYMEX crude oil prices on a nearest-futures basis, after posting a record high of $147 per barrel in July 2008, plunged in the latter half of 2008 on a combination of the commodity bubble bursting and the global financial crisis. Crude oil prices bottomed out at a 6-year low of $32 in December 2008 and then recovered sharply to the $70 per barrel area in the first half of 2009. Oil prices then traded sideways in the range of $70-84 per barrel in the second half of 2009. The recovery in oil prices in early 2009 was due to a sharp cut in OPEC production in the latter half of 2008 and renewed demand from China in particular. World oil demand strengthened by 3.6% from mid-2009 from the 6-year low posted in May 2009 to the 20-month high posted in December 2009. However, that improved demand did not boost oil prices because OPEC members slowly raised their production during 2009. Specifically, OPEC members slowly boosted their production by 5.3% to a 1-year high from the low seen in March 2009. For their part, non-OPEC members boosted their production by 7.3% from the trough seen in September 2008. The rising demand for oil was sufficient to absorb supplies and push inventories lower. U.S. oil inventories, which were 10.5% above their 5-year seasonal average in April 2009, progressively fell and by early 2010 were only 2% above their 5-year seasonal average.

Supply – World crude oil production in 2008 (latest data) rose +1.2% yr/yr to 73.885 million barrels per day, which was a new record high. The world's largest oil producers in 2008 were Russia (with 12.7% of world production in 2006), Saudi Arabia (12.6%), the United States (6.7%), Iran (5.5%), China (5.1%), and Mexico (3.8%). U.S. crude oil production in 2008 fell 2.2% yr/yr to 4.955 million barrels per day, which was the lowest level in over 30 years. Alaskan production in 2008 fell –5.4% yr/yr to 683,000 barrels per day, the lowest level since 1977 and only 34% of the peak level of 2.017 million barrels per day seen in 1988.

Demand – U.S. demand for crude oil in 2008 (latest data available) fell -3.4% yr/yr to 14.645 million barrels per day, below the 2004 record high of 15.475. Most of that demand went for U.S. refinery production of products such as gasoline fuel, diesel fuel, aviation fuel, heating oil, kerosene, asphalt, and lubricants.

Trade – The U.S. is highly dependent on imports of crude oil to meet its energy needs. U.S. imports in 2008 (latest data available) fell 2.7% yr/yr to 9.756 million barrels per day, down from the 2005 record high of 10.126. U.S. imports of petroleum products in 2008 fell –7.4% to 2.557 million barrels per day, imports of distillate fuel oil fell -30.6% yr/yr to 211,000 barrels per day, and imports of residual fuel oil fell -6.5% yr/yr to 348,000 barrels per day.

World Production of Crude Petroleum In Thousands of Barrels Per Day

Year	Canada	China	Indo-nesia	Iran	Kuwait	Mexico	Nigeria	Russia/3	Saudi Arabia	United Kingdom	United States	Vene-zuela	World Total
2000	1,977	3,249	1,428	3,696	2,079	3,012	2,165	6,479	8,404	2,275	5,822	3,155	68,495
2001	2,029	3,300	1,340	3,724	1,998	3,127	2,256	6,917	8,031	2,282	5,801	3,010	68,099
2002	2,171	3,390	1,249	3,444	1,894	3,177	2,118	7,408	7,634	2,292	5,746	2,604	67,158
2003	2,306	3,409	1,155	3,743	2,136	3,371	2,275	8,132	8,775	2,093	5,681	2,335	69,433
2004	2,398	3,485	1,096	4,001	2,376	3,383	2,329	8,805	9,101	1,845	5,419	2,557	72,476
2005	2,369	3,609	1,067	4,139	2,529	3,334	2,627	9,043	9,550	1,649	5,178	2,565	73,719
2006	2,525	3,673	1,019	4,028	2,535	3,256	2,440	9,247	9,152	1,490	5,102	2,511	73,435
2007	2,616	3,729	964	3,912	2,464	3,076	2,350	9,437	8,722	1,498	5,064	2,433	72,975
2008[1]	2,596	3,790	972	4,050	2,586	2,792	2,165	9,357	9,261	1,391	4,950	2,394	73,690
2009[2]	2,564	3,799	945	4,037	2,350	2,601	2,208	9,495	8,250	1,328	5,310	2,239	72,260

Includes lease condensate. [1] Preliminary. [2] Estimate. *Source: Energy Information Administration, U.S. Department of Energy (EIA-DOE)*

Refiner Sales Prices of Residual Fuel Oil In Cents Per Gallon

Year	Jan.	Feb.	Mar.	Apr.	May	June	July	Aug.	Sept.	Oct.	Nov.	Dec.	Average
2004	84.3	80.6	76.3	75.7	80.7	80.5	78.2	81.8	90.3	91.5	96.6	87.2	83.6
2005	86.9	90.8	98.0	106.6	112.2	111.8	116.8	129.2	138.4	142.7	134.3	134.6	116.9
2006	134.6	137.8	136.0	139.7	143.5	148.1	145.1	145.1	132.4	120.1	117.6	119.9	135.0
2007	117.2	121.4	122.1	125.8	135.9	142.1	153.9	158.4	161.0	166.1	183.2	194.8	148.5
2008	203.9	200.3	204.7	221.7	234.8	265.7	294.5	NA	266.6	216.6	165.4	121.1	217.8
2009[1]	116.4	120.4	118.3	117.4	121.3	144.0	148.8	164.1	168.9	171.7	173.9		142.3

Sulfur 1% or less, excluding taxes. [1] Preliminary. *Source: Energy Information Administration, U.S. Department of Energy (EIA-DOE)*

Refiner Sales Prices of No. 2 Fuel Oil In Cents Per Gallon

Year	Jan.	Feb.	Mar.	Apr.	May	June	July	Aug.	Sept.	Oct.	Nov.	Dec.	Average
2004	97.0	93.0	93.6	95.4	103.0	101.9	109.5	118.8	127.0	147.9	139.4	129.9	113.0
2005	131.4	134.4	153.5	155.9	144.4	159.1	164.7	178.4	199.3	207.1	175.2	172.4	164.7
2006	175.6	171.1	179.1	197.2	201.3	198.4	200.6	206.1	179.7	172.2	169.9	175.3	185.5
2007	161.2	172.9	178.1	191.0	194.9	201.4	207.1	202.1	213.3	226.0	256.9	257.0	205.2
2008	256.4	260.7	297.7	319.5	353.6	376.2	380.2	328.7	300.3	240.0	194.7	157.9	288.8
2009[1]	155.0	142.1	135.8	139.7	146.2	174.4	165.6	180.4	177.3	191.8	199.3		164.3

Excluding taxes. [1] Preliminary. *Source: Energy Information Administration, U.S. Department of Energy (EIA-DOE)*

Refiner Sales Prices of No. 2 Diesel Fuel In Cents Per Gallon

Year	Jan.	Feb.	Mar.	Apr.	May	June	July	Aug.	Sept.	Oct.	Nov.	Dec.	Average
2004	96.2	96.8	101.0	107.6	112.1	107.1	115.4	124.4	133.0	153.0	142.2	127.2	118.0
2005	130.6	139.1	158.8	163.8	152.2	167.0	171.5	189.8	212.7	232.3	182.6	175.5	173.0
2006	181.0	180.6	190.1	212.2	218.7	218.7	225.0	234.3	191.3	182.7	186.8	188.6	200.8
2007	169.5	182.4	197.9	211.6	210.1	214.7	222.0	219.3	232.2	242.6	269.8	259.9	219.3
2008	258.0	273.8	315.8	335.6	371.2	385.9	387.6	333.8	316.0	251.4	195.5	146.9	297.6
2009[1]	147.9	132.6	131.3	145.5	152.9	182.8	174.4	193.6	184.8	197.8	203.7		167.9

Excluding taxes. [1] Preliminary. *Source: Energy Information Administration, U.S. Department of Energy (EIA-DOE)*

Refiner Sales Prices of Kerosine-Type Jet Fuel In Cents Per Gallon

Year	Jan.	Feb.	Mar.	Apr.	May	June	July	Aug.	Sept.	Oct.	Nov.	Dec.	Average
2004	99.7	100.0	101.4	103.3	114.9	108.5	115.6	126.9	132.6	155.1	145.2	132.8	119.7
2005	131.7	138.3	158.2	165.5	155.8	165.0	171.2	184.7	206.9	233.5	181.4	173.8	172.2
2006	182.4	182.5	186.2	203.2	213.2	213.3	217.4	221.4	194.7	181.5	177.8	190.6	197.0
2007	172.7	176.6	184.6	202.1	207.9	211.4	216.7	215.1	225.6	235.3	265.6	265.5	214.9
2008	266.5	267.4	310.6	331.5	364.2	391.2	397.8	339.3	327.8	256.9	197.4	147.0	299.8
2009[1]	147.1	134.6	126.5	142.2	146.1	178.0	175.9	189.2	182.1	191.7	204.9		165.3

Excluding taxes. [1] Preliminary. *Source: Energy Information Administration, U.S. Department of Energy (EIA-DOE)*

Refiner Sales Prices of Propane[2] In Cents Per Gallon

Year	Jan.	Feb.	Mar.	Apr.	May	June	July	Aug.	Sept.	Oct.	Nov.	Dec.	Average
2004	71.7	70.1	61.9	60.4	65.5	66.1	72.2	83.0	80.4	88.6	88.3	83.5	74.3
2005	NA	NA	NA	86.0	82.0	83.0	86.0	93.2	108.2	111.6	103.3	106.8	95.6
2006	104.4	97.5	96.7	102.3	102.9	106.7	110.8	111.3	103.2	100.3	101.3	103.3	103.4
2007	99.5	103.3	104.9	106.7	111.2	109.4	115.9	116.7	124.8	135.1	147.1	146.1	118.4
2008	151.9	146.9	149.5	157.1	167.5	176.1	183.3	166.7	156.5	124.2	100.5	91.6	147.7
2009[1]	97.4	90.1	80.5	72.0	73.2	82.1	75.6	83.1	91.4	99.4	108.0		86.6

[1] Preliminary. [2] Consumer Grade, Excluding taxes. *Source: Energy Information Administration, U.S. Department of Energy (EIA-DOE)*

Supply and Disposition of Crude Oil in the United States In Thousands of Barrels Per Day

	Supply						Stock Withdrawal[3]		Disposition		Ending Stocks		
	Field Production		Imports			Unaccounted for Crude Oil							
Year	Total Domestic	Alskan	Total	SPR[2]	Other		SPR[2]	Other	Refinery Inputs	Exports	Total	SPR[2]	Other Primary
	In Thousands of Barrels Per Day										In Millions of Barrels		
2002	5,746	984	9,140	16	9,124	110	134	-94	14,947	9	877	599	278
2003	5,681	974	9,665	0	9,665	54	108	-24	15,304	12	907	638	269
2004	5,419	908	10,088	77	10,010	143	102	46	15,475	27	961	676	286
2005	5,178	864	10,126	52	10,074	76	25	104	15,220	32	1,008	685	324
2006	5,102	741	10,118	8	10,089	8	11	-37	15,242	25	1,001	689	312
2007	5,064	722	10,031	7					15,156	27	983	697	286
2008	4,950	683	9,783	19					14,648	29	1,028	702	326
2009[1]	5,315	645	9,048	NA					14,300	41	1,054	727	327

[1] Preliminary. [2] Strategic Petroleum Reserve. [3] A negative number indicates a decrease in stocks and a positive number indicates an increase.
Source: Energy Information Administration, U.S. Department of Energy (EIA-DOE)

Crude Petroleum Refinery Operations Ratio² in the United States   In Percent of Capacity

Year	Jan.	Feb.	Mar.	Apr.	May	June	July	Aug.	Sept.	Oct.	Nov.	Dec.	Average
2000	85.7	86.4	89.8	92.6	94.7	96.2	96.9	95.9	94.3	92.4	92.7	94.0	92.6
2001	90.2	90.5	89.4	94.9	96.4	95.6	93.9	93.3	92.2	92.0	92.2	90.2	92.6
2002	87.7	86.6	87.9	93.0	91.5	93.1	93.5	92.9	90.4	87.5	92.6	91.1	90.7
2003	87.2	87.4	90.5	94.1	95.8	94.7	94.0	95.0	93.1	92.4	93.6	93.0	92.6
2004	89.1	88.8	88.5	92.5	95.6	97.5	96.8	97.1	90.1	90.2	94.4	95.0	93.0
2005	91.3	90.6	90.2	92.6	94.1	96.7	94.0	92.1	83.9	81.6	89.0	89.0	90.4
2006	87.0	86.5	85.7	88.1	91.1	93.0	92.4	93.2	93.0	88.0	88.2	90.4	89.7
2007	88.1	84.7	87.0	88.2	89.7	88.5	91.2	90.8	88.9	87.4	88.9	88.7	88.5
2008	85.8	85.0	83.2	86.2	88.8	89.5	88.8	87.1	74.6	85.3	85.8	83.9	85.3
2009¹	82.1	81.5	81.5	82.5	83.8	86.1	84.2	84.0	84.8	81.3	80.9	81.3	82.8

¹ Preliminary. ² Based on the ration of the daily average crude runs to stills to the rated capacity of refineries per day. *Source: Energy Information Administration, U.S. Department of Energy (EIA-DOE)*

Crude Oil Refinery Inputs in the United States   In Thousands of Barrels Per Day

Year	Jan.	Feb.	Mar.	Apr.	May	June	July	Aug.	Sept.	Oct.	Nov.	Dec.	Average
2000	13,779	14,028	14,613	15,053	15,494	15,643	15,819	15,640	15,407	15,029	15,023	15,232	15,067
2001	14,789	14,813	14,649	15,536	15,763	15,650	15,369	15,259	15,005	15,002	15,001	14,688	15,128
2002	14,487	14,306	14,526	15,325	15,301	15,397	15,430	15,338	14,861	14,303	15,155	14,900	14,947
2003	14,338	14,381	14,933	15,575	15,910	15,620	15,546	15,693	15,446	15,342	15,455	15,345	15,304
2004	14,782	14,706	14,787	15,541	15,992	16,240	16,142	16,142	14,980	14,941	15,664	15,750	15,472
2005	15,254	15,142	15,214	15,494	15,905	16,401	15,850	15,664	13,986	13,646	15,032	15,046	15,220
2006	14,805	14,581	14,582	14,928	15,516	15,843	15,702	15,792	15,739	15,008	15,009	15,354	15,238
2007	14,992	14,435	14,840	15,045	15,380	15,248	15,671	15,685	15,226	14,933	15,151	15,202	15,151
2008	14,804	14,625	14,364	14,799	15,263	15,417	15,255	14,947	12,759	14,552	14,606	14,352	14,645
2009¹	14,112	14,116	14,091	14,354	14,459	14,845	14,633	14,568	14,684	14,053	13,861	13,823	14,300

¹ Preliminary. *Source: Energy Information Administration, U.S. Department of Energy (EIA-DOE)*

Production of Major Refined Petroleum Products in Continental United States   In Millions of Barrels

			Fuel Oil							Liquified Gasses		
Year	Asphalt	Aviation Gasoline	Distillate	Residual	Gasoline	Jet Fuel	Kero-sene	Natural Gas Plant Liquids	Lubri-cants	Total	at L.P.G.²	AT L.P.G.³
2000	180.6	6.2	1,189.9	234.3	2,664	536.6	20.4	649.4	60.9	788.0	545.5	242.5
2001	177.3	6.5	1,348.4	262.8	2,913	558.2	26.7	680.3	64.1	810.1	569.1	241.0
2002	179.9	6.4	1,309.8	218.8	2,983	552.3	20.8	686.5	63.3	822.5	576.8	245.7
2003	181.0	5.8	1,355.5	241.8	2,992	543.1	20.4	626.7	60.6	766.1	526.4	239.6
2004	185.6	6.2	1,397.6	238.0	3,013	566.3	23.2	662.7	62.0	797.2	561.3	235.9
2005	186.0	6.1	1,441.4	227.9	3,014	561.5	23.6	623.9	60.8	736.9	527.2	209.8
2006	184.8	6.6	1,478.1	231.5	3,036	540.4	17.3	633.4	66.8	757.6	537.8	219.9
2007	166.1	6.0	1,507.7	244.4	3,045	528.6	12.7	648.3	65.1	789.0	552.8	236.2
2008	150.9	5.5	1,569.5	227.1	3,072	539.5	12.0	651.9	63.2	786.1	556.2	229.9
2009¹	131.0	5.0	1,476.7	218.6	3,199	510.2	6.9	688.5	55.4	821.1	591.3	229.8

¹ Preliminary. ² Gas processing plants. ³ Refineries. *Source: Energy Information Administration, U.S. Department of Energy (EIA-DOE)*

Stocks of Petroleum and Products in the United States on January 1   In Millions of Barrels

			Refined Products											
						Fuel Oil							Motor Gasoline	
Year	Crude Petroleum	Strategic Reserve	Total	Asphalt	Aviation Gasoline	Distillate	Residual	Finished Gasoline	Jet Fuel	Kero-sene	Gases²	Lubri-cants	Total	Finished³
2001	826.2	540.7	415.7	25.0	1.3	118.0	36.2	153.0	44.5	4.1	82.5	12.1	207	153
2002	862.2	550.2	445.6	20.6	1.5	144.5	41.0	161.5	42.0	5.4	120.9	13.8	214	161
2003	876.7	599.1	425.1	21.3	1.4	134.1	31.3	161.9	39.2	5.5	105.7	12.0	199	162
2004	906.3	638.4	413.1	19.3	1.2	136.8	37.8	146.8	38.7	5.6	94.4	10.0		147
2005	961.9	675.6	405.6	22.1	1.3	126.0	42.4	143.1	40.2	4.9	111.0	10.4		143
2006	1,007.8	684.5	403.6	21.0	1.2	136.0	37.3	134.8	41.8	5.1	117.6	9.7		135
2007	998.4	688.6	405.9	28.8	1.4	143.7	42.4	118.3	39.1	3.4	125.2	12.4		118
2008	982.8	696.9	374.3	22.2	1.2	133.5	38.6	110.0	39.5	2.8	105.5	10.6		110
2009	1,026.1	701.8	367.8	20.3	1.2	145.9	36.2	98.2	38.2	2.2	126.9	10.7		98
2010¹	1,051.8	726.6	375.1	17.9	1.0	164.7	37.8	85.9	43.4	2.5	113.2	8.9		86

¹ Preliminary. ² Includes ethane & ethylene at plants and refineries. ³ Includes oxygenated.
Source: Energy Information Administration, U.S. Department of Energy (EIA-DOE)

Stocks of Crude Petroleum in the United States, on First of Month In Millions of Barrels

Year	Jan.	Feb.	Mar.	Apr.	May	June	July	Aug.	Sept.	Oct.	Nov.	Dec.
2000	851.6	852.4	855.2	866.5	873.2	864.1	859.5	852.6	858.7	848.2	842.4	833.9
2001	826.2	836.0	824.2	850.8	873.0	871.7	851.5	856.6	851.6	854.1	858.4	859.5
2002	862.2	874.9	887.4	895.0	891.3	898.3	894.1	882.8	878.5	857.8	881.1	884.0
2003	876.7	873.2	870.3	880.8	891.0	888.6	893.1	897.3	897.8	911.1	925.5	914.8
2004	907.3	912.8	931.2	949.4	961.5	965.8	967.2	960.1	947.6	943.3	957.0	961.0
2005	961.3	968.3	985.6	1,007.0	1,022.5	1,026.5	1,025.6	1,018.5	1,012.1	1,000.8	1,006.9	1,007.4
2006	1,007.7	1,006.8	1,027.4	1,028.8	1,035.6	1,029.2	1,024.5	1,019.3	1,020.7	1,020.5	1,027.9	1,023.1
2007	1,000.9	1,012.3	1,006.6	1,020.5	1,026.9	1,038.7	1,045.1	1,028.8	1,015.1	1,008.1	1,002.9	995.0
2008	982.8	994.5	1,001.1	1,015.1	1,021.2	1,008.0	1,001.8	1,002.4	1,009.7	1,006.4	1,014.4	1,023.4
2009[1]	1,027.6	1,056.7	1,060.4	1,078.6	1,089.0	1,083.7	1,072.8	1,071.3	1,061.3	1,059.7	1,058.4	1,063.0

[1] Preliminary. *Source: Energy Information Administration; U.S. Department of Energy*

Production of Crude Petroleum in the United States In Thousands of Barrels Per Day

Year	Jan.	Feb.	Mar.	Apr.	May	June	July	Aug.	Sept.	Oct.	Nov.	Dec.	Average
2000	5,784	5,852	5,918	5,854	5,847	5,823	5,739	5,789	5,758	5,809	5,833	5,855	5,822
2001	5,799	5,780	5,880	5,863	5,829	5,766	5,749	5,725	5,709	5,746	5,881	5,887	5,801
2002	5,848	5,871	5,883	5,859	5,924	5,915	5,770	5,811	5,411	5,363	5,597	5,699	5,746
2003	5,785	5,791	5,817	5,774	5,733	5,701	5,526	5,595	5,683	5,635	5,560	5,579	5,681
2004	5,570	5,556	5,607	5,527	5,548	5,398	5,458	5,333	5,062	5,156	5,396	5,413	5,419
2005	5,441	5,494	5,601	5,556	5,581	5,460	5,240	5,218	4,204	4,534	4,837	4,984	5,179
2006	5,106	5,045	5,045	5,128	5,161	5,160	5,102	5,059	5,037	5,106	5,105	5,166	5,102
2007	5,123	5,125	5,106	5,189	5,197	5,096	5,024	4,914	4,884	5,043	5,017	5,056	5,065
2008	5,100	5,122	5,151	5,117	5,102	5,098	5,133	4,894	3,930	4,669	5,024	5,056	4,950
2009[1]	5,246	5,191	5,270	5,228	5,283	5,183	5,233	5,286	5,444	5,422	5,466	5,519	5,314

[1] Preliminary. *Source: Energy Information Administration, U.S. Department of Energy (EIA-DOE)*

U.S. Foreign Trade of Petroleum and Products In Thousands of Barrels Per Day

	Exports		Imports						Exports		Imports				
Year	Total[2]	Petroleum Products	Crude	Petroleum Products	Distillate Fuel Oil	Residual Fuel Oil	Net Imports[3]	Year	Total[2]	Petroleum Products	Crude	Petroleum Products	Distillate Fuel Oil	Residual Fuel Oil	Net Imports[3]
1990	857	748	5,894	2,123	278	504	7,161	2000	1,040	990	9,071	2,389	295	352	10,419
1991	1,001	885	5,782	1,844	205	453	6,626	2001	971	951	9,328	2,543	344	295	10,900
1992	950	861	6,083	1,805	216	375	6,938	2002	984	975	9,140	2,390	267	249	10,546
1993	1,003	904	6,787	1,833	184	373	7,618	2003	1,027	1,014	9,665	2,599	333	327	11,237
1994	942	843	7,063	1,933	203	314	8,054	2004	1,048	1,021	10,088	3,057	325	426	12,097
1995	949	855	7,230	1,605	193	187	7,886	2005	1,165	1,133	10,126	3,588	329	530	12,549
1996	981	871	7,508	1,971	230	248	8,498	2006	1,317	1,292	10,118	3,517	365	350	12,390
1997	1,003	896	8,225	1,936	228	194	9,158	2007	1,433	1,405	10,031	2,761	304	372	12,035
1998	945	835	8,706	2,002	210	275	9,764	2008	1,802	1,773	9,783	2,570	213	349	11,113
1999	940	822	8,731	2,122	250	237	9,912	2009[1]	2,021	1,980	9,048	2,104	228	346	9,705

[1] Preliminary. [2] Includes crude oil. [3] Equals imports minus exports.
Source: Energy Information Administration, U.S. Department of Energy (EIA-DOE)

Domestic First Purchase Price of Crude Petroleum at Wells[1] In Dollars Per Barrel

Year	Jan.	Feb.	Mar.	Apr.	May	June	July	Aug.	Sept.	Oct.	Nov.	Dec.	Average
2000	23.53	25.48	26.19	23.20	25.58	27.62	26.81	27.91	29.72	29.65	30.36	24.46	26.72
2001	24.58	25.27	23.02	23.41	24.06	23.43	22.94	23.08	22.37	18.73	16.49	15.54	21.84
2002	15.89	16.92	20.04	22.14	23.51	22.59	23.51	24.76	26.08	25.29	23.38	25.29	22.51
2003	28.35	31.85	30.09	25.46	24.96	26.83	27.53	27.94	25.23	26.52	27.21	28.54	27.54
2004	30.35	31.21	32.86	33.23	36.07	34.53	36.54	40.10	40.62	46.28	42.81	38.22	36.90
2005	40.18	42.19	47.56	47.26	44.03	49.83	53.35	58.90	59.64	56.99	53.20	53.24	50.53
2006	57.85	55.69	55.59	62.51	64.31	64.36	67.72	67.21	59.36	53.26	52.42	55.03	59.61
2007	49.32	52.94	54.95	58.20	58.90	62.35	69.23	67.78	73.16	79.32	87.16	85.29	66.55
2008	87.06	89.41	98.44	106.64	118.55	127.47	128.08	112.83	98.50	73.22	53.67	36.80	94.22
2009[2]	35.00	34.14	42.46	45.22	52.69	63.08	60.43	65.28	65.27	69.82	71.98		55.03

[1] Buyers posted prices. [2] Preliminary. *Source: Energy Information Administration, U.S. Department of Energy (EIA-DOE)*

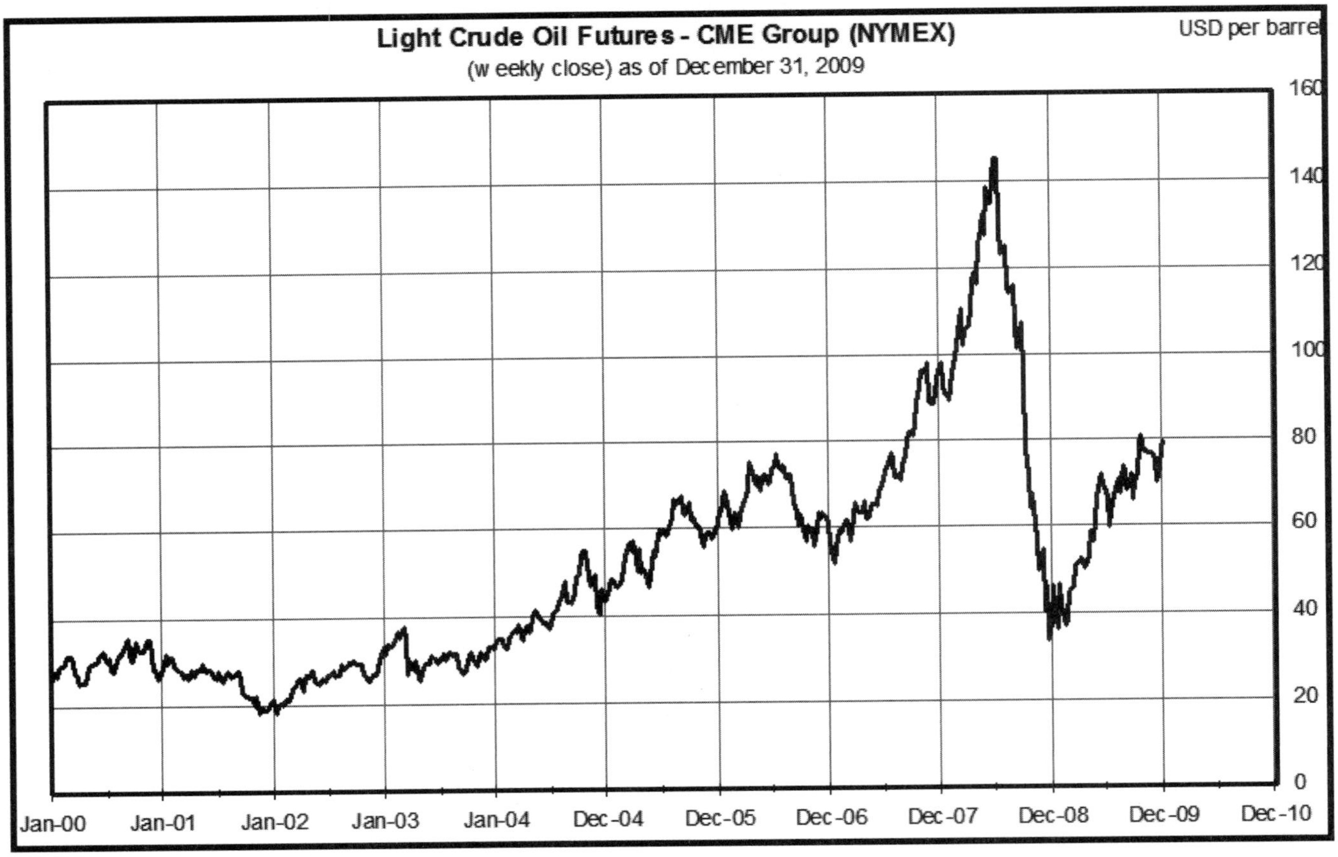

Volume of Trading of Crude Oil Futures in New York In Thousands of Contracts

Year	Jan.	Feb.	Mar.	Apr.	May	June	July	Aug.	Sept.	Oct.	Nov.	Dec.	Total
2000	3,139	3,077	3,380	2,579	3,002	3,232	2,750	3,149	3,712	3,418	2,824	2,620	36,883
2001	3,035	2,855	3,449	3,312	3,469	3,572	3,170	3,316	2,773	2,913	3,210	2,455	37,531
2002	3,481	3,150	3,790	4,315	4,317	3,429	3,466	3,883	3,939	4,397	3,478	4,034	45,679
2003	4,553	4,039	4,151	3,355	3,329	3,534	3,401	3,732	3,826	4,248	3,624	3,646	45,437
2004	4,118	3,887	4,495	4,326	4,250	4,633	4,063	4,987	4,711	4,794	4,510	4,108	52,883
2005	4,352	4,032	5,721	5,404	5,045	5,326	4,629	6,091	5,252	5,022	4,488	4,288	59,650
2006	5,482	5,594	5,937	5,285	5,861	5,134	4,500	5,409	6,067	7,492	7,555	6,739	71,053
2007	10,367	9,092	10,069	9,287	9,487	9,862	9,656	10,647	10,670	12,390	11,307	8,692	121,526
2008	10,815	10,100	12,577	11,066	13,497	12,453	11,321	10,589	11,554	11,638	8,662	9,910	134,183
2009	11,369	11,411	11,340	10,106	9,939	11,367	11,924	11,823	11,462	13,179	11,600	11,906	137,428

Source: CME Group; New York Mercantile Exchange (NYMEX)

Average Open Interest of Crude Oil Futures in New York In Thousands of Contracts

Year	Jan.	Feb.	Mar.	Apr.	May	June	July	Aug.	Sept.	Oct.	Nov.	Dec.
2000	512.0	519.1	513.4	467.3	453.0	462.5	432.6	416.9	461.3	478.2	479.0	438.1
2001	432.9	437.2	432.6	419.9	443.0	462.3	451.0	461.9	435.0	430.8	435.2	436.3
2002	448.1	454.2	497.4	488.1	512.4	474.1	457.0	454.2	505.5	528.5	482.2	531.1
2003	608.3	641.0	568.5	495.5	478.9	494.1	517.5	542.6	507.2	532.0	550.4	580.6
2004	647.7	656.9	673.5	690.0	722.5	705.1	692.9	705.6	684.8	717.0	705.2	676.3
2005	707.9	745.2	829.2	833.8	799.0	785.4	820.1	901.6	870.6	848.7	832.3	841.3
2006	903.5	927.5	954.2	1,000.4	1,055.7	1,016.2	1,068.7	1,164.0	1,181.8	1,168.7	1,176.6	1,200.0
2007	1,284.9	1,281.7	1,314.3	1,328.0	1,390.4	1,431.6	1,523.6	1,477.4	1,483.3	1,447.1	1,451.8	1,362.3
2008	1,393.5	1,384.6	1,428.5	1,393.8	1,396.5	1,351.8	1,277.9	1,224.1	1,171.2	1,076.8	1,139.7	1,160.9
2009	1,232.4	1,223.3	1,190.2	1,163.0	1,159.6	1,180.5	1,170.7	1,176.0	1,174.2	1,231.2	1,207.8	1,200.4

Source: CME Group; New York Mercantile Exchange (NYMEX)

Plastics

Plastics are moldable, chemically fabricated materials produced mostly from fossil fuels, such as oil, coal, or natural gas. The word plastic is derived from the Greek *plastikos*, meaning "to mold," and the Latin *plasticus*, meaning "capable of molding." Leo Baekeland created the first commercially successful thermosetting synthetic resin in 1909. More than 50 families of plastics have since been produced.

All plastics can be divided into either thermoplastics or thermosetting plastics. The difference is the way in which they respond to heat. Thermoplastics can be repeatedly softened by heat and hardened by cooling. Thermosetting plastics harden permanently after being heated once.

Prices – The average monthly producer price index (1982=100) of plastic resins and materials in the U.S. in 2009 fell -11.2% yr/yr to 191.0, down from the 2008 record high of 217.3. The average monthly producer price index of thermoplastic resins in the U.S. in 2009 fell 12.7% yr/yr to 188.5, down from the 2008 record high of 215.9. The average monthly producer price index of styrene plastic materials (also a thermoplastic) in the U.S. in 2003 (latest available data) rose +21.2% to 115.7 from the 25-year low of 95.5 posted in 2002. The average monthly producer price index of thermosetting resins in the U.S. in 2009 fell 2.76% to 217.5, down from the 2009 record high of 233.3.

Supply – Total U.S. plastics production in 2008 (latest data available) fell – 12.3% yr/yr to 101.546, down from the 2007 record high of 115.793 billion pounds. U.S. plastics production has more than doubled in the past two decades. By sector, the thermoplastics sector is by far the largest, with 2008 production falling -11.7% yr/yr to 81.980 billion pounds and accounting for 81% of total U.S. plastic production. Production in the thermosetting plastic sector (polyester unsaturated, phenolic, and epoxy) fell 14.9% yr/yr in 2008 to 7.614 billion pounds and accounted for 7% of total U.S. plastics production. The category of "other plastics" fell -14.7% to 11.952 billion pounds and accounted for 12% of total U.S. plastics production.

Demand – Total usage of plastic resins by important markets in 2008 (latest data available) in the U.S. fell by -10.0% to 74.156 billion pounds. The breakdown by market shows that the largest single consumption category is "Packaging" with 2.097 billion pounds of usage in 2008, accounting for 32% of total U.S. consumption. After packaging, the largest categories are "Consumer and Industrial" (21% of U.S. consumption), and "Building and Construction" (17% of U.S. consumption).

Trade – U.S. exports of plastics in 2008 (latest data available) fell -3.1% yr/yr to 11.962 billion pounds, down from the 2008 record high of 12.346 billion pounds. U.S. exports accounted for 16% of U.S. supply disappearance in 2005.

Plastics Production by Resin in the United States In Millions of Pounds

	Thermosets				Thermoplastics										
Year	Polyester Unsaturated	Phenolic	Epoxy	Total Thermosets	Thermoplastic Polyester	Polyvinyl Chloride	Polystyrene	Polypropylene	Nylon	Low Density Polyethylene[1]	High Density Polyethylene	Total Thermoplastics	Total Selected Plastics	Other Plastics	Total Plastics
1999	2,985	4,388	657	8,030	6,735	14,912	7,075	15,493	1,349	15,807	13,864	78,457	86,487	13,467	99,954
2000	3,149	3,965	669	7,783	7,239	14,364	6,676	15,583	1,395	19,588	16,439	84,553	92,336	13,604	105,940
2001	3,021	3,894	597	7,512	6,972	14,626	6,223	16,135	1,159	18,389	15,195	81,726	89,238	12,720	101,958
2002	3,197	4,076	620	7,893	7,480	15,250	6,768	17,084	1,284	19,515	16,190	86,762	94,655	13,607	108,262
2003	3,152	4,015	587	7,754	7,950	14,938	6,478	17,497	1,306	18,915	15,906	86,071	93,825	12,641	106,466
2004	3,294	4,200	658	8,152	8,632	15,883	6,765	18,523	1,357	20,390	17,519	92,317	100,469	13,471	113,940
2005	3,359	4,689	609	8,657	7,749	15,259	6,293	17,965	1,252	19,736	16,155	87,524	96,181	13,595	109,776
2006	3,430	4,809	624	8,863	8,290	14,919	6,269	18,775	1,270	20,926	17,645	91,204	100,067	13,970	114,037
2007	3,471	4,838	642	8,951	8,745	14,606	6,015	19,445	1,295	21,511	18,222	92,835	101,786	14,007	115,793
2008	2,798	4,233	583	7,614	8,159	12,789	5,220	16,768	1,148	19,061	16,247	81,980	89,594	11,952	101,546

[1] Includes LDPE and LLDPE. *Source: American Plastics Council (APC)*

Total Resin Sales and Captive Use by Important Markets In Millions of Pounds (Dry Weight Basis)

Year	Adhesive, Inks & Coatings	Building & Construction	Consumer & Industrial	Electrical & Electronics	Exports	Furniture & Furnishings	Industrial & Machinery	Packaging	Transportation	Other	Total
1999	1,171	14,794	13,921	2,862	8,353	3,630	1,181	24,130	4,383	2,698	77,123
2000	1,167	14,439	16,487	2,787	9,771	3,572	1,084	20,941	4,389	3,003	77,640
2001	1,143	13,988	16,510	2,501	9,295	3,226	968	22,847	4,207	2,705	77,390
2002	1,165	14,729	17,649	3,037	10,048	3,507	998	24,170	4,738	2,283	82,324
2003	1,170	14,495	17,571	2,862	9,009	3,361	962	24,087	4,732	2,021	80,270
2004	1,196	15,676	18,714	3,096	9,900	3,458	1,042	25,952	4,899	2,168	86,101
2005	1,160	15,483	17,400	2,917	9,790	3,406	1,087	25,144	4,711	2,133	83,231
2006	1,113	15,429	17,735	2,661	9,957	3,332	1,004	26,161	4,558	2,019	83,970
2007	1,069	14,289	17,193	1,980	12,346	3,091	943	26,527	3,312	1,604	82,354
2008	937	12,313	15,461	1,755	11,962	2,671	834	24,097	2,751	1,375	74,156

[1] Included in other. *Source: American Plastics Council (APC)*

Average Producer Price Index of Plastic Resins and Materials (066) in the United States (1982 = 100)

Year	Jan.	Feb.	Mar.	Apr.	May	June	July	Aug.	Sept.	Oct.	Nov.	Dec.	Average
2000	133.2	135.7	139.4	143.7	147.4	147.8	146.4	146.3	142.4	140.7	138.8	137.3	141.6
2001	137.8	139.3	141.4	141.9	139.9	137.6	135.1	131.3	126.8	128.3	126.6	123.9	134.2
2002	122.0	121.3	123.1	125.4	128.0	130.1	135.3	136.4	136.7	138.2	137.0	135.3	130.7
2003	137.2	141.8	149.6	153.2	152.4	149.2	144.9	143.6	144.9	146.2	145.8	144.0	146.1
2004	146.2	150.4	151.4	154.8	156.5	159.6	161.1	164.9	170.6	175.6	181.4	185.2	163.1
2005	190.3	190.8	192.1	192.3	190.3	186.3	185.0	183.4	188.2	203.9	208.6	205.2	193.0
2006	203.9	200.0	198.9	194.3	195.9	198.5	199.2	202.3	202.4	200.0	196.2	189.1	198.4
2007	187.6	185.5	187.0	192.1	193.8	196.9	198.6	198.7	198.0	199.3	205.9	207.5	195.9
2008	209.7	209.6	210.8	212.1	216.4	219.1	229.2	233.3	227.1	222.3	200.3	190.3	215.0
2009[1]	184.6	190.1	188.6	183.5	185.9	185.9	194.4	194.5	196.4	196.5	195.6	199.4	191.3

[1] Preliminary. *Source: Bureau of Labor Statistics, U.S. Department of Commerce (BLS)*

Average Producer Price Index of Thermoplastic Resins (0662) in the United States (1982 = 100)

Year	Jan.	Feb.	Mar.	Apr.	May	June	July	Aug.	Sept.	Oct.	Nov.	Dec.	Average
2000	133.8	136.0	140.4	145.2	149.3	149.6	147.6	147.4	142.7	140.3	137.9	136.0	142.2
2001	136.3	138.0	140.2	140.8	138.4	135.7	133.1	128.6	123.4	125.7	123.9	120.8	132.1
2002	118.4	117.8	120.3	123.8	126.2	128.6	135.0	135.9	136.2	137.6	136.1	133.8	129.1
2003	136.3	142.2	151.4	155.8	153.6	149.5	144.3	142.8	144.7	146.3	146.2	143.9	146.4
2004	146.7	151.9	152.6	156.4	157.5	160.9	162.3	165.5	171.3	176.6	182.3	186.9	164.2
2005	193.2	193.8	195.3	194.9	192.0	187.0	185.4	183.7	189.3	208.4	213.7	209.4	195.5
2006	207.9	202.8	201.5	195.6	197.6	201.1	201.6	205.1	205.0	201.6	196.8	188.1	200.4
2007	186.0	183.4	185.3	190.7	193.0	196.2	198.2	198.4	197.6	199.3	206.6	208.2	195.2
2008	209.9	209.9	211.5	213.2	218.4	221.2	232.4	236.5	229.0	223.5	197.6	187.1	215.9
2009[1]	179.3	187.1	185.9	180.3	183.1	183.2	193.2	192.9	194.5	194.5	193.6	197.3	188.7

[1] Preliminary. *Source: Bureau of Labor Statistics, U.S. Department of Commerce (BLS)*

Average Producer Price Index of Styrene Plastics Materials (0662-06) in the United States (1982 = 100)

Year	Jan.	Feb.	Mar.	Apr.	May	June	July	Aug.	Sept.	Oct.	Nov.	Dec.	Average
1995	129.0	127.0	132.5	134.7	135.9	137.5	135.1	133.2	132.1	130.1	127.9	126.1	131.8
1996	125.7	123.5	125.0	118.3	120.1	122.7	123.4	123.3	123.6	122.8	122.0	120.9	122.6
1997	120.6	123.1	123.0	121.6	121.6	121.6	122.7	117.7	118.0	116.5	113.5	113.7	119.5
1998	113.3	113.9	115.5	114.9	114.1	112.8	111.3	111.2	107.6	107.9	107.1	106.3	111.3
1999	103.5	102.4	103.5	104.7	103.0	102.3	103.1	101.5	101.4	99.8	99.4	100.5	102.1
2000	103.0	104.3	110.5	113.0	116.2	116.9	118.5	116.5	115.0	114.1	112.1	110.4	112.5
2001	110.5	109.2	107.9	108.0	101.8	99.9	97.6	95.7	87.3	89.4	90.0	85.4	98.6
2002	85.7	85.8	87.9	88.5	90.4	91.7	93.7	100.6	100.5	108.9	108.1	103.9	95.5
2003[1]	102.9	110.2	119.5	127.2	126.7	119.1	118.0	113.3	112.8	113.6	113.7	111.6	115.7
2004[1]	Data no longer available												

[1] Preliminary. *Source: Bureau of Labor Statistics, U.S. Department of Commerce (BLS)*

Average Producer Price Index of Thermosetting Resins (0663) in the United States (1982 = 100)

Year	Jan.	Feb.	Mar.	Apr.	May	June	July	Aug.	Sept.	Oct.	Nov.	Dec.	Average
2000	136.8	141.1	141.3	142.8	144.9	146.0	147.6	147.8	147.5	149.5	150.3	151.0	145.6
2001	152.1	152.9	154.5	154.4	154.2	154.2	152.3	151.3	150.4	148.2	146.3	146.1	151.4
2002	146.2	144.6	143.8	141.2	144.1	145.5	145.8	147.6	148.4	150.3	150.3	150.6	146.5
2003	150.4	149.7	151.7	152.0	156.8	157.9	157.1	156.4	155.7	155.6	153.8	153.8	154.2
2004	154.0	154.2	155.9	158.3	162.2	164.3	166.4	173.2	179.0	183.0	189.3	189.8	169.1
2005	189.9	190.3	190.5	193.5	195.8	195.8	195.5	194.6	196.1	197.5	199.9	200.2	195.0
2006	200.0	200.8	200.8	201.7	201.6	200.5	202.1	203.6	204.2	206.3	206.6	206.3	202.9
2007	207.8	208.3	207.8	211.7	210.0	212.6	212.3	212.4	211.9	211.6	214.7	216.8	211.5
2008	221.4	220.7	220.0	219.0	218.5	220.3	224.8	229.3	229.8	229.6	228.3	220.7	223.5
2009[1]	226.7	219.3	216.2	213.5	213.9	213.7	213.5	215.5	219.7	220.1	219.2	223.9	217.9

[1] Preliminary. *Source: Bureau of Labor Statistics, U.S. Department of Commerce (BLS)*

Platinum-Group Metals

Platinum is a relatively rare, chemically inert metallic element that is more valuable than gold. Platinum is a grayish-white metal that has a high fusing point, is malleable and ductile, and has a high electrical resistance. Chemically, platinum is relatively inert and resists attack by air, water, single acids, and ordinary reagents. Platinum is the most important of the six-metal group, which also includes ruthenium, rhodium, palladium, osmium, and iridium. The word "platinum" is derived from the Spanish word platina meaning silver.

Platinum is one of the world's rarest metals with new mine production totaling only about 5 million troy ounces a year. All the platinum mined to date would fit in the average-size living room. Platinum is mined all over the world with supplies concentrated in South Africa. South Africa accounts for nearly 80% of world supply, followed by Russia, and North America.

Because platinum will never tarnish, lose its rich white luster, or even wear down after many years, it is prized by the jewelry industry. The international jewelry industry is the largest consumer sector for platinum, accounting for 51% of total platinum demand. In Europe and the U.S., the normal purity of platinum is 95%. Ten tons of ore must be mined and a five-month process is needed to produce one ounce of pure platinum.

The second major consumer sector for platinum is for auto catalysts, with 21% of total platinum demand. Catalysts in autos are used to convert most of vehicle emissions into less harmful carbon dioxide, nitrogen, and water vapor. Platinum is also used in the production of hard disk drive coatings, fiber optic cables, infra-red detectors, fertilizers, explosives, petrol additives, platinum-tipped spark plugs, glassmaking equipment, biodegradable elements for household detergents, dental restorations, and in anti-cancer drugs.

Palladium is very similar to platinum and is part of the same general metals group. Palladium is mined with platinum, but it is somewhat more common because it is also a by-product of nickel mining. The primary use for palladium is in the use of automotive catalysts, with that sector accounting for about 63% of total palladium demand. Other uses for palladium include electronic equipment (21%), dental alloys (12%), and jewelry (4%).

Rhodium, another member of the platinum group, is also used in the automotive industry in pollution control devices. To some extent palladium has replaced rhodium. Iridium is used to process catalysts and it has also found use in some auto catalysts. Iridium and ruthenium are used in the production of polyvinyl chloride. As the prices of these metals change, there is some substitution. Therefore, strength of platinum prices relative to palladium should lead to the substitution of palladium for platinum in catalytic converters.

Platinum futures and options and palladium futures are traded on the New York Mercantile Exchange (NYMEX). Platinum and palladium futures are traded on the Tokyo Commodity Exchange (TOCOM). The NYMEX platinum futures contract calls for the delivery of 50 troy ounces of platinum (0.9995 fineness) and the contract trades in terms of dollars and cents per troy ounce. The NYMEX palladium futures contract calls for the delivery of 50 troy ounces of palladium (0.9995 fineness) and the contract is priced in terms of dollars and cents per troy ounce.

Prices – NYMEX platinum futures prices started the year 2009 at about $941 per troy ounce and, except for slight dips in May and July, moved steadily higher all year to finally end the year at about $1,460 per troy ounce.

NYMEX palladium futures prices started the year 2009 at about $192 per troy ounce and moved steadily higher all year to finally end the year at about $495 per troy ounce.

Supply – World mine production of platinum in 2009 fell by -5.8% yr/yr to 178,000 kilograms, down from the record high of 216,000 kilograms in 2006. South Africa is the world's largest producer of platinum by far with 79% of world production in 2009, followed by Russia (11%), Canada (3%) and the U.S. (2%). World mine production of palladium in 2009 fell -4.4% to 195,000 kilograms, which was a down from the record high production level of 222,000 in 2006. The world's largest palladium producers are Russia with 41% of world production in 2009, South Africa with 40%, the U.S. with 6%, and Canada with 5%. World production of platinum group metals other than platinum and palladium in 2007 (latest data available) rose by +2.9% yr/yr to a record high of 78,100 kilograms.

U.S. mine production of platinum in 2009 rose by +6.2% yr/yr to 3,800 kilograms, but still down from the record high of 4,390 kilograms posted in 2002. U.S. mine production of palladium in 2009 rose by +5.0% yr/yr to 12,500 kilograms, but still down from the record high of 14,800 kilograms posted in 2002. U.S. refinery production of scrap platinum and palladium in 2007, latest data available, rose +30.4% to 16,340 kilograms, up from the 2005 record low of 11,580 kilograms but still well below the 13-year high of 24,790 kilograms in 2001.

Demand – The total of platinum-group metals sold to consuming industries in the U.S. in 2004 (the latest data available) rose +7.1% to 91,434 kilograms. The two main U.S. industries that use platinum are the auto industry, which accounts for about 74% of U.S. platinum usage, and the jewelry industry, which accounts for about 26% of U.S. platinum usage.

Trade – U.S. imports of refined platinum and palladium in 2009 for consumption fell -41.7% yr/yr to a 15-year low of 195,180 kilograms. U.S. exports of refined platinum and palladium rose by +6.6% to 53,750 kilograms, but still well below the record high of 103,590 kilograms in 2006. The U.S. relied on imports for 47% of its platinum and palladium consumption in 2008.

PLATINUM-GROUP METALS

World Mine Production of Platinum In Kilograms

Year	Australia	Canada	Colombia[3]	Finland	Japan	Russia	Serbia/ Montenegro	Africa	United States	Zimbabwe	World Total
2000	171	6,302	339	441	782	34,000	5	114,459	3,110	505	160,000
2001	174	7,733	674	510	791	27,000	5	130,307	3,610	519	172,000
2002	200	9,202	661	508	762	27,000	5	132,897	4,390	2,306	178,000
2003	225	6,990	828	461	770	28,000	1	148,348	4,170	4,270	195,000
2004	200	1,000	1,209	705	750	28,000	----	153,239	4,040	4,438	194,000
2005	111	7,000	1,082	800	760	29,000	3	163,711	3,920	4,834	212,000
2006	209	7,500	1,438	800	760	29,000	2	168,125	4,290	4,998	217,000
2007	142	7,000	1,526	800	770	27,000	2	160,940	3,860	5,306	208,000
2008[1]	200	7,000	1,500	800	770	23,000	2	146,140	3,580	5,642	189,000
2009[2]		5,000	1,200			20,000		140,000	3,800	6,000	178,000

[1] Preliminary. [2] Estimate. [3] Placer platinum. W = Withheld. *Source: U.S. Geological Survey (USGS)*

World Mine Production of Palladium and Other Group Metals In Kilograms

	Palladium										Other Group Metals		
Year	Australia	Canada	Finland	Japan	Russia	Serbia/ Montenegro	Africa	United States	Zim- babwe	Total	Russia	South Africa	World Total
2000	812	9,949	----	4,712	71,000	25	55,818	10,300	366	153,000	14,100	36,493	51,400
2001	828	8,972	----	4,805	96,000	25	62,601	12,100	371	187,000	14,500	37,005	52,300
2002	810	12,210	----	5,618	96,000	25	63,758	14,800	1,943	196,000	14,500	39,986	57,900
2003	820	12,808	----	5,500	97,000	8	70,946	14,000	3,449	207,000	15,000	46,856	64,400
2004	800	12,000	----	5,300	97,000	19	76,403	13,700	3,564	211,000	15,000	46,759	66,600
2005	550	10,415	----	5,400	97,400	19	82,961	13,300	3,879	216,000	15,500	56,309	77,700
2006	750	10,493	----	5,400	98,400	15	86,265	14,400	4,022	222,000	15,600	53,138	74,600
2007	600	16,000	----	5,500	96,800	15	83,643	12,800	4,180	225,000	14,500	59,449	79,600
2008[1]	700	15,000	----	3,000	87,700	15	75,536	11,900	4,386	204,000	12,500	54,091	72,400
2009[2]		9,000			80,000		79,000	12,500	4,800	195,000			

[1] Preliminary. [2] Estimate. *Source: U.S. Geological Survey (USGS)*

Platinum Group Metals Sold to Consuming Industries in the United States In Kilograms

	Automotive		Chemical		Electrical		Dental & Medical		Jewelry & Decorative		Petroleum		All Platinum Group Metals			
Year	Platinum	Other[3]	Platinum	Other[3]	Platinum	Other[3]	Platinum	Other[3]	Platinum	Other[3]	Platinum	Other[3]	Platinum	Palladium	Other[3]	Total
1996	28,550	19,282	2,115	2,457	4,541	17,665	778	6,285	1,493	1,493	3,514	902	44,489	45,157	----	89,646
1997	28,923	20,402	2,239	2,426	4,945	19,997	840	6,376	2,115	1,617	3,390	871	46,184	50,227	----	96,411
1998	29,483	26,528	2,301	2,488	5,194	20,215	902	6,376	2,333	1,617	3,390	809	47,396	61,827	----	109,223
1999	31,100	29,390	2,364	2,519	5,443	21,148	933	6,065	3,110	1,679	3,514	778	50,310	65,248	----	115,558
2000	32,344	31,100	2,457	2,139	5,691	19,282	964	3,732	3,670	1,400	3,639	660	52,808	61,889	----	114,697
2001	33,411	34,832	2,644	715	5,909	17,354	995	3,670	4,043	1,431	4,199	715	55,399	62,293	----	117,692
2002	17,727	19,904	3,110	2,333	2,955	6,531	1,244	6,687	9,641		1,400		33,433	28,768	----	62,200
2003[1]	27,524	37,476	2,955	2,177	2,644	6,687	778	6,998	9,641		1,244		37,476	47,894	----	85,370
2004[2]	24,880	44,940	2,799	2,644	2,799	6,376	622	7,309	9,019		1,089		33,588	57,846	----	91,434

[1] Preliminary. [2] Estimate. [3] Includes Palladium, iridium, osmium, rhodium, and ruthenium.
Sources: U.S. Geological Survey (USGS); American Metal Market (AMM)

Salient Statistics of Platinum and Allied Metals[3] in the United States In Kilograms

	Net Import Reliance as a % of Apparent	Mine Production		Refinery Pro- duction (Secon-	Total	Refiner, Importer & Dealer Stocks as of Dec. 31				Imports		Exports		Apparent Con-
Year	Consumption	Platinum	Palladium	dary)	Refined	Platinum	Palladium	Other[4]	Total	Refined	Total	Refined	Total	sumptio
2000	83	3,110	10,300	23,780	23,780	5,190	19,000	784	24,974	316,633	----	84,087	----	----
2001	66	3,610	12,100	24,790	24,790	3,680	16,300	784	20,764	267,957	----	67,334	----	----
2002	93	4,390	14,800	20,900	20,900	649	5,870	784	7,303	222,356	----	70,943	----	----
2003	91	4,170	14,000	24,250	24,250	649	1,170	562	2,381	223,653	----	45,124	----	----
2004	92	4,040	13,700	22,180	22,180	649	568	501	1,718	248,705	----	52,897	----	----
2005	93	3,920	13,300	11,580	11,580	261	----	189	450	284,849	----	49,395	----	----
2006	90	4,290	14,400	12,530	12,530	261	----	111	372	287,756	----	103,590	----	----
2007	91	3,860	12,800	16,340	16,340	261	----	18	279	362,733	----	81,100	----	----
2008[1]	89	3,580	11,900	15,050	15,050	261	----	18	279	334,961	----	50,430	----	----
2009[2]	89	3,800	12,500							195,180	----	53,750	----	----

[1] Preliminary. [2] Estimate. [3] Includes platinum, palladium, iridium, osmium, rhodium, and ruthenium. [4] Includes iridium, osmium, rhodium, and ruthenium. W = Withheld. *Source: U.S. Geological Survey (USGS)*

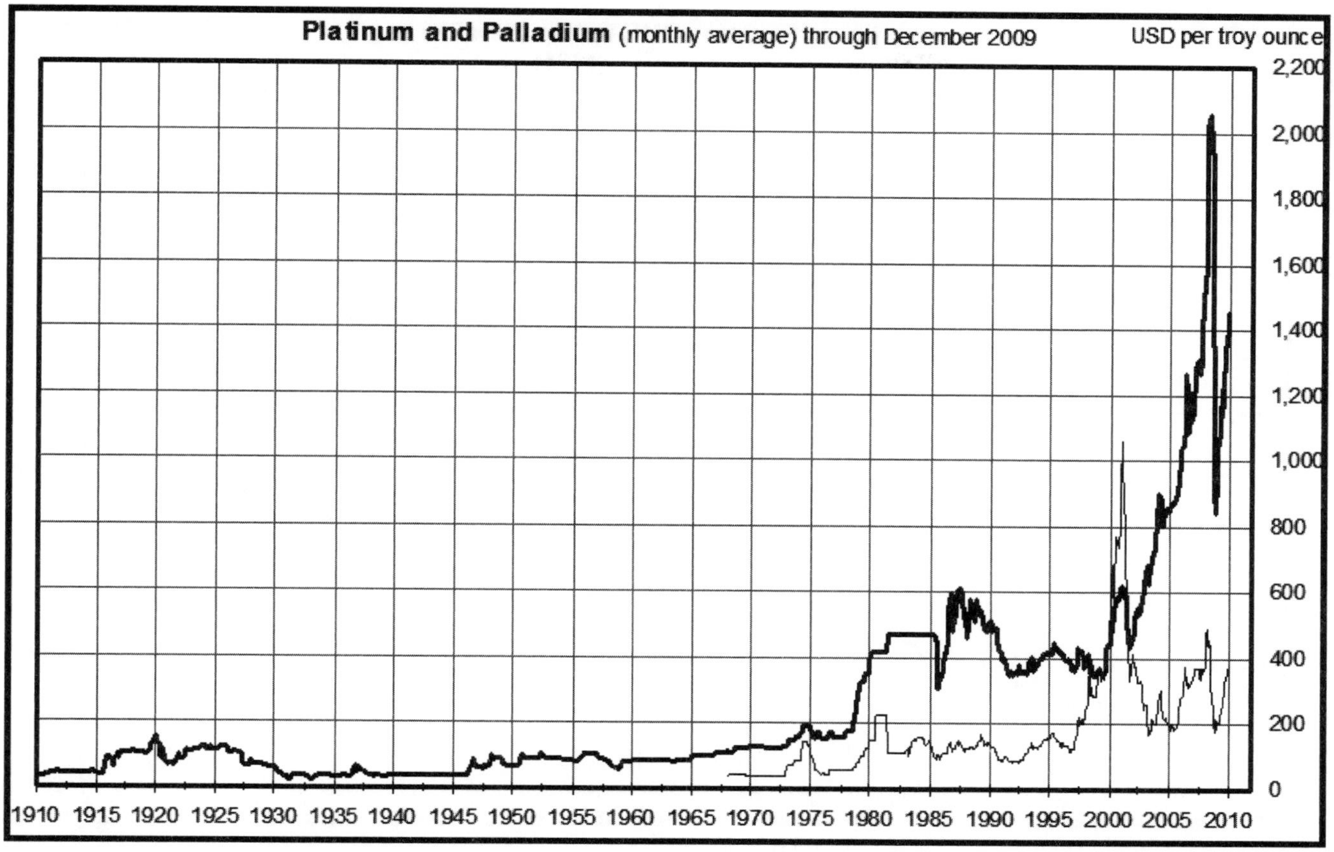

Average Merchant's Price of Platinum in the United States In Dollars Per Troy Ounce

Year	Jan.	Feb.	Mar.	Apr.	May	June	July	Aug.	Sept.	Oct.	Nov.	Dec.	Average
2000	432.95	517.02	478.28	493.53	519.57	557.45	558.53	572.76	592.53	576.91	592.73	608.28	541.49
2001	623.43	453.56	566.67	589.63	611.07	588.91	643.88	457.37	453.50	437.43	427.25	450.24	531.93
2002	471.52	470.68	511.95	539.20	533.66	554.70	526.32	545.48	556.05	580.11	588.15	594.89	539.39
2003	633.09	684.47	677.05	627.19	651.43	664.19	684.68	695.12	707.90	734.91	762.78	810.48	691.78
2004	855.95	849.53	902.78	884.76	814.05	810.59	813.48	851.91	851.05	843.76	856.15	854.55	849.05
2005	861.80	867.40	870.23	867.71	869.00	883.23	876.60	901.04	918.10	933.76	964.00	9,890.48	1,641.95
2006	1,032.48	1,045.16	1,044.39	1,105.00	1,264.05	1,192.73	1,233.03	1,236.74	1,183.30	1,085.32	1,183.73	1,124.79	1,144.23
2007	1,151.90	1,206.47	1,222.77	1,280.90	1,306.50	1,289.14	1,307.38	1,267.30	1,313.00	1,413.87	1,449.45	1,492.47	1,308.43
2008	1,585.09	2,002.55	2,043.65	1,991.32	2,053.57	2,042.24	1,904.68	1,492.52	1,221.71	917.13	841.22	842.40	1,578.17
2009	949.76	1,037.26	1,084.59	1,169.57	1,134.45	1,220.41	1,163.82	1,248.24	1,294.71	1,335.86	1,401.26	1,447.20	1,207.26

Source: American Metal Market (AMM)

Average Dealer Price[1] of Palladium in the United States In Dollars Per Troy Ounce

Year	Jan.	Feb.	Mar.	Apr.	May	June	July	Aug.	Sept.	Oct.	Nov.	Dec.	Average
2000	447.45	607.33	687.72	580.00	574.89	640.80	686.63	759.63	731.15	734.91	778.73	887.33	676.55
2001	1,054.10	984.37	792.68	699.15	663.41	619.67	525.90	459.83	444.47	340.52	333.14	405.95	610.27
2002	412.62	377.79	377.15	372.50	360.00	339.20	325.41	327.55	330.50	319.09	289.20	243.57	339.55
2003	258.41	255.68	226.38	164.76	169.00	181.76	175.27	185.76	214.29	203.74	200.17	200.86	203.01
2004	220.70	237.95	272.43	299.57	249.57	231.32	222.95	217.55	213.95	220.43	215.85	193.00	232.94
2005	188.45	184.15	200.09	200.76	191.38	188.50	186.95	188.13	191.19	209.71	246.35	266.24	203.49
2006	275.95	291.58	312.70	355.74	372.82	319.36	320.21	332.57	324.40	315.18	326.91	328.00	322.95
2007	339.81	344.26	352.27	370.35	369.50	370.76	368.67	344.61	337.63	368.70	366.75	355.42	357.39
2008	376.95	473.65	490.35	449.05	438.29	453.57	428.27	318.29	250.19	193.30	212.61	178.00	355.21
2009	189.81	207.63	203.73	228.29	230.45	247.18	250.64	278.38	295.86	324.45	354.84	376.60	265.66

[1] Based on wholesale quantities, prompt delivery. Source: American Metal Market (AMM)

Volume of Trading of Platinum Futures in New York In Contracts

Year	Jan.	Feb.	Mar.	Apr.	May	June	July	Aug.	Sept.	Oct.	Nov.	Dec.	Total
2000	33,226	31,352	35,013	28,057	22,741	47,197	16,527	14,739	36,643	12,122	12,662	30,645	320,924
2001	19,278	12,885	31,617	14,961	15,714	23,245	14,494	12,477	17,040	9,957	11,401	22,890	205,969
2002	12,848	13,807	24,434	11,066	12,294	27,176	14,198	18,583	29,762	11,834	9,878	33,891	219,771
2003	15,545	15,157	38,170	13,472	18,968	30,961	10,852	11,878	37,686	19,275	14,040	42,301	268,305
2004	16,337	15,574	42,249	29,228	13,125	28,495	15,598	18,180	34,076	24,393	18,606	39,834	295,695
2005	15,410	20,253	41,297	16,267	20,135	55,588	25,132	26,604	52,535	21,827	30,447	50,684	376,179
2006	20,604	27,572	42,804	17,215	34,684	45,985	16,220	21,428	44,000	21,182	46,754	34,671	373,119
2007	20,534	26,975	59,099	26,457	35,525	66,968	35,371	35,975	58,091	34,100	36,126	66,324	501,545
2008	54,479	71,978	84,901	41,283	54,476	66,398	43,127	47,539	74,165	38,107	30,011	69,079	675,543
2009	31,090	35,199	82,949	30,849	34,962	104,413	46,045	48,650	134,462	55,865	63,896	134,504	802,884

Source: CME Group; New York Mercantile Exchange (NYMEX)

Average Open Interest of Platinum Futures in New York In Contracts

Year	Jan.	Feb.	Mar.	Apr.	May	June	July	Aug.	Sept.	Oct.	Nov.	Dec.
2000	10,858	10,952	9,218	8,484	9,057	10,585	9,566	9,731	9,716	8,106	8,163	8,507
2001	8,449	7,311	6,855	6,715	7,436	5,751	6,210	5,996	5,646	5,395	6,102	6,033
2002	6,587	6,213	7,121	6,823	6,031	6,901	5,516	6,405	6,930	7,211	7,406	8,388
2003	8,694	8,132	8,034	6,322	6,599	6,847	7,450	8,556	8,794	8,489	9,421	9,373
2004	8,210	7,379	8,879	7,698	5,555	5,590	5,376	6,282	6,091	6,092	7,208	7,184
2005	6,800	7,486	8,047	8,132	8,496	10,109	8,497	11,729	12,478	13,024	12,377	11,327
2006	10,625	9,995	8,407	9,486	9,681	8,265	8,575	9,889	9,076	7,276	8,332	8,186
2007	8,810	10,752	11,154	13,413	15,173	15,033	16,641	12,347	12,341	15,199	14,427	15,404
2008	17,912	15,770	12,966	12,977	15,869	15,821	14,198	12,325	13,904	15,111	16,530	17,267
2009	18,300	20,041	20,388	20,506	21,045	23,755	21,952	25,303	28,571	31,236	33,730	33,542

Source: CME Group; New York Mercantile Exchange (NYMEX)

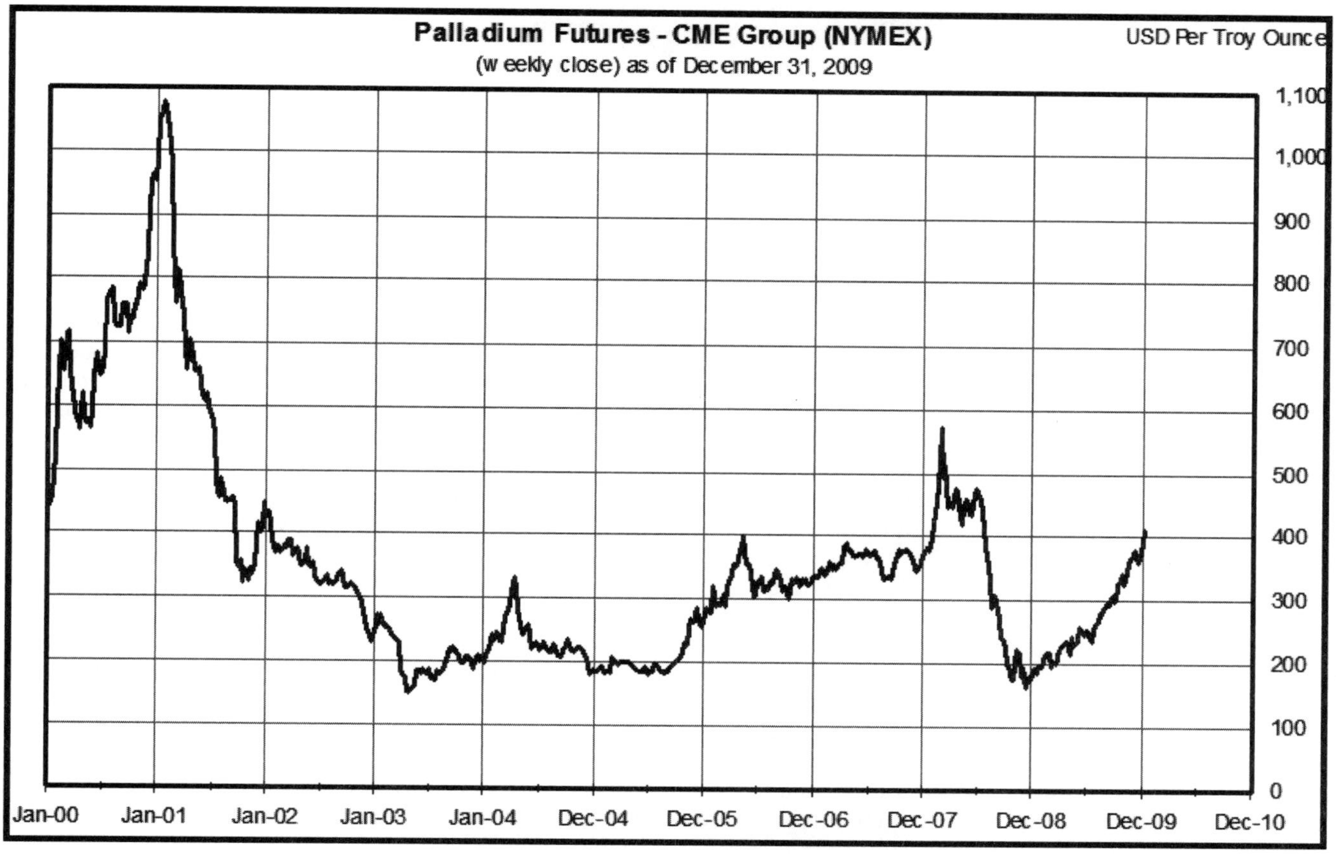

Volume of Trading of Palladium Futures in New York In Contracts

Year	Jan.	Feb.	Mar.	Apr.	May	June	July	Aug.	Sept.	Oct.	Nov.	Dec.	Total
2000	4,584	13,976	2,803	1,833	7,034	2,622	3,120	5,169	2,523	2,460	3,041	1,601	50,766
2001	2,171	6,090	1,397	1,121	3,325	1,013	1,173	3,221	523	1,255	3,261	1,375	25,925
2002	1,275	3,372	1,538	1,527	6,126	2,166	2,154	8,971	1,452	1,710	8,118	2,644	41,053
2003	4,200	7,266	3,256	3,971	8,420	3,430	4,221	15,645	8,152	7,587	18,323	11,142	95,613
2004	17,093	41,036	20,508	30,214	27,343	11,433	7,606	28,895	10,690	15,036	41,269	16,429	267,552
2005	7,728	43,268	16,979	13,316	46,112	13,594	17,185	49,268	17,747	21,680	50,643	24,403	321,923
2006	28,447	59,279	32,573	23,135	64,863	25,857	13,464	41,123	16,222	14,351	47,797	11,005	378,116
2007	23,636	62,815	14,987	25,166	69,089	16,322	15,072	65,106	16,975	26,385	52,411	13,029	400,993
2008	26,954	105,845	49,411	24,750	66,939	18,934	26,245	53,692	25,253	28,627	43,879	13,299	483,828
2009	14,284	41,726	14,509	17,332	51,635	23,403	25,689	57,502	25,393	29,401	71,228	28,719	400,821

Source: CME Group; New York Mercantile Exchange (NYMEX)

Average Open Interest of Palladium Futures in New York In Contracts

Year	Jan.	Feb.	Mar.	Apr.	May	June	July	Aug.	Sept.	Oct.	Nov.	Dec.
2000	3,129	3,101	2,367	2,359	2,628	2,015	2,118	1,974	1,757	1,905	1,859	1,837
2001	1,828	1,666	1,525	1,577	1,613	1,385	1,420	1,318	1,383	1,286	1,477	1,244
2002	1,217	1,208	1,042	1,199	1,554	1,806	2,103	2,298	1,878	1,976	1,977	2,025
2003	2,000	2,039	1,948	1,997	2,315	2,609	2,680	3,605	5,184	5,533	6,096	6,737
2004	9,119	11,878	11,465	11,039	8,828	7,861	8,055	8,688	8,933	9,965	11,192	12,188
2005	12,824	13,821	12,946	13,116	13,345	13,527	13,794	14,465	13,340	13,488	14,676	14,477
2006	14,353	16,632	15,426	17,783	18,002	14,251	14,087	13,166	11,247	11,836	12,511	11,210
2007	13,794	16,132	15,587	18,126	19,682	18,288	18,152	18,035	16,062	16,286	17,194	14,820
2008	18,184	20,999	20,227	19,571	19,197	17,106	15,223	13,821	14,294	14,656	13,435	12,688
2009	12,442	12,596	12,230	14,237	15,594	16,288	17,150	20,669	21,877	21,881	22,650	22,692

Source: CME Group; New York Mercantile Exchange (NYMEX)

Pork Bellies

Pork bellies are the cut of meat from a hog from which bacon is produced. A hog has two belly slabs, generally weighing 8-18 pounds each, depending on the hog's commercial slaughter weight. Total hog slaughter weights average around 255 pounds, equal to a dressed carcass weight of about 190 pounds. Bellies account for about 12% of a hog's live weight, but represent a larger 14% of the total cutout value of the realized pork products. Pork bellies can be frozen and stored for up to a year before processing. The pork belly futures contract at the Chicago Mercantile Exchange calls for the physical delivery of 40,000 pounds of frozen pork bellies, which have been slaughtered at USDA federally inspected slaughtering plants. Each deliverable belly typically weighs 12-14 pounds each.

There are definite seasonal patterns in pork belly prices. Bellies are storable and the movement into cold storage builds early in the calendar year, peaking about mid-year. Net withdrawals from storage then carry stocks to a low around October. The cycle then starts again. Retail bacon demand also follows a time worn trend, peaking in the summer and tapering off to a low during the winter months. While demand patterns would suggest the highest prices in the summer and the lowest in the winter, just the opposite is not unusual. Such contra-seasonal price moves can be partially attributed to supply logistics, notably the availability of frozen storage stocks deliverable against futures at CME exchange-approved warehouses. When stocks prove either too large or small, the underlying demand variables for bacon can be relegated to the backburner as a market-moving factor. The fact that no contract months are traded between August and the following February adds to the late fall futures price distortion.

Belly prices (cash and futures) are sensitive to the inventory in cold storage and to the weekly net movement in and out of storage, which affords some insight to demand, although a better measure is the weekly quantity of bellies being sliced into bacon. Higher retail prices tend to encourage placing more supply into storage because of lower retail bacon demand. Bacon is not a necessary foodstuff so demand can be buoyed by favorable consumer disposable income. However, dietary standards have changed dramatically in recent years and do not favor the consumption of high fat and salt content food, such as bacon. In addition, alternatives to pork bacon have emerged in recent years such as turkey bacon, which has lower fat and calorie content.

Prices – Pork belly futures prices fell sharply during 2009 due to the recession and weak demand and due to the H1N1 swine flu scare, which started to emerge in spring 2009. The swing flu scare caused US pork exports to plunge and caused domestic supplies to back up. Pork belly prices in August 2009 plunged to a 10-year low of 38.50 cents per pound. Pork belly prices then rallied going into late 2009 as pork exports started to recover and as supplies tightened up.

Supply – The average monthly level of frozen pork belly storage stocks in 2009 fell by -0.1% to 60.880 million pounds, down from the 2008 10-year high of 60.932 million pounds. As of December 2009, there were 44.638 million pounds of pork bellies in storage.

Average Retail Price of Bacon, Sliced In Dollars Per Pound

Year	Jan.	Feb.	Mar.	Apr.	May	June	July	Aug.	Sept.	Oct.	Nov.	Dec.	Average
2000	2.75	2.87	2.93	2.95	3.01	3.13	3.17	3.20	3.21	3.07	3.05	3.03	3.03
2001	2.99	3.07	3.16	3.11	3.26	3.25	3.32	3.47	3.49	3.34	3.30	3.30	3.25
2002	3.27	3.32	3.27	3.26	3.18	3.19	3.23	3.29	3.16	3.24	3.21	3.24	3.24
2003	3.20	3.28	3.22	3.29	3.09	3.14	3.16	3.23	3.22	3.16	3.23	3.18	3.20
2004	3.16	3.19	3.13	3.20	3.33	3.42	3.47	3.62	3.59	3.61	3.44	3.37	3.38
2005	3.37	3.40	3.36	3.33	3.56	3.46	3.48	3.44	3.40	3.33	3.26	3.33	3.39
2006	3.36	3.39	3.36	3.34	3.31	3.40	3.51	3.56	3.55	3.61	3.44	3.46	3.44
2007	3.51	3.57	3.46	3.50	3.65	3.66	3.72	3.80	3.78	3.88	3.66	3.69	3.66
2008	3.65	3.62	3.62	3.55	3.64	3.66	3.61	3.84	3.73	3.75	3.60	3.67	3.66
2009[1]	3.73	3.62	3.59	3.58	3.66	3.62	3.64	3.59	3.59	3.60	3.50	3.57	3.61

[1] Preliminary. *Source: Economic Research Service, U.S. Department of Agriculture (ERS-USDA)*

Frozen Pork Belly Storage Stocks in the United States, on First of Month In Thousands of Pounds

Year	Jan.	Feb.	Mar.	Apr.	May	June	July	Aug.	Sept.	Oct.	Nov.	Dec.
2000	40,300	43,802	49,983	60,527	63,461	68,292	60,097	50,515	33,005	21,341	20,589	38,674
2001	47,099	50,145	47,154	45,440	43,878	46,029	39,552	24,996	12,754	8,960	28,216	36,297
2002	44,301	50,849	57,569	60,721	63,293	62,269	51,019	29,925	14,250	9,452	10,354	18,059
2003	28,254	35,354	38,278	42,971	48,542	45,870	43,504	32,075	17,900	10,180	21,135	33,073
2004	49,017	63,095	57,123	50,126	48,363	41,366	37,185	23,383	15,230	11,344	15,970	33,955
2005	56,026	61,528	72,324	77,718	88,367	80,033	66,775	45,254	16,175	8,094	9,421	22,490
2006	40,707	54,902	58,861	61,628	62,665	58,803	46,056	30,506	11,962	10,199	15,597	30,553
2007	41,917	46,227	46,643	55,160	61,796	57,294	47,214	31,619	21,410	17,050	20,356	34,328
2008	54,746	70,647	79,282	98,896	100,189	87,428	74,372	57,964	31,878	21,270	21,696	33,490
2009[1]	51,593	69,166	75,668	72,940	79,543	78,801	76,333	60,238	48,958	38,481	37,127	44,638

[1] Preliminary. *Source: National Agricultural Statistics Service, U.S. Department of Agriculture (NASS-USDA)*

Weekly Pork Belly Storage Movement

Week Ending	In	Out	On Hand	Net Movement	Week Ending	In	Out	On Hand	Net Movement
	Stocks[1] in Thousands of Pounds					Stocks[1] in Thousands of Pounds			
Jan 05, 2008	2,548	-438	39,272	2,110	Jan 03, 2009	3,737	-8	40,167	3,729
Jan 12, 2008	1,519	-492	40,299	1,027	Jan 10, 2009	3,686	-448	43,405	3,238
Jan 19, 2008	2,930	-322	42,907	2,608	Jan 17, 2009	4,841	-156	48,090	4,685
Jan 26, 2008	1,861	-239	44,381	1,622	Jan 24, 2009	3,585	-239	51,607	3,517
Feb 02, 2008	2,487	-44	49,046	2,443	Jan 31, 2009	2,943	-127	54,423	2,816
Feb 09, 2008	2,529	-258	51,317	2,271	Feb 07, 2009	1,561	-159	55,825	1,402
Feb 16, 2008	2,267	-80	53,504	2,187	Feb 14, 2009	827	-191	56,461	636
Feb 23, 2008	1,708	-80	55,132	1,628	Feb 21, 2009	1,448	-367	57,541	1,081
Mar 01, 2008	3,264	-108	58,288	3,156	Feb 28, 2009	812	-156	58,197	656
Mar 08, 2008	2,981	-234	61,035	2,747	Mar 07, 2009	859	-112	58,943	747
Mar 15, 2008	4,814	-121	65,727	4,693	Mar 14, 2009	224	0	59,167	224
Mar 22, 2008	1,678	0	67,405	1,678	Mar 21, 2009	307	0	59,474	307
Mar 29, 2008	5,168	-80	72,493	5,088	Mar 28, 2009	83	-575	58,982	-492
Apr 05, 2008	1,446	0	73,939	1,446	Apr 04, 2009	631	-542	59,071	89
Apr 12, 2008	845	-42	74,742	803	Apr 11, 2009	1,098	-438	59,730	660
Apr 19, 2008	275	-506	74,511	-231	Apr 18, 2009	1,731	0	61,461	1,731
Apr 26, 2008	179	-767	73,923	-588	Apr 25, 2009	1,315	0	62,776	1,315
May 03, 2008	362	-727	73,558	-365	May 02, 2009	955	0	63,731	955
May 10, 2008	501	-2,143	71,916	-1,642	May 09, 2009	204	0	63,935	204
May 17, 2008	620	-2,234	70,302	-1,614	May 16, 2009	0	0	63,935	0
May 24, 2008	687	-5,120	65,869	-4,433	May 23, 2009	84	-1,650	62,369	-1,566
May 31, 2008	441	-3,028	63,282	-2,587	May 30, 2009	13	-369	62,013	-356
Jun 07, 2008	323	-1,943	61,662	-1,620	Jun 06, 2009	7	-960	61,060	-953
Jun 14, 2008	754	-1,554	60,862	-800	Jun 13, 2009	1,572	-1,439	61,194	133
Jun 21, 2008	501	-1,328	60,035	-827	Jun 20, 2009	1,025	-1,222	60,997	-197
Jun 28, 2008	380	-1,802	58,613	-1,422	Jun 27, 2009	286	-1,829	59,298	-1,543
Jul 05, 2008	767	-1,740	57,640	-973	Jul 04, 2009	693	-1,780	58,211	-1,087
Jul 12, 2008	1,366	-3,134	55,872	-1,768	Jul 11, 2009	385	-3,419	55,177	-3,034
Jul 19, 2008	1,119	-3,471	53,520	-2,352	Jul 18, 2009	0	-3,028	52,149	-3,028
Jul 26, 2008	1,192	-4,449	50,263	-3,257	Jul 25, 2009	15	-5,207	46,957	-5,192
Aug 02, 2008	1,560	-3,789	48,034	-2,229	Aug 01, 2009	562	-4,439	43,080	-3,877
Aug 09, 2008	1,426	-4,267	45,193	-2,841	Aug 08, 2009	160	-4,071	39,169	-3,911
Aug 16, 2008	915	-4,044	42,064	-3,129	Aug 15, 2009	1,447	-5,401	35,215	-3,954
Aug 23, 2008	1,688	-4,327	39,425	-2,639	Aug 22, 2009	2,475	-3,712	33,978	-1,237
Aug 30, 2008	1,455	-3,434	21,364	-1,979	Aug 29, 2009	1,535	-4,428	31,085	-2,893
Sep 06, 2008	1,261	-3,176	19,449	-1,915	Sep 05, 2009	1,242	-3,578	28,749	-2,336
Sep 13, 2008	640	-3,111	16,976	-2,471	Sep 12, 2009	392	-1,943	27,198	-1,551
Sep 20, 2008	252	-2,580	14,648	-2,328	Sep 19, 2009	886	-3,315	24,768	-2,429
Sep 27, 2008	136	-1,610	13,174	-1,474	Sep 26, 2009	366	-1,174	23,960	-808
Oct 04, 2008	182	-1,499	11,857	-1,317	Oct 03, 2009	245	-1,184	23,915	-939
Oct 11, 2008	944	-1,319	11,482	-375	Oct 10, 2009	144	-1,190	22,869	-1,046
Oct 18, 2008	1,094	-999	11,577	95	Oct 17, 2009	781	-881	22,769	-100
Oct 25, 2008	1,411	-1,048	11,940	363	Oct 24, 2009	866	-1,030	22,605	-164
Nov 01, 2008	2,168	-1,456	12,652	712	Oct 31, 2009	1,291	-906	22,990	385
Nov 08, 2008	2,555	-509	14,698	2,046	Nov 07, 2009	1,717	-728	23,283	989
Nov 15, 2008	1,939	-403	16,234	1,536	Nov 14, 2009	1,308	-721	23,870	587
Nov 22, 2008	2,904	-735	18,403	2,169	Nov 21, 2009	3,101	-649	26,322	2,452
Nov 29, 2008	3,001	-372	21,032	2,629	Nov 28, 2009	3,137	-293	28,044	2,844
Dec 06, 2008	3,426	-626	23,832	2,800	Dec 05, 2009	2,087	-201	29,930	1,886
Dec 13, 2008	5,292	-283	28,841	5,009	Dec 12, 2009	2,339	-622	31,647	1,717
Dec 20, 2008	4,897	-828	32,910	4,069	Dec 19, 2009	2,381	-1,002	33,026	1,379
Dec 27, 2008	3,618	-90	36,438	3,528	Dec 26, 2009	2,466	-382	35,110	2,084

[1] 60 Chicago and Outside Combined Chicago Mercantile Exchange approved warehouses. *Source: Chicago Mercantile Exchange (CME)*

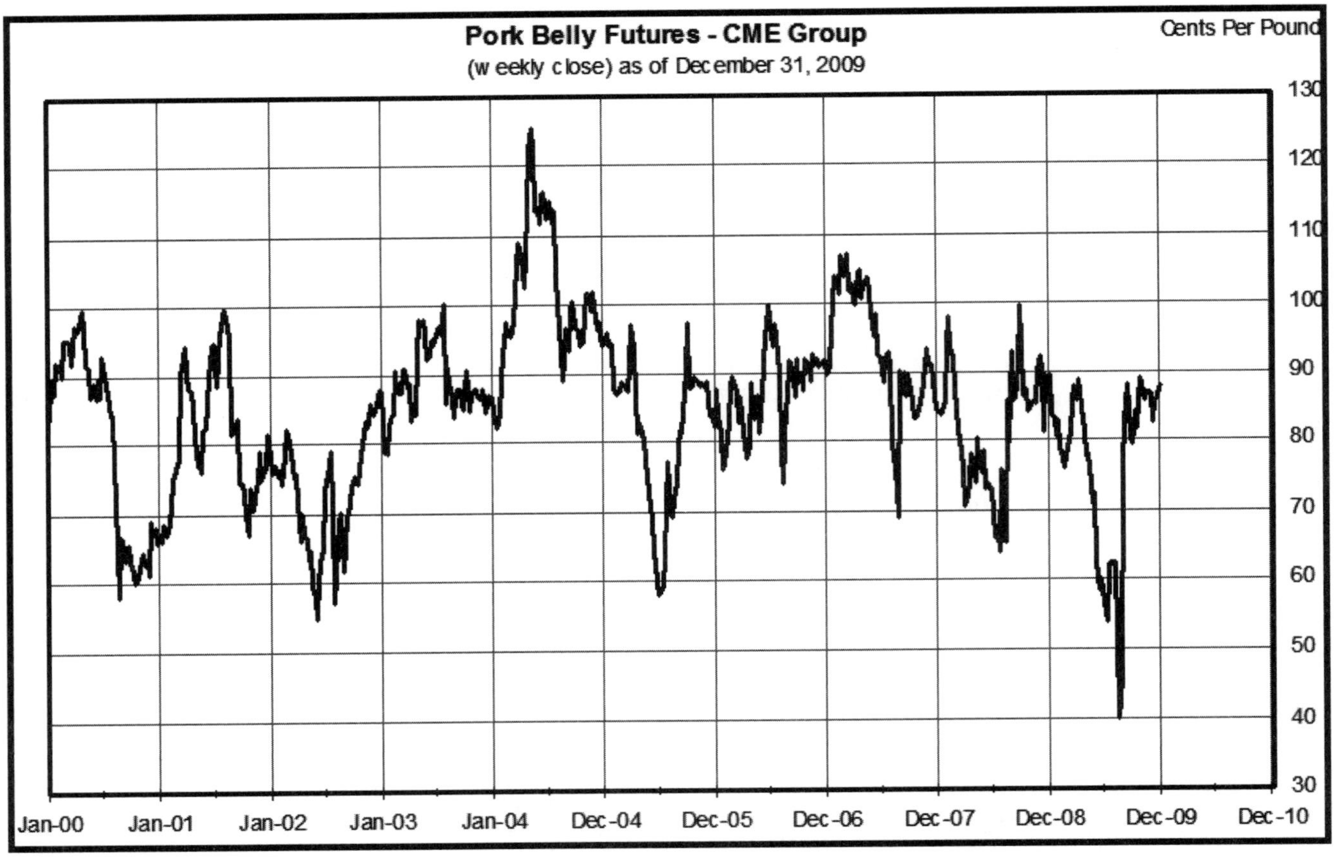

Average Open Interest of Pork Belly Futures in Chicago In Contracts

Year	Jan.	Feb.	Mar.	Apr.	May	June	July	Aug.	Sept.	Oct.	Nov.	Dec.
2000	5,872	6,011	6,320	6,563	5,836	5,306	3,650	1,877	1,860	2,093	2,409	2,610
2001	2,719	2,908	2,935	3,138	2,808	2,354	2,526	2,579	2,695	2,321	2,441	2,451
2002	2,574	2,768	2,879	3,271	3,224	2,821	1,885	986	1,116	1,329	2,020	2,548
2003	2,842	2,805	2,915	3,082	3,383	3,410	2,858	1,632	1,899	1,885	2,075	2,484
2004	2,431	3,213	3,491	3,998	3,880	3,158	2,675	1,473	1,399	1,200	1,491	1,900
2005	2,013	3,010	2,858	2,891	3,743	3,725	2,507	1,599	1,143	1,451	1,323	1,868
2006	2,273	2,407	1,949	2,146	2,049	1,938	1,812	1,006	782	907	1,039	1,069
2007	1,257	1,520	1,391	1,259	1,256	1,369	1,146	851	941	1,532	1,911	1,850
2008	2,047	1,718	1,763	2,051	1,976	2,219	1,816	702	704	805	1,140	1,164
2009	1,192	1,291	1,090	894	860	865	667	573	657	642	595	565

Source: Chicago Mercantile Exchange (CME)

Volume of Trading of Pork Belly Futures in Chicago In Contracts

Year	Jan.	Feb.	Mar.	Apr.	May	June	July	Aug.	Sept.	Oct.	Nov.	Dec.	Total
2000	37,650	38,943	39,061	31,464	40,311	31,229	25,051	17,875	10,711	11,854	11,737	13,690	309,576
2001	15,861	16,200	16,675	18,274	18,708	16,989	20,187	18,823	12,719	12,905	15,984	13,034	196,359
2002	16,495	16,650	14,279	17,758	13,648	15,764	16,773	7,490	6,857	8,107	8,659	9,574	152,054
2003	13,635	13,956	13,137	18,279	18,112	16,993	19,540	9,967	7,909	10,235	8,542	11,024	161,329
2004	11,519	14,738	17,699	18,412	17,366	15,136	16,012	10,518	9,410	5,713	7,643	7,783	151,949
2005	7,736	13,995	10,767	13,713	11,020	15,226	12,869	11,275	5,099	9,370	6,438	6,910	124,418
2006	10,806	12,890	11,682	13,183	10,342	12,616	9,842	9,634	4,885	4,375	4,568	2,741	107,564
2007	7,767	7,117	6,102	6,200	6,072	6,369	6,965	5,873	3,296	4,006	5,140	3,502	68,409
2008	6,159	5,741	5,396	6,289	4,695	5,608	7,993	4,163	2,377	2,463	2,060	3,761	56,705
2009	3,559	3,340	3,400	2,716	2,538	3,610	2,369	1,614	1,211	1,431	776	1,288	27,852

Source: Chicago Mercantile Exchange (CME)

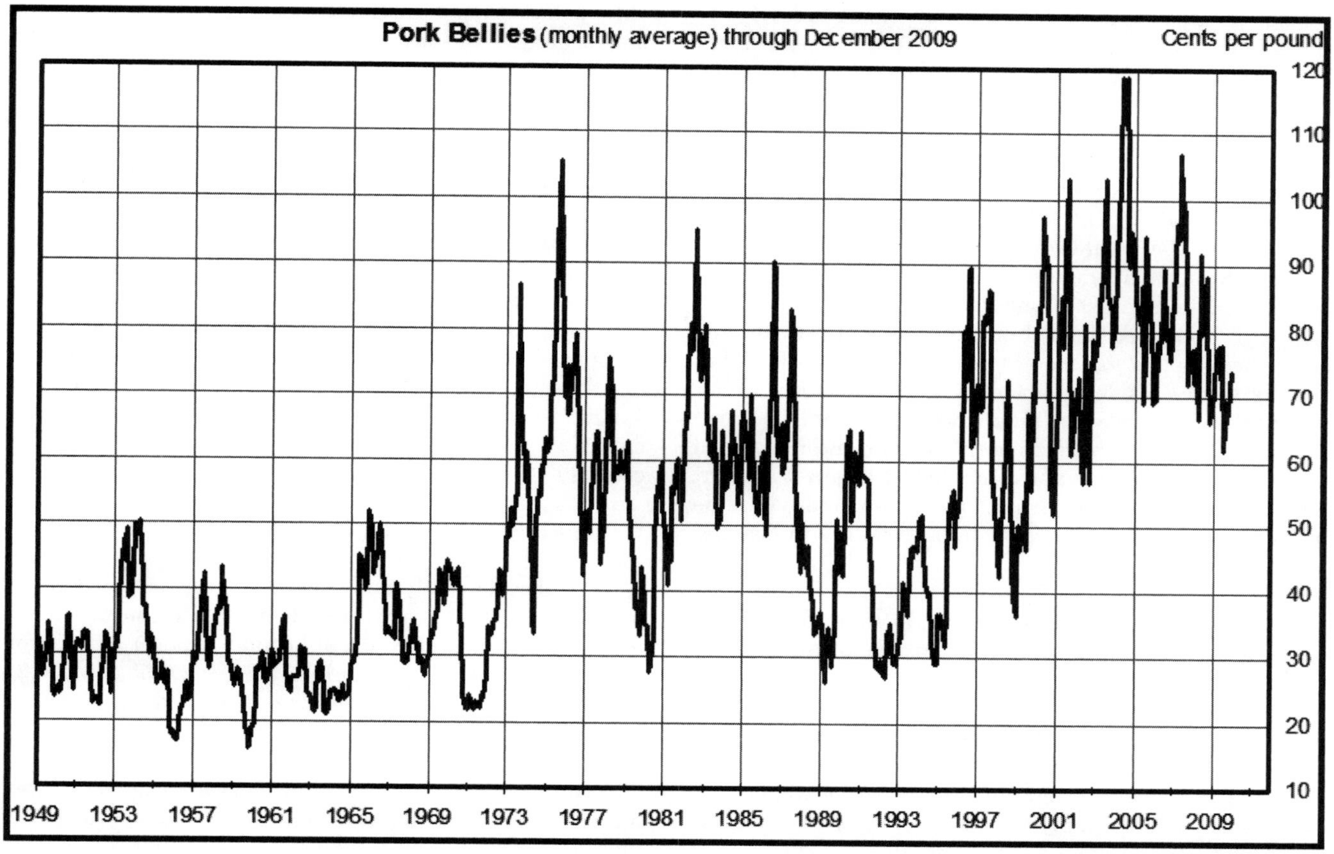

Average Price of Pork Bellies (12-14 lbs.), Central, U.S. In Cents Per Pound

Year	Jan.	Feb.	Mar.	Apr.	May	June	July	Aug.	Sept.	Oct.	Nov.	Dec.	Average
2000	80.45	82.40	85.00	93.70	97.85	91.99	90.38	75.64	63.94	57.83	51.97	58.36	77.46
2001	66.61	66.68	78.04	85.80	77.91	91.50	102.42	98.39	81.91	61.30	63.68	69.13	78.61
2002	70.87	70.75	72.55	63.48	58.65	65.90	81.06	67.98	57.05	76.24	75.50	78.92	69.91
2003	78.02	79.54	85.80	84.94	96.58	97.05	102.37	85.65	83.15	84.46	78.53	81.00	86.42
2004	79.78	90.76	103.67	109.15	117.53	113.00	118.22	99.92	92.00	88.90	91.50	87.81	99.35
2005	78.00	82.13	84.20	78.13	87.31	68.73	77.48	94.00	89.67	84.07	78.82	75.00	81.46
2006	75.00	71.83	78.67	78.83	87.00	101.25	94.29	90.67	82.56	75.44	78.64	79.50	82.81
2007	86.25	96.08	93.25	93.47	106.30	101.06	99.83	86.58	80.42	71.58	75.69	77.08	88.97
2008	75.56	78.94	67.26	61.08	79.00	64.54	78.75	74.17	63.50	77.00	57.25	61.25	69.86
2009[1]	69.88	71.00	65.25	77.50	57.00	50.00	80.36	42.25	45.83	47.33	60.50	64.00	60.91

[1] Preliminary. *Source: Economic Research Service, U.S. Department of Agriculture (ERS-USDA)*

Average Price of Pork Loins (12-14 lbs.)[2], Central, U.S. In Cents Per Pound

Year	Jan.	Feb.	Mar.	Apr.	May	June	July	Aug.	Sept.	Oct.	Nov.	Dec.	Average
2000	99.29	110.66	110.06	127.48	115.38	132.53	131.73	120.45	119.22	119.90	104.19	114.68	117.13
2001	110.80	114.32	128.53	117.98	130.72	132.33	126.41	121.22	116.21	108.69	97.87	98.50	116.97
2002	106.95	105.73	100.08	94.13	101.71	104.80	108.64	97.85	87.17	93.04	82.60	93.03	97.98
2003	91.83	95.75	92.43	96.90	108.93	126.51	102.50	104.85	111.38	97.71	89.06	93.72	100.96
2004	111.98	117.30	110.00	115.48	140.65	130.30	121.36	116.93	119.22	110.00	102.92	109.50	117.14
2005	116.08	114.83	115.88	115.03	133.45	115.62	115.03	119.82	111.31	103.78	96.72	101.12	113.22
2006	95.00	96.21	101.31	107.25	112.77	124.61	114.95	109.35	99.58	99.27	92.02	101.15	104.46
2007	100.96	112.08	101.04	108.99	121.61	113.58	111.78	111.66	100.18	93.41	88.25	86.46	104.17
2008	87.70	90.22	90.33	108.10	130.43	115.19	117.11	128.86	114.54	111.10	92.88	93.10	106.63
2009[1]	94.96	94.83	90.46	92.10	97.73	91.58	101.03	90.33	89.08	85.98	82.63	103.03	92.81

[1] Preliminary. *Source: Economic Research Service, U.S. Department of Agriculture (ERS-USDA)*

Potatoes

The potato is a member of the nightshade family. The leaves of the potato plant are poisonous and a potato will begin to turn green if left too long in the light. This green skin contains solanine, a substance that can cause the potato to taste bitter and even cause illness in humans.

In Peru, the Inca Indians were the first to cultivate potatoes around 200 BC. The Indians developed potato crops because their staple diet of corn would not grow above an altitude of 3,350 meters. In 1536, after conquering the Incas, the Spanish Conquistadors brought potatoes back to Europe. At first, Europeans did not accept the potato because it was not mentioned in the Bible and was therefore considered an "evil" food. But after Marie Antoinette wore a crown of potato flowers, it finally became a popular food. In 1897, during the Alaskan Klondike gold rush, potatoes were so valued for their vitamin C content that miners traded gold for potatoes. The potato became the first vegetable to be grown in outer space in October 1995.

The potato is a highly nutritious, fat-free, cholesterol-free and sodium-free food, and is an important dietary staple in over 130 countries. A medium-sized potato contains only 100 calories. Potatoes are an excellent source of vitamin C and provide B vitamins as well as potassium, copper, magnesium, and iron. According to the U.S. Department of Agriculture, "a diet of whole milk and potatoes would supply almost all of the food elements necessary for the maintenance of the human body."

Potatoes are one of the largest vegetable crops grown in the U.S., and are grown in all fifty states. The U.S. ranks about 4th in world potato production. The top three types of potatoes grown extensively in the U.S. are white, red, and Russets (Russets account for about two-thirds the U.S. crop). Potatoes in the U.S. are harvested in all four seasons, but the vast majority of the crop is harvested in fall. Potatoes harvested in the winter, spring and summer are used mainly to supplement fresh supplies of fall-harvested potatoes and are also important to the processing industries. The four principal categories for U.S. potato exports are frozen, potato chips, fresh, and dehydrated. Fries account for approximately 95% of U.S. frozen potato exports.

Prices – The average monthly price received for potatoes by U.S. farmers in 2009 fell -6.9% to $8.80 per hundred pounds, down from last year's record high of $9.46.

Supply –The total potato crop in 2009 rose by +3.5% to 42.969 billion pounds, but still well below the record high of 50.936 billion pounds posted in 2000. The fall crop in 2009 rose by +3.9% to 39.350 billion pounds and it accounted for 92% of the total crop. Stocks of the fall crop (as of Dec 1, 2008) were 24.330 billion pounds. In 2009, the spring crop rose +5.9% to 2.132 billion pounds, the summer crop rose +4.8% to 1.447 billion pounds, and the winter crop fell -15.7% to 213.20 million billion pounds.

The largest producing states for the fall 2009 crop were Idaho (with 33% of the crop), Washington (7%), Wisconsin (7%), Colorado (6%), and North Dakota (5%). For the spring crop, the largest producing states were Florida with 36% of the crop and California with 34% of the crop. Farmers harvested 1.045 million acres in 2009, down -0.2% from 2008 which was a record low. The yield per harvested acre in 2009 rose +4.3% to 41,300 pounds per acre.

Demand – Total utilization of potatoes in 2008 (latest data available) fell -6.7% yr/yr to an 18-year low of 41.505 billion pounds. The breakdown shows that the largest consumption category for potatoes is frozen French fries with 35% of total consumption, followed closely by table stock (28%), chips and shoestrings (13%), and dehydration (11%). U.S. per capita consumption of potatoes in 2009 rose +0.5% to 121.0 pounds, well below the record high of 145.0 pounds per capita seen in 1996.

Trade – U.S. exports of potatoes in 2007 (latest data available) rose by +3.4% to 621.200 million pounds. U.S. exports hit a record high of 693.196 million pounds in 2002. U.S. imports in 2007 rose sharply by +51.2% to 923.500 million pounds, which was a new record high.

Salient Statistics of Potatoes in the United States

Crop Year	Acreage: Planted (1,000 Acres)	Acreage: Harvested (1,000 Acres)	Yield Per Harvested Acre (Cwt.)	Total Production (In Thousands of Cwt.)	Farm Disposition – Used Where Grown: Seed & Feed (In Thousands of Cwt.)	Farm Disposition – Used Where Grown: Shrinkage & Loss (In Thousands of Cwt.)	Sold[2] (In Thousands of Cwt.)	Farm Price ($ Cwt.)	Value of Production[3] (Million $)	Value of sales (Million $)	Stocks Jan. 1 (1,000 Cwt)	Foreign Trade[4]: Exports (Fresh) (Millions of Lbs.)	Foreign Trade[4]: Imports (Millions of Lbs.)	Consumption[4] Per Capita – In Pounds: Fresh	Consumption[4] Per Capita – In Pounds: Total
1999	1,377	1,332	359	478,216	5,569	35,531	437,116	5.77	2,742	2,519	239,910	579,378	610,581	47.7	136.2
2000	1,384	1,348	381	513,621	5,288	43,688	464,645	5.08	2,590	2,359	275,270	644,190	502,705	47.2	138.0
2001	1,247	1,221	358	437,673	5,387	31,208	401,293	6.99	3,056	2,803	224,680	579,361	487,888	46.6	138.8
2002	1,300	1,266	362	458,171	5,622	30,905	421,644	6.67	3,045	2,812	231,490	647,119	621,461	44.3	132.1
2003	1,273	1,249	367	457,814	5,543	35,294	416,977	5.88	2,686	2,455	233,590	541,775	635,006	46.9	138.4
2004	1,193	1,167	391	456,041	4,796	37,408	413,837	5.65	2,575	2,336	236,700	433,712	575,374	45.9	134.9
2005	1,109	1,087	390	423,926	4,791	28,519	390,616	7.04	2,991	2,750	220,500	586,226	631,251	41.4	125.8
2006	1,139	1,120	393	440,698	4,738	29,852	406,758	7.31	3,209	2,970	225,800	600,715	611,230	38.6	123.5
2007	1,142	1,122	396	444,873	4,105	29,561	411,209	7.51	3,340	3,089	232,300	615,784	923,574	39.1	125.3
2008[1]	1,060	1,047	396	415,053	4,138	26,438	384,478	9.46	3,770	3,494	212,800	615,135	1,072,017	36.7	118.8

[1] Preliminary. [2] For all purposes, including food, seed processing & livestock feed. [3] Farm weight basis, excluding canned and frozen potatoes.
[4] Calendar year. *Source: Economic Research Service, U.S. Department of Agriculture (ERS-USDA)*

Cold Storage Stocks of All Frozen Potatoes in the United States, on First of Month In Millions of Pounds

Year	Jan.	Feb.	Mar.	Apr.	May	June	July	Aug.	Sept.	Oct.	Nov.	Dec.
2000	1,165.4	1,140.9	1,270.1	1,283.4	1,239.4	1,250.4	1,186.3	1,180.3	1,185.7	1,291.5	1,351.5	1,285.9
2001	1,189.7	1,228.6	1,254.7	1,220.9	1,280.4	1,270.3	1,355.0	1,282.6	1,197.5	1,323.8	1,338.5	1,297.4
2002	1,239.8	1,274.2	1,271.5	1,271.4	1,222.7	1,182.3	1,223.5	1,106.6	1,040.6	1,141.4	1,252.2	1,214.4
2003	1,131.2	1,173.1	1,211.0	1,217.4	1,150.5	1,106.6	1,181.8	1,130.4	1,070.4	1,151.7	1,248.0	1,232.8
2004	1,120.4	1,167.3	1,207.4	1,192.5	1,158.7	1,185.9	1,128.7	1,117.1	1,127.0	1,178.6	1,274.9	1,219.3
2005	1,074.8	1,168.8	1,152.8	1,093.7	1,174.3	1,178.1	1,190.5	1,154.9	1,121.3	1,180.4	1,200.0	1,122.5
2006	1,051.1	1,076.2	1,147.0	1,158.9	1,176.6	1,104.9	1,108.1	996.4	964.1	1,009.6	1,066.6	1,052.1
2007	954.8	1,041.3	1,063.6	1,116.2	1,102.2	1,070.7	1,078.2	991.8	1,000.4	1,080.0	1,133.8	1,078.4
2008	1,012.4	1,089.1	1,117.5	1,087.7	1,134.4	1,074.9	1,190.0	1,107.5	1,126.7	1,180.8	1,200.5	1,212.1
2009[1]	1,098.6	1,171.0	1,192.1	1,226.8	1,217.3	1,203.2	1,245.1	1,187.5	1,094.8	1,130.2	1,162.9	1,108.1

[1] Preliminary. *Source: Agricultural Statistics Board, U.S. Department of Agriculture (ASB-USDA)*

Potato Crop Production Estimates, Stocks and Disappearance in the United States In Millions of Cwt.

	Crop Production Estimates						Total Storage Stocks[2]					Fall Crop — 1,000 Cwt.				
	Total Crop			Fall Crop			Following Year									
Year	Oct. 1	Nov. 1	Dec. 1	Oct. 1	Nov. 1	Dec. 1	Jan. 1	Feb. 1	Mar. 1	Apr. 1	May 1	Production	Disappearance (Sold)	Stocks Dec. 1	Average Price ($/Cwt.)	Value of Sales ($1,000)
2000	----	509.4	----	----	463.4	310.3	275.3	234.3	197.7	153.5	109.2	458,827	420,279	310,300	4.55	1,910,952
2001	----	441.8	----	----	400.7	258.8	224.7	192.1	158.6	120.0	81.2	387,033	358,812	258,750	6.54	2,348,006
2002	----	459.7	----	----	415.0	264.5	231.5	199.0	165.2	125.8	83.0	407,085	378,796	264,485	5.89	2,232,627
2003	----	459.2	----	----	413.5	267.9	233.6	200.2	166.3	126.1	85.0	203,566	371,755	267,900	5.23	1,943,986
2004	----	450.2	----	----	407.8	271.1	236.7	203.5	168.0	128.9	88.6	404,017	369,781	271,100	5.08	1,877,912
2005	----	421.3	----	----	382.2	253.8	220.5	189.1	155.5	115.7	75.9	375,118	351,083	253,800	6.53	2,290,850
2006	----	434.8	----	----	390.9	258.9	225.8	192.2	159.5	120.9	79.1	389,527	365,863	258,900	6.68	2,445,026
2007	----	448.0	----	----	408.3	265.5	232.3	199.3	163.4	125.5	84.0	406,800	374,617	265,500	7.04	2,636,885
2008	----	415.1	----	----	373.5	243.7	213.2	183.9	152.7	115.8	78.1	378,586	349,580	243,700	8.49	2,967,871
2009[1]	----	429.7	----	----	391.5	265.8	235.3	203.4	170.1			393,503		265,800		

[1] Preliminary. [2] Held by growers and local dealers in the fall producing areas.
Source: Agricultural Statistics Board, U.S. Department of Agriculture (ASB-USDA)

Production of Potatoes by Seasonal Groups in the United States In Thousands of Cwt.

	Winter	Spring			Summer			Fall								
Year	Total	California	Florida	Total	Mexico	Virgina	Total	Colorado	Idaho	Maine	Minnesota	North Dakota	Oregan	Washington	Wisconsin	Total
2000	4,960	7,426	6,343	21,921	1,050	1,292	19,236	27,972	152,320	17,920	21,240	26,950	30,683	105,000	33,800	458,827
2001	4,115	6,045	7,970	21,814	770	1,386	18,209	21,357	120,200	16,430	18,425	26,400	20,730	94,400	31,955	387,033
2002	4,206	7,695	7,883	22,452	736	1,386	17,932	27,885	133,385	16,960	18,810	23,460	24,936	92,340	30,750	407,085
2003	4,027	8,360	8,008	24,433	532	1,550	18,766	23,652	123,180	17,030	22,330	27,440	20,991	93,150	32,800	203,566
2004	4,818	8,313	7,678	22,663	340	1,200	18,307	23,791	131,970	19,065	18,920	26,765	19,775	93,810	30,450	404,017
2005	4,892	6,116	6,527	18,724	----	1,029	17,567	22,910	118,288	15,455	17,630	20,500	22,023	95,480	27,880	375,118
2006	4,495	6,044	6,441	19,766	----	1,512	18,166	22,686	128,915	17,980	20,400	25,480	18,533	89,900	29,370	389,527
2007	2,258	6,123	7,807	19,817	----	1,134	15,997	20,981	130,010	16,668	21,560	23,660	20,294	100,800	28,160	406,800
2008	2,530	6,930	7,952	20,132	----	1,254	13,805	21,907	116,475	14,769	20,400	22,680	18,674	93,000	25,730	378,586
2009[1]	2,132	7,175	7,700	21,321	----	1,656	14,469	22,080	131,000	15,263	20,700	19,125	21,460	88,450	28,980	393,503

[1] Preliminary. *Source: Agricultural Statistics Board, U.S. Department of Agriculture (ASB-USDA)*

Utilization of Potatoes in the United States In Thousands of Cwt.

	Sales											Non-Sales			
		For Processing							Other Sales						
Crop Year	Table Stock	Chips, Shoestrings	Dehydration	Frozen French Fries	Other Frozen Products	Canned Potatoes	Other Canned Products[2]	Starch & Flour	Livestock Feed	Seed	Total Sales	Used on Farms Where Grown	Shrinkage & Loss	Total Non-Sales	Total
1999	134,130	52,916	50,831	140,196	23,593	3,311	2,394	1,310	3,141	25,294	437,116	4,415	35,531	41,100	478,216
2000	139,590	52,405	54,332	146,869	26,723	2,368	2,709	1,966	14,265	23,345	464,572	3,792	43,685	48,972	513,544
2001	122,552	54,080	40,759	126,711	23,598	2,590	1,722	1,015	3,496	24,537	401,060	4,088	31,227	36,613	437,673
2002	131,889	51,640	51,357	124,875	28,951	2,744	2,089	1,050	3,044	24,005	421,644	4,144	30,905	36,527	458,171
2003	133,143	52,790	48,418	126,515	23,870	3,086	1,168	1,379	2,005	24,603	416,977	4,000	35,294	40,837	457,814
2004	130,418	50,068	48,541	131,592	23,003	2,843	984	1,531	1,942	22,915	413,837	3,601	37,408	42,204	456,041
2005	114,123	52,294	43,387	126,429	25,376	2,174	958	1,622	1,999	22,254	390,616	3,595	28,519	33,310	423,926
2006	113,335	64,377	48,809	126,083	24,229	1,957	930	1,369	1,610	23,610	406,309	3,520	29,639	34,389	440,698
2007	110,860	54,343	49,021	139,624	26,571	2,504	800	4,029	1,160	2,297	411,209	2,986	29,561	33,666	444,875
2008[1]	109,351	50,744	40,714	134,394	19,558	2,156	791	5,067	803	20,900	384,478	3,315	26,438	30,576	415,055

[1] Preliminary. [2] Hash, stews and soups. *Source: Agricultural Statistics Board, U.S. Department of Agriculture (ASB-USDA)*

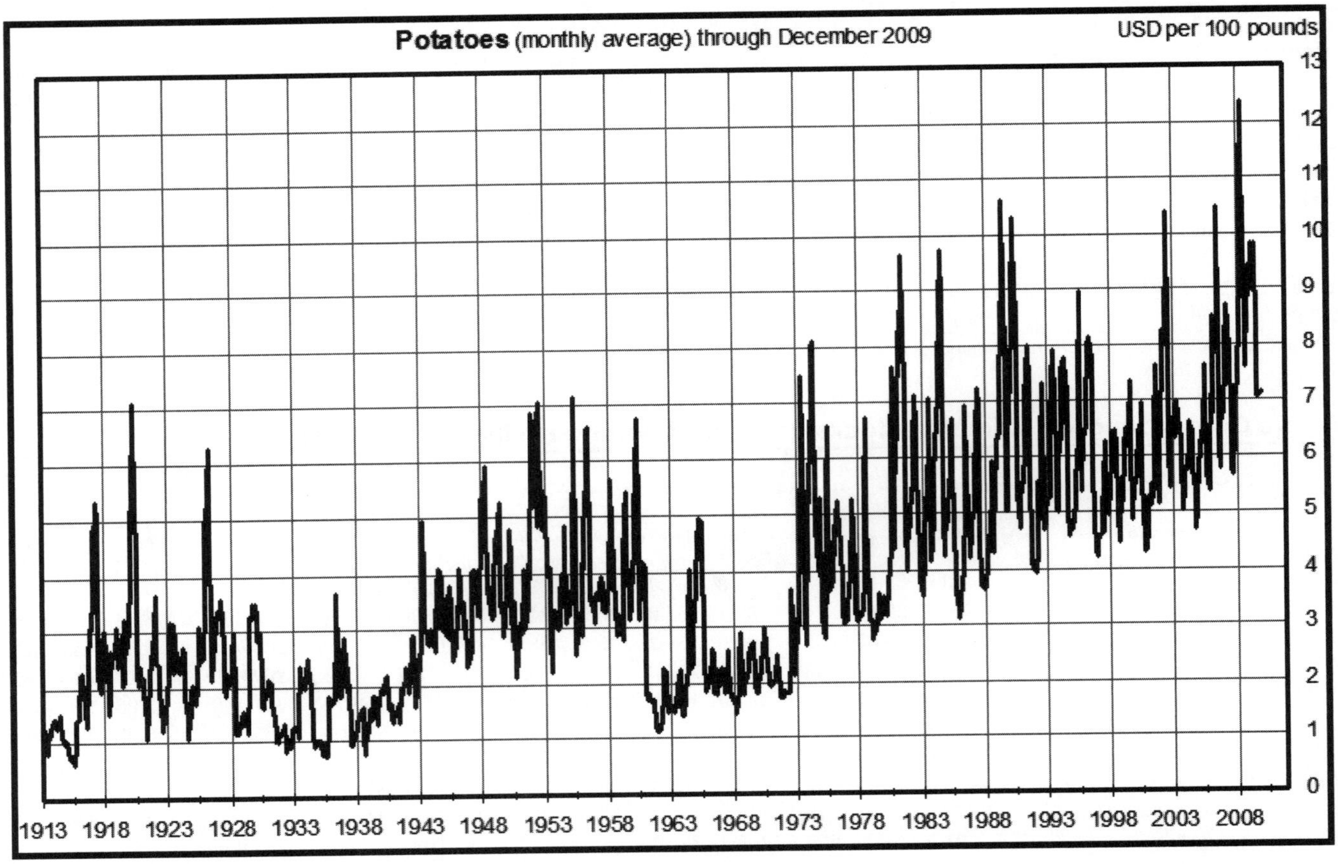

Per Capita Utilization of Potatoes in the United States In Pounds (Farm Weight)

			Processing				
Year	Total	Fresh	Freezing	Chips & Shoe-string	Dehy-drating	Canning	Total Processing
2001	138.8	46.6	58.2	17.6	14.8	1.6	92.2
2002	132.1	44.3	55.2	16.5	14.7	1.4	87.9
2003	138.1	46.8	57.2	17.3	15.5	1.4	91.3
2004	134.8	45.9	57.4	16.6	13.8	1.2	89.0
2005	125.6	41.3	54.4	16.2	12.8	0.9	84.3
2006	123.9	38.6	53.3	18.8	12.5	0.8	85.3
2007	124.6	38.8	53.2	18.7	13.0	0.9	85.9
2008	118.7	37.9	51.6	15.9	12.4	1.0	80.8
2009[1]	117.0	37.5	50.6	16.3	11.7	0.8	79.5
2010[2]	116.8	36.6	50.0	17.0	12.4	0.8	80.2

[1] Preliminary. [2] Forecast. *Source: Agricultural Statistics Board, U.S. Department of Agriculture (ASB-USDA)*

Average Price Received by Farmers for Potatoes in the U.S. In Dollars Per Hundred Pounds (Cwt.)

Year	Jan.	Feb.	Mar.	Apr.	May	June	July	Aug.	Sept.	Oct.	Nov.	Dec.	Season Average
2000	5.68	5.92	6.26	6.46	6.31	6.14	6.93	5.56	4.49	4.27	4.31	4.48	5.08
2001	4.56	5.26	5.12	5.47	5.24	5.75	6.46	7.61	6.04	5.15	5.96	6.66	6.99
2002	6.90	7.34	8.26	8.00	8.62	9.39	10.40	8.00	6.14	5.44	6.38	6.67	6.67
2003	6.67	6.33	6.87	6.94	6.96	6.68	6.30	5.75	5.24	5.03	5.46	5.77	5.88
2004	5.75	5.87	6.09	6.62	6.47	6.16	6.46	5.77	5.32	4.70	5.02	5.36	5.65
2005	5.59	5.79	6.44	6.20	6.23	6.29	7.63	7.02	5.69	5.37	6.26	6.83	7.04
2006	7.07	6.76	8.50	8.35	7.83	8.41	10.46	8.23	6.12	5.76	6.59	6.79	7.31
2007	7.06	7.42	7.93	8.71	7.95	7.75	8.48	6.85	5.81	5.68	6.47	7.02	7.51
2008	7.33	7.51	8.37	8.45	9.16	10.78	12.33	11.33	8.65	7.60	8.77	9.30	8.42
2009[1]	9.40	8.87	9.27	9.81	9.62	9.48	9.81	9.61	8.27	7.03	7.09	7.39	8.00

[1] Preliminary. *Source: Agricultural Statistics Board, U.S. Department of Agriculture (ASB-USDA)*

Potatoes Processed[1] in the United States, Eight States In Thousands of Cwt.

States	Storage Season	to Dec. 1	to Jan. 1	to Feb. 1	to Mar. 1	to Apr. 1	to May 1	to June 1	Entire Season
Idaho and Oregon-Malheur Co.	2001-02	20,940	27,330	33,620	40,860	47,710	54,150	61,200	73,390
	2002-03	28,380	34,860	41,200	48,600	56,240	63,840	71,280	85,390
	2003-04	24,310	30,730	36,260	43,640	49,570	56,380	63,770	77,530
	2004-05	24,360	30,840	36,820	44,610	51,000	58,090	65,800	84,600
	2005-06	22,840	29,300	35,970	43,300	50,820	57,830	65,030	77,360
	2006-07	27,090	34,070	41,350	49,840	56,650	63,680	71,220	85,630
	2007-08	26,230	33,250	40,310	48,660	55,460	63,000	70,700	88,030
	2008-09	22,380	28,980	35,430	42,150	49,030	55,570	62,940	77,340
	2009-10	23,110	29,180	35,170	42,050				
Maine[2]	2001-02	1,975	2,440	3,110	3,700	4,285	4,775	5,515	7,195
	2002-03	2,230	2,715	3,345	3,905	4,505	5,225	5,905	7,835
	2003-04	1,590	2,085	2,720	3,420	4,095	4,740	5,400	7,270
	2004-05	1,540	1,970	2,600	3,135	3,700	4,340	4,910	6,590
	2005-06	1,365	1,880	2,485	3,090	3,800	4,450	5,130	6,825
	2006-07	1,755	2,360	2,910	3,465	4,185	4,810	5,470	7,560
	2007-08	1,700	2,170	2,815	3,440	3,990	4,670	5,240	7,550
	2008-09	1,635	2,240	2,895	3,515	4,005	4,795	5,540	7,545
	2009-10	1,575	2,060	2,680	3,265				
Washington & Oregon-Other	2001-02	29,320	35,310	40,540	47,910	54,970	61,360	69,400	77,180
	2002-03	33,680	39,490	44,190	51,920	58,710	64,300	71,480	79,110
	2003-04	32,670	38,520	43,610	51,210	58,500	64,160	72,350	79,800
	2004-05	32,305	38,130	43,570	50,730	57,140	63,855	71,355	78,680
	2005-06	30,310	35,895	40,545	48,290	55,320	61,855	69,360	78,550
	2006-07	30,980	37,060	41,290	49,930	56,690	63,170	70,410	77,355
	2007-08	30,595	36,940	42,350	50,165	57,160	67,690	72,380	82,770
	2008-09	32,560	38,050	42,795	49,865	56,350	62,635	70,625	81,260
	2009-10	25,350	31,200	36,490	43,750				
Other States[3]	2001-02	13,170	14,925	19,000	22,115	24,655	27,815	30,460	37,740
	2002-03	12,675	15,530	18,735	21,780	24,810	27,405	30,655	38,700
	2003-04	13,835	16,505	19,590	22,685	25,920	29,480	32,845	42,160
	2004-05	12,490	15,000	17,965	20,910	24,150	27,480	30,945	41,175
	2005-06	11,055	14,070	17,005	19,895	22,520	25,270	27,740	35,535
	2006-07	14,355	17,800	21,415	24,690	28,205	31,560	35,040	43,565
	2007-08	15,040	17,535	20,755	23,900	26,650	29,710	32,600	39,430
	2008-09	12,480	15,120	18,165	21,030	24,025	26,515	29,590	37,285
	2009-10	10,605	13,260	16,225	18,945				
Total	2001-02	65,405	80,005	96,270	114,585	131,620	148,100	166,575	195,505
	2002-03	76,965	92,595	107,470	126,205	144,265	160,770	179,320	211,035
	2003-04	72,405	87,840	102,180	120,955	138,085	154,760	174,365	206,760
	2004-05	70,695	85,940	100,955	119,385	135,990	153,765	173,010	211,045
	2005-06	65,570	81,145	96,005	114,575	132,460	149,405	167,260	198,270
	2006-07	74,210	91,320	107,895	127,050	145,760	163,250	182,170	214,225
	2007-08	73,565	89,895	106,230	126,165	143,260	165,070	180,920	217,780
	2008-09	69,055	84,390	99,285	116,560	133,410	149,515	168,695	203,430
	2009-10	60,640	75,700	90,565	108,010				
Dehydrated[4]	2001-02	----	----	----	----	----	----	----	38,581
	2002-03	15,675	19,660	23,710	27,950	31,915	36,105	40,455	48,940
	2003-04	14,250	18,440	22,050	26,090	30,290	34,630	39,070	47,750
	2004-05	14,525	18,540	21,875	25,970	30,020	33,685	38,505	47,805
	2005-06	11,920	15,655	19,225	22,765	26,605	30,065	34,130	41,625
	2006-07	14,590	19,250	23,635	27,885	32,210	36,480	40,915	49,375
	2007-08	12,815	16,785	21,040	25,350	29,500	33,650	37,975	46,660
	2008-09	10,675	14,490	18,335	21,465	24,875	28,195	31,870	39,345
	2009-10	10,945	13,950	17,065	19,800				

[1] Total quantity received and used for processing regardless of the State in which the potatoes were produced. Amount excludes quantities used for potato chips in Maine, Michigan and Wisconsin. [2] Includes Maine grown potatoes only. [3] Colorado, Minnesota, , Nevada, North Dakota and Wisconsin.
[4] Dehydrated products except starch and flour. Included in above totals. Includes CO, ID, NV, ND, OR, WA, and WI.
Source: National Agricultural Statistics Service, U.S. Department of Agriculture (NASS-USDA)

Rayon and Other Synthetic Fibers

World Cellulosic Fiber Production In Thousands of Metric Tons

Year	Brazil	Bulgaria	China	CIS	Czech Republic	India	Indo-nesia	Japan	Mexico	Taiwan	Thailand	United States	World Total
2000	36.2	15.0	552.3	83.7	7.1	297.5	207.0	126.2	14.8	141.5	65.0	158.8	2,215
2001	28.7	12.2	608.6	64.4	7.6	251.9	205.0	107.1	22.6	127.4	65.0	103.0	2,083
2002	34.2	5.6	682.1	72.9	7.3	285.7	214.0	68.1	16.8	114.2	71.1	80.7	2,125
2003	47.2	5.2	800.2	78.8	9.1	283.0	223.0	68.3	8.4	121.5	73.8	75.3	2,249
2004	46.8	5.0	966.1	77.2	9.2	311.5	234.0	67.1	8.4	134.9	79.4	66.8	2,465
2005	40.1	5.0	1,056.0	46.6	9.5	295.4	245.0	66.6	3.8	114.5	78.2	49.1	2,483
2006	34.3	5.0	1,179.0	28.7	9.4	309.5	280.0	65.1	----	132.3	80.2	27.2	2,640
2007	39.7	5.0	1,360.2	27.9	9.3	345.4	325.0	71.5	----	136.3	95.4	25.3	2,920
2008[1]	15.9	5.0	1,203.0	9.2	2.7	301.0	282.0	69.1	----	105.5	80.2	22.8	2,545
2009[2]	43.1	6.0	2,010.0	41.3		471.7	347.0	96.3	----	150.0	142.0	27.0	3,881

[1] Preliminary. [2] Producing capacity. *Source: Fiber Economics Bureau, Inc. (FEB)*

World Noncellulosic Fiber Production (Except Olefin) In Thousands of Metric Tons

Year	Brazil	China	India	Indonesia	Japan	Rep. of Korea	Mexico	Pakistan	Taiwan	Thailand	Turkey	United States	World Total
2000	311.1	6,158.4	1,568.4	1,142.7	1,307.9	2,659.0	586.8	503.9	3,122.9	769.5	744.5	3,149.2	26,219
2001	288.8	7,322.9	1,570.2	1,190.6	1,239.5	2,471.9	536.4	528.4	2,977.5	784.5	669.2	2,687.6	26,243
2002	293.1	8,849.4	1,695.3	1,132.8	1,129.1	2,455.7	509.6	581.5	3,091.3	852.6	728.1	2,805.0	28,052
2003	314.2	10,456.0	1,792.0	1,144.2	1,030.3	2,418.0	474.9	646.8	3,060.9	872.5	766.9	2,719.5	29,450
2004	330.9	12,474.1	1,904.2	1,064.5	989.2	2,194.3	474.9	659.3	2,965.0	905.9	849.5	2,858.2	31,429
2005	255.6	16,097.9	1,849.2	1,072.0	955.4	1,697.4	390.6	565.2	2,587.8	920.7	792.0	2,680.1	33,511
2006	274.2	18,383.1	2,132.5	1,100.7	923.9	1,487.5	271.0	550.7	2,292.4	869.9	788.8	2,479.3	35,098
2007	288.5	21,338.9	2,447.3	1,124.0	901.1	1,479.0	252.6	537.9	2,382.0	826.9	739.3	2,310.9	38,034
2008[1]	279.4	22,012.4	2,261.6	1,081.3	771.1	1,359.3	190.6	483.5	1,928.4	727.9	629.9	1,918.3	36,686
2009[2]	335.5	30,307.0	3,747.0	1,359.0	1,201.6	1,638.6	273.0	731.0	2,277.1	928.0	881.2	2,311.8	50,274

[1] Preliminary. [2] Producing capacity. *Source: Fiber Economics Bureau, Inc. (FEB)*

World Production of Synthetic Fibers In Thousands of Metric Tons

	Noncellulosic Fiber Production (Except Olefin)							Glass Fiber Production							
	By Fibers				World Total										
Year	Acrylic & Mod-acrylic	Nylon & Aramid	Polyester	Other	Yarn & Monofil-aments	Staple & Tow & Fiberfill	Total	Europe	Japan	Other Americas	United States	Total	China	USSR	Cigarette Tow Pro-duction
2000	2,634	4,117	19,155	313	14,771	11,448	26,219	728	280	96	1,143	60	28	2,580	570
2001	2,562	3,784	19,563	335	14,968	11,276	26,243	701	273	93	1,016	67	32	2,431	590
2002	2,713	3,941	21,048	350	15,993	12,059	28,052	718	251	96	1,222	90	34	2,661	612
2003	2,707	3,951	22,365	427	16,853	12,597	29,450	724	250	100	1,307	120	37	2,790	633
2004	2,824	3,976	24,136	492	17,957	13,472	31,429	740	250	104	1,363	150	40	2,903	651
2005	2,698	3,893	26,410	510	19,293	14,218	33,511								665
2006	2,521	3,921	28,070	586	20,554	14,545	35,098								680
2007	2,406	3,891	31,095	642	22,659	15,375	38,034								671
2008[1]	1,913	3,512	30,650	612	22,237	14,448	36,686								689
2009[2]	2,920	5,006	41,514	835	30,111	20,163	50,274								

[1] Preliminary. [2] Producing capacity. [3] Alginate, azion, spandex, saran, etc. *Source: Fiber Economics Bureau, Inc. (FEB)*

Artificial (Cellulosic) Fiber Distribution in the United States In Millions of Pounds

	Yan & Monofilament					Staple & Tow					
	Producers' Shipments					Producers' Shipments					
Year	Domestic	Exports	Total	Imports	Domestic Con-sumption	Domestic	Exports	Total	Imports	Domestic Con-sumption	Glass Fiber Ship-ments
2000	76.7	37.8	114.5	23.2	99.9	162.3	69.3	231.5	37.5	199.7	----
2001	54.3	33.7	88.0	14.5	68.8	117.2	35.5	152.7	33.9	151.2	----
2002	41.2	33.2	74.4	12.7	53.9	91.1	12.6	103.7	56.2	147.4	----
2003	32.5	35.5	68.0	11.7	44.2	86.7	13.1	99.8	44.5	131.2	----
2004	26.7	38.7	65.4	12.2	38.9	77.4	9.9	87.2	63.9	141.3	----
2005	22.6	41.4	64.0	9.3	31.9	40.2	8.1	48.2	91.0	131.2	----
2006	22.4	37.6	60.0	7.7	30.1	----	8.9	8.9	141.4	141.4	----
2007	18.7	41.1	59.8	17.0	35.7	----	5.4	5.4	200.7	200.7	----
2008	15.4	44.5	59.9	11.8	27.2	----	6.8	6.8	179.8	179.8	----
2009[1]	12.7	43.2	55.9	7.4	20.1	----	3.5	3.5	168.3	168.3	----

[1] Preliminary. *Source: Fiber Economice Bureau, Inc.*

Man-Made Fiber Production in the United States In Millions of Pounds

	- Artificial (Cellulosic) Fibers - - Rayon & Acetate -			Synthetic (Noncellulosic) Fibers: Yarn & Monofilament				Synthetic (Noncellulosic) Fibers: Staple & Tow							
Year	Filament Yarn & Monofilament	Staple & Tow	Total Cellulosic	Nylon	Polyester	Olefin	Total Yarn	Nylon	Polyester	Acrylic & Modacrylic	Olefin	Total Staple	Total Noncellulosic Fibers	Total Manufactured Fibers	Total Glass Fiber
2001	----	153	153	1,642	1,188	2,181	5,011	606	2,040	310	721	3,676	8,687	----	2,638
2002	----	104	104	1,772	1,218	2,331	5,321	681	2,050	340	749	3,820	9,141	----	2,759
2003	----	100	100	1,762	1,145	2,349	5,255	697	1,886	270	680	3,533	8,788	----	2,789
2004	----	----	----	1,837	1,242	2,383	5,462	680	2,064	240	676	3,660	9,123	----	----
2005	----	----	----	1,788	1,111	2,395	5,295	598	2,019	140	699	3,455	8,750	----	----
2006	----	----	----	1,739	1,072	2,223	5,034	515	1,864	----	622	3,001	8,035	----	----
2007	----	----	----	1,636	1,017	2,266	4,918	429	1,719	----	588	2,736	7,654	----	----
2008[1]	----	----	----	1,332	915	1,914	4,161	266	1,423	----	488	2,177	6,339	----	----
2009[2]	----	----	----	1,196	830	1,661	3,686	178	1,163	----	410	1,751	5,437	----	----

[1] Preliminary. [2] Estimate. *Source: Fiber Economics Bureau, Inc. (FEB)*

Domestic Distribution of Synthetic (Noncellulosic) Fibers in the United States In Millions of Pounds

	Yarn & Monofilament: Producers' Shipments: Domestic								Staple & Tow: Producers' Shipments: Domestic								
Year	Nylon	Polyester	Olefin	Total	Exports	Total	Imports	Domestic Consumption	Nylon	Polyester	Acrylic & Modacrylic	Olefin	Total	Exports	Total	Imports	Domestic Consumption
2001	1,606	1,211	2,144	4,960	155	5,115	697	5,657	607	1,881	228	673	3,389	308	3,698	757	4,146
2002	1,668	1,139	2,289	5,096	189	5,285	765	5,860	637	1,823	255	723	3,438	353	3,791	875	4,312
2003	1,666	1,088	2,318	5,072	179	5,251	766	5,838	673	1,688	211	635	3,206	246	3,452	829	4,035
2004	1,722	1,119	2,347	5,188	249	5,437	785	5,973	658	1,788	200	641	3,287	296	3,583	766	4,053
2005	1,688	1,014	2,369	5,071	197	5,268	849	5,920	582	1,765	122	650	3,120	292	3,411	914	4,034
2006	1,589	914	2,198	4,702	211	4,913	819	5,520	492	1,624	----	596	2,713	268	2,981	1,007	3,719
2007	1,526	928	2,219	4,672	199	4,871	739	5,411	407	1,506	----	549	2,461	256	2,717	1,029	3,490
2008	1,336	841	1,921	4,098	144	4,242	692	4,790	252	1,279	----	448	1,979	184	2,163	1,038	3,017
2009[1]	1,152	781	1,647	3,580	82	3,661	568	4,148	158	1,080	----	363	1,602	135	1,736	841	2,443

[1] Preliminary. *Source: Fiber Economics Bureau, Inc. (FEB)*

Mill Consumption of Fiber & Products and Per Capita Consumption in the United States In Millions of Pounds

	Cellulosic Fibers				Noncellulosic Fibers								- Per Capita4 Mill Consumption (Lbs.) -				
Year	Yarn & Monofilament	Staple & Tow	Net Waste	Total Cellulosic	Noncellulosic	Net Waste	Total Noncellulosic	Total Manufactured Fibers[2]	Cotton	Wool	Other Fibers[3]	Grand Total	Manmade Finers	Cotton	Wool	Other Fibers[3]	Total
2000	100	200	1.9	302	10,706	190	10,897	11,198	4,754	101	177.9	16,231	47.8	34.9	1.3	2.6	86.6
2001	69	151	2.4	222	10,226	193	10,419	10,641	3,983	87	168.1	14,880	45.8	33.1	1.4	2.1	82.4
2002	54	147	1.8	203	10,149	190	10,339	10,542	3,576	56	110.3	14,284	47.6	34.3	1.3	2.2	85.5
2003	44	131	1.3	177	10,129	177	10,306	10,482	3,210	43	106.3	13,841	49.4	34.8	1.4	2.7	88.3
2004	39	141	1.5	182	10,500	144	10,644	10,826	3,126	44	123.4	14,119	50.4	35.1	1.4	3.4	90.3
2005	32	131	2.0	165	10,467	136	10,603	10,768	3,005	36	141.3	13,950	51.6	37.7	1.4	3.1	93.7
2006	30	141	2.9	174	10,221	73	10,294	10,468	2,729	34	106.7	13,338	51.7	38.3	1.4	2.9	94.4
2007	36	201	2.8	239	9,987	77	10,064	10,303	2,624	32	101.1	13,061	51.3	38.6	1.4	2.6	93.9
2008[1]	27	180	2.9	210	9,169	59	9,228	9,438	2,093	30	96.6	11,658	46.7	34.8	1.3	2.4	85.3

[1] Preliminary. [2] Excludes Glass Fiber. [3] Includes silk, linen, jute and sisal & others. [4] Mill consumption plus inports less exports of semimanufactured and unmanufactured products. *Source: Fiber Economics Bureau, Inc. (FEB)*

Producer Price Index of Grey Synthetic Broadwovens (1982 = 100)

Year	Jan.	Feb.	Mar.	Apr.	May	June	July	Aug.	Sept.	Oct.	Nov.	Dec.	Average
2000	108.1	109.3	110.6	110.6	109.0	107.7	109.6	110.6	109.4	109.3	110.6	110.9	109.6
2001	110.1	111.3	111.8	111.9	109.2	110.1	107.8	108.8	109.2	107.7	107.7	107.5	109.4
2002	106.7	106.4	108.0	108.5	107.7	108.2	107.3	108.1	108.0	107.2	107.3	108.4	107.7
2003	108.2	108.2	107.6	107.7	110.1	106.0	105.7	107.1	106.7	106.0	106.6	107.7	107.3
2004	107.3	106.9	106.2	107.4	108.9	109.0	107.5	106.2	106.3	106.3	106.2	106.2	107.0
2005	108.5	108.8	109.1	110.5	110.2	110.0	110.7	110.9	110.8	112.4	113.3	116.2	111.0
2006	118.2	119.5	119.8	119.2	119.4	119.4	119.5	120.4	119.1	119.5	119.0	118.1	119.3
2007	117.8	118.8	118.9	119.1	119.6	119.8	120.3	121.5	122.9	122.7	123.0	122.9	120.6
2008	122.9	123.0	122.8	123.0	123.3	123.3	123.6	121.8	122.0	121.2	122.0	120.1	122.4
2009[1]	121.7	122.6	122.6	125.9	125.8	127.5	127.2	124.3	124.2	124.6	124.2	124.3	124.6

[1] Preliminary. *Source: Bureau of Labor Statistics, U.S. Department of Commerce (BLS) (0337-03)*

Rice

Rice is a grain that is cultivated on every continent except Antarctica and is the primary food for half the people in the world. Rice cultivation probably originated as early as 10,000 BC in Asia. Rice is grown at varying altitudes (sea level to about 3,000 meters), in varying climates (tropical to temperate), and on dry to flooded land. The growth duration of rice plants is 3-6 months, depending on variety and growing conditions. Rice is harvested by hand in developing countries or by combines in industrialized countries. Asian countries produce about 90% of rice grown worldwide. Rough rice futures and options are traded on the Chicago Board of Trade (CBOT).

Prices – Rough rice prices on the CBOT nearest futures chart at the beginning of 2009 were about $15.00 per hundred pounds but then moved lower to about $12.83 per hundred pounds in March. From there the price moved generally higher to $15.72 in November but then moved lower in December to end the year at about $14.57 per hundred pounds. The downmove continued into 2010 with the price reaching about $14.35 per hundred pounds in February 2010.

Regarding cash prices, the average monthly price of rice received by farmers in the U.S. in the first six months of the 2009-10 marketing year (i.e., August 2009 through July 2010) fell by 14.1% yr/yr to $14.30 per hundred pounds (cwt.).

Supply – World rice production in the 2009-10 marketing year fell -2.5% to 650.616 million metric tons, down from the 20080-09 record high of 657.133 million metric tons. The world's largest rice producers were China with 30% of world production in 2009-10, India with 19%, Indonesia with 9%, Bangladesh with 7%, Vietnam with 6%, and Thailand with 5%. U.S. production of rice in 2009-10 rose +7.9% yr/yr to 219.850 million cwt (hundred pounds), but still well below the 2004-05 record high of 230.818 million cwt.

Demand – World utilization of rice in 2009-10 rose +0.2% to a record high of 434.541 million metric tons. U.S. rice consumption in 2009-10 rose +0.9% yr/yr to 129.5 million cwt (hundred pounds), down from the 2006-07 record high of 128.1 million cwt (hundred pounds).

Trade – World exports of rice in 2009-10 rose +8.6% yr/yr to a new record high of 31.046 metric tons. The world's largest rice exporters are Thailand with 32% of world exports, Vietnam with 18%, Pakistan with 12%, the U.S. with 10%, and India with 6%. U.S. rice imports in 2009-10 rose by +9.4% yr/yr to 21.0 million cwt (hundred pounds), but still below the 2007-08 record high of 23.9 million cwt. U.S. rice exports in 2009-10 rose by +5.8% yr/yr to 99.0 million cwt.

World Rice Supply and Distribution In Thousands of Metric Tons

	Imports							Utilization			Ending Stocks		
Crop Year	Brazil	Indonesia	European Union	Iran	Nigeria	Saudi Arabia	Total	China	India	Total	China	India	Total
2004-05	510	500	1,095	1,200	1,369	1,500	26,074	130,300	80,861	407,251	38,931	8,500	73,390
2005-06	750	539	1,124	1,500	1,650	1,357	26,433	128,000	85,088	412,686	36,783	10,520	75,990
2006-07	732	2,000	1,340	1,500	1,500	958	28,200	127,200	86,700	418,370	35,915	11,430	75,100
2007-08[1]	422	350	1,568	1,500	1,800	961	29,201	127,450	90,466	426,470	38,015	13,000	80,975
2008-09[2]	650	250	1,323	1,700	1,700	1,360	27,363	129,000	93,150	433,706	42,915	17,000	93,344
2009-10[3]	800	250	1,350	1,700	1,600	1,370	28,462	133,500	86,700	434,541	45,265	13,000	92,497

[1] Preliminary. [2] Estimate. [3] Forecast. *Source: Foreign Agricultural Service, U.S. Department of Agriculture (FAS-USDA)*

World Production of Rough Rice In Thousands of Metric Tons

Year	Bangladesh	Brazil	Burma	China	India	Indonesia	Japan	Korea	Pakistan	Philippines	Thailand	Vietnam	World Total
2004-05	38,404	13,229	16,500	179,090	124,707	54,000	10,912	6,737	7,538	14,500	26,303	34,418	597,965
2005-06	43,141	11,579	18,000	180,591	137,699	54,200	11,342	6,435	8,321	15,109	27,576	34,503	623,482
2006-07	43,504	11,316	18,276	181,714	140,039	54,729	10,695	6,306	8,176	15,516	27,652	34,730	627,482
2007-08[1]	43,204	12,057	18,500	186,034	145,050	57,364	10,893	5,962	8,551	16,633	30,000	36,932	648,045
2008-09[2]	46,505	12,601	17,500	191,900	148,740	59,380	11,029	6,545	10,051	17,068	30,076	36,952	667,133
2009-10[3]	45,005	11,500	18,500	195,714	126,763	60,155	10,467	6,635	9,301	16,190	30,909	36,818	650,616

[1] Preliminary. [2] Estimate. [3] Forecast. *Source: Foreign Agricultural Service, U.S. Department of Agriculture (FAS-USDA)*

World Exports of Rice (Milled Basis) In Thousands of Metric Tons

Year	Argentina	Australia	Burma	China	European Union	Guyana	India	Pakistan	Thailand	Uruguay	Vietnam	United States	World Total
2004-05	325	80	190	656	175	243	4,569	2,801	7,274	775	5,174	3,496	28,315
2005-06	485	326	47	1,216	161	182	4,688	3,664	7,376	834	4,705	3,661	29,715
2006-07	452	166	31	1,340	148	250	5,740	2,839	9,557	734	4,522	2,923	31,499
2007-08[1]	420	36	541	969	152	210	4,654	3,000	10,011	778	4,649	3,349	31,241
2008-09[2]	550	20	1,052	760	139	210	2,000	3,000	8,570	900	5,950	2,993	28,597
2009-10[3]	600	40	800	1,500	135	250	2,000	3,800	10,000	750	5,500	3,229	31,046

[1] Preliminary. [2] Estimate. [3] Forecast. *Source: Foreign Agricultural Service, U.S. Department of Agriculture (FAS-USDA)*

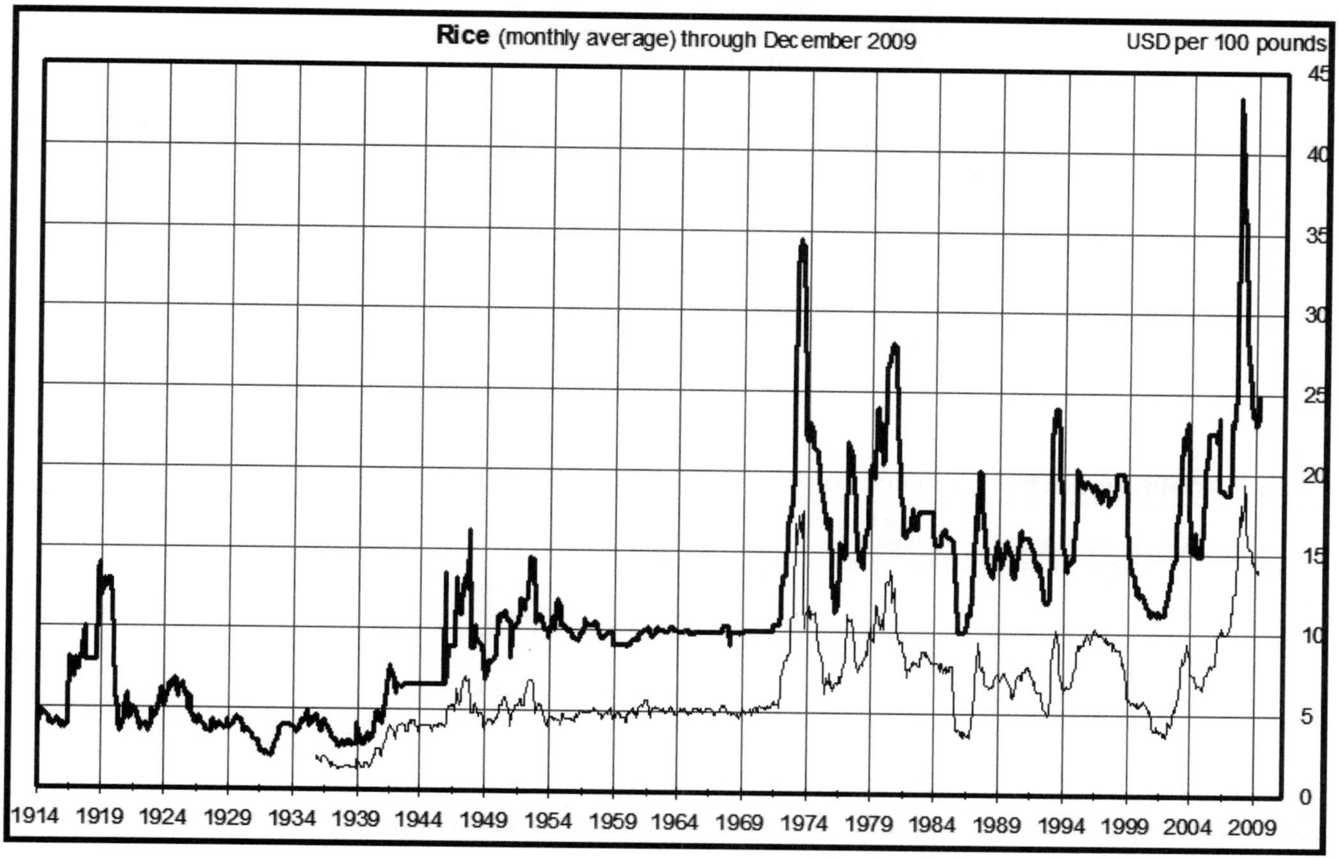

Average Wholesale Price of Rice No. 2 (Medium)[1] Southwest Louisiana In Dollars Per Cwt. Bagged

Year	Jan.	Feb.	Mar.	Apr.	May	June	July	Aug.	Sept.	Oct.	Nov.	Dec.	Average
1999-00	18.60	17.50	14.88	14.70	14.67	14.35	14.00	13.83	13.75	13.40	12.50	12.63	14.57
2000-01	13.00	12.34	12.48	12.41	12.38	12.38	12.25	12.00	11.82	11.53	11.25	11.25	12.09
2001-02	11.06	11.50	11.50	11.50	11.08	11.50	11.50	11.43	10.94	11.13	11.13	11.13	11.28
2002-03	11.13	11.50	12.25	12.25	12.25	12.63	13.50	14.05	14.25	14.44	14.50	14.88	13.13
2003-04	16.75	17.70	19.00	19.95	21.25	21.38	22.30	22.46	22.50	23.00	21.50	21.50	20.77
2004-05	18.60	15.69	15.23	15.13	15.13	16.31	14.88	14.88	14.88	14.88	14.88	14.94	15.45
2005-06	17.00	17.50	18.45	20.13	21.38	22.50	22.50	22.50	22.50	22.50	22.50	22.35	20.98
2006-07	21.94	22.00	22.00	23.50	23.50	23.50	23.50	23.50	23.50	23.50	23.50	23.50	23.12
2007-08	23.50	23.50	23.30	23.25	23.25	23.25	24.31	27.45	34.00	39.00	40.00	40.00	28.73
2008-09[2]	40.63	43.10	43.25	43.06	42.88								42.58

[1] U.S. No. 2 -- broken not to exceed 4%. [2] Preliminary. *Source: Economic Research Service, U.S. Department of Agriculture (ERS-USDA)*

Average Price Received by Farmers for Rice (Rough) in the United States In Dollars Per Hundred Pounds (Cwt.)

Year	Jan.	Feb.	Mar.	Apr.	May	June	July	Aug.	Sept.	Oct.	Nov.	Dec.	Average[2]
2000-01	5.72	5.53	5.57	5.72	5.69	5.86	5.72	5.66	5.68	5.40	5.14	5.32	5.61
2001-02	5.10	4.78	4.36	4.08	4.07	4.30	4.16	3.99	3.94	3.98	3.92	3.81	4.21
2002-03	3.71	3.94	3.69	3.70	4.13	4.66	4.24	4.31	4.61	4.84	5.43	5.31	4.38
2003-04	5.47	6.18	6.44	6.99	7.57	8.57	8.23	8.45	8.65	9.30	9.37	8.79	7.83
2004-05	8.96	8.47	7.60	7.36	7.37	7.39	6.90	6.97	6.98	6.98	6.96	6.82	7.40
2005-06	6.58	6.76	6.99	7.46	7.49	7.80	8.02	8.05	8.16	8.03	8.41	8.18	7.66
2006-07	8.81	9.03	9.65	10.10	9.91	10.40	10.10	10.00	10.20	10.00	10.00	10.10	9.86
2007-08	10.10	10.30	10.70	11.40	11.50	12.40	12.60	13.60	14.60	15.90	16.50	16.80	13.03
2008-09	18.10	16.90	18.10	19.40	18.60	18.20	16.00	15.30	15.30	15.20	14.70	14.30	16.68
2009-10[1]	14.60	14.20	14.20	13.80	14.40	14.40	14.50						14.30

[1] Preliminary. [2] Weighted average by sales. *Source: Economic Research Service, U.S. Department of Agriculture (ERS-USDA)*

Salient Statistics of Rice, Rough & Milled (Rough Equivalent) in the United States In Millions of Cwt.

Crop Year Beginning Aug. 1	Supply: Stocks Aug. 1	Supply: Production	Supply: Imports	Supply: Total Supply	Disappearance: Domestic: Food	Domestic: Brewers	Domestic: Seed	Domestic: Total	Residual	Exports	Total Disappearance	CCC Stocks July 31	Government Support Program: Put Under Price Support	Loan Rate ($ Per Cwt.): Rough[3]: Long	Rough[3]: Medium	Rough[3]: All Classes	Milled Long
2004-05	23.7	230.8	13.2	269.3	118.5	[4]	4.2	122.7	[4]	108.8	231.5	0	----	6.66	6.04	6.50	10.61
2005-06	37.7	223.2	17.1	277.7	116.4	[4]	3.5	119.9	[4]	114.8	234.7	0	----	6.66	6.04	6.50	10.54
2006-07	43.0	193.7	20.6	258.2	124.7	[4]	3.4	128.1	[4]	90.8	218.8	0	----	6.64	6.07	6.50	10.52
2007-08	39.3	198.4	23.9	261.6	123.9	[4]	3.6	127.4	[4]	104.7	232.2	0	----	6.59	6.20	6.50	10.12
2008-09[1]	29.4	203.7	19.2	252.4	124.5	[4]	3.9	128.4	[4]	93.6	222.0	0	----				
2009-10[2]	30.4	219.9	21.0	271.3				129.5		99.0	228.5						

[1] Preliminary. [2] Forecast. [3] Loan rate for each class of rice is the sum of the whole kernels' loan rate weighted by its milling yield (average 56%) and the broken kernels' loan rate weighted by its milling yield (average 12%). [4] Included in Food.
Source: Economic Research Service, U.S. Department of Agriculture (ERS-USDA)

Acreage, Yield, Production and Prices of Rice in the United States

Crop Year Beginning Aug. 1	Acreage Harvested (1,000 Acres): Southern States	Acreage: California	Acreage: United States	Yield Per Harvested Acre (In Lbs.): California	Yield: United States	Production (1,000 Cwt.): Southern States	Production: California	Production: United States	Value of Production ($1,000)	Wholesale Prices ($ Per Cwt.): Arkansas[2]	Wholesale Prices: Houston[2]	Milled Rice, Average C.I.F. Rotterdam ($ Per Metric Ton): U.S. No. 2[4]	Thai "A"[5]	Thai "B"[5]
2004-05	2,735	590	3,325	8,600	6,942	180,059	50,759	230,818	1,701,822	14.46	17.45	316	----	NA
2005-06	2,838	526	3,364	7,380	6,636	184,399	38,836	223,235	1,741,721	20.52	17.53	293	----	NA
2006-07	2,298	523	2,821	7,660	6,868	153,696	40,040	193,736	1,990,783	22.18	21.10			
2007-08	2,215	533	2,748	8,220	7,185	154,704	43,684	198,388	2,600,871	23.18	21.80			
2008-09	2,459	517	2,976	8,320	6,846	160,703	43,030	203,733	3,390,666					
2009-10[1]	2,547	556	3,103	8,600	7,085	172,046	47,804	219,850						

[1] Preliminary. [2] F.O.B. mills, Arkansas, medium. [3] Houston, Texas (long grain). [4] Milled, 4%, container, FAS.
[5] SWR, 100%, bulk. NA = Not available. *Source: Economic Research Service, U.S. Department of Agriculture (ERS-USDA)*

U.S. Exports of Milled Rice, by Country of Destination In Thousands of Metric Tons

Trade Year Beginning October	Canada	Haiti	Iran	Ivory Coast	Jamaica	Mexico	Netherlands	Peru	Saudi Arabia	South Africa	Switzerland	United Kingdom	Total
2003-04	208.4	242.2	0	32.7	44.5	738.0	30.4	3.5	87.7	.0	10.6	100.2	3,690
2004-05	230.8	299.1	0	32.6	48.2	725.8	44.8	45.7	101.4	.6	18.0	130.9	4,248
2005-06	236.9	340.3	0	25.0	53.5	822.3	38.2	1.7	93.4	.0	12.4	118.0	4,014
2006-07	243.9	279.3	0	0	42.6	810.2	4.0	.1	96.8	.7	.2	37.6	3,306
2007-08	251.5	314.1	0	15.0	56.4	783.0	6.2	2.9	150.0	20.2	1.0	63.5	3,899
2008-09[1]	208.1	239.7	31.7	15.3	26.4	798.4	6.9	.3	129.6	8.9	1.3	57.1	3,401

[1] Preliminary. *Source: Economic Research Service, U.S. Department of Agriculture (ERS-USDA)*

U.S. Rice Exports by Export Program In Thousands of Metric Tons

Year	PL 480	Section 416	CCC Credit Programs[2]	CCC African Relief Exports	EEP[3]	Export Programs[4]	Exports Outside Specified Export Programs	Total U.S. Rice Exports	% Export Programs as a Share of Total Exports
2003	263	0	----	0	0	310	4,169	4,478	7
2004	129	0	----	0	0	214	3,484	3,699	6
2005	126	0	----	0	0	150	4,108	4,258	4
2006	53	0	----	0	0	96	3,928	4,024	2
2007	97	0	----	0	0	136	3,180	3,316	4
2008[1]	78	0	----	0	0	108	3,938	4,046	3

[1] Preliminary. [2] May not completely reflect exports made under these programs. [3] Sales not shipments. [4] Adjusted for estimated overlap between CCC export credit and EEP shipments. *Source: Economice Research Service, U.S. Department of Agriculture (ERS-USDA)*

Production of Rice (Rough) in the United States, by Type and Variety In Thousands of Cwt.

Year	Long Grain	Medium Grain	Short Grain	Total	Year	Long Grain	Medium Grain	Short Grain	Total
2000	128,756	59,514	2,602	190,872	2005	177,527	42,408	3,300	223,235
2001	167,555	46,105	1,610	215,270	2006	146,214	43,802	3,720	193,736
2002	157,243	52,201	1,516	210,960	2007	143,235	51,063	4,090	198,388
2003	149,011	48,180	2,706	199,897	2008	153,257	47,166	3,310	203,733
2004	170,445	58,689	3,228	230,818	2009[1]	152,725	63,291	3,834	219,850

[1] Preliminary. *Source: National Agricultural Statistics Service, U.S. Department of Agriculture (NASS-USDA)*

Rubber

Rubber is a natural or synthetic substance characterized by elasticity, water repellence, and electrical resistance. Pre-Columbian Native South Americans discovered many uses for rubber such as containers, balls, shoes, and waterproofing for fabrics such as coats and capes. The Spaniards tried to duplicate these products for many years but were unsuccessful. The first commercial application of rubber began in 1791 when Samuel Peal patented a method of waterproofing cloth by treating it with a solution of rubber and turpentine. In 1839, Charles Goodyear revolutionized the rubber industry with his discovery of a process called vulcanization, which involves combining rubber and sulfur and heating the mixture.

Natural rubber is obtained from latex, a milky white fluid, from the Hevea Brasiliensis tree. The latex is gathered by cutting a chevron shape through the bark of the rubber tree. The latex is collected in a small cup, with approximately 1 fluid ounce per cutting. The cuttings are usually done every other day until the cuttings reach the ground. The tree is then allowed to renew itself before a new tapping is started. The collected latex is strained, diluted with water, and treated with acid to bind the rubber particles together. The rubber is then pressed between rollers to consolidate the rubber into slabs or thin sheets and is air-dried or smoke-dried for shipment.

During World War II, natural rubber supplies from the Far East were cut off, and the rubber shortage accelerated the development of synthetic rubber in the U.S... Synthetic rubber is produced by chemical reactions, condensation or polymerization, of certain unsaturated hydrocarbons. Synthetic rubber is made of raw material derived from petroleum, coal, oil, natural gas, and acetylene and is almost identical to natural rubber in chemical and physical properties.

Natural rubber and Rubber Index futures are traded on the Osaka Mercantile Exchange (OME). The OME's natural rubber contract is based on the RSS3 ribbed smoked sheet No. 3. The OME's Rubber Index Futures Contract is based on a composite of 8 component grades from 6 rubber markets in the world. Rubber futures are also traded on the Shanghai Futures Exchange (SHFE) and the Tokyo Commodity Exchange (TOCOM).

Prices – The average monthly price for spot crude rubber (No.1 smoked sheets, ribbed, plantation rubber), basis in New York, in 2009 fell -25.5% to 97.36 cents per pound, down from the 2008 record high of 130.67 cents per pound. A 3-decade low of 33.88 cents per pound was seen as recently as 2001 during that recessionary year.

Supply – World production of natural rubber in 2009 fell -4.28% to 9.602 million metric tons. The world's largest producers of natural rubber in 2009 were Thailand with 32% of world production, Indonesia (26%), Malaysia (9%), India (9%), Vietnam (8%), and China (7%).

In 2009, world production of synthetic rubber fell by -4.82% to 12.168 million metric tons. The world's largest producers of synthetic rubber in 2009 were the U.S. with 16% of world production, Japan (10%), Russia (9%), and Germany (5%). U.S. production of synthetic rubber in 2009 fell -15.2% to a 23-year low of 1.962 million metric tons. That is down from the record high of 2.708 million metric tons posted in 2007. U.S. production of car and truck tires in 2007 (latest data) fell –6.8% to 186.000 million tires.

Demand – World consumption of natural rubber in 2009 fell -6.0% to 9.547 million metric tons, down from the 2007 record high of 10.224 million metric tons. The largest consumers of natural rubber in 2009 were the U.S. with 7% of consumption, Japan with 7%, Brazil with 3%, and Germany with 2%. The world's consumption of natural rubber has tripled since 1970. World consumption of synthetic rubber in 2009 fell b y -5.9% to 11.878 million metric tons. The largest consumers of synthetic rubber in 2009 were the U.S. with 12% of consumption, Japan with 7%, Germany with 4%, and France with 2%. The world's consumption of synthetic rubber has more than doubled since 1970.

U.S. consumption of natural rubber in 2009 fell by -34.0% to a 26-year low of 687,000 million metric tons, down from the 2000 record high of 1.195 million metric tons. The 2009 U.S consumption is not much greater than in1970. U.S. consumption of synthetic rubber in 2009 fell 16.5% to 1.448 million metric tons. The U.S. consumption of synthetic rubber has remained about the same as it was in 1970.

Trade – World exports of natural rubber in 2009 fell -7.2% to 6.278 million metric tons, down from the 2006 record high of 6.981 million metric tons. The world's largest exporters of natural rubber in 2009 were Thailand with 43% of world exports and Indonesia with 32% of world exports.

U.S. Imports of Natural Rubber (Includes Latex & Guayule) In Thousands of Metric Tons

Year	Jan.	Feb.	Mar.	Apr.	May	June	July	Aug.	Sept.	Oct.	Nov.	Dec.	Total
2001	85.2	69.1	93.9	80.0	74.9	63.8	101.1	109.2	69.9	92.4	69.2	63.4	972.1
2002	104.8	71.2	79.2	90.8	106.1	92.2	108.6	109.7	81.1	94.7	83.0	88.9	1,110.3
2003	104.1	86.2	106.8	99.8	91.4	97.6	94.5	67.4	100.1	70.6	72.3	86.2	1,077.0
2004	116.2	76.6	101.7	96.5	112.6	92.0	87.6	81.7	85.5	120.4	71.0	101.8	1,143.6
2005	99.8	101.9	97.1	115.5	80.9	95.7	84.5	91.7	113.5	92.2	82.7	103.7	1,159.2
2006	113.3	71.8	98.9	80.5	115.6	72.5	72.4	97.3	58.7	83.0	82.0	57.2	1,003.2
2007	86.5	69.5	103.1	91.6	64.1	114.1	74.9	85.0	91.3	82.4	83.9	82.1	1,028.5
2008	75.3	97.3	66.1	115.8	90.2	79.1	97.1	100.7	95.2	78.9	78.4	78.5	1,052.6
2009[1]	84.3	52.3	73.3	49.0	51.8	31.1	61.0	48.5	52.1	64.7	64.9		690.6

[1] Preliminary. *Source: International Rubber Study Group (IRSG)*

World Production[1] of Rubber In Thousands of Metric Tons

	Natural								Synthetic				
Year	China	India	Indonesia	Malaysia	Sri Lanka	Thailand	Vietnam	World Total	Germany	Japan	United States	Russia	World Total
2000	445.0	629.0	1,501.1	927.6	87.6	2,346.4	290.8	6,762	849.2	1,591.7	2,396.8	837.1	10,818
2001	478.0	631.5	1,607.3	882.1	86.2	2,319.5	312.6	7,332	828.4	1,465.5	2,062.1	919.2	10,483
2002	527.0	640.8	1,630.0	889.8	90.5	2,615.1	331.4	7,326	869.2	1,522.0	2,164.4	919.0	10,877
2003	565.0	707.1	1,792.2	985.6	92.0	2,876.0	363.5	8,020	888.0	1,577.4	2,270.1	1,070.0	11,379
2004	573.0	742.6	2,066.2	1,168.7	94.7	2,984.3	419.0	8,746	905.0	1,616.1	2,325.1	1,116.1	11,999
2005	510.0	771.5	2,271.0	1,126.0	104.4	2,937.2	481.6	8,904	855.0	1,626.9	2,365.8	1,146.0	12,136
2006	533.0	853.3	2,637.0	1,283.6	109.2	3,137.0	555.4	9,791	865.0	1,607.0	2,606.3	1,219.0	12,690
2007	590.0	811.1	2,755.2	1,199.6	117.5	3,056.0	605.8	9,801	803.0	1,654.6	2,696.9	1,209.9	13,430
2008[1]	560.0	881.3	2,751.0	1,072.4	129.2	3,089.8	659.6	10,031	791.0	1,651.0	2,314.4	1,139.3	12,784
2009[2]	630.0	817.0	2,534.6	856.2	133.4	3,086.0	723.7	9,602	655.0	1,264.0	1,962.0	1,042.0	12,168

[1] Including rubber in the form of latex. [2] Preliminary. *Source: International Rubber Study Group (IRSG)*

World Consumption of Natural and Synthetic Rubber In Thousands of Metric Tons

	Natural							Synthetic					
Year	Brazil	France	Germany	Japan	United Kingdom	United States	Total	France	Germany	Japan	United Kingdom	United States	Total
2000	226.6	270.0	250.0	751.8	122.5	1,194.8	7,381	481.5	632.0	1,137.5	188.0	2,189.5	10,764
2001	215.9	282.0	246.0	729.2	98.0	974.1	7,333	464.5	613.0	1,085.1	167.0	1,839.5	10,253
2002	233.4	230.6	247.0	749.0	76.0	1,110.8	7,556	469.3	612.0	1,096.0	210.0	1,895.0	10,874
2003	255.5	218.1	258.1	784.2	90.9	1,078.5	7,939	493.2	615.0	1,110.7	203.9	1,926.4	11,386
2004	284.9	230.1	242.3	814.8	86.3	1,143.6	8,718	420.1	624.5	1,146.3	213.5	1,906.8	11,878
2005	301.8	230.0	258.9	857.4	82.3	1,159.2	9,200	354.9	635.0	1,156.0	222.3	2,002.1	11,936
2006	294.3	219.6	268.9	873.7	67.7	1,003.1	9,714	310.8	635.0	1,170.8	200.6	2,000.8	12,691
2007	344.9	220.1	281.7	887.4	90.8	1,018.4	10,224	316.0	599.0	1,162.2	168.7	1,929.3	13,308
2008	357.2	199.6	246.9	877.9	76.8	1,041.0	10,154	316.0	586.0	1,137.6	157.3	1,734.0	12,619
2009[1]	254.3	108.9	170.0	637.0	41.8	687.1	9,547	278.6	450.4	834.0	124.0	1,447.7	11,878

[1] Preliminary. *Source: International Rubber Study Group (IRSG)*

World Stocks[1] of Natural & Synthetic Rubber (by Countries) on January 1 In Thousands of Metric Tons

		In Producing Countries							In Consuming Countries (Reported Stocks)				
Year	Total Synthetic	Africa	Indonesia	Malaysia	Sri Lanka	Thailand	Vietnam	Total Natural	Brazil	India	Japan	United States	Total
1999	1,116	25.3	30	234.2	18.6	209.5	30.0	750	13.0	194.0	58.0	70.4	406
2000	1,103	28.2	33	236.6	18.6	250.9	32.0	929	34.0	215.1	79.1	46.0	475
2001	1,159	11.8	50	151.1	18.7	188.6	15.0	568	40.0	203.3	95.2	44.6	484
2002	1,139	11.4	30	138.3	19.0	214.9	12.0	527	40.0	225.5	46.9	42.6	427
2003	1,161	11.1	20	135.6	19.0	198.5	14.0	460	40.0	151.7	65.0	42.1	299
2004	1,127	10.8	10	162.6	19.0	204.1	19.0	459	40.0	123.3	73.0	40.6	277
2005	1,015	12.0	20	195.0	19.0	234.4	38.0	549	40.0	122.9	58.1	40.6	262
2006	1,004	11.3	60	164.1	19.0	206.1	2.0	497	40.0	114.5	49.3	40.6	244
2007	943	10.7	60	188.0	18.7	251.9	19.0	570	40.0	140.9	60.4	40.6	282
2008[1]	1,223	10.7	60	155.9	18.7	232.0	16.0	516	40.0	195.9	20.4	40.6	297

[1] Preliminary. *Source: International Rubber Study Group (IRSG)*

Net Exports of Natural Rubber from Producing Areas In Thousands of Metric Tons

Year	Cambodia	Guatemala[4]	Indonesia	Liberia	Malaysia	Nigeria	Sri Lanka	Thailand	Vietnam	Other Africa[2]	Other Asia[3]	Total
2000	39.0	31.8	1,379.6	73.5	429.8	36.0	32.6	2,166.2	254.0	207.4	61.8	5,000
2001	38.0	33.0	1,496.9	71.7	345.2	30.0	32.0	2,042.1	270.0	212.4	85.5	5,193
2002	44.3	40.1	1,502.2	109.0	887.0	24.0	36.1	2,354.4	454.8	199.8	91.0	5,158
2003	36.3	41.0	1,660.5	107.0	946.5	22.0	35.2	2,573.5	432.3	211.8	101.2	5,645
2004	32.4	52.9	1,875.1	114.5	1,106.1	29.0	40.3	2,637.1	513.4	220.0	91.9	6,183
2005	28.3	54.6	2,025.0	111.0	1,127.9	25.0	31.6	2,632.4	554.1	250.7	96.6	6,389
2006	25.4	55.4	2,287.0	100.5	1,131.0	24.0	45.8	2,771.6	703.6	275.4	91.8	6,981
2007	24.8	68.7	2,407.4	105.5	1,018.1	24.5	49.5	2,703.8	715.6	292.2	104.1	6,861
2008	14.5	73.4	2,295.6	81.0	916.6	25.9	46.2	2,675.3	658.3	308.3	104.7	6,764
2009[1]	34.1	78.1	2,000.6	77.3	703.6	31.7	53.7	2,684.0	731.4	335.9	94.0	6,278

[1] Preliminary. [2] Includes Cameroon, Cote d'Ivoire, Gabon, Ghana and Zaire. [3] Includes Myanmar, Papua New Guinea and the Philippines.
Source: International Rubber Study Group (IRSG)

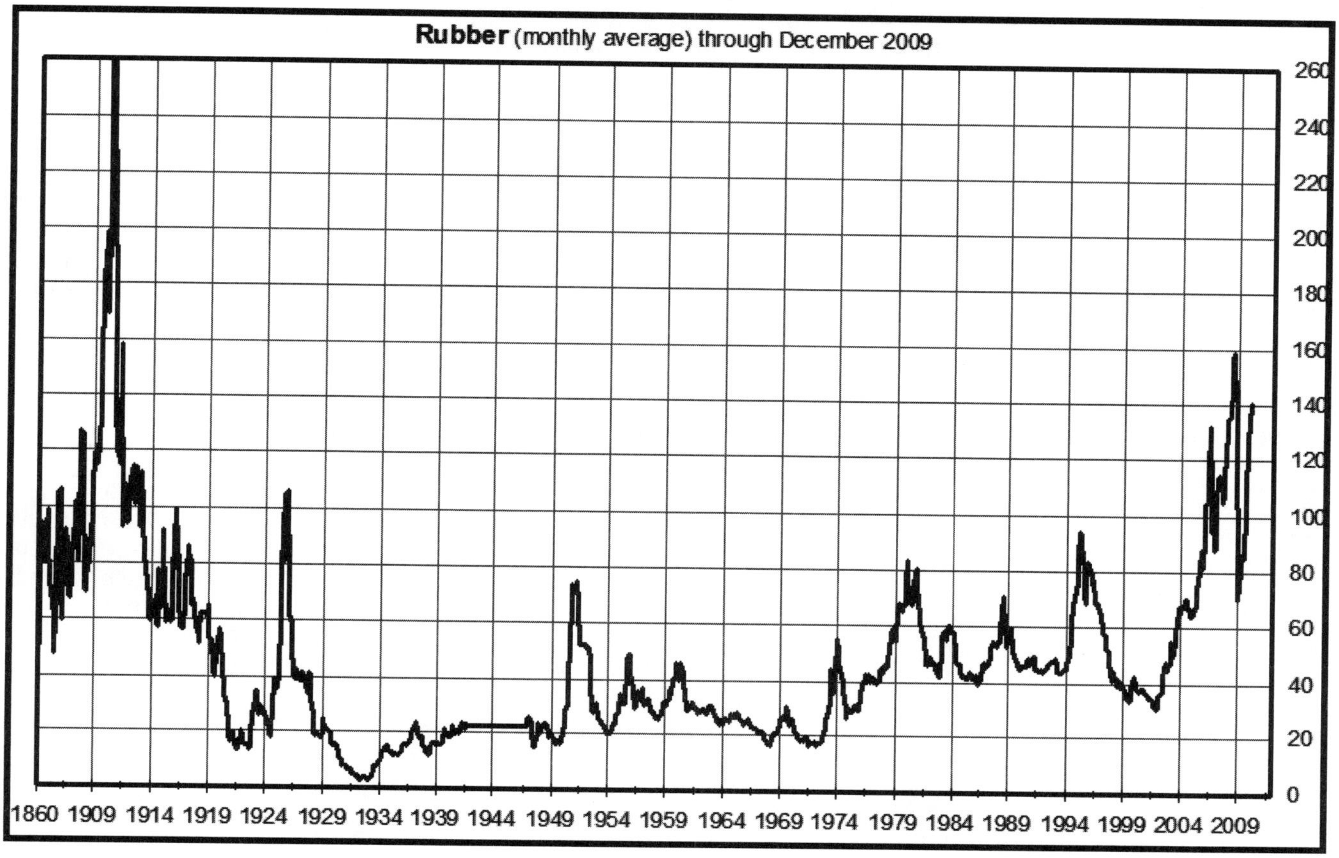

Average Spot Crude Rubber Prices (Smoked Sheets[1]) in New York In Cents Per Pound

Year	Jan.	Feb.	Mar.	Apr.	May	June	July	Aug.	Sept.	Oct.	Nov.	Dec.	Average
2002	32.21	34.45	36.50	36.38	36.93	43.53	44.32	45.20	47.90	45.70	44.97	45.39	41.12
2003	47.95	49.25	54.96	52.04	49.32	51.76	51.99	53.71	57.61	65.88	67.63	65.20	55.61
2004	65.63	67.28	68.09	68.84	70.40	69.90	68.10	66.50	66.39	67.30	66.80	63.90	67.43
2005	64.20	66.18	66.80	66.70	68.07	73.75	80.50	82.34	85.51	87.90	83.75	81.99	75.64
2006	93.04	104.01	104.48	105.20	115.03	131.74	124.01	114.94	95.17	94.77	87.95	88.53	104.91
2007	104.90	113.90	109.86	112.81	114.76	111.72	105.30	106.90	106.49	113.29	123.08	123.85	112.24
2008	127.94	134.87	135.39	136.24	147.26	156.21	158.67	150.99	143.99	110.66	95.41	70.38	130.67
2009	77.06	75.16	73.44	83.31	86.10	85.06	86.81	101.20	112.81	120.12	126.69	140.60	97.36

[1] No. 1, ribbed, plantation rubber. *Source: International Rubber Study Group (IRSG)*

Natural Rubber Prices in London

Year	Jan.	Feb.	Mar.	Apr.	May	June	July	Aug.	Sept.	Oct.	Nov.	Dec.	Average
Buyers' Price RSS 1 (CIF) In British Pounds per Metric Ton													
2005	1,415.4	1,459.1	1,472.7	1,470.5	1,500.7	1,626.0	1,774.7	1,815.2	1,885.2	1,937.8	1,846.4	1,807.5	1,667.6
2006	2,051.1	2,293.1	2,303.3	2,319.2	2,536.0	2,904.3	2,734.0	2,533.9	2,098.2	2,089.4	1,938.9	1,951.7	2,312.8
2007	2,312.7	2,511.1	2,421.9	2,487.0	2,530.1	2,463.0	2,321.5	2,356.8	2,347.6	2,497.5	2,713.5	2,730.4	2,474.4
2008	2,820.6	2,973.3	2,984.9	3,003.5	3,246.6	3,443.7	3,498.1	3,328.7	3,174.4	2,439.6	2,103.5	1,551.6	2,880.7
2009	1,698.9	1,656.9	1,619.1	1,836.7	1,898.1	1,875.2	1,913.9	2,231.1	2,487.0	2,648.2	2,793.1	3,099.6	2,146.5
Buyers' Prices RSS 3 (CIF) In Euro per Metric Ton													
2005	957.2	992.6	1,066.7	1,094.0	1,142.5	1,292.6	1,492.2	1,405.8	1,484.3	1,525.3	1,454.3	1,528.5	1,286.3
2006	1,657.1	1,840.3	1,846.7	1,864.2	2,016.0	2,267.5	2,112.0	1,839.5	1,487.3	1,511.1	1,327.8	1,356.6	1,760.5
2007	1,652.3	1,800.8	1,741.9	1,766.8	1,765.0	1,721.8	1,558.0	1,607.0	1,621.5	1,707.2	1,761.8	1,776.2	1,706.7
2008	1,850.6	1,948.5	1,860.5	1,849.1	2,010.9	2,119.8	2,092.4	2,030.8	2,064.1	1,549.6	1,373.0	952.0	1,808.4
2009	1,178.7	1,197.0	1,138.5	1,273.8	1,286.7	1,246.9	1,284.8	1,487.6	1,530.2	1,629.3	1,749.6	1,963.6	1,413.9
Sellers' Prices SMR 20 (CIF) In Euro per Metric Ton													
2005	950.5	985.8	991.1	1,012.1	1,018.7	1,138.6	1,292.6	1,254.0	1,385.5	1,410.0	1,442.3	1,485.8	1,197.3
2006	1,564.6	1,727.5	1,704.7	1,694.2	1,788.7	1,952.6	1,949.4	1,797.4	1,490.4	1,475.6	1,313.3	1,294.3	1,646.1
2007	1,547.5	1,688.5	1,599.0	1,541.6	1,678.7	1,622.3	1,532.3	1,565.7	1,679.5	1,654.6	1,691.0	1,723.6	1,627.0
2008	1,790.5	1,902.9	1,795.7	1,782.2	1,959.4	2,089.9	2,087.0	2,014.6	2,030.8	1,510.0	1,357.5	947.4	1,772.3
2009	1,121.2	1,066.4	1,029.7	1,174.9	1,196.2	1,143.5	1,182.9	1,342.8	1,465.6	1,580.3	1,713.8	1,957.9	1,331.3

Source: International Rubber Study Group (IRSG)

Consumption of Natural Rubber in the United States In Thousands of Metric Tons

Year	Jan.	Feb.	Mar.	Apr.	May	June	July	Aug.	Sept.	Oct.	Nov.	Dec.	Total
2000	110.0	110.0	110.0	114.0	114.0	114.0	80.0	80.0	80.0	93.0	93.0	93.0	1,194.8
2001	85.5	69.4	94.1	80.2	75.1	64.1	101.2	109.3	70.0	92.4	69.4	63.4	974.1
2002	104.9	71.3	79.2	90.4	106.3	92.3	108.7	109.7	81.2	94.7	83.1	89.0	1,110.8
2003	104.2	86.3	106.9	100.1	91.2	97.7	94.6	67.5	101.3	69.9	72.5	86.3	1,078.5
2004	116.0	76.5	101.5	96.5	112.5	92.5	87.5	82.0	86.0	120.0	71.0	101.8	1,143.8
2005	99.8	101.9	97.1	115.5	80.9	95.7	84.5	91.7	113.5	92.2	82.7	103.7	1,159.2
2006	113.3	71.8	98.9	80.5	115.6	72.5	72.4	97.3	58.7	83.0	82.0	57.2	1,003.2
2007	86.1	67.7	102.1	90.7	63.4	113.3	74.3	83.8	90.6	81.8	80.3	84.3	1,018.4
2008	74.1	96.6	65.3	115.0	89.0	77.8	96.3	99.5	94.0	78.0	77.8	77.6	1,041.0
2009[1]	82.3	51.4	71.7	47.7	50.1	29.2	59.7	46.9	50.6	63.1	63.7	70.6	687.0

[1] Preliminary. *Source: International Rubber Study Group (IRSG)*

Stocks of Natural Rubber in the United States, on First of Month In Thousands of Metric Tons

Year	Jan.	Feb.	Mar.	Apr.	May	June	July	Aug.	Sept.	Oct.	Nov.	Dec.
1998	57.2	61.2	65.5	63.5	60.9	66.7	53.6	57.9	54.7	58.3	58.9	66.5
1999	70.4	68.0	66.0	64.0	62.0	60.0	58.0	56.0	54.0	52.0	50.0	48.0
2000	46.0	63.4	41.6	45.7	39.6	40.5	46.6	32.5	48.7	47.9	51.1	50.3
2001	46.6	44.3	44.0	43.8	43.6	43.4	43.1	43.0	42.9	42.8	42.8	42.6
2002	42.6	42.5	42.4	42.4	42.8	42.6	42.5	42.4	42.4	42.3	42.3	42.2
2003	42.1	42.0	41.9	41.8	41.5	41.7	41.6	41.5	41.4	40.2	40.9	40.7
2004	40.6	40.8	40.9	40.9	40.9	40.9	40.9	40.9	40.9	40.9	40.9	40.9
2005	40.6	40.6	40.6	40.6	40.6	40.6	40.6	40.6	40.6	40.6	40.6	40.6
2006	40.6	40.6	40.6	40.6	40.6	40.6	40.6	40.6	40.6	40.6	40.6	40.6
2007[1]	40.6	40.6	40.6	40.6	40.6	40.6	40.6	40.6	40.6	40.6	40.6	40.6

[1] Preliminary. *Source: International Rubber Study Group (IRSG)*

Stocks of Synthetic Rubber in the United States, on First of Month In Thousands of Metric Tons

Year	Jan.	Feb.	Mar.	Apr.	May	June	July	Aug.	Sept.	Oct.	Nov.	Dec.
1998	377.7	382.2	375.7	379.5	387.5	402.8	394.6	406.8	394.2	398.7	395.7	396.5
1999	409.3	404.0	404.0	406.0	399.0	420.0	410.0	419.0	413.0	390.0	391.0	389.0
2000	406.0	416.0	413.0	402.0	405.0	416.0	409.0	418.0	400.0	412.0	407.0	419.0
2001	433.0	451.0	467.0	4,559.0	448.0	433.0	426.0	420.0	394.0	400.0	394.0	379.0
2002	392.0	377.0	379.0	393.0	398.0	384.0	385.0	381.0	364.0	375.0	364.0	358.0
2003	390.0	325.0	330.0	325.0	336.0	336.0	332.0	332.0	331.0	328.0	317.0	338.0
2004	343.0	347.0	335.0	315.0	310.0	300.0	300.0	290.0	280.0	280.0	280.0	270.0
2005	260.0	255.0	240.0	240.0	235.0	235.0	240.0	245.0	245.0	245.0	245.0	245.0
2006	248.0	240.0	225.0	215.0	210.0	210.0	210.0	210.0	210.0	210.0	210.0	210.0
2007[1]	210.0	210.0	210.0	210.0	210.0	210.0	210.0	210.0	210.0	210.0	210.0	210.0

[1] Preliminary. *Source: International Rubber Study Group (IRSG)*

Production of Synthetic Rubber in the United States In Thousands of Metric Tons

Year	Jan.	Feb.	Mar.	Apr.	May	June	July	Aug.	Sept.	Oct.	Nov.	Dec.	Total
2000	202.0	202.0	214.0	193.0	216.0	202.0	198.0	187.0	193.0	197.0	194.0	184.0	2,382
2001	203.0	188.6	184.3	172.1	175.5	162.3	166.7	164.7	174.3	178.6	155.1	139.2	2,064
2002	176.1	171.9	192.3	190.6	187.0	184.6	183.5	177.3	175.1	175.0	160.4	176.4	2,150
2003	185.6	180.9	193.6	179.8	182.9	166.3	174.2	172.9	188.4	189.7	192.0	185.6	2,192
2004	208.3	199.0	203.5	193.5	187.1	183.5	183.5	184.1	193.5	198.5	202.1	188.5	2,325
2005	206.9	204.8	209.4	202.7	196.9	188.9	187.3	193.7	182.7	185.8	206.9	199.8	2,366
2006	212.9	213.7	212.9	210.2	227.5	217.8	218.1	218.2	218.5	218.3	220.4	214.9	2,603
2007	224.3	223.1	222.6	222.6	227.4	227.8	227.9	227.5	228.4	227.5	224.0	225.0	2,708
2008	220.9	216.3	209.2	211.1	210.9	205.8	200.7	191.1	176.6	170.0	155.8	146.0	2,314
2009[1]	116.5	136.8	146.7	151.1	165.9	176.2	180.9	185.6	190.5	184.9	166.9	160.0	1,962

[1] Preliminary. *Source: International Rubber Study Group (IRSG)*

Consumption of Synthetic Rubber in the United States In Thousands of Metric Tons

Year	Jan.	Feb.	Mar.	Apr.	May	June	July	Aug.	Sept.	Oct.	Nov.	Dec.	Total
2000	173.0	185.0	202.0	178.0	194.0	196.0	177.0	189.0	172.0	182.0	168.0	147.0	2,190
2001	170.8	149.6	166.8	153.3	159.8	148.6	156.4	173.0	145.7	162.7	140.8	112.0	1,840
2002	155.5	146.8	153.0	165.8	173.4	160.4	161.5	169.3	154.8	166.7	148.2	139.6	1,895
2003	166.1	156.4	167.7	157.8	162.0	163.0	163.3	152.3	159.0	175.6	147.3	155.9	1,926
2004	170.0	166.2	176.0	156.5	152.2	141.9	158.8	149.2	152.9	155.0	170.0	158.1	1,907
2005	174.7	184.0	180.6	171.5	156.8	147.9	145.2	148.9	153.7	161.2	166.8	163.3	1,955
2006	173.7	182.7	178.0	170.7	172.2	167.4	157.7	158.1	161.5	161.5	160.9	156.6	2,001
2007	157.8	155.0	155.6	164.6	163.8	166.1	165.6	160.4	166.6	163.6	163.0	158.4	1,941
2008	149.8	145.9	150.1	146.0	148.8	154.6	151.6	150.4	142.2	136.0	133.5	125.2	1,734
2009[1]	118.9	108.7	105.8	114.7	111.0	116.7	112.3	142.5	151.3	133.8	122.7	109.3	1,448

[1] Preliminary. *Source: International Rubber Study Group (IRSG)*

U.S. Exports of Synthetic Rubber In Thousands of Metric Tons

Year	Jan.	Feb.	Mar.	Apr.	May	June	July	Aug.	Sept.	Oct.	Nov.	Dec.	Total
2000	64.3	73.4	83.8	70.2	73.2	72.3	72.4	78.6	78.6	75.2	73.3	70.7	886.0
2001	74.6	67.3	76.4	78.2	75.1	69.6	70.6	71.6	68.1	70.7	62.4	59.4	844.4
2002	67.9	71.6	69.5	74.9	78.5	73.6	74.5	72.8	70.9	73.1	70.8	66.3	864.4
2003	73.1	70.1	80.1	85.2	78.4	75.3	74.4	72.4	73.9	83.7	74.5	79.3	920.4
2004	82.0	87.3	97.0	90.9	96.8	92.6	88.9	91.6	94.8	89.0	87.0	81.6	1,079.5
2005	86.3	89.6	91.8	98.4	98.3	96.9	91.5	100.4	76.4	87.0	101.3	87.5	1,105.4
2006	103.4	97.3	106.7	103.2	109.2	106.8	110.0	112.5	101.3	103.3	97.8	98.5	1,250.0
2007	110.5	108.6	118.0	107.8	116.0	109.7	108.8	112.9	106.3	111.7	104.1	102.1	1,316.5
2008	110.6	113.4	101.4	114.2	111.8	100.9	103.0	101.4	79.9	93.5	69.9	56.5	1,156.5
2009[1]	56.2	59.6	71.3	79.2	84.0	92.2	97.4	88.3	87.7	92.5	83.5	84.0	975.9

[1] Preliminary. *Source: International Rubber Study Group (IRSG)*

Production of Tyres (Car and Truck) in the United States In Thousands of Units

Year	First Quarter	Second Quarter	Third Quarter	Fourth Quarter	Total	Year	First Quarter	Second Quarter	Third Quarter	Fourth Quarter	Total
1988	54,677	52,986	51,195	52,493	211,351	1998	----	----	----	----	270,905
1989	56,716	56,626	50,086	49,444	212,870	1999	----	----	----	----	267,652
1990	55,915	53,856	51,163	49,729	210,663	2000	----	----	----	----	276,765
1991	51,296	52,796	49,183	51,115	202,391	2001	65,367	62,809	62,366	56,106	255,700
1992	57,890	57,319	57,554	57,487	230,250	2002	62,937	64,362	60,524	58,241	246,064
1993	61,809	60,752	57,702	57,184	237,447	2003	62,686	59,311	58,441	55,565	236,003
1994	63,586	63,331	57,018	59,442	243,696	2004	60,272	59,774	58,389	54,824	233,259
1995	63,800	63,800	63,800	63,754	255,521	2005	57,377	58,832	54,920	52,074	223,203
1996	64,000	64,000	64,000	63,700	255,723	2006[1]	56,787	53,452	49,612	39,636	199,487
1997	----	----	----	----	263,860	2007[2]	46,600	44,500	45,700	49,200	186,000

[1] Preliminary. [2] Estimate. *Source: International Rubber Study Group (IRSG)*

U.S. Foreign Trade of Tyres (Car and Truck) In Thousands of Units

	Imports					Exports				
Year	First Quarter	Second Quarter	Third Quarter	Fourth Quarter	Total	First Quarter	Second Quarter	Third Quarter	Fourth Quarter	Total
1998	17,046	17,728	18,016	19,346	72,124	12,840	10,678	10,018	10,372	43,923
1999	19,471	22,295	22,194	23,784	87,768	9,874	9,580	10,480	10,537	40,945
2000	24,200	24,698	23,561	22,123	94,019	11,200	10,200	10,200	10,100	44,164
2001	19,563	22,251	22,072	20,956	84,842	10,087	10,362	11,004	10,691	42,144
2002	21,554	25,831	24,868	24,950	97,203	10,438	10,379	10,167	10,380	41,363
2003	26,310	28,557	28,472	27,536	110,875	9,293	2,648	10,263	10,794	32,998
2004	28,996	31,998	30,788	32,707	124,489	10,272	10,902	10,108	10,299	41,581
2005	32,704	36,924	34,391	33,584	137,603	9,808	10,071	10,659	10,570	41,108
2006[1]	34,562	36,863	34,638	36,136	142,199	9,021	9,328	9,388	9,236	36,973
2007[2]	35,984	39,428	38,778	38,273	152,463	8,922	9,360	9,539	9,417	37,238

[1] Preliminary. [2] Estimate. *Source: International Rubber Study Group (IRSG)*

Rye

Rye is a cereal grain and a member of the grass family. Hardy varieties of rye have been developed for winter planting. Rye is most widely grown in northern Europe and Asia. In the U.S., rye is used as an animal feed and as an ingredient in bread and some whiskeys. Bread using rye was developed in northern Europe in the Middle Ages where bakers developed dark, hearty bread consisting of rye, oat and barley flours. Those were crops that grew more readily in the wet and damp climate of northern Europe, as opposed to wheat which fares better in the warmer and drier climates in central Europe. Modern rye bread is made with a mixture of white and rye flours. Coarsely ground rye flour is also used in pumpernickel bread and helps provide the dark color and course texture, along with molasses. The major producing states are North and South Dakota, Oklahoma, and Georgia. The crop year runs from June to May.

Supply – World rye production in 2009-10 marketing year was rose by +0.04% yr/yr to 17.413 million metric tons, up from the 2006-07 record low of 12.402 million metric tons. The world's largest producers of rye are the European Union with 55% of world production in 2009-10, followed by Russia with 25%, Belarus with 10%, and the Ukraine with 5%. U.S. production of rye accounted for only 1.0% of world production.

U.S. production of rye in 2009 fell -12.4% to 6.993 million bushels but that was far below the production levels of over 20 million bushels seen from the late 1800s through the 1960s. U.S. production of rye fell off in the 1970s, and fell to a record low of 6.488 million bushels in 2002.

U.S. acreage harvested with rye in 2009-10 fell -6.3% to 252,000 acres, down from last year's level of 269,000 acres. U.S. farmers in the late 1800s through the 1960s typically harvested more than 1 million acres of rye, showing how domestic planting of rye has dropped off sharply in the past several decades. Rye yield in 2009-10 fell -6.4% to 27.8 bushels per acre, and that is still well below the record high of 33.1 bushels per acre posted in 1984-85. Modern rye production yields are, however, more than double the levels in the teens seen prior to the 1960s when yields started to rise.

Demand – Total U.S. domestic usage of rye in 2007-08 (latest data) fell 3.4% yr/yr to 12.800 million bushels. The breakdown of domestic usage shows that 26% of rye in 2007-08 was used for food, 23% by industry, 23% as seed, and 3% as feed and residual.

Trade – World exports of rye in the 2009-10 marketing year rose +37.0% yr/yr to 370.000 metric tons, up from the record low of 270,000 metric tons last year. The largest exporters were Canada and the European Union, each with exports of 125,000 metric tons. World imports of rye rose +49.1% to 322,000 metric tons. U.S. imports of rye in 2009-10 rose +27.0% yr/yr to 127,000 metric tons.

World Production of Rye In Thousands of Metric Tons

Crop Year	Argentina	Australia	Belarus	Canada	European Union	Kazak-hstan	Romania	Russia	Switzer-land	Turkey	Ukraine	United States	World Total
2000-01	125	20	1,360	260	10,268	50		5,450	20	260	966	213	19,064
2001-02	81	20	1,294	228	11,956	75		6,600	20	220	1,822	175	22,562
2002-03	80	20	1,600	134	9,255	50		7,150	20	255	1,511	165	20,308
2003-04	37	20	1,200	327	6,972	50		4,200	20	240	625	219	13,983
2004-05	89	20	1,400	398	10,031	50		2,850	20	270	1,600	210	17,036
2005-06	55	20	1,150	330	7,688	50		3,600	20	270	1,050	191	14,520
2006-07	55	20	1,200	383	6,541	50		3,000	20	271	600	183	12,402
2007-08[1]	77	20	1,300	252	7,679	50		3,900	20	265	550	160	14,373
2008-09[2]	55	20	1,600	316	9,234	50		4,500	20	250	1,050	203	17,406
2009-10[3]	55	20	1,700	280	9,503	50		4,300	20	270	950	178	17,413

[1] Preliminary. [2] Estimate. [3] Forecast. *Source: Foreign Agricultural Service, U.S. Department of Agriculture (FAS-USDA)*

World Imports and Exports of Rye In Thousands of Metric Tons

	Imports							Exports					
Year	European Union	Japan	Rep. of Korea	Turkey	Russia	United States	World Total	Belarus	Canada	European Union	Russia	United States	World Total
2000-01	2	337	57	----	193	82	765	50	91	814	----	10	966
2001-02	307	335	121	20	7	126	1,056	30	66	647	4	5	1,046
2002-03	436	414	31	14	----	156	1,356	110	53	669	291	3	1,414
2003-04	99	341	114	43	6	83	845	60	173	506	156	1	907
2004-05	----	261	8	59	172	143	782	50	122	574	----	4	854
2005-06	9	279	7	7	49	139	624	50	132	359	----	----	610
2006-07	25	258	8	5	32	150	568	50	208	424	26	2	712
2007-08[1]	94	83	6	16	----	179	400	75	191	76	119	6	470
2008-09[2]	9	57	7	5	----	100	216	50	76	114	16	8	270
2009-10[3]	25	100	5	10	----	127	322	50	125	125	50	10	370

[1] Preliminary. [2] Estimate. [3] Forecast. *Source: Foreign Agricultural Service, U.S. Department of Agriculture (FAS-USDA)*

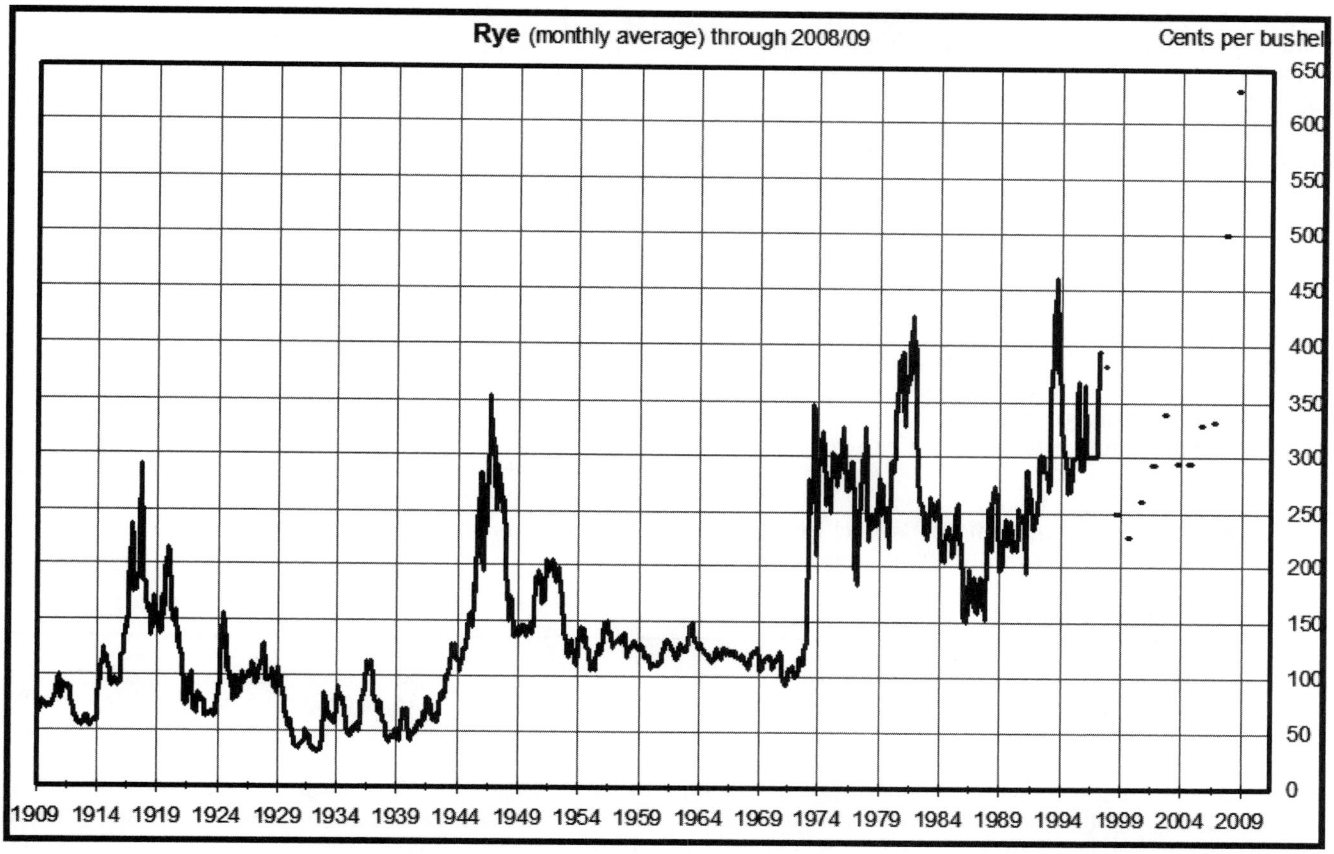

Production of Rye in the United States In Thousands of Bushels

Year	Georgia	Kansas	Mich-igan	Minne-sota	Neb-raska	Dakota	Okla-homa	Penn-ylvania	Carolina	Dakota	Texas	Wis-consin	Total
2000	1,170	[2]	[2]	[2]	[2]	704	1,470	[2]	[2]	546	[2]	[2]	8,386
2001	875	[2]	[2]	[2]	[2]	340	1,150	[2]	[2]	350	[2]	[2]	6,971
2002	560	[2]	[2]	[2]	[2]	210	1,300	[2]	[2]	270	[2]	[2]	6,488
2003	800	[2]	[2]	[2]	[2]	750	1,540	[2]	[2]	672	[2]	[2]	8,634
2004	600	[2]	[2]	[2]	[2]	780	1,620	[2]	[2]	649	[2]	[2]	8,255
2005	810	[2]	[2]	[2]	[2]	[2]	1,400	[2]	[2]	[2]	[2]	[2]	7,537
2006	650	[2]	[2]	[2]	[2]	[2]	1,040	[2]	[2]	[2]	[2]	[2]	7,193
2007	800	[2]	[2]	[2]	[2]	[2]	1,080	[2]	[2]	[2]	[2]	[2]	6,311
2008	1,200	[2]	[2]	[2]	[2]	[2]	1,045	[2]	[2]	[2]	[2]	[2]	7,979
2009[1]	525	[2]	[2]	[2]	[2]	[2]	560	[2]	[2]	[2]	[2]	[2]	6,993

[1] Preliminary. [2] Estimates not published beginning in 2000. *Source: Agricultural Statistics Board, U.S. Department of Agriculture (ASB-USDA)*

Salient Statistics of Rye in the United States In Thousands of Bushels

Crop Year	Supply				Disappearance							Acreage		Yield Per
					Domestic Use						Total		Harvested	Harvested
Beginning June 1	Stocks June 1	Pro-duction	Imports	Total Supply	Food	Industry	Seed	Feed & Residual	Total	Exports	Disap-pearance	Planted (1,000 Acres)	for Grain (1,000 Acres)	Acre (Bushels)
2000-01	1,589	8,386	3,230	13,205	3,300	3,000	3,000	2,325	11,625	390	12,015	1,329	296	28.3
2001-02	1,190	6,971	4,945	13,106	3,300	3,000	3,000	2,970	12,270	193	12,463	1,328	255	27.3
2002-03	568	6,488	6,140	13,196	3,300	3,000	3,000	3,329	12,629	122	12,751	1,355	263	24.8
2003-04	445	8,634	3,286	12,365	3,300	3,000	3,000	2,425	11,725	60	11,771	1,348	319	27.1
2004-05	594	8,255	5,626	14,475	3,300	3,000	3,000	4,237	13,537	145	13,682	1,380	300	27.5
2005-06	793	7,537	5,481	13,811	3,300	3,000	3,000	3,791	13,091	14	13,105	1,433	279	27.0
2006-07	706	7,193	5,899	13,798	3,300	3,000	3,000	3,947	13,247	70	13,317	1,396	274	26.3
2007-08[1]	481	6,311	7,064	13,856	3,300	3,000	3,000	3,909	13,209	251	13,460	1,334	252	25.0
2008-09[2]	396	7,979	3,953	12,328	3,300	3,000	3,000	2,204	11,504	315	11,819	1,260	269	29.7
2009-10[3]	509	6,993	5,000	12,502	3,300	3,000	3,000	2,502	11,802	200	12,002	1,241	252	27.8

[1] Preliminary. [2] Estimate. [3] Forecast *Source: Economic Research Service, U.S. Department of Agriculture (ERS-USDA)*

Salt

Salt, also known as sodium chloride, is a chemical compound that is an essential element in the diet of humans, animals, and even many plants. Since prehistoric times, salt has been used to preserve foods and was commonly used in the religious rites of the Greeks, Romans, Hebrews, and Christians. Salt, in the form of salt cakes, served as money in ancient Ethiopia and Tibet. As long ago as 1450 BC, Egyptian art shows records of salt production.

The simplest method of obtaining salt is through the evaporation of salt water from areas near oceans or seas. In most regions, rock salt is obtained from underground mining or by wells sunk into deposits. Salt is soluble in water, is slightly soluble in alcohol, but is insoluble in concentrated hydrochloric acid. In its crystalline form, salt is transparent and colorless, shining with an ice-like luster.

Prices – Salt prices in 2009 (FOB mine, vacuum and open pan) rose +4.2% yr/yr to $165.00 per ton, which was a new record high.

Supply – World production of salt in 2009 rose +0.8% yr/yr to 260.000 million metric tons. The world's largest salt producers were China with 23% and the U.S. with 18% of world production in 2008. U.S. salt production in 2009 fell -2.8% yr/yr to 46.000 million metric tons.

Demand – U.S. consumption of salt in 2009 fell -6.0% to 56.900 million metric tons, down from the 2008 record high of 60.500 million metric tons.

Trade – The U.S. relied on imports for 19% of its salt consumption in 2009, down from the record high of 23% in 2004. U.S. imports of salt for consumption in 2009 fell -13.7% yr/yr to 12.000 million metric tons, but still below 2003's record high of 12.9 million metric tons. U.S. exports of salt in 2009 rose by +6.8% to 1.100 million metric tons, with the bulk of those exports going to Canada.

World Production of All Salt   In Thousands of Metric Tons

Year	Australia	Canada	China	France	Germany	India	Italy	Mexico	Poland	Spain	United Kingdom	United States	World Total
2002	9,961	12,736	36,024	6,400	15,736	14,500	3,343	7,802	3,558	3,894	5,700	40,300	214,000
2003	10,256	13,718	32,424	6,673	16,424	15,000	2,922	7,547	4,660	3,963	5,900	43,700	225,000
2004	11,088	14,096	37,101	6,910	18,838	15,000	2,876	8,566	5,142	3,993	5,800	46,500	235,000
2005	12,444	13,643	46,610	6,730	19,333	15,500	3,476	9,508	4,885	4,550	5,800	45,200	250,000
2006	11,424	14,389	56,630	8,718	19,846	15,500	3,438	8,371	4,955	4,550	5,800	44,400	261,000
2007	10,855	11,862	59,760	6,140	15,678	16,000	2,214	8,400	4,391	4,550	5,800	44,600	250,000
2008[1]	11,000	14,386	59,520	6,100	16,400	16,000	2,200	8,809	4,390	4,550	5,800	47,300	258,000
2009[2]	11,500	14,000	60,000	6,000	16,500	15,800	NA	8,800	4,400	4,600	5,800	46,000	260,000

[1] Preliminary. [2] Estimate. *Source: U.S. Geological Survey (USGS)*

Salient Statistics of the Salt Industry in the United States   In Thousands of Metric Tons

Year	Net Import Reliance As a % of Apparent Consumption	Average Value FOB Mine Vacuum & Open Pan ($ Per Ton)	Production: Total	Production: Open & Vacuum Pan	Production: Solar	Production: Rock	Production: Brine	Sold or Used, Producers: Open & Vacuum Pan	Sold or Used, Producers: Rock	Sold or Used, Producers: Brine	Sold or Used, Producers: Total Salt	Sold or Used, Producers: Value[3] Million $	Imports for Consumption	Exports: Total	Exports: To Canada	Apparent Consumption
2002	18	120.02	40,300	4,100	3,390	13,500	19,300	4,070	11,400	19,300	37,700	1,010.0	8,160	689	585	45,100
2003	17	124.24	43,700	4,070	3,330	16,300	20,000	4,010	14,100	20,000	41,100	1,130.0	12,900	718	585	53,200
2004	23	128.39	46,500	4,100	3,520	18,300	20,500	4,040	17,400	20,500	45,000	1,270.0	11,900	1,110	971	55,800
2005	20	130.75	45,100	4,170	3,430	17,700	19,900	3,970	18,100	19,800	45,000	1,310.0	12,100	879	686	56,200
2006	17	145.90	44,400	4,450	3,640	16,500	19,800	4,300	13,500	19,800	40,600	1,310.0	9,490	973	775	49,100
2007	15	154.95	44,500	4,420	3,650	16,800	19,700	4,310	18,400	19,600	45,500	1,520.0	8,640	833	588	53,200
2008[1]	21	158.42	47,300	4,470	4,110	19,800	18,900	4,380	21,100	18,800	47,600	1,780.0	13,900	1,030	896	60,500
2009[2]	19	165.00	46,000								45,000		12,000	1,100		56,900

[1] Preliminary. [2] Estimate. [3] Values are f.o.b. mine or refinery & do not include cost of cooperage or containers. *Source: U.S. Geological Survey* (USGS)

Salt Sold or Used by Producers in the U.S. by Classes & Consumers or Uses   In Thousands of Metric Tons

Year	Chemical[2]	Tanning Leather	Textile & Dyeing	Meat Packers[3]	Canning	Baking	Agricultural Distribution	Feed Dealers	Feed Manufacturers	Rubber	Oil	Paper & Pulp	Metal Processing	Water Treatment	Grocery Stores	Water Conditioning Distrib.	Ice Control and/or Stabilization
2001	20,100	87	172	411	213	242	280	1,170	533	61	2,260	100	124	512	824	560	16,800
2002	19,500	79	154	395	230	215	245	1,040	507	61	2,010	93	118	662	781	525	13,300
2003	20,100	71	151	374	231	210	215	1,090	460	67	2,210	88	126	777	802	537	18,500
2004	20,400	56	145	385	225	209	242	1,090	451	69	2,350	86	112	858	794	514	18,000
2005	19,700	55	149	398	211	204	227	1,140	477	65	2,210	81	107	1,140	803	511	21,000
2006	18,400	50	121	380	208	203	211	1,090	502	66	2,150	72	49	952	770	489	12,400
2007	21,500	41	98	305	198	149	385	1,160	457	6	211	61	36	1,030	943	522	20,800
2008[1]	18,600	37	78	283	190	144	436	1,260	405	6	286	77	42	1,330	992	464	22,600

[1] Preliminary. [2] Chloralkali producers and other chemical. *Source: U.S. Geological Survey (USGS)*

Sheep and Lambs

Sheep and lambs are raised for both their wool and meat. In countries that have high wool production, there is also demand for sheep and lamb meat due to the easy availability. Production levels have declined in New Zealand and Australia, but that has been counteracted by a substantial increase in China.

Prices – The average monthly price received by farmers for lambs in the U.S. in 2009 rose by +0.3% to 99.83 cents per pound, but remained well below the record high of 110.67 cents per pound seen in 2005. The average monthly price received by U.S. farmers for sheep in 2009 rose by +20.0% to a 32.90 cents per pound, up from last year's 17-year low of 27.33 cents per pound. The average monthly wholesale price of slaughter lambs (choice) at San Angelo, Texas in 2009 rose by +5.3% to 90.48 cents per pound, but remained below the 2005 record high of 97.76 cents per pound.

Supply – World sheep and goat numbers in 2008 (latest data) rose by +0.6% to a new record high of 1.940 billion head. The world's largest producers of sheep and goats are China with 15% of world production in 2009, India (10%), Australia (4%), and New Zealand (2%). The number of sheep and lambs on U.S. farms in 2009 (Jan 1) fell –3.4% to 5.747 million head. The U.S. states with the most sheep and lambs were Texas (with 15% of the U.S. total), California (12%), Wyoming (7%), Colorado (7%), and South Dakota (5%).

World Sheep and Goat Numbers in Specified Countries on January 1 In Thousands of Head

Year	Argentina	Australia	China	India	Kazakhstan	New Zealand	Romania	Russia	South Africa	Spain	Turkey	United Kingdom	World Total
1999	17,106	115,676	269,309	182,051	9,527	45,866	8,994	15,556	35,137	26,969	37,492	44,736	1,760,535
2000	17,052	118,812	279,461	182,980	9,657	42,443	8,679	14,751	35,257	26,592	38,030	42,341	1,803,865
2001	16,887	111,195	279,667	183,918	9,981	40,173	8,195	14,773	35,350	27,276	35,693	36,792	1,791,779
2002	16,400	106,566	276,413	184,864	10,479	39,725	7,776	15,327	32,452	26,860	33,994	35,909	1,791,076
2003	16,650	99,672	282,565	185,827	11,273	39,707	7,945	16,051	32,178	26,650	31,954	35,939	1,816,525
2004	16,650	101,882	293,239	186,789	12,247	39,424	8,125	17,030	31,732	25,743	32,203	35,937	1,864,264
2005	16,650	101,586	304,169	187,760	13,409	40,035	8,086	17,771	31,690	25,654	31,811	35,345	1,912,308
2006	16,600	91,546	298,119	188,739	14,335	40,253	8,298	18,213	31,383	25,408	31,822	34,820	1,919,192
2007[1]	16,700	86,229	283,880	189,725	15,350	38,572	8,405	19,675	31,347	25,086	31,749	34,041	1,927,660
2008[2]	16,700	79,518	285,813	190,721	16,080	34,184	9,334	20,923	31,974	22,912	29,568	33,226	1,940,081

[1] Preliminary. [2] Forecast. *Source: Food and Agricultural Organization of the United Nations (FAO-UN)*

Salient Statistics of Sheep & Lambs in the United States (Average Live Weight) In Thousands of Head

Year	Inventory, Jan. 1 – Without New Crop Lambs	Inventory, Jan. 1 – With New Crop Lambs	Lamb Crop	Total Supply	Marketings[3] – Sheep	Marketings[3] – Lambs	Slaughter – Farm	Slaughter – Commercial	Slaughter – Total[4]	Net Exports	Total Disappearance	Production (Live Weight) (Mil. Lbs.)	Farm Value – Jan. 1	Farm Value – Jan. 1 – Total
2000	7,032	7,032	4,622	11,654	788	4,827	67	3,460	3,527	329	4,554	508.9	668.8	95.0
2001	6,965	6,965	4,495	11,460	711	4,795	68	3,222	3,290	299	4,303	495.6	694.5	100.0
2002	6,685	6,685	4,357	11,042	855	4,794	66	3,286	3,352	266	4,380	485.1	618.1	94.0
2003	6,300	6,321	4,140	10,461	828	4,387	67	2,979	3,046	105	3,804	470.1	656.6	104.0
2004	6,105	6,105	4,096	10,201	695	4,184	65	2,839	2,904			464.0	723.8	119.0
2005	6,135	6,135	4,117	10,252	669	4,200	64	2,698	2,762			473.3	799.3	130.0
2006	6,230	6,230	4,065	10,295	692	4,196	69	2,699	2,768			463.1	875.4	141.0
2007	6,165	6,273	3,895	10,168	780	3,927	85	2,692	2,777			473.1	823.8	134.0
2008[1]	5,950	6,055	3,710	9,765	736	3,650	92					460.8	836.1	138.0
2009[2]	5,747	5,855	3,690	9,545										

[1] Preliminary. [2] Estimate. [3] Excludes interfarm sales. [4] Includes all commercial and farm.
Source: Economic Research Service, U.S. Department of Agriculture (ERS-USDA)

Sheep and Lambs[3] on Farms in the United States on January 1 In Thousands of Head

Year	California	Colorado	Idaho	Iowa	Minnesota	Montana	Mexico	Ohio	Dakota	Texas	Utah	Wyoming	Total
2002	800	370	260	250	160	335	230	140	400	1,130	365	480	6,685
2003	730	380	260	255	145	310	175	150	380	1,040	310	460	6,300
2004	680	360	260	250	140	300	160	140	370	1,100	265	430	6,105
2005	670	365	270	245	145	305	145	142	375	1,070	270	450	6,135
2006	650	390	260	235	155	295	155	141	385	1,090	280	450	6,230
2007	610	400	260	235	150	290	130	141	380	1,050	295	460	6,165
2008	620	420	235	225	145	270	130	125	340	960	280	425	5,950
2009[1]	660	410	210	200	140	255	120	130	305	870	290	420	5,747
2010[2]	610	375	220	210	130	255	120	128	320	830	290	375	5,630

[1] Preliminary. [2] Estimate. [3] Includes sheep & lambs on feed for market and stock sheep & lambs. *Source: Economic Research Service, U.S. Department of Agriculture (ERS-USDA)*

Average Wholesale Price of Slaughter Lambs (Choice[2]) at San Angelo Texas   In Dollars Per Hundred Pounds (Cwt.)

Year	Jan.	Feb.	Mar.	Apr.	May	June	July	Aug.	Sept.	Oct.	Nov.	Dec.	Average
2001	81.25	87.00	82.63	83.30	86.07	75.21	69.82	54.47	56.50	57.67	59.00	71.60	72.04
2002	65.85	70.00	64.00	65.15	64.06	68.75	75.83	74.35	73.69	76.20	83.00	86.88	72.31
2003	89.25	90.25	96.25	88.13	95.75	97.25	87.88	85.81	91.44	91.31	91.00	96.17	91.71
2004	99.44	99.94	102.50	92.31	97.50	101.37	97.50	91.12	92.25	91.75	95.58	99.12	96.70
2005	107.25	109.69	101.37	99.37	96.94	99.50	95.00	92.14	91.56	93.00	93.33	94.00	97.76
2006	86.75	76.87	67.47	60.60	68.16	70.94	74.00	84.00	85.30	85.18	85.40	83.00	77.31
2007	81.00	82.27	84.50	85.25	84.20	77.40	86.38	86.19	89.44	84.90	84.83	92.92	84.94
2008	86.63	88.82	83.25	74.70	77.75	86.75	88.81	88.13	89.54	85.55	85.46	95.83	85.94
2009[1]	88.74	89.25	92.75	89.38	95.23	93.91	88.00	88.88	88.17	89.50	89.66	92.25	90.48

[1] Preliminary. *Source: Economic Research Service, U.S. Department of Agriculture (ERS-USDA)*

Federally Inspected Slaughter of Sheep & Lambs in the United States   In Thousands of Head

Year	Jan.	Feb.	Mar.	Apr.	May	June	July	Aug.	Sept.	Oct.	Nov.	Dec.	Total
2001	258	236	316	275	227	221	229	258	230	274	273	266	3,065
2002	244	244	311	263	267	216	241	246	259	284	255	262	3,092
2003	227	211	252	280	209	216	225	226	241	251	223	246	2,805
2004	207	199	295	238	175	220	207	219	231	228	228	229	2,676
2005	195	204	268	208	198	210	188	216	219	217	213	219	2,555
2006	210	193	240	234	215	200	191	213	205	223	212	212	2,547
2007	204	194	267	203	205	188	191	212	197	232	223	212	2,529
2008	202	202	219	207	195	181	193	186	207	209	180	213	2,393
2009[1]	179	169	210	213	167	185	189	187	207	201	200	217	2,323

[1] Preliminary. *Source: Economic Research Service, U.S. Department of Agriculture (ERS-USDA)*

Cold Storage Holdings of Lamb and Mutton in the United States, on First of Month   In Thousands of Pounds

Year	Jan.	Feb.	Mar.	Apr.	May	June	July	Aug.	Sept.	Oct.	Nov.	Dec.
2001	13,455	13,833	13,141	13,729	13,551	14,586	15,443	15,744	15,266	13,979	13,238	11,336
2002	11,905	13,110	11,269	10,528	13,172	12,938	13,553	14,215	14,458	11,961	12,004	9,255
2003	7,124	6,232	4,063	3,900	5,016	5,838	5,427	5,929	5,855	6,210	4,485	4,883
2004	3,795	3,671	3,355	3,164	3,251	3,504	3,872	3,376	3,878	4,179	4,166	3,715
2005	3,497	7,549	7,585	7,650	8,739	9,719	9,362	11,756	11,790	10,942	10,137	9,332
2006	9,967	15,730	15,777	15,454	15,247	15,215	15,126	15,254	15,353	15,228	15,452	15,862
2007	15,769	15,640	15,570	15,996	18,206	16,644	15,410	13,811	15,692	14,734	13,944	13,096
2008	12,918	15,177	18,157	17,118	17,783	18,411	19,598	19,723	21,147	20,796	21,331	21,659
2009[1]	21,001	19,469	18,279	19,274	19,801	19,694	21,568	20,062	19,045	17,426	15,301	15,052

[1] Preliminary. *Source: Economic Research Service, U.S. Department of Agriculture (ERS-USDA)*

Average Price Received by Farmers for Sheep in the United States   In Dollars Per Hundred Pounds (Cwt.)

Year	Jan.	Feb.	Mar.	Apr.	May	June	July	Aug.	Sept.	Oct.	Nov.	Dec.	Average
2001	43.30	47.50	46.60	36.90	36.30	31.70	34.10	32.20	29.90	27.20	27.10	34.00	35.57
2002	36.20	34.30	31.80	26.00	25.30	23.50	25.60	25.60	24.50	25.60	31.30	38.70	29.03
2003	41.30	44.00	40.90	31.10	31.30	29.40	28.60	29.20	32.50	35.00	40.50	45.10	35.74
2004	43.80	40.80	36.70	36.70	36.00	31.30	37.10	37.30	41.20	40.40	41.40	44.60	38.94
2005	53.50	52.40	49.00	45.10	43.70	41.20	41.00	43.00	43.70	43.60	46.20	49.30	45.98
2006	47.70	45.90	40.10	35.20	32.50	28.20	27.60	27.90	32.20	31.40	30.30	34.80	34.48
2007	37.10	37.30	36.60	34.20	30.80	28.20	29.20	28.30	26.70	25.50	27.10	30.20	30.93
2008	31.90	29.90	28.70	28.40	25.40	24.50	26.10	26.60	24.50	21.70	27.30	32.90	27.33
2009[1]	31.40	31.90	33.10	35.00	31.90	29.00	29.50	31.40	29.60	30.00	36.80	45.20	32.90

[1] Preliminary. *Source: Economic Research Service, U.S. Department of Agriculture (ERS-USDA)*

Average Price Received by Farmers for Lambs in the United States   In Dollars Per Hundred Pounds (Cwt.)

Year	68.20	67.20	67.40	67.40	82.80	81.30	77.00	80.30	75.30	72.60	76.30	77.60	74.45
2001	74.10	80.10	84.00	84.30	80.00	71.60	64.30	54.80	52.50	51.40	52.80	61.40	67.61
2002	65.50	67.80	66.70	64.70	64.40	72.90	75.60	75.30	76.30	79.60	84.00	87.20	73.33
2003	92.00	92.40	97.10	93.70	97.60	89.30	89.40	88.60	95.10	96.80	99.70	97.70	94.12
2004	104.00	106.00	103.00	100.00	103.00	105.00	101.00	97.90	100.00	97.70	99.90	101.00	101.54
2005	114.00	114.00	114.00	114.00	114.00	114.00	110.00	109.00	110.00	108.00	107.00	100.00	110.67
2006	96.10	97.80	92.10	87.20	88.90	92.10	93.40	95.40	98.30	98.50	95.60	94.00	94.12
2007	96.50	94.80	95.50	97.10	97.10	96.80	98.70	97.90	99.00	97.00	97.10	98.40	97.16
2008	97.50	96.50	97.40	99.40	101.00	102.00	103.00	99.90	99.40	97.40	100.00	101.00	99.54
2009[1]	100.00	100.00	100.00	102.00	101.00	104.00	101.00	97.40	98.40	97.00	98.00	98.10	99.74

[1] Preliminary. *Source: Economic Research Service, U.S. Department of Agriculture (ERS-USDA)*

Silk

Silk is a fine, tough, elastic fiber produced by caterpillars, commonly called silkworms. Silk is one of the oldest known textile fibers. Chinese tradition credits Lady Hsi-Ling-Shih, wife of the Emperor Huang Ti, with the discovery of the silkworm and the invention of the first silk reel. Dating to around 3000 BC, a group of ribbons, threads, and woven fragments was found in China. Also found, along the lower Yangzi River, were 7,000 year-old spinning tools, silk thread, and fabric fragments.

Silk filament was first woven into cloth in Ancient China. The Chinese successfully guarded this secret until 300AD, when Japan, and later India, learned the secret. In 550 AD, two Nestorian monks were sent to China to steal mulberry seeds and silkworm eggs, which they hid in their walking staffs, and then brought them back to Rome. By the 17th century, France was the silk center of the West. Unfortunately, the silkworm did not flourish in the English climate, nor has it ever flourished in the U.S.

Sericulture is the term for the raising of silkworms. The blind, flightless moth, Bombyx mori, lays more than 500 tiny eggs. After hatching, the tiny worms eat chopped mulberry leaves continuously until they are ready to spin their cocoons. After gathering the complete cocoons, the first step in silk manufacturing is to kill the insects inside the cocoons with heat. The cocoons are then placed in boiling water to loosen the gummy substance, sericin, holding the filament together. The filament is unwound, and then rewound in a process called reeling. Each cocoon's silk filament is between 600 and 900 meters long. Four different types of silk thread may be produced: organzine, crepe, tram, and thrown singles. During the last 30 years, in spite of the use of man-made fibers, world silk production has doubled.

Raw silk is traded on the Kansai Agricultural Commodities Exchange (KANEX) in Japan. Dried cocoons are traded on the Chuba Commodity Exchange (CCE). Raw silk and dried cocoons are traded on the Yokohama Commodity Exchange.

Supply – World production of silk in 2005, the latest reporting year, rose +6.6% to 155,549 metric tons, which was a record high and sharply above the 14-year low of 79,458 posted in 1997. China is the world's largest producer of silk by far with 72% of world production in 2005. Other key producers include India with 11% of world production, Vietnam (8%), and Turkmenistan (3%).

Trade – In 2006, the latest reporting year, the world's largest exporters of silk were China with 79% of world exports, Japan with 4.8%, and North Korea with 1.6%. In 2006,the world's largest importers of silk were India (with 48% of world imports), Italy (12%), Japan (10%), and South Korea (8%).

World Production of Raw Silk In Metric Tons

Year	Brazil	China	India	Iran	Japan	North Korea	Rep. of Korea	Kyrgyzstan	Thailand	Turkmenistan	Uzbekistan	Viet Nam	World Total
1999	1,554	70,201	15,544	800	650	150	29	80	1,000	5,000	923	780	97,213
2000	1,389	78,201	15,214	840	650	150	15	67	955	4,700	1,100	7,153	110,996
2001	1,554	94,201	15,857	900	559	150	6	76	1,510	5,000	1,260	10,866	132,496
2002	1,620	100,101	17,347	900	391	200	4	96	1,550	4,500	1,200	12,124	140,551
2003	1,700	95,761	16,319	900	287	320	3	50	1,550	4,500	1,200	11,582	134,816
2004	1,750	104,801	15,742	900	250	350	3	17	1,600	4,500	1,200	12,323	145,930
2005	1,200	111,951	16,500	900	220	350	3	50	1,600	4,500	1,200	13,000	154,043
2006	1,250	111,951	17,305	900	220	350	3	50	1,600	4,500	1,200	13,000	154,924
2007[1]	1,250	111,951	18,475	900	220	350	3	50	1,600	4,500	1,200	13,000	156,094
2008[2]	1,300	111,951	18,475	900	220	350	3	50	1,600	4,500	1,200	13,000	156,144

[1] Preliminary. [2] Estimate. NA = Not avaliable. *Source: Food and Agricultural Organization of the United Nations (FAO-UN)*

World Trade of Silk by Selected Countries In Metric Tons

	Imports							Exports					
Year	France	Hong Kong	India	Italy	Japan	Rep. of Korea	World Total	Brazil	China	Hong Kong	Japan	Rep. of Korea	World Total
1998	454	1,495	2,743	2,436	1,795	1,261	14,963	----	9,171	1,667	----	180	29,611
1999	287	1,059	5,018	2,695	2,596	2,107	18,957	----	12,089	1,048	3	130	35,041
2000	323	561	4,713	3,177	2,581	1,769	17,267	3	12,531	676	9	120	15,183
2001	327	175	6,809	2,760	1,893	1,582	16,410	23	11,266	186	2	90	13,003
2002	262	38	9,054	2,363	2,025	1,845	18,548	4	14,702	102	2	170	16,117
2003	147	67	9,258	2,219	1,949	1,648	18,439	2	13,931	31	96	296	15,866
2004	181	3	7,948	1,983	1,581	1,338	16,607	7	11,288	20	688	227	14,324
2005	262	14	8,383	1,974	1,406	1,359	18,114	36	10,972	11	202	219	13,699
2006	212	3	5,565	2,146	1,295	1,095	14,945	4	6,712	4	11	223	10,012
2007[1]	150	2	7,922	1,463	791	989	15,199	18	13,756	2	10	277	15,429

[1] Preliminary. *Source: Food and Agricultural Organization of the United Nations (FAO-UN)*

Silver

Silver is a white, lustrous metallic element that conducts heat and electricity better than any other metal. In ancient times, many silver deposits were on or near the earth's surface. Before 2,500 BC, silver mines were worked in Asia Minor. Around 700 BC, ancient Greeks stamped a turtle on their first silver coins. Silver assumed a key role in the U.S. monetary system in 1792 when Congress based the currency on the silver dollar. However, the U.S. discontinued the use of silver in coinage in 1965. Today Mexico is the only country that uses silver in its circulating coinage.

Silver is the most malleable and ductile of all metals, with the exception of gold. Silver melts at about 962 degrees Celsius and boils at about 2212 degrees Celsius. Silver is not very chemically active, although tarnishing occurs when sulfur and sulfides attack silver, forming silver sulfide on the surface of the metal. Because silver is too soft in its pure form, a hardening agent, usually copper, is mixed into the silver. Copper is usually used as the hardening agent because it does not discolor the silver. The term "sterling silver" refers to silver that contains at least 925 parts of silver per thousand (92.5%) to 75 parts of copper (7.5%).

Silver is usually found combined with other elements in minerals and ores. In the U.S., silver is mined in conjunction with lead, copper, and zinc. In the U.S., Nevada, Idaho, Alaska, and Arizona are the leading silver-producing states. For industrial purposes, silver is used for photography, electrical appliances, glass, and as an antibacterial agent for the health industry.

Silver futures and options are traded on the Comex division of the New York Mercantile Exchange (NYMEX), the Chicago Board of Trade (CBOT), and the London Metal Exchange (LME). Silver futures are traded on the Tokyo Commodity Exchange (TOCOM). The NYMEX silver futures contract calls for the delivery of 5,000 troy ounces of silver (0.999 fineness) and is priced in terms of dollars and cents per troy ounce.

Prices – NYMEX silver futures prices in 2009 overcame much of the plunge seen in late 2008 when the financial crisis hit. Silver futures prices on a nearest-futures basis, after posting a 29-year high of $21.185 per troy ounce in March 2008, plunged to a 4-year low of $8.40 per ounce in October 2008 due to the financial crisis and fears about deflation. The highest month-end price ever posted for cash silver was about $38 per troy ounce back in January 1980. After the late 2008 plunge, silver prices during 2009 recovered to a 2-year high of $19.43 per ounce in December 2009. Bullish factors in 2009 included (1) worries about inflation, (2) the generally weak dollar seen in 2009 as global financial institutions lightened up their emergency holdings of dollars, (3) the global economic recovery which started in mid-2009 and meant stronger industrial demand for silver, and (4) a continued influx of investor capital into precious metal exchange-traded funds.

Supply – World mine production of silver in 2009 rose +0.5% yr/yr to a new record high of 21,400 metric tons, continuing to show some improvement after flat production figures in 2000-03. The world's largest silver producers in 2009 were Peru with 18% of world production, China (14%), Mexico (12%), Chile (9%), Australia (8%), and the U.S. (6%). U.S. production of refined silver in 2009 (through August, annualized) fell by 20.8% to an 11-year low of 3,899 metric tons.

Demand – U.S. consumption of silver in 2003 (latest data available) fell –1.0% yr/yr to 175.3 million troy ounces. The largest consumption of silver is for photographic materials with 35% of total usage, followed by electrical contacts and conductors (23%), jewelry (9%), coinage (7%), and brazing alloys and solders (5%). The world's largest consuming nation of silver for industrial purposes is the U.S. with 20% of world consumption in 2004, followed by Japan (16%), India (10%), and Italy (7%).

Trade – U.S. exports of refined silver in 2005 (latest data available) fell –21.4% yr/yr to 9.709 million troy ounces, which was less than one tenth of the record high of 99.022 million troy ounces seen in 1997. The major destinations for U.S. silver exports are Canada (38%), Switzerland (29%), and the UK (12%). U.S. imports of silver ore and concentrates in 2005 (latest available data) fell –80.5% yr/yr to 14,000 troy ounces. U.S. imports of refined silver bullion in 2005 (latest data available rose +11.2% yr/yr to 134.387 million troy ounces in 2005. The bulk of those imports came from Mexico (65.908 million troy ounces), Canada (41.474 million troy ounces), and Peru (20.319 million troy ounces).

World Mine Production of Silver In Thousands of Kilograms (Metric Ton)

Year	Australia	Bolivia	Canada[3]	Chile	China	Kazak-hstan	Mexico	Peru	Poland	Russia	Sweden	United States	World Total[2]
2000	2,060	434	1,212	1,242	1,600	927	2,620	2,438	1,148	370	329	1,980	18,100
2001	1,970	411	1,320	1,349	1,910	982	2,760	2,571	1,194	380	306	1,740	18,700
2002	2,077	450	1,408	1,210	2,200	893	2,727	2,870	1,229	400	294	1,350	18,800
2003	1,868	465	1,310	1,313	2,400	827	2,569	2,921	1,237	700	307	1,240	18,800
2004	2,224	407	1,337	1,360	2,450	733	2,569	3,060	1,344	1,277	293	1,250	19,900
2005	2,417	419	1,124	1,400	2,500	832	2,894	3,193	1,306	1,350	310	1,230	20,800
2006	1,727	472	995	1,607	2,600	830	2,970	3,471	1,306	1,250	268	1,160	20,400
2007	1,879	540	862	1,936	2,700	800	3,000	3,494	1,300	1,200	270	1,260	21,100
2008[1]	1,930	1,110	730	1,400	2,800		3,240	3,690	1,190	1,300		1,230	21,300
2009[2]	1,800	1,360	700	2,000	3,000		2,500	3,900	1,200	1,300		1,230	21,400

[1] Preliminary. [2] Estimate. [3] Shipments. *Source: U.S. Geological Survey (USGS)*

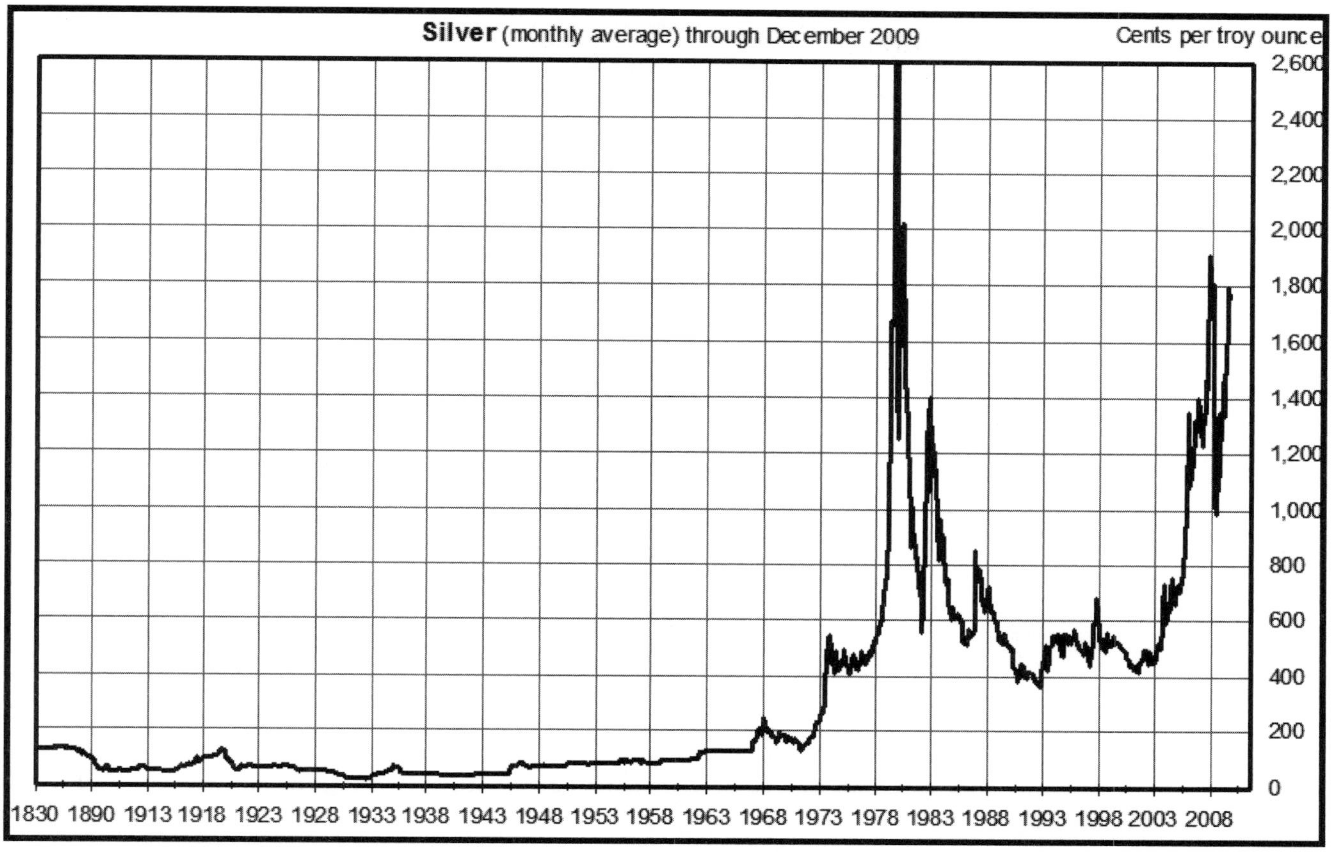

Average Price of Silver in New York (Handy & Harman) In Cents Per Troy Ounce (.999 Fine)

Year	Jan.	Feb.	Mar.	Apr.	May	June	July	Aug.	Sept.	Oct.	Nov.	Dec.	Average
2000	523.47	529.65	510.15	510.37	504.30	505.20	501.82	492.76	494.50	488.14	471.93	466.40	499.89
2001	470.19	457.34	439.93	439.25	443.59	436.79	425.45	420.72	441.09	441.87	412.35	437.98	438.88
2002	450.17	444.79	457.00	460.50	473.55	492.13	494.57	456.16	458.93	442.28	453.87	465.78	462.39
2003	485.62	468.11	454.74	453.40	475.29	455.62	486.48	502.90	520.62	503.91	520.64	565.33	491.06
2004	637.13	647.71	729.48	708.57	589.19	588.38	637.55	670.98	641.93	717.55	751.43	712.43	669.36
2005	665.45	709.18	728.50	715.74	705.29	733.64	704.40	702.72	719.33	769.90	786.35	865.88	733.87
2006	918.48	952.13	1,037.52	1,263.71	1,337.84	1,077.41	1,121.24	1,225.39	1,159.93	1,161.55	1,298.45	1,329.83	1,156.96
2007	1,286.63	1,394.58	1,316.27	1,373.23	1,319.27	1,315.48	1,295.21	1,233.22	1,292.92	1,372.17	1,467.15	1,431.24	1,341.45
2008	1,605.90	1,766.63	1,921.60	1,751.57	1,704.90	1,703.95	1,806.41	1,457.81	1,219.33	1,042.72	986.78	1,031.66	1,499.94
2009	1,139.90	1,343.68	1,311.50	1,252.02	1,411.30	1,465.93	1,338.64	1,443.05	1,648.74	1,726.34	1,787.68	1,765.68	1,469.54

Source: American Metal Market (AMM)

Average Price of Silver in London (Spot Fix) In Pence Per Troy Ounce (.999 Fine)

Year	Jan.	Feb.	Mar.	Apr.	May	June	July	Aug.	Sept.	Oct.	Nov.	Dec.	Average
2000	316.08	327.90	320.87	319.61	330.53	331.24	329.35	327.80	340.75	332.24	327.71	317.47	326.94
2001	315.87	312.57	304.50	304.36	310.19	309.54	300.97	277.97	297.93	289.21	286.92	306.25	302.43
2002	315.08	310.55	318.27	316.61	322.58	329.32	316.07	295.93	292.38	282.49	286.93	291.52	306.48
2003	297.21	289.23	287.39	285.06	292.05	272.79	295.53	313.01	320.30	298.01	306.53	320.48	298.13
2004	347.36	339.49	395.67	391.14	327.03	320.36	342.32	368.78	356.35	392.94	402.52	368.43	362.70
2005	354.28	375.57	382.74	377.48	380.46	403.56	402.10	391.55	397.90	436.23	453.10	496.09	404.26
2006	519.94	544.76	594.70	714.36	715.69	584.44	607.69	647.19	615.09	618.97	678.96	677.31	626.59
2007	656.95	712.03	675.74	690.95	665.15	662.06	636.65	613.19	639.99	670.90	708.45	709.65	670.14
2008	815.50	899.50	960.24	883.98	867.12	866.05	907.89	772.57	677.51	617.03	645.37	693.86	800.55
2009	787.02	931.98	923.81	850.16	912.88	894.99	816.90	872.89	1,010.76	1,065.91	1,076.27	1,087.91	935.96

Source: American Metal Market (AMM)

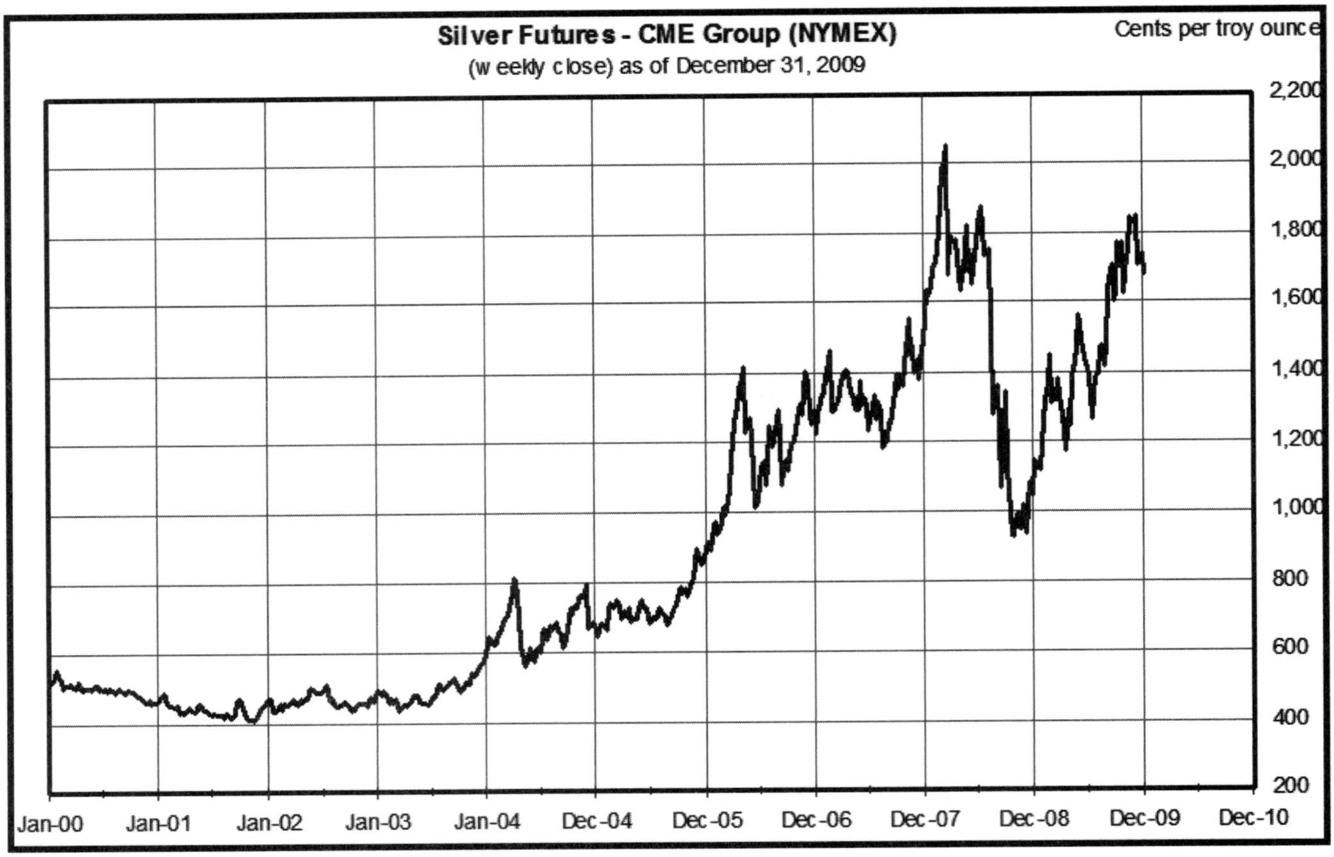

Average Open Interest of Silver Futures in New York (COMEX) In Contracts

Year	Jan.	Feb.	Mar.	Apr.	May	June	July	Aug.	Sept.	Oct.	Nov.	Dec.
2000	76,187	81,398	75,765	76,213	75,001	76,466	75,199	91,083	73,441	78,222	83,142	73,644
2001	69,408	72,798	74,337	71,589	67,328	67,429	75,019	75,830	65,533	66,530	74,228	66,903
2002	67,442	65,355	67,405	76,158	82,525	100,837	94,731	82,349	80,511	89,094	85,434	78,174
2003	98,561	94,472	84,485	87,445	85,232	80,001	91,544	108,118	110,423	92,216	101,303	103,007
2004	109,860	113,764	117,848	113,172	90,493	87,201	89,062	97,844	85,245	108,762	121,221	107,136
2005	97,744	98,644	101,200	103,562	104,680	124,317	124,521	121,133	117,121	135,335	146,409	136,502
2006	131,767	129,928	132,140	137,121	110,400	110,631	98,733	110,635	102,159	105,167	114,132	105,741
2007	105,692	122,515	113,749	118,275	109,070	120,179	117,817	118,292	110,958	123,781	144,897	146,891
2008	174,969	182,076	157,971	143,333	123,649	128,645	136,866	131,931	110,333	97,927	91,983	84,986
2009	87,525	96,902	92,756	93,855	95,420	106,283	99,018	103,076	122,052	133,409	137,261	124,797

Source: CME Group; New York Mercantile Exchange (NYMEX), COMEX Division

Volume of Trading of Silver Futures in New York (COMEX) In Contracts

Year	Jan.	Feb.	Mar.	Apr.	May	June	July	Aug.	Sept.	Oct.	Nov.	Dec.	Total
2000	258,053	425,910	231,336	318,752	216,938	407,455	175,235	370,739	146,007	149,252	303,673	113,667	3,117,017
2001	175,026	302,035	155,658	252,486	204,552	281,846	112,956	267,711	160,329	210,266	266,077	180,256	2,569,198
2002	265,773	271,293	163,898	325,889	243,475	389,798	281,214	296,579	164,537	209,249	292,861	230,998	3,135,564
2003	291,120	409,737	216,660	315,240	251,096	352,729	407,931	442,762	335,508	373,493	464,244	250,835	4,111,355
2004	385,058	544,939	408,447	671,204	278,703	425,501	316,264	427,973	281,737	364,158	541,366	360,775	5,006,125
2005	285,449	513,617	370,338	485,832	392,156	621,647	334,903	600,961	455,033	424,972	652,917	398,526	5,536,351
2006	495,649	624,491	562,330	807,269	513,822	508,746	255,777	452,551	268,393	244,152	424,771	275,112	5,433,063
2007	364,565	589,332	479,896	635,023	417,343	680,612	404,108	783,999	469,459	581,062	1,018,495	393,243	6,817,137
2008	719,308	989,601	881,776	912,952	580,959	859,976	722,663	953,123	792,072	594,307	578,009	332,437	8,917,183
2009	415,581	652,240	433,757	575,714	418,399	869,113	476,592	842,904	657,029	809,637	1,159,284	680,278	7,990,528

Source: CME Group; New York Mercantile Exchange (NYMEX), COMEX Division

Mine Production of Recoverable Silver in the United States In Metric Tons

Year	Arizona	California	Colorado	Idaho	Missouri	Montana	Nevada	New Mexico	South Dakota	Washington	Other States	Total
1998	211	11	W	447	W	W	670	W	2	1	723	2,060
1999	183	8	W	416	W	W	597	W	W	W	748	1,950
2000	W	8	3	W	W	W	734	W	W	2	1,240	1,980
2001	W	8	3	W	W	W	544	W	W	W	1,180	1,740
2002	W	3	W	W	W	W	424	W	W	W	927	1,350
2003	W	1	W	W	W	W	322	W	W	W	916	1,240
2004	W	1	W	W	W	W	302	W	W	W	943	1,250
2005	W	W	W	W	W	W	276	W	W	W	949	1,230
2006	W	W	W	W	W	W	260	W	W	W	895	1,160
2007[1]	W	W	W	W	W	W	194	W	W	W	1,070	1,260

[1] Preliminary. W = Withheld proprietary data; included in "Other States". *Source: U.S. Geological Survey (USGS)*

Consumption of Silver in the United States, by End Use In Millions of Troy Ounces

Year	Brazing Alloys & Solders	Catalysts	Batteries	Mirrors	Electrical Contacts & Conductors	Photographic Materials	Silverplate	Jewerly	Sterling Ware	Total Net Industrial Consumption	Coinage	Total Consumption
1994	7.7	4.2	3.6	1.5	31.6	57.6	3.1	3.7	4.2	130.2	9.5	139.7
1995	8.0	4.9	4.1	1.7	36.0	59.7	3.5	4.1	4.4	138.1	9.0	147.1
1996	8.2	5.5	4.5	2.1	36.3	59.9	3.9	4.4	4.8	140.5	7.1	147.6
1997	8.4	5.7	4.8	2.4	41.9	62.9	4.1	4.9	5.1	150.7	6.5	157.2
1998	8.6	5.9	4.9	2.6	44.1	69.4	4.5	5.5	5.7	163.0	7.0	170.0
1999	9.0	5.9	5.0	2.6	47.1	73.8	4.4	5.7	5.8	175.5	10.7	186.2
2000	8.7	6.3	5.2	2.6	50.6	73.9	4.5	6.1	5.6	181.9	13.4	195.3
2001	8.3	6.1	5.3	2.5	34.1	65.8	4.0	4.9	4.6	157.6	12.3	169.9
2002	8.4	NA	NA	NA	37.6	66.2	[3]	13.7	[3]	162.9	14.2	177.1
2003[1]	7.9	NA	NA	NA	39.5	61.6	[3]	15.1	[3]	162.8	12.5	175.3

[1] Preliminary. [3] Included in Jewelry beginning 2002. NA = Not available. *Source: American Metal Market*

Commodity Exchange, Inc. (COMEX) Warehouse of Stocks of Silver In Thousands of Troy Ounces

Year	Jan.	Feb.	Mar.	Apr.	May	June	July	Aug.	Sept.	Oct.	Nov.	Dec.
2000	75,945	73,948	93,782	104,259	102,589	99,285	102,713	102,291	97,879	99,552	95,749	95,717
2001	93,983	93,195	98,659	96,694	95,745	96,090	98,700	100,494	102,770	101,538	103,982	105,235
2002	104,547	102,395	100,983	102,540	104,526	107,766	105,938	105,563	108,090	107,495	107,440	107,090
2003	107,394	107,610	109,153	108,521	108,168	105,092	107,222	105,406	104,862	106,283	118,238	124,498
2004	124,271	124,181	123,195	122,087	122,687	118,442	118,369	116,253	109,311	107,789	104,624	102,831
2005	103,590	102,390	101,494	103,627	103,995	104,257	104,719	109,467	115,588	116,687	116,257	117,608
2006	119,974	124,793	127,898	125,763	123,627	108,443	102,268	102,086	103,634	105,451	105,313	107,770
2007	111,071	113,970	117,637	126,433	131,343	130,497	139,935	132,106	133,057	133,474	133,891	134,533
2008	130,072	135,414	135,037	135,881	133,512	134,896	135,959	138,061	137,821	135,719	130,204	127,170
2009	NA	123,902	124,121	123,615	119,910	120,879	118,519	117,818	117,796	116,159	116,159	112,494

Source: CME Group; New York Mercantile Exchange (NYMEX), COMEX Division

Production[2] of Refined Silver in the United States, from All Sources In Metric Tons

Year	Jan.	Feb.	Mar.	Apr.	May	June	July	Aug.	Sept.	Oct.	Nov.	Dec.	Total
2000	436	1,177	551	399	431	390	361	402	400	469	386	401	5,780
2001	405	343	405	360	360	331	395	380	338	403	442	383	4,545
2002	544	387	465	532	509	398	398	419	473	437	394	485	5,441
2003	483	426	320	412	357	431	430	373	361	809	363	471	5,235
2004	407	418	460	337	361	177	175	351	433	255	390	678	4,442
2005	402	505	515	568	450	558	556	440	356	376	485	439	5,650
2006	506	434	500	445	381	554	489	431	349	387	209	305	4,990
2007	401	405	445	436	476	452	335	438	290	388	267	339	4,671
2008	325	360	394	460	401	417	420	428	460	445	422	393	4,925
2009[1]	456	181	268	325	336	392	365	495	536				4,471

[1] Preliminary. [2] Includes U.S. mine production of recoverable silver plus imports of refined silver. *Source: U.S. Geological Survey (USGS)*

U.S. Exports of Refined Silver to Selected Countries In Thousands of Troy Ounces

Year	Canada	France	Germany	Hong Kong	Japan	Sing-apore	Rep of Korea	Switzer-land	United Arab Emirates	United Kingdom	Uruguay	Other Countries	Total
1996	489	[2]	2	646	4,662	3,601	383	2,413	15,850	35,366	624	40	93,346
1997	1,861	[2]	2	797	6,044	[2]	547	5,369	16,750	62,693	402	4,557	99,022
1998	669	2,205	347	45	585	210	----	604	3,569	62,693	688	8,760	80,375
1999	2,180	2	1	----	585	37	31	624	4,244	7,716	180	4,205	19,804
2000	1,906	22	2	----	3,504	1	----	727	----	3,311	109	2,634	12,217
2001	1,598	----	----	11	1,202	2	----	354	----	20,029	105	7,659	30,960
2002	466	----	1	4	466	10	----	727	----	14,532	----	11,990	28,196
2003	524	3	----	3	17	2	16	630	----	3,086	----	2,534	6,816
2004	7,009	1	3	24	585	166	1	2,321	----	3	108	2,125	12,346
2005[1]	3,729	----	25	3	1	95	18	2,829	----	1,145	563	1,302	9,709

[1] Preliminary. [2] Included in "Other Countries", if any. NA = Not available. *Source: American Bureau of Metal Statistics, Inc. (ABMS)*

U.S. Imports of Silver From Selected Countries In Thousands of Troy Ounces

Year	Canada	Mexico	Other Countries	Total	Canada	Chile	Mexico	Peru	Uruguay	Other Countries	Total
1996	256	4,662	----	4,918	35,365	1,874	30,285	12,153	[2]	3,122	82,799
1997	7	4,437	90	4,533	29,385	608	28,774	8,873	----	518	68,158
1998	24	5,851	427	6,301	34,722	813	41,152	9,388	----	3,945	90,020
1999	11	334	2	347	43,403	1,048	33,115	5,433	----	2,521	85,519
2000	46	----	----	46	38,902	225	44,689	2,787	----	35,899	122,502
2001	243	----	----	243	44,046	2,054	41,152	5,498	----	1,771	94,521
2002	149	1,813	----	1,961	48,868	2,331	67,837	6,430	----	6,350	131,815
2003	82	----	----	82	41,795	1,987	62,050	18,261	----	12,223	136,316
2004	71	----	----	71	37,616	2,042	59,156	17,297	----	4,774	120,884
2005[1]	14	----	----	14	41,474	2,514	65,908	20,319	----	4,173	134,387

[1] Preliminary. [2] Included in "Other Countries", if any. NA = Not available. Source: American Bureau of Metal Statistics, Inc. (ABMS)

World Silver Consumption In Millions of Troy Ounces

	Industrial Uses										Coinage								
Year	Can-ada	France	Ger-many	India	Italy	Japan	Mex-ico	United Kingdom	United States	World Total	Austria	Can-ada	France	Ger-many	Mex-ico	United States	Total Coinage	World Total
1995	2.0	30.0	43.6	101.3	49.5	112.7	16.9	31.6	148.7	752.7	.5	.7	1.2	2.4	.6	9.0	24.7	777.4
1996	2.0	26.9	41.0	122.2	51.7	112.1	20.3	33.8	155.0	785.8	.5	.7	.3	4.6	.5	7.1	23.3	809.1
1997	2.2	28.3	42.3	122.9	56.1	119.9	23.3	34.9	166.3	828.2	.4	.6	.3	3.7	.4	6.5	28.5	856.7
1998	2.3	28.4	38.4	114.7	55.9	112.8	21.7	38.6	162.6	801.2	.3	1.1	.3	10.0	.2	7.0	27.8	829.0
1999	2.1	26.6	35.1	121.5	61.8	122.5	21.3	39.3	175.2	838.7	.3	1.4	.3	7.0	.4	10.7	29.2	867.8
2000	2.0	28.8	31.8	131.0	65.1	135.0	16.6	42.7	179.1	871.8	.3	1.0	.4	8.8	.6	13.4	32.1	904.0
2001	2.0	28.7	32.4	154.0	58.2	119.3	15.9	45.9	157.3	836.5	.3	.9	.4	8.1	1.1	12.3	30.5	867.0
2002	2.1	27.1	29.4	122.5	56.0	118.7	17.0	43.1	161.6	807.0	.4	1.0	.5	6.0	1.1	15.3	31.6	838.6
2003	2.2	25.6	29.4	122.5	55.0	115.9	18.7	44.1	160.8	817.5	.4	.3	.5	10.3	1.1	14.5	35.8	853.4
2004[2]	2.1	12.0	30.7	79.2	54.8	125.1	18.6	52.2	164.8	807.0	.5	1.3	.5	10.3	.9	15.5	41.1	836.6

[2] Preliminary. NA = Not available. *Source: The Silver Institute*

Soybean Meal

Soybean meal is produced through processing and separating soybeans into oil and meal components. By weight, soybean meal accounts for about 35% of the weight of raw soybeans (at 13% moisture). If the soybeans are of particularly good quality, then the processor can get more meal weight by including more hulls in the meal while still meeting the 48% protein minimum. Soybean meal can be further processed into soy flour and isolated soy protein, but the bulk of soybean meal is used as animal feed for poultry, hogs and cattle. Soybean meal accounts for about two-thirds of the world's high-protein animal feed, followed by cottonseed and rapeseed meal, which together account for less than 20%. Soybean meal consumption has been moving to record highs in recent years. The soybean meal marketing year begins in October and ends in September. Soybean meal futures and options are traded on the Chicago Board of Trade (CBOT). The CBOT soybean meal futures contract calls for the delivery of 100 tons of soybean meal produced by conditioning ground soybeans and reducing the oil content of the conditioned product and having a minimum of 48.0% protein, minimum of 0.5% fat, maximum of 3.5% fiber, and maximum of 12.0% moisture.

Soybean crush – The term soybean "crush" refers to both the physical processing of soybeans and also to the dollar-value premium received for processing soybeans into their component products of meal and oil. The conventional model says that processing 60 pounds (one bushel) of soybeans produces 11 pounds of soybean oil, 44 pounds of 48% protein soybean meal, 3 pounds of hulls, and 1 pound of waste. The Gross Processing Margin (GPM) or crush equals (0.22 times Soybean Meal Prices in dollars per ton) + (11 times Soybean Oil prices in cents/pound) – Soybean prices in $/bushel. A higher crush value will occur when the price of the meal and oil products are strong relative to soybeans, e.g., because of supply disruptions or because of an increase in demand for the products. When the crush value is high, companies will have a strong incentive to buy raw soybeans and boost the output of the products. That supply increase should eventually bring the crush value back into line with the long-term equilibrium.

Prices – Soybean meal futures prices at the Chicago Board of Trade in 2009 started the year at about $301 per ton. After a brief rally, the price moved lower to a low of about $270 per ton in February. The price then rallied to a high of about $423 per ton in June. From there the price move lower, but enjoyed a brief rally in August, to $272 per ton in September. The price then move higher to end the year at about $314 per ton. The price faded into 2010 and reached a low of about $275 in February of 2010. Regarding cash prices, the average price of soybean meal (48% solvent) in Decatur, Illinois in the 2009-10 marketing year (i.e., October 2009 to September 2010) through December of 2009, averaged $329.27 per short ton, down by -0.6% yr/yr.

Supply – World soybean meal production in 2009-10 rose +5.0% yr/yr to a new record high of 160.643 million metric tons. The world's largest soybean meal producers are the U.S. with 23% of world production in 2009-10, China with 22%, Brazil with 15%, and the European Union with 6%. U.S. production of soybean meal in 2009-10 rose +3.4% yr/yr 40.425 million short tons, but that was still below the 2006-07 record high of 43.054. U.S. soybean meal stocks in 2009-10 (Oct 1) fell 20.10% yr/yr to 235,000 short tons, down further from the 2007-08 8-year high of 343,000 short tons.

Demand – World consumption of soybean meal in 2009-10 rose +4.5% yr/yr to a new record high of 159.421 million metric tons. The U.S. accounted for 17% of that consumption and the European Union accounted for 20%. U.S. consumption of soybean meal in 2009-10 fell -0.5% yr/yr to 27.760 million metric tons.

Trade – World exports of soybean meal in 2009-10 rose +5.9% to 55.121 million metric tons. Brazil accounted for 22% of world exports and the U.S. accounted for 16%. World imports of soybean meal in 2009-10 rose +5.9% yr/yr to 54.069 million metric tons. U.S. exports of soybean meal in 2009-10 rose +17.5% yr/yr to 9.072 million short tons. U.S. imports of soybean meal in 2009-10 rose +59.1% yr/yr to 140,000 short tons, remaining well below the record high of 285,000 short tons seen in 2003-04.

World Supply and Distribution of Soybean Meal In Thousands of Metric Tons

Crop Year	Production					Exports			Imports		Consumption			Ending Stocks		
Beginning Oct. 1	Brazil	China	European Union	United States	Total	Brazil	United States	Total	European Union	Total	European Union	United States	Total	Brazil	United States	Total
2000-01	17,725	15,050	13,175	35,730	116,151	10,673	7,335	36,245	17,712	35,930	30,711	28,363	116,042	1,253	348	5,695
2001-02	19,407	16,300	14,042	36,552	125,070	11,862	7,271	41,688	19,961	40,396	33,406	29,545	123,623	1,560	218	5,850
2002-03	21,449	21,000	12,950	34,649	130,647	13,657	5,728	42,781	20,545	42,467	33,335	29,096	130,157	1,647	200	6,026
2003-04	22,360	20,190	11,084	32,953	128,854	14,792	4,690	45,418	22,012	44,894	32,729	28,531	128,401	1,801	191	5,955
2004-05	22,740	24,026	11,300	36,936	139,072	14,256	6,659	47,680	21,910	45,917	32,680	30,446	136,692	1,577	156	6,572
2005-06	21,920	27,296	10,760	37,416	145,816	12,895	7,301	51,781	22,829	51,160	32,875	30,114	145,541	1,469	285	6,226
2006-07	24,110	28,465	11,550	39,037	153,931	12,715	7,987	53,973	22,213	52,601	33,228	31,166	152,244	1,913	311	6,541
2007-08	24,890	31,280	11,715	38,360	158,424	12,138	8,384	55,775	24,074	54,301	35,169	30,148	157,328	2,588	267	6,163
2008-09[1]	25,200	32,475	10,131	35,475	152,954	13,000	7,718	52,033	20,980	51,060	31,579	27,891	152,550	2,453	213	5,594
2009-10[2]	24,500	35,558	9,848	36,764	160,643	12,000	9,072	55,121	22,800	54,069	32,020	27,760	159,421	2,405	272	5,764

[1] Preliminary. [2] Forecast. *Source: Foreign Agricultural Service, U.S. Department of Agriculture (FAS-USDA)*

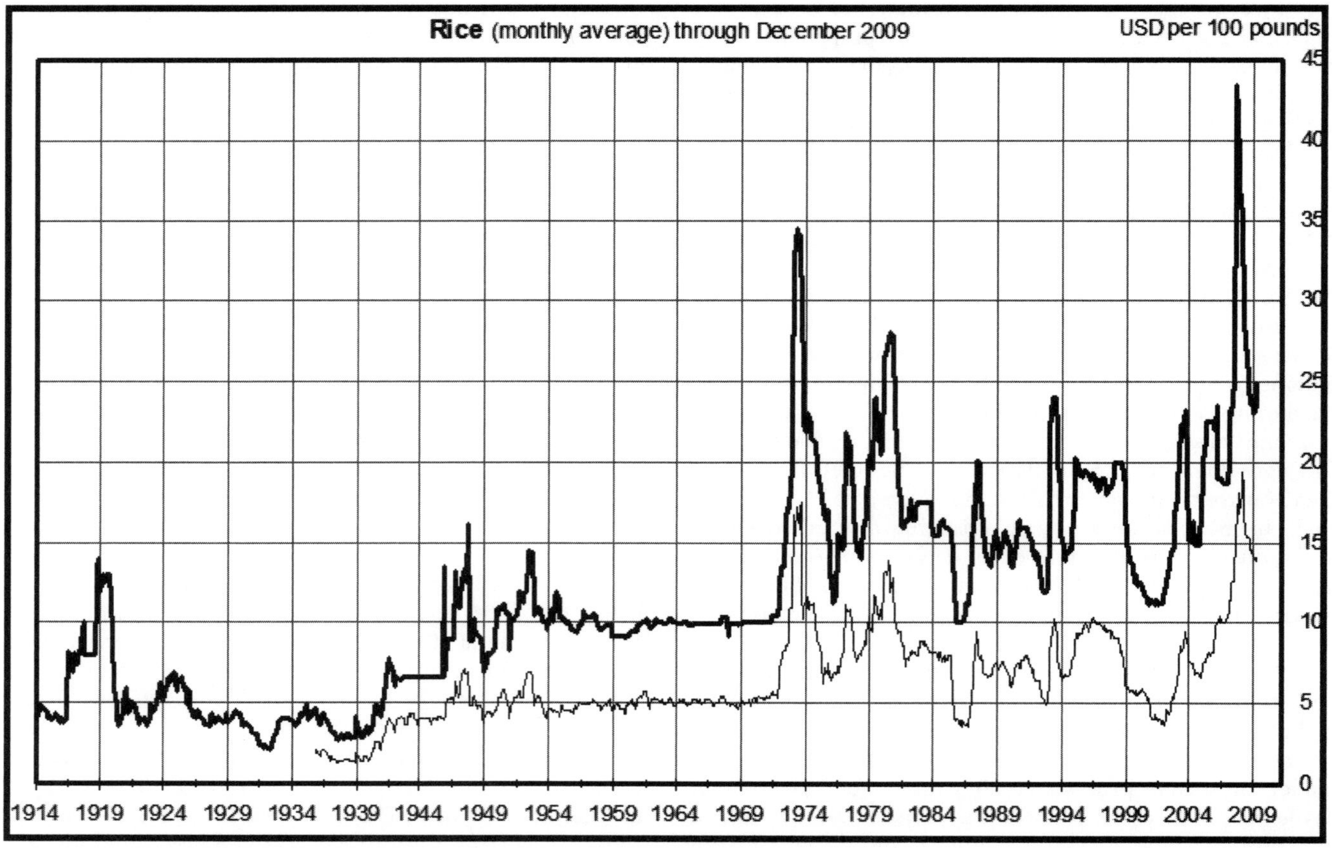

Volume of Trading of Soybean Meal Futures in Chicago In Thousands of Contracts

Year	Jan.	Feb.	Mar.	Apr.	May	June	July	Aug.	Sept.	Oct.	Nov.	Dec.	Total
2000	455.3	537.5	556.0	467.7	566.6	606.2	488.2	469.0	484.6	483.2	690.3	513.3	6,318.0
2001	530.2	431.8	470.6	485.1	584.4	625.1	710.0	630.9	491.4	652.9	659.3	472.1	6,743.8
2002	610.3	398.3	424.7	618.9	567.2	664.7	806.4	673.7	581.2	613.7	657.8	557.7	7,174.5
2003	639.6	551.4	527.7	676.7	599.6	749.8	772.1	692.8	677.2	896.4	700.7	674.3	8,158.4
2004	648.7	767.1	740.7	819.6	795.8	821.6	873.2	638.9	547.3	559.7	703.5	653.2	8,569.2
2005	658.7	857.6	713.4	661.8	571.3	1,025.0	632.8	693.4	602.9	497.9	694.0	715.8	8,324.6
2006	506.9	605.0	575.3	785.6	716.8	976.1	801.5	819.1	807.7	906.1	1,064.2	785.7	9,350.0
2007	768.9	1,018.8	822.1	985.7	798.9	1,217.3	1,107.9	1,025.1	1,028.6	1,016.4	1,218.8	1,204.7	12,213.3
2008	1,260.6	1,235.1	1,240.4	1,257.7	922.5	1,359.0	1,258.6	1,074.5	1,069.3	1,020.3	837.1	818.9	13,354.2
2009	909.2	988.7	841.7	1,195.1	1,071.4	1,390.1	1,146.6	1,071.8	974.6	1,012.1	1,222.7	1,056.6	12,880.8

Contract size = 100 tons. *Source: CME Group; Chicago Board of Trade (CBT)*

Average Open Interest of Soybean Meal Futures in Chicago In Contracts

Year	Jan.	Feb.	Mar.	Apr.	May	June	July	Aug.	Sept.	Oct.	Nov.	Dec.
2000	115,285	124,822	120,157	123,957	123,691	112,425	105,230	94,469	105,240	103,263	120,164	127,529
2001	111,880	108,047	107,253	116,888	119,644	135,046	134,982	129,536	123,644	121,845	145,996	147,576
2002	146,674	137,425	134,880	130,138	132,376	143,956	142,728	132,996	137,799	131,249	137,836	140,902
2003	154,821	168,036	157,670	163,532	163,096	154,985	152,121	146,582	153,505	169,709	170,707	176,191
2004	183,462	186,137	185,647	175,069	162,284	149,584	135,675	134,987	133,045	137,447	152,846	147,307
2005	154,984	165,403	146,326	133,578	129,372	149,882	122,088	109,976	121,833	135,970	140,102	140,959
2006	127,922	132,833	147,837	172,905	181,823	182,940	196,236	230,082	236,351	206,002	216,854	206,762
2007	201,214	227,905	213,708	216,258	212,398	217,576	210,612	201,339	219,046	225,683	248,277	251,133
2008	234,286	234,695	225,607	218,126	199,422	216,039	208,444	178,191	163,511	152,968	138,111	124,898
2009	118,930	121,722	110,580	123,445	160,515	190,481	174,733	167,301	155,388	150,639	159,393	165,141

Contract size = 100 tons. *Source: CME Group; Chicago Board of Trade (CBT)*

Supply and Distribution of Soybean Meal in the United States In Thousands of Short Tons

Crop Year Beginning Oct. 1	Supply: For Stocks Oct. 1	Supply: Production	Supply: Total Supply	Distribution: Domestic	Distribution: Exports	Distribution: Total	Dollars Per Metric Ton: Decatur 48% Protein Solvent	Decatur 44% Protein Solvent	Brazil FOB 45-46% Protein	Rotterdam CIF
2000-01	293	39,385	39,729	31,643	7,703	39,346	173.60	191	187	188
2001-02	383	40,292	40,818	33,070	7,508	40,578	167.73	180	174	174
2002-03	240	38,194	38,600	32,361	6,019	38,380	181.57	200	163	197
2003-04	220	36,324	36,830	31,449	5,170	36,619	256.05	282	211	273
2004-05	211	40,715	41,073	33,559	7,343	40,902	182.90	202	172	231
2005-06	172	41,244	41,557	33,195	8,048	41,243	174.17	192	176	215
2006-07	314	43,054	43,524	34,374	8,804	43,178	205.44	226	199	276
2007-08[1]	343	42,284	42,768	33,232	9,242	42,474	335.94	370	337	469
2008-09[2]	294	39,104	39,486	30,743	8,508	39,251	325.00	365	333	401
2009-10[3]	235	40,425	40,800	30,600	10,000	40,600	250-310			

[1] Preliminary. [2] Estimate. [3] Forecast. *Source: Economic Research Service, U.S. Department of Agriculture (ERS-USDA)*

U.S. Exports of Soybean Cake & Meal by Country of Destination In Thousands of Metric Tons

Year	Algeria	Australia	Canada	Dominican Republic	Italy	Japan	Mexico	Netherlands	Philippines	Russia	Spain	Venezuela	Total
2000	205.6	199.9	828.8	356.8	11.2	255.8	148.0	12.3	943.3	90.7	4.6	247.9	6,219
2001	183.7	190.2	1,023.4	369.5	132.6	297.3	268.1	195.3	720.4	113.7	86.0	136.1	7,290
2002	266.5	294.1	1,100.2	358.7	34.1	157.2	435.1	78.4	756.6	121.3	----	59.8	6,703
2003	184.7	383.9	1,056.4	317.5	0.0	329.0	693.7	10.2	238.5	60.7	0.0	190.5	5,582
2004	176.2	209.2	1,140.6	156.9	0.5	220.3	824.1	2.0	299.0	18.2	0.1	193.4	4,937
2005	63.0	74.9	1,155.9	264.2	0.2	523.4	1,356.3	10.1	442.0	16.8	5.0	112.5	6,352
2006	18.4	54.3	1,390.4	423.6	1.3	481.1	1,705.7	6.5	519.4	31.1	----	27.9	7,479
2007	39.5	1.2	1,467.4	448.7	0.1	451.3	1,638.4	8.2	626.9	31.8	0.6	49.3	7,922
2008	50.1	45.3	1,365.0	368.5	58.5	385.8	1,447.3	36.8	551.2	27.3	0.0	545.0	7,996
2009[1]	----	121.9	1,152.5	362.4	48.5	389.1	1,323.0	0.2	803.4	20.0	90.0	487.1	8,806

[1] Preliminary. *Source: Foreign Agricultural Service, U.S. Department of Agriculture (FAS-USDA)*

Production of Soybean Cake & Meal[2] in the United States In Thousands of Short Tons

Year	Oct.	Nov.	Dec.	Jan.	Feb.	Mar.	Apr.	May	June	July	Aug.	Sept.	Total	Yield in lbs.
2000-01	3,573.9	3,432.8	3,399.4	3,521.6	3,083.0	3,412.5	3,152.3	3,181.0	3,091.6	3,256.6	3,203.6	3,076.8	39,385	48.06
2001-02	3,534.4	3,538.7	3,655.3	3,703.1	3,313.2	3,589.7	3,315.7	3,344.2	3,194.1	3,085.4	3,106.7	2,911.3	40,292	44.27
2002-03	3,499.3	3,424.7	3,526.8	3,358.4	3,048.4	3,360.1	2,994.7	3,072.4	2,873.4	3,064.4	2,966.6	3,023.5	38,213	43.90
2003-04	3,462.1	3,465.9	3,483.7	3,479.3	3,144.9	3,092.4	2,682.4	2,792.4	2,616.2	2,752.2	2,480.2	2,872.6	36,324	44.32
2004-05	3,685.2	3,584.2	3,567.9	3,553.6	3,293.3	3,547.6	3,328.0	3,396.8	3,160.9	3,320.4	3,122.1	3,157.0	40,717	44.26
2005-06	3,700.9	3,562.3	3,518.0	3,589.5	3,215.3	3,504.0	3,212.6	3,474.6	3,250.9	3,507.8	3,351.7	3,354.5	41,242	43.83
2006-07	3,823.2	3,671.9	3,733.0	3,697.5	3,257.2	3,721.5	3,444.5	3,627.3	3,532.6	3,572.4	3,474.6	3,498.2	43,054	43.85
2007-08	3,869.5	3,709.4	3,887.5	3,791.2	3,473.7	3,701.1	3,500.6	3,633.8	3,352.3	3,316.3	3,052.4	2,996.3	42,284	
2008-09	3,519.4	3,413.5	3,346.0	3,439.8	3,203.7	3,425.4	3,335.2	3,502.8	3,323.2	3,066.7	2,844.9	2,683.5	39,104	
2009-10[1]	3,846.0	3,976.5	4,074.7										47,589	

[1] Preliminary. [2] At oil mills; including millfeed and lecithin. *Sources: Economic Research Service, U.S. Department of Agriculture (ERS-USDA)*

Stocks (at Oil Mills)[2] of Soybean Cake & Meal in the United States, on First of Month In Thousands of Short Tons

Year	Jan.	Feb.	Mar.	Apr.	May	June	July	Aug.	Sept.	Oct.	Nov.	Dec.
2000-01	292.9	317.4	343.8	423.7	333.9	325.8	309.1	313.3	286.9	341.3	338.1	273.9
2001-02	383.3	305.5	302.9	393.7	289.7	272.0	336.5	253.8	212.7	343.3	202.4	256.5
2002-03	240.0	285.2	371.7	337.0	299.1	259.5	335.7	263.5	311.8	271.6	228.4	266.9
2003-04	219.9	317.8	432.4	280.7	328.9	415.8	375.0	338.6	465.5	314.9	344.6	196.3
2004-05	210.7	357.7	286.8	271.3	340.9	310.4	248.0	307.5	349.0	244.8	362.3	238.3
2005-06	171.8	316.1	304.9	338.0	326.6	301.6	286.5	415.4	303.5	266.2	372.6	225.8
2006-07	313.8	388.4	373.6	468.9	372.4	289.4	329.9	328.6	279.0	316.8	314.9	231.9
2007-08	343.0	305.1	295.5	421.6	287.4	331.3	395.4	339.9	433.0	424.3	297.4	415.2
2008-09	293.8	372.0	599.1	413.9	448.0	437.2	360.9	421.8	577.6	426.3	328.4	316.3
2009-10[1]	234.7	446.2	627.4	571.6								

[1] Preliminary. [2] Including millfeed and lecithin. *Sources: Economic Research Service, U.S. Department of Agriculture (ERS-USDA)*

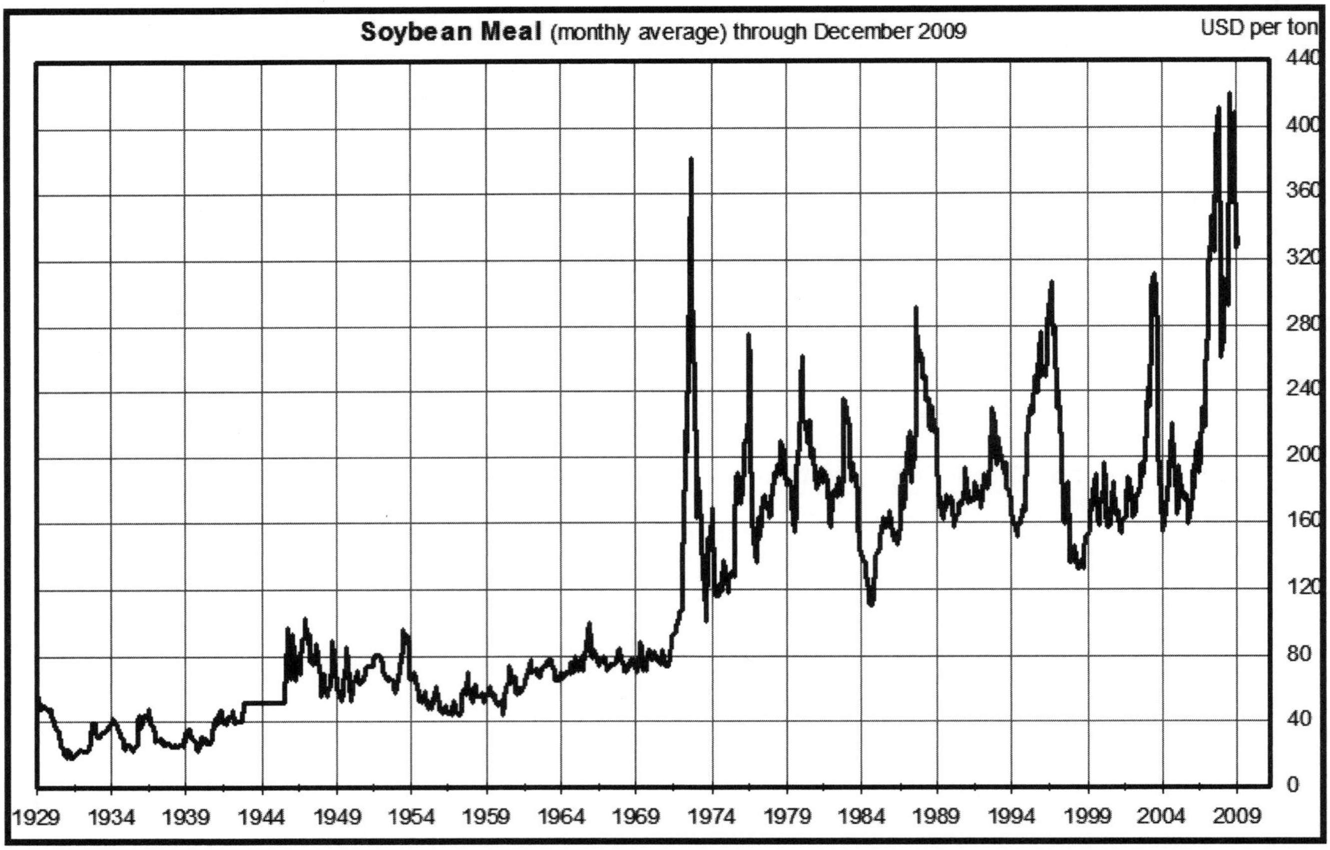

Average Price of Soybean Meal (48% Solvent) in Decatur Illinois In Dollars Per Short Ton -- Bulk

Year	Jan.	Feb.	Mar.	Apr.	May	June	July	Aug.	Sept.	Oct.	Nov.	Dec.	Average
2000-01	171.52	179.95	195.65	183.17	166.08	156.32	158.48	165.14	172.60	184.43	178.46	171.67	173.62
2001-02	165.45	166.10	154.18	158.01	153.11	160.49	161.57	164.28	170.33	187.45	186.25	185.45	167.72
2002-03	168.20	163.20	163.60	167.40	176.80	175.40	182.10	195.40	191.90	187.30	189.70	217.95	181.58
2003-04	225.20	242.00	231.54	252.15	257.39	301.14	311.83	300.69	285.81	284.05	205.34	175.51	256.05
2004-05	155.37	153.90	161.60	167.34	167.95	187.96	193.19	198.68	219.28	215.75	198.43	175.40	182.90
2005-06	166.22	170.32	193.17	183.64	176.73	175.07	174.64	175.77	176.83	168.97	159.76	168.87	174.17
2006-07	177.71	190.67	180.63	190.36	208.81	205.26	189.37	198.66	229.70	222.05	217.63	254.41	205.44
2007-08	260.55	280.76	314.78	331.28	345.87	331.57	329.94	325.48	390.72	412.25	355.35	352.70	335.94
2008-09	260.66	267.37	268.24	306.85	297.42	292.22	324.27	380.37	418.47	373.18	405.27	379.68	331.17
2009-10	325.69	328.18	333.93	314.23									325.51

Source: Economic Research Service, U.S. Department of Agriculture (ERS-USDA)

Average Price of Soybean Meal (44% Solvent) in Decatur Illinois In Dollars Per Short Ton -- Bulk

Year	Jan.	Feb.	Mar.	Apr.	May	June	July	Aug.	Sept.	Oct.	Nov.	Dec.	Average
1992-93	168.6	170.9	176.4	175.6	167.5	172.4	175.6	181.7	181.3	217.6	206.9	186.5	181.8
1993-94	180.6	195.7	192.5	185.9	184.4	182.0	176.4	191.1	183.0	168.1	165.6	162.5	180.7
1994-95	156.4	150.9	145.4	145.1	149.4	145.7	151.0	148.1	149.1	160.1	157.5	171.8	152.5
1995-96	183.4	194.1	213.6	220.5	216.7	215.7	237.9	232.3	227.9	242.3	251.1	265.5	225.1
1996-97	238.0	242.7	240.9	240.7	253.6	270.4	277.7	296.0	275.9	261.5	261.6	265.7	260.4
1997-98	216.0	231.6	214.9	193.1	182.1	165.3	152.8	150.3	157.8	173.3	135.7	126.9	175.0
1998-99	129.4	139.3	139.6	131.0	124.4	127.2	128.6	127.0	131.7	125.7	135.9	144.1	132.0
1999-00	147.2	148.1	145.4	155.0	163.6	166.6	168.1	180.1	170.2	156.8	151.4	166.9	160.0
2000-01	166.0	173.7	187.9	175.6	158.3	149.1	149.7	155.6	163.1	183.9	170.6	163.5	166.4
2001-02	157.7	157.2	146.6	Disc.	Disc.	Disc.	Disc.	Disc.	Disc.	Disc.	Disc.	Disc.	153.8

Source: Economic Research Service, U.S. Department of Agriculture (ERS-USDA)

Soybean Oil

Soybean oil is the natural oil extracted from whole soybeans. Typically, about 19% of a soybean's weight can be extracted as crude soybean oil. The oil content of U.S. soybeans correlates directly with the temperatures and amount of sunshine during the soybean pod-filling stages. Edible products produced with soybean oil include cooking and salad oils, shortening, and margarine. Soybean oil is the most widely used cooking oil in the U.S. It accounts for 80% of margarine production and for more than 75% of total U.S. consumer vegetable fat and oil consumption. Soy oil is cholesterol-free and high in polyunsaturated fat. Soy oil is also used to produce inedible products such as paints, varnish, resins, and plastics. Of the edible vegetable oils, soy oil is the world's largest at about 32%, followed by palm oil and rapeseed oil. Soybean oil futures and options are traded on the Chicago Board of Trade (CBOT).

Prices – Soybean oil futures prices at the Chicago Board of Trade in 2009 were at about 34.00 cents per pound in January. The price fell to about 29.80 in March and then rallied to about 39.73 cents per pound in June. In July the price had fallen to about 32.70 cents per pound but then rallied to end the year at about 40.35 cents per pound. The price faded into the new year and hit about 37.84 in February. Regarding cash prices, for the year 2009-10 (through December 2009), the average monthly price of crude domestic soybean oil (in tank cars) in Decatur (F.O.B.) rose +10.5% yr/yr to 35.52 cents per pound.

Supply – World production of soybean oil in 2009-10 rose +4.6% yr/yr to a new record high of 37.751 million metric tons. The U.S. accounts for 23% of world soybean oil production, while Brazil accounts for 16%, and the European Union accounts for 6%. U.S. production of soybean oil in 2009-10 rose +1.8% yr/yr to 19.085 billion pounds.

Demand – World consumption of soybean oil in 2009-10 rose +5.2% yr/yr to a new record high of 37.666 million metric tons. The U.S. accounted for 20% of world consumption, while Brazil accounted for 13%, the European Union for 78%, and India for 6%. U.S. consumption of soybean oil in 2009-10 rose +0.7% yr/yr to 16.500 billion pounds.

Trade – World exports of soybean oil in 2009-10 rose +3.1% yr/yr to 9.340 million metric tons. U.S. exports of soybean oil in 2009-10 rose +48.1% yr/yr to a record high of 1.474 billion pounds.

World Supply and Demand of Soybean Oil In Thousands of Metric Tons

Crop Year Beginning Oct. 1	Production				Exports			Imports		Consumption					End Stocks[3]	
	Brazil	European Union	United States	Total	Brazil	United States	Total	India	Total	Brazil	European Union	India	United States	Total	United States	Total
2000-01	4,333	2,984	8,355	26,736	1,533	636	7,060	1,400	6,893	2,952	2,137	2,024	7,401	26,301	1,255	3,134
2001-02	4,700	3,198	8,572	28,897	1,775	1,143	8,350	1,479	7,672	2,949	2,291	2,300	7,635	28,237	1,070	3,116
2002-03	5,205	2,950	8,360	30,583	2,394	1,027	9,032	1,197	8,267	2,925	2,304	1,900	7,748	30,166	676	2,768
2003-04	5,588	2,531	7,748	30,246	2,718	425	8,790	906	8,386	2,959	2,112	1,885	7,650	30,102	488	2,508
2004-05	5,630	2,575	8,782	32,631	2,414	600	9,171	2,026	8,883	3,060	2,210	2,627	7,911	31,615	771	3,236
2005-06	5,430	2,460	9,248	34,615	2,466	523	9,844	1,727	9,091	3,113	2,915	2,933	8,147	33,567	1,365	3,531
2006-07	5,970	2,640	9,294	36,359	2,462	851	10,566	1,447	9,929	3,395	3,368	2,600	8,426	35,698	1,399	3,555
2007-08	6,160	2,667	9,335	37,543	2,388	1,320	10,869	733	10,395	3,920	3,377	2,300	8,317	37,608	1,127	3,016
2008-09[1]	6,240	2,314	8,503	36,087	1,910	995	9,063	1,060	8,854	4,274	2,779	2,330	7,432	35,814	1,244	3,080
2009-10[2]	6,060	2,250	8,691	37,751	1,425	1,474	9,340	890	8,908	4,755	2,610	2,243	7,485	37,666	1,010	2,733

[1] Preliminary. [2] Forecast. [3] End of season. *Source: Foreign Agricultural Service, U.S. Department of Agriculture (FAS-USDA)*

Supply and Distribution of Soybean Oil in the United States In Millions of Pounds

Crop Year Beginning Oct. 1	Production	Imports	Stocks Oct. 1	Exports	Domestic Disappearance										
					Total Domestic	Food					Non-Food				
						Shortening	Margarine	Cooking & Salad Oils	Other Edible	Total Food	Paint & Varnish	Resins & Plastics	Total Non-Food	Total Disappearance	
2000-01	3,190	153	4,333	295	3,240	361	2,984	814	675	760	246	8,355	26,736	17,433	
2001-02	3,876	191	4,700	295	3,575	370	3,198	833	695	787	284	8,572	28,897	17,611	
2002-03	4,394	274	5,205	312	4,730	365	2,950	615	770	740	318	8,360	30,583	19,352	
2003-04	4,729	314	5,588	278	4,535	360	2,531	996	645	663	249	7,748	30,246	19,346	
2004-05	5,128	340	5,630	275	5,421	355	2,575	900	579	635	267	8,782	32,631	17,800	
2005-06	5,998	345	5,430	275	6,149	385	2,460	1,070	515	670	252	9,248	34,615	18,763	
2006-07	6,424	313	5,970	278	6,410	380	2,640	1,180	534	685	250	9,294	36,359	19,112	
2007-08	6,627	217	6,160	253	7,045	350	2,667	1,458	528	636	269	9,335	37,543	20,451	
2008-09[1]	6,124	253	6,240	235	7,314	342	2,314	1,340	456	609	254	8,503	36,087	21,235	
2009-10[2]	6,775	264	6,060	251	8,008	352	2,250	1,362	502	626	266	8,691	37,751	18,400	

[1] Preliminary . [2] Forecast. *Source: Economic Research Service, U.S. Department of Agriculture (ERS-USDA)*

Stocks of Crude Soybean Oil in the United States, at End of Month

Year	Oct	Nov	Dec	Jan	Feb	Mar	Apr	May	June	July	Aug	Sept
2003-04	1,236.8	1,329.7	1,390.1	1,737.3	1,797.5	1,675.7	1,452.3	1,410.3	1,296.4	1,198.0	1,001.8	887.7
2004-05	1,019.5	1,013.1	1,111.1	1,348.2	1,425.3	1,588.7	1,560.0	1,658.1	1,622.4	1,715.6	1,525.2	1,505.9
2005-06	1,641.0	1,706.5	2,029.6	2,247.4	2,392.2	2,433.1	2,454.7	2,576.8	2,605.3	2,762.9	2,740.2	2,703.5
2006-07	2,680.0	2,719.5	2,700.0	2,739.4	2,853.0	2,974.9	2,897.9	2,928.5	2,962.3	2,816.3	2,666.4	2,558.1
2007-08	2,701.1	2,736.4	2,713.9	2,860.0	2,713.1	2,714.6	2,573.4	2,633.8	2,554.7	2,482.8	2,265.2	2,200.4
2008-09	2,084.0	2,197.8	2,346.7	2,625.6	2,739.6	2,816.2	2,868.5	2,931.6	3,125.9	3,031.2	2,741.3	2,495.8
2009-10[1]	2,452.0	2,611.1	2,760.0									

Crop year beginning October 1. [1] Preliminary. *Source: Bureau of the Census, U.S. Department of Commerce*

Stocks of Refined Soybean Oil in the United States, at End of Month In Millions of Pounds

Year	Oct	Nov	Dec	Jan	Feb	Mar	Apr	May	June	July	Aug	Sept
2003-04	175.0	200.8	189.9	208.3	190.5	180.2	191.9	241.2	217.7	214.0	178.8	187.8
2004-05	235.8	178.4	200.3	212.6	222.0	222.7	243.4	236.6	216.2	273.8	200.7	193.6
2005-06	254.1	178.9	199.4	251.3	281.2	285.0	300.8	308.2	313.9	343.2	320.9	315.3
2006-07	334.7	355.6	381.7	442.4	427.7	386.5	403.5	382.4	397.9	408.2	380.0	346.1
2007-08	352.1	319.3	364.8	374.5	362.5	360.7	344.1	344.7	338.8	300.8	286.3	282.3
2008-09	307.3	337.6	298.5	282.7	283.1	284.8	294.3	302.8	291.4	298.9	268.8	246.5
2009-10[1]	260.7	275.1	268.2									

Crop year beginning October 1. [1] Preliminary. *Source: Bureau of the Census, U.S. Department of Commerce*

U.S. Exports of Soybean Oil[1], by Country of Destination In Metric Tons

Crop Year Beginning Oct. 1	Canada	Ecuador	Ethiopia	Haiti	India	Mexico	Morocco	Pakistan	Panama	Peru	Turkey	Venezuela	Total
1999-00	22,715	0	13,627	25,214	23,413	118,079	14,091	0	299	66,686	15,680	414	623,651
2000-01	54,909	9,849	5,224	5,793	54,062	72,456	0	62,999	4,558	60,606	0	577	635,493
2001-02	87,047	0	2,225	9,452	88,529	161,760	39,439	59,999	12,616	37,677	85,199	635	1,142,755
2002-03	124,667	0	11,997	1,997	42,727	188,993	26,517	38,215	2,241	20,349	26,500	311	1,026,638
2003-04	96,450	10	3,665	1,298	14,561	97,099	15,518	17	2,834	25,097	0	169	424,554
2004-05	68,162	0	1,529	4,375	29,385	162,913	6,579	15,506	7,247	15,459	21	6,063	600,399
2005-06	76,342	2	3,270	3,972	23,031	108,515	21,951	12,000	1,546	19,588	4,032	38	523,153
2006-07	80,068	3	550	1,962	14,301	151,641	60,347	2	3,409	5,940	16	26,806	851,221
2007-08	90,361	3,009	2,141	14,138	11	269,249	107,323	0	6,817	183	73	82,035	1,320,430
2008-09[2]	41,494	0	840	19,127	146,086	173,041	110,249	0	1,715	37,061	2,598	54,440	994,954

[1] Crude & Refined oil combined as such. [2] Preliminary. *Source: Foreign Agricultural Service, U.S. Department of Agriculture (FAS-USDA)*

Production of Crude Soybean Oil in the United States In Millions of Pounds

Year	Oct.	Nov.	Dec.	Jan.	Feb.	Mar.	Apr.	May	June	July	Aug.	Sept.	Total
2001-02	1,680.1	1,629.0	1,696.4	1,706.7	1,543.7	1,661.9	1,550.6	1,574.0	1,506.1	1,461.2	1,474.8	1,413.8	18,898
2002-03	1,692.6	1,631.5	1,696.0	1,612.8	1,473.6	1,633.3	1,447.5	1,491.7	1,391.0	1,482.4	1,440.4	1,445.2	18,438
2003-04	1,630.8	1,610.6	1,604.6	1,618.3	1,462.4	1,461.4	1,260.3	1,314.6	1,236.0	1,304.0	1,185.9	1,391.7	17,081
2004-05	1,759.6	1,688.0	1,682.3	1,680.2	1,564.1	1,686.4	1,579.6	1,620.1	1,497.3	1,586.7	1,484.4	1,531.1	19,360
2005-06	1,828.6	1,756.7	1,717.3	1,765.2	1,594.8	1,746.5	1,586.3	1,709.3	1,608.7	1,737.6	1,657.7	1,684.1	20,393
2006-07	1,829.5	1,725.0	1,771.0	1,747.2	1,548.3	1,766.9	1,626.3	1,729.9	1,693.5	1,710.7	1,662.8	1,678.0	20,489
2007-08	1,868.6	1,805.4	1,879.4	1,845.2	1,687.7	1,827.8	1,707.0	1,756.4	1,632.8	1,616.4	1,507.5	1,445.5	20,580
2008-09	1,715.9	1,622.9	1,597.0	1,615.6	1,536.5	1,636.4	1,595.9	1,684.2	1,604.3	1,469.2	1,368.6	1,299.9	18,746
2009-10[1]	1,828.5	1,854.0	1,895.2										22,311

Crop year beginning October 1. [1] Preliminary. *Source: Bureau of the Census, U.S. Department of Commerce*

Production of Refined Soybean Oil in the United States In Millions of Pounds

Year	Oct.	Nov.	Dec.	Jan.	Feb.	Mar.	Apr.	May	June	July	Aug.	Sept.	Total
2001-02	1,383.2	1,363.5	1,266.9	1,231.8	1,183.9	1,330.0	1,270.5	1,297.9	1,287.7	1,272.8	1,308.4	1,362.4	15,559
2002-03	1,451.2	1,367.2	1,262.2	1,224.5	1,181.0	1,308.2	1,238.6	1,378.8	1,316.1	1,293.8	1,290.5	1,334.8	15,647
2003-04	1,393.0	1,350.9	1,226.6	1,205.6	1,196.0	1,330.6	1,210.3	1,267.4	1,195.9	1,246.8	1,268.8	1,306.3	15,198
2004-05	1,377.6	1,331.1	1,243.2	1,243.4	1,188.1	1,321.6	1,324.5	1,287.4	1,253.6	1,295.9	1,324.1	1,324.7	15,515
2005-06	1,389.3	1,307.4	1,245.2	1,273.9	1,132.9	1,409.3	1,326.6	1,361.5	1,352.9	1,329.1	1,399.7	1,400.0	15,928
2006-07	1,477.9	1,309.3	1,303.9	1,269.3	1,165.2	1,361.0	1,361.8	1,409.8	1,340.8	1,457.5	1,404.0	1,421.0	16,281
2007-08	1,468.6	1,372.3	1,359.7	1,350.5	1,259.6	1,400.0	1,346.2	1,277.0	1,257.6	1,354.7	1,371.8	1,314.7	16,133
2008-09	1,388.0	1,248.3	1,102.6	1,121.7	1,088.2	1,200.0	1,185.0	1,210.7	1,139.9	1,239.8	1,200.8	1,227.8	14,353
2009-10[1]	1,377.3	1,294.4	1,201.1										15,491

Crop year beginning October 1. [1] Preliminary. *Source: Bureau of the Census, U.S. Department of Commerce*

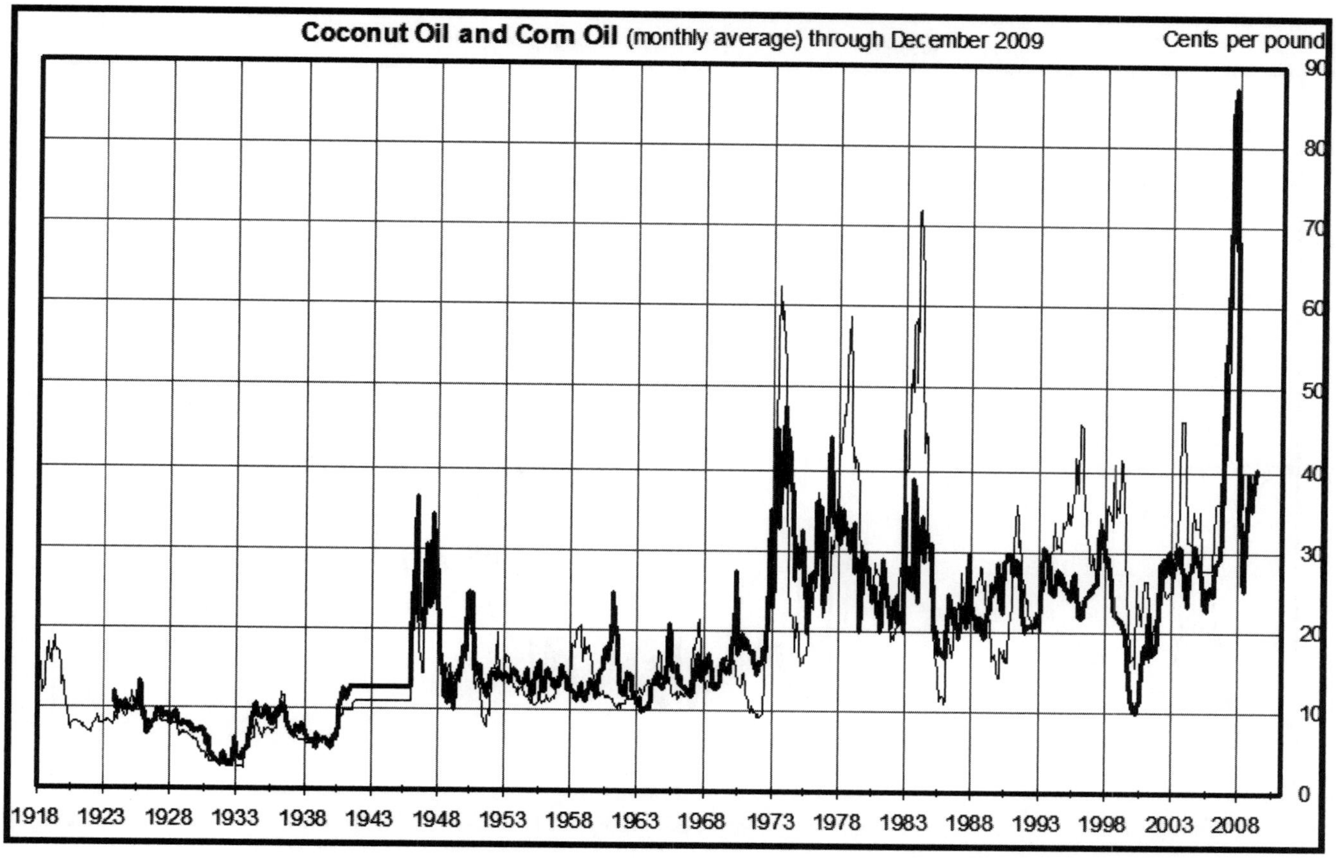

Consumption of Soybean Oil in End Products in the United States In Millions of Pounds

Year	Jan.	Feb.	Mar.	Apr.	May	June	July	Aug.	Sept.	Oct.	Nov.	Dec.	Total
2000	1,096.6	1,050.5	1,217.9	1,158.9	1,183.6	1,102.9	1,121.1	1,226.4	1,163.6	1,306.1	1,139.7	1,079.6	13,847
2001	1,065.9	1,151.7	1,308.8	1,202.4	1,224.2	1,261.6	1,307.6	1,557.5	1,411.0	1,687.3	1,624.0	1,485.8	16,288
2002	1,461.5	1,395.3	1,568.0	1,505.1	1,549.7	1,492.4	1,490.5	1,545.5	1,543.7	1,710.2	1,587.2	1,458.8	18,308
2003	1,418.1	1,347.4	1,490.0	1,494.9	1,552.6	1,493.1	1,509.5	1,483.5	1,577.7	1,660.7	1,544.2	1,451.4	18,023
2004	1,388.1	1,417.6	1,555.2	1,468.0	1,506.7	1,421.1	1,429.2	1,473.6	1,483.2	1,558.3	1,533.7	1,368.9	17,604
2005	1,365.4	1,609.2	1,609.2	1,587.2	1,589.5	1,496.2	1,523.3	1,570.4	1,527.2	1,589.6	1,546.9	1,416.2	18,430
2006	1,505.2	1,368.8	1,661.4	1,561.1	1,634.9	1,653.2	1,575.5	1,746.2	1,727.9	1,775.6	1,638.6	1,571.5	19,420
2007	1,547.3	1,357.8	1,624.8	1,586.7	1,728.6	1,640.3	1,812.9	1,793.1	1,699.5	1,757.8	1,618.9	1,548.4	19,716
2008	1,623.6	1,476.9	1,625.3	1,580.9	1,510.8	1,528.4	1,589.8	1,624.2	1,559.2	1,662.7	1,500.3	1,348.5	18,630
2009[1]	1,251.8	1,245.9	1,346.9	1,282.5	1,275.3	1,283.6	1,357.4	1,374.8	1,397.9	1,606.5	1,468.2	1,374.1	16,265

[1] Preliminary. *Source: Bureau of the Census, U.S. Department of Commerce*

U.S. Exports of Soybean Oil (Crude and Refined) In Millions of Pounds

Year	Jan.	Feb.	Mar.	Apr.	May	June	July	Aug.	Sept.	Oct.	Nov.	Dec.	Total
2000	103.0	146.1	161.3	91.5	48.2	109.8	105.8	57.0	69.0	43.9	115.2	261.6	1,313
2001	130.4	184.5	142.4	105.8	51.2	109.9	89.1	96.3	70.6	233.9	138.6	164.8	1,518
2002	249.9	446.7	233.3	233.3	87.3	345.4	180.8	95.3	109.8	113.5	194.9	210.2	2,501
2003	277.5	319.1	273.9	211.6	109.5	96.6	234.5	116.0	105.9	152.5	111.3	133.2	2,142
2004	71.2	62.8	73.5	38.8	44.0	39.3	53.9	68.8	86.8	59.9	184.5	239.5	1,023
2005	77.0	217.2	74.6	74.8	71.9	68.5	52.4	137.3	65.9	76.3	154.1	107.8	1,178
2006	71.3	67.0	178.2	96.8	53.8	82.0	89.4	64.7	111.8	167.1	120.3	276.7	1,379
2007	176.4	118.2	75.2	102.7	121.3	123.5	202.0	202.3	190.8	132.9	198.0	391.3	2,035
2008	157.7	509.9	385.5	427.1	163.4	171.7	125.5	183.8	64.2	138.1	102.3	119.9	2,549
2009[1]	96.3	145.9	161.3	350.4	277.9	86.5	247.6	302.9	164.3	332.1	241.0	379.3	2,786

[1] Preliminary. *Source: Bureau of the Census, U.S. Department of Commerce*

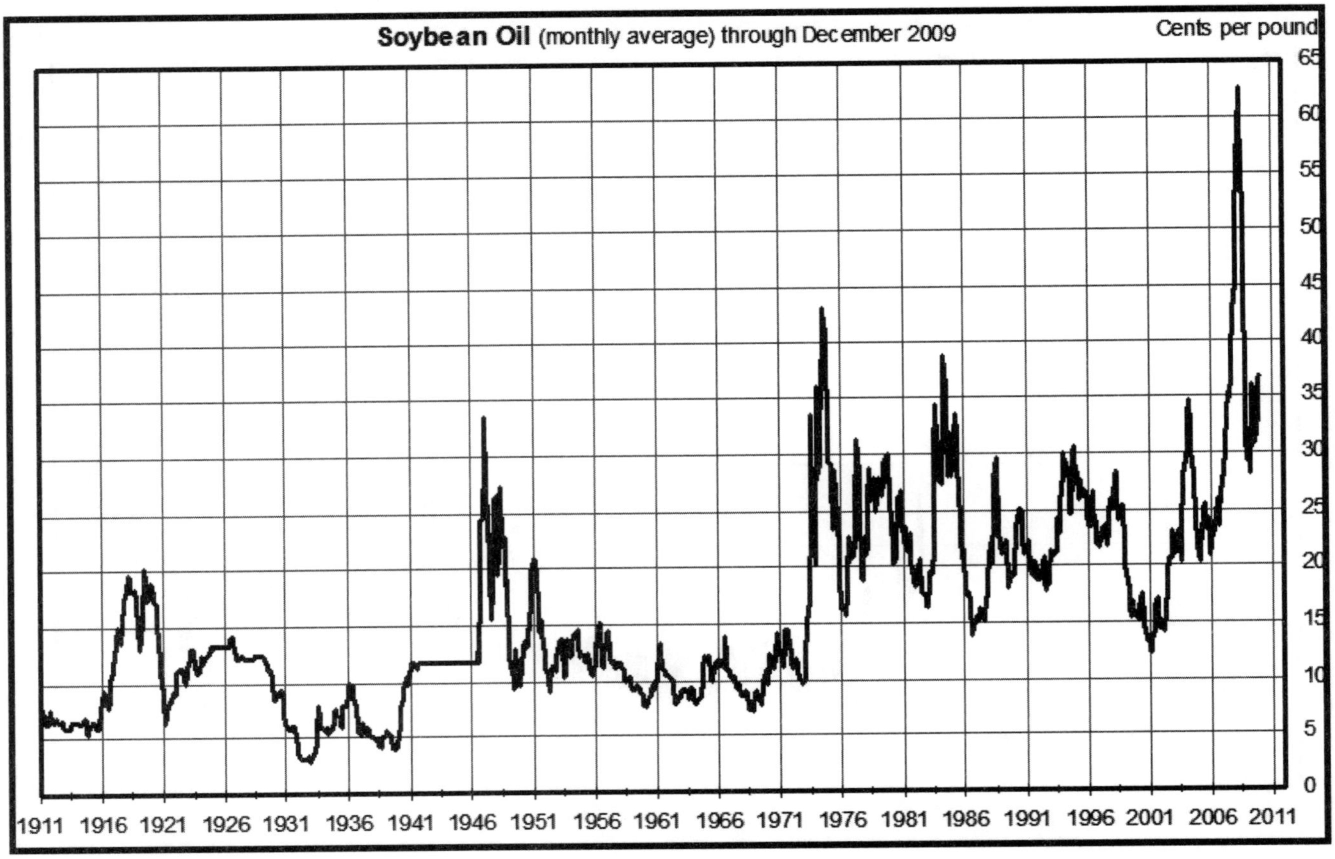

Stocks of Soybean Oil (Crude and Refined) at Factories and Warehouses in the U.S. In Millions of Pounds

Year	Oct.	Nov.	Dec.	Jan.	Feb.	Mar.	Apr.	May	June	July	Aug.	Sept.
2000-01	1,995.3	2,060.8	2,167.5	2,298.0	2,379.7	2,474.0	2,504.0	2,505.8	2,656.1	2,776.7	2,895.5	2,869.9
2001-02	2,877.2	2,724.9	2,787.4	2,868.1	3,038.5	2,896.4	2,952.7	2,856.8	2,943.2	2,735.9	2,529.7	2,521.7
2002-03	2,358.6	2,280.1	2,326.1	2,398.0	2,395.7	2,271.9	2,244.6	2,120.2	2,053.9	1,928.5	1,794.2	1,654.4
2003-04	1,490.6	1,411.8	1,530.4	1,579.9	1,945.6	1,988.0	1,855.9	1,644.1	1,651.6	1,514.0	1,412.0	1,180.6
2004-05	1,075.6	1,269.4	1,191.2	1,311.1	1,560.1	1,646.8	1,812.7	1,797.1	1,888.7	1,838.0	1,988.8	1,727.0
2005-06	1,699.0	1,883.5	1,851.8	2,190.5	2,498.7	2,673.4	2,718.1	2,755.4	2,885.0	2,919.2	3,106.1	3,061.2
2006-07	3,009.8	3,012.3	3,081.9	3,090.6	3,356.7	3,477.7	3,558.4	3,500.0	3,468.7	3,549.8	3,399.6	3,200.4
2007-08	3,085.2	3,224.9	3,235.2	3,277.0	3,408.0	3,278.3	3,083.5	2,925.8	2,989.0	2,906.0	2,793.2	2,567.4
2008-09	2,484.6	2,388.5	2,519.0	2,629.6	2,908.3	3,022.7	3,101.0	3,162.8	3,234.5	3,417.3	3,330.1	3,010.1
2009-10[1]	2,742.3	2,712.7	2,886.2									

On First of Month. [1] Preliminary. *Source: Economic Research Service, U.S. Department of Agriculture (ERS-USDA)*

Average Price of Crude Domestic Soybean Oil (in Tank Cars) F.O.B. Decatur In Cents Per Pound

Year	Oct.	Nov.	Dec.	Jan.	Feb.	Mar.	Apr.	May	June	July	Aug.	Sept.	Average
2000-01	13.50	13.37	13.12	12.53	12.38	13.90	13.53	13.53	14.21	16.49	17.08	15.46	14.09
2001-02	14.38	15.23	15.10	14.82	14.15	14.75	15.31	15.98	17.69	19.12	20.61	20.32	16.46
2002-03	20.75	23.00	22.60	21.50	21.20	21.56	22.40	23.17	22.90	21.80	20.40	23.20	22.04
2003-04	27.40	27.76	29.54	30.34	33.05	34.66	34.19	32.68	30.07	28.05	25.98	25.87	29.97
2004-05	23.23	22.95	21.79	20.46	20.70	23.60	23.09	23.38	24.70	25.46	23.59	23.19	23.01
2005-06	24.26	22.52	21.00	21.63	22.21	23.21	22.98	24.76	24.20	25.86	24.80	23.54	23.41
2006-07	24.80	27.64	27.63	28.00	28.94	29.74	31.06	32.90	34.01	35.74	34.87	36.89	31.02
2007-08	38.10	42.68	45.16	49.77	56.68	57.27	56.58	58.27	62.43	60.54	50.78	46.09	52.03
2008-09	35.50	31.55	29.30	32.16	28.93	28.23	32.76	36.06	35.66	31.08	33.69	30.96	32.16
2009-10[1]	33.15	36.59	36.81	34.88									35.36

[1] Preliminary. *Source: Economic Research Service, U.S. Department of Agriculture (ERS-USDA)*

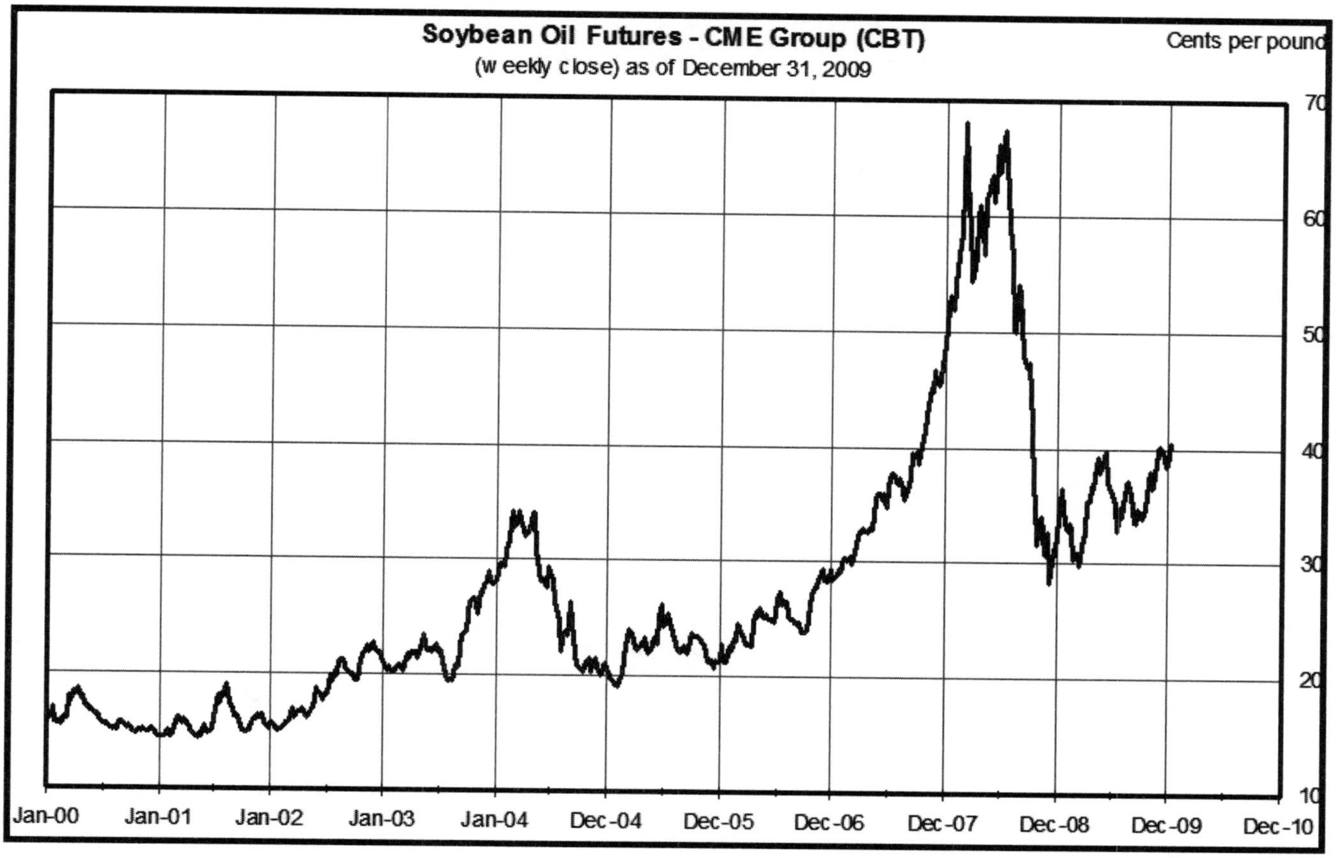

Volume of Trading of Soybean Oil Futures in Chicago In Thousands of Contracts

Year	Jan.	Feb.	Mar.	Apr.	May	June	July	Aug.	Sept.	Oct.	Nov.	Dec.	Total
2000	424.2	451.7	483.2	438.5	451.2	533.4	422.4	456.2	436.8	378.4	507.0	386.8	5,369.9
2001	327.6	458.4	416.7	443.5	403.1	541.2	751.3	612.3	447.4	551.0	579.5	502.3	6,034.3
2002	474.8	497.4	468.9	497.0	526.9	588.4	701.5	648.9	529.4	549.9	705.4	628.0	6,816.5
2003	522.9	540.6	473.7	618.5	520.0	740.5	761.5	594.7	636.5	733.4	656.5	618.5	7,417.3
2004	521.3	722.6	736.2	760.2	631.2	642.9	657.5	549.5	565.4	552.9	654.3	599.3	7,593.3
2005	475.1	799.9	579.6	636.3	565.5	852.3	548.3	637.1	594.8	607.1	672.8	707.4	7,676.1
2006	531.9	611.2	597.6	866.4	688.6	1,024.5	801.2	816.7	729.0	939.3	1,003.3	878.8	9,488.5
2007	784.1	1,091.9	765.0	1,218.3	805.3	1,476.9	1,113.7	1,092.0	947.7	1,213.6	1,324.4	1,337.9	13,170.9
2008	1,294.7	1,541.4	1,291.0	1,551.1	1,107.0	1,467.6	1,624.2	1,386.9	1,441.7	1,414.4	1,252.4	1,455.9	16,828.4
2009	1,211.9	1,518.5	1,189.8	1,429.7	1,202.9	1,993.4	1,543.9	1,400.4	1,217.9	1,342.1	1,527.1	1,554.4	17,132.1

Contract size = 60,000 lbs. *Source: CME Group; Chicago Board of Trade (CBT)*

Average Open Interest of Soybean Oil Futures in Chicago In Contracts

Year	Jan.	Feb.	Mar.	Apr.	May	June	July	Aug.	Sept.	Oct.	Nov.	Dec.
2000	131,948	135,196	143,699	155,114	134,093	140,582	134,392	135,506	136,590	135,584	142,712	134,873
2001	134,677	133,497	123,770	128,360	142,877	151,713	162,395	166,318	159,467	164,521	167,803	154,589
2002	149,103	158,157	149,913	136,198	128,707	129,480	135,762	143,144	146,759	139,626	169,978	155,871
2003	143,607	140,272	131,323	142,123	147,584	143,218	147,610	157,066	141,596	161,556	183,747	191,176
2004	198,361	212,204	186,745	159,478	141,772	136,887	135,649	142,574	132,936	147,046	154,316	151,800
2005	159,229	174,091	161,971	145,808	135,515	155,962	147,542	132,351	139,489	165,634	175,229	186,760
2006	171,317	183,717	192,643	204,132	244,580	241,962	276,251	269,208	259,464	256,153	279,091	273,375
2007	256,800	283,761	285,436	312,454	301,566	309,109	294,005	285,255	277,219	276,874	306,390	298,906
2008	289,892	292,918	287,995	275,016	253,974	259,416	258,412	254,496	256,621	257,226	252,077	220,725
2009	204,502	211,632	206,299	208,101	217,198	246,451	245,978	239,386	217,068	229,387	248,176	229,970

Contract size = 60,000 lbs. *Source: CME Group; Chicago Board of Trade (CBT)*

Soybeans

Soybean is the common name for the annual leguminous plant and its seed. The soybean is a member of the oilseed family and is not considered a grain. The soybean seeds are contained in pods and are nearly spherical in shape. The seeds are usually light yellow in color. The seeds contain 20% oil and 40% protein. Soybeans were an ancient food crop in China, Japan, and Korea and were only introduced to the U.S. in the early 1800s. Today, soybeans are the second largest crop produced in the U.S. behind corn. Soybean production in the U.S. is concentrated in the Midwest and the lower Mississippi Valley. Soybean crops in the U.S. are planted in May or June and are harvested in autumn. Soybean plants usually reach maturity 100-150 days after planting depending on growing conditions.

Soybeans are used to produce a wide variety of food products. The key value of soybeans lies in the relatively high protein content, which makes it an excellent source of protein without many of the negative factors of animal meat. Popular soy-based food products include whole soybeans (roasted for snacks or used in sauces, stews and soups), soy oil for cooking and baking, soy flour, protein concentrates, isolated soy protein (which contains up to 92% protein), soy milk and baby formula (as an alternative to dairy products), soy yogurt, soy cheese, soy nut butter, soy sprouts, tofu and tofu products (soybean curd), soy sauce (which is produced by a fermentation process), and meat alternatives (hamburgers, breakfast sausage, etc).

The primary market for soybean futures is at the Chicago Board of Trade. The CBOT's soybean contract calls for the delivery of 5,000 bushels of No. 2 yellow soybeans (at contract par), No. 1 yellow soybeans (at 6 cents per bushel above the contract price), or No. 3 yellow soybeans (at a 6 cents under the contract price). Soybean futures are also traded at exchanges in Brazil, Argentina, China, and Tokyo.

Prices – Soybean futures prices hit a 2-1/2 year low of $7.77 per bushel in December 2008 but then recovered in the first half of 2009. Bullish factors in the first half of the year included strong Chinese demand and the USDA's early estimates for a 5-year low in the 2009-10 US carry-over. However, soybean prices peaked at a 1-1/2 year high of $12.91 in June 2009 and spent most of the rest of the year trading in the relatively narrow range of $9-11 per bushel. Soybean prices fell back in the latter half of 2009 due to favorable summer growing weather and the record high of 44.0 bushels per acre seen during the summer of 2009, which produced a record US soybean crop of 3.361 billion bushels (+13.3% y/y). Due to relatively strong demand, the record crop was mostly absorbed and the 2009-10 carry-over of 210 million bushels was 33% below the 5-year average of 315 million bushels. On the global stage, world soybean production in 2009-10 hit a record high of 255.020 million metric tons, up sharply by 21% from the year-earlier level. The record level of production pushed the world carry-over up to 59.73 million metric tons, which was the second highest ever behind 62.7 billion in 2006-07. The large global crop and relatively high global carry-over kept a lid on soybean prices in the latter half of 2009 and early 2010. Looking ahead into 2010-11, the USDA is forecasting that the US soybean crop will be just 3% below last summer's record high, thus pushing the carry-over up to 330 million bushels and likely keeping a lid on prices in coming months if the US summer weather is favorable in 2010.

Supply – World soybean production during the 2009-10 marketing year (Sep-Aug) rose by +20.9% yr/yr to a new record high of 255.017 million metric tons. World soybean production has more than tripled from the 81 million metric ton level seen in 1980. The world's largest soybean producers were the U.S. with 36% of world production in 2009-10, Brazil (26%), Argentina (21%), China (6%), and India (3%). China's soybean production has roughly doubled since 1980. Brazil's production has risen by almost four times since 1980.

U.S. soybean production in 2009-10 rose by +13.36% yr/yr to a new record high of 3.361 billion bushels. U.S. farmers harvested a record high of 76.407 million acres of soybeans in 2009-10, which is up +2.31% yr/yr. The average yield in 2009-10 is up +10.8% yr/yr to a new record high of 44.0 bushels per acre. U.S. ending stocks for the 2009-10 marketing year (September 1), fell by -32.6% to 138.2 million bushels but still above the 3-decade low of 112.4 million bushels seen in 2004-05.

Demand – Total U.S. distribution in 2009-10 rose +7.1% to 3.262 billion bushels. The distribution tables for U.S. soybeans for the 2009-10 marketing year show that 52% of U.S. soybean usage went for crushing into soybean oil and meal, 42% for exports, and 6% for seed and residual. The quantity of U.S. soybeans that went for crushing rose +2.9% yr/yr in 2009-10 to 1.710 billion bushels. The world soybean crush rose +5.0% yr/yr in 2009-10 to a new record high of 204.219 million metric tons, which was about double the level seen in 1993-94.

Trade – World exports of soybeans in 2009-10 rose +6.0% yr/yr to a new record high of 81.389 million metric tons. The world's largest soybean exporters in 2009-10 were the U.S. with 47% of world exports, Brazil with 31% of world exports, and Argentina with 10% of world exports. U.S. soybean exports in 2009-10 rose +9.1% yr/yr to a new record high of 38.102 million metric tons. Brazil's soybean exports have more than doubled in the past decade and Canada's exports have almost tripled.

World imports in 2009-10 rose +3.1% yr/yr to a new record high of 79.575 million metric tons. The world's largest importers of soybeans in 2009-10 were China with 53% of world imports, the European Union with 16%, Japan with 5%, and Mexico with 4%. China's imports in 2009-10 rose +3.4% yr/yr to a record level of 42.500 million metric tons, which is way from negligible levels prior to 1994.

World Production of Soybeans In Thousands of Metric Tons

Crop Year[4]	Argentina	Bolivia	Brazil	Canada	China	India	Indonesia	Mexico	Paraguay	Thailand	United States	Russia	World Total
2000-01	27,800	1,150	39,500	2,703	15,400	5,250	1,020	103	3,502	312	75,055	342	175,759
2001-02	30,000	1,245	43,500	1,635	15,410	5,400	870	66	3,547	270	78,672	350	184,815
2002-03	35,500	1,650	52,000	2,336	16,510	4,000	780	89	4,500	250	75,010	423	196,869
2003-04	33,000	1,850	51,000	2,263	15,394	6,800	820	125	3,911	220	66,783	393	186,638
2004-05	39,000	2,027	53,000	3,042	17,400	5,850	825	132	4,040	217	85,019	555	215,777
2005-06	40,500	2,060	57,000	3,161	16,350	7,000	832	185	3,640	226	83,507	689	220,670
2006-07	48,800	1,650	59,000	3,466	15,967	7,690	815	80	5,856	210	87,001	807	237,117
2007-08[1]	46,200	1,050	61,000	2,696	14,000	9,470	780	88	6,900	210	72,859	652	221,141
2008-09[2]	32,000	1,600	57,000	3,336	15,500	9,100	800	153	3,900	180	80,749	744	210,863
2009-10[3]	53,000	1,665	66,000	3,500	14,500	8,800	800	105	7,100	180	91,472	942	255,017

[1] Preliminary. [2] Estimate. [3] Forecast. [4] Spilt year includes Northern Hemisphere crops harvested in the late months of the first year shown combined with Southern Hemisphere crops harvested in the early months of the following year. *Sources: Oil World; Foreign Agricultural Service, U.S. Department of Agriculture (FAS-USDA)*

World Crushings and Ending Stocks of Soybeans In Thousands of Metric Tons

Crop Year	Crushings										Ending Stocks		
	Argentina	Brazil	China	European Union	India	Japan	Mexico	Taiwan	United States	World Total	Brazil	United States	World Total
2000-01	17,300	22,742	18,900	16,728	4,525	3,775	4,450	2,128	44,625	146,602	9,448	6,743	33,696
2001-02	20,859	24,693	20,250	17,819	4,629	3,885	4,610	2,187	46,259	158,018	12,593	5,663	35,526
2002-03	23,533	27,168	26,540	16,480	3,420	4,217	4,335	2,135	43,948	165,634	16,636	4,853	42,870
2003-04	25,040	29,323	25,439	14,084	5,534	3,536	3,889	2,046	41,632	163,965	15,507	3,059	37,885
2004-05	27,313	29,344	30,362	14,350	5,030	3,149	3,729	2,013	46,160	175,856	16,658	6,960	47,473
2005-06	31,888	28,285	34,500	13,670	5,990	2,820	3,823	2,190	47,324	185,188	16,641	12,229	53,207
2006-07	33,586	31,109	35,970	14,670	6,615	2,925	3,900	2,161	49,198	195,659	18,190	15,617	62,885
2007-08[1]	34,607	32,114	39,518	14,870	8,170	2,890	3,620	1,965	49,081	201,874	18,902	5,580	52,947
2008-09[2]	31,911	32,512	41,035	12,860	7,500	2,496	3,465	1,917	45,232	194,550	10,547	3,761	41,638
2009-10[3]	35,300	31,600	44,930	12,500	7,600	2,750	3,560	1,970	46,811	204,219	16,847	5,715	59,727

[1] Preliminary. [2] Estimate. [3] Forecast. *Sources: Oil World; Foreign Agricultural Service, U.S. Department of Agriculture (FAS-USDA)*

World Imports and Exports of Soybeans In Thousands of Metric Tons

Crop Year	Imports							Exports					
	China	European Union	Japan	Rep. of Korea	Mexico	Taiwan	World Total	Argentina	Brazil	Canada	Paraguay	United States	World Total
2000-01	13,245	17,602	4,767	1,389	4,381	2,330	53,052	7,304	15,469	747	2,509	27,103	53,756
2001-02	10,385	18,675	5,023	1,434	4,510	2,578	54,385	5,960	14,504	502	2,285	28,948	52,894
2002-03	21,417	16,943	5,087	1,516	4,230	2,351	62,914	8,624	19,629	726	2,806	28,423	60,973
2003-04	16,933	14,675	4,688	1,368	3,797	2,218	53,999	6,741	20,417	914	2,644	24,128	56,019
2004-05	25,802	14,539	4,295	1,240	3,640	2,256	63,473	9,568	20,137	1,124	2,882	29,860	64,752
2005-06	28,317	13,937	3,962	1,190	3,667	2,498	64,129	7,249	25,911	1,326	2,380	25,579	63,804
2006-07	28,726	15,291	4,094	1,231	3,844	2,436	69,062	9,559	23,485	1,683	4,361	30,386	71,310
2007-08[1]	37,816	15,123	4,014	1,232	3,584	2,148	78,121	13,837	25,364	1,753	5,400	31,538	79,526
2008-09[2]	41,098	13,213	3,396	1,167	3,327	2,216	77,170	5,588	29,986	2,017	2,400	34,925	76,794
2009-10[3]	42,500	13,000	3,950	1,200	3,500	2,250	79,575	7,850	25,300	2,000	5,300	38,102	81,389

[1] Preliminary. [2] Estimate. [3] Forecast. *Sources: Oil World; Foreign Agricultural Service, U.S. Department of Agriculture (FAS-USDA)*

Supply and Distribution of Soybeans in the United States In Millions of Bushels

Crop Year Beginning Sept. 1	Supply					Distribution			
	Stocks, Sept. 1								
	Farms	Mills, Elevators[3]	Total	Production	Total Supply	Crushings	Exports	Seed, Feed & Residual Use	Total Distribution
2000-01	112.5	177.7	290.2	2,757.8	3,052.0	1,640.0	996.0	168.0	2,804.0
2001-02	83.5	164.2	247.7	2,890.7	3,141.0	1,700.0	1,064.0	169.0	2,933.0
2002-03	62.7	145.3	208.0	2,756.1	2,969.0	1,615.0	1,044.0	131.0	2,791.0
2003-04	58.0	120.3	178.3	2,453.7	2,638.0	1,530.0	887.0	109.0	2,525.0
2004-05	29.4	83.0	112.4	3,123.7	3,242.0	1,696.0	1,097.0	193.0	2,986.0
2005-06	99.7	156.0	255.7	3,063.2	3,322.0	1,739.0	940.0	194.0	2,873.0
2006-07	176.3	273.0	449.3	3,188.2	3,655.0	1,808.0	1,116.0	157.0	3,081.0
2007-08	143.0	430.8	573.8	2,675.8	3,261.0	1,803.0	1,159.0	94.0	3,056.0
2008-09[1]	47.0	158.0	205.0	2,967.0	3,185.0	1,662.0	1,283.0	102.0	3,047.0
2009-10[2]	35.1	103.1	138.2	3,361.0	3,507.0	1,720.0	1,400.0	177.0	3,297.0

[1] Preliminary. [2] Estimate. [3] Also warehouses. *Source: Economic Research Service, U.S. Department of Agriculture (ERS-USDA)*

SOYBEANS

Salient Statistics & Official Crop Production Reports of Soybeans in the United States In Millions of Bushels

Year	Acreage Planted (1,000 Acres)	Acreage Harvested (1,000 Acres)	Yield Per Acre (Bu.)	Farm Price ($/Bu.)	Farm Value (Million Dollars)	Yield of Oil (Lbs. Per Bushel Crushed)	Yield of Meal (Lbs. Per Bushel Crushed)	Crop Production Reports In Thousands of Bushels: Aug. 1	Sept. 1	Oct. 1	Nov. 1	Dec. 1	Final
2000-01	74,266	72,408	38.1	4.54	12,548	11.24	48.06	2,988,669	2,899,571	2,822,821	2,777,036	----	2,757,810
2001-02	74,075	72,975	39.6	4.38	12,606	11.14	44.27	2,867,474	2,833,511	2,907,042	2,922,914	----	2,890,682
2002-03	73,963	72,497	38.0	5.64	15,253	11.39	43.90	2,628,387	2,655,819	2,653,798	2,689,691	----	2,756,147
2003-04	73,404	72,476	33.9	7.95	18,014	11.20	44.32	2,862,039	2,642,644	2,468,390	2,451,759	----	2,453,665
2004-05	75,208	73,958	42.2	5.90	17,895	11.33	44.26	2,876,627	2,835,989	3,106,861	3,150,441	----	3,123,686
2005-06	72,032	71,251	43.0	5.63	17,269	11.64	43.83	2,791,133	2,856,449	2,967,075	3,043,116	----	3,063,237
2006-07	75,522	74,602	42.9	6.67	20,468	11.34	44.03	2,927,634	3,092,970	3,188,576	3,203,908	----	3,188,247
2007-08	64,741	64,146	41.7	11.02	26,974	11.54	43.95	2,625,274	2,618,796	2,598,046	2,594,275	----	2,675,822
2008-09[1]	75,718	74,681	39.7	10.13	27,399	11.36	43.93	2,972,577	2,933,888	2,983,023	2,920,589	----	2,967,007
2009-10[2]	77,451	76,407	44.0	9.62				3,199,172	3,245,292	3,250,113	3,319,270	----	3,361,028

[1] Preliminary. [2] Forecast. NA = Not available. *Source: National Agricultural Statistics Service, U.S. Department of Agriculture (NASS-USDA)*

Stocks of Soybeans in the United States In Thousands of Bushels

Year	On Farms: Mar. 1	June 1	Sept. 1	Dec. 1	Off Farms: Mar. 1	June 1	Sept. 1	Dec. 1	Total Stocks: Mar. 1	June 1	Sept. 1	Dec. 1
2000	730,000	370,000	112,500	1,217,000	665,986	404,425	177,662	1,022,791	1,395,986	774,425	290,162	2,239,791
2001	780,000	365,000	83,500	1,240,000	623,908	343,180	164,247	1,035,713	1,403,908	708,180	247,747	2,275,713
2002	687,000	301,200	62,700	1,170,000	648,987	383,721	145,320	943,641	1,335,987	684,921	208,020	2,113,641
2003	636,500	272,500	58,000	820,000	565,528	329,862	120,329	868,653	1,201,028	602,362	178,329	1,688,653
2004	355,900	110,000	29,400	1,300,000	549,947	300,604	83,014	1,004,640	905,847	410,604	112,414	2,304,640
2005	795,000	356,100	99,700	1,345,000	586,364	343,174	156,038	1,157,098	1,381,364	699,274	255,738	2,502,098
2006	872,000	495,500	176,300	1,461,000	797,206	495,199	273,026	1,240,366	1,669,206	990,699	449,326	2,701,366
2007	910,000	500,000	143,000	1,100,000	876,887	592,185	430,810	1,231,860	1,786,887	1,092,185	573,810	2,331,860
2008	593,000	226,600	47,000	1,189,000	840,982	449,543	158,034	1,086,432	1,433,982	676,143	205,034	2,275,432
2009[1]	656,500	226,300	35,100	1,231,500	645,289	369,859	103,098	1,105,180	1,301,789	596,159	138,198	2,336,680

[1] Preliminary. *Source: National Agricultural Statistics Service, U.S. Department of Agriculture (NASS-USDA)*

Commercial Stocks of Soybeans in the United States, on First of Month In Millions of Bushels

Year	Jan.	Feb.	Mar.	Apr.	May	June	July	Aug.	Sept.	Oct.	Nov.	Dec.
2000	34.1	28.3	30.0	23.9	23.8	20.6	17.0	12.3	8.6	15.5	38.2	37.9
2001	34.5	28.8	25.2	22.5	16.3	15.0	12.9	13.4	11.9	9.6	34.7	38.2
2002	29.6	27.0	22.2	21.0	18.4	15.4	14.4	10.2	4.6	8.4	26.9	28.4
2003	25.9	13.2	13.9	12.8	9.7	9.4	11.7	7.6	4.5	7.0	33.0	36.7
2004	35.5	26.2	26.0	19.4	15.7	13.5	8.0	5.9	4.4	10.8	31.1	32.9
2005	26.5	21.5	19.5	16.0	14.8	12.1	11.5	8.8	5.4	17.0	36.7	36.1
2006	36.8	30.2	26.1	25.7	17.6	20.5	14.6	14.5	14.5	19.0	40.1	43.7
2007	42.0	36.5	37.3	34.3	29.7	27.4	26.6	24.6	25.5	32.0	54.0	61.3
2008	51.1	45.5	41.8	36.3	28.2	25.6	19.2	14.8	11.4	19.6	40.5	46.1
2009	44.6	36.8	27.0	15.6	13.9	11.8	10.0	5.8	5.9	24.7	40.5	44.3

Source: Livestock Division, U.S. Department of Agriculture (LD-USDA)

Stocks of Soybeans at Mills in the United States, on First of Month In Millions of Bushels

Year	Sept.	Oct.	Nov.	Dec.	Jan.	Feb.	Mar.	Apr.	May	June	July	Aug.
1999-00	41.7	70.8	162.9	144.7	144.2	140.3	137.8	129.6	98.7	78.7	78.4	52.1
2000-01	52.1	56.8	179.4	166.8	137.8	143.3	127.0	120.6	94.9	86.1	79.3	69.0
2001-02	69.0	41.3	152.8	137.1	121.4	129.6	128.2	112.9	104.2	88.2	67.9	65.4
2002-03	46.4	36.3	114.5	113.5	106.0	109.2	102.9	91.5	91.6	76.0	64.9	55.6
2003-04	35.3	31.9	129.9	121.0	121.7	125.6	124.5	134.3	114.8	91.2	76.0	61.4
2004-05	37.0	74.8	114.1	113.1	100.3	85.6	88.1	88.8	70.9	59.2	66.1	51.7
2005-06	43.7	66.2	158.3	129.7	114.1	117.4	108.0	90.0	69.5	64.0	63.1	51.5
2006-07	52.7	48.7	124.7	132.4	127.0	133.0	121.8	123.8	113.8	102.0	103.5	99.1
2007-08	92.6	101.6	157.2	139.5	117.9	135.5	122.0	104.4	100.8	78.9	74.8	73.7
2008-09[1]	53.3	50.1	130.4	121.7	116.4	104.7	100.1	100.5	98.8	83.0	89.6	75.0

[1] Preliminary. *Source: Economic Research Service, U.S. Department of Agriculture (ERS-USDA)*

Production of Soybeans for Beans in the United States, by State In Millions of Bushels

Year	Arkan-sas	Illinois	Indiana	Iowa	Ken-tucky	Mich-igan	Minn-esota	Miss-issippi	Missouri	Neb-raska	Ohio	Tenn-essee	Total
2000-01	80.3	459.8	252.1	464.6	45.2	73.1	293.2	34.8	175.0	173.9	186.5	28.8	2,757.8
2001-02	91.2	477.9	273.9	480.5	48.8	63.9	266.4	37.0	186.2	223.0	187.8	35.4	2,890.7
2002-03	96.5	453.7	239.5	499.2	42.6	78.5	308.9	43.8	170.0	176.3	151.0	34.7	2,756.1
2003-04	111.3	379.6	204.1	342.9	53.9	54.7	238.4	55.8	146.0	182.3	164.8	47.0	2,453.7
2004-05	122.9	495.0	284.3	497.4	57.2	75.2	232.7	61.5	223.2	218.5	207.7	48.4	3,123.7
2005-06	102.0	439.4	263.6	525.0	53.3	76.6	306.0	58.0	181.7	235.3	201.6	41.8	3,063.2
2006-07	107.5	482.4	284.0	510.1	60.3	89.6	319.0	42.9	191.2	250.5	217.1	44.1	3,188.2
2007-08	101.5	360.2	220.3	448.8	30.3	70.7	267.3	58.3	175.1	196.4	199.3	19.2	2,675.8
2008-09	123.5	428.6	244.4	449.7	47.6	69.9	264.9	78.4	191.1	226.0	161.3	49.6	2,967.0
2009-10[1]	122.6	430.1	266.6	486.0	68.2	79.6	284.8	77.1	230.6	259.4	222.0	68.9	3,361.0

[1] Preliminary. *Source: Agricultural Statistics Board, U.S. Department of Agriculture (ASB-USDA)*

U. S. Exports of Soybeans In Millions of Bushels

Year	Sept.	Oct.	Nov.	Dec.	Jan.	Feb.	Mar.	Apr.	May	June	July	Aug.	Total
2000-01	51.4	141.4	123.0	106.6	103.3	126.5	135.2	52.8	39.8	39.5	33.1	43.4	995.9
2001-02	31.7	158.9	158.0	133.2	157.2	132.0	63.8	46.0	45.6	43.2	56.0	38.0	1,063.7
2002-03	30.9	136.7	152.8	114.7	159.3	151.5	92.1	66.4	35.9	31.9	37.9	34.3	1,044.4
2003-04	34.0	165.3	186.4	143.2	109.3	82.6	69.9	28.7	19.1	20.2	14.8	10.8	884.2
2004-05	47.2	177.7	181.0	155.0	121.9	123.2	96.4	65.2	49.6	35.2	20.0	30.3	1,102.7
2005-06	32.3	143.1	140.1	83.1	111.8	111.3	95.6	43.4	46.5	39.0	47.6	51.0	944.8
2006-07	64.9	182.6	126.4	122.7	147.2	126.5	96.9	71.1	41.9	48.9	37.9	49.6	1,116.6
2007-08	62.0	138.6	127.4	146.0	146.1	139.2	114.8	72.7	56.2	58.7	51.2	45.9	1,158.8
2008-09	34.3	179.3	173.3	170.9	153.1	162.1	101.7	82.7	60.0	60.5	49.9	55.4	1,283.2
2009-10[1]	43.3	196.1	294.4	228.0									2,285.4

[1] Preliminary. *Source: Economic Research Service, U.S. Department of Agriculture (ERS-USDA)*

Spread Between Value of Products and Soybean Price in the United States In Cents Per Bushel

Year	Sept.	Oct.	Nov.	Dec.	Jan.	Feb.	Mar.	Apr.	May	June	July	Aug.	Average
1999-00	48	61	64	58	75	61	70	70	80	81	69	62	66
2000-01	81	76	77	89	85	59	65	72	67	81	96	92	78
2001-02	102	108	106	83	86	65	65	65	57	63	64	89	79
2002-03	77	73	52	60	53	52	61	53	62	59	72	74	62
2003-04	117	88	94	81	84	81	96	96	85	97	150	127	99
2004-05	132	95	70	66	75	76	67	78	69	75	73	82	79
2005-06	100	102	70	91	90	84	94	102	106	104	106	110	97
2006-07	126	105	81	74	73	72	80	64	78	113	110	88	89
2007-08	90	83	100	109	105	103	114	114	84	105	122	114	103
2008-09[1]	195	95	68	72	59	61	61	77	109	106	92	156	95

[1] Preliminary. *Source: Economic Research Service, U.S. Department of Agriculture (ERS-USDA)*

Soybean Crushed (Factory Consumption) in the United States In Millions of Bushels

Year	Jan.	Feb.	Mar.	Apr.	May	June	July	Aug.	Sept.	Oct.	Nov.	Dec.	Total
2000-01	128.9	149.1	143.1	142.3	146.7	128.9	141.8	131.1	132.7	128.0	133.6	133.5	1,640
2001-02	128.2	150.2	149.1	153.4	155.1	139.0	149.8	139.2	140.6	134.6	129.8	130.6	1,700
2002-03	122.3	149.5	145.7	150.2	142.7	129.2	142.8	127.0	129.8	121.4	129.3	125.1	1,615
2003-04	127.6	146.2	145.6	145.8	146.0	131.4	129.6	112.5	117.5	109.4	115.3	103.0	1,530
2004-05	121.0	155.3	151.1	150.0	148.6	137.6	148.5	139.4	142.8	132.0	139.5	130.3	1,696
2005-06	133.2	157.7	151.5	148.4	152.4	136.3	149.5	135.5	146.2	137.4	148.5	142.1	1,739
2006-07	142.4	161.7	155.1	157.4	155.5	136.9	156.1	145.0	152.1	148.9	150.4	146.2	1,808
2007-08	147.3	163.7	156.3	164.1	160.5	146.5	156.0	147.5	152.6	141.0	139.3	128.6	1,803
2008-09	125.7	150.0	144.7	141.3	145.2	135.4	144.4	140.3	146.2	140.1	128.8	119.8	1,662
2009-10[1]	113.3	163.5	168.7	173.0									1,856

[1] Preliminary. *Source: Economic Research Service, U.S. Department of Agriculture (ERS-USDA)*

Volume of Trading of Soybean Futures in Chicago In Thousands of Contracts

Year	Jan.	Feb.	Mar.	Apr.	May	June	July	Aug.	Sept.	Oct.	Nov.	Dec.	Total
2000	1,071.9	1,099.3	1,191.6	1,079.1	1,321.6	1,302.0	883.4	801.4	860.9	1,188.8	932.5	895.3	12,628
2001	935.0	947.4	843.1	916.3	909.5	1,155.6	1,508.1	1,122.0	648.7	1,356.1	964.7	844.1	12,150
2002	1,078.8	899.9	1,065.7	1,238.6	1,048.3	1,311.8	1,762.2	1,346.4	1,002.9	1,486.1	1,070.9	1,163.5	14,475
2003	1,267.3	1,222.9	997.1	1,588.9	1,368.2	1,723.4	1,385.7	1,193.5	1,308.5	2,416.3	1,535.4	1,538.5	17,546
2004	1,509.7	1,879.6	1,957.2	2,036.2	1,593.2	1,601.7	1,551.3	1,107.6	1,052.8	1,635.3	1,395.3	1,526.1	18,846
2005	1,398.6	2,085.8	1,959.9	1,656.5	1,454.6	2,577.3	1,675.4	1,487.2	1,069.1	1,765.0	1,241.5	1,845.1	20,216
2006	1,503.4	1,889.1	1,501.2	1,916.6	1,682.6	2,443.2	1,798.2	1,638.5	1,420.2	2,884.7	2,017.4	1,952.6	22,648
2007	1,976.3	2,620.6	2,251.0	2,641.2	2,107.2	3,461.3	2,734.6	2,323.7	2,315.2	3,680.4	2,521.3	3,093.5	31,726
2008	3,528.7	3,746.2	2,895.0	3,786.1	2,272.2	3,731.2	3,134.9	2,454.4	2,615.1	3,719.0	1,910.5	2,579.7	36,373
2009	2,773.7	2,892.5	2,576.2	3,638.9	2,635.5	3,439.7	2,845.7	2,417.6	2,348.2	3,996.4	2,820.8	3,373.7	35,759

Contract size = 5,000 bu. *Source: CME Group; Chicago Board of Trade (CBT)*

Average Open Interest of Soybean Futures in Chicago In Contracts

Year	Jan.	Feb.	Mar.	Apr.	May	June	July	Aug.	Sept.	Oct.	Nov.	Dec.
2000	149,468	172,494	174,465	195,189	193,500	167,678	140,894	126,952	149,074	183,734	168,023	177,324
2001	160,730	164,017	148,190	156,781	137,227	153,190	181,194	165,630	167,677	195,366	175,522	173,116
2002	156,898	169,242	169,882	164,388	156,548	188,692	220,758	201,494	201,808	210,033	208,099	213,868
2003	201,536	217,680	226,421	251,314	230,325	222,185	190,206	190,533	232,030	265,088	241,320	252,874
2004	258,708	267,482	263,737	262,919	222,310	199,108	172,194	171,791	190,006	242,654	228,700	241,972
2005	244,197	266,745	295,324	268,081	252,582	313,724	278,738	256,853	249,030	285,070	275,308	290,370
2006	315,640	359,379	354,211	374,507	375,124	371,155	336,000	348,321	361,643	384,069	394,259	414,374
2007	416,459	478,579	474,466	470,517	465,303	549,655	536,595	495,302	526,913	580,446	586,635	582,502
2008	563,927	598,278	543,451	506,423	458,047	489,069	446,006	388,939	364,679	348,438	312,905	304,252
2009	297,316	313,704	292,160	358,857	415,599	454,846	410,718	401,752	428,320	461,463	438,531	464,281

Contract size = 5,000 bu. *Source: CME Group; Chicago Board of Trade (CBT)*

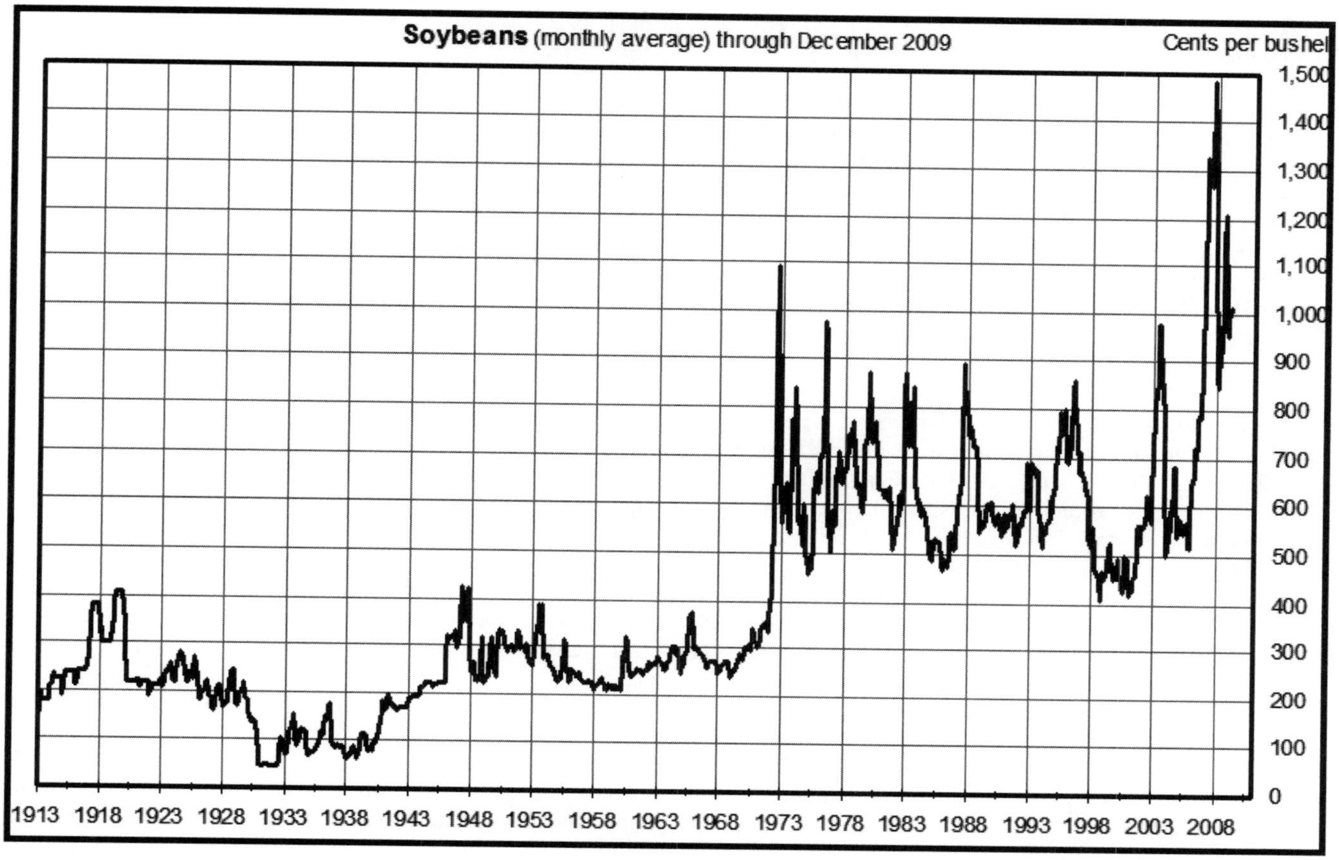

Average Cash Price of No. 1 Yellow Soybeans at Illinois Processor In Cents Per Bushel

Year	Jan.	Feb.	Mar.	Apr.	May	June	July	Aug.	Sept.	Oct.	Nov.	Dec.	Average
1999-00	485	470	464	460	473	500	513	529	542	510	474	463	490
2000-01	484	468	483	506	477	457	451	441	457	474	517	510	477
2001-02	469	430	441	438	437	440	464	471	492	519	575	567	479
2002-03	579	541	575	566	570	590	580	611	640	635	601	589	590
2003-04	639	729	763	772	823	872	975	992	958	890	809	641	822
2004-05	562	519	534	545	539	544	628	622	644	701	703	639	598
2005-06	565	553	574	592	576	575	569	562	581	576	577	542	570
2006-07	535	580	66	657	683	735	730	718	749	792	801	804	704
2007-08	907	944	1,032	1,123	1,216	1,335	1,312	1,292	1,324	1,499	1,516	1,288	1,232
2008-09[1]	1,140	903	893	868	991	938	917	1,025	1,166	1,237	1,096	1,136	1,026

[1] Preliminary. *Source: Economic Research Service, U.S. Department of Agriculture (ERS-USDA)*

Average Price Received by Farmers for Soybeans in the United States In Dollars Per Bushel

Year	Jan.	Feb.	Mar.	Apr.	May	June	July	Aug.	Sept.	Oct.	Nov.	Dec.	Average
2000-01	4.59	4.45	4.55	4.78	4.68	4.46	4.39	4.22	4.33	4.46	4.79	4.85	4.54
2001-02	4.53	4.09	4.16	4.20	4.22	4.22	4.38	4.47	4.64	4.88	5.35	5.53	4.38
2002-03	5.39	5.20	5.46	5.46	5.51	5.55	5.59	5.82	6.07	6.09	5.82	5.68	5.64
2003-04	6.06	6.60	7.05	7.17	7.35	8.28	9.28	9.62	9.56	9.08	8.46	6.83	7.95
2004-05	5.83	5.56	5.36	5.45	5.57	5.42	5.95	6.03	6.21	6.58	6.65	6.15	5.90
2005-06	5.77	5.67	5.62	5.78	5.87	5.67	5.57	5.52	5.68	5.62	5.61	5.23	5.63
2006-07	5.23	5.52	6.08	6.18	6.37	6.87	6.95	6.88	7.12	7.51	7.56	7.72	6.67
2007-08	8.15	8.36	9.42	10.00	9.95	11.70	11.40	12.00	12.10	13.10	13.30	12.80	11.02
2008-09	10.80	9.95	9.39	9.24	9.97	9.54	9.12	9.79	10.70	11.40	10.80	10.80	10.13
2009-10[1]	9.75	9.44	9.53	9.80	9.79	9.40							9.62

[1] Preliminary. *Source: Economic Research Service, U.S. Department of Agriculture (ERS-USDA)*

Stock Index Futures - U.S.

A stock index simply represents a basket of underlying stocks. Indices can be either price-weighted or capitalization-weighted. In a price-weighted index, such as the Dow Jones Industrials Average, the individual stock prices are simply added up and then divided by a divisor, meaning that stocks with higher prices have a higher weighting in the index value. In a capitalization-weighted index, such as the Standard and Poor's 500 index, the weighting of each stock corresponds to the size of the company as determined by its capitalization (i.e., the total dollar value of its stock). Stock indices cover a variety of different sectors. For example, the Dow Jones Industrials Average contains 30 blue-chip stocks that represent the industrial sector. The S&P 500 index includes 500 of the largest blue-chip U.S. companies. The NYSE index includes all the stocks that are traded at the New York Stock Exchange. The Nasdaq 100 includes the largest 100 companies that are traded on the Nasdaq Exchange. The most popular U.S. stock index futures contract is the S&P 500 at the Chicago Mercantile Exchange (CME).

Prices – The S&P 500 index peaked at a record high of 1576.09 in October 2007 and then plunged by a total of -58% in the following 3 years to post a 13-year low of 666.79 in March 2009. The S&P 500 then staged an impressive recovery rally of +73% to post a 15-month high by January 2010. The S&P 500 in early 2010 remained far below the pre-crisis range above 1400, but at least returned to the levels seen in 2004.

The U.S. stock market, starting in March 2009, was able to stage a sharp recovery rally when it became clear that the Federal Reserve had contained the banking crisis and that the U.S. recession was close to bottoming out. In fact, the U.S. recession ended in the summer of 2009 and GDP turned positive in the second half of 2009. The Federal Reserve did its job in preventing an economic depression by flooding the financial system with liquidity and by providing a wide range of guarantees and backstops to halt the panic and capital flight. The other G7 banks also pitched in with massive liquidity injections that softened the blow from the banking system crisis. China was also a big factor in softening the blow from the financial crisis and helping to pull the global economy out of recession. Chinese GDP growth fell only as low as +6.2% in Q2-2009 and then strengthened to a torrid +10.7% by Q4-2009.

U.S. corporations during the worst post-war recession did a remarkable job in preserving profits and limiting losses. The banking system saw massive losses and most of the big banks had to take TARP money from the federal government to ensure their survival. But outside the banking system, the damage was much less severe. U.S. corporations quickly slashed their employee head counts and expenses and downsized their operations to match the lower demand. That produced a better profit picture and also meant that the recovery could begin sooner.

Earnings growth for the S&P 500 companies was negative for nine consecutive quarters from Q3-2007 through Q3-2009. However, earnings growth turned positive in Q4-2009 with growth of about +8% excluding the recovery in bank earnings. As of early 2010, the S&P 500 was trading at a very reasonable price-to-earnings ratio based on forward-looking earnings of 14.2. The reasonable valuation level leaves room on the upside for further gains in stock prices once earnings growth and the economic recovery gain better traction.

Average Value of Dow Jones Industrials Index (30 Stocks)

Year	Jan.	Feb.	Mar.	Apr.	May	June	July	Aug.	Sept.	Oct.	Nov.	Dec.	Average
2000	11,281.3	10,541.9	10,483.4	10,944.4	10,580.3	10,582.9	10,663.0	11,014.5	10,967.9	10,441.0	10,666.1	10,652.4	10,734.9
2001	10,682.7	10,774.6	10,081.3	10,234.5	11,005.0	10,767.2	10,444.5	10,314.7	9,042.6	9,220.8	9,721.8	9,979.9	10,189.1
2002	9,923.8	9,891.1	10,501.0	10,165.2	10,080.5	9,492.4	8,616.5	8,685.5	8,160.2	8,048.1	8,625.7	8,526.7	9,226.4
2003	8,474.4	7,916.2	7,977.7	8,332.1	8,623.4	9,098.1	9,154.5	9,284.8	9,492.5	9,683.6	9,762.2	10,124.7	8,993.7
2004	10,540.1	10,601.5	10,323.7	10,419.9	10,083.8	10,364.9	10,152.1	10,032.8	10,204.6	10,001.6	10,411.8	10,673.4	10,317.5
2005	10,539.5	10,723.8	10,682.1	10,283.2	10,377.2	10,486.6	10,545.4	10,554.3	10,532.5	10,324.3	10,695.3	10,827.8	10,547.7
2006	10,872.5	10,971.2	11,144.5	11,234.7	11,333.9	10,998.0	11,032.5	11,257.4	11,533.6	11,963.1	12,185.2	12,377.6	11,408.7
2007	12,512.9	12,631.5	12,268.5	12,754.8	13,407.8	13,480.2	13,677.9	13,239.7	13,557.7	13,901.3	13,200.5	13,406.9	13,170.0
2008	12,537.4	12,419.6	12,193.9	12,656.6	12,812.5	12,056.7	11,322.4	11,530.8	11,114.1	9,176.7	8,614.6	8,595.6	11,252.6
2009	8,396.2	7,690.5	7,235.5	7,992.1	8,398.4	8,593.0	8,679.8	9,375.1	9,635.0	9,857.3	10,227.6	10,433.4	8,876.1

Source: New York Stock Exchange (NYSE)

Average Value of Dow Jones Transportation Index (20 Stocks)

Year	Jan.	Feb.	Mar.	Apr.	May	June	July	Aug.	Sept.	Oct.	Nov.	Dec.	Average
2000	2,812.2	2,483.4	2,534.5	2,823.9	2,813.2	2,717.2	2,822.3	2,835.6	2,641.5	2,491.0	2,792.3	2,822.9	2,715.8
2001	3,029.9	3,010.2	2,792.5	2,776.6	2,908.2	2,770.4	2,887.3	2,852.1	2,344.8	2,217.3	2,404.6	2,603.0	2,716.4
2002	2,735.3	2,719.1	2,942.9	2,776.0	2,734.8	2,702.2	2,432.1	2,318.5	2,216.0	2,216.6	2,321.6	2,331.7	2,537.2
2003	2,297.3	2,102.5	2,094.6	2,278.7	2,429.9	2,459.6	2,554.5	2,617.3	2,744.7	2,841.3	2,920.0	2,969.3	2,525.8
2004	3,021.0	2,889.4	2,838.3	2,941.1	2,877.1	3,069.0	3,099.8	3,065.8	3,205.1	3,372.6	3,589.4	3,750.0	3,143.2
2005	3,587.0	3,614.5	3,779.4	3,527.8	3,548.8	3,542.1	3,663.1	3,726.1	3,637.0	3,673.1	4,051.7	4,152.1	3,708.6
2006	4,224.5	4,362.5	4,519.5	4,679.6	4,761.4	4,663.1	4,636.1	4,291.1	4,363.3	4,654.7	4,761.6	4,660.0	4,548.1
2007	4,752.2	5,024.6	4,817.3	5,059.2	5,174.8	5,137.2	5,258.8	4,889.0	4,812.7	4,891.2	4,605.9	4,686.4	4,925.8
2008	4,348.7	4,720.0	4,641.9	4,996.9	5,304.5	5,166.7	4,899.2	5,057.0	4,889.3	3,815.4	3,518.5	3,369.2	4,560.6
2009	3,238.3	2,857.3	2,499.9	2,986.8	3,163.7	3,266.6	3,321.5	3,697.2	3,863.1	3,844.4	3,915.2	4,117.2	3,397.6

Source: New York Stock Exchange (NYSE)

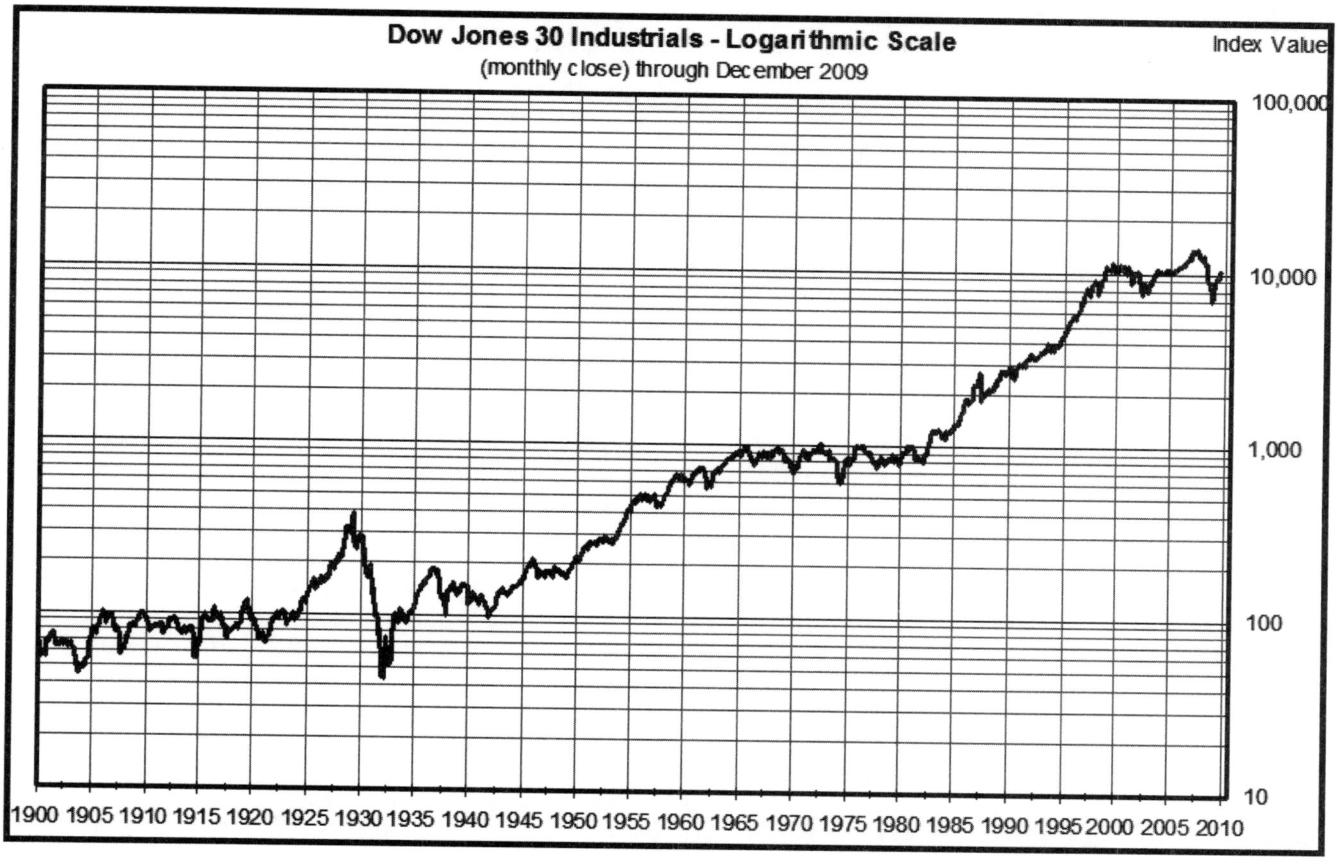

Average Value of Dow Jones Utilities Index (15 Stocks)

Year	Jan.	Feb.	Mar.	Apr.	May	June	July	Aug.	Sept.	Oct.	Nov.	Dec.	Average
2000	300.6	302.3	285.4	307.0	325.2	322.2	325.0	355.6	384.2	386.9	392.5	394.9	340.2
2001	360.9	385.1	375.7	387.0	388.9	367.2	356.8	345.4	321.3	308.8	291.4	284.0	347.7
2002	290.7	279.6	298.4	305.1	297.3	276.1	235.5	241.0	221.7	189.2	200.4	208.5	253.6
2003	217.7	199.5	203.3	215.9	232.3	250.4	240.3	236.8	246.5	253.1	249.2	258.4	233.6
2004	268.8	272.2	278.2	275.6	268.4	275.4	278.8	285.3	293.3	303.3	324.9	327.8	287.7
2005	331.9	351.5	356.3	364.5	364.4	376.3	392.5	397.4	422.7	401.3	395.3	409.0	380.2
2006	416.7	408.2	401.7	392.1	401.0	409.2	424.1	436.9	430.1	439.8	449.1	458.5	422.3
2007	449.9	474.1	486.1	516.9	526.2	498.2	502.3	489.0	499.5	514.0	523.5	540.9	501.7
2008	518.8	499.0	480.3	506.2	516.7	519.1	500.8	472.4	446.3	370.1	368.1	362.7	463.4
2009	371.3	356.3	315.8	331.6	339.3	350.6	361.4	373.3	376.0	375.6	373.4	398.9	360.3

Source: New York Stock Exchange (NYSE)

Average Value of Standard & Poor's 500 Index

Year	Jan.	Feb.	Mar.	Apr.	May	June	July	Aug.	Sept.	Oct.	Nov.	Dec.	Average
2000	1,425.6	1,388.9	1,442.2	1,461.4	1,418.5	1,462.0	1,473.0	1,485.5	1,468.0	1,390.1	1,375.0	1,330.9	1,426.8
2001	1,335.6	1,305.8	1,185.9	1,189.8	1,270.4	1,238.8	1,204.5	1,178.5	1,047.6	1,076.6	1,129.7	1,144.9	1,192.3
2002	1,140.2	1,100.7	1,153.8	1,112.0	1,079.3	1,014.1	903.6	912.6	867.8	854.6	909.9	899.2	995.6
2003	895.8	837.6	846.6	890.0	936.0	988.0	992.5	989.5	1,019.4	1,038.7	1,049.9	1,080.6	963.7
2004	1,132.5	1,143.4	1,124.0	1,133.1	1,102.8	1,132.8	1,105.9	1,088.9	1,117.7	1,118.1	1,168.9	1,199.2	1,130.6
2005	1,181.4	1,199.6	1,194.9	1,164.4	1,178.3	1,202.3	1,222.2	1,224.3	1,225.9	1,192.0	1,237.3	1,262.1	1,207.1
2006	1,278.7	1,276.7	1,293.7	1,302.2	1,290.0	1,253.1	1,260.2	1,287.2	1,317.8	1,363.3	1,388.6	1,416.4	1,310.7
2007	1,424.2	1,444.8	1,407.0	1,463.7	1,511.1	1,514.5	1,520.7	1,454.6	1,497.1	1,539.7	1,463.4	1,479.2	1,476.7
2008	1,378.8	1,354.9	1,316.9	1,370.5	1,403.2	1,341.3	1,257.3	1,281.5	1,217.0	968.8	883.0	877.4	1,220.9
2009	865.6	805.2	757.1	848.2	902.4	926.1	935.8	1,009.7	1,044.6	1,067.7	1,088.1	1,110.4	946.7

Source: Index and Option Market (IOM), division of the Chicago Mercantile Exchange (CME)

Composite Index of Leading Indicators (1992 = 100)

Year	Jan.	Feb.	Mar.	Apr.	May	June	July	Aug.	Sept.	Oct.	Nov.	Dec.	Average
2000	86.8	86.3	86.7	87.2	86.6	86.7	86.5	86.3	86.3	85.9	85.6	85.0	86.3
2001	84.9	84.5	84.2	84.1	84.5	84.6	84.8	84.9	84.2	84.3	85.3	86.6	84.7
2002	87.1	87.7	88.0	88.1	89.0	89.0	89.1	89.3	89.3	89.4	90.2	90.5	88.9
2003	90.6	90.5	90.6	91.1	92.5	93.1	93.8	94.3	95.0	95.8	96.4	96.9	93.4
2004	97.5	97.8	99.1	99.3	100.0	100.2	100.6	100.6	100.8	100.7	101.4	102.0	100.0
2005	101.8	102.2	101.7	101.8	102.1	103.1	102.9	103.1	102.4	103.3	104.2	104.2	102.7
2006	104.7	104.4	104.6	104.4	103.7	103.9	103.7	103.3	103.7	103.9	103.8	104.4	104.0
2007	104.0	103.7	104.1	103.9	104.0	103.9	104.6	103.6	103.7	103.2	102.8	102.6	103.7
2008	102.1	101.9	101.9	102.0	101.9	101.9	101.2	100.3	100.3	99.4	99.0	98.8	100.9
2009[1]	98.5	98.1	97.8	98.9	100.2	101.1	102.1	102.7	103.9	104.2	105.2	106.4	101.6

[1] Preliminary. *Source: The Conference Board*

Consumer Confidence, The Conference Board (2004 = 100)

Year	Jan.	Feb.	Mar.	Apr.	May	June	July	Aug.	Sept.	Oct.	Nov.	Dec.	Average
2000	144.7	140.8	137.1	137.7	144.7	139.2	143.0	140.8	142.5	135.8	132.6	128.6	139.0
2001	115.7	109.3	116.9	109.9	116.1	118.9	116.3	114.0	97.0	85.3	84.9	94.6	106.6
2002	97.8	95.0	110.7	108.5	110.3	106.3	97.4	94.5	93.7	79.6	84.9	80.7	96.6
2003	78.8	64.8	61.4	81.0	83.6	83.5	77.0	81.7	77.0	81.7	92.5	94.8	79.8
2004	97.7	88.5	88.5	93.0	93.1	102.8	105.7	98.7	96.7	92.9	92.6	102.7	96.1
2005	105.1	104.4	103.0	97.5	103.1	106.2	103.6	105.5	87.5	85.2	98.3	103.8	100.3
2006	106.8	102.7	107.5	109.8	104.7	105.4	107.0	100.2	105.9	105.1	105.3	110.0	105.9
2007	110.2	111.2	108.2	106.3	108.5	105.3	111.9	105.6	99.5	95.2	87.8	90.6	103.4
2008	87.3	76.4	65.9	62.8	58.1	51.0	51.9	58.5	61.4	38.8	44.7	38.6	58.0
2009[1]	37.4	25.3	26.9	40.8	54.8	49.3	47.4	54.5	53.4	48.7	50.6	53.6	45.2

[1] Preliminary. *Source: The Conference Board (TCB) Copyrighted.*

Capacity Utilization Rates (Total Industry) In Percent

Year	Jan.	Feb.	Mar.	Apr.	May	June	July	Aug.	Sept.	Oct.	Nov.	Dec.	Average
2000	82.3	82.4	82.4	82.6	82.5	82.3	81.8	81.4	81.5	80.9	80.7	80.1	81.7
2001	79.3	78.6	78.1	77.7	76.9	76.2	75.7	75.2	74.7	74.1	73.6	73.5	76.1
2002	73.7	73.6	74.1	74.2	74.5	75.2	74.9	75.0	75.0	74.9	75.2	74.9	74.6
2003	75.5	75.8	75.7	75.1	75.2	75.3	75.6	75.6	76.0	76.1	76.8	76.7	75.8
2004	77.0	77.4	76.9	77.3	77.9	77.2	77.7	77.9	77.9	78.7	78.8	79.4	77.8
2005	79.7	80.2	80.1	80.0	80.2	80.4	80.3	80.4	78.9	79.7	80.5	80.9	80.1
2006	80.9	80.8	80.8	81.0	80.8	81.1	81.1	81.2	80.8	80.6	80.3	80.9	80.9
2007	80.3	80.8	80.6	80.7	80.7	80.6	80.7	80.6	80.7	80.2	80.5	80.6	80.6
2008	80.5	80.2	79.8	79.2	78.9	78.7	78.6	77.6	74.5	75.4	74.4	72.7	77.5
2009[1]	71.1	70.6	69.5	69.2	68.5	68.3	69.2	70.1	70.6	70.9	71.3	71.9	70.1

[1] Preliminary. *Source: Bureau of Economic Analysis, U.S. Department of Commerce (BEA)*

Manufacturers New Orders, Durable Goods In Billions of Constant Dollars

Year	Jan.	Feb.	Mar.	Apr.	May	June	July	Aug.	Sept.	Oct.	Nov.	Dec.	Average
2000	201.55	184.40	190.94	195.15	189.49	220.42	189.64	189.48	198.70	185.85	189.47	187.55	193.55
2001	178.17	180.50	182.49	172.35	179.24	176.74	170.36	170.98	163.33	171.98	163.46	166.61	173.02
2002	160.56	169.53	168.77	167.56	171.11	163.35	172.96	175.26	165.54	167.16	168.23	162.15	167.68
2003	168.14	172.69	172.19	170.11	170.87	171.78	173.00	171.82	177.28	182.74	180.59	180.27	174.29
2004	173.22	176.96	189.74	182.23	181.29	182.12	184.00	182.12	185.68	183.03	191.14	190.18	183.48
2005	191.30	193.98	189.82	192.26	205.01	207.35	194.43	202.21	202.69	208.84	219.45	218.64	202.16
2006	203.24	213.71	222.58	213.58	213.81	218.39	207.90	207.01	229.08	209.88	217.30	220.67	214.76
2007	210.84	213.05	219.26	222.90	217.62	217.31	223.47	217.10	213.04	214.53	215.92	227.05	217.67
2008	218.02	217.49	218.21	214.83	214.42	214.55	212.67	202.62	203.15	186.39	179.94	173.28	204.63
2009[1]	159.51	160.60	157.96	159.97	163.36	159.99	169.21	164.02	168.19	168.10	167.41	169.01	163.94

[1] Preliminary. *Source: Bureau of Economic Analysis, U.S. Department of Commerce (BEA)*

Corporate Profits After Tax -- Quarterly In Billions of Dollars

Year	First Quarter	Second Quarter	Third Quarter	Fourth Quarter	Total	Year	First Quarter	Second Quarter	Third Quarter	Fourth Quarter	Total
1998	562.9	547.6	554.2	548.6	553.3	2004	909.6	928.7	971.8	953.3	940.9
1999	593.2	592.9	582.1	602.5	592.7	2005	1,003.1	1,033.3	1,051.6	1,086.8	1,043.7
2000	566.2	558.6	560.0	531.8	554.2	2006	1,130.2	1,122.6	1,158.5	1,128.8	1,135.0
2001	558.3	595.6	569.9	599.6	580.9	2007	1,065.9	1,128.4	1,097.1	1,069.3	1,090.2
2002	651.1	666.0	676.0	726.3	679.9	2008	1,136.4	1,086.3	1,149.8	900.4	1,068.2
2003	685.9	723.1	745.5	781.6	734.0	2009[1]	912.4	920.6	1,037.9		957.0

[1] Preliminary. *Source: Bureau of Economic Analysis, U.S. Department of Commerce (BEA)*

Change in Manufacturing and Trade Inventories In Billions of Dollars

Year	Jan.	Feb.	Mar.	Apr.	May	June	July	Aug.	Sept.	Oct.	Nov.	Dec.	Average
2000	69.5	59.5	17.5	38.8	82.8	129.5	8.7	87.4	10.1	77.7	26.4	5.8	63.7
2001	1.7	-40.5	-73.0	-36.6	-38.9	-105.1	-68.2	-34.2	-75.3	-200.6	-139.2	-78.7	-65.2
2002	-0.9	-31.5	-47.8	-20.1	33.6	27.8	78.5	3.5	-106.8	18.5	33.0	-86.0	17.6
2003	-118.4	-60.3	-18.3	0.1	111.8	89.5	24.1	-39.4	78.7	54.4	57.5	45.7	17.6
2004	16.6	108.5	107.0	101.2	88.6	153.5	139.9	373.6	-12.2	54.3	166.0	29.5	72.8
2005	130.5	84.6	60.3	40.0	218.4	-5.7	-66.0	57.9	272.9	81.3	78.8	305.6	54.5
2006	85.9	-49.7	129.5	82.7	169.3	169.3	92.2	93.2	65.9	22.9	28.3	4.2	85.2
2007	37.8	43.6	-17.0	59.5	68.1	55.0	75.6	62.7	87.7	23.8	53.3	96.3	53.4
2008	169.4	78.5	35.6	81.4	66.2	133.3	202.6	34.8	-64.9	-99.6		-250.0	35.2
2009[1]	-212.5	-238.4	-217.7	-216.9	-202.1	-233.4	-181.7	-258.3	-82.2	65.2	64.4		-155.8

[1] Preliminary. *Source: Bureau of Economic Analysis, U.S. Department of Commerce (BEA)*

Productivity: Index of Output per Hour, All Persons, Nonfarm Business -- Quarterly (1992 = 100)

Year	First Quarter	Second Quarter	Third Quarter	Fourth Quarter	Total	Year	First Quarter	Second Quarter	Third Quarter	Fourth Quarter	Total
1998	108.4	108.7	109.9	110.5	109.4	2004	132.9	134.1	134.4	134.6	134.0
1999	111.5	111.7	112.5	114.4	112.5	2005	135.9	135.7	136.7	136.6	136.2
2000	114.5	117.1	117.1	118.3	116.7	2006	137.5	137.7	137.0	137.8	137.5
2001	117.9	120.0	120.7	122.5	120.3	2007	138.2	139.2	141.1	141.8	140.1
2002	125.1	125.2	126.4	126.3	125.7	2008	141.7	142.8	142.8	143.1	142.6
2003	127.4	129.1	132.1	132.6	130.3	2009[1]	143.2	145.6	148.2	150.4	146.8

[1] Preliminary. *Source: Bureau of Economic Analysis, U.S. Department of Commerce (BEA)*

Civilian Unemployment Rate

Year	Jan.	Feb.	Mar.	Apr.	May	June	July	Aug.	Sept.	Oct.	Nov.	Dec.	Average
2000	4.0	4.1	4.1	3.9	4.1	4.0	4.0	4.1	3.9	3.9	4.0	4.0	4.0
2001	4.2	4.2	4.3	4.5	4.4	4.5	4.5	4.9	4.9	5.4	5.7	5.8	4.8
2002	5.6	5.5	5.7	6.0	5.8	5.9	5.9	5.7	5.6	5.7	6.0	6.0	5.8
2003	5.7	5.8	5.8	6.0	6.1	6.4	6.2	6.1	6.1	6.0	5.9	5.7	6.0
2004	5.6	5.6	5.7	5.6	5.6	5.6	5.5	5.4	5.4	5.5	5.4	5.4	5.5
2005	5.2	5.4	5.1	5.1	5.1	5.0	5.0	4.9	5.1	4.9	5.0	4.9	5.1
2006	4.7	4.8	4.7	4.7	4.6	4.6	4.8	4.7	4.6	4.4	4.5	4.5	4.6
2007	4.6	4.5	4.4	4.5	4.5	4.6	4.7	4.7	4.7	4.8	4.7	5.0	4.6
2008	5.0	4.8	5.1	5.0	5.4	5.5	5.8	6.1	6.2	6.6	6.9	7.4	5.8
2009[1]	7.7	8.2	8.6	8.9	9.4	9.5	9.4	9.7	9.8	10.1	10.0	10.0	9.3

[1] Preliminary. *Source: Bureau of Economic Analysis, U.S. Department of Commerce (BEA)*

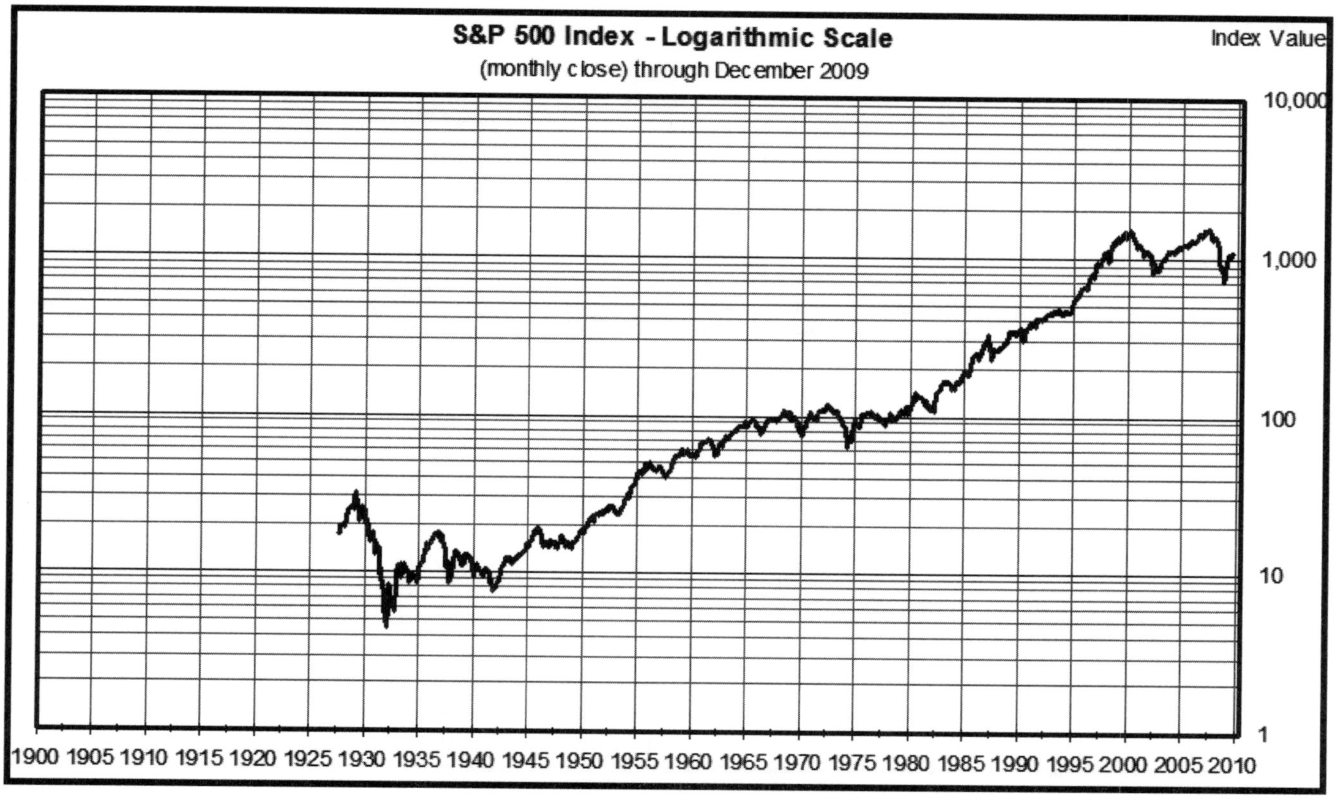

Dow Jones 30 Industrials Index (weekly close) as of December 31, 2009
Index Value
16,000
14,000
12,000
10,000
8,000
6,000
Jan-00
Jan-01
Jan-02
Jan-03
Jan-04
Dec-04
Dec-05
Dec-06
Dec-07
Dec-08
Dec-09
Dec-10

S&P 500 Index (weekly close) as of December 31, 2009
Index Value
1,600
1,400
1,200
1,000
800
600
Jan-00
Jan-01
Jan-02
Jan-03
Jan-04
Dec-04
Dec-05
Dec-06
Dec-07
Dec-08
Dec-09
Dec-10

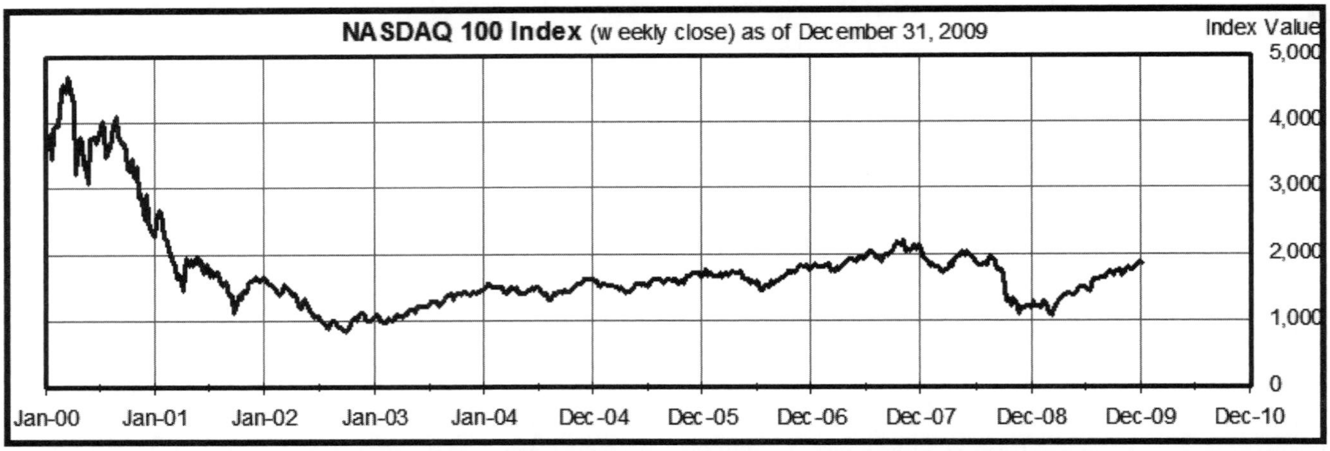
NASDAQ 100 Index (weekly close) as of December 31, 2009
Index Value
5,000
4,000
3,000
2,000
1,000
0
Jan-00
Jan-01
Jan-02
Jan-03
Jan-04
Dec-04
Dec-05
Dec-06
Dec-07
Dec-08
Dec-09
Dec-10

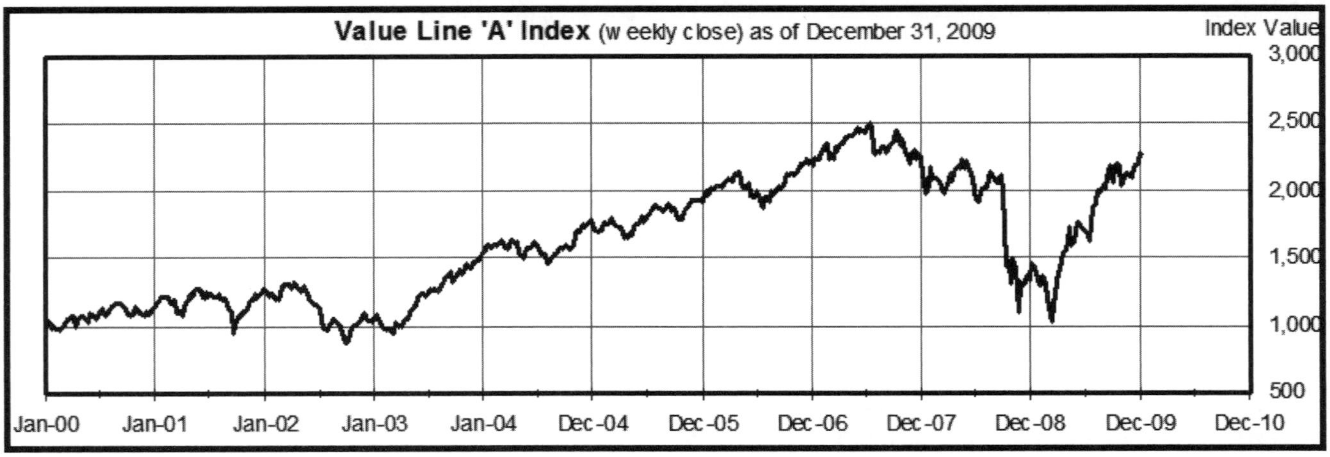
Value Line 'A' Index (weekly close) as of December 31, 2009
Index Value
3,000
2,500
2,000
1,500
1,000
500
Jan-00
Jan-01
Jan-02
Jan-03
Jan-04
Dec-04
Dec-05
Dec-06
Dec-07
Dec-08
Dec-09
Dec-10

Volume of Trading of S&P 500 Stock Index Futures in Chicago In Thousands of Contracts

Year	Jan.	Feb.	Mar.	Apr.	May	June	July	Aug.	Sept.	Oct.	Nov.	Dec.	Total
2000	1,910.7	1,916.6	2,956.5	1,651.4	1,684.9	2,225.6	1,078.9	1,358.5	2,148.8	1,681.3	1,636.0	2,211.6	22,461
2001	1,552.0	1,630.8	2,780.9	1,624.2	1,653.0	2,154.4	1,319.7	1,597.5	2,571.2	1,798.3	1,691.7	2,124.2	22,498
2002	1,459.2	1,677.0	2,251.4	1,472.8	1,584.6	2,720.9	2,205.7	1,615.1	2,943.1	1,930.5	1,374.3	2,465.0	23,700
2003	1,442.8	1,343.0	2,900.2	1,256.8	1,415.6	2,782.4	1,222.9	1,079.4	2,411.7	1,118.1	921.3	2,281.5	20,175
2004	944.8	838.6	2,487.0	880.3	937.7	2,135.8	837.4	964.6	2,076.5	866.3	1,105.3	2,101.3	16,176
2005	764.5	873.6	2,330.2	916.2	891.6	2,090.1	618.4	979.1	2,090.2	902.1	880.2	2,041.4	15,377
2006	711.3	772.9	2,198.8	607.5	1,122.0	2,321.6	726.3	890.8	1,883.1	686.3	935.6	1,988.6	14,845
2007	696.3	765.0	2,341.9	614.6	937.9	2,237.8	803.4	1,546.1	1,941.4	854.5	1,130.8	1,967.9	15,838
2008	1,187.3	907.8	2,374.7	761.0	768.2	1,978.9	921.9	729.7	2,491.2	1,588.1	942.0	2,112.2	16,763
2009	674.4	744.3	2,026.3	555.3	534.7	1,637.5	453.5	427.3	1,338.3	473.3	384.6	1,186.4	10,436

Contract value = $250. *Source: Index and Option Market (IOM), division of the Chicago Mercantile Exchange (CME)*

Average Open Interest of S&P 500 Stock Index Futures in Chicago In Contracts

Year	Jan.	Feb.	Mar.	Apr.	May	June	July	Aug.	Sept.	Oct.	Nov.	Dec.
2000	369,295	374,365	400,089	379,651	383,677	409,448	380,118	391,867	416,600	413,912	447,245	498,049
2001	488,284	495,621	517,666	498,594	490,148	505,063	485,839	501,281	556,737	529,730	550,201	551,175
2002	495,352	519,023	542,358	513,048	542,839	592,888	594,727	621,558	644,806	607,848	631,224	647,022
2003	596,064	619,738	658,749	622,917	643,030	691,003	611,564	611,578	631,509	582,111	589,392	633,997
2004	612,911	614,843	624,209	595,593	587,717	604,154	586,760	597,581	632,050	636,566	686,531	714,420
2005	678,739	686,413	719,141	681,149	697,818	700,618	656,266	653,430	669,849	642,704	657,097	681,868
2006	655,483	668,113	682,218	653,044	664,790	670,449	625,142	634,579	634,817	609,410	640,481	679,221
2007	634,075	639,584	654,891	634,576	662,438	652,951	602,222	643,716	663,165	595,908	623,469	623,631
2008	566,839	602,738	607,396	560,088	559,320	558,810	551,609	565,810	578,027	627,531	633,531	603,664
2009	518,589	583,132	566,284	439,705	467,060	456,209	391,596	393,499	400,489	386,593	398,242	379,761

Contract value = $250. *Source: Index and Option Market (IOM), division of the Chicago Mercantile Exchange (CME)*

Volume of Trading of E-mini S&P 500 Index Futures in Chicago In Thousands of Contracts

Year	Jan.	Feb.	Mar.	Apr.	May	June	July	Aug.	Sept.	Oct.	Nov.	Dec.	Total
2000	1,306	1,388	1,489	1,462	1,676	1,550	1,403	1,439	1,683	2,109	1,843	1,673	19,021
2001	2,226	2,231	3,191	3,067	2,931	2,905	2,925	3,478	3,601	5,255	4,021	3,289	39,119
2002	4,933	5,337	5,609	7,165	7,564	9,772	14,277	11,200	11,765	17,175	11,054	9,892	115,742
2003	13,584	12,631	15,820	13,520	12,846	15,040	14,854	10,860	15,354	14,558	11,002	11,108	161,177
2004	13,087	11,355	18,033	14,993	15,889	12,428	14,361	12,921	12,755	14,636	13,705	13,039	167,203
2005	15,447	12,561	18,478	20,182	16,591	17,371	14,400	17,759	18,786	22,929	16,088	16,503	207,096
2006	18,716	16,095	21,357	18,174	24,750	30,359	21,629	19,107	21,986	22,377	23,616	19,760	257,927
2007	21,632	22,507	37,944	20,399	26,266	39,351	35,295	55,547	37,578	38,649	46,727	33,454	415,348
2008	55,257	40,368	56,108	38,472	36,217	49,724	53,375	36,400	76,696	84,259	56,426	50,587	633,889
2009	45,814	49,498	69,321	49,293	46,060	48,779	42,273	38,448	46,864	46,352	36,951	36,662	556,314

Contract value = $50. *Source: Index and Option Market (IOM), division of the Chicago Mercantile Exchange (CME)*

Average Open Interest of E-mini S&P 500 Index Futures in Chicago In Thousands of Contracts

Year	Jan.	Feb.	Mar.	Apr.	May	June	July	Aug.	Sept.	Oct.	Nov.	Dec.
2000	17.2	25.3	29.6	28.7	38.3	39.9	33.7	45.6	42.4	49.5	66.1	63.1
2001	55.5	68.5	79.9	91.9	110.8	91.6	97.1	126.2	152.3	134.7	224.8	178.7
2002	86.3	120.1	140.0	156.4	225.6	246.3	291.7	349.0	319.3	312.9	419.0	385.2
2003	265.2	356.6	490.0	567.6	741.8	718.5	399.5	492.5	513.4	460.9	467.7	525.3
2004	510.5	576.4	643.1	545.4	579.9	645.8	603.8	698.0	693.5	708.4	979.9	969.3
2005	827.3	901.7	1,013.6	943.3	1,014.9	986.8	932.6	1,060.8	1,110.1	1,042.2	1,166.4	1,211.3
2006	1,149.2	1,194.6	1,334.1	1,211.3	1,402.5	1,525.3	1,371.2	1,512.3	1,582.4	1,549.5	1,754.4	1,810.9
2007	1,625.6	1,825.1	2,037.4	1,943.7	2,088.7	2,060.5	1,735.6	2,105.4	2,151.5	1,972.4	2,095.4	2,172.5
2008	2,208.2	2,418.8	2,442.6	2,076.5	2,180.8	2,311.5	2,405.0	2,467.2	2,566.1	2,987.6	3,114.1	2,942.0
2009	2,512.9	2,896.4	3,123.3	2,489.2	2,680.4	2,690.2	2,429.6	2,622.9	2,582.3	2,397.1	2,593.6	2,688.5

Contract value = $50. *Source: Index and Option Market (IOM), division of the Chicago Mercantile Exchange (CME)*

Volume of Trading of NASDAQ 100 Index Futures in Chicago   In Contracts

Year	Jan.	Feb.	Mar.	Apr.	May	June	July	Aug.	Sept.	Oct.	Nov.	Dec.	Total
2000	349,813	366,408	575,942	503,064	460,085	432,062	296,944	310,549	445,334	490,863	400,412	464,454	5,095,930
2001	422,811	416,445	650,488	498,026	487,334	542,305	369,731	369,845	474,133	516,469	391,042	434,690	5,573,319
2002	380,076	367,561	436,495	378,294	443,579	529,496	454,630	334,242	466,898	367,750	315,925	428,341	4,903,287
2003	360,307	301,454	487,916	301,395	330,640	519,597	350,514	251,058	488,363	322,898	259,960	447,119	4,421,221
2004	271,404	268,590	591,556	321,242	297,320	427,805	286,693	245,050	433,251	286,048	226,853	356,171	4,011,983
2005	254,437	198,956	375,435	217,304	170,882	281,483	125,500	159,789	289,113	200,952	155,141	253,066	2,682,058
2006	186,649	162,841	295,163	113,885	169,399	305,557	132,661	149,906	256,605	136,433	140,407	220,364	2,269,870
2007	122,055	111,962	255,491	73,881	97,857	226,877	94,964	124,717	178,645	112,930	121,891	162,108	1,683,378
2008	137,810	90,886	188,815	72,775	80,472	192,723	103,965	83,158	171,532	125,975	58,023	101,279	1,407,413
2009	61,110	61,943	119,432	47,289	53,465	76,479	46,606	55,012	84,170	45,122	48,519	57,772	756,919

Contract value = $100.   *Source: Index and Option Market (IOM), division of the Chicago Mercantile Exchange (CME)*

Average Open Interest of NASDAQ 100 Index Futures in Chicago   In Contracts

Year	Jan.	Feb.	Mar.	Apr.	May	June	July	Aug.	Sept.	Oct.	Nov.	Dec.
2000	27,242	34,555	37,795	36,512	37,578	35,314	29,974	32,922	34,754	35,559	44,022	48,757
2001	46,582	49,495	59,916	56,328	49,337	54,394	50,854	55,234	61,665	51,977	61,196	67,769
2002	49,992	52,883	52,617	51,157	65,219	73,151	60,625	67,760	84,317	72,229	77,451	76,660
2003	71,219	79,905	87,252	71,636	77,717	88,914	80,002	83,940	91,685	75,191	85,651	86,480
2004	73,805	74,892	89,874	81,220	80,905	83,282	69,818	71,711	84,355	74,161	83,675	87,172
2005	72,299	81,327	78,387	56,668	57,116	56,836	49,357	53,270	61,369	60,918	59,754	63,712
2006	61,254	62,994	69,322	60,603	65,224	65,908	54,289	57,585	54,235	53,832	68,347	61,397
2007	47,832	51,655	55,782	50,905	59,586	63,132	63,492	67,870	64,324	50,761	53,292	50,372
2008	42,272	52,260	51,385	31,738	37,017	34,864	28,456	30,588	27,761	27,770	31,473	29,459
2009	23,558	29,607	29,090	21,525	24,228	21,913	17,299	21,266	22,113	19,389	21,267	18,502

Contract value = $100.   *Source: Index and Option Market (IOM), division of the Chicago Mercantile Exchange (CME)*

Volume of Trading of E-mini NASDAQ 100 Index Futures in Chicago   In Thousands of Contracts

Year	Jan.	Feb.	Mar.	Apr.	May	June	July	Aug.	Sept.	Oct.	Nov.	Dec.	Total
2000	304	382	604	628	745	762	756	883	1,508	1,589	1,446	1,512	11,118
2001	1,845	1,942	2,603	2,873	2,908	2,969	2,529	2,568	2,387	3,935	3,151	2,595	32,304
2002	3,719	3,649	3,652	4,227	4,625	4,713	5,789	4,225	4,337	6,252	4,812	4,490	54,491
2003	5,200	4,620	5,749	5,132	5,075	6,323	6,369	4,816	7,095	6,601	5,254	5,655	67,889
2004	6,157	5,640	8,011	6,387	6,749	5,646	7,139	6,123	6,476	7,322	5,844	5,675	77,169
2005	7,174	6,149	7,336	7,256	5,735	6,233	4,895	5,171	5,624	6,583	5,288	5,008	72,453
2006	6,628	5,803	7,479	5,459	7,386	8,258	6,741	6,315	7,074	6,769	6,333	5,696	79,940
2007	7,122	6,685	8,700	4,976	7,069	8,426	8,122	10,558	6,856	8,916	11,147	6,733	95,309
2008	11,604	8,072	9,677	6,988	7,042	9,912	10,151	7,607	11,523	12,287	7,300	6,571	108,734
2009	5,713	6,789	8,800	6,383	6,241	6,722	6,243	5,959	6,808	7,048	5,686	5,579	77,972

Contract value = $20.   *Source: Index and Option Market (IOM), division of the Chicago Mercantile Exchange (CME)*

Average Open Interest of E-mini NASDAQ 100 Index Futures in Chicago   In Contracts

Year	Jan.	Feb.	Mar.	Apr.	May	June	July	Aug.	Sept.	Oct.	Nov.	Dec.
2000	8,582	9,250	11,117	15,625	23,465	26,095	23,863	31,506	30,956	33,123	58,709	54,420
2001	45,370	65,061	79,962	78,094	90,822	95,236	90,803	131,259	132,349	75,686	115,350	124,023
2002	78,070	94,150	98,159	100,849	153,348	176,394	130,337	171,043	162,133	110,952	154,104	155,987
2003	169,160	227,905	258,023	196,739	240,759	257,390	262,564	316,032	287,936	214,659	279,379	244,333
2004	205,078	251,011	251,486	257,573	304,034	261,067	213,080	256,749	299,794	279,170	374,750	384,492
2005	339,077	419,715	382,805	310,664	331,447	290,759	270,134	325,508	307,007	365,277	382,667	371,388
2006	351,240	361,807	345,533	309,746	381,178	427,387	386,930	421,179	437,975	457,275	498,584	433,456
2007	360,663	354,765	423,270	396,080	463,422	454,010	418,512	429,654	451,180	415,073	439,054	408,021
2008	347,374	410,404	424,513	320,046	377,029	358,774	316,037	333,976	336,525	379,643	359,028	302,534
2009	245,830	281,273	302,750	256,064	286,754	284,962	272,424	332,576	341,802	321,653	329,991	338,692

Contract value = $20.   *Source: Index and Option Market (IOM), division of the Chicago Mercantile Exchange (CME)*

Volume of Trading of S&P 400 Midcap Stock Index Futures in Chicago In Contracts

Year	Jan.	Feb.	Mar.	Apr.	May	June	July	Aug.	Sept.	Oct.	Nov.	Dec.	Total
2000	16,918	15,298	45,942	23,892	19,863	42,514	12,140	12,515	42,658	21,701	25,334	59,265	338,040
2001	21,527	19,884	58,286	18,061	19,258	50,331	22,029	23,805	50,706	23,741	19,591	51,641	378,860
2002	22,322	22,814	43,819	23,019	22,484	51,775	30,607	23,075	52,375	25,593	21,262	48,105	387,250
2003	18,827	18,392	44,454	15,841	15,194	40,603	15,153	12,082	43,112	15,253	13,109	50,797	302,817
2004	13,647	10,361	46,214	13,921	13,078	45,940	12,602	13,582	36,701	7,923	9,824	36,971	260,764
2005	6,486	5,736	36,685	5,130	7,235	39,025	4,603	7,699	42,503	5,736	4,988	39,232	205,058
2006	5,668	3,739	34,668	3,671	4,619	31,924	2,656	3,311	23,289	3,718	6,409	29,596	153,268
2007	2,854	3,205	26,948	3,716	3,937	22,210	3,906	4,271	17,518	3,610	10,570	15,395	118,140
2008	5,581	3,286	14,864	2,796	3,124	15,896	4,670	3,369	19,246	6,432	4,397	13,563	97,224
2009	2,330	4,802	11,017	4,668	1,707	10,037	1,642	1,822	8,854	3,229	2,285	6,967	59,360

Contract value = $500. *Source: Index and Option Market (IOM), division of the Chicago Mercantile Exchange (CME)*

Average Open Interest of S&P 400 Midcap Stock Index Futures in Chicago In Contracts

Year	Jan.	Feb.	Mar.	Apr.	May	June	July	Aug.	Sept.	Oct.	Nov.	Dec.
2000	12,810	13,119	13,965	12,495	13,355	14,040	12,957	13,162	15,026	16,143	16,510	17,479
2001	15,246	15,461	17,235	16,953	15,623	16,606	16,334	16,132	16,718	15,109	15,307	15,337
2002	13,691	14,109	14,954	14,340	16,402	16,611	15,121	16,213	17,006	14,695	15,394	16,432
2003	13,793	13,498	14,530	13,120	13,353	13,986	13,123	13,029	13,726	14,014	15,465	17,446
2004	15,911	15,988	16,554	15,870	15,819	17,148	13,939	13,600	14,213	13,339	14,046	14,755
2005	13,078	13,313	14,861	11,812	11,832	13,811	12,380	12,420	14,477	12,890	12,955	13,822
2006	12,168	11,940	12,409	10,999	10,892	10,447	9,307	9,687	9,194	8,442	9,884	9,794
2007	7,793	8,143	8,267	7,972	9,187	8,425	6,729	6,671	6,951	6,166	8,580	8,839
2008	6,501	7,622	7,512	4,254	5,358	5,700	4,578	5,756	6,847	6,601	6,766	5,761
2009	3,785	4,755	5,227	4,433	4,580	3,781	2,481	2,887	2,847	2,586	2,273	2,437

Contract value = $500. *Source: Index and Option Market (IOM), division of the Chicago Mercantile Exchange (CME)*

Volume of Trading of Dow Jones Industrials Index Futures in Chicago In Contracts

Year	Jan.	Feb.	Mar.	Apr.	May	June	July	Aug.	Sept.	Oct.	Nov.	Dec.	Total
2000	322,046	340,377	472,179	321,026	284,005	270,374	215,234	211,612	277,620	319,636	267,051	268,010	3,569,170
2001	275,814	310,088	594,326	411,767	377,620	389,919	320,335	410,927	573,479	520,885	375,793	329,898	4,890,851
2002	409,009	472,893	538,804	467,571	456,210	616,754	811,518	539,507	639,154	699,005	427,235	407,665	6,485,325
2003	452,579	426,198	559,372	428,972	410,967	473,432	368,277	286,508	367,845	218,394	157,726	266,032	4,416,302
2004	224,713	207,423	362,668	203,745	208,229	246,564	183,469	149,931	230,829	169,627	152,412	237,528	2,577,138
2005	149,353	107,824	226,113	157,010	124,999	192,165	96,885	121,793	188,541	133,636	108,737	180,349	1,787,405
2006	119,593	111,738	220,880	106,325	152,340	272,494	108,053	97,964	237,988	121,736	111,993	258,743	1,919,847
2007	97,032	97,537	231,466	76,661	127,981	197,380	101,710	119,985	135,432	95,101	91,014	112,518	1,483,817
2008	105,901	82,432	135,860	71,571	51,097	121,220	122,305	76,031	170,465	99,607	53,397	57,771	1,147,657
2009	32,235	36,568	54,497	35,502	32,590	50,874	27,114	17,541	47,003	18,659	13,769	29,232	395,584

Contract value = $10. *Source: Chicago Board of Trade (CBT)*

Average Open Interest of Dow Jones Industrials Index Futures in Chicago In Contracts

Year	Jan.	Feb.	Mar.	Apr.	May	June	July	Aug.	Sept.	Oct.	Nov.	Dec.
2000	13,713	16,331	20,443	18,157	19,253	17,394	14,367	15,748	14,840	15,087	19,113	20,966
2001	21,830	23,423	28,340	32,497	33,767	29,357	26,792	33,015	35,451	31,997	30,598	27,018
2002	23,862	35,588	37,582	28,714	32,810	34,482	32,412	32,272	34,665	31,923	34,045	31,892
2003	27,032	30,429	34,371	31,160	34,936	36,352	36,773	43,974	41,747	34,066	37,835	39,727
2004	34,656	44,306	50,172	44,494	45,304	46,641	42,790	42,042	45,940	41,250	43,662	53,469
2005	47,754	48,665	48,423	40,068	41,367	36,909	29,042	30,921	37,232	36,378	37,588	43,819
2006	39,641	39,943	43,595	43,351	45,756	53,833	56,451	58,799	60,497	61,996	63,061	69,927
2007	67,567	72,788	54,933	41,615	48,211	42,631	33,406	37,757	35,894	30,936	35,735	34,375
2008	27,564	32,212	33,736	29,240	31,425	32,987	31,175	34,663	36,423	26,685	27,638	23,708
2009	14,401	22,146	19,045	10,306	15,681	18,781	10,880	11,614	12,693	13,764	16,046	12,915

Contract value = $10. *Source: Chicago Board of Trade (CBT)*

Stock Index Futures - WorldWide

World Stocks – World stock markets in 2009 showed a sharp recovery rally after the debacle seen during the 3-year bear market from mid-2007 to March 2009. The MSCI World Index, a benchmark for large companies based in 23 developed countries, rallied by +27.0% in 2009, reversing part of the –42.1% plunge seen in 2008.

The MSCI World Index peaked at a record high of 1686.32 in October 2007 and then entered a bear market when the U.S. housing and mortgage crisis started to spill over into the banking industry and the real economy. The Index fell by an overall –59.4% to a new 14-1/2 year low in March 2009. However, global stocks started to recover in March 2009 when it became clear that the worst of the financial crisis was over. The MSCI World Index recovered by a total of +49% through early 2010.

The global economy bottomed out in 2009 when the economic recovery began. The World Bank reported that world economic growth in 2009 fell by –1.1%, which was the first decline in global GDP in post-war history. However, the World Bank believes that world economic growth will grow by +3.1% in 2010 and +4.2% in 2011. The global economic recovery was led by China, which saw its GDP improve to +10.7% by Q4-2009. The global economic recovery allowed corporate profits to revive fairly quickly.

Looking ahead, the MSCI World Index as of early 2010 was trading at a reasonable price-to-earnings ratio of 14.8 based on forward-looking earnings. This reasonable valuation level should leave room for stock price gains in coming years as the global recovery picks up steam and as confidence grows in future earnings.

Small-Capitalization Stocks – The MSCI World Small-Cap Index, which tracks companies with market caps between $200 million and $1.5 billion, rose by +41.7% in 2009 following the –42.9% plunge seen in 2008. The 2008 sell-off ended four consecutive years of double-digit gains in 2003-06 (2003 +55.5%, 2004 +22.6%, 2005 +14.2%, 2006 +15.8%). The rise in the MSCI World Small-Cap Index in 2009 of +41.7% was 14.7 percentage points better than the +27.0% gain in the large-cap MSCI World Index, illustrating that small caps during the 2009 recovery rally did much better than large-caps.

World Industry Groups – The MSCI Industry Sectors in 2009 produced the following ranked annual returns: Materials +58.4%, Information Technology +50.9%, Consumer Discretionary +37.3%, Financials +27.7%, Industrials +23.9%, Energy +22.9%, Consumer Staples +18.6%, Health Care +16.4%, Telecom +8.6%, and Utilities +2.0%. The more aggressive cyclical stocks clearly did better during the recovery rally since they got hit harder during the recession. The Materials sector rallied by the most in 2009 at +58.4%, recovering ground after the –51.0% hit taken in 2008. Information Technology rallied by +50.9% in 2009 following the –44.4% loss seen in 2008. Meanwhile, the defensive sectors such as Consumer Staples, Health Care, and Utilities underperformed during the recovery rally. Financials saw a recovery rally of +27.7% after the devastating loss of –55.6% in 2008.

Emerging Markets – Emerging stock markets rallied sharply in 2009 as investors reached for more aggressive stocks during the recovery rally and as China helped lead the world out of recession. The MSCI Emerging Markets Free Index, which tracks companies based in 26 emerging countries, rallied by +74.5% in 2009 following the –54.5% plunge seen in 2008.

G7 – In 2009, all of the seven G7 stock markets saw sharp recovery rallies. The ranked returns for the G7 stock markets are as follows: Canadian Toronto Composite +30.7%, German DAX index +23.8%, U.S. S&P 500 +23.5%, French CAC40 +22.3%, UK FTSE 100 +22.1%, Italian MIB +19.5%, and Japanese Nikkei 225 +19.0%.

North America – In North America, Mexico's Bolsa Index ended 2009 up +43.5%, outperforming the U.S. and Canadian stock markets for the ninth straight year. The Mexican Bolsa index has now posted double-digit gains in six of the last seven years (2009 +43.5%, 2008 –24.2%, 2007 +11.7%, 2006 +48.6%, 2005 +37.8%, 2004 +46.9%, 2003 +43.5%). The Toronto Composite index rallied by +30.7% in 2009, beating the +23.5% gain in the S&P 500 index. The Toronto index has outperformed the S&P 500 for six consecutive years.

Latin America – The large Latin America stock markets showed extraordinary gains in 2009 as investors flocked back to the emerging markets and as Latin America escaped the worst of the damage from the global recession: Argentina's Merval Index +115.0%, Peru's Lima General Index +101.0%, Brazil's Bovespa Index +82.7%, Venezuela's Stock Market Index +57.0%, Columbia's General Index +53.5%, Chile's Stock Market Select Index +50.7%, Jamaica's Stock Exchange Index +4.0%, Ecuador's Guayaqui Bolsa Index –16.2%, and Costa Rica's Stock Market Index –31.6%.

Europe – European stocks in 2009 showed a solid recovery after the debacle in 2008. The Dow Jones Stoxx 50 index closed +24.1% in 2009 following the –43.4% plunge seen in 2008. The rally in 2009 broke the string of two consecutive yearly declines (-0.4% in 2007). All five of the big European countries saw double-digit gains in 2009: Spanish IBEX 35 index +29.8%, German DAX index +23.8%, French CAC 40 index +22.3%, UK FTSE 100 index +22.1%, and Italian MIB index +19.5%.

Asia – The Asian stock markets in 2009 showed a sharp recovery with all the main markets showing double-digit gains. The MSCI Far East Index in 2009 rose by +12.8%, recovering somewhat from the –32.3% decline seen in 2008. The sharp gains in the Asian stock markets illustrated how Asia came out of the global financial crisis in much better shape than the U.S. or Europe. China's Shanghai Composite Index in 2009 rallied by +80.0%, returning to the impressive performance numbers seen in 2006 and 2007 (+130.4% and +96.7%, respectively) after the –65.4% decline seen in 2008.

The ranked closes for the Asian stock markets in 2009 were as follows: Indonesia's Jakarta Composite Index +87.0%, India's Mumbai Sensex 30 index +81.0%, China's Shanghai Composite index +80.0%, Taiwan's TAIEX index of +78.3%, Singapore's Straights Times index +64.5%, Thailand's Stock Exchange index +63.2%, Philippines' Composite index +63.0%, Pakistan's 100 Index +60.0%, Vietnam Stock Index +56.8%, Hong Kong Hang Seng +52.0%, South Korea Composite Index +49.7%, Malaysia's Kuala Lumpur Composite index +45.2%, Australia's All-Ordinaries index +33.4%, Japan's Nikkei 225 +19.0%, and New Zealand's Exchange 50 index +18.9%.

Year	Jan.	Feb.	Mar.	Apr.	May	June	July	Aug.	Sept.	Oct.	Nov.	Dec.	Average
United States													
2003	257.2	252.8	255.0	275.6	289.6	292.9	297.7	303.0	299.4	315.8	318.1	334.2	290.9
2004	340.0	344.2	338.5	332.8	336.9	342.9	331.2	331.9	335.0	339.7	352.8	364.3	340.9
2005	355.1	361.8	354.9	347.7	358.2	358.1	371.0	366.8	369.4	362.8	375.6	375.2	363.1
2006	384.8	385.0	389.2	394.0	381.8	381.8	383.8	391.9	401.5	414.2	421.0	426.3	396.3
2007	432.3	422.9	427.1	445.6	460.1	451.9	437.4	443.1	458.9	465.7	445.2	441.4	444.3
2008	414.4	400.0	397.6	416.5	420.9	384.8	381.0	385.6	350.6	291.2	269.4	271.5	365.3
2009[1]	248.3	221.0	239.8	262.4	276.3	276.3	296.8	306.8	317.7	311.5	329.3		280.6
Canada													
2003	192.0	191.6	185.4	192.5	200.5	204.1	212.2	219.5	216.9	227.2	229.7	240.3	209.3
2004	249.1	256.9	251.0	241.0	246.0	249.8	247.2	244.9	253.4	259.3	264.0	270.3	252.7
2005	269.0	282.6	281.0	273.9	280.8	289.5	304.7	311.9	321.9	303.5	316.4	329.5	297.1
2006	349.2	341.7	354.0	356.7	343.3	339.4	345.8	352.9	343.8	360.8	372.8	377.3	353.1
2007	381.0	381.3	384.8	392.2	410.9	406.5	405.4	399.3	412.1	427.5	400.1	404.3	400.5
2008	384.5	397.0	390.2	407.4	430.1	422.9	397.3	402.5	343.5	285.4	271.0	262.7	366.2
2009[1]	254.2	237.4	254.9	272.6	303.1	303.3	315.3	317.7	333.1	318.9	334.6		295.0
France													
2003	161.6	151.5	144.1	162.5	164.6	169.7	176.6	182.2	172.5	185.6	188.4	195.8	171.3
2004	200.2	205.0	199.5	202.2	201.9	205.4	200.7	197.8	200.3	204.0	206.5	210.2	202.8
2005	215.3	221.6	223.8	215.2	226.7	232.7	244.9	242.1	253.1	244.1	251.3	259.4	235.9
2006	272.2	275.1	287.3	285.5	271.3	273.2	275.6	284.2	288.9	294.3	293.1	304.9	283.8
2007	308.6	303.5	310.0	327.9	335.9	333.2	316.4	311.6	314.5	321.8	312.0	308.9	317.0
2008	267.9	263.6	259.0	274.9	275.9	244.0	241.7	246.6	221.9	191.9	179.5	177.1	237.0
2009[1]	163.6	148.7	154.5	173.9	180.3	172.8	188.5	201.0	208.8	198.5	202.5		181.2
Germany													
2003	162.5	150.6	143.3	173.9	176.4	190.4	206.2	206.0	192.6	216.2	221.5	234.4	189.5
2004	240.0	237.6	228.0	235.6	231.9	239.6	230.3	223.8	230.2	234.1	243.9	251.6	235.6
2005	251.6	257.2	257.1	247.4	263.7	271.2	288.9	285.6	298.2	291.4	307.1	319.8	278.3
2006	335.5	342.7	353.0	355.3	336.6	336.0	335.9	346.4	355.0	370.6	373.0	390.0	352.5
2007	401.4	397.0	409.0	438.0	466.1	473.4	448.4	451.6	464.8	474.1	465.3	477.0	447.2
2008	405.1	399.0	386.4	410.8	419.6	379.5	383.1	379.7	344.8	294.9	276.1	284.4	363.6
2009[1]	256.5	227.3	241.5	282.0	292.1	284.3	315.3	323.1	335.5	320.2	332.6		291.9
Italy													
2003	162.6	166.3	157.2	173.3	180.5	181.1	181.6	184.4	181.5	189.0	196.3	195.6	179.1
2004	201.3	203.3	199.4	204.9	200.5	206.5	202.1	199.1	206.4	212.2	218.6	229.6	207.0
2005	234.9	237.8	241.0	230.5	237.0	241.1	251.9	249.5	261.7	242.9	252.5	261.4	245.2
2006	271.8	282.9	286.3	285.5	269.9	271.5	274.1	283.7	287.2	296.4	304.2	310.9	285.4
2007	317.4	310.9	317.2	331.5	329.5	319.9	307.4	304.6	302.4	307.0	291.2	286.7	310.5
2008	252.1	251.6	236.2	251.1	249.8	221.0	213.6	217.1	190.3	158.0	151.0	146.8	211.6
2009[1]	139.5	121.7	123.5	148.7	154.9	149.1	158.5	169.1	178.2	171.6	168.3		153.0
Japan													
2003	28.9	29.0	27.7	27.2	29.2	31.5	33.2	35.9	35.5	35.5	35.0	37.0	32.1
2004	37.4	38.3	40.6	40.8	39.0	41.1	39.3	38.4	37.5	37.4	37.8	39.9	39.0
2005	39.5	40.7	40.5	38.2	39.1	40.2	41.3	43.1	47.1	47.2	51.6	55.9	43.7
2006	57.8	56.2	59.2	58.6	53.7	53.8	53.6	56.0	55.9	56.9	56.5	59.8	56.5
2007	60.3	61.1	60.0	60.4	62.0	62.9	59.8	57.5	58.2	58.1	54.4	53.1	59.0
2008	47.2	47.2	43.5	48.0	49.7	46.8	46.4	45.4	39.1	29.8	29.5	30.7	41.9
2009[1]	27.7	26.3	28.1	30.6	33.0	34.5	35.9	36.4	35.2	34.8	32.4		32.3
United Kingdom													
2003	159.1	162.5	160.3	174.7	181.9	182.1	189.0	190.7	187.3	196.3	198.3	203.9	182.2
2004	202.0	207.2	202.9	206.7	203.4	205.9	202.5	204.5	209.8	212.2	216.6	222.7	208.0
2005	225.5	230.5	227.0	221.4	229.4	236.5	244.3	245.6	253.6	246.1	253.2	263.0	239.7
2006	270.5	273.1	281.6	284.0	269.4	274.1	277.5	277.8	281.8	290.1	288.2	297.6	280.5
2007	296.7	295.4	303.3	310.0	317.7	314.5	303.8	301.2	306.4	319.1	303.1	303.6	306.2
2008	277.1	278.3	270.4	286.4	284.7	263.8	254.0	265.0	229.4	201.7	197.1	204.1	251.0
2009[1]	192.0	178.3	183.3	200.7	208.1	200.6	217.4	232.8	243.4	238.8	244.7		212.7

[1] Preliminary. Not Seasonally Adjusted. *Source: Economic and Statistics Administration, U.S. Department of Commerce (ESA)*

FT-SE 100 Stock Index (weekly close) as of December 31, 2009
Index Value
7,000
6,500
6,000
5,500
5,000
4,500
4,000
3,500
3,000
Jan-00
Jan-01
Jan-02
Jan-03
Jan-04
Dec-04
Dec-05
Dec-06
Dec-07
Dec-08
Dec-09
Dec-10

Deutscher Aktienindex (DAX) (weekly close) as of December 31, 2009
Index Value
9,000
8,000
7,000
6,000
5,000
4,000
3,000
2,000
Jan-00
Jan-01
Jan-02
Jan-03
Jan-04
Dec-04
Dec-05
Dec-06
Dec-07
Dec-08
Dec-09
Dec-10

Toronto 300 Stock Index (weekly close) as of December 31, 2009
Index Value
16,000
14,000
12,000
10,000
8,000
6,000
4,000
Jan-00
Jan-01
Jan-02
Jan-03
Jan-04
Dec-04
Dec-05
Dec-06
Dec-07
Dec-08
Dec-09
Dec-10

CAC-40 Stock Index (weekly close) as of December 31, 2009
Index Value
7,000
6,000
5,000
4,000
3,000
2,000
Jan-00
Jan-01
Jan-02
Jan-03
Jan-04
Dec-04
Dec-05
Dec-06
Dec-07
Dec-08
Dec-09
Dec-10

Hang Seng Stock Index (weekly close) as of December 31, 2009
Index Value
35,000
30,000
25,000
20,000
15,000
10,000
5,000
Jan-00
Jan-01
Jan-02
Jan-03
Jan-04
Dec-04
Dec-05
Dec-06
Dec-07
Dec-08
Dec-09
Dec-10

Nikkei 225 Stock Index (weekly close) as of December 31, 2009
Index Value
24,000
20,000
16,000
12,000
8,000
4,000
Jan-00
Jan-01
Jan-02
Jan-03
Jan-04
Dec-04
Dec-05
Dec-06
Dec-07
Dec-08
Dec-09
Dec-10

Sugar

The white crystalline substance called "sugar" is the organic chemical compound sucrose, one of several related compounds all known as sugars. These include glucose, dextrose, fructose, and lactose. All sugars are members of the larger group of compounds called carbohydrates and are characterized by a sweet taste. Sucrose is considered a double sugar because it is composed of one molecule of glucose and one molecule of fructose. While sucrose is common in many plants, it occurs in the highest concentration in sugarcane (Saccharum officinarum) and sugar beets (Beta vulgaris). Sugarcane is about 7 to 18 percent sugar by weight while sugar beets are 8 to 22 percent.

Sugarcane is a member of the grass family and is a perennial. Sugarcane is cultivated in tropical and subtropical regions around the world roughly between the Tropics of Cancer and Capricorn. It grows best in hot, wet climates where there is heavy rainfall followed by a dry season. The largest cane producers are Florida, Louisiana, Texas, and Hawaii. On a commercial basis, sugarcane is not grown from seeds but from cuttings or pieces of the stalk.

Sugar beets, which are produced in temperate or colder climates, are annuals grown from seeds. Sugar beets do best with moderate temperatures and evenly distributed rainfall. The beets are planted in the spring and harvested in the fall. The sugar is contained in the root of the beet, but the sugars from beets and cane are identical. Sugar beet production takes place mostly in Europe, the U.S., China, and Japan. The largest sugar beet producing states are Minnesota, Idaho, North Dakota, and Michigan. Sugar beets are refined to yield white sugar and very little raw sugar is produced.

Sugar beets and sugarcane are produced in over 100 countries around the world. Of all the sugar produced, about 25 percent is processed from sugar beets and the remaining 75% is from sugar cane. The trend has been that production of sugar from cane is increasing relative to that produced from beets. The significance of this in that sugarcane is a perennial plant while the sugar beet is an annual, and due to the longer production cycle, sugarcane production and the sugar processed from that cane, may not be quite as responsive to changes in price.

Sugar futures are traded on the Bolsa de Mercadorias & Futuros (BM&F), Kansai Commodities Exchange (KANEX), the Tokyo Grain Exchange (TGE), the London International Financial Futures and Options Exchange (LIFFE), and the ICE Futures U.S. (ICE) exchange. Options are traded on the BM&F, the TGE, the LIFFE and the ICE.

Raw sugar is traded on the ICE Futures U.S. (ICE) exchange while white sugar is traded on the London International Financial Futures Exchange (LIFFE). The most actively traded contract is the No. 11 (World) sugar contract at the ICE. The No. 11 contract calls for the delivery of 112,000 pounds (50 long tons) of raw cane centrifugal sugar from any of 28 foreign countries of origin and the United States. The ICE also trades the No. 16 sugar contract (Domestic), which calls for the delivery of raw centrifugal cane sugar in the United States. Futures on white sugar are traded on the London International Financial Futures Exchange and call for the delivery of 50 metric tons of white beet sugar, cane crystal sugar, or refined sugar of any origin from the crop current at the time of delivery.

Prices – World sugar prices on the ICE No. 11 sugar nearest-futures chart rallied sharply through 2009 and posted a new 29-year high of 30.40 cents per pound in February 2010. Sugar prices closed 2009 at 26.95 cents per pound, up 128% from the 2008 close of 11.81 cents. Bullish factors for sugar that drove the rally included (1) the forecast by the International Sugar Organization for a global sugar production deficit of 9.4 million metric tons in the 2009–10 marketing year, (2) the larger sugar production deficit in India (the world's largest sugar producer and consumer), which was due to a poor crop from the weakest monsoon season since 1972 and caused India to be a net sugar importer for the second straight year, (3) tight sugar supplies in Brazil due to heavy rains which hampered harvesting and caused lower-than-normal sugar concentration in the sugarcane plants. Brazil uses roughly half of its sugar production to distill ethanol. World sugar stocks in the 2009/10 marketing year fell to a 15-year low of 26.0 million metric tons, illustrating the tight sugar supply situation. The sugar stocks/consumption ratio fell to 17.0% in 2009/10, which was a record low for the data series that has history back to 1960.

Supply – World production of centrifugal (raw) sugar in the 2009-10 marketing year (Oct 1 to Sep 30) rose +6.8% to 153.527 million metric tons, further down from the 2006-07 record high. The world's largest sugar producers in 2009-10 were Brazil with 23% of world production, India with 11%, and the European Union with 10%. U.S. centrifugal sugar production in 2009-10 fell -5.0% to 1.625 million metric tons. World ending stocks in 2009-10 fell -5.7% to 26.002 million metric tons. The stocks/consumption ratio fell to 17.0% in 2008-09. U.S. production of cane sugar in 2009-10 rose +3.6% to 3.473 million short tons and beet sugar production rose +5.6% yr/yr to 4.400 million short tons.

Demand – World domestic consumption of centrifugal (raw) sugar in 2009-10 fell by -0.4% yr/yr to 152.854 million metric tons, down from last year's record high of 153.455 million metric tons. U.S. domestic disappearance (consumption) of sugar in 2009-10 fell by -2.3% yr/yr to 10.525 million short tons. U.S. per capita sugar consumption in 2008-09 (latest data) rose +5.9% to 65.79 pounds per year, which is only about two-thirds of the levels seen in the early 1970s.

Trade – World exports of centrifugal sugar in 2009-10 rose +6.4% yr/yr to 51.277 million metric tons, down a little from the 2007-08 record high of 51.433. The world's largest sugar exporter was Brazil, where exports in 2009-10 rose +10.7% to 23.850 million metric tons, which accounted for 47% of total world exports. The next largest exporters are Thailand with 11% of world exports and Australia with 7%. U.S. sugar exports in 2009-10 rose +9.5% yr/yr to 150,000 short tons, but that is down from the 15-year high of 4221,000 seen in 2006-07. U.S. sugar imports in 2009-10 fell -22.9% yr/yr to 2.377 million short tons, down from the 2-decade high of 3.443 in 2005-06.

World Production, Supply & Stocks/Consumption Ratio of Sugar In 1000's of Metric Tons (Raw Value)

Marketing Year	Beginning Stocks	Production	Imports	Total Supply	Exports	Domestic Consumption	Ending Stocks	Stocks As a % of Consumption
2000-01	37,508	130,764	40,404	208,676	38,260	130,147	39,964	30.7
2001-02	39,964	134,398	39,693	214,055	42,332	134,346	36,734	27.3
2002-03	36,734	148,552	41,714	227,000	47,270	138,017	40,664	29.5
2003-04	40,664	142,473	41,226	224,363	46,562	138,970	38,008	27.3
2004-05	38,008	140,674	45,418	224,100	46,909	142,308	33,951	23.9
2005-06	33,951	144,606	45,320	223,877	49,884	142,144	31,076	21.9
2006-07	31,076	164,467	43,975	239,518	51,227	150,317	35,769	23.8
2007-08[1]	35,769	163,297	44,384	243,450	51,433	151,376	39,776	26.3
2008-09[2]	39,776	143,781	46,568	230,125	48,180	153,455	27,570	18.0
2009-10[3]	27,570	153,527	49,921	231,018	51,277	152,854	26,002	17.0

[1] Preliminary. [2] Estimate. [3] Forecast. *Source: Foreign Agricultural Service, U.S. Department of Agriculture (FAS-USDA)*

World Production of Sugar (Centrifugal Sugar-Raw Value) In Thousands of Metric Tons

Year	Australia	Brazil	China	Cuba	European Union	India	Indo-nesia	Mexico	Pakistan	Thailand	United States	Ukraine	World Total
2000-01	4,162	17,100	6,849	3,500	18,519	20,480	1,800	5,220	2,648	5,107	1,687	7,956	130,764
2001-02	4,662	20,400	8,305	3,700	16,153	20,475	1,725	5,169	3,453	6,397	1,790	7,167	134,398
2002-03	5,461	23,810	11,380	2,250	18,675	22,140	1,755	5,229	3,944	7,286	1,550	7,644	148,552
2003-04	5,178	26,400	10,734	2,550	17,132	15,150	1,730	5,330	4,047	7,010	1,580	7,847	142,473
2004-05	5,388	28,175	9,826	1,350	21,648	14,170	2,050	6,149	2,937	5,187	2,054	7,146	140,674
2005-06	5,297	26,850	9,446	1,240	21,373	21,140	2,100	5,604	2,597	4,835	2,054	6,713	144,606
2006-07	5,212	31,450	12,855	1,200	17,757	30,780	1,900	5,633	3,615	6,720	2,850	7,662	164,467
2007-08[1]	4,939	31,600	15,898	1,420	15,614	28,630	1,900	5,852	4,163	7,820	2,020	7,396	163,297
2008-09[2]	4,814	31,850	13,317	1,250	13,570	16,130	2,680	5,260	3,512	7,200	1,710	6,789	143,781
2009-10[3]	4,900	35,750	13,161	1,250	15,485	17,300	2,960	5,400	3,520	7,700	1,625	6,998	153,527

[1] Preliminary. [2] Estimate. [3] Forecast. *Source: Foreign Agricultural Service, U.S. Department of Agriculture (FAS-USDA)*

World Stocks of Centrifugal Sugar at Beginning of Marketing Year In Thousands of Metric Tons (Raw Value)

Year	Australia	Brazil	China	Cuba	European Union	India	Indonesia	Iran	Mexico	Philip-pines	Russia	United States	World Total
2000-01	518	710	1,851	438	3,493	10,710	1,330	207	1,063	330	3,000	2,013	37,508
2001-02	634	860	1,004	350	3,420	11,985	1,415	207	1,548	322	3,100	1,978	39,964
2002-03	507	210	869	360	2,717	11,670	1,385	167	1,172	239	2,130	1,386	36,734
2003-04	662	270	2,021	267	3,581	12,150	1,340	267	1,194	277	1,050	1,515	40,664
2004-05	543	1,030	2,323	275	4,699	8,485	1,170	402	1,237	405	440	1,721	38,008
2005-06	343	585	1,757	215	5,339	4,365	1,120	542	2,045	239	580	1,208	33,951
2006-07	291	-285	703	225	5,088	4,175	1,170	932	1,294	253	470	1,540	31,076
2007-08[1]	402	-485	1,401	150	2,720	9,850	570	1,482	1,718	262	440	1,632	35,769
2008-09[2]	400	215	3,965	45	3,130	9,150	490	1,307	1,975	547	550	1,506	39,776
2009-10[3]	451	-1,135	3,464	55	2,175	3,690	340	407	640	322	750	1,317	27,570

[1] Preliminary. [2] Estimate. [3] Forecast. *Source: Foreign Agricultural Service, U.S. Department of Agriculture (FAS-USDA)*

Centrifugal Sugar (Raw Value) Imported into Selected Countries In Thousands of Metric Tons

Year	Algeria	Canada	China	European Union	Indo-nesia	Iran	Japan	Rep. of Korea	Malaysia	Nigeria	Russia	United States	World Total
2000-01	975	1,211	1,083	1,839	1,591	1,000	1,486	1,574	1,325	714	5,650	1,443	40,404
2001-02	1,015	1,235	1,375	2,025	1,600	1,010	1,407	1,590	1,385	775	4,850	1,393	39,693
2002-03	1,094	1,329	842	2,150	1,600	955	1,483	1,590	1,406	1,000	4,000	1,569	41,714
2003-04	1,185	1,323	1,235	1,900	1,500	760	1,442	1,682	1,484	1,150	3,670	1,591	41,226
2004-05	1,153	1,274	1,360	2,549	1,450	865	1,328	1,652	1,459	1,150	4,300	1,905	45,418
2005-06	1,380	1,133	1,234	2,630	1,800	1,450	1,350	1,669	1,414	1,200	2,900	3,124	45,320
2006-07	1,220	1,191	1,465	3,530	1,800	1,740	1,350	1,518	1,670	1,080	2,950	1,887	43,975
2007-08[1]	1,075	1,416	972	2,948	2,420	855	1,372	1,648	1,430	1,385	3,100	2,377	44,384
2008-09[2]	1,145	1,444	1,077	3,250	1,570	750	1,450	1,550	1,540	1,250	2,800	2,796	46,568
2009-10[3]	1,100	1,450	900	3,500	1,500	693	1,313	1,600	1,530	1,250	2,400	2,200	49,921

[1] Preliminary. [2] Estimate. [3] Forecast. *Source: Foreign Agricultural Service, U.S. Department of Agriculture (FAS-USDA)*

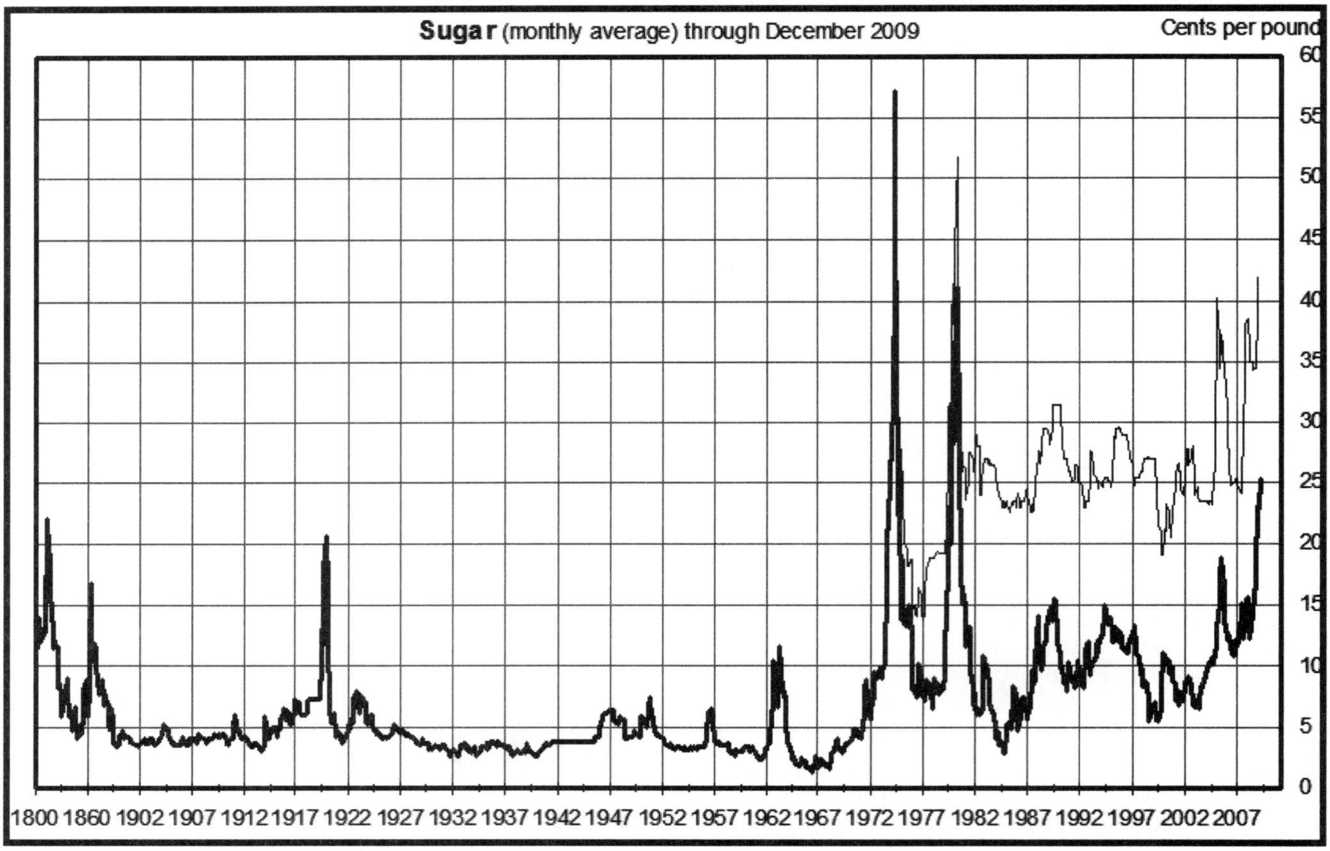

Centrifugal Sugar (Raw Value) Exported From Selected Countries In Thousands of Metric Tons

Year	Australia	Brazil	Colombia	Cuba	Dominican Republic	European Union	Guate-mala	India	Mauritius	South Africa	Swazi-land	Thailand	World Total
2000-01	3,056	7,700	965	2,932	185	6,607	1,190	1,360	555	1,580	287	3,394	38,260
2001-02	3,594	11,600	1,085	3,070	185	4,793	1,310	1,130	628	1,235	208	4,157	42,332
2002-03	4,114	14,000	1,306	1,798	185	5,600	1,335	1,410	542	1,296	278	5,280	47,270
2003-04	4,157	15,240	1,200	1,942	185	4,900	1,335	250	587	1,025	285	4,860	46,562
2004-05	4,447	18,020	1,231	770	185	6,028	1,386	40	581	1,010	298	3,115	46,909
2005-06	4,208	17,090	988	730	251	8,345	1,391	1,510	548	1,230	320	2,242	49,884
2006-07	3,860	20,850	942	800	225	2,439	1,500	2,680	505	1,267	358	4,705	51,227
2007-08[1]	3,700	19,500	661	1,025	217	1,656	1,333	5,830	466	1,154	350	4,914	51,433
2008-09[2]	3,522	21,550	630	730	217	1,105	1,490	190	476	1,000	350	5,500	48,180
2009-10[3]	3,700	23,850	1,035	800	217	1,475	1,515	10	490	900	350	5,800	51,277

[1] Preliminary. [2] Estimate. [3] Forecast. *Source: Foreign Agricultural Service, U.S. Department of Agriculture (FAS-USDA)*

Average Wholesale Price of Refined Beet Sugar[2]--Midwest Market In Cents Per Pound

Year	Jan.	Feb.	Mar.	Apr.	May	June	July	Aug.	Sept.	Oct.	Nov.	Dec.	Average
2000	23.38	22.25	21.50	21.00	19.75	19.00	19.00	19.00	20.70	21.25	21.00	21.80	20.80
2001	23.13	22.75	22.00	20.50	21.38	21.90	22.50	22.50	24.63	25.75	26.20	26.50	23.31
2002	26.75	26.00	25.95	24.63	24.50	24.00	24.00	25.40	26.25	26.75	27.40	27.88	25.79
2003	27.80	26.50	27.13	27.63	28.00	28.00	27.63	25.50	24.00	24.70	23.94	23.63	26.21
2004	23.70	23.50	23.50	23.50	23.50	23.50	23.50	23.50	23.50	23.50	23.38	23.20	23.48
2005	23.50	23.50	23.25	23.80	24.75	25.88	26.00	26.75	40.10	40.00	40.00	36.90	29.54
2006	34.50	36.50	37.10	36.38	35.00	35.00	35.00	34.50	31.20	28.75	27.19	26.10	33.10
2007	25.50	25.00	24.90	25.00	25.00	25.00	25.38	25.60	25.38	25.00	24.50	24.50	25.06
2008	24.13	26.40	28.00	28.00	29.60	33.25	38.00	38.40	38.50	36.20	35.00	35.00	32.54
2009[1]	35.00	35.00	35.00	34.25	34.40	35.50	35.40	38.00	42.00	42.60	45.00	45.00	38.10

[1] Preliminary. [2] These are f.o.b. basis prices in bulk, not delivered prices. *Source: Economic Research Service, U.S. Department of Agriculture (ERS-)*

Average Price of World Raw Sugar[1] In Cents Per Pound

Year	Jan.	Feb.	Mar.	Apr.	May	June	July	Aug.	Sept.	Oct.	Nov.	Dec.	Average
2000	5.64	5.51	5.54	6.48	7.33	8.72	10.18	11.14	10.35	10.96	10.02	10.23	8.51
2001	10.63	10.26	9.64	9.27	9.96	9.80	9.48	8.77	8.60	7.15	7.80	8.02	9.12
2002	7.96	6.81	7.27	7.12	7.33	7.07	8.02	7.86	8.54	8.84	8.87	8.81	7.88
2003	8.56	9.14	8.50	7.92	7.41	6.85	7.18	7.30	6.70	6.74	6.83	6.95	7.51
2004	6.42	7.01	8.23	8.21	8.08	8.41	9.19	8.99	9.10	9.84	9.65	10.19	8.61
2005	10.33	10.51	10.57	10.19	10.23	10.45	10.89	11.09	11.59	12.40	12.86	15.09	11.35
2006	17.27	18.93	18.01	18.21	17.83	16.19	16.61	13.58	12.42	12.09	12.38	12.47	15.50
2007	11.85	11.63	11.44	10.85	10.78	11.05	12.18	11.66	11.61	11.86	11.83	12.47	11.60
2008	13.75	15.16	14.60	13.68	12.23	13.29	14.90	15.58	14.74	12.99	12.87	12.31	13.84
2009[2]	13.09	13.90	13.83	14.43	16.89	16.94	18.57	22.37	23.11	23.22	22.96	25.28	18.72

[1] Contract No. 11, f.o.b. stowed Caribbean port, including Brazil, bulk spot price. [2] Preliminary. *Source: Economic Research Service, U.S. Department of Agriculture (ERS-USDA)*

Average Price of Raw Sugar in New York (C.I.F., Duty/Free Paid, Contract #12 & #14) In Cents Per Pound

Year	Jan.	Feb.	Mar.	Apr.	May	June	July	Aug.	Sept.	Oct.	Nov.	Dec.	Average
2000	17.70	17.24	18.46	19.43	19.12	19.31	17.64	18.12	18.97	21.15	21.39	20.56	19.09
2001	20.81	21.18	21.40	21.51	21.19	21.04	20.64	21.10	20.87	20.90	21.19	21.43	21.11
2002	21.03	20.69	19.92	19.73	19.52	19.93	20.86	20.91	21.65	21.94	22.22	22.03	20.87
2003	21.62	21.91	22.14	21.87	21.80	21.62	21.32	21.26	21.34	20.92	20.91	20.37	21.42
2004	20.54	20.57	20.86	20.88	20.69	20.03	20.14	20.10	20.47	20.31	20.40	20.55	20.46
2005	20.57	20.36	20.54	21.21	21.96	21.89	21.94	20.49	21.10	21.71	21.83	21.74	21.28
2006	23.61	24.05	23.10	23.56	23.48	23.32	22.44	21.38	21.27	20.22	19.66	19.59	22.14
2007	20.03	20.59	20.85	20.91	21.27	21.33	22.72	21.80	21.42	20.56	20.25	20.12	20.99
2008	20.24	20.21	20.65	20.54	20.83	21.80	23.76	23.15	23.10	21.46	19.83	20.00	21.30
2009[1]	20.15	19.83	19.75	21.58	21.64	22.47	23.02	26.18	28.91	30.48	31.86	33.30	24.93

[1] Preliminary. *Source: Economic Research Service, U.S. Department of Agriculture (ERS-USDA)*

Supply and Utilization of Sugar (Cane and Beet) in the United States In Thousands of Short Tons (Raw Value)

	Supply								Utilization						
	Production			Offshore Receipts								Domestic Disappearance			
Year	Cane	Beet	Total	Foreign	Territories	Total	Beginning Stocks	Total Supply	Total Use	Exports	Net Changes in Invisible Stocks	Refining Loss Adjustment	In Polyhydric Alcohol[4]	Total	Per Capita Pounds
2000-01	4,089	4,680	8,769	1,590	0	1,590	2,216	12,575	10,396	141	113	0	33	10,000	65.5
2001-02	3,985	3,915	7,900	1,535	0	1,535	2,180	11,615	10,087	137	-24	0	33	9,785	64.5
2002-03	3,964	4,462	8,426	1,730	0	1,730	1,528	11,684	10,014	142	161	0	24	9,504	63.3
2003-04	3,957	4,692	8,649	1,750	0	1,750	1,670	12,070	10,172	288	23	0	41	9,678	61.0
2004-05	3,265	4,611	7,876	2,100	0	2,100	1,897	11,873	10,542	259	94	0	48	10,019	61.7
2005-06	2,955	4,444	7,399	3,443	0	3,443	1,332	12,174	10,476	203	-67	0	51	10,184	63.2
2006-07	3,438	5,008	8,445	2,080	0	2,080	1,698	12,223	10,424	422	-132	0	53	9,913	62.5
2007-08[1]	3,431	4,721	8,152	2,620	0	2,620	1,799	12,571	10,912	203	0	0	61	10,506	62.1
2008-09[2]	3,318	4,166	7,484	3,082	0	3,082	1,660	12,226	10,775	137	0	0	46	10,479	65.8
2009-10[3]	3,437	4,400	7,837	2,377	0	2,377	1,451	11,665	10,525	150	0	0	60	10,140	

[1] Preliminary. [2] Estimate. [3] Forecast. [4] Includes feed use. *Source: Economic Research Service, U.S. Department of Agriculture (ERS-USDA)*

Sugar Cane for Sugar & Seed and Production of Cane Sugar and Molasses in the United States

			Production					Farm Value		Sugar Production			Molasses Made	
										Raw Value				
Year	Acreage Harvested (1,000 Acres)	Yield of Cane Per Havested Acre Net Tons	for Sugar (1,000 Tons)	for Seed (1,000 Tons)	Total (1,000 Tons)	Sugar Yield Per Acre (Short Tons)	Farm Price ($ Per Ton)	of Cane Used for Sugar (1,000 Dollars)	of Cane Used for Sugar & Seed (1,000 Dollars)	Total (1,000 Tons)	Per Ton of Cane (In Lbs.)	Refined Basis (1,000 Tons)	Edible (1,000 Gallons)	Total[3] (1,000 Gallons)
2000	1,023.3	35.0	34,291	1,823	36,114	----	26.1	895,917	941,791	----	----	----	----	----
2001	1,027.8	33.7	32,775	1,812	34,587	----	29.0	951,813	1,003,046	----	----	----	----	----
2002	1,023.2	34.7	33,903	1,650	35,553	----	28.4	961,896	1,007,142	----	----	----	----	----
2003	992.3	34.1	31,942	1,916	33,858	----	29.5	943,646	998,269	----	----	----	----	----
2004	938.2	30.9	27,243	1,770	29,013	----	28.3	771,734	821,118	----	----	----	----	----
2005	921.9	28.9	24,728	1,878	26,606	----	28.4	701,920	754,529	----	----	----	----	----
2006	897.7	32.9	27,962	1,602	29,564	----	30.4	849,157	897,601	----	----	----	----	----
2007	879.6	34.1	28,273	1,696	29,969	----	29.4	831,218	880,616	----	----	----	----	----
2008[1]	868.0	31.8	26,131	1,472	27,603	----	29.5	771,134	814,479	----	----	----	----	----
2009[2]	877.7	34.5	28,395	1,870	30,265	----								

[1] Preliminary. [2] Estimate. [3] Excludes edible molasses. *Source: Economic Research Service, U.S. Department of Agriculture (ERS-USDA)*

U.S. Sugar Beets, Beet Sugar, Pulp & Molasses Produced from Sugar Beets and Raw Sugar Spot Prices

Year of Harvest	Acreage: Planted (1,000 Acres)	Acreage: Harvested (1,000 Acres)	Yield Per Harvested Acre (Sh. Tons)	Production (1,000 Tons)	Sugar Yield Per Acre (Sh. Tons)	Price[3] (Dollars)	Farm Value (1,000 $)	Sugar Production: Equivalent Raw Value[4] (1,000 Short Tons)	Sugar Production: Refined Basis (1,000 Short Tons)	Raw Sugar Prices: World[5] Refined #5 (In Cents Per Pound)	Raw Sugar Prices: CSCE #11 World (In Cents Per Pound)	Raw Sugar Prices: CSCE N.Y. Duty Paid (In Cents Per Pound)	Wholesale List Price HFCS (42%) Midwest
2000	1,564	1,373	23.7	32,541	----	34.20	1,113,030	----	----	9.97	8.51	19.09	11.32
2001	1,371	1,243	20.7	25,764	----	39.80	1,025,306	----	----	11.29	9.12	21.11	11.90
2002	1,427	1,361	20.4	27,707	----	39.60	1,097,329	----	----	10.35	7.88	20.87	13.05
2003	1,365	1,348	22.7	30,583	----	41.40	1,270,026	----	----	9.74	7.51	21.42	13.24
2004	1,346	1,307	23.0	30,021	----	36.90	1,109,272	----	----	10.87	8.61	20.46	13.20
2005	1,300	1,243	22.2	27,537	----	43.50	1,193,151	----	----	13.19	11.35	21.28	13.58
2006	1,366	1,304	26.1	34,064	----	44.20	1,506,985	----	----	19.01	15.50	22.14	17.03
2007	1,269	1,247	25.5	31,834	----	42.00	1,337,173	----	----	14.00	11.60	20.99	21.22
2008[1]	1,091	1,005	26.8	26,881	----	48.00	1,289,621	----	----	15.96	13.84	21.30	24.50
2009[2]	1,183	1,145	25.8	29,519						22.13	18.72	24.93	25.88

[1] Preliminary. [2] Estimate. [3] Includes support payments, but excludes Gov't. sugar beet payments. [4] Refined sugar multiplied by factor of 1.07. [5] F.O.B. Europe. *Source: Economic Research Service, U.S. Department of Agriculture (ERS-USDA)*

Sugar Deliveries and Stocks in the United States In Thousands of Short Tons (Raw Value)

Year	Quota Allocation	Actual Imports	Deliveries by Primary Distributors: Cane Sugar Refineries Deliveries	Deliveries by Primary Distributors: Beet Sugar Factories Deliveries	Deliveries by Primary Distributors: Importers of Direct Consumption Sugar	Deliveries by Primary Distributors: Mainland Cane Sugar Mills[3]	Total Deliveries	Total Domestic Consumption	Stocks, Jan. 1: Cane Sugar Refineries	Stocks, Jan. 1: Beet Sugar Factories	Stocks, Jan. 1: CCC	Stocks, Jan. 1: Refiners' Raw	Stocks, Jan. 1: Mainland Cane Mills	Stocks, Jan. 1: Total
2000	----	----	5,508	4,433	36	----	9,977	10,091	208	1,554	0	356	1,737	3,855
2001	----	----	5,172	4,680	58	----	9,911	10,075	262	1,500	767	274	1,533	4,337
2002	----	----	5,407	4,291	109	----	9,808	9,994	288	1,472	634	351	1,781	4,525
2003	----	----	5,232	4,219	60	----	9,511	9,713	298	1,300	246	299	1,289	3,432
2004	----	----	4,989	4,668	64	----	9,722	9,901	326	1,817	0	286	1,659	4,088
2005	----	----	5,136	4,710	197	----	10,043	10,212	368	1,753	28	245	1,635	4,029
2006	----	----	5,230	4,195	577	----	10,002	10,162	328	1,429	0	217	1,382	3,357
2007	----	----	5,124	4,707	206	----	10,037	10,265	452	1,792	0	358	1,437	4,039
2008[1]	----	----	5,083	4,867	778	----	10,728	10,912	406	1,806	0	299	1,500	4,012
2009[2]	----	----	5,476	4,324	943	----		10,909	454	1,184	0	446	1,612	3,695

[1] Preliminary. [2] Estimate. [3] Sugar for direct consumption only. [4] Refined. *Source: Economic Research Service, U.S. Department of Agriculture (ERS-USDA)*

Sugar, Refined--Deliveries to End User in the United States In Thousands of Short Tons

Year	Bakery & Cereal Products	Beverages	Confectionery[2]	Hotels, Restar. & Institutions	Ice Cream & Dairy Products	Canned, Bottled & Frozen Foods	All Other Food Uses	Retail Grocers[3]	Wholesale Grocers[4]	Non-food Uses	Non-Industrial Uses	Industrial Uses	Total Deliveries
2000	2,264	168	1,328	71	499	330	817	1,242	2,241	85	3,893	5,491	9,383
2001	2,273	158	1,316	59	484	310	800	1,255	2,250	74	3,927	5,414	9,341
2002	2,075	189	1,223	53	529	297	725	1,322	2,406	99	4,108	5,136	9,244
2003	2,108	214	1,130	52	548	303	632	1,279	2,387	99	4,039	5,034	9,073
2004	2,180	242	1,125	76	603	315	697	1,267	2,398	91	3,956	5,254	9,210
2005	2,297	237	1,131	115	587	336	606	1,262	2,401	92	4,026	5,286	9,312
2006	2,231	228	1,069	88	553	335	535	1,204	2,389	107	3,864	5,057	8,922
2007	2,398	312	1,110	74	609	360	569	1,211	2,412	103	3,877	5,459	9,336
2008	2,312	340	1,108	115	612	427	676	1,212	2,323	97	3,841	5,572	9,414
2009[1]	2,286	351	1,082	127	577	427	572	1,241	2,352	83	3,899	5,377	9,276

[1] Preliminary. [2] And related products. [3] Chain stores, supermarkets. [4] Jobbers, sugar dealers.
Source: Economic Research Service, U.S. Department of Agriculture (ERS-USDA)

Deliveries[1] of All Sugar by Primary Distributors in the United States, by Quarters In Thousands of Short Tons

Year	First Quarter	Second Quarter	Third Quarter	Fourth Quarter	Total	Year	First Quarter	Second Quarter	Third Quarter	Fourth Quarter	Total
1998	2,233	2,428	2,568	2,458	9,686	2004	2,286	2,368	2,520	2,547	9,722
1999	2,208	2,553	2,655	2,580	9,996	2005	2,335	2,471	2,666	2,571	10,037
2000	2,318	2,484	2,611	2,564	9,977	2006	2,436	2,487	2,690	2,389	10,002
2001	2,370	2,486	2,580	2,474	9,911	2007	2,307	2,535	2,682	2,513	10,037
2002	2,227	2,439	2,645	2,497	9,808	2008	2,513	2,665	2,879	2,670	10,727
2003	2,183	2,360	2,464	2,504	9,511	2009[2]	2,470	2,634	2,846		10,600

[1] Includes for domestic consumption and for export. [2] Preliminary. *Source: Economic Research Service, U.S. Department of Agriculture (ERS-USDA)*

Volume of Trading of World Sugar #11 Futures in New York In Contracts

Year	Jan.	Feb.	Mar.	Apr.	May	June	July	Aug.	Sept.	Oct.	Nov.	Dec.	Total
2000	422.5	609.8	501.1	617.6	523.9	717.7	376.8	420.6	622.4	507.6	371.8	242.0	5,934
2001	410.5	545.5	380.6	567.9	427.0	515.6	356.5	419.1	447.3	348.9	414.0	317.4	5,150
2002	568.8	629.5	417.3	693.6	412.2	610.3	529.5	381.0	756.0	402.8	432.1	340.6	6,174
2003	566.0	797.6	443.8	729.5	489.2	719.8	535.9	545.9	760.2	475.3	403.1	674.4	7,141
2004	513.6	1,018.7	1,181.1	993.7	617.3	1,100.6	614.6	679.5	1,248.7	626.5	539.5	632.7	9,767
2005	981.5	1,279.3	957.1	1,258.6	657.6	1,366.8	779.2	1,198.3	1,803.5	915.8	816.6	992.8	13,007
2006	1,444.2	1,601.2	1,092.2	1,467.4	1,147.7	1,459.1	825.0	1,278.6	1,746.7	1,095.7	918.7	1,024.0	15,101
2007	1,322.9	2,189.7	1,659.6	2,023.2	1,819.5	2,679.8	1,559.7	1,326.6	2,175.7	1,565.3	1,452.1	1,489.7	21,264
2008	3,566.7	3,280.8	2,237.7	2,889.5	1,941.8	3,067.4	1,820.2	1,721.4	2,540.9	1,629.9	1,085.5	1,238.1	27,020
2009	1,624.6	2,040.3	1,867.0	2,995.5	2,229.3	3,359.1	1,741.5	2,833.2	3,219.5	1,824.3	1,576.4	1,989.5	27,300

Contract size = 112,000 lbs. *Source: ICE Futures U.S. (ICE)*

Average Open Interest of World Sugar #11 Futures in New York In Contracts

Year	Jan.	Feb.	Mar.	Apr.	May	June	July	Aug.	Sept.	Oct.	Nov.	Dec.
2000	191,464	199,031	193,554	187,810	201,756	200,973	172,361	171,808	160,809	154,101	148,035	145,760
2001	157,478	158,192	158,448	167,555	131,640	126,426	112,483	128,181	139,915	146,058	163,358	170,710
2002	184,096	205,138	194,541	187,415	157,738	158,276	149,202	170,667	202,144	207,456	207,598	217,904
2003	244,036	265,758	220,971	192,497	170,867	184,257	180,898	196,857	195,200	185,917	200,605	207,995
2004	246,347	269,863	268,250	275,423	267,362	282,842	300,961	309,436	292,917	322,079	304,462	332,803
2005	375,713	391,006	357,056	352,521	355,922	366,568	404,141	473,757	468,737	464,829	478,097	523,820
2006	526,575	501,074	462,871	474,241	490,201	453,021	457,301	479,420	493,931	447,817	503,364	563,844
2007	632,783	695,426	652,346	686,648	738,708	695,249	674,318	667,523	656,128	681,403	763,910	835,526
2008	1,035,301	1,013,324	973,541	939,615	915,325	885,082	809,433	804,956	774,839	664,164	636,078	644,852
2009	664,303	656,033	644,829	681,177	703,355	764,799	735,556	838,638	821,646	770,085	772,808	813,238

Contract size = 112,000 lbs. *Source: ICE Futures U.S. (ICE)*

Sulfur

Sulfur (symbol S) is an odorless, tasteless, light yellow, nonmetallic element. As early as 2000 BC, Egyptians used sulfur compounds to bleach fabric. The Chinese used sulfur as an essential component when they developed gunpowder in the 13th century.

Sulfur is widely found in both its free and combined states. Free sulfur is found mixed with gypsum and pumice stone in volcanic regions. Sulfur dioxide is an air pollutant released from the combustion of fossil fuels. The most important use of sulfur is the production of sulfur compounds. Sulfur is used in skin ointments, matches, dyes, gunpowder, and phosphoric acid.

Supply – World production of all forms of sulfur in 2009 rose +1.0% yr/yr to a new record high production of 70.300 million metric tons. The world's largest producers of sulfur are the U.S with 14% of world production, Canada with 13%, China with 12%, and Russia with 10%. U.S. production of sulfur in 2009 rose by +3.7% yr/yr to 9.800 million metric tons. That was up from the 37-year low of 9.070 in 2006.

Demand – U.S. consumption of all forms of sulfur fell by -18.4% in 2009 to 10.200 million metric tons, but still above the 2-decade low of 10.900 million metric tons seen in 2001. U.S. consumption of elemental sulfur rose +2.9% in 2008 (latest data available) to 10.600 million metric tons. U.S. consumption of sulfuric acid fell by -4.8% yr/yr in 2007 to 8.330 million metric tons.

Trade – U.S. exports of recovered sulfur in 2008 (latest data available) rose +3.5% yr/yr to 954,000 metric tons, further up from the 15-year low of 635,000 metric tons in 2006. U.S. imports of recovered sulfur in 2008 rose by +2.4% yr/yr to a new record high of 3.000 million metric tons.

World Production of Sulfur (All Forms) In Thousands of Metric Tons

Year	Canada	China	France	Germany	Iraq	Japan	Mexico	Poland	Russia	Saudi Arabia	Spain	United States	World Total
2002	8,925	5,980	1,030	2,499	----	3,191	1,465	1,220	6,500	2,360	685	9,270	62,000
2003	9,028	6,500	1,420	2,362	----	3,232	1,591	1,231	6,720	2,180	651	9,600	64,100
2004	9,101	7,150	1,405	2,094	----	3,158	1,825	1,271	6,920	2,249	651	10,100	66,200
2005	8,974	7,710	1,372	2,185	----	3,256	1,717	1,252	6,950	2,717	616	9,500	67,000
2006	9,082	7,760	1,366	2,286	----	3,293	1,774	1,280	6,950	2,900	601	9,070	66,900
2007	8,967	8,460	1,306	2,300	----	3,200	1,770	1,324	7,050	3,100	601	9,090	68,400
2008[1]	9,280	8,610	1,310	2,310	----	3,270	1,740	1,280	7,170	3,160	601	9,450	69,600
2009[2]	9,300	8,500	1,300	2,400	----	3,300	1,750	1,200	7,200	3,200	600	9,800	70,300

[1] Preliminary. [2] Estimate. *Source: U.S. Geological Survey (USGS)*

Salient Statistics of Sulfur in the United States In Thousands of Metric Tons (Sulfur Content)

	Production of											Sales Value of Shipments F.O.B. Mine/Plant		
	Elemental Sulfur													
	Native	Recovered												
Year	Sulfur[3] - Frasch	Petroleum & Cole	Natural Gas	Total	Total Elemental Sulfur	By-product Sulfuric Acid[4]	Other Sulf. Acid Compounds	Imports Sulfuric Acid[4]	Exports Sulfuric Acid[4]	Producer Stocks, Dec. 31[5]	Apparent Consumption (All Forms)	Frasch	Recovered	Average Total
2002	----	6,750	1,760	8,500	772	----	9,270	1,060	147	181	11,500	----	----	11.82
2003	----	6,970	1,950	8,970	683	----	9,650	908	205	206	11,900	----	----	28.70
2004	----	7,390	1,990	9,380	739	----	10,100	2,400	204	185	12,800	----	----	32.62
2005	----	6,940	1,850	8,790	711	----	9,500	2,680	338	160	12,400	----	----	30.88
2006	----	6,960	1,440	8,390	674	----	9,050	2,430	248	221	12,000	----	----	32.85
2007	----	7,000	1,280	8,280	817	----	9,100	2,610	336	187	11,900	----	----	36.29
2008[1]	----	7,430	1,160	8,690	753	----	9,450			200	12,500	----	----	262.32
2009[2]	----			9,000	810	----	9,800				10,200	----	----	10.00

Sulfur Consumption & Foreign Trade of the United States In Thousands of Metric Tons (Sulfur Content)

	Consumption			Sulfuric Acid Sold or Used, by End Use[2]						Foreign Trade					
										Exports			Imports		
Year	Native Sulfur (Frasch)	Recovered Sulfur	Total Elemental Form	Pulpmills & Paper Products	Inorganic Chemicals[3]	Synthetic Rubber & Plastic	Phosphatic Fertilizers	Petroleum Refining[4]	Frasch	Frasch	Recovered	Value $1,000	Frasch	Recovered	Value $1,000
2000	W	11,100	11,100	9,620	136	152	68	7,110	497	----	762	53,700	----	2,330	39,400
2001	W	9,520	9,520	9,530	194	158	68	6,840	591	----	675	48,800	----	1,730	22,100
2002	W	10,400	10,400	8,380	122	27	66	6,660	90	----	687	40,000	----	2,560	26,800
2003	W	10,900	10,900	10,100	225	71	82	6,660	140	----	840	54,400	----	2,870	70,600
2004	W	11,300	11,300	9,290	272	154	70	6,870	248	----	949	63,300	----	2,850	76,800
2005	W	10,900	10,900	9,680	267	312	64	7,000	188	----	684	55,200	----	2,820	70,500
2006	W	10,600	10,600	8,750	246	426	250	6,220	262	----	635	43,800	----	2,950	70,400
2007[1]	W	10,300	10,300	8,330	245	245	117	6,280	264	----	922	84,800	----	2,930	79,400

[1] Preliminary. [2] Sulfur equivalent. [3] Including inorganic pigments, paints & allied products, and other inorganic chemicals & products.
[4] Including other petroleum and coal products. W = Withheld proprietary data. NA = Not available. *Source: U.S. Geological Survey (USGS)*

Sunflowerseed, Meal and Oil

Sunflowers are native to South and North America, but are now grown almost worldwide. Sunflower-seed oil accounts for approximately 14% of the world production of seed oils. Sunflower varieties that are commercially grown contain from 39% to 49% oil in the seed. Sunflower crops produce about 50 bushels of seed per acre on average, which yields approximately 50 gallons of oil.

Sunflower-seed oil accounts for around 80% of the value of the sunflower crop. Refined sunflower-seed oil is edible and used primarily as a salad and cooking oil and in margarine. Crude sunflower-seed oil is used industrially for making soaps, candles, varnishes, and detergents. Sunflower-seed oil contains 93% of the energy of U.S. No. 2 diesel fuel and is being explored as a potential alternate fuel source in diesel engines. Sunflower meal is used in livestock feed and when fed to poultry, increases the yield of eggs. Sunflower seeds are also used for birdfeed and as a snack for humans.

Prices – The average monthly price received by U.S. farmers for sunflower seeds in the first five months of the 2009-10 marketing year (September 2009 through August 2010) fell -33.50% to $14.74 per hundred pounds, down from the 2007-08 record high of $23.08 per hundred pounds.

Supply – World sunflower-seed production in the 2008-09 marketing year (latest data available) rose +14.2% yr/yr to 33.198 million metric tons. The world's largest sunflower-seed producers are the former USSR with 43% of world production, Argentina with 9%, China with 6%, U.S with 5%, and France and India both with a little less than 5%.

U.S. production of sunflower seeds in 2008-09 rose by +19.4% yr/yr to 1.553 million metric tons, but that still less than half the record production level of 3.309 million metric tons posted in 1979-80. U.S. farmers harvested 1.954 million acres of sunflowers in 2009-10, down -18.5% yr/yr, further down from the 9-year high of 2.610 million acres posted in 2005-06. U.S sunflower yield in 2009-10 was up +8.8% to a new record high of 15.54 hundred pounds per acre.

Demand – Total U.S. disappearance of sunflower seeds in 2008-09 rose +6.8% yr/yr to 1.501 million metric tons, of which 46% went to crushing for oil and meal, 42% went to non-oil and seed use, and 13% went to exports.

Trade – World sunflower-seed exports in 2008-09 rose +64.6% yr/yr to 2.180 million metric tons. The world's largest exporters are the former USSR which accounted for 40% of world exports in 2008-09 and the U.S. which accounted for 8% of world exports.

World Production of Sunflowerseed In Thousands of Metric Tons

Crop Year	Argentina	Bulgaria	China	France	Hungary	India	Romania	Africa	Spain	Turkey	States	USSR	Total
1999-00	5,760	606	1,765	1,868	793	694	1,301	531	579	820	1,969	7,396	26,718
2000-01	2,970	425	1,954	1,833	484	646	721	638	848	630	1,608	7,824	23,099
2001-02	3,730	405	1,478	1,584	632	726	824	929	871	530	1,551	5,468	21,302
2002-03	3,350	645	1,946	1,497	777	1,060	1,003	643	757	830	1,112	7,836	23,985
2003-04	2,990	789	1,743	1,530	992	1,160	1,506	648	763	560	1,209	10,179	26,984
2004-05	3,730	1,030	1,700	1,462	1,186	1,350	1,220	620	785	640	930	8,830	26,389
2005-06	3,840	8,630	1,830	1,510	1,108	1,490	1,180	520	381	780	1,720	12,132	30,282
2006-07	3,120	1,060	1,850	1,440	1,100	1,450	1,390	300	607	820	997	12,697	30,114
2007-08[1]	4,600	635	1,800	1,311	950	1,460	700	872	703	670	1,309	10,754	29,073
2008-09[2]	2,900	1,000	1,850	1,615	1,450	1,150	1,160	875	822	850	1,553	14,225	33,198

[1] Preliminary. [2] Forecast. *Source: Economic Research Service, U.S. Department of Agriculture (ERS-USDA)*

World Imports and Exports of Sunflowerseed In Thousands of Metric Tons

	Imports						Exports						
Crop Year	France	Germany	Netherlands	Spain	Turkey	World Total	Argentina	France	Hungary	Former USSR	United States	Uraguay	World Total
1999-00	128	124	576	443	486	2,772	265	27	23	1,295	168	28	2,620
2000-01	174	193	413	368	322	2,460	94	11	6	1,865	153	21	2,462
2001-02	43	58	180	172	164	1,202	342	24	14	186	176	130	1,184
2002-03	62	65	148	151	287	1,462	232	3	19	577	123	223	1,586
2003-04	202	60	167	218	630	2,287	45	25	14	1,374	138	127	2,307
2004-05	5	71	24	188	518	1,300	99	20	52	131	117	134	1,186
2005-06	28	63	90	235	391	1,514	45	9	31	664	155	59	1,547
2006-07	49	73	64	233	495	1,947	63	5	42	606	156	13	1,918
2007-08[1]	9	73	55	64	529	1,307	41	5	51	130	167	38	1,324
2008-09[2]	87	64	60	95	460	2,159	32	11	50	865	165	40	2,180

[1] Preliminary. [2] Forecast. *Source: Economic Research Service, U.S. Department of Agriculture (ERS-USDA)*

SUNFLOWERSEED, MEAL AND OIL

Sunflowerseed Statistics in the United States — In Thousands of Metric Tons

Crop Year Beginning Sept. 1	Acres Harvested (1,000)	Harvested Yield Per CWT	Farm Price ($/Metric Ton)	Value of Production (Million $)	Supply: Stocks, Sept. 1	Supply: Production	Supply: Imports	Supply: Total Supply	Disappearance: Crush	Disappearance: Exports	Disappearance: Non-Oil Use & Seed	Disappearance: Total Disappearance
2002-03	2,167	11.31	267	294.6	109	1,112	98	1,319	319	166	634	1,119
2003-04	2,197	12.13	267	316.2	199	1,209	90	1,498	627	170	538	1,335
2004-05	1,711	11.98	302	272.7	163	930	44	1,137	276	140	631	1,047
2005-06	2,610	15.40	267	487.7	90	1,822	39	1,952	566	178	852	1,596
2006-07	1,770	12.11	320	308.8	356	972	112	1,440	659	182	463	1,303
2007-08	2,012	14.26	478	614.7	137	1,301	87	1,526	683	200	523	1,405
2008-09[1]	2,396	14.29	481	704.1	120	1,553	70	1,742	661	183	675	1,519
2009-10[2]	1,954	15.54	320	443.2	223	1,377	54	1,655	680	175	648	1,503

[1] Preliminary. [2] Forecast. *Source: Economic Research Service, U.S. Department of Agriculture (ERS-USDA)*

World Production of Sunflowerseed Oil and Meal — In Thousands of Metric Tons

Year	Oil: Argentina	Oil: France	Oil: Spain	Oil: Turkey	Oil: Ex-USSR	Oil: World Total	Meal: Argentina	Meal: France	Meal: Spain	Meal: Turkey	Meal: United States	Meal: Ex-USSR	Meal: World Total
2001-02	1,308	471	444	299	2,083	7,415	1,268	604	516	336	364	2,104	8,545
2002-03	1,368	487	454	385	2,928	8,653	1,342	599	527	489	173	2,851	9,832
2003-04	1,204	565	459	486	3,394	9,551	1,184	734	534	616	305	3,385	10,982
2004-05	1,507	416	457	451	3,293	9,381	1,509	508	531	572	138	3,431	10,771
2005-06	1,631	400	421	464	4,634	10,969	1,653	494	490	589	299	4,523	12,204
2006-07	1,315	453	410	496	5,004	11,247	1,407	556	476	629	325	4,977	12,686
2007-08[1]	1,575	443	344	459	4,105	10,104	1,609	484	400	601	342	4,225	11,503
2008-09[2]	1,413	503	440	508	5,382	12,047	1,418	595	512	645	328	5,339	13,447

[1] Preliminary. [2] Forecast. *Source: Economic Research Service, U.S. Department of Agriculture (ERS-USDA)*

Sunflower Oil Statistics in the United States — In Thousands of Metric Tons

Crop Year Beginning Sept. 1	Supply: Stocks, Oct. 1	Supply: Production	Supply: Imports	Supply: Total Supply	Disappearance: Exports	Disappearance: Domestic Use	Disappearance: Total Disappearance	Price $ Per Metric Ton (Crude Mpls.)
2002-03	10	134	28	172	51	108	160	721
2003-04	12	264	12	287	107	162	269	736
2004-05	18	116	34	168	57	102	158	938
2005-06	10	238	26	273	95	154	249	893
2006-07	25	277	71	372	77	268	345	1,242
2007-08	27	287	47	361	77	272	349	1,978
2008-09[1]	12	295	30	337	91	196	287	1,170
2009-10[2]	50	276	14	340	82	231	312	1,160

[1] Preliminary. [2] Forecast. *Source: Economic Research Service, U.S. Department of Agriculture (ERS-USDA)*

Sunflower Meal Statistics in the United States — In Thousands of Metric Tons

Crop Year Beginning Sept. 1	Supply: Stocks, Oct. 1	Supply: Production	Supply: Imports	Supply: Total Supply	Disappearance: Exports	Disappearance: Domestic Use	Disappearance: Total Disappearance	Price USD Per Metric Ton 28% Protein
2002-03	5	153	63	221	3	213	221	101
2003-04	5	301	20	326	12	309	326	125
2004-05	5	133	0	138	3	130	138	91
2005-06	5	272	5	282	6	271	282	88
2006-07	5	316	20	341	13	323	341	114
2007-08	5	328	0	333	17	311	333	183
2008-09[1]	5	331	0	336	7	324	336	172
2009-10[2]	5	313	0	318	9	304	118	185

[1] Preliminary. [2] Forecast. *Source: Economic Research Service, U.S. Department of Agriculture (ERS-USDA)*

Average Price Received by Farmers for Sunflower[2] in the United States — In Dollars Per Hundred Pounds (Cwt.)

Year	Jan.	Feb.	Mar.	Apr.	May	June	July	Aug.	Sept.	Oct.	Nov.	Dec.	Average
2004-05	12.90	12.40	12.80	13.40	13.70	15.00	15.00	15.10	15.40	15.20	15.20	14.40	14.21
2005-06	13.20	12.80	12.20	12.20	11.40	11.20	11.50	11.90	11.80	12.30	12.00	12.40	12.08
2006-07	11.70	12.10	12.50	13.60	13.80	14.90	15.60	15.90	16.60	17.00	18.20	18.40	15.03
2007-08	17.70	17.80	18.30	19.20	19.10	24.20	25.90	24.50	27.40	28.10	28.40	26.40	23.08
2008-09	28.20	25.30	23.10	22.80	22.10	22.60	22.60	20.10	21.60	18.60	17.70	20.90	22.13
2009-10[1]	13.90	16.20	14.10	14.70	15.70	14.90							14.92

[1] Preliminary. [2] KS, MN, ND and SD average. *Source: Economic Research Service, U.S. Department of Agriculture (ERS-USDA)*

Tall Oil

Tall oil is a product of the paper and pulping industry. Crude tall oil is the major byproduct of the kraft or sulfate processing of pinewood. Crude tall oil starts as tall oil soap which is separated from recovered black liquor in the kraft pulping process. The tall oil soap is acidified to yield crude tall oil. The resulting tall oil is then fractionated to produce fatty acids, rosin, and pitch. Crude tall oil contains 40-50 percent fatty acids such as oleic and linoleic acids; 5-10 percent sterols, alcohols, and other neutral components. The demand is for the tall oil rosin and fatty acids which are used to produce adhesives, coatings, and ink resins. The products find use in lubricants, soaps, linoleum, flotation and waterproofing agents, paints, varnishes, and drying oils.

Since tall oil and its production are derived from the paper and pulping industry, the amount of tall oil produced is related in part to the pulp industry and in part to the U.S. economy.

Consumption of Tall Oil in Inedible Products in the United States In Millions of Pounds

Year	Jan.	Feb.	Mar.	Apr.	May	June	July	Aug.	Sept.	Oct.	Nov.	Dec.	Total
2001	97.7	96.4	104.4	101.6	105.1	100.7	99.9	98.3	102.4	81.4	87.7	74.4	1,150
2002	93.4	132.9	115.0	121.3	109.3	121.6	128.5	130.2	121.5	141.9	115.5	118.6	1,450
2003	136.1	119.9	136.9	126.3	121.7	121.9	119.3	111.6	131.4	124.1	104.9	120.1	1,474
2004	126.8	109.4	136.1	123.7	135.7	160.5	166.9	140.8	125.3	124.6	129.4	110.7	1,590
2005	134.9	115.4	124.5	97.3	144.4	128.3	125.0	127.5	115.6	137.0	120.3	118.2	1,488
2006	120.4	112.1	135.8	120.2	153.2	131.0	140.6	144.3	134.3	129.6	134.8	133.2	1,590
2007	130.9	126.6	117.7	127.0	130.7	128.7	131.2	129.9	128.5	131.1	128.6	123.8	1,535
2008	135.8	131.8	127.4	130.8	144.0	145.9	144.5	151.0	141.2	148.5	127.6	103.7	1,632
2009[1]	117.1	102.4	103.6	96.2	110.3	110.0	115.0	129.3	115.9	125.8	123.5	107.0	1,356

[1] Preliminary. *Source: Bureau of the Census, U.S. Department of Commerce*

Production of Crude Tall Oil in the United States In Millions of Pounds

Year	Oct.	Nov.	Dec.	Jan.	Feb.	Mar.	Apr.	May	June	July	Aug.	Sept.	Total
2001-02	99.1	100.7	86.5	101.8	93.7	105.5	104.2	96.0	88.5	94.7	103.6	91.4	1,165.6
2002-03	102.5	87.3	101.8	108.7	89.8	111.5	108.3	99.6	91.8	109.2	100.8	97.1	1,208.6
2003-04	102.1	87.9	109.0	113.7	96.1	112.1	102.8	106.8	99.2	94.4	108.9	104.1	1,236.9
2004-05	88.1	93.7	99.6	110.0	97.9	109.4	107.3	109.8	101.5	101.0	101.0	98.9	1,218.1
2005-06	95.5	92.1	100.3	103.9	103.4	108.1	110.4	117.6	101.4	104.6	109.7	99.7	1,246.8
2006-07	104.8	103.7	108.5	107.5	105.0	104.5	121.5	125.5	98.1	108.5	122.2	107.9	1,317.7
2007-08	100.0	99.7	107.2	113.6	112.1	115.9	117.2	112.9	103.2	102.8	107.4	105.0	1,297.0
2008-09	107.6	100.7	87.0	90.3	93.0	107.2	105.9	104.7	103.1	94.0	106.6	102.2	1,202.2
2009-10[1]	105.8	102.0	103.2										1,244.3

[1] Preliminary. *Source: Bureau of the Census, U.S. Department of Commerce*

Stocks of Crude Tall Oil in the United States, on First of Month In Millions of Pounds

Year	Oct.	Nov.	Dec.	Jan.	Feb.	Mar.	Apr.	May	June	July	Aug.	Sept.
2001-02	132.7	125.6	142.1	127.9	135.8	155.2	165.6	177.4	190.7	175.4	161.8	155.1
2002-03	160.2	154.1	155.7	160.5	176.0	167.4	156.3	173.4	163.7	180.3	199.3	209.5
2003-04	210.7	207.3	203.0	210.2	209.6	216.3	205.3	207.1	194.1	190.5	196.1	162.2
2004-05	174.1	140.3	124.4	95.0	109.9	108.8	134.0	132.1	130.5	126.3	122.0	121.8
2005-06	107.5	97.3	83.4	81.5	102.8	118.7	82.6	88.3	94.7	93.9	82.0	92.7
2006-07	73.9	61.7	72.1	75.7	97.8	83.4	115.7	132.5	156.1	162.5	164.3	198.4
2007-08	186.8	185.6	168.5	177.0	176.3	162.9	156.3	187.7	182.2	145.1	137.8	138.6
2008-09	135.7	110.8	95.7	110.8	102.2	112.5	116.2	135.3	134.3	138.3	126.2	108.8
2009-10[1]	98.3	85.9	104.2	87.2								

[1] Preliminary. *Source: Bureau of the Census, U.S. Department of Commerce*

Stocks of Refined Tall Oil in the United States, on First of Month In Millions of Pounds

Year	Oct.	Nov.	Dec.	Jan.	Feb.	Mar.	Apr.	May	June	July	Aug.	Sept.
2001-02	22.4	17.2	17.1	19.9	20.7	20.9	21.5	22.7	20.9	18.6	18.4	16.0
2002-03	13.3	16.5	18.7	20.1	20.1	18.6	20.4	19.7	15.8	14.5	13.5	13.9
2003-04	13.1	20.1	19.6	19.9	19.2	13.7	14.3	12.7	16.3	14.2	16.6	17.7
2004-05	14.8	16.6	16.9	17.0	15.2	20.4	16.0	18.2	16.9	17.2	14.5	17.5
2005-06	18.7	28.1	26.9	32.9	28.5	W	6.1	5.3	6.6	4.5	5.9	6.9
2006-07	7.7	7.5	5.3	5.3	5.8	7.3	7.5	7.3	7.9	9.2	6.6	4.2
2007-08	5.9	6.7	5.2	6.4	6.0	7.5	6.8	7.3	6.5	5.4	5.3	8.2
2008-09	6.6	5.0	6.6	5.2	5.3	4.1	5.0	4.3	3.8	6.0	4.1	5.6
2009-10[1]	5.2	7.4	7.4	6.9								

[1] Preliminary. W = Withheld proprietary data. *Source: Bureau of the Census, U.S. Department of Commerce*

Tallow and Greases

Tallow and grease are derived from processing (rendering) the fat of cattle. Tallow is used to produce both edible and inedible products. Edible tallow products include margarine, cooking oil, and baking products. Inedible tallow products include soap, candles, and lubricants. Production of tallow and greases is directly related to the number of cattle produced. Those countries that are the leading cattle producers are also the largest producers of tallow. The American Fats and Oils Association provides specifications for a variety of different types of tallow and grease, including edible tallow, lard (edible), top white tallow, all beef packer tallow, extra fancy tallow, fancy tallow, bleachable fancy tallow, prime tallow, choice white grease, and yellow grease. The specifications include such characteristics as the melting point, color, density, moisture content, insoluble impurities, and others.

Prices – The monthly average price of tallow (inedible, No. 1 Packers-Prime, delivered Chicago) in 2009 fell -26.4% yr/yr to 25.16 cents per pound, down from last year's record high of 34.18 cents per pound. The wholesale price of inedible tallow in 2009 fell -27.6% yr/yr to 27.54 cents per pound, down from last year's record high of 38.02 cents per pound.

Supply – World production of tallow and greases (edible and inedible) in 2008 (latest data), fell by -0.1% yr/yr to 8.529 million metric tons, down from last year's record high of 8.617 million metric tons. The world's largest producer of tallow and greases by far is the U.S. with 45% of world production, followed by Brazil with 7%, Australia with 6%, and Canada with 3%.

U.S. production of edible tallow in 2008 fell –0.6% yr/yr to 1.779 billion pounds, down from the 2002 record high of 1.974. U.S. production of inedible tallow and greases in 2009 fell -6.1% yr/yr to 5.847 billion pounds, which was well below the record high of 7.156 billion pounds posted in 2002.

Demand – U.S. consumption of inedible tallow and greases in 2009 fell 15.6% yr/yr to 1.769 billion pounds, of which virtually all went for animal feed. U.S. consumption of edible tallow in 2008 (latest data) rose +1.4% yr/yr to 1.423 billion pounds, down from the 2006 record high of 1.583 billion pounds. U.S. per capita consumption of edible tallow in 2007 fell –28.2% to 2.8 pounds per person per year, down from the 2000 and 2004 record high of 4.0 pounds.

Trade – U.S. exports of inedible tallow and grease in 2009 rose +5.2% yr/yr to 335.4 million pounds, and accounted for 5.4% of total U.S. supply. U.S. exports of edible tallow in 2008 (latest data) rose +2.0% yr/yr to 396 million pounds, and accounted for 27.8% of U.S. supply.

World Production of Tallow and Greases (Edible and Inedible) In Thousands of Metric Tons

Year	Argentina	Australia	Brazil	Canada	France	Germany	Korea	Netherlands	New Zealand	Russia	United Kingdom	United States	World Total
1999	160	471	394	285	160	140	18	178	167	186	158	3,979	8,171
2000	161	503	430	293	151	132	17	171	170	178	148	3,948	8,202
2001	142	507	446	296	140	126	15	151	173	171	115	3,503	7,689
2002	147	469	474	305	154	124	14	125	162	178	123	3,826	8,062
2003	154	456	493	289	164	121	15	121	174	183	120	3,707	8,015
2004	178	486	528	343	166	124	15	113	192	181	124	3,714	8,247
2005	184	493	554	339	171	121	15	106	168	176	128	3,797	8,389
2006	181	503	574	314	183	124	16	107	187	178	135	3,808	8,491
2007[1]	194	498	589	306	177	128	16	111	184	184	140	3,818	8,537
2008[2]	188	509	569	292	176	131	16	122	189	182	138	3,804	8,529

[1] Preliminary. [2] Forecast. *Source: Foreign Agricultural Service, U.S. Department of Agriculture (FAS-USDA)*

Salient Statistics of Tallow and Greases (Inedible) in the United States In Millions of Pounds

	Supply				Consumption			Wholesale Prices, Cents Per Lb.	
Year	Production	Stocks, Jan. 1	Total	Exports	Soap	Feed	Total	Edible, (Loose) Chicago	Inedible, Chicago No. 1
2000	7,035	405	7,440	791	146	2,727	2,849	11.7	10.0
2001	6,870	347	7,217	616	107	2,834	2,843	13.7	12.0
2002	7,156	327	7,482	384	W	2,886	2,886	14.8	13.5
2003	6,246	240	6,486	307	W	2,434	2,434	20.3	18.3
2004	6,173	282	6,455	336	W	2,536	2,536	19.8	18.0
2005	6,204	281	6,485	276	W	2,456	2,456	19.0	17.5
2006	6,460	309	6,769	331	W	2,585	2,585	18.6	16.9
2007	6,369	291	6,661	361	W	2,385	2,385	30.7	27.8
2008[1]	6,224	350	6,573	319	W	2,095	2,095	38.0	34.2
2009[2]	5,847	315	6,162	335	W	1,769	1,769	27.5	25.2

[1] Preliminary. [2] Forecast. *Source: Foreign Agricultural Service, U.S. Department of Agriculture (FAS-USDA)*

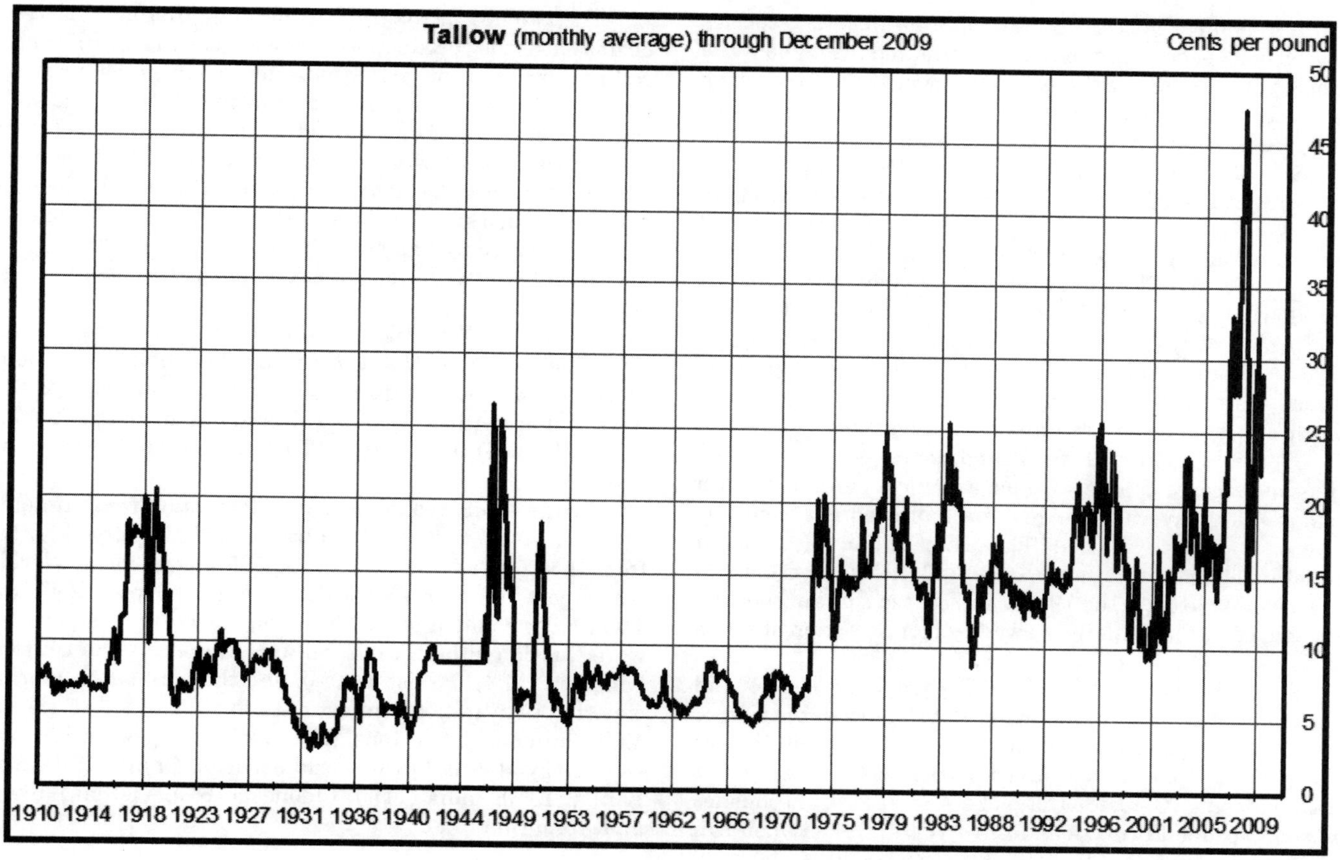

Supply and Disappearance of Edible Tallow in the United States

In Millions of Pounds, Rendered Basis

	Supply			Disappearance					
Year	Stocks, Jan. 1	Production	Total Supply	Domestic Disap-pearance	Exports	Total Disap-pearance	Direct Use	Baking or Frying Fats	Per Capita (Lbs.)
1999	39	1,729	1,775	1,425	317	1,742	998	262	3.6
2000	33	1,825	1,866	1,581	248	1,829	1,125	283	4.0
2001	37	1,792	1,859	1,455	364	1,819	869	W	3.0
2002	40	1,974	2,023	1,486	511	1,998	974	W	3.4
2003	25	1,966	1,996	1,552	420	1,972	1,108	W	3.8
2004	24	1,818	1,842	1,565	255	1,820	1,163	W	4.0
2005	22	1,813	1,836	1,518	293	1,811	1,116	W	3.8
2006	25	1,861	1,893	1,583	275	1,858	1,160	W	3.9
2007[1]	35	1,789	1,831	1,404	388	1,792	889	W	2.8
2008[2]	39	1,779	1,848	1,423	396	1,819	661		

[1] Preliminary. [2] Forecast. W = Withheld. *Sources: Economic Research Service, U.S. Department of Agriculture (ERS-USDA); Bureau of the Census, U.S. Department of Commerce*

Average Wholesale Price of Tallow, Inedible, No. 1 Packers (Prime), Delivered, Chicago

In Cents Per Pound

Year	Jan.	Feb.	Mar.	Apr.	May	June	July	Aug.	Sept.	Oct.	Nov.	Dec.	Average
2000	11.89	10.14	10.67	10.21	11.60	10.74	9.19	9.48	10.07	10.05	9.35	11.23	10.39
2001	12.17	9.46	9.62	10.26	10.19	12.35	15.44	16.83	13.75	11.24	10.60	12.34	12.02
2002	10.00	10.54	12.64	11.06	11.59	15.47	14.80	14.00	14.23	13.98	15.91	18.08	13.53
2003	17.13	15.65	16.60	16.54	16.48	17.30	16.08	15.85	18.70	22.78	23.37	23.08	18.30
2004	23.23	16.72	17.80	21.05	18.01	18.08	19.55	16.92	17.20	14.33	15.61	16.97	17.96
2005	16.20	16.03	18.73	20.95	19.38	18.23	15.11	15.31	17.54	17.40	17.96	16.67	17.46
2006	17.52	17.05	14.98	13.47	14.77	15.27	17.05	17.35	15.59	17.71	20.42	21.46	16.89
2007	22.02	20.78	21.74	25.04	29.16	33.08	32.58	27.67	30.14	31.29	32.87	27.64	27.83
2008	32.19	36.08	40.03	39.66	40.02	45.36	47.55	40.14	36.17	24.39	14.29	14.23	34.18
2009[1]	22.86	19.57	16.72	21.83	25.80	29.53	26.17	31.75	30.44	22.27	25.89	29.09	25.16

[1] Preliminary. *Sources: Economic Research Service, U.S. Department of Agriculture (ERS-USDA)*

Tea

Tea is the common name for a family of mostly woody flowering plants. The tea family contains about 600 species placed in 28 genera and they are distributed throughout the tropical and subtropical areas, with most species occurring in eastern Asia and South America. The tea plant is native to Southeast Asia. There are more than 3,000 varieties of tea, each with its own distinct character, and each is generally named for the area in which it is grown. Tea may have been consumed in China as long ago as 2700 BC and certainly since 1000 BC. In 2737 BC, the Chinese Emperor Shen Nung, according to Chinese mythology, was a scholar and herbalist. While his servant boiled drinking water, a leaf from the wild tea tree he was sitting under dropped into the water and Shen Nung decided to try the brew. Today, half the world's population drinks tea. Tea is the world's most popular beverage next to water.

Tea is a healthful drink and contains antioxidants, fluoride, niacin, folic acid, and as much vitamin C as a lemon. The average 5 oz. cup of brewed tea contains approximately 40 to 60 milligrams of caffeine (compared to 80 to 115 mg in brewed coffee). Decaffeinated tea has been available since the 1980s. Herbal tea contains no true tea leaves but is actually brewed from a collection of herbs and spices.

Tea grows mainly between the tropic of Cancer and the tropic of Capricorn, requiring 40 to 50 inches of rain per year and a temperature ideally between 50 to 86 degrees Fahrenheit. In order to rejuvenate the bush and keep it at a convenient height for the pickers to access, the bushes must be pruned every four to five years. A tea bush can produce tea for 50 to 70 years, but after 50 years, the yield is reduced.

The two key factors in determining different varieties of tea are the production process (sorting, withering, rolling, fermentation, and drying methods) and the growing conditions (geographical region, growing altitude, and soil type). Black tea, often referred to as fully fermented tea, is produced by allowing picked tea leaves to wither and ferment for up to 24 hours. After fermenting, the leaves are fired, which stops oxidation. Green tea, or unfermented tea, is produced by immediately and completely drying the leaves and omitting the oxidization process, thus allowing the tea to remain green in color.

Supply – World production of tea in 2007 (latest available data) rose +5.6% to a record high of 3.871 million metric tons. The world's largest producers of tea in 2007 were China (with 31% of world production), India (25%), Sri Lanka (8%), Kenya (8%), Turkey (5%), and Indonesia (5%).

Trade – U.S. tea imports in 2009 (annualized through May) fell -0.1% to 209,312 metric tons, down very slightly from the 2008 record high of 209,585 metric tons. World tea imports in 2006 (latest data available) rose +2.4% to 1.471 million metric tons. The world's largest tea importers were Russia (with 12% of total world imports), the United Kingdom (11%), Pakistan (9%), and the U.S. (7%). World exports of tea in 2006 (latest data available) fell -5.1% to 1.629 million metric tons. The world's largest exporters were Kenya (with 20% of world exports), China (18%), Sri Lanka (13%), India (11%), Indonesia (6%), Vietnam (6%), and Argentina (4%).

World Tea Production, in Major Producing Countries In Metric Tons

Year	Argentina	Bangladesh	China	India	Indonesia	Iran	Japan	Kenya	Malawi	Sri Lanka	Turkey	Ex-USSR[2]	World Total
2002	70,457	58,000	765,719	854,000	162,194	63,900	84,000	287,045	39,200	310,000	135,000	26,730	3,165,442
2003	69,866	57,500	788,815	838,000	169,818	63,650	91,900	293,670	41,693	303,230	153,800	26,271	3,212,516
2004	70,389	57,580	855,422	878,000	171,200	40,250	100,700	324,600	50,090	308,090	201,663	22,288	3,409,055
2005	67,871	57,580	953,660	893,000	177,700	59,180	100,000	328,500	38,000	317,200	217,540	24,752	3,603,197
2006	72,129	58,000	1,047,345	928,000	146,858	59,180	91,800	310,580	45,009	310,800	201,866	8,405	3,649,170
2007	76,000	58,500	1,183,002	949,220	150,224	60,000	94,100	369,600	46,000	305,220	206,160	8,614	3,902,881
2008[1]	76,000	59,000	1,257,384	805,180	150,851	60,000	94,100	345,800	46,000	318,470	1,100,257	8,643	4,735,961

[1] Preliminary. [2] Mostly Georgia and Azerbaijan. *Sources: Foreign Agricultural Service, U.S. Department of Agriculture (FAS-USDA); Food and Agriculture Organization of the United Nations (FAO-UN)*

World Exports of Tea from Producing Countries In Metric Tons

Year	Argentina	Bangladesh	Brazil	China	India	Indonesia	Kenya	Malawi	Papua New Guinea	Sri Lanka	Vietnam	Zimbabwe	Total
2001	58,110	6,400	4,082	252,204	177,603	99,797	207,244	36,587	8,800	293,524	67,900	6,162	1,450,128
2002	57,643	3,964	3,979	254,875	181,617	100,185	288,300	42,596	5,200	290,500	77,000	18,855	1,580,485
2003	59,062	7,348	4,209	262,663	174,246	88,176	293,751	36,924	6,600	297,003	58,600	13,355	1,529,678
2004	67,819	10,635	3,593	282,643	174,728	98,572	284,309	46,200	8,100	298,909	104,000	14,968	1,634,576
2005	68,270	12,560	3,407	288,814	159,121	102,294	347,971	44,600	6,900	307,793	88,000	4,825	1,718,521
2006[1]	72,056	7,842	3,238	288,625	181,326	95,339	325,066	27,503	6,600	204,240	105,000	11,532	1,629,468
2007[2]	75,767	5,269	3,298	292,199	193,459	83,659	374,329	54,397	6,400	190,203	114,000	6,840	1,701,607

[1] Preliminary. [2] Estimate. *Source: Food and Agriculture Organization of the United Nations (FAO-UN)*

Imports of Tea in the United States In Metric Tons

Year	Jan.	Feb.	Mar.	Apr.	May	June	July	Aug.	Sept.	Oct.	Nov.	Dec.	Total
2004	15,089	14,716	18,355	19,279	18,813	18,782	16,511	14,116	14,530	13,851	14,876	14,698	193,615
2005	16,728	13,977	17,877	20,502	16,696	18,445	15,714	14,146	12,775	14,376	11,276	11,750	184,261
2006	15,660	14,545	17,307	19,003	22,038	20,057	15,690	16,378	14,631	11,807	15,432	13,337	195,885
2007	14,094	12,830	17,312	19,165	19,425	21,156	16,623	15,829	16,136	14,533	15,498	13,964	196,566
2008	15,856	18,000	20,244	21,732	19,547	18,369	17,654	16,458	17,202	16,786	14,354	13,383	209,585
2009[1]	15,448	14,748	19,662	18,148	19,208	18,670	17,093	18,668	17,550	13,216	13,428		202,733

[1] Preliminary. *Source: Foreign Agricultural Service, U.S. Department of Agriculture (FAS-USDA)*

Tin

Tin (symbol Sn) is a silvery-white, lustrous gray metallic element. Tin is soft, pliable and has a highly crystalline structure. When a tin bar is bent or broken, a crackling sound called a "tin cry" is produced due to the breaking of the tin crystals. People have been using tin for at least 5,500 years. Tin has been found in the tombs of ancient Egyptians. In ancient times, tin and lead were considered different forms of the same metal. Tin was exported to Europe in large quantities from Cornwall, England, during the Roman period, from approximately 2100 BC to 1500 BC. Cornwall was one of the world's leading sources of tin for much of its known history and into the late 1800s.

The principal ore of tin is the mineral cassiterite, which is found in Malaya, Bolivia, Indonesia, Thailand, and Nigeria. About 80% of the world's tin deposits occur in unconsolidated placer deposits in riverbeds and valleys, or on the sea floor, with only about 20% occurring as primary hard-rock lodes. Tin deposits are generally small and are almost always found closely allied to the granite from which it originates. Tin is also recovered as a by-product of mining tungsten, tantalum, and lead. After extraction, tin ore is ground and washed to remove impurities, roasted to oxidize the sulfides of iron and copper, washed a second time, and then reduced by carbon in a reverberatory furnace. Electrolysis may also be used to purify tin.

Pure tin, rarely used by itself, was used as currency in the form of tin blocks and was considered legal tender for taxes in Phuket, Thailand, until 1932. Tin is used in the manufacture of coatings for steel containers used to preserve food and beverages. Tin is also used in solder alloys, electroplating, ceramics, and in plastic. The world's major tin research and development laboratory, ITRI Ltd, is funded by companies that produce and consume tin. The focus of the research efforts have been on possible new uses for tin that would take advantage of tin's relative non-toxicity to replace other metals in various products. Some of the replacements could be lead-free solders, antimony-free flame-retardant chemicals, and lead-free shotgun pellets. No tin is currently mined in the U.S.

Tin futures and options trade on the London Metal Exchange (LME). Tin has traded on the LME since 1877 and the standard tin contract began in 1912. The futures contract calls for the delivery of 5 metric tons of tin ingots of at least 99.85% purity. The contract trades in terms of U.S. dollars per metric ton.

Prices – The average monthly price of tin (straights) in New York in 2009 fell by -26.7% yr/yr to \$8.34 per pound, down from the 2008 record high of \$11.38 per pound. The 2009 price of \$8.34 is almost three times the 3-decade low of \$2.83 per pound seen as recently as 2002. The average monthly price of ex-dock tin in New York in 2009 fell -25.9% yr/yr to \$6.37 per pound, and that is over three times the 3-decade low of \$1.99 per pound posted in 2002.

Supply – World mine production of tin in 2009 rose by +2.7% yr/yr to 307,000 metric tons, but still below the 2007 record high of 326,000 metric tons. The world's largest mine producers of tin are China with 37% of world production in 2009, Indonesia with 33%, and Peru with 12%. World smelter production of tin fell -1.4% in 2007 (latest data available) to 346,000 metric tons, down from the 2006 record high of 351,000 metric tons. The world's largest producers of smelted tin are China with 44% of world production in 2007, Indonesia with 22%, and Malaysia with 7%. The U.S. does not mine tin, and therefore supply consists only of scrap and imports. U.S. tin recovery in 2007 rose +2.9% to 7,010 metric tons, up from the 2006 record low of 6,810 metric tons.

Demand – U.S. consumption of tin (pig) in 2008 fell -27.2% to a record low of 31,853 metric tons. The breakdown of U.S. consumption of tin by finished products in 2008 shows that the largest consuming industry of tin is solder (with 33% of consumption), followed by tin plate (23%), chemicals (20%), and bronze and brass (9%).

Trade – The U.S. relied on imports for 80% of its tin consumption in 2008. U.S. imports of unwrought tin metal in 2007 (latest data) fell 20.1% to 34,600 metric tons, which is an 11-year low. The largest sources of U.S. imports in 2007 were Bolivia (13% of total imports), China (12%), Brazil (8%), and Indonesia (5%). U.S. exports of tin in 2007 rose +16.8% yr/yr to 6,410 metric tons.

World Mine Production of Tin In Metric Tons (Contained Tin)

Year	Australia	Bolivia	Brazil	China	Indonesia	Malaysia	Nigeria	Peru	Portugal	Russia	Thailand	United Kingdom	World Total
2000	9,146	12,464	14,200	99,400	51,629	6,307	2,760	70,901	1,227	2,500	1,930	----	278,000
2001	9,602	12,352	13,016	95,000	61,862	4,972	2,870	38,182	1,174	2,000	1,950	----	246,000
2002	7,017	15,242	12,063	62,000	88,142	4,215	790	38,815	574	1,300	1,130	----	235,000
2003	3,864	16,755	12,217	102,000	71,694	3,359	1,800	40,202	218	2,000	793	----	261,000
2004	1,196	17,569	12,202	118,000	65,772	2,745	1,000	67,675	220	2,500	586	----	304,000
2005	2,819	18,640	11,739	126,000	78,404	2,857	1,300	42,145	243	3,000	158	----	305,000
2006	1,478	17,669	8,528	126,000	80,933	2,398	1,400	38,470	25	3,000	190	----	296,000
2007	2,085	17,500	9,500	135,000	102,000	2,500	1,500	39,019	25	2,500	120	----	326,000
2008[1]	1,800	17,000	12,000	110,000	96,000	2,200	----	39,000	100	1,500	100	----	299,000
2009[2]	2,000	16,000	12,000	115,000	100,000	2,000	----	38,000	100	2,000	100	----	307,000

[1] Preliminary. [2] Estimate. *Source: U.S. Geological Survey (USGS)*

World Smelter Production of Primary Tin In Metric Tons

Year	Australia	Bolivia	Brazil	China	Indo-nesia	Japan	Malaysia	Mexico	Russia	South Africa	Spain	Thailand	World Total
1998	655	11,102	14,900	79,300	53,401	500	27,201	1,078	3,000	----	100	15,353	247,000
1999	600	11,166	12,787	90,800	49,105	568	28,913	1,262	4,500	----	50	17,306	267,000
2000	775	9,353	13,825	112,000	46,432	593	26,228	1,204	4,800	----	----	17,076	288,000
2001	1,171	11,292	12,168	105,000	53,470	668	30,417	1,789	4,569	----	----	22,387	289,000
2002	791	10,976	11,675	82,000	67,455	659	30,887	1,748	4,615	----	----	17,548	280,000
2003	597	12,836	10,761	98,000	66,284	662	18,250	1,769	4,100	----	----	15,400	282,000
2004	467	13,627	11,512	115,000	49,872	707	33,914	25	4,570	----	----	20,800	306,000
2005	594	13,841	8,986	122,000	65,300	754	36,924	17	5,000	----	----	31,600	344,000
2006	572	14,100	8,780	132,000	77,400	854	22,850	25	4,980	----	----	27,540	351,000
2007[1]	118	13,500	9,000	151,000	77,600	874	25,000	25	3,800	----	----	20,400	346,000

[1] Preliminary. *Source: U.S. Geological Survey (USGS)*

United States Foreign Trade of Tin In Metric Tons

		Imports for Consumption											
		Concentrates[2] (Ore)			Unwruoght Tin Metal								
Year	Exports (Metal)	Total All Ore	Bolivia	Peru	Total All Metal	Bolivia	Brazil	China	Indo-nesia	Malaysia	Singa-pore	Thailand	Kingdom
1999	6,770	----	----	----	47,500	3,850	4,700	13,900	7,930	944	60	20	60
2000	6,640	----	----	----	44,900	6,330	5,860	10,200	5,320	214	20	----	514
2001	4,350	----	----	----	37,500	6,040	5,510	6,360	3,880	674	145	----	118
2002	2,940	----	----	----	42,200	6,150	4,840	7,600	3,340	122	----	----	2
2003	3,690	----	----	----	37,100	5,720	3,000	4,340	3,070	490	----	----	143
2004	3,650	----	----	----	47,600	5,060	4,330	5,310	4,660	6,600	----	500	97
2005	4,330	----	----	----	37,500	5,400	2,150	4,510	5,220	1,530	194	45	67
2006	5,490	----	----	----	43,300	8,160	1,300	4,440	4,600	245	1,090	210	1,370
2007	6,410	----	----	----	34,600	4,340	2,600	4,230	1,680	14	1,730	15	881
2008[1]	9,800	----	----	----	36,300	4,980	1,570	2,380	2,000	1,740	706	1,670	225

[1] Preliminary. [2] Tin content. *Source: U.S. Geological Survey (USGS)*

Consumption (Total) of Tin (Pig) in the United States In Metric Tons

Year	Jan.	Feb.	Mar.	Apr.	May	June	July	Aug.	Sept.	Oct.	Nov.	Dec.	Total
2000	4,362	4,466	4,430	4,377	4,466	4,470	4,398	4,476	4,397	4,460	4,244	4,157	47,040
2001	4,252	4,185	4,095	4,141	4,148	4,128	4,055	4,163	4,153	4,197	4,129	3,974	49,620
2002	3,965	3,866	3,868	3,819	4,087	3,887	3,887	3,842	3,835	3,966	3,822	3,811	46,655
2003	3,814	3,808	3,851	3,891	3,701	3,814	3,841	3,850	3,803	3,816	3,764	3,887	45,840
2004	3,851	3,632	3,887	3,837	3,874	4,001	3,844	3,871	3,850	3,870	3,947	3,772	46,236
2005	4,097	3,990	4,027	3,874	3,825	3,918	3,806	3,900	3,824	3,833	3,849	3,699	46,642
2006	3,877	3,694	3,508	3,439	3,447	3,580	3,475	3,420	3,456	3,442	3,407	3,356	42,101
2007	3,381	3,342	3,601	3,365	3,716	3,811	3,585	4,070	3,910	3,734	3,586	3,628	43,729
2008	2,653	2,626	2,630	2,693	2,639	2,641	2,665	2,697	2,687	2,607	2,662	2,653	31,853
2009[1]	2,642	2,546	2,610	2,573	2,525	2,521							30,834

[1] Preliminary. *Source: U.S. Geological Survey (USGS)*

Tin Stocks (Pig-Industrial) in the United States, on First of Month In Metric Tons

Year	Jan.	Feb.	Mar.	Apr.	May	June	July	Aug.	Sept.	Oct.	Nov.	Dec.
2000	8,300	8,330	7,960	7,580	7,810	7,930	8,090	8,240	7,820	8,210	7,200	7,970
2001	8,140	8,330	8,360	8,460	8,270	8,640	8,760	8,760	8,920	9,030	7,630	7,470
2002	7,700	7,320	7,020	6,990	6,870	6,600	6,540	6,590	6,670	7,130	6,880	6,950
2003	7,280	6,980	6,690	6,640	6,390	6,400	6,380	6,420	6,250	6,180	6,190	6,340
2004	6,520	6,010	6,130	6,280	5,850	6,000	5,900	6,290	6,110	6,030	5,900	6,410
2005	6,140	5,260	5,570	5,420	5,770	5,400	5,670	5,830	5,540	5,350	5,330	5,410
2006	5,400	5,380	5,330	5,350	5,400	5,380	5,420	5,400	5,740	5,650	5,650	5,830
2007	5,700	5,970	6,030	6,030	5,860	5,570	5,270	5,270	5,260	5,310	5,920	6,000
2008	6,140	8,070	8,280	8,020	8,000	7,970	7,930	7,960	7,980	7,960	7,990	7,940
2009[1]	7,970	7,890	7,660	7,640	7,620	7,640	7,570					

[1] Preliminary. *Source: U.S. Geological Survey (USGS)*

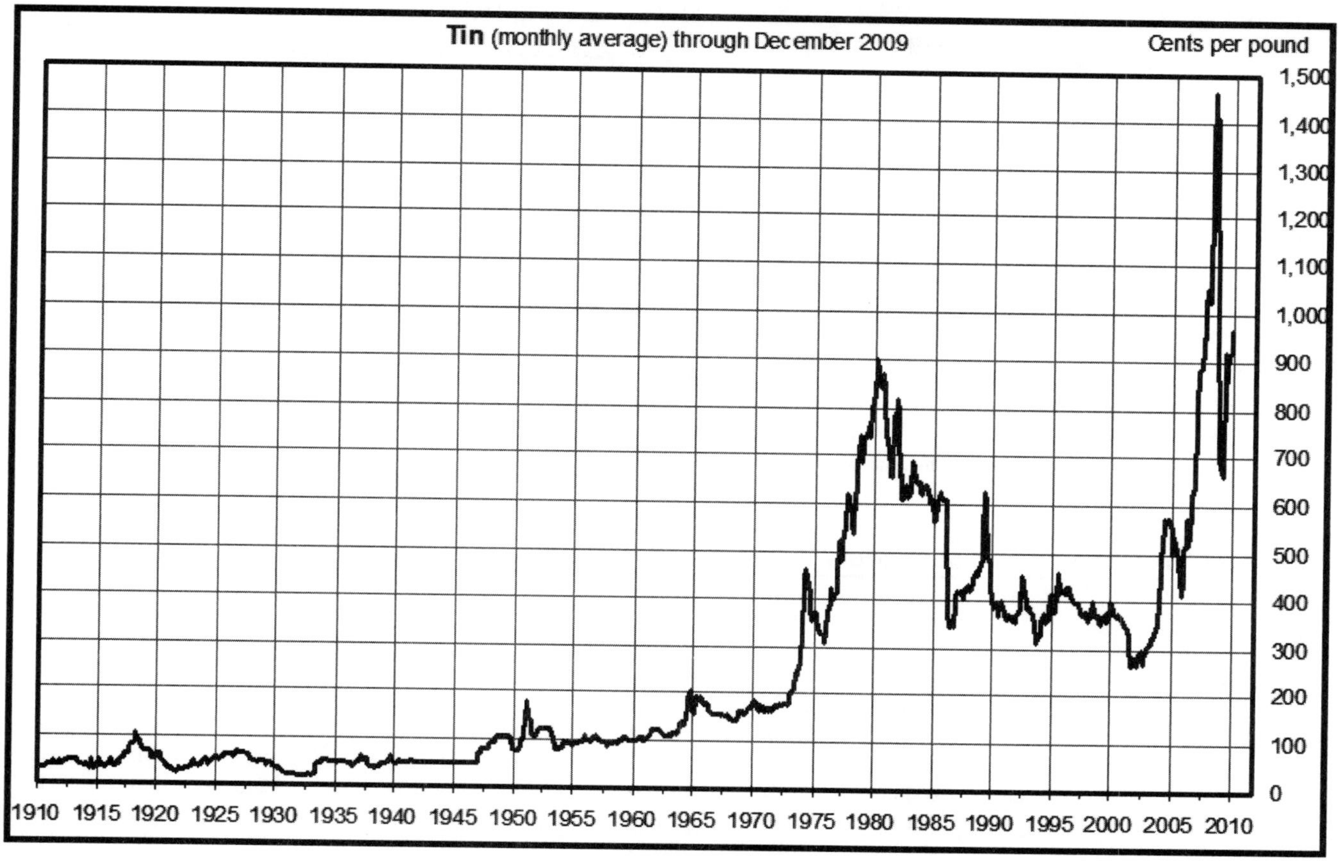

Average Price of Ex-Dock Tin in New York[1] In Cents Per Pound

Year	Jan.	Feb.	Mar.	Apr.	May	June	July	Aug.	Sept.	Oct.	Nov.	Dec.	Average
2000	283.63	271.70	263.42	259.59	259.70	260.16	257.77	255.92	262.54	254.56	253.64	252.19	261.24
2001	249.32	246.91	243.14	238.33	238.53	231.14	210.17	188.42	179.53	181.38	194.77	195.90	216.46
2002	189.23	183.23	187.65	195.36	201.95	208.01	211.51	188.36	193.79	206.67	205.94	206.63	199.15
2003	212.68	217.98	219.58	217.90	225.40	223.69	225.81	229.58	233.59	248.22	252.93	285.40	232.73
2004	305.34	313.55	357.66	418.57	449.29	438.72	439.24	437.68	438.91	436.80	439.24	414.16	407.43
2005	376.37	393.05	408.41	395.40	394.68	367.81	347.78	347.96	331.01	313.73	300.96	323.43	358.38
2006	338.27	373.87	378.76	420.35	420.53	376.76	400.64	404.26	428.83	461.66	475.57	524.69	417.02
2007	535.46	604.14	648.82	656.53	661.04	659.63	689.99	705.01	700.45	748.39	777.74	756.89	678.67
2008	760.82	800.60	917.15	1,001.99	1,108.30	1,027.62	1,070.50	930.65	850.83	672.97	646.77	532.54	860.06
2009	539.32	523.68	508.12	554.44	646.09	702.56	657.47	694.15	695.88	701.13	698.44	721.79	636.92

Source: American Metal Market (AMM)

Average Price of Tin (Straights) in New York In Cents Per Pound

Year	Jan.	Feb.	Mar.	Apr.	May	June	July	Aug.	Sept.	Oct.	Nov.	Dec.	Average
2000	400.90	384.13	372.50	368.42	370.13	370.81	366.49	364.65	375.25	363.54	362.94	360.68	371.70
2001	356.37	352.87	348.19	341.59	340.61	329.68	302.57	276.55	263.17	264.88	281.23	279.46	311.43
2002	271.59	263.91	270.54	280.98	288.74	296.02	299.39	269.30	277.60	293.79	292.40	292.95	283.10
2003	304.44	312.32	314.52	312.26	321.92	319.67	322.10	327.16	332.21	350.90	356.46	396.46	330.87
2004	422.33	433.50	485.99	557.29	575.39	570.99	565.68	568.14	572.72	573.79	577.07	550.97	537.82
2005	500.93	519.61	539.30	522.71	522.18	492.64	467.71	466.67	444.80	426.36	411.23	440.30	479.54
2006	464.54	509.45	519.31	574.53	575.57	517.52	548.29	552.06	583.57	623.07	644.19	705.62	568.14
2007	719.05	811.07	873.03	883.74	886.54	884.67	931.50	954.26	949.21	1,012.46	1,049.78	1,025.36	915.06
2008	1,025.05	1,071.97	1,224.20	1,325.79	1,461.85	1,357.22	1,410.60	1,229.27	1,124.02	887.70	841.86	694.41	1,137.83
2009	711.20	686.02	664.21	724.55	841.83	920.39	862.04	902.14	899.35	911.42	922.75	964.64	834.21

Source: U.S. Geological Survey (USGS)

Tin Plate Production & Tin Recovered in the United States In Metric Tons

Year	----- Tin Content of Tinplate Produced ----- Tinplate Waste	Tinplate (All Forms)	Tin Content (Met. Ton)	Tin per Tonne of Plate (Kilograms)	Tin Recovered from Scrap by Form of Recovery: Tin Metal	Bronze & Brass	Solder	Type Metal	Babbitt	Antimonial Lead	Chemical Compounds	Misc.[2]	Grand Total
	----- Gross Weight -----												
1999	W	1,750,000	9,080	5.2	----	----	----	----	----	----	----	----	----
2000	119,000	1,320,000	8,800	6.7	----	----	----	----	----	----	----	----	----
2001	97,800	2,000,000	7,800	3.9	----	----	----	----	----	----	----	----	----
2002	45,900	2,450,000	7,750	3.2	----	----	----	----	----	----	----	----	----
2003	W	2,500,000	7,750	3.1	----	----	----	----	----	----	----	----	----
2004	W	2,550,000	7,700	3.0	----	----	----	----	----	----	----	----	----
2005	W	2,270,000	7,670	3.4	----	----	----	----	----	----	----	----	----
2006	56,400	2,130,000	6,810	3.2	----	----	----	----	----	----	----	----	----
2007	58,900	1,780,000	7,010	3.9	----	----	----	----	----	----	----	----	----
2008[1]	30,900	2,280,000	6,690	2.9	----	----	----	----	----	----	----	----	----

[1] Preliminary. [2] Includes foil, terne metal, cable lead, and items indicated by symbol "W". W = Withheld. NA = Not available.
Source: U.S. Geological Survey (USGS)

Consumption of Primary and Secondary Tin in the United States In Metric Tons

Year	Net Import Reliance as a % of Apparent Consumption	Stocks, Jan. 1[2]	Net Receipts: Primary	Secondary	Scrap	Total	Available Supply	Stocks, Dec. 31 (Total Available Less Total Processed)	Total Processed	Consumed in Manufacturing Products
1998	85	9,280	39,900	2,490	6,240	48,600	57,900	12,000	45,800	45,700
1999	85	9,290	40,500	2,790	6,360	49,700	58,900	11,900	47,000	46,900
2000	86	8,910	41,400	2,990	6,050	50,400	59,300	12,200	47,100	47,000
2001	88	8,830	34,500	2,180	4,770	41,400	50,200	8,220	42,000	41,900
2002	79	8,500	34,200	1,610	4,230	40,100	48,600	8,550	40,000	39,800
2003	89	8,220	32,400	1,380	3,440	37,300	45,500	7,770	37,700	37,400
2004	92	7,680	40,800	4,160	4,350	49,300	57,000	11,800	45,200	44,700
2005	78	8,060	32,500	5,790	3,840	42,200	50,200	9,120	41,000	40,600
2006	79	7,640	29,900	5,040	4,100	39,000	46,600	8,520	38,100	37,700
2007[1]	81	7,230	25,600	4,950	3,030	33,600	40,800	9,140	31,700	31,100

[1] Preliminary. [2] Includes tin in transit in the U.S. NA = Not available. *Source: U.S. Geological Survey (USGS)*

Consumption of Tin in the United States, by Finished Products In Metric Tons (Contained Tin)

Year	Tinplate[2]	Solder	Babbitt	Bronze & Brass	Tinning	Chemicals[3]	Tin Powder	Bar Tin & Anodes	White Metal	Other	Total	Total Primary	Total Secondary
1999	9,150	18,700	1,610	3,410	905	8,220	W	721	943	3,220	46,900	38,000	8,890
2000	8,800	18,800	1,660	3,360	1,200	8,040	W	714	1,260	3,210	47,000	38,100	8,940
2001	7,800	17,000	770	3,430	1,070	7,590	W	570	1,390	2,230	41,900	34,200	7,630
2002	7,750	13,800	1,310	3,040	679	8,400	W	617	1,320	2,920	39,800	34,000	5,830
2003	7,790	10,600	2,570	2,600	833	8,720	W	852	1,220	2,180	37,400	32,900	4,510
2004	7,700	19,000	728	3,070	798	9,120	W	680	937	2,630	44,700	36,700	7,990
2005	7,250	16,700	554	3,200	790	8,360	W	709	W	3,030	40,600	31,400	9,170
2006	7,110	12,800	484	3,300	696	9,290	W	698	W	1,040	37,700	29,200	8,480
2007	7,010	10,400	604	2,800	451	6,070	W	788	W	1,120	31,100	23,700	7,490
2008[1]	6,690	5,750	459	2,250	322	2,940	227	218	W	389	31,900	21,100	10,800

[1] Preliminary. [2] Includes small quantity of secondary pig tin and tin acquired in chemicals. [3] Including tin oxide.
W = Withheld proprietary data. *Source: U.S. Geological Survey (USGS)*

Titanium

Titanium (symbol Ti) is a silver-white, metallic element used primarily to make light, strong alloys. It ranks ninth in abundance among the elements in the crust of the earth but is never found in the pure state. It occurs as an oxide in various minerals. It was first discovered in 1791 by Rev. William Gregor and was first isolated as a basic element in 1910. Titanium was named after the mythological Greek god Titan for its strength.

Titanium is extremely brittle when cold, but is malleable and ductile at a low red heat, and thus easily fabricated. Due to its strength, low weight, and resistance to corrosion, titanium is used in metallic alloys and as a substitute for aluminum. It is used extensively in the aerospace industry, in desalinization plants, construction, medical implants, paints, pigments, and lacquers.

Prices – The price of the mineral ilmenite, a primary source of titanium, in 2008 rose about +27.4% to $99 per metric ton. The price of titanium metal sponge in 2007 (latest data) traded in the range of $6.33 to $7.06 per pound versus $5.87 to $12.84 in 2006. The price of titanium dioxide pigments (Anatase) in 2005 (latest data available) traded in the range of $.95-$1.00 per pound versus 90-95 cents per pound in 2004.

Supply – World production of titanium ilmenite concentrates in 2008 fell -21.5% yr/yr to 5.640 million metric tons, down from the 2007 record high of 7.180 million metric tons. The world's largest producers of titanium ilmenite concentrates are Australia with 22% of world production in 2008, China (10%), Norway (7%), India (7%), and Vietnam (4%). World production of titanium rutile concentrates in 2008 rose +2.4% yr/yr to 608,000 metric tons, which is a new record high. The world's largest producers are Australia with 51% of world production in 2008 followed by South Africa with 20% and Sierra Leone with 16%.

Demand – U.S. consumption of titanium dioxide pigment in 2008 fell -5.0% yr/yr to 930,000 metric tons, down from 2004's record high of 1.170 million metric tons. U.S. consumption of ilmenite in 2005 (latest data available) fell –12.8% to 1.290 million metric tons, down from 2004's 8-year high of 1.480 million metric tons. U.S. consumption of rutile in 2005 (latest data available) fell 4.7% yr/yr to a 7-year low of 424,000 metric tons.

Trade – U.S. imports of titanium dioxide pigment in 2008 fell by 5.0% yr/yr to 200,000 metric tons, down from the 2005 record high of 341,000 metric tons. U.S. imports of ilmenite in 2005 rose +1.7% yr/yr to 366,000 metric tons.

World Produciton of Titanium Illmenite Concentrates In Thousands of Metric Tons

Year	Australia[2]	Brazil	China	Egypt	India	Malaysia	Norway	Ukraine	United States	Vietnam	World Total	-- Titaniferous Slag[4] --- Canada	Africa
1999	2,008	96	180	130	378	128	600	537	W	91	4,150	950	1,168
2000	2,173	123	250	125	380	125	750	436	400	174	4,940	910	1,090
2001	2,047	165	300	125	430	130	750	485	500	180	5,130	1,010	1,025
2002	1,956	177	750	125	460	106	750	512	400	170	5,400	900	973
2003	2,063	218	800	125	562	95	840	421	500	314	5,950	873	1,010
2004	1,965	242	840	125	621	61	860	370	500	550	6,150	863	1,020
2005	2,080	231	900	125	686	38	860	375	500	523	6,330	860	1,020
2006	2,516	231	1,000	125	690	46	850	470	500	605	7,070	930	1,230
2007	2,506	236	1,100	125	700	45	850	500	400	650	7,180	960	1,295
2008[1]	1,250	130	550		378		380	302	200	215	5,640		

[1] Preliminary. [2] Includes leucoxene. [3] Approximately 10% of total production is ilmenite. Beginning in 1988, 25% of Norway's ilmenite production was used to produce slag containing 75% TiO_2. NA = Not available. *Source: U.S. Geological Survey (USGS)*

Salient Statistics of Titanium in the United States In Metric Tons

	--- Titanium Dioxide Pigment ---			------ Ilmenite ------		-- Titanium Slag ---		------- Rutile[4] --------		------ Exports of Titamium Products ------			
Year	Production	Imports[3]	Apparent Consumption	Imports[3]	Consumption	Imports[3]	Consumption	Imports[3]	Consumption	Ores & Concentrates	Scrap	Dioxide & Pigments	Ingots, Billets, Etc.
1999	1,350,000	225,000	1,160,000	1,070,000	1,280,000	678,000	----	344,000	494,000	9,380	8,130	344,000	3,390
2000	1,400,000	218,000	1,150,000	918,000	1,250,000	533,000	----	438,000	537,000	18,900	5,060	423,000	2,980
2001	1,330,000	209,000	1,100,000	1,060,000	1,180,000	594,000	----	325,000	483,000	7,800	7,500	349,000	3,260
2002	1,410,000	231,000	1,110,000	840,000	1,300,000	445,000	----	390,000	487,000	3,810	6,000	485,000	3,460
2003	1,420,000	240,000	1,070,000	804,000	1,300,000	409,000	----	427,000	489,000	10,300	5,320	518,000	3,960
2004	1,540,000	264,000	1,170,000	701,000	1,480,000	457,000	----	360,000	445,000	8,690	9,760	576,000	4,990
2005	1,310,000	341,000	1,130,000	822,000	1,290,000	667,000	----	366,000	424,000	20,900	20,600	486,000	6,350
2006	1,370,000	288,000	1,080,000							32,800	10,800	513,000	7,900
2007[1]	1,440,000	221,000	979,000										
2008[2]	1,500,000	200,000	930,000										

[1] Preliminary. [2] Estimate. [3] For consumption. [4] Natural and synthetic. W = Withheld. *Source: U.S. Geological Survey (USGS)*

World Production of Titanium Rutile Concentrates In Metric Tons

Year	Australia	Brazil	India	Sierra Leone	South Africa	Sri Lanka	Thailand	Ukraine	World Total
2001	206,000	2,270	19,000	----	134,000	----	----	60,000	421,000
2002	218,000	1,878	18,000	----	138,000	----	----	70,000	446,000
2003	173,000	2,303	18,000	----	108,000	----	----	60,000	361,000
2004	162,000	2,117	19,000	----	110,000	----	----	60,000	353,000
2005	177,000	2,069	19,000	----	115,000	----	----	60,000	373,000
2006	233,000	2,100	19,000	73,802	123,000	----	----	60,000	511,000
2007	297,000	3,000	20,000	79,000	108,000	----	----	57,000	564,000
2008[1]	309,000	3,000	20,000	95,000	121,000	----	----	57,000	608,000

[1] Preliminary. NA = Not available. *Source: U.S. Geological Survey (USGS)*

World Production of Titanium Sponge Metal & U.S. Consumption of Titanium Concentrates

	Production of Titanium (In Metric Tons) Sponge Metal[2]						--- U.S. Consumption of Titanium Concentrates, by Products (In Metric Tons) --- Ilmenite (TiO_2 Content)			Rutile (TiO_2 Content)			
Year	China	Japan	Russia	United Kingdom	United States	Total	Pigments	Misc.	Total	Welding Rod Coatings	Pigments	Misc.	Total
2000	----	----	----	----	----	----	1,240,000	13,900	1,250,000	----	513,000	24,100	537,000
2001	----	----	----	----	----	----	1,160,000	15,400	1,180,000	----	455,000	28,500	483,000
2002	----	----	----	----	----	----	1,280,000	16,000	1,300,000	----	464,000	22,900	487,000
2003	----	----	----	----	----	----	1,280,000	16,700	1,300,000	----	466,000	22,500	489,000
2004	----	----	----	----	----	----	1,460,000	19,300	1,480,000	----	418,000	26,700	445,000
2005	----	----	----	----	----	----	1,260,000	34,000	1,390,000	----	394,000	30,000	424,000
2006	----	----	----	----	----	----	NA	NA	1,510,000	----	----	----	----
2007[1]	----	----	----	----	----	----	NA	NA	1,600,000	----	----	----	----

[1] Preliminary. [2] Unconsolidated metal in various forms. [4] Included in Pigments. NA = Not available. W = Withheld.
Source: U.S. Geological Survey (USGS)

Average Prices of Titanium in the United States

Year	Ilmenite FOB Australian Ports[2]	Slag, 85% TiO2 FOB Richards Bay, South Africa	Rutile Large Lots Bulk, FOB U.S. East Coast[3]	Rutile Bagged FOB Australian Ports	Avg. Price of Grade A Titanium Sponge, FOB Shipping Point	Titanium Metal Sponge	Titanium Dioxide Pigments FOB US Plants Anatase	Titanium Dioxide Pigments FOB US Plants Rutile
	Dollars Per Metric Ton				Dollars Per Pound			
2001	$90 - $110	$419.00	$450 - $500	$475 - $565	----	$3.58	$0.92 - $0.94	$1.00 - $1.09
2002	$85 - $100	$445.00	$430 - $470	$400 - $540	----	$3.64	$0.85 - $0.95	$0.85 - $0.95
2003	$80 - $100	$401.00	$415 - $445	$430 - $540	----	$2.72 - $3.95	$0.85 - $0.95	$0.85 - $0.90
2004	$81.00	$347 - $466	$455.00	$550 - $650	----	$3.55 - $6.44	$0.90 - $0.95	$0.90 - $0.95
2005	$80.00	$390 - $555	$470.00	$550 - $650	----	$3.46 - $12.22	$0.95 - $1.00	$0.95 - $1.00
2006	$80.00	$402 - $454	$475.00	$570 - $700	----	$5.87 - $12.84	----	----
2007[1]	$107.00	$418 - $457	$594.00					
2008[2]	$99.00	$404 - $505	$500.00					

[1] Preliminary. [2] Estimate. NA = Not available. *Source: U.S. Geological Survey (USGS)*

Average Price of Titanium[1] in United States In Dollars Per Pound

Year	Jan.	Feb.	Mar.	Apr.	May	June	July	Aug.	Sept.	Oct.	Nov.	Dec.	Average
2004	3.24	3.24	3.24	NA	NA	NA	NA	NA	NA	NA	NA	NA	3.24
2005	NA	NA	NA	NA	NA	NA	NA	NA	3.33	3.33	3.33	3.33	3.33
2006	3.33	3.33	3.33	3.33	3.33	3.33	3.33	3.33	3.33	3.33	3.33	3.33	3.33
2007	6.09	9.76	9.76	9.76	NA	NA	NA	NA	NA	NA	NA	NA	8.84
2008	NA	NA	NA	NA	NA	NA	NA	NA	NA	NA	NA	NA	NA
2009	NA	NA	NA	NA	NA	NA	NA	NA	NA	NA	NA	NA	NA

[1] Sponge. NA = Not available. *Source: American Metal Market (AMM)*

Average Price of Titanium[1] in United States In Dollars Per Pound

Year	Jan.	Feb.	Mar.	Apr.	May	June	July	Aug.	Sept.	Oct.	Nov.	Dec.	Average
2004	4.90	4.90	5.60	5.75	7.61	7.75	7.89	8.50	8.64	9.25	9.25	9.92	7.50
2005	10.60	11.25	11.25	15.44	17.25	20.25	20.25	20.33	22.00	22.00	22.00	22.13	17.90
2006	24.75	24.75	25.53	26.10	27.50	27.58	27.75	27.75	27.75	27.75	27.75	27.75	26.89
2007	27.21	26.50	26.50	25.69	25.32	24.50	24.50	22.15	21.50	20.63	18.90	17.79	23.43
2008	16.62	16.00	15.60	15.50	15.50	15.14	14.95	14.50	14.50	14.50	13.56	13.17	14.96
2009	12.93	12.50	10.50	9.93	9.20	9.00	9.00	9.00	8.92	8.75	8.75	8.75	9.77

[1] Ingot, 6Al - 4V. NA = Not available. *Source: American Metal Market (AMM)*

Tobacco

Tobacco is a member of the nightshade family. It is commercially grown for its leaves and stems, which are rolled into cigars, shredded for use in cigarettes and pipes, processed for chewing, or ground into snuff. Christopher Columbus introduced tobacco cultivation and use to Spain after observing natives from the Americas smoking loosely rolled tobacco-stuffed tobacco leaves.

Tobacco is cured, or dried, after harvesting and then aged to improve its flavor. The four common methods of curing are: air cured, fire cured, sun cured, and flue cured. Flue curing is the fastest method of curing and requires only about a week compared with up to 10 weeks for other methods. Cured tobacco is tied into small bundles of about 20 leaves and aged one to three years.

Virginia tobacco is by far the most popular type used in pipe tobacco since it is the mildest of all blending tobaccos. Approximately 60% of the U.S. tobacco crop is Virginia-type tobacco. Burley tobacco is the next most popular tobacco. It is air-cured, burns slowly and provides a relatively cool smoke. Other tobacco varieties include Perique, Kentucky, Oriental, and Latakia.

Prices – U.S. tobacco farm prices in 2008 (latest data) rose +9.9% to 186.1 cents per pound from 169.3 cents per pound in 2007. That is, however, far below the record high of 198.4 cents per pound posted in 2004.

Supply – World production of tobacco in 2008 (latest data available) rose by +10.5% yr/yr to an eight year high of 6.881 million metric tons. The world's largest producers of tobacco are China with 41% of world production, followed at a distance by Brazil (with 13% of world production), India (8%), and the U.S. (5%). U.S. production in 2008 rose by +2.0% yr/yr to 360,225 metric tons, where it was down by more than half from the 2-decade high of 810,750 metric tons posted in 1997. Tobacco in the U.S. is grown primarily in the Mid-Atlantic States and they account for the vast majority of U.S. production. Specifically, the largest tobacco producing states in the U.S. are North Carolina (with 51% of U.S. production in 2009), Kentucky (25%), Tennessee (6%), Virginia (6%), South Carolina (5%), and Georgia (3%).

Flue-cured tobacco (type 11-14) is the most popular tobacco type grown in the U.S. and U.S. production in 2009 rose by +5.5% yr/yr to 526.450 million pounds. The second most popular type is burley tobacco (type 31), which saw U.S. production in 2007 rise +6.6% to 214.816 million pounds.

Total U.S. production of tobacco in 2009 rose +1.6% yr/yr to 823.290 million pounds, which is less than half of the 2-decade high of 1.787 billion pounds posted in 1997. U.S. farmers have sharply reduced the planting acreage for tobacco. In 2009, harvested tobacco acreage fell by 0.4% yr/yr to 354.140 acres, which is up from the 2005 record low of 297,080 but still far below the 25-year high of 836,230 posted in 1997. Yield in 2009 rose +2.0% to a 15-year high of 2,325 pounds per acre. The farm value of the U.S. tobacco crop in 2009 rose by +11.5% yr/yr to $1.482 billion.

U.S. marketings of flue-cured tobacco (Types 11-14) in the 2006-07 (latest data) marketing year rose by +18.5% yr/yr to 453.8 million pounds. U.S. marketings of burley tobacco (Type 31) in the 2006-07 marketing year rose by +6.9% yr/yr to 217.4 million pounds.

U.S. production of cigarettes in 2006 (latest data) rose by +1.5% to 496.4 billion cigarettes, which was still down sharply from the record high of 754.5 million posted in 1996. U.S. production of cigars rose by +8.2% yr/yr to 3.977 billion in 2006. U.S. production of chewing tobacco in 2006 fell by 3.1% to 38.0 million pounds, which was a record low.

Demand – U.S. per capita consumption of tobacco products in 2006 (latest data) was unchanged at 3.69 pounds per person but there appears to be a shifting from cigarettes to cigars. The 3.69 pounds per capita consumption of tobacco in 2006 is less than half the record high of 9.68 pounds per person that occurred at the beginning of the series in 1970. Per capita cigarette consumption in 2006 fell 1.5% yr/yr to 1,691 cigarettes per person, which was a record low. Per capita consumption of cigars in 2006 rose +1.9% yr/yr to a record high of 47.80 cigars per person. Per capita consumption of loose smoking tobacco in 2006 fell –6.3% yr/yr to 0.15 pounds.

Trade – U.S. tobacco exports in 2004 (latest data available) rose +3.5% yr/yr to 354.0 million pounds, rebounding further from the record low of 325.8 million pounds seen in 2002. Meanwhile, U.S. tobacco imports in 2004 fell –10.9% yr/yr to 561.7 million pounds from the 11-year high of 630.1 million pounds see in 2003. The U.S. exported 111.3 billion cigarettes and 180 million cigars in 2006.

World Production of Leaf Tobacco In Metric Tons

Year	Brazil	Canada	China	Greece	India	Indo-nesia	Italy	Japan	Pakistan	Turkey	United States	Zim-babwe	World Total
1999	629,525	70,215	2,478,295	139,791	736,200	138,000	126,352	64,727	108,800	243,468	586,360	193,183	6,988,557
2000	578,451	53,010	2,563,854	136,593	520,000	146,100	129,937	60,803	107,700	200,280	477,632	227,726	6,690,506
2001	568,505	58,606	2,358,842	142,000	340,000	201,900	130,487	60,600	85,100	144,786	449,760	195,905	6,152,531
2002	670,309	54,550	2,454,105	133,000	550,000	194,500	122,231	58,200	94,500	152,856	398,520	178,408	6,514,371
2003	656,200	46,338	2,262,658	136,000	490,000	200,875	124,985	50,662	88,200	112,158	364,080	102,683	6,025,602
2004	921,281	42,430	2,411,490	133,937	549,900	165,108	117,882	52,659	86,200	133,913	400,060	78,312	6,532,641
2005	889,426	43,000	2,685,743	125,904	549,100	153,470	115,983	47,000	100,500	135,247	290,170	83,230	6,737,148
2006	900,381	43,000	2,746,193	37,386	552,200	146,265	110,000	38,000	112,592	98,137	329,918	44,451	6,665,802
2007[1]	908,679	44,000	2,397,152	30,783	520,000	164,851	100,000	40,000	103,240	74,584	353,177	79,000	6,228,468
2008[2]	850,421	44,000	2,836,725	28,000	520,000	169,668	100,000	40,000	107,765	100,000	360,225	79,000	6,881,434

[1] Preliminary. [2] Estimate. *Source: Food and Agriculture Organization of the United Nations (FAO-UN)*

Production and Consumption of Tobacco Products in the United States

Year	Cigarettes	Cigars[3]	Plug (Chewing Tobacco)	Twist (Chewing Tobacco)	Loose-leaf (Chewing Tobacco)	Total (Chewing Tobacco)	Smoking Tobacco	Snuff[4]	Cigarettes (Consumption[5] of Per Capita[6])	Cigars[3] (Consumption[5] of Per Capita[6])	Cigarettes (Consumption[5] of Per Capita[6])	Cigars[3] (Consumption[5] of Per Capita[6])	Smoking Tobacco (Consumption[5] of Per Capita[6])	Chewing Tobacco (Consumption[5] of Per Capita[6])	Total Products (Consumption[5] of Per Capita[6])
	- Billions -	- Millions -	In Millions of Pounds						Number		In Pounds				
1997	722.8	2,324	3.5	1.0	53.7	58.1	11.4	64.3	2,422	37.3	4.10	.61	.11	.60	4.85
1998	679.7	2,751	3.1	1.0	49.2	53.3	11.7	65.5	2,275	37.1	3.60	.61	.12	.53	4.32
1999	611.5	2,938	2.8	0.9	47.2	50.9	14.7	67.0	2,101	38.5	3.50	.63	.13	.51	4.23
2000	594.1	2,825	2.5	0.8	46.0	49.4	13.6	69.5	2,049	38.0	3.40	.62	.13	.48	4.10
2001	562.8	3,741	2.4	0.8	43.9	47.0	12.8	70.9	2,051	41.2	3.50	.68	.15	.47	4.30
2002	532.0	3,819	2.0	0.7	40.2	43.0	15.5	72.7	1,982	41.8	3.40	.68	.16	.43	4.16
2003	499.4	4,017	1.7	0.7	37.9	40.3	17.8	73.8	1,890	44.5	3.20	.73	.16	.40	3.97
2004	493.5	4,407	1.7	0.7	37.0	39.3	16.1	79.3	1,814	47.9	3.10	.79	.15	.37	3.87
2005[1]	489.0	3,674	1.4	0.6	37.2	39.2	17.4	86.7	1,716	46.9	2.90	.77	.16	.36	3.69
2006[2]	496.4	3,977	1.3	0.5	36.1	38.0	16.5	81.8	1,691	47.8	2.90	.78	.15	.37	3.69

[1] Preliminary. [2] Estimate. [3] Large cigars and cigarillos. [4] Includes loose-leaf. [5] Consumption of tax-paid tobacco products. Unstemmed rocessing weight. [6] 18 years and older. NA = Not available. *Source: Economic Research Service, U.S. Department of Agriculture (ERS-USDA)*

Production of Tobacco in the United States, by States In Thousands of Pounds

Year	Florida	Georgia	Indiana	Kentucky	Maryland	North Carolina	Ohio	Pennsylvania	South Carolina	Tennessee	Virginia	Wisconsin	Total
2000	11,475	68,820	7,980	283,065	8,265	406,500	13,200	10,170	81,260	95,958	56,613	2,255	1,052,999
2001	11,700	64,206	9,450	254,653	3,300	386,920	11,956	6,166	78,400	86,893	63,415	3,619	991,223
2002	11,960	53,000	7,800	222,991	1,800	347,920	9,625	6,815	59,475	71,331	64,407	3,817	871,122
2003	11,000	59,400	8,190	225,042	1,595	299,995	8,745	7,880	63,000	65,632	38,818	4,255	802,560
2004	9,800	46,690	8,610	235,003	1,870	350,560	10,976	8,100	63,450	65,381	67,285	3,541	881,875
2005	5,500	27,760	----	174,260	----	278,900	6,732	10,700	39,900	51,670	40,351	----	645,015
2006	2,860	30,090	----	186,780	----	330,580	7,000	16,790	48,300	49,135	47,322	----	727,897
2007	----	39,775	----	197,040	----	383,420	7,175	18,310	46,125	38,636	46,142	----	787,653
2008	----	33,600	----	205,850	----	390,360	6,970	17,630	39,900	52,380	45,970	----	800,504
2009[1]	----	28,000	----	206,900	----	423,856	6,800	18,660	38,850	49,960	47,435	----	823,290

[1] Preliminary. *Source: Agricultural Statistics Board, U.S. Department of Agriculture (ASB-USDA)*

Salient Statistics of Tobacco in the United States

Year	Acres Harvested 1,000 Acres	Yield Per Acre Pounds	Production Million Pounds	Farm Price cents Lb.	Farm Value Million $	Exports[2] (Tobacco, June - July)	Imports[3] (Tobacco, June - July)	Cigarettes (U. S. Exports of)	Cigars & Cheroots (U. S. Exports of)	All Tobacco (U. S. Exports of)	Smoking Tobacco[4] (U. S. Exports of)	All Tobacco (Stocks of Tobacco[5])	Fire Cured[6] (Stocks of Tobacco[5])	Cigar Filler[7] (Stocks of Tobacco[5])	Maryland (Stocks of Tobacco[5])
						- Million Pounds -		In Millions				In Millions of Pounds			
2000	472.4	2,229	1,053	191.0	2,002	351.4	457.8	148,300	113	397	136.1	2,388	87.8	9.5	16.0
2001	432.3	2,293	991	195.7	1,940	386.7	568.0	133,900	124	411	118.2	1,893	93.8	12.1	13.4
2002	427.3	2,039	871	193.6	1,687	325.8	549.7	127,400	123	338	144.0	1,738	99.5	12.3	9.7
2003	411.2	1,952	803	196.7	1,576	342.1	630.1	121,500	130	343	121.2	1,584	100.5	10.7	8.2
2004	408.1	2,161	882	198.4	1,750	354.0	561.7	118,700	171	361	45.4	1,529	101.5	9.7	7.2
2005	297.1	2,171	645	164.2	1,059			113,300	301			1,455		9.9	5.0
2006	339.0	2,144	728	166.5	1,211			111,317	180			1,167		10.8	0.8
2007	356.0	2,213	788	169.3	1,329										
2008	354.5	2,258	801	185.9	1,488										
2009[1]	354.1	2,325	823	182.0	1,499										

[1] Preliminary. [2] Domestic. [3] For consumption. [4] In bulk. [5] Flue-cured and cigar wrapper, year beginning July 1; for all other types, October 1. [6] Kentucky-Tennessee types 22-23. [7] Types 41-46. *Source: Economic Research Service, U.S. Department of Agriculture (ERS-USDA)*

Tobacco Production in the United States, by Types In Thousands of Pounds (Farm-Sale Weight)

Year	11-14	21	22	23	31	32	35-36	37	41	41-61	51	54	55	61
2000	598,915	2,548	34,167	14,920	362,788	13,395	15,896	165	5,040	10,205	1,070	1,825	430	1,840
2001	579,091	2,202	30,720	12,377	334,066	5,346	13,949	154	4,120	13,318	3,822	3,042	577	1,757
2002	514,385	1,471	23,292	10,145	293,537	4,205	10,570	116	4,410	13,401	4,021	3,151	666	1,153
2003	456,690	839	23,504	10,165	281,698	4,195	11,230	84	5,280	14,155	3,386	3,472	783	1,234
2004	521,535	1,345	24,800	11,006	292,172	5,830	11,798	124	4,140	13,265	3,767	2,744	797	1,915
2005	380,850	----	----	----	203,383	3,000	----	----	2,860	8,621	4,117	----	----	----
2006	447,190	----	----	----	217,255	2,090	----	----	2,600	8,265	4,434	----	----	----
2007	503,760	----	----	----	216,087	2,420	----	----	4,140	11,442	5,473	----	----	1,829
2008	499,220	----	----	----	201,530	3,780	----	----	3,960	8,444	3,076	----	----	1,408
2009[1]	526,450	----	----	----	214,816	4,830	----	----	4,400	7,229	1,770	----	----	1,059

[1] Preliminary. *Source: Agricultural Statistics Board, U.S. Department of Agriculture (ASB-USDA)*

U.S. Exports of Unmanufactured Tobacco In Millions of Pounds (Declared Weight)

Year	Australia	Belgium-Luxem.	Denmark	France	Germany	Italy	Japan	Netherlands	Sweden	Switzerland	Thailand	United Kingdom	Total U.S. Exports
2000	3.6	23.2	15.3	5.5	86.1	15.8	63.6	19.7	3.4	9.5	7.3	7.3	396.6
2001	3.4	49.7	12.2	11.5	94.8	6.2	51.6	21.6	3.6	14.4	7.7	1.6	410.7
2002	4.5	29.4	13.6	10.3	59.5	8.6	49.6	10.3	1.2	27.3	12.6	6.0	338.2
2003	6.3	61.7	13.5	8.8	55.8	7.6	42.4	9.8	1.6	34.8	3.6	4.8	343.3
2004	3.6	27.4	10.2	16.3	53.5	6.6	34.6	15.8	.6	9.4	8.5	4.0	360.9
2005	2.9	12.7	8.4	10.7	55.3	5.8	21.7	25.4	.7	15.6	4.1	3.2	339.0
2006	4.9	16.8	8.4	7.5	81.2	3.2	3.9	37.0	.7	38.5	3.0	1.1	397.6
2007	3.5	18.0	9.7	13.2	63.1	.7	4.0	24.0	.3	41.7	1.8	.0	411.5
2008	1.3	3.9	6.5	7.0	39.2	.0	.0	46.3	.3	69.3	3.0	.1	372.3
2009[1]	6.4	3.6	6.4	7.1	23.9	.4	.0	37.9	.3	59.1	2.8	.1	378.7

[1] Preliminary. *Source: Economic Research Service, U.S. Department of Agriculture (ERS-USDA)*

U.S. Salient Statistics for Flue-Cured Tobacco (Types 11-14) in the United States In Millions of Pounds

Year	Acres Harvested 1,000	Yield Per Acre Pounds	Marketings	Stocks Oct. 1	Total Supply	Exports	Domestic Disappearance	Total Disappearance	Farm Price cents/Lb.	Placed Under Gov't Loan (Mil. Lb.)	Price Support Level (cents/) Lb.	Loan Stocks Nov. 30	Loan Stocks Uncommitted
2000-01	250.0	2,396	564	1,189	1,754	238	479	717	179.3	27.4	164.0	256.9	135.9
2001-02	238.1	2,432	544	1,036	1,581	276	389	665	185.7	15.0	166.0	93.2	65.0
2002-03	245.6	2,094	565	916	1,481	220	423	643	182.0	24.8	165.6	17.8	12.8
2003-04	233.4	1,957	508	838	1,345	216	307	522	185.1	59.8	166.3	70.6	68.7
2004-05	228.4	2,283	499	823	1,322	189	338	526	184.5	94.9	169.0	108.2	128.5
2005-06	174.5	2,182	383	796	1,179	258	317	575	147.4	----	----	79.0	----
2006-07	213.1	2,095	454	604	1,058	270	248	518	149.6				
2007-08	223.0	2,259							152.7				
2008-09[1]	223.0	2,239							175.7				
2009-10[2]	224.0	2,350							175.7				

[1] Preliminary. [2] Estimate. NA = Not available. *Source: Economic Research Service, U.S. Department of Agriculture (ERS-USDA)*

Salient Statistics for Burley Tobacco (Type 31) in the United States In Millions of Pounds

Year	Acres Harvested 1,000	Yield Per Acre Pounds	Marketings	Stocks Oct. 1	Total Supply	Exports	Domestic Disappearance	Total Disappearance	Farm Price cents/Lb.	Gross Sales[3]	Price Support Level cents/Lb.	Loan Stocks Nov. 30	Loan Stocks Uncommitted
2000-01	193.8	1,957	315	1,040	1,355	142	524	666	196.3	169.7	180.5	420.7	336.5
2001-02	167.6	2,033	344	689	1,033	140	245	385	197.3	258.5	182.6	119.3	74.8
2002-03	157.7	1,861	300	648	948	149	221	370	197.4	217.7	183.5	124.2	46.1
2003-04	152.3	1,850	272	578	1,850	174	136	310	197.7	197.3	184.9	91.7	26.5
2004-05	153.2	1,908	280	540	820	228	100	328	199.4	202.3	187.3	115.1	8.5
2005-06	100.2	2,031	203	493	696	208	84	293	156.4	----	----	78.7	----
2006-07	103.6	2,095	217	403	621	190	56	246	163.8				
2007-08	106.3	2,033							160.1				
2008-09[1]	97.5	2,067							166.9				
2009-10[2]	101.9	2,108							170.8				

[1] Preliminary. [2] Estimate. [3] Before Christmas holidays. NA = Not available.
Source: Economic Research Service, U.S. Department of Agriculture (ERS-USDA)

Exports of Tobacco from the United States (Quantity and Value) In Metric Tons

	Unmanufactured							
Year	Flue-Cured	Value 1,000 USD	Burley	Value 1,000 USD	Total	Value 1,000 USD	Manufactured	Value 1,000 USD
2000	85,562	634,978	38,083	317,375	179,894	1,204,085	101,318	4,012,711
2001	89,930	660,924	42,464	361,567	186,302	1,268,839	104,282	2,734,377
2002	73,125	532,713	40,170	334,621	153,427	1,049,709	110,092	1,950,188
2003	70,669	519,732	41,876	346,504	155,722	1,038,073	102,351	1,843,922
2004	67,183	490,547	58,764	373,001	163,693	1,044,440	60,770	1,566,223
2005	62,779	420,532	61,606	412,588	153,762	989,588	19,364	1,301,834
2006	88,020	569,431	63,214	409,272	180,368	1,141,374	22,261	1,320,283
2007	82,093	541,816	75,905	498,168	186,643	1,207,945	17,552	1,122,176
2008[1]	100,848	730,677	44,506	342,732	168,885	1,238,047	25,474	824,638
2009[2]	86,543	660,678	37,486	301,497	171,785	1,159,991	4,619	489,894

[1] Preliminary. [2] Forecast. *Source: Foreign Agricultural Service, U.S. Department of Agriculture (FAS-USDA)*

Tung Oil

Tung oil is a yellow drying oil produced from the seed of the tung tree. The seeds or nuts of the tung tree are harvested and pressed to yield tung oil. Tung oil is used mostly as an industrial lubricant and drying agent, and is the most powerful drying agent known. It is also used in paints and varnishes, soaps, inks, and electrical insulators. Tung oil is poisonous, containing glycerol esters of unsaturated fats. The oil is also used as a substitute for linseed oil in paints, varnishes, and linoleum, and as a waterproofing agent.

Prices – The price of tung oil in 2008 (latest data) rose by +59.4% yr/yr to a record high of 143.03 cents per pound.

Demand – U.S. consumption of tung oil has fallen sharply over the past decade. In 2008 (latest data annualized) U.S. consumption rose by +1.8% yr/yr to 1.314 million pounds but that 2008 consumption level was only about 7% of 1996's 18-year high of 21.645 million pounds.

Trade – World imports of tung oil in 2008 (latest data) fell –13.3% yr/yr to 16,032 metric tons. U.S. imports of tung oil in 2008 fell by -17.1% to 1,020 metric tons. The world's largest importers of tung oil are South Korea with 12% of world imports, Taiwan with 12%, Japan with 12%, the Netherlands with 11%, and the U.S. with 6%. The world's largest exporter of tung oil by far is China with 12,245 metric tons of exports in 2008, accounting for 76% of total world exports.

World Tung Oil Trade In Metric Tons

	Imports								Exports				
Year	Germany	Hong Kong	Japan	Nether-lands	Rep. of Korea	Taiwan	United States	World Total	Argen-tina	China	Hong Kong	Para-guay	World Total
2002	325	702	1,930	1,793	6,968	5,185	4,166	29,710	916	23,334	589	4,390	30,351
2003	303	306	2,023	1,687	6,396	3,974	4,287	27,419	2,299	19,509	323	2,479	25,951
2004	100	207	1,900	1,778	5,486	3,529	2,975	24,961	1,299	18,850	240	3,626	25,501
2005	43	154	2,067	2,376	3,769	2,938	1,866	22,476	1,035	16,563	171	4,306	23,459
2006	478	104	1,984	2,342	1,828	2,891	2,076	20,183	733	14,668	104	2,876	19,539
2007[1]	1,307	120	1,858	2,119	2,685	2,021	1,230	18,499	956	13,313	100	2,085	18,535
2008[2]	1,251	120	1,937	1,693	1,894	1,884	1,020	16,032	221	12,245	100	2,000	16,048

[1] Preliminary. [2] Estimate. *Source: The Oil World*

Consumption of Tung Oil in Inedible Products in the United States In Thousands of Pounds

Year	Jan.	Feb.	Mar.	Apr.	May	June	July	Aug.	Sept.	Oct.	Nov.	Dec.	Total
2003	685	276	508	317	322	233	270	349	406	269	376	228	4,239
2004	428	400	350	402	264	324	338	310	186	186	101	109	3,398
2005	128	110	144	151	371	127	161	189	92	171	146	110	1,900
2006	174	175	138	103	128	193	198	114	198	134	136	75	1,766
2007	170	81	108	104	176	117	153	83	68	92	75	64	1,291
2008	W	W	141	91	98	W	108	W	W	W	W	W	1,314
2009[1]	W	W	W	W	W	W	W	W	W	W	W	W	W

[1] Preliminary. W = Withheld. *Source: Bureau of the Census, U.S. Department of Commerce*

Stocks of Tung Oil at Factories & Warehouses in the United States, on First of Month In Thousands of Pounds

Year	Jan.	Feb.	Mar.	Apr.	May	June	July	Aug.	Sept.	Oct.	Nov.	Dec.
2003	490	W	858	763	722	790	398	W	W	W	W	W
2004	W	W	W	519	229	209	226	137	91	161	121	117
2005	90	128	107	182	130	141	134	122	114	93	116	70
2006	109	99	98	124	81	116	128	85	128	125	76	98
2007	109	135	109	92	66	110	117	153	101	100	36	59
2008	82	87	94	63	29	79	50	78	86	73	W	W
2009[1]	W	W	W	W	W	W	W	W	W	W	W	W

[1] Preliminary. W = Withheld. *Source: Bureau of the Census, U.S. Department of Commerce*

Average Price of Tung Oil (Imported, Drums) F.O.B. in New York In Cents Per Pound

Year	Jan.	Feb.	Mar.	Apr.	May	June	July	Aug.	Sept.	Oct.	Nov.	Dec.	Average
2003	45.00	45.00	52.80	84.75	85.00	85.00	85.00	85.00	85.00	85.00	85.00	85.00	75.63
2004	85.00	85.00	85.00	85.00	85.00	85.00	85.00	85.00	85.00	85.00	85.00	90.00	85.42
2005	92.50	95.00	97.50	97.50	97.50	97.50	97.50	102.50	105.00	105.00	97.50	95.00	98.33
2006	95.00	95.00	95.00	95.00	95.00	93.75	90.00	90.00	89.00	89.00	89.00	89.00	92.06
2007	85.40	84.33	87.00	85.00	85.00	85.00	85.00	NA	90.00	99.50	100.00	100.71	89.72
2008	107.62	110.79	126.00	130.00	130.00	135.14	139.86	147.62	164.29	175.00	175.00	175.00	143.03
2009[1]	170.00	151.32	135.00	133.33	130.00	130.00	130.00	130.00	130.00	130.00	130.00	130.00	135.80

[1] Preliminary. *Source: Economic Research Service, U.S. Department of Agriculture (ERS-USDA)*

Tungsten

Tungsten (symbol W) is a grayish-white, lustrous, metallic element. The atomic symbol for tungsten is W because of its former name of Wolfram. Tungsten has the highest melting point of any metal at about 3410 degrees Celsius and boils at about 5660 degrees Celsius. In 1781, the Swedish chemist Carl Wilhelm Scheele discovered tungsten.

Tungsten is never found in nature but is instead found in the minerals wolframite, scheelite, huebnertite, and ferberite. Tungsten has excellent corrosion resistance qualities and is resistant to most mineral acids. Tungsten is used as filaments in incandescent lamps, electron and television tubes, alloys of steel, spark plugs, electrical contact points, cutting tools, and in the chemical and tanning industries.

Prices – The average monthly price of tungsten at U.S. ports in 2009 fell by 26.9% yr/yr to $184.51 per short ton, down further from the 2006 record high of $265.68 per short ton.

Supply – World concentrate production of tungsten in 2009 rose by +3.8% yr/yr to 58,000 metric tons. That was down from the 2004 record high of 66,600 metric tons. The world's largest producer of tungsten by far is China with 47,000 metric tons of production in 2009, which was 81% of total world production. Russia is the next largest producer at 4% with only a miniscule production of only 2,400 metric tons.

Trade – The U.S. in 2009 relied on imports for 63% of its tungsten consumption. U.S. imports for consumption in 2009 fell by -4.8% yr/yr to 3,800 metric tons. U.S. exports in 2009 were negligible at 16 metric tons.

World Concentrate Production of Tungsten In Metric Tons (Contained Tungsten[3])

Year	Austria	Bolivia	Brazil	Burma	Canada	China	Mongolia	Korea	Portugal	Russia	Rwanda	Thailand	Total
2002	1,377	399	24	83	2,295	55,100	35	600	693	5,300	153	31	66,200
2003	1,381	441	30	96	3,636	36,200	40	600	715	3,600	69	216	47,200
2004	1,335	403	262	107	----	59,900	77	600	746	2,800	90	187	66,600
2005	1,280	531	577	168	484	51,200	54	600	816	2,900	318	345	59,600
2006	1,153	868	525	197	2,500	45,000	85	600	778	2,900	820	303	56,600
2007	1,200	1,107	537	183	2,700	41,000	250	600	846	3,200	1,534	300	54,500
2008[1]	1,100	1,100	NA	NA	2,300	43,500	NA	NA	850	3,000	NA	NA	55,900
2009[2]	1,000	900	NA	NA	2,000	47,000	NA	NA	850	2,400	NA	NA	58,000

[1] Preliminary. [2] Estimate. [3] Conversion Factors: WO_3 to W, multiply by 0.7931; 60% WO_3 to W, multiply by 0.4758.
Source: U.S. Geological Survey (USGS)

Salient Statistics of Tungsten in the United States In Metric Tons (Contained Tungsten)

Year	Net Import Reliance as a % Apparent Consumption	Total Consumption	Consumption of Tungsten Products by End Uses: Steel: Tool	Steel: Stainless & Heat Assisting	Steel: Alloy Steel[3]	Superalloys	Cutting & Wear Resistant Materials	Products Made From Metal Powder	Miscellaneous	Chemical and Ceramic	Exports	Imports for Consumption	Stocks, Dec. 31 Concentrates: Consumers	Producers
2002	70	W	W	313	W	426	4,820	W	----	133	94	4,090	W	W
2003	63	W	W	312	W	W	5,210	W	----	129	20	4,690	W	W
2004	73	W	W	259	W	W	6,020	W	----	130	43	2,310	W	W
2005	68	W	W	280	W	W	6,020	W	----	130	52	2,080	W	W
2006	68	W	W	292	W	W	6,710	W	----	118	130	2,290	W	W
2007	68	W	W	295	W	W	6,090	W	----	89	109	3,880	W	W
2008[1]	60	W	W		W	W		W	----		496	3,990	W	W
2009[2]	63	W	W		W	W		W	----		16	3,800	W	W

[1] Preliminary. [2] Estimate. [3] Other than tool. [4] Included with stainless & heat assisting. W = Withheld.
Source: U.S. Geological Survey (USGS)

Average Price of Tungsten at U.S. Ports (Including Duty) In Dollars Per Short Ton

Year	Jan.	Feb.	Mar.	Apr.	May	June	July	Aug.	Sept.	Oct.	Nov.	Dec.	Average
2002	----	70.00	70.00	70.00	70.00	68.13	57.88	59.88	60.25	60.25	60.25	60.25	64.26
2003	60.25	61.55	63.00	63.00	63.00	63.00	63.00	63.00	63.00	63.00	63.00	63.00	62.65
2004	63.00	63.00	66.83	89.77	92.50	92.50	88.95	86.09	87.00	89.86	92.00	93.83	83.78
2005	97.08	109.32	134.13	178.21	272.26	277.61	275.25	237.28	232.50	244.05	255.00	255.00	213.97
2006	255.00	265.66	282.50	275.00	266.36	265.00	265.00	265.00	266.13	267.50	262.00	253.00	265.68
2007	252.50	256.71	261.36	262.50	262.50	262.50	262.50	261.63	252.50	252.50	252.50	252.50	257.68
2008	252.50	252.50	252.50	252.50	252.50	252.50	252.50	252.50	252.50	252.50	252.50	252.50	252.50
2009	252.50	215.00	205.00	205.00	165.00	165.00	165.00	165.00	165.00	165.00	166.58	180.00	184.51

U.S. Spot Quotations, 65% WO_3, Basis C.I.F. *Source: U.S. Geological Survey (USGS)*

Turkeys

During the past three decades, the turkey industry has experienced tremendous growth in the U.S. Turkey production has more than tripled since 1970, with a current value of over $7 billion. Turkey was not a popular dish in Europe until a roast turkey was eaten on June 27, 1570, at the wedding feast of Charles XI of France and Elizabeth of Austria. The King was so impressed with the birds that the turkey subsequently became a popular dish at banquets held by French nobility.

The most popular turkey product continues to be the whole bird, with heavy demand at Thanksgiving and Christmas. The primary breeders maintain and develop the quality stock, concentrating on growth and conformation in males and fecundity in females, as well as characteristics important to general health and welfare. Turkey producers include large companies that produce turkeys all year round, and relatively small companies and farmers who produce turkeys primarily for the seasonal Thanksgiving market.

Prices – The average monthly price received by farmers for turkeys in the U.S. in 2009 fell by -11.4% yr/yr to 49.9 cents per pound, down from the 2008 record high of 56.5 cents per pound. The monthly average retail price of turkeys (whole frozen) in the U.S. in 2009 rose by +11.9% yr/yr to a record high of 139.9 cents per pound. Turkey prices have more than tripled from the low 40-cent area seen in the early 1970s.

Supply – World production of turkeys in 2010 is forecasted to rise by 1.9% yr/yr to 5.156 million metric tons. World production of turkeys has grown by more than two and one-half times since 1980 when production was a mere 2.090 million metric tons. The U.S. is the largest producer of turkeys in the world by far with 2.607 million metric tons of production in 2010, which is 50% of world production. The value of U.S. turkey production in the U.S. in 2008 (latest data) was $4.477 billion.

Demand – World consumption of turkeys in 2010 is forecasted to rise by +2.17% to 5.048 million metric tons. U.S. turkey consumption of 2.503 million metric tons in 2010 if forecasted to account for 47% of world consumption. U.S. per capita consumption of turkeys in 2010 is forecasted to fall -0.6% yr/yr to 16.6 pounds per person per year. U.S. per capital consumption of turkeys has been in the range of 17-18 pounds since 1990, but the USDA is projecting that per capita consumption will drop somewhat.

Production and Consumption of Turkey Meat, by Selected Countries   In Thousands of Metric Tons (RTC)

	Production							Consumption						
Year	Brazil	Canada	European Union	Mexico	Russia	United States	World Total	Brazil	Canada	European Union	Mexico	Russia	United States	World Total
2001	165	149	2,100	13	7	2,490	4,938	96	135	1,949	157	171	2,269	4,881
2002	220	147	2,105	13	9	2,557	5,063	130	142	1,932	153	174	2,316	4,959
2003	272	148	2,028	14	12	2,529	5,015	160	137	1,939	170	126	2,301	4,959
2004	315	145	2,032	13	15	2,441	4,974	179	139	1,966	155	112	2,272	4,885
2005	360	155	1,919	14	17	2,464	4,942	199	143	1,888	197	124	2,246	4,865
2006	353	163	1,858	14	19	2,543	4,963	197	144	1,841	200	110	2,295	4,870
2007	458	169	1,790	15	25	2,664	5,137	281	149	1,769	213	100	2,401	5,018
2008	438	180	1,830	15	35	2,796	5,306	234	163	1,835	219	103	2,431	5,073
2009[1]	437	170	1,820	15	40	2,567	5,062	274	156	1,830	185	85	2,348	4,941
2010[2]	480	180	1,815	15	45	2,607	5,156	305	163	1,830	205	95	2,381	5,048

[1] Preliminary. [2] Forecast. *Source: Foreign Agricultural Service, U.S. Department of Agriculture (FAS-USDA)*

Salient Statistics of Turkeys in the United States

			Liveweight			Ready-to-Cook Basis			Consumption		Production Costs (Liveweight Basis)		Wholesale Ready-to-Cook	
Year	Poults Placed[3] (In Thousands)	Number Raised[4] (In Thousands)	Produced Mil Lbs	Price cents Per Lb.	Value of Production Million $	Production (In Millions of Pounds)	Beginning Stocks (In Millions of Pounds)	Exports (In Millions of Pounds)	Total (In Millions of Pounds)	Per Capita Lbs.	Feed	Total	Production Costs	3-Region Weighted Avg Price[5]
1999	297,387	270,494	6,886.4	40.8	2,806.6	5,231	304	378	4,905	17.6	19.00	32.70	57.17	67.81
2000	298,094	269,969	6,942.8	40.7	2,828.5	5,334	254	445	4,903	17.4	19.98	33.68	58.40	68.06
2001	301,721	272,059	7,154.8	39.0	2,796.8	5,489	241	487	5,004	17.5	20.55	34.25	59.11	63.63
2002	296,877	275,477	7,494.9	36.5	2,732.5	5,638	241	439	5,108	17.7	20.85	34.55	59.48	61.09
2003	289,542	274,048	7,487.3	36.1	2,699.7	5,576	333	484	5,074	17.4	22.59	36.29	61.66	60.41
2004	277,717	263,207	7,278.4	42.0	3,054.3	5,383	354	442	5,003	17.0				
2005	293,683	252,053	7,096.0	44.9	3,182.8	5,432	288	570	5,034	16.7				
2006	293,137	262,460	7,463.9	47.9	3,573.7	5,607	206	547	5,065	16.9				
2007[1]	308,402	266,828	7,566.3	52.3	3,954.5	5,880	218	554	5,292	17.5				
2008[2]	297,590	273,088	7,922.1	56.5	4,477.1	6,084	261	605	5,447	17.6				

[1] Preliminary. [2] Estimate. [3] Poults placed for slaughter by hatcheries. [4] Turkeys place August 1-July 31. [5] Regions include central, eastern and western. Central region receives twice the weight of the other regions in calculating the average.
Source: Economic Research Service, U.S. Department of Agriculture (ERS-USDA)

Turkey-Feed Price Ratio in the United States In Pounds[2]

Year	Jan.	Feb.	Mar.	Apr.	May	June	July	Aug.	Sept.	Oct.	Nov.	Dec.	Average
2000	7.6	7.2	7.6	7.9	7.8	8.5	9.5	10.0	10.1	10.0	9.8	8.1	8.7
2001	7.3	7.5	7.7	8.0	8.1	8.3	7.9	7.8	8.3	9.6	9.6	8.1	8.2
2002	7.2	7.2	6.8	6.8	7.3	7.3	6.9	6.3	6.0	6.1	6.5	6.4	6.7
2003	5.7	5.7	5.9	5.9	5.7	5.8	5.9	5.7	6.0	6.3	6.3	5.7	5.9
2004	5.1	4.6	4.5	4.5	4.8	5.2	5.8	7.0	7.9	8.4	8.7	8.2	6.2
2005	6.9	6.9	6.6	6.7	6.9	7.0	7.3	8.0	9.0	9.5	10.0	9.5	7.9
2006	7.0	6.9	6.9	7.3	7.1	7.6	7.7	8.5	9.1	9.6	9.4	5.9	7.8
2007	5.6	5.3	5.5	5.8	5.9	6.1	6.6	6.7	6.6	6.4	6.1	4.9	6.0
2008	4.1	3.6	4.0	4.0	4.3	4.3	4.5	4.7	5.4	5.9	5.6	4.4	4.6
2009[1]	4.1	4.6	4.8	4.7	4.7	4.8	5.1	5.2	5.3	5.6	5.7	5.6	5.0

[1] Preliminary. [2] Pounds of feed equal in value to one pound of turkey, liveweight. *Source: Economic Research Service, U.S. Department of Agriculture (ERS-USDA)*

Average Price Received by Farmers for Turkeys in the United States (Liveweight) In Cents Per Pound

Year	Jan.	Feb.	Mar.	Apr.	May	June	July	Aug.	Sept.	Oct.	Nov.	Dec.	Average
2000	36.4	35.7	38.2	40.0	40.8	41.8	42.2	43.2	44.8	46.1	47.1	40.5	41.4
2001	36.6	36.3	37.1	37.6	38.2	38.3	38.5	38.7	40.5	44.2	44.5	38.7	39.1
2002	34.1	34.1	32.9	32.9	35.8	37.2	38.6	38.2	37.2	37.2	39.8	38.7	36.4
2003	34.6	34.5	35.1	35.6	34.9	34.9	33.6	32.7	36.2	39.1	41.2	38.2	35.9
2004	34.9	35.0	36.6	38.4	40.1	41.7	43.3	45.1	46.2	48.1	48.7	45.9	42.0
2005	39.3	38.0	38.1	38.8	40.7	42.1	44.6	46.5	50.3	52.5	54.5	53.9	44.9
2006	40.8	39.6	40.3	42.5	43.3	45.4	45.9	48.6	53.3	62.7	66.3	42.7	47.6
2007	40.8	42.4	44.3	46.8	48.3	52.0	55.5	57.2	60.4	61.5	61.6	52.6	52.0
2008	44.8	47.5	52.9	55.1	58.1	59.8	60.9	63.2	66.4	64.6	58.6	44.5	56.4
2009[1]	43.8	46.5	47.1	47.6	50.1	52.5	52.0	51.1	48.5	52.1	54.1	53.7	49.9

[1] Preliminary. *Source: Economic Research Service, U.S. Department of Agriculture (ERS-USDA)*

Average Wholesale Price of Turkeys[1] (Hens, 8-16 Lbs.) in New York In Cents Per Pound

Year	Jan.	Feb.	Mar.	Apr.	May	June	July	Aug.	Sept.	Oct.	Nov.	Dec.	Average
2000	61.58	61.84	65.35	67.38	69.18	70.36	71.55	73.61	76.53	78.74	79.58	70.31	70.50
2001	61.50	61.18	62.38	63.45	65.65	66.00	66.10	66.38	68.81	72.86	73.48	67.71	66.29
2002	60.86	60.03	59.00	59.52	63.52	65.68	66.52	66.56	67.15	67.75	69.79	66.96	64.45
2003	61.04	61.13	61.24	61.43	60.36	60.12	58.18	57.74	61.52	66.08	69.33	66.85	62.09
2004	62.13	61.61	62.62	64.52	66.41	68.95	71.21	73.32	74.69	76.89	78.29	76.05	69.72
2005	67.63	65.34	64.68	65.86	67.69	69.50	72.56	75.98	80.90	82.40	85.75	82.60	73.41
2006	68.29	65.84	67.67	69.75	71.27	72.95	74.95	78.70	84.40	95.83	99.51	74.20	76.95
2007	67.63	69.84	71.66	74.45	76.98	82.12	86.89	89.70	93.12	95.20	94.71	82.47	82.06
2008	73.74	76.40	82.20	85.99	89.19	91.45	92.91	96.85	99.62	97.27	87.44	74.88	87.33
2009[2]	71.20	74.32	75.22	76.59	78.71	82.00	82.68	81.33	80.26	82.52	84.96	85.20	79.58

[1] Ready-to-cook. [2] Preliminary. *Source: Economic Research Service, U.S. Department of Agriculture (ERS-USDA)*

Certified Federally Inspected Turkey Slaughter in the U.S. (Ready-to-Cook Weights) In Millions of Pounds

Year	Jan.	Feb.	Mar.	Apr.	May	June	July	Aug.	Sept.	Oct.	Nov.	Dec.	Total
2000	396.9	412.4	466.2	413.5	489.2	479.4	422.8	481.6	423.0	494.7	478.2	396.5	5,354
2001	458.3	405.9	458.7	425.1	485.1	460.7	465.1	481.7	409.2	536.2	477.7	413.2	5,477
2002	477.2	442.1	447.8	487.2	496.7	448.0	474.7	475.9	439.4	519.0	488.2	457.9	5,654
2003	473.6	427.1	464.6	471.1	475.8	478.0	483.9	449.3	453.6	522.8	450.3	436.1	5,586
2004	435.5	389.0	466.6	445.2	445.1	462.8	455.4	462.2	451.2	461.5	479.6	434.4	5,389
2005	439.0	396.3	459.4	439.7	456.3	485.8	427.5	483.7	450.6	479.1	478.2	434.4	5,430
2006	443.0	412.4	487.9	430.3	492.8	504.4	453.5	493.6	456.5	535.8	499.7	423.5	5,633
2007	479.0	442.7	478.8	459.6	507.5	495.7	502.0	517.3	456.4	577.8	520.3	457.3	5,894
2008	544.6	504.0	484.5	515.9	517.9	519.7	544.1	503.8	511.5	570.1	507.9	488.2	6,212
2009[1]	465.5	441.6	467.7	472.2	448.8	490.7	482.3	460.7	463.8	504.4	475.3	453.2	5,626

[1] Preliminary. *Source: Economic Research Service, U.S. Department of Agriculture (ERS-USDA)*

Per Capita Consumption of Turkeys in the United States In Pounds

Year	First Quarter	Second Quarter	Third Quarter	Fourth Quarter	Total	Year	First Quarter	Second Quarter	Third Quarter	Fourth Quarter	Total
1999	3.8	3.8	4.4	5.8	18.0	2005	3.6	3.9	4.2	5.1	16.7
2000	3.7	4.2	4.4	5.5	17.8	2006	3.5	3.9	4.3	5.2	16.9
2001	3.9	3.8	4.3	5.6	17.5	2007	3.8	4.1	4.2	5.5	17.5
2002	3.5	3.9	4.4	5.9	17.7	2008	4.0	4.1	4.3	5.3	17.6
2003	3.6	3.9	4.6	5.3	17.4	2009[1]	3.7	3.9	4.0	5.0	16.7
2004	3.6	4.0	4.5	5.0	17.0	2010[2]	3.6	3.9	3.9		16.6

[1] Preliminary. [2] Estimate. *Source: Economic Research Service, U.S. Department of Agriculture (ERS-USDA)*

Storage Stocks of Turkeys (Frozen) in the United States on First of Month In Millions of Pounds

Year	Jan.	Feb.	Mar.	Apr.	May	June	July	Aug.	Sept.	Oct.	Nov.	Dec.
2000	254.3	319.4	353.9	391.4	416.9	480.3	506.8	524.0	524.9	528.1	473.9	261.1
2001	241.3	291.4	333.5	355.8	392.6	456.0	506.7	534.2	545.3	542.0	497.9	260.0
2002	240.5	327.1	413.2	457.6	515.2	578.2	644.1	706.2	685.6	672.4	624.9	334.3
2003	333.0	451.9	492.7	549.3	573.5	658.8	718.2	722.5	706.5	647.5	582.7	350.7
2004	354.0	420.5	471.7	504.6	548.8	571.1	597.6	599.6	600.2	527.4	472.3	294.9
2005	288.4	332.9	379.4	414.2	440.1	465.9	506.3	518.9	523.1	477.8	417.6	194.7
2006	206.2	260.5	315.7	377.7	423.7	466.5	507.5	512.2	500.3	464.2	404.2	214.5
2007	218.4	293.4	312.9	346.8	360.2	398.0	448.4	503.5	524.4	504.9	417.0	206.9
2008	260.6	327.6	416.7	428.1	491.3	522.4	562.7	620.7	629.2	621.5	578.0	360.4
2009[1]	396.1	446.2	462.4	513.4	571.7	585.7	594.7	641.1	653.5	613.9	509.5	234.5

[1] Preliminary. Source: Economic Research Service, U.S. Department of Agriculture (ERS-USDA)

Average Retail Price of Turkeys (Whole frozen) in the United States In Cents Per Pound

Year	Jan.	Feb.	Mar.	Apr.	May	June	July	Aug.	Sept.	Oct.	Nov.	Dec.	Average
2000	101.3	102.5	101.5	99.7	102.9	106.5	109.5	104.5	104.4	106.7	98.1	99.4	103.1
2001	108.8	112.5	112.7	109.7	109.4	110.9	111.0	113.5	116.2	114.6	98.0	99.5	109.7
2002	102.2	105.1	106.6	104.0	102.5	107.3	108.0	106.8	106.6	111.7	103.8	98.8	105.3
2003	106.6	105.8	105.5	100.1	106.0	110.6	113.4	116.2	116.7	111.2	100.6	105.4	108.2
2004	108.4	109.4	113.4	108.4	109.0	111.7	112.9	114.2	108.8	112.3	99.6	100.3	109.0
2005	105.8	106.3	106.1	105.8	106.9	108.0	116.5	116.6	112.1	113.7	102.3	106.6	108.9
2006	106.9	119.7	120.9	111.1	108.4	112.8	113.0	110.6	115.1	114.9	97.3	99.1	110.8
2007	110.3	113.6	107.9	108.1	114.6	122.3	122.2	122.9	121.6	124.1	111.3	101.0	115.0
2008	120.7	123.0	115.1	117.0	125.8	123.8	127.0	128.8	132.0	122.2	130.9	133.2	125.0
2009[1]	136.5	136.9	134.7	135.4	136.6	141.0	144.5	146.1	145.4	148.0	133.6		139.9

[1] Preliminary. *Source: Economic Research Service, U.S. Department of Agriculture (ERS-USDA)*

Average Retail-to-Consumer Price Spread of Turkeys (Whole) in the United States In Cents Per Pound

Year	Jan.	Feb.	Mar.	Apr.	May	June	July	Aug.	Sept.	Oct.	Nov.	Dec.	Average
1999	29.9	32.7	28.6	21.3	22.5	22.6	23.2	29.1	18.5	17.6	12.0	19.6	23.1
2000	32.1	33.9	29.1	25.9	27.6	29.5	30.9	23.7	21.1	21.7	13.4	23.1	26.0
2001	39.5	43.3	42.5	39.1	37.7	38.7	38.6	40.5	41.0	35.6	18.7	27.0	36.9
2002	34.2	37.9	40.7	38.3	32.9	35.9	35.9	34.9	35.4	40.2	29.8	24.6	35.1
2003	38.4	37.6	36.8	31.2	38.1	42.9	47.1	50.0	47.2	37.8	25.1	33.2	38.8
2004	39.4	40.4	42.5	35.0	33.5	33.9	33.3	32.5	25.7	26.9	14.0	18.0	31.3
2005	31.3	33.4	33.3	31.5	30.9	29.4	25.6	22.4	24.1	22.9	8.7	16.8	25.9
2006	29.4	44.5	44.8	32.8	28.6	30.8	29.6	22.9	21.5	9.3	-11.3	15.9	24.9
2007	33.7	34.3	27.2	25.2	28.7	30.9	26.5	24.6	19.7	20.0	7.4	9.8	24.0
2008[1]	38.0	37.5	23.7	21.6	27.3	23.4	25.1	23.0	23.4	18.0	33.9	48.8	28.6

[1] Preliminary. *Source: Economic Research Service, U.S. Department of Agriculture (ERS-USDA)*

Uranium

Uranium (symbol U) is a chemically reactive, radioactive, steel-gray, metallic element and is the main fuel used in nuclear reactors. Uranium is the heaviest of all the natural elements. Traces of uranium have been found in archeological artifacts dating back to 79 AD. Uranium was discovered in pitchblende by German chemist Martin Heinrich Klaproth in 1789. Klaproth named it uranium after the recently discovered planet Uranus. French physicist Antoine Henri Becquerel discovered the radioactive properties of uranium in 1896 when he produced an image on a photographic plate covered with a light-absorbing substance. Following Becquerel's experiments, investigations of radioactivity led to the discovery of radium and to new concepts of atomic organization.

The principal use for uranium is fuel in nuclear power plants. Demand for uranium concentrates is directly linked to the level of electricity generated by nuclear power plants. Uranium ores are widely distributed throughout the world and are primarily found in Canada, DRC (formerly Zaire), and the U.S.. Uranium is obtained from primary mine production and secondary sources. Two Canadian companies are the primary producers of uranium from deposits in the Athabasca Basin of northern Saskatchewan. Specifically, the companies Cameco accounted for 19% of global mine production in 2000 and Cogema Resources accounted for 15% of world production. Secondary sources of uranium include excess inventories from utilities and other fuel cycle participants, used reactor fuel, and dismantled Russian nuclear weapons.

Prices – The average price of delivered uranium in 2002 (the latest data available) rose by +2.1% yr/yr to $10.36 per pound from $10.15 in 2001. The 2001 price of $10.15 was a record low for the data series that goes back to 1981. The price of delivered uranium in 2002 of $10.36 was roughly one-third of the price of $30 per pound and above seen in the 1980s through 1986 when the price started falling.

Supply – World production of uranium oxide (U308) concentrate in 2003 (the latest data available) rose +7.3% yr/yr to a 13-year high of 56,552 short tons from last 2002's 52,709 short tons. The world's largest uranium producers in 2003 were Canada with 17,050 short tons of production in 2003 (30% of world production), the U.S. with 10,200 short tons of production (18% of world production), and Australia with 9,326 short tons of production (16% of world production). U.S. production in 2003 was the highest since 1983.

U.S. uranium production in 2003 rose +64.4% yr/yr to a 20-year high of 10,200 short tons, up sharply from the record low of 1,315 short tons in 2001. U.S. production had reached a peak of 21,850 short tons in 1980 and production had since fallen steadily to the record low in 2001, which was only 6% of the record level of production.

Trade – U.S. imports of uranium in 2003 (latest data available) rose +0.7% yr/yr to a record high of 53.044 million pounds. The U.S. is being forced to import more uranium as domestic production steadily declines. U.S. exports of uranium fell –14.3% yr/yr to 13.187 million pounds, which was still well above the 7-year low of 8.510 million pounds posted in 1999.

World Production of Uranium Oxide (U_3O_8) Concentrate In Short Tons (Uranium Content)

Year	Australia	Canada	China	Czech Rep. & Slovakia	France	Gabon	Germany	Namibia	Niger	South Africa	United States	Ex-USSR	World Total
1994	3,050	11,950	----	----	1,700	750	----	2,500	3,800	2,250	1,950	----	41,750
1995	4,900	13,600	----	----	1,250	800	----	2,600	3,750	1,850	3,050	----	43,050
1996	6,450	15,250	----	----	1,200	750	----	3,150	4,300	2,200	3,150	----	46,650
1997	7,150	15,650	----	----	940	600	----	3,770	4,500	1,065	2,900	----	46,550
1998	6,350	14,200	----	----	660	950	----	3,590	4,850	1,250	2,435	----	44,110
1999	7,875	10,680	----	----	450	380	----	3,495	3,790	1,195	2,325	----	39,640
2000	9,830	13,875	655	795	525	----	45	2,430	3,270	1,305	1,890	655	43,475
2001	10,035	16,270	650	595	195	----	----	2,910	3,795	1,135	1,315	1,050	47,395
2002[1]	10,857	17,153	W	0	----	W	W	1,082	W	764	6,206	W	52,709
2003[2]	9,326	17,050	W	W	----	0	0	1,034	0	1,438	10,200	W	56,552

[1] Preliminary. [2] Estimate. W = Withheld. *Source: American Bureau of Metal Statistics, Inc. (ABMS)*

Commercial and U.S. Government Stocks of Uranium, End of Year In Millions of Pounds U_3O_8 Equivalent

	Utility		Domestic Supplier		Total	DOE Owned & USEC Held	
Year	Natural Uranium	Enriched Uranium[1]	Natural Uranium	Enriched Uranium[1]	Commercial Stocks	Natural Uranium	Enriched Uranium[1]
1998	42.1	23.7	35.0	35.7	136.5	24.5	----
1999	44.8	13.5	29.5	39.4	127.1	53.1	----
2000	36.0	18.9	12.6	43.8	111.3	53.1	----
2001	34.4	21.2	9.2	39.0	103.8	53.1	----
2002	31.0	22.4	15.0	32.9	102.1	51.8	----
2003	22.7	23.0	[2]	39.9	85.5	W	W
2004	27.9	29.8	[2]	37.5	95.2	W	W
2005	45.3	19.4	[2]	29.1	93.8	W	W
2006	54.3	23.2	[2]	29.1	106.6	W	W
2007	56.0	24.8	[2]	30.8	111.6	W	W

[1] Includes amount reported as UF_6 at enrichment suppliers. [2] Included in Enriched beginning 2003. DOE = Department of Energy
USEC = U.S. Energy Commission *Source: Energy Information Administration, U.S. Department of Energy (EIA-DOE)*

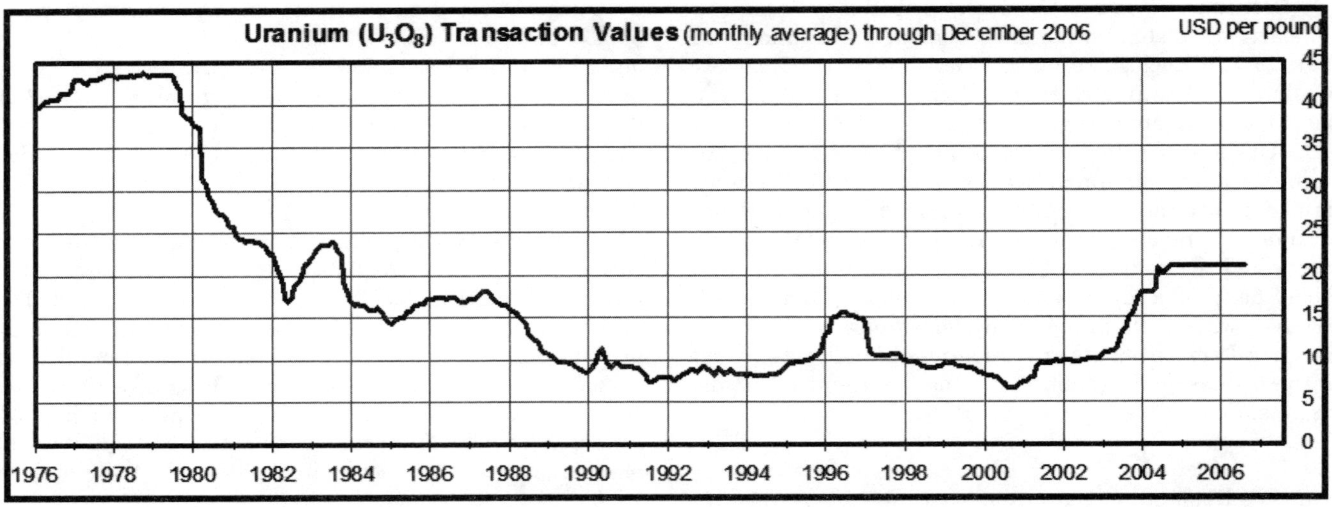

Reported Average Price Settlements for Purchases by U.S. Utilities and Domestic Suppliers In Dollars Per Pound

Year of Delivery	Contract Price	Market Price[1]	Price & Cost Floor	Total	Contract & Market	Year of Delivery	Contract Price	Market Price[1]	Price & Cost Floor	Total	Contract & Market
	Averages of Reported Prices						Averages of Reported Prices				
1998	12.53	9.33	13.50	10.31	12.37	2003	----	----	----	10.81	----
1999	12.72	9.52	14.75	11.16	12.57	2004	----	----	----	12.61	----
2000	12.31	9.11	----	11.04	----	2005	----	----	----	14.36	----
2001	11.72	8.04	----	10.15	----	2006	----	----	----	18.61	----
2002	10.73	9.79	----	10.36	----	2007	----	----	----	32.78	----

[1] No floor. Note: Price excludes uranium delivered under litigation settlements. Price is given in year-of-delivery dollars. *Source: Energy Information Administration, U.S. Department of Energy (EIA-DOE)*

Uranium Industry Statistics in the United States In Millions of Pounds U_3O_8

Year	Production: Mine	Production: Concentrate	Concentrate Shipments	Employment - Person Years: Exploration	Mining	Milling	Processing	Total[1]	Deliveries to U.S. Utilities[2]	Avg Price Delivered Uranium $/lb U_3O_8	Imports	Avg Price Delivered Uranium Imports $/lb U_3O_8	Exports
1998	4.8	4.700	4.900	30	518	160	203	1,120	42.7	12.14	43.7	11.19	15.1
1999	4.5	4.600	5.500	7	310	201	132	848	47.9	11.63	47.6	10.55	8.5
2000	3.1	4.000	3.200	1	157	106	137	627	51.8	11.04	44.9	9.84	13.6
2001	2.6	2.600	2.200	0	81	42	122	423	55.4	10.15	46.7	9.51	11.7
2002	2.4	2.300	3.800	W	W	104	100	426	52.7	10.36	52.7	10.05	15.4
2003	2.2	2.000	1.600	W	W	W	W	321			53.0	10.59	13.2
2004	2.5	2.300	2.300	18	108	W	W	420					
2005	3.0	2.700	2.700	79	149	142	154	648					
2006	4.7	4.100	3.800	188	121	W	W	755					
2007	4.5	4.500	4.000	375	378	107	216	1,231					

[1] From suppliers under domestic purchases. *Source: Energy Information Administration, U.S. Department of Energy (EIA-DOE)*

Month-End Uranium (U3O8) Transaction Values[1] In Dollars Per Pound

Year	Jan.	Feb.	Mar.	Apr.	May	June	July	Aug.	Sept.	Oct.	Nov.	Dec.	Average
1997	15.33	15.08	14.85	14.75	14.43	10.95	10.68	10.45	10.55	10.48	10.43	10.53	12.37
1998	10.63	10.63	10.60	10.05	10.00	9.80	9.80	9.73	9.55	9.35	9.25	9.05	9.87
1999	9.03	9.08	9.20	9.20	9.53	9.48	9.48	9.40	9.35	9.23	9.18	9.13	9.27
2000	9.03	8.70	8.55	8.50	8.40	8.18	8.13	7.98	7.88	7.40	7.15	6.80	8.06
2001	6.78	6.83	6.83	7.25	7.38	7.45	7.83	7.95	9.00	9.47	9.44	9.50	7.97
2002	9.58	9.72	9.90	9.76	9.90	9.90	9.88	9.85	9.79	9.85	9.86	9.97	9.83
2003	10.20	10.10	10.10	10.16	10.84	10.90	10.90	11.13	11.47	12.32	13.18	13.98	11.27
2004	14.85	15.47	16.50	17.52	17.75	17.86	17.90	17.90	18.60	20.80	20.20	20.50	17.99
2005	20.55	21.18	21.20	21.20	21.20	21.20	21.20	21.20	21.20	21.20	21.20	21.20	21.14
2006	21.20	21.20	21.20	21.20	21.20	21.20	21.20	21.20	21.20	21.20	21.20	21.20	21.20

[1] Transaction value is a weighed average price of recent natural uranium sales transactions, based on prices paid on transactions closed within the previous three-month period for which delivery is scheduled within one year of the transaction date; at least 10 transactions involving a sum total of at least 2 million pounds of U3O8 equivalent. *Source: American Metal Market (AMM)*

Vanadium

Vanadium (symbol V) is a silvery-white, soft, ductile, metallic element. Discovered in 1801, but mistaken for chromium, vanadium was rediscovered in 1830 by Swedish chemist Nils Sefstrom, who named the element in honor of the Scandinavian goddess Vanadis.

Never found in the pure state, vanadium is found in about 65 different minerals such as carnotite, roscoelite, vanadinite, and patronite, as well as in phosphate rock, certain iron ores, some crude oils, and meteorites. Vanadium is one of the hardest of all metals. It melts at about 1890 degrees Celsius and boils at about 3380 degrees Celsius.

Vanadium has good structural strength and is used as an alloying agent with iron, steel, and titanium. It is used in aerospace applications, transmission gears, photography, as a reducing agent, and as a drying agent in various paints.

Prices – The price of vanadium in 2009 fell sharply by -59.0% to $6.00 per pound and moving further below the record high of $16.28 per pound in 2005.

Supply – Virtually all (99%) of vanadium is produced from ores, concentrates, and slag, with the remainder coming from petroleum residues, ash, and spent catalysts. World production in 2009 from ore, concentrates and slag fell -2.7% to 54,000 metric tons. World production of all vanadium in 2008 (latest data available) fell -4.1% yr/yr to 56,100 metric tons.

The world's largest producer of vanadium from ores, concentrates and slag is China with 20,000 metric tons of production in 2009 which was 37% of total world production. The two other major producers are South Africa with 19,000 metric tons of production in 2009, which was 35% of world production, and Russia with 14,000 metric tons of production which was 27% of world production. Production in Russia and South Africa has been relatively stable in recent years, while China's production grew sharply in the late 1990s. China's production level of 20,000 metric tons in 2009 is a new record high and almost four times the levels seen in the early 1990s.

Trade – U.S. exports of vanadium in 2009 were in the forms of oxides & hydroxides (270 metric tons, -74.0% yr/yr), ferro-vanadium (740 metric tons, +163.4%), and vanadium pent-oxide, anhydride (360 metric tons, +44.6%). U.S. imports of vanadium in 2009 were in the forms of vanadium pent-oxide, anhydride (1,420 metric tons, -61.6% yr/yr); ferro-vanadium (780 metric tons, -72.1% yr/yr); ore, slag and residues (890 metric tons, -3.3% yr/yr); and oxides & hydroxides (37 metric tons, -74.3% yr/yr).

World Production of Vanadium In Metric Tons (Contained Vanadium)

	From Ores, Concentrates and Slag						From Petroleum Residues Ash, Spent Catalysts			
Year	Australia	China[3]	Kazak-hstan	Russia	South Africa	Total[4]	Japan[5]	United States[6]	Total	World Total
2004	150	16,000	1,000	10,900	23,302	51,400	560	----	560	51,900
2005	100	17,000	1,000	15,100	22,604	55,800	560	----	560	56,400
2006	----	17,500	1,000	15,100	23,780	57,400	560	----	560	57,900
2007	----	19,000	1,000	14,500	23,486	58,000	560	----	560	58,500
2008[1]	----	20,000	1,000	14,500	20,000	55,500	560	----	560	56,100
2009[2]	----	20,000	NA	14,000	19,000	54,000		----		

[1] Preliminary. [2] Estimate. [3] In vanadiferous slag product. [4] Excludes U.S. production. [5] In vanadium pentoxide product. [6] In vanadium pentoxide and ferrovanadium products. Source: U.S. Geological Survey (USGS)

Salient Statistics of Vanadium in the United States In Metric Tons (Contained Vanadium)

	Con-sumer & Producer	Vanadium Consumption by Uses in the U.S.									Exports			Imports			
Year	Stocks, Dec. 31	Tool Steel	Cast Irons	High Strength, Low Alloy	Stainless & Heat Resisting	Super-alloys	Carbon	Full Alloy	Total	Average $ Per Lb. V_2O_5	Vanadium Pent-oxide, Anhydride	Oxides & Hydr-oxides	Ferro-Vana-dium	Ores, Slag, Residues	Vanadium Pent-oxide, Anhydride	Oxides & Hydr-oxides	Ferro-Vana-dium
2004	336	239	W	1,160	60	17	1,300	1,060	4,050	5.99	240	584	285	2,350	1,040	120	3,020
2005	371	402	W	974	60	36	1,170	1,010	3,910	16.28	254	899	505	1,690	1,370	186	11,900
2006	330	323	W	1,020	61	40	1,210	1,030	4,030	7.86	341	832	389	1,000	1,920	129	2,140
2007	323	379	W	1,560	61	44	1,190	1,380	4,970	7.40	327	626	154	920	2,390	42	2,220
2008[1]	310	267	W	1,580	116	5	763	2,070	5,090	14.75	249	1,040	281	920	3,700	144	2,800
2009[2]	320								5,000	6.00	360	270	740	890	1,420	37	780

[1] Preliminary. [2] Estimate. W = Withheld. *Source: U.S. Geological Survey (USGS)*

Average Price of Vanadium Pentoxide In Dollars Per Pound

Year	Jan.	Feb.	Mar.	Apr.	May	June	July	Aug.	Sept.	Oct.	Nov.	Dec.	Average
2004	2.50	3.43	3.74	5.25	5.25	5.25	5.26	4.64	4.40	5.15	7.00	8.63	5.04
2005	9.65	10.24	13.75	15.00	20.36	26.16	19.96	11.63	11.10	13.74	13.75	11.00	14.70
2006	8.73	9.11	8.78	7.92	8.15	8.08	7.40	7.07	7.85	7.70	7.27	6.70	7.90
2007	6.21	6.34	7.22	8.10	7.98	7.67	7.48	7.36	7.64	7.74	7.67	7.40	7.40
2008	8.03	13.11	15.80	14.60	15.85	17.61	15.65	16.39	15.23	12.83	9.85	8.66	13.63
2009	6.50	6.05	5.66	4.75	3.73	4.78	5.25	6.11	6.93	6.69	6.13	6.13	5.73

Source: American Metal Market (AMM)

Vegetables

Vegetables are the edible products of herbaceous plants, which are plants with soft stems. Vegetables are grouped according to the edible part of each plant including leaves (e.g., lettuce), stalks (celery), roots (carrot), tubers (potato), bulbs (onion), fruits (tomato), seeds (pea), and flowers (broccoli). Each of these groups contributes to the human diet in its own way. Fleshy roots are high in energy value and good sources of the vitamin B group, seeds are relatively high in carbohydrates and proteins, while leaves, stalks, and fruits are excellent sources of minerals, vitamins, water, and roughage. Vegetables are an important food for the maintenance of health and prevention of disease. Higher intakes of vegetables have been shown to lower the risks of cancer and coronary heart disease.

Vegetables are best consumed fresh in their raw state in order to derive the maximum benefits from their nutrients. While canned and frozen vegetables are often thought to be inferior to fresh vegetables, they are sometimes nutritionally superior to fresh produce because they are usually processed immediately after harvest when nutrient content is at its peak. When cooking vegetables, aluminum utensils should not be used, because aluminum is a soft metal that is affected by food acids and alkalis. Scientific evidence shows that tiny particles of aluminum from foods cooked in aluminum utensils enter the stomach and can injure the sensitive lining of the stomach.

Prices – The monthly average index of fresh vegetable prices received by growers in the U.S. in 2009 fell by -5.7% to 165.7, down from the 2007 record level of 178.7.

Demand – The leading vegetable in terms of U.S. per capita consumption in 2009 (latest data available) was the potato with 121.0 pounds of consumption. Runner-up vegetables were tomatoes (92.8 pounds), sweet corn (24.63 pounds), lettuce (22.6 pounds), and onions (22.6 pounds). Total U.S. per capita vegetable consumption in 2007 rose +2.2% at 434.2 pounds. That is about 22% higher than the 356.2 pounds consumed in 1980.

Index of Prices Received by Growers for Commercial Vegetables[2] in the United States (1990-92=100)

Year	Jan.	Feb.	Mar.	Apr.	May	June	July	Aug.	Sept.	Oct.	Nov.	Dec.	Average
2004	127	140	111	127	108	107	100	127	129	155	158	119	126
2005	93	117	165	181	135	138	112	118	127	113	113	152	130
2006	128	115	133	151	156	131	119	152	160	123	119	150	136
2007	177	165	192	181	144	133	126	146	155	196	139	138	158
2008	138	118	134	162	154	153	143	143	174	178	154	155	151
2009[1]	173	136	152	177	145	163	147	150	141	169	217	209	165

[1] Preliminary. [2] Includes fresh and processing vegetables. Not seasonally adjusted. *Source: National Agricultural Statistics Service, U.S. Department of Agriculture (NASS-USDA)*

Index of Prices Received by Growers for Fresh Vegetables in the United States (1990-92=100)

Year	Jan.	Feb.	Mar.	Apr.	May	June	July	Aug.	Sept.	Oct.	Nov.	Dec.	Average
2004	143.8	125.9	140.3	133.1	132.9	101.0	102.8	128.3	141.9	200.0	211.1	143.7	142.1
2005	122.0	152.8	168.5	174.7	144.2	160.0	126.8	132.3	153.3	144.0	163.1	200.8	153.5
2006	207.6	138.8	137.6	174.4	147.9	128.7	134.1	179.5	193.1	167.7	138.3	178.4	160.5
2007	175.3	190.3	222.4	222.5	142.1	145.4	146.0	137.8	162.7	218.3	177.4	204.5	178.7
2008	200.2	158.3	194.1	179.3	170.7	191.7	168.3	146.1	158.7	185.1	200.3	155.9	175.7
2009[1]	179.8	163.6	167.4	182.3	134.1	182.5	149.8	144.3	140.4	180.6	197.8	210.4	169.4

[1] Preliminary. Not seasonally adjusted. *Source: National Agricultural Statistics Service, U.S. Department of Agriculture (NASS-USDA)*

Producer Price Index of Canned[2] Processed Vegetables in the United States (1982 = 100)

Year	Jan.	Feb.	Mar.	Apr.	May	June	July	Aug.	Sept.	Oct.	Nov.	Dec.	Average
2004	131.5	131.7	131.9	131.9	131.7	132.8	133.0	133.3	133.4	134.6	135.4	135.5	133.1
2005	135.7	135.9	136.1	136.3	137.6	137.6	137.7	137.7	137.5	137.7	137.6	138.0	137.1
2006	138.0	136.8	137.1	137.3	138.8	140.2	140.0	140.5	141.4	141.5	142.2	142.2	139.7
2007	142.8	142.9	143.1	143.3	143.5	143.6	143.1	143.1	144.0	143.9	144.2	144.6	143.5
2008	147.8	148.4	149.6	151.2	150.2	151.3	153.3	158.6	162.5	163.0	164.2	167.8	155.7
2009[1]	168.9	169.0	170.5	170.7	171.0	171.1	171.3	170.9	170.6	170.3	169.1	167.5	170.1

[1] Preliminary. [2] Includes canned vegetables and juices, including hominy and mushrooms. Not seasonally adjusted. *Source: Bureau of Labor Statistics, U.S. Department of Labor (BLS)*

Producer Price Index of Frozen Processed Vegetables in the United States (1982 = 100)

Year	Jan.	Feb.	Mar.	Apr.	May	June	July	Aug.	Sept.	Oct.	Nov.	Dec.	Average
2004	135.1	136.0	135.3	135.3	134.3	134.7	135.4	135.8	136.8	138.1	137.2	137.0	135.9
2005	137.3	137.3	137.4	137.5	137.5	137.4	137.2	136.8	136.6	136.7	136.1	136.4	137.0
2006	137.3	137.7	138.7	138.6	138.8	139.5	139.4	139.3	139.9	142.0	142.7	142.6	139.7
2007	144.0	144.0	144.0	145.2	145.9	146.7	148.2	149.3	149.9	151.5	152.5	153.2	147.9
2008	153.3	153.8	155.6	156.5	156.7	157.1	158.8	161.1	163.9	170.6	172.7	177.9	161.5
2009[1]	176.5	178.1	178.5	178.1	178.1	178.5	178.1	177.4	179.3	180.7	181.0	180.5	178.7

[1] Preliminary. Not seasonally adjusted. *Source: Bureau of Labor Statistics, U.S. Department of Labor (BLS)*

Per Capita Use of Selected Commercially Produced Fresh and Processing Vegetables and Melons in the United States In Pounds, farm weight basis

Crop	2000	2001	2002	2003	2004	2005	2006	2007	2008	2009[10]	2010[11]
Asparagus, All	1.3	1.2	1.2	1.3	1.4	1.4	1.4	1.4	1.4	1.5	1.5
Fresh	1.0	0.9	1.0	1.0	1.1	1.1	1.1	1.2	1.2	1.2	1.2
Canning	0.2	0.2	0.2	0.2	0.2	0.2	0.2	0.1	0.2	0.2	0.2
Freezing	0.1	0.1	0.1	0.1	0.1	0.1	0.1	0.1	0.1	0.1	0.1
Snap beans, All	7.9	7.8	7.2	7.5	7.6	7.6	7.8	7.8	7.3	7.2	7.2
Fresh	2.0	2.2	2.1	2.0	1.9	1.8	2.1	2.2	2.0	2.1	2.1
Canning	4.0	3.8	3.4	3.7	3.7	4.0	3.9	3.5	3.2	3.2	3.2
Freezing	1.8	1.9	1.8	1.9	2.0	1.8	1.9	2.1	2.0	2.0	2.0
Broccoli, All [1]	8.1	7.4	7.5	7.9	8.0	8.1	8.0	8.3	8.6	8.6	8.6
Fresh	5.9	5.4	5.4	5.4	5.3	5.4	5.8	5.6	5.8	5.6	5.6
Freezing	2.3	2.0	2.1	2.6	2.7	2.7	2.3	2.7	2.8	3.0	3.0
Cabbage, All	10.3	10.1	9.5	8.5	9.2	9.0	9.0	9.1	9.2	9.2	9.2
Fresh	8.9	8.8	8.3	7.4	8.1	7.8	7.8	8.0	8.0	8.0	8.0
Canning (kraut)	1.4	1.3	1.2	1.1	1.1	1.2	1.2	1.2	1.2	1.2	1.2
Carrots, All [2]	13.0	13.0	11.6	11.9	11.7	11.8	11.2	10.7	10.7	10.5	10.5
Fresh	9.2	9.4	8.4	8.8	8.7	8.7	8.1	8.1	8.0	7.8	7.8
Canning	1.1	1.4	1.0	1.1	1.0	1.1	1.0	1.1	1.0	0.9	0.9
Freezing	2.7	2.2	2.1	2.0	2.0	2.0	2.1	1.5	1.7	1.8	1.8
Cauliflower, All [1]	2.3	2.0	1.7	1.9	1.9	2.1	2.1	2.1	2.0	2.1	2.1
Fresh	1.7	1.5	1.4	1.6	1.6	1.8	1.7	1.7	1.7	1.7	1.7
Freezing	0.6	0.5	0.3	0.4	0.4	0.4	0.4	0.4	0.3	0.4	0.4
Celery	6.3	6.4	6.3	6.3	6.2	5.9	6.1	6.3	6.4	6.4	6.4
Sweet Corn, All [3]	27.1	27.2	26.2	26.5	26.3	26.7	26.0	26.1	25.0	24.6	24.6
Fresh	9.0	9.2	9.0	9.2	9.0	8.7	8.3	9.2	8.8	8.7	8.7
Canning	9.0	8.7	7.8	8.3	8.2	8.6	8.4	6.9	6.8	6.5	6.5
Freezing	9.0	9.3	9.3	9.0	9.1	9.5	9.3	10.0	9.5	9.4	9.4
Cucumbers, All	11.2	10.0	12.0	10.6	11.3	10.0	9.1	10.2	10.3	9.8	9.8
Fresh	6.4	6.3	6.6	6.2	6.4	6.2	6.1	6.4	6.3	6.3	6.3
Pickling	4.9	3.7	5.4	4.5	4.9	3.8	3.0	3.7	4.0	3.5	3.5
Melons	27.2	28.2	27.3	26.5	24.9	25.0	26.3	25.9	26.5	26.0	26.0
Watermelon	13.8	15.0	14.1	13.6	13.0	13.6	15.1	14.4	15.0	14.8	14.8
Cantaloupe	11.1	11.2	11.1	10.8	9.8	9.6	9.3	9.6	9.8	9.5	9.5
Honeydew	2.3	2.0	2.2	2.2	2.1	1.9	1.9	1.8	1.8	1.8	1.8
Lettuce, All	31.9	31.0	32.2	33.1	33.3	30.6	32.1	30.0	30.0	30.4	30.4
Head lettuce	23.5	23.0	22.6	22.2	21.3	20.9	20.1	18.4	18.3	18.4	18.4
Romaine & Leaf	8.4	8.0	9.6	10.8	12.0	9.7	12.0	11.6	11.7	11.9	11.9
Onions, All	20.4	19.5	20.4	21.4	23.4	22.0	21.7	22.7	22.0	22.6	22.6
Fresh	18.9	18.5	19.3	19.5	21.9	20.9	19.9	21.6	20.7	21.2	21.2
Dehydrating	1.6	1.0	1.1	1.8	1.5	1.1	1.8	1.0	1.3	1.4	1.4
Green Peas, All [4]	3.7	3.3	2.8	3.1	2.8	2.7	2.7	3.0	2.9	3.0	3.0
Canning	1.5	1.4	1.1	1.3	1.2	1.0	1.1	1.1	1.1	1.1	1.1
Freezing	2.1	2.0	1.7	1.8	1.6	1.6	1.6	1.8	1.9	1.9	1.9
Peppers, All	13.3	13.3	14.1	14.0	14.8	15.3	15.8	15.5	15.7	15.8	15.8
Bell Peppers, All	8.2	8.1	8.3	8.4	8.6	9.2	9.5	9.4	9.4	9.4	9.4
Chile Peppers, All	5.2	5.2	5.8	5.6	6.1	6.1	6.4	6.1	6.3	6.5	6.5
Tomatoes, All	89.1	84.8	89.7	89.3	90.6	93.9	84.4	87.9	92.8	92.8	92.8
Fresh	19.0	19.2	20.3	19.4	20.0	20.2	19.8	19.2	20.0	19.4	19.4
Canning	70.1	65.5	69.4	69.9	70.6	73.8	64.6	68.7	72.7	73.4	73.4
Other, Fresh [5]	18.3	17.2	17.8	18.1	19.1	19.9	19.9	19.3	19.7	19.8	19.8
Other, Canning [6]	2.6	2.8	2.4	2.5	2.9	3.1	2.7	2.7	2.8	2.7	2.7
Other, Freezing [7]	3.2	3.2	4.3	3.9	3.8	3.9	3.9	3.9	4.0	4.0	4.0
Subtotal, All [8]	297.1	288.4	294.1	294.3	299.1	298.9	290.2	292.6	297.1	296.8	296.8
Fresh	173.8	172.2	173.7	172.7	176.1	173.0	174.5	174.0	174.5	174.0	174.0
Canning	100.0	93.9	97.7	98.2	100.0	102.9	92.4	95.2	99.1	99.0	99.0
Freezing	21.8	21.2	21.7	21.6	21.6	21.9	21.5	22.5	22.3	22.5	22.5
Potatoes, All	137.9	138.8	132.1	138.4	134.9	125.8	123.5	125.4	120.4	121.0	121.0
Fresh	47.1	46.6	44.3	46.9	45.9	41.4	38.6	39.1	36.9	37.4	37.4
Processing	90.8	92.2	87.8	91.5	89.0	84.4	84.9	86.3	83.5	83.6	83.6
Sweet Potatoes	4.2	4.4	3.8	4.7	4.6	4.5	4.6	5.1	5.1	5.2	5.2
Mushrooms	4.1	3.9	4.1	4.2	4.2	3.9	4.0	3.9	3.9	3.9	3.9
Dry Peas & Lentils [9]	0.8	0.8	0.8	0.6	0.7	0.8	1.2	0.8	0.6	0.8	0.8
Dry Edible Beans	7.6	6.9	6.8	6.7	6.0	6.1	6.4	6.8	6.3	6.5	6.5
Total, All Items	451.7	443.1	441.7	448.8	449.5	440.0	429.9	434.6	433.4	434.2	434.2

[1] All production for processing broccoli and cauliflower is for freezing. [2] Industry allocation suggests that 27 percent of processing carrot production is for canning and 73 percent is for freezing. [3] On-cob basis. [4] In-shell basis. [5] Includes artichokes, brussels sprouts, eggplant, endive/escarole, garlic, radishes, green limas, squash, and spinach. In 2000, okra, pumpkins, kale, collards, turnip greens and mustard greens added. [6] Includes beets, green limas (1992-2003), spinach, and miscellaneous imports (1990-2001). [7] Includes green limas, spinach, and miscellaneous freezing vegetables. [8] Fresh, canning, and freezing data do not sum to the total because onions for dehydrating are included in the total. [9] Production from new areas in upper midwest added in 1998. A portion of this is likely for feed use. [10] Preliminary. [11] Forecast. NA = Not available. *Source: Economic Research Service, U.S. Department of Agriculture (ERS-USDA)*

Average Price Received by Growers for Broccoli in the United States In Dollars Per Cwt

Year	Jan.	Feb.	Mar.	Apr.	May	June	July	Aug.	Sept.	Oct.	Nov.	Dec.	Season Average
2002	55.30	44.40	33.80	24.00	20.80	28.40	27.00	29.60	40.60	24.00	37.10	35.00	31.40
2003	25.20	40.90	28.10	27.10	29.70	24.60	27.00	29.80	49.10	38.90	48.00	40.00	32.70
2004	33.60	28.50	21.60	24.00	27.20	28.70	24.20	29.70	57.00	43.90	44.20	45.40	33.20
2005	22.60	33.30	42.60	39.80	22.40	39.70	22.40	30.50	27.70	22.40	20.90	34.10	28.50
2006	32.50	23.80	27.60	32.40	29.00	51.10	26.20	56.90	39.40	24.60	27.50	53.10	33.70
2007	69.80	25.40	27.60	36.90	26.70	24.80	28.80	38.20	41.80	61.00	38.10	40.70	36.70
2008	47.90	24.40	30.80	52.10	25.20	29.60	26.70	26.60	41.10	57.50	41.20	33.70	36.20
2009[1]	44.60	29.50	46.50	42.00	32.80	31.00	26.50	29.70	31.60	64.60	57.20	53.50	37.80

[1]Preliminary. *Source: National Agricultural Statistics Service, U.S. Department of Agriculture (NASS-USDA)*

Average Price Received by Growers for Carrots in the United States In Dollars Per Cwt

Year	Jan.	Feb.	Mar.	Apr.	May	June	July	Aug.	Sept.	Oct.	Nov.	Dec.	Season Average
2002	19.30	19.70	21.10	21.20	21.30	21.60	20.60	20.10	18.10	17.90	18.70	19.50	19.10
2003	19.30	19.10	18.70	19.40	19.90	20.00	19.90	20.50	19.80	19.10	21.60	24.30	19.00
2004	24.50	24.90	24.60	24.20	24.90	22.50	20.20	18.00	16.70	16.40	17.20	18.00	20.20
2005	20.30	21.00	21.00	21.10	21.20	21.30	21.80	21.40	20.00	21.40	23.10	22.00	20.90
2006	21.40	21.50	21.50	21.50	20.80	21.40	21.50	22.40	19.30	19.80	20.20	19.10	20.60
2007	21.00	28.10	28.30	29.60	32.00	25.90	19.70	17.10	16.10	15.80	15.80	16.20	22.10
2008	16.20	25.90	25.90	25.50	32.00	25.60	25.60	25.60	25.30	25.20	24.70	25.20	24.50
2009[1]	25.20	25.20	25.20	25.20	25.50	25.80	25.60	24.40	25.20	25.40	27.20	27.80	25.20

[1]Preliminary. *Source: National Agricultural Statistics Service, U.S. Department of Agriculture (NASS-USDA)*

Average Price Received by Growers for Cauliflower in the United States In Dollars Per Cwt

Year	Jan.	Feb.	Mar.	Apr.	May	June	July	Aug.	Sept.	Oct.	Nov.	Dec.	Season Average
2002	65.50	30.80	44.10	25.10	26.40	32.70	27.80	24.00	24.70	22.50	37.60	50.00	32.20
2003	24.60	30.70	30.80	20.70	39.50	46.30	27.60	25.30	40.30	25.80	57.00	75.50	35.10
2004	27.30	42.20	24.20	23.50	28.80	46.20	27.60	26.30	31.10	32.20	43.80	54.40	30.80
2005	27.70	38.20	50.60	36.70	29.70	38.10	25.60	31.50	28.50	19.70	25.50	43.90	30.30
2006	33.10	26.40	31.40	32.80	29.00	51.10	26.20	56.90	39.40	24.60	34.80	41.60	32.30
2007	45.70	29.40	51.40	51.60	24.90	30.00	22.30	27.90	27.20	46.20	26.60	52.40	34.40
2008	51.80	30.00	41.70	63.80	24.90	53.90	38.20	43.20	29.50	48.50	29.50	43.90	40.70
2009[1]	68.20	30.00	51.30	41.90	46.60	43.50	41.70	31.90	26.90	58.10	54.40	47.10	44.40

[1]Preliminary. *Source: National Agricultural Statistics Service, U.S. Department of Agriculture (NASS-USDA)*

Average Price Received by Growers for Celery in the United States In Dollars Per Cwt

Year	Jan.	Feb.	Mar.	Apr.	May	June	July	Aug.	Sept.	Oct.	Nov.	Dec.	Season Average
2002	10.10	19.50	23.50	18.60	12.30	9.37	10.80	10.90	11.70	9.98	15.30	9.50	12.80
2003	8.29	11.80	12.60	17.00	11.00	9.34	12.80	11.90	13.30	15.90	23.40	14.50	13.40
2004	20.80	24.40	13.90	15.60	15.00	13.80	12.00	10.00	11.90	15.10	18.10	13.40	14.80
2005	12.90	22.90	28.40	20.80	15.50	9.62	10.00	10.80	12.80	12.20	13.10	10.70	13.90
2006	9.64	10.80	14.90	16.60	12.70	17.80	21.00	23.30	27.70	27.10	22.00	20.20	18.20
2007	33.90	58.90	31.90	18.80	18.30	11.60	11.60	9.64	13.80	13.30	18.60	13.50	20.40
2008	16.20	13.20	13.40	14.00	37.40	30.10	22.10	12.40	11.90	17.10	16.90	20.30	18.50
2009[1]	35.10	29.70	15.00	17.40	17.40	11.70	11.50	11.30	11.70	21.00	21.10	38.80	18.50

[1]Preliminary. *Source: National Agricultural Statistics Service, U.S. Department of Agriculture (NASS-USDA)*

Average Price Received by Growers for Sweet Corn in the United States In Dollars Per Cwt

Year	Jan.	Feb.	Mar.	Apr.	May	June	July	Aug.	Sept.	Oct.	Nov.	Dec.	Season Average
2002	24.80	23.50	26.30	19.40	20.80	18.80	27.90	21.80	22.50	25.80	15.50	18.30	19.20
2003	29.00	24.00	18.90	14.90	16.60	23.20	21.30	20.10	19.70	23.70	30.70	22.60	19.30
2004	30.80	20.70	20.20	17.60	18.10	22.80	21.80	22.90	24.10	33.50	46.70	36.80	20.80
2005	21.30	28.60	26.10	21.50	18.10	22.60	22.20	20.30	24.70	25.50	37.30	21.20	22.10
2006	36.50	35.00	34.00	27.20	15.40	21.60	21.10	22.70	25.90	21.20	20.00	14.40	23.00
2007	27.40	23.60	30.20	25.60	21.40	17.30	22.20	22.80	23.20	21.40	20.60	34.10	22.70
2008	30.80	23.00	28.60	20.50	21.90	19.90	28.50	27.20	27.10	23.70	30.80	22.20	25.90
2009[1]	24.90	46.40	59.30	32.20	22.70	27.10	37.80	27.90	24.10	25.10	21.00	19.40	29.40

[1]Preliminary. *Source: National Agricultural Statistics Service, U.S. Department of Agriculture (NASS-USDA)*

Average Price Received by Growers for Head Lettuce in the United States In Dollars Per Cwt

Year	Jan.	Feb.	Mar.	Apr.	May	June	July	Aug.	Sept.	Oct.	Nov.	Dec.	Season Average
2000	14.60	9.28	14.10	22.80	23.60	13.50	15.00	19.20	29.40	16.20	19.90	12.00	17.30
2001	13.60	22.80	15.10	21.60	18.80	12.10	16.40	26.90	26.20	11.50	10.90	10.00	17.90
2002	26.20	44.10	86.40	14.10	10.20	10.60	11.30	14.60	14.30	13.50	11.90	30.00	21.10
2003	12.10	11.80	9.64	12.50	21.20	32.20	11.90	21.50	23.90	26.30	31.70	21.30	18.10
2004	15.40	19.80	10.40	14.80	10.50	13.30	10.70	17.10	15.20	24.10	14.90	15.70	16.90
2005	11.50	11.70	27.90	30.10	13.90	17.30	11.00	13.50	12.70	12.40	9.81	16.60	15.50
2006	10.50	12.00	19.10	22.40	33.70	11.80	12.20	20.70	16.30	11.80	12.50	22.40	16.90
2007	20.80	15.50	29.70	17.80	13.60	17.80	17.30	23.10	29.20	44.40	17.40	16.00	21.70
2008	17.60	13.40	14.70	21.60	15.50	17.70	17.30	17.20	31.90	32.90	18.80	23.50	20.10
2009[1]	28.50	17.80	19.60	27.80	18.20	18.90	16.90	16.70	16.60	27.20	49.70	38.70	21.70

[1]Preliminary. *Source: National Agricultural Statistics Service, U.S. Department of Agriculture (NASS-USDA)*

Average Price Received by Growers for Tomatoes in the United States In Dollars Per Cwt

Year	Jan.	Feb.	Mar.	Apr.	May	June	July	Aug.	Sept.	Oct.	Nov.	Dec.	Season Average
2000	21.40	21.10	33.00	34.80	23.10	21.80	24.60	33.90	29.50	42.60	47.80	37.60	30.70
2001	43.80	29.10	56.40	19.00	37.80	28.50	27.40	27.60	23.50	28.60	28.50	25.00	30.00
2002	40.50	26.60	38.50	34.30	29.60	33.00	28.50	25.80	23.70	27.60	40.10	38.00	31.60
2003	47.20	31.70	53.30	30.00	23.70	45.70	37.60	41.00	35.70	30.10	30.50	29.10	37.40
2004	34.50	36.30	42.20	44.20	32.20	21.70	23.40	37.80	38.20	67.90	89.00	47.10	37.60
2005	15.40	40.90	40.70	65.10	49.40	40.00	28.00	26.10	46.10	37.30	36.50	96.80	41.80
2006	79.20	46.50	24.80	34.40	23.30	30.90	25.10	27.80	79.80	53.20	28.10	24.80	43.70
2007	35.60	31.20	26.30	52.60	35.60	29.60	26.70	28.60	33.10	41.60	58.70	81.20	34.80
2008	58.20	45.50	66.10	47.40	48.20	56.80	40.90	29.40	25.60	33.80	64.90	37.90	45.50
2009[1]	29.30	32.70	41.50	45.40	33.20	71.20	32.30	36.60	34.50	40.00	73.70	65.00	40.60

[1]Preliminary. *Source: National Agricultural Statistics Service, U.S. Department of Agriculture (NASS-USDA)*

Frozen Vegetables: January 1 and July 1 Cold Storage Holdings in the United States In Thousands of Pounds

Crop	2005 July 1	2006 Jan. 1	July 1	2007 Jan. 1	July 1	2008 Jan. 1	July 1	2009 Jan. 1	July 1	2010[1] Jan. 1
Asparagus	13,943	9,029	11,929	6,178	9,952	5,409	9,964	7,368	12,353	9,057
Limas, Fordhook	3,502	7,687	2,368	6,543	2,619	7,442	2,209	3,676	1,006	2,973
Limas, Baby	27,360	40,867	21,851	41,849	18,367	40,364	16,213	41,020	20,291	58,390
Green Beans, Reg. Cut	76,655	171,319	24,377	183,610	72,177	183,696	70,854	211,997	97,121	176,371
Green Beans, Fr. Style	8,157	22,341	8,388	27,433	9,303	32,284	12,675	29,298	13,009	25,325
Broccoli, Spears	45,581	35,814	32,699	27,628	23,878	24,078	33,587	36,649	37,721	29,456
Broccoli, Chopped & Cut	62,382	62,561	61,769	46,855	40,715	36,422	49,873	45,513	55,338	41,547
Brussels sprouts	16,028	21,660	10,243	21,650	11,535	21,491	10,392	21,049	12,837	20,789
Carrots, Diced	63,871	128,877	64,540	117,159	53,574	128,121	68,556	156,398	94,151	165,191
Carrots, Other	93,702	150,317	97,528	127,449	51,911	142,063	85,955	150,459	98,764	155,247
Cauliflower	19,916	43,836	18,694	38,196	17,768	36,694	20,334	27,564	16,051	27,066
Corn, Cut	234,965	464,177	188,556	475,671	161,547	461,503	172,494	463,724	203,077	584,048
Corn, Cob	78,525	263,818	71,738	281,694	69,152	256,464	78,251	264,562	96,382	252,108
Mixed vegetables	49,493	55,236	50,856	51,925	43,342	43,868	46,341	47,729	54,659	50,129
Okra	28,097	31,734	26,363	31,507	16,638	23,720	21,505	24,115	21,896	29,030
Onion Rings	6,181	4,757	7,532	7,533	8,136	7,428	5,925	6,628	4,367	3,456
Onions, Other	39,424	43,349	38,192	37,386	26,527	32,010	39,190	29,564	26,498	35,511
Blackeye Peas	1,878	2,348	4,080	4,784	3,136	4,394	2,815	2,737	1,509	3,653
Green Peas	227,162	214,851	222,513	230,351	241,116	232,647	198,133	255,471	249,734	275,625
Peas and Carrots Mixed	5,416	5,227	5,422	4,946	4,654	5,090	4,756	5,109	5,281	6,075
Spinach	87,983	42,464	107,607	52,674	70,443	47,467	80,320	42,505	88,541	47,993
Squash, Summer/Zucchini	39,164	61,518	50,704	64,255	49,275	62,534	46,531	56,537	42,124	52,275
Southern greens	18,905	13,750	17,546	14,826	10,741	12,833	14,231	12,632	15,916	11,621
Other Vegetables	267,205	353,315	238,391	323,249	220,569	373,370	275,882	423,684	292,300	408,829
Total	1,515,495	2,250,852	1,413,886	2,225,351	1,237,075	2,221,392	1,366,986	2,365,988	1,560,926	2,471,765
Potatoes, French Fries	947,971	848,595	877,400	758,254	871,947	820,461	947,666	874,095	1,011,773	847,238
Potatoes, Other Frozen	242,493	202,504	230,710	196,566	206,261	191,894	242,365	224,485	235,394	196,607
Potatoes, Total	1,190,464	1,051,099	1,108,110	954,820	1,078,208	1,012,355	1,190,031	1,098,580	1,247,167	1,043,845
Grand Total	2,705,959	3,301,951	2,521,996	3,180,171	2,315,283	3,233,747	2,557,017	3,464,568	2,808,093	3,515,610

Wheat

Wheat is a cereal grass, but before cultivation it was a wild grass. It has been grown in temperate regions and cultivated for food since prehistoric times. Wheat is believed to have originated in southwestern Asia. Archeological research indicates that wheat was grown as a crop in the Nile Valley about 5,000 BC. Wheat is not native to the U.S. and was first grown here in 1602 near the Massachusetts coast. The common tWheat is a cereal grass, but before cultivation it was a wild grass. It has been grown in temperate regions and cultivated for food since prehistoric times. Wheat is believed to have originated in southwestern Asia. Archeological research indicates that wheat was grown as a crop in the Nile Valley about 5,000 BC. Wheat is not native to the U.S. and was first grown here in 1602 near the Massachusetts coast. The common types of wheat grown in the U.S. are spring and winter wheat. Wheat planted in the spring for summer or autumn harvest is mostly red wheat. Wheat planted in the fall or winter for spring harvest is mostly white wheat. Winter wheat accounts for nearly three-fourths of total U.S. production. Wheat is used mainly as a human food and supplies about 20% of the food calories for the world's population. The primary use for wheat is flour, but it is also used for brewing and distilling, and for making oil, gluten, straw for livestock bedding, livestock feed, hay or silage, newsprint, and other products.

Wheat futures and options are traded on the Mercado a Termino de Buenos Aires (MAT), Sydney Futures Exchange (SFE), London International Financial Futures and Options Exchange (LIFFE), Marche a Terme International de France (MATIF), Budapest Commodity Exchange (BCE), the Chicago Board of Trade (CBOT), the Kansas City Board of Trade (KCBT), and the Minneapolis Grain Exchange (MGE). The Chicago Board of Trade's wheat futures contract calls for the delivery of soft red wheat (No. 1 and 2), hard red winter wheat (No. 1 and 2), dark northern spring wheat (No. 1 and 2), No.1 northern spring at 3 cents/bushel premium, or No. 2 northern spring at par.

Prices – CBOT wheat prices on the nearest-futures chart traded generally sideways during 2009 in the range of $4-$7 per bushel. Wheat prices in 2007 and early 2008 spiked higher due to strong demand, competition for acreage with corn and soybeans, and limited supplies with drought in Australia, Canada, and Russia. However, wheat prices then fell back in 2008 and 2009 due to two years of big global production of a record 683 million metric tons (MMT) in 2008/09 and 677 MMT in 2009-10. Those large crops caused the global carry-over to rise to an 8-year high of 195.9 MMT in 2009-10. World wheat usage in 2009-10 rose by only +0.9% y/y and was unable to absorb the big crops. The stocks-to-use ratio rose to an 8-year high of 30.3% in 2009-10. Regarding the summer 2010 US wheat crop, the USDA is forecasting an 8.4% decline in harvested acres to 45.7 million acres from 49.9 million acres the previous year, a 1.8 bushel per acre decline in yield to 42.6 bushels per acre from 44.4 bushels the previous year, and a 12% decline in US production to 1.945 billion bushels. The USDA expects the lower supply, and small increase in demand, to just slightly cut the US carry-over to 940 million bushels, which would be just slightly below the 22-year high of 981 million bushels posted in 2009-10. The high level of US and global wheat carry-overs expected for 2010-11 are likely to keep a lid on wheat prices in 2010.

Supply – World wheat production in the 2009-10 marketing year fell -0.8% to 677.44 million metric tons, down from last year's record high. The world's largest wheat producers were the European Union with 20% of world production in 2009-10, China (17%), India (12%), the U.S. (9%), Russia (9%), and Canada (4%). China's wheat production in 2009-10 rose +1.8% yr/yr to 114.500 million metric tons, but is still well below its record high of 123.289 million metric tons seen in 1997-98. Australia's wheat production rose +7.5% yr/yr to 22.500 million metric tons in 2009-10, but still well below its record high of 26.132 million metric tons in 2003-04. The world land area harvested with wheat in 2009-10 rose +0.4% yr/yr to 225.8 million hectares (1 hectare equals 10,000 square meters or 2.471 acres), remaining above the 209.6 million hectares in 2003-04, which was the smallest wheat harvest area since 1970-71. World wheat yield in 2009-10 fell -1.0% to 3.00 metric tons per acre, down from the 2008-09 record high of 3.04 metric tons per hectare.

U.S. wheat production in 2009-10 fell -11.3% yr/yr to 2.216 billion bushels, well below the record U.S. wheat crop of 2.785 billion bushels seen in 1981-82. The U.S. winter wheat crop in 2009 fell -18.5% yr/yr to 1.5623 billion bushels, which was well below the record winter wheat crop of 2.097 billion bushels seen in 1981. U.S. production of durum wheat in 2009 rose +30.1% yr/yr to 109.042 million bushels. U.S. production of other spring wheat in 2008 rose +6.6% yr/yr to 584.411 million bushels. The largest U.S. producing states of winter wheat in 2009 were Kansas with 24% of U.S. production, Washington with 6%, Montana with 6%, Oklahoma with 5%, and Texas with 4%. U.S. farmers planted 59.133 million acres of wheat in 2009, which was down -6.4% yr/yr. U.S. wheat yield in 2009-10 was 44.4 bushels per acre, down from the 44.9 record high last year. Ending stocks for U.S. wheat for 2009-10 were at 975.7 million bushels, up +48.6% yr/yr.

Demand – World wheat utilization in 2009-10 rose +1.7% yr/yr to a record high of 644.4 million metric tons. U.S. consumption of wheat in 2009-10 fell -6.2% yr/yr to 1.182 billion bushels, which was below the record high of 1.381 billion bushels seen in 1998-99. The consumption breakdown shows that 80% of U.S. wheat consumption in 2009-10 went for food, 14% for feed and residuals, and 6% for seed.

Trade – World trade in wheat in 2009-10 fell -12.7% yr/yr to 124.3 million metric tons, down from last year's record high of 142.5 million metric tons. U.S. exports of wheat in 2009-10 fell -18.8% yr/yr to 825.0 million bushes, and remained well below the record of 1.771 billion bushels of exports seen in 1981-82. U.S. imports of wheat in 2009-10 fell -13.4% to 110.0 million bushels, down from the 2006-07 record high of 121.9 million bushels.

World Production of Wheat In Thousands of Metric Tons

Crop Year	Argentina	Australia	Canada	China	European Union	India	Iran	Kazakhstan	Pakistan	Russia	Turkey	United States	World Total
2000-01	16,230	22,108	26,519	99,640	131,697	76,369	8,088	9,100	21,079	34,450	18,000	60,641	582,899
2001-02	15,500	24,299	20,568	93,873	123,353	69,680	9,459	12,700	19,024	46,900	15,500	53,001	583,078
2002-03	12,300	10,132	16,198	90,290	132,579	71,810	12,450	12,600	18,227	50,550	16,800	43,705	567,880
2003-04	14,500	26,132	23,049	86,490	110,578	65,100	13,440	11,550	19,183	34,100	16,800	63,805	554,063
2004-05	16,100	21,905	24,796	91,952	146,886	72,150	14,568	9,950	19,500	45,400	18,500	58,698	625,724
2005-06	14,600	25,173	25,748	97,445	132,356	68,640	14,308	11,200	21,612	47,700	18,500	57,243	619,933
2006-07	16,100	10,822	25,265	108,466	124,870	69,350	14,500	13,450	21,277	44,900	17,500	49,217	595,702
2007-08[1]	18,000	13,569	20,054	109,298	120,133	75,810	15,000	16,450	23,300	49,400	15,500	55,821	610,456
2008-09[2]	9,000	20,939	28,611	112,464	151,080	78,570	10,000	12,550	21,500	63,700	16,800	68,016	682,694
2009-10[3]	9,000	22,500	26,500	114,500	138,218	80,580	12,000	17,000	24,000	61,700	17,800	60,314	677,441

[1] Preliminary. [2] Estimate. [3] Forecast. *Source: Foreign Agricultural Service, U.S. Department of Agriculture (FAS-USDA)*

World Supply and Demand of Wheat In Millions of Metric Tons/Hectares

Year	Area Harvested	Yield	Production	World Trade	Utilization Total	Ending Stocks	Stocks as a % of Utilization
2000-01	217.9	2.68	582.9	102.3	583.6	207.3	35.5
2001-02	215.2	2.71	583.1	108.0	587.6	203.2	34.6
2002-03	214.5	2.65	567.9	107.1	602.2	166.6	27.7
2003-04	209.6	2.64	554.1	103.7	580.6	132.0	22.7
2004-05	217.3	2.88	625.7	113.8	605.5	150.2	24.8
2005-06	219.3	2.83	619.9	113.8	617.1	147.5	23.9
2006-07	212.2	2.81	595.7	115.6	618.6	127.6	20.6
2007-08[1]	218.0	2.80	610.5	116.4	613.2	121.1	19.7
2008-09[2]	225.0	3.03	682.7	142.5	633.4	164.0	25.9
2009-10[3]	225.8	3.00	677.4	124.3	644.4	195.9	30.4

[1] Preliminary. [2] Estimate. [3] Forecast. *Source: Foreign Agricultural Service, U.S. Department of Agriculture (FAS-USDA)*

Salient Statistics of Wheat in the United States

Year	Planting Intentions	Acreage Harvested: Winter	Acreage Harvested: Spring	Acreage Harvested: All	Average All Yield Per Acre in Bushels	Value of Production $1,000	Foreign Trade[5]: Domestic Exports[2]	Foreign Trade[5]: Imports[3]	Per Capita[4] Consumption: Flour	Per Capita[4] Consumption: Cereal
	1,000 Acres						In Millions of Bushels		In Pounds	
2000-01	62,549	35,002	18,061	53,063	42.0	5,782,107	1,062.0	89.8	146.3	3.8
2001-02	59,597	31,295	17,338	48,633	40.2	5,440,217	962.3	107.6	141.0	3.8
2002-03	60,318	29,742	16,166	45,824	35.0	5,637,416	850.2	77.4	136.8	3.7
2003-04	62,141	36,753	16,310	53,063	44.2	7,929,039	1,158.3	63.0	136.7	3.7
2004-05	59,674	34,462	15,537	49,999	43.2	7,283,324	1,065.9	70.6	134.5	3.6
2005-06	57,229	33,794	16,325	50,119	42.0	7,171,441	1,002.8	81.4	134.3	3.6
2006-07	57,344	31,117	16,769	46,810	38.7	7,694,734	908.5	121.9	135.7	----
2007-08	60,460	35,938	15,061	50,999	40.5	13,289,326	1,262.6	112.6	138.1	----
2008-09	63,193	39,608	16,091	55,699	44.9	16,625,759	1,015.5	127.0	136.5	----
2009-10[1]	59,133	34,485	15,573	49,868	44.4	10,626,176	825.0	110.0	134.7	----

[1] Preliminary. [2] Includes flour milled from imported wheat. [3] Total wheat, flour & other products. [4] Civilian only. [5] Year beginning June.
Source: Economic Research Service, U.S. Department of Agriculture (ERS-USDA)

Supply and Distribution of Wheat in the United States In Millions of Bushels

Crop Year Beginning June 1	Supply: Stocks, June 1: On Farms	Supply: Stocks, June 1: Mills, Elevators[3]	Supply: Total Stocks	Supply: Production	Supply: Imports[4]	Supply: Total Supply	Domestic Disappearance: Food	Domestic Disappearance: Seed	Domestic Disappearance: Feed & Residual[5]	Domestic Disappearance: Total	Exports[4]	Total Disappearance
2000-01	226.8	723.0	949.7	2,232.5	89.8	3,267.7	949.6	79.5	300.4	1,329.5	1,062.0	2,391.6
2001-02	197.3	678.9	876.2	1,957.0	107.6	2,931.2	926.4	83.4	182.0	1,191.8	962.3	2,154.1
2002-03	216.8	560.3	777.1	1,605.9	77.4	2,460.4	918.6	84.4	115.7	1,118.7	850.2	1,968.9
2003-04	132.1	359.3	491.4	2,344.8	63.0	2,898.9	911.9	79.7	202.5	1,194.1	1,158.3	2,352.4
2004-05	131.9	414.6	546.4	2,158.2	70.6	2,773.8	909.6	77.6	180.6	1,167.8	1,065.9	2,233.7
2005-06	161.3	378.8	540.1	2,104.7	81.4	2,724.8	917.1	77.1	156.6	1,150.8	1,002.8	2,153.6
2006-07	111.0	460.2	571.2	1,812.0	121.9	2,501.5	937.9	81.9	117.1	1,136.8	908.5	2,045.3
2007-08	73.2	383.0	456.2	2,051.1	112.6	2,619.9	947.9	87.6	16.0	1,051.4	1,262.6	2,314.1
2008-09[1]	25.6	280.2	305.8	2,499.2	127.0	2,932.0	926.6	75.1	258.3	1,260.0	1,015.5	2,275.5
2009-10[2]	140.7	515.8	656.5	2,216.2	110.0	2,982.7	940.0	72.0	170.0	1,182.0	825.0	2,007.0

[1] Preliminary. [2] Estimate. [3] Also warehouses and all off-farm storage not otherwise designated, including flour mills. [4] Imports & exports are for wheat, including flour & other products in terms of wheat. [5] Mostly feed use.
Source: Economic Research Service, U.S. Department of Agriculture (ERS-USDA)

Year	Hard Spring Stocks June 1	Hard Spring Pro-duction	Hard Spring Exports[3]	Durum[2] Stocks June 1	Durum[2] Pro-duction	Durum[2] Exports[3]	Hard Winter Stocks June 1	Hard Winter Pro-duction	Hard Winter Exports[3]	Soft Red Winter Stocks June 1	Soft Red Winter Pro-duction	Soft Red Winter Exports[3]	White Stocks June 1	White Pro-duction	White Exports[3]
2000-01	218	502	230	50	110	50	458	846	403	133	471	176	91	303	203
2001-02	210	476	216	45	84	50	411	767	349	135	400	199	75	232	147
2002-03	230	351	259	33	80	32	363	620	309	78	321	105	73	233	148
2003-04	145	500	272	28	97	44	188	1,071	512	55	380	140	75	297	192
2004-05	157	525	314	26	90	31	227	856	388	64	380	122	72	306	207
2005-06	159	467	282	38	101	47	193	930	430	88	309	76	63	298	175
2006-07	132	432	250	40	53	35	215	682	281	106	390	146	78	254	197
2007-08	117	450	305	21	72	42	165	956	538	109	352	209	44	221	170
2008-09	68	512	210	8	84	24	138	1,035	447	55	614	199	37	255	136
2009-10[1]	142	548	200	25	109	50	254	919	300	171	404	105	64	237	170

[1] Preliminary. [2] Includes "Red Durum." [3] Includes four made from U.S. wheat & shipments to territories.
Source: Economic Research Service, U.S. Department of Agriculture (ERS-USDA)

Seeded Acreage, Yield and Production of all Wheat in the United States

Year	Seed Acreage - 1,000 Acres: Winter	Other Spring	Durum	All	Yield Per Harvested Acre (Bushels): Winter	Other Spring	Durum	All	Production (Million Bushels): Winter	Other Spring	Durum	All
2000	43,313	15,299	3,937	62,549	44.6	38.4	30.7	42.0	1,561.7	556.6	109.8	2,228.2
2001	41,078	15,609	2,910	59,597	43.5	35.2	30.0	40.2	1,361.5	512.0	83.6	1,957.0
2002	41,766	15,639	2,913	60,318	38.2	29.1	29.5	35.0	1,137.0	388.9	80.0	1,605.9
2003	45,384	13,842	2,915	62,141	46.7	39.5	33.7	44.2	1,716.7	531.4	96.6	2,344.8
2004	43,350	13,763	2,561	59,674	43.5	43.2	38.0	43.2	1,499.4	568.9	89.9	2,158.2
2005	40,433	14,036	2,760	57,229	44.4	37.1	37.2	42.0	1,499.1	504.5	101.1	2,104.7
2006	40,575	14,899	1,870	57,344	41.7	33.2	29.5	38.7	1,298.1	460.5	53.5	1,812.0
2007	45,012	13,292	2,156	60,460	41.7	37.1	34.1	40.2	1,499.2	479.6	72.2	2,051.1
2008	46,307	14,165	2,721	63,193	47.1	40.5	32.6	44.9	1,867.3	548.0	83.8	2,499.2
2009[1]	43,311	13,268	2,554	59,133	44.2	45.1	44.9	44.4	1,522.7	584.4	109.0	2,216.2

[1] Preliminary. *Source: Economic Research Service, U.S. Department of Agriculture (ERS-USDA)*

Production of Winter Wheat in the United States, by State In Thousands of Bushels

Year	Colorado	Idaho	Illinois	Kansas	Missouri	Montana	Neb-raska	Ohio	Okla-homa	Oregon	Texas	Wash-ington	Total
2000	68,150	63,900	52,440	347,800	49,400	44,550	59,400	79,920	142,800	45,260	66,000	131,400	1,561,723
2001	66,000	51,830	43,920	328,000	41,040	19,140	59,200	60,300	122,100	28,000	108,800	106,750	1,361,479
2002	36,300	48,510	30,870	270,600	33,440	21,840	50,160	50,220	103,600	29,820	78,300	104,400	1,137,001
2003	77,000	57,600	52,650	480,000	53,070	67,340	83,720	68,000	179,400	47,940	96,600	117,000	1,716,721
2004	45,900	63,000	53,100	314,500	48,360	66,830	61,050	55,180	164,500	47,580	108,500	117,250	1,499,434
2005	52,800	66,430	36,600	380,000	29,160	94,500	68,640	58,930	128,000	47,580	96,000	120,600	1,499,129
2006	39,900	54,670	60,970	291,200	49,140	82,560	61,200	65,280	81,600	38,690	33,600	118,800	1,298,081
2007	91,650	51,830	48,950	283,800	37,840	83,220	84,280	44,530	98,000	38,160	140,600	104,780	1,499,241
2008	57,000	60,000	73,600	356,000	55,680	94,380	73,480	74,120	166,500	44,950	99,000	96,320	1,867,333
2009[1]	98,000	56,700	45,920	369,600	34,310	89,540	76,800	70,560	77,000	42,000	61,250	96,760	1,522,718

[1] Preliminary. *Source: Crop Reporting Board, U.S. Department of Agriculture (CRB-USDA)*

Official Winter Wheat Crop Production Reports in the United States In Thousands of Bushels

Crop Year	May 1	June 1	July 1	August 1	September 1	Current December	Final
2000-01	1,648,805	1,621,966	1,588,376	1,594,321	----	----	1,561,723
2001-02	1,341,381	1,321,126	1,366,192	1,385,048	----	----	1,361,479
2002-03	1,300,726	1,237,671	1,178,320	1,158,710	----	----	1,137,001
2003-04	1,563,314	1,626,376	1,715,912	1,712,150	----	----	1,716,721
2004-05	1,550,395	1,530,742	1,469,735	1,489,408	----	----	1,499,434
2005-06	1,590,862	1,545,971	1,525,302	1,520,848	----	----	1,499,129
2006-07	1,322,831	1,263,766	1,280,005	1,283,134	----	----	1,298,081
2007-08	1,615,613	1,609,679	1,561,907	1,537,262	----	----	1,499,241
2008-09	1,777,532	1,817,364	1,864,245	1,874,857	----	----	1,867,333
2009-10[1]	1,502,074	1,491,769	1,524,771	1,537,348	----	----	1,522,718

[1] Preliminary. *Source: Crop Reporting Board, U.S. Department of Agriculture (CRB-USDA)*

Production of All Spring Wheat in the United States, by State In Thousands of Bushels

	Durum Wheat						Other Spring Wheat							
Year	Arizona	California	Montana	North Dakota	South Dakota	Total	Idaho	Minnesota	Montana	North Dakota	Oregon	South Dakota	Washington	Total
2000	8,075	9,700	13,160	78,300	468	109,805	42,750	95,550	77,500	233,600	8,280	60,040	33,480	556,632
2001	7,917	8,505	11,880	54,600	576	83,556	33,320	79,200	65,550	234,600	4,650	64,350	25,830	512,008
2002	8,928	9,000	12,995	48,750	147	79,960	29,900	61,200	75,900	165,200	4,680	24,000	25,370	388,917
2003	11,500	11,500	14,490	58,410	621	96,637	27,060	104,400	60,500	252,800	5,600	56,280	22,345	531,402
2004	9,603	9,000	17,985	52,800	450	89,893	38,710	88,550	88,350	243,950	8,400	71,910	26,250	568,918
2005	7,900	6,555	16,380	68,250	260	101,105	32,400	70,930	81,600	224,400	5,980	67,600	18,700	504,456
2006	7,400	6,435	6,715	31,500	90	53,475	34,310	77,550	63,800	212,350	5,750	42,600	21,250	460,480
2007	8,364	8,000	11,400	43,070	175	72,224	30,600	79,200	55,200	234,000	5,520	52,260	20,562	479,623
2008	14,602	15,225	10,830	42,250	190	83,827	37,440	100,800	59,520	246,400	7,650	68,400	22,470	548,004
2009[1]	12,400	17,000	16,950	61,940	207	109,042	40,810	83,700	70,500	291,200	6,858	64,680	26,325	584,411

[1] Preliminary. *Source: Crop Reporting Board, U.S. Department of Agriculture (CRB-USDA)*

Grindings of Wheat by Mills in the United States In Millions of Bushels -- of 60 Pounds Each

Year	Jan.	Feb.	Mar.	Apr.	May	June	July	Aug.	Sept.	Oct.	Nov.	Dec.	Total
2000-01	-----	244.7	-----	-----	247.7	-----	-----	223.8	-----	-----	221.3	-----	937.5
2001-02	-----	230.2	-----	-----	238.7	-----	-----	217.0	-----	-----	217.6	-----	903.6
2002-03	-----	230.3	-----	-----	224.4	-----	-----	215.8	-----	-----	217.4	-----	888.0
2003-04	-----	231.8	-----	-----	224.2	-----	-----	214.7	-----	-----	214.5	-----	885.2
2004-05	-----	224.8	-----	-----	222.1	-----	-----	214.9	-----	-----	216.5	-----	878.3
2005-06	-----	229.3	-----	-----	223.4	-----	-----	216.1	-----	-----	217.1	-----	885.9
2006-07	-----	233.3	-----	-----	228.0	-----	-----	222.0	-----	-----	226.1	-----	909.5
2007-08	-----	239.3	-----	-----	236.3	-----	-----	223.2	-----	-----	224.3	-----	923.1
2008-09	-----	235.2	-----	-----	225.3	-----	-----	217.5	-----	-----	221.1	-----	899.1
2009-10[1]	-----	233.5	-----	-----		-----	-----		-----	-----		-----	934.1

[1] Preliminary. *Source: Bureau of the Census, U.S. Department of Commerce*

Stocks of Wheat in the United States In Millions of Bushels

	On Farms				Off Farms				Total Stocks			
Year	Mar. 1	June 1	Sept. 1	Dec. 1	Mar. 1	June 1	Sept. 1	Dec. 1	Mar. 1	June 1	Sept. 1	Dec. 1
2000	424.7	226.8	808.4	623.4	991.8	723.0	1,544.3	1,182.7	1,416.5	949.7	2,352.7	1,806.1
2001	384.8	197.3	696.9	517.9	953.6	678.9	1,459.0	1,105.6	1,338.4	876.2	2,155.8	1,623.5
2002	338.5	216.8	580.2	384.8	871.3	560.3	1,170.8	935.1	1,209.8	777.1	1,751.0	1,319.9
2003	236.3	132.1	687.3	491.9	670.3	359.3	1,351.7	1,028.4	906.6	491.4	2,039.0	1,520.3
2004	257.9	131.9	790.6	531.0	762.7	414.6	1,147.8	899.3	1,020.6	546.4	1,938.4	1,430.3
2005	304.7	161.3	721.4	513.0	679.7	378.8	1,201.9	916.4	984.4	540.1	1,923.3	1,429.4
2006	256.0	111.0	572.0	403.3	716.2	460.2	1,178.5	911.4	972.2	571.2	1,750.5	1,314.7
2007	192.5	73.2	495.0	289.5	664.3	383.0	1,221.9	842.4	856.7	456.2	1,716.9	1,131.9
2008	92.0	25.6	635.7	454.0	617.3	280.2	1,222.2	968.1	709.3	305.8	1,857.9	1,422.1
2009[1]	280.4	140.7	836.0	558.8	759.7	515.8	1,373.3	1,206.4	1,040.1	656.5	2,209.3	1,765.2

[1] Preliminary. *Source: National Agricultural Statistics Service, U.S. Department of Agriculture (NASS-USDA)*

Wheat Supply and Distribution in Canada, Australia and Argentina In Millions of Metric Tons

	Canada (Year Beginning Aug. 1)					Australia (Year Beginning Oct. 1)					Argentina (Year Beginning Dec. 1)				
	Supply			Disappearance		Supply			Disappearance		Supply			Disappearance	
Crop Year	Stocks Aug. 1	New Crop	Total Supply	Domestic	Exports[3]	Stocks Oct. 1	New Crop	Total Supply	Domestic	Exports[3]	Stocks Dec. 1	New Crop	Total Supply	Domestic	Exports[3]
2000-01	7.3	26.5	33.8	7.0	17.3	9.7	22.1	31.8	5.3	15.9	.6	16.2	16.8	5.0	11.3
2001-02	9.7	20.6	30.3	7.7	16.3	5.5	24.3	29.8	5.4	16.4	.6	15.5	16.1	4.9	10.1
2002-03	6.5	16.2	22.7	8.0	9.4	8.0	10.1	18.1	6.1	9.1	1.1	12.3	13.4	5.2	6.8
2003-04	5.7	23.0	28.7	7.2	15.8	3.2	26.1	29.3	6.0	18.0	1.5	14.5	16.0	5.2	9.4
2004-05	6.0	24.8	30.8	8.2	14.9	5.4	21.9	27.3	6.0	14.7	1.4	16.1	17.5	5.0	11.7
2005-06	7.9	25.7	33.6	8.2	16.0	6.7	25.2	31.9	6.6	16.0	.7	14.6	15.3	5.0	9.5
2006-07	9.7	25.3	35.0	9.0	19.4	9.4	10.8	20.2	7.6	8.7	.9	16.1	17.0	4.9	10.7
2007-08	6.9	20.1	27.0	6.8	16.1	4.0	13.6	17.6	6.5	7.5	1.4	18.0	19.4	5.1	11.2
2008-09[1]	4.4	28.6	33.0	8.0	18.8	3.7	20.9	24.6	6.9	14.8	3.1	8.4	11.5	5.1	6.0
2009-10[2]	6.6	26.5	33.1	7.3	18.5	3.1	22.5	25.6	7.1	15.0	.4	8.0	8.4	5.2	2.5

[1] Preliminary. [2] Forecast. [3] Including flour. *Source: Foreign Agricultural Service, U.S. Department of Agriculture (FAS-USDA)*

Quarterly Supply and Disappearance of Wheat in the United States In Millions of Bushels

Crop Year Beginning June 1	Supply				Disapperance						Ending Stocks		
					Domestic Use								
	Beginning Stocks	Production	Imports[3]	Total Supply	Food	Seed	Feed & Residual	Total	Exports[3]	Total Disappearance	Gov't Owned[4]	Privately Owned[5]	Total Stocks
1999-00	945.9	2,299.0	78.8	3,323.7	916.1	88.4	302.4	1,306.9	1,060.6	2,367.5	103.9	340.7	444.6
June-Aug.	945.9	2,299.0	30.6	3,275.5	225.9	6.4	275.2	507.5	323.0	830.5	132.2	2,312.8	2,445.0
Sept.-Nov.	2,445.0	----	19.5	2,464.5	241.1	54.6	-6.6	289.2	289.7	578.9	103.0	1,782.6	1,885.6
Dec.-Feb.	1,885.6	----	19.4	1,905.1	219.2	2.3	30.0	251.4	237.1	488.5	108.7	1,307.8	1,416.5
Mar.-May	1,415.3	----	9.3	914.1	229.9	25.1	3.9	258.8	210.8	469.6	103.9	340.7	444.6
2000-01	949.7	2,228.2	89.8	3,267.7	949.6	79.5	300.4	1,329.5	1,062.0	2,391.6	97.0	779.2	876.2
June-Aug.	949.7	2,228.2	20.4	3,198.3	238.8	1.1	317.9	557.8	287.8	845.6	108.9	2,243.8	2,352.7
Sept.-Nov.	2,352.7	----	25.1	2,377.8	253.0	49.8	-24.5	278.4	293.3	571.6	102.9	1,703.2	1,806.1
Dec.-Feb.	1,806.1	----	21.4	1,827.5	228.2	3.5	11.4	243.1	246.1	489.1	104.4	1,234.0	1,338.4
Mar.-May	1,338.4	----	22.9	1,361.3	229.7	25.2	-4.5	250.3	234.8	485.1	97.0	779.2	876.2
2001-02	876.2	1,947.5	107.6	2,931.2	926.4	83.4	182.0	1,191.8	962.3	2,154.1	99.0	678.1	777.1
June-Aug.	876.2	1,947.5	25.7	2,849.3	233.8	3.5	237.9	475.2	218.3	693.5	97.7	2,058.1	2,155.8
Sept.-Nov.	2,155.8	----	29.0	2,184.9	245.1	51.6	-23.1	273.6	287.8	561.4	96.9	1,526.6	1,623.5
Dec.-Feb.	1,623.5	----	27.6	1,651.0	221.1	2.0	-6.6	216.5	224.7	441.2	96.9	1,112.9	1,209.8
Mar.-May	1,209.8	----	25.2	1,235.0	226.4	26.3	-26.2	226.4	231.5	457.9	99.0	678.1	777.1
2002-03	777.1	1,605.9	77.4	2,460.4	918.6	84.4	115.7	1,118.7	850.2	1,968.9	66.4	425.0	491.4
June-Aug.	777.1	1,605.9	26.7	2,409.6	233.2	2.7	184.5	420.4	240.2	660.7	91.4	1,657.6	1,749.0
Sept.-Nov.	1,749.0	----	23.1	1,772.1	237.8	54.6	-74.7	217.7	234.5	454.2	80.9	1,239.0	1,319.9
Dec.-Feb.	1,319.9	----	12.7	1,332.6	218.9	3.1	14.1	236.1	189.8	425.9	74.1	832.5	906.6
Mar.-May	906.6	----	14.9	921.6	228.4	23.9	-8.2	244.5	185.7	430.2	66.4	425.0	491.4
2003-04	491.4	2,344.8	63.1	2,899.3	911.9	79.6	202.9	1,194.4	1,158.1	2,352.5	60.9	485.5	546.4
June-Aug.	491.4	2,344.8	15.7	2,851.9	230.5	2.1	315.3	547.9	264.9	812.8	60.3	1,978.7	2,039.0
Sept.-Nov.	2,039.0	----	17.8	2,056.7	239.6	53.3	-61.9	231.0	305.4	536.4	60.4	1,459.6	1,520.3
Dec.-Feb.	1,520.3	----	12.9	1,533.2	215.9	2.2	3.1	221.2	291.4	512.6	60.0	960.6	1,020.6
Mar.-May	1,020.6	----	16.7	1,037.3	225.9	22.0	-53.6	194.3	296.4	490.7	60.9	485.5	546.4
2004-05	546.4	2,158.2	70.6	2,775.2	904.6	78.9	188.9	1,172.4	1,062.9	2,235.3	54.0	486.1	540.1
June-Aug.	546.4	2,158.2	17.4	2,722.1	227.5	4.1	265.2	496.8	286.8	783.6	61.9	1,876.5	1,938.4
Sept.-Nov.	1,938.4	----	18.7	1,957.1	235.6	48.2	-57.0	226.8	300.0	526.8	61.7	1,369.0	1,430.3
Dec.-Feb.	1,430.3	----	17.8	1,448.1	216.3	2.4	7.7	226.4	237.4	463.8	55.9	928.5	984.4
Mar.-May	984.4	----	16.7	1,001.1	225.2	24.2	-27.0	222.4	238.7	461.1	54.5	485.6	540.1
2005-06	2,105.0	2,104.7	81.0	4,290.7	914.0	78.0	154.0	1,146.0	1,009.0	2,155.0			571.0
June-Aug.	540.1	2,104.7	19.0	2,663.0	231.0	2.0	263.0	496.0	244.0	740.0	48.3	1,875.0	1,923.0
Sept.-Nov.	1,923.0	----	20.0	1,944.0	238.0	51.0	-61.0	228.0	286.0	514.0	44.1	1,385.4	1,429.0
Dec.-Feb.	1,429.0	----	20.0	1,450.0	219.0	1.0	1.0	221.0	257.0	478.0			972.0
Mar.-May	972.0	----	22.0	995.0	226.0	24.0	-49.0	201.0	222.0	423.0			571.0
2006-07	571.0	1,808.0	121.0	2,500.0	937.0	81.0	117.0	1,135.0	908.0	2,043.0			456.0
June-Aug.	571.0	1,808.0	26.0	2,406.0	235.0	2.0	205.0	442.0	214.0	656.0			1,751.0
Sept.-Nov.	1,751.0	----	29.0	1,780.0	243.0	56.0	-47.0	252.0	212.0	464.0			1,315.0
Dec.-Feb.	1,315.0	----	32.0	1,346.0	225.0	1.0	28.0	254.0	235.0	489.0			857.0
Mar.-May	857.0	----	34.0	891.0	234.0	22.0	-69.0	187.0	247.0	434.0			456.0
2007-08	456.0	2,051.0	112.0	2,619.0	947.0	88.0	16.0	1,051.0	1,262.0	2,313.0			306.0
June-Aug.	456.0	2,051.0	30.0	2,538.0	240.0	1.0	257.0	498.0	323.0	821.0			1,717.0
Sept.-Nov.	1,717.0	----	21.0	1,738.0	245.0	60.0	-120.0	185.0	421.0	606.0			1,132.0
Dec.-Feb.	1,132.0	----	24.0	1,156.0	227.0	2.0	-42.0	187.0	261.0	448.0			709.0
Mar.-May	709.0	----	37.0	746.0	235.0	25.0	-79.0	181.0	257.0	438.0			306.0
2008-09[1]	306.0	2,499.0	127.0	2,932.0	924.0	75.0	260.0	1,259.0	1,016.0	2,275.0			657.0
June-Aug.	306.0	2,499.0	28.0	2,833.0	236.0	2.0	392.0	630.0	345.0	975.0			1,858.0
Sept.-Nov.	1,858.0	----	28.0	1,886.0	238.0	54.0	-124.0	168.0	295.0	463.0			1,422.0
Dec.-Feb.	1,422.0	----	36.0	1,459.0	219.0	1.0	28.0	248.0	170.0	418.0			1,040.0
Mar.-May	1,040.0	----	35.0	1,075.0	231.0	18.0	-36.0	213.0	206.0	419.0			657.0
2009-10[2]	657.0	2,216.0	112.0	2,985.0	960.0	92.0	372.0	1,424.0	904.0	2,328.0			976.0
June-Aug.	657.0	2,216.0	28.0	2,900.0	232.0	1.0	259.0	492.0	199.0	691.0			2,209.0
Sept.-Nov.	2,209.0	----	28.0	2,238.0	248.0	45.0	-73.0	220.0	253.0	473.0			1,765.0

[1] Preliminary. [2] Forecast. [3] Imports & exports include flour and other products expressed in wheat equivalent. [4] Uncommitted, Government only. [5] Includes total loans. [6] Includes alcoholic beverages. *Source: Economic Research Service, U.S. Department of Agriculture (ERS-USDA)*

Wheat Government Loan Program Data in the United States   Loan Rates--Cents Per Bushel

Crop Year Beginning June 1	National Average[3]	Target Rate[4]	Farm Loan Prices: Corn Belt (Soft Red Winter)	Central & Southern Plains (Hard Winter)	Northern Plains (Spring & Durum)	Pacific Northwest (White)	Placed Under Loan	% of Production	Acquired by CCC Under Program	Stocks, May 31: Total Stocks May 31	Total CCC Stocks May 31	Outstanding: CCC Loans	Farmer-Owned Reserve	"Free"
							In Millions of Bushels							
1998-99	258	NA	253	257	258	271	363	14.2	30	946	128	140	0	818
1999-00	258	NA	253	257	258	271	154	6.7	13	950	104	62	0	846
2000-01	258	NA	253	257	258	271	181	8.1	27	876	97	42	0	779
2001-02	258	NA	NA	NA	NA	NA	197	10.1	17	777	99	78	0	678
2002-03	280	386	NA	NA	NA	NA	120	7.5	2	491	66	51	0	425
2003-04	280	386	NA	NA	NA	NA	186	7.9	3	546	61	45	0	485
2004-05	275	392	NA	NA	NA	NA	178	8.3	10	540	54	NA	0	486
2005-06	275	392	NA	NA	NA	NA	170	8.1	1	571	43	NA	0	528
2006-07[1]	275	392	NA	NA	NA	NA	94	5.2	0	456	41	NA	0	437
2007-08[2]	275	392								306	24			

[1] Preliminary. [2] Estimate. [3] The national average loan rate at the farm as a percentage of the parity-priced wheat at the beginning of the marketing year. [4] 1996-97 through 2001-02 marketing year, target prices not applicable. NA = Not avaliable.
Source: Agricultural Marketing Service, U.S. Department of Agriculture (AMS-USDA)

Exports of Wheat (Only)[2] from the United States   In Thousands of Bushels

Year	June	July	Aug.	Sept.	Oct.	Nov.	Dec.	Jan.	Feb.	Mar.	Apr.	May	Total
2000-01	88,581	82,739	104,944	113,785	82,716	86,034	94,705	60,743	85,797	71,502	83,157	68,908	1,023,611
2001-02	59,190	64,911	89,582	86,941	94,598	99,800	81,369	72,114	63,446	78,070	84,211	58,449	932,681
2002-03	63,219	78,013	92,345	73,606	78,866	75,678	69,485	62,769	48,618	65,990	55,764	59,438	823,791
2003-04	54,665	88,042	115,869	125,312	101,168	76,222	79,811	109,607	94,480	96,685	102,588	91,917	1,136,366
2004-05	80,599	97,962	103,222	119,965	92,634	83,947	81,718	77,349	73,131	76,612	81,885	75,575	1,044,599
2005-06	64,553	90,760	83,173	102,761	103,423	77,164	91,531	84,659	71,175	74,420	69,050	72,209	984,878
2006-07	63,115	67,846	78,225	76,431	70,752	60,595	72,226	84,629	75,412	76,512	75,130	85,565	886,438
2007-08	73,088	80,285	153,223	149,168	158,064	116,504	82,343	87,539	84,414	92,251	82,781	79,725	1,239,385
2008-09	77,176	119,492	141,173	117,332	93,462	75,311	54,389	56,634	55,825	75,580	61,048	65,884	993,306
2009-10[1]	63,851	58,627	68,321	100,213	77,627	68,117							873,512

[1] Preliminary. [2] Grains. *Source: Economic Research Service, U.S. Department of Agriculture (ERS-USDA)*

United States Wheat and Wheat Flour Imports and Exports   In Thousands of Bushels

Crop Year Beginning June 1	Imports: Wheat: Suitable for Milling	Wheat Unfit for Human Consump.	Grain	Flour & Products[2]	Total	Exports: P.L. 480	Foreign Donations Sec. 416	Aid[3]	Total con-cessional	CCC Export Credit	Export Enhance-ment Program	Total U.S. Wheat
			-- Wheat Equivalent --			In Thousands of Metric Tons						
2002-03	49,741	----	49,741	27,633	77,374	1,475	213	----	2,081	3,633	0	24,295
2003-04	37,156	----	37,156	25,871	63,026	1,211	20	----	1,628	3,791	0	31,179
2004-05	44,499	----	44,499	26,071	70,570	1,867	12	----	2,139	2,554	0	26,505
2005-06	54,073	----	54,073	27,281	81,354	969	17	----	1,191	1,052	0	25,005
2006-07	92,928	----	92,928	28,942	121,870	767	0	----	961	1,008	0	29,413
2007-08[1]			85,806	26,825	112,631	734	12	----	841	1,360	0	32,908
2008-09[1]			101,969	25,013	126,981							

[1] Preliminary. [2] Includes macaroni, semolina & similar products. [3] Shipment mostly under the Commodity Import Program, financed with foreign aid funds. NA = Not available. *Source: Economic Research Service, U.S. Department of Agriculture (ERS-USDA)*

Comparative Average Cash Wheat Prices   In Dollars Per Bushel

Crop Year June to May	Received by U.S. Farmers	No. 2 Soft Red Winter, Chicago	No 1 Hard Red Ordinary Protein, Kansas City	No 2 Soft Red Winter, St. Louis	Minneapolis: No 1 Dark Northern Spring 14%	Minneapolis: No 1 Hard Amber Durum	No 1 Soft White, Portland, Oregon	No 2 Western White Pacific Northwest	No 2 Soft White, Toledo	Export Prices2 (U.S. $ Per Metric Ton): Aust-ralian Standard White	Canada Vancouver No 1 CWRS 13 1/2 %	Argen-tina F.O.B. B.A.	U.S. Gulf No. 2 Hard Winter	Rotterdam C.I.F. U.S. No 2 Hard Winter
2002-03	3.56	3.40	4.22	3.50	4.47	4.25	3.95	4.58	3.34	185	194	158	160	189
2003-04	3.40	3.66	4.03	3.76	4.39	5.31	3.95	4.24	3.59	182	188	161	156	204
2004-05	3.40	3.01	3.99	3.37	4.66	NQ	3.93	4.04	3.10	177	204	127	151	213
2005-06	3.42	3.13	4.45	3.20	4.98	NQ	3.57	4.35	3.15	191	204	140	168	224
2006-07	4.26	3.98	5.38	4.11	5.41	NQ	4.87	5.48	3.85	227	227	189	204	252
2007-08	6.48	7.71	9.11	7.43	10.81	13.08	9.97	8.68	8.06	NQ	NQ	NQ	340	NQ
2008-09	6.78	5.04	7.03	4.86	8.53	NQ	6.25	6.62	4.98	NQ	NQ	NQ	292	NQ
2009-10[1]	4.70-5.00	4.36	5.43	4.05	6.81		5.03	5.18	4.29				213	

[1] Preliminary. [2] Calendar year. NA = Not available. *Source: Economic Research Service, U.S. Department of Agriculture (ERS-USDA)*

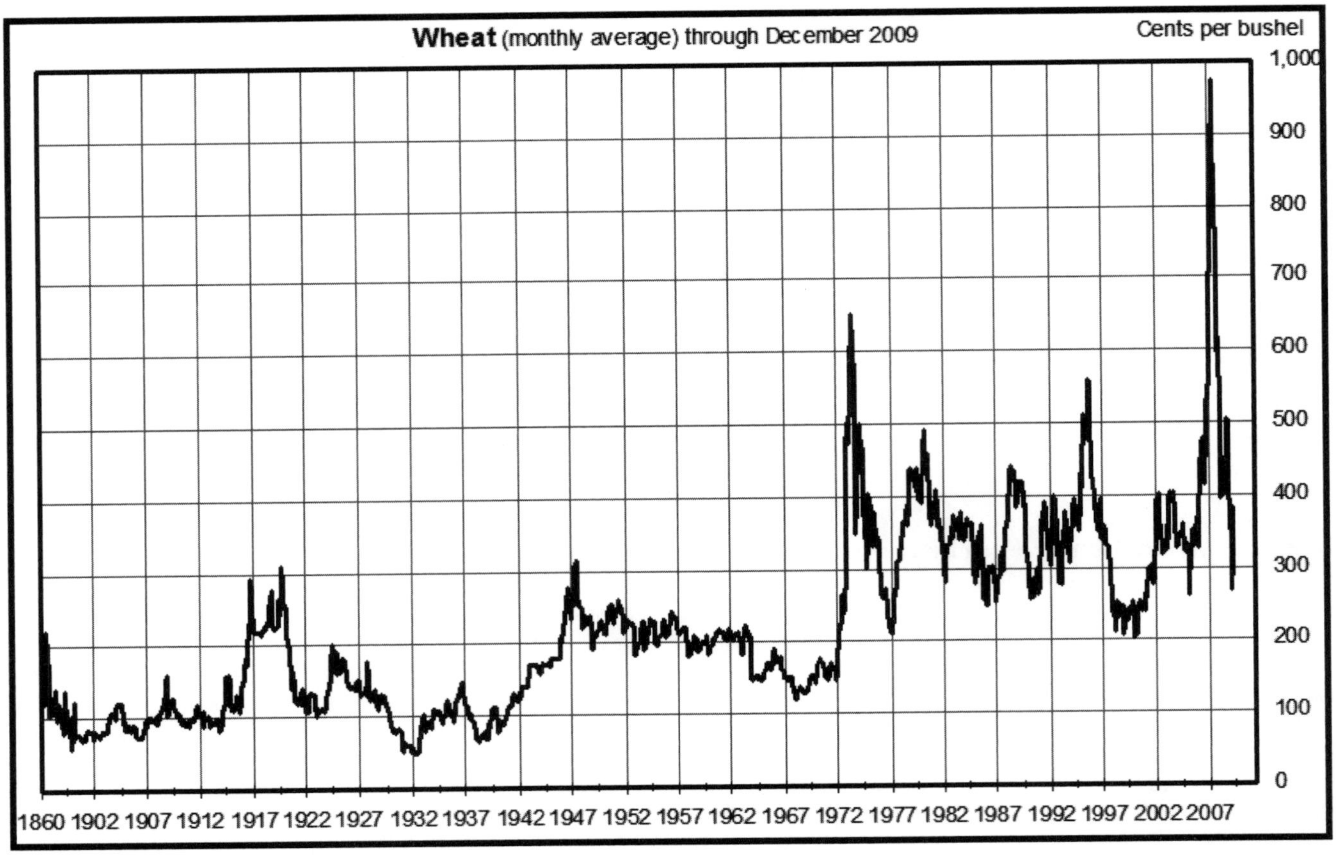

Average Price of No. 2 Soft Red Winter (30 Days) Wheat in Chicago In Dollars Per Bushel

Year	June	July	Aug.	Sept.	Oct.	Nov.	Dec.	Jan.	Feb.	Mar.	Apr.	May	Average
2000-01	2.41	2.14	2.08	2.13	2.36	2.42	2.47	2.57	2.49	2.56	2.52	2.51	2.39
2001-02	2.40	2.56	2.57	2.57	2.68	2.75	2.83	2.96	2.74	2.76	2.75	2.73	2.69
2002-03	2.81	3.19	3.42	3.92	3.89	3.85	3.53	3.32	3.44	3.14	3.08	3.25	3.40
2003-04	3.11	3.23	3.63	3.46	3.42	3.87	3.92	3.90	3.84	3.85	3.92	3.73	3.66
2004-05	3.46	3.26	2.92	2.97	2.82	2.79	2.88	2.93	2.95	3.28	2.92	2.96	3.01
2005-06	3.09	3.22	3.04	2.93	2.99	2.83	2.98	3.11	3.34	3.29	3.21	3.54	3.13
2006-07	3.26	3.43	3.20	3.39	4.40	4.35	4.49	4.19	4.20	4.07	4.25	4.50	3.98
2007-08	5.25	5.52	6.24	7.98	7.89	7.57	8.69	8.55	10.12	10.40	7.72	6.59	7.71
2008-09	7.20	6.87	6.77	5.45	3.76	3.68	4.01	4.62	4.28	4.40	4.43	4.96	5.04
2009-10[1]	4.96	4.45	4.18	3.70	4.01	4.53	4.67						4.36

[1] Preliminary. *Source: Economic Research Service, U.S. Department of Agriculture (ERS-USDA)*

Average Price Received by Farmers for Wheat in the United States In Dollars Per Bushel

Year	June	July	Aug.	Sept.	Oct.	Nov.	Dec.	Jan.	Feb.	Mar.	Apr.	May	Average
2000-01	2.50	2.32	2.41	2.44	2.68	2.83	2.87	2.85	2.83	2.87	2.86	2.98	2.70
2001-02	2.74	2.70	2.73	2.85	2.87	2.87	2.88	2.87	2.83	2.87	2.83	2.81	2.82
2002-03	2.92	3.21	3.63	4.21	4.38	4.25	4.06	3.89	3.70	3.55	3.37	3.33	3.71
2003-04	3.08	2.95	3.35	3.39	3.44	3.61	3.68	3.68	3.77	3.83	3.88	3.82	3.54
2004-05	3.55	3.37	3.27	3.36	3.43	3.46	3.40	3.43	3.36	3.42	3.35	3.31	3.39
2005-06	3.23	3.20	3.24	3.36	3.43	3.45	3.53	3.52	3.66	3.79	3.81	4.09	3.53
2006-07	3.98	3.88	3.91	4.06	4.59	4.59	4.52	4.53	4.71	4.75	4.89	4.88	4.44
2007-08	5.03	5.17	5.64	6.76	7.65	7.39	7.71	7.96	10.10	10.50	10.10	8.87	7.74
2008-09	7.62	7.15	7.61	7.43	6.65	6.29	5.95	6.20	5.79	5.70	5.74	5.84	6.50
2009-10[1]	5.67	5.13	4.83	4.48	4.47	4.79	4.85	4.92	4.67				4.87

[1] Preliminary. *Source: Economic Research Service, U.S. Department of Agriculture (ERS-USDA)*

Average Price of No. 1 Hard Red Winter (Ordinary Protein) Wheat in Kansas City In Dollars Per Bushel

Year	June	July	Aug.	Sept.	Oct.	Nov.	Dec.	Jan.	Feb.	Mar.	Apr.	May	Average
2000-01	3.07	2.97	2.89	3.13	3.41	3.45	3.47	3.54	3.35	3.45	3.41	3.49	3.30
2001-02	3.32	3.20	3.15	3.18	3.28	3.37	3.26	3.29	3.25	3.23	3.24	3.21	3.25
2002-03	3.55	3.92	4.29	5.04	5.10	4.76	4.40	4.06	4.08	3.80	3.79	3.87	4.22
2003-04	3.63	3.34	3.87	3.74	3.79	4.21	4.31	4.32	4.25	4.30	4.35	4.28	4.03
2004-05	4.13	3.97	3.73	4.01	3.95	4.22	4.22	4.14	4.00	4.00	3.76	3.80	3.99
2005-06	3.87	3.83	3.96	4.30	4.57	4.53	4.52	4.46	4.72	4.62	4.86	5.21	4.45
2006-07	5.25	5.27	5.00	5.16	5.62	5.61	5.49	5.29	5.39	5.40	5.52	5.54	5.38
2007-08	6.22	6.28	6.84	8.52	8.89	8.62	9.80	9.97	12.28	12.29	10.29	9.33	9.11
2008-09	9.19	8.68	8.64	7.52	6.17	6.21	6.06	6.59	6.21	6.23	6.10	6.70	7.03
2009-10[1]	6.63	5.58	5.15	4.56	5.06	5.58							5.43

[1] Preliminary. *Source: Economic Research Service, U.S. Department of Agriculture (ERS-USDA)*

Average Price of No. 1 Dark Northern Spring (14% Protein) Wheat in Minneapolis In Dollars Per Bushel

Year	June	July	Aug.	Sept.	Oct.	Nov.	Dec.	Jan.	Feb.	Mar.	Apr.	May	Average
2000-01	3.78	3.50	3.29	3.17	3.69	3.77	3.52	3.79	3.68	3.63	3.73	3.88	3.62
2001-02	3.81	3.72	3.54	3.52	3.71	3.69	3.59	3.55	3.51	3.51	3.55	3.59	3.61
2002-03	3.64	4.03	4.37	5.24	5.20	4.99	4.47	4.34	4.52	4.36	4.22	4.20	4.47
2003-04	4.12	4.00	4.15	4.03	4.31	4.59	4.43	4.44	4.64	4.63	4.69	4.69	4.39
2004-05	4.56	4.31	4.12	4.68	4.87	5.14	4.93	5.01	4.13	4.79	4.69	4.69	4.66
2005-06	5.03	4.71	4.83	4.80	5.11	5.11	5.28	4.87	4.90	4.83	4.94	5.31	4.98
2006-07	5.59	5.65	4.94	4.86	5.36	5.55	5.44	5.27	5.40	5.55	5.65	5.64	5.41
2007-08	6.19	6.60	6.88	8.20	9.27	9.39	11.06	12.59	19.00	15.60	12.93	12.06	10.81
2008-09	11.46	11.46	9.87	8.51	7.37	6.80	7.78	8.02	7.64	7.57	7.72	8.13	8.53
2009-10[1]	7.96	6.82	6.17	6.30	6.36	7.29	6.79						6.81

[1] Preliminary. *Source: Economic Research Service, U.S. Department of Agriculture (ERS-USDA)*

Average Farm Prices of Winter Wheat in the United States In Dollars Per Bushel

Year	June	July	Aug.	Sept.	Oct.	Nov.	Dec.	Jan.	Feb.	Mar.	Apr.	May	Average
2002-03	2.90	3.19	3.63	4.15	4.32	4.18	3.87	3.66	3.52	3.30	3.19	3.19	3.59
2003-04	2.94	2.89	3.28	3.31	3.37	3.56	3.62	3.66	3.67	3.76	3.79	3.72	3.46
2004-05	3.46	3.31	3.19	3.26	3.34	3.39	3.34	3.28	3.27	3.32	3.27	3.23	3.31
2005-06	3.15	3.15	3.16	3.28	3.34	3.27	3.45	3.45	3.59	3.82	3.74	4.06	3.46
2006-07	3.95	3.82	3.77	4.03	4.63	4.67	4.53	4.53	4.67	4.67	4.87	4.77	4.41
2007-08	5.00	5.13	5.66	6.89	7.55	7.31	7.70	7.75	9.17	9.96	9.62	8.17	7.49
2008-09	7.51	7.10	7.30	6.99	6.03	5.65	5.40	5.70	5.26	5.26	5.26	5.52	6.08
2009-10[1]	5.42	4.98	4.67	4.20	4.26	4.60	4.68	4.68	4.36				4.65

[1] Preliminary. *Source: Economic Research Service, U.S. Department of Agriculture (ERS-USDA)*

Average Farm Prices of Durum Wheat in the United States In Dollars Per Bushel

Year	June	July	Aug.	Sept.	Oct.	Nov.	Dec.	Jan.	Feb.	Mar.	Apr.	May	Average
2002-03	3.41	3.44	3.54	4.18	4.43	4.52	4.26	4.23	4.28	4.14	3.93	3.99	4.03
2003-04	3.99	3.85	3.78	3.95	3.89	3.95	3.95	3.96	4.08	4.14	4.19	4.21	4.00
2004-05	4.35	4.09	3.86	3.89	3.87	3.79	3.67	3.64	3.72	3.70	3.63	3.67	3.82
2005-06	3.67	3.72	3.35	3.38	3.39	3.28	3.37	3.29	3.34	3.39	3.41	3.94	3.46
2006-07	3.81	3.83	4.09	4.07	4.55	4.62	4.53	4.71	5.16	5.32	5.46	5.39	4.63
2007-08	5.49	6.69	7.00	8.98	11.70	11.70	11.50	13.10	14.10	15.40	14.30	13.50	11.12
2008-09	8.48	11.70	12.60	11.90	11.50	8.93	8.40	8.26	7.53	7.63	7.28	7.05	9.27
2009-10[1]	7.20	7.57	5.90	4.93	4.97	4.62	4.98	4.95	4.51				5.51

[1] Preliminary. *Source: Economic Research Service, U.S. Department of Agriculture (ERS-USDA)*

Average Farm Prices of Other Spring Wheat in the United States In Dollars Per Bushel

Year	June	July	Aug.	Sept.	Oct.	Nov.	Dec.	Jan.	Feb.	Mar.	Apr.	May	Average
2002-03	2.98	3.31	3.66	4.30	4.45	4.26	4.15	4.03	3.82	3.72	3.48	3.55	3.81
2003-04	3.45	3.31	3.42	3.42	3.53	3.68	3.72	3.67	3.84	3.90	3.94	4.01	3.66
2004-05	3.83	3.55	3.38	3.48	3.50	3.57	3.48	3.61	3.49	3.51	3.39	3.37	3.51
2005-06	3.51	3.45	3.43	3.51	3.61	3.71	3.68	3.70	3.83	3.85	3.95	4.18	3.70
2006-07	4.18	4.41	4.11	4.11	4.48	4.48	4.74	4.51	4.73	4.73	4.87	4.98	4.53
2007-08	5.17	5.43	5.53	6.26	6.99	7.00	7.39	8.01	11.20	10.90	10.50	10.70	7.92
2008-09	10.10	9.52	8.18	7.76	7.20	7.10	6.89	7.02	6.61	6.50	6.48	6.76	7.51
2009-10[1]	6.66	5.96	5.52	4.85	4.99	5.19	5.14	5.29	5.14				5.42

[1] Preliminary. *Source: Economic Research Service, U.S. Department of Agriculture (ERS-USDA)*

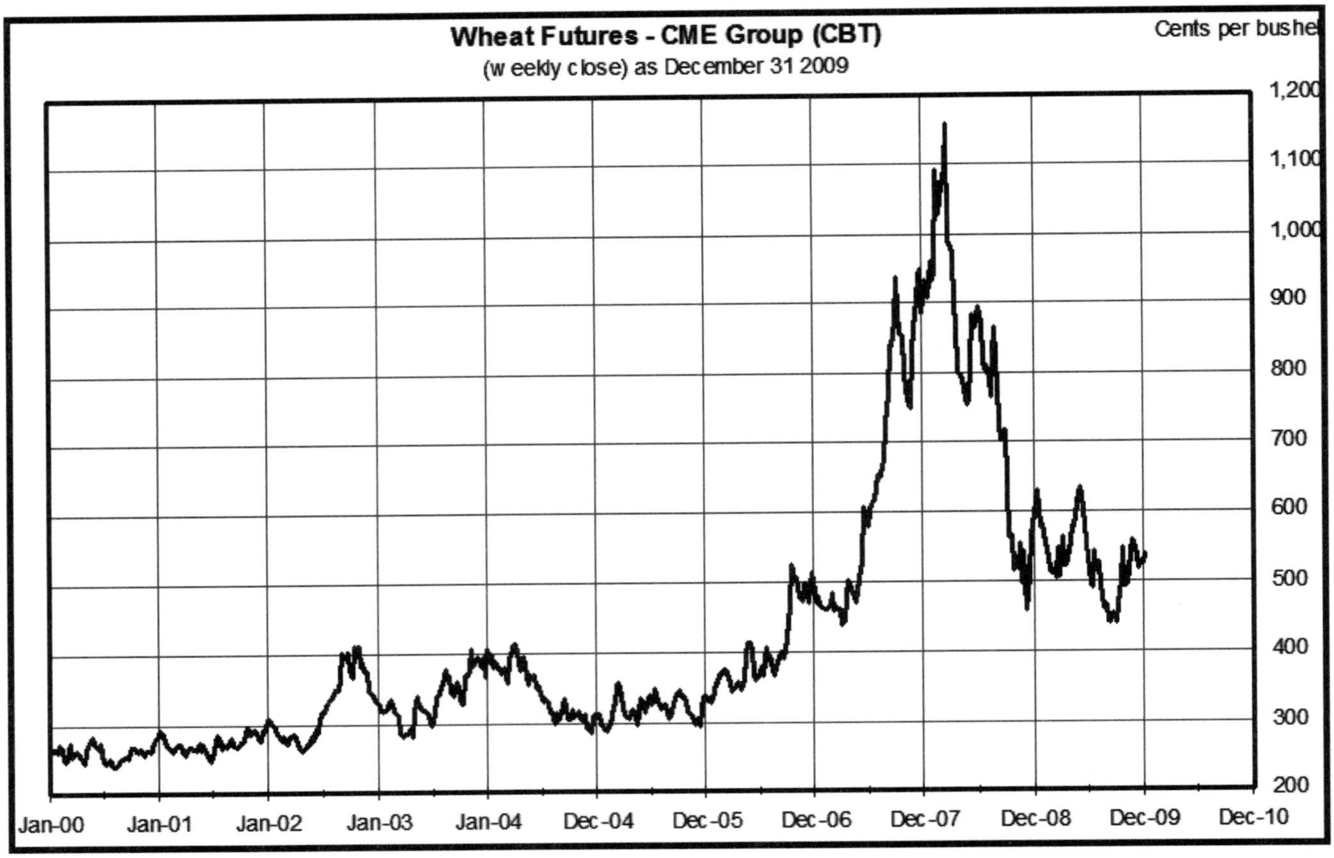

Volume of Trading of Wheat Futures in Chicago In Thousands of Contracts

Year	Jan.	Feb.	Mar.	Apr.	May	June	July	Aug.	Sept.	Oct.	Nov.	Dec.	Total
2000	467.1	691.1	522.4	490.7	627.7	759.4	461.1	572.9	388.2	466.3	596.6	364.1	6,407.5
2001	551.8	595.3	536.1	580.0	537.8	720.4	695.3	600.3	385.9	629.5	614.7	354.3	6,801.5
2002	603.0	593.1	501.1	563.1	419.3	689.8	586.4	651.6	682.9	609.4	594.4	378.8	6,872.9
2003	438.0	526.0	411.0	496.8	638.6	661.8	585.1	689.6	536.5	778.9	739.8	465.4	6,967.4
2004	656.9	771.7	783.1	786.2	606.1	786.5	501.7	747.4	520.9	478.7	913.7	402.3	7,955.2
2005	613.0	1,053.6	827.8	937.5	694.7	1,088.0	690.3	1,024.8	660.0	717.4	1,164.5	642.4	10,114.1
2006	889.2	1,421.3	1,059.6	1,300.0	1,511.6	1,617.1	1,067.4	1,659.9	1,365.9	1,938.1	1,613.7	781.2	16,224.9
2007	1,346.2	1,506.0	1,148.0	2,082.5	1,170.5	2,343.7	1,514.4	2,111.3	1,320.3	1,648.4	2,109.7	1,281.8	19,582.7
2008	1,861.3	2,527.7	1,398.7	1,558.6	1,121.6	2,185.7	1,314.2	2,093.6	1,228.1	1,139.0	1,644.5	939.0	19,011.9
2009	986.9	1,505.7	1,213.8	1,747.8	1,300.1	2,350.9	1,298.1	1,926.4	1,040.0	1,451.2	1,952.5	904.2	17,677.5

Contract size = 5,000 bu. *Source: CME Group; Chicago Board of Trade (CBT)*

Average Open Interest of Wheat Futures in Chicago In Contracts

Year	Jan.	Feb.	Mar.	Apr.	May	June	July	Aug.	Sept.	Oct.	Nov.	Dec.
2000	127,419	135,316	123,980	128,462	130,938	133,527	139,194	144,953	141,803	150,592	153,287	134,997
2001	145,802	146,927	137,377	138,876	134,051	151,951	142,399	143,574	136,514	126,772	113,456	104,975
2002	118,192	118,484	112,469	112,870	96,050	98,047	118,041	131,303	129,913	114,544	101,354	82,934
2003	92,679	99,882	95,464	99,500	97,750	96,230	92,484	119,817	110,703	109,449	125,335	120,376
2004	130,101	137,459	141,239	155,383	127,086	135,322	154,623	166,422	154,431	156,290	172,064	182,402
2005	201,297	223,108	218,153	208,149	207,407	223,014	239,219	256,533	276,741	297,319	301,838	298,523
2006	320,974	380,405	389,284	385,698	466,013	491,343	473,749	459,650	455,755	476,906	435,059	426,976
2007	453,140	441,924	405,383	377,162	363,297	401,509	411,971	404,940	379,871	407,669	414,509	423,198
2008	443,193	440,137	400,426	375,845	362,835	359,429	332,360	331,301	294,696	279,041	283,832	250,914
2009	268,513	297,116	291,831	309,503	302,088	335,407	317,024	327,977	320,607	331,678	355,414	353,774

Contract size = 5,000 bu. *Source: CME Group; Chicago Board of Trade (CBT)*

Commercial Stocks of Domestic Wheat[1] in the United States, on First of Month In Millions of Bushels

Year	July	Aug.	Sept.	Oct.	Nov.	Dec.	Jan.	Feb.	Mar.	Apr.	May	June
2000-01	285.5	310.3	335.3	335.5	306.2	286.6	263.7	251.7	243.2	243.7	224.5	221.0
2001-02	271.0	296.6	318.7	321.9	291.9	251.8	224.5	224.6	217.2	195.6	177.3	176.0
2002-03	193.9	207.7	237.2	241.0	237.7	218.8	195.1	179.7	158.3	133.1	107.2	93.8
2003-04	133.3	171.9	212.0	226.3	220.7	198.1	145.0	126.3	113.1	94.0	89.6	85.4
2004-05	118.3	147.6	174.3	173.5	161.6	137.8	129.8	122.5	113.4	103.8	92.2	88.8
2005-06	127.5	138.6	159.9	163.5	158.5	147.8	137.9	130.9	128.8	122.9	116.7	126.2
2006-07	154.3	172.5	190.3	170.9	166.8	159.5	154.7	146.7	136.3	129.3	116.6	99.2
2007-08	108.6	155.9	173.1	185.7	164.8	151.2	148.3	138.9	123.5	112.3	87.1	78.7
2008-09	98.2	150.4	176.4	214.5	212.9	179.7	167.8	135.9	126.1	124.9	119.5	115.0
2009-10	152.4	198.2	221.3	224.5	219.8	208.8	199.8					

[1] Domestic wheat in storage in public and private elevators in 39 markets and wheat afloat in vessels or barges at lake and seaboard ports, the first Saturday of the month. *Source: Livestock Division, U.S. Department of Agriculture (LD-USDA)*

Stocks of Wheat Flour Held by Mills in the United States In Thousands of Sacks--100 Pounds

Year	Jan. 1	April 1	July 1	Oct. 1	Year	Jan. 1	April 1	July 1	Oct. 1
1998	6,343	6,245	6,210	7,345	2004	4,764	4,666	4,700	4,868
1999	7,544	5,920	5,697	4,265	2005	5,085	4,268	4,637	4,781
2000	5,099	5,217	5,062	5,244	2006	5,211	5,775	5,576	5,587
2001	5,241	5,506	5,178	5,393	2007	5,919	5,884	5,587	6,188
2002	5,377	5,164	4,632	4,184	2008	6,374	6,219	6,157	6,719
2003	4,265	4,707	4,622	4,554	2009[1]	5,831	5,379	5,430	5,250

[1] Preliminary. *Source: Bureau of the Census, U.S. Department of Commerce*

Average Producer Price Index of Wheat Flour (Spring[2]) June 1983 = 100

Year	Jan.	Feb.	Mar.	Apr.	May	June	July	Aug.	Sept.	Oct.	Nov.	Dec.	Average
2000	99.9	99.9	100.2	99.4	100.1	101.7	100.2	100.4	101.2	105.2	103.6	104.4	101.4
2001	104.7	105.1	106.2	105.7	106.9	108.2	107.9	106.8	107.4	110.0	109.5	108.8	107.3
2002	109.6	109.6	110.6	106.5	108.2	108.8	112.6	115.5	120.9	123.0	119.3	116.6	113.4
2003	119.4	121.6	120.2	120.3	122.6	121.6	119.2	122.2	120.4	117.2	121.1	122.4	120.7
2004	123.5	125.1	123.9	124.0	127.6	126.4	125.2	121.0	128.5	127.2	130.2	128.5	125.9
2005	128.5	130.4	130.8	127.6	129.6	130.8	130.3	129.7	130.6	131.4	133.6	131.8	130.4
2006	130.2	134.2	132.8	139.4	142.2	144.2	148.5	141.6	144.2	151.9	151.8	147.5	142.4
2007	144.8	144.6	148.2	153.2	154.3	161.9	167.4	174.0	196.2	209.4	207.1	229.5	174.2
2008	239.6	278.9	293.6	262.8	248.1	246.5	228.5	229.5	214.6	194.8	190.8	181.5	234.1
2009[1]	187.4	185.3	186.5	183.4	185.0	196.2	176.4	171.1	165.2	168.1	169.0	168.5	178.5

[1] Preliminary. [2] Standard patent. *Source: Bureau of Labor Statistics, U.S. Department of Commerce (BLS) (0212-0301)*

World Wheat Flour Production (Monthly Average) In Thousands of Metric Tons

Year	Australia	France	Germany	Hungary	India	Japan	Kazak-hstan	Rep. of Korea	Mexico	Poland	Russia	Turkey	United Kingdom
2000	NA	NA	414.0	73.5	202.5	383.0	120.8	155.9	206.0	125.4	864.0	162.0	374.0
2001	NA	NA	403.1	72.4	197.2	387.2	116.5	142.8	221.1	126.8	866.6	145.2	374.0
2002	NA	473.9	415.3	67.6	211.6	389.4	143.4	151.2	218.3	135.2	797.3	139.6	369.0
2003	NA	467.3	424.4	70.7	234.1	391.0	144.2	149.3	220.6	143.1	821.4	159.8	365.0
2004	NA	465.8	441.8	67.6	238.5	390.1	145.2	157.6	217.4	135.2	799.5	176.8	370.0
2005	NA	464.5	437.9	67.3	205.4	384.6	197.6	153.1	239.1	128.6	765.8	299.0	368.0
2006	NA	472.3	444.2	62.3	180.3	384.6	207.9	154.2	243.8	143.8	776.1	290.0	366.0
2007	NA	478.2	451.3	59.7	180.9	387.8	224.6	146.6	243.8	124.3	757.0	310.0	NA
2008[1]	NA	482.2	453.0	57.6	178.6	387.3	242.0	140.1	244.7	109.8	762.4	327.4	NA
2009[2]	NA	442.8	420.0	59.1	188.3	379.8	255.0	150.7	247.8	143.2	771.1	349.6	NA

[1] Preliminary. [2] Estimate. NA = Not available. *Source: United Nations (UN)*

Production of Wheat Flour in the United States In Millions of Sacks--100 Pounds Each

Year	July	Aug.	Sept.	Oct.	Nov.	Dec.	Jan.	Feb.	Mar.	Apr.	May	June	Total
2000-01	-----	108.8	-----	-----	109.7	-----	-----	99.4	-----	-----	97.2	-----	415.1
2001-02	-----	102.1	-----	-----	105.8	-----	-----	96.0	-----	-----	96.3	-----	400.2
2002-03	-----	102.1	-----	-----	100.3	-----	-----	95.9	-----	-----	96.8	-----	395.0
2003-04	-----	103.1	-----	-----	100.5	-----	-----	96.6	-----	-----	96.8	-----	396.9
2004-05	-----	100.9	-----	-----	99.7	-----	-----	95.9	-----	-----	96.2	-----	392.7
2005-06	-----	102.5	-----	-----	100.3	-----	-----	98.1	-----	-----	98.0	-----	398.9
2006-07	-----	104.9	-----	-----	102.5	-----	-----	100.3	-----	-----	102.5	-----	410.1
2007-08	-----	109.0	-----	-----	107.1	-----	-----	101.4	-----	-----	102.5	-----	420.0
2008-09	-----	108.2	-----	-----	104.2	-----	-----	100.7	-----	-----	103.0	-----	416.1
2009-10[1]	-----	107.6	-----	-----		-----	-----		-----	-----		-----	

[1] Preliminary. *Source: Bureau of the Census, U.S. Department of Commerce*

United States Wheat Flour Exports (Grain Equivalent[2]) In Thousands of Bushels

Year	June	July	Aug.	Sept.	Oct.	Nov.	Dec.	Jan.	Feb.	Mar.	Apr.	May	Total
2000-01	3,620	3,805	1,623	3,174	4,165	2,332	2,741	2,236	2,365	2,200	3,868	2,163	34,292
2001-02	1,412	661	1,990	1,005	3,226	2,534	2,479	2,207	3,294	2,301	2,802	2,759	26,670
2002-03	1,474	1,547	753	1,373	2,437	2,854	4,645	1,049	884	1,146	1,083	541	19,786
2003-04	824	1,074	3,444	1,087	765	1,295	1,673	1,789	1,342	1,020	732	1,386	16,431
2004-05	742	1,220	885	770	834	1,005	1,347	955	617	756	722	781	10,634
2005-06	859	686	839	720	840	871	734	572	620	937	1,188	966	9,832
2006-07	720	488	780	610	532	754	756	786	999	941	1,425	2,711	11,502
2007-08	1,467	1,220	1,277	1,135	1,758	2,515	1,960	1,224	1,544	1,328	1,114	1,126	17,668
2008-09	1,417	1,052	1,093	1,053	856	1,055	958	969	858	750	687	793	11,541
2009-10[1]	865	1,515	1,704	1,473	2,255	1,609							18,842

[1] Preliminary. [2] Includes meal, groats and durum. *Source: Economic Research Service, U.S. Department of Agriculture (ERS-USDA)*

Supply and Distribution of Wheat Flour in the United States

Year	Wheat Ground	Milfeed Production	Flour Production[3]	Flour & Product Imports[2]	Total Supply	Exports: Flour	Exports: Products	Domestic Disappearance	Total Population July 1	Per Capita Disappearance
	-- 1,000 Bu. --	- 1,000 Tons -	In 1,000 Cwt.						-- Millions --	-- Pounds --
1999	917,797	7,040	411,968	9,295	421,263	17,499	1,633	402,131	279.3	144.0
2000	944,868	7,374	421,270	9,666	430,936	16,005	1,693	413,239	282.4	146.3
2001	914,036	7,273	404,521	10,130	414,651	10,507	1,695	402,449	285.3	141.1
2002	889,412	6,893	394,700	11,291	405,991	9,226	2,683	394,082	288.1	136.8
2003	889,188	7,029	396,215	11,145	407,360	5,768	3,953	397,639	290.7	136.8
2004	876,047	6,764	393,925	10,726	404,651	5,152	4,662	394,837	293.3	134.6
2005	884,101	6,826	394,973	11,262	406,235	3,747	4,741	397,748	296.0	134.4
2006	894,527	6,916	403,391	11,740	415,131	3,412	5,867	405,852	298.8	135.8
2007	923,756	7,103	418,836	11,511	430,347	6,707	6,486	417,155	301.7	138.3
2008[1]	906,503	7,103	416,283	10,822	427,105	4,925	6,179	416,001	304.5	136.6

[1] Preliminary. [2] Commercial production of wheat flour, whole wheat, industrial and durum flour and farina reported by Bureau of Census.
Source: Economic Research Service, U.S. Department of Agriculture (ERS-USDA)

Wheat and Flour Price Relationships at Milling Centers in the United States In Dollars

	At Kansas City					At Minneapolis				
	Cost of Wheat	Wholesale Price of		Total Products		Cost of Wheat	Wholesale Price of		Total Products	
Year	to Produce 100 lb. Flour[1]	Bakery Flour 100 lb. Flour[2]	By-Products Obtained 100 lb. Flour[3]	Actual	Over Cost of Wheat	to Produce 100 lb. Flour[1]	Bakery Flour 100 lb. Flour[2]	By-Products Obtained 100 lb. Flour[3]	Actual	Over Cost of Wheat
2002-03	9.66	11.04	1.16	12.20	2.54	9.80	11.03	1.15	12.17	2.38
2003-04	9.43	10.58	1.36	11.95	2.52	9.98	10.67	1.15	11.82	1.84
2004-05	9.33	10.88	.95	11.83	2.50	10.62	11.31	.94	12.25	1.62
2005-06	10.38	11.73	1.03	12.76	2.38	11.35	12.25	.93	13.19	1.84
2006-07	12.41	13.27	1.57	14.85	2.44	12.33	12.92	1.50	14.41	2.08
2007-08	22.67	22.83	2.00	24.83	2.16	24.66	24.94	2.03	26.98	2.32
2008-09	17.14	17.60	2.18	19.77	2.63	19.44	19.18	2.15	21.33	1.89
2009-10	13.55	14.48	1.53	16.01	2.46	15.54	15.74	1.64	17.38	1.84
June-Aug.	14.48	15.00	1.40	16.40	1.92	15.92	15.75	1.53	17.28	1.36
Sept.-Nov.	12.61	13.95	1.66	15.61	3.00	15.16	15.73	1.74	17.47	2.31

[1] Based on 73% extraction rate, cost of 2.28 bushels: At Kansas City, No. 1 hard winter 13% protein; and at Minneapolis, No. 1 dark northern spring, 14% protein. [2] quoted as mid-month bakers' standard patent at Kansas City and spring standard patent at Minneapolis, bulk basis. [3] Assumed 50-50 millfeed distribution between bran and shorts or middlings, bulk basis. *Source: Agricultural Marketing Service, U.S. Department of Agriculture*

Wool

Wool is light, warm, absorbs moisture, and is resistant to fire. Wool is also used for insulation in houses, for carpets and furnishing, and for bedding. Sheep are sheared once a year and produce about 4.3 kg of "greasy" wool per year.

Greasy wool is wool that has not been washed or cleaned. Wool fineness is determined by fiber diameter, which is measured in microns (one millionth of a meter). Fine wool is softer, lightweight, and produces fine clothing. Merino sheep produce the finest wool.

Wool futures and options are traded on the Sydney Futures Exchange (SFE), where there are futures and options contracts on greasy wool, and futures on fine wool and broad wool. All three futures contracts call for the delivery of merino combing wool. Wool yarn futures are traded on the Chubu Commodity Exchange (CCE), the Osaka Mercantile Exchange (OME) and the Tokyo Commodity Exchange (TOCOM).

Prices – Average monthly wool prices at U.S. mills in 2009 (through November) fell by -28.0% yr/yr to $2.20 per pound, down from the 2008 record high of $3.05 per pound. Wool prices in 2009 were about double the 3-decade low of $1.09 posted in 2000. The value of U.S. wool production in 2009 fell -24.9% to $24.387 million, down from the 12-year high of $32.486 million in 2008.

Supply – World production of wool has been falling in the past decade due to the increased use of polyester fabrics. Greasy wool world production in 2008, the latest reporting year for the data series, rose +0.5% yr/yr to 2.191 million metric tons. The world's largest producers of greasy wool in 2008 were Australia with 21% of world production, followed by China (18%), and New Zealand (10%).

U.S. wool production of 10,000 metric tons in 2007 accounted for only 0.9% of world production. U.S. production of wool goods fell 15.8% yr/yr in 2008 (9 months annualized) to a record low of 8.0 million yards. That was less that 4% of the record high of 222.5 million yards of wool goods production seen in 1969. The U.S. sheep herd in 2008 fell 4.8% to a new record low of 4.434 million sheep.

Demand – U.S. consumption of apparel wool has dropped sharply, along with production, and it fell 13.5% yr/yr to a record low of 13.333 million pounds in 2006, which is latest data available. The breakdown of U.S. mill consumption in 2003, the latest data available, showed that wool usage for carpets was 6.017 million pounds, which was a new record low. Wool usage for apparel production in 2003 was 43.869 million pounds, up +21.8%, up from the 2002 record low of 36.015 million pounds.

Trade – U.S. exports of domestic wool in 2006 (latest data) rose +45.2% yr/yr to 18.000 million pounds. U.S. imports in 2006 rose +17.8% to 7.324 million pounds.

World Production of Wool, Greasy In Metric Tons

Year	Argentina	Australia	China	Kazakhstan	New Zealand	Pakistan	Romania	Russia	South Africa	United Kingdom	United States	Uruguay	World Total
1999	65,000	687,600	283,152	22,283	252,000	38,700	18,983	40,243	56,032	66,000	21,130	60,293	2,331,342
2000	58,000	671,000	292,502	22,924	257,200	38,900	17,997	39,241	52,671	64,000	21,070	57,218	2,318,945
2001	56,000	657,000	298,254	23,612	236,661	39,200	16,880	39,210	48,649	55,000	19,510	56,744	2,264,128
2002	65,000	587,274	307,588	24,818	228,300	39,400	16,659	41,428	47,502	60,000	18,633	39,376	2,182,956
2003	72,000	551,107	338,058	26,782	229,600	39,700	16,879	44,586	44,156	60,000	17,372	34,922	2,189,507
2004	60,000	509,473	373,902	28,499	217,700	39,900	17,505	47,111	44,156	60,000	17,065	37,271	2,169,191
2005	60,000	519,660	393,172	30,444	215,500	40,000	17,600	48,033	45,000	60,000	16,888	42,009	2,225,652
2006	60,000	486,726	388,777	32,389	224,700	40,100	17,600	50,276	45,000	60,000	17,000	46,709	2,189,892
2007[1]	60,000	464,736	395,000	34,200	217,900	40,600	17,700	52,022	45,000	62,000	17,500	45,570	2,180,600
2008[2]	60,000	464,736	395,000	35,200	217,900	41,000	17,700	53,491	45,000	62,000	17,500	45,000	2,191,090

[1] Preliminary. [2] Estimate. NA = Not avaliable. *Source: Food and Agriculture Organization of the United Nations (FAO-UN)*

Production of Wool Goods[2] in the United States In Millions of Yards

Year	First Quarter	Second Quarter	Third Quarter	Fourth Quarter	Total	Year	First Quarter	Second Quarter	Third Quarter	Fourth Quarter	Total
2000	17.9	18.0	13.4	17.4	66.7	2005	4.9	6.9	4.2	4.3	20.3
2001	20.8	12.4	11.0	9.0	53.2	2006	4.1	3.9	2.8	2.8	13.7
2002	7.4	8.6	6.2	5.5	27.7	2007	2.6	2.5	2.2	2.1	9.5
2003	6.5	6.4	5.2	4.9	23.0	2008	2.3	2.1	1.7	1.5	7.5
2004	5.5	5.9	4.2	4.2	19.8	2009[1]	1.4	1.2	1.0		4.9

[1] Preliminary. [2] Woolen and worsted woven goods, except woven felts. *Source: Bureau of the Census, U.S. Department of Commerce*

Consumption of Apparel Wool[2] in the United States In Millions of Pounds--Clean Basis

Year	First Quarter	Second Quarter	Third Quarter	Fourth Quarter	Total	Year	First Quarter	Second Quarter	Third Quarter	Fourth Quarter	Total
1997	33.1	33.8	30.6	32.8	130.4	2002	11.0	10.5	6.5	W	36.0
1998	29.3	29.6	21.9	17.5	98.4	2003	W	W	W	W	W
1999	17.3	16.8	15.8	13.6	63.5	2004	W	W	W	W	W
2000	17.4	16.1	14.6	13.9	63.0	2005	2.3	5.2	3.9	4.0	15.4
2001	17.0	13.5	11.6	10.9	53.0	2006[1]	3.7	3.8	2.8	3.0	13.3

[1] Preliminary. [2] Woolen and worsted woven goods, except woven felts. W = Withheld. Source: Bureau of the Census, U.S. Department of Commerce

WOOL

Salient Statistics of Wool in the United States

Year	Sheep & Lambs Shorn[4]	Weight per Fleece	Shorn Wool Production	Price per Lb.	Value of Production	Shorn Wool Support	Shorn Payment Rate	Total Wool Production	Raw Wool (Clean Content): Domestic Production	Domestic Wool Exports	Dutiable Imports for Consumption[3] (48's & Finer)	Total New Supply[2]	Duty Free Raw Imports (Not Finer than 46's)	Mill Consumption: Apparel	Carpet
	-1,000's-	-In Lbs.-	1,000 Lbs.		-$1,000-	-- Cents Per Lb. --		In Thousands of Pounds							
2000	6,135	7.60	46,446	33.0	15,377	----	40.0	46,446	24,413	6,629	23,902	62,785	21,099	62,041	15,205
2001	5,700	7.60	43,000	36.0	15,311	----	----	43,016	22,712	6,154	15,843	52,128	19,727	52,969	13,310
2002	5,476	7.50	41,322	53.0	21,876	100	18.0	41,078	21,689	8,461	10,526	37,913	14,159	36,015	6,891
2003	5,074	7.50	38,229	73.0	28,126	100	20.0	38,299	20,222	11,067	4,986	29,890	15,749	43,869	6,017
2004	5,073	7.40	37,622	80.0	29,921	100	21.0	37,622	19,864	11,168	6,204	31,355	16,455	NA	NA
2005	5,072	7.30	37,232	71.0	26,272	100	19.0	37,232	19,658	12,422	6,220	25,589	12,156	NA	NA
2006	4,852	7.40	36,019	68.0	24,510	100			19,000	18,000	7,324		9,929	NA	NA
2007	4,657	7.50	34,723	87.0	30,242										
2008[1]	4,434	7.43	32,963	99.0	32,486										

[1] Preliminary. [2] Production minus exports plus imports; stocks not taken into consideration. [3] Apparel wool includes all dutiable wool; carpet wool includes all duty-free wool. [4] Includes sheep shorn at commercial feeding yards.
Source: Economic Research Service, U.S. Department of Agriculture (ERS-USDA)

Shorn Wool Prices In Dollars Per Pound

Year	US Farm Price Shorn Wool Greasy Basis[1]	Australian Offering Price, Clean[2]: Grade 70's type 61	Grade 64's type 63	Grade 62's type 64	Grade 60/62's type 64A	Grade 58's-56's 433-34	Market Indicator[3]	Graded Territory Shorn Wool, Clean Basis[4]: 62's Staple 3"& up	60's Staple 3"& up	58's Staple 3 1/4"& up	56's Staple 3 1/4"& up	54's Staple 3 1/2"& up
	-- cents/Lb --	In Dollars Per Pound					- Cents/Kg. -	In Dollars Per Pound				
2000	33.0	2.80	1.50	1.69	1.37	1.30	764	1.08	.75	.65	.57	.53
2001	36.0	2.42	1.66	1.69	1.60	1.54	841	1.21	.91	.77	.66	.65
2002	53.0	2.87	2.68	2.70	2.63	2.55	1,051	1.90	1.41	1.40	1.19	1.02
2003	73.0	3.23	3.14	3.16	3.02	2.81	821	2.41	1.73	1.79	1.48	1.24
2004	80.0	3.21	2.75	2.89	2.49	2.33	NA	2.35	1.59	1.74	1.50	1.25
2005	71.0	2.99	2.57	2.65	2.42	2.23	NA	1.86	1.46	1.39	1.41	1.03
2006	68.0	3.17	2.65	2.75	2.47	2.26	NA	1.79	1.45	1.30	1.00	.94
2007	88.0	4.41	3.73	3.90	3.31	2.77	NA	2.65	2.24	1.82	1.32	1.04
2008	NA	4.48	3.57	3.69	3.27	2.79	NA	3.09	2.45	2.25	1.82	1.20

[1] Annual weighted average. [2] F.O.B. Australian Wool Corporation South Carolina warehouse in bond. [3] Index of prices of all wool sold in Australia for the crop year July-June. [4] Wool principally produced in Texas and the Rocky Mountain States.
Source: Economic Research Service, U.S. Department of Agriculture (ERS-USDA)

Average Wool Prices[1] --Australian-- 64's, Type 62, Duty Paid--U.S. Mills In Cents Per Pound

Year	Jan.	Feb.	Mar.	Apr.	May	June	July	Aug.	Sept.	Oct.	Nov.	Dec.	Average
2000	154	146	144	156	156	154	155	151	149	146	140	148	150
2001	160	168	164	158	164	166	167	172	169	159	166	183	166
2002	218	243	250	251	249	259	255	254	268	312	322	328	267
2003	344	346	326	333	296	326	316	308	306	292	285	290	314
2004	304	294	288	281	261	275	277	263	255	255	270	271	275
2005	273	271	268	242	265	266	270	259	252	244	233	236	257
2006	243	256	259	251	258	254	260	260	258	260	308	315	265
2007	352	344	355	367	381	380	378	359	364	393	405	400	373
2008	416	411	407	404	378	376	386	346	317	257	226	239	347
2009	229	223	230	250	287	295	295	318	339	379	386		294

[1] Raw, clean basis. *Source: Economic Research Service, U.S. Department of Agriculture (ERS-USDA)*

Average Wool Prices --Domestic[1]-- Graded Territory, 64's, Staple 2 3/4 & Up--U.S. Mills In Cents Per Pound

Year	Jan.	Feb.	Mar.	Apr.	May	June	July	Aug.	Sept.	Oct.	Nov.	Dec.	Average
2000	95	95	101	110	125	125	125	120	107	105	105	97	109
2001	95	100	108	129	137	125	127	122	126	130	122	127	121
2002	134	150	170	181	189	200	200	200	198	204	223	233	190
2003	236	260	258	250	223	234	239	243	243	243	232	233	241
2004	233	239	240	240	235	229	233	236	240	236	230	230	235
2005	215	207	200	185	185	185	179	186	195	181	168	140	186
2006	NQ	NQ	162	183	173	171	165	165	165	NQ	212	220	180
2007	186	242	245	279	311	295	285	270	276	NQ	NQ	NQ	265
2008	290	318	319	325	285	295	305	NQ	NQ	NQ	NQ	NQ	305
2009	NQ	NQ	NQ	157	215	226	228	223	NQ	270	NQ		220

[1] Raw, shorn, clean basis. NQ = No quote. *Source: Economic Research Service, U.S. Department of Agriculture (ERS-USDA)*

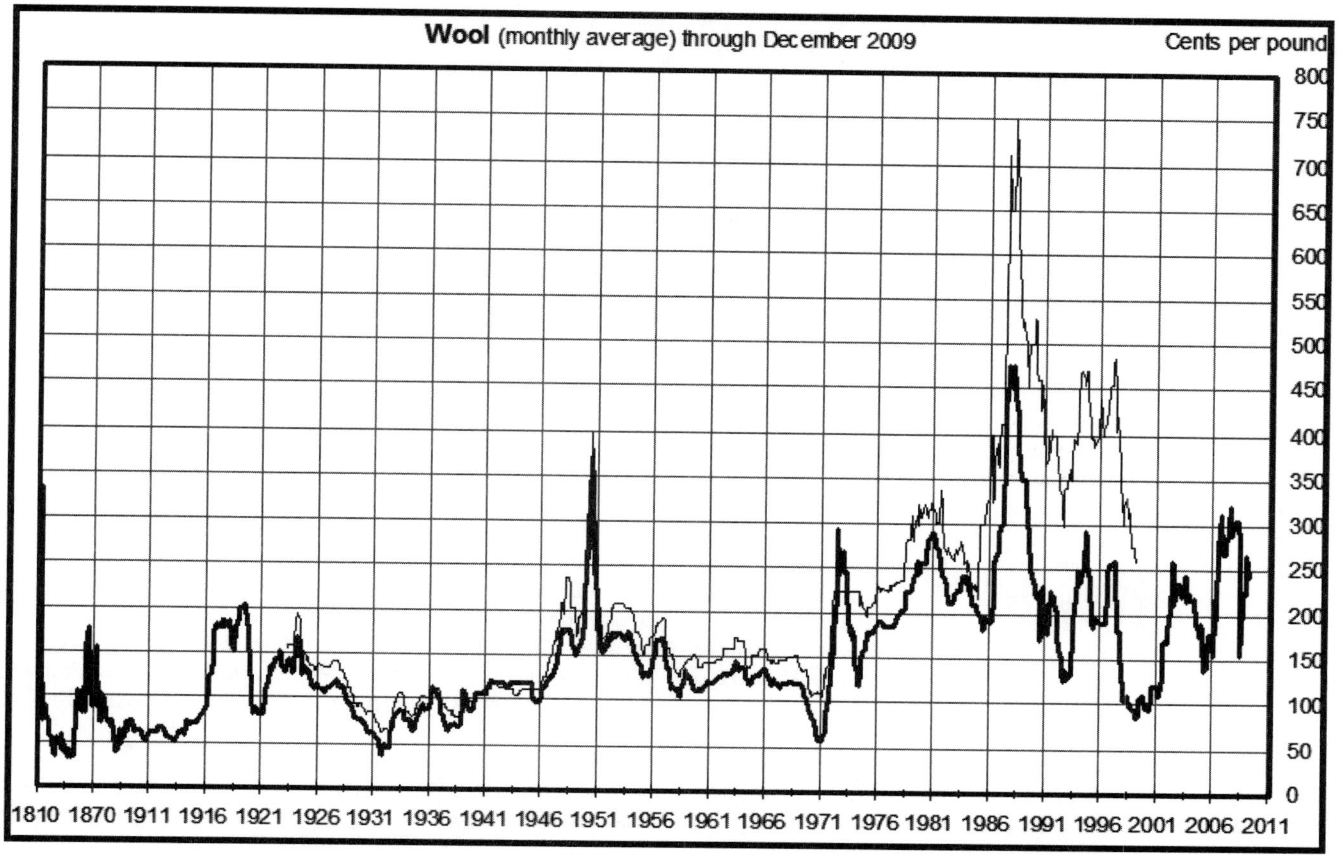

Wool: Mill Consumption, by Grades in the U.S., Scoured Basis In Millions of Pounds

	Apparel Class[1]							
	Woolen System			Worsted System				
Year	60's & Finer	Coarser Than 60's	Total	60's & Finer	Coarser Than 60's	Total	All Total	Carpet Wool[2]
1998	31,258	15,079	46,337	42,243	9,793	52,036	98,373	16,331
1999	18,379	10,772	29,151	27,429	6,955	34,384	63,535	13,950
2000	18,503	13,432	31,935	21,732	8,374	30,106	62,041	15,205
2001	16,062	9,849	25,911	NA	NA	27,058	52,969	13,310
2002	9,627	8,482	18,109	NA	NA	17,906	36,015	6,891
2003	6,681	5,309	11,990	NA	NA	31,879	43,869	6,017
2004	NA	NA	NA	NA	NA	NA	NA	NA
2005	NA	NA	NA	NA	NA	NA	NA	NA
2006[3]	NA	NA	NA	NA	NA	NA	NA	NA
2007[4]	NA	NA	NA	NA	NA	NA	NA	NA

[1] Domestic & duty-paid foreign. [2] Duty-free foreign. [3] Preliminary. [4] Estimate. NA = Not available. *Source: Economic Research Service, U.S. Department of Agriculture (ERS-USDA)*

United States Imports[2] of Unmanufactured Wool (Clean Yield) In Millions of Pounds

Year	Jan.	Feb.	Mar.	Apr.	May	June	July	Aug.	Sept.	Oct.	Nov.	Dec.	Total
2000	4.9	3.8	3.8	4.6	5.1	2.7	3.2	3.7	4.3	3.2	3.5	2.4	45.0
2001	4.9	4.3	4.3	1.5	2.9	2.8	4.0	1.9	2.0	2.8	1.3	1.3	34.1
2002	1.9	1.8	2.6	2.4	2.3	1.5	1.6	1.2	1.9	2.4	2.1	3.1	24.6
2003	2.5	2.8	2.3	2.2	2.1	1.8	1.2	1.1	0.8	1.6	1.1	1.2	20.8
2004	1.3	1.5	2.1	1.8	1.4	2.8	1.6	1.9	2.7	2.4	1.9	1.2	22.7
2005	2.3	1.1	2.0	1.5	1.5	2.0	1.5	1.4	1.0	1.7	1.5	1.0	18.4
2006	1.9	1.0	1.8	1.5	1.3	1.6	0.9	1.5	1.2	1.5	1.6	1.6	17.3
2007	1.3	1.1	1.4	1.4	1.4	1.3	1.1	0.9	0.8	1.3	1.3	1.0	14.3
2008	1.8	0.9	1.4	1.1	1.3	1.1	1.3	0.8	1.2	1.0	0.7	0.7	13.2
2009[1]	1.1	1.0	1.0	0.8	0.8	0.7	0.8	0.8	0.4	0.8	0.6	0.6	9.7

[1] Preliminary. [2] Data are imports for consumption. *Source: Economic Research Service, U.S. Department of Agriculture (ERS-USDA)*

Zinc

Zinc (symbol Zn) is a bluish-while metallic element that is the 24th most abundant element in the earth's crust. Zinc is never found in its pure state but rather in zinc oxide, zinc silicate, zinc carbonate, zinc sulfide, and in minerals such as zincite, hemimorphite, smithsonite, franklinite, and sphalerite. Zinc is utilized as a protective coating for other metals, such as iron and steel, in a process known as galvanizing. Zinc is used as an alloy with copper to make brass and also as an alloy with aluminum and magnesium. There are, however, a number of substitutes for zinc in chemicals, electronics, and pigments. For example, with aluminum, steel and plastics can substitute for galvanized sheets. Aluminum alloys can also replace brass. Zinc is used as the negative electrode in dry cell (flashlight) batteries and also in the zinc-mercuric-oxide battery cell, which is the round, flat battery typically used in watches, cameras, and other electronic devices. Zinc is also used in medicine as an antiseptic ointment.

Zinc futures and options are traded on the London Metals Exchange (LME). The LME zinc futures contract calls for the delivery of 25 metric tons of at least 99.995% purity zinc ingots (slabs and plates). The contract trades in terms of U.S. dollars per metric ton. Zinc first started trading on the LME in 1915.

Prices – Zinc prices in 2009 fell 12.9% to a monthly average of 77.91 cents per pound, down further from the 2006 record high of 158.44 cents per pound.

Supply – World smelter production of zinc in 2009 fell -4.3% to 11.100 million metric tons, down from the 2008 record high of 11.600 million metric tons. The world's largest producer of zinc is China with 25% of world smelter production, followed by Australia with 12%, Canada with 7%, and the U.S. with 6%. China's production of 2.8 million metric tons in 2009 was more than five times its production level of 550,000 metric tons seen in 1990. Australia's production rose dramatically in 2008 to more than double the 2007 level and in 2008 production was at a record high of 1.480 million metric tons. In 2009 the level fell -12.2% to 1.300 million metric tons.

U.S. smelter production in 2009 fell -11.3% to 690,000 metric tons. U.S. mine production of recoverable zinc in 2008 rose +4.92% yr/yr to 780,10 metric tons. U.S. production in 2009 of slab zinc on a primary basis fell -20.0% yr/yr to 100,000 metric tons, while secondary production fell -28.6% yr/yr to 115,000 metric tons.

Demand – U.S. consumption of slab zinc in 2009 fell by -7.8% yr/yr to an 18-year low of 920,000 metric tons. U.S. consumption of all classes of zinc fell by -16.4% yr/yr in 2007 (latest data) to 1.170 million metric tons, which was a new 16-year low. U.S. consumption of slab zinc by fabricators in 2008 fell by 10.3% yr/yr to 251,400 metric tons, which was a new record low.

The breakdown of consumption by industries for 2007 (latest data) showed that 63% of slab zinc consumption was for galvanizers, 8% for brass products, and the rest for other miscellaneous industries. The consumption breakdown by grades for 2007 showed that 50% was for special high grade, 19% for re-melt and other, 17% for high grade, and14% for prime western. Within that grade breakdown, prime Western consumption has fallen by nearly half in the past 7 years.

Trade – The U.S. in 2009 relied on imports for 76% of its consumption of zinc, up sharply from the 35% average seen in the 1990s. U.S. imports for consumption of slab zinc fell by -3.5 yr/yr to 700,000 metric tons in 2009, while imports of zinc ore rose +19.1% yr/yr to 75,000 metric tons. The dollar value of U.S. zinc imports in 2008 fell by -38.5% yr/yr to $1.902 billion, down from the 2007 record high $3.092 billion. The breakdown of imports in 2008 shows that most zinc is imported as blocks, pigs and slabs (725,000 metric tons); followed by ores (63,200 metric tons); dust, powder and flakes (28,500 metric tons); waste and scrap (17,000 metric tons); dross, ashes and fume (13,200 metric tons); and sheets, plates and other (3,330 metric tons).

Salient Statistics of Zinc in the United States In Metric Tons

	Slab Zinc Production		Mine	Imports for Consumption		Exports		Consumption			Net Import Reliance	High-
Year	Primary	Secondary	Production Recovered	Slab Zinc	Ore (Zinc Content)	Slab Zinc	Ore (Zinc Content)	Slab Zinc	Consumed as Ore	All Classes[3]	As a % of Apparent Consumption	Grade, Price -Cents/Lb.-
2000	228,000	143,000	805,000	915,000	52,800	2,770	523,000	1,330,000	----	1,630,000	60	55.61
2001	203,000	108,000	799,000	813,000	84,000	1,180	696,000	1,150,000	----	1,420,000	60	43.96
2002	182,000	113,000	754,000	874,000	122,000	1,160	822,000	1,170,000	----	1,420,000	60	38.64
2003	187,000	150,000	768,000	792,000	164,000	1,680	841,000	1,120,000	----	1,390,000	58	40.63
2004	194,000	156,000	739,000	868,000	231,000	3,300	745,000	1,190,000	----	1,430,000	72	52.47
2005	195,000	156,000	748,000	700,000	156,000	784	786,000	1,080,000	----	1,290,000	67	67.14
2006	113,000	156,000	727,000	895,000	383,000	2,530	825,000	1,190,000	----	1,400,000	78	158.89
2007	121,000	157,000	803,000	758,000	271,000	8,070	816,000	1,040,000	----	1,170,000	74	154.40
2008[1]	125,000	161,000	778,000	725,000	63,000	3,000	725,000	998,000	----		73	88.90
2009[2]	100,000	115,000	690,000	700,000	75,000	3,000	850,000	920,000	----		76	78.00

[1] Preliminary. [2] Estimate. [3] Based on apparent consumption of slab zinc plus zinc content of ores and concentrates and secondary materials used to make zinc dust and chemicals. *Source: U.S. Geological Survey (USGS)*

World Smelter Production of Zinc[3] In Thousands of Metric Tons

Year	Australia	Belgium	Canada	China	France	Germany	Italy	Japan	Kazak-hstan	Mexico	Spain	United States	World Total
2000	494.5	251.7	779.9	1,980.0	350.0	327.5	170.3	698.8	262.2	235.1	386.3	371.0	9,020
2001	558.5	259.3	661.2	2,040.0	347.0	358.3	177.8	684.1	277.1	303.8	418.0	311.0	9,320
2002	573.0	260.0	793.4	2,100.0	350.0	378.6	176.0	673.9	286.3	302.1	488.0	362.0	9,840
2003	613.0	244.0	761.2	2,320.0	268.0	388.1	123.0	686.1	316.7	320.4	519.0	351.0	10,100
2004	538.0	263.0	805.4	2,720.0	268.4	382.0	118.0	667.2	357.1	316.9	525.0	350.0	10,600
2005	532.3	257.0	724.0	2,780.0	267.5	334.9	121.0	675.2	364.8	327.2	501.0	351.0	10,400
2006	548.0	251.0	824.5	3,170.0	120.0	342.6	109.0	654.2	364.8	279.7	503.0	269.0	10,800
2007	584.0	241.0	802.1	3,710.0	115.0	335.0	109.0	597.7	358.2	321.9	479.0	278.0	11,500
2008[1]	1,480.0		750.0	3,200.0					460.0	400.0		778.0	11,600
2009[2]	1,300.0		730.0	2,800.0					490.0	520.0		690.0	11,100

[1] Preliminary. [2] Estimate. [3] Secondary metal included. *Source: U.S. Geological Survey (USGS)*

Consumption (Reported) of Slab Zinc in the United States, by Industries and Grades In Metric Tons

		By Industries					By Grades			
Year	Total	Galvanizers	Brass Products	Zinc-Base Alloy[3]	Zinc Oxide	Other	Special High Grade	High Grade	Remelt and Other	Prime Western
1998	647,000	320,000	60,300	122,000	[4]	145,000	331,000	72,800	51,700	192,000
1999	614,000	308,000	78,200	105,000	[4]	124,000	317,000	58,400	55,400	184,000
2000	640,000	293,000	82,800	123,000	[4]	NA	332,000	60,600	41,500	206,000
2001	543,000	281,000	74,400	91,200	[4]	NA	294,000	54,000	30,300	165,000
2002	496,000	265,000	86,800	103,000	[4]	NA	294,000	61,400	28,000	113,000
2003	506,000	264,000	87,400	113,000	[4]	NA	310,000	60,000	27,600	109,000
2004	510,000	248,000	96,700	W	[4]	NA	321,000	58,800	33,600	96,200
2005	486,000	238,000	83,900	W	[4]	NA	316,000	62,100	40,300	68,000
2006[1]	504,000	259,000	42,300	W	[4]	203,000	315,000	69,100	73,900	75,400
2007[2]	484,000	304,000	39,700	W	[4]	141,000	242,000	80,700	92,700	69,000

[1] Preliminary. [2] Estimated. [3] Die casters. [4] Included in other. W = Withheld. NA = Not applicable. *Source: U.S. Geological Survey (USGS)*

United States Foreign Trade of Zinc In Metric Tons

	Imports for Consumption							Zinc Ore & Manufactures Exported						
								Blocks, Pigs, Anodes, etc.		Wrought & Alloys				
Year	Ores[1]	Blocks, Pigs, Slabs	Sheets, Plates, Other	Waste & Scrap	Dross, Ashes, Fume	Dust, Powder & Flakes	Total Value $1,000	Un-wrought	Un-wrought Alloys	Sheets, Plates & Strips	Angles, Bars, Rods, etc.	Waste & Scrap	Dust (Blue Powder)	Zinc Ore & Con-centrates
1999	74,600	1,060,000	22,600	26,600	20,000	21,300	1,133,890	----	----	----	----	28,200	5,050	531,000
2000	52,800	915,000	9,380	36,500	15,500	26,700	1,272,750	----	----	----	----	36,100	4,830	523,000
2001	84,000	813,000	7,240	39,300	12,000	26,700	937,110	----	----	----	----	44,000	4,690	696,000
2002	122,000	874,000	1,640	31,200	15,500	30,900	887,785	----	----	----	----	47,700	5,660	822,000
2003	164,000	792,000	1,790	10,300	14,100	27,400	839,705	----	----	----	----	50,200	6,550	841,000
2004	231,000	868,000	2,500	10,800	16,100	24,800	1,142,733	----	----	----	----	53,900	7,640	745,000
2005	156,000	700,000	3,630	9,580	15,800	23,400	1,198,040	----	----	----	----	56,000	9,310	786,000
2006	383,000	895,000	2,050	14,200	31,100	30,100	2,771,580	2,530	19,900	3,780	11,200	83,800	16,400	825,000
2007[2]	271,000	758,000	2,160	21,800	18,600	31,300	3,090,910	8,070	22,500	4,310	26,700	102,000	19,400	816,000
2008[3]	63,200	725,000	3,330	17,000	13,200	28,500	1,901,830	3,250	8,550	4,970	28,100	91,000	13,000	725,000

[1] Zinc content. [2] Preliminary. [3] Estimate. *Source: U.S. Geological Survey (USGS)*

Mine Production of Recoverable Zinc in the United States In Thousands of Metric Tons

Year	Jan.	Feb.	Mar.	Apr.	May	June	July	Aug.	Sept.	Oct.	Nov.	Dec.	Total
2000	64.4	56.6	68.5	64.5	70.2	65.3	68.1	71.4	59.6	62.3	63.5	67.2	814.0
2001	68.4	60.5	62.2	65.2	66.9	66.1	66.7	67.6	60.9	67.1	54.0	55.4	799.0
2002	61.3	60.4	67.8	55.2	63.4	63.8	66.0	67.2	54.4	68.3	61.3	65.5	754.6
2003	65.2	60.2	62.7	54.0	65.2	64.0	64.5	59.6	63.3	58.6	61.0	60.5	738.8
2004	60.4	55.3	57.9	58.5	56.1	59.0	60.8	62.0	61.6	61.6	56.8	56.5	706.5
2005	53.6	56.0	64.1	56.7	53.3	64.6	64.5	68.9	61.8	64.4	51.2	62.3	721.4
2006	58.1	51.4	61.5	54.2	54.3	59.8	64.7	62.3	65.8	66.3	51.5	47.4	697.3
2007	60.3	55.8	63.5	56.6	61.2	64.1	63.1	69.5	61.3	64.6	53.9	69.6	743.5
2008	72.4	67.3	72.1	65.6	67.8	72.5	72.4	61.6	58.7	52.2	52.8	64.7	780.1
2009[1]	69.3	54.0	55.2	58.4	56.1	58.6	57.0	62.1	60.5	69.0			720.2

[1] Preliminary. *Source: U.S. Geological Survey (USGS)*

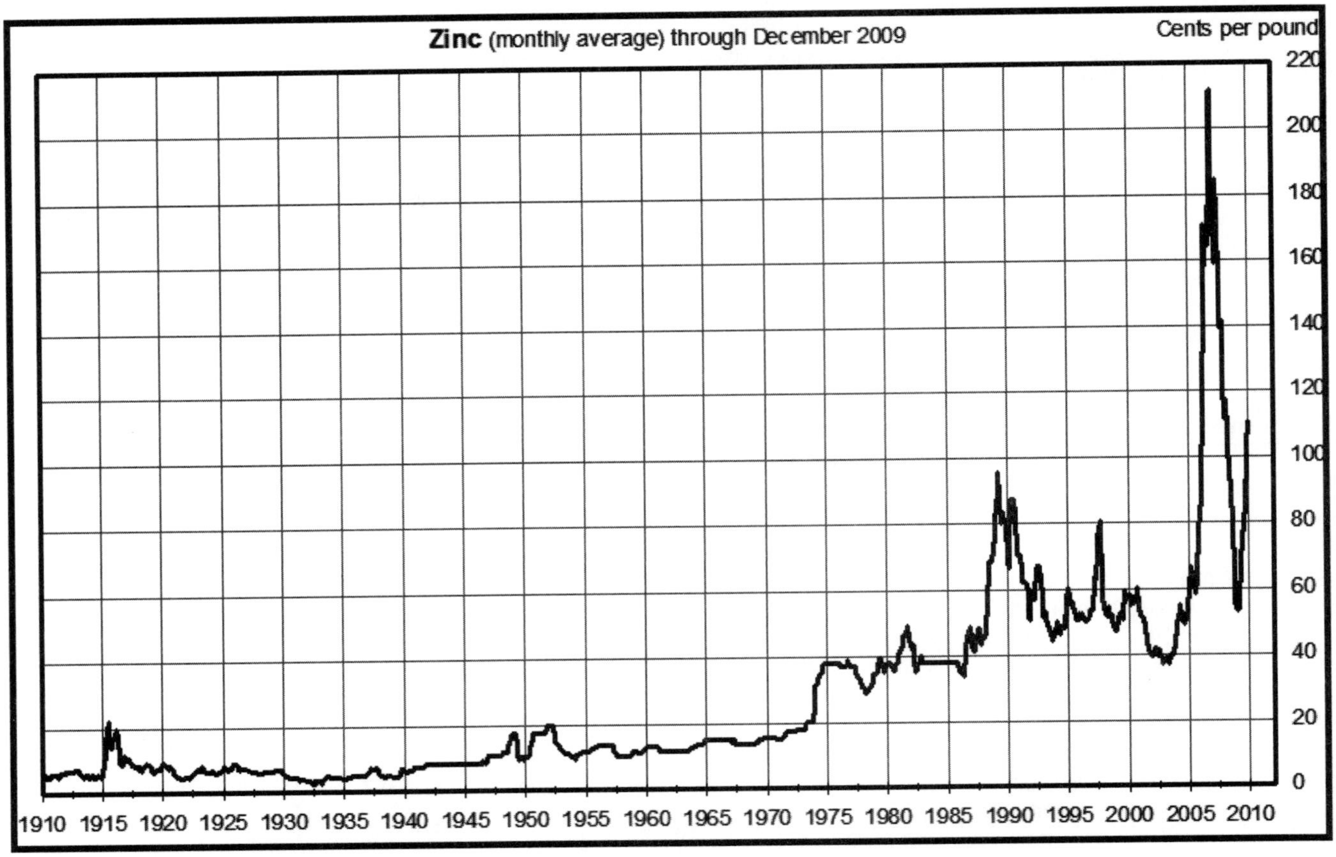

Consumption of Slab Zinc by Fabricators in the United States In Thousands of Metric Tons

Year	Jan.	Feb.	Mar.	Apr.	May	June	July	Aug.	Sept.	Oct.	Nov.	Dec.	Total
2000	41.8	44.6	47.7	45.6	44.4	49.1	42.0	43.3	42.6	47.5	43.8	40.2	640.0
2001	45.4	43.5	44.1	42.7	43.6	38.2	30.6	39.2	37.7	35.7	32.1	27.3	543.0
2002	31.2	31.3	30.4	33.1	34.9	34.4	34.3	35.8	36.1	36.1	32.7	33.3	403.6
2003	33.1	33.1	34.4	35.2	34.7	38.2	34.2	35.5	36.8	36.8	35.3	36.4	423.7
2004	35.1	36.2	36.6	36.7	35.9	37.0	33.7	33.6	33.8	34.6	34.3	33.4	420.9
2005	33.6	33.9	34.1	33.5	33.8	34.1	31.3	33.7	34.8	34.7	33.8	34.1	405.4
2006	34.8	34.5	34.8	34.0	33.1	34.2	32.4	33.4	31.4	32.8	32.0	32.4	399.8
2007	33.0	23.1	22.3	23.1	22.7	23.5	22.3	22.7	23.2	23.4	23.4	17.4	280.1
2008	19.7	19.8	21.0	18.6	24.8	23.3	21.5	21.5	22.1	20.2	19.5	19.4	251.4
2009[1]	18.8	20.5	17.4	16.5	17.3	17.3	17.8	20.2	21.0	20.3			224.5

[1] Preliminary. *Source: U.S. Geological Survey (USGS)*

Average Price of Zinc, Prime Western Slab (Delivered U.S. Basis) In Cents Per Pound

Year	Jan.	Feb.	Mar.	Apr.	May	June	July	Aug.	Sept.	Oct.	Nov.	Dec.	Average
2000	58.44	54.67	55.60	56.14	57.44	55.67	56.52	58.04	60.53	54.67	53.07	53.00	56.15
2001	51.82	51.29	50.55	48.95	47.54	45.56	43.62	42.53	41.14	39.53	39.99	39.25	45.15
2002	40.98	39.97	42.15	41.66	39.97	39.70	41.01	38.91	39.26	39.08	36.99	38.52	39.64
2003	38.88	38.46	38.48	36.99	37.86	38.57	40.30	39.77	39.84	43.44	44.11	47.60	40.36
2004	49.61	53.31	54.63	51.89	51.88	51.53	49.85	49.31	49.37	53.36	54.61	58.32	52.31
2005	61.10	64.57	66.59	63.55	60.70	61.97	58.26	62.76	67.73	72.10	77.60	87.45	67.03
2006	100.02	106.57	116.10	147.28	170.57	158.11	163.89	164.23	166.56	185.80	210.32	211.82	158.44
2007	183.91	161.21	158.81	171.08	184.68	173.23	169.81	155.93	139.28	140.84	122.63	112.65	156.17
2008	111.49	115.37	117.27	107.07	102.59	89.16	87.44	81.53	81.83	62.25	55.26	53.22	88.71
2009	57.28	53.96	57.96	65.19	69.91	73.34	74.38	85.30	88.25	97.11	102.32	109.97	77.91

Source: American Metal Market (AMM)

CRB Yearbook CD

Contents

Chapter 1: Installation

Installing QuickSearch

To run QuickSearch, you will need:
- A computer with a 120 Mhz or faster processor, running any current Windows 2000®, XP®, Vista® or Mac OS X running Parallels or Boot Camp
- At least 32 MB of total RAM installed on your computer; for best performance, we recommend at least 64 MB
- A CD-ROM drive

To Install:
1) Place the disc in the CD-ROM drive. If installation does not start automatically proceed to step 2.
2) Click Start; Select Run
3) Type D:\Autoplay, where D is the letter representing your CD-ROM drive. Press the enter key and follow the instructions.

Chapter 2: Searching and Browsing

Selecting Text to Search

Searches can be conducted across all the text in a *QuickSearch* document (full-text), restricted to a specific field (fielded search), or restricted to a selected table of contents section.

Everywhere in text – searches the full text of the *QuickSearch* document (except for user-defined notes and bookmarks). Choose **Everywhere in text** in the Search dialog box to specify a full-text search.

Fielded Search – searches a specific field and ignores all text outside of that field. To specify a fielded search:

1) Click **Selected field** under **Select where to search**.
2) Select a field from the list of available fields.

Current Table of Contents section – restricts a research only to a Table of Contents (TOC) section.

1) Click the TOC section in the TOC window.
2) Click the Search button on the toolbar OR select Search/Search from the main menu.
3) Click *Current Table of Contents section* under *Select where to search.*

Note: Search results will represent the selected TOC Section and its sublevels.

Types of Searches

Search for Phrase

Type an exact phrase you wish to find, e.g. "Business is the key." Use quotation marks around the search text to distinguish a *phrase search* from a *word search* or choose *Search for phrase* in the **Search/More>>** dialog box. The QuickSearch default setting is a phrase search.

Search for Words

Two types of word searches may be conducted – single words or words in proximity as determined by **Search Operators**. To conduct a word search, choose *Search for word(s)* in the **Search/More>>** dialog box.

1) **Single Word** – Enter any single word, e.g. BUSINESS, to find all occurrences in the document.
2) **Words in Proximity** – Enter any series of words that you wish to find near each other (e.g. BUSINESS INCREASE). Before conducting a *proximity search*, define a search range/proximity in the **Search/ More>>** dialog box. The default setting is 4 words. A typical sentence has 10 words, a typical paragraph has 25 words, and a typical page has 500 words.

Refine Last Search

The **Refine last search** feature can be used to modify your most recent search. (See the Advanced Searching section of this chapter.)

Search Operators

Boolean, wildcard and phrase search operators are available by selecting **MORE>>** in the **Search** dialog box. Double-click on any operator to add it to the Search command line ***or*** type the operator in the **Type the text to find** box.

To see example of each operator:

- Click the **Search** button and then the **More>>** button.

OR

- Select **Search/Search** from the main menu and **More>>**.
- Click once on the operator you wish to view.

The following operators are available for a word search:

AND (&) – BUSINESS AND INCREASE - Returns all occurrences of BUSINESS and INCREASE in the specified search range that are near each other. "Near" is defined using the Word Proximity setting in the **Search/ More>>** dialog box.

OR (|) – BUSINESS OR INCREASE - Returns all occurrences of the words in the specified search range without regard to proximity.

NOT (~) – BUSINESS NOT INCREASE - Returns all occurrences of the word BUSINESS that are not near the word INCREASE in the specified search range. "Near" is defined using the Word Proximity setting in the **Search/ More>>** dialog box.

Wildcard (*) – Use the asterisk (*) at the end of any part of a word to represent any character or combination of characters. For example, BUSI* may return hits such as *business*, *businesses*, *busing*, and *Businowski*. The wildcard operator cannot be used in a phrase search.

Conducting a Search

Basic Searching

1) Click the Search button on the Reader toolbar OR select Search/Search from the main menu.
2) In the **Search** dialog box, select where to search choosing one of the following:
- Everywhere in text
- Selected field*
- Current Table of Contents

*Note: Click a field or a TOC entry before choosing Selected field or Current Table of Contents section.

3) Type the search text (word, words within proximity or phrase) in the *Type the text to find* box or double click on any entry in the **Word Wheel** to select it as search text.
4) Click **Search** in the dialog box. "Hits" will be highlighted in the text and displayed in context in a separate **Hit List** window. The number of hits also will be displayed on the status bar at the bottom of the screen.

Advanced Searching

Search for Words

1) Begin a search by completing steps 1-3 of a Basic Search.
2) Select **More>>** to expand the Search dialog box and change to a *Search for Word(s)* and/or select other **Search Operators** which alter the nature of the search to be conducted. A *Search for Phrase* is conducted unless you select another type of search.
3) Specify the **Word Proximity** in the **Search/ More>>** dialog box, if you are conducting an AND or NOT search. The default proximity is 4 words.
4) Click **Search** in the dialog box. "Hits" will be highlighted in the text and displayed in context in a separate **Hit List** window. The number of hits also will be displayed on the status bar at the bottom of the screen.

Refine Last Search

To refine the last research:
1) Begin a search by completing steps 1-3 of a Basic Search. Click the **More>>** button on the **Search** dialog box to access all search parameters.
2) Click the **Refine last search** box in the lower left corner of the **Search** dialog box.
3) Select the **Boolean** operator to be applied to the refined search (just to the right of the *Refine last search* check box).
4) Preview the format for the refined search in the *Refined Search box* at the bottom of the **Search** dialog box.
5) Type the **[New text to Find]** word(s) in the *Type the text to find box* at the top of the **Search** dialog box.
6) Click **Search**.

Example:

Your first search in the Constitution was for the word "House." If you want to narrow the search results to include only hits of "House" which are not near "senate," you can return to the **Search** dialog box, select **Refine last search**, select the *NOT* operator, specify the word proximity, type "Senate" in the *Type the text* to find box at the top of the **Search** dialog box and click the **Search** button. The **Hit List** will display only hits of "House" which were not located near "Senate" ("near" depends on the proximity that you specified). The final search command would look as follows:

(House) ~ (Senate)

This search could be further refined by selecting **Refine last search** and repeating the steps above.

Example:

If you want to find only occurrences of "House *NOT* Senate" which are near "Representative," return to the Search dialog box, select **Refine last search**, select the *AND* operator, specify the word proximity, type "Representatives" in the Type the text to find box at the top of the **Search** dialog box and click on the **Search** button. The **Hit List** would display only hits of "House" which were near "Representatives" but not located near "Senate" ("near" depends on the proximity that you specified). The final search command would look as follows:

[(House) ~ (Senate)] & (Representatives)

Search Results

Browsing Search Results

Hit List

After conducting a search, each occurrence of the e search text in the document will be displayed in context in a separate **Hit List** window. Double click on any entry in the **Hit List** to move to the corresponding section of text.

Highlighted Hits in the Text

After conducting a search, each occurrence of the search text is highlighted in the text of the document.

1) Click the **First/Previous/Next/Last (Hit)** buttons to move between highlighted hits in the text.
2) The number of the current hit being viewed and the total number of hits are displayed in the Status bar at the bottom of the screen.

Removing the Hit List

1) Click the **Clear** button on the toolbar ***OR*** select **Search/Clear Search** from the main menu to remove the current **Hit List** window and the highlighting from the hits in the text.
2) Turn off the **Hit List** for future searches by selecting **Edit/Preferences** to open the **Document Preferences** dialog box. Click the **Reader** tab to open **Reader Preferences**. Deselect *Show Hit List?*.

Reader Preferences

Select **Edit/Preferences** from the main menu to open the **Document Preference** dialog box. The box includes three tabs: **Reader**, **Author**, and **Stopper Word List**.

Reader Preferences include:

CD-ROM Drive Letter

Every CD-ROM player is assigned a drive letter. (It is usually the last drive letter after your other drives.)

Default Word Search Proximity

Set the default proximity (the number of words between selected words) to be applied in multiple word (non-phrase) searches.

Show Hit List?

Click **Show Hit List?** to open a **Hit List** automatically after conducting a Search. The Hit List shows "hits" - items found - when you do a search. Browse hits by clicking the **Next/Previous Hit** buttons on the toolbar or selecting **Search/Search** from the main menu. All hits will be highlighted in the text even if a **Hit List** is not activated.

TOC Window Color

Click the **TOC Window Color** button to open a dialog box containing table of Contest background color options. Select from a present color chart, or create a custom color and select it. Click **OK**.

SAVE YOUR DOCUMENT after you select preferences!

Table of Contents Browsing

Hyperlinks

The Table of Contents (TOC) provides a convenient method for accessing any section of the ***QuickSearch*** document. Each TOC entry is hyper-linked to the corresponding section of text; just click on an entry and ***QuickSearch*** automatically will move the corresponding section to the text window.

Multiple Levels

QuickSearch TOC's may include up to 32 levels. If there are sublevels in a TOC section, a "+" will appear in front of the TOC entry. To open the next level, click on the "+".

Automatic Tracing

As you move through a ***QuickSearch*** document (scroll, Next Hit, Previous Hit, etc.) the Table of Contents will "track" your location in the document automatically. A box outline indicates the current TOC section.

Chapter 3: Viewing Images

A ***QuickSearch*** document may contain ***hyperlinked*** or ***embedded*** images. Different methods are used for finding and viewing each type of image

Finding Images

Finding Hyperlinked Images

You can find hyperlinked images in a QuickSearch document by using any of the following options:

- **List** of images
- **Next/Previous Image** buttons or menu selections
- **Search** feature
- **Special formatting**/camera icon

Image List - Open a comprehensive list of hyperlinked images in the document.

1) Click the **Image List** button on the Toolbar ***OR*** select **Search/Image List** from the main menu.
2) Double click on an image title in the **Image List** to open the image.

Browsing Images - You can browse through images using the **Next/Previous Image** buttons or menu selections.

1) Select **Nest/Previous Image** buttons ***OR*** Search/ First (Nest, Previous, Last) Image from the main menu.
2) The **Next and Previous Image** buttons or menu selections move the reader sequentially through images in the document.
3) The **First** and **Last Image** menu selections move only to the first or last image in the document.

Searching for Words in Hyperlinked Image Titles – As each hyper-linked image file is added to a ***QuickSearch*** document, it is given an ***Image Title***. The Image Title appears with an optional camera icon at the point you have chosen in the text window. The Image Title is indexed with other text and may be found using a word or phrase search (see Chapter 1 – *Searching & Browsing*).

Look for Special Formatting/Camera Icon – Hyper-linked images can be found by looking for words that have special formatting (the default is double-underlined text). Double click on the specially formatted text to open the image. A camera icon may precede the specially formatted image title. The image can also be opened by clicking on the camera icon.

Finding Embedded Images

Embedded images appear in the text at the point you have chosen. They may be found by:

- Scrolling through text
- Conducting a search for words/phrases that appear near the image.

Scrolling for an Embedded Image

Use the vertical scroll bar to scan text and locate embedded images.

Searching for an Embedded Image*

Search for text that has been placed near an image and marked as hidden.

*Note: **Titles of embedded images will *NOT* appear on an Image List**. The Image List feature is only for hyper-linked images.

Zooming Hyper-linked Images

Marquee Image Zooming*

Marquee Image Zooming allows you to select a portion of a **hyper-linked image** and enlarge it to the size of the image window. ***QuickSearch*** allows you to zoom to a single pixel.

*Note: Marquee Image Zooming **is available *ONLY* for hyper-linked images**.

1) Click a hyperlinked image title or camera icon to open the image window.
2) Click on and hold the left mouse button and drag a box around the image area you want to enlarge.
3) When the area is defined, release the mouse button. The area selected will fill the Image Window.
4) Steps 2 and 3 may be repeated to continuing zooming.
5) To return the image to its original size, click once on the image with the left mouse button.

Image Panning

Image Panning allows you to use the horizontal/ vertical scroll bars* to move around a **hyperlinked** image that has been enlarged by Marquee zooming.

Click an arrow on the scroll bar ***OR*** click and drag the horizontal or vertical scroll bar button to move the image across the screen.

*Note: **Scroll bars do not appear on-screen until an image has been zoomed**.

Scale to Gray

Some 1 bit (black & white) hyperlinked images can be sharpened by using the **Scale to Gray** feature. **Scale to Gray** will fill in missing pixels to improve the quality of an image. This feature is particularly useful for viewing scanned document images.

To use Scale to Gray:

1) Open a hyperlinked image
2) Select **View/Scale to Gray** from the main menu
3) **Scale to Gray** will remain active until it is deselected.

Chapter 4: Printing

The **Print** feature will print text and images in the following forms:

- Highlighted lines or blocks of text
- Selected Tables of Contents section(s)
- Search results ("hit" lists)
- Embedded images
- Hyper-linked images
- Zoomed portions of Hyper-linked images

Print Hints

Highlighted text, images and TOC sections will print in order as they are found in the document.

The printed size of Zoomed and Hyper-linked images may vary between portrait and landscape page orientation settings (found via **File/Print Setup**).

You can print *multiple* TOC sections by:

- Using the **Shift** key to select a series of adjacent TOCs.
- Using the **CTRL** key to individually select specific TOCs.
- Using the **Shift** and **CTRL** keys alternately to select specific TOC groupings.

Printing specifications can be set from the Windows Print Manager utility.

Make **Print Setup** modifications *before* you **Print**.

Printing Text or Images

To Print portions of a document:

1) Highlight lines and/or block(s) of text.
2) Click the **Print** button on the toolbar.

OR

Select the **File/Print** from the main menu.

OR

Press **CTRL+P**.

To Print a *Single* TOC section:

1) Click the TOC heading in the **Table of Contents** window.
2) Click the **Print** button on the toolbar.

OR

Select the **File/Print TOC selection(s)** from the main menu.

OR

Click the **right mouse** button and select **Print TOC selection(s)**.

OR

Press **CTRL+P**.

*Note: All the sublevels in the TOC section will be printed.

To Print Multiple TOC sections:

1) Click the first TOC section you want to print from the **Table of Contents** window.
2) Press and hold the **CTRL** key while you click the order TOC sections you want to print. They do not have to be adjacent.
3) When you have finished selecting TOCs, click the **Print** button on the toolbar.

OR

Select **File/Print TOC selection(s)** from the main menu.

OR

Click the **right mouse** button and select **Print TOC selection(s)**.

OR

Press **CTRL+P**.

To Print adjacent TOC sections:

1) Click the *first* TOC section you want to print from the **Table of Contents** window.
2) Press and hold the **Shift** key, and click the last TOC section in the series (all TOC sections between the first and last will be selected automatically).
3) Click the **Print** button on the toolbar.

OR

Select **File/Print TOC selection** from the main menu.

OR

Click the **right mouse** button and select **Print TOC selection(s)**.

OR

Press **CTRL+P**.

*Note: **Multiple TOC Selection functions (highlighting using the** Shift **and/or** CTRL **keys) can be used in combination to select specific TOC groupings**.

To Print Embedded Images:

1) Highlight (double click) the embedded image(s) you want ant to print.
2) Click the **Print** button on the Toolbar.

OR

Select **File/Print** from the main menu.

OR

Press **CTRL+P**.

To Print a Hyperlinked Image:

You can print a **Hyperlinked Image** or a zoomed portion of a Hyperlinked Image.

1) Open the image by double clicking the **Image title** and/or the **camera icon**.

OR

Click the Image List button on the toolbar and double click the Image title from the list.

2) Click the Print button on the Toolbar.

OR

Select File/Print from the main menu.

OR

Press **CTRL+P**.

Print Setup

The Print Setup option allows you to select printer type, page orientation, paper size, paper source, and printer properties (paper, graphics, fonts, device options). Make these selections **before** you print.

To change the Print Setup:
1) Select **File/Print Setup** from the main menu.
2) In the **Print Setup** dialog box, click the down arrow in the **Name** pull down menu, select a printer type and enter it in the **Name** window (or click **Network** to access Network printer options).
3) To select new printer properties select **Properties** and make modifications.
4) Select **Landscape** or **Portrait**.
5) Select **OK** to exit.

Page Layout

You can adjust the top, bottom, left, and right margins of a printed page as follows:
1) Select **File/Page Layout** from the main menu.
2) In the **Page Parameters** dialog box, set margins (in inches) and click **OK**.

Chapter 5: User Annotations

The reader may customize a ***QuickSearch*** document by adding "margin" Bookmarks and Notes.

Annotate functions enable the reader to make customized **Bookmarks** in the text and make private, unsearchable comments about a document with **Notes**. The **Bookmark** feature enables the reader to "save his place," while the **Notes** feature allows the reader to "write in the margins" of the text.

Using Bookmarks

To add a Bookmark to a document:
1) Highlight a portion of text or place the cursor where you would like to add the Bookmark.
2) Click on the **Bookmark** icon on the Reader toolbar ***OR*** select **Annotate/Bookmark** from the main menu or select **Insert Bookmark** from the **right mouse** button menu. If text has been highlighted, it is shown in the **Edit Bookmark/Name** text box. If not, enter a name for the bookmark in the text box.
3) Click **Add** to place the selected text in the **Current Bookmarks** list.
4) Click **Go to** to scroll text to the point where the bookmark appears.
5) Click **Close** to close the Bookmark dialog box.

To go to a Bookmark:
1) Click on the **Bookmark** button on the toolbar ***OR*** select **Insert Bookmark** from the **right mouse** button menu to open the list of Current Bookmarks.
2) Highlight the bookmark you want to move to in the text.
3) Click **Go to**. The selected text will move to the top of the text window.

To edit a Bookmark:
1) Click on the **Bookmark** icon on the toolbar ***OR*** select **Annotate/Bookmark** from the main menu ***OR*** select **Insert Bookmark** from the **right mouse** button menu to open the dialog box containing current bookmarks.
2) In the **Current Bookmarks** list, click on the bookmark you wish to edit. It will appear in the **Edit Bookmark/Name** window.
3) Make changes and click **Add**.

To remove a Bookmark:
1) Click the **Bookmark** icon on the Reader toolbar or select **Insert Bookmark** from the **right mouse** button menu to open the dialog box containing current bookmarks.
2) In the **Current Bookmarks** list, click on the bookmark you wish to remove. It will appear in the **Edit Bookmark/Name** text box.
3) Click **Remove**.

Using Notes

To add a Note to a document:
1) Place the cursor in the text window where you want the note to appear.
2) Click on the **Notepad** button ***OR*** select **Annotate/Notes/Insert** from the main menu ***OR*** select **Insert Note** from the **right mouse** button menu to open the **Notepad** dialog box.
3) Type in the note and click **Save**; a Notepad icon appears in the left margin next to the specified line of text.

To View a Note:
1) Double click the **Notepad** icon in the left margin.
2) The **Notepad** dialog box displays the note.

To Edit a Note:
1) Double click the icon of the note you want to edit.
2) Make changes to text.
3) Click **Save**.

To Remove a Note:
1) Place the cursor on the **Notepad** icon and select **Annotate/Note/Delete** from the main menu ***OR*** select **Delete Note** from the **right mouse** button menu.
2) A dialog box will ask you to confirm the note deletion.
3) Click **Yes**. The icon will disappear after scrolling in the document.